Business Ethics for the 21ˢᵗ Century

Business Ethics for the 21st Century

David M. Adams
California State Polytechnic University, Pomona

Edward W. Maine
California State University, Fullerton

Mayfield Publishing Company
Mountain View, California
London ■ Toronto

Library of Congress Cataloging-in-Publication Data

Adams, David M.
    Business ethics for the 21st century / David M. Adams, Edward W.
Maine.
      p.   cm.
    ISBN 1-55934-560-8
    1. Business ethics. I. Maine, Edward L. II. Title.
    HF5387.A335   1997
    174'.4—dc21
                                        97-21283
                                          CIP

Manufactured in the United States of America
10 9 8 7 6 5 4 3

Mayfield Publishing Company
1280 Villa Street
Mountain View, California 94041

Sponsoring editor, Kenneth King; production, Rogue Valley Publications; manuscript editor, Elizabeth von Radics; art director, Jeanne M. Schreiber; text and cover designer, Terri Wright; manufacturing manager, Randy Hurst. The text was set in 9/11 Palatino and printed on 45# Quebecor Matte by Quebecor Printing Book Group.

Cover photo: the London International Financial Futures Exchange, Steve Benbow/ Stock Boston

For Jani,
and Aubrey, Aaron, and Erin Kathleen
and
for Patti, Emily, and Elizabeth

Preface

A COURSE IN BUSINESS ETHICS FACES MANY CHALLENGES BEYOND DEALING WITH THE FAMIL-
iar quip that the phrase itself describes an oxymoron. Most students enrolled in introductory-level business ethics courses come from a variety of disciplinary backgrounds, and
most have had little if any exposure to philosophy or moral theory. Consequently, students
often view the standard material assigned in such a course as dry and difficult. The principal tasks set by these circumstances for the instructor are to find a way to acquaint students
with the primary issues and problems in the field, immerse them in at least the basic
vocabulary of moral philosophy, and teach in a way that is lively and inviting to a diverse
group of students. This book has been written with those principal tasks preeminently
in mind.

Our aim is to engage students as early as possible in ethical reflection upon issues that
arise in all aspects of the contemporary workplace. Both in the selection and sequencing of
the readings and in the topics covered, *Business Ethics for the 21st Century* aims to be user-
friendly as well as comprehensive. The content and the organization of the text reflect
these aims.

Content and Orientation

Business Ethics for the 21st Century is oriented toward issues, with greater attention paid to a
number of specific problems and less concern given to providing an in-depth survey of
moral philosophy and social theory. Our aim has been, wherever possible, to emphasize
issues that students will perceive to be of interest as they graduate and enter the workforce,
whether as secretaries, middle managers, or corporate CEOs. Accordingly, we have given
relatively less attention to, for example, debates about corporate identity or competing theories of economic justice, with a greater focus instead upon emerging issues, such as those
involving cyberspace, information technology, and the globalization of the economy. Our
experience has been that students in introductory-level business ethics courses often have
difficulties when hit with too much theory at the outset. We have found that much better
headway can be made if the more theoretical content is introduced incrementally, in conjunction with particular topics. Thus, although the book opens with a chapter on ethical
theory, that chapter does not aim to be exhaustive. Rather, we have chosen to integrate
certain ideas and concepts—for example, ethical relativism and cost/benefit analysis—into
the discussion of concrete issues, as these arise throughout the text. Our hope is that students will better grasp these concepts if they are presented within a concrete setting, and
that they will more clearly appreciate the theoretical implications of ethics for business
practice.

Issues and Coverage

The issues selected for coverage also reflect our desire to engage the attention of students with material that is topical, as well as substantive. As the title implies, we focus particularly upon recent cases and emerging controversies. Full-chapter coverage is given to such topics as multinational corporate activity, business and the environment, and women in the workplace. In addition, the text incorporates material on many of the most recent developments in a whole range of areas: labor conditions in the Third World; hazardous waste export; environmental racism; sustainable development and business growth; negligent hiring; genetic testing and identification; mass torts and product liability; and so on. Recent and high-profile cases dealing with the marketing of and liability for tobacco-related injuries; affirmative action; workplace discrimination and disabilities; and sexual harassment, among others, are also included. A chapter entitled "Moral Dimensions of Information Technology" attempts to survey the array of issues emerging from cyberspace: computer crime; intellectual property and software piracy; online services and liability for user conduct; privacy and information technology; the impact of technology on the quality of work life, and so on. The epilogue, on the globalization of the economy, examines forces driving the emerging world economy, questions of competitiveness, free-trade and tariff issues, wealth creation, and so on.

Organization and Pedagogy

The overall structure of the book, and of each of the chapters within it, seeks to make it as readily "teachable" as possible. Accordingly, we begin with an introductory chapter covering the basics of ethical theory as applied to business practice. We introduce and explain several systematic approaches to normative philosophical ethics that have dominated the Western tradition: consequentialism, deontology, and virtue-based ethical moral theories. Students need at least a rudimentary understanding of such concepts as "goodness," "rights," and "utility" to be part of the conversation about what constitutes a good life and what makes for right action; and efforts to apply normative concepts to business practices presupposes exactly these concepts. In order to fully grasp, for example, moral issues concerning the activities of multinationals, a preliminary discussion of human rights is relevant; to understand the moral justification of a free market, the concept of welfare utilitarianism is of importance. As in other chapters, our aim has been to make access to the nuts-and-bolts of ethical theory as straightforward as possible without sacrificing coverage.

Immediately following the chapter on ethical theory, we turn to the multinational activities of corporations, as an exploration of this issue affords a particularly useful way to broach another basic moral theory familiar to students: the topic of moral relativism. The next four chapters focus on specific moral issues concerning conditions in the contemporary workplace: downsizing, layoffs, and job security; privacy, health, and safety in the workplace; discrimination and affirmative action; and women in the workplace. The following two chapters—on advertising and consumer safety—broaden the focus from conditions in the office or factory to the moral and policy dimensions of business dealings with consumers. The final two chapters expand the focus again to the global level, exploring the impact of business practices upon the environment and reviewing the moral issues raised by the explosion in information technologies. The epilogue examines questions of justice and wealth-creation in a global economy. Although the chapters have been sequenced to present basic ideas, each unit is nonetheless largely self-contained, giving instructors flexibility to pursue alternative paths through the material.

Business Ethics for the 21st Century incorporates several pedagogical devices.

- Each chapter opens with one or more case studies. These have been chosen both to engage students' interest and to serve as useful vehicles for class discussion.
- Sidebars appear throughout each chapter, highlighting recent cases or emerging issues of particular interest.
- The study questions, following the readings for each chapter, are designed to test students' comprehension of the readings and guide their reflections upon them.
- Each chapter concludes with several case scenarios, many drawn from actual events or court cases. These can be used to elicit further discussion or as the basis for written work.

Acknowledgments

We are indebted to a number of colleagues who have helped, in one way or another, to bring this text into being: Darrell Moellendorf, University of Witwatersrand; Marshall Osman, Laurie Shrage, and Dale Turner, California State Polytechnic University, Pomona; Jeff Vanderpool, California State University, Fullerton; and Jim Bull and Ken King, both of Mayfield Publishing Company. Thanks are also due to the following people for their thoughtful reviews of the manuscript: Mark Alfino, Gonzaga University; James J. Brummer, University of Wisconsin–Eau Claire; Michael Davis, Illinois Institute of Technology; John W. Dienhart, St. Cloud State University; John Hasnas, Georgetown University School of Business; A. Pablo Iannone, Central Connecticut State University; Michael Kerlin, La Salle University; William Langenfus, John Carroll University; Neil Luebke, Oklahoma State University; J. David Newell, Washington College; Michael A. Payne, University of Dayton; Benjamin A. Petty, Southern Methodist University; Franklin E. Robinson, Murray State University; David Schmidt, Fort Hayes State University; and Anne Waters, Albuquerque Technical-Vocational Institute.

Contents

CHAPTER 3
Downsizing and Layoffs: Employee Job Security 109

CHAPTER 4
Working Conditions and Employee Rights   166

CHAPTER 5
Discrimination and Affirmative Action   224

CHAPTER 6
Women in the Workplace   284

CHAPTER 7
Advertising and Marketing   354

CHAPTER 8
Consumer Safety and Product Liability   411

CHAPTER 9
Business and the Environment   456

CHAPTER 10
The Moral Dimensions of Information Technology   525

EPILOGUE
International Competition and Corporate Social Responsibility   581

APPENDIX:
Information on the World Wide Web   589

 CHAPTER 1

Ethics and Business

This is a book about business. It is also a book about ethics. There is a widespread feeling in our society, of course, that many people in business are not very "ethical" (whatever that means), and this leads many to conclude that "business ethics" is a contradiction in terms, not worth much thought, and certainly not worth a whole book. We hope to convince you that this conclusion does not follow, despite however unscrupulous some people in business can be. But first some terminology.

As we use the term here, *business* refers to all aspects of the world of work in contemporary society. The word *ethics* refers both to the standards and values that people use to judge what is right or good or worthwhile—their *moral* standards—as well as to the serious study of such standards and values. To see what all this means, imagine yourself facing this dilemma: Let's say that you are the general manager of a small computer firm. You recently sent your top sales representative to a seminar. Attending the seminar were sales reps from a number of companies that vie with yours for business, including Acme Computing, one of your fiercest competitors. You have been especially irritated with Acme lately, because of ads it is running that are highly critical of your products. Now it is the morning after the seminar, and your sales rep comes into your office and hands you an envelope.

"What's this?" you ask.

"I found it lying on the chair next to me after the seminar ended," the rep says. "It belonged to the guy from Acme."

You open the envelope and remove the contents. Glancing at the document, you see that it is a comprehensive outline of Acme's entire marketing plan for the upcoming year. The cover page is marked *confidential.*

"The Acme guy must have forgot and left it there," the rep confides. " I wasn't sure whether I should open it or not."

You immediately realize the significance of this accident: With knowledge of Acme's plans, you can exploit their weaknesses, adjust your marketing accordingly, and get the better of Acme once and for all. Another realization, however, leaves you uneasy: Even though you didn't buy or steal Acme's plan, is it ethical for you to read it?

Assuming you were faced with this situation, what should you do? And what thinking would support your decision? These questions ask about the "ethics" of the situation in at least two ways: First, they ask about what standards of right and wrong you would use to decide what to do; and, second, the dilemma forces you to critically examine your own beliefs and convictions about what is right or good—to reason ethically, in other words. For example, you might think to yourself that it's okay to study Acme's plan, now that you have it, since they would surely do the same thing were the situation reversed. This is a form of ethical reasoning (though whether it is good reasoning is not so clear). Some of the most profound and challenging questions any of us can put to ourselves involve such ethical questioning: How should I live my life? What are the things I should value? What is the best way of life? A life of pleasure? A life spent seeking wealth? By what principles should I live? Are the principles or values I follow valid for everyone?

Now, all of this sounds very nice, you may be thinking, and perhaps ethics is important sometimes. But what can such philosophizing really have to do with business? Isn't it still true that "business ethics" is a contradictory idea? It is not. And the reason is plain: Dilemmas like the one we just imagined occur all the time. They can arise daily, whenever a company can exploit confidential information; whenever an employer secretly monitors its workers; whenever a corporation creates a toxic waste dump; whenever a business condones sexual harassment; whenever a multinational corporation uses child labor; whenever an advertising company tries to sell alcohol or tobacco to teenagers; whenever an automaker builds a car with a defective gas tank. In short, ethical problems in business can arise out of any of the various ways in which business can touch and affect our lives. Each of the examples just given raises fundamental questions about what practices are morally right or wrong; about what values are important; about the responsibilities of corporations to society and to their employees; about truthfulness and deception; about loyalty, privacy, and fairness. Moreover, these are not issues that can be brushed aside as "academic" or otherwise pointless to debate or to think about; such issues must be and are being addressed by businesses and corporations, by lawmakers and governmental leaders, and by the courts.

Business ethics, then, is concerned with examining these issues, understanding what they involve, exploring different ways to judge and resolve them, and arguing about which resolution seems best. And it is vitally important that you who will be entering the business and professional world, in whatever capacity, be aware of and alive to the ethical dimensions of the business.

THE CORPORATION, SOCIAL RESPONSIBILITY, AND THE WORLD MARKET

To get a clearer picture of what business ethics is about, let's start by looking at one of the most pressing moral and social controversies facing the business world: How much, if any, responsibility does a corporation have to "make the world a better place"?

The issue of what general responsibilities, if any, a corporation has to society and the world isn't new. It has been a staple of public policy debate since the inception of modern capitalism. The debate concerns just what these societal responsibilities should be. Corporations do produce goods and services that benefit society. But their function is to generate profits or dividends for their owners.

Many people think that the interests of society and the shareholders are harmonious. Profitability benefits society in terms of better technology, cheaper goods, and more jobs. Others believe that these interests are not necessarily consistent. Higher profits might mean poor working conditions or exploitation; cheaper goods through, say, automation may mean the elimination of jobs entirely. Debates about corporate social responsibility generally occur between these two poles: corporate profitability and the effects of that quest.

Those who believe that the interests of business and society are not necessarily consistent demand that business do more than simply generate wealth for the shareholders. Historically, that is the exclusive role of the corporation in our society. Its interests are purely economic: If a product line is unprofitable, it is shut down; if labor costs are too high, cheaper labor is sought elsewhere. The corporation's essence is profitability, and whatever benefit its operation brings to society is coincidental. It does not offer high wages and benefits to workers because it is benevolent, but rather because doing so is a business necessity; it is necessary to attain the goal of highest profitability.

Critics of this conception of corporate activity argue that the corporation should voluntarily adopt non-economic goals. Rather than passively engage in non-discrimination (as required by law), the corporation should strive for diversification in its workplace and alter its hiring practices to guarantee equal opportunity for all workers; it should actively promote environmental stewardship rather than simply obey existing environmental regulations; it should adhere to exemplary standards of product and worker safety beyond what is required by the government agencies; it should maintain the highest standards of morality in dealing with national and international markets; it should contribute to the communities in which it operates; and it should protect its workforce even during economic downturns. The corporation should, in effect, adopt the role of a "good citizen" who attempts to satisfy both its own economic interests and those of society at large. This is what corporate social responsibility requires.

Recently, a new corporate social responsibility issue has appeared on the horizon. This has come about with the globalization of the marketplace, a phenomenon that really began shortly after the Second World War. The issue concerns what relationship the multinational corporation should have to its mother country and to its host nation. This is an important question, as America presently exports jobs in large numbers, and existing wages in the manufacturing and service industry in the United States are declining. The relationship between national economic productivity and national welfare has come into question perhaps for the first time in our history.

Since World War II, the giant corporation has been proof of what U.S. capitalism could achieve. It generated vast wealth for shareholders and consistently dominated foreign competitors. But perhaps more important, the corporation provided a reliable avenue for many workers to substantial social goods. Even without the benefit of a college education, many Americans were virtually guaranteed the opportunity to own a house and car and have job security if they did their work competently. Of course the salary and benefits were not the result of corporate largesse. They were bought with hard work and hard bargaining. Still, corporations such as General Motors, U.S. Steel, DuPont, and Standard Oil helped sponsor the emergence of the middle class in this century—even if it was the by-product of their quest for higher profits.

Some argue that these changes were the result of an implicit contract between the corporation and society. In exchange for profitability, government and society would provide certain goods for the corporation and its proper functioning. Government would maintain a lenient regulatory posture toward corporate behavior. It might attempt to regulate lending rates in order to keep inflation manageable, but it would not intrude on business operations nor would it engage in Depression era–type industrial planning. It might regulate pollution, but it would not make the regulation too burdensome. In addition, government would provide for a national defense that would protect business interests abroad, and it would provide a pool of educated workers through the public education system.

With the signing of GATT (the General Agreement on Tariffs and Trade) in 1948, international marketplaces ravaged by World War II opened up to U.S. commerce, American corporations were happy to fill the vacuum, and American products and know-how spread throughout the Free World. Capitalism became a worldwide phenomenon, and foreign corporations began to follow the U.S. example. Foreign corporations learned the ropes quickly and well, with the result that by the late sixties they were competing ably in U.S. domestic markets with high-quality goods which they were able to manufacture at lower prices.

Former Labor Secretary Robert Reich put the matter this way: "The truly humbling discovery was that they [foreign competitors] could build and manage factories as effectively as could the executives of America's national champions . . . By the late 1960's, America's core corporations could no longer set their prices. They were now subject to fierce foreign competition . . ."[1]

An important reason for this (but certainly not the only reason) was lower labor costs. Labor is a significant portion of production costs. The cost of labor was much cheaper in the new competitor countries, and in many cases the competitor had easier access to the natural resources needed for production. Add to that the fact that the foreign countries typically didn't have the history of collective bargaining that existed in the United States, and the result was cheaper goods. Americans benefited from these less expensive products, but the American middle class, which enjoyed a large increase in income as a result of corporate expansion into international markets, was now threatened. The very corporations that provided that income were now engaged in a fierce battle for the steel, automobile, and electronics *domestic* markets. The competition meant a loss of profitability, of course, but it also meant that the existence of U.S. industries was threatened.

The United States reacted to these incursions in various ways: U.S. manufacturers complained of "dumping"; former free-market ideologues argued that formal tariffs and quotas were necessary to protect U.S. domestic markets; corporations undertook to merge and acquire other companies, only to sell off the most valuable assets in order to enhance their bottom lines; manufacturers closed U.S. facilities to cut labor costs, only to reopen them in foreign host countries at one-twentieth of the wages of domestic workers. This latter point is significant. With competitive pressures, profit-maximizing managers found that they could no longer afford the implicit social contract with labor; if the corporation was to enjoy its previous high profits, it had to find a way to lower labor costs. This could be done voluntarily, as, for example, when workers make wage cut concessions to their employers. But the more popular method to recoup profits was (and still is) disinvestment, for example, close the U.S. facility and reopen in a foreign country.

According to Bary Bluestone, "The solution was capital mobility. If labor was unwilling to moderate its demands, the prescription became 'move'—or at least threaten to do so. For one enterprise, this entailed disinvestment. When entire industries adopted this strategy, the result was deindustrialization."[2]

■ *The Multinational Corporation*

With the competitive furor of the 1970s and 1980s, a new type of corporation emerged—the "multinational" corporation, a kind of international composite. For our purposes, its most important feature, in contradistinction to earlier U.S. corporations, is that it has no national identity and no substantial commitment to the country of its origin. Its workforce and production facilities are wherever the greatest profits can be made. Its shareholders and management are U.S. nationals and citizens of other countries. Its mode of operation is to invest in the country that can return the greatest profit.

Most giant corporations whose names are traditionally affiliated with the United States are multinationals and have been for some time. In the 1970s General Motors (G.M.) increased its labor force by 5,000 employees. It did this by laying off some 25,000 U.S. workers and adding 30,000 foreign jobs. By 1990, 20 percent of the output of U.S.-owned firms was produced by foreign workers. An example of the composite nature of multinationals is instructive. Throughout the 1980s, U.S. automobile consumers were continually told to "buy American." But during this same time, U.S. auto manufacturers were busily disinvesting U.S. facilities and essentially setting up the same shops elsewhere in the Free World or buying substantial interests in foreign companies. A Pontiac Le Mans is a nice, domestically made car. "Buy American" if you want to save jobs in Detroit, right? As you put down your money, you enter the international market. Of, say, $10,000 paid to G.M. for your new Pontiac:

- about $3,000 goes to South Korea for routine labor and assembly
- $1,750 goes to Japan for engines, transaxles, and electronics
- $750 goes to Germany for design and engineering
- $400 goes to Japan, Singapore, and Taiwan for small components
- $250 goes to Great Britain for advertising and promotion
- $50 goes to Ireland and Barbados for data processing

The rest goes to shareholders, lobbyists, and managers—most of whom live in the United States.[3]

As the social and economic atmosphere of the United States changed, so did the public's perception of the corporation. Instead of (to use Robert Reich's phrase) a "national champion"—a means for national welfare—the multinational came to be seen as part of the cause of serious social problems. Millions of U.S. citizens lost their jobs and suffered unemployment or underemployment at diminished salaries (e.g., in the service sector of the economy). Some corporate leaders reacted with sympathy, others with plans to save U.S. employees through retraining. But the problem was economywide. Little could be done to stem the flow of jobs overseas. The phenomenon was simply the result of global capitalism: Corporations try to maximize profits, and profits go to whoever can produce goods the most quickly and cheaply.

Some corporate leaders told labor that the lost jobs and lower salaries were simply something that workers would have to get used to. Donald Fites, then chairman and CEO of Caterpillar, said in an interview that American workers would have to accept lower wages and that they could expect them to continue to go down. "There is a narrowing of the gap between the average American's income and that of the Mexicans . . . As a human being, I think what is going on is positive. I don't think it is realistic for 250 million Americans to control so much of the world's GNP."[4]

Wages would continue to decline until U.S. workers' salaries were in line with those of poorer nations. Then U.S. labor would be competitive. In 1992 Caterpillar announced that it would permanently replace 13,000 unionized striking workers if they didn't accept a bargaining agreement of a 13 percent wage increase over three years—probably less than the rate of inflation. Caterpillar's reasoning: a contract that will enable it to be globally competitive. Perhaps we can applaud Fites for his desire to share world GNP (gross national product) more equitably. But his compensation between 1989 and 1991 was estimated at $2,014,000—equal to the GNP share of some 426 average Mexicans.[5] In the end, the union capitulated to Caterpillar's demands. How could it refuse, given the amount of cheaper and willing labor abroad? What undermines organized labor today is the "iron law" of supply and demand—the supply of able and trainable world laborers now exceeds the demand. Capital is fluid and can be moved to the country with the cheapest labor and best conditions for profitable investment. But labor is static; workers can't move to countries that offer the best wages. Hence wages are driven down in the United States while investment soars in poorer countries. Given the massive world market of available labor, some wonder whether unionized labor (presently about 10 percent of the U.S. workforce), whose essence is in its power to limit the supply of workers, won't be put out of business by burgeoning oversupply.[6]

The fallout of global capitalism is not restricted to U.S. workers. Nineteen thousand of Mattel's 25,000-person workforce are foreign, 11,000 workers in China alone. The company that delivers Ken and Barbie dolls on Christmas Day pays its Indonesian workers $2.25 per day. It would take a Bekasi worker one month to buy Mattel's Calvin Klein Barbie. It was reported by the Christian Industrial Committee (a group that monitors international labor rights) that in China a major Mattel subsidiary pays workers only $0.25 per hour.[7] Compare that to Mattel CEO John Amerman's salary of $7 million in 1995. According to Eyal Press, who reported this story in *The Nation,* some of these Chinese workers complained of headaches, dizziness, and skin rashes, presumably from the molding process used to produce the dolls. They also reported that they received sometimes only two days off per month and sometimes no leave time when the workload was heavy.[8] Chinese imports to the United States have swelled to more than $5 billion thanks to M.F.N. (Most Favored Nation) trade status—a status they received despite China's record on human rights.

Such issues are not restricted to one industry. Working conditions in the largely unregulated garment industry abroad (and even domestically) are abominable. Improper ventilation and sanitary facilities and the absence of fire exits top the list of offenses. Laborers work eighty-hour weeks in sweatshops whose working conditions conjure images of Charles Dickens's mills. Child labor is not uncommon. In 1996 activists discovered that Honduran children were making clothing for Kathie Lee Gifford's line of garments sold at WalMart.[9] Labor activists and some manufacturers have complained. A White House task force (of which Gifford is a member) is presently engaged in an effort to eliminate sweatshop labor and plans to make recommendations on wages and overtime. But, in the eyes of some, these standards fall well short of those in the United States (e.g., they propose a sixty-hour regular work week). Efforts have begun to unionize foreign labor; consumer advocates attempt to educate U.S. consumers about how toys and other products are made and try to get companies to adopt enforceable safety standards and codes of labor. But most of these efforts have been piecemeal and have run aground against the irresistible impetus of profit maximization fueled by cheap labor.

As the stock market climbs above the 7,000 mark and investors become wealthier, critics of unbridled capitalism have begun to question the wisdom of the old saying that profitability benefits everyone. They wonder what arguments can be given to justify the enormous corporate wealth at the source of U.S. jobs and dismal working conditions abroad.

As we will see later, the kinds of arguments concerning corporate social responsibility that are called for here are, at their root, *philosophical* arguments. They are arguments that call upon us to question our beliefs and assumptions, that try to envision what should be and how the world should work. Given how complicated the business world has become, it is hard for many people to accept that philosophizing about these matters can be at all helpful—or even relevant. Nonetheless, it is. To see why, we need to look more closely at what philosophy is and its connection with ethics and business. This is the subject of the next several sections.

PHILOSOPHY AND ETHICS

Before we can explore the moral problems of business, it is important to understand just what ethical thinking is and what role philosophical reflection has within it. Being philosophical, as most people know, means asking some pretty deep questions. Philosophers wonder what any of us is doing here, about the ultimate purpose of life. Why, philosophers ask, does the universe exist at all? How much, if anything, can we truly know about the world around us? What is truth? Love? Time? Philosophy is concerned with these kinds of fundamental questions and is an attempt to reflect upon them in a sustained and critical way.

Some of the most profound of these philosophical questions fall within the field of ethics—philosophical reflection upon the values and standards that shape our lives and guide our actions. What makes life worthwhile? What are the really important values? Being honest? Being wealthy? Being successful? Or is having fun what we're really after? Why should I care about being a moral person anyway? Is there anything in it for me? Is it moral even to ask that question? Is morality simply a matter of self-interest, obeying the rules and doing what you should do simply to avoid hassles or punishment? Does being moral lead to happiness? And, assuming we do care about being moral, by what rules, principles, or standards should we live? How can I decide what to do in a particular situation? What validates or justifies the principles I choose to follow? Are those standards relative to my culture or time or place? Or are there "objective" or universal moral truths applicable to all cultures and times? Facing up to these questions and trying to think them through as carefully as possible constitutes the task of philosophical ethics.

As you can imagine, much can and has been said by philosophers about each of these questions. Because this is not a book dealing comprehensively with ethics per se, we do not explore all of these issues or the theories philosophers have developed to help us understand them. Yet some of the questions raised previously are particularly relevant to the kinds of moral problems that arise in the working world. Questions about what makes an action "right" in a given situation, for example, have a direct bearing on a dilemma facing an employee or manager. We do need, then, to spend at least some time examining the basic distinctions and concepts central to a philosophical view of morality.

■ *Egoism, Facts, and Values*

To begin our exploration of ethical theory, let's return for a moment to the case of the confidential marketing plan belonging to your competitor. Earlier we said that the question of whether to make use of the information poses a genuine moral dilemma for you, as the general manager, whose sales rep discovered the document. But some of you might want to debate this claim. "What's the big deal?" you might say. "Why is there a moral issue here? It's obvious that the manager should make use of the competitor's information, assuming it is to his or her benefit to do so. There's no moral question at all. Everyone in business knows that you do what is in your own best interest—that's the reality of the business world." The view summed up by this reaction is not uncommon, and it might seem that philosophers are completely out of touch with reality if they don't realize this. Although the philosophers may not *agree* with this assessment, they certainly have thought about its underlying assumptions. The idea that everyone is always looking out for himself has been around a long time; philosophers refer to it as *egoism.*

There are actually at least two distinct views that fall under the general umbrella of egoism. The first might best be called *psychological egoism.* This view claims that the only motive from which anyone ever acts is self-interest. Note that this is a claim about how people, as a matter of fact, *do* behave. Hence, this theory is different from one that insists that the only obligation anyone *ought* to have is to pursue his or her own interests. This latter view is a claim about how people *should* behave, even if they don't actually do so. This view is *ethical egoism.* Is either of these views correct?

Defenders of psychological egoism point to what they take to be the many obvious cases in which human beings act either to please themselves or to get something from others. Equally obvious cases where people cooperate with each other are explained by the egoist on the basis of sheer necessity: We are more afraid of a "war of all against all," which would be a likely outcome of everyone pursuing self-interest exclusively, than we are of putting up with a few, minimal social rules. Nonetheless, the psychological egoist would insist, no matter what people do, they are doing it because they *want* to—because it gives them self-satisfaction. This holds even for apparently altruistic acts. So, when the owner of a local ice-cream company decides to donate money to build a children's hospital, or when the CEO of a major oil company supports funding for the broadcast of ballet, the actions taken are purely self-interested—designed, no doubt, to enhance public relations and improve the image of the owner or manager.

Critics of psychological egoism make several points. First, it is simply false that people always do things because they want to do them. Often, for example, we do things because we believe we must—because we are under an obligation to do them. If the boss promises his workers a bonus at the end of the year, the fulfillment of that promise is what explains the checks he places on their desks at Christmas. But doesn't giving a bonus make the boss feel good? And isn't that really why he hands out the checks? The critic of egoism would not agree. Egoists, the critic would say, wrongly assume that fulfilling a desire (such as the desire to keep a promise or to help others) is necessarily a *selfish* exercise, and this is not the case. Ordinarily, when we say that someone is "selfish," we mean that she is thinking only of her own interests and needs and desires, having little or no regard for the interests, needs, or desires of others. Such a person *is* selfish; but a person who gets satisfaction from being kind to others is not acting selfishly, even if she is fulfilling a desire to be kind.

Suppose the egoist now takes the discussion one step further. "All right," he says, "I'll concede that people sometimes act unselfishly. But there is no reason why they *should* act this way." The egoist is now endorsing *ethical egoism*. Even if the boss decides to give out the bonuses or to donate to charity as an act of compassion and kindness, he is under no obligation to do so, for, according to the ethical egoist, the only moral requirement incumbent upon anyone is to pursue his own self-interest. Of course, in many situations it may be in my self-interest to respect the wishes of others, because doing so will make it easier in the long run for me to get my way. But on those occasions when he can get away with it, the egoist should pursue his own self-interest even if it conflicts with the interests of others.

To many people ethical egoism has too much ego and not enough ethics. It is hard for most of us to accept the single-minded pursuit of self-interest as a moral ideal, because we believe that morality has essentially to do with treating others in certain ways, even if doing so does not fulfill one's own interests. To see this, recall the case of your competitor's marketing plan. Let us modify the facts slightly and suppose that your sales representative attended the seminar and deliberately removed the plan from the briefcase of the person sitting next to him. The rep then brings the stolen envelope to you.

"I can't look at this," you say. "It's stolen property."

"But the guy will never know it's gone," the rep counters.

"I don't care. It's wrong to steal it and you should know that."

Here, says the critic of egoism, you have recognized a moral duty not to steal and not to profit by thievery. Even though you might want very much to know the information in the plan, self-interest is overshadowed by other, different considerations. But the argument isn't over yet.

"Look," says the sales rep, "why are you so worried about the ethics of this anyway? Who is to say it's wrong to slip the plan out and take a look at it? That kind of thing is done all the time. Corporations hire spies to infiltrate factories, and they try to reverse-engineer products so they can figure out the process used to make them. Are these things wrong? It's all a matter of opinion."

What the sales rep is saying here strikes a chord with many people in contemporary culture—people who say that all talk about ethics and morality is a waste of time, not because everyone is egoist, but rather because morality is inherently *subjective;* that is, that moral judgments and opinions are merely matters of taste over which no meaningful discussion is possible. Let's look at this view more carefully.

It is common to see newspaper columnists and TV commentators bemoaning the cynicism of most people when it comes to questions of values. The reaction of the sales rep to the boss's refusal to read the competitor's marketing plan reflects deep skepticism about morality. His view both reflects and reinforces the idea that morality lacks any objectivity and that moral or value judgments cannot be "proven." This cynicism is, in turn, grounded in large part upon a distinction that many people in our contemporary culture draw, almost unthinkingly, between "facts" on the one hand and "values" on the other. The assumption is that some areas of human inquiry—science, for example—are factual and objective, but that morality can be neither of these. If two people of roughly equal intelligence and education initially disagree on some matter that is "scientific," they can usually study the facts more carefully and come to an agreement. When the issue is a moral one, however, they may still disagree no matter how carefully the "facts" are weighed. This seems to show that when the question is a moral one, the people are not disagreeing about any facts "out there" in the world, but instead are merely indicating that they have differing attitudes.

As you might guess, this sharply drawn distinction between facts and values relies upon several questionable assumptions. It is not very clear, of course, just what a "fact" is, and, even more important, it is not obvious that the "moral" facts are any less clear than the "scientific" ones. Consider, for example, a claim entailed by modern particle physics. The current view is that physical matter is actually composed of discrete, subatomic particles (with names like *quarks* and *muons*), none of which can be seen directly. The existence of such particles is inferred on the basis of various kinds of indirect observations and theoretical predictions. The claim that Adams's desk is made of quarks is far removed from his daily experience—it is certainly a claim for which no commonsense "proof" exists. Yet it appears to be a "fact." Now compare the claims of particle physics with the moral judgment that torturing human beings is wrong. This moral judgment would likely receive widespread assent—indeed, it would probably seem more obvious to most than the strange postulations of physics. If called upon to "prove" the judgment that torture is wrong, one could reason that torture involves the infliction of pain and injury, that pain and injury are bad or evil, and that evil should not be done. This "proof" will not satisfy the cynic, of course. He may insist, as have some philosophers, that no claim should be accepted as making sense unless it can be verified—shown by observation to be true (or falsified—shown by observation to be false). But the cynic now has a serious problem: The statement that claims make sense only if they are verifiable is not *itself* verifiable in the way the cynic demands.

There are other reasons for doubting the claim that moral judgments are inherently subjective. The moral subjectivist believes that when Adams says something is wrong or bad, all he means is "I don't like it." In much the same way, of course, there are many things that Adams doesn't care for—the taste of lima beans, for example. One reason sometimes given for rejecting the subjectivistic theory of morality is that it doesn't fully capture or accurately reflect the degree of seriousness that most of us commonly attach to moral issues and value judgments. People argue and debate, protest and march, even resort to violence to defend their moral views. No one holds a rally about how good or bad lima beans taste. The ways in which people actually behave with regard to moral claims belies the view of the subjectivist that judgments like "sexual harassment is wrong" are no different from "I don't like broccoli." The manner in which moral judgments are actually made and treated suggests that they are not mere expressions of taste. When office workers complain that drug testing invades their privacy or that hiring and firing decisions are discriminatory, they are not simply expressing preferences about which further debate or discussion is pointless. We take these kinds of moral issues more seriously than our thieving sales rep's cynicism assumes.

But let's suppose the sales rep doesn't give up. "I don't care at all about morality," he confesses. "I just do what I want. I don't see anything wrong in that." At this point you may want to consider getting rid of this guy, for now our salesperson seems to have moved beyond skepticism about morality to complete *amoralism*—the absence of any concern for or interest in a moral outlook on life. Fortunately, such people are rare, as our ability to argue with them is now more limited. How can we convince someone who is seemingly blind to moral concepts and distinctions to take those concepts and distinctions seriously? Why should he bother with a moral way of life at all? To this question, philosophers have given different responses. The ancient Greeks, for example, insisted that to live a completely amoral and self-absorbed life is to choose a path that is deeply damaging to oneself, to the essence of what one is. Plato and Socrates argued that the soul of an amoral person would be corrupted and distorted through actions that hurt others. Some philosophers have claimed that a life of amorality precipitates a kind of psychic turmoil and disintegration, an unbalanced and disorderly existence plagued by anxiety, nightmares, and an obsessive quest for momentary pleasures and amusements to fill the void of an otherwise empty life. Still other philosophers have concluded that it is impossible to prove to an amoralist that he is wrong; all one can do is realize that acknowledging the importance of a moral outlook on life is a matter of personal commitment and choice of the most abiding and significant sort.

But these reflections shouldn't worry us further, for almost all of us, whatever our place in the workforce, whatever our career or salary, acknowledge that we must think of the welfare of others on at least some occasions. But it is just because we take morality seriously that we face many questions more troubling than the ones we have looked at so far. To begin our exploration of these questions and the attempts philosophers have made to address them, let's look at the facts of another case. The following reading, "Cooking the Books" presents a case with several moral dimensions.

CASE STUDY   Cooking the Books

Doug Wallace

It was on the third shot to the wastepaper basket of a crumpled up spreadsheet that Debra Duncan's hand froze in mid-air. Her eyes narrowed, as if honing in on a distant enemy. At that moment, she knew she had to make a tough decision, one that could cost co-workers their jobs.

Ben Wiley, her boss and division's general manager, was a charming man who could calm customers' anxieties no matter what the situation. Debra had been impressed with how easily he came to the rescue when her $50 million contract—representing two-thirds of the division's revenues—would occasionally weaken due to manufacturing delays. But with this new matter, she felt Ben and his can-solve-anything methods were going too far.

The two worked for Congent, a producer of high-tech components used in the transportation industry. Ben had been with the company ten years, Debra four. Congent's parent company had recently been acquired, and its new owners immediately began selling off divisions. Ben and Debra's division was cut in half for two separate sales: The sister half sold first, while her unit languished unsold, leaving its employees fearing the new owner would close its doors if a buyer didn't come along soon. Finally, a potential buyer materialized. Ben and his fellow executives felt extreme pressure from Congent's new owners to make sure a sale happened.

The only hitch was Debra. In conducting its due diligence, the possible buyer asked Debra

Business Ethics, July/Aug. 1995. Reprinted with permission from *Business Ethics* Magazine, 52 S. 10th St. #110, Minneapolis, MN 55403, (612) 962-4700.

for a status report on her current project—specifically profit and loss projections, as well as a schedule. All of the information was tied into important payments that affected the company's cash flow.

Ben's executive team was hustling, rounding up information demanded in the due diligence process. Debra discovered, however, that Ben was going even further by fabricating financial numbers and dates. The problem came home to roost in Debra's office, as Ben knocked on the frame of her open door and asked, "Can I talk with you for a moment?"

Gracious as ever, his request seemed to Debra innocuous. But she soon realized the real reason for the visit: Ben came to ask her to falsify documents. She was furious, all the more so because it was Ben, whom she had trusted. She winced as he delivered his final parry: "Debra, you would be doing a noble thing by repairing these numbers. It will probably mean that a lot of people here will end up with jobs instead of pink slips; you'll save a lot of folks.

"Well, gotta go into a meeting with the buyer. Let's see, I can't remember which made-up number I gave him last time," Ben said, pausing, then adding with a smile, "Oh, now I remember." He turned and walked out.

Debra felt numb. She tried to put it out of her mind, but two days later the revised projections were due. She picked up page one of an earlier draft of her numbers, crumpled it up into a ball, and tossed it absentmindedly toward the wastebasket on the other side of the room, groaning, "What am I going to do?"

Gabe Barton
Production and Logistics Manager
Hunter Industries, San Marcos, California

I would provide the real numbers. I would speak to Ben and tell him why I was doing that, that it was the ethical thing to do.

Any deception would likely be discovered very soon after the company was sold and at that point, where would an operations manager stand? There is no "win" in engaging in deception; it will eventually be discovered. If necessary, I would argue my case on this point, but I would hold firm to my belief that it's the right thing to do.

Also, there are many ways of presenting information. Assuming that Debra has not already presented the figures in the best light, one option might be to go back and place the figures in a more favorable form, while still putting the truth on the table. If that still was not acceptable to Ben, I would resign.

Kevin Gildart
Assistant to the President
Bath Iron Works, Bath, Maine

Debra has only one way to go: to provide the numbers she knows to be accurate. The last thing that would be helpful in a situation like this would be to provide numbers that give buyers a false impression, have them make a purchase based on what they think the returns should be, and have those returns come in less than expected. For the sake of short-term gain—that you found a willing buyer you're comfortable with in terms of reputation and financial capability—you could quickly find after the acquisition that your division couldn't pay its bills. In that case you've caused the downfall of the division, unwittingly.

The interesting part of this case is that Ben's the guy who is most able to confront the issue: He's the general manager. The problem that Debra has with her contract is that things are not going through the manufacturing process in a timely manner. It's suffering delays which are probably adding costs and creating customer problems. Ben has the ability to correct that and, therefore, make the numbers come out well. But rather than do that, he's asking for someone to change the numbers.

The important message here is that we really need to be looking at both short term and long term. The wiser decisions are made when we seriously consider the long term, and not allow short-term gains or problem solving to keep us from asking where this is going.

Doug Wallace
Corporate ethics consultant
Minneapolis

In contrast with other ethical conflicts written in this column, there is virtually no ambiguity in the dilemma that Debra is facing, and no competing ethical claims with which she is struggling.

Our guest commentators are clear about that fact. There are no shades of gray in truth-telling, especially when misleading others will result in harm to them, and eventually, to Debra's own company. So the problem here is not one of moral reasoning. It's one of moral courage.

What do we do when we need to say "no" to someone up the chain of command? How do we say "no" and make it a learning opportunity for others rather than an occasion of moral self-righteousness? What are effective ways of raising a question so others have a chance to reflect upon and rethink their own actions?

Debra has something to teach us in this regard by what she chose to do. She created a way by which Ben was invited to travel down a new road, and in the process transformed the way in which the whole acquisition team behaved.

WHAT ACTUALLY HAPPENED?

Debra struggled with what she should do. "I was torn between doing what was 'right' for the company and its employees (namely, assisting the sale by falsifying documents), and my own personal value of telling the truth," she says. "After a great deal of thought over a one-day period, I decided to compose a letter to my boss. The letter stated I would not participate in such activity and that he could remove me from my position if he felt my action was insubordinate. I then asked him to come into my office, closed the door, and handed him the letter. He read it, thought for a brief time, and said, 'OK, keep on doing what you have been doing. Thank you for the letter.' He also said he was happy it was not a letter of resignation. I told him he had the only copy of the letter and that he could destroy it."

Two days later in an internal strategy meeting, Ben said he was unwilling to alter any documents, and added that he would not ask any of his staff to do so. The president agreed and made sure that only accurate numbers were reported.

An ironic postscript: The prospective buyer did not acquire the company. A year later it was sold to another organization, and eventually, it went out of business.

UTILITARIANISM AND THE GREATER GOOD

The moral problem confronting Debra in the preceding case study is not one that too many of us face routinely, but neither is it uncommon in the workplace. It is therefore a good case with which to assess the relative merits of differing ways of thinking philosophically about moral questions.

One place to start is with the outlook of Debra's immediate supervisor, Ben. Ben is being pressured by company executives to ensure that his division of Congent is acquired by the new buyer. The buyer naturally wants to know as much as possible about the division's fiscal health. Ben has been giving the buyer misleading information, making the numbers appear more favorable than perhaps they otherwise would, and he wants Debra's help in continuing this deception. The closest Ben comes to providing a justification for perpetrating the fraud is found in his remarks to Debra in her office: "Debra, you would be doing a noble thing by repairing these numbers. It will probably mean that a lot of people here will end up with jobs instead of pink slips; you'll save a lot of folks." Let's explore the reasoning that seems to underlie Ben's remarks.

On the most basic level, Ben seems to be appealing to the *good consequences* that would flow from deceiving the potential buyer. The division for which Ben and Debra work has been struggling; many employees are rightly concerned that if the deal falls through and the division is not acquired, the unit will be shut down and they will lose their jobs. Ben's reasoning, then, would appear to assume that he and Debra ought to do what will have the best results for everyone in the long run, or, more generally, that *the morally right act is that which will produce the best consequences for all affected.* Philosophers call such an outlook *consequentialist,* because it makes the consequences of an act the key to understanding its moral status. To understand what this means in direct terms, consider and contrast the following two cases.

CASE ONE   You and your friend are both attending the university and taking some of the same courses. It is the night before your big final exam in biology, and your friend has called you in a panic. She has lost her textbook and wants to know if she can borrow yours. You have already studied thoroughly and feel ready for the test, so you agree to loan your friend the book. "I'll bring it right over," you say.

"Do you promise?" your friend pleads. "I need the book or I might flunk the test."

You reassure your friend that you will get the book to her tonight. But, as luck would have it, things don't work out as planned. Driving to your friend's house takes you down a long, back-country road; after driving down this road for some time, you come upon an accident. A car is off the side of the road and the driver appears to be injured. You pull over and stop. The driver is unconscious and needs immediate medical attention. You have no car phone, no other phones are close by, and there are no other cars on the road to flag down for assistance. It is apparent that you are the only person who can rescue the injured driver. To do so, however, means that you will not be able to get the textbook to your friend as you promised. Knowing that you will be unable to keep your promise, you carefully move the injured driver to your car, turn around, and head back into town.

CASE TWO   Your friend is sitting at the edge of a small lake, enjoying some relaxing sun and trying to forget the biology exam that she just flunked. It is a weekday afternoon; she seems to be alone at the lake. But then she notices a figure down at the shore—a small child who appears to be in trouble in the water. No one else is around. Your friend is an excellent swimmer and the water in the lake is quite shallow. Though she could easily help the child, your friend decides to leave, telling herself that she doesn't want to get involved. The child survives but is injured.

Most of us would likely say, upon reflection, that you did the right thing in the first case, but that your friend acted wrongly in the second. Helping the injured driver, we might reason, is more important than arriving on time with the textbook; and pulling the child out of the water is something your friend could have done with little or no inconvenience to herself. In each of these cases, it seems natural to say that what makes the actions taken right or wrong from a moral standpoint depends upon what the consequences will be for all of those affected. *Consequentialism* takes this familiar and plausible way of thinking and reflecting on moral questions and decisions and systematizes it into a formal moral theory. In the first case, the act of coming to the aid of the injured motorist was right, because it had the best consequences of all the alternatives open to you—it produced the most good, we would say, since a life was saved (even though your promise was broken); whereas, in the second case, the inaction of your friend might be judged to be wrong, because it was not the course that would produce the most good.

This basic statement of consequentialism still leaves it quite abstract. There are several ways in which philosophers have attempted to make the basic idea behind consequentialist thinking more precise, but for our purposes it will suffice to focus on just one of these attempts: the theory called *utilitarianism.*

The most prominent philosophers to formulate and write extensively on utilitarianism were Jeremy Bentham (1748–1832) and John Stuart Mill (1806–1873). Bentham regarded utilitarianism as an important tool for social and legal reform—a blueprint for legislation. He ridiculed the criminal justice system of England at the time, calling it excessively brutal and outdated. A person's action should be criminal, Bentham reasoned, only if it produces genuinely harmful consequences for others. Bentham's cause was taken up by Mill, whose book *Utilitarianism,* published in 1863, became a classic statement of the view.

■ The Principle of Utility

According to utilitarianism, the central moral requirement, sometimes called the *principle of utility,* can be stated this way: *Always act so as to bring about the greatest net good for all of those affected by your actions.* Several aspects of this statement need to be carefully examined. To begin with, the principle of utility demands that we strive for the greatest *net* good. This reference is meant, of course, to recognize that we may on some occasions be forced to choose between alternatives that have both good and bad consequences. In such a case, the utilitarian says, we must choose the course of conduct that produces the greatest amount of good or the least amount of bad. Also, utilitarianism insists we do that which will produce the most good. But what do *good* or *bad* mean here? Just what is the "good" that is to be maximized? Plainly, the utilitarian must answer this question, and Bentham, Mill, and later utilitarians have realized this, though not all have agreed on the best response.

Bentham and Mill both believed that the good we must seek to maximize and the bad that we must minimize reduce, in the final analysis, to pleasure and pain. The theory that explains the good in terms of pleasure and the bad in terms of pain is called *hedonism.* Hedonism holds that pleasure (and the avoidance of pain) is the only thing of intrinsic value or worth—that is, the only thing worth having just for what it is. All the other things that we humans want—money, cars, fame—are valuable only as a means to obtain pleasure or avoid pain. Imagine, for example, asking someone to explain why he wants a university degree. "To get a good job," he answers. But why do you want that? "So I can make more money." But why do you want more money? "So I can buy things that give me pleasure." Why do you want more pleasure? Most people would find the last question rather strange: Everybody wants pleasure just because it is what it is—pleasurable. Here we seem to come to a point where the thing we desire or seek is sought just for itself, not as a means to get something further. This is the good that Bentham and Mill believed all of us want, ultimately, to get the most of.

Not all utilitarians are hedonists, however, and this is explained by the fact that hedonism itself raises further questions, not all of which have found satisfactory answers. For example: Are all pleasures to be regarded as on a par? Is the pleasure derived from donating money to a museum or writing a great novel really no better than the pleasure associated with getting drunk or staring vacantly at the television for hours? While Bentham seemed willing to accept this consequence, Mill and other hedonistic utilitarians were less comfortable with it. Mill tried to distinguish between "higher" and "lower" pleasures, insisting that the higher pleasures were more desirable. Philosophers are divided over whether Mill's effort to establish this point is convincing. Others have accused hedonists of placing the cart before the horse. What human beings truly seek, these critics would argue, are those things that enable us to lead genuinely and uniquely human lives—for example, friendship, love, and the pursuit of knowledge. These are the good things of life that human beings need, and pleasure usually accompanies them. But the pleasure such things bring is not what we ultimately seek; and, in fact, it is often only when we don't specifically aim at getting pleasure that we experience it.

If pleasure is not the good that the principle of utility instructs us to maximize, what, then, is the good to which it refers? Some utilitarians have tried to avoid the problematic implications of hedonism by speaking in terms of "happiness" and "unhappiness": the principle of utility entreats us always to act so as to produce the "greatest happiness," leaving it undetermined exactly how happiness is to be cashed out. Other utilitarians have spoken of "satisfying people's preferences" as the good to be maximized in the utilitarian calculus. *Preference utilitarianism,* as it is sometimes called, asks us to take account of the preferences or interests of all of those affected by our conduct; the goal is then to bring about the greatest net satisfaction of preferences. To take a simple example, suppose that you are the chair of the board of directors of a large corporation. You have recently been approached regarding two possible acquisitions your firm could make. The stockholders of the corporation, to whom you are answerable, naturally prefer to get the greatest possible return on their investment; and you, of course, have an interest in seeing to it that the stockholders' preferences are satisfied. If the acquisitions have consequences for the firm's employees, their preferences (to retain their jobs, benefits, and so on) must also be considered. According to preference utilitarianism, you should take the course of action (pursuing one or the other acquisition, or rejecting both) that would maximize the satisfaction of all the relevant preferences (knowing, of course, that it won't be possible to satisfy everyone).

The case of the two potential acquisitions is instructive in another way, as it forces us to look at other aspects of the principle of utility. As the case reveals, utilitarianism requires that it be possible, at least in principle, to identify and add up all of the relevant preferences (or, in the hedonistic version, pleasures and pains) of all those affected by one's actions. This may strike you as not being terribly realistic, and for several reasons. For one thing, how can my preference for the merger (assuming that is how I feel) be compared with your preference to keep your job (assuming the merger would threaten your position with the company)? Are people's preferences really comparable items? The same problem faces the hedonistic utilitarian: How can the pleasure I derive from one course of action really be compared with the pain you might derive from it? How is the chair of the board of directors supposed to know whose preference is stronger? Or whose pain is greater? Moreover (and this raises a related concern for the utilitarian), how can any of us know the precise impact that our actions will have? Wouldn't I need to have the power to see far into the future to know just what consequences my actions might have? To these kinds of questions, utilitarians have responded variously. Some, most notably Bentham, thought it actually possible to quantify episodes of pain and pleasure and devise an interpersonal scale or metric against which to compare one person's pleasure with that of another. By assigning numerical values to differing episodes of pain and pleasure, Bentham hoped, a common currency could be devised with which everyone's good could be measured.

■ *Utilitarianism and Cost/Benefit Analysis*

Suppose that your friend will receive ten units of pleasure from receiving the biology textbook you promised to deliver to her, and that the injured motorist you encounter on the way to your friend's house will receive one hundred units of pleasure from being rescued. Being able to express the situation in this way makes it clear that, all things being equal, greater "good" will come from the rescue than from the delivery of the book. Yet to many, Bentham's calculus seems to require heroic assumptions that are just not realistic. How, for example, is a "unit" of pleasure or pain to be identified and standardized? Other utilitarians have responded more circumspectly, claiming only that it is possible to make at least some assumptions allowing for comparisons (for example, that most people prefer the pleasure of friendship or good health over the pleasure of scratching an itch or watching TV). And many utilitarians would insist that omniscience or clairvoyance are not necessary to apply the principle of utility: Though no one can appreciate in advance all of the consequences of his or her actions, the best anyone can be expected to do is to judge in light of the best understanding possible at the time. We are all human, after all, and we have to live with our limitations.

One of the most successful responses by utilitarians to these questions of measurement and comparison has involved the use of something called *cost/benefit analysis*. Indeed, cost/benefit analysis has become, in the business world, one of the major implementations of the principle of utility. To understand how this kind of analysis might work, take another simple example. Suppose you are the chief administrator for a major, research-oriented medical facility. One of your research teams has just developed a new artificial-heart device and wants to start a program of operations to test it. The equipment and support staff needed to perform these operations and conduct these tests are very expensive, however. Funding for the artificial-heart project would have to be diverted from other research programs—programs which might otherwise have helped a larger group of people. Moreover, the staff needed for the artificial-heart program would have to be reassigned from these other areas, so fewer medical staff personnel would be covering other needs at the facility. Should you approve the artificial-heart program? Some utilitarians would instruct you to base your decision on an assessment of the consequences of approval versus nonapproval. One way you might naturally approach this problem would be to look at the pros and cons of the artificial-heart project, restricting yourself to *economic* costs and benefits. These, of course, can be measured in monetary terms, providing a convenient medium by which all sorts of differing preferences could be translated and compared. Here you would look at the benefits of the program (the value of the program to the hospital, the amount of additional revenue it might bring, and so on) weighed against its costs (the money needed to buy the equipment, the pay for any extra staff, the cost of a decline in patient census in other units due to a decrease in staffing, and so on) and select the course of action that had the greatest net economic benefit (or the least economic cost). We examine cost/benefit analysis later in this book in more detail, but the idea should be clear enough.

The classical utilitarian theory (either in its hedonistic or preference-based version) has several significant attractions as a moral theory, and it might be well to note these before moving on to some of the criticisms that have been raised against it. To begin with, utilitarianism does not presuppose any commitment to theological views that say that what is morally right or wrong is determined by the dictates of God. Theories that ground moral principles by appeal to a transcendent, divine reality face the problem of first establishing that such a divine being exists, and then showing what moral demands such a being makes. Obviously, there are many, incompatible views on both of these questions. Utilitarianism, since it is a secular moral view, does not suffer from these problems. Also, identifying the good with happiness (or pleasure or satisfaction of desires) seems to many to be quite reasonable; after all, everyone wants to be happy, and aiming at as much happiness as possible surely makes sense. Finally, utilitarianism promises to make the process of reaching particular moral judgments fairly straightforward, since all one need do is calculate the likely consequences of any given course of action and do what will produce the best results.

■ Objections to Utilitarianism

One of the most common objections to the moral theory of utilitarianism concerns what the principle of utility might allow—or even require—people to do, under certain circumstances. One complaint is that the principle of utility might, on some occasions, ask too much of us. Suppose that you are old and sick. You have been hospitalized for some time, and, though you are not terminally ill, the doctors don't hold out much hope for any real improvement in your health. Meanwhile, your family is suffering greatly. They are deeply troubled to see you in this condition, and they have spent nearly all of their life savings to pay your escalating medical bills. Under these (admittedly somewhat vague) circumstances, it might seem that it would be better for everyone concerned (though certainly not for you in particular) if you were simply to end your own life. The greater good, in other words, might be best served through the self-sacrifice of your life. Yet, even if the principle of utility would appear to demand this course of action, this would seem to many to be asking too much. In fact, some might object that you have a *duty* to live, and that any principle is just wrong if it seems to suggest otherwise. (We return to the subject of duty in the following section.)

The flipside of the complaint that utilitarianism may require too much of us is that it may demand a course of action that seems simply to be wrong. This, of course, is a serious charge for any moral theory—that is, any theory that purports to capture and explain what is most important in moral life. To understand this charge, let's look at another case. Let's imagine that the owner of a local retail store, Mr. O, is looking at ways in which to cut costs. Mr. O has a number of employees, most of whom have been hired recently on a part-time basis. Mr. O likes hiring part-time employees, because he can control the hours they work and thus ensure that he does not have to pay them overtime or provide them with costly benefits (such as medical and dental insurance). In fact, Mr. O now has only a handful of full-time employees—including you. You have been working full-time for Mr. O for many years. You have been a hardworking and dedicated employee, and you are now earning a handsome wage (plus benefits). Some years ago, when Mr. O began hiring part-time help, he promised that he would keep you on in your present, full-time status. Mr. O knew at the time that he probably would not keep this promise; but he also realized that you would not stay unless the promise was made. Now the time has come for Mr. O to act. His business has been falling lately, victim to fierce competition from Target, WalMart, and other discount retailers (which also rely heavily on cheap, part-time labor). Mr. O calculates that the cost of your current salary, benefits, and pension could easily buy many hours of less expensive part-time labor. He must decide what action to take regarding your continued employment. Given these facts, a utilitarian cost/benefit calculation might reveal to Mr. O that he should break his promise and dismiss you, despite your years of loyal service. The greater good would be best served, Mr. O might reason, if the money used to employ you were used instead to invest in part-time labor. In effect, the principle of utility might require that you be sacrificed to the greater good. Yet, as with the case in the previous example, most of us would insist that to sacrifice you in this way, thereby breaking a promise, is wrong, regardless of the benefits to be gained. Mr. O ought not to fire you, even if it might be more cost-effective to replace you with cheaper labor.

How might a utilitarian respond to these charges? Each of these major arguments against the principle of utility turns on showing that the principle can require that people do something that would otherwise be believed to be wrong. The utilitarian might reply that utilitarianism, properly understood, does not lead to these counterintuitive results. Demanding that people kill themselves or that they be sacrificed in some way to the greater good would not, in fact, be legitimated or condoned by the principle of utility, despite what critics say. Utilitarians who make this move often insist that careful attention be paid to the level on which the principle of utility is applied. The weighing of costs and benefits is not to be undertaken merely on a case-by-case, short-term basis. Any rational person, the utilitarian might claim, must realize the importance of looking at the larger picture. Breaking promises and sacrificing others to the common good would not have overall positive consequences in the long run. Breaking one's word or using people as scapegoats in the name of the greater good in fact won't maximize happiness over time. This is because much unhappiness and distress would characterize a society in which no one could feel safe or secure—in which no one could rely upon the promises of others. The utilitarian in this way argues that the principle of utility applies not so much to individual actions at a particular time and place, but rather to social rules or conventions that are broadly applicable. Rules like "Keep your promises," which set standards valid in all situations, are justified on utilitarian grounds, since the general observance of such rules will produce the most good overall in the long run. This version of utilitarianism, often called *rule utilitarianism*, contrasts with *act utilitarianism*, the view that the principle of utility is to be applied to individual actions in specific situations.

Let's now return, finally, to the case study of Debra and Ben, presented earlier in this chapter. Ben seems to be urging Debra to think like a utilitarian. He wants her to weigh the costs of deceiving the buyer with false figures (for example, the risk of getting caught, the knowledge that one is participating in a lie) against the benefits of doing so (the purchase of the division, the job security thereby afforded fellow employees). Ben seems to be arguing that the benefits (either in terms of pleasure, happiness, or preference satisfaction) outweigh the pain or unhappiness of having to resort to deception to secure the deal. Should Debra follow this line of thinking? She appears to be frustrated by Ben's maneuvering to place her in this dilemma, and she seems shocked that Ben would actually lie to achieve his objective. What would explain her reaction? What alternative moral theories might Debra look to in attempting to resolve her dilemma? With these questions in mind, let's consider a different approach to moral reasoning.

DEONTOLOGY, KANT, AND RIGHTS

Our exploration of moral theory began with a hypothetical case in which a sales representative hands his boss an envelope containing sensitive information belonging to a competitor. The employee urges the boss to disregard the *confidential* stamp and use the classified information to their company's best advantage. Returning to that point in the story, let's imagine that the boss answers this way: "Look, I know it would be great to see what's inside this report, but we can't. Knowingly disregarding the stamp on the report and reading the confidential document just isn't right. Like it or not, we have a duty to respect the other guy's work, just as he has a duty to respect ours. You wouldn't want him to look at our marketing strategies if the situation were reversed, would you?"

In this exchange, the boss articulates some of the main ideas underlying an approach to moral thinking that contrasts sharply with utilitarianism. This view, often called *deontology*, insists that the central fact about moral life is that we all have *duties* or *obligations* to treat others in certain ways, and that these duties are based upon something other than the consequences of our or others' actions. The word *deontology* comes from the Greek root *deon*, which meant "to bind" and suggests what we mean by *duty*. What makes a decision or an action morally worthwhile or right, according to deontologists, is not the effect it has or the consequences it produces, but rather the fact that it was the right decision to make, the right thing to do. Where consequentialists tend to be forward-looking—estimating the future impact of present actions—deontologists are more likely to look another way: examining actions already undertaken or relationships already formed as a basis for obligations in the present. That I have made a promise or commitment to someone in the past, for example, might be, for the deontologist, grounds for a moral duty that I must fulfill to that person, regardless of whatever consequences would result from my keeping or breaking the promise.

Deontology is a way of thinking about morality that has a long history, though we cannot examine that history here. It is enough to point out that the writings of contemporary deontologists have been influenced by several sources. One such source is the natural-law philosophy of the Greek and Roman Stoic philosophers—a school of thought that flourished a few centuries before and after the birth of Christ; another source is the Hebrew and Christian moral traditions. The common thread running throughout these views is the belief that there exist moral rules or standards of conduct that are universally valid and applicable to all human beings, and which can be ascertained by us, at least in principle, through the use of our ability to reason. This universal or common moral code was variously referred to as the "moral law" or the "natural law." Many Jewish and Christian philosophers explicitly linked this idea of a moral law valid for everyone with their own religious doctrines of God, creation, and human destiny. According to these views, the supreme principle of morality might be "Do whatever God commands." Other deontological philosophers, however, have tried to argue that the validity of these ultimate principles could be seen independently of specific religious beliefs. One of the most influential of these philosophers was Immanuel Kant (1724–1804). It is especially instructive to consider Kant's version of deontology, because he tried with great care to reconstruct this traditional way of thinking about morality and make explicit what it says and the assumptions upon which it rests. Moreover, Kant's theory has been enormously influential.

Several concepts are important in understanding the deontological ethic defended by Kant. A review of these will make his theory more understandable and the contrast between deontology and consequentialism sharper. To begin with, Kant disagreed strongly with the hedonism of some of the utilitarians. Pleasure is not, Kant claimed, of intrinsic or inherent value; nor does the moral value or worth of an action lie in the effects or results it produces, whether these are measured by units of pleasure or satisfaction of preferences, or what have you. Suppose the boss decides not to read the confidential report handed him by the sales representative: He is afraid of the negative publicity that might flow from the disclosure that he obtained such secret information. Instead, the boss places the envelope in the mail back to the competitor. It might seem that the boss did a good deed, and his actions may actually wind up having better consequences for his firm in the long run than had he disregarded the *confidential* stamp and made use of the report's contents. But, Kant maintains, the boss's actions deserve no praise: He is due no moral credit for what he has done, since he did not act for a moral reason but for a purely prudential one. Consider another of the cases we discussed earlier. Your friend, lounging by the lake, sees a child in trouble in the shallow water. Let's modify the original scenario and suppose that your friend wades into the water and rescues the child. Later we discover that the apparent heroine in fact acted only because the child's parents owe her money, and she believed the "good deed" would hasten the repayment. Outwardly, Kant would say, your friend may have done the right thing, but surely she did not do it for the right reason. She acted selfishly, and hence her actions really have no moral value. An action is right, Kant claims, only if it is done just because it is the right thing to do, not because doing so will get you something you want, whether that be money, fame, or the pleasure of thinking yourself heroic.

But how, according to the deontologist, can I know that my actions are right? How can I know what my moral duties to others are? To grasp Kant's answers to these questions, we need to explore another aspect of his view.

■ *Deontology and the Categorical Imperative*

Kant assumed that whenever any of us does something deliberately, it is as though we are endorsing a private rule that we are choosing to follow. If I discover that my employer is in violation of state pollution laws and I decide to "blow the whistle" on him by writing to state authorities, I am effectively operating on the basis of a rule that says, "When I am convinced that my employer is violating the law, I will alert the law enforcement authorities." I may not say such a rule to myself in so many words, of course, but that is the rule I am implicitly endorsing. Kant called all such private rules *maxims,* and he believed that those who take morality seriously would never follow a maxim that did not conform to the most basic of all moral principles, which he called the *categorical imperative.*

An *imperative* is a command of the form "You should to this" or "You ought not to do that." Some commands or imperatives, Kant observed, are *hypothetical,* that is, conditional upon some fact or preference. Examples of hypothetical imperatives would include: "If you want to get hired, you should dress professionally"; "If you desire a raise, you ought to increase your productivity"; "If you want to avoid liability, you should improve your product design." Each of these hypothetical imperatives takes as given some end or goal already accepted or desired. Kant believed, however, that moral principles cannot command us in these merely hypothetical ways, since the demands of morality are not dependent upon how we feel or what we want. Feelings and desires are far too flimsy a basis for morality. After all, if the only reason you should act morally is that you feel like doing so or that you desire something in return, what happens when your feelings change (as they often do) or when your desire dissipates? Feelings and preferences are transient, and thus too undependable a foundation for genuine moral principles. Hypothetical imperatives can even take the form of immoral demands, followed by people pursuing their own ends, as when the unscrupulous corporate executive reasons that "If we are to stay competitive, we must break any laws that get in our way." For all of these reasons, Kant concluded, a moral imperative must be categorical or absolute: It must be unconditional, providing an enduring incentive to act rightly. It is a genuine moral command that says what we must do regardless of whether we want to do it.

The moral duties we have, as delineated in the deontological theory of Kant, are defined by the categorical imperative. Although Kant's discussion of the categorical imperative is notoriously complicated (he reformulated the idea in several ways throughout his writings), the essence of his thinking can be stated fairly straightforwardly. According to Kant, the basic and unconditional rule behind all moral thinking is that one ought *always to act only on that maxim which one can, without contradiction, will to be a universal law,* or, more simply, *act only in ways that you can, without contradiction, imagine everyone acting.* This basic principle, which is sometimes called the test of *universalizability,* is one that Kant was convinced we all rely upon, whether we are conscious of it or not, in our everyday moral thinking. This is the principle we have in mind when we reprove people who act wrongly with the question "How would you like it if everyone did that?" The moral education of children often proceeds on this basis, getting the child to place herself in the other person's shoes.

To determine whether an action is morally right, I must determine the maxim upon which it relies and then ask whether I could conceive of this maxim being a "universal law," that is, a rule for everyone similarly situated that could be followed without contradiction. So, for example, the general manager with his competitor's confidential report in his hand might pause to consider whether, if the situation were reversed, he would want the competitor to appropriate his confidential work product. Recall the case of Mr. O, the retail employer who calculates that he can save money by breaking a promise to his loyal, full-time worker and firing him, replacing him with cheap, part-time labor. As we saw, Mr. O's original promise of continued employment was a deceitful one, as he had known at the time he would not likely keep it. Kant would argue that his deontological conception of morality convincingly explains the judgment that Mr. O was acting wrongly in making just such a sham commitment. Mr. O acted on the basis of a maxim that could be expressed this way: "If it is to the advantage of my business, I will extend promises to my employees that I do not intend to keep." Remember that Kant's idea is to determine whether someone's action is morally right by asking what it would be like if their maxim were to be universalized, that is, if everyone were to act upon it. Kant observed that no one could, without contradiction, will the maxim of deceitful promising to be a universal practice; after all, if everyone followed this maxim, everyone would attempt to gain an advantage from a false promise. But, since no one would be fooled by such pretense, promises would no longer exist in such a world, and thus the making of a "false promise" would be impossible.

Consider one other example, involving the ethical standards of medical professionals. Imagine that you are a physician and that you have an elderly patient whose illness you have diagnosed as terminal. You have just told the members of the patient's immediate family the truth about her condition; they now request that you keep the truth from the patient herself. "It will make her final days easier," they plead. Uncertain how to proceed, you delay informing the patient of her status. The patient soon realizes she is not improving, however, and one day she confronts you: "What's going to happen to me, doctor? Am I going to die?" What should you say? To act as the family had requested would be tantamount to acting on a maxim that could be expressed this way: "If deceiving my patient will keep him or her from possible suffering and make others happy, I will do so." Could you "will" this maxim to be a universal practice? A Kantian moralist might well respond that you could not, that no rational person would want to live in a world where this practice was the norm. To see why the Kantian would likely give such an answer, we must look at one last aspect of Kant's deontology.

■ Deontology and Autonomy

We began our discussion of Kant by noting that acting morally, in his view, means doing what is right just because it is right: This is the only basis for action that has intrinsic worth and unconditional value. Kant tried to connect this idea with the claim that humans are rational beings in order to explain the value and importance of human life. Kant claimed that each person has an absolute worth, that each rational being exists as an "end in itself," that is, as a being valuable simply by virtue of being what it is. Each of us has an intrinsic value; we do not exist or have importance only because others can use us to suit their purposes. It is for this reason that Kant restates the categorical imperative as follows: *Always act so as to treat others as an end and never only as a means.* Notice that Kant is not saying that we may *never* use others as a means to something we might want. In fact, we use others all the time: Commuters use the bus driver to get them to work; shoppers use manufacturers to supply goods for purchase; workers use their employers as a source of income; and so on. What Kant says is forbidden is treating others *only* as a means: You may use the bus driver as a way to get around, but you must also acknowledge the driver as a person, not just a body in a uniform—as an individual with a life that matters. Kant is saying here that we must always respect the *autonomy* of others—the ability to take charge of one's own life and to live in accordance with valid moral principles rather than being led around by desires. Kant maintained that only human beings have the capacity to intentionally act in ways that are motivated by an awareness of moral duties. Autonomy is also often expressed in terms of the idea of self-determination: An autonomous person is a determiner of his or her own destiny; and moral relationships depend upon mutual respect for the autonomy of all rational beings. This suggests that respect for others involves, for example, helping them to further their own ends and goals.

The demand that we respect the dignity and worth of each and every person as autonomous beings may explain why no rational being could conceive of living in a world where lying to the dying person is a universal practice; for to deceive the patient in this way, a deontologist could argue, is an affront to his or her dignity as an autonomous person. We can now fully appreciate the contrast between Kant's deontology and the consequentialism of the utilitarians. The centerpiece of Kant's ethic is that to act morally is to act on principle—to do the right thing because it is right. This kind of deontological view insists that certain acts simply must not be done, regardless of the consequences that might flow from them. Even if it would make others extremely happy, it might still be wrong to conceal the truth or break a promise. To lie to or deceive another would be to use that person as a means to the happiness of others—and this one must not do. This last point connects with another that is often made by deontologists. What Kant says about autonomy and respecting the dignity of other persons is frequently expressed in the language of *rights:* To say that we must respect the lives of other autonomous beings is to say that they are entitled to or have a right to be so treated. A right typically is a claim that others do something for the person who holds the right (or that they refrain from doing something to him), and thus it correlates with a duty or obligation to act accordingly. For example, if X owes money to Y, Y has a right to the money and X has a duty to pay; if Mr. O promised that he would retain you in a certain job, we would say that Mr. O has a duty not to fire you, and you have a right not be fired. The language of rights seems to presuppose a division between the public boundaries limiting your actions—boundaries set by everyone's respective rights—and a private realm of choice within which each of us is free to develop and pursue our own plans and projects in life. To have a right is to occupy a kind of moral space within which one can operate as one pleases, to enjoy a sphere of autonomy or a realm of protected choices and interests.

When we speak of rights, of course, we are sometimes talking about legal rights, that is, rights secured and protected by the courts. Corporations have a number of legal rights, including the right to enter into contracts, the right to advertise products, and the right to sue others in court. Corporations, like other "persons," can also have moral rights, that is, rights supported by moral duties incumbent upon others, even though not necessarily recognized by the law. The exact nature of the rights held by corporations in our society bears directly on the issue of corporate social responsibility, and this can be seen by noting the distinction between *negative* and *positive* rights. A negative right, according to many social and political philosophers, is a right to be free of interference of others in the pursuit of one's goals and interests—a right that others *not* hinder that pursuit. So, for example, you and I each have the negative (legal) right to freedom of expression: We can express our views and speak our minds, and others are bound not to prohibit us from doing so. Corporations also have such negative rights: A corporation that enters into a contract with a supplier has the right to expect that others will not interfere with its freedom to make such business arrangements. Corporations also have the right to advertise and market their wares, free from the interference of others. No such rights are absolute, however. We are all familiar with certain limitations upon freedom of speech: I am not free to start a riot, for example; and the speech of corporations is also restricted in certain ways (which we discuss in chapter 7).

Negative rights are pretty straightforward. But what of positive rights? A positive right is a claim or an entitlement to be given some good or benefit—a right to the affirmative assistance of others. A worker may have the freedom to enter into employment contracts without interference, but if she cannot find work this negative right will be of little help. Under such circumstances, some philosophers have argued, workers have a positive claim upon society for some level of material or monetary assistance—until they can land a job. Similarly, I may have the right to express my views without interference; but if I am a political candidate with modest means, I may argue that I am entitled to have some broadcast time allotted to me, a claim necessitated by the fact that the airwaves are a limited resource which society controls. Whether workers or citizens have such positive rights is a question hotly debated among moral and political philosophers; and it is clear that the resolution of this issue relates directly to the question of corporate social responsibility. As we explore in later chapters, when workers claim that they have positive rights to a decent living wage and safe working conditions, or when citizens insist that they are entitled to a clean environment, it is plain that the duties and obligations of corporations are directly affected.

An important moral feature of rights is that they often counteract just those considerations that would be important from a consequentialist point of view: The fact of Mr. O's promise to you confers upon you a right that he keep you in his employ, and this is so even if Mr. O is persuaded that the greater good will be served by firing you. Just this feature of promises is reflected, for example, in the law of contracts, which empowers parties to whom certain kinds of promises have been made to have them enforced by a court. Deontologists sometimes describe this power of rights by saying that rights are like trump cards in a game of bridge—they take priority over other factors. (This is not always the case, of course, and few deontologists would declare that any given right is absolute, taking priority over everything else, including other rights.)

Before we look at some criticisms of deontological ethics, let's return again to the "Cooking the Books" case study involving Ben and Debra and see what role deontological reasoning might play in the moral dilemma Debra is facing. As we discussed earlier, Ben's remarks suggest that his thinking is proceeding largely along utilitarian lines: Lying to the prospective buyer is justified by the greater good that will come of such deception. Debra is deeply troubled by Ben's actions, and her misgivings may reflect the pull of deontological ethics. How might Kant's ethics analyze the situation? Suppose Debra were to go along with Ben and falsify the status report of the division. The basis for such a course of action might be expressed in the following maxim: "If lying to a potential buyer will improve my situation and that of my colleagues, I will do it." Could a rational person conceive of this rule being a universal practice? The bite of this question, of course, lies in forcing us to consider the possibility that the situation might one day be reversed—we might be the buyer about to be duped. Since we would not wish to be so cheated, it would appear that we could not will for such deception to be a universally sanctioned practice. In this way, Kant's deontology dictates that Ben's actions are wrong and that the buyer must not be deceived.

■ *Objections to Deontological Ethics*

Deontology, like consequentialism, has its critics. One of the most common complaints concerning Kant's version of deontology centers on what some perceive to be the excessive formality and abstractness of his view. Insisting that moral credit is to be awarded only to those who act solely for the sake of duty is often scorned as an arid, puritanical position, unconnected to any of the particular duties that arise out of the richness and diversity of human relationships; and though Kant may have shown us what morality is to be like if it is to be based on reason alone, few people actually live their moral lives in this fashion. Defenders of Kant respond that, though an action must be done from duty to be morally worthy, this is not incompatible with being a compassionate and loving individual. The happiness and satisfaction that comes from doing good for others is not banned from Kantian deontology, so long as they are accompanied by the proper motive for moral action.

More-specific criticisms focus on the categorical imperative itself. Critics question, for example, whether the categorical imperative always recommends one best course of action as the "right" one under the circumstances. Isn't it possible that different people, evaluating the same situation (evaluating, that is, the same maxim) might conclude that the categorical imperative demands two or more different actions? Kant seems to have thought that this would not happen, and in this he doubtless shared in the belief of many living during the

Enlightenment that human reason is universal, with requirements that are the same for everyone. But these are overly optimistic assumptions, say the critics, and the categorical imperative is so general and abstract that its requirements can easily be read in differing ways. Kant famously argued, for example, that suicide is morally impermissible when motivated by self-interest, since it is just that self-interest that is designed to ensure one's continued survival. Yet others have found suicide to be morally acceptable even when so motivated (for example, in the case of those who are ill and in terrible pain). Of course, Kant might insist that it depends on how the maxim for any given case is formulated; yet this too has attracted the ire of critics, who maintain that, without a means to determine the morally correct way to state a maxim, the possibility remains open that different people might evaluate a situation very differently. Again, to take another example, Kant seems to have thought that a maxim of the form "When it suits my interests, I will tell a lie" cannot pass the test of the categorical imperative. Yet suppose that if I tell a lie, I can save the life of my child. The maxim "When doing so will save a life, I will tell a lie" is one that some critics, at least, would insist *can* be universalized.

Nor does it help matters here for Kant to invoke the language of rights. Much of contemporary moral and social life is punctuated by appeals to "his right to this" and "her right to that," without any clear sense of how these often conflicting rights are to be weighed or measured against each other, or how conflicts between them are to be resolved. Utilitarians point out that a moral world in which people think only of exercising their rights is not necessarily a better world: A wealthy corporate executive may have the right to donate large amounts of money to the Ku Klux Klan or to groups of neo-Nazis; this fact, of course, is no guarantee that doing so would be the right thing to do. Rights can be exercised in a way that actually *increases* the unhappiness and disvalue in the world. Utilitarians might question whether the value of individual autonomy and choice is always such as to outweigh the disvalue that exercising rights can create.

VIRTUE AND THE ETHICS OF CHARACTER

Our discussion thus far has presented consequentialist and deontological theories as competing views of morality proceeding from very different starting points. It would be wrong to conclude, however, that consequentialism and deontology have nothing in common; for, as some philosophers, both ancient and contemporary, have observed, consequentialist and deontological accounts of moral life share a common assumption, one that reveals further shortcomings of each view, beyond the criticisms already discussed. What is this assumption and what could the shortcomings be?

Put most succinctly, both of the main ethical theories we have so far reviewed assume that morality is built upon some central rule or principle, which is claimed to be true or correct and which we must understand and follow if we are to be moral persons. It is true, as we have seen, that the principle of utility and Kant's categorical imperative do appear to identify quite different courses of action as "moral" under certain circumstances. Nonetheless, both theories take the most important fact about moral life to be identifying and following the right principle. This common assumption is one that some philosophers and moralists have challenged. This *principle-based* understanding of morality, the critics claim, often does not recommend a clear course of action in "real-life" situations. In this connection, we have already seen the limitations of the principle of utility and of the categorical imperative in picking out the "right thing to do." Moreover, the principle-based moral outlook suffers from the absence of any conclusive argument that one or the other purportedly "supreme" principle of morality is the "true" one. Neither the consequentialist nor the deontologist seems able to make a definitive case for his or her favored moral theory. Finally, critics allege, principle-based ethical theories tend to give rise to the cynicism of the amoralist at which we looked earlier. The inability of principle-based moralists to agree on much of substance invites the demand of the amoralist to be shown why he or she—or indeed anyone—should take morality seriously in the first place.

All of foregoing criticisms of principle-based moral views lead, so the critics imagine, to one further consequence of particular importance for the subject of ethics and business. This is that looking at ethics from the standpoint of principles makes it difficult to know how anyone in the world of business can be brought to take ethics more seriously. If the philosophers of principle-based morality cannot agree among themselves on which principle is the true basis of moral life, nor upon what implications the contending rules have in many real-life situations, it is hard to know what, for example, it would mean for a corporation to be a more responsible member of society, or what makes someone a "good" employer or employee. The central failing of the morality of rules and principles, according to the critics, is that it focuses only upon what people *do* and not upon what they *are:* It looks only at conduct and not at character. These critics, who support an ethics of character, claim that the most important moral question one can ask is not "What is the moral thing to do?" but rather "What kind of person should I be?" This character-based approach to ethics dominated the moral thinking of the ancient Greeks and Romans, in the western tradition, and has some contemporary defenders as well. Perhaps the most influential work on this view, now often called *virtue ethics,* was written by the Greek philosopher Aristotle. Let's look at Aristotle's efforts to elucidate a virtue-based approach to understanding morality.

■ *Virtue, Aristotle, and* Eudaimonia

According to Aristotle, the most basic question facing any of us is *What is the way of life that is valued in itself?* or (put another way), *What is the highest good for human beings?* For Aristotle, ethics is a branch of practical philosophy, which is concerned not with knowing for the sake of knowing, but knowing for the sake of doing—knowing how one should live. Aristotle used the Greek term *eudaimonia* to describe the state of well-being that he took to be the highest good for human beings. What is *eudaimonia?* Aristotle was well aware that opinions vary greatly on this score: Some (such as the hedonists) insist that the highest good is pleasure (and the avoidance of pain); some say it is wealth; others insist that it is honor. Aristotle rejected each of these views. Undistracted pleasure-seeking is beneath the station of human beings, as even animals can experience pleasure. Success, honor, and wealth, on the other hand, must be rejected because they each depend too heavily upon external circumstances: I cannot be honored unless others care about knowing who I am; I cannot be wealthy unless I can get and keep lots of money. But these contingencies may or may not come to pass. True well-being cannot be so transient and unreliable; it must be a constant that comes from within. The highest good, Aristotle believed, must be self-sufficient and something chosen for its own sake; it cannot be simply a means to something else, but something which by itself makes life desirable.

So what is the highest good? Aristotle tried to answer this question by appealing to one of the ideas of his teacher, the Greek philosopher Plato. Both Plato and Aristotle assumed that anything that does something has a function: The function of a carpenter is to build with wood; the function of a flute-player is to play the flute; the function of a plant or an animal is to live the kind of life that is appropriate to it. By the term *function,* Aristotle meant to refer to whatever can be done only by the individual or thing in question or, at least, what can be done by it better than by anything else. The function of any living thing, Aristotle reasoned, is to live. But life can be manifested at different levels: The ways in which a vegetable, for instance, shows that it is alive (by taking in water and nutrients, growing, and so on) are quite different from the activities of a human being. Human beings are rational: We are capable consciously of directing our lives by our own thought, and this, Aristotle believed, is the key to the highest good for us. The way to attain the highest good is to live in a way that is uniquely human, and this, for Aristotle, meant two things. It meant, first, that each of us must live in accordance with some kind of plan—a plan of life. As we grow older, more mature and more purposeful, we look further into the future and we try (or should try) to fit our various purposes into a coherent scheme for living. This imparts meaning to our lives. In saying that we must live rationally in this way, Aristotle is not maintaining that we become cold-hearted and calculating, empty of feeling. This itself would be a denial of an important part of our own nature. He is claiming that the best way of life is one in which each of us seeks to fit our feelings and desires into some coherent pattern. Living rationally also meant, for Aristotle, that we seek to live in a way calculated to lead to the most complete realization of our specifically human needs, capacities, and abilities—living a life that will allow us to flourish as human beings. There are some things, Aristotle believed, that humans need in order to live a good life. Biological necessities (food, clothing, shelter, and so on) clearly are required; but these are not sufficient. Human beings also have a need for love, friendship, and the acquisition of knowledge. Of course, we do not always seek such things, even if we do need them; and it is for this reason that many people do not lead happy lives: The quest for money and success, for example, may obscure our vision, thus preventing us from getting those things that we really need.

We began this discussion of Aristotle's ethics with the idea that morality has essentially to do with character, and we are now in a position to see what this meant for Aristotle and why he believed it to be the central fact of moral life. *Moral virtue*, according to Aristotle, is the habit of making right and wise choices. And each of us must know how to make such choices in order to ensure that we realize our needs and capacities as human beings. *Eudaimonia*, Aristotle concludes, is *an activity of the soul in conformity with moral virtue.* True well-being consists in becoming a person who habitually chooses wisely. This view reflects the claim that moral virtue and character are the product of habit. We are not morally virtuous by nature; we become so by acting or feeling virtuously. But what habits should we cultivate? How are we to be sure that we are choosing wisely?

The first and most fundamental guideline here, Aristotle says, is that we must learn to avoid extremes in our conduct and feelings. We often have the tendency to overindulge in pleasures or give in to the temptation to seek more of something than is good for us. One reason why bodily pleasures tempt us is that they can be enjoyed immediately. But the best way of life is one in which a person cultivates the ability to resist what appears to be good in the short run for the sake of what is really good in the long run. Similarly, the best way of life is one in which a person cultivates the habit to see money only as a means to other genuine goods, not as an end in itself. Aristotle thinks such habits reflect and reinforce the virtue of *temperance* or self-control: The habitual disposition to resist the temptation of immediate pleasure for the sake of more important goods that overindulgence in pleasure might prevent us from attaining. The virtue of temperance, then, lies between the extremes of over- and underindulgence. In the same way, Aristotle claims, all moral virtues are a mean or middle ground between the extremes that he labels vices. Courage, for example, is the disposition to undergo the hardships and struggles necessary to obtain what is really good for us and, as such, it avoids both the extremes of timidity or cowardice, on the one hand, and those of rashness or recklessness, on the other.

In explaining this doctrine of the mean, Aristotle is careful to point out that not all feelings and actions have a mean that we should seek to hit. Aristotle is not saying, for example, that it is permissible to become a thief or adulterer just so long as one does so in moderation.

The very names of these actions, he says, convey that they are already extremes and thus wrong. Theft, for example, is wrongful excess in the accumulation of wealth; adultery is wrongful excess of sexual expression; and so on. Habituating ourselves to choose the mean involves training our impulses and feelings to manifest themselves on the proper occasions, in the proper manner, and to the proper degree. In this Aristotle differed markedly from Kant. As we saw, Kant held that moral worth and value attaches only to actions done from a sense of duty, a sense that has nothing to do with our natural inclinations or feelings. Aristotle, on the other hand, claims that the way for people to become morally virtuous is precisely to train and refine their natural human responses and feelings in order to develop good moral character.

■ Objections to Virtue Ethics

It may seem, given all of his focus on character and moral virtue, that Aristotle's ethical theory recommends a life of self-absorption, the single-minded cultivation of personal character traits. But Aristotle argues against drawing such a conclusion. Many of the virtues Aristotle discusses—justice, friendship, "liberality" (or the willingness to give to others)—deal specifically with how one interacts with others. The person of fully cultivated virtues is one who must live in a community with others in order to live a truly full life, and the life of the community is vital to promoting human well-being.

An additional criticism of Aristotle's ethics raises a more significant issue. The ethics of virtue, critics argue, doesn't tell us what to do—it fails to provide any clear answer to what we should do in specific situations. A defender of Aristotelian ethics might agree with this point, but insist that this is not a fair objection. After all, Aristotelian ethics is not principle-based in the way that consequentialism and deontology are; and Aristotle might well say that looking to his view for specific guidelines on how to act is a mistake in the first place. The proper course of conduct is that which would be taken by the person of *practical wisdom*—the person of experience and good judgment. Practical wisdom is not something for which there exists a specific recipe or rule book—it is rather a matter of cultivating insight into how best to live. To see what this means, let's recall one last time the case of Debra and Ben and the sale of their division of Congent. Aristotle's ethics would have Debra ask the following questions: "What sort of person do I want to be? Do I want to be the kind of person who would deceive a potential buyer in a business transaction? Or do I want to be the kind of person who is honest even at the cost of my welfare and the welfare of others?" Ultimately, Debra must answer these questions for herself.

Still, it may seem that Aristotelian ethics offers too little guidance. What, for example, are the specific virtues that Debra, or you, or any of us, should seek to develop? In his writings Aristotle outlined his own list of specific virtues: One must be courageous, but not rash; one must be temperate, but not foolish; one must be "liberal" but not stingy; one must have proper pride, but not vanity; and one must be righteously indignant, but not malicious. In many ways this specific list of moral virtues reflects the culture of the ancient Greek world in which Aristotle lived. The principal Greek city-states of Aristotle's time, such as Athens, were not democratic and egalitarian, but elitist. There was a privileged class of citizens in the Athens of Aristotle's day, and in fact it was to that privileged group that Aristotle was primarily writing. It is not surprising, then, that his list of moral virtues reflects those traits most admired by the cultivated nobleman or gentleman of Athens. The quasi-military virtues of courage and self-control are prominent throughout Aristotle's writings on ethics, for example; and certain of his virtues, such as "liberality" and "magnificence" (living well materially) would not apply to the lives of the poor. Finally, it is clear that the complete cultivation of the moral virtues on Aristotle's list would require a degree of leisure and income not shared by all. The moral virtues esteemed by Aristotle also differ sharply from those advocated in a later era by the Christians of the Middle Ages: Faith, hope, charity, and humility (the vice of deficiency of self-respect for Aristotle) would not have been regarded by Aristotle himself as ennobling traits of character.

Contemporary defenders of virtue ethics have tried to move away from Aristotle's own particular list of virtues and approach understanding virtues in a more general way. Crucial to the notion of a moral virtue, these contemporary Aristotelians argue, is the social context to which they are necessarily linked. Some of the most valued and prized "goods" in life can be obtained only when one joins with others in activities that have a value all their own. When someone joins a club or performs in a musical band, for example, she is participating in something larger than herself that is valuable and enjoyable just for what it is, not simply as a means to something else (money, for instance). To be viable, such essentially social activities require a shared recognition of the goal to be achieved, and every participant shares in the common project of creating and sustaining that activity. In this way, the virtue-ethicist says, we can say that a moral virtue is any character trait or excellence necessary to the ongoing viability of the activity. Cooperative human activity always requires bonding with others, the forging of relationships among those participating. And there will be certain traits—for example, truthfulness, courage, justice—without which the activity could not continue: When musicians perform they cannot be antagonistic or distrustful, as this will undermine their joint ability to create something of value.

How might the understanding of virtue ethics of these contemporary Aristotelians apply to the business world? One suggestion would be to think of a business as a cooperative venture, the aim of which is to supply goods and services to the wider community, and within which the roles of each person contribute to the intrinsic value of the business as a supplier of goods and services. One does not work merely to earn money, in this view; instead, one's work becomes valuable just because it contributes to the greater project. And those character traits necessary to the attainment of that intrinsic end are the virtues important in the business world. Critics of this view point out that the precise nature of the virtues appropriate to business is still unclear; and they question the degree to which business can be compared to such cooperative endeavors as music. Though we may agree that the creation of a wonderful piece of music is an end in itself, is the same really true of doing business? Is business an end in itself? Or only a means to a paycheck and material comfort?

THE CANONICAL VIEW OF BUSINESS SOCIAL RESPONSIBILITY

We began earlier by examining what we can now see to be a basic moral question: Does a corporation have a moral responsibility to be a "good citizen"? Now that we understand the dimensions of moral reasoning a bit more clearly, let's turn to this question and explore it further.

The idea that business should behave socially like a "good citizen" and implement livable wages, provide safe working conditions, and protect domestic workers, is not necessarily applauded by businesspersons and economists. In fact, the claim that business social responsibility *ends* with profit maximization and obeying the law is a well-received view— so well received that we refer to it as the *canonical view* of business social responsibility.

The view is composed of two tenets of neoclassical economics—the kind of economics you typically study in your "econ" classes. The first is an assumption about human nature. Human beings are self-interested, we are told, and they are motivated to do whatever it takes to satisfy their individual desires. Further, human beings are relatively indifferent about how their actions affect others. This does not imply that they are mean or spiteful, just that they tend to be disinterested about those effects. Given what we learned in the previous sections, you should recognize this theory as a form of psychological egoism. As a theory of human motivation, it has a long and distinguished pedigree, going back to the philosopher Thomas Hobbes in the seventeenth century and even before. The second tenet is based on the first, and it has to do with the nature of corporations. These comprise individuals who are self-interested. The shareholders want a return on investment, which is produced by labor for compensation. Hence, corporations involve relationships that are essentially self-interested also. The goal of a corporation is to maximize net returns or profits (profit maximization).

These tenets appear to be a descriptive claim about how firms and people actually work. People attempt to better themselves and do attempt to satisfy their desires. One way of doing this is by working for compensation, which gives you the means of satisfying those desires. Another way is by investing money in a corporation that is dedicated to maximizing profits for the people who invest the money. Money provides the means of satisfying those preferences which in the end make you happy. What about corporations? If you could look at the daily workings of an industrial giant like I.B.M. and of your local video store, they would have this feature in common: They're about making money, and their efforts are coordinated to achieving that end.

As a statement about how economic institutions and consumers in our society function, these tenets seem plausible (i.e., from "the armchair," to use a phrase from Daniel Hausman, this appears to be reasonable approximation). Some economists have complained that there is scant empirical evidence to show that these statements are in fact true.[10] But that doesn't bother most economists and business theorists. The canonical view of business social responsibility extends this descriptive claim into a moral claim about how things ought to be. It says that at least with respect to the economic aspects of people's lives, they ought to be self-interested and that firms ought only to maximize profits while obeying the law. This is a value claim of some significance. The reason for making it is the belief that if firms are allowed to maximize profits and obey the law, society as a whole will be better off (we considered this claim in the last section of the introduction). This view of business is connected with a view about society. An efficient society should divide the labor among its institutions. A society's economic institutions should generate capital and wealth; a society's political institutions should determine how the wealth should be distributed (e.g., through taxation for social programs) and address those social problems created by the economic institutions by means of laws and regulations. In other words, law and, in particular, regulation hold the reins on the profit-maximizing behavior of individuals and corporations.

Often we hear the platitude that it would be much better if government kept out of the way of business entirely. The canonical view does not suggest this. Imagine an economy in which government did not protect corporate property rights, or allowed corporations to engage in deception and coercion in their dealings with consumers, or in which there were no environmental regulatory agencies. The result would be chaotic. There would be no reason to believe that economic activity would lead to society's welfare. Hence, there have to be some limitations on corporate activity. So government must protect the interests of society, on the one hand, while at the same time make the economic environment conducive to commercial interests, on the other. It does this through regulation and corporate law, which are written to protect individuals, property, and natural resources. In effect, society through the law moralizes corporate behavior. Here's where business social responsibility enters into the discussion: According to the canonical view of business, business social responsibility means obeying these societal laws. So a socially responsible business maximizes profits but is limited in this pursuit. This is essentially how morality and commerce are seen to relate. As you can see, this approach to business responsibility is quite a bit different from the one we sketched in the beginning of this section—the "good citizen" view—which imputes to business certain non-economic social responsibilities. According to the canonical view, business's moral obligations to society are simply legal constraints on profit maximization ordained by society.

■ *Milton Friedman on Corporate Social Responsibility*

One of the clearest examples of this canonical view of business social responsibility and its implications is found in a short essay written by the Nobel Prize–winning economist Milton Friedman. This now classic article entitled "The Social Responsibility of Business Is to Increase Its Profits" appeared first in the *New York Times* magazine in 1970.[11] It is so influential that it is reprinted or mentioned prominently in almost every business ethics text. In this article Friedman presents moral arguments that attempt to justify the canonical view of business social responsibility. In a nutshell, Friedman argues that management's single moral duty is to maximize shareholder wealth—but within certain limitations such as obeying the law. Managers who attempt to do anything else (e.g., by adopting any of the broad aims of social responsibility mentioned above) are either unfair to the firm's investors or act irresponsibly toward society at large. This section examines Friedman's arguments that attempt to establish this thesis.[12] It is important to note to his credit that Friedman, unlike other proponents of the canonical conception of business social responsibility, *does* offer arguments for his position rather than simply assert that his position is true. Doing the latter is uninteresting, since exactly what we want to know is *why* the canonical view should be adopted over the "good citizen" view. Additionally, his arguments are interesting to us, as students of ethics, because they are arguments about the nature of business moral responsibility (as opposed to arguments about economic efficiency and the like). Finally, his arguments are interesting because they have an initial plausibility resting on appeals to commonsense notions of fairness and responsibility. In what follows we use Friedman as a spokesperson for the canonical view of business social responsibility.

Friedman begins his article by claiming that the proponents of the broad view of corporate social responsibility (i.e., the idea that "corporate social responsibility" means more than profit maximization and obeying the law) are guilty of an intellectual incongruity. The very phrase *social responsibility of business*, which is what the debate is supposed to be about, is an oxymoron, since only human beings can have moral responsibilities. Corporations may consist of the interactions of human beings in various roles, but they are not human beings themselves. Hence, they cannot be the bearer of the weighty notion of moral responsibility. If that phrase is meaningful, says Friedman, it must refer to those individuals charged with the operation of the corporation—its owners or those who act for them, the individual managers. Because most corporations are run by hired managers, and most corporate actions are at least the indirect result of this latter class of people, his discussion is limited to them.

The claim that corporations cannot have moral responsibilities is subject to debate. Against Friedman, some philosophers have thought that it is indeed possible to speak of corporations as moral persons themselves—at least in some sense.[13] After all, we do speak this way. We say, for instance, that Exxon was responsible for the *Exxon Valdez* oil spill disaster, and that a firm should be punished for damages it causes, and so on. When we make such statements, they may not be directed at a particular person employed by Exxon. Instead they may be directed at the corporation itself, whose actions are the object of our moral criticism. Friedman implies that when we talk about moral responsibility, those statements that have as their subject a corporation do not make sense and need to be paraphrased[14] into statements about the people in charge of corporate operations (e.g., Exxon's

CEO, the corporate officers in charge of transportation, or the ship's captain). After all, Friedman might point out, even though we may say things like "Exxon is responsible for the oil spill," we nevertheless cannot put Exxon in prison. Which view is appropriate is subject to debate, and we won't try to settle it here.

■ The Agent/Principal Model

What kind of individuals are managers and what is their special relationship to corporate social responsibility? A corporate executive is like any other individual whose private life is structured around clusters of commitments and interests. She may have duties to family, religion, and political and social allegiances that give meaning to her life and which might involve considerable expenditure of time and money. But in her role as a corporate executive, her obligations are different and much narrower. As a manager she is an employee of the shareholders and owes the shareholders a certain moral duty. A manager has, as Friedman puts it, a "direct responsibility" to the employers. That responsibility is to conduct business in accordance with the employers' desires and in compliance with the law.

And what is it that the employers (i.e., the shareholders) desire? Friedman is explicit in his answer. He says that they desire to make as much money as possible while, of course, conforming to the regulations of society both explicitly mentioned in the law and also embodied in ethical custom.[15] The whole debate about corporate social responsibility for him concerns the activities of those individuals who manage corporations by acting to fulfill the desires of the owners. Corporate social responsibility is a three-part relationship of the shareholders, their desires, and the manager.

Friedman's article is probably as concise a statement of corporate social responsibility as exists in print. It implies, in accord with both traditional common law and economic theory, that managers are *agents* who act for the interests of their *principals* (i.e., the employers or shareholders). Although you may not have heard the words *agent* and *principal* so used, this agent/principal model is probably familiar to everyone. Agents are individuals with special knowledge and powers, who provide services for the benefit of the individuals they represent. In return they are remunerated with material compensation. Doctors, lawyers, engineers, and auto mechanics fall into this category. A doctor, for instance, can make recommendations about a patient's health or treat an illness by virtue of knowledge and skills he has acquired through formal education, training, and experience; an attorney can navigate a client through the rocky shoals of the legal system, an auto mechanic can repair an engine with problems, and so on.

Because the interests of their clients are vested in them, and since clients cannot typically act in their own behalf, professionals owe certain duties to their clientele—above all, not to violate their trust or harm their interests. Thus almost every professional organization (e.g., the American Medical Association, the American Society of Mechanical Engineers, and the American Bar Association) has established professional codes of conduct which articulate the duties and responsibilities of its members.[16]

As we've suggested, Friedman believes that managers and shareholders are in an agent/principal relationship similar to these other professionals. But there are some significant differences. Typically, a doctor or a lawyer has one or a small number of principals, who are called upon to solve a single medical or legal problem. But a multinational corporation has perhaps many thousands of principals, and these spread over many lands. This fact will be seen as significant later in this discussion. A doctor's activities on behalf of her client can affect the patient and his family. But multinational corporate actions can affect a wide range of individuals—more than just the principals. Imagine that a production line is shut down in some facility. The shareholders might be made wealthier because of the savings in labor costs, but people other than shareholders are affected by a production line closing. Workers, consumers, and the local community that supports the product line can be displaced and have their economic prospects threatened or dashed.

Most people believe that the interests of others are important and should provide a constraint upon action at least insofar as those interests are given consideration before action. So, the effect of the closure on the interests of the affected parties should be considered. But the agent/principal model seems to favor the interests of the principals over those of everyone else. That this seems to be so invites the complaint that the scope of the agent/principal model is too narrow to provide a basis for corporate social responsibility, at least in the context of modern global capitalism. A commonsense moral consideration would have people responsible for the parties affected by their intentional actions (assuming that they can foresee those effects). The consequences of your action on others, even your action on behalf of someone else, *is* an important moral consideration (as utilitarianism rightly points out). In terms of the agent/principal model, this would imply that the manager as agent must consider the effect of the corporate action on those parties who will be affected by that action. But the agent/principal model in the context of multinational management is silent about these other parties—in fact, it seems to ignore their interests altogether. It says that the agent should strive to maximize profits because that is what all the principals want. Presumably, the other parties' interests would be protected by law. This, of course, assumes the existence of law—in many poorer countries there is scant legal protection for laborers. Furthermore, as we indicate in the following section, there is much harm a corporation can do while still being in compliance with corporate law and regulation. So if this commonsense moral consideration is correct, there would have to be a compelling argument made by proponents of applying the agent/principal model to corporations to show that ignoring these other parties is morally justifiable.[17]

■ *Agents and Conflicts of Interest*

There are other criticisms regarding the efficiency of the agent/principal model. One common problem is conflict of interest. These are cases in which professional judgment is warped by the agent's interests. The result of this might be a bad judgment for the principal in which she suffers harm by having her interests frustrated. Again, this is a common problem. An auto mechanic might make unnecessary repairs in order to line his pockets. A judge might decide a case in favor of a corporation in which the judge has substantial holdings. Both of these cases entail satisfying the agent's economic desires and frustrating the principals'.

But conflict of interest doesn't necessarily imply an economic motive on the part of the agent. Another common case of conflict of interest occurs when an agent's "moral preferences" interfere with the interests of the principal. Imagine, for instance, that you are an engineer who is ordered by your employers to design a product using inferior materials. As an engineer you have internalized certain moral values about the practice of engineering. You believe that you have a moral obligation in your role as engineer to produce products that are safe for the public, and you believe, further, that the production of this product will endanger the public. In this case, there is a conflict between the agent's interest in being dutiful to the employer and the agent's interest in pursuing the moral ideals of the practice of engineering. The result of this tension might be an act of whistleblowing to some public agency. That act may not be in the interest of a firm that is concerned solely with profit maximization.

The advice that professional organizations typically offer their membership is to avoid even potential conflicts of interest or at least to disclose them to the principals (e.g., rather than whistleblow, report your concerns to the proper corporate officials). The agent is to be a pure tool of the principal. Whether or not it is psychologically possible for an agent to strip herself entirely of self-interests—economic or moral—is an interesting question. But doing just that is what seems to be required by this model.

The agent/principal model in the context of the corporate life is rife with conflict-of-interest problems. Remember that according to economic theory, individuals are self-interested, so employees, including managers, are assumed to be self-interested. In its most general form, the problem is this: How can one get an employee to set aside her set of interests and to act in the interest of her principal? How can a firm prevent a manager from stealing trade secrets and taking them to a competitor who has hired him? How can it keep an employee from whistleblowing? How can the corporation prevent an employee from taking sick days for recreational outings, or from standing around, idly chatting at the watercooler? Actions such as these impose costs on the firm, some of them significant. There is copious literature suggesting solutions to these difficulties. Two suggested solutions loom large: the stick and the carrot. Both of these methods appeal to the self-interested nature of the agent. The firm can attempt to bar such behavior by supervision of employees or by contracts that prevent these cost-imposing actions. Or the firm can attempt to promote employee loyalty through generous benefit packages, ethical-training seminars, and so forth. Both of these methods are only moderately successful and, as you might imagine, they tend to be very expensive. An agent might decide to be disloyal and even suffer legal sanctions if she judges that such actions are in her best interest. Or she might gamble that the contract will not hold up in court. The problem of aligning the interests of agents and principals has led some to be skeptical of any workable solution. Ironically, the assumption of individual self-interest made by the canonical view requires that one appeal to self-interest in order to make an individual act in a non–self-interested manner.[18] In the end, the problem is that you cannot extract loyalty from self-interest. Moral admonitions about duty and professional ideals are hollow against that background.

■ *The Ideal of Profit Maximization*

Like most economists, Friedman claims that the single interest of shareholders is maximum profitability and that this is the goal management and employees are morally obligated to pursue. Most managers embrace this ideal. After all, profitability is what allows you to keep your job and what allows for those generous compensation packages. If this is a moral principle, it would seem that it should apply in all circumstances; but some managers apply it only selectively. A manager justifies cutting wages and benefits to employees or relocates a facility in a country where labor is cheaper by appeal to "business necessity." Labor is, after all, expensive. Usually, this means that the decision maximizes profits although it imposes significant costs on the employees. But the directive of profit maximization would also seem to imply reducing wage costs in other sectors of the corporation. Imagine that the manager takes a hefty salary for her efforts to direct the firm, say, ten million per year. This is not far-fetched—many managers in the United States make considerable salaries. Imagine that the manager could do well at half that amount—after all, she has asked the employees to do well on less than their former wage. Shouldn't the principled manager give back $5 million to the shareholders in dividends? This, of course, rarely happens. The manager is considered essential personnel. Anything less than $10 million a year would be an insult and a motive for the manager to begin looking for a different corporation to manage. (After all, managers are self-interested.) If she has an established reputation in the industry, this might be easy. So the directive to maximize profits with respect to labor seems limited in its scope. Employees are expected to give back wages, but managers rarely are.

Friedman does suggest that the principals *could* offer directives to management other than profit maximization. Remember that the fundamental moral obligation of the agent is to pursue the interests of the principal. This is what is owed the principal in that model. It is conceivable that the principals' desire is not maximum profitability—or not profitability at all. Friedman is aware of this, and he mentions in passing the example of a managed charity. But, of course, running a charity and running a business are different matters. Business should apply itself to economic goals, not social ones, according to the canonical view of social responsibility. People are self-interested at least in their economic relations. So shouldn't the firm maximize profits?

Without denying that business should apply itself to economic ends, it is at least questionable why the goal of every business and every manager should be to maximize profits. It's easy to think of other possibilities. Maybe the goal should be to produce goods and services for society at a reasonable return for shareholder investment. This is consistent with social responsibility in the "good citizen" sense. Is it possible that this more modest economic imperative is one that shareholders might endorse?

One reason why you might answer no is that you believe that people are rabid egoists. So in all their dealings, including economic matters, they would want to satisfy their desires maximally regardless of the effects. If they desire profit, it would ideally be maximum profit. But most of us aren't like that. We don't conduct ourselves in our personal relationships on the economic model of agent and principal. We do not conceive of our relationships to our spouses and children as economic quid pro quos, in which we agree to do things for them only if they do comparable things for us. We do not endorse ethical principles after first performing a cost/benefit analysis. People's conception of morality permeates all facets of their life—even the economic aspects. They react with sympathy to the plight of others, even if those others are not members of their immediate family. They keep promises, even though keeping them results in personal costs. They don't try to extort money, even if they believe that they can get away with it. They don't lie, even though they won't get caught. The general tendency toward morality is what keeps civil society civil. But that general tendency is also what allows markets and capitalism to work. Imagine that businesspersons committed fraud and coercion, broke contracts, and so on whenever it furthered their self-interest. The chaos that ensued would destroy commerce. Sure, there are laws that prohibit these activities, but these have force only because businesspeople honor them, not out of fear of detection and sanctions, but because they think it's the right thing to do.

All of this suggests that the assumption of self-interest, which is the central tenet of the canonical view, is false. There is no denying that people invest in corporations because they seek a high rate of return on their investments. It is not a moral fault to try to enhance your financial well-being or put away some money for your retirement or your children. But do all investors require maximized profits as Friedman suggests? Some may not if those actions involve harming others. Here's where the law is supposed to enter in. The law regulates corporate behavior; but, unfortunately, the law does not provide a shield against harm. There are many corporate actions that are profit-maximizing and legal and can still injure the prospects of nonshareholders. Legal scholar Christopher D. Stone has cited several reasons why this is the case. Some of these are as follows:

- **Time-lag problems:** The law is primarily a reactive institution. Regulative law often comes *after* some social ill has occurred. In creating it lawmakers have to respond to problems that managers anticipated long before, for example, that the drugs their corporations are about to produce can alter consciousness or damage the gene pool of the human race, that they are on the verge of multinational expansion that will endow them with the power to trigger a worldwide financial crisis in generally unforeseen ways, and so on.

- **Limitations on lawmaking:** Corporations play a large role in the creation of law itself. They lobby for laws protecting their interests and against laws injurious to them. In certain sectors of the economy (e.g., food, drug, and cosmetic markets), the overseeing government agency might simply adopt the safety rules worked out by industry, whether or not these rules are effective barriers to harm; the regulating agency may be staffed with industry personnel who are charged with regulating the industry; or the regulating body simply may not have the information (which might not be forthcoming from the corporation) or the technical expertise to answer questions concerning the health risks to workers exposed to, for example, asbestos or pesticides.

- **Limitations connected with implementing the law:** Even if legislation is created and plaintiffs file suit under the respective regulations, the cases the courts or agencies hear may be overly technical and complex, or too expensive to enforce properly; and the law may be badly written.

Stone comments that there is something grotesque and socially dangerous in encouraging corporate managers to believe that they have no responsibilities other than obeying the law.[19] Laws restricting the economic activities of firms are created through legislative processes that occur only after court battles and the lobbying efforts of businesses are defeated. What results is usually the product of a compromise between private and public interests.

An example might help make this clear. In its quest for profit maximization, a firm may disinvest a U.S. facility, leaving many workers without jobs and without reasonable prospects for gainful employment. Or a firm might relocate a facility in a country that has few or no child labor laws, or it might arrange to dump its toxic waste unsafely in a cash-poor Third World country. Or a firm might find it advantageous to close a U.S. facility entirely and reopen another in the Third World. Are these steps profit-maximizing? Quite possibly. Labor costs are considerable, especially union labor. Are such closings consistent with public interests? The argument that they are claims that the profits will be reinvested in the U.S. economy, meaning more jobs, and the decreased labor costs mean cheaper goods for U.S. consumers. So the closures are justifiable and the corporation's responsibilities might consist only in a mandatory advisement of an impending closure.

But, say critics like Stone, the unemployed workers must now find new jobs or retrain. If the disinvestment is industrywide, finding new jobs might be impossible. Workers who haven't the financial resources may not be able to retrain. A similar situation exists in cases of shutdowns and mergers. In February 1996, AT&T announced that it would downsize its operations and lay off forty thousand employees. A similar loss of employment (ten thousand jobs) occurred in the same year when Wells Fargo Bank announced the takeover of First Interstate Bank. First Interstate's top management got "golden parachutes" amounting to millions of dollars. The other employees were not so lucky. In both cases, stocks soared and the investors became wealthier.

Corporate actions can lead to significant reduction of costs and higher profitability and be perfectly legal. Yet they can also impose considerable harm on employees and innocent third parties. Layoffs and shutdowns are, of course, subject to some regulation, and perhaps no business manager takes delight in unemployment and pollution. But for the most part, these actions are seen by business and policy makers as business necessities—part of the social cost of capitalism which serves the interests of shareholders and management.

But reflecting on the foregoing discussion suggests that awareness of cases like this might give even a prudent investor pause. Is maximum profitability worth these social costs? Do I want a few dollars more in dividends—or even a lot more—if the cost is unemployment for thousands? Do I want to send my kids to college on profits resulting from the exploitation of children (albeit in some other country) or of the environment? Would any of us direct the corporation to maximize profits if this is what resulted? That is an open question. Some would say yes and rest easy. There is unemployment insurance. They're not my children. But some individuals might be willing to sacrifice maximum profitability to avoid these social ills. When thinking about the implications of profit maximization, some would discover that what they really want is simply a good return on their investment, and this return should be made without harming others. The suggestion here is that at least some investors may not be indifferent to the plight of others affected by their corporate investments. They might not desire that profits be maximized if the result is unemployment or exploitation. Or they may desire profit maximization but insist that it come about without harming the interests of others.[20] Note that even this possibility is consistent with the canonical view's core assumption of self-interest. What these investors discover is that they have a moral interest that supercedes their economic interests; that is, that there are moral considerations that constrain the desire for profit maximization even if the harmful corporate actions are legal and exist with the blessings of our legislators and economic planners.

■ *The Forums for Corporate Social Responsibility*

If we assume that the people described in the preceding discussion are direct investors in a corporation (or perhaps vested in a mutual fund or are contributors to a pension fund), it would seem that a manager's moral duty, according to the canonical view of business responsibility, is to heed those desires, or at least consider them when they direct corporate actions. After all, they are the principals. So one would expect that managers would regularly question their shareholders about what they desire, or at least that there would be some mechanism through which the issue of social responsibility could be addressed by the principals.

But there are virtually none. Part of the problem has to do with investment. Typical investors have very little information about how their dividends have been produced. And many investors simply don't care. To those who believe in expanding the range of corporate social responsibility, this fact is deplorable. If you are investing in a corporation, you ought to know what it's doing to bring you your dividends. If you disagree with the manner in which the corporation gets its profits, say, by exploiting child labor in a poor country, you should abandon it and invest somewhere else. A corporation that lost a lot of investors this way would probably rethink the way it does business.

By far the most popular investment tool today for most people is the mutual fund, which accounts for roughly 50 percent of investments in the stock market (this figure is climbing). Investors in Fidelity Investments, American, or Mutual Series Fund, Inc., will find that their contributions are distributed over hundreds of international companies, about the business of which investors know little and of which they may never have heard. To keep track of their business practices here and abroad would be impossible. So why not invest in a socially responsible mutual fund? By all accounts, these make up about 10 percent of the mutual fund market today and can be as highly diversified as commercial mutuals. It is hard to tell if the corporations of the fund are really acting in a socially responsible manner, or whether they've acquired new profit-maximizing management, or whether they've fallen victim to a hostile takeover or a merger. Furthermore, the effects of socially responsible mutual funds on the business practices of large multinational corporations are minimal. They can call upon a multinational to exercise responsibility, but that doesn't mean that it will listen. Usually, socially responsible investors must content themselves with symbolic gestures and not a change of corporate conduct.

In February 1997 Disney's stockholders were called upon to approve what some took to be CEO and Chairman Michael Eisner's engorged salary; at the same time, they were to vote upon two resolutions tied to social and environmental causes and to the monitoring of the potential use of sweatshops abroad. Management opposed these socially responsible efforts. A floor fight over the resolutions was led by some socially progressive mutual funds. But the best they expected from it was publicity—and that depended on the press and whether it deemed the floor fight worth reporting. "If successful," said Conrad MacKerron, director of social research of Progressive Asset Management, which holds 265,000 shares of Disney, "the business press might write that 97 percent voted a resolution down. We say that if we can get 3 percent to focus on it, given how hard it is to get the attention of shareholders, it's a kind of victory."[21] Instead, the press reported only on Eisener's raise.

Another natural forum for shareholders' interests is the board of directors, which is elected at annual stockholder meetings. Couldn't a firm's board of directors act as a kind of watchdog over corporate improprieties? By law the board is supposed to select management and supervise the conduct of the managers. These powers seem enormous. The board's actions could provide an internal check on the activities of the corporation through such supervision. So you could try to elect those members of the board who would represent your conception of corporate social responsibility. Assuming you were successful, and this is a big assumption as we will see, there are reasons to think that there would likely be no practical impact.

According to business theorist Peter Drucker, one thing that all modern boards of directors have in common regardless of their legal position is that they do not function.[22] Most big corporations have disinvested their boards of directors of any real supervisory powers. Myles Mace discussed this issue after interviewing hundreds of corporate officials. His findings: The board of directors rarely establishes corporate objectives and strategies; in fact, it almost always gives blanket approval to the recommendations of management. John C. Coffee makes the same point more forcefully: "Boards do not set policy, do not veto management, seldom intervene short of major crisis, and do not even select their own successors or the next chief executive officer."[23] This fact should not be surprising, since board members are usually nominated by management (as in the Disney example), which is free to use corporate funds to see that its candidates are elected. Let's say you wanted to elect social activist Ralph Nader to the board of the corporation in which you are vested. You could try. You would have to run your campaign out of your own pocket. If management disapproved, it would probably have a lot more resources available to finance the original solicitation to shareholders and the followups.

The active participation of shareholders in corporate decision making is just what Friedman's model of corporate social responsibility would seem to call for. Managers and shareholders, or their representatives, should have a forum in which they can raise their concerns and express their interests about how dividends are produced and how people are affected by those decisions. The critics of Friedman's model claim that this does not happen and, practically speaking, cannot happen; and, they argue, this implies that there is something wrong with Friedman's model of corporate social responsibility. If managers as agents are unconnected in this important respect with their clientele, how can they pursue their clients' interests?

Let's return to our first question: Why hold that a manager's duty is to maximize profit? One reason, of course, is the presumption that shareholders are greedy because people are self-interested and indifferent to the fate of others. This assumption about human nature may be false, since many investors indeed seem concerned about how their dividends are produced. If this is so, profit maximization should not be seen as carte blanche to act as one pleases; the interests of others affected by corporate action are important. So the argument must be made that managers have a moral responsibility to maximize profits and this case must be made independent of the truism that shareholders always seek maximum profits. This argument is made by Friedman.

■ *Friedman's Arguments for Profit Maximization*

Friedman argues that managers have no other choice *but* to maximize profits. He provides two arguments for the conclusion that pursuing anything other than profit maximization is either being irresponsible to society or unfair to shareholders and is morally objectionable on the grounds of "consequences and principle."

Let us consider, first, the argument about consequences. Suppose a manager wishes to promote a social good by way of some corporate action. Friedman uses the example of inflation. Assume that inflation is skyrocketing and the manager sees this phenomenon as a social evil that should be addressed by an action of the corporation. So the manager holds down the prices of goods. Friedman asks how the manager will know that this action will reduce inflationary pressures. Although the manager is presumably an expert at conducting a business, she is not an expert on inflation. The low product prices might result only in more consumer money going toward other goods and services in the economy—in which case inflation would still spiral upward. Or it might result in product shortages, in which case consumers' preferences will be frustrated. To use a more contemporary example, suppose that a manager wishes to prohibit child labor in an offshore facility where child labor is a current practice. Would this individual action on the part of the manager really help protect the interest of children in the host country? What if the unemployed children are then left with nothing to do, since in this nation there are no care facilities or schools where they can be looked after? The host nation might then have to invest in such institutions or else be faced with hordes of children engaging in acts of hooliganism or left to the influence of predators. Furthermore, although one company banishes child labor, it doesn't follow that other companies will. Won't the cheap labor give those companies a competitive advantage? Although these consequences might be unintentional, they are nonetheless real possibilities. The point, according to Friedman, is that a socially responsible act by a manager might well lead to bad consequences for a society (this society or another). Presumably, this will be true regardless of what her objectives are and even if she had the full support of the shareholders. The implication is that managers simply don't have the social or economic knowledge required to guide the corporation in a socially responsible manner, if that expression means more than maximizing profits and obeying the law. Managers should rather apply themselves to profit maximization—something they do know about. To do anything else can cause harm to both corporation and society.

To critics of Friedman, this argument is not convincing. You cannot derive a general conclusion about the ills of social responsibility, they insist, from a consideration of a few cases. It is perfectly possible that a manager could act in a socially responsible manner and not damage the firm or society. Imagine that the manager decides to invest in equipment that reduces pollution below what is regulated by law. Perhaps the motive is that existing regulation is too lax. Assuming the investment is not too burdensome to the firm and does not threaten its financial well-being, society will benefit. By forbidding the host country from using child labor in its facilities, a U.S. firm may lose a temporary competitive advantage. Indeed, it might not maximize profits. But it might be to the overall advantage of the firm not to be singled out by consumer and child advocates as one that uses child labor or whose foreign facilities are sweatshops. So, the critics conclude, whether an action by the ethically motivated manager is destructive depends upon the circumstances: One would have to decide on a case-by-case basis.

Friedman's second argument concerns the unfairness of socially responsible actions.

Think again of the socially responsible manager who wishes to curb inflation or to enforce U.S. work standards. Doing this or some other socially responsible action could benefit some people. But, according to this argument, not the right people. To use the inflation example, some consumers might benefit from the reduced price of goods. But someone has to pay for it, and in this case it is the shareholders, who, according to Friedman, expect maximized profits. This cost imposition, suggests Friedman, is like a tax on the shareholders. Of course, there is nothing wrong with reasonable taxes; they provide for public goods that are otherwise unobtainable (for example, national defense). Friedman's point is not that taxation is necessarily bad; the problem is rather that the manager in the exercise of social responsibility is making the decision unilaterally. The shareholder is not represented in this decision. As Friedman says of such cases, the manager is simultaneously legislator, executive, and jurist. It is she who decides whom to tax, by how much, and for what purpose. For any tax to be justified, it must result from democratic legislative, judicial, and executive processes which ensure that the taxes are imposed in accordance with the desires of the public. Anything else is taxation without representation. By analogy, the socially responsible manager who wishes to promote social causes other than profit maximization imposes costs without the representation of the shareholders. If taxation without representation is unfair, so is social responsibility without representation.

Once again, proponents of greater corporate social responsibility are not convinced. Friedman compares the socially responsible manager to an autocratic sovereign who can arbitrarily impose taxes at will without the checks of a legislature or a judiciary. And, naturally, mention of taxes is likely to get anybody's hair up. But remember, the critics urge, what we are really talking about here is the imposition of a cost on the shareholders. Could Friedman mean that *any* cost imposition by a manager is bad? This can't be right. Managers who are *commited* to profit maximization impose costs all the time by beginning new product lines, acquiring other firms, investing in research and development, commencing advertising campaigns, and so on. All such efforts cost money. And typically, managers do this without consulting the shareholders first. For example, although there is a nominal ban on corporate contributions to federal elections, it is estimated that corporations opened their coffers to the pretax tune of $250 million in 1996.[24] The reason for these contributions is obvious enough: softer regulations, relief from antitrust pressures, and the like. Of course, these monies could have been used for investment, or to raise wages, and add to dividends. Nobody asked the shareholders. So, the critics say, the answer can't be that cost impositions are bad because the manager is acting unilaterally, or else many business decisions that entail profit maximization are socially irresponsible.

Rather it must be that only *certain* cost impositions are wrong, that is, those made on the basis of social responsibility and not profit maximization. But why are these wrong? The answer must be that they are not profit-maximizing. Yet, say Friedman's critics, *that* shareholder imperative is merely assumed if in fact the shareholders are not consulted. Friedman's arguments based on principle and consequences are supposed to establish that corporate social responsibility is either irresponsible or unfair. Their purpose is to show that profit maximization is the only alternative for profit-minded corporations. But to make those arguments effective, we can't bring in considerations of profit maximization as our trump cards, since the arguments are intended to show that profit maximization *is* the trump card to begin with. To show that acting in a way that is socially responsible is actually irresponsible or unfair, one must use arguments independent of any appeal to profit maximization. Otherwise, we beg the question by assuming what we have set out to prove.

Friedman's arguments do not show that profit maximization must be a moral ideal of business, say opponents of the canonical view; it is more of a sacred cow, an assumption we have not questioned, since in our recent economic history its adoption has led to prosperity for most Americans. But the economic situation of the world economy is different. Our citizens and citizens of the world are affected by the not-so-benign actions of the multinationals. Further, the critics suggest, the agent/principal model on which the principles of individual social responsibility are said to rest is itself too narrow a model, given these new conditions of international commerce.

CONCLUSION

This chapter has covered much ground, and you may be feeling even more bewildered now than when you began. You may be thinking: This is all so abstract, and there seems to be an argument for everyone's position. It is true that there are many arguments for and against the various theories and claims we examine in this chapter; but it does not follow that all of these argument are *equally good:* Some are better than others, and it is the task of philosophical reflection, in large part, to learn to distinguish which is which. It is also true that much of what we discuss in this introductory chapter is abstract. Nonetheless, it is important, for it equips you with a basic understanding of how questions of ethics are framed and debated in the office and in life. Nor is it uncommon to come away from such discussion feeling uneasy. The study of ethics is not (as you can see by now) a job of memorizing dates or digesting facts. It is rather a process of immersing yourself in a set of issues and problems—many of which have direct and immediate consequences in the "real world"—and trying to find your way through them as best you can. On this journey you are now well on your way.

NOTES

1. Robert B. Reich, *The Work of Nations: Preparing Ourselves for 21st-Century Capitalism* (New York: Vintage Books, 1992), 70.

2. Bary Bluestone and Bennett Harrison, *The Deindustrialization of America,* (New York: Basic Books, 1982), p. 17.

3. Reich, *Work of Nations*, 113.

4. Cited in Edward N. Luttwak, *The Endangered American Dream* (New York: Touchstone, 1993), 184.

5. Ibid.

6. See William Greider, *One World, Ready or Not: The Manic Logic of Global Capitalism* (New York: Simon & Schuster, 1997).

7. The *Financial Times* in 1994 reprinted a list of manufacturing labor costs for rich and poor countries. Here is an extrapolation.

	Pay per Hour		*Pay per Hour*
West Germany	$24.90	Singapore	$5.10
Former East Germany	$17.30	South Korea	$4.90
Japan	$16.90	Hong Kong	$4.20
United States	$16.40	Hungary	$1.80
United Kingdom	$12.40	China	$0.50

8. Eyal Press, "Barbie's Betrayal: The Toy Industry's Broken Workers," *The Nation* (Dec. 30, 1996).

9. They presented their evidence to Gifford on her television show. She tearfully explained that she had no knowledge of the child labor.

10. See Daniel M. Hausman, *The Inexact and Separate Science of Economics* (Cambridge: Cambridge University Press, 1992), 159, for citations.

11. Milton Friedman, "The Social Responsibility of Business Is to Increase Its Profits," reprinted in *Contemporary Issues in Business Ethics,* 2d ed., edited by J. DesJardins and J. McCall (Belmont, Calif.: Wadsworth Publishing Co., 1985).

12. Additionally, we will use this piece to explore some other matters pertinent to social responsibility and commerce.

13. Peter A. French, "The Corporation as a Moral Person," reprinted in *Business Ethics: A Philosophical Reader,* edited by Thomas I. White (New York: Macmillan, 1993); and Kenneth A. Goodpaster and John B. Matthews, Jr., "Can a Corporation Have a Conscience?" reprinted in DesJardins and McCall, *Contemporary Issues.*

14. An argument for this approach is made plausibly by Manuel Velasquez in "Why Corporations Are Not Responsible for Anything They Do," reprinted in DesJardins and McCall, *Contemporary Issues.* To say that "Exxon is responsible" is really an elliptical way of saying that some agents of Exxon are responsible. We use the term "Exxon" in lieu of individuals whom we do not know.

15. He also mentions that managers have a duty to avoid deception and fraud, which, we take it, might fall under the heading of ethical custom. Friedman is a proponent of free-market capitalism, and fraud would undermine its efficiency.

16. This issue, and others pertaining to the nature of professional responsibility, is the focus of an anthology edited by Albert Flores entitled *Professional Ideals* (Belmont, Calif.: Wadsworth, 1988).

17. For some interesting and important variations on this these, see Lisa Newton, "Agents for the Truly Greedy," in *Ethics and Agency Theory: An Introduction,* edited by Norman E. Bowie and R. Edward Freeman (Oxford: Oxford University Press, 1992).

18. See the provocative paper by Ronald J. Duska, "Why Be a Loyal Agent? A Systematic Ethical Analysis," in Bowie and Freeman, *Ethics and Theory.*

19. Christopher D. Stone, *Where the Law Ends: The Social Control of Corporate Behavior* (Prospect Heights, Ill.: Waveland Press, 1991).

20. Presently, there does exist a number of socially responsible mutual funds, which concern themselves with a wide range of issues including environmental conservation, animal welfare, and labor rights. These amount to more than $600 billion or 10 percent of the mutual fund market, according to the *Los Angeles Times* (2/25/97).

21. *Los Angeles Times* (2/25/97).

22. "The board, whatever its name and whatever its legal structure, has become a fiction. The law may still treat it as the sovereign organ of the corporation—but, then, English legal rhetoric still treats the Queen as an absolute monarch whose every whim is a command," Peter Drucker, *Management: Tasks, Responsibilites, and Practices* (New York: Harper and Row, 1974), 628.

23. John C. Coffee, "Beyond the Shut-Eyed Sentry: Toward a Theoretical View of Corporate Misconduct and Effective Legal Response," *Virginia Law Review* 63 (1977), 1131.

24. As reported by Richard C. Leone, president of the Twentieth Century Fund, in *The Nation* (Feb. 17, 1997).

THE SOCIAL RESPONSIBILITY OF BUSINESS IS TO INCREASE ITS PROFITS

Milton Friedman

When I hear businessmen speak eloquently about the "social responsibilities of business in a free-

enterprise system," I am reminded of the wonderful line about the Frenchman who discovered at the age of 70 that he had been speaking prose all his life. The businessmen believe that they are defending free enterprise when they declaim that business is not concerned "merely" with profit but also with promoting desirable "social" ends; that business has a "social conscience" and takes seriously its responsibilities for providing employment, eliminating discrimination, avoiding pollution and whatever else may be the catchwords of the contemporary crop of reformers. In fact they are—or would be if they or anyone else took them seriously—preaching pure and unadulterated socialism. Businessmen who talk this way are unwitting puppets of the intellectual forces that have been undermining the basis of a free society these past decades.

The discussions of the "social responsibilities of business" are notable for their analytical looseness and lack of vigor. What does it mean to say that "business" has responsibilities? Only people can have responsibilities. A corporation is an artificial person and in this sense may have artificial responsibilities, but "business" as a whole cannot be said to have responsibilities, even in this vague sense. The first step toward clarity in examining the doctrine of the social responsibility of business is to ask precisely what it implies for whom.

Presumably, the individuals who are to be responsible are businessmen, which means individual proprietors or corporate executives. Most of the discussion of social responsibility is directed at corporations, so in what follows I shall mostly neglect the individual proprietor and speak of corporate executives.

In a free-enterprise, private-property system a corporate executive is an employee of the owners of the business. He has direct responsibility to his employers. That responsibility is to conduct the business in accordance with their desires, which generally will be to make as much money as possible while conforming to the basic rules of the society, both those embodied in law and those embodied in ethical custom. Of course, in some cases his employers may have a different objective. A group of persons might establish a corporation for an eleemosynary purpose—for example, a hospital or a school. The manager of such a corporation will not have money profit as his objective but the rendering of certain services.

In either case, the key point is that, in his capacity as a corporate executive, the manager is the agent of the individuals who own the corporation or establish the eleemosynary institution, and his primary responsibility is to them.

Needless to say, this does not mean that it is easy to judge how well he is performing his task. But at least the criterion of performance is straightforward, and the persons among whom a voluntary contractual arrangement exists are clearly defined.

Of course, the corporate executive is also a person in his own right. As a person, he may have many other responsibilities that he recognizes or assumes voluntarily—to his family, his conscience, his feelings of charity, his church, his clubs, his city, his country. He may feel impelled by these responsibilities to devote part of his income to causes he regards as worthy, to refuse to work for particular corporations, and even to leave his job, for example, to join his country's armed forces. If we wish, we may refer to some of these responsibilities as "social responsibilities." But in these respects he is acting as a principal, not an agent; he is spending his own money or time or energy, not the money of his employers or the time or energy he has contracted to devote to their purposes. If these are "social responsibilities," they are the social responsibilities of individuals, not of business.

What does it mean to say that the corporate executive has a "social responsibility" in his capacity as businessman? If this statement is not pure rhetoric, it must mean that he is to act in some way that is not in the interest of his employers. For example, that he is to refrain from increasing the price of the product in order to contribute to the social objective of preventing inflation, even though a price increase would be in the best interests of the corporation. Or that he is to make expenditures on reducing pollution beyond the amount that is in the best interests of the corporation or that is required by law in order to contribute to the social objective of improving the environment. Or that, at the expense of corporate profits, he is to hire "hardcore" unemployed instead of better-qualified available workmen to contribute to the social objective of reducing poverty.

In each of these cases, the corporate executive would be spending someone else's money for a general social interest. Insofar as his actions in accord with his "social responsibility" reduce returns to stockholders, he is spending their money. Insofar as his actions raise the price to customers, he is spending the customers' money. Insofar as his actions lower the wages of some employees, he is spending their money.

The stockholders or the customers or the employees could separately spend their own money on the particular action if they wished to do so. The executive is exercising a distinct "social responsibility," rather than serving as an agent of the stockholders or the customers or the employees, only if he spends the money in a different way than they would have spent it.

But if he does this, he is in effect imposing taxes, on the one hand, and deciding how the tax proceeds shall be spent, on the other.

This process raises political questions on two levels: principle and consequences. On the level of political principle, the imposition of taxes and the expenditure of tax proceeds are governmental functions. We have established elaborate constitutional, parliamentary and judicial provisions to control these functions, to assure that taxes are imposed so far as possible in accordance with the preferences and desires of the public—after all, "taxation without representation" was one of the battle cries of the American Revolution. We have a system of checks and balances to separate the legislative function of imposing taxes and enacting expenditures from the executive function of collecting taxes and administering expenditure programs and from the judicial function of mediating disputes and interpreting the law.

Here the businessman—self-selected or appointed directly or indirectly by stockholders—is to be simultaneously legislator, executive and jurist. He is to decide whom to tax by how much and for what purpose, and he is to spend the proceeds—all this guided only by general exhortations from on high to restrain inflation, improve the environment, fight poverty and so on and on.

The whole justification for permitting the corporate executive to be selected by the stockholders is that the executive is an agent serving the interests of his principal. This justification disappears when the corporate executive imposes taxes and spends the proceeds for "social" purposes. He becomes in effect a public employee, a civil servant, even though he remains in name an employee of a private enterprise. On grounds of political principle, it is intolerable that such civil servants—insofar as their actions in the name of social responsibility are real and not just window-dressing—should be selected as they are now. If they are to be civil servants, then they must be selected through a political process. If they are to impose taxes and make

expenditures to foster "social" objectives, then political machinery must be set up to guide the assessment of taxes and to determine through a political process the objectives to be served.

This is the basic reason why the doctrine of "social responsibility" involves the acceptance of the socialist view that political mechanisms, not market mechanisms, are the appropriate way to determine the allocation of scarce resources to alternative uses.

On the grounds of consequences, can the corporate executive in fact discharge his alleged "social responsibilities"? On the one hand, suppose he could get away with spending the stockholders' or customers' or employees' money. How is he to know how to spend it? He is told that he must contribute to fighting inflation. How is he to know what action of his will contribute to that end? He is presumably an expert in running his company—in producing a product or selling it or financing it. But nothing about his selection makes him an expert on inflation. Will his holding down the price of his product reduce inflationary pressure? Or, by leaving more spending power in the hands of his customers, simply divert it elsewhere? Or, by forcing him to produce less because of the lower price, will it simply contribute to shortages? Even if he could answer these questions, how much cost is he justified in imposing on his stockholders, customers and employees for this social purpose? What is his appropriate share and the share of others?

And, whether he wants to or not, can he get away with spending his stockholders', customers' or employees' money? Will not the stockholders fire him? (Either the present ones or those who take over when his actions in the name of social responsibility have reduced the corporation's profits and the price of its stock.) His customers and his employees can desert him for other producers and employers less scrupulous in exercising their social responsibilities.

This facet of "social responsibility" doctrine is brought into sharp relief when the doctrine is used to justify wage restraint by trade unions. The conflict of interest is naked and clear when union officials are asked to subordinate the interest of their members to some more general social purpose. If the union officials try to enforce wage restraint, the consequence is likely to be wildcat strikes, rank-and-file revolts and the emergence of strong competitors for their jobs. We thus have the ironic phenomenon that union leaders—at least in the U.S.—have objected to government interference with the market far more consistently and courageously than have business leaders.

The difficulty of exercising "social responsibility" illustrates, of course, the great virtue of private competitive enterprise—it forces people to be responsible for their own actions and makes it difficult for them to "exploit" other people for either selfish or unselfish purposes. They can do good—but only at their own expense.

Many a reader who has followed the argument this far may be tempted to remonstrate that it is all well and good to speak of government's having the responsibility to impose taxes and determine expenditures for such "social" purposes as controlling pollution or training the hardcore unemployed, but that the problems are too urgent to wait on the slow course of political processes, that the exercise of social responsibility by businessmen is a quicker and surer way to solve pressing current problems.

Aside from the question of fact—I share Adam Smith's skepticism about the benefits that can be expected from "those who affected to trade for the public good"—this argument must be rejected on grounds of principle. What it amounts to is an assertion that those who favor the taxes and expenditures in question have failed to persuade a majority of their fellow citizens to be of like mind and that they are seeking to attain by undemocratic procedures what they cannot attain by democratic procedures. In a free society, it is hard for "good" people to do "good," but that is a small price to pay for making it hard for "evil" people to do "evil," especially since one man's good is another's evil.

I have, for simplicity, concentrated on the special case of the corporate executive, except only for the brief digression on trade unions. But precisely the same argument applies to the newer phenomenon of calling upon stockholders to require corporations to exercise social responsibility (the recent G.M. crusade, for example). In most of these cases, what is in effect involved is some stockholders trying to get other stockholders (or customers or employees) to contribute against their will to "social" causes favored by the activists. Insofar as they succeed, they are again imposing taxes and spending the proceeds.

The situation of the individual proprietor is somewhat different. If he acts to reduce the returns of his enterprise in order to exercise his "social responsibility," he is spending his own money, not someone else's. If he wishes to spend his money on such purposes, that is his right, and I cannot see that there is any objection to his doing so. In the process, he, too, may impose costs on employees and customers. However, because he is far less likely than a large corporation or union to have monopolistic power, any such side effects will tend to be minor.

Of course, in practice the doctrine of social responsibility is frequently a cloak for actions that are justified on other grounds rather than a reason for those actions.

To illustrate, it may well be in the long-run interest of a corporation that is a major employer in a small community to devote resources to providing amenities to that community or to improving its government. That may make it easier to attract desirable employees, it may reduce the wage bill or lessen losses from pilferage and sabotage or have other worthwhile effects. Or it may be that, given the laws about the deductibility of corporate charitable contributions, the stockholders can contribute more to charities they favor by having the corporation make the gift than by doing it themselves, since they can in that way contribute an amount that would otherwise have been paid as corporate taxes.

In each of these—and many similar—cases, there is a strong temptation to rationalize these actions as an exercise of "social responsibility." In the present climate of opinion, with its widespread aversion to "capitalism," "profits," the "soulless corporation" and so on, this is one way for a corporation to generate goodwill as a by-product of expenditures that are entirely justified in its own self-interest.

It would be inconsistent of me to call on corporate executives to refrain from this hypocritical window-dressing because it harms the foundations of a free society. That would be to call on them to exercise a "social responsibility"! If our institutions, and the attitudes of the public make it in their self-interest to cloak their actions in this way, I cannot summon much indignation to denounce them. At the same time, I can express admiration for those individual proprietors or owners of closely held corporations or stockholders of more broadly held corporations who disdain such tactics as approaching fraud.

Whether blameworthy or not, the use of the cloak of social responsibility, and the nonsense spoken in its name by influential and prestigious businessmen, does clearly harm the foundations of a free society. I have been impressed time and again by the schizophrenic character of many businessmen. They are capable of being extremely far-sighted and clear-headed in matters that are internal to their businesses. They are incredibly short-sighted and muddle-headed in matters that are outside their businesses but affect the possible survival of business in general. This short-sightedness is strikingly exemplified in the calls from many businessmen for wage and price guidelines or controls or income policies. There is nothing that could do more in a brief period to destroy a market system and replace it by a centrally controlled system than effective governmental control of prices and wages.

The short-sightedness is also exemplified in speeches by businessmen on social responsibility. This may gain them kudos in the short run. But it helps to strengthen the already too prevalent view that the pursuit of profits is wicked and immoral and must be curbed and controlled by external forces. Once this view is adopted, the external forces that curb the market will not be the social consciences, however highly developed, of the pontificating executives; it will be the iron fist of government bureaucrats. Here, as with price and wage controls, businessmen seem to me to reveal a suicidal impulse.

The political principle that underlies the market mechanism is unanimity. In an ideal free market resting on private property, no individual can coerce any other, all cooperation is voluntary, all parties to such cooperation benefit or they need not participate. There are no "social" values, no "social" responsibilities in any sense other than the shared values and responsibilities of individuals. Society is a collection of individuals and of the various groups they voluntarily form.

The political principle that underlies the political mechanism is conformity. The individual must serve a more general social interest—whether that be determined by a church or a dictator or a majority. The individual may have a vote and a say in what is to be done, but if he is overruled, he must conform. It is appropriate for some to require others to contribute to a general social purpose whether they wish to or not.

Unfortunately, unanimity is not always feasible. There are some respects in which conformity appears unavoidable, so I do not see how one can avoid the use of the political mechanism altogether.

But the doctrine of "social responsibility" taken seriously would extend the scope of the political mechanism to every human activity. It does not differ in philosophy from the most explicitly collectivist doctrine. It differs only by professing to believe that collectivist ends can be attained without collectivist means. That is why, in my book *Capitalism and Freedom,* I have called it a "fundamentally subversive doctrine" in a free society, and have said that in such a society, "there is one and only one social responsibility of business—to use its resources and engage in activities designed to increase its profits so long as it stays within the rules of the game, which is to say, engages in open and free competition without deception or fraud."

Study Questions

1. Based on your understanding of the readings, sketch alternative moral perspectives on Debra's problem in the "Cooking the Books" case study. Do the analyses of the commentators at the conclusion of the case match any of the perspectives introduced in the selections? Explain.

2. What does it mean to say that human beings are "self-interested"? Do you agree?

3. State the two basic assumptions constituting the canonical view of corporate social responsibility.

4. Distinguish in your own words between rule utilitarianism and act utilitarianism. Do you think that rule utilitarianism is really a disguised version of act utilitarianism? Explain with examples.

5. As completely as possible, explain the principle of utility. Imagine that a corporation used this principle to conduct its commercial affairs. How would the shareholders (or Wall Street) respond to this? If utilitarianism were the operative principle of business, would the point of commerce be different from what it is presently? What is the point presently?

6. Explain the distinction between psychological egoism and ethical egoism.

7. Find an example in the newspaper or in a newsmagazine of a conflict of interest facing an agent with respect to his or her principal.

8. What two arguments does Friedman give to show that managers ought to concern themselves only with profits?

9. Do you agree that a manager's sole moral duty is to maximize corporate profits? If not, what other moral responsibilities or duties does the manager have, in your view? And on what basis would you affirm the existence of such duties?

10. Explain the difference between a hypothetical and a categorical imperative. Give two examples of each.

11. How could the categorical imperative be used as a test of business practices? Explain.

12. Kant places a great deal of importance on the duty of respect for other persons. Given this emphasis, how would a proponent of Kant's philosophy view cost/benefit analysis in those cases in which a value is placed on a human life? Does your answer entail that Kantian ethics is impracticable in the context of business?

13. Find a magazine or newspaper story on a current moral debate or issue. Identify an example of consequentialist, deontological, or virtue-based reasoning in the story. Which of the arguments—consequentialist, deontological, or virtue-based—do you find most convincing? Why?

14. State in your own words the critique of principle-based ethical theories given by defenders of virtue ethics.

 CHAPTER 2

Multinational Corporations and Ethical Relativism

It is now nearly a cliché to say that we live and work in a global economy. More and more corporations are doing business in two or more parts of the world. Many U.S.-based corporations, for example, now have subdivisions and factories, contractors and customers spread throughout much of the globe. And it is certainly a cliché to say that we live in a time of tremendous cultural diversity, in which hundreds of cultures and peoples seem to operate with divergent systems of beliefs and values. The convergence of the truisms these clichés represent, however, has produced results hardly mundane. Because they operate in varying cultural contexts, many multinational enterprises have had to confront moral problems caused by the clash of different standards and norms governing everything from workers' rights to environmental protection to consumer safety. Moreover, governments, like that of the United States, now increasingly debate whether foreign trade policy should be driven principally by the commercial interest in opening new markets, or in order to promote American concepts of human rights, including freedom of expression, the right to organize, and the right to a livable environment.

These issues are further complicated by the fact that a multinational's holdings, shareholders, and facilities may be distributed over several countries with different cultural and ethical standards. There may be no literal "home" country (in fact, the language of "host," "home," and "visiting" corporation may presently be relevant only for historical purposes). Because it would seem arbitrary to pick one locale over another (for example, the country in which the corporation is incorporated or headquartered), the canonical position on business social responsibility might recommend adhering to the norms and standards that exist in the host country, that is, in the country in which business is actually conducted. According to the canonical position, laws moralize corporate behavior and the existing laws in the host nation, although they may diverge from those customary in the United States. Yet these laws express that country's statement of what constitutes morally legitimate business practices. The same point could be made with respect to the informal business customs of the host nation.

Also according to the canonical position, management must respect the desires of the shareholders. If these laws and customs are indeed abhorrent to the shareholders, it is management's obligation to look for another international business partner. But it is more than likely that management, and many shareholders, would view the existing laws and practices as consequences of rational, self-interested choices made by the host nation. For instance, although an eighty-hour workweek for low pay is unattractive to many of us in the United States, it is a labor alternative chosen by those in many poorer nations. The host

The "Good Guys" of the Garment Industry

Each year the U.S. Labor Department issues a list of those manufacturers in the garment industry that it considers to have taken extra measures to ensure that their goods have been manufactured under labor conditions that are legal and ethical. The list released in December 1995 contained the following companies:

Abercrombie & Fitch	Galyans Trading	Liz Claiborne
Baby Superstore	Gerber Childrenswear	Mast Industries
Bath & Body Works	Guess	Nicole Miller
Bergner's	Henri Bendel	Nordstrom
Boston Stores	Jessica McClintock	Patagonia
Brylane	Land's End	Penhaligon's
Cacique	Lane Bryant	Structure
Carson Pirie Scott	Lerner New York	Superior Surgical Mfg.
Dana Buchman	Levi Strauss	Victoria's Secret
Elisabeth	Limited	
Express	Limited Too	

Source: *Los Angeles Times* 12/7/95: D1, D11.

nation might choose this practice because it thinks it necessary as a means of increasing its wealth and ensuring its competitiveness. With the eventual increase of wealth, the standard of living for all persons of the host nation will increase. Or the host nation might reason that employment, albeit at poor wages, is a better economic option than underemployment or unemployment. In either case, the choice of laws and customs must fall upon the host nation. To attempt to foist on the host nation standards informed by our sense of morality is moral arrogance insofar as it assumes that we know what matters are in the best interest of the host nation. The canonical position notwithstanding, a policy debate rages over the nature of morally justifiable labor practices in poorer countries.

Wage and labor standards, for example, differ widely around the globe. Practices tolerated or even encouraged in one part of the world may be illegal elsewhere. In 1995 many Americans were appalled at the discovery that a group of workers from Thailand had been held in conditions of virtual slavery at a seedy textile sweatshop in southern California. Yet both prison and child labor are sometimes tolerated and widely practiced in other nations. Had the Thai workers been confined in a factory located in Thailand itself, would anyone have cared? And if such an overseas factory were owned by an American textile manufacturer, could the company defend such servile conditions by noting that they are common throughout much of Southeast Asia? Just such questions faced TV celebrity Kathie Lee Gifford and giant retailer WalMart when, in 1996, allegations were raised by an independent human rights organization that Gifford's line of women's apparel originated in part from a sweatshop in Choloma, Honduras, where girls as young as thirteen were allegedly forced to work twelve-hour shifts. Gifford denied any knowledge of abuse and quickly denounced such practices.[1] Such highly publicized cases illustrate a basic moral dilemma facing many corporations in an expanding global economy: Should a corporation operating in a number of different nations shape its policies and practices in each country to suit that nation's culture and practices? Or should it adhere to the standards and norms prevalent in its home country, regardless of where it operates? In this chapter we explore several dimensions of this basic dilemma.

If a practice is, for example, forbidden by U.S. law but is not illegal in a foreign nation, should an American multinational pursue that practice in that foreign country? Here are some specific examples of this general question: Company X manufactures a pesticide that is now banned in the United States due to the hazard it poses to human health. The pesticide is not illegal, however, in other parts of the world. Should Company X sell its pesticide abroad? Company Y opens an electronics assembly plant in a country where child labor is practiced. Should Company Y follow the customary practice of its host nation and employ child laborers? Company Z used to operate a number of strip mines in North America; however, because of the environmental damage it causes, strip-mining is now severely curtailed in the United States and Canada. Many lesser developed countries in Asia and South America have few, if any, restrictions on strip-mining. Should Company Z seek to open strip mines overseas? Since they involve the intersection of often very different views about the morality of various aspects of business, the dilemmas posed by these questions are, not unexpectedly, hard to answer. A further example of such dilemmas concerns the use of bribes in international business transactions, to which we turn shortly.

Many of the specific questions raised so far in this introduction ride on the surface of an even deeper issue: If a business operating in several different cultures must choose which among competing moral beliefs and practices it will follow concerning working conditions, environmental degradation, or product safety, does this mean that all moral beliefs are relative to particular cultures? And does that mean that there are no moral absolutes, no values or beliefs that transcend the specific histories and traditions of people living in different parts of the world? If a company closes up its operations in a country in Southeast Asia, for example, citing human rights violations by the country's rulers, has it appealed to a universally valid ethical standard? Or has it merely imposed its own moral views on another nation? These questions, as we will see, involve the debate over what philosophers call "ethical relativism," and its relevance to the world of international business.

WHAT'S WRONG WITH BRIBERY?

Bribery is a practice involving the payment or remuneration of an agent of some organization to do things that are inconsistent with the purpose of his or her position or office. Good examples of this kind of practice include paying a judge to be partial to your case, paying a policeman to forgo giving you a speeding ticket, or paying a buyer to use your company's services.

It's clear that something illegitimate happens in these cases. Purchasing agents are supposed to use criteria for buying that turn on the price and quality of the products and services offered. To buy poor-quality or overpriced merchandise because one has been bribed can result in harm to customers and can deprive owners of their rightful profits. Judges are required to administer the law impartially; to do otherwise is to harm those citizens who come before them seeking fairness. And a hundred-dollar bill is not supposed to override a posted speed limit; the speed limits apply to all drivers regardless of how much money happens to be in one's pocket. In these cases, the offices of the individuals accepting the bribes have been compromised. Their jobs require that they protect the interests of the public or their principals; to fail to do that is to both break the law and violate the canons of professional responsibility. If bribes were regularly accepted by these officials, we would soon lose trust in their positions and their ability to reach objective judgments. That would obviously be bad for the society in which these officials are judges or police officers. Furthermore, the consequences of accepting the bribe might affect the safety and economic well-being of the public at large. The purchasing agent might purchase less-than-acceptable components, resulting in the production of defective products that threaten consumer

---

✑   **Ethical Decisions at Levi's**

Often cited for its forward-looking approach to thorny moral and social problems, Levi Strauss, in 1992, adopted a set of global-sourcing guidelines, *Business Partner Terms of Engagement*, to be applied to all of its domestic and overseas contractors. The guidelines forbid child and prison labor, set maximum weekly work hours (sixty per week, and one day off in seven), permit union activity, and stipulate certain environmental requirements. Some in the business community praised Levi's for its level of social and moral concern. Others pointed to the impracticality of enforcing such guidelines worldwide. Levi's cannot adequately inspect its nearly seven hundred contract factories, critics observed; and abuses are still being tolerated: The company apparently looked the other way, for example, when a factory in Malaysia engaged in forms of union busting, practices legal in that country though nominally prohibited by the guidelines.

Supporters of Levi's point to its creativity in resolving cases of clashing cultures and values, such as the recent discovery that two of Levi's manufacturing contractors—one in Turkey, the other in Bangladesh—employed underage workers. Levi's CEO Robert Haas reported:

> It appeared we had two options: instruct our contractors to fire these children, knowing that many are the sole wage earners for their families and if they lost their jobs, their families would face extreme hardships; or continue to employ the underage children, ignoring our company's stance against the use of child labor.

Avoiding these alternatives, Levi's chose instead to negotiate with the contractors: Levi's would continue to do business with the contractors if they agreed to pay the children's salaries while they completed school. Once of working age, the children would be offered full-time jobs, though they would not have to take them.

SOURCE: *Wall Street Journal,* 7/28/94: pp. A1, A5.

---

safety. Even when a product is acceptable, the purchasing agent might buy it at a higher-than-market price, thereby diminishing returns to the corporation's investors. It is for all of these reasons, many would contend, that bribery is generally against the law.

What about the perpetrator of the bribe? From both the consequentialist and respect-for-persons perspectives, there is something morally problematic about offering bribes, and this is so even if the bribe is not accepted. Assessed from the standpoint of consequences, bribery is wrong because it undermines the objective, professional judgments of the bribe's target. If the bribe is accepted, the official is partial or biased where exactly the opposite is called for. Moreover, one instance of bribery may lead to others in the future, perhaps becoming a habit. In this way a bribe contributes to actions that are not in the public interest. And what if the bribe is not accepted? Even if refused, there is still something morally problematic about offering a bribe. You offer the bribe to an official to obtain a judgment that favors you. But, of course, you wouldn't want others to engage in the same kind of conduct with such officials. This is because you wouldn't want payments to become so routine that they simply become part of normal business practice, for then your tender of money would no longer stand out as an extra inducement for official action. Were everyone to make bribes, this might hike up the costs to you, competing with other would-be bribers in a bidding war. That there be a generally observed prohibition against such conduct seems to

---

✑ Human Rights and Doing Business in Myanmar

Over the years, many U.S. multinationals set up business in the Southeast Asian nation of Myanmar, formerly known as Burma. Petro-chemical giants such as Unocal and Texaco began exploring for oil and natural gas; PepsiCo, Inc., had invested in a plant, as had garment industry leaders like Levi Strauss, Eddie Bauer, and Liz Claiborne. Recently, however, most of these companies have left Myanmar, which has become an example of corporate concern over doing business in a country that seems to have violated widely held ethical standards. The regime in Myanmar has been accused of "systematically murdering and imprisoning its opponents, selling off virgin rain forest, dealing in the heroin trade, and enslaving ethnic minorities." When it pulled out of Myanmar in 1994, an executive of Liz Claiborne stated that, "though the facilities with which we work [in Myanmar] have complied with our strict human rights standards, we cannot support the activities of this country's current government." Virtually alone in refusing to leave Myanmar has been California-based Unocal Corporation. Unocal is a partner with the state-owned Myanma Oil & Gas Co. in the construction of the controversial $1.2 billion Yadana pipeline project. Two recent developments may dramatically affect Unocal's ability to continue business in Myanmar. In the spring of 1997, President Clinton, under pressure from human rights groups, decided to ban new U.S. investments in the country. More serious, a federal district judge in California recently ruled that Unocal could be held criminally liable for abuses allegedly committed by the government of Myanmar through its operation of Myanma Oil & Gas. Unocal reportedly paid Myanmar's military leaders to provide both labor and security for the pipeline project; human rights groups claim that farmers and their families were forced to relocate and work on the project, and that they were beaten and abused by troops assigned to protect the pipeline.

SOURCE: *Business Ethics*, Mar./Apr. 1995: 8.

---

be a necessary condition for your attempt at bribery to be successful. The effectiveness of your bribe depends on such an observance. So to offer a bribe is to be partial to your own interests: You want bribery to be allowable for *you* in this circumstance, but you also desire that no one else have that advantage. To make an exception of yourself in this way is, according to Kantian ethicists, a constituent element of immoral behavior.

BRIBERY AND RELATIVISM

Talking about what the law or the canons of professional responsibility require suggests a social context in which judges are supposed to be objective and policemen equitable in their application of the law. That's simply a part of the job for which they are paid. But what if the social context is different? What if those actions that North Americans condemn as unprofessional and immoral are, from the perspective of another society, business as usual? After all, it is clear that not all societies share the same beliefs and values; and if this is so, shouldn't it be possible that conduct found objectionable in one culture might be thought unobjectionable in another?

The idea implicit in the foregoing questions has a long and distinguished history, both in the social sciences and in philosophy. We might call this position *relativism,* but we must be cautious, because relativism can take different forms. One form we might call *belief rela-*

tivism. This position starts with an undoubted truth: that beliefs about the world may vary to some degree across distinct cultures and societies, and that such differences in belief may well translate into differences in practices and conventions. In some societies, accordingly, we can expect to find people who would regard beliefs prevalent in our society as false. So, for example, one group of people, afflicted by what we would term "psychological problems," might seek help from a local shaman, whose incantations are believed to remedy what our psychiatrists might characterize as a physical ailment treatable with drugs instead of prayers. Belief relativism was popular during the nineteenth century, when reports of activities in previously uncharted lands abounded.

Concurrent with the emergence of belief relativism was the appearance of what might be termed *value relativism.* Along with reports of the activities of shamans, European and North American explorers and missionaries returned to their homes with exciting (and often titillating) reports of the sexual, social, and religious behaviors to be found in far-off places. Polygamy, cannibalism, infanticide, and other practices widely proscribed (if not abhorred) in North Atlantic cultures were viewed as unproblematic (or at least as lesser moral evils) by the members of these newfound cultural groups. In fact, in some cases it looked to the missionaries and explorers that such actions were morally required in the societies in which they occurred.

Such reports led many to value relativism: the view that an action, performed by a member of a given society, is morally right when it is permitted by the conventions of that society. This conclusion abandons the idea that there is some universal and absolute moral code that applies to everyone across cultures. Whenever we use moral terms like *right, wrong,* or *duty,* we must, according to value relativism, be careful to note that the term applies only to the moral canon of some particular society. In other words, a "right action" is right only within the context of a society's normative conventions; it makes no sense to speak of an action being right in general, or of a duty incumbent upon all persons. To illustrate this, let's go back to the case of bribery. The value relativist would say that there could be no general condemnation of bribery, since presumably there are (or could be) societies in which bribery is tolerated, if not encouraged. It follows, according to the value relativist, that there can be no universal moral standards. If we can speak of the moral rightness or wrongness of an action only from the context of some given society, the value relativist might say, we would be wrong to condemn acts of bribery engaged in by those whose culture tolerates it.

The consequences of value relativism are far-reaching. Intersocial moral criticism, for example, would seem impossible. We could not condemn another society for (what we would term) vicious practices like slavery, apartheid, or genocide. But, further, moral criticism from within a society would also appear to be impossible. Imagine a person who wished to call into question a prevailing moral position in her own society. She believes that those moral conventions are wrong and she exhorts the citizenry to moral reform. It certainly seems that the individual could be right about this; in other words, it seems possible that the "moral truth" is indeed on her side. But, according to the value relativist, she must be wrong, since "right action" must mean "action in accord with the prevailing moral conventions." The reformer must then be mistaken; and if she acts in ways inconsistent with those conventions, <u>her</u> conduct would be immoral.

What can the opponent of relativism do when faced with the claims of the value relativist? Essentially, there are two strategies for responding to the relativist. The critics could examine certain practices within the context of a given society and argue that the relativist has mistaken the character of the actions that seem to conflict with the critic's preferred canon of morality. What appears to be bribery, for example, might really be a practice that has a more apt description consistent with what we and the critic would regard as innocent behavior. In this way what seems to be an example of people who permit bribery turns out in fact not to be so. Similarly, what appears to be moral indifference to, say, infanticide, might really not be indifference at all: Perhaps a given society condones infanticide only in the harshest circumstances, when overpopulation threatens the survival of the society.

A second strategy for responding to the claims of the value relativist involves granting that the practitioners believe that their practices are right, but asserting that it does not follow from the *belief* that something is right that it *is*, in fact, right. This response amounts to insisting that what is truly good or right is simply not determined by what people believe to be the case. To make this anti-relativist argument persuasive, of course, would compel the critic to explain just what the basis of "true" rightness or goodness is, if it is not the attitudes and beliefs of particular people. And this, as you might guess, is not an easy task.

BRIBERY, SCANDALS, AND THE FCPA

The discussion of value relativism is intended to put into context an issue that multinationals face regularly: What code of ethics is appropriate in business dealings with another country? Is it good business to "when in Rome, do as the Romans do"? Is it "moral imperialism" to assume that the moral standards of the multinational's home society are the only appropriate rules of commercial conduct? This issue came to public attention in the 1970s, when the general public discovered that multinationals had regularly engaged in bribery in their dealings with trade partners overseas. For instance, Lockheed Aircraft Corporation offered $22 million in bribes to foreign officials over a five-year period in the 1970s. The payoffs were intended to secure contracts for the purchase of commercial airliners and military aircraft. In 1976 disclosure of Lockheed's bribery led to the arrest of former Japanese prime minister Kukeo Tanaka and the resignation of Holland's Prince Bernhardt from his government position. Both had been the beneficiaries of $3 million in Lockheed bribes. Lockheed defended the payments to Tanaka as simply another among similar transactions occurring throughout the Japanese business world and argued that the bribes did not violate any American laws. Nor was bribery restricted to the aircraft industry. Exxon Corporation said that it paid $59 million to Italian officials to promote business objectives; and United Brands paid more than $1 million in bribes to a Honduran official to win a reduction in that country's import tax. In all it was discovered that close to four hundred U.S. companies had paid $300 million to agents of foreign countries for business favors. Bribery, it seemed, was indeed a U.S. business practice.

Congress responded quickly to these scandals. In 1977, during the Carter administration, Congress passed the Foreign Corrupt Practices Act (FCPA), which provided for stiff fines and penalties for corporate officials engaging in bribery when doing business abroad. The passage of this legislation led to strong criticism from proponents of business interests: The law, they argued, imposes U.S. moral standards on its trading partners, since bribery is a common business practice in other nations; the prohibitions against bribery put the United States at a disadvantage with other international competitors, who have no such prohibitions; and, moreover, the FCPA seeks to draw distinctions among bribery, extortion, and "facilitating" or "expediting" payments where the lines of demarcation are fuzzy at best. So, for example, the FCPA would forbid XYZ Corp. from making a payment to a government minister with the intention that the minister interfere with the work of customs officials; yet the act does not prohibit XYZ from making a so-called grease payment to the customs official directly, so long as the payment is intended merely to expedite the official's compliance with the law, providing a service that XYZ is entitled to receive but which the

---

    The FCPA and Global Anticorruption Initiatives

The year 1997 marks the twentieth anniversary of the Foreign Corrupt Practices Act (FCPA), which prohibits U.S. citizens and companies from bribing officials of foreign governments to obtain business favors. Although prosecutions under the FCPA were, until recently, quite rare, many legal experts predict that the rapid expansion of U.S. businesses into such new markets as China, Southeast Asia, and the former Soviet Union will bring greater scrutiny of overseas business practices by U.S. firms and increased prosecutions. Penalties under the FCPA can be harsh. In 1995 Lockheed Martin Corporation pleaded guilty to charges that it violated the FCPA when executives of the company paid Egyptian officials to guarantee purchase of several C-130 cargo planes made by Lockheed. A criminal fine of $21.8 million was reportedly levied against the company, along with a $3 million civil settlement. At least one Lockheed official is serving a prison sentence in connection with the scandal. Stiff fines and punishments are not the only reason members of the business community have been unhappy with the FCPA. Until quite recently, the United States was the only major industrialized nation to penalize bribery of foreigners. Since 1995, however, international support for multilateral anti-bribery agreements has strengthened. In 1996 the Organization for Economic Cooperation and Development (OECD) approved resolutions calling on member states to ban bribery of foreign officials; and the Organization of American States (OAS) in 1996 finished work on a Convention on Corruption. Not yet ratified by all member states, the OAS convention would impose a wider ban than even the FCPA, prohibiting receiving a bribe as well as giving one, and permitting the seizure of assets of violators.

SOURCE: *National Law Journal,* 3/3/97: B9–B17.

---

customs worker might otherwise delay. Drawing distinctions between cases like these in practice is quite difficult, however, and such difficulties have led some to complain that the strictures of the FCPA are unworkable.

THE READINGS

The selections included here examine the moral dimensions of international business generally and investigate as well the specific moral issues raised by cases of bribery and the moral status of the FCPA.

The readings open with three case studies, one hypothetical, the others involving U.S. companies operating in Central America. The dilemma facing Steve Riley in the fictional case "Worlds Apart" is discussed briefly by several commentators. Ask yourself when reading this selection how you would have acted and why.

The second case study involves H. B. Fuller and pursues the difficult issues raised by the sale of one of its products overseas. Resistol is a solvent-based contact glue, used primarily in shoe manufacturing, leatherwork, and carpentry. Resistol is made and marketed by Fuller. Beginning in the early 1980s, reports began to surface that Resistol was being used by street kids in Honduras, who would sniff the fumes of the glue to get high. As the abuse of its product spread, Fuller was presented with various options for approaching the problem. As the case study explores, none of the options seemed to impress executives at Fuller.

Nor have the problems posed by Resistol been resolved since the case study included here was written. As recently as late 1995, Resistol was still available for purchase in a number of Latin American countries, though Fuller has since stopped retail distribution in two nations and modified its warning labels. Pending developments may bring the issue of Resistol to a head: It was reported in July 1995 that a group of U.S. attorneys, critical of Fuller's inaction, is prepared to file a wrongful death suit against the company on behalf of the family of a Guatemalan boy who died, allegedly as a result of sniffing Resistol. Fuller still maintains that it is not the guilty party. "We're no different from people who make Glade air freshener or gasoline," stated a company spokesperson. "We make a legitimate product that is sold for legitimate purposes. We distribute it as controlled as we can, and we do everything we're expected to do."[2]

The last of the three case studies concerns the manufacture and marketing of DBCP, a pesticide made and sold both by Dow Chemical and Shell Oil. Banned in the United States after the late 1970s due to evidence linking it to sterility, DBCP continued to be sold in other countries. Workers abroad injured by the product sought to sue Dow and Shell in a U.S. court for injuries they claimed were brought on by exposure to the pesticide. The opinion of the Supreme Court of Texas reveals sharp differences of opinion as to the legality and morality of selling dangerous products outside U.S. borders.

The readings by Thomas Donaldson and by Ellen Frankel Paul each look at aspects of the larger question of international business practices and the meaning and scope of moral standards. Donaldson begins with an overview of ethical issues confronting multinational businesses. He articulates a set of what he takes to be the most basic moral responsibilities of international business entities, and then reviews a number of specific examples in an effort to illustrate the duties incumbent upon multinational companies by virtue of the basic rights he thinks they must respect. Paul offers a general assessment of international commerce from the three traditional perspectives of moral philosophy. She argues that the best approach to international trade would combine elements of both natural rights theory and utilitarianism.

The final selections for this chapter turn to two more particular issues: controversy over the Foreign Corrupt Practices Act, and the growing problem of international trade in hazardous materials.

Mark Pastin and Michael Hooker provide a moral analysis of the FCPA using two moral perspectives they describe as "end-point assessment" and "rule assessment." Judged from the former perspective, the FCPA has meant a loss of business for U.S. manufacturers and has had a negligible effect on moralizing commercial conduct. Viewed from the latter perspective, the prohibition against bribery is only a prima facie rule (that is, a rule that allows exceptions), and the costs to U.S. businesses are the exception that "weighs against the prima facie obligation not to bribe." In fact, far from being a duty, the legislation may be immoral. Robert E. Frederick disputes the conclusions reached by Pastin and Hooker, arguing that an end-point assessment of the FCPA indicates only that the legislation is morally neutral. He admits the possibility that the FCPA should be revised, but not for the reasons that Hooker and Pastin suggest—that is, that bribery is only prima facie wrong. Frederick concludes with a discussion of an issue troubling to both critics and proponents of the FCPA: the distinction between bribery and extortion.

In the final selection included here, authors Jang Singh and V. C. Lakhan review the alarming increase in shipments of hazardous waste material across international borders. Singh and Lakhan examine the extent of the trade and the principal motivations behind it, both on the part of those countries generating the waste and on those receiving it. The authors explain how market forces have shaped an international practice that arguably violates basic human rights, and they address the claim that the practice has racist implications.

NOTES

1. *Los Angeles Times* (6/14/96), A1.
2. *Business Ethics* (July/Aug. 1995), 21.

CASE STUDY   Worlds Apart

Doug Wallace

The exact time Steve Riley's mind went blank was 10:59 a.m., Monday, September 6. His eyes had just glanced at an antique, walnut-framed clock, its wrought iron and brass hands moving like miniature medieval swords about to strike 11:00. And then he was given a piece of linen paper, on which was printed the name of a Swiss bank, an account number, and a name. "The contract is yours. We just have one additional request," he was told, "that your company make a contribution to this account."

Steve was the general manager of Flight Food International Inc. (nicknamed "Fifi" by its competitors), a U.S.-based catering organization that provides meals for use on major airlines. He reported to Ted Wright, regional vice president of the United Kingdom and an accessible colleague respected for his professionalism, as well as his performance record. Ted's group generated more than $100 million in annual revenue. Both his bonus and Steve's were tied to revenue goals.

Competition was tight, with caterers in several countries bidding for business from airlines landing in England. Steve had hit several sales home runs in the last two years, and the care that he took in developing effective food and financial presentations attracted attention. This morning's pitch was no exception. It was to Western Winds, a large African airline. This was the first opportunity that Steve had for going after Western Winds, and Ted was impressed with his presentation plan. Also at the meeting were Flight Food's chief financial officer and head chef—a nice touch, Ted told Steve.

On the other side of the large wooden conference table sat nine members of Western Winds' entourage. Steve was impressed with the colorful robes that several company representatives wore—including a key financial manager and the director of customer service. Dressed in more traditional Western garb was Devon Litergan, Western Winds' British representative, and the person leading the day's discussion.

Flight Food figured that about three competitors were also vying for the contract. Steve thought that a superior food and financial package would give him an edge toward landing this $8 million dollar contract. Flight Food's chef put together a splendid presentation on the china and crystal used in Western Wind's first class cabin. The financial numbers were tight and attractive. Devon's smile was encouraging. He began by complimenting the presentations, and then went on to say, "We believe that the business should be yours."

Then came the rest. "Make a contribution to this account and then add twice the amount to the price of your contract," Devon said. Steve was unclear on what was being said and asked for Devon to explain. "Say you make a contribution of $1 million. We would expect that you would add to the total price of your contract twice that amount, or $2 million," Devon explained. "This is the custom of our organization."

Steve was shocked. Though he was accustomed to "contract sweeteners" used in many foreign negotiations, he had never before experienced a situation similar in magnitude. He froze.

Business Ethics, Nov./Dec. 1995. Reprinted with permission from Business Ethics Magazine, 52 S. 10th St. #110, Minneapolis, MN 55403, (612) 962–4700.

Everyone's eyes turned toward him as time slipped into a slow motion nightmare sequence. "I can't believe this is happening," he thought to himself. "I feel like Rod Serling will reach out and put his hand on my shoulder at any moment."

As he regained his composure, Steve suggested the group take a brief break. Once out in the hallway, he told Ted he couldn't believe Western Winds could be so unethical. "I can't move any further on these negotiations," Steve said. But to his surprise, the only thing Ted was worried about was how big of a contribution Flight Food should make to the Swiss bank account. "This is purely a financial arrangement. As long as it is not illegal—which it isn't—we shouldn't interject our Western ideas about what is right or wrong," Ted said. "They want to do business in their traditional manner."

Realizing that the argument wouldn't get resolved at that moment, Steve excused himself and started walking toward the men's room. Mixing pleasant smiles with "hellos" to those he passed, he fought back his anxiety as he thought to himself, "What should I do?"

Bob Page
Corporate Vice President of Purchasing Services,
Northwest Airlines,
St. Paul, Minnesota

Ted, Steve's boss, is skirting the law. Technically, this is not a bribe, but from my reading of the Foreign Corrupt Practices Act, a U.S. citizen can not go along with the arrangement of contributing money to a Swiss bank account as part of a business deal.

But aside from legal considerations, from an ethical perspective, I wouldn't do it. Hopefully, if I were Steve, I would be working for a company that knew better than to even consider the offer. I'd say, "Sorry, this isn't the way we do business." Steve must be willing to walk away from the deal. The guy should be supporting Steve, applauding him, instead of considering the offer from the business agent.

This case points to an issue that isn't going away. There are countries that don't insist on maintaining standards of conduct that many of us take for granted. As the economy becomes increasingly global, more businesses should be prepared to confront the kind of problems described in this case. It's a topic that's going to get hotter.

Dennis Christ
President, Transportation Division,
Unisys,
Blue Bell, Pennsylvania

Maybe it's where I'm at in my life or where I'm at in my company, or all the stuff that we have been through in the past with regard to meeting stiff ethical requirements with government contracts. But to me, it seems more straightforward than it may to Steve, Ted, or other people. There's nothing in this situation that would warrant going through with the request.

To me it's an obvious situation of providing grease for the skids. Whether it's a way of life in that part of the world, or not, I can't be party to it. I recognize that in taking this stand there are all sorts of implications in terms of impact on the company, impact on the people in that room, and for the boss, Ted. But I don't feel that I have to play that game. I know I could walk away from it and if it meant my job, so be it.

Ted's argument that this is purely a financial arrangement doesn't ring true. If it is purely a financial arrangement, let's put it all on the table, identify who is getting what, and make it part of a contract. Let's state clearly and above board that this is money going for so-and-so.

If everybody is prepared to make it part of the legal, contractual document, then maybe there is some rationale to do it.

Doug Wallace
Corporate ethics consultant
Minneapolis

The advice, "When in Rome, do as the Romans do," has for centuries opened up a vast sea of misuse and misinterpretation. But never more so than in our current explosive growth in international trade.

In working with many businesses, I've found that the topic of business ethics stays rational as long as people talk about U.S. operations. Once it moves into an international context, the discussion suddenly turns to murky situational ethics, where adaptation to "reality" is promoted as the highest virtue. In those cases, one's own moral principles are judged irrelevant.

Falling into this trap is easy to do because the habit of facilitating payments in some countries is woven into the fabric of their market culture. It starts with small-scale matters: an individual wanting to get through a customs check without hassle, or a company wanting a commodity shipment unloaded off the dock today instead of next week. But it then escalates: "Well, if they don't have pollution laws, who are we to insist on adding additional costs to our new plant that will meet *our* domestic requirements. It's *their* country."

The underlying question here is whether we can get beyond moral relativism or imperialism. More people are beginning to think so.

WHAT ACTUALLY HAPPENED?

Steve told his boss that he would step aside if they each presented their case up the chain of command and the answer supported Ted's position. Ted's boss took it to the president of the division. His comment was "I'll take it to the CEO myself." Within forty-five minutes the CEO called Ted's boss, who in turn asked Steve and Ted to meet. "The CEO told us we don't do this kind of deal, now or ever. Case closed."

CASE STUDY   H. B. Fuller in Honduras: Street Children and Substance Abuse

Norman Bowie and Stefanie Ann Lenway

In the summer of 1985 the following news story was brought to the attention of an official of the H. B. Fuller Company in St. Paul, Minnesota.

GLUE SNIFFING AMONG HONDURAN STREET CHILDREN IN HONDURAS:
CHILDREN SNIFFING THEIR LIVES AWAY

An Inter Press Service Feature
    BY PETER FORD
Tegucigalpa July 16, 1985 (IPS)—They lie senseless on doorsteps and pavements, grimy and loose limbed, like discarded rag dolls.

Some are just five or six years old. Others are already young adults, and all are addicted to sniffing a commonly sold glue that is doing them irreversible brain damage.

Roger, 21, has been sniffing "Resistol" for eight years. Today, even when he is not high, Roger walks with a stagger, his motor control wrecked. His scarred face puckers with concentration, his right foot taps nervously, incessantly, as he talks.

From *Ethical Issues in Business*, 5th Edition, T. Donaldson and P. Werhane, eds., Prentice-Hall, 1996, 78–90. Reprinted by permission of Columbia University Graduate School of Business.

Since he was 11, when he ran away from the aunt who raised him, Roger's home has been the streets of the capital of Honduras, the second poorest nation in the western hemisphere after Haiti.

Roger spends his time begging, shining shoes, washing car windows, scratching together a few pesos a day, and sleeping in doorways at night.

"Sniffing glue," he says, "makes me feel happy, makes me feel big. What do I care if my family does not love me? I know it's doing me damage, but it's a habit I have got, and a habit's a habit. I cannot give it up, even though I want to."

No one knows how many of Tegucigalpa's street urchins seek escape from the squalor and misery of their daily existence through the hallucinogenic fumes of "Resistol." No one has spent the time and money needed to study the question.

But one thing is clear, according to Dr. Rosalio Zavala, Head of the Health Ministry's Mental Health Department, "these children come from the poorest slums of the big cities. They have grown up as illegal squatters in very disturbed states of mental health, tense, depressed, aggressive."

"Some turn that aggression on society, and start stealing. Others turn it on themselves and adopt self-destructive behavior . . ."

But, he understands the attraction of the glue, whose solvent, toluene, produces feelings of elation. "It gives you delusions of grandeur, you feel powerful, and that compensates these kids for reality, where they feel completely worthless, like nobodies."

From the sketchy research he has conducted, Dr. Zavala believes that most boys discover Resistol for the first time when they are about 11, though some children as young as five are on their way to becoming addicts.

Of a small sample group of children interviewed in reform schools here, 56 percent told Zavala that friends introduced them to the glue, but it is easy to find on the streets for oneself.

Resistol is a contact cement glue, widely used by shoe repairers and available at household goods stores everywhere . . .

In some states of the United States, glue containing addictive narcotics such as toluene must also contain oil of mustard—the chemical used to produce poisonous mustard gas—which makes sniffing the glue so painful it is impossible to tolerate. There is no federal U.S. law on the use of oil of mustard, however . . .

But even for Dr. Zavala, change is far more than a matter of just including a chemical compound, such as oil of mustard, in a contact cement.

"This is a social problem," he acknowledges. "What we need is a change in philosophy, a change in social organization."

Resistol is manufactured by H. B. Fuller S. A., a subsidiary of Kativo Chemical Industries, S. A., which in turn is a wholly owned subsidiary of the H. B. Fuller Company of St. Paul, Minnesota.[1] Kativo sells more than a dozen different adhesives under the Resistol brand name in several countries in Latin America for a variety of industrial and commercial applications. In Honduras the Resistol products have a strong market position.

Three of the Resistol products are solvent-based adhesives designed with certain properties that are not possible to attain with a water-based formula. These properties include rapid set, strong adhesion, and water resistance. These products are similar to airplane glue or rubber cement and are primarily intended for use in shoe manufacturing and repair, leatherwork, and carpentry.

Even though the street children of each Central American country may have a different choice of a drug for substance abuse, and even though Resistol is not the only glue that Honduran street children use as an inhalant, the term "Resistolero" stuck and has become synonymous with all street children, whether they use inhalants or not. In Honduras Resistol is identified as the abused substance.

Edward Sheehan writes in the *Agony in the Garden:*

> Resistol. I had heard about Resistol. It was a glue, the angel dust of Honduran orphans. . . . In Tegucigalpa, their addiction had become so common they were known as los Resistoleros. (p. 32)

Honduras[2]

The social problems that contribute to widespread inhalant abuse among street children can be attributed to the depth of poverty in Honduras. In 1989, 65 percent of all households and 40 percent of urban households in Honduras were living in poverty, making it one of the poorest countries in Latin America. Between 1950 and 1988, the increase in the Honduran gross domestic product (GDP) was 3.8 percent, only slightly greater than the average yearly increase in population growth. In 1986, the Honduran GDP was about U.S. $740 per capita and has grown only slightly since. Infant and child mortality rates are high, life expectancy for adults is 64 years, and the adult literacy rate is estimated to be about 60 percent.

Honduras has faced several economic obstacles in its efforts to industrialize. First, it lacks abundant natural resources. The mountainous terrain has restricted agricultural productivity and growth. In addition, the small domestic market and competition from more industrially advanced countries has prevented the manufacturing sector from progressing much beyond textiles, food processing, and assembly operations.

The key to the growth of the Honduran economy has been the production and export of two commodities—bananas and coffee. Both the vagaries in the weather and the volatility of commodity markets had made the foreign exchange earned from these products very unstable. Without consistently strong export sales, Honduras has not been able to buy sufficient fuel and other productive input to allow the growth of its manufacturing sector. It also had to import basic grains (corn and rice) because the country's traditional staples are produced inefficiently by small farmers using traditional technologies with poor soil.

In the 1970s the Honduran government relied on external financing to invest in physical and social infrastructures and to implement development programs intended to diversify the economy. Government spending increased 10.4 percent a year from 1973. By 1981, the failure of many of these development projects led the government to stop financing state-owned industrial projects. The public sector failures were attributed to wasteful administration, mismanagement, and corruption. Left with little increase in productivity to show for these investments, Honduras continues to face massive budgetry deficits and unprecedented levels of external borrowing.

The government deficit was further exacerbated in the early 1980s by increasing levels of unemployment. By 1983, unemployment reached 20–30 percent of the economically active population, with an additional 40 percent of the population underemployed, primarily in agriculture. The rising unemployment, falling real wages, and low level of existing social infrastucture in education and health care contributed to the low level of labor productivity. Unemployment benefits were very limited and only about 7.3 percent of the population was covered by social security.

Rural-to-urban migration has been a major contributor to urban growth in Honduras. In the 1970s the urban population grew at more than twice as fast a rate as the rural population. This migration has increased in part as a result of a high birth rate among the rural population, along with a move by large landholders to convert forest and fallow land, driving off subsistence farmers to use the land for big-scale cotton and beef farming. As more and more land was enclosed, an increasing number of landless sought the cities for a better life.

Tegucigalpa, the capital, has had one of the fastest population increases among Central American cities, growing by 178,000 between 1970 and 1980, with a projected population of

975,000 by the year 2000. Honduras' second largest city, San Pedro Sula, is projected to have a population of 650,000 by 2000.

The slow growth in the industrial and commercial sectors has not been adequate to provide jobs for those moving to the city. The migrants to the urban areas typically move first to cuarterias (rows) of connected rooms. The rooms are generally constructed of wood with dirt floors, and they are usually windowless. The average household contains about seven persons, who live together in a single room. For those living in the rooms facing an alley, the narrow passageway between buildings serves both as sewage and waste disposal area and as a courtyard for as many as 150 persons.

Although more than 70 percent of the families living in these cuarterias had one member with a permanent salaried job, few could survive on that income alone. For stable extended families, salaried income is supplemented by entrepreneurial activities, such as selling tortillas. Given migratory labor, high unemployment, and income insecurity many family relationships are unstable. Often the support of children is left to mothers. Children are frequently forced to leave school, helping support the family through shining shoes, selling newspapers, or guarding cars; such help often is essential income. If a lone mother has become sick or dies, her children may be abandoned to the streets.

Kativo Chemical Industries S.A.[3]

Kativo celebrated its 40th anniversary in 1989. It is now one of the 500 largest private corporations in Latin America. In 1989, improved sales in most of Central America were partially offset by a reduction of its sales in Honduras.

Walter Kissling, chairman of Kativo's board and senior vice president for H. B. Fuller's international operations, has the reputation of giving the company's local managers a high degree of autonomy. Local managers often have to respond quickly because of unexpected currency fluctuations. He comments that, "In Latin America, if you know what you are doing, you can make more money managing your balance sheet than by selling products." The emphasis on managing the balance sheet in countries with high rates of inflation has led Kativo managers to develop a distinctive competence in finance.

In spite of the competitive challenge of operating under unstable political and economic conditions, Kativo managers emphasized in the annual report the importance of going beyond the bottom line:

> Kativo is an organization with a profound philosophy and ethical conduct, worthy of the most advanced firms. It carries out business with the utmost respect for ethical and legal principles, and its orientation is not solely directed to the customer, who has the highest priority, but also to the shareholders, and communities where it operates.

In the early 1980s the managers of Kativo, which was primarily a paint company, decided to enter the adhesive market in Latin America. Their strategy was to combine their marketing experience with H. B. Fuller's products. Kativo found the adhesive market potentially profitable in Latin America because it lacked strong competitors. Kativo's initial concern was to win market share. Resistol was the brand name for all adhesive products including the water-based school glue.

Kativo and the Street Children

In 1983, Honduran newspapers carried articles about police arrests of "Resistoleros"—street children drugging themselves by sniffing glue. In response to these newpaper articles, Kativo's Honduras advertising agency, Calderon Publicidad, informed the newspapers that Resistol was not the only substance abused by street children and that the image of the manufacturer was being damaged by using a prestigious trademark as a synonym for drug abusers. Moreover glue sniffing was not caused by something inherent in the product but was a social problem. For example, on one occasion the company complained to the editor, requesting that he "make the necessary effort to recommend to the editorial staff that they abstain from using the brand name Resistol as a synonym for the drug, and the adjective *Resistolero,* as a synonym for the drug addict."

The man on the spot was Kativo's vice president, Humberto Larach ("Beto"), a Honduran, who headed Kativo's North Adhesives Division. Managers in nine countries including all of Central America, Mexico, the Caribbean and two South American countries, Ecuador and Columbia, reported to him. He had become manager of the adhesive division after demonstrating his entrepreneurial talents managing Kativo's paint business in Honduras.

Beto had proven his courage and his business creativity when he was among 105 taken hostage in the Chamber of Commerce building in downtown San Pedro Sula by guerrillas from the Communist Popular Liberation Front. Despite fire fights between the guerrillas and government troops, threats of execution, and being used as a human shield, Beto had sold his product to two clients (fellow hostages) who had previously been buying products from Kativo's chief competitor! Beto also has a reputation for emphasizing the importance of "making the bottom line," as a part of Kativo corporate culture.

By summer 1985, more than corporate image was at stake. As a solution to the glue sniffing problem, social activists working with street children suggested that oil of mustard, allyl isothiocyanate, could be added to the product to prevent its abuse. They argued that a person attempting to sniff glue with oil of mustard added would find it too powerful to tolerate. Sniffing it has been described like getting an "overdose of horseradish." An attempt to legislate the addition of oil of mustard received a boost when Honduran Peace Corps volunteer, Timothy Bicknell, convinced a local group called the "Committee for the Prevention of Drugs at the National Level," of the necessity of adding oil of mustard to Resistol. All members of the committee were prominent members of Honduran society.

Beto, in response to the growing publicity about the "Resistoleros," requested staff members of H. B. Fuller's U.S. headquarters to look into the viability of oil of mustard as a solution with special attention to side effects and whether it was required or used in the United States. H. B. Fuller's corporate industrial hygiene staff found 1983 toxicology reports that oil of mustard was a cancer-causing agent in tests run with rats. A 1986 toxicology report from the Aldrich Chemical Company described the health hazard data of allyl isothiocyanate as:

ACUTE EFFECTS

May be fatal if inhaled, swallowed, or absorbed through skin.
Carcinogen.
Causes burns.
Material is extremely destructive to tissue of the mucous membranes and upper respiratory tract, eyes, and skin.

PROLONGED CONTACT CAN CAUSE

Nausea, dizziness, and headache.
Severe irritation or burns.
Lung irritation, chest pain, and edema that may be fatal.
Repeated exposure may cause asthma.

In addition the product had a maximum shelf-life of six months.

To the best of our knowledge, the chemical, physical, and toxicological properties have not been thoroughly investigated.

In 1986, Beto contacted Hugh Young, president of Solvent Abuse Foundation for Education (SAFE), and gathered information on programs SAFE had developed in Mexico. Young, who believed that there was no effective deterrent, took the position that the only viable approach to substance abuse was education, not product modification. He argued that reformulating the product was an exercise in futility because "nothing is available in the solvent area that is not abusable." With these reports in hand, Beto attempted to persuade Resistol's critics, relief agencies, and government officials that adding oil of mustard to Resistol was not the solution to the glue sniffing problem.

During the summer of 1986 Beto had his first success in changing the mind of one journalist. Earlier in the year Marie Kawas, an independent writer, wrote an article sympathetic to the position of Timothy Bicknell and the Committee for the Prevention of Drugs in Honduras. In June, Beto met with her and explained how both SAFE and Kativo sought a solution that was not product-oriented but that was directed at changing human behavior. She was also informed of the research on the dangers of oil of mustard (about which additional information had been obtained). Kawas then wrote an article:

EDUCATION IS THE SOLUTION FOR DRUG ADDICTION

LA CEIBA. (BY MARIE J. KAWAS).
A lot of people have been interested in combating drug addiction among youths and children, but few have sought solutions, and almost no one looks into the feasibility of the alternatives that are so desperately proposed . . .

Oil of mustard (allyl isothiocyanate) may well have been an irresponsible solution in the United States of America during the sixties and seventies, and the Hondurans want to adopt this as a panacea without realizing that their information sources are out of date. Through scientific progress, it has been found that the inclusion of oil of mustard in products that contain solvents, in order to prevent their perversion into use as an addictive drug, only causes greater harm to the consumers and workers involved in their manufacture . . .

Education is a primordial instrument for destroying a social cancer. An effort of this magnitude requires the cooperation of different individuals and organizations . . .

Future generations of Hondurans will be in danger of turning into human parasites, without a clear awareness of what is harmful to them. But if drugs and ignorance are to blame, it is even more harmful to sin by indifference before those very beings who are growing up in an environment without the basic advantages for a healthy physical and mental existence. Who will be the standard bearer in the philanthropic activities that will provide Honduras with the education necessary to combat drug addiction? Who will be remiss in their duty in the face of the nation's altruism?

At first, Beto did not have much success at the governmental level. In September 1986, Dr. Rosalio Zavala, Head of the Mental Health Division of the Honduran Ministry of Health, wrote an article attacking the improper use of Resistol by youth. Beto was unsuccessful in his attempt to contact Dr. Zavala. He had better luck with Mrs. Norma Castro, Governor of the State of Cortes, who after a conversation with Beto became convinced that oil of mustard had serious dangers and that glue sniffing was a social problem.

Beto's efforts continued into the new year. Early in 1987, Kativo began to establish Community Affairs Councils, as a planned expansion of the worldwide company's philosophy of community involvement. These employee committees had already been in place in the United States since 1978.

A company document gave the purpose of Community Affairs Councils:

To educate employees about community issues.
To develop understanding of, and be responsive to, the communities near our facilities.
To contribute to Kativo/H. B. Fuller's corporate presence in the neighborhoods and communities we are a part of.
To encourage and support employee involvement in the community.
To spark a true interest in the concerns of the communities in which we live and work.

The document goes on to state, "We want to be more than just bricks, mortar, machines, and people. We want to be a company with recognized values, demonstrating involvement and commitment to the betterment of the communities we are a part of." Later that year, the Honduran community affairs committees went on to make contributions to several organizations working with street children.

In March 1987, Beto visited Jose Oqueli, Vice-Minister of Public Health, to explain the philosophy behind H. B. Fuller's Community Affairs program. He also informed him of the health hazards with oil of mustard; they discussed the cultural, family, and economic roots of the problem of glue sniffing among street children.

In June 1987, Parents Resource Institute for Drug Education (PRIDE) set up an office in San Pedro Sula. PRIDE's philosophy was that through adequate *parental* education on the drug problem, it would be possible to deal with the problems of inhalant use. PRIDE was a North American organization that had taken international Nancy Reagan's "just say no" approach to inhalant abuse. Like SAFE, PRIDE took the position that oil of mustard was not the solution to glue sniffing.

Through PRIDE, Beto was introduced to Wilfredo Alvarado, the new Head of the Mental Health Division in the Ministry of Health. Dr. Alvarado, an advisor to the Congressional Committee on Health, was in charge of preparing draft legislation and evaluating legislation received by Congress. Together with Dr. Alvarado, the Kativo staff worked to prepare draft legislation addressing the problem of inhalant addicted children. At the same time, five congressmen drafted a proposed law that required the use of oil of mustard in locally produced or imported solvent-based adhesives.

In June 1988, Dr. Alvarado asked the Congressional Committee on Health to reject the legislation proposed by the five congressmen. Alvarado was given 60 days to present a complete draft of legislation. In August 1988, however, he retired from his position and Kativo lost its primary communication channel with the committee. This was critical because Beto was relying on Alvarado to help insure that the legislation reflected the technical information that he had collected.

The company did not have an active lobbying or government monitoring function in Tegucigalpa, the capital, which tends to be isolated from the rest of the country. (In fact, the company's philosophy has generally been not to lobby on behalf of its own narrow self-interest.) Beto, located in San Pedro Sula, had no staff support to help him monitor political developments. Monitoring, unfortunately, was an addition to his regular, daily responsibilities. His ability to keep track of political developments was made more difficult by the fact that he traveled about 45 percent of the time outside of Honduras. It took over two months for Beto to learn of Alvarado's departure from government. When the legislation was passed in March, he was completely absorbed in reviewing strategic plans for the nine-country divisions, which report to him.

On March 30, 1989, the Honduran Congress approved the legislation drafted by the five congressmen.

After the law's passage Beto spoke to the press about the problems with the legislation. He argued:

This type of cement is utilized in industry, in crafts, in the home, schools, and other places where it has become indispensable; thus by altering the product, he said, not only will the drug addiction problem not be solved, but rather, the country's development would be slowed.

In order to put an end to the inhalation of Resistol by dozens of people, various products that are daily necessities would have to be eliminated from the marketplace. This is impossible, he added, since it would mean a serious setback to industry at several levels . . .

There are studies that show that the problem is not the glue itself, but rather the individual. The mere removal of this substance would immediately be substituted by some other, to play the same hallucinogenic trip for the person who was sniffing it.

H. B. Fuller: The Corporate Response

In late April 1986, Elmer Andersen, H. B. Fuller Chairman of the Board, received the following letter:

Elmer L. Andersen
H. B. Fuller Co.

Dear Mr. Andersen

I heard part of your talk on public radio recently and was favorably impressed with your philosophy that business should not be primarily for profit. This was consistent with my previous impression of H. B. Fuller Company since I am a public health nurse and have been aware of your benevolence to the nursing profession.

However, on a recent trip to Honduras, I spent some time at a new home for chemically dependent "street boys" who are addicted to glue sniffing. It was estimated that there are 600 of these children still on the streets in San Pedro Sula alone. The glue is sold for repairing *tennis shoes* and I am told it is made by H. B. Fuller in *Costa Rica*. These children also suffer toxic effects of liver and brain damage from the glue . . .

Hearing you on the radio, I immediately wondered how this condemnation of H. B. Fuller Company could be consistent with the company as I knew it before and with your business philosophy.

Are you aware of this problem in Honduras, and, if so, how are you dealing with it?

That a stockholder should write the 76-year-old Chairman of the Board directly is significant. Elmer Andersen is a legendary figure in Minnesota. He is responsible for the financial success of H. B. Fuller from 1941–1971 and his values reflected in his actions as CEO are embodied in H. B. Fuller's mission statement.

H. B. Fuller Mission Statement

The H. B. Fuller corporate mission is to be a leading and profitable worldwide formulator, manufacturer, and marketer of quality specialty chemicals, emphasizing service to customers and managed in accordance with a strategic plan.

H. B. Fuller Company is committed to its responsibilities, in order of priority, to its customers, employees, and shareholders. H. B. Fuller will conduct business legally and ethically, support the activities of its employees in their communities, and be a responsible corporate citizen.

It was also Elmer Andersen, who as President and CEO, made the decision that foreign acquisitions should be managed by locals. Concerning the 1967 acquisition of Kativo Chemical Industries Ltd., Elmer Andersen said:

We had two objectives in mind. One was directly business related and one was altruistic. Just as we had expanded in America, our international business strategy was to pursue markets where our competitors were not active. We were convinced that we had something to offer Latin America that the region did not have locally. In our own small way, we also wanted to be of help to that part of the world. We believed that by producing adhesives in Latin America and by employing only local people, we would create new jobs and help elevate the standard of living. We were convinced that the way to aid world peace was to help Latin America become more prosperous.

Three years later a stockholder dramatically raised the Resistol issue for a second time directly by a stockholder. On June 7, 1989, Vice President for Corporate Relations, Dick Johnson, received a call from a stockholder whose daughter was in the Peace Corps in Honduras. She asked, "How can a company like H. B. Fuller claim to have a social conscience and continue to sell Resistol, which is 'literally burning out the brains' of children in Latin America?"

Johnson was galvanized into action. This complaint was of special concern because he was about to meet with a national group of socially responsible investors who were considering including H. B. Fuller's stock in their portfolio. Fortunately Karen Muller, Director of Community Affairs, had been keeping a file on the glue sniffing problem. Within 24 hours of receiving the call, Dick had written a memo to CEO Tony Andersen.

In that memo he set forth the basic values to be considered as H. B. Fuller wrestled with the problem. Among them were the following:

1. H. B. Fuller's explicitly stated public concern about substance abuse.
2. H. B. Fuller's "Concern for Youth" focus in its community affairs projects.
3. H. B. Fuller's reputation as a socially responsible company.
4. H. B. Fuller's history of ethical conduct.
5. H. B. Fuller's commitment to the intrinsic value of each individual.

Whatever "solution" was ultimately adopted would have to be consistent with these values. In addition, Dick suggested a number of options including the company's withdrawal from the market or perhaps altering the formula to make Resistol a water-based product, eliminating sniffing as an issue.

Tony responded by suggesting that Dick create a task force to find a solution and a plan to implement it. Dick decided to accept Beto's invitation to travel to Honduras to view the situation firsthand. He understood that the problem crossed functional and divisional responsibilities. Given H. B. Fuller's high visibility as a socially responsible corporation, the glue sniffing problem had the potential for becoming a public relations nightmare. The brand name of one of H. B. Fuller's products had become synonymous with a serious social problem. Additionally, Dick understood that there was an issue larger than product misuse involved, and it had social and community ramifications. The issue was substance abuse by children, whether the substance is an H. B. Fuller product or not. As a part of the solution, a community relations response was required. Therefore, he invited Karen to join him on his trip to Honduras.

Karen recalled a memo she had written about a year earlier directed to Beto. In it she had suggested a community relations approach rather than Beto's government relations approach. In that memo Karen wrote:

This community relations process involves developing a community-wide coalition from all those with a vested interest in solving the community issue—those providing services in dealing with the street children and drug users, other businesses, and the government. It does require leadership over the long-term both with a clear set of objectives and a commitment on the part of each group represented to share in the solution . . .

In support of the community relations approach Karen argued that:

1. It takes the focus and pressure off H. B. Fuller as one individual company.
2. It can educate the broader community and focus on the best solution, not just the easiest ones.
3. It holds everyone responsible, the government, educators, H. B. Fuller's customers, legitimate consumers of our product, social service workers and agencies.
4. It provides H. B. Fuller with an expanded good image as a company that cares and will stay with the problem—that we are willing to go the second mile.
5. It can de-politicize the issue.
6. It offers the opportunity to counterbalance the negative impact of the use of our product name Resistol by re-identifying the problem.

Karen and Dick left on a four-day trip to Honduras September 18. Upon arriving they were joined by Beto, Oscar Sahuri, General Manager for Kativo's adhesives business in Honduras, and Jorge Walter Bolanos, Vice President Director of Finance, Kativo. Karen had also asked Mark Connelly, a health consultant from an international agency working with street children, to join the group. They began the process of looking at all aspects of the situation. Visits to two different small shoe manufacturing shops and a shoe supply distributor helped to clarify the issues around pricing, sales, distribution, and the packaging of the product.

A visit to a well-run shelter for street children provided them with some insight into the dynamics of substance abuse among this vulnerable population in the streets of Tegucigalpa and San Pedro Sula. At a meeting with the officials at the Ministry of Health, they reviewed the issue of implementing the oil-of-mustard law, and the Kativo managers offered to assist the committee as it reviewed the details of the law. In both Tegucigalpa and San Pedro Sula, the National Commission for Technical Assistance to Children in Irregular Situations (CONATNSI), a country-wide association of private and public agencies working with street children, organized meetings of its members at which the Kativo managers offered an explanation of the company's philosophy and the hazards involved in the use of oil of mustard.

As they returned from their trip to Honduras, Karen and Dick had the opportunity to reflect on what they had learned. They agreed that removing Resistol from the market would not resolve the problem. However, the problem was extremely complex. The use of inhalants by street children was a symptom of Honduras' underlying economic problems—problems with social, cultural, and political aspects as well as economic dimensions.

Honduran street children come from many different circumstances. Some are true orphans, while others are abandoned. Some are runaways, while others are working the streets to help support their parents. Children working at street jobs or begging usually earn more than the minimum wage. Nevertheless, they are often punished if they bring home too little. This creates a vicious circle; they would rather be on the street than take punishment at home—a situation that increases the likelihood they will fall victim to drug addiction. The street children's problems are exacerbated by the general lack of opportunities and a lack of enforcement of school attendance laws. In addition, the police sometimes abuse street children.

Karen and Dick realized that Resistol appeared to be the drug of choice for young street children who were able to obtain it in a number of different ways. There was no clear pattern, and hence the solution could not be found in simply changing some features of the distribution system. Children might obtain the glue from legitimate customers, small shoe repair stalls, by theft, from "illegal" dealers or from third parties who purchased it from legitimate stores and then sold it to children. For some sellers the sale of Resistol to children could be profitable. The glue was available in small packages, which made it more affordable, but the economic circumstances of the typical legitimate customer made packaging in small packages economically sensible.

The government had long been unstable. As a result there was a tendency for people working with the government to hope that new policy initiatives would fade away within a few months. Moreover there was a large continuing turnover of government, so that any knowledge of H. B. Fuller and its corporate philosophy soon disappeared. Government officials usually had to settle for a quick fix, for they were seldom around long enough to manage any other kind of policy. Although it was on the books for six months by the time of their trip, the oil-of-mustard law had not yet been implemented, and national elections were to be held in three months. During meetings with government officials, it appeared to Karen and Dick that no further actions would be taken as current officials waited for the election outcome.

Kativo company officers, Jorge Walter Bolanos and Humberto Larach, discussed continuing the government relations strategy hoping that the law might be repealed or modified. They were also concerned with the damage done to H. B. Fuller's image. Karen and Dick thought the focus should be on community relations. From their perspective, efforts directed toward changing the law seemed important but would do nothing to help with the long-term solution to the problems of the street children who abused glue.

Much of the concern for street children was found in private agencies. The chief coordinating association was CONATNSI, created as a result of a seminar sponsored by UNICEF in 1987. CONATNSI was under the direction of a general assembly and a Board of Directors elected by the General Assembly. It began its work in 1988; its objectives included (a) improving the quality of services, (b) promoting interchange of experiences, (c) coordinating human and material resources, (d) offering technical support, and (e) promoting research. Karen and others believe that CONATNSI had a shortage of both financial and human resources, but it appeared to be well-organized and was a potential intermediary for the company.

As a result of their trip, they knew that a community relations strategy would be complex and risky. H. B. Fuller was committed to a community relations approach, but what would a community relations solution look like in Honduras? The mission statement did not provide a complete answer. It indicated the company had responsibilities to its Honduran customers and employees, but exactly what kind? Were there other responsibilities beyond those directly involving its product? What effect can a single company have in solving an intractable social problem? How should the differing emphases in perspective of Kativo and its parent, H. B. Fuller, be handled? What does corporate citizenship require in situations like this?

NOTES

1. The Subsidiaries of the North Adhesives Division of Kativo Chemical Industries, S. A. go by the name "H. B. Fuller (Country of Operation)," e.g., H. B. Fuller S. A. Honduras. To prevent confusion with the parent company we will refer to H. B. Fuller S. A. Honduras by the name of its parent, "Kativo."

2. The following discussion is based on *Honduras: A Country Study,* 2nd ed., James D. Rudolph, ed. (Washington, D.C.: Department of the Army, 1984).

3. Unless otherwise indicated all references and quotations regarding H. B. Fuller and its subsidiary Kativo Chemical Industries S. A. are from company documents.

RESOURCES

Acker, Alison, *The Making of a Banana Republic* (Boston: South End Press, 1988).

Rudolph, James D., ed., *Honduras: A Country Study,* 2nd ed. (Washington, D.C.: Department of the Army, 1984).

H. B. Fuller Company, *A Fuller Life: The Story of H. B. Fuller Company: 1887–1987* (St. Paul: H. B. Fuller Company, 1986).

Schine, Eric, "Preparing for Banana Republic U.S." *Corporate Finance* (December, 1987).

Sheehan, Edward, *Agony in the Garden: A Stranger in Central America* (Boston: Houghton Mifflin, 1989).

CASE STUDY   *Dow Chemical Company and Shell Oil Company*
v. Domingo Castro Alfaro, et. al.

Supreme Court of Texas, 1990
786 S.W.2d 674

The following excerpt from an opinion of the Supreme Court of Texas concerns the pesticide Dibromochloropropane ("DBCP"), widely used in the United States through the late 1970s, when further sale and use was prohibited by the Environmental Protection Agency (EPA), based on evidence linking exposure to DBCP to a variety of injuries and illness, including sterility. Dow Chemical and Shell Oil, among other companies, continued to manufacture and sell DBCP abroad. Standard Fruit Company, an American subsidiary of a company headquartered in Florida, purchased DBCP for use in Costa Rica. In 1984, Domingo Castro Alfaro, a Costa Rican plantation worker, along with many other employees of Standard Fruit, filed suit against both Dow and Shell for DBCP-related injuries. The suit was filed in a state court in Houston, Texas. Shell's world headquarters is located in Houston, and Dow maintains a large presence in Texas. Dow and Shell both sought to have the case against them dismissed on procedural grounds under a doctrine known as *forum non conveniens.* This is a legal claim that asks a court to decline to hear a case on the grounds that to defend itself in that court would cause the defendants undue hardship. The companies wanted to have the plaintiffs in the case forced to bring their suit in a "more convenient" location, which in this case would be Costa Rica. The law in Costa Rica was far more favorable to Dow and Shell, since it severely limited the amount of damages that could be awarded in such a case and would not force Dow or Shell employees to travel to Costa Rica to appear in court. The issue before the Supreme Court of Texas was whether to grant the defendants' request for a dismissal.

DOGGETT, Justice, concurring.

. . . In their zeal to implement their own preferred social policy that Texas corporations not be held responsible at home for harm caused abroad, these dissenters refuse to be restrained by either express statutory language or the compelling precedent, previously approved by this very court, holding that *forum non conveniens* does not apply in Texas. To accomplish the desired social engineering, they must invoke yet another legal fiction with a fancy name to shield alleged wrongdoers. . . . The refusal of a Texas corporation to confront a Texas judge and jury is to be labelled "inconvenient" when what is really involved is not convenience but connivance to avoid corporate accountability.

. . . The dissenters are insistent that a jury of Texans be denied the opportunity to evaluate the conduct of a Texas corporation concerning decisions it made in Texas because the only ones allegedly hurt are foreigners. Fortunately Texans are not so provincial and narrow-minded as these dissenters presume. Our citizenry recognizes that a wrong does not fade away because its immediate consequences are first felt far away rather than close to home. Never have we been required to forfeit our membership in the human race in order to maintain our proud heritage as citizens of Texas.

The dissenters argue that it is inconvenient and unfair for farmworkers allegedly suffering permanent physical and mental injuries, including irreversible sterility, to seek redress by suing a multinational corporation in a court three blocks away from its world headquarters and another corporation, which operates in Texas this country's largest chemical plant. Because the "doctrine" they advocate has nothing to do with fairness and convenience and everything to do with immunizing multinational corporations from accountability for their alleged torts causing injury abroad, I write separately.

Shell Oil Company is a multinational corporation with its world headquarters in Houston, Texas. Dow Chemical Company, though headquartered in Midland, Michigan, conducts extensive operations from its Dow Chemical USA building located in Houston. Dow operates this country's largest chemical manufacturing plant within 60 miles of Houston in Freeport, Texas. The district court where this lawsuit was filed is three blocks away from Shell's world headquarters, One Shell Plaza in downtown Houston.

Shell has stipulated that all of its more than 100,000 documents relating to DBCP are located or will be produced in Houston. Shell's medical and scientific witnesses are in Houston. The majority of Dow's documents and witnesses are located in Michigan, which is far closer to Houston (both in terms of geography and communications linkages) than to Costa Rica. The respondents have agreed to be available in Houston for independent medical examinations, for depositions, and for trial. Most of the respondents' treating doctors and co-workers have agreed to testify in Houston. Conversely, Shell and Dow have purportedly refused to make their witnesses available in Costa Rica.

The banana plantation workers allegedly injured by DBCP were employed by an American company on American-owned land and grew Dole bananas for export solely to American tables. The chemical allegedly rendering the workers sterile was researched, formulated, tested, manufactured, labeled, and shipped by an American company in the United States to another American company. The decision to manufacture DBCP for distribution and use in the third world was made by these two American companies in their corporate offices in the United States. Yet now Shell and Dow argue that the one part of this equation that should not be American is the legal consequences of their actions.

. . . Both as a matter of law and of public policy, the doctrine of *forum non conveniens* is without justification. The proffered foundations for it are "considerations of fundamental fairness and sensible and effective judicial administration. . . ." In fact, the doctrine is favored by multinational defendants because a *forum non conveniens* dismissal is often outcome-determinative, effectively defeating the claim and denying the plaintiff recovery. . . .

. . . The abolition of *forum non conveniens* will further important public policy considerations by providing a check on the conduct of multinational corporations. . . . The misconduct of even a few multinational corporations can affect untold millions around the world. For example, after the United States imposed a domestic ban on the sale of cancer-producing TRIS-treated children's sleepwear, American companies exported approximately 2.4 million pieces to Africa, Asia, and South America. A similar pattern occurred when a ban was proposed for baby pacifiers that had been linked to choking deaths in infants. . . .

. . . The allegations against Shell and Dow, if proven true, would not be unique, since production of many chemicals banned for domestic use has thereafter continued for foreign marketing. . . .

During the mid-1970s . . . the EPA began to restrict the use of some pesticides because of their environmental effects, and OSHA established workplace exposure standards for toxic and hazardous substances in the manufacture of pesticides. . . . [I]t is clear that many pesticides that have been severely restricted in the United States are used without restriction in many third world countries, with resulting harm to fieldworkers and the global environment. . . .

. . . Some United States multinational corporations will undoubtedly continue to endanger human life and the environment with such activities until the economic consequences of these actions are such that it becomes unprofitable to operate in this manner. At present, the tort laws of many third world countries are not yet developed. . . .

. . . The doctrine of *forum non conveniens* is obsolete in a world in which markets are global and in which ecologists have documented the delicate balance of all life on this planet. The parochial perspective embodied in [it] enables corporations to evade legal control merely because they are transnational. This perspective ignores the reality that actions of our corporations affecting those abroad will also affect Texans. Although DBCP is banned from use within the United States, it and other similarly banned chemicals have been consumed by Texans eating foods imported from Costa Rica and elsewhere. . . . In the absence of meaningful tort liability in the United States for their actions, some multinational corporations will continue to operate without adequate regard for the human and environmental costs of their actions. This result cannot be allowed to repeat itself for decades to come. . . .

HECHT, Justice, dissenting.

. . . [F]or this Court to give aliens injured outside Texas an absolute right to sue in this state inflicts a blow upon the people of Texas, its employers and taxpayers, that is contrary to sound policy.

The United States does not give aliens unlimited access to its courts. Indeed, one federal district court in California and two in Florida have already dismissed essentially this same lawsuit which the Court now welcomes to Texas. No state has ever given aliens such unlimited admission to its courts. The United States Supreme Court, the District of Columbia, and forty states have all recognized what has come to be called the rule of *forum non conveniens.* Simply stated, the rule is that "[a] state will not exercise jurisdiction if it is a seriously inconvenient forum for the trial of the action provided that a more appropriate forum is available to the plaintiff. . . ." The rule is founded in "considerations of fundamental fairness and sensible and effective judicial administration. . . ." Until now, no state has ever rejected this rule. This Court, however, does not even acknowledge the collective wisdom of the entire country. . . .

The dearth of authority for the Court's unprecedented holding is disturbing. Far more disconcerting, however, is the Court's silence as to why the rule of *forum non conveniens* should be abolished in personal injury and death cases, either by the Legislature or by the Court. . . . The benefit to the plaintiffs in suing in Texas should be obvious: more money. . . . This advantage to suing in American courts has not escaped international notice. England's Lord Denning, for example, has observed, "As a moth is drawn to the light, so is a litigant drawn to the United States. If he can only get his case into their courts, he stands to win a fortune. . . ."

. . . But what purpose beneficial to the people of Texas is served by clogging the already burdened dockets of the state's courts with cases which arose around the world and which have nothing to do with this state except that the defendant can be served with citation here? Why, most of all, should Texas be the only state in the country, perhaps the only jurisdiction on earth, possibly the only one in history, to offer to try personal injury cases from around the world? Do Texas taxpayers want to pay extra for judges and clerks and courthouses and personnel to handle foreign litigation? If they do not mind the expense, do they not care that these foreign cases will delay their own cases being heard? As the courthouse for the world, will Texas entice employers to move here, or people to do business here, or even anyone to visit? . . . Who gains? A few lawyers, obviously. But who else? . . .

Moral Minimums for Multinationals[1]

Thomas Donaldson

When exploring issues of international ethics, researchers frequently neglect multinational corporations. They are prone to forget that these commercial leviathans often rival nation-states in power and organizational skill, and that their remarkable powers imply nonlegal responsibilities. Critics and defenders agree on the enormity of corporate multinational power. Richard Barnet and Ronald Mul-

From *The Ethics of International Business* by Thomas Donaldson, 1989, Oxford University Press. Reprinted by permission.

ler, well-known critics of multinationals, remark that the global corporation is the "most powerful human organization yet devised for colonizing the future"[2] The business analyst, P. P. Gabriel, writing in the *Harvard Business Review,* characterizes the multinational as the "dominant institution" in a new era of world trade.[3] Indeed, with the exception of a handful of nation-states, multinationals are alone in possessing the size, technology, and economic reach necessary to influence human affairs on a global basis.

Ethical issues stemming from multinational corporate activities often derive from a clash between the cultural attitudes in home and host countries. When standards for pollution, discrimination, and salary schedules appear lower in a multinational's host country than in the home country, should multinational managers always insist on home-country standards? Or does using home standards imply a failure to respect cultural diversity and national integrity? Is a factory worker in Mexico justified in complaining about being paid three dollars an hour for the same work a U.S. factory worker, employed by the same company, is paid ten dollars?[4] Is an asbestos worker in India justified in criticizing the lower standards for regulating in-plant asbestos pollution maintained by a British multinational relative to standards in Britain, when the standards in question fall within Indian government guidelines and, indeed, are stricter than the standards maintained by other Indian asbestos manufacturers? Furthermore, what obligations, if any, do multinationals have to the people they affect indirectly? If a company buys land from wealthy landowners and turns it to the production of a cash crop, should it ensure that displaced farmers will avoid malnutrition?

I

It is well to remember that multinational power is not a wholly new phenomenon. Hundreds of years ago, the East India Company deployed over 40 warships, possessed the largest standing army in the world, was lord and master of an entire subcontinent, had dominion over 250 million people, and even hired its own church bishops.[5] The modern multinational is a product of the post–World War II era, and its dramatic success has stemmed from,

among other factors, spiraling labor costs in developed countries, increasing importance of economies of scale in manufacturing, better communication systems, improved transportation, and increasing worldwide consumer demand for new products.[6] Never far from the evolution of the multinational has been a host of ethical issues, including bribery and corrupt payments, employment and personnel issues, marketing practices, impact on the economy and development of host countries, effects on the natural environment, cultural impacts of multinational operations, relations with host governments, and relations with the home countries.[7]

The formal responsibilities of multinationals as defined in domestic and international law, as well as in codes of conduct, are expanding dramatically. While many codes are nonbinding in the sense that noncompliance will fail to trigger sanctions, these principles, taken as a group, are coming to exert significant influence on multinational conduct. A number of specific reasons lie behind the present surge in international codes and regulations. To begin with, some of the same forces propelling domestic attempts to bring difficult-to-control activities under stricter supervision are influencing multinationals.[8] Consider, for example, hazardous technology, a threat which by its nature recognizes no national boundaries yet must be regulated in both domestic and foreign contexts. The pesticide industry, which relies on such hazardous technology (of which Union Carbide's Bhopal plant is one instance), in 1987 grossed over $13 billion a year and has been experiencing mushrooming growth, especially in the developing countries.[9] It is little surprise that the rapid spread of hazardous technology has prompted the emergence of international codes on hazardous technology, such as the various U.N. resolutions on the transfer of technology and the use of pesticides.

Furthermore, just as a multiplicity of state regulations and laws generates confusion and inefficiency, and stimulates federal attempts to manage conduct, a multiplicity of national regulations stimulates international attempts at control. Precisely this push for uniformity lies behind, for example, many of the international codes of ethics, such as the WHO Code of Marketing Breast Milk Substitutes. Another well-known instance illustrating the need for uniformity involved the collision of French and U.S. law in the sale of equipment by

Dresser Industries to the Soviets for the planned European pipeline. U.S. law forbade the sale of such technology to the Soviets for reasons of national security while French law (which affected a Dresser subsidiary) encouraged it in order to stimulate commercial growth. It was neither to the advantage of Dresser Industries nor to the advantage of the French and U.S. governments to be forced to operate in an arena of conflict and inconsistency. For months the two governments engaged in a public standoff while Dresser, and Dresser's public image, were caught in the middle.

National laws, heretofore unchallenged in authority, are now being eclipsed by regulatory efforts falling into four categories: namely, inter-firm, inter-government, cooperative, and world-organizational efforts.[10] The first category of "inter-firm" standards is one that reflects initiatives from industries, firms, and consumer groups, and it includes the numerous inter-industry codes of conduct that are operative for international business, such as the World Health Organization's Code on Pharmaceuticals and Tobacco, and the World Intellectual Property Organization's Revision of the Paris Convention for the Protection of Industrial Patents and Trademarks. The second category of "inter-government" efforts includes specific-purpose arrangements between and among nation-states, such as the General Agreement on Tariffs and Trade (GATT), the International Monetary Fund (IMF), and the World Bank.[11] "Cooperative" efforts, which comprise the third category, involve governments and industries coordinating skills in mutual arrangements that regulate international commerce. The European Community (EC) and the Andean Common Market (ANCOM) are two notable examples of such cooperative efforts.[12]

Finally, the fourth or "world-organizational" category includes efforts from broad-based global institutions such as the World Court, the International Labor Organization (ILO), the Organization for Economic Cooperation and Development (OECD), and the various sub-entities of the United Nations.

II

The growing tradition of international business codes and policies suggests that the investigation of ethical issues in international business is press-

ing and proper. But what issues deserve attention?

One key set of issues relates to business practices that clearly conflict with the moral attitudes of most multinationals' home countries. Consider, for example, the practice of child labor, which continues to plague developing countries. While not the worst example, Central America offers a sobering lesson. In dozens of interviews with workers throughout Central America conducted in the fall of 1987, most respondents said they started working between the ages of 12 and 14.[13] The work week lasts six days, and the median salary (for all workers including adults) is scarcely over a dollar a day. The area is largely non-unionized, and strikes are almost always declared illegal. There is a strong similarity between the pressures compelling child labor in Central America and those in early nineteenth-century England during the Industrial Revolution. With unemployment ranging from a low of 24 percent in Costa Rica to a high of 50 percent in Guatemala, and with families malnourished and older breadwinners unable to work, children are often forced to make growth-stunting sacrifices.[14]

Then, too, there are issues about which our moral intuitions seem confused, issues which pose difficult questions for researchers. Consider an unusual case involving the sale of banned goods abroad—one in which a developing country argued that being able to buy a banned product was important to meeting its needs. Banned pharmaceuticals, in contrast to other banned goods, have been subject to export restrictions for over 40 years. Yet, in defense of a recent Reagan initiative, drug manufacturers in the United States argued by appealing to differing cultural variables. For example, a spokesman for the American division of Ciba-Geigy Pharmaceuticals justified relaxing restrictions on the sale of its Entero-Vioform, a drug he agrees has been associated with blindness and paralysis, on the basis of culture-specific, cost-benefit analysis. "The government of India," he pointed out, "has requested Ciba-Geigy to continue producing the drug because it treats a dysentery problem that can be life threatening."[15]

III

The task for the international ethicist is to develop or discover concepts capable of specifying the obligations of multinational corporations in cases such as these. One such important concept is that of a human right.

Rights establish minimum levels of morally acceptable behavior. One well-known definition of a right construes it as a "trump" over a collective good, which is to say that the assertion of one's right to something, such as free speech, takes precedence over all but the most compelling collective goals, and overrides, for example, the state's interest in civil harmony or moral consensus.[16] Rights are at the rock bottom of modern moral deliberation. Maurice Cranston writes that the litmus test for whether something is a right or not is whether it protects something of "paramount importance."[17] Hence, it may help to define what minimal responsibilities should be assigned to multinational corporations by asking, "What specific rights ought multinationals to respect?"

The flip side of a right typically is a duty.[18] This, in part, is what gives aptness to Joel Feinberg's well-known definition of a right as a "justified entitlement *to* something *from* someone."[19] It is the "from someone" part of the definition that reflects the assumption of a duty, for without a correlative obligation that attaches to some moral agent or group of agents, a right is weakened—if not beyond the status of a right entirely, then significantly. If we cannot say that a multinational corporation has a duty to keep the levels of arsenic low in the workplace, then the worker's right not to be poisoned means little.

Often, duties associated with rights fall upon more than one class of moral agent. Consider, for example, the furor over the dumping of toxic waste in West Africa by multinational corporations. During 1988, virtually every country from Morocco to the Congo on Africa's west coast received offers from companies seeking cheap sites for dumping waste.[20] In the years prior, dumping in the United States and Europe had become enormously expensive, in large part because of the costly safety measures mandated by U.S. and European governments. In February of 1988, officials in Guinea-Bissau, one of the world's poorest nations, agreed to bury 15 million tons of toxic wastes from European tanneries and pharmaceutical companies. The companies agreed to pay about $120 million, which is only slightly less than the country's entire gross national product. In Nigeria in 1987, five European ships unloaded toxic waste in Nigeria containing

dangerous poisons such as polychlorinated biphenyls, or PCBs. Workers wearing thongs and shorts unloaded the barrels for $2.50 a day, and placed them in a dirt lot in a residential area in the town of Kiko.[21] They were not told about the contents of the barrels.[22]

Who bears responsibility for protecting the workers' and inhabitants' rights to safety in such instances? It would be wrong to place it entirely upon a single agent such as the government of a West African nation. As it happens, the toxic waste dumped in Nigeria entered under an import permit for "nonexplosive, nonradioactive, and non-self-combusting chemicals." But the permit turned out to be a loophole; Nigeria had not meant to accept the waste and demanded its removal once word about its presence filtered into official channels. The example reveals the difficulty many developing countries have in creating the sophisticated language and regulatory procedures necessary to control high-technology hazards. It seems reasonable in such instances, then, to place the responsibility not upon a single class of agents, but upon a broad collection of them, including governments, corporate executives, host-country companies and officials, and international organizations.

One list receiving significant international attention is the Universal Declaration of Human Rights.[23] However, it and the subsequent International Covenant on Social, Economic, and Cultural Rights have spawned controversy, despite the fact that the Declaration was endorsed by virtually all of the important post–World War II nations in 1948 as part of the affirmation of the U.N. Charter. What distinguishes these lists from their predecessors, and what serves also as the focus of controversy, is their inclusion of rights that have come to be called, alternatively, "social," "economic," "positive," or "welfare" rights.

Many have balked at such rights, arguing that no one can have a right to a specific supply of an economic good. Can anyone be said to have a "right," for example, to 128 hours of sleep and leisure each week? And, in the same spirit, some international documents have simply refused to adopt the welfare-affirming blueprint established in the Universal Declaration. For example, the European Convention of Human Rights omits mention of welfare rights, preferring instead to create an auxiliary document (The European Social Charter of 1961), which references many of what earlier had been treated as "rights," as "goals." Similar objections underlie the bifurcated covenants drawn up in an attempt to implement the Universal Declaration: one such covenant, entitled the Covenant on Civil and Political Rights, was drawn up for all signers, including those who objected to welfare rights, while a companion covenant, entitled the Covenant on Social, Economic, and Cultural Rights, was drawn up for welfare rights defenders. Of course, many countries signed both; but some signed only the former.[24]

Many who criticize welfare rights utilize a traditional philosophical distinction between so-called negative and positive rights. A positive right is said to be one that requires persons to act positively to *do* something, while a negative one requires only that people not directly deprive others. Hence, the right to liberty is said to be a negative right, whereas the right to enough food is said to be a positive one. With this distinction in hand, the point is commonly made that no one can be bound to improve the welfare of another (unless, say, that person has entered into an agreement to do so); rather, they can be bound at most to *refrain* from damaging the welfare of another.

Nonetheless, Henry Shue has argued persuasively against the very distinction between negative and positive rights. Consider the most celebrated and best accepted example of a negative right: namely, the right to freedom. The meaningful preservation of the right to freedom requires a variety of positive actions: for example, on the part of the government it requires the establishment and maintenance of a police force, courts, and the military, and on the part of the citizenry it requires ongoing cooperation and diligent (not merely passive) forbearance. The protection of another so-called negative right, the right to physical security, necessitates "police forces; criminal rights; penitentiaries; schools for training police, lawyers, and guards; and taxes to support an enormous system for the prevention, detention, and punishment of violations of personal security."[25]

This is compelling. The maintenance and preservation of many non-welfare rights (where, again, such maintenance and preservation is the key to a right's status as basic) require the support of certain basic welfare rights. Certain liberties depend upon the enjoyment of subsistence, just as subsistence sometimes depends upon the enjoyment of some liberties. One's freedom to speak freely is meaningless if one is weakened by hunger to the point of silence.

What list of rights, then, ought to be endorsed on the international level? Elsewhere I have argued that the rights appearing on such a list should pass the following three conditions:[26] (1) the right must protect something of very great importance; (2) the right must be subject to substantial and recurrent threats; and (3) the obligations or burdens imposed by the right must satisfy a fairness-affordability test.[27]

In turn, I have argued that the list of fundamental international rights generated from these conditions include: (1) the right to freedom of physical movement; (2) the right to ownership of property; (3) the right to freedom from torture; (4) the right to a fair trial; (5) the right to nondiscriminatory treatment (e.g., freedom from discrimination on the basis of such characteristics as race or sex); (6) the right to physical security; (7) the right to freedom of speech and association; (8) the right to minimal education; (9) the right to political participation; and (10) the right to subsistence.

This seems a minimal list. Some will wish to add entries such as the right to employment, to social security, or to a certain standard of living (say, as might be prescribed by Rawls's well-known "difference" principle). The list as presented aims to suggest, albeit incompletely, a description of a *minimal* set of rights and to serve as a point of beginning and consensus for evaluating international conduct. If I am correct, many would wish to add entries, but few would wish to subtract them.

As we look over the list, it is noteworthy that, except for a few isolated instances, multinational corporations have probably succeeded in fulfilling their duty not to actively deprive persons of their enjoyment of the rights at issue. But correlative duties involve more than failing to actively deprive people of the enjoyment of their rights. Shue, for example, notes that three types of correlative duties (i.e., duties corresponding to a particular right) are possible: (1) to avoid depriving; (2) to help protect from deprivation; and (3) to aid the deprived.[28]

While it is obvious that the honoring of rights clearly imposes duties of the first kind, i.e., to avoid depriving directly, it is less obvious, but frequently true, that honoring them involves acts or omissions that help prevent the deprivation of rights. If I receive a note from Murder, Incorporated, and it looks like business, my right to security is clearly threatened. Let's say that a third party (X) has relevant information, which, if revealed to the police, would help protect my right to security. In this case, there is no excuse for X to remain silent, claiming that it is Murder, Incorporated, and not X, who wishes to murder me.

Similarly, the duties associated with rights often include ones from the third category, i.e., that of aiding the deprived, as when a government is bound to honor the right of its citizens to adequate nutrition by distributing food in the wake of famine or natural disaster, or when the same government, in the defense of political liberty, is required to demand that an employer reinstate or compensate an employee fired for voting for a particular candidate in a government election.

Which of these duties apply to corporations, and which apply only to governments? It would be unfair, not to mention unreasonable, to hold corporations to the same standards for enhancing and protecting social welfare to which we hold civil governments—since frequently governments are formally dedicated to enhancing the welfare of, and actively preserving the liberties of, their citizens. The profit-making corporation, in contrast, is designed to achieve an economic mission and as a moral actor possesses an exceedingly narrow personality. It is an undemocratic institution, furthermore, which is ill-suited to the broader task of distributing society's goods in accordance with a conception of general welfare. The corporation is an economic animal; although its responsibilities extend beyond maximizing return on investment for shareholders, they are informed directly by its economic mission. Hence, while it would be strikingly generous for multinationals to sacrifice some of their profits to buy milk, grain, and shelter for persons in poor countries, it seems difficult to consider this one of their minimal moral requirements. If anyone has such minimal obligations, it is the peoples' respective governments or, perhaps, better-off individuals.

The same, however, is not true of the second class of duties, i.e., to protect from deprivation. While these duties, like those in the third class, are also usually the province of government, it sometimes happens that the rights to which they correlate are ones whose protection is a direct outcome of ordinary corporate activities. For example, the duties associated with protecting a worker from the physical threats of other workers may fall not only upon the local police but also upon the employer. These duties, in turn, are properly viewed as correlative duties of the right—in this instance, the worker's right—to personal security. This will become clearer in a moment when we discuss the correlative duties of specific rights.

The following list of correlative duties reflects a second-stage application of the fairness-affordability condition to the earlier list of fundamental international rights, and indicates which rights do, and which do not, impose correlative duties upon multinational corporations of the three various kinds.[29]

Minimal Correlative Duties of Multinational Corporations

Fundamental Rights	*To Avoid Depriving*	*To Help Protect from Deprivation*	*To Aid the Deprived*
Freedom of physical movement	X		
Ownership of property	X		
Freedom from torture	X		
Fair trial	X		
Nondiscriminatory treatment	X	X	
Physical security	X	X	
Freedom of speech and association	X	X	
Minimal education	X	X	
Political Participation	X	X	
Subsistence	X	X	

Let us illustrate the duty to protect from deprivation with specific examples. The right to physical security entails duties of protection. If a Japanese multinational corporation operating in Nigeria hires shop workers to run metal lathes in an assembly factory, but fails to provide them with protective goggles, then the corporation has failed to honor the workers' moral right to physical security (no matter what the local law might decree). Injuries from such a failure would be the moral responsibility of the Japanese multinational despite the fact that the company could not be said to have inflicted the injuries directly.

Another correlative duty, to protect the right of education, may be illustrated through the example mentioned earlier: namely, the prevalence of child labor in developing countries. A multinational in Central America is not entitled to hire an eight-year-old for full-time, ongoing work because, among other reasons, doing so blocks the child's ability to receive a minimally sufficient education. While what counts as a "minimally sufficient" education may be debated, and while it seems likely, moreover, that the specification of the right to a certain level of education will depend at least in part upon the level of economic resources available in a given country, it is reasonable to assume that any action by a corporation that has the effect of blocking the development of a child's ability to read or write will be proscribed on the basis of rights.

In some instances, corporations have failed to honor the correlative duty of protecting the right to political participation from deprivation. The most blatant examples of direct deprivation are fortunately becoming so rare as to be nonexistent, namely, cases in which companies directly aid in overthrowing democratic regimes, as when United Fruit, Inc., allegedly contributed to overthrowing a democratically elected regime in Guatemala during the 1950s. But a few corporations have continued indirectly to threaten this right by failing to protect it from deprivation. A few have persisted, for example, in supporting military dictatorships in countries with growing democratic sentiment, and others have blatantly bribed publicly elected officials with large sums of money. Perhaps the most celebrated example of the latter occurred when the prime minister of Japan was bribed with $7 million by the Lockheed Corporation to secure a lucrative Tri-Star Jet contract. The complaint from the perspective of this right is not against bribes or "sensitive payments" in general, but against bribes in contexts where they serve to undermine a democratic system in which publicly elected officials are in a position of public trust.

Even the buying and owning of major segments of a foreign country's land and industry have been criticized in this regard. As Brian Barry has remarked, "The paranoia created in Britain and the United States by land purchases by foreigners (especially the Arabs and the Japanese, it seems) should serve to make it understandable that the citizenry of a country might be unhappy with a state of affairs in which the most important natural resources are in foreign ownership."[30] At what point would Americans regard their democratic control threatened by foreign ownership of U.S. industry and resources? At 20 percent ownership? At 40 percent? At 60 percent? At 80 percent? The answer is debatable, yet there seems to be some point beyond which the right to national self-determination, and in turn national democratic control, is violated by foreign ownership of property.[31]

Corporations also have duties to protect the right to subsistence from deprivation. Consider the following scenario. A number of square miles of land in an underdeveloped country has been used for years to grow black beans. The bulk of the land is owned, as it has been for centuries, by two wealthy landowners. Poorer members of the community work the land and receive a portion of the crop, a portion barely sufficient to satisfy nutritional needs. Next, imagine that a multinational corporation offers the two wealthy owners a handsome sum for the land, and does so because it plans to grow coffee for export. Now if—and this, admittedly, is a crucial "if"—the corporation has reason to *know* that a significant number of people in the community will suffer malnutrition as a result—that is, if it has convincing reasons to believe either those persons will fail to be hired by the company and paid sufficiently or, if forced to migrate to the city, will receive wages insufficient to provide adequate food and shelter—then the multinational may be said to have failed in its correlative duty to protect persons from the deprivation of the right to subsistence. This despite the fact that the corporation would never have stooped to take food from workers' mouths, and despite the fact that the malnourished will, in Coleridge's words, "die so slowly that none call it murder."

In addition to articulating a list of rights and the correlative duties imposed upon multinational corporations, there is also a need to articulate a practical stratagem for use in applying the home-country norms of the multinational manager to the vexing problems arising in developing countries. In particular, how should highly placed multinational managers, typically schooled in home-country moral traditions, reconcile conflicts between those traditions and ones of the host country? When host-country standards for pollution, discrimination, and salary schedules appear substandard from the perspective of the home country, should the manager take the high road and implement home-country standards? Or does the high road imply a failure to respect cultural diversity and national integrity?

What distinguishes these issues from standard ones about corporate practices is that they involve reference to a conflict of norms, either moral or legal, between home and host country. Consider two actual instances of the problem at issue.

Case #1: A new American bank in Italy was advised by its Italian attorneys to file a tax return that misstated income and expenses and consequently grossly underestimated actual taxes due. The bank learned, however, that most other Italian companies regarded the practice as standard operating procedure and merely the first move in a complex negotiating process with the Italian internal revenue service. The bank initially refused to file a fallacious return on moral grounds and submitted an "American-style" return instead. But because the resulting tax bill was many times higher than what comparable Italian companies were asked to pay, the bank charged policy in later years to agree with the "Italian style." [32]

Case #2: In 1966 Charles Pettis, employee of an American multinational, became resident engineer for one of the company's projects in Peru: a 146-mile, $46 million project to build a highway across the Andes. Pettis soon discovered that Peruvian safety standards were far below those in the United States. The highway design called for cutting through mountains in areas where rock formations were unstable. Unless special precautions were taken, slides could occur. Pettis blew the whistle, complaining first to Peruvian government officials and later to U.S. officials. No special precautions were taken, with the result that 31 men were killed by landslides during the construction of the road. Pettis was fired and had difficulty finding a job with another company. [33]

One may well decide that enforcing home-country standards was necessary in one of the above cases, but not in the other. One may decide that host-country precautions in Peru were unacceptable, while at the same time acknowledging that, however inequitable and inefficient Italian tax mores may be, a decision to file "Italian style" is permissible.

Thus, despite claims to the contrary, one must reject the simple dictum that whenever the practice violates a moral standard of the home country, it is impermissible for the multinational company. Arnold Berleant has argued that the principle of equal treatment endorsed by most U.S. citizens requires that U.S. corporations pay workers in less developed countries exactly the same wages paid to U.S. workers in comparable jobs (after appropriate adjustments are made for cost of living levels in the relevant areas). [34] But most observers, including those from the less developed countries, believe this stretches the doctrine of equality too far in a way that is detrimental to host countries. By arbitrarily establishing U.S. wage levels as the benchmark for fairness, one eliminates the role of the international market in establishing salary levels, and this in turn eliminates the incentive U.S. corporations have to hire foreign workers. Perhaps U.S. firms should exceed market rate for foreign labor as a matter of moral principle, but to pay strictly equal rates would freeze less developed countries out of the international labor market. [35] Lacking a simple formula such as "the practice is wrong when it violates the home country's norms," one seems driven to undertake a more complex analysis of the types and degrees of responsibilities multinationals possess.

What is needed is a more comprehensive test than a simple appeal to rights. Of course the earlier rights-based approach clarifies a moral bottom line regarding, say, extreme threats to workers' safety. But it leaves obscure not only the issue of less extreme threats, but of harms other than physical injury. Granted, the celebrated dangers of asbestos call for recognizing the right to workers' safety no matter how broadly the language of rights is framed. But what are we to say of a less toxic pollutant? Is the level of sulphur-dioxide air pollution we should tolerate in a struggling nation, one with only a few fertilizer plants working overtime to help feed its malnourished population, the same we should demand in Portland, Oregon?

In the end, nothing less than a general moral theory working in tandem with an analysis of the foundations of corporate existence is needed. But at the practical level a need exists for an interpretive mechanism or algorithm that multinational managers could use in determining the implications of their own moral views.

The first step in generating such an ethical algorithm is to isolate the distinct sense in which the norms of the home and host country conflict. If the practice is morally and/or legally permitted in the host country, but not in the home country, then either: (1) the moral reasons underlying the host country's view that the practice is permissible refer to the host country's relative level of economic development; or (2) the moral reasons underlying the host country's view that the practice is permissible are independent of the host country's relative level of economic development.

Let us call the conflict of norms described in (1) a type 1 conflict. In such a conflict, an African country that permits slightly higher levels of thermal pollution from electric power generating plants, or a lower minimum wage than prescribed in European countries, would do so not because higher standards would be undesirable per se, but because its level of economic development requires an ordering of priorities. In the future, when it succeeds in matching European economic achievements, it may well implement the higher standards.

Let us call the conflict of norms described in (2) a type 2 conflict. In such cases, levels of economic development play no role. For example, low-level institutional nepotism, common in many developing countries, is justified not on economic grounds, but on the basis of clan and family loyalty. Presumably the same loyalties will be operative even after the country has risen to economic success—as the nepotism prevalent in Saudi Arabia would indicate. The Italian tax case also reflects an Italian cultural style with a penchant for personal negotiation and an unwillingness to formalize transactions, more than a strategy based on level of economic development.

The difference in norms between the home and host country, i.e., whether the conflict is of type 1 or 2, does not determine the correctness, or truth value, of the host country's claim that the practice is permissible. The practice may or may not be permissible, whether the conflict is of type 1 or 2. This is not to say that the truth value of the host country's claim is independent of the nature of the conflict. A different test will be required to determine whether the practice is permissible when the conflict is of type 1 as opposed to type 2. In a type 1 dispute, the following formula is appropriate:

> The practice is permissible if and only if the members of the home country would, under conditions of economic development similar to those of the host country, regard the practice as permissible.

Under this test, excessive levels of asbestos pollution would almost certainly not be tolerated by the members of the home country under similar economic conditions, whereas higher levels of thermal pollution would be tolerated. The test, happily, explains and confirms our initial moral intuitions.

Since in type 2 conflicts the dispute between the home and host country depends upon a fundamental difference of perspective, a different test is needed. In type 2 conflicts, the opposing evils of ethnocentricism and ethical relativism must be avoided. A multinational must forego the temptation to remake all societies in the image of its home society, while at the same time rejecting a relativism that conveniently forgets ethics when the payoff is sufficient. Thus, the ethical task is to tolerate cultural diversity while drawing the line at moral recklessness.

Since in type 2 cases the practice is in conflict with an embedded norm of the home country, one should first ask whether the practice is necessary to do business in the host country, for if it is not, the solution clearly is to adopt some other practice that is permissible from the standpoint of the home country. If petty bribery of public officials is unnecessary for the business of the Cummins Engine

Company in India, then the company is obliged to abandon such bribery. If, on the other hand, the practice proves necessary for business, one must next ask whether the practice constitutes a direct violation of a basic human right. Here the notion of a fundamental international right outlined earlier, specifying a minimum below which corporate conduct should not fall, has special application. If Toyota, a Japanese company, confronts South African laws that mandate systematic discrimination against nonwhites, then Toyota must refuse to comply with the laws. In type 2 cases, the evaluator must ask the following questions: (1) Is it possible to conduct business successfully in the host country without undertaking the practice? and (2) Is the practice a clear violation of a fundamental international right? The practice would be permissible if and only if the answer to both questions is "no."

What sorts of practice might satisfy both criteria? Consider the practice of low-level bribery of public officials in some developing nations. In some South American countries, for example, it is impossible for any company, foreign or national, to move goods through customs without paying low-level officials a few dollars. Indeed, the salaries of such officials are sufficiently low that one suspects they are set with the prevalence of the practice in mind. The payments are relatively small, uniformly assessed, and accepted as standard practice by the surrounding culture. Here, the practice of petty bribery would pass the type 2 test and, barring other moral factors, would be permissible.

The algorithm does not obviate the need for multinational managers to appeal to moral concepts both more general and specific than the algorithm itself. It is not intended as a substitute for a general theory of morality or even an interpretation of the basic responsibilities of multinationals. Its power lies in its ability to tease out implications of the moral presuppositions of a manager's acceptance of "home" morality, and in this sense to serve as a clarifying device for multinational decision-making. The algorithm makes no appeal to a universal concept of morality (as the appeal to fundamental rights does in type 2 cases), save for the purported universality of the ethics endorsed by the home-country culture. When the home country's morality is wrong or confused, the algorithm can reflect this ethnocentricity, leading either to a mild paternalism or to the imposition of parochial

standards. For example, the home country's over-sensitivity to aesthetic features of the environment may lead it to reject a certain level of thermal pollution, even under strained economic circumstances. This results in a paternalistic refusal to allow such levels in the host country, despite the host country's acceptance of the higher levels and its belief that tolerating such levels is necessary for stimulating economic development. It would be a mistake, however, to exaggerate this weakness of the algorithm; coming up with actual cases in which the force of the algorithm would be relativized is extremely difficult. Indeed, I have been unable to discover a single, nonhypothetical set of facts fitting this description.

IV

How might multinational corporations improve their moral performance and come to embody the normative concepts advanced in this article? Two classes of remedies suggest themselves: external remedies, i.e., those that rely on international associations or agreements on the one hand; and internal remedies, i.e., those that rely on internal, corporate initiative on the other.

Earlier we discussed the dramatic expansion of external remedies in the form of international laws, agreements, and codes of conduct. Again, while many of these are nonbinding in the sense that noncompliance will fail to trigger sanctions, they are as a group coming to exert significant influence on multinational conduct. One of the principal advantages of such global and industry-wide initiatives is that they distribute costs more fairly than initiatives undertaken by individual corporations. When, in line with the WHO Code of Marketing Breast Milk Substitutes, Nestle curtails questionable marketing practices for the sale of infant formula, it does so with the confidence that the other signers of the WHO Code will not be taking unfair advantage by undertaking the same questionable practices, for they must adhere to its provisions. Still another advantage of external remedies stems from the fact that many nation-states, especially developing ones, are unable to gather sufficient information about, much less control, the multinational corporations that operate within their borders. Thus, the use of supranational entities, whether of an international or inter-industry form, will sometimes augment, or supplement, the power and information-gathering abilities of developing nations. It seems difficult to deny that the growth and maturation of such entities can enhance the ethical conduct of multinational corporations.

The most important change of an internal nature likely to enhance the ethical behavior of multinationals is for multinationals themselves to introduce ethical deliberation, i.e., to introduce factors of ethics into their decision-making mechanisms. That they should do so is a clear implication of the preceding discussion, yet it is a conclusion some will resist. Those who place great confidence in the efficacy of the market may, for example, believe that a corporate policy of moral disinterest and profit maximization will—*pace* Adam Smith's invisible hand—maximize overall global welfare.

This kind of ideological confidence in the international market may have been understandable decades ago. But persisting in the belief that market mechanisms will automatically ensure adequate moral conduct today seems recklessly idealistic. Forces such as Islamic fundamentalism, the global debt bomb, and massive unemployment in developing countries have drastically distorted the operation of the free market in international commerce, and even though a further selective freeing of market forces may enhance global productivity, it cannot automatically solve questions of fair treatment, hazardous technology, or discrimination.

Even adopting the minimal guidelines for corporate conduct advanced here would involve dramatic changes in the decision-making mechanisms of multinational corporations. Such firms would need to alter established patterns of information flow and collection in order to accommodate new forms of morally relevant information. The already complex parameters of corporate decision-making would become more so. Even scholarly research about international business would need to change. At present, research choices tend to be dictated by the goals of increased profits, long-term access to basic commodities needed for manufactured items, and increased global market share; but clearly these goals sometimes conflict with broader moral ends, such as refraining from violating human rights. Revised goals call for a revised program of research. And although we have rejected the view that multinational corporations must shoulder the

world's problems of poverty, discrimination, and political injustice because, as economic entities, they have limited social missions, their goals nonetheless must include the aim of not impeding solutions to such problems.

Are such changes in the decision-making of multinational corporations likely or even possible? Resistance will be intense; clearly, there should be no delusions on this score. Yet, without minimizing the difficulties, I do not think the task impossible. At a minimum, corporations are capable of choosing the more ethical alternative in instances where alternative courses of action yield equal profits— and I believe they are capable of even more. Corporations are run by human beings, not beasts. As multinationals continue to mature in the context of an ever-expanding, more sophisticated global economy, we have reason to hope that they are capable of looking beyond their national borders and recognizing the same minimal claims made in the name of our shared humanity that they accept at home.

NOTES

1. Much of this article is extracted from Thomas Donaldson's book, *The Ethics of International Business* (Oxford: Oxford University Press, 1989). The book provides a framework for interpreting the ethics of global business. Excerpts reprinted by permission of Oxford University Press.
2. Richard Barnet and Ronald Muller, *Global Reach: The Power of Multinational Corporations* (New York: Simon and Schuster, 1974), p. 363.
3. P. P. Gabriel, "MNCs in the Third World: Is Conflict Unavoidable?" *Harvard Business Review,* Vol. 56 (March–April 1978), pp. 83–93.
4. An example of disparity in wages between Mexican and U.S. workers is documented in the case study by John H. Haddox, "Twin-Plants and Corporate Responsibilities," in *Profits and Responsibility,* eds. Patricia Werhane and Kendall D'Andrade (New York: Random House, 1985).
5. Barnet and Muller, *Global Reach,* p. 72.
6. J. R. Simpson, "Ethics and Multinational Corporations vis-à-vis Developing Nations," *Journal of Business Ethics,* Vol. 1 (1982), pp. 227–37.
7. I have borrowed this eight-fold scheme of categories from researchers Farr and Stening in Lisa Farr and Bruce W. Stening's "Ethics and the Multinational Corporation" (an unpublished paper), p. 4.
8. An analysis of such reasons, one which also contains many observations on the evolution of international

public policy, is Lee E. Preston's "The Evolution of Multinational Public Policy Toward Business: Codes of Conduct," a paper read at the annual meeting of the American Academy of Management, New Orleans, August 1987.

9. Jon R. Luoma, "A Disaster That Didn't Wait," *The New York Times Book Review,* November 29, 1987, p. 16.

10. While I personally have coined the terms, "inter-industry," "inter-government," etc., the basic four-fold division of international initiatives is drawn from Preston, *op. cit.*

11. See, for example, Raymond J. Waldman, *Regulating International Business through Codes of Conduct* (Washington, D.C.: American Enterprise Institute, 1980).

12. See, for example, P. S. Tharp, Jr., "Transnational Enterprises and International Regulation: A Survey of Various Approaches to International Organizations," *International Organization,* Vol. 30 (Winter 1976), pp. 47–73.

13. James LeMoyne, "In Central America, the Workers Suffer Most," *The New York Times,* October 26, 1987, pp. 1 and 4.

14. *Ibid.*

15. Quoted in "Products Unsafe at Home Are Still Unloaded Abroad," *The New York Times,* August 22, 1982, p. 22.

16. Ronald Dworkin, *Taking Rights Seriously* (Cambridge: Harvard University Press, 1977). For other standard definitions of rights, see: James W. Nickel, *Making Sense of Human Rights: Philosophical Reflections on the Universal Declaration of Human Rights* (Berkeley: University of California Press, 1987) especially chapter 2; Joel Feinberg, "Duties, Rights and Claims," *American Philosophical Quarterly,* Vol. 3 (1966), pp. 137–44. See also Feinberg, "The Nature and Value of Rights," *Journal of Value Inquiry,* Vol. 4 (1970), pp. 243–57; Wesley N. Hohfeld, *Fundamental Legal Conceptions* (New Haven: Yale University Press, 1964); and H. J. McCloskey, "Rights—Some Conceptual Issues," *Australasian Journal of Philosophy,* Vol. 54 (1976), pp. 99–115.

17. Maurice Cranston, *What Are Human Rights?* (New York: Taplinger, 1973), p. 67.

18. H. J. McCloskey, for example, understands a right as a positive entitlement that need not specify who bears the responsibility for satisfying that entitlement. H. J. McCloskey, "Rights—Some Conceptual Issues," p. 99.

19. Joel Feinberg, "Duties, Rights and Claims," *American Philosophical Quarterly,* Vol. 3 (1966), pp. 137–44. See also Feinberg, "The Nature and Value of Rights," pp. 243–57.

20. James Brooke, "Waste Dumpers Turning to West Africa," *The New York Times,* July 17, 1988, pp. 1 and 7.

21. *Ibid.*

22. *Ibid.,* p. 7. Nigeria and other countries have struck back, often by imposing strict rules against the acceptance of toxic waste. For example, in Nigeria officials now warn that anyone caught importing toxic waste will face the firing squad.

23. See Ian Brownlie, *Basic Documents on Human Rights* (Oxford: Oxford University Press, 1975).

24. James W. Nickel, "The Feasibility of Welfare Rights in Less Developed Countries," in *Economic Justice: Private Rights and Public Responsibilities,* eds. Kenneth Kipnis and Diana T. Meyers (Totowa, N. J.: Rowman and Allenheld, 1985), pp. 217–26.

25. Henry Shue, *Basic Rights: Subsistence, Affluence, and U. S. Foreign Policy* (Princeton: Princeton University Press, 1980), pp. 37–38.

26. Donaldson, *The Ethics of International Business,* see especially chapter 5. My formulation of these three conditions is an adaptation from four conditions presented and defended by James Nickel in James W. Nickel, *Making Sense of Human Rights: Philosophical Reflections on the Universal Declaration of Human Rights* (Berkeley: University of California Press, 1987).

27. The fairness-affordability test implies that in order for a proposed right to qualify as a genuine right, all moral agents (including nation-states, individuals, and corporations) must be able under ordinary circumstances, both economically and otherwise, to assume the various burdens and duties that fall fairly upon them in honoring the right. "Affordable" here means literally capable of paying for; it does not mean "affordable" in the vernacular sense that something is not affordable because it would constitute an inefficient luxury, or would necessitate trading off other more valuable economic goods. This definition implies that—at least under unusual circumstances—honoring a right may be mandatory for a given multinational corporation, even when the result is bankrupting the firm. For example, it would be "affordable" under ordinary circumstances for multinational corporations to employ older workers and refuse to hire eight-year-old children for full-time, ongoing labor, and hence doing so would be mandatory even in the unusual situation where a particular firm's paying the higher salaries necessary to hire older laborers would probably bankrupt the firm. By the same logic, it would probably not be "affordable" for either multinational corporations or nation-states around the world to guarantee kidney dialysis for all citizens who need it. The definition also implies that any act of forbearance (of a kind involved in not violating a right directly) is "affordable" for all moral agents.

28. Shue, *Basic Rights,* p. 57.

29. It is possible to understand even the first four rights as imposing correlative duties to protect from dep-

rivation under highly unusual or hypothetical circumstances.

30. Brian Barry, "The Case for a New International Economic Order," in *Ethics, Economics, and the Law: Nomos XXIV*, eds. J. Roland Pennock and John W. Chapman (New York: New York University Press, 1982).

31. Companies are also charged with undermining local governments, and hence infringing on basic rights, by sophisticated tax evasion schemes. Especially when companies buy from their own subsidiaries, they can establish prices that have little connection to existing market values. This, in turn, means that profits can be shifted from high-tax to low-tax countries, with the result that poor nations can be deprived of their rightful share.

32. Donaldson and Werhane, eds., *Ethical Issues in Business*, 4th ed. (Englewood Cliffs: Prentice-Hall, 1993).

33. Charles Peters and Taylor Branch, *Blowing the Whistle: Dissent in the Public Interest* (New York: Praeger, 1974), pp. 182–85.

34. Arnold Berleant, "Multinationals and the Problem of Ethical Consistency," *Journal of Business Ethics*, Vol. 3 (August 1982), pp. 182–95.

35. Some have argued that insulating the economies of the less developed countries would be advantageous to the less developed countries in the long run. But whether correct or not, such an argument is independent of the present issue, for it is independent of the claim that if a practice violates the norms of the home country, then it is impermissible.

Business Abroad

Ellen Frankel Paul

Introduction

An area of commerce that poses ethical as well as public policy challenges is foreign trade. With the phenomenal rise of multinational commerce, people in the business world need to think clearly about proper conduct and sound public policy in foreign trade.

Should corporate executives sanction payoffs to government officials of foreign countries in order to secure contracts to sell or purchase goods within those countries? Is it permissible for United States corporations to engage in business activities within countries that practice racial discrimination and deprive blacks of basic human rights as a matter of governmental policy?

Questions like these have dominated the public media and its treatment of international business, particularly in the post-Watergate era, for Watergate brought to public awareness the fact that multinational corporations often acted in ways that did not conform to our intuition about how moral individuals ought to act. When it was revealed that corporations often kept slush funds to make contributions of a dubious nature to domestic politicians, and that corporations also engaged in activities that

smacked of bribery of foreign officials, big business suffered a tremendous loss in public esteem.

But how are we to determine whether such seemingly dubious business activities are actually unjustifiable from a moral point of view? Given that we live in a world in which moral codes conflict, how ought these issues be decided? After all, we are not simply engaged in an idle, albeit interesting, academic discussion, but rather in an enterprise with direct implications for public policy. While virtually all moral systems developed in our Western tradition have condemned such activities as murder, theft, bribery, or lying, they have done so from different foundational principles, and sometimes these principles have led their practitioners to differ about the classification of the same sorts of activities. For example, some moral theorists might claim that stealing another person's property is always to be categorized as theft and condemned, while another theorist, operating from different principles, might declare that if a person were starving and another had an abundance of goods, then the destitute man would be justified in stealing from the rich man, while still a third moralist might claim that private property is illegitimate by its very nature, and therefore everyone should receive from society what he needs.

It might be helpful in examining these troublesome issues relating to international business to pause for a moment to examine several ethical systems that have shaped the thinking of moralists in the Western tradition, especially during the last three centuries. Three systems appear to have dominated the field of ethics during this period: (1) utilitarianism, (2) natural rights theory, and (3) Kantianism.

Utilitarianism is an ethical system devised principally by Jeremy Bentham, a British moral philosopher who wrote in the late eighteenth and early nineteenth centuries. Although utilitarianism was modified by Bentham's illustrious successor, John Stuart Mill, to allow for more conformity to conventional ethical judgments, its essential character has remained constant to this day, and many contemporary philosophers and public policy analysts are still adherents of utilitarianism. In fact, the currently popular notion of cost/benefit analysis owes its inspiration to this doctrine. Utilitarianism is based on the perception that human beings are pain-avoiders and pleasure-seekers. More importantly, utilitarians conclude from this observation of how individuals actually behave that they *ought* to act in this way. Thus, if one wishes to behave morally and be a good utilitarian, one should seek to maximize one's pleasure and minimize one's pain. From this moral precept, utilitarians seek to generalize from the behavior of single individuals to how people ought to behave in society, and how their governments ought to legislate. The famous utilitarian maxim proclaims—act to achieve the greatest happiness for the greatest number. Therefore, when a government examines a proposal for, let us say, building a new hospital, it should consider the pleasure to be gained by the likely beneficiaries and balance that against the harm to be suffered by the projected losers. Also, the onerousness of any legislative action must be taken into account and the advantages and disadvantages of using public funds for a different purpose. It is easy to see how modern cost/benefit analysis developed from this approach to morality.

In contrast to utilitarianism, which tends to be very pragmatic because it weighs harms and benefits to reach its moral and policy prescriptions, natural rights theory is more abstract and theoretical. John Locke's *Second Treatise of Government* is the veritable bible of natural rights theory. Written in the late seventeenth century, again by an English author, it proclaimed the importance of individualism and the protection of individuals from gov-

ernmental oppression in their pursuit of property and in their exercise of liberty. Locke went so far as to proclaim a novel thesis, that government exists for the protection of the property—and he meant by property, life, liberty, and estates—of individuals, and, indeed, that government is nothing more than a trustee established by the consent of individuals for the purpose of protecting their rights. Government, consequently, can be overthrown if it acts in ways that violate the rights of men.

Our third moral system was developed by a German philosopher, Immanuel Kant, in the late eighteenth century. Kant argued that to act morally an individual ought to conceive the principle upon which he acts as one upon which everyone should act. An example might help clarify his position. Let us imagine that you are thinking about murdering your rich uncle, who also happens to be a genuinely despicable character. But if we apply the principle embodied in this proposal—that everyone ought to eliminate rich people who also happen to be nasty—one can foresee some really horrendous consequences for the future welfare of society. Kant called this principle the "categorical imperative." Another element of Kantianism has remained influential—his precept that one ought to treat people as ends only and never simply as means to the pursuit of one's own ends. What this principle captures is the notion of the moral autonomy and importance of every living person, that is, the idea that people ought not be treated as tools to be used for another person's pleasure. If these Kantian ideas sound familiar, it is not surprising, for Kant acknowledged that what his moral principles amounted to was the Christian precept that one ought to treat others as one wished to be treated—the Golden Rule.

In what follows, we will examine two major issues of controversy regarding American business practices abroad: (1) the payment of allegedly illicit payments to foreign government officials, and (2) the practice of doing business in countries with objectionable social practices. It is my hope that the three ethical positions adumbrated above might prove helpful in refining our intuitive reactions to each of these practices.

Foreign Bribery

In December 1977, Congress passed the Foreign Corrupt Practices Act (FCPA) without a single dissenting vote. This remarkable unanimity was the result of a series of revelations of bribery engaged in by some of America's leading corporations in their business dealings around the world. It was revealed that officials of Lockheed, Gulf Oil, Northrop, and Boeing (among others) had made payments to officials of foreign governments in order to secure business for their firms. In an orgy of self-revelation, some 450 United States corporations revealed to the Securities and Exchange Commission that they had made three hundred million dollars worth of under-the-table payoffs.

The FCPA made it a criminal offense for any United States corporation to make any payment to a foreign official or foreign political party or its official for the purpose of influencing that person to exercise his authority or connections to affect decisions of his government. In other words, United States corporations were prohibited from paying bribes to foreign officials to solicit their assistance in securing contracts. Companies caught violating the Act would be subject to a fine of up to one million dollars, while officers or directors of the offending companies could receive sentences of up to five years in jail and ten thousand dollars in fines. In addition, the Act called for detailed disclosure in the accounting records submitted by companies to the SEC in an attempt to eliminate double bookkeeping that could hide secret payments. This provision, too, carries criminal penalties. As of April 1983, twenty-six cases had been brought against companies by the SEC and another eight cases by the Justice Department, which shares enforcement powers with the SEC.

Despite the unanimous support that the FCPA garnered in Congress in 1977, it has provoked widespread objections in the business community. Since 1981, lobbying for amendments to the legislation has been intense, with business groups pressuring congressmen to eliminate what they feel to be some of the more onerous elements of the Act. While their efforts had not met with success (as of 1984) as the result of some powerful opposition in the House, the Senate did pass amendments to the act in November 1981, but that effort failed to reach the House floor. These efforts at amending the FCPA have continued. The principal objectives of these proposed amendments is to remove the criminal penalties attached to the accounting disclosure requirements and to weaken the liability placed on corporate officers for payments made by third-

party intermediaries. This latter objective would be achieved by diluting the original language of the Act, which placed liability on officers if they had "reason to know" that payments might be made by intermediaries. This provision would be replaced by one that limited liability to instances in which the executive directed or authorized the payment "expressly or by a course of conduct." Representative Timothy Wirth (D., Colorado) the leading opponent of this reform in the House considers such language to be much too vague, and he condemns the effort at reform as an attempt to emasculate the Act and evade its intent.

Businessmen who favor modifications of FCPA and their congressional allies—most conspicuously Senators John Chafee (R., Rhode Island) and John Heinz (R., Pennsylvania), and Representative Dan Mica (D., Florida)—view the matter quite differently. While no one goes so far as to endorse bribery or urge the outright repeal of FCPA, they do point to its tendency to undermine our exporting effort both by discouraging companies from actively pursuing foreign contracts because of uncertainty about when they might fall afoul of the vaguely defined prohibitions of FCPA, and by placing even the willing companies at a competitive disadvantage. If European companies, for example, can enter a country like Saudi Arabia and pay bribes disguised as "commissions" to members of the royal family, how, these critics ask, can American companies compete? Indeed, no other country has followed our lead, they point out, in prohibiting such payoffs so scrupulously, and this despite the fact that the United States, ever since the passage of the FCPA, has been working through diplomatic channels to achieve such an international agreement on the prohibition of these questionable practices. In West Germany, such payments are fully tax deductible; in Italy, a 1980 law established that payments to foreign officials to secure business are legal; and in France no law exists to curb foreign bribery.[1] In a Louis Harris poll conducted in the Fall of 1983 among corporate officials, 78 percent of the respondents agreed that the law makes it difficult to sell in countries in which bribery is a way of life and that U.S. exports are, therefore, hindered. About one-fifth of the respondents also felt that they had lost business as a result of the Act, a figure only slightly less than the 30 percent who claimed losses two years earlier in a General Accounting Office survey.[2] What the Harris Poll also indicated was a division of opinion about what ought to be done about some controversial elements of the FCPA, with opinion divided over the elimination of criminal penalties for violating the accounting provisions and the effort to ease executives' accountability for payments made by intermediaries.

While it is difficult to quantify a nonevent such as the loss of potential business, some evidence does exist that the U.S. export effort has been adversely affected by the Act. For example, the Emergency Committee for American Trade surveyed its 65 member-companies and they reported an estimated two billion dollars in lost business. This translates into 60,000 to 80,000 lost jobs in the United States, according to Commerce Department estimates.[3] Norman Pacun, vice-president and general counsel of Ingersoll-Rand, a company with over one billion dollars in foreign sales per year, testified before the Senate Banking Committee that while it is difficult to quantify such lost business, many experts have pointed to the negative impact of the FCPA in the OPEC countries in particular. As confirmation of this conjecture, he pointed to the much slower growth of our exports to OPEC countries than throughout the rest of the world after the passage of the Act.[4] And President Carter's task force on export promotion concluded that the FCPA constitutes the second most serious legal disincentive for U.S. exports, with only the tax code presenting a graver barrier.

Business critics, like Mr. Pacun, have also pointed to the fact that America's scrupulousness in policing its own corporations has not significantly ameliorated the problem of bribery around the world. While American companies have undeniably been curtailed from committing these "shady" acts, foreign companies have not been so constrained. Some critics even argue that if our objective is to greatly constrain such activities throughout the world, our unilateral attempt serves to hamper that effort rather than encourage it because other countries realize that by refusing to sign an international prohibition they can still reap the benefits of eliminating American competitors. Thus, the only true beneficiaries of the FCPA would be our foreign competitors, and we will have accomplished little or nothing for the cause of international morality.

Critics have also pointed to the deleterious for-

eign policy implications of the FCPA. Foreign governments, they maintain, are often offended by our "holier than thou" attitude and deeply resent our attempt to foist our values upon them. Curiously, in May 1981 a former State Department official who handled the attempts at negotiating an international agreement on the prohibition of bribery testified before the Senate Banking Committee that "it is hard to overestimate the potential damage to U.S. relations with another country if we find ourselves investigating and disclosing misconduct by the head of government or other senior officials of that country. It is likely that one day the policies of this Act and critical U.S. foreign policy interests will come into sharp conflict."[5] Little more than two years later former Japanese Prime Minister Kakuei Tanaka was found guilty of taking nearly two million dollars in bribes from Lockheed to get All Nippon Airlines to purchase a fleet of planes from Lockheed. When these payments were revealed in the 1970s, they weakened the Japanese government, and the aftereffects are still being felt.

In addition to these more weighty objections, opponents point to the vagueness of the Act's requirements, and their consequent inability to distinguish a permissible payment—so-called "grease" payments to minor officials such as customs agents to facilitate the entry of goods—from impermissible acts of bribery. Given that the Act excluded such trivial payments to minor governmental functionaries, the problem of where to draw the line is rife for differences of opinion. Thus, the ambiguity of the law has engendered much confusion. And finally, the detailed recordkeeping and the lack of precise standards for the information required in these disclosures has disturbed some businessmen and added to their accounting costs.

Those who favor the Act tend not to go into such great detail as their critics. For them, the Act's necessity is nearly self-evident, given the unacceptably immoral practices that many businesses perpetrated prior to its passage. While they might concede that some technical clarification to the wording of the Act would be acceptable, and even Representative Wirth has seemed more accommodating, they bitterly resent any attempts to dilute the criminal liability elements imposed on executives by the FCPA. Although some supporters deny that American businesses have suffered loss of trade as a result of the Act, most acknowledge that this might well be the case, yet they hold morality to be more imperative in this case than the marginal promotion of the U.S. export-import business.

Now that we have perused some of the arguments for and against the FCPA and its modifications, let us proceed as moralists to examine this Act. It is difficult, indeed, to discover a moral system that explicitly and unqualifiedly endorses bribery. But as Mark Pastin and Michael Hooker have pointed out in their article "Ethics and the Foreign Corrupt Practices Act,"[6] there may well be countervailing considerations of a moral nature that can modify a general prohibition against bribery in the types of cases covered by the FCPA. They examined the Act from two different moral positions, one utilitarian and the other, more or less Kantian. As they examined the law from a utilitarian moral perspective, they concluded that it might be preferable to have no law at all. In reaching this conclusion, they cited the Act's adverse effect on our balance of payments, the loss of business and jobs, the fact that American bribes have simply been replaced by bribes given by businesses from other developed countries, and the bureaucratic infighting between the SEC and the Justice Department. On a utilitarian, cost/benefit analysis, then, they found that the gains in heightened moral conduct by American businesses did not outweigh the losses from the other factors just mentioned. On another moral framework, which the authors called "rule assessment" a law is morally sound if and only if it accords with a code of correct ethical rules, they also found the FCPA wanting. For the rule against bribery is merely a prima facie rule (that is, one that can be overridden by a conflicting rule) not a categorical rule (one that can't be overridden), and in this case the rule against bribery can be overridden by corporate obligations to shareholders and workers to make a profit for the former and to retain the jobs of the latter. If a little bribery is necessary to keep these promises, then so be it. And besides, the authors argue, such payments are usually extorted by the foreign official from the American businessman, so he may not be involved in the evil of promoting deception, particularly when these practices accord with recognized local practices. Many of the business critics of FCPA, by the way, also make this point: that in many areas of the world such practices are accepted as standard business procedures.

Not surprisingly, Pastin and Hooker's position generated much controversy, as it seemed to place the moral onus more on the FCPA itself than on so-called corrupt business practices. Kenneth Alpern, in his "Moral Dimensions of the Foreign Corrupt Practices Act: Comments on Pastin and Hooker,"[7] took them to task. He concentrated his fire on their application of the "rule assessment" model, arguing that corporations are the agents of their individual shareholders and, as such, promise only to work to increase the value of their investments, but not by any means whatsoever. Thus, he sees no conflict between the moral rule against bribery and the promise of a corporation to its shareholders, merely a conflict between the antibribery injunction and the self-interest of the shareholders. And moral rules must always take precedence over self-interest, for that is the whole purpose of having moral rules. The FCPA, thus, is perfectly compatible with morality, according to Alpern.

We have seen how a utilitarian analysis might lead to the repeal of the FCPA, or at the very least its modification. For a utilitarian, the weight of its negative consequences is simply too great to bear when measured against its dubious benefits in promoting international morality. But what might a natural rights moralist make of this law? He might proceed to reason in this fashion. Corporations are simply the agents of individuals who pool their assets, they hope, to augment them through the production and sale of commodities or services that consumers desire to purchase. As an agent, the corporation is not entitled to commit any acts that would be immoral if committed by an individual. If it is immoral for you to bribe a purchasing agent for a large corporation in order to induce that man to buy your inferior product for his company's use at an inflated price, then it is wrong for a corporation to do the same thing. But why is it wrong for an individual to engage in such a practice? It is wrong because it deprives the shareholders of the bribed official's company of a portion of their assets because the official will not make the decision on the basis of the only relevant considerations— price and quality. The moral question seems to be decided against bribery when we are dealing with a case of trade between two privately held companies.

However, the issue becomes somewhat clouded when we examine the kinds of cases addressed by the FCPA, that is, where a private U.S. company is having dealings with a third world government for the construction of some public works project or for the purchase of some raw materials native to that country. One might argue that the government official in the third world country is an agent, now, not of shareholders, but rather of the citizens of his country and, as such, the same argument ought to hold against bribing him. But things are not as simple as they might first appear. In most such countries, the governments are dictatorships or even Marxist regimes who in no sense can be analogized to our system of government, which is based on the theory that the government is the agent of the people. Rather, these governments have usurped authority, usually by force of arms. Such governments are more like thieves than representatives of the people, for they oppress their people, deprive them of their property, and claim the right to make business decisions for the whole country as though they owned it exclusively for themselves. In such a situation, what does morality dictate? It seems that two sets of circumstances need to be differentiated: (1) if the government is really thoroughly treacherous, even to the extent that it exterminates its own citizens, then we ought not deal with such murderers; or (2) if the government is less oppressive and marked by corruption more than outright villainy, then we can either deal with it or not, and from a natural rights perspective, morality does not seem to favor one of the courses of action over the other.

A bit of explanation is in order. In the first case, if an American company proceeded to sell arms, computers, film, or whatever to that treacherous government, it would be abetting the persecution and slaughter of innocent people. Thus, to have traded with Idi Amin's bloodthirsty regime in Uganda by the use of bribes or not would be morally reprehensible. In the second type of case, for example, a decision of whether or not to do business with the Saudi princes who control their country's oil reserves—it seems more a matter of personal taste than a question of natural rights whether one should or should not conform to local customs and submit bribes in order to do business there. The American company would be entitled to its resources, having received them initially from shareholders and later through profits reaped from the sale of merchandise to willing customers, while

the Saudi princes would not be entitled to their resources, having gotten them through conquest and by treating the resources found within their territory almost as the personal property of the royal family. If the American company determines that the most profitable use of its assets, the use most likely to produce the greatest profits, lies in consummating a deal with the princes, even when the bribe is factored in, then I see no reason in rights theory to deny them that pursuit. It should be purely a matter of corporate choice whether they wish to use their assets in that way, and chalk up the bribe or the extortion payment, whatever one wishes to call it, to a cost of doing business. Other companies, when faced with a similar circumstance, may find it too offensive to engage in that type of activity, and that is their privilege. Where natural rights theory leaves the option to the individual in this kind of ambiguous case (or "gray" area), utilitarian considerations of cost/benefit might be advantageously employed to reach a decision. But what is unambiguous is that on this moral foundation of natural rights, the FCPA appears as an unjustifiable intrusion upon individual and corporate decision-making.

Undoubtedly, a Kantian moralist would see things differently when applying a golden-rule standard. "If you do not wish to be subject to the temptations of corruption by others, then don't engage in bribery yourself"—so their categorical imperative might read. This moral absolutism is, however, difficult to justify when applied to business activities in a less than perfect world, and a world in which moral precepts and customs differ so greatly from country to country. While I do not wish to endorse moral relativism—the position that everyone and every culture is entitled to make up its own moral rules and we are incapable of judging which are better—I do see the adaptability of natural rights theory, here, as preferable to the absolutism of the Kantian position. It seems preferable in these murky situations to leave the decision to individuals and not have government dictate *the* one and only moral course.

How helpful have our three moral systems proven in resolving . . . [the] issue of the legitimacy of bribing foreign officials in the pursuit of contracts? Kantian principles being absolutist have, I think, little usefulness in resolving these issues, since they take too little account of what goes on in the real world. Given the fact that few governments in the world adhere to Western democratic standards even in rough approximation, and no government, our own included, ever behaves in a manner beyond reproach, it is unduly utopian to demand that businessmen adhere to principles so lofty that, if followed, they could never engage in business anywhere in the world.

The solution that I prefer would involve a combination of natural rights moral theory and, in those ever troublesome "gray" cases—where natural rights theory does not direct a clear-cut answer—an infusion of utilitarian considerations. My test would go like this.

1. Establish whether Company X has legitimate claim to its resources; that is, did it acquire them by noncoercive means, by original acquisition of unowned land or voluntary transfer from individuals who originally had title to land or goods.
2. Inquire into the status of the government within whose territory Company A wishes to do business. Is the government a massive violator of the rights of life, liberty, and property of its citizens, is it a "gray" government that violates rights but is not murderous, or is it a rights-observing government? If it falls within the first category, no dealings with it would be morally permissible because such dealings would be analogous to an individual acting as an accessory to murder; if it falls within the third category, no problem arises and business may proceed; if it falls within the second, "gray" category, then apply a further test.
3. This further test involves weighing the advantages and disadvantages of doing business with that government or under the laws of that government. Such a balance might include both pragmatic considerations and the personal sensibilities of the businessmen making the decision.

Admittedly, this framework still leaves a lot of room for personal differences in reaching decisions, especially in the application of the third criterion, for utilitarian weighing always involves subjective judgments about how much weight ought to be assigned to each factor. But this may not be as big a liability as it at first may seem because these "gray" cases we have examined are

precisely the kind that should be left to individual conscience where people of goodwill can differ. What these criterion do provide is a way of differentiating these tough cases from ones that invariably ought to be denied American business involvement.

Perhaps, these criteria will be clearer if we examine some instances in which they would prohibit any involvement of American businesses with foreign governments. If we look at the issue of making bank loans to Eastern Bloc countries, an endeavor much favored by our international bankers during the 1970s and the era of détente, our second criterion appears to eliminate such activities as immoral. The reason for this prohibition is that these Communist countries have systematically and as a declared party and governmental policy acted to deprive their citizens of basic human rights, including the right to own productive property; the rights to move freely, to engage in business activities of one's choice, to speak one's opinions without fear of persecution, and in many cases, the right to life. The Soviet Union, for example, exterminated an estimated twenty million people during the Great Purges of the 1930s, and the policy of incarcerating political dissidents in slave labor camps and psychiatric institutions continues to this day. To buttress such regimes with Western loans at below market rates, loans that in all likelihood will never be repaid, makes little sense as pragmatic policy, and offends our second criterion because it places our bankers in the positions of subsidizing murderers. As of June 1983, Eastern European countries, excluding the Soviet Union, owed Western bankers and countries almost sixty-two billion dollars. It seems curious, indeed, that our system rallies to legislate against bribe payments to foreign officials, yet our government encourages such loans to Communist regimes.

One more example of a clear-cut case where our criteria can direct businessmen to avoid foreign ventures lies in the area of technology transfer. Recently, there have been some dramatic revelations of Western businessmen serving as intermediaries for the Eastern Bloc in its attempt to circumvent United States export restrictions and acquire advanced computers.[8] Aside from being illegal, such actions are morally culpable, for they endanger American lives by bolstering the Soviet military establishment, to say nothing of their impact on strengthening the organs of internal repression within the Soviet Union.

In conclusion, while the criteria enunciated above can provide moral guidance to businessmen by offering a framework in which to proceed toward making a decision, the "gray" cases can still lead to some companies choosing to continue doing business in South Africa or not, and to offering payoffs to foreign officials or not. But in cases like the banking and spying examples, our moral criteria lead to a decisive conclusion that they are always wrong. Admittedly, the conclusions reached in this chapter diverge rather radically from contemporary legal requirements.

NOTES

1. "Big Profits in Big Bribery," *Time,* March 16, 1981, p. 67.
2. "The Antibribery Act Splits Executives," *Business Week,* September 19, 1983, p. 16.
3. *Congressional Record,* July 14, 1982, S8263, testimony by Edward T. Pratt, Jr., chairman, Emergency Committee for American Trade, before the Subcommittee on International Finance and Monetary Policy.
4. *Congressional Record,* August 5, 1982, S9984, testimony of Norman Pacun, vice-president, Ingersoll-Rand Company, before Senate Banking Committee.
5. *Congressional Record,* July 22, 1982, S9083, testimony of Mark B. Feldman to the Senate Banking Committee.
6. Mark Pastin and Michael Hooker, "Ethics and the Foreign Corrupt Practices Act," in Tom L. Beauchamp and Norman E. Bowie, eds., *Ethical Theory and Business* (Englewood Cliffs, N.J.: Prentice-Hall, 1983), pp. 280–84.
7. Kenneth D. Alpern, "Moral Dimensions of the Foreign Corrupt Practices Act: Comments on Pastin and Hooker," in W. Michael Hoffman and Jennifer Mills Moore, *Business Ethics: Readings and Cases in Corporate Morality* (New York: McGraw-Hill, 1984), pp. 468–75.
8. TK

Ethics and the Foreign Corrupt Practices Act

Mark Pastin and Michael Hooker

Not long ago it was feared that as a fallout of Watergate, government officials would be hamstrung by artificially inflated moral standards. Recent events, however, suggest that the scapegoat of post-Watergate morality may have become American business rather than government officials.

One aspect of the recent attention paid to corporate morality is the controversy surrounding payments made by American corporations to foreign officials for the purpose of securing business abroad. Like any law or system of laws, the Foreign Corrupt Practices Act (FCPA), designed to control or eliminate such payments, should be grounded in morality, and should therefore be judged from an ethical perspective. Unfortunately, neither the law nor the question of its repeal has been adequately addressed from that perspective.

Business Horizons, Dec. 1980. Reprinted with permission of Jai Press Inc.

History of the FCPA

On December 20, 1977, President Carter signed into law S.305, the Foreign Corrupt Practices Act (FCPA), which makes it a crime for American corporations to offer or provide payments to officials of foreign governments for the purpose of obtaining or retaining business. The FCPA also establishes record-keeping requirements for publicly held corporations to make it difficult to conceal political payments proscribed by the Act. Violators of the FCPA, both corporations and managers, face severe penalties. A company may be fined up to $1 million, while its officers who directly participated in violations of the Act or had reason to know of such violations, face up to five years in prison and/or $10,000 in fines. The Act also prohibits corporations from indemnifying fines imposed on their directors, officers, employees, or agents. The Act does not prohibit "grease" payments to foreign government employees whose duties are primarily ministerial or clerical, since such payments are sometimes required to persuade the recipients to perform their normal duties.

At the time of this writing, the precise consequences of the FCPA for American business are unclear, mainly because of confusion surrounding the government's enforcement intentions. Vigorous objections have been raised against the Act by corporate attorneys and recently by a few government officials. Among the latter is Frank A. Weil, former Assistant Secretary of Commerce, who has stated, "The questionable payments problem may turn out to be one of the most serious impediments to doing business in the rest of the world."[1]

The potentially severe economic impact of the FCPA was highlighted by the fall 1978 report of the Export Disincentives Task Force, which was created by the White House to recommend ways of improving our balance of trade. The Task Force identified the FCPA as contributing significantly to economic and political losses in the United States. Economic losses come from constricting the ability of American corporations to do business abroad, and political losses come from the creation of a holier-than-thou image.

The Task Force made three recommendations in regard to the FCPA:

- The Justice Department should issue guidelines on its enforcement policies and establish procedures by which corporations could get advance government reaction to anticipated payments to foreign officials.
- The FCPA should be amended to remove enforcement from the SEC, which now shares enforcement responsibility with the Department of Justice.
- The administration should periodically report to Congress and the public on export losses caused by the FCPA.

In response to the Task Force's report, the Justice Department, over SEC objections, drew up guidelines to enable corporations to check any proposed action possibly in violation of the FCPA. In response to such an inquiry, the Justice Department would inform the corporation of its enforcement intentions. The purpose of such an arrangement is in part to circumvent the intent of the law. As of this writing, the SEC appears to have been successful in blocking publication of the guidelines, although Justice recently reaffirmed its intention to publish guidelines. Being more responsive to political winds, Justice may be less inclined than the SEC to rigidly enforce the Act.

Particular concern has been expressed about the way in which bookkeeping requirements of the Act will be enforced by the SEC. The Act requires that company records will "accurately and fairly reflect the transactions and dispositions of the assets of the issuer." What is at question is the interpretation the SEC will give to the requirement and the degree of accuracy and detail it will demand. The SEC's post-Watergate behavior suggests that it will be rigid in requiring the disclosure of all information that bears on financial relationships between the company and any foreign or domestic public official. This level of accountability in record keeping, to which auditors and corporate attorneys have strongly objected, goes far beyond previous SEC requirements that records display only facts material to the financial position of the company.

Since the potential consequences of the FCPA for American businesses and business managers are very serious, it is important that the Act have a rationale capable of bearing close scrutiny. In looking at the foundation of the FCPA, it should be noted that its passage followed in the wake of intense newspaper coverage of the financial dealings of corporations. Such media attention was engendered by the dramatic disclosure of corporate slush funds during the Watergate hearings and by a voluntary disclosure program established shortly thereafter by the SEC. As a result of the SEC program, more than 400 corporations, including 117 of the Fortune 500, admitted to making more than $300 million in foreign political payments in less than ten years.

Throughout the period of media coverage leading up to passage of the FCPA, and especially during the hearings on the Act, there was in all public discussions of the issue a tone of righteous moral indignation at the idea of American companies making foreign political payments. Such payments were ubiquitously termed "bribes," although many of these could more accurately be called extortions, while others were more akin to brokers' fees or sales commissions.

American business can be faulted for its reluctance during this period to bring to public attention the fact that in a very large number of countries, payments to foreign officials are virtually required for doing business. Part of that reluctance, no doubt, comes from the awkwardly difficult position of attempting to excuse bribery or something closely resembling it. There is a popular abhorrence in this country of bribery directed at domestic government officials, and that abhorrence transfers itself to payments directed toward foreign officials as well.

Since its passage, the FCPA has been subjected to considerable critical analysis, and many practical arguments have been advanced in favor of its repeal.[2] However, there is always lurking in back of such analyses the uneasy feeling that no matter how strongly considerations of practicality and economics may count against this law, the fact remains that the law protects morality in forbidding bribery. For example, Gerald McLaughlin, professor of law at Fordham, has shown persuasively that where the legal system of a foreign country affords inadequate protection against the arbitrary exercise of power to the disadvantage of American corporations, payments to foreign officials may be required to provide a compensating mechanism against the use of such arbitrary power. McLaughlin observes, however, that "this does not mean that taking advantage of the compensating mechanism would necessarily make the payment moral."[3]

The FCPA, and questions regarding its enforcement or repeal, will not be addressed adequately until an effort has been made to come to terms with the Act's foundation in morality. While it may be very difficult, or even impossible, to legislate morality (that is, to change the moral character and sentiments of people by passing laws that regulate their behavior), the existing laws undoubtedly still reflect the moral beliefs we hold. Passage of the FCPA in Congress was eased by the simple connection most congressmen made between bribery, seen as morally repugnant, and the Act, which is designed to prevent bribery.

Given the importance of the FCPA to American business and labor, it is imperative that attention be given to the question of whether there is adequate moral justification for the law.

Ethical Analysis of the FCPA

The question we will address is not whether each payment prohibited by the FCPA is moral or immoral, but rather whether the FCPA, given all its consequences and ramifications, is itself moral. It is well known that morally sound laws and institutions may tolerate some immoral acts. The First Amendment's guarantee of freedom of speech allows individuals to utter racial slurs. And immoral laws and institutions may have some beneficial consequences, for example, segregationist legislation bringing deep-seated racism into the national limelight. But our concern is with the overall morality of the FCPA.

The ethical tradition has two distinct ways of assessing social institutions, including laws: *end-point assessment* and *rule assessment*. Since there is no consensus as to which approach is correct, we will apply both types of assessment to the FCPA.

The end-point approach assesses a law in terms of its contribution to general social well-being. The ethical theory underlying end-point assessment is utilitarianism. According to utilitarianism, a law is morally sound if and only if the law promotes the well-being of those affected by the law to the greatest extent practically achievable. To satisfy the utilitarian principle, a law must promote the well-being of those affected by it at least as well as any alternative law that we might propose, and better than no law at all. A conclusive end-point assessment of a law requires specification of what constitutes the welfare of those affected by the law, which the liberal tradition generally sidesteps by identifying an individual's welfare with what he takes to be in his interests.

Considerations raised earlier in the paper suggest that the FCPA does not pass the end-point test. The argument is not the too facile one that we could propose a better law. (Amendments to the FCPA are now being considered.[4]) The argument is that it may be better to have *no* such law than to have the FCPA. The main domestic consequences of the FCPA seem to include an adverse effect on the balance of payments, a loss of business and jobs, and another opportunity for the SEC and the Justice Department to compete. These negative effects must be weighed against possible gains in the conduct of American business within the United States.

From the perspective of foreign countries in which American firms do business, the main consequence of the FCPA seems to be that certain officials now accept bribes and influence from non-American businesses. It is hard to see that who pays the bribes makes much difference to these nations.

Rule assessment of the morality of laws is often favored by those who find that end-point assessment is too lax in supporting their moral codes. According to the rule assessment approach: A law is morally sound if and only if the law accords with a code embodying correct ethical rules. This approach has no content until the rules are stated, and different rules will lead to different ethical assessments. Fortunately, what we have to say about rule assessment of the FCPA does not depend on the details of a particular ethical code.

Those who regard the FCPA as a worthwhile expression of morality, despite the adverse effects on American business and labor, clearly subscribe to a rule stating that it is unethical to bribe. Even if it is conceded that the payments proscribed by the FCPA warrant classification as bribes, citing a rule prohibiting bribery does not suffice to justify the FCPA.

Most of the rules in an ethical code are not *categorical* rules; they are *prima facie* rules. A categorical rule does not allow exceptions, whereas a prima facie rule does. The ethical rule that a person ought to keep promises is an example of a prima facie rule. If I promise to loan you a book on nuclear energy and later find out that you are a terrorist building a private atomic bomb, I am ethically obligated not to keep my promise. The rule that one ought to keep promises is "overridden" by the rule that one ought to prevent harm to others.

A rule prohibiting bribery is a prima facie rule. There are cases in which morality requires that a bribe be paid. If the only way to get essential medical care for a dying child is to bribe a doctor, morality requires one to bribe the doctor. So adopting an ethical code that includes a rule prohibiting the payment of bribes does not guarantee that a rule assessment of the FCPA will be favorable to it.

The fact that the FCPA imposes a cost on American business and labor weighs against the prima facie obligation not to bribe. If we suppose that American corporations have obligations, tantamount to promises, to promote the job security of their employees and the investments of shareholders, these obligations will also weigh against the obligation not to bribe. Again, if government legislative and enforcement bodies have an obligation to secure the welfare of American business and workers, the FCPA may force them to violate their public obligations.

The FCPA's moral status appears even more dubious if we note that many of the payments prohibited by the Act are neither bribes nor share features that make bribes morally reprehensible. Bribes are generally held to be malefic if they persuade one to act against his good judgement, and consequently purchase an inferior product. But the payments at issue in the FCPA are usually extorted *from the seller.* Further it is arguable that not paying the bribe is more likely to lead to purchase of an inferior product than paying the bribe. Finally, bribes paid to foreign officials may not involve deception when they accord with recognized local practices.

In conclusion, neither end-point nor rule assessment uncovers a sound moral basis for the FCPA. It is shocking to find that a law prohibiting bribery has no clear moral basis, and may even be an immoral law. However, this is precisely what examination of the FCPA from a moral perspective reveals. This is symptomatic of the fact that moral conceptions that were appropriate to a simpler world are not adequate to the complex world in which contemporary business functions. Failure to appreciate this point often leads to righteous condemnation of business, when it should lead to careful reflection on one's own moral preconceptions.

NOTES

1. *National Journal,* June 3, 1978: 880.
2. David C. Gustman, "The Foreign Corrupt Practices Act of 1977," *The Journal of International Law and Economics,* Vol. 13, 1979: 367–401, and Walter S. Surrey, "The Foreign Corrupt Practices Act: Let the Punishment Fit the Crime," *Harvard International Law Journal,* Spring 1979: 203–303.
3. Gerald T. McLaughlin, "The Criminalization of Questionable Foreign Payments by Corporations," *Fordham Law Review,* Vol. 46: 1095.
4. "Foreign Bribery Law Amendments Drafted," *American Bar Association Journal,* February 1980: 135.

Bribery and Ethics: A Reply to Pastin and Hooker

Robert E. Frederick

In their article on the Foreign Corrupt Practices Act, Mark Pastin and Michael Hooker used both "end-point assessment" and "rule assessment" to evaluate the FCPA from a moral point of view.[1] They argue that neither method of assessment supports the FCPA and hence that it "has no clear moral basis, and may even be an immoral law."[2] It seems to me, however, that Pastin and Hooker's arguments are not compelling and that there is a sense in which the FCPA does have a sound moral basis. Thus in the remainder of this paper I will give reasons why I think Pastin and Hooker are mistaken. I will begin with their end-point assessment of the FCPA and then turn to the rule assessment. In the final section I will have some brief comments about extortion and the FCPA.

I

End-point assessment is based on the moral theory of utilitarianism. If we use end-point assessment to evaluate a law, then according to Pastin and Hooker it is a morally sound law "if and only if the law promotes the well-being of those affected by the law to the greatest extent practically achievable."[3] They argue that the FCPA has not promoted the well-being of those affected by the law to the greatest extent practically achievable, since it has led to a loss of business and jobs, it has unfavorably affected the balance of payments, and it is a source of discord between government agencies.[4] Hence, they suggest that the FCPA does not pass the end-point test of moral soundness.

It is difficult to judge the strength of this argument against the FCPA, since it is very difficult to find and evaluate objective empirical evidence that either confirms or disconfirms the economic harm allegedly caused by the FCPA. There is anecdotal evidence that the FCPA has caused some firms a loss of business.[5] In a 1983 study of the data, how-

ever, John L. Graham finds that "the FCPA has not had a negative effect on U.S. trade," and in a 1987 analysis of U.S. trade in the Mideast, Kate Gillespie concludes that "The FCPA potential to hurt U.S. exports remains unproved."[6] These studies do not show that the FCPA has promoted the well-being of those affected by it to the greatest extent practically achievable, so they do not show that the FCPA passes the end-point assessment test of moral soundness. Perhaps the best we can say about the studies is that they seem to show, not that we are economically any better off for having the FCPA on the books, but rather that we are not any worse off.

Let us suppose, however, that there is good evidence that the FCPA has caused a loss of U.S. exports and a loss of jobs in U.S. export-related industries. Would this show that the FCPA does not pass the end-point assessment? It seems to me it would not. One of the central tenets of utilitarianism is that the well-being of any one person or group of persons is not to count more or be of more moral weight than the well-being of some other person or group of persons. Thus the well-being of people in the United States does not count more than the well-being of people in France or Uganda or China. Now, if the FCPA causes a U.S. firm to lose an export contract, then some foreign competitor must have gotten that contract. Thus it could be that a loss of exports and jobs in the United States would be offset by an increase in exports and jobs in some foreign country. Assuming the people receiving the goods are as well off with either vendor, and since the well-being of people in the United States does not count more than the well-being of people in the country that got the contract, the net effect of the FCPA on economic well-being, once we consider *everyone* affected by it, might be entirely neutral.

If this argument is correct, it shows that from a utilitarian point of view the FCPA is morally neutral. It neither harms nor enhances total economic well-being. Thus, as long as we consider only economic well-being, end-point assessment does not provide moral grounds for either favoring

From *Business Ethics*, Hoffman and Moore, eds., 1990, 542–547. Reprinted with permission of the author.

or opposing the law. Of course, it is possible that the FCPA affects well-being in noneconomic ways. For example, one might argue that insofar as the FCPA discourages the corrupt practice of bribery, people both in the United States and abroad are better off. But it seems to me that considerations of well-being, although important, do not address the central moral issues raised by the FCPA. For that we have to turn to rule assessment.

II

Pastin and Hooker claim that a law passes the rule assessment test of moral soundness "if and only if the law accords with a code embodying correct moral rules."[7] They then try to show that the FCPA does not pass the rule assessment test regardless of the actual content of the moral code. This may seem a little extreme, since it may be that the correct moral code contains a rule such as "under no circumstances is bribery morally permissible." But Pastin and Hooker circumvent this problem by claiming that the rule against bribery is always a prima facie rule, i.e., it can be overridden by other moral considerations in appropriate circumstances. They then seem to claim that in the arena of international competition other moral considerations frequently override the rule. And since the FCPA makes no allowance for such instances—it prohibits bribes even in cases where it is morally permissible to offer a bribe—it does not accord with the moral code and does not pass the end-point assessment.

But is the rule against bribery a prima facie rule? And even if it is, are there moral considerations that frequently override it? I will try to show that for certain types of bribery the moral rule against bribery is not a prima facie rule and that in other cases the considerations Pastin and Hooker mention are not overriding. I will begin with a brief description of what I take to be a central case of bribery, and then, using that case as a focal point for discussion, I will say something about why I think bribery is morally wrong.

Suppose you find yourself in the following situation: You are taking a difficult course required for your major. You work hard, go to class, do all the homework, and are well satisfied with the B you

receive for a final grade. You happen to find out, however, that an acquaintance of yours made an A in the course even though he missed most of the classes, didn't do the homework, and didn't even show up for the final exam. You know this person is no genius, so you wonder how he did it. You are so curious, in fact, that you decide to ask him. "Well," he replies, "let's just say I know how to spread some money around where it will do the most good."

You are outraged, since the clear implication is that your acquaintance bribed the professor to give him an A. But exactly why are you outraged? Exactly what is wrong with bribery?

The best way to begin to answer that question is to get as clear as we can about the main characteristics of a central case of bribery, such as the one just described. The first thing to note is that the above situation is a kind of social practice, which is governed in all essential respects by an agreement or understanding between the participants. This understanding, parts of which may be explicit and parts implicit, is voluntary, at least in the sense that no one is threatened with unjustifiable harm if he or she does not take the class, and the understanding does not require that any of the participants engage in morally impermissible behavior. In addition, the agreement defines the role, position, or function of each participant in the practice and delineates the kinds of behaviors that are acceptable or unacceptable for each role or position in certain circumstances. For example, even though it may never be explicitly stated, it is a part of the understanding, and undoubtedly a part of your expectations for the course, that all students will be graded, solely on the amount and quality of work that they do.

The understanding can be broken in a number of ways, some of which are innocuous and do not involve immoral behavior. But the case of bribery in question is not innocuous. It is an attempt by one student to gain an unfair advantage over the other students by offering the professor something of value in return for the professor violating the understanding by giving the student special treatment. It is, in effect, an attempt by one of the participants to subvert the original understanding by entering into a new one with terms that are incompatible with the terms of the original.

If we put all these things together we can give a complete, although somewhat complex, characterization of central cases of bribery:

> In central cases bribery is a violation of an understanding or agreement that defines a social practice. It is an attempt by one person(s) X to secure an unfair advantage over another person(s) Y by giving a third person(s) Z something of value in exchange for Z giving favorable treatment to X by violating some prima facie duty Z has in virtue of Z's position, role, or function in a morally permissible understanding in which X, Y, and Z are all voluntary participants.

Thus, if my analysis is correct, central cases of bribery always involve social practices in which there are voluntary and morally permissible agreements or understandings, always involve a three-term relationship, and are always attempts to gain an unfair advantage. Noncentral cases of bribery deviate from central cases in that they apparently either do not involve morally permissible agreements, or voluntary agreements, or there is no three-term relationship, or they are not attempts to gain an unfair advantage.

We are finally in a position to say something about what is wrong with central cases of bribery. To give someone an unfair advantage is to give them special treatment that others do not receive, treatment that cannot be justified under the terms of the original understanding, and treatment that the other parties of the understanding would not acquiesce to if they were to know about it. And to give someone such an advantage is, it seems reasonable to say, morally wrong. To paraphrase Aristotle, it is not to treat equals equally. Hence to *accept* a bribe is morally wrong. This does not explain why *offering* a bribe is morally wrong. But I suggest, as a general moral principle, that if one person attempts to get another person to do something morally wrong, then the attempt is also morally wrong. Hence, if I attempt to bribe you to do something that is morally wrong, my attempt to bribe you is morally wrong regardless of whether you accept the bribe or not.

If the rule against bribery is a prima facie rule, then, even for central cases of bribery, there must be some possible circumstances in which it can be overridden. But what circumstances might those be? Under what conditions is it morally permissible to give someone an unfair advantage over others? It seems to me there are no such conditions. It is never morally permissible to give someone an unfair advantage, nor is it morally permissible to induce someone to provide an unfair advantage. Hence, for central cases, the rule against bribery is not a prima facie rule. Thus, the FCPA does have a clear moral basis since it prohibits a type of bribery that is always morally wrong.

III

There are two ways that Pastin and Hooker might respond. We concede, they might say, that central cases of bribery are always wrong. Given your characterization of central cases it could hardly be otherwise. Yet in foreign competition such cases hardly ever occur. Noncentral cases are much more common, and in these cases the rule against bribery is prima facie. Their second response would probably be to point out, as they do in their article, that many of the payments prohibited by the FCPA are not bribes at all, but extortions. And, they might continue, since the FCPA as it is presently formulated prohibits noncentral cases of bribery, and since it prohibits most types of extortion, it lacks a completely sound moral basis. The reason is that in many instances it is morally permissible to pay bribes in noncentral cases, or to make extortion payments. Thus, the FCPA does not pass the rule assessment test after all, since the FCPA is not in *complete* accord with the correct moral code.

To some extent I am sympathetic with these responses. They do show, I believe, that there are considerations in favor of *revising* the law.[8] This is not too surprising, since there are many laws that could be improved. But it is important to see that, as long as the FCPA is on the books in its present form, the responses I have attributed to Pastin and Hooker give no justification whatever for violating the law by offering a bribe. Let me explain.

Suppose for a moment that we have not made the distinction between central and noncentral cases of bribery, and suppose Pastin and Hooker are correct about the rule against bribery always being a prima facie rule. If it is, then if one has other moral obligations that override the obligation not to bribe, it is morally permissible to offer a bribe. So, in order to determine whether it is permissible, we need to know something about what kinds of obligations might override the rule against bribery.

It is beyond the scope of this article to examine all the different obligations that might override the rule against bribery, but Pastin and Hooker do mention one that deserves discussion. It is the obligation businesspeople have to protect the financial interests of corporate investors. Pastin and Hooker seem to say that in order to protect these interests businesspeople must sometimes offer bribes. I believe, however, that this mistakes the obligations businesspeople actually have. Except in very unusual circumstances they are only obligated to protect the interests of investors *within* the limits established by law. They simply have no obligation to protect those interests by breaking the law. Thus, investors can have no *moral* complaint against a businessperson if they suffer a financial loss because the businessperson refused to break a law.

There are occasions on which it is morally permissible or obligatory to break the law. If the law is flagrantly unjust, or if following the law is likely to cause severe and irremediable harm, then our moral obligations may outweigh our legal ones. But it has not been established that the FCPA is flagrantly unjust or that following it is likely to cause severe and irremediable harm. Hence, there is no justification for concluding that businesspeople are morally required to violate the FCPA by offering bribes, even assuming the rule against bribery is always prima facie.[9]

IV

One aspect of the FCPA that I have only touched on is the prohibition of most types of extortion payments. Typically extortion is an attempt by one person(s) X to gain from another person(s) Y something of value to which X has no rightful claim by an actual or implied threat to harm unjustifiably Y's legitimate interests unless Y yields the thing of value to X. For example, if your professor makes it known to you that she will not grade your work fairly unless you give her $100, then she is attempting extortion.

Although there are clear differences between extortion and central cases of bribery, extortion and noncentral cases of bribery are often confused. For example, an illustration Pastin and Hooker use—"bribing" a doctor to get essential medical treatment for a child—seems to me a form of extortion instead of bribery.[10]

It is important to distinguish carefully between extortion and bribery, since the moral relationships in extortion are quite different from the moral relationships in bribery. For example, in extortion, but not in bribery, there is a threat to vital interests. And since, I believe, it is always morally wrong to threaten unjustifiably vital interests, demanding extortion is always morally wrong. But it is sometimes morally permissible to make an extortion payment provided that no other reasonable alternative is available to protect threatened vital interests. Paying the doctor to treat the child is a good example. Thus, there is a sense, absent in cases of bribery, in which someone making an extortion payment is a victim of morally improper behavior.

Pastin and Hooker appear to argue that since it is at least sometimes morally permissible to make extortion payments, and since the FCPA prohibits most types of extortion payments, the FCPA is defective from a moral point of view. But I suggest that we look at the FCPA in a different light. Businesspeople who are forced to make extortion payments to protect threatened interests are victims of a corrupt and immoral practice. We do have moral obligations to protect people from such victimization. How should we do it? It is unlikely that businesspeople acting individually would be able to prevent extortion. What is needed is concerted action, and one effective way to achieve concerted action is through regulation and law.[11] If the FCPA prohibition of extortion payments is strictly enforced, then U.S. firms will not do business in countries where extortion is common. And if we can encourage other countries strictly to enforce laws against extortion, or to pass such laws if they do not have them, then businesspeople in those countries will respond similarly. This will eventually bring pressure on the remaining countries where extortion is common, since it will close them off from products and services that are needed for their economies. And this, in turn, should make them much more likely to enforce laws against demanding extortion. Thus, instead of the FCPA being morally defective, if it is strictly enforced, and if other countries enforce similar laws, the FCPA can advance a worthwhile moral purpose by helping stop the victimization imposed by extortion.

It would be naive to think that extortion can be completely eliminated via the sort of concerted action I have proposed, but I believe it is morally unacceptable to take no action against it at all. Enforcing the FCPA and similar laws is one way to help the international business community avoid falling victim to extortionists' demands. Hence, in my view the FCPA should not be revised to permit extortion payments. If anything, the prohibition of such payments should be strengthened.

There is one misunderstanding I would like to forestall. It might be suggested that prohibiting extortion payments is *imposing* morality. As long as we are concerned with a rule assessment of the FCPA, this is a completely mistaken view. The correct moral code, on which rule assessment is based, is a moral code that applies to everyone at all times. It exempts no one. Thus if a practice is a violation of the code, as I have claimed demanding extortion always is, to refuse to pay extortion is not in any sense imposing morality. It is refusing to participate in and make possible behavior prohibited by the moral code, behavior that is immoral for anyone in any country.

In conclusion I would like to emphasize that my analysis and discussion of bribery and extortion is by no means complete. I have not tried to address many issues that could be raised, and with many others I have undoubtedly raised more questions than I have answered. But I do think I have shown that Pastin and Hooker are incorrect in claiming that the FCPA does not pass either endpoint or rule assessment tests of moral soundness. The FCPA may not be a perfect law, but it is not entirely without moral justification.[12]

NOTES

1. Mark Pastin and Michael Hooker, "Ethics and the Foreign Corrupt Practices Act," in *Business Ethics: Readings and Cases in Corporate Morality,* ed. W. Michael Hoffman and Jennifer Mills Moore, 2d ed. (New York: McGraw-Hill Book Company, 1989), p. 551.
2. *Ibid.,* p. 555.
3. *Ibid.,* p. 553.
4. It is beyond my expertise to say whether, in this case, discord between agencies is a good thing or a bad one, so I will not comment on it.
5. Suk H. Kim, "On Repealing the Foreign Corrupt Practices Act: Survey and Assessment," *Columbia Journal of World Business,* Fall 1981, pp. 16–20. Also see Justin G. Longenecker, Joseph A. McKinney, and Carlos W. Moore, "The Ethical Issue of International Bribery: A Survey of Attitudes Among U.S. Business Professionals," *Journal of Business Ethics,* vol. 7, no. 5, May 1988, pp. 341–346.
6. John L. Graham, "Foreign Corrupt Practices: A Manager's Guide," *Columbia Journal of World Business,* Fall 1983, p. 89. Kate Gillespie, "Middle East Response to the Foreign Corrupt Practices Act," *California Management Review,* vol. 29, no. 4, Summer 1987, p. 28.
7. Pastin and Hooker, p. 554.
8. I will argue later that the FCPA prohibition of extortion payments should not be revised.
9. The same sort of argument applies against making extortion payments. However, extortion is more complex, since in some cases severe harm may be caused by refusing to make an extortion payment. The FCPA makes provision for some of these cases.
10. There are a number of more difficult cases. For example, it is often said that in some countries bribery is a common practice. But are payments made in such countries bribes or extortion payments? Can bribery be a common practice, or after a certain point does it become institutionalized extortion?
11. Longenecker, McKinney, and Moore, p. 346.
12. My thanks to W. Michael Hoffman and Jennifer Mills Moore for their comments on an earlier draft of this paper.

Business Ethics and the International Trade in Hazardous Wastes

Jang B. Singh and V. C. Lakhan

The export of hazardous wastes by the more developed countries to the lesser developed nations is escalating beyond control. The ethical implications and environmental consequences of this trade in hazardous wastes highlight the need for international controls and regulations in the conduct of business by corporations in the more developed countries. In the late 1970s, the Love Canal environmental tragedy awakened the world to the effects of ill conceived and irresponsible disposal of hazardous by-products of industries. Today, the media focuses its attention on the alleged illegal dumping of hazardous wastes in the lesser developed countries (see Barthos, 1988, and Harden, 1988). The most recent dramatic case so far is that of Koko, Nigeria where more than eight thousand drums of hazardous wastes were dumped, some of which contained polychlorinated biphenyl (PCB), a highly carcinogenic compound and one of the world's most toxic wastes (Tifft, 1988). . . .

The International Trade in Hazardous Wastes and Attendant Problems

Miller (1988) defined hazardous waste as any material that may pose a substantial threat or potential hazard to human health or the environment when managed improperly. These wastes may be in solid, liquid, or gaseous form and include a variety of toxic, ignitable, corrosive, or dangerously reactive substances. Examples include acids, cyanides, pesticides, solvents, compounds of lead, mercury, arsenic, cadmium, and zinc, PCBs and dioxins, fly ash from power plants, infectious waste from hospitals and research laboratories, obsolete explosives, herbicides, nerve gas, radioactive materials, sewage sludge, and other materials that contain toxic and carcinogenic organic compounds.

Since World War II, the amount of toxic by-products created by the manufacturers of pharmaceuticals, petroleum, nuclear devices, pesticides,

chemicals, and other allied products has increased almost exponentially. From an annual production of less than 10 million metric tonnes in the 1940s, the world now produces more than 320 million metric tonnes of extremely hazardous wastes per year. The United States is by far the biggest producer, with "over 275 million metric tonnes of hazardous waste produced each year" (Goldfarb, 1987). The total is well over one tonne per person. But the United States is not alone. European countries also produce millions of tonnes of hazardous wastes each year (Chiras, 1988). Recent figures reported by Tifft (1988) indicate that the twelve countries of the European Community produce about 35 million tonnes of hazardous wastes annually. . . .

The United States and certain European countries are now turning to areas in Africa, Latin America, and the Caribbean to dump their wastes. Historically, the trade in wastes has been conducted among the industrialized nations. A major route involving industrialized nations is that between Canada and the United States. The movement of wastes from the United States into Canada is governed by the Canada-U.S.A. Agreement on the Transboundary Movement of Hazardous Waste, which came into effect on November 8, 1986 (Environment Canada). In 1988, the United States exported 145,000 tonnes. Of this amount, only one-third was recyclable, leaving approximately 96,667 tonnes of hazardous organic and inorganic wastes such as petroleum by-products, pesticides, heavy metals, and organic solvents and residues for disposal in the Canadian environment. Of interest is the fact that Canada restricts the import of nuclear waste, but not toxic, flammable, corrosive, reactive, and medical wastes from the United States.

Most of the United States' hazardous wastes are shipped from the New England states, New York, and Michigan, and they enter Ontario and Quebec, which in 1988 received approximately 81,899 and 62,200 tonnes respectively. The neutralization and disposal of the imported hazardous wastes are done by several Canadian companies, with the two largest being Tricil and Stablex Canada Inc. Tricil, with several locations in Ontario,

Journal of Business Ethics, 1989, vol. 8. Reprinted by permission of Kluwer Academic Publishers.

imports wastes from more than 85 known American companies, which it incinerates and treats in lagoons and landfill sites. Stablex Canada imports a wide variety of hazardous wastes from more than 300 U.S. companies. It uses various disposal methods, including landfills and cement kilns, which burn not only the components needed for cement but also hazardous waste products. With the established Canada-U.S. Agreement on the Transboundary Movement of Hazardous Waste, companies like Tricil and Stablex may increase their importation of hazardous wastes generated in the United States. As it stands, the United States Environmental Protection Agency estimates that over 75 percent of the wastes exported from the U.S. are disposed of in Canada (Vallette, 1989). This estimate will likely have to be raised in the near future. Canada–United States trade in hazardous wastes is not a one-way route. It is believed that all of the hazardous wastes imported by the United States (estimated at 65,000 tonnes in 1988) is generated in Canada (Ibid).

An especially controversial trend in the international trade in hazardous wastes is the development of routes between industrialized and "lesser developed countries." For example, according to the United States Environmental Protection Agency, there have been more proposals to ship hazardous wastes from the United States to Africa during 1988 than in the previous four years (Klatte et al., 1988).

African nations have recently joined together to try to completely ban the dumping of toxic wastes on their continent. They have referred to the practice as "toxic terrorism" performed by Western "merchants of death." Some African government officials are so disturbed by the newly exposed practices that they have threatened to execute guilty individuals by firing squad. Recently, Lagos officials seized an Italian and a Danish ship along with fifteen people who were associated with transporting toxic wastes in the swampy Niger River delta into Nigeria. This occurred shortly after the discovery of 3,800 tonnes of hazardous toxic wastes, which had originated in Italy. Local residents immediately became ill from inhaling the fumes from the leaking drums and containers that were filled with the highly carcinogenic compound PCB, and also radioactive material.

Companies in the United States have been re-sponsible for sending large quantities of hazardous wastes to Mexico. Although Mexico accepts hazardous wastes only for recycling, which is referred to as "sham recycling," there are numerous reports of illegal dumping incidents. . . .

Given the fact that hazardous wastes are:

1. Toxic
2. Highly reactive when exposed to air, water, or other substances that they can cause explosions and generate toxic fumes
3. Ignitable that they can undergo spontaneous combustion at relatively low temperatures
4. Highly corrosive that they can eat away materials and living tissues
5. Infectious
6. Radioactive

Miller (1988) has, therefore, emphasized correctly that the proper transportation, disposal, deactivation, or storage of hazardous wastes is a grave environmental problem, which is second only to nuclear war.

The practice of transporting and dumping hazardous wastes in lesser developed nations, where knowledge of environmental issues is limited, is causing, and will pose, major problems to both human health and the environment. Several comprehensive studies have outlined the detrimental impacts that hazardous waste can have on humans and natural ecosystems. Epstein et al., (1982) have provided a thorough and dramatic coverage of the impacts of hazardous wastes, while Regenstein (1982), in his book *America the Poisoned*, gives a good overview of the implications of hazardous wastes. Essentially, hazardous wastes not only contaminate ground water, destroy habitats, cause human disease, and contaminate the soil, but also enter the food chain at all levels, and eventually damage genetic material of all living things. . . .

The hazardous wastes can also directly threaten human health through seeping into the ground and causing the direct pollution of aquifers, which supply "pure" drinking water. Today, in the United States, a long list of health related problems are caused by hazardous chemicals from "leaking underground storage tanks" (LUST). Investigations now show that human exposure to hazardous wastes from dumpsites, water bodies, and processing and storage areas can cause the disposed synthetic compounds to interact with particular enzymes or other chemicals in the body and result in altered functions. Altered functions have been shown to include mutagenic (mutation-causing), carcinogenic (cancer-causing), and teratogenic (birth-defect causing) effects. In addition, they may cause serious liver and kidney dysfunction, sterility, and numerous lesser physiological and neurological problems (see Nebel, 1987). . . .

The Ethical Implications

The international trade in hazardous wastes raises a number of ethical issues. The rest of this paper examines some of these.

The Right to a Livable Environment

The desire for a clean, safe, and ecologically balanced environment is an often expressed sentiment. This is especially so in industrialized countries where an awareness of environmental issues is relatively high—a fact that is gaining recognition in political campaigns. However, expression of the desire for a clean, safe environment is not the same as stating that a clean, safe environment is the right of every human being. But the right of an individual to a livable environment is easily established at the theoretical level. Blackstone (1983) examines the right to a livable environment from two angles—as a human right and as a legal right. The right to a clean, safe environment is seen as a human right since the absence of such a condition would prevent one from fulfilling one's human capacities.

> Each person has this right qua being human and because a livable environment is essential for one to fulfill his human capacities. And given the danger to our environment today and hence the danger to the very possibility of human existence, access to a livable environment must be conceived as a right that imposes upon everyone a correlative moral obligation to respect. (Blackstone, 1983, p. 413)

Guerrette (1986) illustrates this argument by reference to the Constitution of the United States. He proposes that people cannot live in a chemically toxic area, they cannot experience freedom in an in-dustrially polluted environment, and they cannot be happy worrying about the quality of air they breathe or the carcinogenic effects of the water they drink (Guerrette, 1986, p. 409). Some even argue (e.g., Feinberg, 1983) that the right to a livable environment extends to future generations and that it is the duty of the present generation to pass on a clean, safe environment to them.

Establishing the right to a livable environment as a human right is not the same as establishing it as a legal right. This requires the passing of appropriate legislation and the provision of a legal framework that may be used to seek a remedy if necessary. Such provisions are more prevalent in the industrialized countries, and this is one of the push factors in the export of hazardous wastes to the lesser developed countries. This points to the need for a provision in international law of the right to a decent environment, which with accompanying policies to save and preserve our environmental resources would be an even more effective tool than such a framework at the national level (Blackstone, 1983, p. 414). As ecologists suggest, serious harm done to one element in an ecosystem will invariably lead to the damage or even destruction of other elements in that and other ecosystems (Law Reform Commission of Canada, 1987, p. 262) and ecosystems transcend national boundaries. . . .

A more direct harmful effect of the international trade in hazardous wastes is the damage to the health of workers involved in the transportation and disposal of these toxic substances. For example, prolonged exposure to wastes originating in Italy and transported by a ship called Zanoobia is suspected of causing the death of a crew person and the hospitalization of nine others (Klatte et al., 1983, p. 12). Whereas worker rights in workplace health and safety are gaining wider recognition in many industrialized nations, this is not so in the "less developed" countries, which are increasingly becoming the recipients of hazardous wastes. Widespread violation of workers' rights to a clean, safe work environment should therefore be expected to be a feature of the international trade in hazardous wastes.

Racist Implications

The recent trend of sending more shipments of hazardous wastes to third world countries has led to charges of racism. *West Africa*, a weekly magazine, referred to the dumping of hazardous wastes as the latest in a series of historical traumas for Africa. . . . Charges of racism in the disposal of wastes have been made before at the national level in the United States. A study of waste disposal sites found that race was the most significant among variables tested in association with the location of commercial hazardous waste facilities. The findings of this national study, which were found to be statistically significant at the 0.0001 level, showed that communities with the greatest number of commercial hazardous wastes facilities had the highest concentration of racial minorities (Lee, 1987, pp. 45–46). The study found that although socioeconomic status appeared to play a role in the location of commercial hazardous wastes facilities, race was a more significant factor.

In the United States, one of the arguments often advanced for locating commercial waste facilities in lower income areas is that these facilities create jobs. This is also one of the arguments being advanced for sending wastes to poor lesser developed countries. . . . Nearly all the countries receiving hazardous wastes have predominantly coloured populations. This is the reason why charges of racism are being made against exporters of wastes. However, it must be noted that even though the trend of sending wastes to other countries . . . has recently gained strength, the bulk of the international trade in hazardous wastes is still within industrialized Europe and North America, which have predominantly noncoloured populations.

For example, the United States Environmental Protection Agency estimates that as much as 75 percent of the wastes exported from the United States is disposed of in Canada (Klatte et al., 1988, p. 9). Another striking example is that a dump outside Schonberg, East Germany, is the home of well over 500,000 tons of waste a year from Western Europe (Rubbish Between Germans, March 1, 1986, p. 46). Thus, while charges of racism in the export of hazardous wastes are being made by some third world leaders, figures on the international trade in such substances do not substantiate these claims.

Corporate Responsibility

The international trade in hazardous wastes basically involves three types of corporations—the generators of wastes, the exporters of wastes, and the importers of wastes. These entities, if they are to act

in a responsible manner, should be accountable to the public for their behaviour.

> Having a corporate conscience means that a company takes responsibility for its actions, just as any conscientious individual would be expected to do. In corporate terms, this means that a company is accountable to the public for its behaviour not only in the complex organizational environment but in the natural physical environment as well. A company is thus responsible for its product and for its effects on the public. (Guerrette, 1986, p. 410)

Using Guerrette's definition of corporate responsibility, it seems clear that a corporation involved in the international trade in hazardous wastes is not likely to be a responsible firm. The importer of hazardous wastes is clearly engaged in activities that will damage the environment while the exporter being aware that this is a possibility, nevertheless sends these wastes to the importer. However, it is the generator of hazardous wastes that is the most culpable in this matter. If the wastes are not produced then obviously their disposal would not be necessary. Therefore, in view of the fact that virtually no safe method of disposing hazardous wastes exists, a case of corporate irresponsibility could easily be formulated against any corporation involved in the international trade in these substances.

Government Responsibility

Why do countries export wastes? A major reason is that many of them are finding it difficult to build disposal facilities in their own countries because of the NIMBY syndrome. Other reasons are that better technologies may be available in another country, facilities of a neighboring country may be closer to a generator of waste than a site on national territory, and economies of scale may also be a factor. However, to these reasons must be added the fact that corporations may be motivated to dispose of waste in another country where less stringent regulations apply (Transfrontier Movements, March 1984, p. 40). It is the responsibility of governments to establish regulations governing the disposal of wastes. In some countries these regulations are stringent while in others they are lax or nonexistent. Moreover, some countries have regulations governing disposal of wastes within national boundaries as well as regulations relating to the export of hazardous wastes. For example, companies in the United States that intend to export hazardous wastes are requested to submit notices to the Environmental Protection Agency (EPA) and to demonstrate that they have the permission of the receiving country (Porterfield and Weir, 1987, p. 341). However, the effectiveness of these controls is in question. The General Accounting Office has found that "the E.P.A. does not know whether it is controlling 90 percent of the existing waste or 10 percent. Likewise it does not know if it is controlling the wastes that are most hazardous" (Ibid). Moreover, there is evidence indicating that other U.S. government agencies are encouraging the export of hazardous wastes. The Navy, the Army, the Defense Department, the Agriculture Department, and the Treasury Department are some government agencies that have provided hazardous wastes to known exporters. Also, major U.S. cities, sometimes with the approval of the State Department, have been suppliers to the international trade in hazardous wastes (Porterfield and Weir, 1987, p. 342).

While more stringent regulations, higher disposal costs, and heightened environmental awareness are pushing many companies in industrial countries to export hazardous wastes, it must be, nevertheless, realized that the governments of lesser developed countries are allowing such imports into their countries because of the need for foreign exchange. These governments are willing to damage the environment in return for hard currency or the creation of jobs. One must assume that on the basis of cost-benefit analysis these governments foresee more benefits than harm resulting from the importation of hazardous wastes. However, these benefits go mainly to a few waste brokers while the health of large numbers of people is put at risk. In some cases decisions to import wastes are made by governments that hold power by force and fraud. For example, Haiti, which has imported wastes, is ruled by a military dictatorship, and Guyana, which is actively considering the importation of industrial oil wastes and paint sludge, is ruled by a minority party that has rigged all elections held in that country since 1964. The ethical dilemma posed by this situation is that of whether or not an unrepresentative government of a country could be trusted to make decisions affecting the life and health of its citizens. In fact, a larger question is whether or not any government has the right to permit business activity that poses a high risk to human life and health.

Generally, governments of waste generating countries, in reaction to political pressure, have imposed stringent regulations on domestic disposal and some restrictions on the export of hazardous wastes. However, as the examples above illustrate, the latter restrictions are not strictly enforced, hence, indicating a duplicitous stance on the part of the generating countries. The governments of importing countries, in allowing into their countries wastes that will disrupt ecosystems and damage human health, deny their citizens the right to a livable environment.

Conclusion

Hazardous wastes are, in the main, by-products of industrial processes that have contributed significantly to the economic development of many countries. Economic development, in turn, has led to lifestyles that also generate hazardous wastes. To export these wastes to countries that do not benefit from waste generating industrial processes or whose citizens do not have lifestyles that generate such wastes is unethical. It is especially unjust to send hazardous wastes to lesser developed countries, which lack the technology to minimize the deleterious effects of these substances. Nevertheless, these countries are increasingly becoming recipients of such cargoes. The need for stringent international regulation to govern the trade in hazardous wastes is now stronger than ever before. However, this alone will not significantly curb the international trade in hazardous wastes. International regulation must be coupled with a revolutionary reorganization of waste generating processes and change in consumption patterns. Until this is achieved the international trade in hazardous wastes will continue and with it a plethora of unethical activities.

RESOURCES

Barthos, G.: 1988, "Third World Outraged at Receiving Toxic Trash," *Toronto Star*, June 26, pp. 1, 4.

Blackstone, W. T.: 1983, "Ethics and Ecology," in Beauchamp, T. L. and Bowie, N. E. (Eds), *Ethical Theory and Business*, 2nd. edition (Prentice-Hall, Englewood Cliffs, New Jersey), pp. 411–424.

Brooke, J.: 1988, "Africa Fights Tide of Western Wastes," *Globe and Mail*, July 18, p. A10.

Chiras, D. D.: 1988, *Environmental Science* (Benjamin Cummings Publishing Co. Inc., Denver).

Environment Canada: 1986, *Canada-U.S.A. Agreement on the Transboundary Movement of Hazardous Waste* (Environment Canada, Ottawa).

Epstein, S. S., Brown, L. O., and Pope, C.: 1982, *Hazardous Waste in America* (Sierra Club Books, San Francisco).

Feinberg, J.: 1983, "The Rights of Animals and Unborn Generation," in Beauchamp, T. L. and Bowie, N. E. (eds), *Ethical Theory and Business*, 2nd. edition (Prentice-Hall, Englewood Cliffs, New Jersey), pp. 428–436.

Goldfarb, T. D.: 1987, *Taking Sides: Clashing Views on Controversial Environmental Issues* (Dushkin Publishing Co., Inc., Connecticut).

Guerrette, R. H.: 1986, "Environmental Integrity and Corporate Responsibility," *Journal of Business Ethics*, Vol. 5, pp. 409–415.

Harden, B.: 1988, "Africa Refuses to Become Waste Dump for the West," *Windsor Star*, July 9, p. A–6.

Klatte, E., Palacio, F., Rapaport, D., and Vallette, J.: 1988, *International Trade in Toxic Wastes: Policy and Data Analysis* (Greenpeace International, Washington, D.C.).

Law Reform Commission of Canada: 1987, "Crimes Against the Environment" in Poff, D. and Waluchow, W., *Business Ethics in Canada* (Prentice-Hall, Canada Inc., Scarborough), pp. 261–264.

Lee, C.: Summer 1987, "The Racist Disposal of Toxic Wastes," *Business and Society Review*, Vol. 62, pp. 43–46.

Miller, T.: 1988, *Living in the Environment* (Wadsworth Publishing Co., California).

Montreal Gazette: April 27, 1987, "Mexico Sends Back U.S. Barge Filled with Tonnes of Garbage," p. F9.

Morrison, A.: 1988, "Dead Flowers to U.S. Firms that Plan to Send Waste to Guyana," *Catholic Standard*, Sunday, May 8.

Nobel, B. J.: 1987, *Environmental Science* (Prentice-Hall, New Jersey).

OECD Observer: March 1984, "Transfrontier Movements of Hazardous Wastes: Getting to Grips with the Problem," pp. 39–41.

Porterfield, A. and Weir, D.: 1987, "The Export of U.S. Toxic Wastes," *The Nation*, Vol. 245, Iss. 10 (Oct. 3), pp. 341–344.

Regenstein, L.: 1982, *America the Poisoned* (Acropolis Books, Washington, D.C.).

The Economist: March 1, 1986, "Rubbish Between Germans," p. 46.

Tifft, S.: 1988, "Who Gets the Garbage," *Time*, July 4, pp. 42–43.

Vallette, J.: 1989, *The International Trade in Wastes: A Greenpeace Inventory*, 4th edition (Greenpeace International, Luxembourg).

Study Questions

1. Suppose Steve Riley came to you for advice on what he should do about his predicament in the case "Worlds Apart." How would you advise Steve and why?

2. What different solutions to the abuse of H. B. Fuller's Resistol product were proposed by government officials and Fuller stockholders and personnel? Which, if any, seems to you to be the best? Why? How would you recommend that Fuller handle the problem of Resistol?

3. In *Dow Chemical Co. and Shell Oil Co. v. Alfaro*, the defendants, because they are American companies, are open to lawsuit in Texas. Had they been Costa Rican firms, the only forum for a lawsuit would have been Costa Rica, where the law is decidely pro-business. Is there a moral justification for allowing citizens of Costa Rica to sue American defendants in the United States, where the potential for recovery is much greater than in their home country? If there is such a justification, what is it?

4. List some of the basic rights that Donaldson argues multinational companies ought to respect. Which of these rights are what Donaldson calls "negative rights"? Which are "positive rights"? How would you rank these rights in order of their relative importance?

5. Summarize the three ethical perspectives Paul says have dominated the Western tradition in philosophy. What is her analysis of the utilitarian understanding of the FCPA? Do you agree with the analysis?

6. Paul recommends application of the utilitarian perspective for ambiguous or "gray" area cases. Explain, with an example, what this might be like.

7. Explain in your own words as clearly as you can what Pastin and Hooker mean by "end-point assessment" and "rule assessment."

8. Comment critically on Pastin and Hooker's argument that labor and business costs weigh against the prima facie obligation to avoid bribery.

9. Sketch Frederick's argument to the conclusion that the FCPA "might be entirely neutral," that is, have no net effect if one considers all the parties affected by the legislation. Should everyone's welfare be considered when the morality of a nation's legislation is assessed?

10. Explain how Frederick distinguishes between bribery and extortion.

11. As explained by Singh and Lakhan, how have some ethicists argued that enjoyment of a livable environment is a basic human right? What do these ethicists seem to think such a right encompasses?

12. According to Singh and Lakhan, why have some argued that the disposal of hazardous waste amounts to environmental racism? How do the authors rebut such charges?

CASE SCENARIO 1   **International Business and Sex Discrimination**

High-Tech Industries, Inc., is a London-based telecommunications firm. The company has operated successfully in a number of eastern European countries and has recently expanded to the Persian Gulf region. Because many of the Gulf states have a shortage of local personnel to fill technical positions, they need to rely on a fairly large body of foreign workers. When High-Tech could not recruit sufficiently qualified Gulf residents for its marketing positions, the company advertised in London. Catherine Jenkins, a native of England, was hired along with several men and sent to the Gulf to spearhead the company's operations there.

Problems began immediately for Ms. Jenkins. Because she was a single woman, her entry into some Arab states was delayed for weeks. Saudi Arabia, at least initially, refused to allow her entry at all. Where she could enter, Jenkins often was required to stay only in hotels that government officials had approved for foreign women. She was prohibited from eating in the dining room unless accompanied by the hotel manager. Her efforts to hire assistants were frustrated by various forms of harassment. Predictably, Jenkins's job performance lagged due to these many restrictions and frustrations. Her male co-workers, on the other hand, managed to move about in Arab culture much more easily and, consequently, were more successful at securing new business for High-Tech. When it became apparent to upper management that Jenkins was not doing as well as they expected, Bill Philips, vice president for marketing and sales at High-Tech, met with Jenkins to discuss the matter. It was then that Philips made suggestions that angered Jenkins.

"You need to make some compromises here," Philips told her, "so you can be more efficient." Philips suggested that, when traveling, Jenkins eat meals in her room; he said she should conduct meetings in conference rooms rather than in public, and have incoming calls screened by the hotel operator. She should wear long-sleeved blouses and full-length skirts in a dark color. Last, Philips suggested that Jenkins wear a wedding ring and register at hotels as a married woman.

"It's demeaning to have to act like that," Jenkins responded. "You don't tell the guys what to wear or how to eat."

"But it's the culture here," Philips pointed out. "That's what they expect. You won't get anywhere if you don't bend."

"You mean compromise my values and pretend to be something I'm not?" Jenkins replied. "It's discrimination against me because I'm a woman. And you're telling me to go along with it."

"I'm telling you what you need to do to succeed with High-Tech," Philips answered, "but if you don't want the job, the choice is yours."

1. What should a woman in Catherine Jenkins's position do? How would you advise her? Based on your readings, what advice do you believe Jenkins would receive from Paul? From Donaldson?
2. Has Jenkins been discriminated against on the basis of her gender? And if so, by whom? High-Tech? Arab culture? Both?
3. Did Philips and High-Tech make unreasonable and improper demands on Jenkins concerning how to conduct herself while working in the Gulf region? How would you suggest that High-Tech approach the problem of Jenkins's poor performance?

CASE SCENARIO 2   Product Labels and Human Rights

Manville Corporation (formerly Johns-Manville) emerged from bankruptcy in the late 1980s, after massive litigation over injuries sustained from the company's manufacture and sale of asbestos. Among other items, Manville now markets fiberglass and fiberglass products. The Hazard Communication Standard of the Occupational Safety and Health Administration (OSHA) requires that products that have been found to be cancer-causing must carry a warning label to that effect. In 1987 the International Agency for Research on Cancer suggested that fiberglass was a "possible carcinogen." Subsequently, Manville affixed warning labels on all of its fiberglass products shipped within the United States.

Manville does business in Japan and ships fiberglass to Japanese distributors. OSHA regulations did not mandate that warnings about the carcinogenic potential of fiberglass be placed on material shipped overseas; nonetheless Manville's top management discussed just such a course of action. Some people within Manville objected to placing any warnings on items bound for Japan. Manville's business customers were fearful of scaring their workers; and architects worried about alerting lawyers by calling attention to a possibly carcinogenic building material. Most important, the Japanese government itself recommended that Manville not affix the warning labels. Government officials warned Manville against using "the C word," pointing out that the Japanese public is especially fearful of cancer—a legacy of the bombing of Hiroshima and Nagasaki. The contemplated warnings, officials believed, would unduly frighten Japanese citizens. "We'll tell them what the risks are," Japanese officials told Manville; there was no need for the labels.

After some debate, Manville elected to go ahead with the warning labels despite the objections. Manville President and CEO Tom Stevens explained the company's decision: "A human being in Japan is no different from a human being in the U.S. We told them we had a policy. We had to have a label." According to Stevens, the Japanese ministers remarked that Manville was "very brave" to choose such a course, referring to the potential risk to Manville's Japanese business. Indeed, the company lost 40 percent of its usual sales to Japan in only one year; some, though not all, of Manville's Japanese business was later rebuilt.

1. Did Manville make the right decision in choosing to affix the warning labels to its fiberglass products exported to Japan?

2. Should Manville have followed the advice of the Japanese government and refrained from labeling its goods as carcinogenic? Some argue that U.S. corporations should not impose American values and standards on the governments and people of other countries. Would you agree even if the company claimed to be acting out of concern for the human rights of those abroad, and not simply the company's own self-interest?
3. What recommendation would the authors in this chapter make to Manville in this situation? Give reasons for your answer.

CASE SCENARIO 3   Bribery and Local Customs

Dick Smith is the president and CEO of a small domestic civil engineering firm. The slow economy in the nineties has not been kind to his firm, and Smith has begun looking for overseas business to boost the firm's sagging revenues. Smith has done some overseas assignments in the past, but now he finds himself negotiating some government contracts in a country in which he has not previously worked. During the course of the negotiations, he is advised by a high-ranking government source of the host country that, in this country, it is customary for those awarded contracts to make personal gifts to those officials authorized to award the contracts. It is further explained to Smith that such a practice is entirely legal in this country; furthermore, Smith is told that such gifts are often the major source of personal income for those officials. Finally, Smith is informed that, although the gift is not a condition of the contract, his failure to make a gift to these officials would likely end any hope of future business for Smith's firm and that Smith could expect poor cooperation in executing even those contracts he does land. Smith responds that these unstated conditions sound like bribery, a practice which he finds repugnant and in which his firm has never engaged. Smith's source, however, is not impressed by this objection and points out that other U.S. and international firms have adhered to the local practice in regard to the gifts.

1. If Smith does give a gift to the foreign officials, would such a gift amount to bribery? Extortion? Explain the difference between these two characterizations. Does the issue turn on the size of the gift?
2. Do you think that the practice of bribery of foreign officials, if unchecked by legislation like the FCPA, might make U.S. firms more likely to offer bribes in the domestic market? If you answer yes, do you think that this might be another argument for the legitimacy of the FCPA?
3. Would it be best for Smith to simply withdraw his bids in this case? Why or why not?
4. How, in your view, would Pastin and Hooker assess this case? How would Frederick?

CASE SCENARIO 4   Labor Conditions, the Third World, and Profitability

Peter Jacob stormed into the office of his colleague, Oscar White, at TGG Connector. Jacob had just completed a sourcing expedition in the Far East and a visit with some of TGG's assembly plants in that region of the world. A small assembler of D-subminiature connectors, TGG purchases connectors and pins from Korea and cable from Great Britain and the United States; it then assembles the connectors for distribution to U.S. retailers, as well as to original equipment manufacturers (OEMs) in the Far East. The connectors end up as hardware for personal computers and printers. Only recently has TGG established assembly facilities in the Far East. The company intends to use these new facilities to save on labor and distribution costs, allowing it to chip away business from its competitors.

On his recent trip abroad, Jacob was startled to find a large number of children, some not more than twelve years old, working in TGG's assembly plants. When he questioned factory supervisors, Jacob was told that the use of children was a common labor practice in the host country. Adequate child care is simply not available, and parents who themselves work in the factories prefer to have their children near them, rather than have them playing in the streets. Jacob was quite upset. The idea of child labor was abhorrent to him. These kids should be in school, he thought, or at least be able to spend their time outside rather than be stuck in here.

Now back in Oscar White's office, Jacob is still angry. "What kind of work were the kids doing?" White asked.

"Sorting cable and counting out pins," Jacob replied. "Some were sweeping up. But it's not the kind of work they were doing that bothers me so much. It's that those kids shouldn't be working at the plant at all. They should be in school or at least at a daycare facility. How can the supervisors and parents allow this kind of thing? And how can TGG continue to support it? It reminds me of the old days of the industrial revolution. There are child labor laws in this country, you know, and for good reason. I think we should cancel our contracts with these factories and move the assembly work back here to the United States."

"Hold on a minute, Peter," cautioned White. "If we do the assembly work here in the States, we'll be out of business in a few months. We can't handle the labor costs. The big U.S. and international firms will crush us. Besides, you know what the assemblers over there are paid. They need every bit of income they can get; and, as you noted, the children are paid for their service. These assembly plants are not in the United States. They have a different view of work and education over there. There's no daycare to speak of, so why shouldn't the parents want their kids alongside them in the plant? At least they can keep an eye on them. And as you say, they're not doing anything dangerous. If we cancel the contracts, those kids and their parents will be out on the streets—but they won't be playing, they'll be begging. Unemployment there runs 25 percent."

Jacob rubbed his brow. "So what do you think should be done?"

"Well," answered White, "I think we should start by refusing to impose U.S. conventions and values on a third world nation. When their economy develops, they can start worrying about education and labor laws and the like. For the time being, they have to dance to the tune the international market is playing."

1. Do you think that Jacob's view is an instance of "moral imperialism" between an international corporation and a host country? Is White correct in claiming that the need for labor laws and daycare are a matter of "convention"? What does that term imply?
2. Should the restrictions of child labor generally be a concern for multinationals with facilities in the Third World? Or is this really a matter for the host country or parents?
3. Try to formulate a plan that could address the concerns of both Jacob and White. Is such a plan feasible?

CHAPTER 3

Downsizing and Layoffs: Employee Job Security

A significant shift in the attitudes and expectations of American workers seems to be taking place as the end of the century approaches. A generation or two ago, the principal concern of Americans was to get a "good job," to be "upwardly mobile," and to realize the dream of a house in the suburbs. But increasingly, those entering the job market today voice a more basic concern: Merely to get a job and keep it has, for many, become a distant goal. Those who believe that the sole objective of a corporation is to pursue profits (without breaking the law) would argue that such phenomena are a lamentable but unavoidable fact of the global economy. Defenders of this canonical view of business responsibility claim that if the global market presents an opportunity for cheaper resources, it is economically rational to pursue that opportunity, regardless of whether it be for raw materials or human labor. Downsizing and layoffs do cause palpable if temporary harms to employees. But this is a cost that must be endured by the affected parties or nation if the multinational is to maintain its competitiveness in global markets and if it is to return to its shareholders maximum profitability. If profitability is the ideal of commerce, downsizing and layoffs are a business necessity. Finally, say the defenders of the canonical view, since such actions as downsizing, shutdowns, and so on are legal, this indicates that our society believes that they are in its interests. Hence, there is no question of their moral legitimacy. Is this argument correct? This chapter explores this and other questions concerning job security that have become a predominant concern for many workers.

CHANGES IN THE JOB MARKET

The worries many have over keeping a job are well founded. A recent report found that, while nearly 80 percent of workers in 1980 rated their job security as "good" or "very good," only slightly more than 50 percent of workers gave the same rating in 1994.[1] These results doubtless reflect in large measure the substantial wave of corporate downsizing that took place throughout the 1980s and into the 1990s: AT&T laid off 140,000 workers; Chevron, Inc., reduced its workforce by almost 50,000 after its merger with Gulf Oil in 1984; IBM let go over 85,000 workers, and General Motors eliminated 75,000 jobs. The U.S. Bureau of Labor Statistics's occupational forecast for the coming decade projects substantial and continuing declines in traditional, skilled, or semi-skilled union jobs; aside from technical and professional positions, the only sector of the workforce projected for large increases are in so-called service-sector jobs—minimum-wage jobs in such venues as convenience stores

---

 Vegetarianism and Religious Freedom in the Workplace

Bruce Anderson worked as a bus driver for the Orange County Transportation Authority until 1996. He was dismissed from his job for insubordination and disobeying a direct order of his supervisor. Anderson, who is a strict vegetarian, refused to hand out coupons for free fast-food hamburgers, part of a promotional campaign arranged between the Transit Authority and Carl Jr.'s restaurants. The campaign, Anderson claimed, violated his moral convictions that animals should not be killed or eaten. A suit was brought against the Transit Authority on Anderson's behalf, alleging discrimination. The Equal Employment Opportunity Commission (EEOC) sided with Anderson, finding that the Transit Authority had violated laws against religious discrimination by failing to make "reasonable accommodations" for Anderson's beliefs. Though his beliefs were not religious in a strict sense, the EEOC found that Anderson's ethical convictions concerning use of animals for food was "held with the strength of traditional religious views."

SOURCE: Los Angeles Times 2/7/97.

---

and fast-food restaurants, typically the least secure forms of regular employment. Last, the number of part-time and contract workers is also projected to rise sharply into the next century.[2]

THE EMPLOYMENT-AT-WILL DOCTRINE

As with many other aspects of conducting business, corporate practices and policies concerning the hiring, retention, or firing of workers have been shaped significantly by the law.

The basic approach of American law to questions of job security is markedly different in its underlying assumptions from the law in other nations, particularly the nations of western Europe. In France, Germany, and other European nations, workers are assumed to

---

 Violence in the Workplace

Data available from the U.S. Bureau of Labor Statistics reveals a growing and disturbing pattern of workplace violence emerging in recent years. For example, in 1993, more than one thousand homicides occurred on the job in the United States; over twenty-two thousand separate acts of violence were reported by the Bureau in 1993. Workplace deaths that year included: a shooting at a Chuck E. Cheese restaurant in a Denver suburb in which a fired kitchen worker killed four employees; the deaths of three men by an ex-employee of Fireman's Fund Insurance Co., at an office in Tampa; and an attack by a disgruntled postal worker at a post office in Dearborn, Michigan, which left one worker dead. What steps should employers take to protect those in their employ from violence? Do employers have a duty to hire "safe" employees? Can employers meet that duty without violating the rights of workers and job applicants?

✑ Protection for Paid Union Organizers

Under the National Labor Relations Act (NLRA) it is an unfair labor practice to "interfere with . . . employees in the exercise of their rights," including rights "to self-organization, to form, join, or assist labor organizations." Clearly, these rights apply to an employer's current workers. But what about job applicants who also work (and are paid) as union organizers? Town & Country Electric, a nonunion company, advertised for a position with the firm. Of eleven union members who applied for the position, ten were refused even an interview. The applicant who was interviewed was hired, but was terminated after a few days. The unsuccessful applicants filed a complaint with the National Labor Relations Board. Town & Country argued that the union was trying to seed nonunion companies with union members who might then seek to harm the company. But in November 1995, the U.S. Supreme Court rejected this argument. Paid union organizers are no less employees than those who don't work for a union, the Court held. Because union organizing is protected under the law, the Court argued, even if such activities are disloyal, the employer cannot prohibit workers from engaging in them. Employers can still discipline workers who are disruptive, and they can exclude nonemployee union members from their premises. Town & Country complained that union organizers are more likely than regular employees to quit without notice, openly disparage the firm, or even engage in efforts to sabotage the company or its products. The Court found no merit in these contentions. Employees quit for all kinds of legitimate reasons, and even unpaid union members can try to hurt the company. Is the Court's ruling unfair to employers?

have a right to the continuation of their employment and cannot be laid off or fired except for a good reason or "just cause," as it is sometimes called. The assumption of American law is just the reverse: Employers are assumed to have the right to terminate an employee at any time and for whatever reason. This *employment-at-will* doctrine forms the baseline from which business and employers in America begin; the employer is assumed to have the ability to hire, fire, promote, or demote "at will" unless some specific exception to the general assumption is applicable. In other words, an employer is presumed free to terminate an employee; but there are some grounds upon which or circumstances in which this is not permitted. For example, an employee may not be fired as a result of discrimination based upon her gender, religion, or ethnicity. Failing to hire a worker because he is disabled, though otherwise capable of performing the job tasks assigned to him, is also a form of unlawful discrimination.

Many employers, of course, offer contracts to their employees, and these contracts often spell out certain protections for job security. A contract might stipulate, for example, that workers will be given notice before a pink slip is issued; they may be accorded rights to a pretermination hearing or to severance benefits. Such procedural safeguards, generally comprehended under the notion of due process, are an important part of employment security, though they fall far short of guaranteeing that one will not be terminated. Though employment-at-will remains a basic presumption of employment law, some changes are beginning to occur. In 1987, for example, the State of Montana became the first state to prohibit employers from firing employees where such action is without "good cause," as defined by statute or as specified by promises made in employee handbooks or other express provisions of the employer's own written personnel policy. The Wrongful Discharge from Employment Act requires that an employer have "reasonable job-related grounds for dismissal based on a failure to satisfactorily perform job duties, disruption of the employer's operation, or other legitimate business reasons." Even this legislation does not protect workers from layoffs, however: A Montana court recently ruled that an oil company executive who had been let go from his company during a period of decline in oil prices had been discharged for "legitimate business reasons."

What moral arguments might be made in support of the employment-at-will doctrine? As the readings for this chapter reveal, some have argued for a policy of employment-at-will on the grounds that it represents the most economically efficient arrangement. Others claim that this policy most fully respects the autonomy and liberty of each party, since the employee is just as free to quit "at will" as the employer is to discharge him. But others see serious weaknesses in these arguments. Efficiency should not be achieved at the cost of using people, some maintain; and employment-at-will really only protects the liberty of the employer, as there are frequently fewer alternative jobs for the employee than there are substitute workers for the employer.

UNIONS AND PERMANENT REPLACEMENTS

From the late nineteenth century through the middle of the twentieth, labor unions were a powerful voice for working men and women in America. Despite resorts to violence by industry in an effort to break labor strikes, and in the face of adverse rulings by courts, the labor movement prevailed by the mid-thirties with the passage of the National Labor Relations Act (also known as the Wagner Act). This law established the National Labor Relations Board (NLRB) to regulate union organizing; gave employees the right to organize and bargain collectively; and prohibited various unfair labor practices. Later statutes set minimum-wage rates and required premium pay for overtime work.

In recent decades, however, the influence of labor unions has waned. The decline of the labor movement has been viewed positively by some. They claim that collective bargaining agreements interfere with the rights of employers and employees to form mutually advantageous agreements; moreover, it is urged, unions force workers to join their ranks, thereby violating their right to work. Supporters of unions are quick to point out, however, that so-called right-to-work laws, outlawing both "closed shops" (where employers are required to hire only union members) and "union shops" (where union membership is a necessary

---

✌ Presidential Ban on Permanent Striker Replacements

In March 1996 President Bill Clinton signed Executive Order 12954, barring federal contractors from permanently replacing striking workers. Covering all contracts for $100,000 or more, the order subjects firms doing business with the government to two penalties for violating the ban. Any firm found to have replaced strikers with permanent employees can be prohibited from doing any future business with the government; and the U.S. Labor Department can act to cancel any existing contracts. Clinton's order followed the defeat by Congress of a bill that would have banned permanent replacements. Does the order represent good policy?

condition of continued employment) have effectively killed trade unions. As Mancur Olson has noted, "A rational worker will not voluntarily contribute to a large union providing a collective benefit since he alone would not perceptibly strengthen the union, and since he would get the benefits of any union achievements whether or not he supported the union."[3] Right-to-work laws promote "free-riding," a form of getting the benefit without paying the associated costs. With respect to consent, it is argued that collective bargaining is a means of protecting workers from serious harm. For example, many nonunion workers are at-will employees. As we have already seen, this legal status allows employers to terminate the employment agreement for good reason, for no reason at all, or even for a reason that many might see as morally wrong (so long as it doesn't violate anti-discrimination or other laws). Most union-initiated collective bargaining agreements restrict this legal right and require that no employee will be disciplined or discharged without just cause. The employer must have legitimate reason to justify the action, and the action itself must conform to certain specified procedures.[4]

For most people, work is a great asset. Labor unions are often seen as a means of balancing an unequal and sometimes coercive relationship between employer and employee. Collective action by employees (particularly a strike or the threat of one) can help balance that relationship and further the interests of the individual employee. Because a strike can effectively stop the production of goods and services, management must at least give due consideration to union demands. But, say pro-unionists, a management strategy used with increasing frequency threatens to undercut the economic threat of the strike. Employers are legally entitled to hire permanent replacement workers, filling the spots of those who go out on strike. President Reagan did this in 1981, when he fired some eleven thousand members of Patco, a union of air-traffic controllers employed by the federal government. According to some, this strategy (permitted under earlier Supreme Court rulings) eliminates the right to strike and consequently imperils the workers' ability to negotiate contracts and wages.

◈   Liability for References

If an employer chooses to terminate a worker and then provide the former employee with job references, an employer may face liability for injuries or damage caused by the worker in his or her new job. In a decision handed down in early 1997, the Supreme Court of California ruled that employers may be sued for omitting in job references any information showing that the worker poses "a foreseeable and substantial risk of harm" to others. The case arose out of an allegation of molestation, brought against the defendant, a school vice principal. The family of the victim filed suit against the perpetrator and against several other school districts that had previously employed the molester and had provided him with positive recommendations, despite their knowledge of similar allegations of molestation while the defendant had been in their employ. In holding in favor of the victim, the Court asserted that providing recommendations while leaving out facts amounting to an "affirmative misrepresentation" of a worker's potential danger can make the recommender liable for the worker's future misconduct. "The writer of a letter of recommendation owes to prospective employers and third persons a duty not to misrepresent fact in describing the qualifications and character of a former employee."

༄ം **WARN**

In 1988 Congress enacted the first federal law designed to limit the ability of employers to shut down plants and factories. The Worker Adjustment and Retraining Notification Act (WARN) applies to any business that employs one hundred or more workers. The law defines a "plant closing" as a shutdown at a single job site that results in a loss of work for at least fifty employees. Employers cannot engage in such a shutdown without giving sixty days' notice to the plant's union (if there is one), as well as to each worker (when there is no union), and to representatives of both state and local government. Workers laid off without appropriate notification are entitled to back pay and any fringe benefits they may have lost. Under exceptional circumstances, an employer can give less than sixty days' notice, as (for example) when closing is required by unforeseeable business circumstances or is brought on by a natural disaster.

HOSTILE TAKEOVERS AND PLANT CLOSINGS

It is clear that corporate downsizing or other forms of restructuring—takeovers and mergers, as well as plant closures—can harm employees. The worker, to begin with, faces the financial hardship of a potentially long term of unemployment, costly retraining in a new field of work, and the inevitable stress of being out of work for an uncertain period. Those remaining employees who do keep their jobs after restructuring may suffer as well, since they will naturally speculate about whether their jobs will be the next to be eliminated. According to proponents of the free market, these employee costs are externalities of the market which must be borne. They point out that the shareholders who benefit from such events (through the increase of stock value) have the right to benefit from property to which they have a legal entitlement. If anyone owns the corporate property, it is the shareholders who have a right to these profits, since they assume the risk of losing their investment. Further, it might be argued on utilitarian grounds that, although a hostile takeover might harm employees and the community, it is nonetheless best for the economy as a whole, since these actions prune from the market corporations that have been managed inefficiently.

THE READINGS

The readings for this chapter open with a case study prompting you to examine the ethical quandary of a middle manager forced to report on the profitability of a plant closure to which he is personally opposed. Several commentators debate how to weigh the moral costs of undermining a community's livelihood versus the imperative to remain competitive and solvent in a world economy.

The selection by Patricia Werhane looks critically at the employment-at-will doctrine. Such a doctrine is often supported, Werhane observes, by an appeal to several considerations: the freedom of the employee to choose his or her working conditions, the right to private property, and the demand for economic efficiency. Werhane then challenges attempts to use these considerations in support of employment-at-will. Employees are people, not property; and the theoretical parity of workers and their employers under employment-at-will is actually a fiction: The employment-at-will doctrine puts employees at a significant disadvantage by placing them in a coercive position. In the course of defending these claims, Werhane tries to develop a case in favor of due process protections for those in the workplace. Such protections are, she reasons, a necessary corrective to the employer's otherwise unrestricted right to fire or demote workers arbitrarily.

Werhane's stance is contested by Ian Maitland. Due process and other job security measures are counterproductive for workers themselves, Maitland insists. This can happen because of the way a free-market economy compensates workers for jobs that are more or less meaningful, secure, and so on. Some workers and employers, for instance, may both have an interest in some jobs being repetitive and with little in the way of security; and such jobs might draw workers with the incentive of greater pay. Those who want the protections of due process and a more meaningful job may take the trade-off of lower pay. Maitland's point is that the freedom of employers and employees to make these trade-offs freely, unhampered by mandated salaries and safeguards, must be preserved.

The selections by Werhane and Maitland debate a core question: How much freedom should an employer have to terminate a worker? The final reading for this section switches our focus to the opposite issue: When (if ever) is an employer obligated either not to hire a worker or not to continue retaining him once he is hired? Marian Extejt and William Bockanic review the meaning and development of the employer liability for negligent hiring and negligent retention, liability imposed when the employer hires or retains a worker that it knew (or should have known) posed a danger to others. Among the questions the authors explore are: To what extent should prior criminal activity on a worker's part be used as evidence of unfitness for a job? Should the employer be liable where the worker caused an injury to another after hours or away from the job site? How are employers properly to balance the moral imperative to protect others from dangerous employees against the need not to violate the worker's rights to privacy and against discrimination?

The selection by Brian Steverson turns to the recent and well-documented rise of the ranks of temporary workers. Temporary employment practices, Steverson argues, have serious moral implications. The shift away from more-traditional, permanent jobs and toward independent contracting and temporary assignments cannot, Steverson argues, be justified morally.

The readings next turn to the issue of replacement of striking workers. Former Labor Secretary Robert Reich argues that the use of permanent replacements (and the threat of their use) makes labor disputes bitter and unproductive and that a ban on such practices will help promote a balance of power between otherwise opposed camps. But David Warner, in his selection, argues that businesses are often the victims of unreasonable strikes, which jeopardize the existence of the firm. Without the threat of permanent replacements, labor would exert an unacceptable degree of control over business operations. Furthermore, Warren states, under current law "permanent" replacements are not necessarily permanent. After the termination of a strike, unions can petition the NLRB to reinstate their members, thereby displacing replacement workers. This, he claims, is unfair to nonunion laborers, who might themselves then face the prospect of unemployment.

The final set of readings for this chapter examine the ethics of corporate restructuring and downsizing. Lisa Newton argues against the prevailing view on Wall Street; takeovers, she insists, are in fact inefficient. The current flurry of mergers and takeovers actually undermines, she believes, the traditional concept of ownership by which an owner has an interest in the stewardship of the property to which he or she lays claim. Newton ends her selection with some provocative observations about the status of corporations, suggesting that the corporation, as an entity, might in fact have a right to self-preservation. Judith Lichtenberg's essay highlights some of the moral problems surrounding the phenomenon of plant closures for the purpose of lowering labor costs. She argues against the consequentialist claim that allowing corporations to move when they see fit will produce more wealth overall and that the wealth will be distributed in ways that benefit workers. Finally, by means of an ingenious analogy, she casts doubt on the truism that ownership entails the freedom to relocate whenever the owner sees fit.

NOTES

1. See "The New Deal," *Fortune* (June 13, 1994).
2. See "The New World of Work," *Business Week* (Oct. 17, 1994).
3. Mancur Olson, *The Logic of Collective Action* (Cambridge: Harvard University Press, 1975).
4. See Burton Hall, "Collective Bargaining and Workers' Rights," in *Moral Rights and the Workplace*, edited by Gertrude Ezorsky (Albany: State University of New York Press, 1987).

CASE STUDY   Southern Discomfort

Doug Wallace

Jim Malesckowski remembers the call of two weeks ago as if he just put down the telephone receiver: "I just read your analysis and I want you to get down to Mexico right away," Jack Ripon, his boss and chief executive officer, blurted in his ear. "You know we can't make the plant in Oconomo work anymore—the costs are just too high. So go down there, check out what our operational costs would be if we move, and report back to me in a week."

At that moment, Jim felt as if a shiv had been stuck in his side, just below the rib cage. As president of the Wisconsin Specialty Products Division of Lamprey Inc., he knew quite well the challenge of dealing with high-cost labor in a third-generation, unionized manufacturing plant. And although he had done the analysis that led to his boss's knee-jerk response, the call still stunned him. There were 520 people who make a living at the Oconomo facility, and if it closed, most of them wouldn't have a journeyman's prayer of finding another job in the town of 9,900 people.

As he changed planes in Houston on his way to the Mexican border town, Jim remembered the words of Smiley, one of author John Le Carre's protagonists: "It's true that we are obliged to sup with the Devil, and not always with a very long spoon." The words gnawed at him as he went about his assignment.

Instead of the $16.00-per-hour average wage paid at the Oconomo plant, the wages paid to the Mexican workers—who lived in a town without sanitation and with an unbelievably toxic effluent from industrial pollution—would amount to about $1.60 an hour on average. That's a savings of nearly $15 million a year for Lamprey, to be offset in part by increased costs for training, transportation, and other matters.

After two days of talking with government representatives and managers of other companies in town, Jim had enough information to develop a set of comparative figures of production and shipping costs. On the way home he started to outline the report, knowing full well that unless some miracle occurred, he would be ushering in a blizzard of pink slips for people he had come to appreciate.

Since 1921, the Oconomo plant had made special apparel for persons suffering injuries and other medical conditions. Jim had often talked with employees who would recount stories about their fathers or grandfathers working in the same Lamprey plant—the last of the original manufacturing operations in town.

Business Ethics, Mar./Apr. 1996. Reprinted with permission from Business Ethics Magazine, 52 S. 10th St. #110, Minneapolis, MN 55403, (612) 962–4700.

But friendship aside, competitors had already edged past Lamprey in terms of price and were dangerously close to overtaking it in product quality. Although the plant manager and Jim had tried to convince the union to accept lower wages, union leaders resisted. In fact, on one occasion when Jim and the plant manager tried to discuss a cell manufacturing approach, which would cross-train employees to perform up to three different jobs, local union leaders could barely restrain their anger. Yet probing beyond the fray, Jim sensed the fear that lurked under the union reps' gruff exterior. He sensed their vulnerability, but couldn't break through the reactionary bark that protected it.

It was Jim's empathy that kept the fire of concern alive. That and his ethical belief in the dignity of life. He knew what closure would mean to employees and their families. Countless times in the past six months, he could have easily recommended that Lamprey walk away—with the jobs. But he continued to hope that somehow, the operation could be turned around.

A week has passed and Jim just submitted his report to his boss. Although he didn't specifically bring up the point, it was apparent that Lamprey could put its investment dollars in a bank and receive a better return than what its Oconomo operation was currently producing.

Tomorrow, he'll discuss the report with the CEO. Jim doesn't want to be responsible for the plant's dismantling, an act he personally believes would be wrong as long as there's a chance its costs can be lowered. "But Ripon's right," he says to himself. "The costs are too high, the union's unwilling to cooperate, and the company needs to make a better return on its investment if it's to continue at all. It sounds right but feels wrong. What is my responsibility?"

Fred Wagner
President,
Minnesota Wire and Cable,
Minneapolis

Jim's ethical belief in the dignity of life has to include the understanding that what "dignity" means in Wisconsin is not the same as in Mexico or in other developing countries. Would the people in Third World countries be better off without jobs, or with low-paying jobs? A good ethical argument can be made that the jobs are needed more elsewhere in the world than they are in Wisconsin, for example. There are places in the world (Central America, India, etc.) where 40- or 50-percent unemployment is not unheard of.

Also, the prospect of closing the plant hasn't sunk in yet with its employees. If they were convinced of the tenuousness of the situation, they might very well overrule their union leaders and vote to de-unionize. I've seen that happen.

In his meeting with the CEO, Jim should offer potential solutions and viable alternatives. He could propose that the company (1) schedule a mass meeting with a thorough explanation to employees and key local suppliers of the consequences of a decision to move; (2) consider a management-led buyout offer with serious potential for an employee stock ownership plan and de-unionization; (3) investigate potential outsourcing for the most costly aspects of production; (4) explore what percent of overall costs are represented by wages; and (5) make a request for a trial period of recovery with set measurable goals to be attained.

Jim has an ethical obligation to go beyond his identification with friends and neighbors in Wisconsin. His empathy may get in the way of a good decision.

Richard Clapp
Director of Product Development,
Cross Point Paper,
West Chicago, Illinois

When I read the question, "What is my responsibility?" my first reaction is that his responsibility is to all of his company's stakeholders—owners, employees, the communities in which the plants are located, and the customers. Jim needs to consider all of them when he looks at what's best to do.

Starting with that point of view, I would say the Wisconsin operation has to be competitive if it's going to survive. The question is how? Jim needs to get the workers' understanding of the facts so that they can become part of the solution to make that plant competitive. Without their help, the plant will die a slow death, which is worse than if it was cut off quickly.

Possible ways to get their input might involve getting employee leaders to look at labor costs in Mexico, and to look at the competitors' products and prices and how that is affecting the marketplace. The company needs to do a better job of keeping all stakeholders—especially employees—informed and involved in business strategy and issues such as competitiveness and product quality.

If change at home can't occur, then they need to consider manufacturing their products elsewhere. But obviously they need to do a better job of communicating so change *can* occur at home. That's key to Jim's ethical and managerial responsibility.

Doug Wallace
Corporate ethics consultant,
Minneapolis

This case raises important ethical questions about the ongoing trend of globalizing production. Information technology and real-time electronic communication now make it relatively easy to set up and manage company production and sales operations all over the world, operations that only a few years ago would not have been possible. This is especially true in manufacturing.

Just what should be the ethical standards that shape decision making in this brave new world? While our guest commentators work through this case, they are, at the same time, exploring this question themselves. It is not an easy one to puzzle through.

Richard Clapp suggests that a basic threshold criterion needed to shape decisions of this sort is competitiveness. This test makes all other considerations secondary. Using this yardstick, the manager's first ethical responsibility is to do everything possible to develop and execute action that makes an operation competitive. Both of our commentators point out that invariably this will involve active participation of employees who are closest to how the work is organized, and whose buy-in (or lack of it) will make or break the success of new initiatives.

If this argument is valid, it implies that there is a marriage of managerial and ethical competency, that one cannot exist without the other. If an executive or manager cannot effectively develop and implement a plan to make an operation competitive, he or she also fails his or her ethical obligation to all stakeholders, especially employees. How Jim handles this situation, then, is as much of a morality play as it is a test of managerial competence.

WHAT ACTUALLY HAPPENED

Jim bought some time from the CEO and went to work. One of the first things he did was to call in leaders from the national union office. Once they became aware of the facts they were alarmed at the position of the local union leaders and set them straight. National union officials then helped find some "best practice" operations around the country which opened the eyes of the local employees.

Jim also laid the competition's products and their prices next to the plant's own products for employees to examine. The discussion moved to the need for restructuring and reorganizing the production process into teams. Employees developed a strategy of selecting their own teams and leaders. Jim also established "open-book management" practices and set up weekly plant meetings.

As a result, the plant became more competitive and improved its financial performance as employees took on more responsibility. Cycle times—from start to finish in the making of a single item—went from six weeks to six hours. And product delivery time improved dramatically.

The Right to Due Process

Patricia H. Werhane

Employment at Will

The principle of Employment at Will, . . . is an unwritten common-law idea that employers as owners have the absolute right to hire, promote, demote, and fire whom and when they please. The principle, hereafter abbreviated as EAW, was stated explicitly in 1887 in a document by H. G. Wood entitled *Master and Servant.* Wood said, "A general or indefinite hiring is prima facie a hiring at will."[1] But the principle behind EAW dates at least to the seventeenth century and perhaps was used as early as the Middle Ages. EAW has commonly been interpreted as the rule that all employers "may dismiss their employees at will . . . for good cause, for no cause, *or even for causes morally wrong,* without being thereby guilty of legal wrong."[2]

The principle of EAW is not self-evident and stands in need of defense. The most promising lines of defense involve appeals to the right to freedom, to the common notion that property is defined as private ownership (for example, of land, material possessions, or capital), to the supposed moral right to dispose freely of one's own property as one sees fit, or to the utilitarian benefits of freely operating productive organizations. Let us briefly characterize the main elements of each defense.

The first justification for EAW in the workplace, at least in the private sector of the economy, involves both appeals to the right to freedom and considerations about the nature of places of employment in a free society. Places of employment are privately owned, voluntary organizations of all sizes, from small entrepreneurships to large corporations. As such, it is claimed, they are not subject to the same restrictions governing public and political institutions. And, as they are voluntary organizations, employees join freely and may quit at any time. Political procedures, needed to safeguard citizens against arbitrary exercise of power in society at large, do not apply to voluntary private insti-

tutions. Any restriction on the principle of EAW, those who argue in this way conclude, interferes with the rights of persons *and* organizations not to be coerced into activities that either are not of their own choosing or limit their freedom to contract.

The principle of EAW is also sometimes defended purely on the basis of property rights. The rights to freedom and to private ownership, we are assuming, are equally valid claims, and the latter right entitles owners, it is argued, to use and improve what they own, including all aspects of their businesses, as they wish. According to this view, when an employee is working for another, this activity affects, positively or negatively, the employer's property and production. Because employers have property rights, and because these rights entitle them to control what happens to what they own, the employer has the right to dispose of the labor of employees whose work changes production. In dismissing or demoting employees, the employer is not denying *persons* political rights; rather, the employer is simply excluding their *labor* from the organization.

Finally, EAW is often defended on practical grounds. Viewed from a utilitarian perspective, hiring and firing "at will" is necessary in productive organizations if they are to achieve their goal of maximum efficiency and productivity. To interfere with this process, it is claimed, would defeat the purpose of free enterprise organizations. We shall consider each of these arguments more fully in the following section.

The Right to Due Process in the Workplace

Due process is a procedure by which one can appeal a decision or action in order to get a rational explanation of the decision and a disinterested, objective review of its propriety. In the workplace due process is, or should be, the right to grievance, arbitration, or some other fair procedure to evaluate hiring, firing, promotion, or demotion. For example, Geary and Alomar were fired without a hearing. Should they have been given some warning, a hearing by peers, a chance to appeal? The call

From *Just Business: New Introductory Essays in Business Ethics,* Tom Regan, ed., McGraw-Hill, 1984, 1–113, 124–126. Used with permission of the publisher.

to recognize the right to due process in the workplace extends the widely accepted view that every accused person, guilty or innocent, has a right to a fair hearing and an objective evaluation of his or her guilt or innocence. Those who deny due process in the workplace could argue (a) that this right does not extend to every sector of society, or (b) that rights of employers sometimes override those of employees and do so in this case. However we decide the merits of these arguments, the absence of due process in the workplace is not merely an oversight, as witness the principle of Employment at Will discussed in the last section. An employer, according to this principle, need not explain or defend its employee treatment in regard to dismissal nor give a hearing to the employee before he or she is dismissed.

In order to support the validity of the claim to the right to due process in the workplace, we must examine the defenses of the principle of EAW given in the previous section. First, EAW was defended on the ground that every person has the right to own and accumulate private property and, relatedly, every person, and analogously every corporation, has the right to dispose of what they own as they see fit. To say that employers have the right to dispose of their property "at will" is a legitimate claim, which follows from the right to ownership. To say that employers have this same right to "dispose of," that is, to fire for *any* reason, their employees is quite another sort of claim. The right to private ownership gives one the right to dispose of *material possessions* as one pleases, but it in no sense implies that one has the right to dispose of *persons* as one pleases. Employees, although they work on, and labor to improve, the business of their employers, are not themselves property. They are autonomous persons. Their employers do not own them, just as the employers do not own members of their own families. So the right of an employer to hire or demote "at will" cannot be defended simply by appealing to employer ownership rights, because employees are not the property of employers.

A second attempted justification of EAW, we saw earlier, appeals to an employer's right to freedom. Voluntary private organizations in a free society rightly argue that they should be as free as possible from coercive and restrictive procedures. Due process might be thought of as such a procedure, since it requires checks for arbitrariness on the part of employers. However, one needs to evaluate the role of the employer and the coercive nature of "at will" employment in voluntary organizations more carefully before accepting a negative view of due process in the workplace.

Though private businesses are voluntary organizations which employees are free to leave at any time, employers are in a position of power relative to individual employees. This by itself is not a sufficient reason to restrict employer activities. But the possible abuse of this power *is* what is at issue when we question the principle of EAW. By means of his or her position, an employer can arbitrarily hire or fire an employee. The employee can, of course, quit arbitrarily too. But an "at will" employee is seldom in a position within the law to inflict harm on an employer. Legally sanctioned "at will" treatment by employers of employees, on the other hand, frequently harms employees, as the following observations confirm.

When one is demoted or fired, the reduction or loss of the job is only part of an employee's disadvantage. When one is demoted or fired, it is commonly taken for granted that one *deserved* this treatment, whether or not this is the case. Without an objective appraisal of their treatment, employees are virtually powerless to demonstrate that they were fired, demoted, and so forth, for no good reason. Moreover, fired or demoted employees generally have much more difficulty than other persons in getting new jobs or rising within the ranks of their own company. The absence of due process in the workplace places arbitrarily dismissed or demoted employees at an *undeserved* disadvantage among persons competing for a given job. Viewed in this light, the absence of due process is unfair because workers who do not deserve to be fired are treated the same as those who do, with the result that the opportunities for future employment for both are, other things being equal, equally diminished.

To put the point differently, a fired employee is harmed, at least prima facie. And this raises the question, Do employers exceed their right when they fire or demote someone arbitrarily? For it is not true that one has the right to do just anything, when one's activities harm those who have not done anything to deserve it. In order to justify the harm one does to another as a result of the exercise of one's freedom, one must be able to give good reasons. And good reasons are precisely what are lacking in cases where employers, by firing those in their employ, prima facie harm these people for "no cause, or even for causes morally wrong." It is difficult to see how a defense of EAW can elicit our rational assent, if it is based exclusively on an appeal to an employer's liberty rights, because the unrestrained exercise of such rights may cause undeserved harm to those employees who are the victims of its arbitrary use.

Worse, "at will" practices violate the very right the principle of EAW is based on. Part of the appeal of the the principle of EAW is that it protects the employer's right not to be coerced. According to the libertarian thinker Eric Mack, a coercive act is one that renders individual or institutional behavior involuntary.[3] Due process might be thought of as a coercive procedure because it *forces* employers to justify publicly their employment practices. But some of the employment practices sanctioned by EAW also are, or can be, coercive, according to Mack's definition. Persons who are fired without good reason *are involuntarily* placed in disadvantageous, undeserved positions by their employer. It is, therefore, difficult to defend "at will" employment practices on the basis of avoidance of coercion, since these practices themselves can be, and often are, coercive.

Defenders of EAW might make the following objection. EAW, they might claim, balances employee and employer rights because, just as the employer has the right to dispose of its business and production, so the employee has the right to accept or not to accept a job, or to quit or remain in a job once hired for it. Due process creates an imbalance of rights, this defense continues, because it restricts the freedom of the employer without restricting the freedom of the employee.

This objection lacks credibility. It supposes that the rights of employees and employers are equal when EAW prevails, but this is not the case. The principle of EAW works to the clear advantage of the owner or employer and to the clear disadvantage of the employee, because the employee's opportunity to change jobs is, other things being equal, significantly impaired when the employee is fired or demoted, while the employer's opportunity to hire is not similarly lessened. The employee's decreased opportunity to dispose of his or her labor, in other words, normally is *not* equal to the

employer's decreased ability to carry on his business activities. So the operation of EAW, judged in terms of the comparative losses normally caused to employers and employees, does not treat the two, or their rights, equally.

"At will" treatment of employees is also advocated on the basis of maximizing efficiency. Unproductive or disruptive employees interfere with the business of the employer and hamper productivity. Employers must have the liberty to employ whom and when they wish. But without due process procedures in the workplace, what is to prevent an employer from making room for a grossly unqualified son-in-law by firing a good employee, for example, an action which is itself damaging to efficiency? And how inefficient *is* due process in the workplace really? Due process does not alter the employee-employer hierarchical arrangement in an organization. Due process does *not* infringe on an employer's prima facie right to dispose of its business or what happens in that business. The right to due process merely restricts the employer's alleged right to treat employees arbitrarily. Moreover, would not knowledge that employees are protected against arbitrary treatment go some way toward boosting employee morale? And will anyone seriously suggest that employee morale and employee efficiency are unrelated? In spite of the fears of some employers, due process does not require that employees never be dismissed on grounds of their inefficiency. Due process merely requires that employees have a hearing and an objective evaluation before being dismissed or demoted.

Finally, proponents of EAW will argue as follows. Ours is a free-market economy, they will say, and government should keep out of the economy. To heed the call for legally mandated due process in the workplace, which is what most critics of EAW seek, is to interfere with the free enterprise system. The government and the courts should leave employees and employers to work out matters on their own. Employees have the freedom to quit their jobs "at will." Therefore, the freedom of the employer to fire "at will" should be protected.

This is a peculiar defense. The plain fact is that employers, at least when they have the status of corporations, have not been reluctant to involve the government and the courts in the name of protecting *their* interests. The courts have recognized the right of corporations to due process while by and large upholding the principle of EAW for employees in the workplace. This at least appears to contravene the requirement of universality. . . . For if corporations have a moral right to be treated fairly, and this moral right grounds legal rights to due process for them, then one would naturally expect that employees would also have this moral right, and that the law should protect employees by requiring fair grievance procedures in the workplace, including, in particular, legal protection against arbitrary dismissals or demotions. Yet the situation is not as expected. *Employers* have a legally protected right to due process. Employees hired "at will" do *not*. The universality we expect and require in the case of moral rights is missing here.

The difference in the status of employers and employees under the law is defended by the courts by the claim that corporations, all of which have state charters, are "public entities" whose activities are "in the public interest." Employees, on the other hand, are not public entities, and, at least in private places of employment, the work they perform is, so the courts imply, *not* in the public interest. Now there are celebrated problems about conceiving of corporations as public entities, and one might want to contest this defense of EAW by challenging the obscurity of the difference on which it is based. The challenge we should press in this essay, however, is not that the distinction between what is and what is not a public entity is too obscure. It is that the distinction is not relevant. The *moral* importance of due process—of being guaranteed honest attempts at fair, impartial treatment—has nothing to do with who is or is not a public entity. Fundamentally, it has to do with the rights of the private citizen. The right to due process is the right to a fair hearing when the acts or accusations of others hold the promise of serious harm being done to a person who does not deserve it. To deny due process of employees in the workplace, given the prima facie harm that is caused by dismissal or demotion, and given that those who are harmed in these ways may not deserve it, is tantamount to claiming that *only some* persons have this right. Such a conclusion conflicts with the view, widely held in our society, that due process is a *moral* right, one that is possessed by *everyone* in *all* circumstances.

To make what is an obvious point, due process is an essential political right in any society that respects just treatment of every person. When people

who do not deserve it are put at risk of being significantly harmed by the arbitrary decisions of others, the persons put at risk ought to be protected. Indeed, if those who make decisions are powerful, and those who are the recipients of these decisions are, by comparison, both weak and in danger of significant harm, then we must insist *all the more* on measures to protect the weak against the strong. Paradoxically, therefore, precisely in those cases where workers are individually weak—precisely, that is, in those areas where EAW prevails—is where it should not. Thus, the democratic political ideal of fairness is threatened if the principle of EAW is allowed.

There is, then, for the reasons given, a very strong presumptive case to be made against EAW and in favor of the right of employees to impartial grievance procedures in the workplace, independently of the presence of a contractual guarantee of such procedures. Let us give a summary statement of the right.

> Every person has a right to a public hearing, peer evaluation, outside arbitration or some other mutually agreed upon grievance procedure before being demoted, unwillingly transferred or fired.

The arguments given in favor of recognizing the right of employees to due process in the workplace were characterized as being strong presumptive arguments. It was not contended that the reasoning given "proves" this right conclusively. Rather, the arguments collectively provide a set of reasons that make it logical to recognize this right, while allowing that objections might be raised that show that there are better reasons against recognizing the right to due process in the workplace.

According to strong advocates of employee rights, the right to due process does not go far enough. It does not give an employee much in the way of *rights*. It simply precludes dismissal without a formal hearing. However, the worker's right to due process would, if appropriately institutionalized, make progress in the area of employee rights. This is because due process helps to prevent arbitrary treatment of persons in the workplace by making the cause and reason for the employee treatment public and by guaranteeing the opportunity to appeal. Respect for the rights of employees as persons will not be satisfied with anything less, even if it is true, as some contend, that genuine respect requires much more.

Conclusion: Guaranteeing Rights in Employment

The widespread and persistent non-recognition of employee rights in this country is inconsistent with the primary importance our nation places on the rights of the individual. This non-recognition remains one of the most questionable elements in the political and economical structure of our society. If the arguments in this essay are sound, standardly accepted individual rights need to be recognized and honored in the workplace. The rights to due process . . . are moral rights honored politically in public life. To deny them a place in the workplace is to assume that employer rights or economic interests always take precedence over the rights of employees. Neither assumption is tenable.

How does one institutionalize the recognition of rights in employment? In many European countries employee rights are recognized by law and enforced by the government. In West Germany, for example, after a trial period, employees acquire a right to their jobs. Persons may be dismissed for job-related negligence, absences, or disruptive and criminal activities, but the grounds for dismissal must be documented and hearings must be conducted before an employee can be fired. The United States is the only major industrial nation that offers little legal protection of the rights of workers to their jobs. It has been suggested that what is needed in this country is statutory protection for employees against unjust firing, an idea that embodies some of the principles of the German model. It has been further suggested that this statutory protection should include rights to expenses incurred in finding a new job, and rights to back pay for those unjustly dismissed.[4]

A second fruitful way to institutionalize recognition of employee rights is through written contracts between employers and employees, contracts that state the exchange agreement, the rights of each party, and the means for enforcing these rights (for example, arbitration, peer review, or outside negotiators). If properly done, such con-

tracts could be relied upon to help give meaning to the sometimes loose talk about the moral rights of each party and would help settle, without the intervention of the courts, many disagreements about employee *and* employer rights.

A third, most propitious and less coercive way to institutionalize recognition of employee rights is simply for employers to do this voluntarily. This suggestion is not as preposterous as it may seem. Increasingly, employees are demanding rights in the workplace. Correspondingly, employers are beginning to recognize the expediency and, sometimes, the fairness of such employee demands. And the courts are beginning to take interest in employee rights. There is an obvious way for employers to avoid "coercive intervention" by government and the courts. This is for employers *voluntarily* to institute programs that respect and protect employee rights on their own.

There are many employee rights that remain to be considered in another essay. The rights to work safety, information, and participation in management decision-making, for example, are essential for employee autonomy and job development. And the question of meaningful work cannot be dismissed if employees are to be considered as autonomous individuals. . . . The continuation of a private free enterprise economy set within a democratic free community where individual rights are viewed as fundamental requires that employee rights be fully and fairly recognized *and* protected in the workplace.

NOTES

Some notes have been deleted and the remaining ones renumbered.

1. H. G. Wood, *A Treatise on the Law of Master and Servant* (Albany, N.Y.: John D. Parsons, Jr., 1877), p. 134.
2. Lawrence E. Blades, "Employment at Will versus Individual Freedom: On Limiting the Abusive Exercise of Employer Power," *Columbia Law Review* 67 (1967), p. 1405, quoted from *Payne* v. *Western*, 81 Tenn. 507 (1884), *Hutton* v. *Watters*, 132 Tenn. 527, S.W. 134 (1915).
3. Eric Mack, "Natural and Contractual Rights," *Ethics* 87 (1977), pp. 153-159.
4. Clyde W. Summers, Individual Protection Against Unfair Dismissal: Time for a Statute," *Virginia Law Review* 62 (1976), pp. 481-532.

Rights in the Workplace: A Nozickian Argument

Ian Maitland

There is a growing literature that attempts to define the substantive rights of workers in the workplace, a.k.a. the duties of employers toward their workers. Thus it has been proposed that employers have (at least *prima facie*) duties to provide workers with meaningful/fulfilling/self-actualizing work, some degree of control over work conditions, advance notice of plant closures or layoffs, due process before dismissal, etc. (See, for example, Goldman, 1980; Schwartz, 1984; Donaldson, 1982; Werhane, 1985.)

The argument of this paper is that in a competitive labor market these standards are superfluous and, indeed, may interfere with workers' rights to freely choose their terms of employment. Furthermore, these supposed moral rights in the workplace may come at the expense of non-consenting third parties—like other workers or consumers.

Nozick on Meaningful Work

Since my argument basically extends Nozick's (1974, pp. 246 ff) discussion of meaningful work, let us start with that. Assuming that workers wish to have meaningful work, how does and could capitalism respond? Nozick notes that if the productivity of workers *rises* when the work tasks are segmented so as to be more meaningful, then individual employers pursuing profits will reorganize the production process in such a way out of simple self-interest. Even if productivity were to remain the same, competition for labor will induce employers to reorganize work so as to make it more meaningful.

Accordingly, Nozick says, the only interesting case to consider is the one where meaningful work leads to reduced efficiency. Who will bear the cost of this lessened efficiency? One possibility is the employer. But the individual employer who unilaterally assumes this cost places himself at a competitive disadvantage and eventually—other things equal—will go out of business. On the other hand,

Journal of Business Ethics, 1989, vol. 8. Reprinted by permission of Kluwer Academic Publishers.

if *all* employers recognize their workers' right to meaningful work (and if none cheats), then consumers will bear the cost of the industry's reduced efficiency. (Presumably, too, we would have to erect trade barriers to exclude the products of foreign producers who do not provide their workers with meaningful work, otherwise they would drive the domestic industry out of business.)

What about the workers? If they want meaningful work, they will presumably be willing to give up something (some wages) to work at meaningfully segmented jobs:

> They work for lower wages, but they view their total work package (lower wages plus the satisfactions of meaningful work) as more desirable than less meaningful work at higher wages. They make a trade-off. . . .

Nozick observes that many persons make just such trade-offs. Not everyone, he says, wants the same things or wants them as strongly. They choose their employment on the basis of the overall package of benefits it gives them.

The Market for Meaningful Work

Provided that the firm's lessened efficiency is compensated for by lower wages, then the employer should be indifferent between the two packages (meaningful work at lower wages or less meaningful work at higher wages). Indeed, if workers prize meaningful work highly, then they might be prepared to accept *lower* wages than are necessary simply to offset the firm's lower productivity. In that case, entrepreneurial employers seeking higher profits should be expected to offer more meaningful work: they will, by definition, reduce labor costs by an amount greater than the output lost because of less efficient (but more meaningful) production methods. In the process, they will earn higher profits than other firms (Frank, 1985, pp. 164-5).

In other words, there is a market for meaningful work. The employer who can find the combination of pay and meaningful work that matches workers' desires most closely will obtain a competitive advantage. Thus Goldman (1980, p. 274) is wrong when he claims that "profit maximization may . . . call . . . for reducing work to a series of simple menial tasks." On the contrary, profit maximization creates pressures on employers to offer workers meaningful work up to the point where workers would prefer higher pay to further increments of meaningfulness. Goldman's claim holds only if we assume that workers place no value at all on the intrinsic rewards of their work.

To "legislate" moral rights in the workplace to a certain level of meaningfulness, then, would interefere with workers' rights to determine what package of benefits they want.

Extending the Logic (1): Employment at Will

In her discussion of employment at will (EAW), Werhane (1985, p. 91) says "[i]t is hard to imagine that rational people would agree in advance to being fired arbitrarily in an employment contract." According to her estimate, only 36% of the workforce is covered by laws or contracts which guarantee due process procedures with which to appeal dismissal. Werhane regards EAW as a denial of moral rights of employees in the workplace.

But, is it inconceivable that a rational worker would voluntarily accept employment under such conditions? Presumably, if the price is right, some workers will be willing to accept the greater insecurity of EAW. This may be particularly true, for example, of younger, footloose and fancy-free workers with marketable skills. It is also likely to be truer in a metropolitan area (with ample alternative employment opportunities) than a small town and when the economic outlook is good.

Likewise, some employers may value more highly the unrestricted freedom to hire and fire (smaller businesses, for example) and may be willing to pay higher wages for that flexibility. There may be other employers—larger ones in a position to absorb the administrative costs or ones with more stable businesses—who will find it advantageous to offer guarantees of due process in return for lower wages. Such guarantees are also more likely to be found where employees acquire firm-specific skills and so where continuity of employment is more important (Williamson, 1975).

According to this logic, wage rates should vary inversely with the extent of these guarantees, other things equal. In other words, workers purchase their greater security in the form of reduced wages. Or, put another way, some firms pay workers a premium to induce them to do without the guarantees.

If employers were generally to heed business ethicists and to institute workplace due process in cases of dismissals—and to take the increased costs or reduced efficiency out of workers' paychecks—then they would expose themselves to the pirating of their workers by other (less scrupulous?) employers who would give workers what they wanted instead of respecting their rights.

If, on the other hand, many of the workers not currently protected against unfair dismissal would in fact prefer guarantees of workplace due process—*and* would be willing to pay for it—then such guarantees would be an effective recruiting tool for an entrepreneurial employer. That is, employers are driven by their own self-interest to offer a package of benefits and rights that will attract and retain employees. If any employer earns a reputation for treating workers in a high-handed or inconsiderate way, then he (or she) will find it more difficult (or more expensive) to get new hires and will experience defections of workers to other employers.

In short, there is good reason for concluding that the prevalence of EAW does accurately reflect workers' preferences for wages over contractually guaranteed protections against unfair dismissal. (Of course, these preferences may derive, in part, from most workers' perception that their employers rarely abuse EAW anyway; if abuses were widespread, then you would expect the demand for contractual guarantees to increase.)

Extending the Logic (2): Plant Closure/Layoff Notification

Another putative workplace right is notice of impending layoffs or plant closures. The basis for such a right is obvious and does not need to be rehearsed here. In 1988 Congress passed plant-closing notification provisions that mandate 60-days notice. Earlier drafts of the legislation had provided for 6 months' advance notification.

But the issue of interest here is employers' moral responsibilities in this matter. The basic argument is by now familiar: if employers have not universally provided guarantees of advance notice of layoffs, that reflects employers' and workers' choices. Some workers are willing to trade off job security for higher wages; some employers (e.g., in volatile businesses) prefer to pay higher wages in return for the flexibility to cut costs quickly. If employers have generally underestimated the latent demand of workers for greater security (say, as a result of the graying of the baby boomers), then that presents a profit opportunity for alert employers. At the same (or lower) cost to themselves, they should be able to put together an employment package that will attract new workers.

A morally binding workplace "right" to X days' notice of a layoff would preempt workers' and employers' freedom to arrive at an agreement that takes into account their own particular circumstances and preferences. In Nozick's aphorism, the "right" to advance notice may prohibit a capitalist act between consenting adults.

It would mean, for example, that workers and managers would be (morally) barred from agreeing to arrangements that might protect workers' jobs by enhancing a firm's chances of survival. This might be the case if, say, the confidence of creditors or investors would be strengthened by knowing that the firm would be free to close down its operations promptly if necessary.

Likewise, the increased expenses associated with a possible closure might deter firms from opening new plants in the first place—especially in marginal areas where jobs are most needed. In that case workers won't enjoy the rights due them in the workplace because there won't be any workplace. As McKenzie (1981, p. 122) has pointed out, "restrictions on plant closings are restrictions on plant openings."

The effects of rights to notice of layoffs are not limited to the workers. If resources are diverted from viable segments of a (multiplant) firm in order to prolong the life of the plant beyond its useful economic life, then the solvency of the rest of the firm may be jeopardized (and so too the jobs of other workers).

If the obstacles to plant shutdowns are serious enough and if firms are prevented from moving to locations where costs are lower, then (as McKenzie, p. 120, points out) "Workers generally must pay higher prices for the goods they buy. Further, they will not then have the opportunity of having paying plants moving into their areas. . . ." And if such restrictions reduce the efficiency of the economy as a whole (by deterring investment, locking up resources in low-productivity, low-wage sectors of the economy), then all workers and consumers will be losers. Birch (1981, p. 7) has found that job creation is positively associated with plant closures: "The reality is that our most successful areas [at job creation] are those with the highest rates of innovation and failure, not the lowest." Europe has extensive laws and union agreements that make it prohibitively expensive to close plants, order layoffs, or even fire malingerers and, not coincidentally, it has barely added a single job in the aggregate in the 1980s (as of 1987). Europe's persistent high unemployment is usually attributed to such "rigidities" in its labor market—what the London *Economist* picturesquely terms "Eurosclerosis."

It may be objected by some that workers' "rights claims cannot be overridden for the sake of economic or general welfare" (Werhane, 1985, p. 80; see also Goldman, p. 274). This is probably not the place to debate rights vs. utilities, but this discussion raises the question of whether workplace rights may sometimes violate the rights of third parties (other workers, consumers).

Respecting Workers' Choices

The argument of this paper has been that to set up a class of moral rights in the workplace may invade a worker's right to freely choose the terms and conditions that he (or she) judges are the best for him. The worker is stuck with these rights no matter whether he values them or not; they are inalienable in the sense that he may not trade them off for, say, higher wages. *We* might not be willing to make such a trade, but if we are to respect the worker's autonomy, then *his* preferences must be decisive.

Along the way the paper has tried to indicate how competition between employers in the labor market preserves the worker's freedom to choose the terms and conditions of his employment within constraints set by the economy. This competition means that employers' attempts to exploit workers (say, by denying them due process in the workplace without paying them the "market rate" for forgoing such protections) will be self-defeating because other would-be employers will find it profitable to bid workers away from them by offering more attractive terms. This point bears repeating because many of the accounts of rights in the workplace seem to assume pervasive market failure which leaves employers free to do pretty much what they want. Any persuasive account of such rights has to take into account the fact that employers' discretion to unilaterally determine terms and conditions of employment is drastically limited by the market.

REFERENCES

Birch, David: 1981, 'Who creates jobs?', *Public Interest* (vol. 65), fall.

Donaldson, Thomas: 1982, *Corporations and Morality* (Prentice-Hall, Englewood Cliffs, N.J.).

Frank, Robert: 1985, *Choosing the Right Pond* (Oxford University Press, New York).

Goldman, Alan. 1980, 'Business ethics: profits, utilities, and moral rights', *Philosophy and Public Affairs* 9, no. 3.

McKenzie, Robert: 1981, 'The case for plant closures', *Policy Review* 15, winter.

Nozick, Robert: 1974, *Anarchy, State and Utopia* (Basic Books, New York).

Schwartz, Adina: 1984, 'Autonomy in the workplace', in Tom Regan, ed., *Just Business* (Random House, N.Y.).

Werhane, Patricia H.: 1985, *Persons, Rights and Corporations* (Prentice-Hall, N.Y.).

Williamson, Oliver E.: 1975, *Markets and Hierarchies* (Free Press, N.Y.).

Issues Surrounding the Theories of Negligent Hiring and Failure to Fire

Marian M. Extejt and William N. Bockanic

Discussions in law[1] journals and management periodicals[2] have focused on the issue of negligent hiring, and its related cause of action—failure to fire. Typically, these articles have concentrated on either legal principles and precedents, or on managerial actions necessary to avoid such liability. The purpose of this article is to blend these two perspectives, and to introduce a third—an ethical analysis—as a means of presenting an interdisciplinary view of an issue that will increasingly affect corporate personnel practices in the future. The principles of negligent hiring and failure to fire are examined from a legal, managerial, and ethical perspective. Common law and court rulings are examined to determine the basis for such actions. Management practices and policies designed to reduce the probability of such actions are discussed. Finally, the ethics of employers' liability for employees' actions are explored.

Legal Definition of Negligent Hiring

Negligent hiring suits may be filed against a firm when one of its employees causes injury to a customer, fellow employee, or other person. Injuries are most often physical in nature, but recently this liability was extended in a case where an employee illegally discriminated against a customer.[3] Courts have held that an employer may be directly liable for negligent hiring or retention of an employee where the employer knew, or should have known, of the employee's dangerous tendencies and the employer's negligence was the proximate cause of the plaintiff's injuries (Walker, 1984).

There is some confusion among three related but distinct causes of action that have been employed to define employers' liability for their employees' actions. The first and oldest principle is that of *respondeat superior*. Under this doctrine, the employer is held vicariously liable for the negligent acts of the employee (agent) committed within scope and course of employment.

The other two causes of action, negligent hiring and negligent entrustment, are very similar. Negligent hiring subjects employers to liability for the risk created by exposing members of the public to potentially dangerous individuals. Negligent entrustment involves the same liability, but does not require proof of an employer-employee relationship.

In a suit predicated upon a negligent hiring theory, the liability of the employer occurs because

Reprinted from *Business & Professional Ethics Journal*, Vol. 8, No. 4 with permission of the authors.

the employee is being used to accomplish the employer's goals. Under negligent entrustment, however, the employee is not necessarily accomplishing the goals of the employer, but is using the employer's property to accomplish some objective.

A major difference between *respondeat superior* and negligent hiring stems from a difference in their perspectives on fault and compensation. *Respondeat superior* focuses more on determining fault and punishing the employer of the party causing the damage. Negligent hiring liability is based on a justice principle; who can best bear the financial burden of compensating the victim—the deep pocket theory. Companies are typically in a better financial position to pay for damages than the individual employee who caused them (Susser and Jett, 1987).

All three theories of liability are based on the common law concept of Master and Servant, where there has been a breach of the duty owed by the master to his servants and to the public to make an inquiry about the competence and qualifications of employees.[4] Employers must exercise great caution in a number of human resource management practices as all three principles may be used to establish an employer's liability for an employee's actions.

History

A cause of action predicated upon negligent hiring is based on the theory of the Master-Servant relationship. This cause of action has a long history. Under common law, certain types of employers were felt to have a greater duty than others to screen prospective employees as to their qualifications. These groups included carriers, innkeepers, and hospitals (Loftus, 1967). Their liability was based upon the fiduciary responsibility that existed between the employer and customers. Under the common law, however, these employers were only liable for their employees' intentional torts made while on the employer's premises and during employment.

The common law fellow-servant doctrine provides that an employer has the duty to select competent employees who can perform the job without being a danger to fellow employees. As early as 1941, in *Country Club of Jackson v.Turner*,[5] the court stated that:

Compliance with the duty to use reasonable care to maintain working conditions that are reasonably safe involves the duty to use such care in avoiding the employment or retention of a servant who is known to be dangerous or vicious where such propensities are calculated to expose co-employees to greater dangers than the work necessary entails. This principle no longer needs cited authority.

Before 1950, employers' liability was limited to actions taken by employees while in the course and scope of employment. Beginning in the 1950s, courts began using the principle of negligent hiring to broaden the scope of this liability.[6] Some courts have upheld the tort theory that an employer may be liable for damage or injury even if it occurs *outside the scope* of the unfit worker's employment, *after* regular work hours, *away* from the job site, and under circumstances clearly removed from job-related tasks (Green and Reibstein, 1988).

The trend in the number of negligent hiring actions has increased over the past 15 years. A highly publicized case occurred in 1979 when Avis Rent-A-Car was required to pay $800,000 ($750,000 to the victim and $50,000 to her husband) after a male employee raped a female employee. The jury found Avis negligent because it had hired the man without thoroughly investigating his background. In another case, a passenger sued American Airlines for negligent hiring after being kicked and bitten by a boarding agent who allegedly later tested positive for the AIDS virus.

An increase in the number of negligent hiring cases is occurring because a number of advantages are offered to an injured party.

First, negligent hiring theory does not limit the employer's liability to actions taken during the course of employment. Kasandra Gaines was employed as a secretary at Monsanto Company. Burton Woods, who had previously been convicted of rape and robbery, also worked at the Monsanto site as a mail clerk. Woods killed Gaines at her apartment. Her parents filed a negligent hiring case against Monsanto and won.[7]

Second, the level of compensation arising out of a negligent hiring case may be much higher than that resulting from other cases. Employers have more assets and typically more insurance than an individual. Thus, if a firm is found liable, the amount awarded and the amount actually recovered is characteristically much greater. Juries are well aware of the assets of corporations and typically assess punitive damages as well as compensatory damages in cases of negligent hiring.

Third, the statute of limitations for negligent hiring claims is much longer than other claims, such as workers' compensation or assault.

Finally, evidence of prior specific acts of negligence of the employee, as well as the employee's reputation, may be introduced in a negligent hiring case. Most state courts would not allow either in an action brought against the individual who caused the injury.

At this writing, the authors were unable to find any legislation at the Federal, state or local level which deals with negligent hiring. However, there is an abundance of case law to guide employers in their hiring decisions.

Basis for Negligent Hiring Actions

In order for a claim of negligent hiring to be successful, two elements must be established. First, the plaintiff must prove that the employer owed a duty of care to the injured party. Second, if a duty of care has been established, then the injured party must show that the employer was negligent in its hiring practices and that this negligence proximately resulted in the plaintiff's injury.

Different states have different requirements to establish an employer's duty of care to an injured party, but generally three factors are used:

1. Were both the employee and the injured party in a place where they had the right to be when the injury occurred?
2. Did the injured party meet the employee as a direct result of the employment? and
3. Did the employer receive some benefit (maybe only potential) from the encounter between the employee and the injured party? (Susser and Jett, 1987)

To establish negligence on the employer's part, the injured party must prove five elements. The degree of proof and the exact nature of these elements differs from state to state, but a basis for all five must be established.

1. An employment relationship must exist between the employer and the employee at the time of the injury.
2. The employee was unfit for the position.
3. The employer knew or should have known that the employee was unfit for the position.
4. The employee intentionally or negligently caused the third party's injury.
5. The employer's negligence was the proximate cause of the third party's injury.

The plaintiff must prove the fact of employment, but does not have to show that the employee was acting within the scope of employment. The employer is not liable in all employment relationships, however. A Connecticut Court of Appeals[8] limited an employer's liability to exclude liability for acts of employees of independent contractors. If a firm hires an independent contractor and one of the contractor's employees causes harm to a fellow employee, the employer is not liable. This is in accord with the principle that an employer of an independent contractor has no right to direct the actions of the independent contractor's employees and, thus, should not be held legally accountable for their actions.

In order to establish that the employee was incompetent, prior specific acts of negligence may be introduced. In addition, proof of the employee's general reputation may be submitted. The plaintiff must show that prior acts or elements of the employee's reputation demonstrated inadequacy of a similar nature to the act causing the injury. Unfitness to perform a job has been shown by habitual drinking and drug use, habitual carelessness, forgetfulness, inexperience, mental and physical defects, and a propensity for recklessness or viciousness.

Past criminal activity is one of the strongest proofs of unfitness. Hiring an apartment manager who has previously been accused of robbery or rape was strong evidence of negligent hiring.[9] In *Foster v. The Loft, Inc. et al*[10] the Appeals Court of Massachusetts upheld a jury verdict against an employer (The Loft) and its former employee, Rida. The Loft hired Rida as a bartender. A dispute between Foster, a customer, and Rida over an allegedly improperly mixed drink resulted in an altercation. After Rida responded with obscene language and gestures to a request for a new drink, a companion of Foster's threw a drink into Rida's face. Rida then punched both Foster and his companion; Foster suffered a fractured cheekbone and an injured eye. During the trial it was disclosed that The Loft, prior to this incident, had knowledge of Rida's past criminal record.[11] The Court commented that mere knowledge of a past criminal record standing alone may not be sufficient to establish negligence; it did state the following:

> The evidence disclosed that The Loft was not a quiet cocktail lounge but rather a large complex of bars that served alcoholic beverages to a rather young crowd. . . . The jury from the evidence could infer that the atmosphere in which Rida worked was volatile and there was a high potential for violence. . . . In these circumstances it was open to the jury to decide The Loft was negligent in retaining Rida in his position as bartender, and that its action in doing so was the proximate cause of plaintiff's injuries.[12]

Rida's previous criminal record included such offenses as (1) assault and battery with a dangerous weapon (a knife), (2) assault with intent to commit rape and (3) kidnapping.[13] Therefore, taking into account The Loft's knowledge of Rida's prior criminal record and the volatile nature of the employment, the Court found the employer liable under the theories of negligent hiring and negligent retention. An employer should analyze the circumstances of the position and decide whether the applicant's history has a high probability of recurrence under the current conditions.

Employees do not have to be negligent in order to be unfit for a job. Lack of experience or training that results in an injury may also be the basis of a negligent hiring action.

In order for the plaintiff to prove that the employer should have known of the employee's background or reputation, the principle of the prudent man exercising reasonable care must be considered. *Black's Law Dictionary* defines due care as "just and sufficient care, so far as the circumstances demand it; the absence of negligence. That care which an ordinarily prudent person would have exercised under the same or similar circumstances."[14] Due care and reasonableness vary with the type of business. In a situation where the employee must work without supervision, or has access to persons or property, a higher standard of care is necessary.

Additionally, employers may be obligated to secure current information from credible sources, and to use that information in the selection decision. In *Welsh Mfg., Div. of Textron v. Pinkertons,*[15] Pinkertons, a security guard agency, hired a person who later participated in the theft of a large amount of gold from Welsh. Pinkertons had asked for personal references, but had never used them. When they contacted previous employers, they made only cursory inquiries ('Would you recommend the applicant without reservation?') of persons who did not know the employee for a reasonable period. When checking for past criminal activity, they limited their search to the records of one state. Pinkertons was found guilty of negligent hiring for a position as sensitive as that of a security guard.

Employers complain that they are caught in a catch-22 situation. Potentially, as ex-employers, they can be sued for providing references (invasion of privacy; defamation of character) and now they can be sued for not checking the references of potential employees.

Usually, the easiest element of a negligent hiring action to prove is that the employee negligently or intentionally caused the injury. It is this same element that the employer has the least control over.

Finally, it must be shown that the employer's negligence was not necessarily a direct cause of the injury, but it must have been at least a proximate cause of the action. A variety of evidence has been introduced to prove this element. Not only have the employer's hiring practices come under attack, but proper training, supervision, and performance appraisal techniques and policies have also been questioned. Some courts have held that it is sufficient to show that a negligent action on the part of the employer was the efficient cause which set in motion a chain of events and circumstances that led to the injury. The real test of the proximate cause of injury is whether, after the occurrence, the injury appears to be a reasonable and probable consequence of the act or omission of the employer, not whether a reasonable person could have foreseen the particular injury (Walker, 1984).

Managerial Considerations

Managers must apply basic human resources management principles and practices to avoid negligent hiring liability. First, a thorough job analysis for each position should be conducted. This analysis must include a current list of tasks and qualifications, and detail the working conditions for the position. Qualifications should not exceed those necessary, because the employer may (1) lose potentially qualified applicants in a tight labor market and (2) be guilty of adverse impact against a protected group.

Second, hiring procedures should be tailored to each job. The level of background investigation may differ for each position. The background check on a person who has little or no access to customers or their property would be more limited to a person whose actions can directly influence the safety of third parties. Pre-employment testing, work sampling, and reference checks are all a part of the hiring process.

Training may be necessary for certain classes of employees. In *Welsh Mfg. v. Pinkertons,* Pinkertons did not provide adequate training for its guards. Injuries which can be traced to lack of training may result in negligent hiring actions.

Supervision is another responsibility of the employer in such cases. While employees may be free to direct their own actions and make decisions, the employer may still be liable for injuries resulting from such decisions. A reasonable amount of supervision based on the level of skill and experience of the employee is necessary to limit liability.

Finally, performance review procedures should be timely and valid. They should concentrate on job behaviors, not personal traits of the employee. Consistent consequences for failure to perform should be part of the employer's employment policy. This does not necessarily mean that employees who cannot perform the job in an acceptable manner should be dismissed. Training programs, EAP's and progressive discipline may all be employed as methods of rehabilitation.

Ethical Considerations

Whether an employer should be held liable for the actions of his/her employees, especially when the actions resulting in injury do not occur in the course of employment, is a major ethical question. In analyzing the ethical aspect of the negligent hiring dilemma, three approaches will be employed. First, employers' and employees' actions will be considered from a cost-benefit perspective. Next these actions will be analyzed based on various rights and responsibilities held by the parties. Finally, questions of justice will be raised.

From the injured parties' point of view, making employers liable for negligent hiring practices has a number of benefits. As previously discussed, the plaintiffs have a greater chance of recovery of damages under this cause of action, than if they were to sue the individual who caused the injury.

The costs of employers' liability in hiring are both direct and indirect. A potential employee may suffer because the employer is so strict in determining qualifications for the job that the otherwise qualified employee will not be considered for the job. Indirectly, additional costs of hiring, training and supervision will be passed along to the customer, or result in lower wages for the employees.

Employers contend that the costs of preventing negligent hiring liability far outweigh the benefits. Validating information on application blanks and resumes is a time consuming activity. Surveys of human resources personnel reveal that the vast majority have encountered embellishment and fraud in pre-employment data supplied by applicants. Firms specializing in applicant background checks prosper. Employers must weigh the costs of background checks against the potential costs of negligent hiring suits in order to make this decision.

By making employers liable for the injuries caused by their employees, actions may be taken on the part of the employer which result in the violation of applicants' and employees' rights. For example, in conducting a background check, an employee's privacy may be invaded. Employers may feel forced to use questionable means of gathering information. When obtaining certain pieces of negative information which cannot be validated easily, i.e. hearsay information, the employer may decide to take the conservative action of not hiring an individual rather than incur the costs of verification.

An employee's rights to be free from discrimination may also be violated. This is especially true for physically and mentally handicapped individuals. Firms which fail to have an accurate and thorough job analysis behind each position description may fail to hire handicapped individuals because the firm fears the individual may be considered incompetent later by a jury.

Discrimination may also occur when persons belonging to one group (based on age, sex, race, etc.) are subjected to different background checks, medical or psychological testing, than applicants belonging to different groups. If an employer believes pre-employment conditions are necessary for a job they should be applied equally to all applicants.

Finally, if employers believe that they have a responsibility to determine the psychological fitness of an applicant, a variety of testing methods may be employed. Although there are many valid psychological testing methods, employers often use less valid, less costly, and less time consuming methods to make a determination. An employee's right to a job may be abridged by the use of such methods in the name of screening.

It has been determined that the public has a right to protection from unfit employees. There is significant social value in supervision, and the basic trust between an employer and employees and the trust between a firm and its customers and community must be preserved. The employer is in the best and most efficient position to preserve such trust.

Finally, is it just to make an employer liable for such a broad scope of employee actions? On the one hand, a distributive justice argument would state that an employer is better able to pay for the mistake than the employee. If an injured party is to be compensated, a more equitable compensation can be extracted from a firm than from the individual. On the other hand, simple ability to pay without some level of responsibility and duty of care is not a just criterion.

A somewhat different view of justice occurs when one considers the 'failure to fire question.' Suppose that an individual is hired, performs the job in a satisfactory manner, and then the employer learns of some past actions on the part of the employee. If the employer had known these facts during the pre-employment period, an offer of employment would never have been extended. Is it just for an employer to fire the employee at this point? In order to make this decision, an employer should take into consideration several factors.

1. What was the nature of the past offense? Is it reasonable to assume that, given the nature of the employee's current work demands and condition, that the actions will be repeated?
2. When was the past action committed? Actions committed as a juvenile are rarely, in and of themselves, considered predictive of a mature adult's behavior. If an employee has performed adequately for 10 years without incident, it is a much different case from someone who committed the previous injury six months ago.
3. What was the pattern of the past offense? An individual who had three traffic violations in one year, six years ago may be considered different from someone who has had one violation every two years for the past six.
4. Finally, have rehabilitative actions been taken? A person who has undergone alcohol or drug abuse rehabilitation should be considered different from an individual who had the same problem but apparently has taken no constructive action to deal with the problem. In some situations, recovering alcoholics or drug abusers are legally considered a protected class. Employers would be guilty of discrimination if such an applicant's past behavior was the sole basis for not hiring them.

In this paper, the legal, managerial and ethical questions dealing with an employer's liability for negligent hiring have been explored. Although the legal principles supporting this liability are clear, the standards of duty of care, reasonable investigation of background, and proximate cause of injury will continue to be debated in the courts. Ethical issues regarding the rights of employees, the duty of employers to customers and the public, and the application of justice will also continue to be questioned.

NOTES

1. See Walker (1984) and Loftus (1967).
2. See Susser and Jett (1987) and Cook (1988).
3. In the case of *Totem Taxi v. N.Y. State Human Rights Appeal Board*, 491 N.Y.S. 2d 293 (Ct. App. 1985) the

firm was found guilty of negligent hiring based on the racially discriminatory actions of one of its employees.

4. Restatement (Second) of Agency Section 213 (1958).
5. 192 Miss. 510, 4 So. 2d 718, 719 (1941).
6. See for example *Fleming v. Bronfin,* 80 A. 2d 915 (D.C. Munic. Ct. App. 1951); *Boland v. Love,* 222 F. 2d 27 (D.C. Cir. 1955) and *Murray v. Modoc state Bank,* 181 Kan. 642, 313 P. 2d 304 (1957).
7. *Gaines v. Monsanto,* 655 S.W.2d 568 (Mo. App. 1983).
8. *Ray v. Schneider* 548 A. 2d 461 (Conn. App. 1988).
9. *Ponticas v. K.M.S. Investments,* 331 N.W. 2d 907 (Minn. 1983).
10. 526 N.E. 2d 1309 (Mass. App. Ct. 1988)
11. Id. at 1312.
12. Id. at 1312 - 1313.
13. Id. at 1312 n.5.
14. *Black's Law Dictionary* 448 (5th edition. 1979).
15. 474 A. 2d. 436 (R.I. 1984).15.

REFERENCES

Cook, S. (1988) How to Avoid Liability for Negligent Hiring. *Personnel* 65(11) 32–36.

Green, R. M. and Reibstein, R. J. (1988) *Negligent Hiring, Fraud, Defamation and Other Emerging Areas of Employer Liability.* Washington, D.C.: Bureau of National Affairs, Inc.

Libbin, A., Mendelsohn, S. R. and Duffy, D. P. (1988) *Employee Medical and Honesty Testing* 65(11) 39–48.

Loftus, M. R. (1967) Employer's Duty to Know Deficiencies of Employees. *Cleveland-Marshall Law Review* 16 143–149.

Susser, P. A. and Jett, D. H. (1987) Negligent Hiring: What You Don't Know Can Hurt You. *Employment Relations Today* 14(3), 279–286.

Walker, S. (1984) Negligent Hiring: Employer's Liability for Acts of an Employee. *American Journal of Trial Advocacy* 7 603–610.

Temporary Employment and the Social Contract

Brian K. Steverson

A recent article in *Fortune* magazine, entitled "The Temp Biz Boom: Why It's Good," opens with this "realistic" assessment of the much discussed, unprecedented rise in temporary/contingent employment (Aley, p. 53). After noting that the number of temporary workers has nearly doubled in the past five years (from 1.2 million to more than 2 million), the author remarks,

> Reactions to this rather stunning piece of information tend to be either dismissive ("but they're not real jobs") or cynical ("the cheaper the labor, the higher the profits"). Commentary on the temp industry tends to focus on business ethics, not business reality.
>
> In fact, looking at the temp phenomenon simply as a struggle between good and evil can lead you to overlook its larger and more fascinating implications. The growth and increasing sophistication of the temporary employment industry is creating a national

> trading floor for talent. . . . Just as an exchange floor provides a fluid, efficient forum for clearing the market for stocks, gold, and pork bellies, the temp industry is becoming a clearinghouse for buyers and sellers of skill.

That the temporary employment *industry* treats individual workers akin to the fashion in which other markets treat stocks, gold and pork bellies is, indeed, a "fascinating implication," and one which we clearly should not "overlook."

Setting aside the serious ethical issues raised by the rhetoric of such a view, the fact that the traditional nature of employment in America has been undergoing a significant transformation over the past decade should attract the attention of business ethicists. Given the importance of employment to individual well-being in a free-market, economic system, large-scale changes in the manner in which employment is created, structured, and distributed will inevitably, and rightfully, elicit ethical concern. In this paper I would like to examine the possibility that the recent boom in temporary employment has serious ethical implications which weigh against

From *Online Journal of Ethics.* Used with permission of Institute of Business and Professional Ethics.

employers' reliance on it. I will argue that an employer-initiated shift in traditional employment patterns away from permanent employment to temporary employment, even if it results in financial benefits for the business sector, disadvantages those workers forced to rely on temporary work instead of permanent employment to such a degree that the practice is at least morally suspicious, if not outright unacceptable. I will rely on a social contract approach such as that extensively developed by Donaldson to establish my conclusion.

I should, at least briefly, explain my choice of a social contract approach as the philosophical standard by which to judge the moral adequacy of an employer-initiated increase in the use of temporary employment. There is an overarching reason, namely, that I find a contractarian approach to business ethics much more fruitful than other traditional approaches such as utilitarianism or Kantianism. This essay is not, however, the place to attempt an overall defense of the superiority of the social contract approach to business ethics (e.g., see Dunfee and Donaldson). A more specific reason for approaching employment issues like that of temporary employment from the contractarian perspective is that such a perspective more adequately captures the artifactual and historical nature of employment relationships and the role which employment has and continues to have in the pursuit of individual well-being in a capitalistic society. In the abstract, Bandow is probably correct to say that, "a potential employee has no moral claim to be hired—or, if hired, to be guaranteed forty years of employment, receive a certain level of health insurance, or expect anything else" (Bandow, p. 16). But such an ahistorical, noncontextual view fails to recognize that historically a range of social goods and opportunities are distributed in American society mainly via employment, so that a diminishing of employment opportunities entails a loss of those goods or opportunities, or at least makes them extremely difficult to secure. Some of those goods and opportunities (e.g. health care, continued income, food, housing) are essential to an individual mapping out anything remotely like a stable and satisfying life. We recognize the value of these goods and opportunities inasmuch as we have taken on the social burden of providing them to those who are unable to secure them on their own. To say that no one has a "right" to the means

by which such goods and opportunities are acquired is, in effect, to say that no one has a right to pursue the very ideal which free-market capitalism is supposed to provide us with.

A social contract approach frames the question of individual entitlement in terms of those agreed upon expectations of social, political, and economic institutions which give birth to and sustain them. The method is to examine the legitimacy of claims individuals can make regarding employment, and, consequently, employers, in the light of the motivation for an initial movement out of a world of individual production to a world populated by productive organizations (as Donaldson does) or, in the context of a procedural attempt to adjust such initial expectations to the known realities of current historical contexts in order to generate specific, applicable standards by which to judge the justness of historical practices (Rawls' "reflective equilibrium"). Whether such expectations constitute "natural rights" or some derivative thereof, misses the point that expectations like those that individuals currently have of employment and employers have emerged as part of the evolution of employment in our society, and have come to occupy a prominent place in the "American Dream." In fact, such expectations have been historically fostered by productive organizations when it was to their advantage to do so (e.g. IBM, until very recently, and the automotive industry during the fifties and sixties). Thinking about the obligations that employers are subject to in this way, rather than against the background of abstract, ahistorical, "inherent" rights that potential employees might possess, in my opinion, more adequately reflects the actual role and importance that employment has for the vast majority of individuals.

The designation "temporary employee" can be quite vague, inasmuch as the calculations of the number of temporary or contingent workers can vary depending on who gets included. For instance, most analysts lump together government data on part-timers and the self-employed to arrive at an estimate of the overall number of temporary workers. Others simply use data on the number of individuals working for temporary-employment agencies like Manpower and Kelly Services. A difference in the data used can result in quite different impressions of the growth of temporary employment. If one compares government statistics on part-timers and the self-employed over the past decade, one discovers that the percentage of the American workforce they occupy has remained relatively stable. On the other hand, the number of people working for temporary-employment agencies has risen 240% during the same time (Fierman, p. 31, as well as Golden and Appelbaum, p. 474). Whether the last two decades has or has not experienced a significant rise in the overall level of temporary employment is not nearly as important an issue as is the experience of those who have found themselves forced to opt for temporary employment in the absence of permanent. And, with this group, the key question still is not whether its size is large or growing, although if both were the case that would make even more serious any ethical worries one would have about temporary employment in the first place, but whether or not they are unjustly disadvantaged by their circumstances. This is where a Rawlsian understanding of the social contract is especially relevant.

Temporary employment is often extolled as a great boon for the labor force, or at least certain segments of it, because of the flexibility it provides. As the argument goes, over the past few decades, the demographic make-up of the American workforce has changed dramatically. The introduction of large numbers of working mothers into the labor pool, the rise in the number of younger workers seeking employment, and the re-entrance of older workers (e.g. retirees) into the workforce, to name a few, has significantly altered the demography of the labor market. Since, as a neoclassical analysis of labor markets predicts, shifts in occupational preferences in the labor pool itself will effect corresponding changes in the nature of work offered within the market, one should both expect and not be alarmed at the fact that as worker preferences for nontraditional work schedules and impermanent work contracts increases, so too will the availability of temporary employment arrangements. The phenomenon of growth in temporary employment is but another instance of a market responding to demand. As such, the growth in temporary employment over the past decade and a half ought to be conceived of as a good thing inasmuch as it serves to satisfy current individual preferences regarding work conditions.

Apart from general concerns about such market analyses (e.g. the extent to which market choices are autonomous, the ability of markets to actually satisfy preferences, the appropriateness of assigning the procurement of certain goods to the market, etc.), such an assessment of the value of temporary employment is dependent upon the assumption that in this particular case, the growth in temporary employment is a reaction to an increased demand within the labor pool for such work arrangements. If there is a significant correlation between labor preferences and growth in temporary employment, there is a great deal of plausibility to the idea that temporary employment is actually a desirable outcome. If such a correlation does not exist, however, then one might be suspicious, at least initially, about the desirability of the present and predicted continued growth in temporary employment. Unfortunately for the neoclassical assessment of the temporary employment boom, there is evidence that no such correlation exists. In a 1992 study by Lonnie Golden and Eileen Appelbaum, a number of independent variables related to variations in temporary employment levels were studied in an effort to isolate positive associations between particular variables and temporary employment levels. The variables were grouped into five classes: (1) variables expected to affect the desire by firms to hire temporary workers, (2) variables which indicate the ability of labor to resist an increase in temporary jobs, (3) variables which measure the share of the labor force held by groups thought to prefer temporary employment, (4) a single variable representing the decrease in the availability of permanent jobs, and (5) variables responsible for secular trends and seasonal variations in the labor force. The results of their study were these: (a) a strong positive association between the growth in temporary employment and those variables related to employers' desire to hire temporary workers, as well as those variables related to the ability of labor to resist temporary work, and (b) no positive association between the growth in temporary employment and those variables related to the share of the labor force presumably disposed to seeking temporary work. In other words, those forces leading employers to pursue an increase in the percentage of their workforce composed of temporary workers, predominate, and no support exists for the claim that changes in the composition of the labor force are responsible for the increase in temporary employment. Relatedly, they discovered that a decline in labor bargaining power has contributed significantly to that increase. Supporting the findings of this study, Bureau of Labor Statistics data show that, though the overall size of the contingent work force broadly defined to include both part-time workers and the self-employed has not actually risen over the past decade, the number of Americans working in temporary positions who say they would rather have permanent employment has risen to its highest level since the BLS began keeping such data (Fierman, p. 31). What this indicates is that employee preferences have in fact changed over the past decade, but not in the fashion advanced by the neoclassical account. Rather than shifting toward temporary employment, employee preferences have shifted the other way, toward permanent employment. Again, the neoclassical explanation simply seems to fail.

The rationale put forth by the business sector to justify their shift to temporary employment is, of course, the claim that competition requires that they cut costs wherever they can. Since labor costs typically constitute a large portion of their overhead, that is a likely place to swing the axe. It is far from clear, however, that as a general rule, shifting to temporary employment actually saves businesses money. Independent contingent workers, depending on their skill level, sometimes command higher wages than permanent workers, and the wages paid to temporary workers supplied by agencies, who have to cover the costs of recruiting, screening, and employment taxes, can run higher than those of regular workers. Also, companies discover that temporary workers require training and must be managed differently from their regular workers. If the costs of such training and management are not incurred, excessive turnover and low productivity often result. It is true that employing temporary workers allows companies to cut benefits costs (e.g. employment taxes like Social Security, health insurance, paid sick and vacation leaves), which typically add up to about 30% of their total labor costs. If a company can minimize the cost of using temporary employees, then they stand to benefit financially. There is also the added benefit of freeing oneself from the burdens imposed by labor and equal-opportunity requirements. Nonetheless, even if one grants that the pursuit of such benefits by companies is legitimate in itself, the value of pursuing them must be weighed against the real and potential harm that

can result for employees from such practices. To that I now turn.

Generally speaking, a contractarian approach requires that rational agents weigh the overall impact on their individual welfare that would occur as a result of agreeing to enter into some type of "social contract." The grounding assumption is that the various institutions and practices that would be created or allowed to exist via the social contract are legitimate only if each party to the contract can reasonably expect to benefit from their existence. For the Donaldsonian application of the contractarian approach to business, the comparison to be made by rational agents is that between their overall welfare in a "state of individual production" (SIP) and their expected level of welfare in a society where productive organizations dominate. For the latter arrangement to represent a better state of affairs for individual agents, several conditions must be imposed upon productive organizations and their activity. One of the conditions which Donaldson believes rational agents would impose upon productive organizations is that they act so as to enhance the long-term welfare of their employees. Such a condition is sensible enough, since the point of granting the various social, legal, and economic privileges necessary for productive organizations to exist and function is that their existence is judged beneficial for the parties involved in the social contract. Judging whether productive organizations meet this condition requires that one be more precise about the components of an individual's well-being which productive organizations can either enhance or diminish. In the present context, the specific concern is with the effects that productive organizations have on individuals as employees when they alter employment practices in such a way as to lead to a significant increase in the percentage of the workforce unwillingly accepting temporary rather than permanent employment. The best way to assess these effects on long-term employee welfare is to begin by examining the particular benefits which employees seek from the kind of employment made possible by the existence of productive organizations.

Donaldson lists three such *prima facie* benefits: (1) increased income potential, and, because of that, the capacity for social contribution, (2) diffusion of personal liability, and (3) the chance for adjusting personal income allocation. As regards income potential, the idea is that the increased productive efficiency resulting from the cooperative specialization fostered by productive organizations will result in opportunities for levels of personal income not achievable in an "economic state of nature" where the necessary conditions for such cooperative specialization do not exist. Apart from expectations of *increased* personal income, it should also be noted that the existence of productive organizations can create an extensive market for labor which itself provides greater opportunities for converting one's labor into income, opportunities which may be much less available in their absence. The second of Donaldson's *prima facie* benefits captures the fact that productive risks in the form of product liability are more easily borne by productive organizations than by individual producers. Finally, the existence of productive organizations and their increased resources allows for individuals to secure income over the span of their life in a fashion which does not always directly link income and individual productivity. For example, during periods of illness, or as one ages, one's productivity may decline to an extent that if income were directly tied to productivity, one's ability to address economic needs would greatly diminish. Guaranteed income during illness and salary levels based on seniority are examples of the ways in which productive organizations can create an "income-allocation scheme" more suitable to an individual's actual needs than one based purely on individual productivity. The first and third of these expected benefits are of special importance in the context of temporary employment.

At the same time, however, as Donaldson notes, procuring such benefits via the introduction of socially sanctioned productive organizations has drawbacks which must be weighed against these benefits. As regards workers, Donaldson lists three such drawbacks: (1) worker alienation, (2) lack of worker control over work conditions, and (3) monotony and dehumanization of the worker. In general, all three drawbacks issue from the introduction of highly specialized, largely technologized work structures on the part of productive organizations, in the name of productive efficiency, which have the political/economic power to set the conditions under which work occurs and employment is tendered. This last point is of special impor-

tance in the context of temporary employment. The extent to which productive organizations can control work conditions goes beyond simply structuring the physical setting in which work occurs. They are equally effective at establishing and manipulating the many factors which shape the nature of employment opportunities. They set wages, establish criteria for raises and bonuses, control the dispensing of the many amenities which are typically associated with employment (e.g. health care benefits, pensions, vacation time), determine conditions for advancement, and have the power to impose upon workers a range of contractual obligations as preconditions for hiring (e.g. requiring notice prior to terminating employment, restricting secondary employment, regulating extra-workplace activities). It is the purpose of a social contract to recognize that trade-offs between expected benefits and drawbacks must be made, and any viable social contract must express at least general criteria for which trade-offs are acceptable and which are not. At least, as Donaldson notes, productive organizations should *minimize* the existence of the three harms previously mentioned, though it would be unreasonable to demand as a condition for the social contract that they be *nonexistent*. At the same time, it would be equally unreasonable to require that productive organizations fully maximize the interests of workers, come what may. There must be practical limits on the extent to which productive organizations are obligated to satisfy worker interests.

Donaldson includes one more general consideration. Since individuals opting to live in a post-SIP world will exist there both as workers and as consumers, the gains and losses they might incur as workers due to the introduction of productive organizations must be weighed against the gains and losses they might incur as consumers. As Donaldson describes it,

> Because trade-offs must be made, it remains logically possible that people in the state of individual production would choose to introduce productive organization and to establish the social contract, even when they expected either worker interests or consumer interests to be less satisfied than in the state of nature— so long as *overall* welfare were enhanced. In other words, the inhabitants might believe

that, on balance, people as workers stand to lose from the introduction of productive organizations, and that potential alienation, loss of control, and other drawbacks make the overall condition of the worker worse than before. But if the benefits to people as consumers fully *overshadowed* these drawbacks, we should still expect the contract to be enacted (Donaldson, 1982, pp. 52–53).

In its most succinct form, Donaldson's social contract for business imposes these three conditions on productive organizations.

1. They should enhance the long-term welfare of employees and consumers
2. They should minimize the drawbacks associated with moving beyond the state of nature to a state containing productive organizations, and
3. They should refrain from violating minimum standards of justice and of human rights (Donaldson, 1989, p. 54).

Condition (1) has two dimensions. The fixed dimension requires that productive organizations avoid acting so as to lower the overall welfare of employees and consumers below that level which they enjoyed prior to the introduction of productive organizations. The fluctuating dimension requires that productive organizations act so as to enhance the relative welfare of employees and consumers through time. Setting aside condition (3) by allowing, at least for this argument, that the mass introduction of temporary employment into the world of work does not violate any minimal standards of justice or human rights, and just focusing on the first two conditions, we can now turn to an evaluation of temporary employment in that light.

Given Golden and Appelbaum's findings that no positive association exists between the recent increase in levels of temporary employment and variables related to the share of the labor force presumably disposed to seeking temporary employment, and that a strong positive association does exist between the growth in temporary employment and those variables related to employers' desire to hire temporary employees, it would appear that an increase in temporary employment, rather than providing employees with greater control over

work conditions, actually provides them with significantly less. Golden and Appelbaum's finding that a decrease in the power and activity of labor unions is positively correlated with the rise in temporary employment levels is especially revealing in this regard. Couple this with the fact that the rationale given by businesses for replacing permanent, full-time jobs with temporary help has to do with their desire to gain greater control over the costs and obligations imposed upon them by permanent employment, and it becomes quite clear that from the perspective of employees, temporary employment represents a greatly undesirable manipulation of one of the most basic features of employment. As regards worker alienation, there exists a great deal of anecdotal evidence to indicate that temporary workers are often thought of as less valuable than their full-time colleagues, and, consequently, are ostracized within the work setting. An example that all academics ought to be familiar with is the status of adjunct instructors and professors in university departments. They typically have no voice in departmental affairs, are not eligible for university committees, are not present at departmental meetings, and are generally thought of as disposable resources to be hired and let go at will. IBM even refers to their temporary/contingent workers as "peripherals." As one manager puts it: "We don't count them. They're not here long enough to matter" (Castro, p. 46). It should come as no surprise that given the role that our work plays in defining our sense of self, an inability to secure full-time employment coupled with the perception that temporary workers are "second-class citizens" has the potential for deeply affecting an individual's sense of self-worth (Karen Mendenhall, a "career temp" described part of the experience of temping as "horrible, demeaning, thankless, and boring").

There are reasons to worry that a market-wide shift from permanent employment to temporary employment has a negative impact on income potential, though detailed numbers are difficult to obtain. Again, stories abound of individuals losing well-paying jobs due to corporate "downsizing" who are forced to accept temporary work at a much lower level of pay. At the same time, temporary workers are usually paid less than their permanently employed counterparts for the same tasks. Census Bureau statistics show that since 1989, the real median income of self-employed Americans, a category which includes many temporary workers, fell 12.6%, a figure 11.5% higher than that of the general category of employed Americans (Fierman, p. 32). In addition to worries about income levels, temporary employment raises serious concerns about the security and stability of income. The use of temporary employment extends the power productive organizations have always had to set and distribute wages in a way which allows them to establish temporary income as a contractual precondition for employment. It has always been the case that even with permanent employment, income may cease due to economic factors and poor job performance. But the assumption was that in the absence of these intervening factors income would continue indefinitely. Large corporations, in fact, often used such an "employment promise" as part of their public relations campaigns. With temporary employment, however, no such assumption is realistic. That income *will be* temporary is part of the employment contract. If it is sensible to assume that the potential for increased personal income would be one of the primary expected benefits of a social contract creating the existence of productive organizations, it is equally sensible to assume that the potential for permanent or stable income would also be an expectation. In fact, it is at least *prima facie* reasonable to believe that an arrangement which better guarantees a stable source of income, even if the potential for larger levels of income is sacrificed because of that arrangement, is better than one with a greater potential for higher levels of income if the latter arrangement involves a commitment to a system with much less stability in terms of that income. The general fear expressed by temporary workers regarding future income testifies to the importance we place on income stability.

As mentioned earlier, the primary reason employers have for shifting to temporary employment is to reduce that portion of their labor costs involving the various benefits associated with permanent employment. The anecdotal evidence is quite clear that the loss of such benefits, especially health insurance, is the greatest concern which temporary workers have. It is rare that temporary workers receive benefits packages of any kind, and when benefits are given it is almost exclusively in the professional and technical fields which constitute less than twenty percent of the overall pool of temporary employees (Aley, p. 53). For the vast majority

of temporary workers, their wage level makes it extremely difficult, if not impossible, for them to afford private insurance. The possibility exists that some form of nationalized health care system may materialize in the future, thereby alleviating this particular drawback to temporary employment. However, if, as President Clinton has proposed, a nationalized health care system were to be subsidized via an employer tax, that may create an added incentive for employers to convert an even larger percentage of their workforce to temporary employees as a way of avoiding that extra labor cost. Given that other moral concerns apart from the lack of health care benefits are associated with temporary employment, the even greater rise in levels of temporary employment that could be expected in such a scenario would only heighten moral concern about temporary employment.

Strictly in terms of the welfare of employees affected by temporary employment, then, available evidence seems to indicate that the losses for temporary employees *as a group* far outweigh the gains that some segments of the group might experience. Is it plausible, nonetheless, to believe that consumers benefit economically from the presence of mass temporary employment, and that such benefits *"fully overshadow"* the drawbacks for employees? An argument that it does might go like this. A conversion of a significant portion of a productive organization's workforce to temporary employment makes it more flexible and efficient, able to respond to consumer demand in a more sensitive and timely fashion. It allows producers to respond to changes in financial markets and the international business climate more quickly. Further, the cost of maintaining a large permanent workforce is quite high given all of the costs that employers must bear in addition to wages. This cost might even become prohibitive at times. Cutting such costs would, of course, result in lower consumer prices, all else being equal. In general, the thrust of the argument would be that a shift to temporary employment represents a way for producers to lower significantly the cost of production, a savings which would "trickle down" to consumers in the form of lower prices.

In theory, such a conclusion does follow from neoclassical assumptions about how producers would behave in an ideal market. But arguments based on assumptions about ideal markets are just that, *ideal.* The question is whether there exists any evidence to believe that in fact such an outcome has resulted from the existence of temporary employment. It is obviously the case that consumers have not experienced anything remotely like a noticeable drop in prices of goods during the last fifteen years, the "boom" period in temporary employment. And, even if it were the case that the shift to temporary employment had resulted in cost savings for many productive organizations, those savings in productive costs may very well have been eaten up by cost increases in other areas of production. The point is, the "trickle-down" argument would have to be shown to be empirically valid, not just assumed to be correct based on ideal assumptions. My guess is that it would be nearly impossible to identify anything like a simple causal link between rises in levels of temporary employment and consumer savings. In the absence of positive evidence to the effect that such a link exists, the "trickle-down" argument is entirely unconvincing. In fact, there exists *prima facie* evidence that changes in employment patterns similar to that represented by a large shift to temporary employment are far from a guarantee of increased productivity and efficiency, and in many cases are counterproductive. A 1991 survey of 1,005 companies, with a total workforce of approximately 4 million, which had pursued a program of downsizing and related restructuring, showed that such moves did not necessarily produce an upswing in productivity and profitability (Bennett, p. B1). Only 46% of companies surveyed met their cost reduction targets, only 32% showed an increase in profits, only 22% became more productive; and only 19% experienced an increase in their competitive advantage. A more recent 1994 survey of 140,000 manufacturing plants employing approximately 12.7 million workers by the Center for Economic Studies at the Census Bureau found that during a ten year period ending in 1987, 32% of those companies had experienced productive growth while "upsizing," compared to only 26% of the companies which had downsized (Rose, p. A2, and Noble, p. F21). Though growth in labor productivity was almost the same for "successful upsizers" and "successful downsizers," value added growth of successful upsizers was more than eight times that of their downsizing counterparts. And in a third study, it was found that the shares of downsizing companies outperform the Standard & Poor's 500 index only during the six months follow-

ing the news of their restructuring (*The Economist*, p. 59). Three years down the line, their performance actually lags behind the S&P 500. What this indicates is that major cuts in the permanent workforce is no sure ticket to increased productivity and profitability. Consequently, the simple argument that "leaner and meaner" entails greater productivity and profitability, which itself then entails price benefits for consumers falls quite a bit short of being a law of economics. It can not be denied that in many instances, reducing its workforce issues in productivity gains for companies, but available data indicates that phenomenon is not at all the rule, and in as many cases has just the opposite effect.

Combine these findings with the fact that, as mentioned earlier, a move to temporary employment quite often requires additional training and reordering of management patterns, and it becomes quite clear that sufficient reasons exist to doubt any general claim that benefits for consumers can be expected to result from the mass introduction of temporary employment. I think that the best that can be said is that the benefits for consumers from temporary employment are uncertain, while the losses that employees suffer are real and quite significant. Given that Donaldson's criterion is that consumer benefits "fully overshadow" the losses to employees, the case for the acceptability of mass temporary employment as a part of the "business social contract," when seen from the perspective of employees and consumers, appears very difficult to make. Gillian Brock has suggested to me an even stronger version of a contractarian argument against temporary employment. She suggests that if we take the inhabitants of the SIP to have the kind of bargaining power requisite for insisting that, as a condition of their existence, productive organizations be committed to improving the overall welfare of individuals, it would be of greatest advantage to the inhabitants of the SIP that they obtain guarantees that productive organizations not act so as to lower their overall welfare below some threshold. Minimally, that threshold would be equivalent to the level of welfare they currently enjoy in the SIP. Now, *ex hypothesi*, as individual producers, presumably one can either produce individually that which is necessary to maintain a certain level of welfare, or obtain it through bartering with other individual producers. In either case, the assumption is that in the SIP individuals are able to sustain themselves at some level of well-being. Given this, one obvious restraint individuals would place on productive organizations is that they not act so as to deprive individuals of the means by which to sustain themselves. The large-scale introduction of temporary employment on the part of productive organizations clearly violates this prohibition, at least as long as many of the goods necessary for sustaining oneself in contemporary society are distributed via permanent, full-time employment.

The strength of this argument is dependent on the assumption that in the SIP all individuals are able to produce a livelihood for themselves. As Brock notices, by definition, that does seem to be a valid description of the SIP. If so, then, not only is it the case that there is scant reason to believe that the benefits for consumers from the large-scale introduction of temporary employment come close to approximating the losses suffered by employees, it is also the case that in and of itself a world in which temporary employment exists as an option for employers to impose unilaterally represents a worse state of affairs for employees than that existing in the SIP. Together, these two considerations show that temporary employment fails the first two of the conditions placed on productive organizations by a Donaldsonian version of the social contract. It neither enhances the long-term welfare of employees and consumers, nor does it minimize the drawbacks of moving from the SIP to a state with productive organizations. The fact that evidence shows that the existence of growth in temporary employment is attributable to employer desires to restructure work conditions, and not to a demand by the workforce that such restructuring take place, further weakens any claim that temporary employment somehow contributes to or enhances the welfare of individuals subject to it. These considerations, brief though they are, are sufficient to show that, from the perspective of a social contract theory like Donaldson's, the phenomenon of market-wide increases in involuntary, employer-initiated temporary employment runs afoul of the ethical requirements placed on productive organizations by the social contract. If nothing else, this should prompt us to examine closely the supposed economic necessity of large-scale shifts to temporary employment. If it is the case that temporary employment only minimally cuts costs for employers, or that the "savings" resulting from

temporary employment could be obtained through other cost-cutting measures, then the fact that temporary employment represents a greatly undesirable state of affairs for the majority of individuals caught in the practice (perhaps even a "harm") weighs against the moral acceptability of an employer-initiated shift to temporary employment. Assessing this phenomenon from the perspective of social contract theory is especially helpful since it allows one to focus specifically on the role that employment plays in shaping individual welfare in a free-market system and how significant alterations of traditional employment patterns and practices can negatively impact the success individuals have at procuring the various goods that a free-market system distributes via employment. Given that traditional, full-time, permanent employment continues to be the only effective means by which the vast majority of individuals can secure even a minimally satisfying life, and given that in the absence of specific laws to the contrary, employers continue to hold the upper hand in controlling the conditions of work which employees must agree to, a social contractarian might be justified in believing that the phenomenon of temporary employment represents, as Secretary of Labor Reich has put it, a "fraying of the social contract."

RESOURCES

Aley, James. 1995. "The Temp Biz Boom: Why It's Good." *Fortune* (October 16): 53–56.

Bandow, Doug. 1993. "Should We Even Bother to Mourn?" *Business and Society Review* (Fall 1993): 16–17.

Bennett, Amanda. 1991. "Downsizing Doesn't Necessarily Bring an Upswing in Corporate Profitability." *Wall Street Journal* (June 16): B1.

Castro, Janice. 1993. "Disposable Workers." *Time* (March 29): 43–47.

Donaldson, Thomas. 1982. *Corporations & Morality*. Englewood Cliffs, Prentice-Hall, Inc.

Donaldson, Thomas. 1989. *The Ethics of International Business*. New York, Oxford University Press.

Dunfee, Thomas W. and Thomas Donaldson. 1995. "Contractarian Business Ethics: Current Status and Next Steps." *Business Ethics Quarterly* 5: 173–186.

Fierman, Jaclyn. 1994. "The Contingency Work Force." *Fortune* (January 24): 30–36.

Goldman, Lonnie and Eileen Appelbaum. 1992. "What Was Driving the 1982–88 Boom in Temporary Employment? Preference of Workers or Decisions and

Power of Employers." *American Journal of Economics and Sociology* 51: 473–491.

Mendenhall, Karen. 1993. *Making the Most of the Temporary Employment Market*. BetterwayBooks.

Noble, Barbara Presley. 1994. "Questioning Productivity Beliefs." *The New York Times* (July 10): F21.

Rose, Frederick. 1994. "Job-Cutting Medicine Fails to Remedy Productivity at Many Companies." *Wall Street Journal* (June 7): A2.

"When Slimming is Not Enough." 1994. *The Economist* (September 3): 59–60.

Business Should Not Be Allowed to Permanently Replace Striking Workers

Robert B. Reich

As our national economy becomes, increasingly, a global and technological economy, America's ability to be competitive will depend on how well we have invested in developing a skilled and motivated workforce. To succeed in this new economy, we cannot afford to waste any of our resources, especially the resource most firmly rooted within our borders: our people, their ideas, their education, and their skills.

But to compete effectively on a world-class level, we need even more than a high-skill, high-wage workforce. We also need a new framework for labor relations—one that stimulates employee productivity and enables management to get the most out of its employees' skills, brainpower, and effort.

An Invaluable Asset

Workers on the front line have unique perspectives on production and immediate access to information that smart businesses depend on for quick response and high quality. So it is not surprising that an increasing number of companies are finding that they profit when they treat their workforce not as just another cost to be cut—but as an invaluable asset to be developed.

The Clinton Administration is committed to fostering practices that improve productivity. I have seen many illustrations that both productivity and profitability increase when workers have a

voice—whether through collective bargaining or other means of promoting cooperation between workers and management and fostering employee involvement and participation in workplace decision-making. We cannot afford to limit American competitiveness by any practices that inspire workers and managers to work at cross purposes. What will make us most competitive is a dedicated and innovative workforce—and this requires a partnership between workers and employers, predicated on teamwork and mutual respect.

In short, good labor-management relations make good business—and a healthy economy. But in the most recent chapter of American labor history, productive relations between some companies and their unions have been thwarted by increasing distrust, hostility, and litigation. The permanent replacement of strikers exemplifies practices and attitudes that make real cooperation between labor and management impossible, by undermining the basic foundations of the collective bargaining system. As an editorial pointed out, labor cannot approach negotiations with trust and a sense of shared purpose when management has a gun pointed at the union's head. Management that has the option of simply eliminating the other side has little commitment to finding a mutually satisfactory resolution of differences.

The practice of permanent striker replacement became a prominent feature of American labor relations only since 1981. I believe many employers were emboldened when, in 1981, 11,400 PATCO (Professional Air Traffic Controllers Organization) strikers were fired and permanently barred from reinstatement. Although PATCO was considered an illegal strike involving public sector employ-

From Robert B. Reich's testimony before the U.S. Senate Committee on Labor and Human Resources, Subcommittee on Labor, March 30, 1993, regarding S.R. 55, the Workplace Fairness Act.

ees—which differentiates it from the work stoppages addressed by proposed legislation [called the Workplace Fairness Act, designed to prevent employers from firing striking workers]—the action taken in 1981 sent a loud signal to the business community that the hiring of permanent replacement workers was an acceptable way of doing business. This, coupled with a distorted focus on short-term performance at the expense of long-term interests, began a decade characterized by a wave of labor disputes in which thousands of employees lost their jobs after they engaged in completely lawful economic strikes.

CONTRARY TO THE NATIONAL INTEREST

The *Mackay* doctrine [*Labor Board v. Mackay Co.* is the Supreme Court case that upheld employers' ability to permanently replace striking workers] is contrary to the national interest in long-term labor and management relationships, and in investment in our human resources. Permanent replacement is not a means of building a quality workforce, of investing in workers' skills, or of developing relationships built on mutual respect. It betrays a management approach whose premise is that workers are a disposable resource, to be exploited for short-term profit, and then, if the worker questions the employer's unilateral authority, discarded.[1]

Strikes are usually an act of desperation, a last resort which employees undertake at great economic and often personal risk to themselves and their families. When workers enter negotiations, the last thing they want to do is strike. But the availability of that option is a crucial counter-weight to the economic powers that business owners and managers bring to the fundamental premise of American labor law.

At its best, collective bargaining is a win-win process. But without a viable right to strike, employers have less incentive to engage in serious bargaining with their unions, to hammer out mutually satisfactory solutions. And unions see no point in trying to work cooperatively with management when there is no real avenue for dialogue.

In the changed climate of labor relations, more employers have been willing to choose intimi-

dation over serious negotiation. Some companies even advertise for permanent replacement workers before they begin negotiations—stockpiling them just like raw materials.

Successful bargaining is made even less likely if the workers do take on this added risk and strike—and are permanently replaced. The rehiring of the strikers, and the fate of their replacements, add highly charged, problematic issues that replace and obscure the original dispute.

A study conducted in 1989 indicated that the use of permanent replacements not only complicates the dispute, but also prolongs the strike. Productivity is reduced by prolonged strikes—as well as by the permanent displacement of skilled and experienced workers.

Although permanent replacements have been used only by a minority of employers, the practice affects even those employers who would never use, or even threaten to use, this weapon. All employees receive the message that they are disposable, each time a workforce is permanently replaced or threatened with permanent replacement. This undermines, throughout the economy, the trust necessary for true cooperation between workers and managers.

The Workplace Fairness Act would enable us to close the book on this counterproductive recent chapter in American labor law. The legislation would restore balance in collective bargaining, allowing management to operate during a strike through alternate means, but not destroying fundamental union rights. The Clinton Administration supports this legislation, because it would foster the equilibrium and stability in industrial relations which are critical to the health of our economy. The sooner that we can conclude this chapter, the sooner we can turn our attention from the past and begin, together, to write the next chapter.

But we risk failing to meet the challenges that await us if—as Louis Brandeis said nearly 90 years ago—we "assume that the interests of employer and employee are necessarily hostile—that what is good for one is necessarily bad for the other. The opposite is more likely to be the case. While they have different interests, they are likely to prosper or suffer together." We need to remember that management doesn't "win" when labor "loses," just as workers don't triumph when businesses fail. Maintaining a balance of power that promotes labor-management cooperation promotes our long-term economic strength; undermining that balance puts us all at risk.

NOTE

1. Thomas R. Donahue, testimony given before the Labor Subcommittee of the Senate Labor and Human Resources Committee on March 30, 1993.

Business Must Be Allowed to Permanently Replace Striking Workers

David Warner

William A. Stone was on the shop floor of his business, Louisville Plate Glass Co., along with 3 salesmen and 2 supervisors, cutting glass to fill customers' orders. Outside the Louisville, Kentucky, plant, 15 of his 25 employees—members of Local 1529 of the Glass Glazers and Painters International Union—were on strike for higher wages and benefits. The union was seeking an increase that would double Stone's labor costs over three years, he says.

The strike occurred in June 1977, in the midst of double-digit inflation and high interest rates. Stone and the 5 management employees continued to run the company's normally 15-man shop floor operation for almost a month, hoping the striking workers would back off from their position. "But they hardly gave," Stone says.

After six months on the picket line, the union was still seeking an 80 percent increase in wages and benefits.

The company started losing orders—it lost 50 percent of its volume in the first month of the strike. "It became apparent that either we replaced our [striking] employees or we would be out of business," says Stone.

So the firm hired 7 new employees as permanent replacements for strikers. Eventually, 8 of the strikers crossed the picket line to return to work. Because only seven of the 15 workers who went on strike were replaced, the 8 who returned were given back their jobs.

Stone's company survived that labor unrest, primarily because he was able to replace the strikers. And the company has since expanded to three

plants—two were added in Georgia—and 100 employees.

[But proposed] legislation would bar employers from permanently replacing employees who walk off the job for economic reasons, such as wages and benefits.

The Wagner Act

Employers have been able to hire permanent replacements for economic strikers since 1935, when Congress passed the Wagner Act—also known as the National Labor Relations Act—which governs union organizing and collective bargaining.

The U.S. Supreme Court affirmed that ability as a "right" in a 1938 case, *NLRB [National Labor Relations Board] vs. Mackay Radio & Telegraph Co.* The high court also ruled in that case that permanent replacements were prohibited if the employer had committed an unfair labor practice, such as provoking a strike to "bust" the union.

The Workplace Fairness Act, or striker-replacement bill—it's one of the top priorities of organized labor—would reverse the Supreme Court ruling dealing with economic strikes.

The Clinton administration supports the legislation.

The AFL-CIO [American Federation of Labor–Congress of Industrial Organizations] and Labor Secretary Robert Reich maintain the legislation is needed to level the playing field between management and labor during contract negotiations. And Reich states that banning permanent replacements is a step toward ending what he and the unions assert has been years of growing distrust between labor and management.

At House and Senate hearings on the striker-replacement bill, the labor secretary told lawmakers that "employees suffer as a result of strikes; they are putting their jobs and their livelihoods on the line."

A CORE PRINCIPLE

The Strike Bill [the Workplace Fairness Act] . . . would prohibit employers from defending their businesses by offering permanent jobs to replacement workers during a strike over economic issues such as pay raises and benefits.

Proponents of the Strike Bill claim that employers' use of permanent replacement workers during an economic strike is a recent phenomenon. This simply is not true. The National Labor Relations Act, enacted in 1935, provided a delicate balance that allows unions to strike over wage demands and allows employers to defend their businesses by hiring permanent replacement workers.

The striker-replacement legislation would destroy this core principle of United States labor law, which has been consistently supported by Democratic and Republican presidents and federal courts for over half a century.[1]

Many labor-law experts, however, believe barring permanent replacements would have grave effects on the collective-bargaining process.

Daniel Yeager, a labor lawyer with the Labor Policy Association, a business-supported Washington, D.C., group focusing on human-resources issues, says the ability of the union to strike and the capability of management to hire permanent replacements are weapons whose "mere presence has the effect of bringing the parties to agreement at the bargaining table." If management lost its weapon, "unions would be able to call virtually risk-free strikes over any issue," says Yeager.

Republican Sen. Nancy Landon Kassebaum of Kansas says that denying employers the ability to continue operations during a strike would foster more labor-management strife.

The legislation "will turn the clock back to the era of bitter, prolonged, and divisive strikes, where everyone loses—not only the workers but the economy as well," she says. Kassebaum is the ranking minority member of the Senate Labor and Human Resources Committee.

The Harm of No-Risk Strikes

Management would have to accede to the union's demands or try to weather a strike, says John Irving, a partner in the Washington, D.C., law firm of Kirkland & Ellis and general counsel to the National Labor Relations Board from 1975 to 1979. Irving also believes that in the absence of any risk that their members would be replaced, unions would be likely to strike more often and for longer periods.

Some industries can afford to take a strike for a while, says Irving. "But there are many, many others that . . . simply can't afford to do that; they must continue to operate, or their competitors will be all too happy to permanently take their customers."

Reich and the unions argue that employers have other means, such as hiring temporary replacements, to continue operations during a strike.

While employers in some businesses—mostly those requiring low-skilled workers—can use temporary replacements as long as there's no violence by strikers on the picket line, says Irving, many others cannot. "If they can't," he says, "and they need to hire permanent replacements, . . . they should have that right. Otherwise, the union just sits out there [on the picket line], and employees dictate when they're going to come back.

"Employers permanently replace their workers only as a last resort. No employer in his right mind wants to get rid of his skilled workers and have to train a bunch of 'green' people."

In addition to the costs of training temporary replacements, under state and federal laws employers could owe these workers unemployment and health benefits once a strike is resolved and they are let go.

Health care is one industry in which hiring temporaries often is not a viable option and where the ability to replace striking workers can literally be a matter of life or death.

For the 110 residents of the Jewish Home for the Aged, in Cincinnati, that certainly was the case in early 1993 when 80 of the nursing home's 95 employees, members of District 1199 of the Service Employees International Union, went on strike for, among other things, higher wages.

The nonprofit health-care facility was able to use temporary replacements for the first three weeks of the strike. But because it had to hire some high-priced temporary-agency workers and because of certain state-mandated staffing and training requirements, permanent replacements were later hired.

"The union recognizes how vulnerable health-care institutions are," says Alan Lips, a partner with Taft, Stettinius & Hollister, a Cincinnati law firm representing the Jewish Home. "If [union members] can hold the residents hostage to the boycott of their labor . . . and they can prevent the hiring of replacement labor, then the employer has to capitulate quickly [to union demands] because he's got an overriding, moral imperative to take care of the residents."

The Replacement Workers

Stone, who is president and CEO of Louisville Plate Glass, points out that replacement workers take physical and emotional risks when they agree to work for a company being struck. "They're going to be insulted and called 'scabs'; they're going to be threatened and intimidated. You couldn't get most people to cross a picket line in any kind of intense negotiation situation unless the carrot of permanent replacement were available."

Under current law, even "permanent" replacements aren't necessarily permanent. Striking unions often file charges of unfair labor practices with the NLRB against a company that hires such replacements. If the labor board agrees with the charges, the employer would be prohibited from hiring permanent replacements.

Strike settlement agreements often provide for reinstatement of all strikers at the expense of the replacement workers' jobs.

A March 1992 survey by the Bureau of National Affairs, a private research and publishing company in Washington, D.C., found that 75 percent of replaced strikers return to their jobs after a strike.

Under current law, striking workers cannot be fired; they can return to their jobs even during a strike; and, at the end of a strike, they must be given first priority when job vacancies occur.

The striker-replacement measure would require employers to favor returning strikers over nonstrikers—both replacements and those who did not strike—for jobs and to ensure that the strikers' seniority remained unaffected by their absence. . . .

Nonunion and union small companies that supply goods and services to companies could also suffer financially if their customers are unable to continue operations during a strike, say several business organizations.

"The little guy can really be hurt by having his customer shut down," says Irving.

Labor unions are looking to the striker-replacement bill not only as a way to help secure higher wages and benefits but also as an organizing tool, says Irving. If a union can guarantee workers' jobs even when they strike for unreasonably high wages and benefits, chances are good the union's organizing efforts will be successful, he says.

And the unions are eager to achieve such success. Union membership has been declining steadily since it reached its peak of 35.5 percent of the work force in 1945. In 1994, organized workers make up just 11.5 percent of the nation's work force.

Kassebaum sums up the stakes involved in the striker bill this way: "At a time when we should be enhancing our competitiveness, we ought to be looking for ways not to destroy but to encourage labor and management cooperation."

Says Stone of the striker-replacement measure: "Had there not been the right to hire permanent replacements [during the 1977 strike], I would be doing something else, somewhere else." And 100 more Americans might be without jobs.

NOTE

1. Howard Jenkins and John A. Penello, *The Christian Science Monitor*, July 11, 1994.

The Hostile Takeover: An Opposition View

Lisa H. Newton

1. Rights and Consequences

Given the nature and prestige of the players, we might be tempted to think that the *hostile takeover* is just one more game businessmen play. But the business literature on the subject sounds atypically harsh notes, describing this activity in the unbusinesslike language of threat and attacks, followed by occasionally desperate and increasingly sophisticated defenses—the junk-bond bust-up takeover versus the Pac-Man, Poison Pill, Crown Jewel Option defenses ranged against the two-tier tender offer and finally the launching of the golden parachutes.

In this colorful literature, the most noticeable feature of a corporate takeover is its terrible human cost. *Fortune* magazine entitled a 1984 article, "Help! My Company Has Just Been Taken Over," and began the article with the story of the suicide of a corporate executive precipitated by his termination following a takeover. "There are more mergers than ever these days," the author warns, "and their human toll is higher than ever too."[1] A more recent *New York Times* article, entitled "'People Trauma' in Mergers" documents the anxiety and feelings of betrayal experienced by employees—increasingly, down to the hourly level—when the prospect of takeover looms into view. Trust is broken, loyalty ebbs, and, if none of the above is of any interest to managers, productivity plummets.[2] The fact that these alarms come from publications inside the business world is significant; outsiders might be expected to see human effects more clearly than the economic realities that underlie the takeover activity, yet here are the insiders suddenly concluding that the realities of profit may actually be less important than the injuries to the people caught up in it against their will. The hostile corporate takeover

is simply *not* business as usual. It is assault with a deadly weapon; and the question seems to be, how can it be right?

Let us backtrack for the moment. A practice requires moral scrutiny if it regularly derogates from human dignity, causes human pain, or with no apparent reason treats one class of human beings less well than another. Any practice that regularly throws people out of work does at least the first two of those (work being possibly the largest factor in self-worth and the major instrument to creature satisfactions), and unless we find the raider's urgent need for self-aggrandizement as a worthy reason for dismembering working units, it probably does the third also. To be sure, all manner of evil things can happen to people in non-takeover situations; part of the fun of being alive is the risk, and part of being in business is knowing that your livelihood may depend on the next quarter's earnings. But as a general moral principle, if I, by my voluntary act and for my own profit, increase the riskiness of your life, no matter how high the base risk and no matter how small the increment by which I raise it for you, then I owe you an explanation. The hostile takeover regularly disemploys at least some people who would not have been unemployed absent the takeover; that makes it, by the above, a proper candidate for moral scrutiny, without presumption one way or another on the results of the scrutiny.

A further problem, if it is a problem, is that a takeover deliberately destroys something—a company, corporation, an instance of human association. In the other cases, it can be said that the association itself "decided" to do something to make itself better, or more efficient. But when it is taken over, it does nothing—it is killed, and the atmosphere of the threat of death hangs over the entire proceeding, from the raider's first phone call to the final resolution (usually the acquisition of the company by some party other than the raider). Does it make any difference, that a company is destroyed? Is that an evil over and above all the other disruptions that takeovers occasion? Or is it,

---

From Lisa H. Newton, "The Hostile Takeover: An Opposition View," in *Ethical Theory and Business*, 3d ed., edited by Tom L. Beauchamp and Norman Bowie (Englewood Cliffs, NJ: Prentice Hall, 1988), 301–310. Reprinted by permission of the author.

strictly speaking, meaningless, beyond the suffer-
ings of the individuals?

We have, in short, two very separate and distinct questions. First, does the hostile corporate
takeover serve some ordinary and necessary role
in the economy? Whatever the present injuries, is
the practice justified in the long run as improving
the economic condition of the greatest number?
That very pragmatic question is accompanied by a
second, metaphysical one: Is the corporation the
type of thing whose demise could or should be re-
gretted? Could it have some right to live, to persevere in existence—a right appropriately exercised
in management's series of "defenses"? Ordinarily
we assume that only individual human beings have
dignity, worth, or rights (beyond the uninteresting
legal "rights" bestowed on the corporation to permit it to conduct business). But that assumption fits
poorly with the fact that people will willingly die
for their associations when they will not willingly
sacrifice their lives for personal interests; that fact
needs further examination before we dismiss the
association as a merely instrumental good. We will
pursue, then, two separate and logically independent lines of inquiry: First, on straightforward utilitarian reasoning, does the business practice that we
know as the *hostile takeover* serve the public interest
by performing some useful role in the economy, or
are there good utilitarian reasons for limiting or
prohibiting it? Second, does the corporation have
some right to exist that is violated by any business
practice that ends it existence without the consent
of its present governors? Along the line of the first
inquiry, we will argue, first, that the hostile takeover is damaging to the economy (and the people
in it) in the short and middle run and, second, that
this practice is a deadly symptom of a long-term
process in our relation to material goods, a loss of
"ownership," which ought to be noted and, as far
as possible, reversed. On the line of the second inquiry, we will argue that "the association," usually
the political association, has been invested with
dignity since Aristotle's day, and that its right to
self-defense is firmly grounded in individual rights
of undisputed worth. Therefore, the corporation,
acting through its present management, has the
right and (sometimes) the duty to defend itself
when its existence is threatened, apart from any
arguments about immediate effects on the wealth
of individuals.

II. Responsible Ownership Profits

Takeovers are generally defended on the utilitarian
grounds that they are in the public interest. The
"takeover" is simply capital flowing from one sector of the economy to a more profitable one, in this
instance, to buy up the stock of a company the
value of whose assets is significantly greater than
the value of its outstanding stock. Where stock is
undervalued, an inefficiency exists in the economy;
whether through management ineptness or other
market conditions, the return on the shareholder's
investment is not as high as it could be. It would
be maximized by selling off the assets and distributing the proceeds among the owners; but then,
by the above, it is management's duty to do that.
The takeover merely does the job that the managers were supposed to do, and the prospect of a
takeover, should the stock become undervalued, is
an excellent incentive to management to keep the
shareholders' interest in mind.

Moreover, defenses against takeovers often involve managers in apparent conflicts of interest.
They are protecting their jobs rather than meeting
their fiduciary obligations to stockholders. Theory
in this instance concurs with current case law; there
should be no regulation of takeovers beyond (not
very rigorous) anti-trust scrutiny, and defensive
moves on the part of management are morally and
probably legally illegitimate. To be sure, people get
hurt in takeovers, but the shareholders profit, and
control of the corporation belongs by statute to
them. Against these considerations, what arguments can be raised that unregulated takeover activity is harmful, wrong, contrary to the public
interest, and ought to be stopped by new legislation?

The best approach to a response may be to peel
an onion: All of the evils seem to be related, differing primarily in the level of analysis suited to elicit
them. Beginning with the surface, then, we may
note the simple disruption caused by hostile takeover activity: The raider's announcement that a certain percentage of shares of a company have been
purchased, more to follow, immediately puts the
company in play in a deadly game from which it
will not emerge intact. Productive activity, at least
at the upper levels of the target (where salaries
are highest), stops. Blitzkrieg raider tactics are met
with poison pills, sales of crown jewels and other

defenses—often of questionable legality. Orderly planning disappears. Employees, terrified for their jobs, spend their days in speculation and the search for another job.[3] Other bidders emerge from the Midwest, from abroad, from next door. Nobody sleeps. All the players hire lawyers, financiers, banks, and start paying them incredible amounts of money. (In the takeover of Revlon by Pantry Pride in the fall of 1985, the investment bankers' share alone came to over $100 million, legal fees to over $10 million, and the negotiated "golden parachutes" to $40 million. Added up, the costs of the takeover—not one penny of which went to shareholders—came to close to 9 percent of the $1.83 billion deal.)[4] However the game ends, people are exhausted, betrayed, out of work, and demoralized. The huge debt incurred by the acquiring company, secured by the assets of the target (by the infamous *junk bonds),* requires the immediate dismemberment of the company for financial survival (more on this later), and financial health, under those circumstances, is out of the question. And all this to what end?

"Hostile takeovers create no new wealth," Andrew Sigler pointed out to the House Committee on Energy and Commerce, "They merely shift ownership, and replace equity with large amounts of debt." He continues:

> More and more companies are being pushed—either in self-defense against the raiders or by the raiders once they achieve control—into unhealthy recapitalizations that run contrary to the concepts of sound management I have learned over thirty years. This type of leveraging exposes companies to inordinate risks in the event of recession, unanticipated reverses, or significant increases in interest rates. . . . Generation after generation of American managers have believed that there *must* be a solid equity basis for an enterprise to be successful in the long term. This long-term equity base absorbs—in exchange for the expectation of higher returns—the perils of depression, product failure, strikes, and all the other dangers that characterize business in a free economy. That healthy conservatism is now being replaced by a new game in which the object is to see how far that equity base can be squeezed down by layers of debt. And too much of this debt is carrying interest rates far

in excess of those a prudent manager can possibly be comfortable with.[5]

At a second level, then, the takeover has two deleterious effects on the management of corporations: First, when the takeover materializes, equity is inevitably transformed into debt, leaving the company terribly vulnerable to foreseeable reverses, second anticipating takeover attempts, management may well be tempted to aim for short-term profits and engage in aggressive accounting practices to show higher current earnings. These practices may weaken the company and deceive long-term investors, but they will be reflected in a higher stock price and thus one more resistant to attack.[6] As Peter Drucker put it, "Fear of the raider and his unfriendly takeover bid is increasingly distorting business judgment and decisions. In company after company the first question is no longer: Is this decision best for the business? But, will it encourage or discourage the raider?"[7] Fear of the raider may encourage the managers of a company to put up their own money as well as to incur debts well beyond prudence, to take the company privately in a "leveraged buyout." All the same risks, including bankruptcy in the event of any reversal, attend the buyout as attend the takeover.[8] Nor is it clear that the damaging effects of these maneuvers are limited to the domestic scene: As Harold Williams (chairman of the Securities and Exchange commission during the Carter administration) points out,

> The pursuit of constantly higher earnings can compel managers to avoid needed write-downs, capital programs, research projects, and other bets on the long term. The competitiveness of U.S. corporations has already been impaired by the failure to make long-term commitments. To compound the problem because of fears of takeovers is a gift to foreign competitors that we cannot afford.[9]

The alarms, confusions, and pains first noted as the result of hostile takeover activity, are then compounded by what seems to be very imprudent business practice. But imprudent for whom? Do the target shareholders, at least, get some profit from the takeover—and if they do, does that not justify it? Michael Jensen, one of a new breed of scholar known as the "shark defenders," argues that they do and it does. He dismisses worries about shareholders' welfare as "folklore," and insists that "science" shows otherwise.[10] His evidence for this claim is interesting:

> More than a dozen studies have painstakingly gathered evidence on the stock price effect of successful takeovers. . . . According to these studies, companies involved in takeovers experience abnormal increases in their stock prices for approximately one month surrounding the initial announcement of the takeover. . . . The evidence shows that target company shareholders gain 30% from tender offers and 20% from mergers.[11]

But isn't the raider's effect pure artifice? Let his initiative be withdrawn—because of government opposition, or because he has agreed to purchase no more stock for whatever reason—and the same studies show that the stock immediately reverts to its previous value.[12] So it was not, really, that the company's stock was too low. It was rather that the flurry of activity, leading to speculation that the stock might be purchased at an enormous premium, fueled the price rise all by itself. Or could it be that certain professional investors find out about the raid before the public does, buy the target's stock at the lowest point, sending it up before the announcement, wait for the announcement, ride the stock to the top, then sell off before the defense moves, government action, or "targeted repurchase" (see the section on "greenmail," below) stop the takeover bid and send the stock back down to its true market value? As Jensen's figures confirm,[13] that value is often a bit *lower* than the starting value of the stock; after all those payouts we are dealing with a much poorer company. Nothing but evil, for all concerned except professional fund managers and investment bankers, seems to come of this takeover activity.

Hence, at the first level there is disruption and tens of millions of dollars' worth of unproductive expense; at the second level there is very dubious business practice. At a third, there is the betrayal of the stakeholders. Current laws, as discussed earlier, force the directors of the target company to consider only shareholder rights and interests, to the probable disadvantage of the other stakeholders: employees, retirees, creditors, host communi-

ties, customers, and suppliers. But each of these has helped to build the company to its present state, relying on the company's character and creditworthiness; the employees and retirees, especially, have worked in expectation of future benefits that may depend in part on the good faith of management, good faith that can hardly be presumed in a raider.[14] The mid-career, upper middle-level managers are especially vulnerable to redundancy and the least likely to be able to transfer their acquired skills and knowledge elsewhere.

Some elimination of positions resulting from duplication is inevitable in any merger, of course, hostile or otherwise, and when carried out under normal conditions succeeds at least in making the company more efficient, even if the cost to the individual is very high. But only some of the people-cutting in these extravagant takeovers stems from real redundancy. Companies are paying such high takeover prices that they have to engage in deep cost-cutting immediately, even to the elimination of personnel crucial to continued operations. The "efficiency" achieved may not serve the company well in the long run, but the raider's calculations rarely run very long. As a consequence, middle-management employees (who are, on the whole, not stupid, and read the same business publications as we do) seem to have taken all this into account and reoriented their work lives accordingly.

> Management turnover at all levels is on the rise and employee loyalty is at a low, according to consultants, executive recruiters and the companies themselves. And there is growing evidence, they say, that merger mania is an important reason for both problems, spreading fear about layoffs and dissatisfaction with other changes in the corporate environment. These problems, in turn, promise to make it harder for companies to realize the anticipated efficiencies that many of them pointed to in justifying their acquisitions. . . . Critics of the takeover binge maintain that the short shrift given to 'people issues' . . . [is] one reason why perhaps half to two-thirds of mergers and acquisitions ultimately fail.[15]

Do we owe anything to people who have worked for a company and who may actually love the company and may be devastated by its dismemberment or transformation? At present, our law does not recognize, or even have any language to describe, the rights possessed by those who have contributed to the growth of an association, have participated in it and loved it, and now see it threatened. The fact that such rights are by no means absolute does not mean they are not there. Classical political theory has the vocabulary to discuss them, under the rubric of the "just war"; discussion of the implications of that doctrine for the hostile takeover issue will occupy the final section of this paper. Rights or no rights, and prudential considerations (as discussed earlier) aside, the condition of the stakeholders ought not, in charity, to be ignored; yet our institutions make no provision for them. Here we have, in the center of the most civilized sector of the civilized world, an open wound, a gap of institutional protection most needed by those who have worked hardest, which we struggle to paper over with the "unemployment benefits" fashioned for different people in different circumstances. Law and business practice seem to require a callousness toward human need and human desert that is incompatible with our notions of justice.

Inevitable disruption, mandated imprudence, and legally required injustice are the first three levels of palpable wrong in the hostile takeover phenomenon. It may be that the fourth layer, the last under consideration in this section, has more worrisome implications than all of the above. The thesis is simple: At primary risk in all of this is our concept of ownership. For all of human history, we have been able to trust property owners (individuals or groups) to take care of their property, because it was in their interest to do so, and outside of military and government property, that was how the property of the world was cared for. With the corporate takeover, that may no longer be the case for the kind of property that looms too large in Western economics, the publicly held corporation. And this development is very alarming.

To begin with the concepts: Ordinarily we use the concepts of *ownership* and *property* interchangeably; even etymologically, they are indistinguishable. But the concept does have two distinct aspects: the primary aspect of a legally protected complex of rights and duties obtaining between the owner and other *persons* and the less prominent aspect of a diffuse set of nonlegal duties, or imperatives, incumbent upon the owner to take care of the *owned thing*, itself. This duty of care has a history of its own; the duty to the thing, analogous to the duty of *stewardship* when the property of others is in question, attaches naturally to the legal owner.

Ownership has the longest history of any concept still extant in the West, certainly longer than its ultimate derivative, *personhood.* Aristotle assumed that the union of man and property, along with the union of man and woman, lay at the foundation of the household and hence of all society. Ownership is presupposed, and discussed, throughout the earliest books of the Bible. The list of *what* was owned was very short: animals, people (slaves), land, tools, buildings, and personal effects. Except for the last item, all were essential to survival, and all required care. The duty arises from that fact.

Whether ownership is single or shared, the duty corresponds to personal interest. If I own a sheep, it is very much in my interest, and incumbent upon me, to take care of the beast and see that it thrives. If you and I together own a sheep, the same interest applies to both of us, the same imperative follows, and we shall divide up the responsibilities of caring for it. If you and I and 998 others own it, enormous practical difficulties attend that care. But however small my interest in that sheep, it is still in my interest that the animal should thrive. Similarly, partial ownership in a whole herd of sheep, or a farm, or a factory, or a business that owns several factories, does not necessitate a change in the notion of *ownership.*

Liquidation consumes something that is owned, or turns it into money that can be spent on consumption. The easiest way to liquidate a sheep is to eat it. The way to liquidate most owned things is to sell them. Then you no longer own the thing, and your responsibilities terminate; but so, of course, does all future good you might have gotten of the thing. Part of the cultural evolution of ownership has been the elaboration of a tension between retention and liquidation, saving and spending, with the moral weight of the most successful cultures on the side of thrift and preservation. The business system probably depends as much on Ben Franklin's "A penny saved is a penny earned" as it does on Adam Smith's "invisible hand." The foreseen result of the *hand,* we may remember, was to increase the wealth, the assets, of a nation. For the herdsman it is self-evident that if you slaughter or sell all your sheep, you will starve in the next year; for Smith, it was equally self-evident that it is in a businessman's interest, whatever business he may be in, to save his money and invest it in clearing more land, breeding more beasts, or building more plants, to make more money in the future. Hence the cleared land, the herds, and the factories—the assets of the nation—increase without limit, and all persons, no matter how they participate in the economy, in fact share in this increased wealth. Presupposed is the willingness of all players in the free enterprise game to acquire things that need care if they are to yield profit, hence to render that care, and to accept that responsibility, over the long run. Should that willingness disappear, and the population suddenly show a preference for liquidation, all bets are off for the wealth of the nation.

And the problem is, of course, that the developments of ownership made possible in the last century create excess tendencies toward liquidation. If several thousand of us jointly own several thousand shares of stock, we may in theory bear the traditional responsibilities of owners for those companies, but we shall surely not *feel* them. And if we purchased those shares not for the sake of investing in the companies, but for the sake of having money available to us at some future time (say, in a pension fund), we will have acquired them for a purpose that is directly contrary to our concerns as owners. We will be involved in a conflict of interest and obligation with ourselves: On the one hand, we should be protecting and nurturing the company(s) we (partially) own, plowing profit back into improvements in plant on occasion, even if that means no profit this year; on the other, if it seems we could get more money if the company were liquidated and the proceeds shared around, we should work toward that end. Suppose that we several thousand owners hire a fund manager to make sure our pension fund provides us with as much pension as possible. That manager, hired with those instructions, is not an owner, and has *no* responsibility toward the companies. On the contrary, his entire obligation is to us and the increase of our money. Where liquidation serves that purpose, it is his job to bring it about. Ownership, for such a manager, is no more than present legal title to property, a way station between sums of money, and its whole moral framework has become totally

irrelevant. To complete the picture, let only the tax structure subsidize that liquidation in cases of takeover:

> Accounting procedures and tax laws . . . shift much of the cost of acquisitions to taxpayers through the deductibility of interest payments and the revaluation of assets in ways that reduce taxes . . . I suspect that many of the acquisitions that proved profitable for acquirers did so largely because of tax benefits and the proceeds from busting up the target company. If liquidation is subsidized by the tax system, are we getting more liquidations than good business would dictate? [16]

The answer is probably yes.

Institutional investors—those gargantuan funds—now own up to 70 percent of the stock of the publicly owned corporations. It must be unprecedented in human history that majority ownership of such entities lies with "owners" whose interests may be best served by the destruction of the object owned. In the case of companies that own large holdings of natural resources, forests, or oil reserves, it is usually the case that the assets sold separately will yield more than the companies' stock. (As Minow and Sawyier grimly put it, under current practices such companies "are worth more dead than alive.") [17] Any company, in fact, that regularly works for the long term (funding research and development, for example) can be profitably liquidated: Whatever those raiders may be, they do not need to be geniuses to figure out which companies to attack. The only limits on the process of liquidation of the country's assets by the managers hired by those investors, or by the raiders that cater to their own interests, might be the success of new and inventive defenses.

The evils of the takeover market, then, go to the philosophical base of our market system, striking at the root of moral habits evolved over 2500 years. The corporate raiders have yet to make their first widget, grow their first carrot, or deliver their first lunch. *All* they do is turn money into money, cantilevering the profit off the shell of responsible ownership. No doubt capital is more productively lodged in some places than others, but it follows from no known economic theory that it is more beneficial to the world when lodged in T. Boone Picken's bank account than when lodged wherever it was before he got it. Possibly it will end up facilitating some industrial projects—he has no intention of keeping it in a mattress, after all—but only in those that promise quick profits. We need not look to him to revitalize our smokestack industries and make them competitive on the world markets. The whole productive capacity of the American economy seems at the mercy of moneymen on the rampage, with all productive companies under threat of being taken over, taken apart, and eradicated. Surely this condition cannot be healthy or good.

In sum: This section has tried to provide a series of pragmatic arguments that the present rash of corporate takeover activity is harmful to the stakeholders, to the economy, and to the general public, from all of which it would follow that regulation is justified. In the next section we attempt to provide a defense for the proposition that a corporation has a real right to exist, hence to resist takeover.

III. The Association as Worth Keeping

Individuals may be hurt by the corporate takeover. The corporation, on the other hand, is usually killed. Does this fact add anything to the list of injuries, or is it simply a shorthand way of saying that the individuals are no longer part of it? Does the corporation have a right to life—a right to persevere in existence, as itself, under its own laws and practices, at least to the extent that would give it a presumptive right to mount a defense against hostile takeover?

The disutility of unregulated takeover activity, implying the desirability of some regulation in the public interest, was the theme of the last section. In this section we ask a different question: Can the corporation be seen as an entity analogous to an individual human being, with rights, including the right to defend itself (through the actions of its officers) regardless of the utilities involved in each case? The law is unsympathetic to defensive moves in takeover situations, suggesting that the right in question here is not derivable from any acknowledged legal rights or present powers of the corporation. It must be found, if it is to be found

anywhere, as a logical derivation from other recognized rights of the corporation or, more likely, of the individuals who make it up.

We may begin the inquiry by noting that over the last decade, philosophical students of the corporation have been moving cautiously in the direction of grounding their moral discourse, in the assumption that the corporation is a moral individual like other moral individuals.

It is possible, however, that a corporation may be capable of assuming moral responsibility and still not have rights, but it is not likely. Our attribution of rights rests heavily on the attribution of moral agency, which alone confers worth or dignity on the human, and moral agency is the condition for attribution of moral responsibility. In the literature, the development continues, and recent work (e.g., Patricia Werhane's *Persons, Rights, and Corporations*) accepts that corporations have, indeed, moral rights, even if only "secondarily."[18]

There is, however, one body of literature precisely on the point of our question, albeit not one that deals with "the corporation" as this paper understands the corporation. Since Saint Augustine, the right of a nation to defend itself against foreign aggression has been recognized. While the political association, as Aristotle and Augustine understood it, may seem an odd model for Phillips Petroleum and Continental Group, it is possible that the literature articulating any collectivity's right of defense may help us formulate one for the modern corporation.

The queerness of attributing a "right" to a collectivity rather than to an individual was not generally noticed in discussions of the Just War, most likely because its recognition predates the theory of individual rights by several centuries; nations had rights long before we did. But if we are to make sense of this right in a modern political context, it must be restated in terms compatible with individual rights theory. Michael Walzer undertakes this task in *Just and Unjust Wars*. For Walzer, the right of the political association to exist comes from the general right of *social contract*—the right of people to join together in any voluntary association, preeminently the state, the association charged with the whole governance of a people. (This is the right primarily challenged in *aggression*, which threatens to abrogate it permanently.) Like Burke before him,

Walzer does not understand the agreement that binds the state as a set of real "contracts."

> What actually happens is harder to describe. Over a long period of time, shared experiences and cooperative activity of many different kinds shape a common life. . . . The moral standing of any particular state depends on the reality of the common life it protects and the extent to which the sacrifices required by that protection are willingly accepted and thought worthwhile.[19]

Again,

> The right of a nation or people not to be invaded derives from the common life its members have made . . . and not from the legal title they hold or don't hold.[20]

So the fact of the common life, which has been made by the participants in it, is the immediate source of the right to defend it, presumably necessarily mediated by the desire of participants to defend it. Walzer is likely correct that the right of the state to defend itself stems from the right of a people to create a common life, to adorn and embellish it, to examine and reform it, and by spending themselves on it, to make it valuable—a variety of the rather prosaic right of association. And the reason why people exercise that right in the formation of permanent associations, which build up a history for themselves, is that associations extend individual life in dimensions that the individual otherwise cannot control—in time, in space, in power. To the limited and partial individual, participation in an association provides immortality, global reach, and collective power. The individual needs the association for these benefits, and in this way the right of association is grounded in human nature. When my association is attacked, my basic security in these insecurity-ridden areas is very much endangered, and that is why I so justifiably resent any attacks on it.

Has this argument any validity for the corporation? Here the relatively recent moves to articulate the internal order of a corporation precisely as a historical culture, with a set of values and commitments all its own, may have some relevance. It would be tempting to argue that a corporation that has, as have the best companies of the recent litera-ture, earnestly pursued excellence in all respects, taken care of its employees, stayed close to its customers, produced the highest quality product, and really cared about its communities, has somehow earned the right to exist, while the others have not.[21] Temptation must be resisted: the difficulties of discerning the "excellent" companies from the others are insurmountable. But maybe we don't have to make that judgment: If a corporation, even in theory, can be the kind of collectivity that the state is, and can serve the purposes in human life that a state can serve, then good or bad, it shares in the state's presumptive right to defend itself.

To summarize this section: The association provides those individuals who voluntarily and fully participate in it with goods they can not get elsewhere—social recognition, material reward, and above all the extension of the limited self in space, time, and power. These are the reasons why the right of association exists and is exercised, and why the result of that exercise has, derived from that right, the right to stay in being and to expect its officers to mount a defense for it should that turn out to be necessary. But that is all we need to establish the right to defend itself against hostile takeover attempts.

That conclusion does not entail, of course, that present officers may do anything they like in the course of a defense; as Walzer points out, there are standards of justice in war as well as standards to determine if a war as a whole is just. (At present, for instance, the payment of greenmail to a raider—a premium price to obtain his stock and only his stock, to persuade him to go away and leave the company alone—raises questions of acceptable practice in the event of a takeover, more than the poison pills, ESOPs, and Crown Jewel Options designed to make a company significantly poorer in the event of takeover.)

Conclusion

We have argued that as a matter of right, and as a matter of utility, the takeover game should be ended. Capital is not unlimited; in a country rapidly losing out to foreign competition in part because of outdated plant, and declining in its quality of urban life in part because of obsolete and crumbling infrastructure, there are plenty of worthwhile uses for capital. Law that turns the attentions of restless rich away from cannibalizing productive corporations, toward investing in the undercapitalized areas of the economy, would be a great public service.[22]

NOTES

1. Myron Magnet, "Help! My Company Has Just Been Taken Over," *Fortune*, July 9, 1984, pp. 44–51. See also Joel Lang, "Aftermath of a Merger," *Northeast Magazine*, April 21, 1985, pp. 10–17.
2. Steven Prokesch, "People Trauma' in Mergers," *New York Times*, November 19, 1985.
3. *Ibid.*
4. *Wall Street Journal*, November 8, 1985.
5. Testimony of Andrew C. Sigler, Chairman and Chief Executive Officer of Champion International Corporation, representing the Business Roundtable, before hearings of the Subcommittee on Telecommunications, Consumer Protection and Finance of the House Committee on Energy and Commerce, Thursday, May 23, 1985.
6. Some of these considerations I owe to conversations and correspondence with S. Bruce Smart, Jr.
7. Drucker, *Wall Street Journal*, January 5, 1983.
8. Leslie Wayne, "Buyouts Altering Face of Corporate America," *New York Times*, November 23, 1985.
9. Harold M. Williams, "It's Time for a Takeover Moratorium," *Fortune*, July 22, 1985, pp. 133–136.
10. Michael Jensen, "Takeovers: Folklore and Science," *Harvard Business Review* 62 (November–December 1984): 109–121.
11. P. 112. The footnote on the studies cites. For a summary of these studies, Michael C. Jensen and Richard S. Ruback, "The Market for Corporate Control: The Scientific Evidence," *Journal of Financial Economics* (April 1983). The studies are cited individually in the same footnote; *ibid.*, p. 120.
12. *Ibid.*, p. 116.
13. *Ibid.*
14. Another point owed to conversations and correspondence with S. Bruce Smart, Jr.
15. Prokesch, "'People Trauma' in Mergers."
16. Williams, "'It's Time for a Takeover Moratorium," pp. 133–136.
17. Newton Minow and David Sawyier, "The Free Market Blather Behind Takeovers" Op-ed, *The New York Times*, December 10, 1985.
18. Patricia H. Werhane, *Persons, Rights, and Corporations* (Englewood Cliffs, N.J.: Prentice-Hall, 1985), p. 61.
19. Michael Walzer, *Just and Unjust Wars* (New York: Basic Books, 1977), p. 54.
20. *Ibid.*, p. 55.
21. Criteria freely adapted from Thomas J. Peters and Robert H. Waterman, Jr., *In Search of Excellence* (New York: Harper and Row, 1982).
22. In developing ideas for this paper. I have profited enormously from conversations with Lucy Katz, Philip O'Connell, Stuart Richardson, Mark Shanley, Andrew Sigler, S. Bruce Smart, Jr., and C. Roger Williams.

On Alternatives to Industrial Flight: The Moral Issues

Judith Lichtenberg

Staughton Lynd writes: "Workers in Youngstown and elsewhere are beginning to ask: Why is the company allowed to make a shutdown decision unilaterally? Since the decision affects my life so much, why can't I have a voice in the decision? The communities in which shutdowns occur are starting to ask the same questions."[1]

The thrust of Lynd's questions is moral, not practical. He is asking why companies *ought* to be allowed to exclude workers and communities from shutdown decisions, and he is suggesting that the latter have a *right*—a moral right, which ought perhaps to be made a legal right—to participate in these decisions.

From some perspectives, these questions seem to answer themselves. The free market defender may say: "It is the company that owns the factory, makes the investments and takes the risks; in accepting jobs, workers freely consent to certain ground rules." Thus, the firm has the right to move whenever it chooses. The committed democrat, on the other hand, may insist that in matters that crucially affect a person's life, that person ought to have some say. "What touches all must be decided by all."[2] A shutdown decision touches deeply the

Institute for Philosophy and Public Policy's newsletter, QQ v. 4, No. 3 (Fall 1984). Permission for publication granted by the author.

lives of workers, their families, and their communities; they ought to have a say in what happens to the factory on which their livelihoods depend.

These are polar views, framed in the strongest terms—in terms of rights, moral "musts." But there are positions short of poles that, though expressing some of the same underlying concerns, do not state the issues as inescapable moral imperatives. Defenders of laissez-faire may think not that firms have a natural or God-given *right* to make shutdown decisions unilaterally, only that our kind of economic system is preferable (for which they may have a variety of reasons), and for it to work, firms must completely control investment decisions. Similarly, advocates of workers' participation in company decisions may think not that they have a *right* to participate, but simply that the possibly disastrous consequences of plant closings make a moral claim on our concern.

How can we adjudicate between these conflicting points of view? Suppose we go back to Lynd's questions and the view implicit in his essay—one that challenges the status quo, in which workers have no voice in shutdown decisions. What reasons are there for thinking that the status quo is not as it should be, that workers and communities ought to have some say in decisions about whether a plant stays or goes?

At least two basic kinds of arguments support worker participation. One focuses on the idea that, although in our legal system factories belong to stockholders, workers may acquire a kind of moral property right, a moral claim to some control over their workplaces. The other emphasizes that, through their relationships over time with workers, firms have incurred obligations to them that preclude unilateral shutdown decisions.

The first view rests on the labor theory of property, originally developed by John Locke.[3] The germ of the theory is that property rights are acquired by "mixing one's labor" with, and thereby adding value to, external objects. To make this view workable requires many qualifications, but its essential core is persuasive: Having worked on an object and transformed it into a socially valuable commodity gives one *some* claim to the fruits of one's labor. How much of a claim, and how it compares to that of the entrepreneur who has mixed a different kind of labor and has taken risks the worker has

not, are questions a complete theory of property must address.

The second argument for workers' rights to a say in shutdown decisions expresses the idea that when a company has dug deep over generations into people's lives, perhaps affecting a whole community, it incurs obligations to those people and that community. Although the company may have entered freely, it is no longer at liberty simply to withdraw from relationships that have developed over years or even generations.

These are mere sketches of arguments, and I shall not flesh them out here. For some, no elaborate argument is necessary; for others, none will be convincing. Here I shall assume that, as matters of abstract moral right, these views seem persuasive; it seems plausible at least in the abstract that workers have some moral claim to the factories in which they labor and that companies have incurred obligations to these workers and communities that they are not free simply to renounce.

The sticking point is in the phrase *in the abstract*. I said earlier that the thrust of Lynd's questions is moral, not practical. But this is too simple; moral questions are not altogether separable from practical ones. Indeed, much of the controversy about employee versus management claims in plant shutdowns rests precisely on disagreement about what would in fact happen if owners were not free to make such decisions unilaterally. To decide, then, whether the abstract moral arguments for worker participation are plausible when concrete, we need to know more about the consequences of such legal and institutional changes.

What obstacles, then, do abstract moral right and obligation encounter? What arguments can be made against the rights of workers or the duties of owners?

One important argument is that plants like those in the Youngstown area are no longer sufficiently profitable; therefore, it is both natural and right (or at least not wrong) to abandon them for more profitable ventures.

Not sufficiently profitable; that looks like an easy cover for greed. What profits are sufficient? What the traffic will bear?

But this cynical response may be misguided—or at least premature. The idea that a company can be profitable, yet not sufficiently profitable, can be explained in terms other than sheer avarice; it can be explained by the economics of investment. Unless a plant's rate of return equals the standard rate—that is, unless it is competitive with other ventures in which investment might be made—it will not endure beyond the short run.

This is not to deny that corporations may seek profits above the standard rate of return. It may be their natural tendency to seek the highest profits possible; to suppose so is not to ascribe to them base motives, only the desire for gain often found among human beings. But many economists argue that the tendency to seek higher profits, though it may be motivated only by self-interest, benefits others too. They say that the profit motive leads to the creation of more wealth, and in the long run, not only firms and corporations, but also workers and the general population benefit. The wealth spreads or trickles down. If companies are prevented from closing and seeking higher profits elsewhere, it is argued, in the long run the total pie will shrink, and everyone, workers included, will suffer.

Two claims are implicit here. First, permitting companies to move when they deem fit is *efficient*, that is, will produce more wealth overall.[4] Second, this greater overall wealth will be *distributed* in a way that benefits workers. Each of these claims needs to be considered more carefully.

Does Management's Freedom to Move Increase Efficiency?

The idea that if owners, rather than workers, are legally entitled to make shutdown decisions, the economy will be more efficient, is refuted by a well-known theorem of economics. According to this theorem, if the two parties (in this case, owners and workers) are free to bargain with each other, and each is guided only by economic motives, the most efficient outcome will be reached no matter who possesses the legal entitlement.[5] For whichever side stands to benefit most will simply buy out the other side's entitlement if it doesn't possess the entitlement itself.

Take a simple example. Suppose a company will realize savings in labor costs of $4 million a year if it moves a plant from Ohio to South Caro-

lina. Suppose also that the Ohio workers will lose $3 million, the difference between their present wages and their income, from other jobs or from unemployment compensation if the plant moves. In this case, it is efficient for the factory to move, for efficiency is a matter of realizing the greatest net benefit overall. Now whoever is legally entitled to make the shutdown decision, the plant will move. Suppose the owners have the entitlement. It won't be in the workers' interests to pay more than $3 million to get the plant to stay, and it won't be in the owners' interests to accept less than $4 million. No agreement will be reached, and the plant will move. Now suppose the workers possess the entitlement. Then it will be in the owners' interests to pay up to $4 million to the workers to be allowed to move, and it will be in the workers' interests to accept something above $3 million to allow the plant to move. Owners and workers will reach an agreement under which the plant moves—the efficient outcome.

Now imagine instead that the owners will realize savings of $4 million if the plant relocates, but the workers will lose $5 million. Then it is efficient for the plant to stay. Suppose the workers possess the entitlement. It won't be in the owners' interests to pay more than $4 million to be permitted to move, and it won't be in the workers' interest to accept less than $5 million. No agreement will be reached, and the plant will stay. What if the owners possess the entitlement? Then it will be in the workers' interests to pay up to $5 million to keep the plant from going, and it will be in the owners' interests to accept something above $4 million. Owners and workers will come to an agreement under which the plant stays—again, the efficient outcome.

There is, then, no merit to the claim that allowing workers to have some control over shutdown decisions is bad for the economy because it is inefficient. The difference between the system in which owners are entitled to make these decisions and the system in which workers are is not a difference in the *total* amount of wealth produced, but in *who* gets the better economic deal. So, for example, in the first case, where owners will save $4 million if the plant moves, but workers will lose $3 million, if the owners have the entitlement, they will move straightaway, saving $4 million while the workers lose $3 million; whereas if the workers have the en-titlement, they will be able to bargain for a better deal. The question is not how much wealth, but in whose hands?

Does Management's Freedom To Move Benefit Workers?

Now if it is a question of improving the lot of al-ready well-off owners as against much less well-off workers, many people will see no dilemma. And yet it will be argued that the issue is not so simple. For it is often said that if the company realizes higher profits, it will invest them in ways that are good for the economy, and so in the long run for all Americans. But if it pays out what would have been those profits in the form of higher wages, the in-come will not be saved and invested. Since work-ers do not have enough income to save, they will spend it on consumer goods, groceries and the like, which do the economy no good.

This argument depends on the assumption that income spent on consumer goods is not invested. True, it is not invested by the consumer. But money spent on groceries increases the profits of the super-market, which in turn may invest those profits. Some would argue that this sort of investment does not benefit the economy in the way investment by steel companies (and similar producers) does. But this is a disputed question among economists, and it ought not to be assumed without argument, there-fore, that money spent on consumer goods has no effect on savings and investment.

There is a more important argument for the view that corporate autonomy benefits workers. When factories close down in the old industrial centers of the North and Northeast, they move to places that have traditionally been poorer: to the South, now fashionably called "the Sunbelt," or to Third World countries whose standard of living is much below that of the average American. The new factories create jobs for workers in these places and may greatly improve their standard of living. This fact seems to confront us with a discomforting di-lemma. We are now forced to weigh not the welfare of workers against that of owners, but rather the welfare of Youngstown workers against that of workers in South Carolina or Korea. And framed in these terms, it may seem there are good grounds

for preferring South Carolinians or Koreans. For these people, especially those in the Third World, are generally much poorer than workers in Ohio, even laid-off workers. Shouldn't we give more weight to the welfare of the worse off than the bet-ter off?

So the concern with Youngstown workers might appear to rest on a partial view; when we extend our vision beyond one town or one region, a differ-ent picture seems to emerge.

Or does it? Will workers worldwide be better off on balance if plants are permitted to move when they choose, or not? We are interested in what will happen *in the long run*, and predicting what will happen far in the future is extremely difficult. The controversy is at this point in danger of degener-ating to mere assertion and counterassertion, for we do not have the tools to settle this dispute empirically.

The argument must proceed at a different level. We can begin by asking why it is that Ohio workers are better off now than their counterparts in the American south or in the Third World. There seem to be several reasons. When the Northeast became industrialized in the nineteenth century, practical necessity dictated the location of factories; they were built close to the source of raw materials, or convenient to waterways or railroads. Labor was relatively scarce, so workers were in an advan-tageous bargaining position compared to most modern factory workers. But the position of these earlier American workers was improved immeas-urably by the facts of their coexistence under the same management, their similar interests, and the forces making it necessary for factories to be where they were. It became clear that collectively they could exert a power they didn't possess as individ-uals. They formed unions and were able to extract concessions from the companies. Owners and man-agers were no longer able to say, "take what we of-fer or leave it." They were forced to operate partly on workers' terms.

So the situation remained as long as there was no viable alternative to the factories staying where they were; companies could not set the terms of work unilaterally. But as technology developed the situation changed; the reasons keeping factories in the Northeast (such as convenience to waterways) were less weighty, and the attractions of moving (primarily, cheap, unorganized labor elsewhere) became increasingly compelling. There was at this point only one way the company could avoid having to come to a mutually satisfactory agreement with its employees, and that was to move, or threaten to, if workers did not accept management's terms.

Now it is obvious what the effects of shutdowns or relocations are on workers in threatened factories. But we are at the moment considering their effects on workers elsewhere; we are considering the claim that such workers, in greater need, may benefit by such actions. But the two issues are not separate. When Ohio workers have achieved a certain degree of power, companies undermine that power in the only way now available to them: by threatening not to "play the game" anymore. But this has consequences far beyond Ohio. It means undermining the hard-won strides labor has made over the years, and that affects not only the communities in which shutdowns occur, but workers elsewhere as well. For there will always be unorganized workers to act as a magnet for companies when their own employees get into a position to make unwelcomed demands.

Thus, even though in the short-run workers in South Carolina or Korea might benefit from Ohio plant closings—and might benefit from them more, economically, than Ohio workers are harmed—over time, corporate autonomy in shutdown decisions is a setback for labor, not an advance. This is even more obvious if we think not only in the narrowest economic terms, not simply in terms of dollars, but also in terms of self-respect and the ability to determine important aspects of one's own life. What workers benefiting from plant closings would gain in the short-run are jobs and money—nothing to sneeze at, to be sure. But what they would not gain and what Ohio workers and ultimately all workers would lose is the power to affect in any way a crucial aspect of their lives, their work and livelihood. For they would be forever at the mercy of employers who can say: "take it or leave it."[6]

Freedom to Move and Fair Play

"Take it or leave it" is not only *harmful* to workers, but also *unfair* to them.

Consider an analogy. A child with a Monopoly game offers to play with other children. They play contentedly for a while, but eventually some of the other children are putting hotels on Pennsylvania Avenue and Boardwalk, and the game's owner is broke. He's a bad sport, declares the game at an end ("It's my game"), takes his game and goes home.

Obviously, the child is acting unfairly. He was free to play or not play. But having agreed to play, he is not free to quit simply because the terms no longer suit him. (It would be different if he began to feel sick or had to finish his homework.) Similarly, we may conclude that the company is acting unfairly if it says, "You play our way or not at all." But the analogy may appear to have its limits. For although in quitting, the child is clearly being unfair, most people would probably say that it would be wrong to force him to continue to play. Would it be similarly wrong to force the company to stay? If so, our conclusion may seem innocuous: the company is acting unfairly, but nothing can be done about it. (After all, "life is unfair.")

The question is this: What is the difference between those situations in which we think, "He's being unfair, but it would be wrong to force him not to," and those in which we conclude, "He's being unfair and should be made to act otherwise"? There are, I think, two conditions relevant to answering this question. One has to do with the costs of various sorts—economic, moral, political—of forcing people to be fair. It may be literally too expensive to force them, or it may involve trampling on other values, like privacy or personal freedom. The other condition concerns how much is at stake for the participating players.

Obviously, it would be ludicrous to consider bringing the coercive power of the state down upon our poor, unsporting child. It would be ludicrous because not enough is at stake for anyone and because the implications of such a policy in terms of state interference in people's private lives would be monstrous.

What about prohibiting companies from making unilateral decisions to abandon factories? We have argued above that there are no clear economic costs of doing so in terms of efficiency and the like. Nor would it seem to be especially expensive or unwieldy to set into motion the necessary enforcement apparatus. Already existing government agencies, as well as the negotiation structures of management and labor unions, can perform the relevant tasks. Without a compelling argument for owners' exclusive property rights to factories, there do not seem to be any other obvious costs of enforcement. As for the other condition, it seems clear that the stakes for participating players are very high. Obviously some people (company stockholders, perhaps) may be made worse off by the decision, but workers in the affected plants will be spared grave economic and personal hardships. And, in the long run, we have argued, so will workers in general.

There is a further similarity between the Monopoly case and plant closings. Although it would be absurd to force children legally to fulfill agreements to play Monopoly, it is at least plausible that parents would be justified in forcing them. The difference between the Monopoly case and the plant closings case, then, seems to be not that it is wrong to force in one case and not the other, but rather that the morally appropriate agents of force are different.

These considerations bring us back to our earlier discussion. We began by mentioning two (not unrelated) kinds of arguments for the conclusion that workers ought to have a say in decisions about plant shutdowns and relocations. The first, rooted in the labor theory of property, supports the view that not only owners but workers may come to have property rights in their workplaces. The other argues that in view of relationships developed over years and even generations, companies come to have certain obligations to workers that are incompatible with abrupt withdrawal. We abandoned these matters of "abstract moral right and obligation," in the belief that the controversy about factory closings hangs mostly in more pragmatic considerations. Having, we hope, dispelled some of these concerns, we have returned, in these last arguments about fairness, to the more purely moral substance of the earlier arguments. For the idea that it is unfair for companies to "play the game" only as long as it suits them and that it is legitimate to force them to do otherwise, really amounts to the view that, having agreed to play the game at all, companies have incurred obligations they are not at liberty to abandon, and workers have as a result of their investments of labor acquired rights. The Monopoly example and our inquiry into the conditions under which it is legitimate to "coerce fairness" are steps toward fleshing out further the arguments for owners' obligations and workers' rights.

The connection between fairness and the earlier arguments can now be made more explicit. In the Monopoly case as in the plant closings case, the response of "It's mine" (my game, my factory) is no longer an argument stopper. We can interpret this in either of two ways: (1) It may be yours, but that doesn't mean you can do with it whatever you please; or (2) it may have been all yours once, but other people have now acquired rights to it, so it is no longer just yours to do with as you please. The first interpretation grants the original owner an exclusive property right, but asserts that it has been limited or qualified by his own actions;[7] the second interpretation denies the original owner an exclusive property right. The difference between these may be more semantic than substantive, but which interpretation we choose may determine whether we frame the argument in terms of workers' rights or just companies' obligations.

The practical conclusion is the same in either case: Companies should not be permitted to make decisions about plant closings and relocations unilaterally. This conclusion is supported by a variety of moral considerations having to do with fairness, self-respect, autonomy, and the interests of workers in general over the long run. It is, in addition, a conclusion that seems to survive the harsh scrutiny of economics. . . .

NOTES

1. Staughton Lynd, *The Fight Against Shutdowns: Youngstown's Steel Mill Closings* (San Pedro, Calif.: Singlejack Books, 1983), 3.
2. See Michael Walzer, *Radical Principles: Reflections of an Unreconstructed Democrat* (New York: Basic Books, 1980), 275.
3. *Second Treatise of Government,* chap. 5.
4. It is important to realize that the economist's notion of efficiency concerns the total amount of wealth irrespective of how it is distributed. The situation where A has $100 and B has $1 is more efficient in this sense than the situation where A and B each have $50.
5. This is Coase's theorem. R. H. Coase, "The Problem of Social Cost," *Journal of Law and Economics* 3 (1960). The theorem assumes also that transaction costs—in this case the costs of bargaining—are zero. Since the structures for collective bargaining are already in place, transaction costs will in fact be close enough to zero in this case to make the theorem practically applicable.

6. George Steinbrenner, owner of the New York Yankees and chairman of the board of American Ship Building, told shipbuilding union leaders in Lorain, Ohio, that if they did not agree to wage and other concessions, he would close down the shipyard and throw union members out of work. "I don't know about you boys, but *I'll* be eating three meals a day," Steinbrenner said. (*Washington Post*, 5 February 1984, Fl.) What is disturbing is that the same outcome can be achieved without the assumption of maliciousness; it results naturally from structural features of the situation.

7. Property rights are, of course, always limited and qualified: To say "It's mine" never means "I can do with it anything I please." I am not at liberty to burn down my house.

Study Questions

1. Imagine that you are Jim Malesckowski in the "Southern Discomfort" case. What would you do in this situation and why?

2. In what ways, according to Werhane, are employees in a position of relative disadvantage with regard to employers? Do you agree?

3. What does Werhane identify as the moral ground for the due process requirement?

4. Do you agree with Maitland that there may be circumstances in which it is rational for an employee to accept a position with little job security?

5. Maitland speaks of workers deciding to make trade-offs, for example, by ranking job security against an increase in wages. Do workers actually make such trade-offs? How would Maitland deal with the argument that workers often begin from a position of comparative disadvantage?

6. According to Extejt and Bockanic, what are the two main elements of a negligent hiring claim? Be specific.

7. According to Extejt and Bockanic, how might a claim against an employer for negligent hiring result in the violation of the employee's rights? Be specific about what rights might be violated.

8. In what ways, according to Steverson, does temporary employment raise serious ethical questions? Do you agree with Steverson that such practices are morally unacceptable?

9. Do you agree with Reich's claim that good labor/management relations make for good business? Defend your answer.

10. According to Warner, what is the harm of "no-risk strikes"?

11. Do you believe that workers have a right to collective bargaining? What would be the foundation for that right?

12. Newton argues that takeovers undermine the traditional view of ownership, which she claims entails stewardship. Do you agree? How might Newton respond to the objection that the right to liquidate or to dispose of property as one sees fit is at least as fundamental as the obligation of stewardship?

13. Assuming that a corporation has a right to survive, does that mean it has the further right to ban unionized labor strikes, since strikes can threaten survival of the firm? Why or why not?

14. Explain how, according to Lichtenberg, the right to relocate might benefit workers. How does Lichtenberg respond to this conclusion?

15. What is the point of the Monopoly analogy with which Lichtenberg ends her essay? Is the analogy a good one? In what ways is it not a good analogy?

CASE SCENARIO 1   Wrongful Demotion

Engineers C. Byron Scott and Al Johnson had worked for the Pacific Gas & Electric Company in California since the early 1970s. By 1989 both had risen to senior managerial positions in PG&E's technical and ecological services unit, an in-house engineering consulting service. In 1977 Scott and Johnson started an independent corporation, S&J Engineering, to which they devoted time on weekends and holidays. The existence of S&J was well known within PG&E. Near the end of 1988, PG&E's internal auditors began a review of Scott and Johnson's supervisorial duties and their outside business interests. The company later alleged that the two engineers were negligent supervisors and that their ownership of S&J created conflicts of interest that detrimentally affected PG&E. Scott and Johnson believed that the investigation was in retaliation for their earlier intervention on behalf of a worker in their department who had been accused of time card fraud. In August 1989 Scott and Johnson were abruptly suspended; two months later they were stripped of all supervisory authority and reassigned to entry-level positions; their salaries and benefits were reduced by approximately 25 percent.

Scott and Johnson sued the utility, claiming that the company had breached an implied promise, given to PG&E employees, not to demote them without good cause. PG&E countered that no such promise had been made, and that even if it had, the law does not recognize a claim of "wrongful demotion." A jury awarded Scott and Johnson damages; and the California Supreme Court, in November 1995, upheld the verdict. Justice Stanley Mosk, writing for the majority, acknowledged PG&E's claim that "there is . . . a strong common-law presumption that an employee may be demoted at will. Since it is presumed that an employee may be discharged at will, the at-will presumption would surely apply to lesser quantums of discipline, as well." But, Mosk countered, "the employer's right to demote, like the right to discharge, is not absolute . . . We perceive no reason . . . why the presumption that an employer has the right to demote an employee at will may not also be rebutted by evidence of a contractual agreement, express or implied, to limit the employer's power of demotion." Just such an implied agreement had in fact been made by PG&E with its employees, the Court determined. Relying upon the utility's "Positive Discipline Guidelines," the Court observed that the company had established and publicized a procedure of "progressively more serious, but constructively oriented responses to employee misconduct," which ensured that workers could not be subjected to disciplinary action until the steps in the process had been taken. Such guidelines, Justice Mosk concluded, amounted to an agreement not to demote without good cause.

PG&E had claimed that the practical effect of allowing employees to sue based on actions short of termination would "open the floodgates of litigation," swamping the courts with lawsuits and involving the courts in every aspect of employer/employee relations, from performance evaluations to transfers. Such a level of judicial intrusion into areas of legitimate "managerial discretion" runs counter, the company argued, to the core principles of liberty and market-based capitalism. Justice Mosk responded that courts have long been charged with supervising aspects of employment contracts (as with other contracts), and that there is no reason that implied contractual terms concerning demotion should be any different. If employers don't want to be caught up by such implied terms, they ought simply to ensure that no such promises are made.

1. What might be the likely response of employers to this ruling? Do you agree that permitting courts to enforce implied promises not to demote without good cause will inevitably lead to judicial interference with what are properly business decisions?

2. What other arguments could PG&E make to support its position? Do you find them convincing?
3. Explain how you think Werhane and Maitland would evaluate the actions of PG&E in this case. What resolution would each suggest and why?

CASE SCENARIO 2   *Yunker v. Honeywell Inc.*

Randy Landin worked for Honeywell Corporation in Minnesota from 1977 to 1979 and then again from 1984 to 1988. In 1979 Landin had been imprisoned for the strangulation death of a co-worker, Nancy Miller. Upon being released, Landin reapplied to Honeywell and was rehired as a custodian in the company's general office facility in South Minneapolis. Landin was subsequently transferred twice: first to the firm's Golden Valley plant, and then to the plant in St. Louis Park. At each of these last two sites, Landin was involved in several confrontations. He sexually harassed female employees and challenged a male co-worker to a fight; at St. Louis Park, Landin threatened to kill a co-worker during an angry confrontation following a minor car accident. He also became hostile and abusive toward a female colleague after problems developed in their friendship. Kathleen Nesser was assigned to Landin's maintenance crew in April 1988. The two became friends and spent time together away from work. When Landin expressed romantic interest in Nesser, however, she stopped seeing him. Landin then began to harass and threaten Nesser both at work and at home. By the end of June, Nesser sought help from a supervisor and requested a transfer. On July 1, Nesser found a death threat scratched on her locker door. Landin did not come to work after July 1, and Honeywell accepted his resignation on July 11. On July 19 Landin shot and killed Nesser in her driveway. He was convicted of murder and sentenced to life imprisonment. Jean Yunker, a trustee of Nesser's heirs, brought a lawsuit against Honeywell, alleging that the firm was liable for the wrongful death of Nesser by virtue of negligence in hiring, retaining, and supervising Landin.

The state district court granted summary judgment for Honeywell, effectively asserting that Honeywell could not be held liable under existing law, even given all the facts. Yunker appealed. The state appellate court examined each allegation separately. The court first determined that Honeywell could not be liable for negligent supervision of Landin, since the killing did not take place on the company's property and Landin did not use an instrumentality in Honeywell's possession. Negligent hiring occurs, according to the court, "when, prior to the time the employee is actually hired, the employer knew or should have known of the employee's unfitness," in the form, for example, of tendencies toward violence. But the employer's duty is dependent, the court reasoned, upon the types of responsibilities associated with the employee's job. On this basis, the court concluded, Honeywell did not owe a duty to Nesser at the time it hired Landin:

> Landin was employed as a maintenance worker whose job responsibilities entailed no exposure to the general public and required only limited contact with coemployed . . . Landin's duties did not involve inherent dangers to others, and . . . Nesser was not a reasonably foreseeable victim at the time Landin was hired.[1]

The court also expressed the concern that the law not encourage the perception that all ex-felons are inherently dangerous and not to be trusted. "Such a rule would deter employers from hiring workers with a criminal record" and undermine efforts to rehabilitate ex-offenders.

The court reached a different conclusion on the claim of negligent retention. An employer can be held liable for negligent retention when it was aware that an employee posed a threat and

---

[1] 496 N.W. 2d 419.

failed to take reasonable steps to ensure the safety of others. Here Honeywell had been negligent, the appellate court concluded: Given Landin's history of confrontation and harassment after being rehired in 1984, it was foreseeable that he could act violently against a co-worker.

1. Do you agree with the court's analysis of the negligent hiring allegation?
2. Should employers be allowed greater latitude in investigating the personal histories of job applicants who have a prior criminal record?

CASE SCENARIO 3   The Wall Street Effect: A Case Study

First Interstate Bancorp of Los Angeles had been ailing for years. The bank—which has more than 500 branches in thirteen states, most of them in California—had failed to see the high-tech future of the industry, priding itself instead on old-fashioned teller service. So last October 18, when Wells Fargo & Co., a San Francisco-based banking company beloved by Wall Street for replacing traditional branches with supermarket ATM sites, announced a hostile takeover of First Interstate, the move was seen by many financiers as a logical step in the evolution of banking.

But First Interstate chairman William Siart and the rest of the bank's executives spurned Wells Fargo's first offer—$10.1 billion in Wells Fargo stock—and began searching for a "white knight"—another bank whose bid might be more palatable, even if somewhat lower. They found one in the Minneapolis-based First Bank System Inc., which offered $9.9 billion worth of its stock for First Interstate. Although Wells Fargo promptly upped its offer to $10.7 billion, First Interstate executives announced that they preferred to merge with First Bank, and signed a "poison pill" pledge that would force First Interstate to pay First Bank a $200 million penalty if First Interstate merged with Wells Fargo.

First Interstate's shareholders were considering two very different deals. One offered instant gratification; the other, a long-term commitment. Wells Fargo's plan for First Interstate was to save $700 million a year by firing up to 10,000 people (mostly First Interstate employees in California) and closing more than 350 branches. Shareholders' profits would be substantial and immediate.

First Bank, on the other hand, proposed a more long-term approach. To produce $500 million in annual savings, 6,000 jobs would be eliminated. But since the two banks had overlapping operations only in Colorado, Montana, and Wyoming, few of their combined 1,500 branches would be closed, cuts would be thinly spread across twenty-one states, and many of the cuts could be accomplished through attrition.

The CEOs of First Interstate and First Bank began to crisscross the country, making their pitch to shareholders that although Wells Fargo was offering more per share, the First Bank merger would be the best opportunity for growth. They also pointed out that fewer jobs would be lost.

That turned out to be a tactical error. Although concern over jobs buoyed the plan's favor with California politicians—Los Angeles mayor Richard Riordan had denounced the proposed Wells Fargo merger as a "job killer" and a "disaster for lower-income communities" where branches would close—it angered stockholders. "First Interstate shareholders are not at all happy," analyst Thomas Brown noted at the time. "I have talked to four of the five largest holders, and the reaction ranges from modestly negative to violently negative. The shareholders are saying that they have no obligation to the state of California." Some shareholders went so far as

---

to sue First Interstate's directors, accusing them of a breach of fiduciary responsibility by spurning Wells Fargo's offer.

More than 80 percent of First Interstate's shares were held by fifty large financial institutions—mutual funds, pension funds, and investment partnerships such as Kohlberg, Kravis, Roberts & Co. The pressure on fund managers is to maximize investor returns—now. Their responsibility is, out of necessity, to the bottom line. First Interstate's institutional shareholders were not concerned by the prospect of layoffs; they wanted the bank's stock price boosted quickly. In fact, many managers favored the Wells deal precisely *because* of the proposed layoffs and branch closings. Those moves would guarantee profit, at least in the short term.

In hearings before the Federal Reserve, California politicians and community activists made their case against the Wells Fargo deal, arguing that poor neighborhoods in L.A. need more, not less, access to banking services, and that promises of techno-banking nodes in supermarkets were of little consolation to communities that didn't have supermarkets. They also pointed out that Wells Fargo had recently stopped offering home mortgages and was the only major regional bank that had not provided financial support to the Southern California Business Development Corporation.

Wall Street investors made their feelings known in their own, more convincing way. They signaled their enthusiasm for the Wells Fargo deal by trading up its stock dramatically. The increase in the price of Wells stock automatically increased the value of its offer to First Interstate's investors. By January 15 the gap between the two deals was almost $1.5 billion. Ten days later, First Interstate executives announced that Wells Fargo's merger offer had been accepted.

Layoffs were expected to begin in April. Terminated First Interstate employees will get four weeks' pay for every year of service. Thirty-nine First Interstate executives fared better; they will receive golden parachutes worth a total of about $29 million. The top five will receive at least $2 million each. Chairman Siart will get $4.57 million.

1. How would you assess the decision of First Interstate stockholders to accept the takeover offer from Wells Fargo? How would the stockholders actions be defended morally?
2. How would Lisa Newton's analysis of hostile takeovers apply to the First Interstate case?

CHAPTER 4

Working Conditions and Employee Rights

For those who do not have a job, getting one is often a priority. But whether an employer will hire you and how much it will pay are not the only dimensions of the relationship between employers and employees: The conditions under which one works will likely mean the difference between a job that is fulfilling and one that is dreadful. The specific nature of one's duties; the possibilities for promotion; the degree of freedom and privacy one has in the workplace; the safety of the job site; the degree to which the employer conducts itself ethically and legally—all of these factors can have a profound impact on the satisfaction one derives from work. And problems arising in any of these areas can be the source of difficult moral issues. This chapter explores moral issues that deal with a broad range of working conditions. As we will see, many of these issues turn on the tension between employer interests in controlling the conditions of employment, and employee rights that seek to limit that interest.

Why are employers interested in controlling the conditions of employment? The main reason is probably productivity, which is seen to be causally connected with profitability. Corporations will rightly argue that they have a legitimate interest in productivity. According to the canonical position of corporate social responsibility, introduced in chapter 1, the role of the employee is to help satisfy the interest in productivity. Employees can be viewed as "human resources" or "assets," and like other assets they must perform to the best of their abilities. Practices like drug and genetic testing can assist employers by allowing them to weed out potentially unproductive workers or those who might expose the corporation to liability. Increasingly, employers insist that they must be able to cut soaring insurance costs. Again, of course, defenders of the canonical position would maintain that any such testing must be legal. Ideally, notice of such testing should be a part of the job description every prospective employee sees before a job offer is made. If such notice appears in the job description or job contract, and the employee is aware of it and signs the contract, on the canonical position, there is no moral problem. Drug, genetic, and other possible forms of employee testing are just one more condition of employment, which the employee has voluntarily accepted. Still, even if notice is made, many critics of current corporate culture think that the interest in productivity too often overrides another legitimate right: that of employee privacy.

PRIVACY IN THE WORKPLACE

One familiar example of the tension just mentioned involves the value we all place upon privacy. Consider this case involving the retailer Kmart.[1] The female plaintiff, a checker, rang up purchases for a customer—Mrs. Golden—who subsequently complained that one of the items she purchased was on sale. Golden left the checkout lane with another clerk for a price check. Upon returning to the checkout area, Golden began accusing the plaintiff of taking money which the customer claimed to have left on the counter. The plaintiff denied having seen any money; but Golden was not satisfied and sought out the manager. After a short discussion, the manager walked up to the plaintiff, pulled out her jacket pockets, looked inside them, and found nothing. The register and immediate area were checked, whereupon the manager told the plaintiff to accompany a female assistant manager to the restroom for the purpose of a strip search. The manager asked if Golden wanted to watch. She replied, "You had better believe I do—it is my money." The plaintiff stripped to her underwear; no money was found. When asked if more clothing needed to be removed, the customer replied that this would not be necessary as she could see through the plaintiff's underwear anyway. (The money was later found in Golden's own purse.)

Such outrageous conduct is surely one extreme; though, as we shall see, invasions of worker privacy far more commonplace can still constitute significant intrusions and form the basis for important moral debate. In 1997, for example, public attention was focused on the degree of latitude employers should have over workplace romances. After U.S. Air Force Lt. Kelly Flinn resigned under threat of court-martial for seeking to conceal reported violations of Air Force bans on adultery and "fraternization," public debate shifted to the moral justification for scrutinizing a subordinate's love life. Civilian employers had in the past sought to restrict office romances on the grounds that such relationships could lead to favoritism and charges of discrimination, and that relationships turned sour could lead to allegations of harassment. Yet many employers no longer enforce such rules with regularity, citing both difficulty in drafting overall policies and an unwillingness to do the kind of snooping into the private affairs of workers that consistent enforcement of such policies

---

 Privacy, Genetic Identification, and the Military

In 1995 two marines refused to undergo a medical procedure mandated by the Defense Department's DNA Identification Program. Corporals Joseph Vlacovsky and John Mayfield indicated they would not comply with a request to extract blood and tissue samples used to obtain samples of their DNA. The two were charged with disobeying a direct order and face courts-martial for their stand. The DNA program represents an effort to collect and store as many as 18 million genetic specimens for up to seventy-five years. The government maintains that such a registry is necessary in order to ensure proper identification of battlefield casualties, noting that reliance on such traditional methods as medical and dental records is inadequate. Vlacovsky and Mayfield argued that genetic information, once on file, can be misused, for example, by future employers who elect not to hire persons with certain genetic traits in order to save on health insurance costs, or by military scientists performing genetic research on the sample without consent. A U.S. district court judge in Hawaii dismissed these complaints as hypothetical and held that the genetic sampling is a "minimal intrusion" justified by the "compelling interest" of the military in properly accounting for all service personnel.

would seem to require. Flinn, for example, had complained that Air Force officials had scrutinized her past sex life, even determining what method of birth control she used. What are the proper moral limits of an employer's authority to probe the after-hours aspects of an employee's life?

Some of the most hotly debated issues in worker privacy today revolve around the use (or abuse) of emerging technologies. Listening in on an employee's telephone line or reading her fax messages are obvious forms of snooping. But technologies are currently coming on line that give businesses far greater potential for information gathering about their workers. Computerized performance monitoring, for example, involves the systematic use of personal data systems to collect, store, and evaluate an employee's productive activity. Programs like these can be used to count the number of keystrokes on a worker's keyboard; track the time, destination, and length of telephone calls; or allow a supervisor to view directly from his own office an employee's computer screen. Computerized locator badges that allow employers to pinpoint a worker's whereabouts, and micro-lens cameras, concealed behind pinholes, are just some of the other monitoring methods employers have used. One recent study found that, of three hundred companies surveyed in 1993, more than 30 percent of the largest employers admitted to routine searches of employee computer files, voice mail, and e-mail.[2]

As legal scholars Terry Halbert and Elaine Ingulli observe, employers try to justify electronic surveillance in a number of ways:

> It allows them to discover whether training programs are effective. It is a form of quality control, enabling supervisors to better correct and improve employee performance. It measures efficiency. It enhances the completeness and fairness of employee evaluations. It can uncover employee disloyalty.

Employees contend that:

> electronic monitoring puts them in a dehumanizing pressure-cooker, where computers instead of people judge their output. They say the systems are overrated: Because computers measure quantity better than quality . . . employees who work fast might look better than those who work best. The "electronic sweatshop" . . . causes psychological stress and physical symptoms.[3]

Perhaps the most contentious area of high tech and privacy concerns the status of voice mail and e-mail communications. The law generally forbids listening in on phone calls or wiretapping phone lines. The Electronic Communications Privacy Act of 1986 prohibits "the interception of any wire, oral or electronic communication. "A significant exception to this prohibition, however, is made for messages conveyed by electronic communication devices or services provided by the employer "in the ordinary course of business." Just what such an exception covers is contested. Courts often try to solve difficult cases by asking whether an employee had a "reasonable expectation of privacy" with regard, for example, to restrooms, desks, or lockers. In a 1993 California case,[4] a supervisor reviewed an employee's e-mail messages, including messages of a personal and sexual nature. The court held that the employee had no reasonable expectation of privacy since she had signed a computer-user registration form stating that it was company policy that employees restrict use of office equipment to work-related matters. The employee argued that, by giving all employees passwords and instructing workers to safeguard them, the employer had created an expectation of privacy. In 1995 a supervisor working for McDonald's accessed the voice-mail messages of an employee. The messages had been sent to the employee by a woman with whom he was having an affair. The supervisor listened to the messages, forwarded them to upper-management personnel, and he even played them for the employee's wife. The employee argued that, even if McDonald's had the right to monitor company voice-mail accounts, the supervisor had no right to continue listening after it was apparent that the content was not business related. Who is right in these cases? And what does the potential for invading a worker's privacy in these ways tell us about the meaning and value of privacy?

INFORMATION GATHERING AND THE VALUE OF PRIVACY

Many of the cases that raise questions about an employee's right of privacy come about as a result of efforts by employers to collect, use, and in some cases disperse information about workers. Employers seek personnel information in a number of ways. Businesses seeking to hire workers must, of course, request some information of them. Application forms and job interviews are obvious sources of information about potential employees. But how much and what kind of information may an employer elicit? Existing law prohibits questions about one's religious beliefs, race, or age (except to determine if the applicant is under eighteen or over seventy). California prohibits asking applicants about arrests not leading to conviction and about marijuana convictions more than two years old; New Jersey forbids an employer from inquiring into draft or marital status. Should a company concerned to limit insurance costs be allowed to ask if an applicant is a smoker? Should interviewers be permitted to ask if a female applicant is considering having children?

Employers may also obtain information about current or prospective employees through a variety of tests, ranging from medical questionnaires and examinations to polygraphs, personality inventories, and "honesty" tests. In the past, inquiries into an applicant's health were routinely conducted as a way of ensuring that the candidate was free of diseases or other conditions that might impair his or her ability to do the job; increasingly, however, such diagnostic tests have been replaced by tests that are prognostic—tests designed to predict whether a person might be at risk of ill health in the future. The use of genetic screening to identify traits linked to heritable diseases illustrates one such prognostic tool, which is of natural interest to companies seeking to minimize their insurance costs and hire workers with the greatest potential longevity and productivity. Polygraph (or

---

✑ Privacy and Hair Samples

A case filed in Boston in November 1996 concerns a method of genetic sampling to which employers are increasingly turning. Two employees of Global Access Telecommunications, a high-tech firm, were fired when they refused to provide samples of their hair to their employer. Global required workers to provide the strands of hair for what it called "medical research" as well as for drug testing. Traces of drugs can be detected in human hair for up to 90 days after the substances were ingested; by contrast, more-common urine testing is typically effective for only three or four days. The two workers, who did provide urine specimens, refused to comply with the request for hair samples, stating that the hair could also be used to test for genetic conditions or predispositions, which might later become the basis for adverse decisions, for example, the denial of insurance benefits. The case was scheduled for trial in early 1997.

"lie-detector") machines were widely used in the past on the theory that they could accurately measure a worker's veracity. Some employers believed that the devices could help assess an applicant's overall "character"; others sought specifically to determine whether the applicant had, for example, used drugs. The questionable reliability of such devices, however, coupled with the demeaning and distrustful nature of the test and frequent cases of abuse, resulted in legislation dramatically curtailing polygraph use. The federal Employee Polygraph Protection Act of 1988 bans nearly all preemployment use of polygraphs, and permits testing of current employees only where there is a "reasonable suspicion" that a worker may have been involved in a specific workplace incident (for example, theft of company property).

For most businesses, polygraphs have given way to a variety of written tests. So-called honesty or integrity tests typically consist of questions gauged to ascertain an applicant's honesty through indirect questioning. Such a test might, for example, ask an applicant to respond yes or no to such questions as: "Have you ever told a lie in your life?" or "Have you ever stolen anything in your life?" A job candidate yearning to land a job may well respond in the negative to these queries—but this could well be the "wrong" answer, according to the employer. Since most people have, at some point in their lives, failed to be fully truthful, the employer assumes, an applicant who answers "no" is not being honest. The use of broad-gauged personality inventories is even more common. One such test, given by the retailer Target, is described in Case Scenario 1 at the end of this chapter.

Many of us are made uncomfortable by the prospect of our employer acquiring the quantity and kind of information about us detailed here. But why is that? Why do we value privacy? Some philosophers have answered this question by insisting that each of us typically needs to exercise a certain degree of control over facts about ourselves that others come to know. What makes personality inventories and various forms of "cyber snooping" by employers threatening to many is the fear that use of these information-gathering tools will compromise our ability to decide how much people will know about us and whom those people will be. And this ability is crucial to structuring one's social relationships. I don't

---

✍ **Drug-Testing Methods and Privacy**

In a recent decision, a federal court in Delaware held that it did not violate the constitutional rights of city firefighters in requiring that they provide urine samples in the presence of a monitor for random drug testing. Beverly Wilcher and other firefighters working for the city of Wilmington sued their employer, challenging the city's procedure whereby the provision of urine samples is directly supervised by a monitor. Wilcher and her colleagues insisted that being forced to urinate in front of a stranger was an undue intrusion into their privacy and that less invasive means of collecting a urine sample are possible. The city relied upon prior rulings upholding drug testing in cases of police officers and prison guards, nurses, railway workers, and persons employed at nuclear facilities. In cases such as these, where workers are responsible for handling emergency situations or operating potentially dangerous machinery or hazardous materials, the interest in health and safety takes priority over concerns of privacy. The district court agreed with the city, observing that firefighters have a reduced expectation of privacy since they work in such a heavily regulated industry. The use of the monitor, the court reasoned, was necessary to ensure integrity of the urine samples and was not constitutionally impermissible.

Wilcher v. City of Wilmington.

want just anyone to know my "private" thoughts or beliefs or to overhear a conversation between me and my therapist. I might, of course, choose to let certain people know about such things, but it is just that choice that allows me to form special bonds of friendship or intimacy with selected people. Other philosophers might argue that the world would be a worse place to live if workers couldn't feel free to confide in colleagues or friends for fear that the information conveyed would find its way into the company's master database.

DRUG TESTING

One of the most controversial of recent employment practices believed to have a significant impact on employee privacy is the use of testing for drug and substance use. Businesses have several important incentives to acquire information concerning drug use. Federal law currently places upon all employers doing business with the government an obligation to make employees aware of the dangers of workplace drug use and to penalize violations; and various categories of federal and state workers have been required to submit to mandatory testing. Employers are understandably concerned about maintaining a safe workplace and enhancing the productivity of their employees. And, as noted in chapter 3, employers can now be held liable for negligence in hiring a worker who endangers co-workers or the public. Substance abusers can often fall into that category. For employers who test for drug use, several types of testing are possible. Preemployment drug testing seeks to identify substance abusers at the outset, before they are hired. Testing can also be conducted subsequent to hiring: "post-accident" testing involves screening employees as part of an overall investigation of an accident or similar incident (as in, for example, screening of railway workers after a train derailment); "reasonable suspicion" testing limits testing to those workers for whom there is well-founded evidence of actual drug use; random drug testing, by contrast, is performed on all employees regardless of individualized suspicion. Which, if any, of these forms of drug testing ought to be allowed is a debated moral and legal question.

Courts have generally upheld drug-testing requirements predicated upon ensuring the health and safety of workers and the public. Thus testing is frequently held to be permissible for those who handle emergency situations (police officers, firefighters, nurses) or who operate potentially dangerous equipment (railway engineers, pilots) or hazardous materials (operators of nuclear power plants). How far should the category of those legitimately tested be extended? In 1996, for example, the California Supreme Court held that state and local governments could require drug and alcohol testing for all job applicants. Because employers have not had a previous opportunity to observe a new applicant in an everyday working situation, the Court reasoned, employers have a legitimate interest in testing at the hiring stage, regardless of the nature of the position for which the candidate has applied. As the readings in this chapter show, the questions raised by workplace drug testing cannot be settled until we take a careful look at the interests of employers in using the information testing provides, and the rights of employees in terms of access and use of such information. The readings in this chapter begin that examination.

HEALTH AND SAFETY

It is common knowledge that many workers face various hazards on the job, including risks to their own health and safety. These risks can come in the form of accident or injury— anything from broken limbs to ear damage to a decrease in sperm count. Moreover, certain types of work have given rise to so-called occupational diseases: lung disorders linked to

Secrecy and Worker Safety

The experience of aerospace workers at Lockheed and at Boeing in the late 1980s and early 1990s dramatized a difficult problem: how to balance the rights of workers to health and safety with the need for national security. Workers assigned to the assembly of the stealth bomber began to complain of an unusual increase in a variety of health problems: rashes, cramps, bloody urine, open sores, memory loss, and fainting spells. Many of those afflicted alleged that their problems began when they started working with the chemicals used to create the composite plastics out of which the "skin" of the plane was made. Since the plastic-carbon composites, representing the latest in high-tech design, were new, little was known of the long-term effects of exposure to them. Employees of the companies involved in assembling parts of the stealth were told by industrial insurance carriers that they did not have serious problems; and though they were not prohibited from talking with their own personal physicians about chemical exposure at the work site, workers in many cases knew the substances only by code names that would be meaningless to ordinary health-care practitioners. Though supporters of the workers alleged that a number of deaths were ultimately attributable to toxic chemicals, the aerospace industry continued to dismiss such claims. The Clinton administration eventually cut funding for the program.

Source: *National Law Journal* 3/6/89: 45–47.

inhalation of cotton or coal dust or asbestos fibers; neurological disorders brought on by exposure to chemical solvents and heavy metals. Emphasis upon these familiar examples may, however, give the false impression that worker health and safety is primarily a "blue collar" problem, confined to members of labor unions and those working in service industries. The reality is that even those working in upscale office buildings downtown may face a variety of workplace hazards: eye damage from video display terminals, nerve damage in the wrist due to excessive time at a keyboard, even "indoor pollution" from such sources as secondhand cigarette smoke and improperly filtered air-conditioning systems.

Reflection on the fact that the health and safety of workers can be threatened in these ways raises many questions: What are the responsibilities of employers for worker health and safety? How much should an employer be obligated to do in alleviating the risks of workplace accident or injury? What factors may it permissibly consider in deciding these questions? And what rights do employees have? Do workers have a right to a safe workplace? What does that mean? To what level of safety do workers have a right? And should the government enforce that right? Suppose a worker is willing to accept the risk associated with a dangerous job. Should she have a right to accept that risk, even if the cumulative effect of the hazard in question is not one that society is prepared to tolerate? Should jobs with unreasonable risks continue to be available if the only alternative is unemployment? Should workers have a right to refuse hazardous work assignments? How can society effectively make the workplace safer?

OSHA

One of the earliest forms of comprehensive protection for the safety and health of American workers came in the form of so-called worker's compensation laws. Prior to their enactment, many employees injured or ill as a result of a job were unable to obtain compensation. The law at that time afforded employers many protections: the "contributory negligence" doc-

---

⌘   **OSHA, the FDA, and Smoking Bans**

In April 1994 OSHA announced a proposed workplace safety rule, prompted by concerns over the risk of secondhand cigarette smoke, that would ban smoking at more than 6 million job sites across the country. Only rooms ventilated directly to the outdoors would be exempt from the proposed regulation. Many states, including California and Washington, already banned workplace smoking. The proposed OSHA rule ran into stiff industry opposition and, as of late 1996, was still languishing due to inaction by the Clinton administration. While OSHA's proposal stalled, recent rules issued by the FDA concerning the marketing of tobacco products to children gained broad support. The FDA rule would prohibit tobacco-brand sponsorship of sporting events, ban billboards within a thousand feet of schools, and limit print advertising of tobacco products to black-and-white text.

---

trine held that employers had no responsibility to employees injured through the conduct of co-workers; and the "assumption of risk" rule was frequently invoked to argue that workers had agreed to live with any injury or illness that might befall them as a result of their job. Worker's compensation laws, enacted in the early part of this century, required workers to forfeit most of their rights to sue employers in court; in exchange workers received a much greater chance of receiving some compensation, usually in the form of modest medical benefits, payments for disability or disfigurement, and costs for hospitalization and for treatment of some occupational diseases. For all of their virtues, worker's compensation schemes did have weaknesses, not the least of which was that they did nothing directly to prevent work-related injuries or make the factory or plant a safer place to work. Designed to address just these kinds of concerns, Congress in 1970 passed the Occupational Health and Safety Act (OSHA).

Under OSHA, employers must keep their places of employment free of recognized hazards likely to cause injury to workers, and they must comply with promulgated standards designed, for example, to regulate exposure to dangerous substances or mandate safety precautions that must be taken at the work site. Employers also have a duty to ensure the compliance of their employees with applicable OSHA standards and rules, though they are not liable for injuries arising out of "unpreventable employee misconduct." OSHA affords workers numerous rights. Workers may petition for the adoption of safety standards, file complaints against their employers, and request OSHA inspections. Workers are protected from discharge or discriminatory treatment in retaliation for exercising their rights under the act. Perhaps most important, OSHA grants employees the right to know about hazards at the workplace and the right to refuse particular assignments based on that knowledge. Employees exposed to harmful physical agents have the right to certain forms of risk information. Records of exposure levels for those working with toxic substances, for example, must be open to the employee. Employees also have the right to refuse to perform certain forms of dangerous work. A hazardous-work refusal must be based on a good faith belief, supported by reasonable evidence, that the assignment would pose a serious risk of injury or death.

ECONOMICS AND THE VALUE OF HEALTH

Much of the discussion of workplace health and safety is framed in terms of the employee's rights. Doing so emphasizes the importance of protecting the employee's interests; for when we say that something is my "right," we often want to underscore that my interests must take priority over other considerations. Being able to speak freely, for example, is a right because the interest we all have in being able to express our own views as autonomous citizens is more important than the concerns of others that they might hear something they don't like. But questions of health and safety in the workplace can also be discussed in terms other than that of rights—they can, for example, be couched in terms of economic costs. A worker in a textile plant may claim that she has a right to breathe air free of cotton dust; the textile company operating the plant might want to determine the least amount of money it can spend to attain a certain level of safety in the plant—a given amount in the reduction of cotton dust in the air. Employers often seek to use cost/benefit analysis to identify the level of safety that can affordably be achieved.

Whether we look at workplace safety as a right or as a good to be purchased at a certain cost may in turn depend upon how we understand the value and importance of health. Philosophers often distinguish between two ways in which something can be said to have value. Many things have what has been called *instrumental value*. To say that something has instrumental value is to say that it is valuable just insofar as it can be used for some purpose; it is valuable, in other words, because it can get you something else that you want. The computer on which this book was written has instrumental value, since it can be used for a variety of office tasks; the TV in the living room has instrumental value because it can be used to provide (albeit poor quality) entertainment. The dollar bill in your purse or wallet also has instrumental value; in and of itself, the dollar bill is a nearly worthless piece of paper—it is useful only because you can use it as a form of exchange, getting something else you want. Contrasted with instrumental value is *intrinsic value*. To say that something has intrinsic value means that it is important and worthwhile just for what it is, not because it can get you something further. Examples of things with intrinsic value are, as you might guess, harder to find. Into that category have been put such things as love, friendship, and the appreciation of beauty. Some philosophers have claimed that the life of a person is something that has intrinsic value: I am valuable not just because I can be used by others—my life has value apart from any ways in which others might try to use or exploit me.

Having said all of this, what is the value of health? On the face of it, being healthy would seem to share in both of the forms of value just explained. Health is certainly an important instrumental value—for without health it is difficult to enjoy much of anything in life. Yet sometimes people will say that they simply like being healthy—they prize it just for itself. It is important to see that this is not merely a semantic dispute; for depending upon which conception of health one adopts, one might be more or less inclined to accept trade-offs between health and other things. Someone who viewed health as an instrumental good, for instance, might be inclined to accept a slightly diminished prospect of good health in order to obtain some other benefit—hazard pay or a shorter work week, for example. An employer with this view might realize that the cost of ensuring a maximally safe working environment for those in its employ would cut too deeply into its profits and thus might bargain with its employees concerning wages and benefits from that standpoint. Those who regard health as of intrinsic importance, however, may be less willing to accept such trade-offs, insisting that all feasible means of protecting workers on the job must be adopted regardless of cost.

EMPLOYEE OBLIGATIONS

What do you owe your employer? The question may sound strange. Most people assume (if they think about it at all) that they owe nothing to their employer except to show up to work on time and do what they are paid to do. Although this common assumption is not incorrect, things are somewhat more complicated. For example, the law has traditionally taken the position that employees have a duty of confidentiality with regard to their employers. Often workers can come to possess information about trade secrets—information concerning details of a manufacturing process, for example—which, if disclosed, could seriously hamper the company's ability to compete in the marketplace. What other duties might an employee have? Our society has customarily assumed that workers have, in addition to obligations of confidentiality, duties of obedience and loyalty. To say that working people have such duties is, however, to invite questions: To whom must I be loyal? The president or CEO of the company for which I work? The corporation itself? The shareholders? And what does loyalty mean in this context, anyway? Surely not that I do whatever my employer asks: I don't, for example, have a duty to do something that would be obviously illegal. What are the limits of my responsibility?

The classical view of business social responsibility, as espoused by such figures as economist Milton Friedman, implies that managers have a moral duty of loyalty and obedience to the owners of the firms that employ them, that is, the shareholders. This relationship has been captured in a traditional model of corporate moral responsibility called the *agent/principal* model, as discussed in chapter 1. Derived from English common law and the law of torts, the model was first posited to answer questions concerning liability of masters for damages caused by servants. In a contemporary context, the model implies that principals have a right to control (or monitor) the activities of a person who renders services for them, and that agents have reciprocal obligations of loyalty and obedience to the principals for whom they work. In contemporary discussions the moral implications of this neoclassical model are gone: Most of us no longer assume the worst about human behavior, namely, that managers and shareholders (agents and principals) are motivated only by self-interest. This leads to the interesting problem of how to motivate the essentially self-interested to act in a manner that is not self-interested; in other words, how to motivate a manager to act in the interests of the firm when those interests are not consistent with her own self-interests. Both the stick (the law) and the carrot (generous compensation packages) are usable here. But, as Ronald Duska points out in a provocative essay, this leads to a double standard: The owners of a firm are interested only in maximizing profit, yet they require of their agents (management) selflessness and loyalty on their behalf. In order to pursue this end, they engage management's self-interest with either the threat of legal sanctions or by generous compensation. In effect, the principal engages management's self-interest in order not to act self-interestedly.

WHISTLEBLOWING AND LOYALTY

One of the most obvious ways in which an employee's duty of loyalty can be challenged is through being confronted by conduct on the part of his or her employer that is illegal or unethical. What should a worker do under such circumstances? Is "blowing the whistle" on one's employer—disclosing practices that one considers illegal, unjust, or harmful to the public—ever morally justified? If so, under what circumstances?

Those who have studied whistleblowing often distinguish between several different forms that such an activity might take. Whistleblowing can be *internal* if the questionable practice is disclosed only to those within the employee's organization. This happened in the tragic case of the *Challenger* space shuttle, for example, when engineers for Morton Thiokol, the company who built the solid-rocket boosters that failed, stressed to their supervisors, prior to launch, the seriousness of their concerns about launching the shuttle in low temperatures. *External* whistleblowing, by contrast, occurs when the employee goes outside the company with the information he or she has acquired, as would happen, for instance, when an employee notifies a newspaper reporter of wrongdoing at a plant. Whistleblowing can also be either *open* or *anonymous,* depending upon whether the worker openly identifies herself or chooses to communicate her concerns in a way that shields her identity. Some of the difficult questions regarding whistleblowing can be understood in light of these concepts. For example, is it ever permissible for a worker to go public with potentially damaging information about his employer without first having at least attempted to pursue internal channels of complaint or protest? And how serious must the wrongdoing be before any kind of whistleblowing is appropriate? How much evidence of wrongdoing must a potential whistleblower have? And, finally, what about the duty of loyalty to one's employer? How is that to be factored into the situation? At least some of these hard questions are taken up in the readings for this chapter.

✒ The Costs of Whistleblowing

One of the most recent and highly publicized cases of whistleblowing dramatically illustrates the costs whistleblowers face in bringing the truth to light. In January 1988 Merrell Williams was hired by the Louisville, Kentucky, law firm of Wyatt, Tarrant & Combs to work on what turned out to be a document-coding project for the Brown & Williamson tobacco company (B&W). Williams, twice divorced and in and out of jobs for nearly two decades, had himself smoked as a young man and later admitted that he knew little if anything about lawsuits brought against the tobacco makers by consumers. Williams was assigned to sift through a huge collection of internal company records—memos and research studies sought by plaintiffs in lawsuits—and code them as to their sensitivity. Williams became increasingly incensed at what he saw: documents from as early as 1957, admitting that the company knew its product caused cancer; the now-famous 1963 memo stating that the industry was "in the business of selling nicotine, an addictive drug"; he even found plans to funnel all research data to company lawyers so the attorney/client privilege could be invoked to keep the results from coming out. Williams began stealing the documents, copying, and then returning them. Fearful of retaliation, Williams shipped boxes of the papers to friends in Florida. By 1990 he began seeking out avenues to make the documents public, but the task was difficult. One freelance reporter for the *Washington Post* refused to look at the papers, afraid he would become embroiled in a lawsuit. Williams eventually connected with anti-tobacco lawyers in Mississippi, who funneled the documents to a congressional subcommittee investigating nicotine and addiction. Though finally public, the purloined documents gave little consolation to Williams. The stress of four years' deception left his third marriage in financial and emotional trouble: It brought on a heart attack and a bypass operation, and one of his daughters was told that a hit man was after her dad. Attorneys helped Williams purchase a home in Florida, but his third wife refused to move and divorced him. His daughters also refused to stay with him. By 1996 Williams was described as depressed and lonely, and was now facing a lawsuit filed by B&W, alleging he had stolen confidential information and sold it for a house. Williams was recently quoted: "There's a certain point in life when you realize you're a total failure. I mean, in my opinion, I'm a total failure."

SOURCE: *Los Angeles Times* 6/23/96: D1.

THE READINGS

The reading selections for this chapter begin with two cases. The first case study deals with a difficult dilemma: how to balance concerns for worker safety in an area where clear standards do not yet exist, and where failure to move quickly on producing a new product may jeopardize a worker's future. The second case study, taken from a federal court opinion handed down in 1992, explores some of the basic arguments concerning monitoring of employee phone conversations.

The readings then turn to explore two dimensions of employee privacy: drug testing and genetic screening. Joseph DesJardins and Ronald Duska consider two arguments in support of drug testing in the workplace: that the employer needs to know if its workers are abusing drugs, as such abuse can affect job performance; and that testing is necessary for the employer to comply with its duty to prevent harm to others. DesJardins and Duska attack both of these arguments, insisting that information about drug use is either unnecessary for or irrelevant to job performance issues, and that the duty to prevent harm does not license much of the testing currently conducted. In their view drug testing is permissible in only a few, restricted contexts.

Joseph Kupfer discusses the recent technology of genetic screening and the uses to which it can be put in employment. Kupfer is critical of genetic testing for a variety of reasons. To begin with, our ability to directly detect genes responsible for heritable disorders is limited. Genetic tests often pick out only genetic "markers," the presence of which does not ensure the existence of the gene for the defect itself. Additionally, more than one gene can be a causal factor in the manifestation of a disorder, and nongenetic factors can contribute as well. Genetic screening is especially suspect in the workplace, Kupfer argues, due to the relative powerlessness of workers, both over their genes and over their employers. Because such screening often reveals mere susceptibility to disease, it is not justifiable to base potentially life-changing employment decisions upon them.

The readings turn next to the issue of health and safety. Tibor Machan takes up the general issue of the right to worker safety. While all people have certain basic rights, Machan maintains, there are no rights workers have to special benefits, such as those granted by OSHA. Employers have property rights in their places of business, and thus the right to set terms and working conditions as they see fit; equally, Machan insists, workers have the freedom to accept such working conditions or not to do so. Machan defends this view and argues that much of the paternalistic agenda of those who support special protections and rights for workers is unfounded and unnecessary. We already possess rights not to be defrauded or killed, Machan observes, so no special rights are needed.

Norman Daniels takes up the tension between the competing demands of safety and economics. Daniels's concern is illustrated by OSHA's efforts to clean up the textile industry. Byssinosis, or "brown lung disease," affected workers in the textile industry for decades, where they were exposed to air filled with microscopic cotton fibers. Many were permanently disabled or died from the disease. In an effort to regulate exposure to toxic substances in the workplace, OSHA requires that a standard be set that "most adequately assures, to the extent feasible, on the basis of the best available evidence" that no employee will suffer impairment of health. In a decision upheld in court, OSHA imposed a very stringent standard upon the textile industry in an effort to crack down on brown lung. The agency demanded that the industry do everything technologically possible to alleviate the problems of the dust. This strong feasibility criterion, as he calls it, is the subject of Daniels's essay.

Is such a criterion justifiable? The textile industry argued that "feasible" means "economically feasible" under prevailing market conditions, and suggested that workers might accept the added risk of disabling disease in exchange for better pay or other benefits.

Daniels considers a central argument in support of OSHA's position on feasibility: Workers must be protected to the greatest degree possible where they might be asked to trade their health for hazard pay; and this is because placing workers in such a position and asking them to weigh their own health against a need for money is to coerce them unfairly. Daniels carefully analyzes the nature of coercion in such contexts in order to show that workers are better protected when their employers are expected to live up to strong standards like those set by OSHA.

The final set of readings for this chapter addresses the issue of whistleblowing. Ronald Duska argues that acts of whistleblowing are morally permissible, since the relationships in a commercial enterprise are not the kinds of relationships to which the concept of loyalty even applies. The relationship of an agent to a principal in a commercial venture is self-interested, and this leaves no room for loyalty. Duska examines the conditions for the presence of loyalty in human interactions and finds that they are characterized by properties of mutual enrichment and reciprocity—properties not present in the typical employment setting. But it is one thing to say that whistleblowing is morally permissible and another to say that it is morally obligatory. Whistleblowing involves grave costs. Most whistleblowers in the private sector are unprotected by whistleblowing laws. The price of their actions may entail severe financial and psychological hardships on themselves and their families. Given these realities, whistleblowing clearly ought to be undertaken only in the most serious of situations. Duska ends his essay with some suggestions regarding when whistleblowing might be morally obligatory.

The article by Daryl Koehn is based on events surrounding Mark Whitacre's act of whistleblowing on the Archer Daniels Midland Corporation. Koehn argues that whistleblowing undermines personal, corporate, and public trust by creating the impression that corruption is widespread; and she points to the many dangers connected with a central assumption behind the argument of whistleblowers: namely, that their actions are justified because they serve the greater good of the public interest. Koehn argues that often whistleblowers are an integral part of the "corporate culture on which they blow the whistle"; yet by assigning responsibility to the corporation, whistleblowers tend to distance themselves from the alleged corruption upon which they report.

NOTES

1. *Bodewid v. Kmart, Inc.,* 635 p.@d 657 (1981).
2. Charles Pillar, "Bosses With X-Ray Eyes," *MacWorld* (July 1993).
3. Terry Halbert and Elaine Ingulli, *Law and Ethics in the Business Environment,* 2d ed. (Minneapolis: West Publishing, 1996), 76.
4. *Bourke v. Nissan Motor Corp.* (unpublished).

CASE STUDY   The Letter of the Law

Doug Wallace

Shifting her weight off of her tired left foot, Celest Benedeto squinted down the wet pavement in front of her company's headquarters, searching for her ride home. The rain had stopped, leaving

Business Ethics, Mar./Apr. 1995. Reprinted with permission from Business Ethics Magazine, 52 S. 10th St. #110, Minneapolis, MN 55403, (612) 962-4700.

behind a faint fragrance of an early spring warmed by a low-slung sun peering through clouds. She recognized the blue Plymouth Voyager just as it sent a puddle of water spraying diamonds in all directions. It pulled up; she climbed aboard. No one pressed her for conversation, which was just as well: She wanted time to close her eyes and think.

Celest was a chemical engineer at Salinsten Inc., a major West Coast producer of adhesives and other chemically based products. Her lab researched, developed, and tested new products for several of the company's business units. Restructuring had slashed the jobs of several of her colleagues and underlings, and assignments had piled up. One had Celest especially concerned.

It came from Ned Olson, director of a troubled wood products business unit that came in $3 million, or 10 percent, behind its revenue goal last year. In December, he was told this year's numbers would have to come in $5 million above last year's—a directive that followed the loss of two major accounts worth more than $1 million each.

Celest could see his morale sinking and his anger rising. Ned was seeking out those to blame, and on the top of his list was the research and development laboratory. Since Celest was in the lab section that serviced his unit, she felt the heat of his indignation.

The last time he had checked on the testing of a critical product, he couldn't get agreement on a completion date. Celest tried to get Ned to understand the demands that her unit was under, but he was in no mood to listen. "My competitors are eating me alive. They already have similar advanced products on the market. Most of our customers would prefer to buy it from us because of our history of good technical service and high customer commitment. But they can't wait forever. I need this product in four months. And to sweeten the pot, I've decided to provide you a bonus of $3,000, and each of your chemists a bonus of $2,000, if you finish testing it by May."

Celest knew making that goal would improve her odds of being promoted to technical director. It also would give her staff a solid chance at winning thousands of dollars in bonuses. But she also knew there were serious faults with this new adhesive—stability and toxicity. If not applied shortly after mixing, the nearly identical product made by competitors became unusable. And worse, workers were getting sick, some sensitized, because of isocyanate given off by the product. But customers were still demanding the product because its use meant faster production and lower costs.

Celest and her crew went at it, working evenings and weekends. The product was finally finished and tested, performing with far better stability than the competitor's version. There was, however, still a toxicity issue with the product—3 percent free isocyanate, the maximum amount allowed by the Occupational Safety and Health Administration (OSHA). She told Ned her concern and recommended that the lab do more work to reduce the level of free isocyanate before marketing the product.

Although Salinsten would be meeting the letter of OSHA's rules, Celest strongly suspected that because the technology was relatively new, OSHA had not developed sufficient data on safe limits of free isocyanate. Workers were still getting sick, and no one knew whether there could be long-term health effects.

Then Ned dropped his bomb shell. "I've already accepted a huge order, which must be shipped within four weeks to an important customer. As long as we meet OSHA requirements, just as our competitors have, I'm not waiting. We're not violating any laws." Celest pleaded with him to reconsider, reminding him of the importance of the company's historical commitment to safety in all products, but Ned was past the point of listening.

Sitting in the back of the van, Celest opened her eyes long enough to glance at an accident on the opposite side of the freeway. She closed them again, this time tight, and silently repeated the mantra, "What should I do?"

Katherine Dickinson
Clinical Research Manager,
UltraCision Inc.,
Smithfield, Rhode Island

First off, Celest should let Ned know what her department could produce realistically and safely, indicating a firm schedule. This would allow him to manage his customers' expectations and handle them throughout the waiting period.

If Celest's concerns about the product's safety are founded, she should discuss a plan with her supervisor to allocate personnel to fulfill the current order—provided a percent of their time is devoted to finding a way to make a safer product. This would win greater market share in the long run.

It's important that she fully communicates her department's goals and priorities. If projects have to be postponed, then marketing and administration should support her efforts to reprioritize her work load. They have to realize that some things are just not going to get done. But it is her responsibility to communicate that, and to make sure that priorities are agreed upon.

Celest should maintain test records to document that the free isocyanate remains within OSHA limits, in case any health hazard does result and the company needs to defend itself. In addition, she could determine whether there are other ways of handling the product to minimize worker exposure. She could recommend something like hood ventilation or increased air flow in areas it is used. And she could work with her company's regulatory and marketing departments to expedite such things, and to educate customers on safe handling techniques.

If she doesn't receive support from her superiors, she's up against a pretty hard decision. She has to live with herself. She has to document that she's done everything that she could to make sure everything is handled as properly as possible. And she needs to document conversations and communications with other members of her company.

Earl Hess
Chairman,
Lancaster Laboratories,
Lancaster, Pennsylvania

This falls into what Rush Kidder calls one of his right-right dilemmas, truth versus loyalty. Celest needs to be concerned about the truth of this situation—there is still a safety problem—but she has loyalty to an internal client who is really bearing down on her. Using Kidder's approach, we could apply three decision-making guidelines. The rule-based approach would say there is a safety problem, and as a rule, you don't put human life at risk for economic advantage. The consequentialist viewpoint—the greatest good for the greatest number—again, would say a large number of workers would possibly be harmed by this product for the good of a few within the company. The care-based orientation, which can be summarized with the question, "How would you want to be treated if the roles were reversed," is more complicated. Applied here, it comes down to how you would want to be treated. If you were Celest's associate, you would want her to look the other way and let you go ahead with the product. But if you were an ultimate user of the product, you would want additional research done.

Celest hasn't been given the tools that would help her reduced staff become more productive. A similar thing could be said for Ned, who basically is caught in a catch-22; he is working his tail off and in return, he's receiving higher and higher goals. Where does top management bear responsibility for creating these situations?

Even though the company is staying within OSHA limits, people could still get sick when using its product. The human health problem here demands the truth and should override economic considerations.

I would advise Celest to call Ned on his decision to go ahead with manufacturing. She could say to Ned, "You've done this without my approval, but I, as the chemist, am knowledgeable about the health effects of this thing, and I have to go on record with you and with your superiors. I can't sign off on this product. I have one of your two problems licked, but you haven't allowed me to complete work on the second one." If he doesn't back down, she should write a very strong letter to him and send a copy to his supervisor. Hopefully, someone up the line would say, "We can't allow our reputation to suffer from this one product; we have to go back and do more work."

Doug Wallace
Corporate Ethics Consultant,
Minneapolis, Minnesota

Guest commentator Earl Hess' observations about this case are unusual. He reverse-engineered the problem, looking for what I and my colleagues refer to as "the drivers." And as Mr. Hess follows the trail in this case to its origins, he finds the company's senior management wanting.

Regardless of whether the executives of Salinsten are aware of the consequences from the environment they have created, in the end they are responsible for the ethical dilemmas in which they put the Neds and Celests of the company. Either they are held accountable for reaching sales goals they have not determined for themselves (Ned), or they are expected to do more with fewer resources without receiving training needed to streamline inefficient processes (Celest). In both cases, employees are left holding the bag, and it's one that doesn't smell very good.

There are fortunately some executives who go to the root of ethical issues that surface when changes are made in the face of increasing competition. And they don't begin with a code of ethics or educational program. Instead, they almost always start with a systems perspective—a view that all parts and processes in an organization are interconnected, and that changes in one part have an impact on all other areas. For example, if higher ethical standards are promulgated, while at the same time greater financial performance is expected, when push comes to shove, you can count on the ethical standards getting the short end of the stick. That is, unless a company's executive committee takes a hard look at aligning the company's reward system with the higher ethical standards that it wants employees to honor. In making such a change, everything must be reviewed, from decision making to promotion criteria.

If those changes are not taken, despite the best published and audited codes of ethnics, the company will inevitably be plagued with problems it never intended, and more employees will become as frustrated as Celest and Ned.

WHAT ACTUALLY HAPPENED?

Celest went to her boss and explained her safety concerns. Her manager was sympathetic, but he agreed with Ned's view, that as long as the company was abiding by the strict language of the regulations, personal concerns should be set aside. Celest found that trying to separate her personal values from business responsibilities was painful. She continued to believe that separating such values from corporate responsibility causes more problems than it solves.

CASE STUDY   *Deal v. Spears*

Eighth Circuit Court of Appeals
980 F.2d 1153 (1992)

Bowman, Circuit Judge.

Newell and Juanita Spears have owned and operated the White Oak Package Store near Camden, Arkansas, for about twenty years. The Spearses live in a mobile home adjacent to the store. The telephone in the store has an extension in the home, and is the only phone line into either location. The same phone line thus is used for both the residential and the business phones.

Sibbie Deal was an employee at the store from December 1988 until she was fired in August 1990. The store was burglarized in April 1990 and approximately $16,000 was stolen. The Spearses believed that it was an inside job and suspected that Deal was involved. Hoping to catch the suspect in an unguarded admission, Newell Spears purchased and installed a recording device on the extension phone in the mobile home. When turned on, the machine would automatically record all conversations made or received on either phone, with no indication to the parties using the phone that their conversation was being recorded. Before purchasing the recorder, Newell Spears told a sheriff's department investigator that he was considering this surreptitious monitoring and the investigator told Spears that he did not "see anything wrong with that."

Calls were taped from June 27, 1990, through August 13, 1990. During that period, Sibbie Deal, who was married to Mike Deal at the time, was having an extramarital affair with Calvin Lucas, then married to Pam Lucas. Deal and Lucas spoke on the telephone at the store frequently and for long periods of time while Deal was at work. (Lucas was on 100% disability so he was at home all day.) . . . [T]he trial court concluded that much of the conversation between the two was "sexually provocative." Deal also made or received numerous other personal telephone calls during her workday. Even before Newell Spears purchased the recorder, Deal was asked by her employers to cut down on her use of the phone for personal calls, and the Spearses told her they might resort to monitoring calls or installing a pay phone in order to curtail the abuse.

Newell Spears listened to virtually all twenty-two hours of the tapes he recorded, regardless of the nature of the calls or the content of the conversations, and Juanita Spears listened to some of them. Although there was nothing in the record to indicate that they learned anything about the burglary, they did learn, among other things, that Deal sold Lucas a keg of beer at cost, in violation of store policy. On August 13, 1990, when Deal came in to work the evening shift, Newell Spears played a few seconds of the incriminating tape for Deal and then fired her. . . .

Mike Deal testified that Juanita Spears told him about the tapes, and that she divulged the general nature of the tapes to him. Pam Lucas testified that Juanita Spears intimated the contents of the tapes to her but only after Pam asked about them, and she also testified that Juanita told her to tell Sibbie to drop a worker's compensation claim she had made against the store or "things could get ugly." Pam Lucas also testified that Juanita Spears "never told me what was on the tapes." Juanita testified that she discussed the tapes and the nature of them, but only in general terms.

Under the relevant provisions of the [Omnibus Crime Control and Safe Streets Act], a federal civil cause of action arises when a person intentionally intercepts a wire or electronic communication or intentionally discloses the contents of the interception. . . .

The Spearses first claim they are exempt from civil liability because Sibbie Deal consented to the interception of calls that she made from and received at the store. Under the statute, it is not unlawful "to intercept a wire, oral, or electronic communication . . . where one of the parties to the communication has given prior consent to such interception . . ." The Spearses contend that Deal's consent may be implied because Newell Spears had mentioned that he might be forced to monitor calls or restrict telephone privileges if abuse of the store's telephone for personal calls continued. They further argue that the extension in their home gave actual notice to Deal that her calls could be overhead, and that this notice resulted in her implied consent to interception. We find these arguments unpersuasive.

There is no evidence of express consent here. . . . [A]ctual consent may be implied from the circumstances. Nevertheless, "[c]onsent under title III is not to be cavalierly implied. . . . [K]nowledge of the capability of monitoring alone cannot be considered implied consent."

We do not believe that Deal's consent may be implied from the circumstances relied upon in the Spearses' arguments. The Spearses did not inform Deal that they were monitoring the phone, but only told her they might do so in order to cut down on personal calls. Moreover, it seems clear that the couple anticipated Deal would not suspect that they were intercepting her calls, since they hoped to catch her making an admission about the burglary, an outcome they would not expect if she knew her calls were being recorded. As for listening in via the extension, Deal testified that she knew when someone picked up the extension in the residence while she was on the store phone, as there was an audible "click" on the line.

The Spearses also argue that they are immune from liability under what has become known as an exemption for business use of a telephone extension. . . .

[T]here are two essential elements that must be proved before this becomes a viable defense: the intercepting equipment must be furnished to the user by the phone company or connected to the phone line, and it must be used in the ordinary course of business. The Spearses argue that the extension in their residence, to which the recorder was connected, meets the equipment requirement, and the listening-in was done in the ordinary course of business. We disagree.

First, we are not . . . convinced . . . that an extension telephone is exempt equipment . . . when a recording device is attached to the extension to record calls for later listening. The calls would not have been heard or otehwise acquired—that is, intercepted—at all but for the recording device, as the Spearses did not spend twenty-two hours listening in on the residential extension. When turned on, the recorder was activated automatically by the lifting of the handset of either phone, even though it was connected only to the extension phone. Further, Deal ordinarily would know (by the "click" on the line) when the residential extension was picked up while she was using the store phone; thus her calls likely would not have been intercepted if the recorder had not been in place.

It seems far more plausible to us that the recording device, and not the extension phone, is the instrument used to intercept the call. We do not believe the recording device falls within the statutory exemption. The recorder was purchased by Newell Spears at Radio Shack, not provided by the telephone company. Further, it was connected to the extension phone, which was itself the instrument connected to the phone line. . . .

We hold that the recording device, and not the extension phone, intercepted the calls. But even if the extension phone intercepted the calls, we do not agree that the interception was in the ordinary course of business.

We do not quarrel with the contention that the Spearses had a legitimate business reason for listening in: they suspected Deal's involvement in a burglary of the store and hoped she would incriminate herself in a conversation on the phone. Moreover, Deal was abusing her privileges by using the phone for numerous personal calls even, by her own admission, when there were customers in the store. The Spearses might legitimately have monitored Deal's calls to the extent necessary to determine that the calls were personal and made or received in violation of store policy.

But the Spearses recorded twenty-two hours of calls, and Newell Spears listened to all of them without regard to their relation to his business interests. Granted, Deal might have mentioned the burglary at any time during the conversations, but we do not believe that the Spearses' suspicions justified the extent of the intrusion. . . . We conclude that the scope of the interception in this case takes us well beyond the boundaries of the ordinary course of business.

Spears also contends that she did not communicate the information on the tapes, and thus she is not liable for disclosure under the statute. Liability attaches when a party "intentionally discloses . . . to any other person the contents of any wire, oral, or electronic communication, knowing or having reason to know that the information was obtained" through an interception illegal under Title III. . . . The statutory definition of "contents," a term of art under Title III, brings Juanita's alleged disclosures within the purview of the statute; she need not play the tapes or repeat conversations to be liable. " '[C]ontents', when used with respect to any wire, oral, or electronic communication, includes any information concerning the substance, purport, or meaning of that communication. . . ."

Finally, Deal and Lucas cross-appeal the District Court's failure to award punitive damages. . . . Punitive damages are unwarranted under Title III unless Deal and Lucas can prove "a wanton, reckless or malicious violation. . . ." It is difficult to conceive of a case less appropriate for punitive damages than this one.

The Spearses had lost $16,000 by theft in what must have been a serious blow to their business, and installed the recorder in hopes that they would be able to recover their loss, or at least catch the thief. They suspected an inside job and naturally they were anxious to find out whether the burglar was one of their employees. Further, despite warnings about abuse of the phone, the Spearses were paying a salary to an employee for the hours she spent on personal calls, including (as it turned out) her conversations with her lover. She sometimes carried on these conversations in the presence of the store's customers and apparently not infrequently used salacious language. The Spearses were not taping to get "dirt" on Lucas and Deal, but believed their business interests justified the recording. Moreover, before installing the recorder, Newell Spears inquired of a law enforcement officer and was told that the officer saw nothing wrong with Spears tapping his own phone. While the Spearses' reliance on the officer's statement does not absolve them of liability, it clearly demonstrates that the taping was neither wanton nor reckless. As for the disclosures, Sibbie Deal was the only person for whom any of the tapes were played, and even then Newell Spears played the tape for only a few seconds, just enough to let Deal know why she was being fired. There was no evidence that taped conversations were repeated verbatim, or that anything but vague substance was revealed. Other than Sibbie Deal, those who testified as to direct knowledge of the disclosures apparently believed Juanita Spears had their best interests at heart and that the disclosures were in the manner of a warning to them and not malicious.

We agree with the District Court that defendants' conduct does not warrant the imposition of punitive damages.

Drug Testing in Employment

Joseph DesJardins and Ronald Duska

We take privacy to be an "employee right," by which we mean a presumptive moral entitlement to receive certain goods or be protected from cer-

From *Business and Professional Ethics Journal* (1989) vol. 6, no. 3. Reprinted by permission of the authors.

tain harms in the workplace.[1] Such a right creates a prima facie obligation on the part of the employer to provide the relevant goods or, as in this case, refrain from the relevant harmful treatment. These rights prevent employees from being placed in the fundamentally coercive position where they must choose between their jobs and other basic human goods.

Further, we view the employer–employee relationship as essentially contractual. The employer–employee relationship is an economic one and, unlike relationships such as those between a government and its citizens or a parent and a child, exists primarily as a means for satisfying the economic interests of the contracting parties. The obligations that each party incurs are only those that it voluntarily takes on. Given such a contractual relationship, certain areas of the employee's life remain his or her own private concern, and no employer has a right to invade them. On these presumptions we maintain that certain information about an employee is rightfully private, in other words, that the employee has a right to privacy.

The Right to Privacy

George Brenkert has described the right to privacy as involving a three-place relation between a person A, some information X, and another person B. The right to privacy is violated only when B deliberately comes to possess information X about A and no relationship between A and B exists that would justify B's coming to know X about A.[2] Thus, for example, the relationship one has with a mortgage company would justify that company's coming to know about one's salary, but the relationship one has with a neighbor does not justify the neighbor's coming to know that information.

Hence, an employee's right to privacy is violated whenever personal information is requested, collected, or used by an employer in a way or for any purpose that is *irrelevant to* or *in violation of* the contractual relationship that exists between employer and employee.

Since drug testing is a means for obtaining information, the information sought must be relevant to the contract if the drug testing is not to violate privacy. Hence, we must first decide whether knowledge of drug use obtained by drug testing is job relevant. In cases in which the knowledge of drug use is *not* relevant, there appears to be no justification for subjecting employees to drug tests. In cases in which information of drug use is job relevant, we need to consider if, when, and under what conditions using a means such as drug testing to obtain that knowledge is justified.

Is Knowledge of Drug Use Job-Relevant Information?

Two arguments are used to establish that knowledge of drug use is job-relevant information. The first argument claims that drug use adversely affects job performance, thereby leading to lower productivity, higher costs, and consequently lower profits. Drug testing is seen as a way of avoiding these adverse effects. According to some estimates $25 billion are lost each year in the United States through loss in productivity, theft, higher rates in health and liability insurance and similar costs incurred because of drug use.[3] Since employers are contracting with an employee for the performance of specific tasks, employers seem to have a legitimate claim upon whatever personal information is relevant to an employee's ability to do the job.

The second argument claims that drug use has been and can be responsible for considerable harm to individual employees, to their fellow employees, and to the employer, and third parties, including consumers. In this case drug testing is defended because it is seen as a way of preventing possible harm. Further, since employers can be held liable for harms done to employees and customers, knowledge of employee drug use is needed so that employers can protect themselves from risks related to such liability. But how good are these arguments?

The First Argument: Job Performance and Knowledge of Drug Use

The first argument holds that drug use lowers productivity and that consequently, an awareness of drug use obtained through drug testing will allow an employer to maintain or increase productivity. It is generally assumed that the performance of people using certain drugs is detrimentally affected by such use, and any use of drugs that reduces productivity is consequently job relevant. If knowledge of such drug use allows the employer to eliminate production losses, such knowledge is job relevant.

On the surface this argument seems reasonable. Obviously some drug use, in lowering the level of performance, can decrease productivity. Since the employer is entitled to a certain level of performance and drug use adversely affects performance, knowledge of that use seems job relevant.

But this formulation of the argument leaves an important question unanswered. To what level of performance are employers entitled? Optimal performance, or some lower level? If some lower level, what? Employers have a valid claim upon some *certain level* of performance, such that a failure to perform at this level would give the employer a justification for disciplining, firing, or at least finding fault with the employee. But that does not necessarily mean that the employer has a right to a maximum or optimal level of performance, a level above and beyond a certain level of acceptability. It might be nice if the employee gives an employer a maximum effort or optimal performance, but that is above and beyond the call of the employee's duty and the employer can hardly claim a right at all times to the highest level of performance of which an employee is capable. . . .

If the person is producing what is expected, knowledge of drug use on the grounds of production is irrelevant since, by this hypothesis, the production is satisfactory. If, on the other hand, the performance suffers, then to the extent that it slips below the level justifiably expected, the employer has preliminary grounds for warning, disciplining, or releasing the employee. But the justification for this action is the person's unsatisfactory performance, not the person's use of drugs. Accordingly, drug use information is either unnecessary or irrelevant and consequently there are not sufficient grounds to override the right of privacy. Thus, unless we can argue that an employer is entitled to optimal performance, the argument fails.

This counterargument should make it clear that the information that is job relevant, and consequently is not rightfully private, is information about an employee's level of performance and not information about the underlying causes of that level. The fallacy of the argument that promotes drug testing in the name of increased productivity is the assumption that each employee is obliged to perform at an optimal or at least quite high level. But this is required under few if any contracts. What is required contractually is meeting the normally expected levels of production or performing the tasks in the job description adequately (not optimally). If one can do that under the influence of drugs, then on the grounds of job performance at least, drug use is rightfully private. An employee who cannot perform the task adequately is not ful-

filling the contract, and knowledge of the cause of the failure to perform is irrelevant on the contractual model.

Of course, if the employer suspects drug use or abuse as the cause of the unsatisfactory performance, then she might choose to help the person with counseling or rehabilitation. However, this does not seem to be something morally required of the employer. Rather, in the case of unsatisfactory performance, the employer has a prima facie justification for dismissing or disciplining the employee. . . .

The Second Argument: Harm and the Knowledge of Drug Use to Prevent Harm

The performance argument is inadequate, but there is an argument that seems somewhat stronger. This is an argument that takes into account the fact that drug use often leads to harm. Using a variant of the Millian argument, which allows interference with a person's rights in order to prevent harm, we could argue that drug testing might be justified if such testing led to knowledge that would enable an employer to prevent harm.

Drug use certainly can lead to harming others. Consequently, if knowledge of such drug use can prevent harm, then knowing whether or not an employee uses drugs might be a legitimate concern of an employer in certain circumstances. This second argument claims that knowledge of the employee's drug use is job relevant because employees who are under the influence of drugs can pose a threat to the health and safety of themselves and others, and an employer who knows of that drug use and the harm it can cause has a responsibility to prevent it.

Employers have both a general duty to prevent harm and the specific responsibility for harms done by their employees. Such responsibilities are sufficient reason for an employer to claim that information about an employee's drug use is relevant if that knowledge can prevent harm by giving the employer grounds for dismissing the employee or not allowing him or her to perform potentially harmful tasks. Employers might even claim a right to reduce unreasonable risks, in this case the risks involving legal and economic liability for harms caused by employees under the influence of drugs, as further justification for knowing about employee drug use.

This second argument differs from the first, in which only a lowered job performance was relevant information. In this case, even to allow the performance is problematic, for the performance itself, more than being inadequate, can hurt people. We cannot be as sanguine about the prevention of harm as we can about inadequate production. Where drug use may cause serious harms, knowledge of that use becomes relevant if the knowledge of such use can lead to the prevention of harm and drug testing becomes justified as a means for obtaining that knowledge.

Jobs with Potential to Cause Harm

In the first place, it is not clear that every job has a potential to cause harm—at least, not a potential to cause harm sufficient to override a prima facie right to privacy. To say that employers can use drug testing where that can prevent harm is not to say that every employer has the right to know about the drug use of every employee. Not every job poses a threat serious enough to justify an employer coming to know this information.

In deciding which jobs pose serious-enough threats, certain guidelines should be followed. First the potential for harm should be *clear* and *present.* Perhaps all jobs in some extended way pose potential threats to human well-being. We suppose an accountant's error could pose a threat of harm to someone somewhere. But some jobs—like those of airline pilots, school bus drivers, public transit drivers, and surgeons—are jobs in which unsatisfactory performance poses a clear and present danger to others. It would be much harder to make an argument that job performances by auditors, secretaries, executive vice-presidents for public relations, college teachers, professional athletes, and the like could cause harm if those performances were carried on under the influence of drugs. They would cause harm only in exceptional cases.[4]

Not Every Person Is to Be Tested

But, even if we can make a case that a particular job involves a clear and present danger for causing harm if performed under the influence of drugs, it is not appropriate to treat everyone holding such a job the same. Not every jobholder is equally threatening. There is less reason to investigate an airline pilot for drug use if that pilot has a twenty-year record of exceptional service than there is to investigate a pilot whose behavior has become erratic and unreliable recently, or one who reports to work smelling of alcohol and slurring his words. Presuming that every airline pilot is equally threatening is to deny individuals the respect that they deserve as autonomous, rational agents. It is to ignore their history and the significant differences between them. It is also probably inefficient and leads to the lowering of morale. It is the likelihood of causing harm, and not the fact of being an airline pilot per se, that is relevant in deciding which employees in critical jobs to test.

So, even if knowledge of drug use is justifiable to prevent harm, we must be careful to limit this justification to a range of jobs and people where the potential for harm is clear and present. The jobs must be jobs that clearly can cause harm, and the specific employee should not be someone who has a history of reliability. Finally, the drugs being tested should be those drugs that have genuine potential for harm if used in the jobs in question.

Limitations on Drug-Testing Policies

Even when we identify those situations in which knowledge of drug use would be job relevant, we still need to examine whether some procedural limitations should not be placed upon the employer's testing for drugs. We have said when a real threat of harm exists and when evidence exists suggesting that a particular employee poses such a threat, an employer could be justified in knowing about drug use in order to prevent the potential harm. But we need to recognize that so long as the employer has the discretion for deciding when the potential for harm is clear and present, and for deciding which employees pose the threat of harm, the possibility of abuse is great. Thus, some policy limiting the employer's power is called for.

Just as criminal law imposes numerous restrictions protecting individual dignity and liberty on the state's pursuit of its goals, so we should expect that some restrictions be placed on employers to protect innocent employees from harm (including loss of job and damage to one's personal and professional reputation). Thus, some system of checks upon an employer's discretion in these matters seems advisable.

A drug-testing policy that requires all employees to submit to a drug test or to jeopardize their jobs would seem coercive and therefore unacceptable. Being placed in such a fundamentally coercive position of having to choose between one's job and one's privacy does not provide the conditions for a truly free consent. Policies that are unilaterally established by employers would likewise be unacceptable. Working with employees to develop company policy seems the only way to ensure that the policy will be fair to both parties. Prior notice of testing would also be required in order to give employees the option of freely refraining from drug use. Preventing drug use is morally preferable to punishing users after the fact, because this approach treats employees as capable of making rational and informed decisions.

Further procedural limitations seem advisable as well. Employees should be notified of the results of the test, they should be entitled to appeal the results (perhaps through further tests by an independent laboratory), and the information obtained through tests ought to be kept confidential. In summary, limitations upon employer discretion for administering drug tests can be derived from the nature of the employment contract and from the recognition that drug testing is justified by the desire to prevent harm, not the desire to punish wrongdoing.

The Illegality Contention

At this point critics might note that the behavior which testing would try to deter is, after all, illegal. Surely this excuses any responsible employer from being overprotective of an employee's rights. The fact that an employee is doing something illegal should give the employer a right to that information about his or her private life. Thus it is not simply that drug use might pose a threat of harm to others, but that it is an *illegal* activity that threatens others. But again, we would argue that illegal activity itself is irrelevant to job performance. At best, *conviction* records might be relevant, but since drug tests are administered by private employers we are not only ignoring the question of convic-

tion, we are also ignoring the fact that the employee has not even been arrested for the alleged illegal activity.

Further, even if the due process protections and the establishment of guilt are acknowledged, it still does not follow that employers have a claim to know about all illegal activity on the part of their employees.

Consider the following example: Suppose you were hiring an auditor whose job required certifying the integrity of your firm's tax and financial records. Certainly, the personal integrity of this employee is vital to adequate job performance. Would we allow the employer to conduct, with or without the employee's consent, an audit of the employee's own personal tax return? Certainly if we discover that this person has cheated on a personal tax return we will have evidence of illegal activity that is relevant to this person's ability to do the job. Given one's own legal liability for filing falsified statements, the employee's illegal activity also poses a threat to others. But surely, allowing private individuals to audit an employee's tax returns is too intrusive a means for discovering information about that employee's integrity. The government certainly would never allow this violation of an employee's privacy. It ought not to allow drug testing on the same grounds. Why tax returns should be protected in ways that urine, for example, is not, raises interesting questions of fairness. Unfortunately, this question would take us beyond the scope of this paper.

Voluntariness

A final problem that we also leave undeveloped concerns the voluntariness of employee consent. For most employees, being given the choice between submitting to a drug test and risking one's job by refusing an employer's request is not much of a decision at all. We believe that such decisions are less than voluntary and thereby hold that employers cannot escape our criticisms simply by including with the employment contract a drug-testing clause.[5] Furthermore, there is reason to believe that those most in need of job security will be those most likely to be subjected to drug testing. Highly skilled, professional employees with high job mobility and security will be in a stronger position to resist such intrusions than will less skilled, easily replaced workers. This is why we should not anticipate surgeons and airline pilots being tested and should not be surprised when public transit and factory workers are. A serious question of fairness arises here as well.

Drug use and drug testing seem to be our most recent social "crisis." Politicians, the media, and employers expend a great deal of time and effort addressing this crisis. Yet, unquestionably, more lives, health, and money are lost each year to alcohol abuse than to marijuana, cocaine, and other controlled substances. We are well advised to be careful in considering issues that arise from such selective social concern. We will let other social commentators speculate on the reasons why drug use has received scrutiny while other white-collar crimes and alcohol abuse are ignored. Our only concern at this point is that such selective prosecution suggests an arbitrariness that should alert us to questions of fairness and justice.

In summary, then, we have seen that drug use is not always job relevant, and if drug use is not job relevant, information about it is certainly not job relevant. In the case of performance it may be a cause of some decreased performance, but it is the performance itself that is relevant to an employee's position, not what prohibits or enables that employee to do the job. In the case of potential harm being done by an employee under the influence of drugs, the drug use seems job relevant, and in this case drug testing to prevent harm might be legitimate. But how this is practicable is another question. It would seem that standard motor dexterity or mental dexterity tests given immediately prior to job performance are more effective in preventing harm, unless one concludes that drug use invariably and necessarily leads to harm. One must trust the individuals in any system for that system to work. One cannot police everything. Random testing might enable an employer to find drug users and to weed out the few to forestall possible future harm, but are the harms prevented sufficient to override the rights of privacy of the people who are innocent and to overcome the possible abuses we have mentioned? It seems not.

Clearly, a better method is to develop safety checks immediately prior to the performance of a job. Have a surgeon or a pilot or a bus driver pass a few reasoning and motor-skill tests before work.

The cause of the lack of a skill, which lack might lead to harm, is really a secondary issue.

NOTES

1. "A Defense of Employee Rights," Joseph DesJardins and John McCall, *Journal of Business Ethics* 4 (1985). We should emphasize that our concern is with the *moral* rights of privacy for employees and not with any specific or prospective *legal* rights. Readers interested in pursuing the legal aspects of employee drug testing should consult "Workplace Privacy Issues and Employer Screening Policies" by Richard Lehr and David Middlebrooks in *Employee Relations Law Journal,* vol. 11, no. 3, 407–421; and "Screening Workers for Drugs: A Legal and Ethical Framework," Mark Rothstein, in *Employee Relations Law Journal,* vol. 11, no. 3, 422–436.

2. "Privacy, Polygraphs, and Work," George Brenkert, *Journal of Business and Professional Ethics,* vol. 1, no. 1 (Fall 1981). For a more general discussion of privacy in the workplace see "Privacy in Employment" by Joseph DesJardins, in *Moral Rights in the Workplace,* edited by Gertrude Ezorsky (SUNY Press, 1987). A good resource for philosophical work on privacy can be found in "Recent Work on the Concept of Privacy" by W. A. Parent, in *American Philosophical Quarterly,* vol. 20 (Oct. 1983), 341–358.

3. *U.S. News and World Report,* 22 Aug. 1983; *Newsweek,* 6 May 1983.

4. Obviously we are speaking here of harms that go beyond the simple economic harm that results from unsatisfactory job performance. These economic harms are discussed in the first argument above. Further, we ignore such "harms" as providing bad role models for adolescents, harms often used to justify drug tests for professional athletes. We think it unreasonable to hold an individual responsible for the image he or she provides to others.

5. It might be argued that since we base our critique upon the contractual relationship between employers and employees, our entire position can be undermined by a clever employer who places within the contract a privacy waiver for drug tests. A full answer to this would require an account of the free and rational subject that the contract model presupposes. While acknowledging that we need such an account to prevent just any contract from being morally legitimate, we will have to leave this debate to another time. Interested readers might consult "The Moral Contract between Employers and Employees" by Norman Bowie in *The Work Ethic in Business,* edited by W. M. Hoffman and T. J. Wyly (Cambridge, MA: Oelgeschlager and Gunn, 1981), 195–202.

The Ethics of Genetic Screening in the Workplace

Joseph H. Kupfer

Today we are witnessing the onslaught of "testing" in the workplace. We test for personality, aptitude, competence, "truthfulness," drugs, and now genetic make-up. Clearly, some of this testing may well be warranted, but genetic "screening" as it's called raises some peculiar questions of its own—questions of meaning and questions of morality. In what follows, I shall spell out the nature of genetic screening, its possible purposes or values, and then raise some moral questions about it.

The Issue and Its Background

Genetic research is one of those areas of science which has clear practical benefits. If we know that we are carrying a gene for an inheritable illness, such as Huntington's disease, we can make a more informed choice about procreation. Knowledge of our genetic disposition toward heart disease or high blood pressure can prompt us to change our patterns of eating and exercise. And once informed of our genetically based vulnerability to lung disease, we are able to avoid threatening work conditions. Indeed, this was the first goal of genetic screening in the workplace: to enable the employee to steer clear of work situations which were liable to call forth a disabling condition or disease (henceforth, simply "disorder").

Obviously, businesses also had an interest in this goal. Fewer disabled workers means reduction in costs caused by illness, absenteeism, health insurance, workers' compensation, and turnover. In addition, the first workplace screening was a response by business to 1970's legislation making business responsible for health in the workplace. DuPont, Dow Chemical and Johnson and Johnson were among the first companies to implement genetic screening.[1] The tests were voluntary and there was no threat of job loss, rather, "warning" and "relocating" to less hazardous conditions or func-

tions were the procedure. Indeed, DuPont's testing for sickle cell trait was requested by its own black workers! So, at its inception, genetic screening of workers seemed to be a mutually agreed upon practice aimed at mutual benefits—workers and owners cooperating for the good of all.

If this were all there was to genetic screening in the workplace, obviously there would be little need for moral discussion. But, corporations have an interest in extending the purpose of screening beyond its original scope—to deny people work. What began as a benign program can be modified to serve only the interests of business. After all, relocating workers or modifying existing conditions so that they will be less hazardous takes time, effort, and money. It's just plain cheaper to fire or not hire a worker who is at "genetic risk." The facts of the matter, however, make the whole issue more complicated. They also point to moral difficulties with the use of genetic screening to exclude workers from jobs, what we shall consider "discriminatory genetic screening."

Before investigating the moral issues involved, we must get clear on the scientific ones concerning *how* genetic screening, in fact, works. There are serious limitations to what we can learn from genetic screening and they have moral implications. The limitations on the knowledge afforded by genetic screening are of two sorts—technical and causal. Technical limitations are determined by the level of sophistication of our techno-scientific understanding. Causal constraints depend upon how genes actually bring about disorders.

Each kind of limitation itself involves two sets of variables. Technical restrictions on genetic knowledge turn on (1) whether the gene itself has been located or simply correlated with other DNA material, and (2) whether knowledge of other family members is necessary to determine the presence of the affecting gene. Causal restrictions on genetic knowledge involve (1) whether the affecting gene requires other genes to produce the disorder, and (2) whether the gene causes the disorder with inevitability or just creates a vulnerability to it. We shall consider the two sorts of limitations on ge-

Reprinted from Joseph H. Kupfer, "The Ethics of Genetic Screening in the Workplace," *Business Ethics Quarterly* vol. 3, no. 1 (1993), 17–25. Reprinted by permission.

netic knowledge by examining in order these sets of variables for their significance for the practice of genetic screening.

Technical Limitations

First is the question of whether the gene itself has been located. Hemophilia, Duchenne muscular dystrophy, and cystic fibrosis are among the few exceptions where the genetic test actually identifies the gene in question. What is more typical are DNA "probes" or "markers" which indicate the likelihood of the gene's presence. "Most of today's probes aren't capable of pinpointing a bad gene. They can only detect sequences of healthy genes called markers, that are usually found near a bad one."[2] When "restriction" enzymes are introduced into the chromosome material, DNA fragments are generated: specifically, strips of genetic material called restriction fragment length polymorphisms (RFLPs), whose patterns can be statistically associated with the occurrence of a particular disorder.[3] In the case of Huntington's disease, for example, the probe detects "a piece of DNA that is so close to the as yet unidentified Huntington's gene that it is inherited along with the gene."[4]

This technical limitation—inability to locate the particular gene in question—means that we are usually dealing with statistical correlations. The marker can be inherited without the defective gene; therefore, uncovering the marker must be treated with caution. Conversely, Marc Lappe warns,[5] failure to turn up the marker does not guarantee the gene's absence!

In order to establish the correlation between the marker and the disorder, collateral data may be needed. One kind, "linkage analysis," points to our second set of variables—whether or not reference to family members is needed. Linkage analysis is comparing a given individual's DNA pattern with both affected and unaffected family members. The marker for Huntington's disease, for example, is useless if there are no living family members *with* the disease. This is because what is needed is to identify the piece of DNA material *as* a marker for Huntington's disease. Its association with the disease must be ascertained by comparison with DNA fragments of surviving relatives.

This is obviously very time consuming and expensive, prohibitively so for workplace application. It also requires the consent of family members who may not be employed by the company (over whom the company can exert little leverage). In contrast, "direct markers" indicate a genetic connection with a disorder without linkage analysis. The marking of the genes for hemophilia, cystic fibrosis, and adult polycystic kidney disease can be ascertained directly. These are more feasible for workplace screening.

Causal Limitations

Our third set of variables concerns how the genetic material generates the disorder: whether the disorder is caused by one or several genes. When a disorder is coded for by more than a single gene, the gene in question must interact with these other genes in order to be expressed (as a disorder). For screening to have predictive value it must indicate the presence (or absence) of these auxiliary, "modifier" genes. For instance, in the case of Gaucher's disease, the gene marked by the DNA probe is associated with three forms of the disease. While one of the varieties of this neurological disorder is severe, the other two are fairly mild.[6] Without corroboration from modifier genes, which form of Gaucher's disease the individual will develop can't be determined.

One interesting combination of variables occurs in Huntington's disease. It is caused by a single gene; however, that gene has not yet been located. Therefore, it is identified by means of other DNA material, *and* correlation of the material with the disease requires linkage analysis. Because it is caused by a single gene, if that gene can be identified, then linkage analysis won't be needed. In addition, it will be known with virtual certainty that the individual will be afflicted. As with adult polycystic kidney disease, all carriers of the gene for Huntington's disease develop the disorder. The causal tie between the gene and the disorder is virtually absolute.

But this is the rare exception. The great majority of genes do not lead inevitably to the disorder. They create a susceptibility or vulnerability, not a certainty of expression. Our last set of variables concerns this—the nature of the gene's causal efficacy. Conditions such as high cholesterol levels and high blood pressure, and diseases such as Alzheimer's disease and diabetes, are determined by "contingency" genes. Certain contingencies must be met before these genes bring about their respective disorders.

One of these contingencies is the presence of other genes, as we have just noted. In addition, the expression of most genetically based disorders requires the influence of biological, social, or psychological factors. It is already common knowledge that diet and exercise (biological and social influences) can affect the onset of coronary artery disease and high blood pressure. The same also holds for diabetes and back arthritis.

What does it *mean* to say that the gene produces a disposition or susceptibility to a disorder? One fourth of the people with the genetic marker for "ankylosing spondylitis" develop this debilitating back arthritis. Put another way, someone with the marker is between forty and one hundred times more likely to develop ankylosing spondylitis than is someone without this genetic material.[7] Even in such "high odds" cases like this one, however, 75 percent of the people with the genetic marker do *not* develop the arthritis. Work and work conditions, for instance, contribute greatly to its onset. For many genetically determined disorders, the individual may have considerable control over whether and how severely the disorder occurs. Knowledge of our genetic constitution can be helpful in making practical decisions rather than simply forecasting our fate.

Considerations of Privacy

We come now to the moral questions of whether and to what extent genetic screening in the workplace is justified. Recall that we are talking about discriminatory screening which is designed to exclude workers from jobs, rather than to "warn and relocate." I shall argue that considerations of privacy and justice mitigate against screening or at least its untrammeled deployment.

Let's begin with considerations of privacy. When information is gathered about us our privacy may be infringed upon in varying degrees. Whether our privacy is violated depends on such things as whether we consent to the gathering of the information, the nature of the information, and what happens as a result of its gathering. What I would like to focus on here is the issue of control

and autonomy. Many different sorts of information can be obtained, most of it valuable to the company. Some information concerns such things as credit ratings or religious affiliations, other involves ascertaining physical facts by monitoring drug use. Is genetic screening any different in principle from drug screening, polygraph tests, or surveillance? In at least one regard it seems to be. Although in most cases, we have some control over whether a gene is expressed as a disorder, we cannot control whether we *have* the gene in the first place. Whether we have the disposition, the vulnerability to the disorder, is out of our hands.

We have some say over our work, religion, credit rating, and most of us can choose to use drugs or not. But not so with genes. They are in and of us, forever. This lack of control is especially compounded in the workplace because of related lack of power in this context. First, most workers are not in a position to refuse to cooperate with demands for screening. When this is the case, they have no control over the gathering of information about which they also lack control. This lack of power is magnified by workers' overall status in the workplace. In spite of unionization, most workers have little say over working conditions, product manufacture, wages, promotions, and firing.

We need to see testing in general, and genetic screening in particular, within the context of the employer-employee relationship. Testing workers gives employers and managers still greater control over workers' lives. Screening of all sorts would be different, and experienced differently, in a context in which power were more equitably distributed in the workplace. This seems especially important in the area of testing for genetically based disorders, precisely because we have no control over our genetic makeup.

This sense of powerlessness is critical to the special type of stigmatization associated with genetic defects. When screening uncovers a genetic abnormality, the individual can feel morally defective—cursed or damned. This could and has happened simply from acquiring genetic information under the most benign circumstances. Thus, Madeleine and Lenn Goodman found considerable stigmatization among Jewish people identified as carriers of Tay-Sachs disease even though no obvious disadvantages followed from such identification.[8] But when the information is used prejudicially, as in the workplace discrimination we are here considering, the likelihood and intensity of stigmatization increases. As Thomas Murray notes, diagnosing an illness as genetically caused may *label* the person as *constitutionally* weak, making finding another job difficult.[9]

All of these aspects of the situation help explain why the loss of privacy suffered in genetic screening in the workplace is serious. The screening is for properties over which the worker has no control and is not responsible; it occurs in a context of relative powerlessness; and it is likely to result in stigmatization with profound costs to his or her life-chances. The genetic screening as described here involves loss of privacy, but the stigmatization and its repercussions, as we shall see, are a matter of *injustice*. Loss or forfeiture of privacy is less defendable the less just the situation under which it occurs and the less just the purposes for which it is used.

The invasion of privacy is greater when the genetic screening is "across the board" rather than selective. When businesses screen for *any* potential disease or debilitating condition, it is like having the police come and search your house just to see what they'll turn up. In both cases, there is clearly an "interest" in uncovering the relevant danger. The state and employer reduce their respective risks. But such interests are not overriding, not in a society which claims to value the individual's autonomy and privacy. The employer has no more right to a total genetic profile than he has to information about one's sexual habits, recreational activities, or religious and political beliefs—even though knowledge of these and other details of our lives might well be of use to him.

Testing for job-specific susceptibilities is more warranted since directly connected to the work context and the employer's role in bringing about the disorder. It is more like searching someone's home for specific items, such as guns or counterfeit money. Presumably, there is a good reason for looking in both sorts of case. Since screening for just a *few*, job-related genetic dispositions, less of the self is being "searched." Therefore, there is probably less sense of being violated or stigmatized. The individual is told that she is unfit to do this particular job, for example, heavy lifting because of the disposition to back arthritis. She is not labelled as constitutionally weak due to some general condition, such as vulnerability to heart disease.

Even here, however, another threat looms. It is all too likely that employers will tend to use such information to fire employees rather than improve workplace conditions. It's cheaper. But perhaps it's the employer's responsibility to make the workplace safe, even for those with susceptibilities to environmentally-triggered disorders. People who have a disposition to lung disease, for example, might be able to work in this particular factory at no increased risk *if* the employer provided better air ventilation and circulation. This issue seems to be a matter of justice: who should bear the burden of workplace danger.

Considerations of Justice

We turn now directly to considerations of justice. The first sort of consideration focuses on the individual and the nature of genetic causation. The second concerns these individuals as members of a paying public.

In the great majority of cases, genetic markers indicate merely a predisposition for a disorder, not the inevitability of its onset. (Even when inevitable, in many cases the degree of severity remains unpredictable.) It seems unjust to penalize an individual for something that has not yet come to pass and which may well be prevented by him. It is unjust to act as if the individual is already diseased or disabled, especially when he may run a lower risk than others without the marker because of healthful life-choices made on the basis of this information.

It is like treating someone as though guilty until proven innocent. In the case of genetically caused susceptibility to a disorder, it is worse because carrying the gene is beyond the person's control. Considerations of justice suggest that there is something wrong in penalizing people for conditions which are beyond their control. Of course, sometimes people are justly denied benefits or privileges on account of uncontrollable considerations. Thus, we don't allow blind people to drive or people who have slow reaction times to be air-traffic controllers. But this is not penalizing someone so much as finding them unqualified for performance of a task. Public safety certainly does and should operate as a constraint on opportunity. However, this kind of consideration is rare in the case of genetically based disorders; moreover, it should come into play only with the onset of the disabling condition, not with the mere discovery of a genetic propensity toward it. In a society proclaiming commitment to egalitarian principles, we shouldn't further handicap people who may become disabled by depriving them of work while they are still able to do the job.

The question of the justness of discriminatory genetic screening can also be posed from the larger, social perspective. It arises from the social nature and purpose of genetic research. Genetic research, including testing individuals and groups, was developed to help people. By diagnosing genetic predispositions, testing could enable people to make beneficial decisions concerning themselves, family members, and potential offspring. When individuals already manifested certain disorders, voluntary genetic counselling was designed to help provide diagnosis, prognosis, and information for vital decisions.

This is analogous to diagnostic reading tests conducted in the public schools. These are designed to help students get remedial help when needed. Instead, imagine a situation where such tests were used to "weed out" the weakest students so that they didn't clutter up the classroom and drain teaching resources. Surely we would find such a policy unjust, if not outrageous! This would be similar to the discriminatory use of genetic screening. Like individuals with contingency markers, slow readers often can *alter* their futures. In both cases, the diagnostic tests can be used to assist the individual deal with his problem and make life-enhancing choices. On the other hand, the tests can be used to exclude the individual from certain beneficial opportunities: jobs in the case of genetic screening, and instruction to improve reading skills in the case of the reading tests.

Each use of the diagnostic test can be viewed as part of a larger model. The "diagnostic-therapeutic" model takes as primary the interests of the individuals being tested. The "competition" model, however, takes as primary the interests of some other group or institution: the business in the case of genetic testing, the school or superior students in the case of reading diagnosis. On the competition model, the "defective" worker or student is displaced in favor of the competing interests.

My analogy between the school reading test and genetic screening being used against the diagnosed individuals faces the following objection. In the case of the reading test, public education is paid for by public monies; therefore, everybody has an equal right to instruction, including those with reading disabilities. But in the case of genetic screening, the employer is operating privately. She is under no obligation to serve the interests of the employee (or prospective employee). The parallel between people with reading disabilities and those genetically marked for disorders would then break down on the basis of the public/private distinction.

My reply is that genetic research and the procedures employed in genetic screening were developed with public monies. They were carried out by means of government grants and publicly financed facilities such as state universities. Even private universities and research institutes rely greatly on government monies for equipment and salaries, as well as the findings generated by the public institutions. Moreover, these public funds were allocated for the expressed purposes of increasing scientific knowledge and helping society's members. Promotion of these social goods was used to legitimate if not justify investing society's taxes in genetic research. For private businesses to use the knowledge and technology developed through this research in order to deny some of its members employment seems unjust. This is so even if private companies market instruments and procedures for the genetic screening; the technologies *these* private companies are selling could only have been developed on the shoulders of publicly financed (and publicly available) research.

This brings us to the importance of health. Health is unlike most other goods because it is a prerequisite for so many things we value. Without it, we are cut off from the joys of recreation, travel, the arts, work, socializing, sometimes even life itself. Depending on the degree of infirmity, even such simple, apparently available delights as reading, talking, or walking may be denied the individual. The economic benefits of work are usually needed for people to receive adequate long-term health care, so that depriving them of work is likely to be condemning people to lack of health.

Denying a person work on the basis of the *disposition* to develop a disorder may, ironically, increase its likelihood of occurrence. Prevention of its occurrence might require repeated diagnostic tests, treatment, or therapy; it might require the economic wherewithal for a particular health regimen, such as exercise. Even if the lack of work doesn't contribute to the onset of the genetically marked disorder through economic deprivation, it compounds the individual's plight. He not only suffers from the potential to develop this particular disorder, but is now unemployed (and probably uninsured) to boot. He is now economically unprotected against *other* misfortunes and subjected to the psychological stress which could foster other disorders.

What should we conclude from all this? It seems to me that these considerations of privacy and justice argue strongly against general, discriminatory genetic screening in the workplace. Thomas Murray has a list of requirements that a morally defensible exclusion policy must meet. Among them are two that especially turn on considerations of justice.[10] The policy must exclude workers from but a few jobs so that those affected stand a good chance of finding other employment. Otherwise, we'd be treating them unjustly by virtually denying them the opportunity to work at all. In addition, the exclusion shouldn't single out groups that have already been unjustly treated. This is important since genetic dispositions are often inherited along racial and ethnic lines such as the high black incidence of sickle cell anemia and the high Jewish incidence of Tay-Sachs. This, too, is a matter of justice. We shouldn't compound prior injustices with present ones.

I would qualify Murray's conditions with the following restrictions. Corporate screening should be confined to work-specific disorders, rather than probe for a general genetic profile. Moreover, the company should make it a policy to try to relocate the employee to a less hazardous work site or activity, just as the first companies engaged in screening did. This degree of constraint seems minimal in light of the importance of privacy and justice.

NOTES

1. William Pat Patterson, "Genetic Screening: How Much Should We Test Employees?," *Industry Week,* June 1, 1987, pp. 47–48.
2. Kathleen McAuliffe, "Predicting Diseases," *U.S. News and World Report,* May 25, 1987, p. 65.
3. Kathleen Nolan and Sara Swenson, "New Tools, New Dilemmas: Genetic Frontier," *The Hastings Center Report,* October/November, 1988, p. 65.
4. Gina Kolati, "Genetic Screening Raises Questions for Employers and Insurers," *Research News,* April 18, 1986, p. 317.
5. Marc Lappe, "The Limits of Genetic Inquiry," *The Hastings Center Report,* August, 1987, p. 7.
6. Ibid., p. 8.
7. Marc Lappe, *Genetic Politics* (New York: Simon and Schuster, 1979), p. 61.
8. Madeleine and Lenn Goodman, "The Overselling of Genetic Anxiety." *The Hastings Center Report,* October, 1982, p. 249. There was, however, fear of loss of marriage eligibility among many of the people tested. The Goodmans also cite a study of sickle cell trait in Greece, where "possession of sickle cell trait had become a socially stigmatized status, introducing new anxieties into this rural community," p. 26.
9. Thomas Murray, "Warning: Screening Workers for Genetic Risk," *The Hastings Center Report,* February, 1983.
10. Ibid., p. 8. Murray also includes the following: sound scientific basis linking anomaly to exposure to disease; risk should be very large and the disease should be severe and irreversible; and that the number of people excluded should be very small. This last stricture doesn't strike me as all that convincing. It isn't the number of people affected that *makes* a policy unjust. Although many suffering an injustice is worse than few suffering it, injustice done even to few is still injustice and weighs against the policy.

Human Rights, Workers' Rights, and the "Right" to Occupational Safety

Tibor R. Machan

Human Rights[1]

Our general rights, those we are morally justified to secure by organized force (e.g., government), are

Reprinted from *Moral Rights in the Workplace* by Gertrude Ezorsky; by permission of the State University of New York Press.

those initially identified by John Locke: life, liberty, and property. That is, we need ask no one's permission to live, to take actions, and to acquire, hold, or use peacefully the productive or creative results of our actions. We may, morally, resist (without undue force) efforts to violate or infringe upon our rights. Our rights are (1) absolute, (2) unalienable, and (3) universal: (1) in social relations no excuse legitimatizes their violation; (2) no one can lose these rights, though their exercise may be restricted (e.g., to jail) by what one chooses to do; and (3) everyone has these rights, whether acknowledged or respected by others or governments or under different descriptions (within less developed conceptual schemes).[2]

I defend this general rights theory elsewhere.[3] Essentially, since adults are rational beings with the moral responsibility to excel as such, a good or suitable community requires these rights as standards. Since this commits one to a virtuously self-governed life, others should respect this as equal members of the community. Willful invasion of these rights—the destruction of (negative) liberty—must be prohibited in human community life.

So-called positive freedom—that is, the enablement to do well in life—presupposes the prior importance of negative freedom. As, what we might call, self-starters, human beings will generally be best off if they are left uninterfered with to take the initiative in their lives.

Workers' Rights

What about special workers' rights? There are none. As individuals who intend to hire out their skills for what they will fetch in the marketplace, however, workers have the right to offer these in return for what others, (e.g., employers) will offer in acceptable compensation. This implies free trade in the labor market.

Any interference with such trade workers (alone or in voluntary cooperation) might want to engage in, with consent by fellow traders, would violate both the workers' and their traders' human rights. Freedom of association would thereby be abridged. (This includes freedom to organize into trade associations, unions, cartels, and so forth.)

Workers' rights advocates view this differently. They hold that the employee-employer relationship involves special duties owed by employers to employees, creating (corollary) rights that governments, given their purpose, should protect. Aside from negative rights, workers are owed respect of their positive rights to be treated with care and consideration.

This, however, is a bad idea. Not to be treated with care and consideration can be open to moral criticism. And lack of safety and health provisions may mean the neglect of crucial values to employees. In many circumstances employers should, morally, provide them.

This is categorically different from the idea of enforceable positive rights. (Later I will touch on unfulfilled reasonable expectations of safety and health provisions on the job!) Adults aren't due such service from free agents whose conduct should be guided by their own judgments and not some alien authority. This kind of moral servitude (abolished after slavery and serfdom) of some by others has been discredited.

Respect for human rights is necessary in a moral society—one needn't thank a person for not murdering, assaulting, or robbing one—whereas being provided with benefits, however crucial to one's well-being, is more an act of generosity than a right.

Of course moral responsibilities toward others, even strangers, can arise. When those with plenty know of those with little, help would ordinarily be morally commendable. This can also extend to the employment relationship. Interestingly, however, government "regulation may impede risk-reducing change, freezing us into a hazardous present when a safer future beckons."[4]

My view credits all but the severely incapacitated with the fortitude to be productive and wise when ordering their affairs, workers included. The form of liberation that is then vital to workers is precisely the bourgeois kind: being set free from subjugation to others, including governments. Anti-bourgeois "liberation" is insultingly paternalistic.[5]

Alleging Special Workers' Rights

Is this all gross distortion? Professor Braybrooke tells us, "Most people in our society . . . must look for employment and most (taking them one by one) have no alternative to accepting the working conditions offered by a small set of employers—perhaps one employer in the vicinity."[6] Workers need jobs and cannot afford to quibble. Employers can wait for the most accommodating job prospects.

This in part gives rise to special workers' rights doctrines, to be implemented by government occupational safety, health and labor-relations regulators, which then "makes it easier for competing firms to heed an important moral obligation and to be, if they wish, humane."[7]

Suppose a disadvantaged worker, seeking a job in a coal mine, asks about safety provision in the mine. Her doing so presupposes that (1) she has other alternatives, and (2) it's morally and legally optional to care about safety at the mine, not due to workers by right. Prior to government's energetic prolabor interventions, safety, health, and related provisions for workers had been lacking. Only legally mandated workers' rights freed workers from their oppressive lot. Thus, workers must by law be provided with safety, health care, job security, retirement, and other vital benefits.

Workers' rights advocates deny that employers have the basic (natural or human) private property rights to give them full authority to set terms of employment. They are seen as nonexclusive stewards of the workplace property, property obtained by way of historical accident, morally indifferent historical necessity, default, or theft. There is no genuine free labor market. There are no jobs to offer since they are not anyone's to give. The picture we should have of the situation is that society should be regarded as a kind of large team or family; the rights of its respective parts (individuals) flow not from their free and independent moral nature, but from the relationship of the needs and usefulness of individuals as regards the purposes of the collective.

By this account, everyone lacks the full authority to enter into exclusive or unilaterally determined and mutual agreements on his or her terms. Such terms—of production, employment, promotion, termination, and so on—would be established, in line with moral propriety, only by the agency (society, God, the party, the democratic assembly) that possesses the full moral authority to set them.

Let us see why the view just stated is ultimately unconvincing. To begin with, the language of rights does not belong within the above framework. That language acknowledges the reality of morally free and independent human beings and includes among them workers, as well as all other adults. Individual human rights assume that within the limits of nature, human beings are all efficacious to varying degrees, frequently depending upon their own choices. Once this individual-

ist viewpoint is rejected, the very foundation for rights language disappears (notwithstanding some contrary contentions).[8]

Some admit that employers are full owners of their property, yet hold that workers, because they are disadvantaged, are owed special duties of care and considerateness, duties which in turn create rights the government should protect. But even if this were right, it is not possible from this position to establish enforceable *public* policy. From the mere existence of *moral* duties employers may have to employees, no enforceable public policy can follow; moral responsibilities require freely chosen fulfillment, not enforced compliance.

Many workers' rights advocates claim that a free labor market will lead to such atrocities as child labor, hazardous and health-impairing working conditions, and so forth. Of course, even if this were true, there is reason to think that OSHA-type regulatory remedies are illusionary. As Peter Huber argues, "regulation of health and safety is not only a major obstacle to technological transformation and innovation but also often aggravates the hazards it is supposed to avoid."[9]

However, it is not certain that a free labor market would lead to child labor and rampant neglect of safety and health at the workplace. Children are, after all, dependents and therefore have rights owed them by their parents. To subject children to hazardous, exploitative work, to deprive them of normal education and health care, could be construed as a violation of their individual rights as young, dependent human beings. Similarly, knowingly or negligently subjecting workers to hazards at the workplace (of which they were not made aware and could not anticipate from reasonable familiarity with the job) constitutes a form of actionable fraud. It comes under the prohibition of the violation of the right to liberty, at times even the right of life. Such conduct is actionable in a court of law and workers, individually or organized into unions, would be morally justified, indeed advised, to challenge it.

A consistent and strict interpretation of the moral (not economic) individualist framework of rights yields results that some advocates of workers' rights are aiming for. The moral force of most attacks on the free labor market framework tends to arise from the fact that some so-called free labor market instances are probably violations of the detailed implications of that approach itself. Why would one be morally concerned with working conditions that are fully agreed to by workers? Such a concern reflects either the belief that there hadn't been any free agreement in the first place, and thus workers are being defrauded, or it reflects a paternalism that, when construed as paternalism proper instead of compassion, no longer carries moral force.

Whatever its motives, paternalism is also insulting and demeaning in its effect. Once it is clear that workers can generate their own (individual and/or collective) response to employers' bargaining power—via labor organizations, insurance, craft associations, and so on—the favorable air of the paternalistic stance diminishes considerably. Instead, workers are seen to be regarded as helpless, inefficacious, inept persons.

The "Right" to Occupational Safety

Consider an employer who owns and operates a coal mine. (We could have chosen any firm, privately or "publicly" owned, managed by hired executives with the full consent of the owners, including interested stockholders who have entrusted, by their purchase of stocks, others with the goal of obtaining economic benefits for them.) The firm posts a call for jobs. The mine is in competition with some of the major coal mines in the country and the world. But it is much less prosperous than its competitors. The employer is at present not equipped to run a highly-polished, well-outfitted (e.g., very safe) operation. That may lie in the future, provided the cost of production will not be so high as to make this impossible.

Some of the risks will be higher for workers in this mine than in others. Some of the mineshafts will have badly illuminated stairways, some of the noise will be higher than the levels deemed acceptable by experts, and some of the ventilation equipment will be primitive. The wages, too, will be relatively low in hopes of making the mine eventually more prosperous.

When prospective employees appear and are made aware of the type of job being offered, and its hazards they are at liberty to (a) accept or reject, (b) organize into a group and insist on various terms not in the offing, (c) bargain alone or together

with others and set terms that include improvements, or (d) pool workers' resources, borrow, and purchase the firm.

To deny that workers could achieve such things is not yet to deny that they are (negatively) free to do so. But to hold that this would be extraordinary for workers (and thus irrelevant in this sort of case) is to (1) assume a historical situation not in force and certainly not necessary, (2) deny workers the capacity for finding a solution to their problems, or (3) deny that workers are capable of initiative.

Now suppose that employers are compelled by law to spend the firm's funds to meet safety requirements deemed desirable by the government regulators. This increased cost of production reduces available funds for additional wages for present and future employees, not to mention available funds for future prospect sites. This is what has happened: The employee-employer relationship has been unjustly intruded upon, to the detriment not only of the mine owners, but also of those who might be employed and of future consumers of energy. The myth of workers' rights is mostly to blame.

Conclusion

I have argued that the doctrine of special workers' rights is unsupported and workers, accordingly, possess those rights that all other humans possess, the right of life, liberty, and property. Workers are not a special species of persons to be treated in a paternalistic fashion and, given just treatment in the community, they can achieve their goals as efficiently as any other group of human beings.[10]

NOTES

1. I wish to thank the Earhart, Jon M. Olin, and Reason Foundations for making it possible, in part, for me to work on this project. I also wish to thank Bill Puka and Gertrude Ezorsky for their very valuable criticism of an earlier draft of this essay, despite their very likely disapproval of my views.
2. This observation rests, in part, on epistemological insights available, for example, in Hanna F. Pitkin, *Wittgenstin and Justice* (Berkeley, Calif.: University of California Press, 1972).
3. Tibor R. Machan, "A Reconsideration of Natural Rights Theory," *American Philosophical Quarterly* 19 (January 1980): 61–72.

4. Peter Huber, "Exorcists vs. Gatekeepers in Risk Regulation," *Regulation* (November/December 1983), 23.

5. But see Steven Kelman, "Regulation and Paternalism," *Rights and Regulation,* ed. T. R. Machan and M. B. Johnson (Cambridge, Mass.: Ballinger Publ. Co., 1983), 217–48.

6. David Braybrooke, *Ethics in the World of Business* (Totowa, N.J.: Rowman & Allanheld, 1983), 223.

7. Ibid., 224.

8. For an attempt to forge a collectivist theory of rights, see Tom Campbell, *The Left and Rights* (London and Boston: Routledge & Kegan Paul, 1983).

9. Huber, "Exorcists vs. Gatekeepers," 23.

10. Ibid. Huber observes that "Every insurance company knows that life is growing safer, but the public is firmly convinced that living is becoming ever more hazardous" (p. 23). In general, capitalism's benefits to workers have simply not been acknowledged, especially by moral and political philosophers! It is hardly possible to avoid the simple fact that the workers of the world believe differently, judging by what system they prefer to emigrate to whenever possible.

Does OSHA Protect Too Much?

Norman Daniels

The Occupational Safety and Health Act (OSHA) of 1970 requires the Secretary of Labor to set *standards* for dealing with toxic or harmful materials in the workplace. Such standards specify permissible exposure levels and require various practices, like the wearing of air masks, and means, like monitoring devices, for insuring that exposure does not exceed these levels. . . .

A centrally important feature of the 1970 Act is the *criterion* it specifies for acceptable standards: a standard should "most adequately assure, *to the extent feasible,* on the basis of the best available evidence," that no employee will suffer material impairment of health. . . .

OSHA has taken "feasibility" to mean *technological (or technical) feasibility.* A standard must protect workers to the degree it is technologically feasible to do so. . . . We shall refer to the criterion as the *strong* or *technological feasibility criterion.* . . .

I shall consider two lines of argument . . . for OSHA's strong feasibility criterion. . . . Both develop . . . worries about the voluntariness of the choices workers make when they trade daring in handling hazardous materials for hazard pay. . . .

Is it *coercive* to propose that a worker take

Reprinted from Norman Daniels, *Just Health Care,* Philosophy and Health Series, edited by Daniel Wikler (New York: Cambridge University Press, 1985) by permission of Cambridge University Press. Copyright © 1985 by Cambridge University Press.

hazard pay for accepting certain technologically reducible risks in handling carcinogens or breathing dust?

Consider a central case of coercion, the mugger who threatens, gun in hand, "Your money or your life!" The standard analyses all agree that the coercion consists in the fact that the mugger (1) changes the range of options open to the victim, and (2) the change makes the victim much worse off than he would be in some relevant baseline situation.

Suppose we take the case of a worker who has a "clean," non-risky job. His employer wants to change the work process and proposes, "Accept hazard pay for these risks or lose your job." Is the proposal coercive? Our first problem is to specify the "normally expected" course of events. . . . Shall we construe the normal course of events quite *locally,* as the continuation of the clean job now held by this worker? Or should we specify the normal course of events by reference to a more *global* baseline, the normal practices and prerogatives of employers, which include the powers to hire and fire in accord with decisions about the profitability of production processes?

If we construe the baseline *locally,* the proposal begins to look coercive. The employer's proposal changes the particular worker's options in a way that makes the worker much worse off. But this result is quite sensitive to the actual array of alternatives (and their utilities) open to this particular worker: it does not just depend on the employer's action. If there is ready access to comparable clean jobs elsewhere, and shifting jobs entails no great losses of benefits, pensions, and so on, then we may just have a case of an unpleasant offer. The "lose your job" part of the employer's proposal loses its sting, and the employer has not really seriously altered the worker's options for the worse. That is, conditions (1) and (2) of the standard analysis fail to obtain, so the proposal is just an (non-coercive) offer. However, if the alternatives really are "starve your family (go on welfare) or accept hazard pay for cancer risks," then the proposal again meets conditions (1) and (2) and may well be coercive.

Notice how specific this result is to the details of our example. If the worker were already unemployed, and the proposal was, "Accept hazard pay or stay unemployed," then we again have a case that does not meet conditions (1) or (2). After all, the employer's proposal does not worsen the unemployed worker's situation: were the proposal not made, his options would not be improved (just as the victim is no better off if Mugger A refrains and B acts). But there seems to be something wrong with an account that makes the coerciveness of the offer depend on whether the employer is proposing unemployment which is new or merely continued. The employer's more explicit causal role in firing rather than not hiring does not seem to be just what worries us here. To be sure, the proposal to the unemployed worker might be judged exploitive, even if it is not coercive. But intuitions will differ about whether it is *thereby* coercive.[1] For our purposes, if we could agree the offer was exploitive, we might have grounds for viewing it as morally objectionable in ways that might provide a rationale for the strong feasibility criterion. But then the argument would turn on showing why the exploitive conditions undermine autonomy and not on the narrower, more direct judgment that the employer's offer is coercive.

To avoid the charge that the *local* baseline is unduly sensitive to accidental details of the example (e.g., making hazard pay offers to employed workers coercive, but not those to unemployed workers), we might consider shifting to a *global* baseline. Such a baseline builds into our description of the normally expected course of events an account of normal practices of employers. Specifically, suppose that normally workers are presented with such choices as are embodied in the employer's

proposal because the employer's normal practices include the making of decisions which force such proposals. Though our employed worker now faces an unhappy choice, between taking unpleasant risks or not having work, and though his particular options are worse than the ones he happened to enjoy before the proposal, they are not worse than the normally expected options specified by the global baseline. That is, workers normally have such poor options, and the employed and unemployed workers are treated similarly. However, conditions (1) and (2) are now not met in either case, and the offer is not coercive.

Unfortunately, in making the baseline less sensitive to putatively irrelevant details, such as whether new or continued unemployment is threatened, we have also made it hostage to the status quo. If the general practices defining the baseline are, intuitively speaking, coercive, proposals which are no more coercive than these practices will be camouflaged: they will blend in and will not appear coercive at all. Indeed, proposals which (intuitively) seem coercive may be welcomed by people who "normally" suffer from practices that are part of a "coercive" (global) baseline. Nozick discusses the example of a slave owner who beats his slaves daily.[2] One day he proposes that the slave can avoid his usual beating if he does something disagreeable that the slave master wants done. The proposal seems coercive, but we cannot show it is by baseline of normally expected options: the change from the baseline is here welcomed by the slave. So, if we do not modify or supplement our account of the "normally expected" baseline, we cannot accommodate this kind of example. And yet, it is the kind of example that seems most relevant to our case: the offer of hazard pay for facing cancer risks is most likely to be welcomed by the otherwise unemployed worker.

There are . . . ways to supplement the account of the baseline to accommodate the example of the slave. The first, (one) which Nozick and others adopt, is to suggest we need a second baseline, specified by what is *morally required*. In the slave example, it is morally required that the slave not be beaten, or not be a slave at all. By reference to this preproposal baseline, the master's proposal is coercive, even if the slave welcomes the offer. . . .

The two-baseline theory faces some serious difficulties. First, where the baselines conflict and yield different judgments about the presence of coercion, we need to know which baseline to use, which is problematic in some cases.[3] Second, and more important from our perspective, is the fact that the two-baseline theory makes the concept of coercion an intrinsically moral one.[4] That is, on this view, we cannot decide whether a proposal is coercive or not unless, in key cases, we can agree on other judgments, about what is morally required. For these cases, our judgment about the coerciveness of the proposal is no more basic and no more secure than our judgment about what is morally required at the baseline.

Consider the effect of this point on our hazard pay example. Nozick would probably believe that the normal—unregulated—hiring and firing practices of employers do not violate the morally required baseline. Such practices break no prohibitions derived from what is morally required, since they are within the employers' rights, as specified by Nozick's view of individual rights. Others, however, might argue that if the distribution of income or other social goods, like opportunity, is not fair or just, despite compliance with a framework of Nozickian rights, then hazard pay proposals will make workers worse off than what is morally required. Of course, the background injustice may not be the result of actions by the particular employer making the proposal at all: they are systematic and institutional in origin. Notice what has happened: by making coercion a moral notion, we are required to make judgments about justice. The result is that we cannot hope to appeal to agreement on coerciveness, and its *prima facie* wrongness, to undercut moral disagreement about these other issues. Thus we lose one of the advantages that might have resulted if we could provide a rationale for strong OSHA standards that rested on straightforward claims about coercion.

I shall sketch an argument . . . now which, I believe, provides a plausible rationale for OSHA's strong feasibility criterion. To state the argument I will introduce a bit of terminology which will help us capture the underlying intuition. Let us call a proposal *quasi-coercive* if it imposes or depends on a restriction of someone's alternatives in a way that is unfair or unjust; that is, a just or fair social arrangement would involve a range of options for the individual both broader than and strongly preferred to the range in the proposal situation.

The intuition underlying calling unfair or un-

just restrictions of options "quasi-coercive" is that they involve a diminished freedom of action of the same sort which is glaring in the central cases of coercion. A central difference may be in the mechanism through which freedom of action is diminished. We do not have the direct and invasive intrusion into the choice-space of the individual which is present in the central cases of coercion, for example, when the mugger exceeds his rights by pointing a gun at my head. Instead, we have an indirect, yet pervasive, erosion of that space as a result of unjust or unfair social practices and institutions. The two share the feature that the restriction is socially caused. It is not the kind of restriction that results merely from misfortune; it is an act or institution of man, not God or nature, that produces it. Moreover, there are just, feasible alternatives.

Notice an important fact: like the slave in Nozick's example, people who standardly suffer from an unfair or unjust restriction of their options may welcome a quasi-coercive proposal. That is, from their perspective, it may represent an offer and not a threat. Locally considered, the proposal may advance their interest. Moreover, its quasi-coerciveness may even seem to be invisible. Not everyone living under an unjust arrangement may be aware of its injustice. Some may even deny its injustice, say through "false consciousness." Indeed, against the background of a familiar and psychologically accepted range of options, however unfair or unjust it is, jumping at the new "opportunity" embodied in such a proposal, say by trading daring in handling carcinogens for hazard pay, may seem the essence of autonomous action. After all, no one is holding a cocked pistol to one's head or threatening prison if one does not take the offer. The quasi-coerciveness of unjust arrangements works in a more subtly restrictive fashion.

There is another way in which the quasi-coerciveness of some proposals may be hidden: it may be only potential, not actual. That is, if we imagine institutionalizing such proposals, then their effect *over time* will be to produce, or to contribute to, actual quasi-coerciveness, even if initially, and viewed locally, there seems to be nothing worrisome about them, and they seem to be the essence of autonomous exchange. There is just such a worry about a hazard pay market for certain kinds of risks when the market is aimed at workers with a severely restricted range of options. Such proposals might seem unquestionably fair at one time: they are the local manifestation of a process of market exchange which seems procedurally fair under certain circumstances. But such markets will tend to greater inequality over time, especially where there is substantial inequality in bargaining power because workers have highly restricted alternatives. Workers who might at one point be able to sell their daring at a relatively high price—as do, say, movie stuntmen—will find that it is worth little or nothing over time. Risk-taking then becomes a condition of getting a job at all, a price only one with an unfair or unjust range of options—one who is quasi-coerced—would accept. This outcome has historically been the lot of the textile mill worker involved in the Cotton Dust Case, and other low-skill workers whose typical work choices involve exposure to health hazards.

The argument for OSHA's strong feasibility criterion can now be sketched as follows (and this is only a sketch): (1) Hazard pay proposals for technologically reducible risks in the contexts OSHA regulated are quasi-coercive or would tend to be over time. (2) Eliminating such proposals (and the market for them) protects workers from harmful consequences, viz. the destruction of their health at a price that only someone under quasi-coercion would accept. (3) Though hazard pay proposals of the sort involved here may be *offers* welcomed by certain workers, the autonomy embodied in accepting them is only illusory, for quasi-coercion undermines true autonomy in much the same way coercion does. (4) Just as people would reasonably contract to permit paternalistic interventions which protect them against the harmful decisions they would make when they are not, or cannot be, adequately informed, competent, or free to make autonomous ones, so too they would reasonably contract to protect themselves against quasi-coerced decisions of the sort involved here. Thus, OSHA's strong feasibility criterion can be viewed as a social insurance policy against quasi-coercive proposals to trade health for other benefits.

I shall restrict my defense of this sketch to comments on several of its controversial features. One issue of considerable concern is that the argument not prove too much: . . . Specifically, it is important to see that the claim about quasi-coerciveness, or potential quasi-coerciveness, assuming we can apply it to OSHA contexts, does not extend readily to hazard pay proposals involving some other kinds of risky work, where we endorse no such stringent regulation. Does the argument cover the right cases? . . .

Consider that the kinds of risks we are most concerned with, the handling of toxins, carcinogens and other hazardous materials, are not risks which are likely to be chosen for their intrinsic desirability, for the satisfaction that might derive from facing danger or using special skills to survive, or for their instrumental connection to highly desirable consequences, like saving lives. Rather, the motivation to take these risks derives entirely from the extrinsic rewards associated with them, rewards like hazard pay or steady employment in areas of limited employment opportunity. Partly as a result of this difference, the choice to be a fireman or stuntdriver is *exceptional*, reflecting a high degree of self-selection: such choices could readily have been foregone for many other kinds of work. In contrast, the choice to be a miner, millworker, or industrial worker facing health hazards subject to OSHA's strong criterion is *typical*. For a large class of workers, these are the primary forms of available employment. Indeed, these are the typical options, or the sole or most attractive ones, facing a class of workers with a significantly restricted range of options. The restrictions on workers' options are the result of various factors: their limited educational opportunity, their array of marketable skills and talents, accidents of geographical location, or their limited economic resources for financing job mobility.

Moreover, this narrowness of the range of options open to the typical worker is compounded by another factor. The riskiness of exceptional jobs (stuntdriver, fireman) can be viewed as stable over time: the worker knows more or less what he is getting into over a standard period of employment. But in 'typical' jobs, changes in manufacturing processes can expose workers to risks not anticipated at the inception of an employment period. To impose the burden of dodging these risks on the worker, given possible losses in benefits, pensions, family disruption, is to overestimate his effective options, to assume he has job mobility where it does not exist.

What this point about exceptional versus typical choices means, then, is that hazard pay proposals in one setting, made to one group of workers, may be, or will tend to be, quasi-coercive without all hazard pay proposals being so. The difference will depend on judgments about the range of alternatives open to one group, rather than the other, and on the reasons for the restricted options. Thus the argument does not force us to treat dissimilar groups similarly.

Moreover, nothing in this argument for strong OSHA regulation implies we ought to intervene similarly in lifestyle choices affecting health, even though by doing so we might prevent comparable harms. Like the stuntdriver's choices, these lifestyle choices are also not generally or potentially quasi-coerced. . . .[5] (There are) some worries about the voluntariness of certain lifestyle choices, noting, for example, the effect of strong sub-cultural influences. But these threats to autonomy are different from quasi-coercion, and arguments based on these more diffuse kinds of influence are not likely to justify comparable interventions. Indeed, they are just the sorts of influence we are fearful of undermining if we respect diversity.

The argument sketched here for the OSHA criterion thus appears to avoid the worries of the libertarian lament that OSHA must be compatible with the liberty to consent to risk, we recognize in other contexts. It turns out that only the appropriate hazard pay proposals are quasi-coercive, or potentially so. It is important to remember that the argument does not require that we already think the range of options open to regulated workers is unjustly or unfairly restricted. It is sufficient that we believe the restricted range of options such workers enjoy, though fair or just now, would tip in the direction of injustice and unfairness over the long run. Moreover, we should be concerned that the "tipping" might be hard to detect and therefore that the quasi-coerciveness would remain hidden and invisible to many participants in the hazard pay market. Consequently, we should be reluctant to rely on our perceptions of fairness once faced with such situations. Just as some incompetent or uninformed individuals may not be in the best position to detect their diminished capacity for making autonomous decisons, so too we should not wait till we are quasi-coerced to protect ourselves against diminished autonomy. Rather, it is prudent to impose prior, protective constraints on the framework of markets built on exchanges between workers and employers. These constraints are designed to insure that market changes remain within the requirements of justice or fairness.

An important objection to this argument sketch is . . . that the argument straddles a fence. The appropriate reaction to complaints about an injustice, or potential injustice, in the distribution of social goods should be to alter the fundamental institutional arrangements which lead to the unjust distribution. Yet our argument leads us merely to intervene narrowly to block one sort of consequence of such (potential) injustice, the harm that might result from quasi-coerced decisions. This intervention seems to add insult to injury, if the premise about quasi-coercion is correct. We leave all the factors intact which create, or tend to create, the unjust, quasi-coercive setting. Instead, we intervene to stop a vulnerable class of individuals from exercising its own discretion. This paternalism seems vexing because it leaves intact the background conditions which seem to make the intervention necessary. The objection, then, is that worries about injustice should not lead to narrow constraints on autonomy. If the objection is correct, step (4) of the argument sketch is dubious.

I should like to make three points in response to this objection. First, the autonomy that is restricted here is only an illusion if the claim about quasi-coercion is correct. To be sure, the interventions may remain offensive to those who want to accept the offers involved, but if the discussion in earlier sections is correct, we have reason to think the voluntariness of quasi-coerced decisions is diminished in morally significant ways. Second, contrary to the premise of the objection, arguments from justice often involve restrictions on free exchanges among individuals: the restrictions take the general form of restricting some free exchanges to preserve the fairness of others. Does a market which permits quasi-coerced exchanges respect liberty more than one that restricts some exchanges in order to make all exchanges free from quasi-coercion? I would suggest not, but the answer would take us afield into some central questions in the general theory of justice.

My third point is that the modification of distributive institutions involved in OSHA regulations does have an effect on distributive justice, at least if arguments I have made elsewhere about the nature of health care as a social good are at all plausible. No doubt, the importance of health might be argued for in various ways, all of which might justify viewing the trading of health for too low a price as unfair. But on my own view . . . health is of direct relevance to worries about justice because it contributes directly to the distribution of opportunity in society. Compromising health through quasi-coerced hazard pay bargains thus compromises the ability to maintain fair equality of opportunity in a society. The restricted opportunity range of poor or worst-off classes of workers would act, in hazard pay markets, to further undermine fair equality of opportunity. Earlier, I had argued that claims about the special importance of health or health care will not show by themselves why we should not rely on consent to distribute risks to health: health is not so important we refuse to let people compromise it in various contexts. The argument sketch for the strong OSHA criterion shows, however, why certain hazard pay proposals would depend on a highly questionable form of consent, consent under quasi-coercion, and that is the crux of the rationale offered here.

There is a deeply troubling consequence of the argument offered in the last section, one that is important to bring out in the open. The rationale I offered turned on concern about the actual or potential quasi-coerciveness of certain hazard pay proposals. The quasi-coerciveness of the proposals depended on the fact that the class of workers facing such proposals have, or are likely to have, unfairly or unjustly restricted alternatives. But what if we could agree that the distribution of income and opportunity were really fair or just, and that the distribution would not be tipped toward unfairness over time through the operation of a market for such risk-taking. Suppose, that is, that we lived in a just social arrangement, one that were stable over time. If the rationale for OSHA's strong criterion depends on the claim about quasi-coerciveness, then there would be no need for the strong OSHA feasibility criterion. Perhaps the class of workers receiving these hazard pay proposals might still face a range of options more restricted than more fortunate groups of workers or professionals, but the inequalities here are no threat to justice (we are supposing). In such circumstances, we would still have a role for OSHA: guaranteeing adequate information is present for informed decision-making about risk-taking, and guaranteeing that costs are

internalized, so that hazard pay bargains do not free-load on other parties. But the strong OSHA criterion now lacks a rationale.

Some proponents of the strong OSHA criterion might readily agree to this restriction on its applicability: for them, the rationale I have offered would seem to capture their underlying moral view. But some proponents of strong regulation might feel uneasy about the restriction: indeed, I feel uneasy about it myself. It is not clear to me just what follows from this sort of unfocused uneasiness. It could be that there are other components to a rationale which are not captured at all in this argument from justice. Yet, it is not obvious at all what they are. On the other hand, the problem may lie with this methodology for testing a philosophical argument. Intuitions or considered moral judgments about the rightness of a practice, like stringent OSHA regulations, arise in a particular social setting, one which has many forms of injustice or threats of injustice. It is notoriously difficult to clean up and make the principles underlying these intuitions explicit merely by forming counter-factual test contexts in which to deploy them. To be sure, this is standard philosophical method, but its results are often less clear than what we take them to be. Nevertheless, if one cannot show why one is dissatisfied with the kind of "test" of the rationale this hypothetical case involves, then the dissatisfaction will linger to infect the rationale itself. This result should worry proponents of strong OSHA regulation, who must offer an alternative, or more complete, rationale than the one sketched here.

The rationale I have offered, despite these deeper worries that there are still *other* components needed for a complete account, does carry weight wherever we have reason to worry about quasi-coerciveness in our own society. That is, we *do* get a plausible argument for the OSHA criterion as long as we have reason to worry about the fairness or justice of the distribution of options available to the workers most likely to receive the hazard pay proposals in question. But, of course, just such worries are themselves controversial. And differences in moral judgment here depend not only on different estimates of empirical facts, but on different underlying conceptions of what is just or fair. So my rationale also has the strength of locating clearly a source of controversy about the acceptability of the

OSHA criterion itself. My rationale will be controversial just where moral controversy about regulation is sharpest in our society. The rationale cannot by itself resolve this dispute. Still, it may help make it clearer what might be needed to do so, given the source of conflict.

Does OSHA protect too much? The answer depends on other moral judgments we make about the justice and fairness of choices open to workers in certain hazard pay markets.

NOTES

1. Cf. David Zimmerman's summary of the dispute, "Coercive Wage Offers," *Philosophy and Public Affairs* 10 (1981): 133–34.
2. Robert Nozick, "Coercion," *Philosophy, Politics and Society,* ed. P. Laslett, W. G. Runciman, and Q. Skinner (New York: Barnes & Noble Books, 1972), 450.
3. For example, Nozick considers the example of the drug supplier who proposes that he give an addict his usual dose for $20 only if the addict, in addition, performs a disagreeable task. Nozick suggests the proposal is a threat because here the addict's preference is for the normally expected baseline (the $20 dose), not the morally required baseline (no drug). We need to know why the addict's preference is here (always?) decisive. Cf. Nozick, "Coercion," 451 and Zimmerman, "Coercive Wage Offers," 129.
4. This objection is effectively argued by Zimmerman, "Coercive Wage Offers."
5. The elderly who have to eat dog food may be a case of quasi-coercion.

Whistleblowing and Employee Loyalty

Ronald Duska

Three Mile Island. In early 1983, almost four years after the near meltdown at Unit 2, two officials in the Site Operations Office of General Public Utilities reported a reckless company effort to clean up the contaminated reactor. Under threat of physical retaliation from superiors, the GPU insiders released evidence alleging that the company had rushed the TMI cleanup without testing key maintenance systems. Since then, the Three Mile Island mop-up has been stalled pending a review of GPU's management.[1]

The releasing of evidence of the rushed cleanup at Three Mile Island is an example of whistleblowing. Norman Bowie defines whistleblowing as "the act by an employee of informing the public on the immoral or illegal behavior of an employer or supervisor."[2] Ever since Daniel Ellsberg's release of the Pentagon Papers, the question of whether an employee should blow the whistle on his company or organization has become a hotly contested issue. Was Ellsberg right? Is it right to report the shady or suspect practices of the organization one works for? Is one a stool pigeon or a dedicated citizen? Does a person have an obligation to the public which overrides his obligation to his employer or does he simply betray a loyalty and become a traitor if he reports his company?

There are proponents on both sides of the issue—those who praise whistleblowers as civic heroes and those who condemn them as "finks." Glen and Shearer who wrote about the whistleblowers at Three Mile Island say, "Without the *courageous* breed of assorted company insiders known as whistleblowers—workers who often risk their livelihoods to disclose information about construction and design flaws—the Nuclear Regulatory Commission itself would be nearly as idle as Three Mile Island . . . That whistleblowers deserve both gratitude and protection is beyond disagreement."[3]

Still, while Glen and Shearer praise whistleblowers, others vociferously condemn them. For example, in a now-infamous quote, James Roche, the former president of General Motors said:

> Some critics are now busy eroding another support of free enterprise—the loyalty of a management team, with its unifying values and cooperative work. Some of the enemies of

business now encourage an employee to be *disloyal* to the enterprise. They want to create suspicion and disharmony, and pry into the proprietary interests of the business. However this is labelled—industrial espionage, whistle blowing, or professional responsibility—it is another tactic for spreading disunity and creating conflict.[4]

From Roche's point of view, whistleblowing is not only not "courageous" and deserving of "gratitude and protection" as Glen and Shearer would have it, it is corrosive and not even permissible.

Discussions of whistleblowing generally revolve around four topics: (1) attempts to define whistleblowing more precisely; (2) debates about whether and when whistleblowing is permissible; (3) debates about whether and when one has an obligation to blow the whistle; and (4) appropriate mechanisms for institutionalizing whistleblowing.

In this paper I want to focus on the second problem, because I find it somewhat disconcerting that there is a problem at all. When I first looked into the ethics of whistleblowing it seemed to me that whistleblowing was a good thing, and yet I found in the literature claim after claim that it was in need of defense, that there was something wrong with it, namely that it was an act of disloyalty.

If whistleblowing was a disloyal act, it deserved disapproval, and ultimately any action of whistleblowing needed justification. This disturbed me. It was as if the act of a good Samaritan was being condemned as an act of interference, as if the prevention of a suicide needed to be justified. My moral position in favor of whistleblowing was being challenged. The tables were turned and the burden of proof had shifted. My position was the one in question. Suddenly instead of the company being the bad guy and the whistleblower the good guy, which is what I thought, the whistleblower was the bad guy. Why? Because he was disloyal. What I discovered was that in most of the literature it was taken as axiomatic that whistleblowing was an act of disloyalty. My moral intuitions told me that axiom was mistaken. Nevertheless, since it is accepted by a large segment of the ethical community it deserves investigation.

In his book *Business Ethics,* Norman Bowie, who presents what I think is one of the finest presentations of the ethics of whistleblowing, claims that "whistleblowing . . . violate[s] a *prima facie* duty of loyalty to one's employer." According to Bowie, there is a duty of loyalty which prohibits one from reporting his employer or company. Bowie, of course, recognizes that this is only a *prima facie* duty, i.e., one that can be overridden by a higher duty to the public good. Nevertheless, the axiom that whistleblowing is disloyal is Bowie's starting point.

Bowie is not alone. Sisela Bok, another fine ethicist, sees whistleblowing as an instance of disloyalty.

> The whistleblower hopes to stop the game; but since he is neither referee nor coach, and since he blows the whistle on his own team, his act is seen as a *violation of loyalty* [italics mine]. In holding his position, he has assumed certain obligations to his colleagues and clients. He may even have subscribed to a loyalty oath or a promise of confidentiality . . . Loyalty to colleagues and to clients comes to be pitted against loyalty to the public interest, to those who may be injured unless the revelation is made.[5]

Bowie and Bok end up defending whistleblowing in certain contexts, so I don't necessarily disagree with their conclusions. However, I fail to see how one has an obligation of loyalty to one's company, so I disagree with their perception of the problem, and their starting point. The difference in perception is important because those who think employees have an obligation of loyalty to a company fail to take into account a relevant moral difference between persons and corporations and between corporations and other kinds of groups where loyalty is appropriate. I want to argue that one does not have an obligation of loyalty to a company, even a *prima facie* one, because companies are not the kind of things which are proper objects of loyalty. I then want to show that to make them objects of loyalty gives them a moral status they do not deserve and in raising their status, one lowers the status of the individuals who work for the companies.

But why aren't corporations the kind of things which can be objects of loyalty? . . .

Loyalty is ordinarily construed as a state of being constant and faithful in a relation implying trust or confidence, as a wife to husband, friend to friend, parent to child, lord to vassal, etc. According to John Ladd "it is not founded on just *any* casual relationship, but on a specific kind of relationship or tie. The ties that bind the persons together provide the basis of loyalty."[6] But all sorts of ties bind people together to make groups. I am a member of a group of fans if I go to a ball game. I am a member of a group if I merely walk down the street. I am in a sense tied to them, but don't owe them loyalty. I don't owe loyalty to just anyone I encounter. Rather I owe loyalty to persons with whom I have special relationships. I owe it to my children, my spouse, my parents, my friends and certain groups, those groups which are formed for the mutual enrichment of the members. It is important to recognize that in any relationship which demands loyalty the relationship works both ways and involves mutual enrichment. Loyalty is incompatible with self-interest, because it is something that necessarily requires we go beyond self-interest. My loyalty to my friend, for example, requires I put aside my interests some of the time. It is because of this reciprocal requirement which demands surrendering self-interest that a corporation is not a proper object of loyalty.

A business or corporation does two things in the free enterprise system. It produces a good or service and makes a profit. The making of a profit, however, is the primary function of a business as a business. For if the production of the good or service was not profitable the business would be out of business. Since non-profitable goods or services are discontinued, the providing of a service or the making of a product is not done for its own sake, but from a business perspective is a means to an end, the making of profit. People bound together in a business are not bound together for mutual fulfillment and support, but to divide labor so the business makes a profit. Since profit is paramount if you do not produce in a company or if there are cheaper laborers around, a company feels justified in firing you for the sake of better production. Throughout history companies in a pinch feel no obligation of loyalty. Compare that to a family. While we can jokingly refer to a family as "somewhere they have to take you in no matter what," you cannot refer to a company in that way. "You can't buy loyalty" is true. Loyalty depends on ties that demand self-sacrifice with no expectation of reward, e.g., the ties of loyalty that bind a family together. Business functions on the basis of enlightened self-interest. I am devoted to a company not because it is like a parent to me. It is not, and attempts of some companies to create "one big happy family" ought to be looked on with suspicion. I am not "devoted" to it at all, or should not be. I *work* for it because it pays me. I am not in a family to get paid, but I am in a company to get paid.

Since loyalty is a kind of devotion, one can confuse devotion to one's job (or the ends of one's work) with devotion to a company.

I may have a job I find fulfilling, but that is accidental to my relation to the company. For example, I might go to work for a company as a carpenter and love the job and get satisfaction out of doing good work. But if the company can increase profit by cutting back to an adequate but inferior type of material or procedure, it can make it impossible for me to take pride in my work as a carpenter while making it possible for me to make more money. The company does not exist to subsidize my quality work as a carpenter. As a carpenter my goal may be good houses, but as an employee my goal is to contribute to making a profit. "That's just business!"

This fact that profit determines the quality of work allowed leads to a phenomenon called the commercialization of work. The primary end of an act of building is to make something, and to build well is to make it well. A carpenter is defined by the end of his work, but if the quality interferes with profit, the business side of the venture supercedes the artisan side. Thus profit forces a craftsman to suspend his devotion to his work and commercializes his venture. The more professions subject themselves to the forces of the marketplace, the more they get commercialized; e.g., research for the sake of a more profitable product rather than for the sake of knowledge jeopardizes the integrity of academic research facilities.

The cold hard truth is that the goal of profit is what gives birth to a company and forms that particular group. Money is what ties the group together. But in such a commercialized venture, with such a goal there is no loyalty, or at least none need be expected. An employer will release an employee and an employee will walk away from an employer when it is profitable to do so. That's business. It is perfectly permissible. Contrast that with the ties between a lord and his vassal. A lord could not in good conscience wash his hands of his vassal, nor could a vassal in good conscience abandon his lord. What bound them was mutual enrichment, not profit.

Loyalty to a corporation, then, is not required. But even more it is probably misguided. There is nothing as pathetic as the story of the loyal employee who, having given above and beyond the call of duty, is let go in the restructuring of the company. He feels betrayed because he mistakenly viewed the company as an object of his loyalty. To get rid of such foolish romanticism and to come to grips with this hard but accurate assessment should ultimately benefit everyone.

One need hardly be an enemy of business to be suspicious of a demand of loyalty to something whose primary reason for existence is the making of profit. It is simply the case that I have no duty of loyalty to the business or organization. Rather I have a duty to return responsible work for fair wages. The commercialization of work dissolves the type of relationship that requires loyalty. It sets up merely contractual relationships. One sells one's labor but not one's self to a company or an institution.

To think we owe a company or corporation loyalty requires us to think of that company as a person or as a group with a goal of human enrichment. If we think of it in this way we can be loyal. But this is just the wrong way to think. A company is not a person. A company is an instrument, and an instrument with a specific purpose, the making of profit. To treat an instrument as an end in itself, like a person, may not be as bad as treating an end as an instrument, but it does give the instrument a moral status it does not deserve, and by elevating the instrument we lower the end. All things, instruments and ends, become alike.

To treat a company as a person is analogous to treating a machine as a person or treating a system as a person. The system, company, or instrument get as much respect and care as the persons for whom they were invented. If we remember that the primary purpose of business is to make profit, it can be seen clearly as merely an instrument. If so, it needs to be used and regulated accordingly, and I owe it no more loyalty than I owe a word processor.

Of course if everyone would view business as a commercial instrument, things might become more difficult for the smooth functioning of the organization, since businesses could not count on the "loyalty" of their employees. Business itself is well served, at least in the short run, if it can keep the notion of a duty to loyalty alive. It does this by comparing itself to a paradigm case of an organization one shows loyalty to, the team.

Remember that Roche refers to the "management team" and Bok sees the name "whistleblowing" coming from the instance of a referee blowing a whistle in the presence of a foul. What is perceived as bad about whistleblowing in business from this perspective is that one blows the whistle on one's own team, thereby violating team loyalty. If the company can get its employees to view it as a team they belong to, it is easier to demand loyalty. The rules governing teamwork and team loyalty will apply. One reason the appeal to a team and team loyalty works so well in business is that businesses are in competition with one another. If an executive could get his employees to be loyal, a loyalty without thought to himself or his fellow man, but to the will of the company, the manager would have the ideal kind of corporation from an organizational standpoint. As Paul R. Lawrence, the organizational theorist says, "Ideally, we would want one sentiment to be dominant in all employees from top to bottom, namely a complete loyalty to the organizational purpose."[7] Effective motivation turns business practices into a game and instills teamwork.

But businesses differ from teams in very important respects, which makes the analogy between business and a team dangerous. Loyalty to a team is loyalty within the context of sport, a competition. Teamwork and team loyalty require that in the circumscribed activity of the game I cooperate with my fellow players so that pulling all together, we can win. The object of (most) sports is victory. But the winning in sports is a social convention, divorced from the usual goings on of society. Such a winning is most times a harmless, morally neutral diversion.

But the fact that this victory in sports, within the rules enforced by a referee (whistleblower), is a socially developed convention taking place within a larger social context makes it quite different from competition in business, which, rather than being defined by a context, permeates the whole of society in its influence. Competition leads not only to winners but to losers. One can lose at sport with precious few serious consequences. The consequences of losing at a business are much more serious. Further, the losers in sport are there voluntarily, while the losers in business can be those who are not in the game voluntarily (we are all forced to participate) but are still affected by business decisions. People cannot choose to participate in business, since it permeates everyone's life.

The team model fits very well with the model of the free-market system because there competition is said to be the name of the game. Rival companies compete and their object is to win. To call a foul on one's own teammate is to jeopardize one's chances of winning and is viewed as disloyalty.

But isn't it time to stop viewing the corporate machinations as games? These games are not controlled and not over after a specific time. The activities of business affect the lives of everyone, not just the game players. The analogy of the corporation to a team and the consequent appeal to team loyalty, although understandable, is seriously misleading at least in the moral sphere, where competition is not the prevailing virtue.

If my analysis is correct, the issue of the permissibility of whistleblowing is not a real issue, since there is no obligation of loyalty to a company. Whistleblowing is not only permissible but expected when a company is harming society. The issue is not one of disloyalty to the company, but the question of whether the whistleblower has an obligation to society if blowing the whistle will bring him retaliation. I will not argue that issue, but merely suggest the lines I would pursue.

I tend to be a minimalist in ethics, and depend heavily on a distinction between obligations and acts of supererogation. We have, it seems to me, an obligation to avoid harming anyone, but not an obligation to do good. Doing good is above the call of duty. In-between we may under certain conditions have an obligation to prevent harm. If whistleblowing can prevent harm, then it is required under certain conditions.

Simon, Powers and Gunnemann set forth four conditions:[8] need, proximity, capability, and last resort. Applying these, we get the following.

1. There must be a clear harm to society that can be avoided by whistleblowing. We don't blow the whistle over everything.
2. It is the "proximity" to the whistleblower that puts him in the position to report his company in the first place.
3. "Capability" means that he needs to have some chance of success. No one has an obligation to jeopardize himself to perform futile gestures. The whistleblower needs to have access to the press, be believable, etc.
4. "Last resort" means just that. If there are others more capable of reporting and more proximate, and if they will report, then one does not have the responsibility.

Before concluding, there is one aspect of the loyalty issue that ought to be disposed of. My position could be challenged in the case of organizations who are employers in non-profit areas, such as the government, educational institutions, etc. In this case my commercialization argument is irrelevant. However, I would maintain that any activity which merits the blowing of the whistle in the case of non-profit and service organizations is probably counter to the purpose of the institution in the first place. Thus, if there were loyalty required, in that case, whoever justifiably blew the whistle would be blowing it on a colleague who perverted the end or purpose of the organization. The loyalty to the group would remain intact. Ellsberg's whistleblowing on the government is a way of keeping the government faithful to its obligations. But that is another issue.

NOTES

1. Maxwell Glen and Cody Shearer, "Going after the Whistle-blowers," *The Philadelphia Inquirer*, Tuesday, Aug. 2, 1983, Op-ed Page, p. 11a.
2. Norman Bowie, *Business Ethics* (Englewood Cliffs, N.J.: Prentice-Hall, 1982), 140. For Bowie, this is just a preliminary definition. His fuller definition reads, "A whistle blower is an employee or officer of any institution, profit or non-profit, private or public, who believes either that he/she has been ordered to perform some act or he/she has obtained knowledge that the institution is engaged in activities which a) are believed to cause unnecessary harm to third parties, b) are in violation of human rights or c) run counter to the defined purpose of the institution and

who inform the public of this fact." Bowie then lists six conditions under which the act is justified. 142–143.

3. Glen and Shearer, "Going after the Whistleblowers," 11a.

4. James M. Roche, "The Competitive System, to Work, to Preserve, and to Protect," *Vital Speeches of the Day* (May 1971), 445. This is quoted in Bowie, 141 and also in Kenneth D. Walters, "Your Employee's Right to Blow the Whistle," *Harvard Business Review,* 53, no. 4.

5. Sisela Bok, "Whistleblowing and Professional Re-

sponsibilities," *New York University Education Quarterly,* vol. II, 4 (1980), 3.

6. John Ladd, "Loyalty," *The Encyclopedia of Philosophy,* vol. 5, 97.

7. Paul R. Lawrence, *The Changing of Organizational Behavior Patterns: A Case Study of Decentralization* (Boston: Division of Research, Harvard Business School, 1958), 208, as quoted in Kenneth D. Walters, op. cit.

8. John G. Simon, Charles W. Powers, and Jon P. Gunnemann, *The Ethical Investor: Universities and Corporate Responsibility* (New Haven: Yale University Press, 1972).

Whistleblowing and Trust:
Some Lessons from the ADM Scandal

Daryl Koehn

The 1980s witnessed a flurry of articles regarding the ethics of whistleblowing. These articles tended to focus on three issues: (1) the definition of whistleblowing; (2) whether and when it was permissible to violate one's obligations of loyalty to colleagues or one's profession/corporation; and (3) whether a threat to the public interest actually obligates someone with knowledge of this threat to make this knowledge public.[1] These same issues have surfaced in recent discussions of the act of whistleblowing by Mark Whitacre at Archer Daniels Midland. While I do not think these three issues are morally irrelevant to a discussion of whistleblowing, I am troubled by the fact that the entire discussion to date has focused on the issue of duty. In this commentary, I want to focus less on the question of duty and more on the question of personal, corporate, and public trust: Does whistleblowing foster or destroy moral trust? What makes whistleblowers and the companies for whom they work worthy of employee and public trust?

I shall use the alleged events at ADM to explore these questions. The reader should keep in mind that I am not writing a case history of whistleblowing at ADM. At the time of this writing, we have yet to hear much of the company's side of the story nor do we know exactly what evidence Whitacre

has to support his allegation that the company engaged in price-fixing with their competitors. What matters for my purposes here is not that these events did occur but that they could have occurred and they raise serious and interesting questions for corporate, individual and public behavior.

Part One: Whistleblowing and Its Effects on Trust

It will be helpful to begin with a working definition of a whistleblower. Following Sisela Bok, I shall define whistleblowers as persons who "sound an alarm from within the very organization in which they work, aiming to spotlight neglect or abuses that threaten the public interest.[2] Several features of this definition are relevant to thinking about trust. First, the whistleblower claims to be acting in the public interest. He or she tries to occupy the moral highground by calling attention to some matter the whistleblower thinks the public will be, or should be, concerned about. I say "concerned about" rather than simply "interested in" because the whistleblower claims to be more than a mere tattler. If I were to disclose the religious preferences of my boss, we would not think such disclosure constituted whistleblowing because it is hard to see what public interest is involved. Given the very real risks of being fired, demoted, ostracized, or at-

Reprinted with permission of *The Online Journal of Ethics,* http://condor.depaul.edu/ethics/ethg1.html

tacked by those the whistleblower is accusing of negligence or abuse, the whistleblowers generally must think of themselves as on something akin to a mission. They try to portray themselves as acting on behalf of an interest higher than their own—the public interest.

I dwell on this point to emphasize that the whistleblower has made some assumptions as to what constitutes the public interest. He may have erred in his assessment of the nature of the public interest. Or he may have misevaluated his "facts". The facts may be unsound, or they may be sound yet irrelevant to the public interest. If we take trust as the trustor's belief that he or she is the recipient of the good will of the trusted party, the whistleblower can be thought of as portraying himself as a trustworthy person who has acted in good will toward the public and who merits the public's trust. Mark Whitacre, for example, portrayed himself as the white knight of the consumer, a consumer whom ADM had allegedly declared to be the enemy.[3] However, if Whitacre's accusations result in the demise of ADM and the loss of a major supplier of consumer goods, we may well wonder whether Whitacre has acted in fact in the public's interest. Moreover, Whitacre himself arguably has something of a skewed view of public interest since he seems perfectly willing to engage in predatory, monopolistic pricing.[4] According to his own account, he balked at his company's pricing policy only when his colleagues tried to engage in price-fixing.[5] Given that the customer is hurt by monopolistic pricing as well as price-fixing, his whistleblowing at this late date may be less an attempt to aid the customer and the public than to save his own skin. More generally, if and when a whistleblower's motives are mixed, we have some reason to wonder, on the one hand, whether he is trustworthy and, on the other hand, to perhaps be more sympathetic to a company who charges that the whistleblower has betrayed it and the public as well.

Second, the whistleblower believes that there is a substantial audience who will attend to her disclosures. If an employee calls up the press and discloses that the CEO wears blue shirts to work every day, his announcement is likely to be greeted by the reporter with a stifled yawn, if not a burst of profanity. To say that the whistleblower's disclosure is in the public interest just is to say that it has the makings of a good story. The tale, therefore, will likely attract the press and maybe the regulatory authorities as well. It can quickly become sensationalized as people begin to speculate on the extent and magnitude of the alleged corporate misconduct. Furthermore, the regulatory authorities may begin an elaborate investigation on the theory that any abuse known by one individual may just be the tip of the iceberg. The Federal authorities, for example, are not merely subpoenaeing many of ADM's records; they have also asked for the records of many of ADM's competitors.[6] There is a very real danger of a witchhunt, for as Bok reminds us, secret police almost always rely on informers and have a history of widening the charges against those accused.[7] Such reflections suggest that it is incumbent upon a whistleblower who truly wants to merit the public's trust to try to explore issues internally before going public with her accusations.

There are, of course, difficulties associated with going public internally. I shall say more about these shortly. My point here is that whistleblowing may harm public trust in our institutions, rather than restore it, if whistleblowing creates a whirlwind of suspicion and the impression that corruption is everywhere. Fellow employees of whistleblowers may be justifiably irritated at a colleague who makes accusations to the press without ever running these same charges by them or without seeking their interpretation of actions and events within the corporation. It may be unfair for the corporation to try to dismiss a whistleblower as a troublemaker with few social skills. On the other hand, the whistleblower may very well be someone who is overly suspicious or inclined to make wild accusations without verifying her facts. Moreover, if the whistleblower does not try to work internally first to try to resolve what she perceives as a problem, it is difficult to see how she can claim to be trying to right the problem. It is striking that Whitacre, by his own account, had heard allegations of price-fixing for many years and had simply ignored them,[8] treating them as though they were someone else's problem. But if he really cared for the company and for the public interest, why did he not investigate these charges when he first heard them? Given that he was in line to be president of ADM, he surely should have worried about this problem and taken steps to address a problem that he was bound to inherit. Conversely, one wonders why he would have wanted to be president of a company that was in his judgment engaged in dastardly deeds. At a minimum, it seems as though he should have interested himself many years ago in the question of whether and why ADM had a history of tolerating price-fixing.

Another way of putting the point is as follows: Whistleblowers are part and parcel of the corporate culture on which they blow the whistle. They are often rather senior because it is those issuing orders who usually have the most control over and the most knowledge about what is occurring within the corporation. At the point of public disclosure, the whistleblower assigns responsibility for the abuse to someone else and thereby distances himself from any responsibility. But matters are rarely so clean. If one has worked many years for a company, taken a salary from them, followed their policies, then one is arguably complicitous in the practices of that corporation. The traditional discussion of whistleblowing pits the individual's loyalty to the company against his loyalty to himself. But this formulation presupposes that that self is a private self, totally independent of the company. I am saying that the self is a company self as well. And while it may be convenient for the whistleblower to talk as though it is him against the big bad company, such talk is suspect to the extent that the whistleblower has supported the company. Blowing the whistle may not increase public trust to the extent the public is rightly suspicious of the whistleblower's own history within the corporation.

Third, the whistleblower is levelling an accusation of neglect or abuse at particular persons within the corporation. These accusations are not pleasant for the accused whose lives may be permanently disrupted by what may turn out to be false charges. At a minimum, the lives of the accused will be unsettled for a substantial amount of time as the press picks up the story and as investigations run their course. While no one should be above the law, we also should not be insensitive to the need for due process. We should also remember that passions almost always run high around whistleblowers' accusations because the whistleblower's charge applies to present activities of a corporation or profession.[9] No one blows the whistle or shows much interest in past abuses with few present effects or in remote, unlikely future events. The alleged danger is present and a person's emotions are engaged, which is all the more reason for exercising extreme caution in making charges and in evaluating them.

The above observations suggest that corporate employees and leaders rightly are concerned about the effect of whistleblowing not merely on corporate morale but on the ability of employees to work together in relative harmony. This harmony becomes close to impossible when the atmosphere is a highly charged one of mutual suspicion. Note that I am not saying that an employee has an overriding loyalty of duty to the group for which he works. It may well be, as Ronald Duska has argued, that the corporation is not the kind of group to which one can be loyal.[10] In any case, there is no prima facie duty to be loyal to any group. A profession such as medicine is worth serving not because it is a group but because its end—the health of individuals—is a genuine good. The end, not the group per se, commands group members' loyalty. We do not, for example, say that agents have a prima facie duty to the Ku Klux Klan or the mafia. The person who leaves such a group does not override a prima facie duty. Rather, there never was a duty to be a part of a group engaged in unethical behavior.

My point then is not that the employee acts wrongly because whistleblowing is disloyal. The wrongness in the whistleblowing consists instead in acting to destroy workplace atmosphere if and when this destruction could have been avoided by adopting a less accusatory stance or by working within the corporation. Whistleblowing may destroy trust. And trust within a corporation is good when the trust is a reasoned trust, born of open and probing discussions with one's peers regarding matters of joint concern. Whistleblowing should be evaluated in light of its consequences for this reasoned trust not in light of its effects on irrational loyalty or its relation to a non-existent prima facie duty of group loyalty.

Part Two: Responsibilities of Both Whistleblower and Corporation

This last comment raises what I take to be the central moral issue connected with whistleblowing: What can both whistleblower and corporation do to foster reasoned trust and to avoid a situation in which employees feel they have to go outside the company to get their concerns addressed?

Given the very real dangers associated with whistleblowing and the all-too-human propensities toward self-righteousness and misinterpretation, it is clear that the would-be whistleblower and corporation alike should make every effort to discuss perceived abuses and negligence before it gets to the point where the whistleblower thinks a public accusation must be made. The corporation thus has a responsibility to provide a regular forum for free and open discussion of possible abuses. Participants should have equal and reciprocal rights to question one another, to bring evidence, etc. They should not be penalized in any way for participation in this forum. It is striking that ADM had no such forum. In fact, communication was so bad within the company that the CEO's own son apparently did not know until after the fact that the father had called in the FBI to help investigate whether production at ADM was being sabotaged.[11]

Conversely, the whistleblower must be willing to come forward and be identified. It is close to impossible for the accused to mount a defense or even seek clarification when the accuser is anonymous. This requirement to publicly participate increases the odds that the would-be whistleblower will doublecheck her facts before going public. Discussion will also tend to dispel employees' perception that corruption is everywhere. In fact, regular discussion should deflate a good deal of the anger and anxiety regarding corporate problems. Employees will come to see that, yes, their corporation has problems and oversights but, yes, their corporation is routinely and professionally addressing these difficulties. Participation in such a forum will require a good deal of courage on the part of employees and a good bit of restraint on the part of a corporate hierarchy tempted to retaliate against any and all perceived threats.

Second, it is incumbent on corporate leadership to examine the tasks they impose on their employees. An employee can only be morally required to do that which is possible. If the employee is placed in an untenable position, then he will feel anxious, trapped, and may be driven to try to escape from this position by taking his predicament public in an effort to gain public sympathy and support. Whitacre, for example, apparently was expected to do cutrate pricing with a view to grabbing a large market share while at the same time showing either minimal losses or a profit.[12] Price-fixing becomes a temptation in a corporate environment with these

unreasonable expectations, and reasoned trust is not given much of a chance to flourish. For their part, the employees must critically examine the position they are being asked to assume. It is curious that Whitacre professed unease about recruiting competitors for their expertise when he himself seems to have been recruited from a German competitor precisely for his expertise![13] Uncritical naivete on the part of employees becomes morally culpable to the extent that they fail to raise objections that would promote in-house discussion of possibly unethical practices.

Third, a company that desires the reasoned trust of its employees must grant the employees access to information about the company's practices. When a whistleblower accuses a company of malpractice, all employees of the corporation feel slightly tainted and anxious. They may feel betrayed not just by the whistleblower but also by the company whom they perceive as having hid relevant information from them. Secrecy encourages corporate paranoia. One of the best ways to combat it is to run as open a corporation as possible. The more access employees have, the more the corporation can legitimately hold them accountable for their actions and the more responsibility the employees will feel for actions they have known about and have had a chance to discuss. If there is genuine access to information about corporate practices, employees have a responsibility to seek out and to consider the implications of this information. It becomes less legitimate for them to bury their heads in the sand and then at some late date cry "Foul!" And this is how it should be in a corporation where all parties are genuinely committed to acting well.

Fourth, and finally, all members of the corporation have a responsibility to critically examine their actions, even if they have been taught to perform these acts and rewarded for doing so. A recent study comparing Japanese and American managers' attitudes toward ethics showed that the American managers were far more focussed on marketing than their foreign competitors and tended to think of immorality as occurring largely within marketing. This focus is problematic in several ways. It encourages managers to overlook ways in which they are treating their employees badly (e.g., by imposing unreasonable job requirements upon them). Furthermore, to the extent that American managers see only particular marketing practices as immoral, they fail to consider whether marketing itself may not be in some ways immoral. For example, does the idea of "targeting" specific groups of people for specific products wind up instrumentalizing the customer? If this customer is little more than a means to selling this product, it is not much of a leap to begin to think (as ADM allegedly did) of the customer as an enemy whose demand for low prices is keeping the company from attaining maximal profit.[14] More thought needs to be given to the nature of the core practices of business and less attention devoted to the bribery, price-fixing, etc. which may merely be symptoms of a sick practice. Unless and until these practices are well-scrutinized by the people who are engaged in them and who have the most knowledge about them, we should expect to continue to have a series of nasty abuses springing up and surprising us.

The corporate atmosphere also should be scrutinized. ADM's anti-bureaucratic rhetoric is a case in point. Whitacre mentions it several times and indicates that ADM has historically prided itself on its ability to get things done.[15] However, what gets dismissed as bureaucracy is often the system of checks and balances within the firm. Anti-bureaucratic rhetoric may encourage, at worst, an attitude of lawlessness and at best, a "can-do" approach which may, as in the case of Whitacre, breed enthusiasm but not do much for thoughtfulness.

Conclusion

While whistleblowing sometimes may be the only way to call attention to serious abuses by professions or corporations, whistleblowing is not un-

ambiguously ethically good. It is perhaps best seen as an option of last recourse. Rather than concentrating on when whistleblowing is moral, our time would be better spent thinking about how to improve corporate and professional environments so that employees and clients will not be driven to adopt this strategy.

NOTES

1. Ronald Duska, "Whistleblowing and Employee Loyalty," in Tom L. Beauchamp and Norman E. Bowie, *Ethical Theory and Business* (Englewood Cliffs, NJ: Prentice Hall, 1993), pp. 312–316.
2. Sisela Bok, "Whistleblowing and Professional Responsibility," in Beauchamp, op. cit.
3. Mark Whitacre as told to Ronald Henkoff, "My Life as a Corporate Mole for the FBI," in *Fortune,* Sept. 4, 1995, pp. 56–62.
4. Ibid.
5. Ibid. Ronald Henkoff comments that Whitacre's preferred approach to pricing "sounds a lot like predatory pricing," in Henkoff, "So Who Is This Mark Whitacre, and Why Is He Saying These Bad Things about ADM?," in *Fortune,* Sept. 4, 1995, pp. 64–67.
6. See "Suicide Hurts Government's ADM Case," Monday, August 14, 1995 at clari.news.crime.murders on the Worldwide Web.
7. Bok, op. cit.
8. Whitacre, op. cit.
9. Bok also discusses the fact that the charges apply to present wrongdoing. Bok, op. cit.
10. Duska, op. cit.
11. Whitacre, op. cit.
12. Ibid.
13. Ibid.
14. Ibid.
15. reference still missing--cited on p. 344.

Study Questions

1. What would the canonical position imply about the issue of safe working conditions?

2. Is it possible that an employer's demand for drug testing can be coercive even if the employee had notice of it before taking the job?

3. Imagine that you are a close friend of Celest Benedeto and that she comes to you for advice on what she should do to resolve the problem she faces in the "Letter of the Law" case. What would your advice to her be and why?

4. In *Deal v. Spears*, what was the "legitimate business interest" that the Spearses invoked to justify listening in on the phone conversations of Deal? How could the Spearses argue that their listening falls within the "ordinary course of business"?

5. How did the court in *Deal v. Spears* argue that Deal's consent to the monitoring of phone conversations could not be inferred from the circumstances invoked by the Spearses? Do you agree with the court's reasoning?

6. What reasons do DesJardins and Duska give to show that employers need not have access to information about drug use by employees in order to evaluate job performance? Do you agree with their reasons?

7. Can you think of cases in which you would want to permit drug testing of employees where DesJardins and Duska would rule it out? If so, what case would this be?

8. Kupfer claims that the intrusiveness of genetic screening is exacerbated by the feeling of relative powerlessness experienced by most employees in the typical workplace setting. Would such screening be permissible in a setting far more cooperative and egalitarian? Why or why not?

9. Near the end of his essay, Kupfer endorses severe limitations upon genetic screening in the workplace. What are these restrictions? Do you agree with them?

10. What grounds could be given to support Machan's claim that all people have rights to life, liberty, and property?

11. How does Machan respond to the objection that workers would routinely be faced with a "take it or leave it" situation if, as Machan proposes, government has no right to require employers to provide a safe workplace?

12. Is Daniels right in his assertion that offers to give workers hazard pay to accept unsafe or risky work are "quasi-coercive"?

13. Summarize Duska's position on loyalty. Is he correct in arguing that employees owe no obligation of loyalty to their firm? What about loyalty to co-workers whose careers may be negatively affected by the act of whistleblowing?

14. Critically assess the conditions Duska suggests need to be met for there to be an obligation to whistleblow. Given the serious personal costs, how do you interpret the first condition?

15. What, according to Koehn, are some of the attendant moral dangers of whistleblowing?

16. Koehn argues that the whistleblower must be willing to come forward and be identified. Would this practice have a chilling effect on whistleblowing? If so, what might be the larger effect on society?

17. Should the public be obligated to protect whistleblowers by insisting on legislation that would at least allow legitimate whistleblowers to keep their jobs? Would such a law really protect whistleblowers?

CASE SCENARIO 1   *Soroka v. Dayton Hudson Corp.*

The following opinion was handed down by a California appellate court in 1992. Justice Timothy Reardon wrote for the court majority.

Respondent Dayton Hudson Corporation owns and operates Target Stores throughout California and the United States. Job applicants for store security officer (SSO) positions must, as a condition of employment, take a psychological test that Target calls the "Psychscreen." An SSO's main function is to observe, apprehend and arrest suspected shoplifters. An SSO is not armed, but carries handcuffs and may use force against a suspect in self-defense. Target views good judgment and emotional stability as important SSO job skills. It intends the Psychscreen to screen out SSO applicants who are emotionally unstable, who may put customers or employees in jeopardy, or who will not take direction and follow Target procedures.

The Psychscreen is a combination of the Minnesota Multiphasic Personality Inventory and the California Psychological Inventory. Both of these tests have been used to screen out emotionally unfit applicants for public safety positions such as police officers, correctional officers, pilots, air traffic controllers and nuclear power plant operators. The test is composed of 704 true-false questions. At Target, the test administrator is told to instruct applicants to answer every question.

The test includes questions about an applicant's religious attitudes, such as: "[¶] 67. I feel sure that there is only one true religion. . . . [¶] 201. I have no patience with people who believe there is only one true religion. . . . [¶] 477. My soul sometimes leaves my body. . . . [¶] 483. A minister can cure disease by praying and putting his hand on your head. . . . [¶] 486. Everything is turning out just like the prophets of the Bible said it would. . . . [¶] 505. I go to church almost every week. [¶] 506. I believe in the second coming of Christ. . . . [¶] 516. I believe in a life hereafter. . . . [¶] 578. I am very religious (more than most people). . . . [¶] 580. I believe my sins are unpardonable. . . . [¶] 606. I believe there is a God. . . . [¶] 688. I believe there is a Devil and a Hell in afterlife."

The test includes questions that might reveal an applicant's sexual orientation, such as: "[¶] 137. I wish I were not bothered by thoughts about sex. . . . [¶] 290. I have never been in trouble because of my sex behavior. . . . [¶] 339. I have been in trouble one or more times because of my sex behavior. . . . [¶] 466. My sex life is satisfactory. . . . [¶] 492. I am very strongly attracted by members of my own sex. . . . [¶] 496. I have often wished I were a girl. (Or if you are a girl) I have never been sorry that I am a girl. . . . [¶] 525. I have never indulged in any unusual sex practices. . . . [¶] 558. I am worried about sex matters. . . . [¶] 592. I like to talk about sex. . . . [¶] 640. Many of my dreams are about sex matters."

An SSO's completed test is scored by the consulting psychologist firm of Martin-McAllister. The firm interprets test responses and rates the applicant on five traits: emotional stability, interpersonal style, addiction potential, dependability and reliability, and socialization—i.e., a tendency to follow established rules. Martin-McAllister sends a form to Target rating the applicant on these five traits and recommending whether to hire the applicant. Hiring decisions are made on the basis of these recommendations, although the recommendations may be overridden. Target does not receive any responses to specific questions. It has never conducted a formal validation study of the Psychscreen, but before it implemented the test, Target tested 17 or 18 of its more successful SSO's.

Appellants Sibi Soroka, Susan Urry and William d'Arcangelo were applicants for SSO positions when they took the Psychscreen. All three were upset by the nature of the Psychscreen questions. Soroka was hired by Target. Urry—a Mormon—and d'Arcangelo were not hired. In August 1989, Soroka filed a charge that use of the Psychscreen discriminated on the basis of race, sex, religion and physical handicap with the Department of Fair Employment and Housing.

Having exhausted their administrative remedies, Soroka, Urry and d'Arcangelo filed a class action against Target in September 1989 to challenge its use of the Psychscreen. The complaint was amended twice. The second amended complaint alleged that the test asked invasive questions that were not job-related. Soroka alleged causes of action for violation of the constitutional right to privacy, invasion of privacy, disclosure of confidential medical information, fraud, negligent misrepresentation, intentional and negligent infliction of emotional distress, violation of the Fair Employment and Housing Act, violation of sections 1101 and 1102 of the Labor Code, and unfair business practices. This complaint prayed for both damages and injunctive relief.

In June 1990, Soroka moved for a preliminary injunction to prohibit Target from using the Psychscreen during the pendency of the action. A professional psychologist submitted a declaration opining that use of the test was unjustified and improper, resulting in faulty assessments to the detriment of job applicants. He concluded that its use violated basic professional standards and that it had not been demonstrated to be reliable or valid as an employment evaluation.

The trial court denied Soroka's motion for preliminary injunction. It ruled that he had not demonstrated a reasonable probability of prevailing on the merits of the constitutional or statutory claims at a trial. The court found that Target demonstrated a legitimate interest in psychologically screening applicants for security positions to minimize the potential danger to its customers and others. It also found that Target's practice of administering this test to SSO applicants was not unreasonable. Finally, the trial court denied both parties' motions for summary adjudication. This appeal followed.

•   •   •

The California Constitution explicitly protects our right to privacy. Article I, section 1 provides: "All people are by nature free and independent and have inalienable rights. Among these are enjoying and defending life and liberty, acquiring, possessing, and protecting property, and pursuing and obtaining safety, happiness, and privacy." "By this provision, California accords privacy the constitutional status of an inalienable right, on a par with defending life and possessing property." Before this constitutional amendment was enacted, California courts had found a state and federal constitutional right to privacy even though such a right was not enumerated in either constitution, and had consistently given a broad reading to the right to privacy. Thus, the elevation of the right to privacy to constitutional stature was intended to expand, not contract, privacy rights.

Target concedes that the Psychscreen constitutes an intrusion on the privacy rights of the applicants, although it characterizes this intrusion as a limited one. However, even the constitutional right to privacy does not prohibit *all* incursion into individual privacy. The parties agree that a violation of the right to privacy may be justified, but disagree about the standard to be used to make this determination. At trial, Target persuaded the court to apply a reasonableness standard because Soroka was an applicant, rather than a Target employee. On appeal, Soroka and the ACLU contend that Target must show more than reasonableness—that it must demonstrate a compelling interest—to justify its use of the Psychscreen.

•   •   •

We are satisfied that any violation of the right to privacy of job applicants must be justified by a compelling interest. This conclusion is consistent with the voter's expression of intent when they amended article I, section 1 to make privacy an inalienable right and with subsequent decisions of the California Supreme Court.

Soroka and the ACLU also argue that Target has not demonstrated that its Psychscreen questions are job-related—i.e., that they provide information relevant to the emotional stability of its SSO applicants. Having considered the religious belief and sexual orientation questions carefully, we find this contention equally persuasive.

Target concedes that the Psychscreen intrudes on the privacy interests of its job applicants. Under the legislative history and case law, Target's intrusion into the privacy rights of its SSO applicants must be justified by a compelling interest to withstand constitutional scrutiny. Thus, the trial court abused its discretion by committing an error of law—applying the reasonableness test, rather than the compelling interest test.

While Target unquestionably has an interest in employing emotionally stable persons to be SSO's, testing applicants about their religious beliefs and sexual orientation does not further this interest. To justify the invasion of privacy resulting from use of the Psychscreen, Target must demonstrate a compelling interest and must establish that the test serves a job-related purpose. In its opposition to Soroka's motion for preliminary injunction, Target made no showing that a person's religious beliefs or sexual orientation have any bearing on the emotional stability or on the ability to perform an SSO's job responsibilities. It did no more than to make generalized claims about the Psychscreen's relationship to emotional fitness and to assert that it has seen an overall improvement in SSO quality and performance since it implemented the Psychscreen. This is not sufficient to constitute a compelling interest, nor does it satisfy the nexus requirement. Therefore, Target's inquiry into the religious beliefs and sexual orientation of SSO applicants unjustifiably violates the state constitutional right to privacy. Soroka has established that he is likely to prevail on the merits of his constitutional claims.

1. How would DesJardins and Duska's criteria for use of drug testing apply to the Soroka case?
2. The court insisted that Target must show a "compelling interest" in using a test like Psychscreen in order to overcome the interest of job applicants in their privacy. Do you agree? Why should a compelling interest be necessary?
3. Soroka and the other plaintiffs in this case expressed the concern that inquiries into such matters as sexual orientation and religious beliefs could be the basis for discriminatory hiring. Assuming that Target could show that no pattern of discrimination was evident as a result of its having used the Psychscreen test, should the entire test be banned? Should Target be required only to eliminate questions dealing with sex and religion?
4. Suppose Target defends its use of such tests by insisting that it has a duty to ensure that those individuals it hires as security personnel, due to the nature of their jobs, must be psychologically stable. Assuming that Target does have such a duty, how can it best discharge it?

CASE SCENARIO 2   *City of North Miami v. Kurtz*

The following case was decided by the Supreme Court of Florida in April, 1995. Justice Overton wrote the opinion for the court majority.

The record establishes the following unrefuted facts. To reduce costs and to increase productivity, the City of North Miami adopted an employment policy designed to reduce the number of employees who smoke tobacco. In accordance with that policy decision, the City issued Administrative Regulation 1–46, which requires all job applicants to sign an affidavit stating that they have not used tobacco or tobacco products for at least one year immediately preceding their application for employment. The intent of the regulation is to gradually reduce the number of smokers in the City's work force by means of natural attrition. Consequently, the regulation only applies to job applicants and does not affect current employees. Once an applicant has been hired, the applicant is free to start or resume smoking at any time. Evidence in the record, however, reflects that a high percentage of smokers who have adhered to the one year cessation requirement are unlikely to resume smoking.

Additional evidence submitted by the City indicates that each smoking employee costs the City as much as $4,611 per year in 1981 dollars over what it incurs for non-smoking employees. The City is a self-insurer and its taxpayers pay for 100% of its employees' medical expenses. In enacting the regulation, the City made a policy decision to reduce costs and increase productivity by eventually eliminating a substantial number of smokers from its work force. Evidence presented to the trial court indicated that the regulation would accomplish these goals.

The respondent in this case, Arlene Kurtz, applied for a clerk-typist position with the City. When she was interviewed for the position, she was informed of Regulation 1–46. She told the interviewer that she was a smoker and could not truthfully sign an affidavit to comply with the regulation. The interviewer then informed Kurtz that she would not be considered for employment until she was smoke-free for one year. Thereafter, Kurtz filed this action seeking to enjoin enforcement of the regulation and asking for a declaratory judgment finding the regulation to be unconstitutional . . . .

The trial judge noted that Kurtz had presented the issue in the narrow context of whether she has a right to smoke in her own home. While he agreed that such a right existed, he concluded that the true issue to be decided was whether the City, as a governmental entity, could regulate smoking through employment. Because he found that there is no expectation of privacy in employment and that the regulation did not violate any provision of either the Florida or the federal constitutions, summary judgment was granted in favor of the City.

The Third District Court of Appeal reversed. The district court first determined that Kurtz' privacy rights are involved when the City requires her to refrain from smoking for a year prior to being considered for employment. The district court then found that, although the City does have an interest in saving taxpayers money by decreasing insurance costs and increasing productivity, such interest is insufficient to outweigh the intrusion into Kurtz' right of privacy and has no relevance to the performance of the duties involved with a clerk-typist.

• • •

Florida's constitutional privacy provision, which is contained in article I, section 23, provides as follows:

> Right of privacy.—Every natural person has the right to be let alone and free from governmental intrusion into his private life except as otherwise provided herein. This section shall not be construed to limit the public's right of access to public records and meetings as provided by law.

This right to privacy protects Florida's citizens from the government's uninvited observation of or interference in those areas that fall within the ambit of the zone of privacy afforded under this provision.

Although Florida's privacy right provides greater protection than the federal constitution, it was not intended to be a guarantee against all intrusion into the life of an individual.

• • •

In this case, we find that the City's action does not intrude into an aspect of Kurtz' life in which she has a legitimate expectation of privacy. In today's society, smokers are constantly required to reveal whether they smoke. When individuals are seated in a restaurant, they are asked whether they want a table in a smoking or non-smoking section. When individuals rent hotel or motel rooms, they are asked if they smoke so that management may ensure that certain rooms remain free from the smell of smoke odors. Likewise, when individuals rent cars, they are asked if they smoke so that rental agencies can make proper accommodations to maintain vehicles for non-smokers. Further, employers generally provide smoke-free areas for non-smokers, and employees are often prohibited from smoking in certain areas. Given that individuals must reveal whether they smoke in almost every aspect of life in today's society, we conclude that individuals have no reasonable expectation of privacy in the disclosure of that information when applying for a government job and, consequently, that Florida's right of privacy is not implicated under these unique circumstances.

In reaching the conclusion that the right to privacy is not implicated in this case, however, we emphasize that our holding is limited to the narrow issue presented. Notably, we are not addressing the issue of whether an applicant, once hired, could be compelled by a government agency to stop smoking. Equally as important, neither are we holding today that a governmental entity can ask any type of information it chooses of prospective job applicants.

• • •

KOGAN, Justice, dissenting.

As the majority itself notes, job applicants are free to return to tobacco use once hired. I believe this concession reveals the anti-smoking policy to be rather more of a speculative pretense than a rational governmental policy. Therefore I would find it unconstitutional under the right of due process. *See Department of Law Enforcement v. Real Property,* 588 So.2d 957 (Fla.1991).

The privacy issue is more troublesome, to my mind. There is a "slippery-slope" problem here because, if governmental employers can inquire too extensively into off-job-site behavior, a point eventually will be reached at which the right of privacy under article I, section 23 clearly will be breached. An obvious example would be an inquiry into the lawful sexual behavior of job applicants in an effort to identify those with the "most desirable" lifestyles. Such an effort easily could become the pretext for a constitutional violation. The time has not yet fully passed, for example, when women job applicants have been questioned about their plans for procreation in an effort to eliminate those who may be absent on family leave. I cannot conceive that such an act is anything other than a violation of the right of privacy when done by a governmental unit.

Health-based concerns like those expressed by the City also present a definite slippery slope to the courts. The time is fast approaching, for example, when human beings can be genetically tested so thoroughly that susceptibility to particular diseases can be identified years in advance. To my mind, any governmental effort to identify those who might eventually suffer from cancer or heart disease, for instance, itself is a violation of bodily integrity guaranteed by article I, section 23. Moreover, I cannot help but note that any such effort comes perilously close to the discredited practice of eugenics.

The use of tobacco products is more troubling, however. While legal, tobacco use nevertheless is an activity increasingly regulated by the law. If the federal government, for instance, chose to regulate tobacco as a controlled substance, I have no trouble saying that this act alone does not undermine anyone's privacy right. However, regulation is not the issue here because tobacco use today remains legal. The sole question is whether the government may inquire into off-job-site behavior that is legal, however unhealthy it might be. In light of the inherently poor fit between the governmental objective and the ends actually achieved, I am more inclined to agree with the district court that the right of privacy has been violated here. I might reach a different result if the objective were better served by the means chosen.

1. Do you agree with the court that "privacy is not implicated" in the facts of this case?
2. The court mentions several contexts in which society legitimately seeks information about smoking habits—restaurants, motels, and the like. All of these could be called "public places." The city of North Miami, in this case, sought to inquire into the habits of job applicants in their homes, which most people would distinguish from a public place. Does this fact undermine the court's argument? Why or why not?
3. The majority opinion notes that the policy in question applied only to new job applicants; once hired, a city employee could smoke at home and not be forced to disclose that fact. Could Kurtz argue that the policy is thus discriminating against job candidates?

CASE SCENARIO 3   Whistleblowing at ADM

In 1992 Mark Whitacre was a corporate star. At thirty-five, he headed the fast-growing Biochem Product Division of Archer Daniels Midland Corporation (ADM). An $11.5 billion company and self-described "supermarket to the world," ADM is the nation's largest processor of agricultural commodities. Whitacre had overseen ADM's expansion into the world lysine market. Lysine is a feed additive, and the market is extremely competitive and capital-intensive; but it can also be extremely profitable. ADM estimates that a full one-third of its earnings will be generated by this division in 1997. But in 1992 the picture was bleaker. Owing to entrenched Asian competition, ADM had to establish market share by drastically cutting prices. A spectacular price war ensued, with the price of lysine dropping from $1.30 to $0.60 per pound. ADM felt that Whitacre needed a mentor. He was told to work closer with Terry Williams of the corn-processing division, who would teach him, Whitacre states, "how ADM does business." Williams proposed to the competitors that they form an association to promote and expand the lysine business. Later, Williams instructed Whitacre to convene the major competitors to discuss the market. At one of these meetings, Williams indicated that the price-cutting was benefiting the customer too much and not the people who had spent billions building the plants. Then he said something, a common phrase around ADM according to Whitacre: "The competitor is our friend, and the customer is our enemy." Whitacre believed that Williams was hinting at price-fixing, a practice he reports hearing about in other ADM divisions. He was uncomfortable with the idea, not only because it's illegal, but because it violated his view of how free-market capitalism should proceed: "My philosophy was to get the plant going full ahead, become the low-cost producer and kick butt."

In the meantime, ADM was having difficulty keeping down production costs because of a persistent contamination problem. Management suspected sabotage and called in the FBI. During the course of this investigation, Whitacre got to know several of the FBI agents and conveyed to them his allegations of price-fixing. He agreed to tape meetings with key ADM players, and over the course of the FBI investigation collected almost sixteen thousand hours of tape. ADM discovered that Whitacre was the "mole" after the Justice Department began its public investigation; in August 1995, ADM fired Whitacre. The company also accused him of stealing at least $2.5 million from the company during the time he was acting as an agent for the FBI. Whitacre denies ADM's allegation, saying that the money represents part of his compensation. Whitacre expressed pain and disappointment at ADM's allegations. He didn't know that ADM would react so bitterly to his cooperation with the FBI. In fact, according to one associate, Whitacre thought he would be seen by folks at ADM as a hero.

1. Put yourself in the place of Mark Whitacre. Would you have handled this situation any differently? If so, how?
2. What would the analyses of whistleblowing by Duska and by Koehn imply about whether Whitacre did the right thing in agreeing to work with the FBI and in making price-fixing allegations against ADM?

CASE SCENARIO 4   Privacy at Pacific Refining Company

Amanda Lee is a thirty-five-year-old employee of Pacific Refining Company in San Pedro. On her first day back on the job after a week of sick leave, Amanda is ushered into the ladies' room, where an employee of a drug-testing lab holds open the stall door and watches Amanda lower her pants and urinate into a cup. Amanda leaves the room feeling humiliated and fearful that medication she takes for a peptic ulcer might show up in the urinalysis and be mistaken for something else. She worries she may lose her job. Pacific Refining tests as many as ninety other employees for drugs in a similar fashion. Company representatives point out that the refinery processes and stores large quantities of oil and gas, and that the plant is located in close proximity to residential neighborhoods.

While Amanda is busy in the ladies' room, David Fung, Amanda's boss, enters her office and leaves a stack of material for her to review on her desk. As he does so, he happens to glance at Amanda's computer screen, on which is an e-mail message from Amanda to her best friend. David is about to turn away when he catches the word 'AIDS' on the screen. Curious, David reads on. When he is finished, he leaves Amanda's office in shock. Amanda, the message revealed, has tested positive for HIV, the virus that causes AIDS. Though she is well now, Amanda had explained to her friend, she is concerned that her health may begin to deteriorate at any time, forcing her out of work and leaving her without health insurance. The news of Amanda's condition is not all that worries David. He also knows that one of his closest friends, Brian, is engaged to Amanda; they are to be married next month. David wonders, Does Brian know about this?

Returning to her office, Amanda finishes her e-mail message and begins to look through the material David had left. The material consists of documents the company must submit to the Air Quality Management District (AQMD) on pollution emissions from the refinery. Quite by chance, Amanda stumbles upon a subtle but disturbing pattern in the figures, and she spends most of the day scrutinizing the documents and cross-checking against other files. The result is clear: Pacific Refining is systematically falsifying its environmental reports in order to make it appear that the plant is operating within legal pollution limits, when in fact this is not the case. What should I do about this? Amanda asks herself. Should I go to my supervisors? Alert the AQMD?

Amanda is still worrying about what she should do when the phone rings. It's David. "I need to see you right away," he says. Puzzled, Amanda walks down the hall to David's office. He shuts the door behind her. "I'll get right to the point," David says, taking a seat. "I was in your office this morning to leave some things on your desk, and I inadvertently saw your e-mail message—and I read it after I saw the reference to AIDS."

"You had no right!" Amanda exclaims. "That's *my* mail."

"The company provides the account and the Internet access," David reminds her.

"The company also owns the building," Amanda shouts back. "Does that mean it can install a camera in the bathroom? My mail is not your business."

"Is it Brian's business?"

Amanda bristles at the question. "No, it's mine," she fumes.

"Do you intend to tell him you are HIV-positive?"

Amanda pauses, draws a deep breath, and looks straight at David. "No, I don't," she answers firmly. "Brian is all I have, and I won't lose him." Amanda rises and leaves the room.

David, alone now in his office, agonizes over some tough questions. Now that he believes she may contract AIDS and that AIDS patients frequently require long and expensive medical treatment, should he take steps to minimize what the company will have to pay out for Amanda's health insurance coverage? Should he call his best friend with the news that his fiancée is HIV positive?

1. How would the authors you read for this chapter analyze the issues raised in this case? Be specific.
2. What are the central ethical issues raised by the events depicted in this scenario?
3. How would you argue for a position on how each of the issues raised by this story should be resolved? Base your argument on the concepts and arguments raised in the readings for this chapter.

CHAPTER 5

Discrimination and Affirmative Action

In a workplace all employees should be treated fairly. That is something almost everyone would say that they both believe and expect. And doubtless part of what is meant in affirming a belief in fair treatment is a commitment to equal treatment. This basic ethical principle—that people should be treated equally—lies at the root, both of our moral thinking about fairness and at the center of much controversy and uncertainty in today's workplace. These controversies are explored in this chapter.

Discrimination in employment is illegal. Furthermore, it is arguable that discrimination on the basis of sex, color, or creed is economically irrational, as proponents of the canonical position on business social responsibility, introduced in chapter 1, might point out. What color of skin a person has or what religion he or she practices is a very weak indicator of the productivity or potential productivity of an individual. These factors would be better predicted by a person's occupational credentials (for example, work experience or education), on the assumption that the best-qualified employee is typically the most productive. Hence, a racist manager would actually be cheating the shareholders of the corporation for which he works by discriminating against a qualified black or Asian candidate in favor of a lesser-qualified white candidate. It would generally be in the best interests of the firm if it maintained a posture of strict equal opportunity and hired what it took to be the most talented job candidates. But, of course, neither managers nor corporations always act in ways that are "efficient"; nor are any of us free of biases. When these biases are translated into discriminatory employment practices, however, problems arise.

What counts as "discriminatory" is sometimes unclear; and existing anti-discrimination laws do not cover all employment practices that might be thought unfair. Title VII of the Civil Rights Act of 1964 makes it unlawful

> to fail or refuse to hire or to discharge any individual, or otherwise to discriminate against any individual with respect to his compensation, terms, conditions, or privileges of employment, because of such individual's race, color, religion, sex, or national origin.

Other federal laws, such as the Age Discrimination in Employment Act (ADEA) and the American with Disabilities Act (ADA) prohibit employers from discriminating against older workers or those who are disabled in any number of ways. Laws such as these clearly prohibit patent forms of discrimination in hiring, promotion, and pay. Refusing to hire a black man because "he's a n-----," or failing to promote a Latina because "she's a dirty Mexican," would be obvious examples. Occasionally, examples of such blatant forms of

---

The ADA and Mental Disability

The Americans with Disabilities Act (ADA) covers mental as well as physical impairments. Recent ADA cases of concern to employers involve employees with mental disabilities who may become disruptive, or even violent, in the workplace. Discharging such a potentially disruptive worker confronts the employer with a possible lawsuit for discrimination under the ADA; yet refusing to remove such a person from the workplace can mean lawsuits by co-workers placed at risk by the disabled worker, alleging negligent retention of an unfit employee. How do you think such conflicts should be resolved? What steps should an employer take when faced with this situation? What kind of accommodations are employers morally obligated to make for mentally disabled workers who, though able to perform, may pose a risk to the health and safety of others?

---

discrimination come to light. In November 1996 Texaco, Inc., agreed to a settlement in one of the largest racial discrimination lawsuits brought to date. The suit, filed by six Texaco employees on behalf of themselves and nearly fifteen hundred other African American workers, alleged that Texaco systematically denied promotions to qualified black employees. The case was settled only days after the release of tape recordings of Texaco executives making disparaging remarks about the company's black employees and plotting to destroy incriminating evidence.

Conduct less glaring than that of Texaco can also be discriminatory. In *Price Waterhouse v. Hopkins*,[1] the plaintiff, a female office manager at Price Waterhouse, alleged that she was refused a partnership at the firm because of the sexist attitudes of the (male) partners. Hopkins had been told that she was "macho," that she needed "a course at charm school," that her male colleagues objected to "a lady using foul language," and that she should "walk more femininely, talk more femininely, dress more femininely, wear makeup, have her hair styled, and wear jewelry." Discrimination on the basis of race and sex can take more subtle forms, often proceeding under a practice or policy that, on the face of things, might appear neutral and unbiased. A company might have height or weight requirements, for example, which adversely affect job applicants who are female or who are of certain ethnic backgrounds. Should such requirements be viewed as discriminatory? What considerations should the employer be allowed to use in defense of its requirements? Sometimes an allegation of discriminatory practices will be made on the basis of statistical evidence. In one recent case, for example, aerospace giant Lockheed Martin agreed to a $13 million settlement in one of the largest age discrimination cases on record, affecting nearly two thousand former employees of Martin Marietta Corp. The suit was brought by the Equal Employment Opportunity Commission (EEOC), alleging on the basis of statistical evidence that layoffs and forced retirements at the company since 1990, while seemingly neutral, had in fact targeted employees over the age of forty.

Differing forms of race and sex discrimination, and possible remedies for them, are explored fully in this and the following chapter.

DISCRIMINATION AND DISABILITIES

Increasingly, employers recognize that persons with disabilities can be valued workers. Discrimination against people with disabilities is still common, however. The Americans

---

✎ AIDS in the National Guard

Oscar Charles served for more than twenty years in the Puerto Rico Air National Guard. When it learned that Charles had tested positive for HIV, the Guard discharged him, pursuant to a regulation that members of the Guard testing positive for HIV cannot serve in deployable positions but must be transferred to the stand-by reserve unless a non-deployable position is available. Charles filed suit in federal court, arguing that the regulation violated his rights to due process and equal protection under the law. The Guard's actions were unjustifiable, Charles contended, since reservists with HIV can still lead normal lives.

The First Circuit Court of Appeals decided the case in 1995. The readiness of armed forces is important, the court stated, and there was reasonable ground to believe that persons with HIV who are asymptomatic are nonetheless not deployable due to their restricted capacity to be immunized, their inability to donate blood, and the unpredictability of the onset of symptoms.

---

with Disabilities Act, enacted in 1990, prohibits discrimination in employment on the basis of various physical and mental disabilities. The ADA also mandates that employers make "reasonable accommodations" for those workers who are disabled but otherwise qualified for a job. Such accommodation can include, for example, job restructuring, modification of schedules or equipment, job reassignment, or making the workplace accessible to and usable by individuals with disabilities. Such accommodations must be made unless they impose an "undue hardship" upon the employer. Precisely what conditions are covered by the term *disability* is in some cases controversial, or at least unclear. The ADA defines a disability as "(a) a physical or mental impairment that substantially limits one or more of the major life activities of such individual; (b) a record of such an impairment; or (c) being regarded as having such an impairment." Conditions excluded by the act from the category of disabilities include "homosexuality, bisexuality . . . compulsive gambling . . . [and] kleptomania," among others. Whether the act covers such conditions as drug dependence, alcoholism, or obesity remains unclear. Nor is it always clear what it means to "accommodate" a worker who suffers from a disability. This problem is very apparent with workers who suffer from AIDS or AIDS-related conditions. The first set of readings in this chapter focuses on AIDS in the workplace.

Are there any legitimate grounds on which an employer could refuse to hire someone it knew to have AIDS? What if the person is infected with HIV, the virus known to cause AIDS, but has yet to develop any symptoms of the disease? Assuming the hire is made, can the employer satisfy its duty to accommodate the needs of a worker with AIDS without breaching a duty of confidentiality to that employee? Should an employer invest greater resources (say, through extra training or a promotion) on an employee who may shortly become seriously ill? These questions are explored in "A Case of AIDS," a hypothetical case study later in this chapter in which three commentators develop and defend their views.

AFFIRMATIVE ACTION

The moral and legal justification for programs of affirmative action has recently become an area of great controversy. Since the early 1960s, affirmative action programs have been a mainstay of efforts to address the economic and educational status of minorities. But in the mid-1990s, such programs seemingly fell into disfavor. A Republican presidential candidate promised to rescind all affirmative action programs within his powers, if elected. The Board of Regents of the University of California—one of the largest public educational systems in the United States—decided in 1995 to abolish so-called set-aside programs for the acceptance of students and hiring of faculty, programs that reserve a certain number of positions or jobs for which only members of certain groups may compete. And an initiative intended for submission to voters on the 1996 California ballot attempted to prohibit the use of preferences in public employment, education, and contracting (see the "California Civil Rights Initiative" sidebar). Finally, the Supreme Court, in *Adarand v. Pena*, decided in 1995, declared that racial classifications are generally unconstitutional, even when they are intended to benefit minority groups who have suffered injustices in the past. This section attempts to characterize affirmative action programs and reviews various arguments for and against such programs.

Affirmative action is typically taken to refer to a body of social programs in both the public and private sectors that are intended by their proponents to ensure that certain segments of society have the opportunity to participate fully in the benefits of citizenship. These benefits might include the opportunity to succeed in the most prestigious medical schools and law schools, or the chance to get a good job. The nature of the programs varies greatly and ranges, for example, from advertising employment opportunities to minority groups to numerical quotas for hiring individuals from target groups. The basic rationale of those programs is taken to be the need to correct imbalances in employment and education that exist as a result of past discrimination.

✐⁀⁊ California Civil Rights Initiative

In 1996 California voters approved the following initiative, known as Proposition 209, after a divisive and closely followed election battle:

> Neither the State of California nor any of its political subdivisions or agents shall use race, sex, color, ethnicity or national origin as a criterion for either discriminating against, or granting preferential treatment to, any individual or group in the operation of the State's system of public employment, public education or public contracting. . . .
>
> Nothing in this section shall be interpreted as prohibiting classifications based on sex which are reasonably necessary to the normal operation of the State's system of public employment or public education . . . . If any part or parts of this section are found to be in conflict with federal law or the United States Constitution, this section shall be implemented to the maximum extent federal law and the United States Constitution permit. . . .

Implementation of the initiative was almost immediately blocked by a federal court injunction; that injunction was lifted, however, in April 1997, by a panel of the Ninth Circuit Court of Appeals. "Impediments to preferential treatment do not deny equal protection," that court wrote. "While that Constitution protects against obstructions to equal treatment, it erects obstructions to preferential treatment by its own terms." Both backers and opponents of the initiative expected it to have a significant impact statewide, especially upon admission to the campuses of the University of California.

RECENT FACTS AND STATISTICS

Although all U.S. citizens are protected from unwarranted discrimination by both the Fourteenth Amendment to the Constitution and the 1964 Civil Rights Act, those favoring affirmative action point to significant evidence of continued underrepresentation of blacks and women in both labor and educational institutions. *Fortune* magazine found only one black CEO among its Fortune 1000 and only one African American among its top five hundred industrial firms in 1988.[2] *Business Week*'s directory of one thousand publicly held companies lists only one black and two female executive officers.[3] Of 2 million engineers in America, only 2 percent are Hispanic. Of 225,000 physical scientists, 3 percent are black and less than 2 percent Hispanic. Blacks and Hispanics make up less than 2.5 percent of the lawyers in the nation's largest law firms. According to another recent survey, seven out of ten Latinos and African Americans remain in low-level jobs, and only one architect in five is a woman. Nearly 80 percent of all skilled jobs are still held by white males.[4] Nor have women fared

---

> ### ✑⊃   The "Old Boys Network" Is Still Around
>
> According to *Business Week*, in 1989 about 5 percent of all managers in the United States were black. Although this is a fivefold increase from 1966 and a 30 percent increase since 1978, 97 percent of senior executives in the biggest U.S. firms are white. In fact, only 5 percent of all professionals are black. Some say that part of the problem is the so-called old boys network, which excludes many non-whites and women from participation in professional positions. Jason Wright, a black vice president at RJR Nabisco at the time of the *Business Week* study, says: "The reality of life in America is that if you're white, most of the people you know are white. If someone says to you, 'Do you know anyone for this job?' the people you recommend will probably be white." Even when affirmative action programs are mandated by law, similar problems afflict minorities and women. In contracting, for example, established white male contractors and procurement officers often prefer to do business with established companies that they know, most of them owned by other white males.
>
> According to a recent study by the *Los Angeles Times*, the State of California had set numeric targets of 15 percent for minorities and 5 percent for women in the awarding of some $6 billion in annual contracts for the years 1993–1994; but although a full half of California's population is made up of women and more than one-third are non-white, only 6 percent of the contracts had been awarded to women and 9 percent to non-whites. In 1993 public hearings regarding affirmative action contracting were held in Los Angeles, and large numbers of minority and women contractors testified that they were shut out of public work by white male contractors who do business primarily with firms they know. The net result, according to one city official, is that non–white male contractors are dissuaded from doing business with the city. Others point to evidence that some white male–controlled companies create corporate "fronts," posing as women- or minority-owned firms in order to benefit from affirmative action plans. Certification as a minority- or female-owned firm often takes little more than the word of the contractor; but even legitimate firms must endure long delays in certification, because of the application process. The result, say supporters of affirmative action plans, is that minority- and female-owned companies frequently drop out of the competition.
>
> SOURCE: *Business Week* 7/8/91; *Los Angeles Times* 9/11/95.

much better. Many women continue to be relegated to poor-paying "pink-collar" jobs or are stranded in entry-level positions at the bottom of the corporate ladder. According to one university study, 25 percent of thirteen hundred women polled earn a poverty-level income. It is estimated by a Rand Corporation study that women can expect to earn 75 percent of the average for working men by the year 2000.[5] With respect to education, as noted by Margie Burns in the readings in chapter 6, the Department of Education estimates that male full-professors outnumber female full-professors by a margin of close to six-to-one; in 1988 Latinos and African Americans constituted just 15 percent of the total college enrollment nationwide.

The foregoing figures are taken to reveal significant and continuing disparities in material resources and prestige between whites and non-whites, and between men and women. The reasons for these disparities are rarely overt or blatant discrimination; proponents of affirmative action suggest that the disparities are much more likely the result of institutional barriers: the use of qualification requirements, employment networks and tradition, and the after-effects of previous legal segregation. Employers who use race- or gender-neutral qualifications as the basis for their hiring practices might disadvantage minorities. Everyone claims, for example, that they want to hire the most qualified candidates; yet the qualifications justifiable on grounds of ensuring productivity may also put to a comparative disadvantage those individuals whose education was second-rate. This problem is particularly acute for African Americans in the labor force who attended legally segregated schools in which there was likely a presumption of black inferiority, or for women who were taught that analytical and scientific reasoning were unfeminine and that their proper role in society was to get married and have babies. Moreover, in employment, the old adage "It's not what you know, but who you know" is often true. The more-prestigious job opportunities may not even be announced publicly in trade journals and newspapers, but instead communicated to likely candidates by word of mouth through employee networks. For this reason employment and job search agencies constantly emphasize the importance of personal connections (see "The 'Old Boys' Network Is Still Around" sidebar). Individuals who are excluded from such networks are again at a disadvantage. This is as problematic for a white woman seeking to enter a traditionally male-dominated field as it is for a black man who lives in conditions of virtual exclusion from the better economic opportunities because of prior legalized racial segregation.

ARGUMENTS FOR AND AGAINST AFFIRMATIVE ACTION

On the basis of the trends and employment practices pointed out already, proponents of affirmative action believe that such programs are necessary for remedying past injustices and addressing present inequalities. Thus, for some, affirmative action policies are necessary for a just society.

An important aspect of justice is embodied in the idea of equality, the idea that individuals who are equals under the law should be treated in the same manner (or at least there should be good reasons for disparity of treatment). As it applies to social justice, this principle implies that all individuals who are governed by the same laws must have the same rights and obligations. So although some citizens may, for instance, have greater economic power than others, that fact will have no bearing on whether and how the law applies to each. From the perspective of justice, they are all citizens and the law is partial to neither the wealthy nor the poor.

The principle of treating equals as equals, then, requires that one's race and sex (and

---

✑ Affirmative Action and "Minority Set-Aside" Programs

In a series of recent rulings, the U.S. Supreme Court has held to be unconstitutional affirmative action programs that have a direct impact on the business community. During the late 1970s and early 1980s, many local and state governments created "minority enterprise" laws designed to remedy what were perceived to be discriminatory practices in the allocation of public contracting jobs and money. Typically, such laws required governments to "set aside" a certain percentage of government work for "disadvantaged business enterprises," defined as businesses largely or entirely owned by African Americans, Latinos, Asian Americans, or women. In December 1996 the Supreme Court ruled against such a program in Philadelphia which had been challenged in court by a coalition of white contractors. Justice Sandra Day O'Connor, writing for the Court, agreed with the white contractors that the Philadelphia plan was discriminatory: "The guarantee of equal protection of the law cannot mean one thing when applied to one individual and something else when applied to a person of another color." The Court's ruling reaffirmed an earlier decision striking down a set-aside program in Richmond, Virginia. There, Richmond had sought to defend its plan on the grounds that it remedied the effects of past discrimination in the construction industry. The Court viewed such claims as speculation: "To accept Richmond's claim that past societal discrimination alone can serve as the basis for rigid racial preferences would be to open the door to competing claims for "remedial relief" for every disadvantaged group. The dream of a nation of equal citizens . . . would be lost in a mosaic of shifting preferences based on inherently unmeasurable claims of past wrongs."

---

perhaps other characteristics as well) be deemed irrelevant to possessing the opportunity to participate equally in the benefits and burdens of society. A controversial point about affirmative action programs, however, is that they seem to some to imply a violation of this very principle; and, indeed, opponents of affirmative action often declare that it is nothing more than reverse discrimination. If it was a violation of equality to discriminate *against* persons in the past, the critics say, it is also wrong to discriminate *in favor* of them now by means of programs that give preferential treatment. Affirmative action destroys equality under the law, say the opponents, and in so doing might even open the door to further discrimination. The result could be the unraveling of social justice—an ironic result, so critics contend, since affirmative action programs were created with the intention of securing social justice.

Proponents of affirmative action respond variously to the foregoing criticism. Some say that the objection misses the mark, because it misconstrues the intention of affirmative action. Advocates might point to the history of racism in our country and argue that its effects unfairly placed intolerable burdens on segments of our society. It is one thing to discriminate against a group where the intention is to oppress that group and concentrate power into the hands of a powerful majority. But it is quite another thing to wrest a share of privilege and power from a majority who benefited from past injustices and restore it to citizens whose rights have been violated. The United States Commission on Civil Rights made the point this way:

> What distinguishes such "preferential treatment" attributable to affirmative action plans from "quotas" used in the past is the fact that the lessened opportunities for white males [resulting from affirmative action] are incidental and not generated by

prejudice and bigotry. The purpose of affirmative action plans is to eliminate notions of racial, gender, and ethnic inferiority or superiority, not perpetuate them.

Those critical of affirmative action raise further questions. Will those people who benefit from preferences be stigmatized? Will the attitudes of their colleagues and co-workers be that they don't deserve their jobs and that they are less competent? Will the beneficiaries of preferential hiring programs themselves believe or come to believe that they could not have made it on their own? Without satisfying answers to these questions, the critics maintain, affirmative action plans may do more harm than good.

Still other critics of preferential treatment programs claim that such programs represent an unwarranted intrusion of government into the workplace. As Gertrude Ezorsky notes in the readings later in this chapter, individual remedies for discrimination may be impracticable; but, critics say, this means that affirmative action gives government a significant influence over private institutions, including many businesses. The government can require, for instance, that certain target quotas be met by contractors before a government contract is awarded or a project funded. The effect is to politicize the workplace. As Charles Fried, former Reagan administration solicitor general, points out:

> If jobs were handed out according to membership in a group that has managed to attract political power, then the private sector and private institutions are not responsible to themselves or to the market, but to politics. If the job market is thus distorted, not only do employers have to play a political game in order to get employees but also people seeking jobs do so through politics, not their own capabilities.[6]

The objection here is that government-administered affirmative action programs will intrude on the efficient workings of the marketplace, and that this will lead to inefficiency, since jobs would be acquired not through qualifications, but by virtue of membership in a group that has managed to capture the political spotlight. Affirmative action might then lead to a shoving match among different groups, all of whom claim to have been harmed by past discrimination.

THE READINGS

The readings for this chapter begin with a hypothetical case study concerning a worker with AIDS. Several commentators reflect on a series of decisions made by the worker's employer as it tries to deal with changes in the worker's health. The case raises questions about what it means to discriminate against and to make accommodations for workers with AIDS. Arthur Leonard's essay reviews current legal protections for HIV-infected workers. Leonard argues that gaps in the law, together with lax enforcement and the social stigma still attaching to AIDS and HIV, make it possible for an employer to discriminate against persons with AIDS with little risk of getting caught. Thus, Leonard argues, employers face the ethical challenge of deciding how they *ought* to proceed in dealing with those with AIDS. Leonard sets out several ethical principles he thinks should guide such decisions and reviews their likely consequences for specific employment practices. Karen Clifford and Russel Iuculano argue that AIDS testing for new employees must be allowed, because otherwise insurance companies, who might bear the burden of health-care costs for the treatment of AIDS, will not be able to assess risk and adjust premiums fairly and in a way that protects their economic interests. They put some of the important moral and legal issues surrounding affirmative action into perspective.

The next selection switches the focus away from AIDS to explore a basic question: What counts as a disability? Terrah Elynn Alfred had a slight facial disfigurement as a result of treatment she received for blindness in one eye. She worked for Chico Dairy as an assistant manager in a market. After being passed over twice for promotion, Alfred discovered that company officials refused to advance her to store manager because of what they took to be her "unsavory appearance." Alfred filed a complaint. State law forbade discrimination on the basis of disability (or "handicap"), and the state human rights commissioner found that the same law also prohibited discrimination against an individual who, like Alfred, is *perceived to have* a disability. On appeal, the state supreme court, however, in an opinion included in the readings, rejected that argument, insisting that Alfred never proved she was passed over for being blind, but rather merely because her employers didn't like the way she looked—and that, the court concluded, is not against the law. A dissenting judge takes issue with the majority view, and a debate is joined on what it means to have a disability and how society should frame its laws to ensure fair treatment for those with disabilities.

The remaining readings in this chapter seek to put into perspective some of the important moral and legal issues surrounding affirmative action. This section begins with excerpts from one of the most recent rulings on affirmative action by the U.S. Supreme Court. Handed down in June 1995, the decision in *Adarand Constructors v. Pena*[7] is one with potentially far-reaching implications for all government-sponsored affirmative action programs.

Many opponents of affirmative action find it objectionable either because it is an over-inclusive remedy, since targeted quotas benefit individuals who have not been harmed by discrimination, or because compensation cannot be extended to groups, since a collection of individuals is not enough like a person to be the beneficiary of a legal remedy. They argue that the only suitable way of addressing discriminatory harms, when they do occur, is by allowing an individual person to make a complaint that he or she was denied an opportunity because of racial or sexist bias. Gertrude Ezorsky attacks this strategy of individual remedy by suggesting that it fails to address the underlying social injustices exhibited in the fabric of our society. She suggests that individual remedies are for the most part impracticable when the victim of discrimination is black.

Herman Belz contends that equality of opportunity should not be viewed as it has been by civil rights activists since the 1960s—as a guarantee of equality of results. Such activists have relied on what Belz calls "disparate impact discrimination," whereby statistical disparities in certain sectors of the labor market are interpreted as evidence of discrimination. The acceptance of this theory provides a justification for affirmative action, which, according to Belz, is a "policy of resource allocation and social redistribution" that has not been approved by the voters. Affirmative action is undesirable because it undermines qualifications and places the courts in the unfortunate position of deciding whether a group has been harmed, turning the courts into a political arena.

Laura Purdy addresses two persistent themes in the affirmative action debate: the nature of qualifications and the issue of compensation. For some, affirmative action is taken to undermine a moral entitlement—that the "best qualified" person should always be awarded the job. But, says Purdy, determining what counts as a "qualification" is not an easy matter, and our conception of an appropriate qualification may sometimes be "too high, too narrow, or just plain unwarranted." Arguments concerning the issue of compensation presuppose that widespread discrimination no longer exists. But, Purdy notes, even if the incidence of overt discrimination is negligible, its effects are still present in existing social institutions, such as social services, schooling, and health care. Like Ezorsky, Purdy suggests that the debate about affirmative action fails to address an underlying question about what social conditions are necessary for a just society.

NOTES

1. 109 S.Ct. 1775 (1989).
2. See *Fortune* (1/19/88).
3. See *Business Week* (10/19/90).
4. See *Los Angeles Times* (9/10/95).
5. Ibid.
6. See Charles Fried, *Order and Law* (New York: Simon & Schuster, 1991), 100.
7. (1995) 132 L Ed 2d 158.

CASE STUDY   A Case of AIDS

Richard S. Tedlow and Michele S. Marram

I. The Hiring Decision, 11-1-89

Greg van de Water leafed through the applications one more time. After weeks of interviewing, he had narrowed the field to two young men, both of them internal candidates seeking promotion to Greg's sales and customer service team.

Hiring, he believed, was the most important decision he made as team leader. Since taking over three years ago, he had hired four of the six team members, and he had chosen well. Now again he was faced with a choice that would affect team performance for better or worse. Subjective judgments about how people would work together, how they would feel about each other, how deeply they would buy into company values like openness, honesty, mutual respect, and support were just as important as the sales ability, communication skills, knowledge of the industry, energy, and enthusiasm that the job called for on paper. Greg also knew that teamwork and attitude produced results and that members of a sales team could easily become destructively competitive unless their commitment to each other was genuine.

The folder on top belonged to Peter Kroll. Peter had worked his way up through the company and understood its products and its product strategy. He was bright, eager, and came highly recommended. Greg was confident that he could handle the job and handle it well.

The second folder was Joe Collins. On paper, Joe and Peter looked much the same, but after meeting them both, Greg preferred Joe. On the minus side, Joe hadn't been with the company as long—only two years. On the plus side, Joe had worked well under the kind of group-compensation system Greg's sales team utilized. Moreover, Joe seemed to have more self-confidence than Peter. Joe also struck him as a better listener and a more sensitive person—important qualities in teamwork and communication. Finally, although neither had much sales experience, Joe somehow seemed a natural salesman.

So that was that—except for one thing. In the strictest confidence, Joe had revealed that he was HIV infected. Greg was not panicked by the news. He knew there was no danger of contagion from casual office contact, and he knew an HIV-positive person could live and work productively for years without developing an active case of AIDS. Moreover, the company guidelines

---

From *Harvard Business Review,* November/December, 1991. Used with permission.

stated clearly that "physical disabilities and chronic health conditions" were not to be considered in hiring and promotion decisions unless they interfered directly with performance.

But was it really that simple? Joe had shown no symptoms yet, but Greg was worried about hiring him and then having his health deteriorate. How could Joe work up to speed if he was recovering from a bout of pneumonia? Wasn't there at least a chance that the pace and the pressure of this job would be detrimental to his health? Moreover, how could Joe keep his secret from the other people on the team?

Except for HIV, the choice was easy: hire Joe. But was there any such thing as "except for HIV"?

Jonathan Mann

Greg van de Water should hire Joe Collins—with or without his HIV infection. Like all other people, some HIV infected are excellent workers and some are not. It is wrong to assume that when people become HIV infected, they immediately and irrevocably fall into a category of people who can't work well. Joe proves that HIV infection need not handicap one's performance.

Obviously, the "hidden" issue here is transmission. Will other workers be safe in the workplace? In this case, the answer is absolutely unanimous and unequivocal: there should be no concern for transmission in the workplace. (The exceptions are professions that involve exposure to blood and, in two instances that transcend the workplace but that I mention for the sake of completeness, people having sexual intercourse and sharing needles.) So it's important to put that concern to rest.

It's also important to put the hiring decision into the context of the expected lifespan of a person who is infected with HIV. The facts are that ten years after being infected, half of HIV-positive people will develop AIDS, while half will not—and this is without treatment. With treatment, depending on a number of factors related to individuals that we don't fully understand, that picture is improved in several ways.

There is an issue of a potentially reduced work life. While that's a real concern, consider how important any condition—HIV infection, hypertension, smoking, a family history of cancer—should weigh upon a hiring decision where there is a clear, or felt, superiority of a candidate. HIV infection doesn't tell you whether someone can or can't do a job well.

The employee's ability counts most. Greg should hire Joe because Joe is the most qualified candidate. At the same time, he should discuss the future with Joe. Finally, having the information that he does, Greg should find out if the company has an AIDS policy in place. If it doesn't, he should push for one. Because in the United States, with over one million people who are HIV infected, the idea that it won't happen in your company is fantasy. It's just a matter of time.

James W. Nichols

Greg van de Water should not take Joe Collins's HIV infection into account when hiring him. He should hire on abilities, not disabilities. Besides, who is to say that Peter Kroll, the other candidate, isn't HIV positive as well?

I know that many of the roughly 1.2 million people infected with the AIDS virus in this country are productive workers. For five and a half years after receiving my HIV diagnosis, I continued to contribute to my company as an employee and a manager. My company knew my health status throughout. In allowing me to continue working, the company not only benefited from my work but also fueled my will to live.

My experience taught me that the only way for companies to handle the issue of HIV infection is for the company and the employee to work together. Like work, AIDS takes place in the context of personal relationships. It needs to be *comanaged,* not merely managed. When Greg hires Joe, then, he should establish that he will work with Joe as his illness develops or when other considerations arise. Greg could say, "Joe, I can't tell you how important your honesty has been to me, and I believe that knowledge of your HIV status should be held in the strictest confidence.

"But when you are ready to tell people you have HIV, or if your productivity slips to the point that people approach me, I would hope, Joe, that you and I can work together to solve the problem."

It is absolutely critical for HIV-positive employees to know that they're going to have the support of their company. When I tested positive, I had a very good relationship with the head of my division. After I told him of my infection shortly after I was diagnosed in the spring of 1985, he said to me, "Jim, I have to tell you this makes me very sad."

He went on to say that the bank was ready to deal with AIDS. It had already rewritten its life-threatening illness policy to include AIDS. It was willing to support me in my work. My boss said: "We want the decisions made about you to be decisions that *we* make about you, not decisions that the bank is going to make for you, not decisions that you're going to make on your own."

As I began living and working with HIV, my company continued doing its work behind the scenes. The bank produced an AIDS-in-the-workplace training program for all employees. It provided brochures on AIDS for the home and workplace, directed toward both singles and families, and produced them in several languages.

All this made me feel like a million dollars. I don't believe the bank kept me because it liked me—but because keeping me was fair.

Lee Smith

Joe Collins should get the job. In terms of professional skills and "fit," he is the most qualified. And perhaps as important, there is no reason *not* to pick Joe. His HIV status should not count against him for the same reason we don't consider the projected health status of an older employee or the possibility of pregnancy for a female employee. Also, the Americans with Disability Act of 1990 now includes HIV infection as a disability, which means it is illegal for Greg to use HIV as a basis for not hiring Joe.

Once Greg hires Joe, he must respect Joe's confidentiality. Unfortunately, HIV-positive individuals today are subject to terrible discrimination in the workplace and in the rest of their lives. They face fear and stigmatization from colleagues, friends, even family, and as a direct or indirect result, they lose their jobs, their insurance, and other work-related benefits.

On the other hand, disclosure represents the first step for a company and an individual to manage HIV together. I encourage people like Joe to be open about their illness. A partnership of concerned individuals can manage this illness far more effectively than can individuals on their own.

Disclosure is not a easy step: I am not sure that I could follow my own good advice if faced with this situation. Disclosure, moreover, doesn't work without a supportive and well-informed workplace. Levi Strauss & Co. took its first steps toward establishing its AIDS corporate policy in 1982, when the epidemic was in its early stages. It was evident that an appropriate AIDS strategy had to be included in Levi's philosophy about the treatment of employees with any life-threatening illness: all employees are to be treated with dignity and respect. This clearly included an employee with HIV. Employee groups began volunteer activities and fundraising to support people with AIDS. This effort created opportunities for communication and education about the disease, about fear, and about people living and working with the virus.

Since then, we have rolled out a companywide policy of education, support, and involvement in AIDS causes. These education efforts go beyond the company to the employees and their families, to other businesses and community organizations. Initially, we designed a program for managers and employees that we customized to regional and cultural differences.

Today AIDS education is ongoing: most Levi employees in the United States have attended, on company time, a minimum of a one-hour education program about AIDS in the workplace. New employees attend AIDS awareness trainings. Managers and work groups receive specialized training and consultation as needed.

II. The Confidentiality Crisis 11-1-90

Greg van de Water looked up in surprise. Harry Lopez, who'd been a member of the sales team for four years, had come into Greg's office and was closing the always-open door.

"Greg," he began as he turned to face him, "I've got to talk to you about Joe."

"Sit down, Harry," Greg said casually, trying to remain expressionless and hide his concern. "What seems to be the trouble?"

"Well, I don't know exactly, but something's wrong. I hate to say it, but Joe's been letting us down. Now, don't get me wrong. We all like him. We liked him the moment he came on board last year. He was fun and easy to work with, he contributed more than his share of new leads, he knows the merchandise. He pulled his weight and then some. He made us look better than we'd ever looked before. And with sales up, we were making more money than ever before."

Lopez paused, took a deep breath, and went on. "But that's all changed. I want to be fair, but lately he's been, well, taking advantage of the team. You know what I'm talking about. He comes in late or he leaves early—not every day but two or three times a week. A couple of times last month, and again yesterday, he didn't come in at all. No phone call, no explanation, just never showed up.

"Worse yet, he's preoccupied and unpredictable. I heard him yell at a customer last week, and Friday we had a real argument about who would take care of one last caller. I ended up handling it myself.

"It's reached the point where we're all having to work harder because of Joe's behavior. We're still a team, so we still cover for him, but nobody likes doing it. And nobody can talk to him anymore. Greg, he's just not himself. You know what I'm talking about. You've got eyes."

Harry paused for a moment and cleared his throat. "In fact," he went on, "I wonder if you know something about Joe that you're not telling the rest of us."

"Like what?" Greg said lamely. He'd been trying hard not to see Joe's increasing delinquencies. He dreaded the prospect of talking to Joe and addressing the issue of his apparently emerging illness—if that's what it was. And then there was the issue of Joe's privacy to consider. Of course he'd known when he hired him that this day would probably come sooner or later, but who would have thought Joe would get sick so soon?

"You tell me," Harry said. "Maybe there's a family crisis. Maybe he's got a drinking problem. For all I know, he could have AIDS—and I've been sharing a cubicle with him for a year. Whatever it is, you owe us an answer. This team lives and dies on honesty and openness and mutual respect. We've never kept secrets from each other. Whatever it is that's going on violates everything we stand for."

Greg needed time. "You're right, Harry," he said. "I'm glad you brought it up. I have noticed some of the things you're talking about, but I didn't know it was this serious. I'll talk to Joe. Thanks, Harry. We'll work it out."

Jonathan Mann

Forget HIV infection for a second. Greg's got an employee who's dysfunctional. The question is: What's really going on? Jumping to the conclusion that Joe has AIDS is premature. Though his behavior could be related to the symptoms of HIV infection, I can think of many reasons why someone would be unreliable or irritable—and they have nothing to do with HIV.

The point is that Greg does not have to diagnose the condition. He just has to help Joe do his job. As a first step, he needs to open up the channel of communication. Greg could approach Joe in a supportive way and point out that his work has been suffering. It's unlike him to miss work, Greg could say. Is there anything he could do to help? Greg thus begins a process of easing Joe toward the evaluation and care he might need.

At the same time, Greg needs to become what I call "literate about AIDS." People at his level in a corporation should know what the disease is, how it spreads, how it acts in the body. Most important, Greg should know how and where to learn about AIDS. He needs access to accurate and updated AIDS information independent of Joe—a doctor, for instance, whom he can call to ask any and all questions without embarrassment. Because AIDS is a constantly evolving health and social issue, it mandates access to sound and up-to-date technical information in order to make informed decisions.

Facts are important; leadership is equally vital. Harry's aside shows that Greg should also start pushing the company to develop an ongoing educational program on AIDS in the workplace. He needs to take a leadership role so that company discussion is a coming together and not a witch hunt. Greg might make a symbolic gesture such as walking into the educational meeting with his arm around Joe.

Greg should not tell Harry about Joe's situation without Joe's consent. First of all, Joe deserves to have his immediate problem evaluated and brought under control. Then he and Greg can discuss disclosure. Given that transmission is not an issue here, neither Greg nor Joe has a legal or public health obligation to disclose that Joe is HIV infected. But for the sake of group dynamics, Greg and Joe might want to consider informing the team about Joe's health status, which can be done in a way that builds on the supportive environment of the team.

James W. Nichols

Greg van de Water needs some fundamental training on how to manage people. No one can make a positive contribution to AIDS in the workplace unless teamwork already exists. And teams are built by professional managers who respect and build the self-esteem of their employees. Clearly, Greg has not learned this.

As a general rule, managers should attack problems, not employees. Greg did the opposite by agreeing with Harry that Joe's work has suffered. He should have merely thanked Harry for offering his opinion. And rather than playing the paternalistic manager who fixes employees' problems, Greg could have asked Harry for his solution.

When Greg does talk to Joe he should focus on his failing productivity and show him the same respect he shows Harry—that is, give him the chance to solve the problem. Asking Joe what he thinks should be done may force him to concede that HIV has slowed him down, but it also respects his abilities.

Let me add that Joe's declining productivity may be AIDS related but does not necessarily reflect his own health. My own productivity dropped so low at one point that the bank could have fired me in 30 seconds. I was performing so poorly primarily because I was suffering from bereavement overload.

Bereavement overload and grief are two of the biggest problems for employees who have AIDS. My brother was the thirty-fifth person I knew who died of AIDS. After him I quit counting. It got to the point where one day I exploded at work over an incident that had nothing to do with work and everything to do with my anger; it took a sympathetic worker to say to me, "Jim, it's not the teller you can't take. You can't take having lost so many friends." Her reaction, which was to gather the troops and tell them I was having personal troubles—without mentioning my health— helped me immensely.

You don't have to be infected to be affected by AIDS. The HIV factor is a hidden productivity crippler to the brothers, sisters, parents, friends, and lovers of those who have the disease. Unfortunately, the stigma associated with AIDS forces those people to cope with AIDS privately, secretively, and from a distance.

Lee Smith

Greg van de Water's missed opportunities are coming back to haunt him. Because Greg didn't develop a plan, educate his work team, or work with Joe more openly, he now faces a volatile situation.

He has abrogated the stated company standards of honesty, openness, and forthrightness and chosen the path of avoidance. There's absolutely no question that the best approach with this disease is proactive rather than reactive. It is easier for people to grapple with the issues surrounding an HIV-infected coworker before he or she begins showing symptoms and performing poorly.

Of course Greg is dealing with a thorny issue: balancing Joe's right to confidentiality with the expectations, needs, and rights of the other team members. First of all, Greg should talk with Joe about his situation; after all, Greg can't be sure that the recent performance delinquencies are due to the illness. Then Greg should use all his skills to convince Joe of the benefits of confiding in the work group. Much can be gained by sharing this information. A team can manage this situation far better than one individual fighting it quietly, secretly, alone. Work teams really mount an effort to help individuals in trouble: there are times in all of our lives when colleagues cover for us, whether the problem is AIDS or something else. Sharing information that affects the work group can bring out the best in everyone.

At Levi Strauss, I work with an HIV-positive man by the name of Alan Philip. Right now he is asymptomatic. In fact, he's a marathon runner. With his input and participation, we disclosed Alan's HIV status to selected managers and are running small, informal meetings with Alan and his close coworkers to discuss any issues involving HIV and their own work group. We want to provide a safe place for everyone on the staff to be informed and to be able to explore their own feelings.

Greg and Joe shouldn't miss this opportunity to teach the work team about HIV infection in all its complexities. Talking about AIDS is very different from watching it happen to someone you know. Few people turn their backs on the person who sits next to them day after day.

I remember how Keith Coppin, a Levi Strauss employee who recently died of complications related to HIV infection, was apprehensive about telling his work group about his illness. When he did, people were initially scared and uncertain; some were angry with his manager for not revealing his condition earlier. But Keith and his manager, Paula Dueball, worked to create an environment where people could talk about their feelings and clarify assumptions they had made about what Keith could and should do. Eventually, Keith felt there was a normalcy to his daily working life.

III. The Long-term Question 11-1-91

Joe Collins was sitting in Greg van de Water's office, grinning broadly. "Tell me the truth, Greg," he said. "Have you ever had a better sales team? Or a better salesperson? Admit it, I'm 110% of my old self, and those numbers prove it!"

Greg laughed at Joe's good humor as he scanned Joe's most recent sales figures. "No question about it, Joe," he said. "You've really bounced back from last year. I don't know if it's the medication or if it's just you and your attitude, but I have to admit, the work you've done in the last six months has been super."

"I was hoping you'd say that," Joe said. "As a matter of fact, that's what I came to talk to you about." He paused briefly to signal the beginning of a more serious discussion. "I've been here two years now, and frankly, Greg, I think that I'm ready for a change."

Greg nodded attentively, so Joe went on. "I feel as though I've pretty much done everything I can do here. I was looking through the job listing sheets, and I think I came across one that's right up my alley. It's right here," Joe said, handing him the internal job listings. "I've got it circled."

Greg read the job description: "Senior Sales Representative, Western States Region. Top-level sales and customer service job covering our fastest growing markets. Requires full knowledge of our product line. Candidate must be prepared for extensive travel and fast-paced customer demands. As the company grows, we will look to this individual—and the team that comes together under his/her leadership—to form long-term relationships with Western customers and to steer us into the markets of the future. Compensation commensurate with contribution to the company's future! Who wants it???"

Greg looked up. "I don't know, Joe." he said slowly, trying to hide his surprise. "When you said you wanted a change . . . I was expecting . . . well, I kind of thought that after the rough time you had last year, you might want to slow down a bit."

Greg knew he had to be gentle. Joe had confirmed he had AIDS and was likely to get sick again, and he seemed to be in denial. But Greg also knew he couldn't recommend Joe for a job he couldn't handle. That would hurt the company, and it wouldn't do much for Greg's reputation, either.

"It seems to me," Greg said carefully, "that this job calls for the kind of long-term commitment you might not want or be able to make right now. Tell me the truth, Joe, do you really want to add all this stress to your life? And all that travel?

"You're such a good salesman," he went on, "I was thinking we could design a special job just for you—maybe a training and teaching job so you could help some of our younger people. You know, a chance for you to pass along some of your ideas and techniques. The hours would be flexible, you could work whenever you felt like it, and you could design the course to meet your own health needs. But this job," Greg looked back down at the job description in his hands. "I don't know about this job. This isn't slowing down, Joe. This is going into overdrive."

Joe fixed Greg with a long, searching look. "Greg," he said, "I know what you're thinking, but I'm not kidding myself. I'm just a long, long way from giving up—or from having to. I've still got a life to live. God knows I've still got drive. And I still do terrific work, which matters a lot to me and ought to matter to the company. I want my career."

He sat back in his chair and grinned. "I'll tell you what, Greg. Stop and think about it again. I'm going to give you another chance."

Jonathan Mann

HIV workers who are not ill should be handled like all other workers who are not ill; HIV infected workers who are ill should be handled like all other workers who are ill. Greg's problem is that he is operating on what he expects rather than what the facts of the disease and the infection indicate. He sees a worker working well. Why should Greg assume Joe wants to slow down?

Even for people who have developed clinical AIDS, survival can be quite long. I have a friend who had clinical AIDS diagnosed almost ten years ago. And though he is the exception rather than the rule, it is important to know that exceptions exist. We're talking about biology, not mathematics.

If Joe can do the job and is the most qualified, Greg should recommend him. For Joe's sake, if he believes he'll be happy with the extra work and travel, if he'll be satisfied and fulfilled, then this job might actually be more important than eight hours of sleep. Stress is *not* necessarily unhealthy for Joe: some people work better and are in fact happier with a certain amount of external stress.

Greg's alternative comes across as a way of "parking" Joe. The real question is: What does Joe's future look like? Will he live longer and be healthier if he feels his career's over or if he's working extra hours as the head of a team? I think the answer lies somewhere between the two extremes: maybe what works for him now is the high-stress travel, and later he'll take another position with less stress and fewer hours.

Above all, Greg and Joe must use the facts of Joe's condition to make the decision. Now if Joe is clinically ill and can work only two days a week, the situation is easier to resolve: How could he possibly take this job? But until then, I recommend Greg follow this principle: if Joe's clinically sick, treat him like any other sick worker. If he's well, treat him that way.

Can Joe handle a long-term commitment? The question for me is, How long is long term? In today's work force, where mobility has become the norm, even a five-year commitment is considered long term. When you start to think about a job with a ten-year or fifteen-year commitment, then I would ask another question: How do you make decisions about the long term? Would it matter if Joe smoked or had hypertension? We don't figure those questions into the equation now, why should we with AIDS?

That is especially true today, as one can legitimately offer hope to a person who develops AIDS. It used to be that a person diagnosed with AIDS had an average life expectancy of about one year. Now it's a couple of years. And with the ability to prevent some life-threatening illnesses, it is becoming quite common to see people who have suffered their first AIDS-related illness return to relative health for a long period of time.

James W. Nichols

Greg has offered Joe the ultimate in reasonable accommodation. Again, I speak from the perspective of an employee with HIV and AIDS. Greg has offered Joe a training position with flexible hours, with no cut in pay or benefits, without the stress of sales goals, and without competition from his peers.

As manager, Greg's role is to assess Joe's work performance and then provide choices. It certainly is his right to offer, or push for, reasonable accommodation. I was appalled when Joe offered Greg "a second chance." Joe has got it backwards. Employees don't give managers second chances. Besides, Greg has already given Joe a second chance. When his productivity declined, Greg gave him the opportunity to stay with the company and keep his job.

Joe appears to be very poorly educated about how HIV operates. I say this because I agree with Greg's original assumption: Joe is in serious denial. Joe seems to be denying the spiraling health-care costs associated with AIDS. He appears not to know that stress is a major cofactor in the replication of the virus and that fatigue is a major symptom. Beyond that, if he takes the new job and fails, he could be fired on the spot—losing his salary and benefits. Joe's hope for the future is overshadowing his assessment of the present.

Greg has given Joe options—and only with options can Joe still maintain control. In fact, Greg's offer sounds exactly like the deal my bank offered me two and a half years ago. At that time, my boss said I had a decision to make. My productivity had gone to hell, and I was not acting as a good manager. I had the choice of quitting—or turning my attitude around and keeping a job at the bank. I was not given the choice of keeping my old job, however. The bank offered me a new job, at the same salary and benefits, yet without the stress of managing people or meeting sales goals.

The way the bank handled my illness was vital to my continued productivity. If employees want to work and can, companies should let them. If you take away a person's job unnecessarily, you not only rob the company of potentially valuable work, you also take away much of what sustains that person's will to live.

Lee Smith

Greg should take the "second chance" Joe's offering him by putting Joe up for the promotion. If Joe can perform, has shown the ability to do so, and is qualified for the promotion, I can think of no other relevant consideration. AIDS or not, he is entitled to his career.

Joe may not be able to work indefinitely, but I'm betting that he can perform well in this job for a reasonable amount of time, providing a return on the investment. If he becomes too ill to work, then reasonable accommodation can be worked out by all parties.

But it's not only Joe that worries me. I'm also concerned about Greg. He talks about the company's openness and honesty, and yet he still seems to be acting solely to protect himself. Although I applaud him for being more explicit with Joe, he is still making assumptions about Joe's *future* health.

Ultimately, this situation is an opportunity for the company to find out whether it really cares about individuals in the organization or whether it cares strictly about output. Joe's situation presents the company with a tremendous chance to educate fellow employees, to bring compassion to the workplace, and to treat people with dignity in the face of a life-threatening illness.

There are also solid business reasons to keep and promote people in Joe's condition. First of all, employees in companies such as ours stay for an average of five or more years. We have a huge investment in those people, and losing them suddenly to disease means an absolute loss. We also incur the expense of training replacements. So it is cost-effective to leave HIV-positive workers in place as long as they continue to be productive. And we benefit in terms of insurance and medical outlays by intervening earlier to help individuals stave off the higher costs of the later stages of the disease.

Additionally, we have an opportunity to educate people about the disease and in so doing help prevent the spread of AIDS. For many adults, the workplace is the only place they receive this lifesaving information. We gain financially if we save even one employee from becoming infected. And by creating a more supportive work environment, we allow people who might otherwise be fearful to get on with their jobs and work side-by-side with someone who is HIV positive.

Ethical Challenges of HIV Infection in the Workplace

Arthur S. Leonard

Introduction

Infection with the Human Immunodeficiency Virus (HIV) associated with Acquired Immune Deficiency Syndrome (AIDS) poses significant ethical challenges for employers and employees in America's workplaces. As new medications make it physically possible for persons infected by HIV to participate in normal workplace activities for longer periods of time in greater numbers and as more workers respond to the urgings of public health officials to be tested and submit to prophylactic treatment to prevent the development of physical symptoms, many more known HIV-infected persons than heretofore will be asserting their legal rights to continue working. Employment of persons with life-threatening medical conditions will predictably have a significant impact on work-

places, affecting morale and productivity, as well as imposing direct financial burdens both due to claims on employee benefit systems and to necessary accommodations for impaired persons. Employers will have to make decisions that respond to these impacts.

While the issue of legal workplace rights of HIV-infected persons is by no means finally settled, there is an emerging trend in administrative, judicial and legislative forums toward protection of HIV-infected persons from unjustified employment discrimination. However, the slow pace of administrative and judicial processes, the emphasis on monetary settlements of claims by administrative agencies, and the reluctance of HIV-infected people to expose themselves to publicity and stress by asserting their legal rights, combine to make it possible for many employers to eliminate known HIV-infected persons from their workplaces if they are willing to bear the costs involved. Thus, an ethical dilemma is posed for employers, who must decide whether to take the possibly unlawful but practical

Reprinted from *Notre Dame Journal of Law, Ethics & Public Policy* 5 (1990), 53–73. Used with permission.

course of termination of employment or forced exclusion from the workplace, or to retain the employee, with the attendant problems that retention will entail, and if the employee is retained, the employer must further decide how to proceed to accommodate the employee.

Neither is the issue of workplace confidentiality settled. While some states have legislated specific confidentiality requirements regarding information about HIV infection to supplement existing provisions in some jurisdictions which generally protect the confidentiality of medical records[1] and some courts have held that government agencies will be constitutionally liable for damages for unjustified disclosure of such information,[2] many persons injured by breaches of confidentiality may decide not to assert claims, and monetary damages will not in most instances suffice to repair the emotional and reputational damage imposed by such breaches. The employer may imagine conflicting imperatives with regard to confidentiality, including concerns about protecting co-workers and customers from danger (whether real or perceived). The infected employee may even present a different confidentiality issue: by not desiring confidentiality, the employee may create circumstances which prove disruptive of normal workplace routine. Thus, both employers and employees face serious ethical issues about confidentiality.

Costs of employee benefits constitute one of the most significant workplace expenses associated with HIV infection. Drugs now in common use for prophylaxis against development of symptoms are expensive, and hospitalization for serious opportunistic infections is also quite expensive. Most employees rely on job-based group health programs to pay for their health care expenses. HIV-infected persons encounter great difficulty obtaining individual insurance coverage outside of employment-based groups. Existing gaps in federal and state law may make it possible for employers to avoid major costs of covering HIV-related illness while inflicting considerable injury on their affected employees, including a shortened lifespan of inferior quality when lack of insurance coverage results in denial of access to acceptable health care. Once again, the employer is faced with an ethical dilemma, balancing economic and human issues.

In this article, I propose to discuss these ethical issues using principles described by medical ethicists Carol Levine and Ronald Bayer in their analysis of HIV screening policies.[3] They identify four "widely accepted ethical principles . . . derived from secular, religious, and constitutional traditions" which are "commonly applied to medicine, research, and public health":[4]

1. the principle of respect for persons (an autonomy principle);
2. the harm principle (acknowledging that limits may be placed on individual rights when others will be harmed by the exercise of those rights);
3. the beneficence principle (the requirement that individuals act on behalf of the interests and welfare of others, taking into account a realistic risk/benefit analysis); and
4. the justice principle (requiring equitable distribution of benefits and burdens and forbidding invidious discrimination).[5]

These principles may come into conflict in considering each of the ethical dilemmas posed above. The justice principle may present the most difficulties, since the negative impact, both psychological and economic, of employing a person with HIV-infection in a society which has refused to take collective responsibility for health care costs may be considerable. I will suggest how I would resolve these conflicts in proposing an ethical solution to the challenges of HIV infection in the workplace.

I begin with the premise that ethical obligations of individuals and businesses exist independently from minimal legal requirements, but that such requirements are a starting point for analyzing the appropriate response to HIV-related problems, since they are one representation of society's consensus regarding minimally acceptable conduct. Serious inefficiencies in civil rights enforcement enhance the ethical dilemmas, since employers may coldly calculate that violation of the law is justified by cost/benefit analysis. A conscious decision to violate the law based on cost/benefit analysis (rather than, for example, on a sincerely held belief that a law is unconstitutional or otherwise invalid or inapplicable) does not constitute ethical conduct. I will also make some arguments about the ethical obligations of society, transcending those of individual employers or employees.

I. The State of the Law

A. Discrimination

Until the Americans With Disabilities Act is enacted and its employment provisions become effective,[6] the legal obligations of most employers with regard to HIV-infected employees and job applicants will differ depending upon the nature and location of their operations. Private and state and local government employers who receive federal financial assistance or who are federal contractors, as well as federal agency employers, are bound by nondiscrimination requirements of the Rehabilitation Act of 1973,[7] which requires that "otherwise qualified handicapped individuals" not suffer invidious employment discrimination.[8] Under *School Board v. Arline*[9] and subsequent Civil Rights Restoration Act amendments to the Rehabilitation Act,[10] persons whose handicapping condition is contagious are not excluded from protection, provided that their condition does not present a substantial risk of contagion in the workplace. Employers covered by the Rehabilitation Act are required to make "reasonable accommodations" to the handicapping conditions of their employees. State and local laws in many jurisdictions impose similar requirements on employers who may not be covered by the federal law.

Persons suffering gross physical impairments resulting from HIV infection would clearly be "handicapped individuals" under the Act, but those most significantly impaired are least likely to be qualified to work. Less obvious but very real physical impairments, such as a compromised immune system, would also qualify persons for Rehabilitation Act protection, and these individuals are more likely to be found qualified. Most of the caselaw to date has dealt with persons in this latter category, and has concluded that such individuals who are able to work may not be excluded from the workplace solely because of their medical condition.

The legal requirements with regard to asymptomatic HIV-infected persons are less clear. In *Leckelt v. Board of Commissioners*,[11] a federal trial court concluded that Kevin Leckelt, a hospital employee discharged after he refused to reveal his HIV antibody status to his employer, was not protected from discrimination by the Rehabilitation Act. Although acknowledging the accumulating authority that "HIV seropositivity is itself an impairment protected" by the Rehabilitation Act, the court found that Leckelt was discharged not for being seropositive or even for being perceived as seropositive, but rather for refusing to comply with the hospital's Infection Control Program by failing to inform the hospital of his antibody status after having obtained confidential HIV testing outside the hospital. The disingenuity of this opinion was exposed in a subsequent letter from the Regional Director of the Office of Civil Rights of the United States Department of Health and Human Services (OCR) to Leckelt's attorney, which concluded that the employer's "overriding concern was not the complainant's insubordination, but his HIV status. There is no suggestion that the type of discipline applied here was the norm for insubordination."[12] OCR also concluded that the hospital's "Infection Control Program" appeared contrived primarily to get rid of Leckelt, whose roommate had died after treatment at the hospital.

Disreputable as it is, the *Leckelt* court opinion is the only published federal court ruling concerning employment discrimination against an *employee* assertedly perceived to be seropositive. Although cases cited by the *Leckelt* court show the widening consensus that HIV seropositive persons are protected from discrimination under the Rehabilitation Act, that proposition cannot be considered fully established with regard to the workplace until a better reasoned decision on the merits issues from another court, or the Fifth Circuit rejects the *Leckelt* view on appeal.

B. Confidentiality

Legal obligations of confidentiality vary widely. There is no federal law mandating confidentiality about HIV-related information, although the federal Office of Personnel Management has adopted a confidentiality policy for federal executive branch agencies (apart from the military and security agencies) that restricts access to such information on a need-to-know basis and leaves it mostly to the infected individual to determine who knows about his or her condition beyond that small circle.

Many states have enacted laws dealing specifically with HIV or AIDS-related information in the workplace or more generally with confidentiality of such information in the world at large. New York, for example, in Article 27-F added to its

Public Health Law in 1988, provides strict rules for access to information about HIV infection, which leave up to the infected individual the decision whom to inform, with enumerated exceptions relating primarily to health care providers. An employer who came into possession of such information might be subject to misdemeanor prosecution for passing the information to others without appropriate written consent from the infected individual.

California, Hawaii, Massachusetts, Missouri, New Mexico, and Texas, to take a broad geographical sample, have all passed laws dealing specifically with the confidentiality of HIV-related information, all differing in details from the New York approach but all typically barring dissemination of such information without the consent of the infected individual.

Existing statutory and common law principles governing the confidentiality of medical information in general are also relevant in considering the legal ramifications of HIV confidentiality. Some states specifically provide for the confidentiality of medical records while others have developed constitutional, statutory or common law tort principles concerning personal privacy rights of employees.

However, confidentiality laws may be characterized more as pious hopes than effective enactments. Direct penalties for their violation are minor, and injunctive relief does not seem a very effective device for addressing breaches of confidentiality after they occur. Legal protections for confidentiality do not appear to have a particularly great deterrent effect, as illustrated by a recent study showing widespread violations of privacy and confidentiality respecting HIV-related information in health care institutions which are technically subject to such laws. Consequently, ethical concerns about confidentiality may loom much larger than legal requirements in discussing the roles of employers and employees with respect to sensitive information about HIV.

C. *Employee Benefits*

HIV infection can present significant expenses for employee benefit plans. As newer drugs go into wider use among infected asymptomatic persons, either to retard viral replication or to forestall the development of particular opportunistic infections, the associated expenses may replace hospitali-

zation as the main AIDS expense, because the overwhelming number of HIV-infected persons drawing on employee benefit plans may be asymptomatic. This could lengthen the period of time over which expenses occur, without necessarily reducing the overall expense.

Legal regulation of the substance of employee benefit plans is complicated. The principal federal law, the Employee Retirement Income Security Act (ERISA),[13] does not address substantive issues of benefit coverage. Rather, it provides a general framework within which employers (or employers and unions in collective bargaining situations) determine what actual benefits will be afforded to employees. Most of ERISA deals with the administration of pension plans. Those portions dealing with other benefit plans, such as health and disability benefits, are concerned mainly with broad issues of eligibility for participation, including continued eligibility for participation after termination of employment.

•   •   •

II. Ethical Issues

The ethical issues raised by the HIV epidemic and the reality of existing workplace law can be dealt with at several levels. I will first discuss the ethical issues for individual employers, and then briefly consider the broader ethical issues facing society.

Employers confronting the reality or perception of HIV infection can select from an array of responses. The ideal response from the point of view of a person infected with HIV would be for the employer to undertake an objective evaluation of the individual's ability to work, taking into account a realistic assessment of the risk of infection to others; to base employment decisions upon the results of such evaluation, taking into account the expressed desires of the affected employee, without regard to the possible reactions of managers and supervisors, co-workers, customers or members of the public or to costs which might be incurred as a result of employing an HIV-infected person. This response would include a commitment to maintain confidentiality to the extent requested by the employee and consistent with the company's actual needs, a commitment to maintain full employee benefits to the extent consistent with the continued economic viability of the business, and appropriate workplace educational programs to deal with employee fears. This approach would constitute a plausible means of compliance with existing handicap discrimination law and ERISA principles applicable to most workplaces.

The employer might widen the range of consideration, taking greater account of reactions of others or financial implications. One would be surprised to find an employer making such decisions without considering the wider impact, because an employer has responsibilities to a variety of constituencies. Part of that impact will be psychological: the effect on the workplace of having an employee whose physical and mental condition may deteriorate alarmingly if available medications prove unable to contain the impairing effects of opportunistic infections, and the impact on co-workers, clients or customers, or other members of the public of knowing that an HIV-infected person will be dealing with them, should such information become known. Such an evaluation would require a realistic assessment of the current level of knowledge in the workplace and the community, and the ability and willingness of the employer to commit resources to increase that level of knowledge. Such an evaluation might also consider the possibility of accommodating the special needs of an HIV-infected person, and how the employer's handling of such issues as confidentiality and employee benefits administration might affect the reactions of others.

Having considered these factors, how might an ethical employer proceed?

One response could be to determine the employer's legal obligations in the situation and to proceed strictly in accordance with those obligations, doing no more and no less than the employer's legal counsel advises is required, but the equation of ethical behavior with mere obedience to law is unsatisfactory in this context, for the law provides at best a floor of minimally acceptable behavior. Furthermore, strict compliance without a more affirmative response is likely to have a negative effect on the employer's business, since some of the negative impact of AIDS on the atmosphere and productivity of a workplace can be avoided through a more active, positive response.

An ethical employer will be concerned with respecting the autonomy of the individual and with preventing harm to the individual and others with whom the individual will come into contact in the workplace. This requires a realistic assessment of workplace transmission risk as well as workplace risk of exposures for the HIV-infected employee with a weakened immune system, especially in a health care institution (where the employee's job could require exposure to contagious conditions) or a manufacturing job with heightened exposure to toxic substances. There may seem to be a significant clash between the principle of respect for persons and the principle of beneficence, as the former would dictate letting the HIV-infected employee decide whether to expose himself to workplace risks, given full knowledge of those risks, while the latter might justify a more paternalistic approach of the employer deciding to "do what is right" for the HIV-infected employee against the employee's wishes. An employer desiring to pursue the paternalistic course would have a duty to base such a course on knowledge rather than speculation. The ethical employer will want to surmount negative or fearful emotional reactions in accordance with the beneficence principle, which would require a rational response based on a careful weighing of benefits and risks. Finally, an ethical employer will seek a fair distribution of benefits and burdens in line with the justice principle.

How might this play out in a workplace where an ethical approach is affirmatively sought? First, the employer would resolve to make decisions which will not exacerbate the problems the HIV-infected individual confronts, to the extent this can be done without endangering the viability of the business. Second, the employer would resolve to involve the HIV-infected person in the decision-making process to the extent this is feasible, since the principle of respect for persons requires that individuals be accorded the right to participate in determinations about their status and opportunities. Effectuating the harm and beneficence principles, the employer would undertake appropriate educational programs in the workplace about HIV infection, employee benefits and personnel policies, so that employees will know their rights and obligations and make decisions in light of such information. Respect for individual autonomy would require the employer to safeguard the confidentiality of HIV-related information, restricting knowledge about an employee's HIV status consistent with the employee's wishes, except to the extent that such knowledge is necessary for others to do their jobs properly. (For example, the reasonable accommodation requirements of disability discrimination law may not be implemented effectively if a supervisor does not know about the need to accommodate and the reasons for it.) The justice principle will require the ethical employer to undertake a realistic assessment of the costs dictated by the other principles, and to attempt a fair allocation of costs.

The justice principle poses difficult issues. How much expense may an employer fairly be expected to assume to accommodate an HIV-infected employee? The concept of reasonable accommodation found in most handicap discrimination laws has not received extensive caselaw development. In the *Arline* case, the Supreme Court commented that accommodation responsibilities do not include changes in the basic function or mission of the operation, or even job redesign or transfers not normally available under the employer's personnel policies. Regulations suggest that the accommodation duty will vary depending upon the size and scope of the employer's operation. But beyond what the law may require, which may really be quite minimal, what is the right thing for an employer to do? Incurring a major expense to accommodate an employee with symptomatic HIV infection may present undue financial hardship to a small employer, but for many employers the real expenses of accommodation may, upon sober consideration, be over-balanced by the continued productive participation of an individual in whom the employer has a significant training investment. The accommodation requirement under existing disability laws seems to strike an appropriate balance between the beneficence principle, respect for persons, and the justice principle, by recognizing that people with disabilities should be integrated into the workforce, but only to the extent that is consistent with the legitimate interests of employers and fellow employees in the practical ability to get the job done, safety concerns, and the economic health of the business.

Ethical questions are more starkly drawn in the current economic climate surrounding employee benefits. Premiums for health insurance have been escalating, and conversion to self-insurance will

undoubtedly grow as a cost saving measure. Such conversions may provide an escape route from state insurance regulations forbidding caps or benefit limits for particular diseases, but an ethical employer will surely resist the temptation to take advantage of this opportunity to discriminate against HIV-infected employees. Health benefit expenses related to HIV infection are not necessarily greater than those related to other life-threatening illnesses normally covered without question by health plans, so singling out HIV infection but not other conditions for exclusions or caps does not have an objective justification.

Those employers who have justified HIV exclusions as a "self-inflicted problem" because of its association with IV drug use or promiscuous sexual behavior are displaying ignorance about the spectrum of behaviors in which viral transmission may take place, or the state of knowledge of individuals at the time of their infection. It seems likely, given the long period which may elapse between infection and symptoms, that the overwhelming majority of HIV-infected employees became infected when the danger of HIV was unknown to them and information about safer sex practices was unavailable. Also, some portion of HIV-infected employees will have acquired their infection through other behaviors, such as use of tainted medications or receipt of tainted blood transfusions. Even if one were to grant employers the right to allocate health care benefits based on their normative evaluation of the conduct which led to infection, one would question why HIV-related claims should be excluded while illnesses arising from other behaviors, such as smoking, drinking, or poor dietary habits, were not similarly treated. Exclusion of some "lifestyle" claims but not others seems based arbitrarily on employer dislike or disapproval of the people involved, and violates the justice principle by discriminating in compensation, since some employees would be covered for their "lifestyle" illnesses and others would not, regardless of their contribution to workplace productivity.

HIV infection raises ethical issues beyond the individual workplace. The epidemic, together with the phenomenon of rising health insurance premium rates, refusals by insurance companies to sell group policies to employers in particular industries, and the significant number of Americans who are individually considered uninsurable, raises ethical problems for our whole society. Is it consistent with the principles of beneficence and justice for our nation, alone among the great Western democracies, to relegate a large portion of our population to the inferior quality of health care available to the uninsurable? Is it consistent with the principle of respect for persons to tolerate a system in which access to health care turns on the decisions of individual employers about how to allocate their assets, or in which access to health care for uninsurable persons may require them to deplete their assets to qualify for public assistance programs which carry stigmatizing connotations?

The substitution of a system which cuts health care access free from any workplace tie would seem a more appropriate approach for a society which embraces an equitable distribution of benefits and burdens as suggested by the justice principle. Halfway proposals to supplement or perpetuate the current employment-based system do not achieve this equitable distribution, since they still leave a significant portion of the burden on individual employers. A full discussion of the arguments for and against a national health insurance program are beyond the scope of this article, but it is certainly relevant to note that a substantial portion of the ethical issues raised by HIV and the workplace just does not occur in other countries which have chosen to deal with access to health care as primarily a public sector concern.

Another ethical issue for society is raised by our employment at will system, under which employers have no obligation to maintain the employment relationship with employees who are unable to work due to illness or other long-term disabilities. Disability laws only provide protection for those who are able to work. So long as quality health care access is closely tied to employment status, a system which affords no protection to that status once an employee is too disabled to perform falls down on the obligation of beneficence. Without contending that employers should be required to continue compensating employees who can no longer work, our society must address the ethical problem raised by the severance of workplace ties.

The continuation coverage provisions of ERISA are a half-hearted step in this direction, and a further step is the action being taken by some states to authorize their Medicaid systems to help former employees pay the premiums to maintain their health coverage under the ERISA continuation entitlement. Because HIV infection has proven to be an unpredictable phenomenon in terms of the long-term outlook for individual physical well-being, the maintenance of some workplace tie might be useful in assisting HIV-infected persons to have gainful employment upon recovery from significant opportunistic infections, and might help provide a psychological lift that would be helpful in the recovery process. In addition, governmental assistance to employers in meeting the expenses of maintaining regular health insurance coverage for temporarily disabled HIV-infected employees might deter unnecessary terminations of employee status.

Conclusion

Many American employers have responded ethically to the epidemic of HIV disease with compassion and understanding. Others have placed regard for the bottom line over the ethical principles of respect for persons, beneficence, justice and avoidance of harm, or, with disregard for basic principles of individual autonomy, have made decisions, albeit well-intentioned, without consulting the involved employee.

The developing law of HIV and the workplace suggests minimum standards of an ethical approach, but our society needs to reach beyond the notion of compliance with minimal legal standards if people affected by the epidemic are to be treated in a way consistent with our collective sense of ethical behavior. The ethical approach may also be the most rational approach, since appropriate health education for workforces and compassionate assistance for HIV-infected employees and their family members may result in the least workplace disruption while enabling the employer to continue tapping the skills and experience of infected employees.

More significantly, employers can help form the vanguard of those arguing that our society should radically restructure our health care financing system to more equitably distribute the benefits and burdens of providing quality health care to employees and the unemployed alike. Such a fundamental restructuring could more equitably spread the burdens of a new epidemic while preserving that respect for individual human dignity which lies at the heart of ethical concerns.

NOTES

1. *E.g.,* N.Y. Pub. Health Law § 2781 (McKinney Supp. 1990); Calif. Health & Safety Code § 199.21 (West Supp. 1990); Hawaii. Rev. Stat. § 325–101(a) (1989 Supp.); Mass. Gen. Laws Ann. ch. 111, § 70F (West Supp. 1990); Mo. Ann. Stat. § 191.653 (Vernon Supp. 1990); Tex. Health & Safety Code Ann. § 81.103 (Vernon Supp. 1990). *See also* U.S. Office of Personnel Management, AIDS Guidelines, Bulletin No. 792–42 (1988).

2. Woods v. White, 689 F. Supp. 874 (W.D. Wis. 1988) (disclosure of prisoner's HIV status to non-medical personnel actionable under 42 U.S.C. § 1983); *accord* Doe v. Borough of Barrington, 729 F. Supp. 376 (D.N.J. 1990). *See also* Zinda v. Louisiana Pac. Corp., 149 Wis. 2d 913, 440 N.W. 2d 548 (1989).

3. Carol Levine is Executive Director of the Citizens Commission on AIDS for the New York City Metropolitan Area. Ronald Bayer is a professor at the Columbia University School of Public Health. *See* Levine & Bayer, *The Ethics of Screening for Early Intervention in HIV Disease*, 79 Am. J. Pub. Health 1661 (1989).

4. *Id.* at 1663.

5. *Id.*

6. The Americans With Disabilities Act [U.S. House of Representatives, 101st Cong., 2nd Sess., H.R. 2273] was awaiting final passage as this article went to press. The Act would eventually cover all employers with fifteen or more employees, but for the first two years following the effective date of the employment title, it would cover only employers with twenty-five or more employees, section 101, and the entire employment title does not take effect until 24 months after enactment, section 107. The Act would forbid discrimination against a "qualified individual with a disability" concerning "job application procedures, the hiring, advancement, or discharge of employees, employee compensation, job training, and other terms, conditions, and privileges of employment." *Id.* § 102(a). The employment title of the Act incorporates by reference the "remedies and procedures" of the Civil Rights Act of 1964. *Id* § 106.

7. 29 U.S.C. §§ 701–796i. The Act exempts certain federal agencies in the national security and defense realms. *See* Doe v. Ball, 725 F. Supp. 1210 (M.D. Fla. 1989) (HIV-infected Navy employee not covered by Rehabilitation Act non-discrimination requirements). This was recently affirmed on appeal *sub nom.* Doe v. Garrett, 903 F. 2d 1455 (11th Cir. 1990).

8. *See* 29 U.S.C. §§ 791, 793, 794. "Handicapped individuals" are defined in section 706(7)(B) to include those with physical or mental impairments, records of such impairments, or who are perceived as having such impairments. A handicapped individual will be considered "otherwise qualified" if the individual is physically and mentally capable of participation in the activity, with reasonable accommodation, despite the handicapping condition. *See* Southeastern Community College v. Davis, 442 U.S. 397 (1979).

9. 480 U.S. 273 (1987).

10. 29 U.S.C. § 706(8)(C), *enacted by* Pub. L. No. 100–259 (1988).

11. 714 F. Supp. 1377 (E.D. La. 1989).

12. Letter from Regional Manager Davis A. Sanders to R. James Kellogg, Esq., of New Orleans, attorney for Kevin Leckelt, date (Dec. 1989), *quoted in* 1990 Lesbian/Gay Law Notes 7 (Feb. 1990).

13. 29 U.S.C. §§ 1001–1461.

AIDS and Insurance: The Rationale for AIDS-Related Testing

Karen A. Clifford and Russel P. Iuculano

Acquired Immune Deficiency Syndrome (AIDS) is potentially the most serious health threat the United States has ever faced. The disease, although unknown in this nation until 1981, may afflict as many as 270,000 Americans by 1991, causing an estimated 179,000 deaths.[1] Most of these deaths will

occur among the 1 to 1.5 million Americans already infected with the virus, many of whom do not yet show signs of illness.[2]

Although the immediate danger posed by AIDS to Americans has understandably attracted a great deal of attention, the epidemic also threatens the country's economic well-being and the solvency of its health care system. In the rush to ensure that persons with AIDS are treated fairly, some legislatures have enacted and others are considering laws which, by mandating the abandonment of time-honored and sensible underwriting principles, endanger the financial stability of many insurers.

The United States Public Health Service estimates that the annual direct cost of health care for the estimated 171,000 AIDS patients expected to be alive in 1991 will be between eight billion and sixteen billion dollars.[3] This figure assumes a per case cost of $46,000 to $92,000.[4] Some studies predict considerably higher costs.[5] A large portion of these health care costs will be borne by insurance companies. Yet, high as they are, these figures underestimate the total impact of AIDS on the insurance industry because they do not include the cost of outpatient health care, including counseling and home health care costs. Moreover, these studies do not reflect claims incurred for loss of income due to disability, and they do not in any way measure the impact on the life insurance business. Insurers expect to pay billions of dollars for AIDS-related claims over the next several years as they fulfill contractual responsibilities to policyholders who are or become AIDS patients.[6] Estimates indicate that the insurance community has already paid a significant portion of the health care costs associated with AIDS, from thirteen to sixty-five percent in some hospitals.[7]

Insurance is founded on the principle that policyholders with the same expected risk of loss should be treated equally. Infection with the AIDS virus is now known to be a highly significant factor, one that cannot be ignored by any actuarially sound insurance system. Yet some lawmakers, understandably motivated by sympathy for persons with AIDS, are giving serious consideration to a prohibition on any use of AIDS-related testing for insurance purposes, a ban that would seriously distort the fair and equitable functioning of the insurance pricing system.

This commentary argues that insurers must be allowed to continue using AIDS-related testing to determine insurability. Part I begins with an explanation of some fundamental principles of insurance and examines how these principles might apply to individuals at risk for developing AIDS. Parts II and III then review both the legal and medical rationales behind testing by insurers and set forth recent actions by several jurisdictions that have

prohibited AIDS-related testing for insurance purposes. [We] conclude that such actions present potential dangers to both insurers and the insurance-buying public. Finally, [we] suggest an alternative means of financing the AIDS-related costs of individuals who are denied insurance.

I. Basics of Insurance Underwriting

Even a cursory review of the fundamentals of insurance underwriting underscores the unprecedented challenges and implications the AIDS crisis holds for the life and health insurance industry. Underwriting is generally defined as the "process by which an insurer determines whether or not and on what basis it will accept an application for insurance."[8] The primary goal of underwriting is the accurate prediction of future mortality and morbidity costs.[9] An insurance company has the responsibility to treat all its policyholders fairly by establishing premiums at a level consistent with the risk represented by each individual policyholder. As one observer has noted, "[b]asic to the concept of providing insurance to persons of different ages, sexes, . . . occupations and health histories . . . [is] the right of the insurer to create classifications to recognize the many differences which exist among individuals."[10] Individual characteristics that have an impact on risk assessment, such as age, health history and general physical condition, gender,[11] occupation, and use of alcohol and tobacco, are analyzed separately and in combination to determine their effects on mortality.[12] "It is the understanding of the way these various [characteristics] influence mortality that enables companies to classify applicants into groups or classes with comparable mortality risks to be charged appropriate premium rates."[13]

At last count, some 158 million Americans under the age of sixty-five were covered by some form of group health insurance, and nine million more were covered soley by individual health insurance.[14] About ninety percent of the insured population is covered by group health insurance and forty-seven percent is covered by group life insurance.[15] Group insurance underwriting involves an evaluation of the risk of a *group*—for example, employees, members of a labor union, or members of an association—to determine the terms on which the insurance contract will be acceptable to the insurer.[16]

In contrast to underwriting for individual insurance, insurers underwriting group life insurance and health insurance consider only the relevant characteristics of the *group,* not of the individuals who comprise the group. Such an approach operates "on the premise that in any large group of individuals there will only be a few individuals who have medical conditions of [significant] severity and frequency which would, using individual underwriting standards, make them either a substandard or noninsurable risk."[17] Thus, the issue of testing for the presence of the AIDS virus, its antibodies, AIDS-related complex (ARC), or the active presence of AIDS relates only to new coverage for which evidence of insurability is required.[18]

II. Fairness and Equity Required by Insurance Law

The insurance industry has long been subject to statutory rules requiring the fair and equitable treatment of insured parties in the underwriting process. The Unfair Trade Practices Act (UTPA), developed by the National Association of Insurance Commissioners (NAIC), was, by 1960, enacted in some form in all states and the District of Columbia.[19] The central tenet of the UTPA is its distinction between fair and unfair discrimination. State insurance laws modeled on the NAIC Act both compel discrimination in certain situations and prohibit unfair discrimination in others.[20] For example, the Act deems it inequitable to charge identical premiums for life insurance to a sixty-year-old man in poor health and a twenty-year-old woman in good health.[21] In such a case, an insurer must differentiate between the two to determine an equitable premium: "[r]ates should be adequate but not excessive and should discriminate fairly between insureds . . . so that each insured will pay in accordance with the quality of his risk."[22]

Likewise, section 4(7)(a) of the UTPA prohibits any insurer from "making or permitting any *unfair* discrimination between individuals of the same class and equal expectation of life in the rates charged for any contract of life insurance." Section 4(7)(b) contains a similar provision for health insurance that proscribes "unfair discrimination between individuals of the same class and having essentially the same hazard."[23] We contend that persons who have been infected by the AIDS virus are not of the same class and risk as those who have not been infected.

The proper definition of "fairness" in the underwriting context has been the subject of litigation. In *Physicians Mutual Insurance Co. v. Denenberg,*[24] for example, the Pennsylvania Insurance Commissioner had revoked his approval of several of Physicians Mutual's health insurance policy forms.[25] Each of the policy forms in question provided for an initial premium of one dollar, regardless of the type of risk insured.[26] The Commissioner's action was based on his determination that the policy forms "effected unfair discrimination and . . . were not in accord with sound actuarial principles."[27] Agreeing with the Commissioner's ruling, a Pennsylvania state court found that "[t]he $1.00 premium in the first month in no way relate[d] actuarially to the risk involved and [was] discriminatory."[28] To underwrite within the spirit of state antidiscrimination laws, an insurer is bound to accord similar treatment in the underwriting process to those representing similar health risks.[29]

Last year, Washington became the first state to address the practical application of its Unfair Trade Practices Act to the underwriting of AIDS. The state's insurance department had promulgated a rule establishing minimum standards to be met by insurers in underwriting the AIDS risk. The regulation construed the state's UTPA "to *require* grouping of insureds into classes of like risk and exposure" and the "charg[ing of] a premium commensurate with the risk and exposure."[30] The department's rule stresses the Act's mandate that underwriting considerations for AIDS be consistent with underwriting considerations for other diseases. It notes, by way of example, that "policies issued on a standard basis should not be surcharged to support those issued to insureds suffering from an ailment."[31]

The Washington regulation illustrates that although, on its face, the UTPA seems to impose only a negative duty on insurers, closer examination reveals that under the Act insurers have a positive duty to separate insureds with identifiable, serious health risks from the pool of insureds without those risks. Failure to do so represents a forced subsidy from the healthy to the less healthy. To meet the fundamental fairness requirements of the UTPA and to address the concern for unfair discrimination, insurers must continue to use objective, accurate, and fair standards for appraising the risk of AIDS. As will be shown below, the tests for infection by the AIDS virus indisputably identify an actuarially significant risk of developing AIDS. If the insuring process is to remain fair to other applicants and policyholders, insurers must be permitted to treat tests for infection by the AIDS virus in the same manner as they treat medical tests for other diseases.[32] To ignore risk levels associated with infection and treat a seropositive individual on the same terms as one not similarly infected would constitute unfair discrimination against noninfected insureds and, therefore, violate the state's Unfair Trade Practices Acts.[33]

III. AIDS Antibody Tests Are Valid Underwriting Tools

AIDS is caused by a virus that has been given various scientific designations but is chiefly known as HTLV-III. When the HTLV-III virus enters the bloodstream, it begins to attack certain white blood cells (T-lymphocytes) which are vital to the body's immune defenses. In response to infection with the virus, the white blood cells produce antibodies. A person generally develops antibodies two weeks to three months after infection.[34]

A protocol of tests, known as the ELISA-ELISA-Western blot (WB) series, is considered highly accurate for determining the presence of infection with the HTLV-III virus. A person with two positive ELISA tests and a positive WB is a true confirmed positive with 99.9% reliability.[35] The insurance industry and the medical profession commonly administer the ELISA-ELISA-WB series of tests.[36]

Several developments have established the reliability of the series of AIDS antibody tests used by insurers. The blood test series is consistent with the Centers for Disease Control's (CDC) definition of HTLV-III infection, which provides that "[f]or public health purposes, patients with repeatedly reactive screening tests for HTLV-III/LAV anti-

body (e.g. [ELISA]) in whom antibody is also identified by the use of supplemental tests [including the Western blot test] should be considered both infected and infective."[37]

Further evidence of the reliability of these tests comes from the findings of the Wisconsin State Epidemiologist, who was recently directed by state law to determine whether any test or series of tests was "medically significant and sufficiently reliable" for detecting the presence of antibodies to HTLV-III.[38] The epidemiologist concluded, after a comprehensive review of the relevant medical literature, that two positive ELISA tests followed by a positive WB are "medically significant and sufficiently reliable" for detecting the presence of HTLV-III antibody.[39]

Nonetheless, when analyzing a test's validity for underwriting purposes, reliability, in and of itself, is not sufficient. A test must also be established as an effective and accurate predictor of future mortality and morbidity costs. In June 1986, the CDC estimated that 20% to 30% of those infected will develop the invariably fatal disease over the next five years.[40] In July of the same year, the National Institutes of Health predicted that, over the next six to eight years, as many as 35% of HTLV-III antibody positive persons may develop AIDS.[41] On October 29, 1986, the Institute of Medicine of the National Academy of Sciences issued a 374-page report, *Confronting AIDS*, which estimated that up to 50% of all those infected with the virus might develop full-scale AIDS within ten years.[42]

Quite apart from signaling the risk of developing AIDS itself, HTLV-III infection may herald the onset of other illnesses such as ARC or neurological disease. Studies cited by the CDC found that 25% of those who were confirmed positive with the HTLV-III antibody developed ARC within two to five years.[43] An individual suffering from ARC may have a weakened immune system and manifest such symptoms as night sweats, weight loss, fatigue, fever, gastrointestinal symptoms, and enlargement of the lymph nodes, and may become disabled as a result.[44] Due to the chronic nature of these ailments, ARC may, in and of itself, give rise to substantial medical expenses.

Despite the wealth of medical data that lends support to AIDS-related testing for insurance purposes, utilization of such tests is sometimes questioned because there are a significant number of individuals who have tested positive but have not yet developed AIDS. This viewpoint, however, demonstrates a fundamental lack of familiarity with basic insurance principles. Underwriting is, by its very nature, concerned with probabilities, not certainties; no one knows how many infected people will eventually develop AIDS. Even assuming that "only" twenty percent will contract AIDS during the first five years, there is a demonstrable risk that a large percentage of infected individuals will develop AIDS in year six and beyond.

A twenty percent assumption implies that 200 of each 1000 applicants testing positive on the ELISA-ELISA-WB series will develop AIDS within five years and, therefore, die within approximately seven years.[45] In comparison, life insurance mortality tables estimate that, of a standard group of 1000 persons aged thirty-four, only about seven and one-half (as opposed to 200 in 1000) will die within the first seven years from any cause.[46]

The substantially greater risk represented by persons who test positive for HTLV-III infection is obvious. The comparison of 200 deaths to seven and one-half deaths indicates that a person infected with the AIDS virus is, over a seven-year period, twenty-six times more likely to die than is someone in "standard health."[47] The actuarial significance of these percentages is overwhelming and cannot be ignored. Because such tests are reliable, accurate, and effective predictors of risk, they must be considered appropriate as underwriting tools. . . .

Conclusion

To operate in a voluntary market, insurance underwriting must appraise the risk of an unknown and unanticipated occurrence and spread that risk over a large number of individuals. The risk must be assessed as accurately as possible because the whole price structure of insurance depends on the principle that individuals who present the same expected risk of loss pay the same premium. When an insurer is able to estimate accurately the risk to which it is exposed, it can, in turn, be more precise in pricing the cost of the insurance.

Contrary to this principle, several jurisdictions have imposed legal constraints which place AIDS

outside the normal medical and regulatory rules pertaining to underwriting for other diseases. Although it is legally permissible for an insurer to obtain medical information about an applicant who may contract any other disease, such as heart disease or cancer, some states grant AIDS carriers special treatment by completely exempting them from relevant tests.

The tests for infection by the AIDS virus are extremely accurate in the same sense that any tests used in the insurance business can be accurate: they provide a basis for an objective determination of significantly higher risks and, hence, risk-based pricing. Legislation intended to force life and health insurers to ignore reliable, scientific evidence of a person's increased risk of contracting a fatal disease will result in significant inequities to policyholders. Given the potential magnitude of the AIDS epidemic and the substantial likelihood that gay rights advocates will seek additional legal constraints on AIDS-related testing by insurers, the financial consequences of AIDS to all involved—insurers, policyholders, and the public—will become even more severe.

Because the life and health insurance industry's livelihood is dependent on insuring persons against premature death and the costs of disability, it is as concerned as the public health community with curbing this tragic disease. Although the industry is fully cognizant of the concerns of those who have been infected with the AIDS virus, it must also consider its responsibility to those who have not been infected. If projections of AIDS cases materialize, public policy makers will be faced with an increasingly pressing need to achieve a balance between competing concerns. This balance need not, and indeed should not, be achieved at the expense of an industry that will inevitably bear a substantial amount of the costs associated with the AIDS crisis.

NOTES

1. See *U.S. Public Health Service, Public Health Service Plan for the Prevention and Control of AIDS and the Aids Virus* 5 (Report of the Coolfont Planning Conference, June 4–6, 1986) [hereinafter *Public Health Service Plan*].
2. See *id.*
3. See Institute of Medicine, National Academy of Sci-

ences, *Confronting AIDS, Directions for Public Health, Health Care, and Research* 21 (1986) [hereinafter *Confronting AIDS*]. This figure substantially underestimates actual expenses associated with AIDS because it does not include aggregate medical expenses associated with AIDS-related complex (ARC) patients or infected individuals. These expenses may outstrip all other costs associated with AIDS because of the large number of ARC or seropositive individuals and because of the length of treatment they undergo. One study estimated the average hospital stay for AIDS patients to be between 13 and 25 days, at an average charge of from $740 to $950 per hospital day. See Scitovsky and Rice, "Estimates of the Direct and Indirect Costs of Acquired Immunodeficiency Syndrome in the United States, 1985, 1986, & 1991," 102 *Pub. Health Rep.* 10 (1987).

4. See *Public Health Service Plan, supra* note I. at 15.

5. See, e.g. Hardy, Rauch, Echenberg, Morgan & Curran, "The Economic Impact of the First 10,000 Cases of Acquired Immunodeficiency Syndrome in the United States," 255 *J. Am. Med. Ass'n.* 209, 210 (1986) (estimating hospitalization costs of approximately $147,000 per case for the first 10,000 AIDS cases).

6. If, in the year 1991, 54,000 people die of AIDS, as has been projected by the United States Public Health Service, see *Public Health Service Plan, supra* note I, at 5, and if one-half of those people owned $50,000 of individual life insurance—a conservative estimate—the resulting claim liability of the insurance industry would be $2.7 billion.

7. See *Confronting AIDS, supra* note 3, at 165.

8. Health Insurance Association of America, *A Course In Group Life and Health Insurance* pt. A, at 379 (1985) [hereinafter HIAA 1985 ed.].

9. "Mortality" is defined as "the death rate at each age as determined from prior experience." "Morbidity" is the "incidence and severity of sickness and accidents in a well-defined class or classes of persons." *Id.* at 366.

10. Bailey, Hutchison & Narber, "The Regulatory Challenge to Life Insurance Classification," 25 *Drake L. Rev.* 779, 780 (1976) (footnote omitted).

11. In *Manufacturers Hanover Trust Co. v. United States,* 775 F.2d 459 (2nd Cir. 1985), *cert. denied,* 106 S. Ct. 1490 (1986), the Second Circuit upheld the Internal Revenue Service's use of gender-based mortality tables to compute the value of reversionary trust interests. The court concluded that categorizing individuals by gender and calculating different costs and benefits on the basis of this group characteristic did not discriminate against individuals and did not involve any intent to discriminate against men and women. See *id.* at 465, 469.

12. See R. Mehr, E. Cammack & T. Rose, *Principles of Insurance* 657–59 (8th ed. 1985), C. Will, *Life Company Underwriting* 6, 8–19 (1974); Bailey, Hutchison & Narber, *supra* note 10, at 785.

13. C. Will, *supra* note 12, at 6.

14. See Letter from Thomas D. Musco, HIAA Director of Statistics, to the *Harvard Law Review* (Mar. 31, 1987) (citing unpublished 1986 Health Insurance Association of America Survey) (on file at Harvard Law School Library).

15. See Public Relations Division, Health Insurance Association of America, *Source Book of Health Insurance Data:* 1986 Update 6; Letter from Suzanne K. Sternnock, ACLI Program Director, to the *Harvard Law Review* (Apr. 16, 1987) (citing a forthcoming 1984 Life Insurance Marketing and Research Association Survey) (on file at Harvard Law School Library).

16. Groups must have characteristics that permit the insurance company to predict, within reasonable limits, the probable claim costs under the contracts issued. The underwriting of a new group involves a general assimilation and evaluation of all the relevant factors to be considered. Common factors include, but are not limited to, the size of the group, type of industry, number of eligible lives, cost sharing involved, type of insurance plan, and previous coverage and experience. See *HIAA* 1985 ed., *supra* note 8, at 153.

17. *Id.* Although no screening takes place in most group situations, there are at least three instances in which a group plan may require evidence of insurability. These exceptions include: (1) small groups, (2) late entrants to a group plan, and (3) large amounts of life insurance that are used to supplement basic coverage. It is common to use individual underwriting standards in these situations due to the increased danger of adverse selection—the tendency of persons with poorer than average health expectations to apply for insurance to a greater extent than persons with average or better health expectations. Underwriting standards are stricter for small groups, for example, because the size of the group is insufficient to spread the risk broadly enough to absorb the effect of adverse selection. The same rationale supports the use of evidence of insurability in the group area for "late entrants." These are employees who decline coverage when first eligible but later seek to be covered. Finally, every group life insurer has a "guaranteed issue" amount, the maximum face amount it will approve without requiring evidence of insurability. Individuals seeking coverage above the guaranteed issue amount may be required to furnish a statement of health or to undergo a medical examination. See *id.* at 204–7.

18. In the United States, individual health insurance accounts for 10% of the health insurance in force, see Health Insurance Association of America, *HIAA Annual Survey of Health Insurance Coverage* (1984) [hereinafter *HIAA Annual Survey*], and individual life insurance approximately 58% of the life insurance in force, *see* American Council of Life Insurance, *1986 Life Insurance Fact Book* 30.

19. See Bailey, Hutchison & Narber, *supra* note 10, at 782.

20. See *id.* at 782.

21. See *id.*

22. *Id.* quoting A. Mowbray, R. Blanchard & C. Williams, *Insurance* 411 (6th ed. 1969) (emphasis omitted); accord *Thompson v. IDS Life Ins. Co.*, 274 Or. 649, 654, 549 P.2d 510, 512, (1976) (en banc) ("[I]nsurance, to some extent, always involves discrimination, to a large degree based on statistical differences and actuarial tables. The legislature specifically intended . . . to only prohibit *unfair* discrimination in the sale of insurance policies." (emphasis in original) [footnote omitted]).

23. National Association of Insurance Commissioners, *An Act Relating to Unfair Methods of Competition and Unfair and Deceptive Acts and Practices in the Business of Insurance*, 1972 Proc. NAIC I 493, 495 (as amended).

24. 15 Pa. Commw. 509, 327 A.2d 415 (1974).

25. See *id.* at 511, 327 A.2d at 416.

26. See *id.*

27. *Id.* at 515, 327 A.2d at 418.

28. *Id.* at 516, 327 A.2d at 419.

29. *Cf.* S. Huebner & K. Black, *Life Insurance* 4 (10th ed. 1982) (stating that equitable principles require those with more serious health risks to be charged higher premiums).

30. *Wash. Admin. Code?* 284-90-010(2) (effective Nov. 14, 1986) (emphasis added).

31. *Id.*

32. In opposing AIDS-related testing by insurers, gay rights advocates have placed particular emphasis on laws prohibiting consideration of the sickle cell trait. Sickle cell *trait*, however— as opposed to the disease of sickle cell *anemia*—presents only a minimal increased risk of mortality or morbidity. As a study prepared by the National Academy of Sciences noted, "[s]ickle-cell trait (AS) has been considered—except in situations that involve exposure to significant hypoxia, dehydration, or acidosis—as a benign and relatively innocuous condition." National Research Council, National Academy of Sciences, *The S-Hemoglobinopathies: An Evaluation of Their Status in the Armed Forces* 1–2 (1973) (footnote omitted).

33. A different interpretation of the Unfair Trade Practices Act was made in Massachusetts when the Commissioner of Insurance, on December 12, 1986, issued a "Policy Statement," which announced that the use of AIDS antibody tests by life and health insurers constituted an unfair trade practice under that state's version of the Act, see *Mass. Gen. L.* ch. 176D, §3(7) (1984), and that violators would be subject to an enforcement action. See Letter from Peter Hiam, Commissioner of Insurance to All Life / Health Insurance Companies (Dec. 12, 1986) (Policy Statement Re: Application Form Questions Inquiring About AIDS and ARC). The validity of the Policy Statement may be subject to legal challenge because the Massachusetts Legislature expressly declined to enact legislation in 1986 that would have prohibited life and health insurers from requiring AIDS antibody tests as a condition of insurability. See S. 489, Reg. Sess., §2(1986). Moreover, the Policy Statement was issued without any prior notice, opportunity for comment, or public hearing as required by the Massachusetts Administrative Procedures Act, *See Mass. Gen. L.* ch. 31 §4 (1984).

34. See U.S. Dep't of Health and Human Services, *Surgeon General's Report on Acquired Immune Deficiency Syndrome* 10 (1986).

35. See J. Slaff & J. Brubaker, *The AIDS Epidemic* 201 (1985) (citing Dr. Robert Gallo, National Institutes of Health researcher and a co-discoverer of the HTLV-III virus).

36. See American Council of Life Insurance & The Health Insurance Association of America, *AIDS Survey of Member Companies* 2 (Aug. 19, 1986) (unpublished survey) [hereinafter AIDS Survey of Member Companies].

37. "CDC Classification System for HIV Infections," 35 *Morbidity & Mortality Weekly Rep.* 334, 335 (1986).

38. *Wis. Stat. Ann.* §631.90(3)(a) (West Supp. 1986).

39. J. Davis, *Serologic Tests for the Presence of Antibody to Human T-Lymphotropic Virus Type III: Information Pursuant to the Purposes of Wisconsin Statute §631.90 Regarding Their Use in Underwriting Individual Life, Accident and Health Insurance Policies* 22(Wis. Dep't of Health and Social Servs., 1986) [hereinafter Report of Wisconsin Epidemiologist].

40. See *Public Health Insurance Plan, supra* note 1, at 5. In 1985, the CDC cited studies in which 5% to 19% of those infected with the AIDS virus were found to develop AIDS over a period of two to five years. See "Provisional Public Health Service Inter-Agency Recommendations for Screening Donated Blood and Plasma for Antibody to the Virus Causing Acquired Immunodeficiency Syndrome," 34 *Morbidity & Mortality Weekly Rep.* 5 (1985) [hereinafter] *Recommendations for Screening.*

41. See National Institutes of Health, "The Impact of Routine HTLV-III Antibody Testing on Public Health," 6 *Consensus Development Conference Statement* 10 (1986).

42. See *Confronting AIDS, supra* note 3, at 7.

43. See *Recommendations for Screening, supra* note 40, at 5.

44. See *Report of Wisconsin Epidemiologist, supra* note 39, at 3.

45. See *Confronting AIDS, supra* note 3, at 7. ("Most patients die within two years of the appearance of clinical disease; few survive longer than 3 years.").

46. *See* Society of Actuaries, Transactions: 1982 *Reports of Mortality and Morbidity Experience* 55 (1985). That is the approximate mortality upon which the premium cost of an individual standard class life insurance policy for such a person is based.

47. See Affidavit of Warren L. Kleinsasser, M.D. at 6, American Council of Life Ins. v. District of Columbia, 645 F. Supp. 84 (D.D.C. 1986).

Chico Dairy Company, Store No. 22 v. West Virginia Human Rights Commission and Terrah Elynn Alfred.

No. 18317. Supreme Court of Appeals of West Virginia. June 27, 1989.

A. The Facts

The complainant, Ms. Terrah Elynn Alfred, had been employed, as an assistant manager, by Chico Dairy Company (the "employer") at its Chico Dairy Mart Store No. 22 in Fairmont, West Virginia. The complainant is blind in her left eye. That eye was removed when she was an infant to abate cancer. She wears a prosthesis, or artificial, replacement eye. The socket around that eye is somewhat sunken or hollow.

As the assistant manager of a Chico Dairy Mart the complainant's duties included opening the store, getting the cash registers ready, preparing deposits, keeping track of inventory, ordering goods from vendors and dealing with customers and the vendors. The manager of a Chico Dairy Mart store performs essentially the same duties as the assistant manager and also has the final responsibility for running the affairs of the store, including supervising, hiring and firing subordinate personnel.

On each of two separate occasions, the first time in July, 1980 and the second time on July 24, 1981, a male, part-time clerk with a Chico Dairy Mart who had less experience than the complainant was promoted to store manager at her store, instead of the complainant. The complainant was at least as well qualified as the first of these men and undoubtedly better qualified than the second for the promotion to store manager.

The employer employed many women as managers of its various stores. One of these female store managers, a Ms. Vandergrift, who had previously been the store manager at the complainant's store, testified that the employer's area supervisor, who is responsible for selecting store managers, told Ms. Vandergrift, in August, 1980, that the complainant would not be his choice for a store manager's position because of the complainant's noticeable "facial deformity." According to Ms. Vandergrift, he also stated that it would not be wise to promote the complainant to the position of store manager, strictly on the basis of her physical *appearance*, because, in his opinion, the complainant's "facial deformity" was not something a vendor or customer "would like to encounter."

After being "passed over" the second time for a promotion to the position of store manager, the complainant was so upset that she, on July 25, 1981, submitted her resignation from employment. Her resignation was effective on August 1, 1981.

B. Proceedings before the Commission

The complainant thereafter timely filed a complaint against the employer with the West Virginia Human Rights Commission (the "Commission"), alleging that her resignation was a constructive discharge based upon unlawful discrimination on account of her sex. Much later, but as soon as she learned from Ms. Vandergrift about the area supervisor's statements concerning his opinion of the complainant's physical appearance, the complainant amended her complaint to add an allegation of unlawful discrimination against her by the employer on account of her alleged "handicap," expressly referring to the manner in which the employer *regarded* her physical appearance, not to her blindness in one eye. In her amended complaint the complainant stated that she was able to perform the job, and she did *not* mention any actual handicap for which the employer should have made reasonable accommodations.

•   •   •

A case from another state which is virtually identical to the case now before us is *Kirby v. Illinois Cent.* 454 N.E.2d 816 (1983). The complaint there was under the Illinois Equal Opportunities for the Handicapped Act (the "EOHA"), then in effect. The complainant in that case alleged an unlawful refusal to hire him on the basis that the potential employer "perceived" that the complainant had spina bifida, a back condition. The complaint did not allege any existing back condition which was a handicap, and, instead, alleged the complainant's ability to perform the work in question. The statute prohibited unlawful employment discrimination because of an individual's physical or mental handicap, defined by the statute, in relevant part, as "'a handicap unrelated to one's ability to perform jobs or positions available to him for hire or promotion[.]'"

The court in *Kirby* examined prior cases under the statute and held: "Plaintiff's theory that only the perception of a handicap need be alleged was previously rejected by" state precedents. "The EOHA does not provide a remedy to persons who are not in fact handicapped. The complaint under consideration did not state a cause of action under the Act." Restating its holding, the court said: "We hold that pleading the existence of a handicap is a threshold requirement for stating a cause of action under the EOHA. Secondly, it is necessary to allege that the complained-of discriminatory employment practice occurred because of the perception of the handicap."

The complainant here likewise failed to allege and prove unlawful discrimination on account of an actual, existing "handicap," defined by *W.Va.*

Code, 5-11-3(t), as amended, as "any physical or mental impairment which substantially limits one or more of an individual's major life activities." The complaint was not premised upon the fact that the complainant was blind in one eye but upon the fact that the socket around that eye was somewhat sunken or hollow and was *regarded* by the employer as "unsavory and unacceptable" for a store manager who dealt with vendors and customers. In short, the complaint in the present case, as in *Kirby,* alleges the unimpaired ability to do the work in question, as well as work in general, without any accommodations and was based upon the mere perception of a handicap by the employer, which is not actionable under the Act as written.

C. Invalidity of Rule Under West Virginia Human Rights Act

The definition of "handicap" under the West Virginia Human Rights Act is more restrictive than the federal definition of "handicapped individual." The West Virginia statute requires an actual, existing handicap. In obvious contrast, the federal statute, and the Commission's rule taken verbatim therefrom, include—in addition to an actual, existing handicap—a past handicap and a perceived handicap.

•   •   •

This Court now decides the issue left open in *Ranger Fuel* and holds that the rule of the West Virginia Human Rights Commission, defining a "handicapped person" to include a person who does not in fact have a "handicap," as defined by *W.Va.Code,* 5-11-3(t), as amended, but who "is regarded as having such a handicap," is invalid because that rule clearly conflicts with the *legislative* intent by expressly enlarging upon the substantive rights created by the statute. It is an unlawful discriminatory practice under the West Virginia Human Rights Act for an employer to refuse to offer a job promotion to an employee on account of the person's "handicap." However, where a complainant never alleges, and the evidence does not indicate, that the discrimination was on account of the complainant's "handicap," as statutorily defined, but solely because the employer regarded the complainant's physical appearance to be unacceptable, the conduct of the employer is not actionable under the clearly restrictive definition of "handicap" contained in the West Virginia Human Rights Act.

• • •

Workman, Justice, dissenting:

The opinion of the majority is not only unconscionable, but wrong as a matter of law.

This is a simple case and the result should be clear: Terrah Elynn Alfred is blind in her left eye and therefore clearly handicapped as that term is defined by the West Virginia Human Rights Act, *W.Va.Code* § 5-11-3(t), as amended. She wears a prosthesis, or glass eye. She was denied a promotion to which she was entitled because of the "deformed" appearance of her eye which resulted from and is part of her handicap. It is unlawful for any employer to discriminate against an individual with respect to compensation, hire, tenure, terms, conditions or privileges of employment if such individual is able and competent to perform the services required even if such individual is blind or handicapped.

Therefore, Terrah Elynn Alfred should be compensated for the damages she suffered as a result of such unlawful discrimination.

The majority, however, mistakenly classifies this as a case of "perceived handicap," as that concept is delineated in a rule of the W.Va. Human Rights Commission. That rule in pertinent part expands the definition of handicapped person to include a person who does not in fact have a handicap, but who is "regarded as having such a handicap." The majority at great length and in scholarly depth analyzes whether that rule was validly promulgated. Such an analysis, while probably correct, is completely unnecessary. Terrah Alfred is handicapped.

This is a handicap (not perceived handicap) discrimination case. Even explanatory footnotes to the perceived handicap rule make it clear that the instant case is not one involving perception of handicap. Footnote 8 to the rules (published therewith) states in pertinent part:

> This regulation follows the federal [statutory] definition and expands upon the [West Vir-

ginia] statutory definition of 'Handicap' by including persons who are regarded as having a substantially limiting impairment and persons with a history of such impairment. This extension is necessary to make it clear that the law prohibits discrimination against persons who are *incorrectly perceived as handicapped* as well as persons who are correctly perceived as handicapped. . . .

> . . . [D]iscrimination against persons who are regarded as being substantially impaired *even though they are not actually impaired* is discrimination rooted in prejudices or mistaken ideas about the capacities of persons who are not physically or mentally normal. . . . Examples of discrimination against persons who are regarded as being substantially impaired include . . . *denial of employment to a person with a florid face on the mistaken assumption he or she has high blood pressure.*

(emphasis added)

The majority fails to preceive what is meant by the concept of perception of handicap, despite the fact that the rule makes clear that it involves the *incorrect* perception that the person has a handicap when in fact the person does not have a handicap. Terrah Alfred *does* have a handicap, so it is impossible to bring the circumstances of her case within the definition of perceived handicap as enunciated by the rule. Likewise, had the employer perceived the complainant could not perform the duties of the job due to her handicap, when in fact she could, that would also have been a mistaken perception on the part of the employer. But that certainly would not render it a perceived handicap case. The employer here did not mistakenly perceive that Terrah Alfred had a handicap. He discriminatorily perceived it as unsavory and he wrongfully denied her a promotion on that basis.

It is beyond comprehension why the majority goes through nineteen tortuous pages to determine whether the rule on perceived handicap was properly adopted. This woman was denied a promotion for which she was qualified and to which she was entitled—not because her employer mistakenly perceived she was handicapped, but because she is handicapped and the employer did not like the way she looks as a result of that handicap. That is clearly discrimination on the basis of handicap which is unlawful under *Code,* 5-11-9(a).

The majority's opinion explicitly permits the employer to decline to promote the complainant because her supervisor considered her appearance unacceptable for dealing with customers and vendors. This determination is insensitive, outrageous and wrong as a matter of law. As pointed out in a brief of amicus curiae, employers in the early days of civil rights litigation frequently argued that their customers would not frequent a store if they were to be served by a black person. The courts have uniformly rejected customer preference as a defense to human rights actions.

Despite the fact that "customer preference" has been held by the United States Supreme Court not to be a valid defense against handicap discrimination actions, and despite the fact that the majority says in a footnote that they don't approve of such a defense, they go on to condone it in this case.

•   •   •

Many handicaps leave their victims with a physical appearance that may seem "unsavory" to non-handicapped people. Blind people may be glassy-eyed or have involuntary eye movements. People with spina bifida or other crippling diseases may walk with a pronounced limp. People with cerebral palsy may drool or have other involuntary body movements. Non-handicapped people often feel "uncomfortable" around handicapped people—a person in a wheelchair, an amputee, one with a withered hand . . . or a sunken eye. These examples are not given to over-dramatize. They are the real-life experience of many physically handicapped people, as graphically pointed out by the affidavit of Jim Dickson, executive director of the Disabled Rights Equal Access Movement, a national coalition of disabled organizations, and himself a blind person.

One of the chief underlying reasons for anti-discrimination laws is to require employers to base their employment decisions on an individual's qualifications, as opposed to irrational conclusions about their limitations or deep-seated anxieties about their physical appearance. As the United States Supreme Court said in *School Bd. of Nassau County, Fla. v. Arline*, 480 U.S. 273, 284, (1987), "society's accumulated myths and fears about disability and disease are as handicapping as are the physical limitations that flow from actual impairment."

The majority opinion permits this most blatant and insidious form of handicap discrimination. Their mistake is tragic and wrong.

Adarand Constructors v. Pena [1]

The United States Supreme Court

In 1989 the federal Department of Transportation awarded a contract for a Colorado highway construction project to Mountain Gravel & Construction Company. Mountain Gravel solicited bids from a variety of subcontractors specializing in guardrail work. Among the firms submitting subcontracting bids were Adarand Constructors and Gonzales Construction. Adarand submitted the lowest bid; but Mountain awarded the guardrail work to Gonzales. Gonzales had been certified by the Small Business Administration (SBA), a federal agency, as a business 51 percent controlled by "socially and economically disadvantaged individuals," and un-der the terms of federal law, Mountain Gravel would receive extra federal money if it hired an SBA-certified concern. The SBA presumed that "Black, Hispanic, Asian Pacific, Subcontinent Asian, and Native Americans" are "socially and economically disadvantaged." After losing the guardrail subcontract to Gonzales, Adarand filed suit against various federal officials, claiming that the SBA's presumptions of disadvantage based on race violated Adarand's right to "equal protection of the laws," guaranteed by the Fifth and Fourteenth Amendments to the U.S. Constitution. Lower federal courts, relying on some of the Supreme Court's recent rulings, denied Adarand's claim. But the Supreme Court reversed the lower courts and held that Adarand had a legitimate complaint under the Constitution. The lower courts had rejected Adarand's claim because they found that the SBA rules were designed to achieve the "significant governmental purpose" of providing subcontracting opportunities for small disadvantaged business enterprises. O'Connor argued that Adarand had to be given another day in court, this time focusing on whether the ways in which the government uses subcontracting compensation rules can meet the test of strict scrutiny.

Writing for the majority of the Court, Justice O'Connor explained that a central point of controversy in Adarand *turned on the level of scrutiny appropriate to racial classifications included in the federal subcontracting law. As O'Connor explained, any local, state, or federal law classifying people according to their racial identity is automatically suspect because of the risk that the law may be the result of bigotry and prejudice. Consequently, the courts must look carefully at such laws to ensure their validity. How carefully the courts must scrutinize or examine such laws, however, has been unclear. Two differing levels of examination, or standards of review, had previously been endorsed by the courts, according to O'Connor. One standard was articulated by the Supreme Court in* Richmond v. Croson, *decided in 1989. As O'Connor wrote in* Adarand,

> [a] majority of the Court in *Croson* held that the standard of review under the Equal Protection Clause is not dependent on the race of those burdened or benefited by a particular classification, and that the single standard of review for racial classifications should be 'strict scrutiny,'

meaning that the law in question must be shown to be necessary to the furtherance of a "compelling governmental objective," something of such overriding importance that it outweighs the dangers of race-based laws. The Croson *opinion held*

> that the Fourteenth Amendment requires strict scrutiny of all race-based action by state and local governments. But *Croson* . . . had no occasion to declare what standard of review the Fifth Amendment requires for such action taken by the Federal Government.

A competing interpretation of the appropriate standard of review had been announced by the Court in the year following Croson. *The decision in that case, O'Connor argued, was a mistake.*

> *Metro Broadcasting, Inc. v. FCC* involved a Fifth Amendment challenge to race-based policies of the Federal Communications Commission. In *Metro Broadcasting*, the Court repudiated the long-held notion that it would be unthinkable that the same Constitution would impose a lesser duty of the Federal Government than it does on a State to afford equal protection of the laws. . . . It did so by holding that 'benign' federal racial classifications need only satisfy intermediate scrutiny, even though *Croson* had recently concluded that such classifications must satisfy strict scrutiny. 'Benign' federal racial classifications, the Court said, 'even if those measures are not 'remedial' in the sense of being designed to compensate victims of past governmental or societal discrimination—are constitutionally permissible to the extent that they serve *important* governmental objectives within the power of Congress and are *substantially related* to achievement of those objectives.'

This more relaxed standard of review, O'Connor argued, which some courts had used to justify programs of preferential treatment, is inappropriate in all cases where people are being distinguished by race. This conclusion and its implications for programs of affirmative action were hotly debated among members of the Court.

Justice O'Connor

. . . [According to precedent] the basic principle is that the Fifth and Fourteenth Amendments to the Constitution protect persons, not groups. It follows from that principle that all governmental action based on race—a group classification long recognized as "in most circumstances irrelevant and therefore prohibited" . . . should be subjected to detailed judicial inquiry to ensure that the personal right to equal protection of the laws has not been infringed. These ideas have long been central to this Court's understanding of equal protection, and holding "benign" state and federal racial classifications to different standards does not square with them. [A] free people whose institutions are founded upon the doctrine of equality . . . should tolerate no retreat from the principle that government may treat people differently because of their race only for the most compelling reasons. Accordingly, we hold today that all racial classifications, imposed by whatever federal, state, or local governmental actor, must be analyzed by a reviewing court under strict scrutiny. In other words, such classifications are constitutional only if they are narrowly tailored measures that further compelling governmental interests.

Justice Scalia, concurring in part and concurring in the judgment.

. . . In my view, government can never have a "compelling interest" in discriminating on the basis of race in order to "make up" for past racial discrimination in the opposite direction. . . . Individuals who have been wronged by unlawful racial discrimination should be made whole; but under our Constitution there can be no such thing as either a creditor or a debtor race. That concept is alien to the Constitution's focus upon the individual . . . and its rejection of dispositions based on race. . . . To pursue the concept of racial entitlement—even for the most admirable and benign of purposes—is to reinforce and preserve for future mischief the way of thinking that produced race slavery, race privilege and race hatred. In the eyes of government, we are just one race here. It is American. . . .

Justice Thomas, concurring in part and concurring in the judgment.

. . . I believe that there is a "moral [and] constitutional equivalence" . . . between laws designed to subjugate a race and those that distribute benefits on the basis of race in order to foster some current notion of equality. Government cannot make us equal; it can only recognize, respect, and protect us as equal before the law.

That these programs may have been motivated, in part, by good intentions cannot provide refuge from the principle that under our Constitution, the government may not make distinctions on the basis

of race. As far as the Constitution is concerned, it is irrelevant whether a government's racial classifications are drawn by those who wish to oppress a race or by those who have a sincere desire to help those thought to be disadvantaged. There can be no doubt that the paternalism that appears to lie at the heart of this program is at war with the principle of inherent equality that underlies and infuses our Constitution. . . .

These programs not only raise grave constitutional questions, they also undermine the moral basis of the equal protection principle. . . .

. . . [T]here can be no doubt that racial paternalism and its unintended consequences can be as poisonous and pernicious as any other form of discrimination. So-called "benign" discrimination teaches many that because of chronic and apparently immutable handicaps, minorities cannot compete with them without their patronizing indulgence. Inevitably, such programs engender attitudes of superiority or, alternatively, provoke resentment among those who believe that they have been wronged by the government's use of race. These programs stamp minorities with a badge of inferiority and may cause them to develop dependencies or to adopt an attitude that they are "entitled" to preferences. . . .

In my mind, government-sponsored racial discrimination based on benign prejudice is just as noxious as discrimination inspired by malicious prejudice. . . . In each instance, it is racial discrimination, plain and simple.

Justice Stevens, with whom Justice Ginsburg joins, dissenting.

. . . There is no moral or constitutional equivalence between a policy that is designed to perpetuate a caste system and one that seeks to eradicate racial subordination. Invidious discrimination is an engine of oppression, subjugating a disfavored group to enhance or maintain the power of the majority. Remedial race-based preferences reflect the opposite impulse: a desire to foster equality in society. No sensible conception of the Government's constitutional obligation to "govern impartially" . . . should ignore this distinction. . . .

The consistency that the Court espouses would disregard the difference between a "No Trespassing" sign and a welcome mat. It would treat a Dixiecrat Senator's decision to vote against Thurgood Marshall's confirmation in order to keep African Americans off the Supreme Court as on a par with President Johnson's evaluation of his nominee's race as a positive factor. . . . An attempt by the majority to exclude members of a minority race from a regulated market is fundamentally different from a subsidy that enables a relatively small group of newcomers to enter that market. An interest in "consistency" does not justify treating differences as though they were similarities.

. . . As a matter of constitutional and democratic principle, a decision by representatives of the majority to discriminate against the members of a minority race is fundamentally different from those same representatives' decision to impose incidental costs on the majority of their constituents in order to provide a benefit to a disadvantaged minority. . . .

Justice Souter, with whom Justice Ginsburg and Justice Breyer join, dissenting.

. . . When the extirpation of lingering discriminatory effects is thought to require a catch-up mechanism, like the racially preferential inducement under the statutes considered here, the result may be that some members of the historically favored race are hurt by that remedial mechanism, however innocent they may be of any personal responsibility for any discriminatory conduct. When this price is considered reasonable, it is in part because it is a price to be paid only temporarily; if the justification for the preference is eliminating the effects of a past practice, the assumption is that the effects will themselves recede into the past, becoming attenuated and finally disappearing. . . .

Justice Ginsburg, with whom Justice Breyer joins, dissenting.

. . . The statutes and regulations at issue, as the Court indicates, were adopted by the political branches in response to an "unfortunate reality": "[t]he unhappy persistence of both the practice and the lingering effects of racial discrimination against minority groups in this country. . . ." The United States suffers from those lingering effects because, for most of our Nation's history, the idea that "we are just one race" was not embraced. For generations, our lawmakers and judges were unprepared to say that there is in this land no superior race, no race inferior to any other. In *Plessy v. Ferguson,* 163 U.S. 537 (1896), not only did this Court endorse the oppressive practice of race segregation, but even Justice Harlan, the advocate of a "color-blind" Constitution, stated: "The white race deems itself to be the dominant race in this country. And so it is, in prestige, in achievements, in education, in wealth and in power. So, I doubt not, it will continue to be for all time, if it remains true to its great heritage and holds fast to the principles of constitutional liberty. . . ." Not until *Loving v. Virginia,* 388 U.S. 1 (1967), which held unconstitutional Virginia's ban on interracial marriages, could one say with security that the Constitution and this Court would abide no measure "designed to maintain White Supremacy. . . ."

. . . [The lingering effects of discrimination], reflective of a system of racial caste only recently ended, are evident in our workplaces, markets, and neighborhoods. Job applicants with identical resumes, qualifications, and interview styles still experience different receptions, depending on their race. . . . White and African-American consumers still encounter different deals. . . . People of color looking for housing still face discriminatory treatment by landlords, real estate agents, and mortgage lenders. . . . Minority entrepreneurs sometimes fail to gain contracts though they are the low bidders, and they are sometimes refused work even after winning contracts. . . . [B]ias both conscious and unconscious, reflecting traditional and unexamined habits of thought . . . keeps up barriers that must come down if equal opportunity and nondiscrimination are ever genuinely to become this country's law and practice. . . .

Although the Court in Adarand *did not actually invalidate any federal affirmative action laws, it did clearly announce its intention in the future to subject such programs to the strictest possible scrutiny—a level of examination which, as Justice O'Connor noted, has a reputation for being "strict in theory but fatal in fact." Many legal experts believe that existing programs that do not seek to redress specific instances of* past, overt discrimination and look merely to the non-remedial goal of expanding diversity will almost certainly be illegal under Adarand. *A memorandum issued by the Department of Justice in 1995 states that affirmative action programs justified "solely by reference to general societal discrimination, general assertions of discrimination in a particular sector or* industry, or a statistical underrepresentation of minorities in a sector or industry . . . without more" will be "impermissible bases for affirmative action." [2]

NOTES

1. (1995) 132 L Ed 2d 158.
2. See *National Law Journal,* July 17, 1995, A12.

Individual Candidate Remedies: Why They Won't Work

Gertrude Ezorsky

Discrimination against blacks in America has exemplified a caste system, marked by fear of contamination from "inferior" caste members, their segregation into the lowest paid, most miserable occupations and their consequent impoverishment.

Today the laws banning white contact with blacks in personal facilities are gone, but race prejudice has far from disappeared. The disinclination of most whites to form friendships and intimate relationships with blacks, and the widespread resistance to neighborhood and school integration, causing violence in some cities, are indicators of a pervasive racial bias. Although a few blacks have moved up, occupational segregation into the lowest jobs, and even into unemployment, is still fundamentally intact. Today a white high-school dropout is less likely to be unemployed than a black with some college education.[1] Where employed, blacks are overrepresented at the bottom of the occupational ladder.

Nathan Glazer warns us that unrepresentative racial distribution in occupations may only reflect ways in which racial groups have "expressed themselves."

> Distinctive histories have channeled ethnic and racial groups into one kind of work or another, and this is the origin of many of the "unrepresentative" work distributions we see. These distributions have been maintained by an occupational tradition linked to an ethnic

community which makes it easier for the Irish to become policeman, the Italians fruit dealers, Jews businessmen, and so on.[2]

But Glazer fails to note the kind of work that blacks have traditionally performed: hot, heavy, and dirty jobs in the foundries and paint pits of the automobile plants, the boiler rooms of utilities, the dusty basements of the tobacco factories, and in the murderous heat of the coke ovens of the steel mills. Today every other person involved by occupation with dirt or garbage is black.

I suggest that black people have not "expressed themselves" by such labor. Moreover, while Glazer reminds us that the Irish have by historic tradition been policemen, he fails to mention the "distinctive" history that has "channelled" blacks into their "kind of work"; that history is slavery.

Two ways of reducing occupational segregation may be distinguished: the group method—known as affirmative action—and the individual candidate method. Affirmative action is exemplified when an employer sets a numerical goal for hiring, promoting, or retaining black employees during layoffs. Taking affirmative action does *not* require that the blacks who benefit from its use be victims of past discrimination by this same employer. The point of affirmative action in employment is to reduce occupational segregation of blacks as a group; as U.S. civil rights enforcement officials learned—before the drastic decline of affirmative action enforcement began in the seventies—the notable absence of blacks from a work force is remedied not by vague employer promises to look for blacks, but by setting a reasonable, *specific* numerical goal for hiring them.

The individual candidate method is exemplified when a black applicant makes a legal complaint proving that he was denied a position because of an employer's bias. The black applicant is then restored to the position he would have held with the employer, but for discrimination. Thus, unlike affirmative action, the individual candidate method [hereafter, the individual method] requires that the blacks *prove* that they were discriminated against by the employer.

Some persons who agree that occupational segregation is unfair, also think that it can be undone without affirmative action. They believe that use of the individual method to rectify specific acts of discrimination will eliminate occupational segregation. I shall confine myself here to criticizing that belief in the effectiveness of the individual method. As I shall show, that method has inherent weaknesses. Moreover, it is often irrelevant to situations where the consequences of social practices, past and present, sustain occupational segregation.

Inherent Weakness of the Individual Method

First, the black complainant must prove that the employer denied him a position because of race prejudice. But the existence of pervasive race prejudice is compatible with great difficulty in proving prejudice in an individual case, a difficulty due in part to effective counter-strategies by employers. How does a black applicant know whether the job has really "just been filled"? How can a qualified black driver prove that a delivery company's new policy—hiring only college graduates—was devised to exclude black candidates? How can an experienced black worker demonstrate that announcement of a managerial opening was canceled because the employer learned that she—a *black* employee—was clearly the most qualified candidate. The difficulty of proving biased intent, when employers have power to cover up such bias, reduces the effectiveness of the individual method.

A second weakness of that method is that employees who assert their rights are often labeled "troublemakers" by their supervisors. (Many of the rights we now take for granted were won by such troublemakers.) However, that label can damage a person—especially a black person—for her

entire working life. A realistic assessment of that damage to themselves and to the families they support often stops black people from initiating perfectly justified discrimination complaints.

Two Societies

Contemporary social practices contribute to occupational segregation. White and black people still live, for the most part, in two different societies. They have personal and intimate relationships with persons of their own color. Such social separation from whites creates disadvantages for blacks in the world of work that cannot be dispelled by the individual method. Here is why:

As vocational counselors know, "connections" —friends, family and neighbors—lead people to jobs. "It isn't what you know, but who you know" expresses a profound social truth. Today the better jobs are still held predominantly by whites. They tell their white associates about vacancies in their line of work; such hiring through social connections, although a disadvantage for blacks, is for employers a cheap form of personnel recruitment.

Blacks also lack access to the white gatherings where political candidacies and well-paying patronage jobs are dispensed over lunch, dinner, and drinks. As a prominent U.S. official said recently, "To get a job" in Washington, "you have to know someone."

Thus, the existence of two societies, a white and a black, reinforces occupational segregation. However, the individual method cannot remove the damage to blacks caused by their exclusion from white society. First, because choice of one's personal associates is rightfully exempt from the laws that prohibit racially biased acts. Even prejudiced persons have a moral right to choose their own friends and spouses. Second, because the individual method presupposes the *candidate* model of discrimination: A black candidate competing for a position is rejected because of race. His discrimination complaint granted, he is awarded the position that he should have been given in that competition. But where positions are dispensed behind the scenes in white society, no competition exists. Hence, blacks have no opportunity to become candidates for such jobs. When a white employer gives his nephew a comfortable position with the firm, usually no one knows which individual would have been hired in a fair competition. Therefore, no black individual can complain that he or she should have been given that position. Since the individual method is usually irrelevant to hiring through white social connections, that method cannot reduce the adverse impact of such behind-the-scenes hiring on black people, an impact that serves to reinforce occupational segregation.

Another social practice that contributes to such segregation is racial separation by neighborhoods. That separation is a palpable barrier to establishing white connections that lead to better jobs. Moreover, excluded from residence in distant white suburbs, ghetto blacks have no access to many jobs in newly created suburban enterprises. In some cases, where openings exist, no public transportation is available, or the carfare is prohibitively expensive for a black youth. But the individual method is an ineffective tool for opening up all white neighborhoods to black residents. Landlords and realtors, like employers, use effective strategies to defeat individual complaints of housing bias. Does a black apartment seeker have *proof*, or the time to assemble proof, that a landlord's excuses ("The apartment isn't available because it needs repair") are conjured up to exclude blacks, or that a real estate agent is steering black clients away from white neighborhoods? Moreover, the individual method cannot eliminate ostensibly race-neutral practices that tend to exclude blacks from white areas, such as zoning laws that ban multiple unit dwellings— more affordable by blacks—or the prohibition by public referendum of government subsidized housing where, as it happens, more black people live. Complaints of biased acts against specific individuals are irrelevant to such practices. Yet the segregated housing they sustain cuts off employment possibilities for blacks.[3]

Nor can individual complaints create effective vocational training for black youths in ghetto schools, which as segregated are visible targets for inadequate state funding.

Consequences of Past Discrimination

Black people, as the saying goes, have been the "last hired and first fired." Hence, they have usually been overrepresented among job losers during economic recessions. However, that higher job-loss rate has persisted into the present, a persistence that is due in part to the consequences of past discrimination. But as I shall show, the individual method is of no use in remedying this situation.

After the 1965 Civil Rights Act, many public and private employers, because of affirmative action regulations, hired more than their usual token (or zero) number of blacks. However, due to the employer's *past* hiring discrimination, blacks still remained noticeably absent among the more senior workers. Thus, during the economic recessions beginning in the seventies, the jobs of the more recently hired black workers tended to be eliminated by seniority-based layoffs. (In the mid-seventies the black male job-loss rate was twice their work force ratio.) Thus, where blacks have been hired as municipal police, teachers, fire fighters, and in private enterprises because of recent affirmative action measures, layoffs by seniority tend to make the work force—as before the Civil Rights Act—all white.[4] However, although a seniority system in fact tends to sight blacks first for layoff, it is race blind. Hence, individual complaints of biased acts cannot reduce its devastating impact in employment on black people.

When blacks lose their jobs during an economic recession, they usually move down the occupational ladder into unskilled, temporary jobs or no jobs at all. Once again the individual method is irrelevant to the reinforcement of occupational segregation.

NOTES

1. The Caste System: See William Ryan, *Equality* (New York: Pantheon Books, 1981), 140. The unemployment comparison between blacks with some college education and white high-school dropouts: See "Students, Graduates and Dropouts in the Labor Market," *Special Labor Force Reports, Monthly Labor Review* (October 1979). (Table reprinted in *State of Black America*, National Urban League, 1982.)

2. Nathan Glazer, *Affirmative Discrimination,* (New York, Basic Books, 1975), 203.

3. Housing discrimination. *Racism in America and How to Combat It*, U.S. Commission on Civil Rights (January 1970); J. and C. Feagin, *Discrimination, American Style* (Englewood Cliffs, N.J.: Prentice-Hall), chap. 4.

4. Seniority and affirmative action. *Last Hired, First Fired; Layoffs and Civil Rights*, U.S. Commission on Civil Rights (February 1977), chap. 2.

Affirmative Action Does Not Promote Equality

Herman Belz

Analysis of the affirmative action debate begins with the idea of equality of opportunity on which traditional anti-discrimination law rests. Based on the natural rights principles of the Declaration of Independence, equal opportunity rejects distinctions of legal status and privilege defined by race, religion, ethnicity, language, sex, and family inheritance that formed the basis of premodern societies. Defined by the guarantee of equal treatment regardless of superficial differences such as race, it is a means by which individuals, through talent, ability, and other personal attributes, take responsibility for themselves and pursue their interests. The rule of equal opportunity does not guarantee equal results. Because it values liberty and gives scope to differences among individuals with respect to interest and ability, it recognizes the impossibility of achieving perfect equality in the distribution of social and economic goods.

In comparative historical terms, the promise of equal opportunity inherent in the American Revolution was broadly realized in nineteenth-century America. Even in a country like the United States, however, where feudal or aristocratic institutions were never firmly established, equal opportunity was seriously restricted by the existence of slavery. Nevertheless the idea of equality of opportunity possessed unquestioned political legitimacy, even among groups that were excluded from its full benefits. This fact explains why equal opportunity was the aim of democratic political reformers, abolitionists, and women's rights advocates in the nineteenth century as well as progressive reformers in the early twentieth century.

From Equal Opportunity to Group-Based Equality

In race relations, equal opportunity—long denied by the system of legalized segregation—was guaranteed in the Civil Rights Act of 1964. The law commanded indifference to race in private employment in order to reinforce the government's own constitutionally required indifference to race under the equal protection clause of the Fourteenth and (by judicial construction) Fifth Amendments. In a political sense, Title VII [of the Civil Rights Act] reflected an interest-group outlook, insofar as the right of individuals not to be discriminated against because of race was intended to improve economic conditions for blacks in general. Under the law, however, the rights of individuals were the basis for any group concern. The Civil Rights Act recognized that individuals are morally prior to rather than dependent upon groups.

The civil rights establishment and the equal employment opportunity bureaucracy in the 1960s rejected equal opportunity because it did not lead to equality of condition. In their view, the legal capacity to participate and the right to equal treatment in a procedural sense—the central meaning of equal opportunity—were insignificant compared to the socially determined meaning of opportunity. The social and cultural deprivation suffered by blacks and other minority groups was seen as constituting an inseparable obstacle to the advancement of their interests and socioeconomic status. Civil rights policymakers therefore infused the equal opportunity law with the new meaning of group-based equality of result.

Disparate Impact Discrimination

The theory of disparate impact discrimination [that the unintentional exclusion of blacks from jobs constituted discrimination] provided the means for this transformation. Under pre-Title VII fair employment practice legislation, an inference—though not a conclusive finding—of intentional discrimination could be drawn from statistics of racial imbalance or exclusion. In enforcing Title VII, civil rights strategists persuaded the courts to accept statistical racial disparity, completely apart from an employer's intent, as *prima facie* evidence of unlawful discrimination. The *prima facie* evidence became a conclusive finding of discrimination if the employer could not prove that the employment practice that caused the disparate impact was a business necessity. Accordingly, in order to avoid discrimination charges under the disparate impact theory of liability, employers were forced to have a sufficient number of blacks in their work force. This method of enforcing or complying with Title VII focused attention on the results of the employment process, or on the bottom line, rather than on equality of opportunity defined as the removal of procedural barriers to the equal treatment of individuals. The civil rights lobby argued that focusing on bottom-line results was a way of monitoring the extent to which an employer was providing equal opportunity in employment. In reality, employers were forced to guarantee equal or racially proportionate results in disregard of equal opportunity for individuals irrespective of race—as was required by Title VII.

Under disparate impact theory routine business practices could be found unlawful. The theory served the liberal purpose of expanding government regulation of business and forcing private employers and white workers to bear the cost and responsibility of compensating blacks for societal discrimination. Liberals were able to pursue the goal of restricting the operation of the labor market for social redistributive purposes while justifying it simply as a means of securing equal opportunity.

Disparate impact theory also provided a rationalization for preferential treatment, whether voluntary or coerced, as a remedy for unlawful discrimination. Preferential treatment as public policy was adopted in the absence of informed national discussion of the remedial concept [of providing a remedy for discrimination to people not directly victimized by discrimination] or of the theory of disparate impact discrimination on which it rested. No one in Congress supported quotas in the Title VII debate; when affirmative action preferences were introduced, policymakers deliberately obscured their coercive, race-conscious character. Objections had been raised against compensatory preference since the idea was first proposed in the early 1960s;

not until the early 1970s, however, when defenders of the new civil rights ideology undertook to justify race-conscious measures, did the affirmative action debate really take shape.

Affirmative action preferences were initially justified as a legal remedy for past discrimination. . . . Courts proceeded to exercise broad remedial authority and elaborate the remedial rationale as an instrument of social reform. From the standpoint of public opinion, remedying past unlawful discrimination remains the principal justification of preferential treatment. . . .

Race as Merit

Two basic elements of affirmative action have remained constant. The first is the idea that individual merit should be defined in social terms, in relation to the principle of racial group equality of result. The second is the idea that reverse discrimination differs from traditional racial discrimination in being non-stigmatic. . . .

The affirmative action vision identifies race as a major component of the concept of merit. According to sociologist Benjamin Ringer, in a true merit society each group will be represented at each occupational level according to its numbers in the total work force. Most defenders of affirmative action reject the traditional idea of individual merit as culturally biased and redefine it in terms of racial and ethnic diversity. Psychologist Craig Haney contends that test-based selection should be supplemented by "recognition of the special merit that racial minorities bring to the work place by virtue of their unique perspectives and experiences." Linda S. Greene views individual merit as "a visionary ideal" that should not be embodied in legal doctrine before it is actually realized in social practice. Asserting that the concept of merit is political, Randall Kennedy reasons that since the elevation of blacks is a response to pressing social needs, race is rightly to be considered one of the primary traits that constitutes merit. Jeffrey Prager explains that under affirmative action, race *per se* is a merit deserving of reward, expressed in the rhetoric of diversity and representation rather than intelligence and achievement. Affirmative action rejects the idea of a hierarchy of merit: instead it argues for the concept of a pool of candidates who are equally qualified—that is, who are all equally likely to succeed on the job. Prager contends that companies operating under affirmative action plans should be permitted to set an absolute minimum standard of merit, rather than in effect be forced to accept the higher standards set by the abilities of candidates competing under a rank-ordered free-market concept of qualifications. Affirmative action merit is thus collectivistic, sociological, and relativistic.

ENFORCING DISCRIMINATION

Ironically, just as socialism has collapsed across the globe, the leading capitalist power has adopted a peculiarly American neosocialism, putting politics (and lawyers) in command of its workplace, albeit on the pretext of equity rather than efficiency. . . .

Quotas are not the law of the land, exactly. They are explicitly banned in both the 1964 and 1991 Civil Rights Acts. Nevertheless, corporate America has been terrorized by the legal legerdemain whereby any statistical disparity between work force and population is equated with intentional discrimination. Throughout American business, newly entrenched affirmative action bureaucrats are enforcing discrimination by race and sex—in favor of the "protected classes" (women, minorities, and, most recently, the disabled)—as decreed by Washington.[1]

The non-stigmatic nature of affirmative action preferences is a second feature of the policy that is consistently asserted. This argument rests on the presumption that in a democratic political system governed by a white majority, it is not possible for policy outcomes to be antagonistic to the interests of members of the dominant group. Because of this fact, racial classifications may be used in relation to whites without the suspicion of unconstitutionality that ordinarily attaches to racial criteria. . . .

Basic Rights

Analyzing the quota controversy, a defender of affirmative action in a judicious moment said there were two major reasons for opposing preferential treatment: it denied basic rights, and it might not serve the good of the community. This comment aptly summarizes the position of critics of preferential treatment through two decades of controversy.

Opponents of preferential treatment argued, to begin with, that the Constitution guarantees equal protection of the laws to all persons, and that Title VII prohibits discrimination against any individual on account of race, color, religion, national origin, or sex. In their view, the anti-discrimination principle of the Civil Rights Act was effective in eliminating racial barriers to equal opportunity, enabling blacks to achieve social and economic gains. Urging that the policy of individual rights and equal opportunity be continued, critics held that preferential treatment did not address the problem of unlawful discrimination and economic deprivation. On the contrary, they contended, it exacerbated racial tension, impeded the formulation of sound social policy, and undermined equality of opportunity. . . .

A more systematic argument against affirmative action developed in the later 1970s. Its fundamental premise is that the constitutional equal protection principle prohibits the distribution of benefits and costs by government on racial and ethnic grounds. Richard A. Posner states that to use race for constructive social purposes in non-stigmatizing or non-invidious ways, as affirmative action policy professes to do, requires courts to decide whether race-conscious measures harm a group. This involves weighing competing claims of racial groups on a subjective political scale that deprives the equal protection principle of its precision and objectivity. According to William Van Alstyne, determining that racial classification favoring certain groups can be justified under the Fourteenth Amendment by a compelling governmental interest rests on questionable judgments about motive and purpose. "That is not . . . a constitutional standard at all," Van Alstyne declares. "It is, rather, a sieve . . . that encourages renewed race-based laws, racial discrimination, racial competition, racial spoils systems, and mere judicial sport." . . .

An Over-Inclusive Remedy

Opponents contend that preferential treatment is not only wrong in principle, it is also ineffective for achieving its intended purpose. It does not provide a remedy for discrimination, as its legal justification asserts. Anglo-American jurisprudence holds that where the law creates an injury, the law must afford a remedy. The corollary, reflecting the principle of individual moral autonomy, is that no one can be made part of the remedy who is not part of the injury. Under quota orders, however, those who receive preferential treatment often are not victims of discrimination, and those who are victims receive no benefit. In addition, members of excluded non-minority groups are unlikely to have perpetrated or benefited from the discrimination, while the employer guilty of discrimination bears none of the burden. The idea of group discrimination implies that individual members of the group suffer injury because of their race. Yet compensation to the group as a whole in the form of preferential hiring is directed at the wrong target. If past discrimination is the reason for giving compensatory preference, the recipients are deserving because they are victims of discrimination, not because of their race. And assuming that personal qualifications count even minimally in affirmative action, the beneficiaries of racial preference are those who suffer the least discrimination and are most qualified. Race-conscious affirmative action is thus over-inclusive. Any reason given for group preference, Alan Goldman points out, such as compensating for injury or giving opportunity to persons in need, provides grounds for defining the preference more narrowly than race.

Contradicting Social Science and History

Critics further aver that insofar as preferential remedies are aimed at attaining racial balance or proportional representation, affirmative action rests on erroneous social science. Disparate impact theory holds that racial group differences in income, occupation, educational achievement, test scores, and other indicators are the result of discrimination. Opponents of preference contend, on the contrary, that to a considerable extent group differences are based on aptitude, ability, taste, and opportunity. Questioning the notion that members of minority groups can actually be placed in the position they would have occupied but for discrimination, critics claim that education, cultural values, age, geo-

graphical location, and the character of the labor market are causes of racial group disparities. Moreover, it is false to assume that without discrimination, one can expect a nearly random distribution of women and minorities in all jobs. Economist Walter Williams says there is no known theory indicating the "correct" number of minorities that should be found in an activity or organization.

Affirmative action not only contradicts social science, it disregards the lesson of history that race and ethnicity as principles of social organization result in hostility and repression. If discrimination along racial lines divides societies into oppressors and oppressed, observes Barry Gross, "it is scarcely reasonable to hope to heal the split and redress the wrongs by further reference to those things." In his view, the main argument against preferential treatment is the historical fact that racial, religious, and ethnic discrimination have led to social disorder, war, and mass slaughter. Alan Goldman notes that whereas the historic achievement of liberalism was to eliminate native differences like race as determinants of social roles and benefits, affirmative action reversed this trend. According to critics, the affirmative action strategy of using racial criteria to eliminate racial discrimination is inherently contradictory and futile. "We shall not now see racism disappear by employing its own ways of classifying people and of measuring their rights," declares William Van Alstyne. Douglas Rae expresses the fallacy of affirmative action thus: "The trouble with compensatory inequality—'inequality in the name of equality'—is that it is akin to 'killing for peace' or 'lying in the name of the truth.'"

Achievement Obscured

Still another argument against affirmative action is that it obscures the genuine achievement of those who receive preferential treatment. In 1973, business writer Daniel Seligman reported the observation of a black corporate equal employment opportunity officer that all minorities are stigmatized when less qualified applicants are hired. Reverse discrimination denies minorities the satisfaction of having their ability validated if they otherwise would have made it on their own. Criticism of this feature of affirmative action gained force as the policy spread. According to Charles Murray, under affirmative action a market premium attaches to race, with the result that every black professional, no matter how able, is tainted. Some black supporters of preferential treatment concede its stigmatizing effect, but believe it is less than the stigma associated with exclusion. Other blacks insist on standards that judge individuals by ability and achievement. If the worst feature of slavery was the dishonor it imposed on blacks, Glenn C. Loury asserts, then affirmative action preferences will not resolve but only prolong this destructive legacy. Neither white guilt, special favors, nor racial proportionalism decreed by government can secure the freely conveyed respect of one's peers that signifies real equality, Loury concludes. . . .

According to Harvey C. Mansfield, Jr., the most obvious meaning of affirmative action is that certain groups of people are not sufficiently capable of helping themselves and so require assistance. In order not to hurt the pride of the minority groups, however, this fact cannot be publicly admitted. It is not the injustice of preferential treatment that is its worst feature, Mansfield contends, but its evil and underhanded means. In essence, affirmative action categorically accuses the American people of racial discrimination in order to avoid telling the truth that minorities, in the eyes of the civil rights bureaucracy, are incapable of competing in society. By focusing on equality of result instead of equal opportunity, Mansfield charges, preferential treatment encourages indifference to means as long as the end is achieved. The consequence is indifference to morality. This is seen in the "immoral moralism" of the consent decree, wherein a defendant employer who does not admit he is guilty agrees under compulsion to act as if he were. Mansfield warns that under the rule of affirmative action, government by consent decree threatens to replace government by consent.

The ultimate criticism of race-conscious affirmative action, therefore, is that it lacks political legitimacy. While it purports to enforce civil rights and remedy discriminatory injury, it is in reality a policy of resource allocation and social redistribution that in a substantial sense has not been approved by democratic decision-making. Although most Americans supported the goal of bringing minority groups into the economic mainstream,

they were divided on the problem of means. The question of whether measures going beyond the anti-discrimination principle were needed, the identification of alternative principles on which preferential treatment rested, and the reconciliation of conflicting values and interests provoked by affirmative action proposals were political questions that should have been decided by representative institutions. It is true that some preferential programs were adopted by legislative bodies, but these were by far the exception rather than the rule and occurred long after the courts and administrative agencies had fundamentally installed a new policy in place of the Civil Rights Act. . . .

Affirmative action is often viewed as simply a strong means of enforcing traditional equal opportunity that can be used temporarily without weakening the principle of individual rights. Even so persistent a critic as Nathan Glazer says that preferential treatment has helped institutionalize non-discrimination laws. The longer racial criteria are employed, however, the more likely they are to become permanent. This result can only be at the expense of genuine equality of opportunity.

The chief historical significance of affirmative action has therefore been to promote statist intervention into the free market and weaken political and social institutions based on individual rights. In an era when proposals of social reform based on the rationale of class conflict have generally been rejected by the electorate, affirmative action attempts to achieve the redistributive and anti-capitalist purposes of contemporary liberalism by other means. Instead of promising liberty through social welfare and security, it promises substantial racial equality. To carry out its promise, it attacks individual liberty. Describing the obstacles to a policy of more far-reaching equality of result, Judge Damon J. Keith expresses the essential spirit of affirmative action when he critically observes: "Despite the progress of the past two decades, an entrenched belief in the sanctity of individual rights remains. Our courts have time and again explicitly or implicitly shied away from intruding too far into the rights of private individuals."

Affirmative action requires ever-expanding government regulation if the new American dilemma perceived by radical egalitarians—the unwillingness of democratic majorities to adopt measures necessary to achieve equality of condition for racial minorities—is to be resolved. Ultimately, then, the struggle to define American equality will determine whether the United States will remain a free society.

NOTE

1. Peter Brimelow and Leslie Spencer, *Forbes*, February 15, 1993.

Why Do We Need Affirmative Action?

Laura M. Purdy

Why is affirmative action sometimes morally required? Three general strategies for defending affirmative active have been suggested. One is that it appropriately compensates members of disadvantaged groups for past discrimination, another is that it counteracts current and ongoing discrimination, and a third is that it helps to secure more equality in society.

Affirmative action has been the subject of a great deal of controversy and confusion. Part of it has arisen because of conflicting definitions of affirmative action, and of the related notions of preferential treatment and reverse discrimination. A second problem has been that the populations for which it has been pressed vary in significant ways among themselves. Thus, for example, points which might be relevant to the situation of white middle class women might not be so for members of certain ethnic minorities. Hence, remedies that make sense for the one will not necessarily do so for the other. Thirdly, even for the same group, some proposals address the particular problem better than others and so, even where some action is well warranted, not every remedy will be equally justifiable. Accordingly, steps that would seem morally reasonable or even mandatory for one situation (admission to higher education, for instance) might be thoroughly inappropriate for another (such as tenuring a faculty member). These problems would create some obstacles to intelligent discussion, even if affirmative action were not such a deeply political issue. But it is such an issue, not only because it involves fundamental concepts in ethics and polit-

ical philosophy (concepts that bear upon our most basic ways of looking at the world and about which there is substantial debate), but also because it appears to be a zero-sum game: any victory for members of one class appears to be a loss for another. That the debate is mostly conducted by those with something to lose, whether it be a job, or just the satisfaction of knowing they deserve their job, helps to keep tempers hot.

Whatever the reasons for controversy, many people seem to have reached the conclusion that little more can usefully be said about the issue: we shall simply have to agree to disagree, and attempt to find compromises—fighting it out in schools, workplaces, legislatures, and courts. Given the prevailing political winds, however, existing affirmative action programs are clearly in jeopardy. In any case, it is doubtful that anything worthwhile remains to be said about this issue; consequently, despite this pessimism about further reasoned debate here, I believe it is worth another look. This paper starts with definitions and moves on to questions about qualifications; compensation arguments raise additional issues about how this society allocates social resources and the values that drive such allocations.

What Is Affirmative Action?

Some people distinguish between the kind of procedural practices that increase the probability of finding qualified individuals in the relevant classes, and the substantive ones that advantage members of such classes. I take it for granted that such procedural practices are morally necessary, as do most people: the rancor here is focused on substantive rules that benefit individuals who are members

Journal of Social Philosophy, vol. 25, no. 1 (Spring 1994), 133–143. © 1994 *Journal of Social Philosophy*. Reprinted by permission of the publisher.

of certain groups like white women, African-Americans, and the disabled.

Substantive affirmative action principles can take various forms. One ("weak" affirmative action), involves selecting members of disadvantaged groups (hereafter "Ds") whenever their qualifications are as good as those of their competitors; another ("strong"), involves selecting them even when they are somewhat less qualified. Both of these practices may be known as "preferential treatment." Preferential treatment is used both by proponents and by opponents of affirmative action to describe what it requires in practice. "Reverse discrimination," on the other hand, tends to be used by opponents of affirmative action, and seems generally intended to convey the idea that systematically preferring candidates in certain classes is as unjust as the kind of discrimination that spurred affirmative action policies in the first place.

These definitions immediately raise some questions. First and foremost, how do we judge "qualifications"?

Qualifications

Opponents of affirmative action programs often assume that we know what the right qualifications are for any given enterprise, and that judgments about them are generally unproblematic. But there are good reasons for doubting whether these beliefs are as solid as they are taken to be: our conception of appropriate qualifications may be too high, too narrow, or just plain unwarranted.

There are surely enterprises for which we can be reasonably confident that we know what it takes to do a job well, since they require clearly definable and measurable skills. A good typist, for example, needs speed and accuracy and these abilities are easily and reliably measured by means of a typing test.

But requirements for many other ventures are a good deal less clear. In question may be both what it takes to achieve a given result, and what result is desirable. We like to think, for instance, that only the most literate students can think philosophically. Yet I have often been surprised at the acuity of otherwise quite savage students, as well as by untutored children. In fact, students at all levels are sometimes clearly capable of doing well in courses for which they lack prerequisites. This is not to say that having certain skills and knowledge is not desirable, but that we may sometimes overlook alternative ways to acquire them, judge them necessary when they are not, or mistakenly link them with others.

Another example of debatable standards of qualification comes from the heart of the affirmative action debate, admission to professional schools. One might reasonably infer from discussions of *Bakke,* for instance, that the standards for admission to medical school are valid and clear; at most, there seem to be a few questions about the relevance of social issues like the importance of role models for white women or the probability of practicing in underserved populations for minorities. Thus discussion centers on whether it is unjust to select traditionally less qualified students rather than more qualified ones in order to promote these nontraditional ends. But what about even the relatively prosaic decision-making difficulties that admissions committees face with several non-commensurable measures, like GPA, MCATs, recommendations, prestige of school, and so forth? And, as I have argued elsewhere, it also fails to take account of bias embedded in those measures.[1]

But that is just the tip of the iceberg. Do the MCATs really measure what an individual knows? More to the point, do their scales validly portray the relationship between someone's score and success in medical studies? Worse yet, what do we know about the relationship between success in medical school and good doctoring? The inadequacies of the contemporary medical establishment are becoming increasingly evident, and the education of physicians plays no small role in the crisis. For this and other reasons, medical education clearly needs fundamental rethinking, a process pursued more or less actively at any given time by those involved. Some changes would make quite a difference in our conception of who is most qualified for medical school. What, for example, about a requirement that aspiring doctors first work as nurses, in order to test and reinforce their capacity for conscientious caring?[2] Until such issues are better settled, why confine the debate to the narrow questions now so often regarded as central? Medicine is not the only field where this point is relevant.

Examples of the widespread tendency to set unnecessary and hence overly restrictive standards for opportunities and performance can easily be found in legal cases. For example, in the 1971 *Griggs v. Duke Power Company*, the Supreme Court found that the company's employment standards (a high school diploma, and certain scores on an aptitude test) unreasonably excluded blacks from its better paying jobs, for those requirements hadn't been shown to be relevant to the jobs in question.[3] Height and weight rules have similarly operated to exclude white women and members of small ethnic groups from some occupations. They have been found unconstitutional under Title VII when potential employers could neither show why the requirement was relevant nor would let applicants attempt to prove that they could do the job anyway. Interestingly, as Judith Baer points out, in some situations "the relevance of these requirements could not be proved even in instances where common sense might suggest that they were sound: height requirements for police officers, for example. The assertion that taller officers are more impressive authority figures than their shorter counterparts may seem plausible, but there is no evidence to support this hypothesis."[4] Recourse to such notions as "authority figure" might also suggest unjustifiable assumptions about how to understand a given job, perhaps giving undue priority to specific ways of dealing with people.[5]

That in turn raises the more general point that what is considered important or desirable is often a contestable moral or political issue. Examples that will be familiar to academics are the relative valuation of different areas of specialization within a discipline, or the ranking of different approaches to certain problems. For example, as Sheila Ruth has pointed out, the discipline of philosophy has had—and still has to a considerable extent—a hierarchy by which such "central" areas as metaphysics, epistemology, philosophy of language, and logic are considered the most prestigious, as well as a hierarchy of abstractness valuing more theoretical work above the more applied.[6] These judgments create a network of effects, ranging from what gets published, to who and what wins the prestigious positions and prizes. Yet, it is hardly clear that the initial premises of this system are justified, and hence at least some judgments about who is better qualified will be seriously questionable.

This issue becomes especially pressing as we make decisions about the aims of enterprises for which individuals are being selected. Education, for example, is currently being torn by debate about whether it should be passing on "traditional wisdom" or helping to create a more just world. Yet that choice bears fundamentally on who is most qualified for many jobs. In particular, overtly "political" work, long anathema in academe, must now in some cases be taken seriously. Doing so is especially difficult for those who see the status quo as politically neutral since they are used to rejecting politically aware scholarship without having to distinguish good from bad.

The upshot of all this is that we should be much warier of the view that takes it for granted that we know how to evaluate qualifications. What follows is that there needs to be a great deal more to affirmative action decisions than whether it is ever defensible to prefer those with "worse" qualifications.

Compensation

Arguments from compensation assume that although Ds have suffered discrimination in the past, it no longer keeps them from deserved positions. Hence, such arguments focus on whether Ds deserve special help because of that past discrimination. Whether they do so or not seems to me to depend on the present effects of that discrimination, and what kind of special help might be at issue.[7]

There is no space here to address the interesting and voluminous debate on this topic. However, there are a couple of general points about the issue worth noting. First, compensation arguments tend to assume that discrimination no longer occurs and that merit is now the basis of all competitive selection. That assumption changes our conception of the affirmative action debate and makes it seem less pressing and more theoretical than it really is. It is also, as I will argue shortly, unrealistic.

But second, even if such discrimination disappeared tomorrow, that would not compensate African-Americans, for instance, for the injustices done to them. Merit-based decision-making rewards achievement, but downplays factors that lead to lack of achievement even where they are compounded by further injustice. The more relevant issue here is not the old injustice of enslavement, but a second and ongoing injustice that magnifies it, namely inequality of social services. Especially significant here are those that, like health care and schooling, help prepare children for higher education and the job market. As long as parents' unequal resources play so large a role in children's access to such services, equality of opportunity will not exist.[8] Such inequality is bad enough when it rests on bad luck; it is surely even more intolerable when it is built on prior injustice. However, it is, unlike slavery, something that could be remedied. And if it were, it seems to me that compensation arguments based solely on past injustice, such as slavery, might, like its other legacies, wither away.

In short, many of the intriguing moral questions raised by affirmative action could well be rendered moot by a minimally just society that allocated resources more fairly than does ours to create true equality of opportunity.[9] Wouldn't it therefore be more sensible for philosophers and lawyers to wait to cross some moral bridges once the issue has been situated in its larger context? Without that context, papers rejecting this remedy or that remedy may be quite right, but nevertheless fall short of articulating just social policy.

This analytical approach is symptomatic of the more general fragmentation of our social thinking, such that if one remedy is rejected, perhaps appropriately, there is no guarantee that another better one will be promoted instead. Thus, for example, it may be true that some children's schooling has been so inadequate that they cannot benefit from university work. At present, institutions of higher education may admit them to make amends, knowing that they are likely to fail. It would be more sensible to provide comprehensive special programs to help them cope; in a time of scarcity, however, such programs may divert scarce resources from the central (and defensible) mission of the school. Yet failing to admit them, or refusing to provide programs—in themselves perhaps justifiable policies—could well mean that nothing at all will be done. That is a morally untenable consequence.

Also responsible in part for current situations that seem to call for affirmative action is the overall scarcity of resources devoted to human needs. Such scarcity means that competition for education, jobs, and basic well-being is far more ferocious than nec-

essary. If the stakes were lower, affirmative action measures would not be seen as the winner-take-all, zero-sum game that now provokes such bitterness. More spending on education would help provide everybody with excellent educational opportunities, and getting into a prestige school would become less important. If there were enough jobs for all, and each guaranteed a living wage, access to the most attractive positions would not be such a desperate matter. So here, as elsewhere, questions about affirmative action deflect our attention from the larger picture, leading us to downplay or ignore altogether morally untenable social arrangements.[10]

Ongoing Discrimination

Opponents of affirmative action programs generally suppose that discrimination against Ds is now only a trivial factor in social choices. Thus to take race, sex, or any other non-merit based characteristic into account constitutes the same kind of discrimination—this time against members of the mainstream—that was originally rejected for Ds. Implicit in this argument is the assumption that in the absence of affirmative action programs, merit is the driving force behind competitive choices. Hence affirmative action constitutes objectionable reverse discrimination.

This argument collapses if the underlying premise about ongoing discrimination is false, however. Yet that premise seems dubious, at best, as there is much evidence of both continuing direct prejudice and institutional discrimination against members of certain ethnic minorities, women, gays, lesbians, and the disabled.

It is surely undeniable that many people are still very prejudiced, and that sexism, racism, and a variety of other isms are flourishing.[11] Although relatively few educated people would now admit to such prejudice, that does not mean that they are free of it, and overt manifestations of it are still quite common. Consider, for instance, the kinds of harassment and insults women, ethnic minorities, and gay people still face in public places when they overstep the bounds sanctioned by tradition: even conservative opponents of speech codes cannot deny the existence of the hate speech that has triggered those policies. More subtle, but still powerful, opposition to the most basic tenets of equality for Ds is still widespread. For example, I recently gave a talk on women's and men's social roles at a nearby Rotary Club. Its members, mostly middle-aged white males, and prime movers in the town, so far from disputing my claims that women are not yet free to define their own nature, were clearly upset at that prospect. This talk was given, not in 1952, but in 1992.

Feminists have been documenting the inequalities between females and males for years, and while perhaps not every such inequality is a result of discrimination, many obviously do result from it.[12] A similar case could be made with respect to certain other groups.[13]

Ignoring the evidence here makes the lives of non-Ds more comfortable, as they can then enjoy their privilege in good conscience: if, after all, differences in well-being are merely a result of free choices, they are justifiable.

However, there is good reason for thinking that the status quo is often not the result of free and informed choices, and that, even if it were, some of the enormous discrepancies in well-being that now exist would be indefensible. Take, for instance, the handicaps women often suffer as a result of their responsibility for childrearing. Suppose Josie opts for the "traditional" route in life, perhaps finishing high school or college, marrying Joe, and staying at home to care for their children. If she is lucky, she will be happy in her marriage, and her husband will provide for her and the children. But what if her marriage doesn't work out? The best-case scenario is that her ex-husband continues to take some responsibility for the children, as well as for her support. But how many ex-wives find themselves in that position? Far more frequently, Joe's child support does not even cover the children's needs, let alone her own. So, out to work she must go. But because she lacks job skills and experience, and must be on call for the children, her job will most likely be poorly paid, quite possibly without such benefits as health insurance. From these meager earnings she must also pay for daycare, if her children are young. Anybody who doubts the ubiquity of this scenario should consult the literature on the feminization of poverty.[14]

Are the choices that led to this outcome free and well informed? It is arguable that women's decision to choose this traditional path is both less

free than it seems, and less free than it ought to be. Despite considerable progress toward the idea that women, like men, should be free to choose the nature of the life they will lead, many girls are still brought up to believe that they are to be nurturers of men and children. This message is reinforced by a variety of powerful vehicles like movies, books, magazines, and advertisements. They are also a conduit of the pronatalism that encourages girls and women to think that having and rearing children is natural, inevitable and fun: when was the last time you saw a dirty diaper in a Pampers ad? Or a sulky child in a plug for baby food?[15] Politicians and pundits who blame society's ills on working women are common enough these days, too; the evils of daycare is a perennial topic of debate.[16] Of course, even the apparently free and informed choices girls and women now make will become more obviously less free as abortion becomes ever more unavailable, especially if contraception follows in its footsteps.[17]

The power of these influences certainly shows up in many women students. Even if they are aware of divorce statistics, they resist the idea that their own marriage is as likely to collapse as succeed; the feminization of poverty might as well be happening in Timbuktu. Sadly, the social cover-up of these trends plus the "it-can't-happen-to-me" syndrome prevents many from building what protection they can for these contingencies into their planning. These are not informed choices.

But suppose they were? Opponents of progressivism, including certain forms of affirmative action, seem to believe that the social arrangements that make these choices so imprudent for women are natural and immutable. That is not the case. Tax policy and social programs are routinely used by governments to encourage people to behave in ways that are perceived as desirable. Instead of leaving women and children to suffer impoverishment, they could be used here to protect women who stay at home with their children. That they aren't suggests that society doesn't really value women's homemaking activities, or else that it cynically figures that women can be persuaded to do them at their own risk.

Keeping women in the home full or part-time under the present circumstances has many benefits for society taken as a whole, despite the drawbacks for women themselves. First, when women put husbands and children first, they do not compete for more desirable places in the work world. Second, men benefit from women's domestic work, for they will provide otherwise unobtainable or prohibitively expensive services. The military, corporations, and educational institutions have long assumed that when they hire a man, a woman's services are included. Third, when women are in charge of children, society is spared the expense of making other arrangements for their care. Last, but not least, society benefits from a reasonable number of children. This last point is often rejected by those who claim that children are a personal luxury and that women ought therefore to take full responsibility for the ones they produce. The real agenda here is revealed, however, when women have fewer children than is thought necessary, whether for cannon fodder, business interests, or "racial purity": women's choices are then described as selfish or sick.[18]

Given these perceived social benefits, it is surely wrong to penalize the women who have provided them. A just social policy would support women who choose to do this work so that they do not risk impoverishment. However, even were such a policy in place, affirmative action might be necessary to recognize the disvalued skills women have acquired, and to help ensure that their time at home does not hold them back for the rest of their lives. Comparable issues may well exist for people in other categories.

Conclusion

This paper has considered some rather general issues relevant to affirmative action. It suggests that coming up with a just affirmative action policy will require a more comprehensive understanding of social issues than is yet evident in much of the debate. Because the issues are broad, but also presuppose detailed knowledge of specific situations, compelling solutions to contemporary problems will not be forthcoming anytime soon. Nor, even where they are, can we expect immediately to right underlying injustices and therefore render moot affirmative action controversies now resting upon them.

Affirmative action decisions must therefore—like others—be made in unjust contexts. Unfortunately, debate about how to make the best of bad circumstances is still necessary; it is also valuable, so long as it does not obscure the need for larger analysis. Perhaps emphasizing the need for that larger analysis will help temper the tone of the debate, whether philosophical or legal, even if it does not give us instant answers.

NOTES

1. I have argued elsewhere both that past prejudice biases much evidence and that present prejudice can bias perception of the evidence. See "In Defense of Hiring Apparently Less Qualified Women," *Journal of Social Philosophy,* Vol. 15 (Summer 1984), 26–33.
2. That would also help democratize the profession.
3. Judith A. Baer, *Women in American Law,* (New York: Holmes and Meier Publishers, Inc., 1991), pp. 88–89.
4. Baer, p. 89.
5. The social reluctance to question such matters is demonstrated in at least two other cases. In *Boyd v. Ozark Airlines,* 568 F. 2d 50 (8th Circ. 1977), an appellate panel let stand a height requirement for pilots because of the cockpit design of aircraft—despite the fact that airplanes are, like cars, often redesigned (Baer, p. 89). And, in *Dothard v. Rawlinson,* whereas the Court held height and weight requirements to be unconstitutional for Alabama prison guards, it refused to strike down a same-sex rule adopted instead—even though other states successfully guard male inmates with females (Baer, p. 90).
6. Sheila Ruth, "Methodocracy, Misogyny and Bad Faith: The Response of Philosophy," *Men's Studies Unmodified: The Impact of Feminism on the Academic Disciplines,* ed. Dale Spender (London: Pergamon Press, 1980).
7. For a useful discussion, see Bernard Boxill, *Blacks and Social Justice,* (Totowa, NJ: Rowman and Allenheld, 1984), especially chap. 7.
8. Skeptics might start by skimming Jonathan Kozol's *Savage Inequalities,* with its hungry and ill children, housed in rotting buildings where classes are lucky to have teachers or books. They should pay special attention to the Appendix, which lays out the disparities in school funding among districts. To deny that Manhasset's $15,084 per capita buys a better education than New York City's $7,299 is less than plausible. (Jonathan Kozol, *Savage Inequalities* [New York: Crown Publishers, Inc., 1991.])
9. A related, but perhaps more utopian point, is that positions of at least modest security and comfort

would be accessible to everybody. And, a better society would redistribute both positions and income in such a way that more enjoyable jobs would be available, so that the competition for them would be reduced. No doubt most of my readers will object that these ideals are hopelessly unrealistic, but that shouldn't stop us from doing what we can.

10. My comments here presuppose very different social possibilities from those currently taken for granted by many people in the United States. Obviously, this is not the place to argue in detail about those issues. However, the following points should provide some preliminary food for thought on the part of those who find my suggestions utopian. There is considerable literature on the economic feasibility of converting defense spending to civilian uses. The current resistance to cutting military spending ignores studies that show that only 17,000 jobs in missile production are created from $1,000,000,000 in industrial investment, whereas it creates respectively 25,000 jobs in petrochemicals, 48,000 jobs in the health sector, 62,000 jobs in educational services, or 65,000 retail jobs. (Alan S. Miller, *Gaia Connections* [Savage, Maryland: Rowman & Littlefield, 1991], pp. 63–69.)

11. For disheartening examples of misogyny, see Fidelis Morgan, *A Misogynist's Sourcebook* (London: Jonathan Cape, 1989). To believe that such deeply embedded attitudes, and ones that are so openly expressed, no longer exert any influence on society, would be implausible. Considerable evidence about other Ds is easily available.

12. For useful summaries, see *The American Woman 1990–91: A Status Report*, ed. Sara E. Rix for the Women's Research and Education Institute (NY: Norton and Norton, 1990) and *Sisterhood is Global*, ed. Robin Morgan (NY: Anchor Books, 1984).

   She first notes in the Introduction that "in this country many women are double- or triple-working in families, jobs, and public roles, and they are often stretched to the limit. . . . Many women are alone—with children, but without jobs or adequate support. Many are ill-housed, undereducated, and underemployed. There are not only glass ceilings atop women who have risen part way in corporate life; plenty of steel caps still hold the lid on initial opportunities" (p. 22). The rest of the book provides support for these claims.

   Morgan's introduction to the second is still more shocking. She begins her lengthy description of the inferior position of women with a quotation from Kurt Waldheim's "Report to the UN Commission on the Status of Women": "While women represent half the global population and one-third of the labor force, they receive only one-tenth of the world income and own less than one percent of world prop-

erty. They also are responsible for two-thirds of all working hours" (p. 1).

   Since these are not states of affairs that would be chosen by anybody, they strongly suggest the failure of societies to safeguard women's interests equally with those of men. Against such a failure the objection that women's plight is just the result of their own choices rings hollow.

13. See for example, Gertrude Ezorsky, *Racism and Injustice* (Ithaca: Cornell University Press, 1991), chap. 1; also, Tom L. Beauchamp, "The Justification of Reverse Discrimination," *Social Justice and Preferential Treatment: Women and Racial Minorities in Education and Business,* ed. William T. Blackstone and Robert D. Heslep (Athens, GA: University of Georgia Press, 1977), especially part 2; and my "In Defense of Hiring Apparently Less Qualified Women," *Journal of Social Philosophy*, Vol. 15 (Summer 1984), 26–33. Prejudice against such Ds as the disabled and homosexuals could also be documented.

14. For more information see Hilda Scott, *Working Your Way to the Bottom: The Feminization of Poverty* (London: Pandora Press, 1984).

15. For a compelling argument about the nature and force of pronatalist messages, see *Pronatalism: The Myth of Mom and Apple Pie*, ed. Ellen Peck and Judith Senderowitz (New York: Thomas Y. Crowell, 1974).

16. See, for example, George Gilder, *Sexual Suicide* (NY: Bantam Books, 1973), Robert D. McCracken, *Fallacies of Women's Liberation* (Boulder: Shields Publishing, Inc., 1972), or Michael Levin, *Feminism and Freedom* (New Brunswick, NJ: Transaction Books, 1987).

17. Consider the interesting statistic that some 30 percent of first year college men and 20 percent of first year women still think that women's place is the home! See "This Year's College Freshmen: Attitudes and Characteristics," *Chronicle of Higher Education*, 37, n. 20 (30 January 1991): A30–31.

18. A glance or two at history provides evidence for this claim. A good place to start is with the 19th century debate about education for women: if women got too much education, their reproductive organs would shrivel and they wouldn't have enough children. (Edward H. Clarke, *Sex in Education: A Fair Chance for the Girls* (Boston: James R. Osgood and Co., 1873) This theme surfaces periodically, especially in the literature on eugenics. For an excellent overview of the nineteenth century, see Carroll Smith-Rosenberg and Charles Rosenberg, "The Female Animal: Medical and Biological Views of Woman and Her Role in Nineteenth-Century America," *Concepts of Health and Disease,* ed. Arthur L. Caplan, H. Tristram Engelhardt, Jr., and James L. McCartney (Reading, MA: Addison-Wesley Publishing Co., 1981).

Study Questions

1. Put yourself in the position of Greg van de Water in "A Case of AIDS." Would you have hired Joe Collins, who tested HIV-positive? When Joe's declining work performance became apparent to his co-workers, would you have shared with them the truth about Joe's situation? Would you support Joe in pursuing more-advanced positions within the company even after the onset of AIDS? Give reasons for your answers.

2. List some of the ways in which, according to Leonard, persons who are HIV-positive or who have AIDS are subject to workplace discrimination.

3. What specific steps does Leonard recommend an ethical employer take with regard to dealing with HIV-infected employees?

4. Clifford and Iuculano argue that, since companies that write group health insurance must act fairly by grouping individuals according to the health risks they represent, such companies would be guilty of unfair discrimination if they did *not* require AIDS-related testing as evidence of insurability for those seeking new coverage. How, exactly, does this argument go? Do you find it convincing? Why or why not?

5. The court opinion in *Chico Dairy* relies on a sharp distinction between *being disabled* and *being perceived in a certain light as a consequence of that disability.* Is it always possible to clearly distinguish these? What, for example, of a case involving a burn victim whose facial features are distorted from skin grafts? Note also that the Americans with Disabilities Act includes "being regarded as having . . . an impairment" as itself a "disability." What conditions might fall within the scope of that definition?

6. As the dissenting judge in *Chico Dairy* points out, the fact that a store's customers might prefer to deal with workers of a certain gender, ethnicity, or other status cannot generally be used to discriminate against employees. Can you think of any case in which customer preference ought to be a legitimate defense to a charge of workplace discrimination?

7. The justices writing in *Adarand* all agree on the result, though each gives different reasons. What do you see as the principal differences between the reasoning of Justices O'Connor, Scalia, and Thomas? Which of the arguments seems to you to be the most persuasive?

8. In what way do the dissenting justices distinguish discriminatory acts deserving of strict scrutiny from cases of affirmative action?

9. What is wrong with the individual method of addressing injuries inflicted by discrimination, according to Ezorsky?

10. Summarize Ezorsky's argument that blacks and whites live in two separate societies. Do you find her reasoning convincing?

11. What is the "disparate impact discrimination" theory? How does it affect normal business practices? Why does Belz think it in conflict with social science?

12. Why does Belz hold that affirmative action is an overinclusive remedy? How do you think he would respond to the charge that all women and minorities are injured by harms committed against individuals?

13. How does affirmative action interfere with the free market? Are all interferences with the free market unacceptable? Why is an interference like affirmative action so damaging in this view?

14. According to Purdy, what is the difference between substantive and procedural affirmative action plans or practices?

15. What evidence does Purdy present to support the claim that the "status quo" is not the result of free choices?

CASE SCENARIO 1   Religious Practices and the Employer's Duty to Accommodate

Mr. Toledo lived in Farmington, New Mexico, and applied there for a job as a truck driver with Nobel-Sysco, Inc. Toledo was interviewed by Nobel's Albuquerque office manager, Rodney Plagmann. After the interview Plagmann told Toledo that he had the necessary experience for the job and would probably be hired, assuming Toledo passed some routine tests. One of these tests was a polygraph to determine the applicant's truthfulness regarding prior use of illegal drugs. Nobel's policy was to refuse to hire anyone who had used illegal drugs within a two-year period prior to the application. At this point Toledo revealed that he was a member of the Native American Church and that he had used the drug peyote twice in the past six months as part of church ceremonies, typically held on the weekend. It was undisputed by Nobel that the Native American Church is a bona fide religion, that Toledo was indeed a member and sincere believer in the church's teachings, and that he used peyote only as part of church ceremonies. Plagmann subsequently informed Toledo that Nobel could not hire him because of his drug use. Toledo then filed a complaint, charging that Nobel had made no effort to accommodate his religious practices.

Nobel argued that hiring Toledo would have meant hiring an illegal drug user, violating laws against operating a motor vehicle while in possession or under the influence of a powerful drug, and would expose Nobel to the risk of increased tort liability should Toledo cause an accident while in its employ. The court rejected these arguments and sided with Toledo, ruling that Nobel discriminated against Toledo on the basis of his religion by not trying to accommodate his religious practices.

The court pointed out that religious use of peyote by members of the Native American Church had been made legal by an exception to the federal Controlled Substances Act, and that religious use of peyote was legal by state law in both New Mexico and Colorado, the states where Toledo would have been driving. Finally, the court insisted that "accommodating Toledo's practices by requiring him to take a day off after each ceremony would virtually eliminate the risk that the influence of peyote would cause an accident or be a factor in subsequent litigation." The court here relied on the testimony of experts that a person should not drive a truck for twenty-four hours after ingesting peyote in the quantities Toledo normally used.

1. How far should employers like Nobel be required to go in accommodating the religious beliefs and practices of its potential employees?
2. Did the court take sufficiently seriously the safety concerns raised by Nobel? Suppose Toledo were to attend church ceremonies where peyote was used more than once a week? Or during the week instead of on weekends? Would Nobel have to accommodate these practices? Under the court's ruling, would Nobel be required to hire an applicant who regularly used medication that rendered him unable to drive safely? Why or why not?
3. Suppose a Muslim woman applies for a position as a flight attendant with an airline. She is required by her religion to wear a headdress that covers her hair whenever she is in public. She is qualified for the job, but the airline refuses to hire her as she would not conform to the dress code, which specifies uniform clothing for all flight attendants. The company

is not willing to permit her to wear the headdress. Has the airline discriminated against her on the basis of religion? Why or why not?

CASE SCENARIO 2   Obesity, Disability, and Discrimination

Catherine McDermott applied for a job as a systems consultant with Xerox Corp. The company offered her a job contingent upon passing a preemployment medical exam. The examining physician found that McDermott was five feet six inches tall and weighed 249 pounds. On the examining form, the physician wrote that McDermott was "obese" and thus medically "not acceptable." Xerox withdrew the employment offer; McDermott filed a complaint with the state, charging Xerox with employment discrimination in violation of a law prohibiting employers from refusing to hire persons with disabilities.

McDermott testified that she had always been overweight, but that this had not prevented her from performing most normal life tasks. She had raised five children after her husband's death, and she had held down other jobs similar to the one Xerox offered her. Xerox argued that it refused to hire McDermott, not because of any present limitation, but because of the statistical likelihood that her obesity would produce impairments in the future. Xerox was concerned about the impact on disability and life insurance programs as a result of employing people like McDermott.

Laws in effect at the time stated that employment could be refused only if the applicant's disability related to the performance of the duties of the position. Xerox did not dispute that McDermott's obesity in no way restricted her ability to perform as a systems consultant. Assuming that obesity is a disability, the court thus concluded, Xerox had discriminated against her. The court then determined that obesity was indeed a "medical impairment."

1. Should the condition of obesity be considered a disability? Would it qualify as a disability under the language of the Americans with Disabilities Act? What other conditions should qualify as disabilities? Should alcoholism, for example, be treated as a disability?
2. Should it be relevant whether McDermott's obesity was caused by a glandular condition or by her "lifestyle," that is, by overeating?
3. Is it fair to allow companies like Xerox to consider the additional insurance costs they might have to bear should they hire a person with a particular condition? Should Xerox be allowed to rely on general statistical evidence of impairments associated with disabilities in making hiring decisions? Or should the company be required to judge each case individually?

CASE SCENARIO 3   Affirmative Action
and the *Hopwood* Case

In June 1996 the U.S. Supreme Court, in a move widely viewed as further repudiation of affirmative action, refused to hear an appeal from a lower federal court ruling in the case of Cheryl Hopwood. Hopwood worked about twenty hours a week to pay her way through college. Her father left the family when she was small, and her mother worked at several jobs to support the family. Hopwood raised a severely disabled child of her own. In 1992 Hopwood applied for admission to the University of Texas law school. She had a 3.80 grade-point average (GPA) and scored in the eighty-third percentile on the LSAT. The Texas law school admits five hundred students per year, accepting those who score better than 85 percent of all college graduates who take the LSAT and have a 3.50 GPA. Texas, like other law schools, seeks to recruit a "diverse" class of incoming students. In 1992, however, only eighty-eight African American and fifty-two Mexican American students in the entire nation satisfied these standards. To achieve diversity, Texas therefore segregated its admissions process, reviewing separately applications from African American and Mexican American students. Hopwood, who is white, was denied admission and filed suit, alleging racial discrimination by the law school.

Hopwood argued that only one of the forty-one African American students and three of the Mexican American students admitted to Texas in 1992 had scores that matched hers. Hopwood insisted that the university operated a virtual "quota system" for certain students. University officials countered that the African American and Mexican American students it admitted were qualified, with average GPAs of around 3.30. It also pointed out that the population of the state of Texas is nearly 50 percent African American and Mexican American, and that the university would not be doing its job if it enrolled students strictly on the numbers alone.

In March 1996, the Fifth U.S. Circuit Court of Appeals accepted Hopwood's arguments and struck down the University of Texas plan. Any government action predicated on race, the court said, must be subject to "strict scrutiny," meaning that the state (the university, in this case) must have a "compelling" purpose to justify classifying people by race, and its use of race must be necessary to achieve that purpose. The Court also referred to the Supreme Court's earlier opinion in the *Bakke* case, in which a divided court ruled against the use of quotas for admission to schools and colleges, but cited race as one of the "factors" that could be considered in making admissions decisions. Part of the Court's argument is excerpted as follows.

> With the best of intentions, in order to increase the enrollment of certain favored classes of minority students, the University of Texas School of Law ("the law school") discriminates in favor of those applicants by giving substantial racial preferences in its admissions program. The beneficiaries of this system are blacks and Mexican Americans, to the detriment of whites and non-preferred minorities. The question we decide today in [Case] No. 94-50664 is whether the Fourteenth Amendment permits the school to discriminate in this way.
>
> We hold that it does not. The law school has presented no compelling justification, under the Fourteenth Amendment or Supreme Court precedent, that allows it to continue to elevate some races over others, even for the wholesome purpose of correcting perceived racial imbalance in the student body.
>
> Here, the plaintiffs argue that diversity is not a compelling governmental interest under superseding Supreme Court precedent. Instead, they believe that the Court finally has recognized that only the *remedial* use of race is compelling. In the alternative, the plaintiffs assert that the district court misapplied Justice Powell's *Bakke* standard, as the law school program here uses race as a strong determinant rather than a mere "plus" factor and, in any case, the preference is not narrowly applied. The law school maintains, on the other hand, that Justice Powell's formulation in *Bakke* is law and must be followed— at least in the context of higher education.
>
> We agree with the plaintiffs that any consideration of race or ethnicity by the law school for the purpose of achieving a diverse student body is not a compelling interest under the Fourteenth Amendment. . . .
>
> As the *Adarand* Court states, the *Bakke* Court did not express a majority view and is questionable as binding precedent. ("The Court's failure in *Bakke* . . . left unresolved the proper analysis for remedial race-based government action.").
>
> Since *Bakke,* the Court has accepted the diversity rationale only once in its cases dealing with race. Significantly, however, in that case, *Metro Broadcasting, Inc. v. Federal Communications Comm'n,* 497 U.S. 547, 564-65 (1990), the five-Justice majority relied upon an

intermediate scrutiny standard of review to uphold the federal program seeking diversity in the ownership of broadcasting facilities. In *Adarand,* the Court squarely rejected intermediate scrutiny as the standard of review for racial classifications, and *Metro Broadcasting* is now specifically overruled to the extent that it was in conflict with this holding. No case since *Bakke* has accepted diversity as a compelling state interest under a strict scrutiny analysis.

Indeed, recent Supreme Court precedent shows that the diversity interest will not satisfy strict scrutiny. Foremost, the Court appears to have decided that there is essentially only one compelling state interest to justify racial classifications: remedying past wrongs. . . .

In short, there has been no indication from the Supreme Court, other than Justice Powell's lonely opinion in *Bakke,* that the state's interest in diversity constitutes a compelling justification for governmental race-based discrimination. Subsequent Supreme Court case law strongly suggests, in fact, that it is not.

Within the general principles of the Fourteenth Amendment, the use of race in admissions for diversity in higher education contradicts, rather than furthers, the aims of equal protection. Diversity fosters, rather than minimizes, the use of race. It treats minorities as a group, rather than as individuals. It may further remedial purposes but, just as likely, may promote improper racial stereotypes, thus fueling racial hostility.

The use of race, in and of itself, to choose students simply achieves a student body that looks different. Such a criterion is no more rational on its own terms than would be choices based upon the physical size or blood type of applicants. Thus, the Supreme Court has long held that governmental actors cannot justify their decisions solely because of race.

Accordingly, we see the case law as sufficiently established that the use of ethnic diversity simply to achieve racial heterogeneity, even as part of the consideration of a number of factors, is unconstitutional. Were we to decide otherwise, we would contravene precedent that we are not authorized to challenge. . . .

A university may properly favor one applicant over another because of his ability to play the cello, make a downfield tackle, or understand chaos theory. An admissions process may also consider an applicant's home state or relationship to school alumni. Law schools specifically may look at things such as unusual or substantial extracurricular activities in college, which may be atypical factors affecting undergraduate grades. Schools may even consider factors such as whether an applicant's parents attended college or the applicant's economic and social background. For this reason, race often is said to be justified in the diversity context, not on its own terms, but as a proxy for other characteristics that institutions of higher education value but that do not raise similar constitutional concerns. Unfortunately, this approach simply replicates the very harm that the Fourteenth Amendment was designed to eliminate. The assumption is that a certain individual possesses characteristics by virtue of being a member of a certain racial group. This assumption, however, does not withstand scrutiny. . . . To believe that a person's race controls his point of view is to stereotype him. The Supreme Court, however, has remarked a number of times, in slightly different contexts, that it is incorrect and legally inappropriate to impute to women and minorities "a different attitude about such issues as the federal budget, school prayer, voting, and foreign relations." Social scientists may debate how people's thoughts and behavior reflect their background, but the Constitution provides that the government may not allocate benefits or burdens among individuals based on the assumption that race or ethnicity determines how they act or think. Instead, individuals, with their own conceptions of life, further diversity of viewpoint.

Plaintiff Hopwood is a fair example of an applicant with a unique background. She is the now-thirty-two-year-old wife of a member of the Armed Forces stationed in San Antonio and, more significantly, is raising a severely handicapped child. Her circumstance would bring a different perspective to the law school. The school might consider this an advantage to her in the application process, or it could decide that her family situation would be too much of a burden on her academic performance. We do not opine on which way the law school should weigh Hopwood's qualifications; we only observe that "diversity" can take many forms. To foster such diversity, state universities and law schools and other governmental entities must scrutinize applicants individually, rather than resorting to the dangerous proxy of race.

The Court also has recognized that government's use of racial classifications serves to stigmatize. See, e.g., Brown v. Board of Educ., 347 U.S. 483, 494 (1954) (observing that classification on the basis of race "generates a feeling of inferiority"). While one might argue that the stigmatization resulting from so-called "benign" racial classifications is not as harmful as that arising from invidious ones, the current Court has now retreated from the idea that so-called benign and invidious classifications may be distinguished. As the plurality in Croson warned, "[c]lassifications based on race carry the danger of stigmatic harm. Unless they are reserved for remedial settings, they may in fact promote notions of racial inferiority and lead to the politics of racial hostility." 488 U.S. at 493. Finally, the use of race to achieve diversity undercuts the ultimate goal of the Fourteenth Amendment: the end of racially-motivated state action. Justice Powell's conception of race as a "plus" factor would allow race always to be a potential factor in admissions decision-making. . . . In sum, the use of race to achieve a diverse student body, whether as a proxy for permissible characteristics, simply cannot be a state interest compelling enough to meet the steep standard of strict scrutiny. These latter factors may, in fact, turn out to be substantially correlated with race, but the key is that race itself not be taken into account.

1. Do you agree with the arguments of the court in this case? Why or why not?
2. Do you think a state-supported university has an obligation to admit a diverse pool of students to a professional school?
3. How would the arguments of Ezorsky, Belz, and Purdy apply to this case? What position would each of them be likely to take and why? Be specific.
4. What implications do you think the Supreme Court's ruling in *Adarand v. Pena* might have for the kind of preferential admissions program run by the University of Texas Law School?

CASE SCENARIO 4   *O'Connor v. Consolidated Coin Caterers, Inc.*

James O'Connor worked for Consolidated Coin Caterers from 1978 until August 19, 1990, when, at age fifty-six, he was fired. Believing that he had been fired because of his age, O'Connor filed a suit in federal court, alleging that Coin Caterers had violated the Age Discrimination in Employment Act (ADEA). The court dismissed his suit. The ADEA limits its protection to individuals forty years of age and older and this, the court reasoned, meant that to prove discrimination, plaintiffs like O'Connor must show that they were replaced by someone with comparable qualifications who was *under* forty years old. Because the person who replaced O'Connor was exactly forty, a prima facie case of discrimination could not be made. O'Connor appealed to the U.S. Supreme Court.

In April 1996 the Court ruled in O'Connor's favor. Justice Scalia, writing for the majority, gave the following argument:

As the very name "prima facie case" suggests, there must be at least a logical connection between each element of the prima facie case and the illegal discrimination for which it establishes a "legally mandatory, rebuttable presumption." The element of replacement by someone under 40 fails this requirement. The discrimination prohibited by the ADEA is discrimination "because of [an] individual's age," 29 U.S.C. §623(a)(1), though the prohibition is "limited to individuals who are at least 40 years of age," §631(a). This language does not ban discrimination against employees because they are aged 40 or older; it bans discrimination against employees because of their age, but limits the protected class to those who are 40 or older. The fact that one person in the protected class has lost out to another person in the protected class is thus irrelevant, so long as he has lost out *because of his age.* Or to put the point more concretely, there can be no greater inference of *age* discrimination (as opposed to "40 or over" discrimination) when a 40 year-old replaced by a 39 year-old than when a 56 year-old is replaced by a 40 year-old. Because it lacks probative value, the fact that an ADEA plaintiff was replaced by someone outside the protected class is not a proper element of the prima facie case.

Perhaps some courts have been induced to adopt the principle urged by respondent in order to avoid creating a prima facie case on the basis of very thin evidence—for example, the replacement of a 68 year-old by a 65 year-old. While the respondent's principle theoretically permits such thin evidence (consider the example above of a 40 year-old replaced by a 39 year-old), as a practical matter it will rarely do so, since the vast majority of age-discrimination claims come from older employees. In our view, however, the proper solution to the problem lies not in making an utterly irrelevant factor an element of the prima facie case, but rather in recognizing that the prima facie case requires *"evidence adequate to create an inference that an employment decision was based on a[n] [illegal] discriminatory criterion. . . . "* In the age-discrimination context, such an inference can not be drawn from the replacement of one worker with another worker insignificantly younger. Because the ADEA prohibits discrimination on the basis of age and not class membership, the fact that a replacement is substantially younger than the plaintiff is a far more reliable indicator of age discrimination than is the fact that the plaintiff was replaced by someone outside the protected class. The judgment of the Fourth Circuit is reversed, and the case is remanded for proceedings consistent with this opinion.

It is so ordered.

1. Do you agree with Justice Scalia's argument? Why or why not?
2. How much of a disparity in ages must be present before you would be persuaded that discrimination on the basis of age has occurred? Is ten years' difference sufficient? Five? Three?
3. Suppose O'Connor had been thirty-five years old and that he was fired and replaced with someone who was twenty. Would this suggest to you age discrimination?

CHAPTER 6

Women in the Workplace

DISCRIMINATION, WOMEN, AND JOBS

More women are part of the workplace now than ever before, and their earnings, status, and visibility continue to grow. In 1979 women's earnings were 62 percent of that of the average for men; by 1995 that figure had grown to more than 75 percent. Women now hold more than 40 percent of managing jobs in the United States. The number of women-owned businesses is also rapidly escalating, numbering more than 7 million.[1] Such gains are a far cry from the status of women in the nineteenth century, when the law was used to justify widespread discrimination against women in business and the professions.

The history of legalized sexual discrimination in the United States was justified by what were thought to be "legitimate" or "real" differences between the sexes. Throughout the nineteenth and early part of the twentieth century, the law treated women as separate and distinct from men. Women were thought to possess a separate, distinct, and immutable "nature" that made them unfit for many of the jobs traditionally held by men. Women, it was believed, belonged to a separate social and legal sphere, focused on domestic life and child rearing. This ideology was succinctly expressed by the Supreme Court in 1873, when it ruled that Myra Bradwell could not be admitted to the practice of law in Illinois. Concurring in the court's decision, Justice Bradley wrote:

> [T]he civil law as well as nature itself has always recognized a wide difference in the respective spheres and destinies of man and woman. Man is, or should be, woman's protector and defender. The natural and proper timidity and delicacy which belongs to the female sex evidently unfits it for many of the occupations of civil life . . . The paramount destiny and mission of women are to fulfill the noble and benign offices of wife and mother. This is the law of the Creator.[2]

With increasing industrialization many states passed legislation regulating a variety of working conditions for women. Typical of these was a law challenged in *Muller v. Oregon*,[3] which upheld restrictions on the number of hours women could work.

> [T]hat woman's physical structure and the performance of maternal functions place her at a disadvantage in the struggle for subsistence is obvious . . . Differentiated by these matters from the other sex, she is properly placed in a class by herself, and legislation designed for her protection may be sustained, even when the legislation is not necessary for men . . .[4]

Discrimination at Nabisco

In January 1995 the Equal Opportunity Employment Commission (EEOC) was asked to investigate complaints made by female employees of a Nabisco food plant in Oxnard, California. The employees alleged that the employer severely restricted so-called bathroom privileges, to the point where certain women resorted to wearing diapers on the job site. "It's humiliating to have to walk in there like a baby," a fifty-nine-year-old employee said. Other women reported using toilet paper and Kotex; those caught sneaking off to the bathroom said they were threatened with being sent home without pay. Female workers claimed that Nabisco limited their restroom visits to work breaks; male employees, on the other hand, were allowed trips to the restroom whenever needed. Women workers insisted that the practice amounted to discrimination and complained of resulting bladder and urinary tract infections. The women first took their complaint to their local union, but were told initially that nothing could be done because bathroom regulations are a matter of company policy. Later the union opted to support the workers in their fight against Nabisco. Said a local attorney representing the employees: "Hearing the stories that these women have told, I'm saddened and angered. I feel embarrassed that our community would permit this. I'm embarrassed this is how we treat people."

Los Angeles Times 1/9/95: A1.

The blatant stereotyping of and discrimination against women exemplified by the foregoing cases is no longer legal. As discussed in chapter 5, even the canonical position on business social responsibility implies that discrimination is economically irrational. What should count in hiring decisions is the estimate of how productive an employee will be, not her sex. Sexual harassment, in any of its forms, leads to an unproductive labor force by creating an atmosphere in which women are unable to compete with their male counterparts on the basis of their qualifications, thereby damaging the productivity of the firm or, worse, creating a situation in which their own abilities are diminished by the harassment. So it is certainly appropriate that it is illegal, although the question of exactly what constitutes sexual harassment is difficult to answer. But despite legal protections and real gains in the business world, many women still encounter barriers reflecting sexist assumptions and prejudices—barriers that have given rise to a new set of moral and social issues involving women in the workplace. Many women, for example, perceive that their work is still undervalued relative to that of men. Traditional women's professions, such as nursing, teaching, and social work, have become targets of recent efforts to cut budgets and trim spending; and more women than men are relegated to part-time work with little job security and few benefits.

Stereotyped views about women also still prevail. In the late 1980s, for example, a group of female workers at Johnson Controls, a Milwaukee-based manufacturer of automotive batteries, accused the company of sex discrimination. Car batteries are made with lead, and studies had shown that exposure to certain levels of lead can seriously impair female reproductive abilities and injure developing fetuses. Johnson Controls, along with many other large manufacturing corporations, instituted a fetal protection policy. Under the policy, all female employees, unless they provided proof of sterility, were barred from any job with a level of lead exposure alleged to pose reproductive hazards; no such restrictions were placed on male employees, regardless of their fertility and level of lead exposure. The policy

---

✑ Gender Stereotyping, Discrimination, and Hooters

Hooters of America, Inc., operates a chain of restaurants. For years the company has had a strict policy of hiring only women to work as servers in its restaurants. The women hired by the company are called "Hooters Girls" and are chosen (among other things) for their large bust size and how well they look in a skimpy uniform. In late 1995 the Equal Employment Opportunity Commission filed a gender bias complaint against Hooters. The company reportedly was willing to invest as much as $10 million in resisting the complaint. "A little good clean wholesome female sexuality," according to a company spokesperson, "is what our customers come for." Company supporters argued that the EEOC's bias suit was misplaced and that its reasoning would dictate that "men would have to be allowed to try out for the Dallas cheerleaders." Critics of Hooters responded that similar arguments were once used by airlines to justify hiring only women as flight attendants (women's unique "nurturing" abilities were essentially to comfort passengers); they also argued that female waiters make up a disproportionately large segment of servers in the poorly paying fast-food sector. Should customer preferences be used to justify sex-based hiring? And does such hiring necessarily reflect a negative stereotype?

---

had the effect of excluding women workers from virtually all of the typically higher-paying assembly-line positions in the company. The women who challenged the company in court claimed that the policy reflected some of the same paternalistic and condescending attitudes toward women prevalent a century ago, evident, for example, in the assumption that women, unlike men, are not capable of deciding for themselves whether to accept a job that poses certain risks.

SEXUAL HARASSMENT

Sexual harassment is increasingly recognized as a serious problem in the workplace. Often such harassment has been regarded by victims as something beyond their control—an unavoidable consequence of the fact that employees are also sexual beings. But to many, sexual harassment is a clear indication of discrimination, a harm to the victim based on the victim's gender.

Concern over sexual harassment and what to do about it has drawn much notable media attention, fueled by recent controversies. In 1996 numerous female U.S. Army recruits stationed at Ft. Leonard Wood, Missouri, and at the Aberdeen Proving Ground in Maryland, filed complaints against their cohorts and superiors, alleging various forms of sexual misconduct, from fondling to rape. As the Army's investigation broadened, so did the number of complaints filed. The scandal brought comparisons with the notorious Tailhook incident, in which similar allegations were made against Navy personnel several years earlier. In 1995 Oregon senator Bob Packwood was forced to resign as a result of complaints lodged by a number of female co-workers, accusing him of harassing behavior over a period of years. The 1991 confirmation hearings for a justice of the U.S. Supreme Court saw Anita Hill make detailed sexual harassment allegations against her former boss, Clarence Thomas. The increased attention given to the problem of sexual harassment has converted an issue rarely discussed in the past into a matter of broad public concern. More women are speaking out about abuses to which they have been subjected. According to a 1991 *Time* magazine poll conducted during the Thomas hearings, 34 percent of all working women reported that they had been sexually harassed. Most large corporations have put the topic of sexual harassment at the top of their executive education programs. The *Los Angeles Times* has reported that, between 1989 and 1994, the number of complaints of sexual harassment received by the Equal Employment Opportunity Commission (EEOC) has tripled and monetary awards have quadrupled, even though the number of court decisions for plaintiffs dropped from 30 percent in 1990 to 23 percent in 1994.[5]

Corporate concern over sexual harassment is not surprising, since lawsuits against a company can be extremely expensive. A 1994 sexual harassment suit brought by a female secretary against a veteran partner of the international law firm Baker & McKenzie cost the firm $7 million in damages. In 1995 Del Laboratories in New York settled a harassment complaint brought against its CEO for $1 million. Claims by men of sexual harassment are rare, but in 1993 a jury awarded more than $1 million to a man who claimed he was sexually harassed by a firm's female financial officer.[6]

■ Definitions of Sexual Harassment

What exactly is sexual harassment? And just what harm does it cause? The EEOC first attempted to define sexual harassment in 1980. It defined the conduct as follows:

> unwelcome sexual advances, requests for sexual favors, verbal and physical contact of a sexual nature when (a) submission to such is either explicitly or implicitly a condition of an individual's employment and submission to or rejection of such conduct is used as a basis for employment decisions regarding that individual; (b) when such harassing behavior has the purpose of or results in interfering with the individual's work performance or creates a hostile, intimidating, or offensive work environment.

The EEOC stipulated that the employer is responsible for all harassment engaged in by employees "where the employer (its agents or supervisory employees) knows or should have known of the conduct, unless it can show that it took immediate and effective corrective action."

✑ Harassment at Mitsubishi

Workers at a Mitsubishi Motors Corp. plant in Illinois became the focus of an intense government investigation of alleged sexual harassment in 1996, one of the largest of its kind on record. Several private lawsuits and a class-action suit brought against Mitsubishi by the Equal Employment Opportunity Commission accused low-level supervisors of threatening retaliation against women who refused to perform oral sex. Nearly thirty women complained of numerous incidents in which male workers allegedly grabbed female colleagues' breasts, buttocks, and genitals. Pictures of nude women and lewd graffiti, the women claimed, regularly adorned work areas. In one assembly area, men routinely hooted like monkeys at young women; female workers stated that they were blasted by air guns normally used to tighten screws in metal. Mitsubishi was scheduled to file its response to the class-action suit by June 1996.

Los Angeles Times. February 3, 1996.

According to the EEOC, sexual harassment can take one of several forms. The first is usually called "quid pro quo" harassment. In these cases, the harasser uses his or her more powerful position at the workplace to obtain sexual favors from a subordinate. The harasser may threaten the victim's position ("Either sleep with me or you will lose your job") or the harassment make take the form of an offer ("If you will sleep with me, your employment situation will be improved"). Both of these forms of quid pro quo harassment are proscribed by the EEOC guidelines.

A third form of harassment is noted in section (b) of the EEOC definition. This has been called "condition of work" or "hostile environment" harassment. This category includes behaviors of a sexual nature that may interfere with an individual's work performance because that individual finds such behavior to be, for example, intimidating or offensive. Quid pro quo harassment always involves a threat or an offer and is directed at a particular victim; hostile-environment harassment refers to a pattern of behavior found in the day-to-day circumstances of employment though not necessarily directed at a particular employee to gain sexual favors. Various gestures, jokes, and lewd remarks; patting, fondling, or other offensive touching; comments about women's bodies; posting pictures of nude women—all can constitute a "hostile environment" amounting to sexual harassment.

Although the EEOC guidelines have provided a basis for the definition of sexual harassment in legal contexts, some ethicists have attempted to refine the definition in various ways. The guidelines state that sexual conduct is harassing when such conduct has the purpose of interfering with the individual's work performance. Some ethicists argue that, to be a moral offense, sexual harassment must be intentional; that is, the perpetrator must have had the intention of harassing the victim and must have viewed his own conduct as harassment and not, for example, as a compliment. This suggestion presupposes that an indi-

---

✐ Examples of Sexual Harassment?

- Unwanted statements or innuendoes that sexual favors will lead to job favors
- Retaliation by a supervisor or co-worker whose unwanted sexual advances were previously rejected
- Unwanted pressure for sexual favors
- Unwanted sexual looks or gestures
- Unwanted letters and telephone calls
- Catcalls
- Referring to an adult as "girl," "hunk," "babe," or "honey"
- Asking about sexual preferences, fantasies, or history
- Kissing sounds, howling, and smacking lips
- Neck massage
- Touching an employee's clothing, hair, or body
- Hanging around a person
- Looking up and down [elevator eyes]
- Staring at someone
- Giving personal gifts

vidual can be held morally responsible only for things that he intended to do. Certainly, this is at least part of what we mean by moral responsibility. It is conceivable that what appears on the surface to be quid pro quo harassment might be intended by the actor as mere banter, or as a joke. On this reading, a necessary condition for the occurrence of sexual harassment is that the perpetrator have had the proper mental state. Further, it might be argued that it is necessary that the alleged victim also interpret the behavior as harassment and not something else, for example, that the individual takes the behavior as harassment and not as a "career opportunity." Of course, proving that the victim or the perpetrator had the appropriate state of mind when the conduct occurred may not be easy.

For this reason, some philosophers have opted for a behavioral definition of sexual harassment. From this perspective "sexual harassment" simply refers to a range of behaviors the presence of which is sufficient to conclude that sexual harassment has occurred—the mental state of either the victim or perpetrator is irrelevant. This eliminates the difficult issue of assessing intention, and allows the possibility that a victim could be sexually harassed even though she claims not to have been bothered and shrugs it off. This possibility is of importance to those who believe that women should not be made to endure harassing behaviors, even though they have been socialized into passively accepting such behaviors as a consequence of intractable male attitudes toward women and sexuality. A woman who accepts such behavior with the justification that "boys will be boys" is still a victim, just as is a person of color who is hardened to racial slurs. These views and their implications are discussed further in the reading by Vaughana Feary, later in this chapter.

WHY IS SEXUAL HARASSMENT WRONG?

What is morally wrong about sexual harassment? At the very least, it shows disrespect for the victim; but some forms of harassment are objectionable on other grounds as well. John Hughes and Larry May, in their seminal article "Is Sexual Harassment Coercive?"[7] argued that quid pro quo harassment takes away the victim's freedom to choose. In cases of sexual threats, the victim is presented with a dilemma: Either engage in sexual behavior or be fired, demoted, sorry . . . If the victim accepts, she is forced into a sexual relationship that was unchosen. But if the victim refuses, she runs the risk of losing a job or of facing reprisals. In neither case can it be said that the victim's choice is voluntary. Sexual offers have the same formal features. Here the perpetrator presents an offer to the victim: Engage in this behavior and I'll see, for example, that you are promoted, given a bonus, or receive some other benefit. If the victim accepts, she risks being viewed henceforth only in terms of sexual value, that is, the victim's continuing willingness to be sexually available would be the "qualification" for this and future positions. Should she refuse, the victim risks retaliation from the perpetrator in a position of greater power. But even if there is no hint of retaliation, the employee's work environment has changed in undesirable ways and in both cases the victim is in a worse position than before the proposition was made. It seems clear that the victim in both cases has been harmed.

Hostile-environment harassment is the most problematic form sexual harassment can take, insofar as the range of potentially harassing conduct is very broad and given that a great deal depends on how such conduct is interpreted by the victim. The EEOC guidelines mention several behaviors that might constitute sexual harassment—off-color jokes, neck rubs, "elevator eyes," and so on—but notes that the crucial question is whether these behaviors are construed as harassing by the victim. Clearly, some people enjoy off-color jokes and do not construe them as attempts to demean anyone's gender. Similarly, certain forms of touching may or may not be offensive or intimidating given the circumstances and the people involved. According to the EEOC, whether these behaviors are offensive depends on the judgments of the persons exposed to them. To some, this seems intolerably subjective and indicates the need for more-objective standards to determine what behaviors are proscribed. To others, evaluating possibly harassing conduct from the perspective of those affected by it—most often women—is a necessary corrective to years of gender stereotyping and male dominance of women in the workplace.

The courts, for their part, have proposed at least two standards for assessing what counts as sexual harassment: a standard based on the perspective of a *reasonable person,* and a standard based on the perspective of a *reasonable victim.* The first standard asks whether a reasonable person would find such things as sexual humor or certain forms of touching to be unwelcome and offensive. Feminist critics of the law have repeatedly argued against such a standard. The typical image of the reasonable person, they argue, is really that of the reasonable *male* person; yet men and women do, such critics contend, see the world differently: What a man might pass off as a harmless joke, a woman might find very offensive or even threatening. These theorists favor judging harassing conduct from the standpoint of the reasonable *victim,* or, more specifically, the reasonable *woman;* and at least one U.S. court has endorsed this view, as is explained in the readings.

Finally, further issues concerning the scope of sexual harassment prohibitions lie on the horizon. Why, for example, should legitimate harassment complaints be restricted to those involving persons of different sexes? Should same-sex harassment be an actionable wrong in the workplace? In one case, a male press operator at an Iowa muffler factory was verbally abused by other male co-workers, who repeatedly "bagged" the victim: grabbing or squeezing his testicles. The worker filed suit against his employer alleging sexual harassment.[8] Critics of the suit argued that there was no evidence of an antimale environment at the factory and that the physical grabbing was just "crude horseplay"; defenders insisted that the central question in harassment cases is whether members of one sex are exposed to disadvantageous conditions of employment to which members of the other sex are not: Since only men can be "bagged," the conduct is genuine harassment. Other cases involving harassment allegedly committed against heterosexual men by gays have engendered similar disputes. How should such cases be resolved?

THE READINGS

The reading selections included in the first part of this chapter begin with a hypothetical case study focusing on the harassment of women on the job. A disturbing e-mail message is discovered by a supervisor, who then must decide how best to help a female co-worker. Several commentators offer their views on how the situation should be handled. The selection by Margie Burns turns to what she claims is continuing discrimination against women in the workplace. Burns's specific focus is on the academic world, and, using stories from her own career, she argues that women remain in many ways marginalized in the academy. Burns pays particular attention to the growing phenomenon of "part-timers," and insists that the high proportion of women in such temporary positions is not coincidental.

The *Johnson Controls* case illustrates the difficulties that sometimes arise when employers attempt to implement safety measures. The plaintiffs in the case, a group of female workers, challenged Johnson Controls's fetal-protection policy, under which all female employees, absent proof of sterilization, were barred from any job with a level of lead exposure alleged to pose reproductive problems. When reading Justice Blackmun's majority opinion, ask yourself whether protecting the health and safety of third parties such as fetuses is properly part of a company's concern. Does the policy in question constitute sex discrimination, in your view? Why wasn't the company concerned with potential impacts upon the reproductive capacities of its male employees? Hugh Finneran and George Annas debate the issue of fetal protection policies. They discuss the *Johnson Controls* case and debate whether placing restrictions on the employment of women is unjustifiably discriminatory or legitimate and necessary for the purpose of protecting unborn life.

The readings then turn to discuss conceptual questions concerning the reasonable-person standard and the general issue of the moral wrongness of sexual harassment. The majority opinion of the Ninth Circuit Court of Appeals in *Ellison v. Brady* outlines the case for recognition of the reasonable-woman standard in sexual harassment cases; the dissenting opinion questions how this approach would preserve a gender-neutral prohibition on harassment. Deborah L. Wells and Beverly J. Kracher argue that a sexually hostile work environment must be determined from the perspective of the reasonable victim. An analysis of sexual harassment from this perspective fulfills a natural duty of mutual respect for persons and the duty to refrain from harming other innocent parties. Their essay concludes with a discussion of sexual harassment training and the reasonable victim standard. Vaughana Macy Feary argues that the issue of sexual harassment has not been taken seriously by the business community, in part because it fails to see the problem as a moral problem. Part of the reason for this is that the concept of sexual harassment is dismissed by some (including some philosophers) as murky and confused. Feary defends the clarity of the existing EEOC guidelines and suggests several reasons why sexual harassment remains a moral problem. Finally, Ellen Frankel Paul argues that the scope of sexual harassment, especially in work environments, has been exaggerated to include mere sexual annoyances which should not be actionable in court.

NOTES

1. *Los Angeles Times* (9/12/95).
2. *Bradwell v. Illinois* 83 U.S. 130 (1873).
3. 208 U.S. 412 (1908).
4. Ibid.: 421–422.
5. *Los Angeles Times* (9/12/95).
6. *San Francisco Chronicle* (5/20/93).
7. Reprinted in *Ethical Theory and Business*, 4th ed., edited by Tom L. Beauchamp and Norman E. Bowie (Englewood Cliffs, N.J.: Prentice Hall, 1993), 415–420.
8. See *Quick v. Donaldson Co. Inc.*, 90 F.3d 1372 (1996).

CASE STUDY   The Case of the Hidden Harassment

Daniel Niven

Jerry Tarkwell, a real estate lending manager at Filmore Trust, marched out of his office toward the associate's wing of the bank's eighteenth-floor offices. "I need the Thompson Properties file right away," Tarkwell said to the associates' secretary. "Do you know where I can find it?"

"It's probably on Jill's computer table. I was helping her enter the new figures this morning."

"Thanks." Tarkwell headed down the hallway and knocked on the door marked "Jill McNair, Associate." McNair didn't answer, so he opened the door and walked over to the computer table piled high with folders. As he shuffled through the files, Tarkwell glanced at what was written on the computer screen. It was an electronic mail message McNair had sent earlier.

Can you walk me out again tonight? He's in today and I'm sure he'll be waiting for me. He leaned up against me when I was at the coffee machine this morning and whispered some disgusting stuff about how great he is in bed. I don't want another episode like the one in the hallway Monday night. I should have left when you did, but I thought he'd already gone.

I'm sorry you have to put up with this. Get back to me. I'll be ready to go whenever you are.

"Oh, that's awful." Tarkwell felt sickened as he got up to leave. "God, I wonder who's doing this?" He grabbed the Thompson Properties file, returned to his own office, and called the company's equal employment officer.

"Tarkwell was in your office a little while ago looking for the Thompson file," shouted the secretary as Jill McNair walked briskly down the hall.

"Damn, I was supposed to hand that over to him an hour ago," McNair thought as she opened her door. The computer screen immediately caught her eye. "Oh no," she gasped, "I can't believe I left that on." The ring of her phone made her jump.

"Hi, Jill, it's Jerry. I'd like to talk to you right away. Can you come down to my office?"

"Sure," she said weakly and then hung up the phone. "I'll bet he read it," she thought. "What am I going to do now?"

McNair knocked on Tarkwell's door and went in. "Sit down, Jill. I have something rather disturbing to discuss with you," Tarkwell began. "I went into your office to pick up the Thompson file. I'm afraid I read what was on your computer screen."

Jill looked at him angrily. She clenched her fists in her lap.

"Let me tell you first how sorry I am that you've been . . . put in that kind of situation." Tarkwell shifted uncomfortably. He was having trouble finding words that wouldn't embarrass them both. "I need to know who's been doing this to you so we can put a stop to it. I called the equal employment officer, and she explained the steps to resolving a case of this sort. First you . . ."

McNair cut him off. "You had no right to read my personal e-mail, and you had no right to call EEO before talking to me. This is my problem not yours, and I don't want this getting around. Do you have any idea what can happen to me and to my career if people find out about this?"

"I didn't tell them who'd be bringing the complaint," Tarkwell said. "You just have to write a letter, and they do an investigation."

"Don't you understand?" she asked, seething. "It would be his word against mine, and he's senior to me." She wished she hadn't let that slip. "I'm the one who's going to get hurt. If this gets investigated by EEO, everyone in this building could be questioned. I'll probably get transferred, and then I won't have a chance at promotion. And who'd want to work with me? Every man in the company would be afraid I'd report him if he so much as opened a door for me."

"Look," Tarkwell reasoned, "nobody here has to find out. I'm sure the EEO will do whatever you feel is best. You know you can't go on working under these conditions."

"I won't have my privacy invaded," McNair said flatly. "There's nothing you can do."

"But it's a federal law," Tarkwell demanded. "This company has to maintain a workplace free of sexual coercion, and as your manager, I have to report this. It's company policty."

"I've got too much at stake here," McNair answered, reaching for the door. "So just stay out of it, Jerry. I can take care of it myself."

HOW CAN TARKWELL BEST RESOLVE THIS ISSUE?

Mary Wang
Public Television
Producer

Jerry, although I know you will be talking to lawyers, people from human resources, and equal employment officers about Jill McNair's case, perhaps I can offer you another perspective—the perspective of someone who understands what Jill is going through. I too was a victim of sexual harassment.

In my case, however, the managers were not as enlightened as you are. They heard my harasser make comments like "let's go see a porno film" or "let me pet your sweater." They knew that intelligent women like me weren't getting assigned to exciting, high-visibility projects. They saw that women were leaving the department, one by one. And they did nothing. You, on the other hand, have recognized that what Jill is experiencing is sexual harassment. And, most important, you are treating this as a serious problem.

Unlike the managers I encountered, you want to help. But you won't be helping Jill by forcing her to bring a complaint against the harasser. She is already a victim of someone else's unwanted actions. Don't compound her sense of victimization by pushing her into another situation she doesn't want to be in.

Perhaps the best way to help Jill is to show her how to take control. Show her that there *are* options. But first make damn sure that those options really do exist.

Find out what the sexual harassment policy in your office is. Does the message that sexual harassment is illegal and will not be tolerated come through loud and clear? Does that message come from top management? Are seminars held so that all employees understand what sexual harassment is and what to do if they encounter it? Is there a complaint system in place? If so, does it work? Do the employees trust it?

I suspect that the answer to these questions is no. If Filmore Trust did have an effective way of dealing with sexual harassment, Jill wouldn't feel as if she had to accept harassment as a necessary evil of her job. And managers like you would know specific steps to take that wouldn't jeopardize the victim or the company.

If you really want to help Jill and Filmore Trust, you must convince the company to educate its employees and to establish a good system of handling sexual harassment complaints. Ultimately, you will be helping not only Jill but other potential victims as well. The chances are good that Jill is not the only person at Filmore Trust experiencing sexual harassment.

These are long-term solutions that will take time to implement; however, you and Jill also need immediate help. Two options for the short-term are:

☐ Call a meeting of your department and discuss sexual harassment. Tell your employees that Filmore Trust and you will not tolerate any behavior that is sexual in nature, unwelcome, or unreasonably disruptive.

☐ Find an expert on sexual harassment who doesn't have any ties to Filmore Trust and give his or her name to Jill. Obviously, Jill doesn't trust the way your company would handle a sexual harassment complaint. Perhaps she might have greater confidence in advice coming from someone on the outside.

In the meantime, let Jill know your concerns but don't dismiss hers. The unfortunate truth is that a sexual harassment victim who makes a formal complaint to management without the protection of an established, trusted complaint procedure risks losing his or her reputation, job, or even career.

I know. When I brought my complaint to senior management, one of my greatest fears was retaliation. I wrote a letter, just like the one you are suggesting Jill write. In response, management thanked me for bringing sexual harassment to its attention and told me not to worry. I was promised it would be "business as usual" around the department.

But it wasn't. Instead of starting an investigation of my harasser, managment started an investigation of me. It stole positive performance reviews out of my employee file and then told me my work was unsatisfactory because there weren't any good reviews on record. Colleagues who had once been sympathetic now didn't want to get involved. Others just stopped talking to me. Conversation would halt when I entered a room. So I sympathize with Jill when she wonders who will want to work with her if she brings a complaint. The answer often is no one.

And don't think that "nobody here has to find out." Long after I left my company, I heard that people were gossiping about the financial settlement I had received—and this in spite of a gag order.

Like other victims of sexual harassment, Jill hopes that the problem will eventually go away. Unfortunately, sexual harassment doesn't stop on its own. It simply goes somewhere else, finds someone else—unless people like you step in.

Mary P. Rowe
Special assistant to the president, ombudsman, and adjunct professor at the
Sloan School of Management at Massachusetts Institute of Technology

People who feel harassed need options and choices—especially if they lack conclusive proof of the harassment. This case appears to present two unacceptable choices for manager Jerry Tarkwell and no desirable options for Jill McNair. Moreover, Filmore Trust's policy will not work in the company's interests either. No party's interests are served well here.

Let's start with the company. Filmore Trust needs an environment where sexual harassment is absent or at least rare. This will occur where employees can and do speak up and get incipient harassment stopped on the spot, where managers offer options so people who feel harassed have some control over what happens, and where reporting harassment and asking for help will not damage someone's career.

My research and experience indicate that while a mandatory investigation policy may appear to be helpful to harassed people, it actually discourages reports of harassment. Mandatory investigation especially threatens careers when the only evidence is "he said/she said" (though more evidence might be found in the Filmore Trust case). This is because responsible managers hate to take action in such a case, so no one gets punished, and the alleged offender does not feel truly acquitted.

What about McNair's interests? They are the same interests I listed for Filmore Trust. In addition, McNair values her privacy and fears reprisal. Tarkwell's interests are probably similar.

How can Filmore Trust meet the interests of all parties? The company should offer four sets of options for dealing with harassment:

1. *Counseling for Direct Negotiation.* Filmore Trust should offer off-the-record counseling so that employees can learn to negotiate the problem effectively. With the help of an employee assistance program or an ombudsman, for example, McNair might choose to learn how to confront the harasser directly and/or write that person a private letter. Drafting a clear, factual letter will help McNair think through her evidence, compose her mind and feelings, and help her select and pursue an option for action. Sending or hand delivering (and keeping a copy of) a letter is statistically likely to end the harassment, at no cost to privacy. It also provides more evidence, if harassment continues or the offender retaliates, that the alleged sexual approach actually happened and was unwelcomed.

2. *Informal, Third-Party Intervention.* McNair should be able to seek informal assistance from a human resources manager or other appropriate person. The third party would intervene as a

shuttle diplomat or mediator. Informal intervention usually does not include adverse administrative action. The third party could deliver a warning and write a memo to his or her own file.

3. *Formal Investigation and Action.* McNair should be able to request fact-finding and judgment. If she knows she has choices, she will be more likely to make formal complaint, but this option should not be pursued against her wishes.

4. *Generic Approach.* McNair should be able to ask Tarkwell or another appropriate manager—off the record and without providing the name of the alleged offender—for a harassment prevention effort. This choice could trigger an apparently routine training program in the relevant department. Or McNair could ask that the department head send a departmental letter that includes examples of sexual harassment and a strong statement of company policy. If McNair has the option to ask for such action without anyone's name being used, then the harassment can be stopped at no cost to anyone's privacy or rights. In my experience, the generic approach will stop the alleged harassment about four-fifths of the time, and it helps to affirm company policy. It also fosters an atmosphere where people can feel comfortable taking a direct approach if they are harassed and where they will feel less afraid to ask for an investigation.

There should be no adverse administrative action against an alleged offender without a fair—probably formal—process. If any of the informal options are chosen by McNair, then Tarkwell must follow up immediately, several months, and one year later to be sure that the alleged harassment has ceased and that there has been no retaliation.

Mikiko Taga
Freelance Journalist

Jerry Tarkwell does not have to choose between respecting Jill McNair's privacy and putting a stop to sexual harassment. His accidental knowledge of McNair's harassment has given him, whether he likes it or not, the responsibility to do both.

It would be irresponsible to follow blindly "company policy" if to do so would undermine its original intent (presumably to help employees deal with harassment). Doing nothing, however, is also not an option. Sexual harassment involves the entire company, not just two people. Tarkwell therefore cannot let the issue go now that he knows something is going on.

As long as McNair refuses to report her case, Tarkwell will, by definition, be threatening her privacy in any attempts to talk to her about it. But McNair has already crossed the line between private and company life by using company equipment (e-mail) to tell her colleague about her sexual harassment. While Tarkwell must get McNair to report her case, he must refrain from reporting it to the company's EEO until she assents.

Regardless of whether or not McNair utimately reports her case, Tarkwell must make this his opportunity to attack the problem of sexual harassment and to raise company consciousness about it. Anything less would be shirking his responsibility of creating a safe working environment for his staff.

In Japan, on the other hand, a Jerry Tarkwell would have no cause to even mention his knowledge of Jill McNair's case to her, and the ethical problem presented by this situation would not have surfaced. Few Japanese companies have any sexual harassment policy in place.

Indeed, consciousness of sexual harassment here is so undeveloped that the very issue of the protection of privacy has yet to surface. For women, Japanese companies are still hotbeds of harassment.

The first sexual harassment suit filed in Japan was in 1989. The woman, who was being harassed by her immediate supervisor, complained to his boss, only to find that his boss condoned his actions and blamed her for inviting them. In other words, the men stuck together.

Within such a context, a woman must go beyond those immediately involved in order to be heard. But once she does, the rest of the company eventually finds out, she is further harassed, and generally, she ends up quitting.

If she does file suit, she will most likely do so out of a desire for revenge than of a feeling that her rights have been violated. Japan has such a long history of male dominance that there is no collective belief that a woman should be the equal working partner of a man.

I endured two years of sexual harassment—though at the time I did not know the term—while I was employed at a large manufacturing company. The older female employees taught the younger women that it was a mark of "female maturity" to respond to harassment by smiling and ignoring it.

During my stay in the United States (1983 to 1988), I was shocked to learn that there was a name for such hateful behavior. In 1989, when I published my book *Single Mind,* I was able to introduce the term sexual harassment to Japan.

In the three years since, the term *seku hara* has gained currency as the media has legitimized its usage. (In fact, seku hara is a trivialization of the term sexual harassment, further proof of the widespread insensitivity to this issue.) There have been three sexual harassment suits filed in Japan that I have followed; two have been won, and the other is still pending. Though this sounds promising, and though anti-seku hara campaigns would seem to indicate substantial change, the situation is, in fact, far from progressive. In effect, the message is "Watch out, guys. We know women are emotional, so we will have to step lightly for our own protection."

Ultimately, sexual harassment is less an issue of company policy than one of personal responsibility in a management position. Tarkwell has shown that he takes the company's policy seriously; now he should follow through on his commitment by ensuring that McNair's situation is justly resolved and by raising office consciousness about harassment.

Judith P. Vladeck
Senior partner at Vladeck, Waldman, Elias & Engelhard,
Counsellors at Law in New York City

Jerry Tarkwell should respect Jill McNair's request for privacy. She is not obliged by law to press charges of harassment and should not be required to do so against her own better judgment. McNair is probably realistic about the potential damage to her career. She has no doubt seen the lack of sympathy and support available to a woman who complains about harassment. She should not be pressured into becoming an unwilling martyr.

If Tarkwell is concerned about McNair's complaining later that she was not protected by the company, he could ask her to provide a memo stating that she had considered her options and rejected the company's offer of assistance. If she declines to provide such a memo, Tarkwell should write his own memo to that effect and place it in McNair's personnel file. It would likely protect the company in the future.

Tarkwell, having alerted the EEO of his knowledge that a company employee was imposing on other workers, is in the difficult position of any good citizen who learns of a malfeasant in his community. If the victim refuses to press charges, the bystander cannot do so. Having encouraged the victim to do what he thinks is correct, he must accept her decision.

Obviously, a conscientious person such as Tarkwell could suggest that the company's harassment policy, with assurances of confidentiality, be circulated and posted again.

Whether McNair can be disciplined for refusing to cooperate in an investigation is a more difficult question. While reporting harassment is protected by law and retaliation against a person who does so violated federal law, failing to report is *not* protected by an clear statutory language. It might be argued that discipline for failing to report is a form of discrimination in itself. A woman who is required to report sexual harassment is being deprived of equal terms and conditions of employment, in that, unlike the men who are not subjected to the harassment, she is burdened with an obligation to come forward and place herself at risk.

Unfortunately, in many jurisdictions, a woman in McNair's position is at risk of discipline or termination for failing to disclose information requested by the company. In New York, for example, an employer who fired McNair for remaining silent could do so with impunity.

A subsidiary question arises concerning Tarkwell's conduct. If Tarkwell had not looked at McNair's computer screen, he would not have known about the problem. While it may be understandable that Tarkwell went into her office while she was not there to look for documents that he needed at once, his reading of her electronic mail message was inappropriate and an invasion of her privacy. McNair, unfortunately, has no right to the privacy of her personal e-mail, unless the company has some rules protecting the privacy rights of its employees.

Jill McNair is in the unenviable position of a woman trying to make a career for herself, who is likely to get battered for not publicly fighting back against the sexual harassment she is suffering and who risks ostracism and abuse from her colleagues if she does complain.

Lee Chester Garron
Equal employment office/affirmative action training manager for
Digital Equipment Corporation in Maynard, Massachusetts

Like many companies, Digital doesn't deny that sexual harassment exists in the workplace. Digital encourages managers and employees to take advantage of sexual harassment training, which examines the issue and develops solutions to harassment in any given work situation.

At Digital, 90% of all sexual harassment claims involve individuals who are not aware that their behaviors are offensive or unwelcome. And 90% of these claims are settled by an apology and a promise by the harasser to correct permanently his or her behavior. The remaining 10% might be settled with some disciplinary action.

A great deal of consideration should be given to validating any claim of sexual harassment, even before a full-fledged investigation takes place. This allows for the possibility that an employee should be filing a claim to offset poor performance or getting revenge for a personal relationship "gone sour." Evidence must be secured to avoid a "his word against mine" situation.

In the case of Jerry Tarkwell and Jill McNair, Tarkwell did exactly what I would recommend by first contacting Filmore Trust's EEO for instructions. Even though McNair demands that no further steps be taken, Tarkwell should continue to consult with the company EEO so a decision can be made about how to react to McNair's requests for anonymity. Only there can it be determined if the potential harm to the victim or other employees outweighs the complainant's concern for privacy. Tarkwell is responsible for acting on any issues that affect his employees, so McNair's situation cannot be ignored. At Digital, Tarkwell would be held accountable for his employees' behavior.

Tarkwell must pursue the issue, first to find out if the complaint is merited and then to ensure that no other incidents of harassment occur. Tarkwell can suggest that McNair seek the advice of another manager if she feels uncomfortable talking about it with him, and he must convince her that a company policy exists that will protect her. Every company's sexual harassment policy must contain a "no retaliation" stipulation promising that the complainant will not incur any kind of reprisal as a result of a claim.

Programs and policies assuring employees of their right to bring forth, without reprisal, issues that they feel are affecting them negatively are paramount to any positive or reasonable resolution in issues of sexual harassment. Many cases are resolved with simple, positive intervention— when the offended employee is convinced that the company will stand behind its policies, standards, and values. Helping employees understand not only their right to utilize the internal open-door process but also federal EEOC guidelines on sexual harassment and their right to use these avenues to find a resolution is very important. The prevention of sexual harassment in the workplace is the employer's responsibility.

To implement this policy successfully, Digital managers and supervisors are encouraged to know their environment and subordinates—as well as raise their level of awareness through sexual harassment training courses. The training involves role playing of actual sexual harassment situations and lively follow-up discussion in which attendees share their thoughts and ideas about the implications of sexual harassment. Digital's EEO also offers "Train the Trainer" seminars for human resource professionals to learn more about the issue and prepare them to train others. Digital's goal is to bring resolution to a sexual harassment claim and ensure the investigative process satisfies both the employee and management.

Women and Part-time Employment: Discrimination in Academia

Margie Burns

It is widely known that women have made significant gains in higher education over the past 20 years, with increasing numbers of women in faculty and other professional positions, women undergraduates, women graduate students and holders of graduate degrees, and women entering branches and disciplines of academia from which they were virtually barred in earlier decades. This is all good news—but it hardly tells the whole story.

Again, the most recent, and relevant, numerical surveys expose significant disparities. In these figures, all women faculty combined—full-time and regular part-time—total 263,657—a sizable number. But it is exceeded by the number of women employed in clerical or secretarial positions in higher education: 391,164. This number in turn is augmented by the other ranks of "nonprofessional" women in service, maintenance, and related fields: 95,792.

Indeed, in all the ranks of women employed full- or part-time, in higher education, "nonprofessionals" outnumber "professionals" in public institutions across the board, in private institutions across the board, and in four-year institutions across the board. Only in two-year institutions do professional women somewhat outnumber non-

professional women—by about 61,000 to 58,000—a distinction that undoubtedly reflects the lesser prestige of two-year institutions.

It goes without saying that women employees—professional and nonprofessional—are outnumbered by men, in all the institutions across the board. The extent of the gender disparity is actually masked by the inclusion of part-time jobholders—some of whom (mostly men) are genuine moonlighters and others of whom (mostly women) are unwillingly underemployed.

Among women with full-time positions in postsecondary education, 149,874 are faculty; another 48,285 are "executive/administrative/managerial"—a total of 198,159. However, another 321,532 full-time women are employed in "clerical/secretarial" positions, and another 74,192 in "service and maintenance"—totalling 395,724.

In other words, despite all the ballyhoo over women's gains in recent years, and despite all the genuine gains beneath the hype, a woman employed full-time on a college campus is (almost exactly) twice as likely to be found behind a typewriter or the cafeteria counter as in front of a classroom or administrative gathering. And this disparity persists even though, of all the professional fields, higher education is that most closely linked to one of women's traditional occupations (teaching).

Incidentally, the disparity is (predictably) even greater in the most prestigious category of higher education institution, the four-year institution.

From *Thought and Action,* vol. 10, #1, 1994. Used with permission of Thought and Action, the NEA Higher Education Journal.

In four-year institutions, the number of full-time women faculty/administrators is 150,233; but the number of full-time women clerical/service workers is 348,111—more than double.

Moreover, any suggestion that women are overcompensated or even comparably compensated, relative to their male peers, once they do break into professional ranks, can be quickly subjected to a reality check. In its comprehensive faculty survey, the NCES found that male "regular faculty" were paid, on average, 25 percent more than female "regular faculty." (This figure, again, masks the far greater disparity which the nature of nominally part-time teaching would reveal). This income disparity, furthermore, is found at all ranks of the professoriate: full professor, associate professor, assistant professor, instructor, and lecturer. The agency's own summary statement is as follows:

Among full-time regular faculty, women received less income in all categories than did their male counterparts (table 3.7). On the average, compared to men, women received 25 percent less basic salary ($42,322 versus $31,755), 37 percent less income from the academic institution ($3,966 versus $2,501), 75 percent less consulting income ($4,124 versus $1,049), 62 percent less other outside income ($2,876 versus $1,093), and 32 percent less total income ($53,318 versus $36,398). (Some of these differences may be explained by the relative preponderance of men in research universities.)

Predictably, monetary compensation accompanies promotion to higher rank, with the concomitant increased prestige and budgetary clout. Once again, the pattern established by rank, like that established by income, displays a gender disparity at all levels. On college faculties across the board, men outnumber women at every level—down to, but not including, the lowest level of "lecturer" (where, however, men are still paid more).

The gender disparity is neatly and strikingly displayed in ascending order corresponding to ascending rank: male instructors outnumber female instructors by five to four; male assistant professors outnumber their female counterparts by 88,001 to 27,843; and male full professors outnumber female full professors by a truly impressive 142,418 to 19,105.

Much of this disparity, still in place after the gains made by women over the last 20 years, stems from conditions in place long before: existing "tra-

ditions, customs and institutions," in the old code words for segregation. It is only to be expected that most senior faculty members and administrators, at the highest ranks, are men, and that these personnel are paid the most.

Likewise, it is only to be expected that the gender gap in faulty compensation is intensified by the disproportionate number of women in liberal arts, where compensation is lower than in the sciences. In the most recent comprehensive faculty surveys, full-time engineering faculty were still 97 percent male, natural sciences faculty were still 85 percent male, and even social sciences faculty were still 77 percent male.

The division is modifying only gradually, if student degrees are any indication. According to the *Digest,* where men's degrees in engineering still swamp those earned by women (by over six to one in bachelor's degrees, seven to one in master's degrees, and 13 to one in doctorates), women's degrees in education still outnumber those earned by men (by over three to one in bachelor's and master's degrees, though by only four to three in doctorates).

Women have for years received the most degrees at all levels in area studies, foreign languages, and "letters"—English, American studies, classics. Men have consistently received the most degrees at all levels, and still do, in mathematics and physical sciences. Life sciences and health sciences are somewhat more mixed.

Interestingly, women receive more degrees at all levels in psychology, but men receive more degrees at all levels in the social sciences. (When I was an undergraduate, psychology used to be lumped with the "social sciences"; in the more recent demarcation, male students seem to have gravitated more toward economics and political science, which overlap more with government or public affairs).

What is more disheartening, at least to me, are the distribution problems that have newly arisen in the last 20 years, especially in a sector of academia where the problem cannot be explained by seniority or tradition. I refer to the current, widespread practice of hiring so-called "part-timers" to teach lower-level humanities courses, especially in English, foreign languages, and English as Second Language programs.

Part-time faculty hiring has increased exponentially in universities across the board, with most part-time faculty—like most full-time faculty—male. But the practice of part-time hiring in humanities service courses is especially pernicious, characterized ineluctably by caste and gender, consistently intertwined.

Even after gains made through affirmative action, full-time faculty in the humanities are still 70 percent men—69.95 percent, to be exact—and 30 percent—30.03 percent—women. This is in the humanities, where there are no job-description pretexts for gender discrimination (driving a forklift, engaging in hand-to-hand combat), where the majority of the undergraduate majors are women, and have been the majority for many years, and where—depending on discipline—a substantial proportion and often a majority of the graduate degrees are awarded to women.

Women have gotten a majority of the doctorates in letters for more than 10 years; in foreign languages, for more than 15 years. Even in English—traditionally a "girls" major—the disproportion is almost as great: full-time faculty in English departments, as of the most recent count, are still 66 percent men, 34 percent women.

The Truth About "Part-timers"

The disparity is thrown into greater relief by the almost mirror-image figures for part-time faculty in the humanities: 32.86 percent men, 67.14 percent women (and 31 percent men to 69 percent women in English departments). By the way, it should be pointed out here that the term "part-time" is a misnomer: nontenured faculty often teach a heavier course load than tenured faculty. The usual—and false—explanation for this gender disparity is that women "choose" part-time work more than men, for "family reasons."

This explanation contains a kernel of empirical validity—many women working part-time do so because of the lack of child care. But this explanation also contains unexamined assumptions. As already mentioned, one such unexamined assumption concerns the nature of teaching defined as "part-time" in higher education.

A number of faculty in higher education are genuinely moonlighting, purely by choice—for the intellectual challenge or "just for fun." Most of these genuine moonlighters, however, teach in business, law, architecture—they are either retirees or full-time professionals elsewhere, having a change of pace from their day jobs by teaching a college class. Not surprisingly, most of these genuine part-timers are men, on the whole satisfied with their lot as college instructors.

Their situation differs greatly from that of their counterparts in the humanities—a pool two-thirds women—routinely assigned much of the most taxing part of teaching: the writing and paper-grading courses; introductory foreign language classes; large introductory-survey classes. (Only when these same functions are performed by the hapless graduate student TA's, as a rule, are the nontenured instructors released from them—if unemployment is a release).

Both of the large public research institutions in the Washington, D.C., suburbs employ part-time instructors and graduate students in large numbers to perform these functions. Not that the situation is unique to the metropolitan D.C. area. Everywhere one looks, in higher education—to private or public institutions, large or small, open-admissions or highly selective (or anything in between)—one can see the same pools of overqualified and always underpaid staff, mostly women, teaching the lower-division service courses.

The situation has become so much a matter of course that a friend of mine, a senior faculty member himself in a loaded-with-clout English department, was recently asked by a colleague whether they couldn't "just hire a few housewives to teach composition."

Obviously, the purpose of doing so is to save money. But the economy practiced by establishing a second tier of faculty has had grotesquely caste- and gender-ridden side effects. As the "housewives" comment reveals, what facilitates these practices is a convenient assumption that the secondary tier of faculty are somehow innately inferior—an assumption facilitated, in turn, by the fact that this secondary tier is mostly female.

In other words, second-tier status has little to do with actual qualifications. As studies of nontenured faculty show, among the part-timers who are so only reluctantly, who are teaching at two or more campuses simultaneously to make ends meet or to attain professional status—"freeway flyers" and the like—and who have doctorates and who attempt to publish for advancement, women are disproportionately represented.

Unfortunately, the desire for advancement is seldom met: although writing programs especially (part of the "core curriculum" at most sizable institutions) are overwhelmingly staffed by women, most heads of writing programs are men—creating a truly unpleasant rooster-in-the-henhouse effect. And when some "part-timer" does miraculously break through the emotional and other barriers and attain full-time status, according to the studies, it's more often a man (whose gender presumably helps separate him perceptibly from the flock).

Second-Tier Faculty

The situation is compounded by the ways the second-tier faculty are prevented from accruing credentials in the first place. Given the conditions of part-time teaching in service courses—the frequent student overloads and heavy paper loads in introductory and other writing courses; the necessity to teach extra sections for extra money with piecework compensation; the lack of job security and benefits such as health insurance and retirement pensions; the lack of travel money; the lack of participation in departmental or institutional processes leading to recognition—substantial numbers of women in a highly visible occupation are denied equal access to the means of professional development and advancement.

Even well-meant efforts to focus more on "teaching" (as opposed to "research") do not help much. Second-tier faculty are indeed essentially forced to focus on "teaching," given the conditions just listed, but the effect on a part-time individual's teaching record is not benign. The instructor who teaches the same lower-division course, over and over, loses the pleasure of tracking with the same students in progressively more challenging classes; she also loses the recognition factor in having her students select her again (except when, as a student of mine once did, they choose her again after having failed her class once—something of a rarity).

Students sometimes resent these required courses and their paper loads in the first place, setting up an initial barrier of resistance. And instructors teaching such courses are often *de facto* and sometimes *de jure* barred from "teaching awards"; nor do they usually direct senior theses, teach honors sections or—of course—direct graduate work.

Not surprisingly, these external factors take their toll on morale; they become internalized, both for the "regular" faculty and for the second-tier

faculty themselves. The institutionalized regimen of less pay, less benefits, less recognition, and less promotion (usually, none) eventually institutionalizes an atmosphere of de-entitlement, of de-professionalization. And while the term "atmosphere" may seem nebulous, its effects are anything but.

At a panel in which I participated last year, a member of the audience rose, and referred casually and in passing to the "intellectual poverty" of part-time faculty (his question was how the situation of such could possibly be improved). As a prime example of Freudian projection, his remark had merit; in existing circumstances, it overlooks the actual credentials of part-time or nontenured faculty. (Aside from on-paper credentials, a master's-degree instructor with 10 plus years of experience can often outmotivate a newly hired doctoral graduate with every incentive to scamp his teaching in pursuing publications; this observation has by now become a truism of academic life).

Along similar lines, a would-be-helpful senior faculty member advised a part-timer, "You know, you people are like migrant laborers; if you all left, we could replace you in a minute." In today's job market, of course, the remark applies equally to the speaker, a point perhaps unnoticed by him (the *Chronicle of Higher Education* once ran an article on the "lost generation" of humanities Ph.D.s from the 1970s). Such remarks are more often, and more easily, directed against women—who seemingly present fertile fields—unprotected by tenure or by unionization—for colonialist protection.

Professional Barrier-Making

Academic discourse abounds with comparison of composition instruction to domestic labor (a topic being researched by one woman). More generally, the atmosphere surrounding the usual forms of privilege is formed by all the usual kinds of gas.

Perhaps it will come as no surprise that one department chair I know of found it amusing to give his female faculty a pat on the butt—even in front of their students. Another chair I knew of had a habit of picking his nose, when in conference with women colleagues; but it was hard to tell whether that was indirect aggression or just a nervous habit.

The former chair also engaged in other forms of overt sexual harassment—with (according to him) the encouragement of his dean, and in tandem with the head of the department's personnel search committee. This activity, by the way, is by no means restricted to the backwaters; as lawsuits around the country testify, it has been sited at some of academia's most prestigious institutions. During the Hill-Thomas hearings, a petition on sexual harassment in academia collected 700 signatures, as I heard, in two days.

Overt sexual harassment, however, is only one form of professional barrier-making, and sometimes the least dangerous because of its overtness. The more pernicious barriers in the processes of hiring, promotion and other advancement sometimes have effects discernible only indirectly or in the aggregate. I myself have the following (polite) atrocity story to relate, in regard to the realm of "publications."

I had sent an article to a journal editor and another under different cover to the same man, who happened to be chairing a session at a learned conference. The paper for the conference was quickly accepted; that for the journal was held for months (not unusual, in academic publishing). Just before the conference, I received a last-minute note from the session chair/editor, to give me pointers about the session—and to remind me that he still had my other article, about which—he said—he would talk to me at the conference.

When I met the fellow, I felt too much delicacy about seeming to pressure him to bring the matter up (such was my naivete at the time); but he mentioned it, again reminding me that he was still waiting to make up his mind. He then suggested we discuss it over dinner. I declined; the conference ended; and within two or three days, I received the rejected manuscript in the mail.

The whole story—not, by a long shot, among the worst—illustrates the nebulousness of attainment in the realm of publications in general, and that for women trying to get published in particular. I have revised articles to editors' specifications and then had them rejected; I have also had articles lost or otherwise mislaid; kept for months (and years); or belatedly returned with intemperate, unprofessional letters of rejection (even in connection with articles I subsequently published in other journals). I have also had my ideas used without proper attribution, although fortunately very seldom.

None of the above is peculiar to the experience of women in the academy, but there is every indication that women suffer rejection of their writing, relative to men, disproportionately. Michael Korda, whose me-generation self-help books were at least written with wit and energy, wrote amusingly of woman's fate in writing: A woman is best off negotiating face-to-face, second best on the phone, and least likely to succeed in writing—a poor prognostication for women in academia, where the most important credentials are publications.

Early studies such as the "Joan Green-John Green" test displayed, some years back, the different responses to writing identified as a woman's and to writing identified as a man's. This study might be regarded as primitive today, but the basic difference in credibility accorded to the sexes remains.

I can remember a tiny instance: A professor characterized a facetious comment in one of my papers as "cutesy" (and wrote that he didn't like "cutesy" remarks), but gently characterized facetious remarks by a male classmate as "talky" (and wrote that he personally liked them). The basic problem is—or at least was—that a reader of ill will, or bad faith, can read anything written by a woman in a sort of mental falsetto. I would think that traces of the same problem persist in print journalism.

My own experience and observation in academia, while no means uphappy (I enjoyed my years in teaching), yield abundant indications of the gender differential relating to matters of professional development, at every level. When I first discussed my plans to attend graduate school with a faculty member, I was told categorically that my gender could cause extra difficulties in being admitted to an Ivy League program (though I was also assured that a local program would let me in, with all the money they could give me).

A woman friend of mine, who transferred into an Ivy League program, was told straightforwardly that her graduate fellowship would be less than that given a man entering the program. The explanation: the wives of male graduate students had less income than the husbands (supposedly) of female graduate students. (This is the administrative version of killing both parents and throwing yourself on the court's mercy as an orphan).

Needless to say, the whole husbands-and-wives ball of wax is ever rife with potential tensions. One liberal arts program yanked the fellowships of two women graduate students after their second year, to award the fellowships to two men entering at the time. This transfer of resources from two proven students to two unknown quantities was widely perceived as an attempt to beef up the masculinity of the program. It was officially justified on the ground that both women had "husbands who worked." Just for the record, both women continued, and completed their doctorates; neither of the men did so.

"You'll Get the Job, You're a Woman"

Despite the "double shift" for women trying to develop professionally while also maintaining a marriage and family, the lot of such women is often perceived as "easy" by people in different situations, and envied as such. And intense envy is roused by any slight movement in the direction of affirmative action.

Despite the abysmal academic job market (during the middle 1970s, the unemployment rate for humanities Ph.D.s was 83 percent), I can still remember being told, "You'll get the job, because you're a woman." Sadly enough, this mythology persists; I recently heard an almost identical remark about women in mathematics, another area where jobs have declined just when traditional practitioners have changed somewhat.

The tensions connected with a dreadful job market are, in the abstract, predictable; in combination with affirmative-action efforts, they can become Behavioral Sink City. Experiments show that, in a hypothetical hiring situation, where the (hypothetical) job is given to a woman or minority member, each of 500 other applicants will assume that he would have gotten the job without undue or reverse discrimination—a mathematical impossibility.

Unreasoning prejudice is unleashed and intensified by a block-from-the-top hiring structure. I can remember male graduate students referring angrily, and openly, to a female faculty member as a "stupid . . ."—this on campus; I can remember a male faculty member disparaging female graduate students behind their backs, to other graduate students; I can remember the token hiring of a woman followed by one senior faculty member's joking (again on campus), "Well, thank God we don't have to do that again for another 20 years!"

Happily, the worst abuses would not be replicated as easily today. But persistent bias is often projected onto women indirectly. For example, the lesbian-cat-fight stereotype of competition between women can be projected onto a woman by a male colleague ("I'll bet other women are terribly jealous of you because of those . . ." whatever). Actually, in my experience, women have tended to be rather supportive of each other.

Credentials and Employment

Moving right along—from graduate school to a job—the tensions are, if anything, exacerbated. Anyone, on any kind of job, can get crossed with his/her boss. When the gender differential is combined with the power differential in the boss-subordinate relationship, however, it's really a stacked deck.

Department chairs, especially, can wield tremendous discretion in the professional development of their subordinates. Teaching schedules can be manipulated (every administrator knows that the instructor teaching at 3:00 p.m. gets worse teaching evaluations than one teaching the same course/students at 10:00 a.m.); student evaluations can be used selectively—misfiled, or lost, or culled for the best or worst; credentials can be misplaced, mischaracterized, or overlooked.

One woman in literature, applying for a job to a department less than receptive to women, took the precaution of submitting her credentials in two separate packets—one to the main department itself and another to the search committee. Her foresight was for naught. Not one, but both, packets of application credentials were "lost in the mail." Footnote: The department hired a man, in this case with several publications but very poor teaching, for the position.

When Admiral James Stockdale was, in effect, ousted from a department in one institution for being too popular a teacher, the fact was widely reported—and rightly so. When the same thing happens to a faculty member of less independent renown—and it happens more often to women—the event receives no press attention. I have certainly heard of departments reconstituting themselves as a lynch-mob-of-the-whole, and, in general, when such a dynamic develops, the hapless job/tenure candidate has little recourse. This particular dynamic is not new: C.P. Snow represented it (not targeted at a woman) in *The Masters*, decades ago.

Given the other forms of waspishness, the job-market pressures and the status anomaly of junior faculty especially, it is hardly surprising that the theoretically objective sphere of "publications" should be subject to its own problems. One is that, as noted, there is nothing objective about it. On average, men's writing will be adjudged clearer, more "factual," more evidentiary, and more "theoretical" than women's.

More generally, any publication (even once achieved) can be discounted, if the will to do so exists. Poetry and other "creative writing" sometimes does not count as "real" publication. Feminist or socially oriented scholarship can be devalued as "ideological." Anything co-authored can be devalued (and women co-author more than men, in the humanities), and, of course, anything interdisciplinary or "outside the field" can also be devalued (and women do more interdisciplinary and discipline-boundary work than men).

Perhaps the most blatant undervaluing of a woman's writing in literary history occurred when the young Charlotte Bronte wrote to the elder Wordsworth for advice—enclosing, poor creature, a manuscript. In the remarkable letter in response (which has been preserved), Wordsworth literally told Bronte to stick to her needlework and to forget about writing.

While a deterrent this blatant is less likely in today's academic realm (or at least less likely to be in writing), women still get published less than do their male counterparts. Across the board, they also serve less often as "principal investigator" in research projects. This cannot simply be the result of women's writing less (I have seen too many grant applications by women turned down, to credit the idea that women aren't trying to engage in research).

Interestingly, however, NCES figures do show that, on average, women faculty spend more time in teaching and with students than do men faculty, on average. This is partly because women are represented in larger numbers in the humanities, where more hours are engaged in teaching (as opposed to laboratory research). But, even in the sciences, women faculty are more likely to be assigned the lower-level and higher-contact job of student advising than men. The perception in all occupations, after all, is still that women do better in face-to-face, personal-interaction functions than men. This perception is by no means absent from higher education.

Actually, there may be some genuine difference in willingness to nurture. Certainly, the women who, in large part, staff writing programs spend a relatively high proportion of their time on teaching and attendant activity (paper-grading). At worst, the gender-and-workload demarcation within faculty ranks can become so apparent that one will see a composition bullpen full of dedicated (mostly) middle-aged women conferring with students over papers—passing, to approach the bullpen, empty offices of senior faculty away doing research.

But the segregation of regular faculty from the nontenured is typically intense, in any case; frequently they hardly see each other in the halls of academia, until the end-of-the-semester party given by the writing program—at which the women typically provide refreshments (assisted by the secretaries).

Racism and Sexism Far From Over

Abusive situations and abusive discourse reinforce each other. I would hardly try to settle the question of which causes which—a chicken-and-egg question. However nebulous a term "atmosphere" seems, discourse remains a sign of other, material problems. Given recent media attention (mostly, but not entirely, in conservative publications) to "free speech" issues on campus, I wonder whether the commentators assume that abusive speech—straightforward verbal abuse, ethnic, religious, sexual slurs—is a thing of the past. I write to reassure them on this point.

Perhaps, as I would hope, the day is past when a department chair can scribble on a job-application letter "We don't need another Polack" (as did a department chair I knew of). Perhaps the days of overtly rank ethnic prejudice, with male-bonding evenings of colleagues drinking and exchanging ethnic jokes, are mostly past. But I know from firsthand hearing that jokes about rape on campus are still with us ("doing a train—whoowhoo" for gang rape). Obscene references to women and women's body parts are widespread—not only in recreation places, or in the dorms or the frat houses, but in classrooms.

As one example, I was told about an anthropology professor who decided to ventilate the speech or epithet issues in a class. This particular professor taught at a well-regarded but not elite private institution, formerly all-male, where the student population is still male-majority (meaning that effectively the competition is stiffer for women in the admissions process—as with unofficial quotas limiting Asian-American students on various campuses).

Unfortunately, the invitation to openness opened a Pandora's box of gleefully sexist recitals, reflecting the underlying tensions implicit in the fact that the highest standings in each class were held mostly by women. Thus, the women on their campus were termed by the male students "psycho-dykes from hell"; the women they dated from a nearby women's college were "road cheese," (an obscene reference to sex in parked cars). Interestingly, in this atmosphere of defensive testosterone, men at a nearby military academy were consistently referred to as "fags."

I have not myself had a similar discussion in a classroom, and, on the whole, I think the behavior of my students has compared favorably to that of adults in responsible positions on campus. The worst single ethnic joke I can remember from the classroom was, "UCLA stands for United Caucasians Lost Among Asians." And the speaker noticed (after speaking) an Asian-American student in the same class, flushed, and so obviously felt distressed that there was no call to drive home any point about sensitivity. But my own relatively be-

nign experience does not alter the fact that hate crimes, racial, religious, other ethnic slurs, and related hate incidents, have become far too frequent on college campuses in recent years, and seem to be on the rise (surely in connection with a worsening economy).

Some Final—For This Paper—Thoughts

It is not within the scope of this article to exhaust all examples of bigotry or discrimination in higher education today. After all, it would be impossible to do so in one article. I have hardly touched on the topic of violence against women on college campuses—date rape and the rest; or the persistent association of "Greek systems" with violent hazing; or the perennial incidents of gay-bashing; or the abuses in athletic programs, which often bear hardest on those young athletes whose race or class make them most dependent on athletics for some upward mobility. But merely the politer abuses I have mentioned—endangering people's livelihoods rather than their lives—should be cause for concern.

•   •   •

International Union, UAW v. Johnson Controls, Inc.

111 S. Ct. 1196 (1991) United States Supreme Court

Justice Blackmun delivered the opinion of the Court.

In this case we are concerned with an employer's gender-based fetal-protection policy. May an employer exclude a fertile female employee from certain jobs because of its concern for the health of the fetus the woman might conceive?

I

Respondent Johnson Controls, Inc., manufactures batteries. In the manufacturing process, the element lead is a primary ingredient. Occupational exposure to lead entails health risks, including the risk of harm to any fetus carried by a female employee.

Before the Civil Rights Act of 1964 . . . became law, Johnson Controls did not employ any woman in a battery-manufacturing job. In June 1977, however, it announced its first official policy concerning its employment of women in lead-exposure work:

> "[P]rotection of the health of the unborn child is the immediate and direct responsibility of the prospective parents. While the medical profession and the company can support them in the exercise of this responsibility, it cannot assume it for them without simultaneously infringing their rights as persons.

. . .

". . . Since not all women who can become mothers wish to become mothers (or will become mothers), it would appear to be illegal discrimination to treat all who are capable of pregnancy as though they will become pregnant."

Consistent with that view, Johnson Controls "stopped short of excluding women capable of bearing children from lead exposure," but emphasized that a woman who expected to have a child should not choose a job in which she would have such exposure. The company also required a woman who wished to be considered for employment to sign a statement that she had been advised of the risk of having a child while she was exposed to lead. The statement informed the woman that although there was evidence "that women exposed to lead have a higher rate of abortion," this evidence was "not as clear . . . as the relationship between cigarette smoking and cancer," but that it was, "medically speaking, just good sense not to run that risk if you want children and do not want to expose the unborn child to risk, however small . . ."

Five years later, in 1982, Johnson Controls shifted from a policy of warning to a policy of exclusion. Between 1979 and 1983, eight employees became pregnant while maintaining blood lead levels in excess of 30 micrograms per deciliter. This appeared to be the critical level noted by the Occupational Health and Safety Administration (OSHA) for a worker who was planning to have a family. The company responded by announcing a broad exclusion of women from jobs that exposed them to lead:

> ". . . [I]t is [Johnson Controls'] policy that women who are pregnant or who are capable of bearing children will not be placed into jobs involving lead exposure or which could expose them to lead through the exercise of job bidding, bumping, transfer or promotion rights."

The policy defined "women . . . capable of bearing children" as "[a]ll women except those whose inability to bear children is medically documented." It is further stated that an unacceptable work station was one where, "over the past year," an em-

ployee had recorded a blood lead level of more than 30 micrograms per deciliter or the work site had yielded an air sample containing a lead level in excess of 30 micrograms per cubic meter.

II

In April 1984, petitioners filed . . . a class action challenging Johnson Controls' fetal-protection policy as sex discrimination that violated Title VII of the Civil Rights Act of 1964. Among the individual plaintiffs were petitioners Mary Craig, who had chosen to be sterilized in order to avoid losing her job, Elsie Nason, a 50-year-old divorcee, who had suffered a loss in compensation when she was transferred out of a job where she was exposed to lead, and Donald Penney, who had been denied a request for a leave of absence for the purpose of lowering his lead level because he intended to become a father.

• • •

III

The bias in Johnson Controls' policy is obvious. Fertile men, but not fertile women, are given a choice as to whether they wish to risk their reproductive health for a particular job. Section 703(a) of the Civil Rights Act of 1964 . . . prohibits sex-based classifications in terms and conditions of employment, in hiring and discharging decisions, and in other employment decisions that adversely affect an employee's status. Respondent's fetal-protection policy explicitly discriminates against women on the basis of their sex. The policy excludes women with childbearing capacity from lead-exposed jobs and so creates a facial classification based on gender. Respondent assumes as much in its brief before this court. . . .

Nevertheless, the Court of Appeals assumed, as did the two appellate courts who already had confronted the issue, that sex-specific fetal-protection policies do not involve facial discrimination. . . . That assumption, however, was incorrect.

First, Johnson Controls' policy classifies on the basis of gender and childbearing capacity, rather than fertility alone. Respondent does not seek to protect the unconceived children of all its employees. Despite evidence in the record about the debilitating effect of lead exposure on the male reproductive system, Johnson Controls is concerned only with the harms that may befall the unborn offspring of its female employees. . . . Johnson Controls' policy is facially discriminatory because it requires only a female employee to produce proof that she is not capable of reproducing.

Our conclusion is bolstered by the Pregnancy Discrimination Act of 1978 . . . in which Congress explicitly provided that, for purposes of Title VII, discrimination "on the basis of sex" includes discrimination "because of or on the basis of pregnancy, childbirth, or related medical conditions." . . . In its use of the words "capable of bearing children" in the 1982 policy statement as the criterion for exclusion, Johnson Controls explicitly classifies on the basis of potential for pregnancy. Under the PDA, such classification must be regarded, for the Title VII purposes, in the same light as explicit sex discrimination. Respondent has chosen to treat all its female employees as potentially pregnant; that choice evinces discrimination on the basis of sex.

IV

Under § 703(e)(1) of Title VII, an employer may discriminate on the basis of "religion, sex, or national origin in those certain instances where religion, sex, or national origin is a bona fide occupational qualification reasonably necessary to the normal operation of that particular business or enterprise." . . . We therefore turn to the question whether Johnson Controls' fetal-protection policy is one of those "certain instances" that come within the BFOQ exception. . . .

The wording of the BFOQ defense contains several terms of restriction that indicate that the exception reaches only special situations. The statute thus limits the situations in which discrimination is permissible to "certain instances" where sex discrimination is "reasonably necessary" to the "normal operation" of the "particular" business. Each of these terms—certain, normal, particular—prevents the use of general subjective standards and favors an objective, verifiable requirement. But the most telling term is "occupational"; this indicates that these objective, verifiable requirements must concern job-related skills and aptitudes.

Johnson Controls argues that its fetal-protection policy falls within the so-called safety exception to the BFOQ.

•　•　•

V

We have no difficulty concluding that Johnson Controls cannot establish a BFOQ. Fertile women, as far as appears in the record, participate in the manufacture of batteries as efficiently as anyone else. Johnson Controls' professed moral and ethical concerns about the welfare of the next generation do not suffice to establish a BFOQ of female sterility. Decisions about the welfare of future children must be left to the parents who conceive, bear, support, and raise them rather than to the employers who hire those parents. Congress has mandated this choice through Title VII, as amended by the Pregnancy Discrimination Act. Johnson Controls has attempted to exclude women because of their reproductive capacity. Title VII and the PDA simply do not allow a woman's dismissal because of her failure to submit to sterilization.

Nor can concerns about the welfare of the next generation be considered a part of the "essence" of Johnson Controls' business.

•　•　•

VI

A word about tort liability and the increased cost of fertile women in the workplace is perhaps necessary. One of the dissenting judges in this case expressed concern about an employer's tort liability and concluded that liability for a potential injury to a fetus is a social cost that Title VII does not require a company to ignore. . . . It is correct to say that Title VII does not prevent the employer from having a conscience. The statute, however, does prevent sex-specific fetal-protection policies.

•　•　•

The tort-liability argument reduces to two equal unpersuasive propositions. First, Johnson Controls attempts to solve the problem of reproductive health hazards by resorting to an exclusionary policy. Title VII plainly forbids illegal sex discrimination as a method of diverting attention from an employer's obligation to police the workplace. Second, the spectre of an award of damages reflects a fear that hiring fertile women will cost more. The extra cost of employing members of one sex, however, does not provide an affirmative Title VII defense for a discriminatory refusal to hire members of that gender. . . . Indeed, in passing the PDA, Congress considered at length the considerable cost of providing equal treatment of pregnancy and related conditions, but made the "decision to forbid special treatment of pregnancy despite the social costs associated therewith." . . .

We, of course, are not presented with, nor do we decide, a case in which costs would be so prohibitive as to threaten the survival of the employer's business. We merely reiterate our prior holdings that the incremental cost of hiring women cannot justify discriminating against them.

•   •   •

Title VII and Restrictions on Employment of Fertile Women

Hugh M. Finneran

During the decade of the 1970s, there was a rapid expansion of the female work force accompanied by a simultaneous expansion of scientific knowledge concerning hazards of exposure to toxic substances in the workplace. Health hazards in industry present serious legal, medical, and sociological issues.

Recently, a dramatic awareness of the hazards to the employee's reproductive capacity, i.e., miscarriage, stillbirth, and birth defects, has materialized. The hazard to the reproductive capacity and fetal damage is not a unique problem for female workers. Rather, it is a problem which may impact upon all workers. This article, however, will restrict its analysis to factual situations where the employer considers the problems of exposure to chemicals as uniquely, or primarily, arising out of the female physiology and either restricts or refuses to hire females with childbearing ability. Physical conditions other than chemical substances may also be harmful to the fetus, i.e., radiation, heat stress, vibration, and noise, but will not be treated in this article. . . .

Title VII of the Civil Rights Act of 1964 incorporates two theories of discrimination which must be considered in a legal analysis of restrictions (the term "restriction" includes a refusal to hire) placed on females because of health hazards. These are:

disparate treatment and policies, practices, or procedures with disparate impact not justified by business necessity.

Two types of substances will be considered in this article: teratogens and mutagens. Teratogens are substances that can harm the fetus after conception by entering the placenta. Mutagens are substances that can cause a change in the genetic material in living cells.

Disparate Treatment

The Supreme Court in *International Brotherhood of Teamsters v. United States* stated: "Disparate treatment . . . is the most easily understood type of discrimination. The employer simply treats some people less favorably than others because of their race, color, religion, sex, or national origin. Proof of discriminatory motive is critical, although it can in some instances be inferred from the mere fact of differences in treatment. . . ."

The Equal Employment Opportunity Commission and the United States Department of Labor on February 1, 1980, issued, for comment, Interpretive Guidelines on Employment Discrimination and Reproductive Hazards. "An employer/contractor whose work environment involves employee exposure to reproductive hazards shall not discriminate on the basis of sex (including pregnancy or childbearing capacity) in hiring, work assignment, or other conditions of employment."

An employer's policy of protecting female em-

Reproduced with permission from *Labor Law Journal*, vol. 31, no. 4 (April 1980). Published and copyrighted © 1980 by Commerce Clearing House, Inc., 2700 Lake Cook Road, Riverwoods, IL 60015, 1-800-TELL-CCH.

ployees from reproductive hazards by depriving them of employment opportunities without any scientific data is a per se violation of Title VII. The Guidelines' position, however, is that the exclusion of women with childbearing ability from the workplace is a per se violation. To arrive at such a conclusion without an analysis of the precise scientific and medical evidence is an erroneous and indefensible legal standard. Thus, an employer's exclusion of females on the basis of their susceptibility to the mutagenic effects of a toxic substance should not be a per se violation but should be analyzed under the rubric of disparate treatment or adverse impact.

One line of inquiry under the disparate treatment analysis would be whether the mutagenic substance has reproductive hazards for male and female employees. If the particular chemical substance has a mutagenic effect on male and female employees, the obvious question is why female workers are treated differently. The answer may be scientifically explained, but it raises the issue of disparate treatment. Indeed, the employer should consider whether there are any other substances in the workplace, other than the substance relied on to exclude the female, which have mutagenic effects on males.

In essence, if the basis for the exclusion is the mutagenic characteristics of a substance, the employer would have to treat all employees, male and female, who are exposed to mutagenic effects in the same manner. The employer may face a serious possibility of a Title VII violation for disparate treatment unless the scientific justification for the differential treatment is very persuasive.

In establishing a prima facie case of sex discrimination, under the principles of *McDonnell Douglas Corp. v. Green* a female must show that: she belongs to a protected class; she applied or was qualified for a job for which the employer was seeking applicants; and despite her qualifications, she was rejected. She also must prove that, after her rejection, the employer continued to seek applicants with her qualifications.

Applying the *McDonnell Douglas* principles to a restriction on female employment, the female could establish a prima facie case of sex discrimination if a chemical substance has a mutagenic effect on the males but only females are excluded from exposure to the hazard by the employer's restrictive policy. In this assumed factual situation,

the very basis for the restriction would be applicable to either of sex discrimination, the employer has the burden of proving the existence of a business necessity or a bona fide occupational qualification. Of course, proof of compelling scientific data that the degree or severity of risk was substantially greater might alter the existence of a prima facie case, but the court more likely would consider such evidence as an affirmative defense.

Gender-Based Classification

Varying the factual assumptions, let us consider the existence of a work environment in which the chemical substance is a teratogen and an employer restricts the employment of females with childbearing ability. In these circumstances, the employer could argue that the exclusion is based on a neutral health factor rather than sex-based criteria. Since teratogens by definition harm a fetus after conception, the safety hazard is present only for females with childbearing ability and cannot affect males or females without childbearing ability. Thus a strong argument could be presented that the exclusion of females based upon the teratogenic effect of a chemical substance is a health classification and is not gender based.

In *Geduldig v. Aiello*, the Supreme Court ruled that the exclusion of pregnancy-related disabilities from a state disability system was not sex discrimination but was a distinction based on physical condition "by dividing potential recipients into two groups—pregnant women and non-pregnant persons." Likewise, *General Electric Co. v. Gilbert* viewed pregnancy classifications as not being gender based.

At least one commentator has criticized the relevance of *Gilbert* and *Aiello* to the restriction of female employment in toxic workplaces, because the classification suffers from overinclusiveness since "many women in the excluded class delay or plan to avoid childbearing and thus face no additional risk at all." This contention is small comfort to an employer, however, since women have been known to change their plans and birth-control techniques are not universally effective.

Furthermore, some teratogens are cumulative and remain in the body long after the exposure has ceased. The legal issue is more complex where there is a restriction on the employment of a woman with childbearing ability where teratogens are present but mutagens with adverse reproductive effects present in the workplace affect males on whom no restrictions are placed.

The Pregnancy Disability Amendment to Title VII may have a bearing on the issue of whether the classification is gender based. "The terms 'because of sex' or 'on the basis of sex' include, but are not limited to, because of or on the basis of pregnancy, childbirth, or related medical conditions. . . ."

The Pregnancy Amendment to Title VII does not state expressly that the terms "because of sex" or "on the basis of sex" includes a woman's childbearing ability or potential. The Guidelines, however, interpret "childbearing capacity" as prohibited by the Amendment. Such an interpretation is not without some doubt as to its validity. Nevertheless, if the Guidelines' construction is correct, a distinction based on childbearing ability would be considered gender-based disparate treatment. The practical consequences may be minimal since exclusions or restrictions on the employment of females with childbearing ability has a disparate impact and is best analyzed in this context.

Disparate Impact

The Supreme Court in *Griggs v. Duke Power Co.* held: "Under the Act, practices, procedures, or tests neutral on their face, and even neutral in terms of intent, cannot be maintained if they operate to 'freeze' the status quo of prior discriminatory employment practices." Thus, *Griggs* ruled that the employer's requirement of a high school diploma or passage of a test as a condition of employment was a prima facie race violation of Title VII, unless these requirements are a "business necessity." "The Act proscribes not only overt discrimination but also practices that are fair in form but discriminatory in operation. The touchstone is business necessity."

In *Dothard v. Rawlinson,* the Supreme Court held that the employer violated Title VII by requiring a minimum height of five feet two inches and a weight of 120 pounds for prison guards since the policy had a disparate impact on women. Likewise, *Nashville Gas Co. v. Satty* is relevant to the issue. In *Satty,* the employer denied accumulated seniority

to female employees returning from pregnancy leaves of absence. The Court held that an employer may not "burden female employees in such a way as to deprive them of employment opportunities because of their different role." The conclusion appears inescapable that an employer's restriction on the employment of women with childbearing ability, and this includes restrictions limited to specific jobs, is a prima facie violation of Title VII's proscriptions against sex discrimination under *Griggs, Dothard,* and *Satty.*

Bona Fide Occupational Qualification

Two affirmative defenses must be considered: bona fide occupational qualification [BFOQ] and business necessity. Title VII provides an affirmative defense to a charge of sex discrimination where sex "is a bona fide occupational qualification reasonably necessary to the normal operation of that particular business or enterprise. . . ."

The Guidelines state: "narrow exception [for BFOQ] pertains only to situations where all or substantially all of the protected class is unable to perform the duties of the job in question. Such cannot be the case in the reproductive hazards setting, where exclusions are based on the premise of danger to the employee or fetus and not on the ability to perform." Under *Weeks v. Southern Bell Telephone & Telegraph Co.,* an employer relying on the bona fide occupational qualification exception "has the burden of proving that he had reasonable cause to believe, that is, a factual basis for believing, that all or substantially all women would be unable to perform safely and efficiently the duties of the job involved."

In the absence of medical evidence to the contrary, an employer's assumption is that all, or substantially all, females have the capacity of bearing children. Thus, the area of controversy will probably center on the issue of whether the safety of the fetus or future generations is reasonably necessary to the normal operation of the employer's business. However, plaintiffs may argue that all or substantially all females are not at risk since not all females plan to have a family.

Courts have sustained decisions by bus companies not to hire drivers over specified ages as being a BFOQ justified by increased safety hazards for third persons. In *Hodgson v. Greyhound Lines, Inc.,* the company refused to consider applications for intercity bus drivers from individuals thirty-five years of age or older. The Seventh Circuit held that the company was not guilty of age discrimination, since its hiring policy was a BFOQ justified by the increased hazards to third persons caused by hiring older drivers. "Greyhound must demonstrate that it has a rational basis in fact to believe that elimination of its maximum hiring age will increase the likelihood of risk of harm to its passengers. Greyhound need only demonstrate however a minimal increase in risk of harm for it is enough to show that elimination of the hiring policy might jeopardize the life of one more person than might otherwise occur under the present hiring practice."

The Fifth Circuit in *Usery v. Tamiami Trail Tours, Inc.,* in upholding the company's refusal to hire bus drivers over forty years of age, found that the policy was a BFOQ. The company had demonstrated "that the passenger-endangering characteristics of over-forty job applicants cannot practically be ascertained by some hiring test other than automatic exclusion on the basis of age."

The language of the BFOQ exception under the Age Discrimination Act is essentially the same as the language of the BFOQ exception under Title VII of the Civil Rights Act. Cases in the airline industry also have considered third-party safety as a sufficient BFOQ in situations involving involuntary pregnancy leaves of absence for flight attendants.

The concept of concern for third parties is sufficiently elastic to include the unborn. It is submitted that society, including employers, has an obligation to avoid action which will have an adverse effect on the health and well-being of future generations. With all the present concerns about the protection of our environment and endangered species, an enlightened judiciary should not callously turn its back on generations unborn. Indeed, on the more mundane and pragmatic basis, it is of the essence of a business venture to operate safely in a manner which avoids costly tort liability.

Business Necessity

The business necessity defense may also justify the exclusionary or restrictive practice. In order to prove this defense, the employer has the burden of establishing that: the practice is necessary to the safe and efficient operation of the business; the purpose must be sufficiently compelling to override the adverse impact; and the practice must carry out the business purpose. The employer also must establish that there are not acceptable alternative policies or practices which would better accomplish the business purpose or accomplish it with lesser adverse impact on the protected class.

Prenatal Injury

Since the safe and efficient operation is premised on the need to protect the fetus, tort law relating to prenatal injuries is pertinent. The potential tort liability bears on the necessity for the exclusion. The law of Texas will be reviewed in regard to prenatal injuries. Texas was selected because of its large petrochemical industry.

The parents of a child suffering prenatal injuries resulting in its death have cause of action under the Texas wrongful death statute, provided the child was born alive and was viable at the time the injury was inflicted. In so ruling, the court stated that the statutory requirement of the Texas wrongful death statute, that the deceased has suffered an injury for which he could have recovered damages had he survived, was met. This holding of necessity implied that the Texas Supreme Court recognized a cause of action for a surviving child who is born alive with a birth defect caused by prenatal injuries. For a child born with birth defects, the cause of action exists for prenatal injuries at any time during pregnancy.

The Texas courts apparently have not yet decided whether parents have a cause of action under the wrongful death statute in cases where a child is stillborn due to prenatal injuries. The inquiry in such a case would revolve around the issue of whether a fetus is a person within the meaning of the wrongful death statute. Other state courts interpreting their wrongful death statutes have split on the issue.

Assuming the liability is established, Texas courts allow surviving parents to recover damages under the wrongful death act to compensate them for the pecuniary value of the child's service that would have been rendered during minority, less the cost and expense of the child's support, education, and maintenance, as well as economic benefits reasonably expected to have been contributed after reaching majority.

While it is generally held that some evidence of pecuniary loss is necessary to support a wrongful death judgment, the Texas courts have recognized that such proof cannot be supplied with any certainty or accuracy in cases involving young infants. Therefore, they leave the damages question largely to the discretion of the jury. Of course, a prenatally injured infant who manages to survive would be able to sue for his own personal injuries, including pain and suffering, loss of earning capacity, and any other damages, if applicable. Recognizing the "deep pocket syndrome," employers have a reasonable basis for being concerned about large tort recoveries.

The female employee's willing and informed consent to the assumption of the risk is not binding to the unborn child. Hence, obtaining a waiver from the female employee is an act with no legal significance other than documenting the employer's awareness of the unavoidably unsafe condition of the workplace for the fetus for use against the employer in tort litigation.

The employer should not be required to assume the risk of significant tort liability which could threaten the very existence of the enterprise, depending on the financial assets of the employer and the severity of injuries. Courts have required employers in discrimination cases to assume additional expense to achieve compliance with Title VII (costs of validation studies, loss of customer patronage, and training costs), but it is submitted that the magnitude of the risks of exposure to prenatal injuries and reproduction hazards should result in a different decision. The financial impact on the employer is important but certainly not the most important factor. A lifetime of suffering by future generations is worthy of societal concern. The Civil Rights Act does not exist in a vacuum.

Whether the purpose of the restriction is sufficiently compelling to override the adverse impact on women and is necessary to accomplish the employer's business purpose of ensuring a safe workplace without reproductive hazards will be decided by the scientific and medical data relating to the severity of the health hazard of the particular substance.

Less Restrictive Alternatives

Under the business necessity principles of *Robinson v. Lorillard*, the employer must demonstrate the absence of "less restrictive alternatives" before relying on the affirmative defense. The Guidelines indicate that four factors should be considered. These are: whether the employer is complying with applicable occupational federal, state, and local safety and health laws; respirators or other protective devices are used to minimize or eliminate the hazard; product substitution is used; and affected employees are transferred without loss of pay or other benefits to areas of the plant where the reproductive hazard is minimal or nonexistent.

The employer's obligation to comply with its safety obligations under the Occupational Safety and Health Act is eminently reasonable, provided that it is recognized that the employer's obligation under OSHA only requires the use of technologically and economically feasible engineering and administrative controls. If engineering and administrative controls are not feasible, the employer must protect his employees by the use of personal protective devices. It is fair and reasonable to require an employer to satisfy his legal obligations under safety and health laws before excluding females from the workplace.

To suggest, however, that the employers change their products or provide rate retention for employees restricted from hazardous exposure is extreme and without legislative support. If Congress had intended to require substitution of products and rate retention for employees under Title VII, it would have done so explicitly. When, as here, these matters are at best tangentially related to nondiscrimination, Title VII is silent on the subject, and wages and rates of pay and seniority of workers transferred to jobs other than their usual jobs are mandatory subjects of collective bargaining, then a reasonable interpretation of the legislation is that Title VII does not impose this obligation of management.

If an employer intends to sustain his business necessity defense, there must be evidence that the employer has explored the feasible alternatives to imposing restrictions on the employment of fertile females. One alternative which must be considered is a system for individual screening and evaluation with restrictions imposed on the female only if she becomes pregnant. Serious medical questions are posed by this alternative. Indeed, for some teratogenic substances the first weeks of pregnancy are the most critical. During this period, a woman may not know that she is pregnant, and sophisticated tests may not reveal the pregnancy. The administration of such a program might raise serious personnel problems since female employees might object to continuous monitoring to determine whether they are pregnant.

Conclusion

The decade of the 1970s was the era of the testing cases under Title VII. The decade of the 1980s wil be the era of large class actions involving the exclusion of fertile females from exposure to reproductive hazards.

On the extreme of one side will be those arguing that Title VII rejects these protections as Victorian, romantic paternalism which deprives the individual woman of the power to decide whether the economic benefits justify the risks. On the other extreme, some employers will argue that any possible risk of harm to the female's offspring require her exclusion.

An informed judiciary should consider not only the economic interests of the female employee and the employer but the societal concern for the quality and happiness of future generations as well. The Supreme Court in *Roe v. Wade* recognized that a state may properly assert important interests in protecting potential life. After evaluating the level, duration, and manner of exposure in the specific employer's workplace, if there is reputable scientific evidence of a recognized reproductive hazard, either from a mutagen with significantly greater risk for female workers or a teratogen, the employer should be allowed to exclude females from that workplace if the business necessity criteria are satisfied. The employer should have the right and, indeed, the duty and obligation to operate his facility with due concern for the safety and health of future generations.

Fetal Protection and Employment Discrimination—The *Johnson Controls* Case

George J. Annas

Employers have historically limited women's access to traditionally male, high-paying jobs.[1] In one famous case early in this century, the U.S. Supreme Court upheld an Oregon law that forbade hiring women for jobs that required more than 10 hours of work a day in factories. The Chief Justice explained that this restriction was reasonable because "healthy mothers are essential to vigorous offspring" and preserving the physical well-being of women helps "preserve the strength and vigor of the race."[2] This rationale was never particularly persuasive, and women's hours have not been limited in traditionally female, low-paid fields

From George J. Annas, "Fetal Protection and Employment Discrimination—The *Johnson Controls* Case," *The New England Journal of Medicine*, vol. 325, no. 10 (September 5, 1991), 740–743. Copyright © 1991 by The Massachusetts Medical Society. All rights reserved.

of employment, such as nursing. Although such blatant sex discrimination in employment is a thing of the past, the average man continues to earn "almost 50 percent more per hour than does the average woman of the same race, age, and education."[3]

The contemporary legal question has become whether employers can substitute concern for fetal health for concern for women's health as an argument for limiting job opportunities for women. The U.S. Supreme Court decided in March 1991 that the answer is no and that federal law prohibits employers from excluding women from job categories on the basis that they are or might become pregnant.[4] All nine justices agreed that the "fetal-protection policy" adopted by Johnson Controls, Inc., to restrict jobs in the manufacture of batteries to men and sterile women was a violation of law, and six of the nine agreed that federal law prohibits any discrimination solely on the basis of possible or actual pregnancy. The ruling in *International Union* v. *Johnson Controls* applies to all employers engaged in interstate commerce, including hospitals and clinics.

Title VII of the Civil Rights Act of 1964 forbids employers to discriminate on the basis of race, color, religion, sex, or national origin. Explicit discrimination on the basis of religion, sex, or national origin can be justified only if the characteristic is a "bona fide occupational qualification." The federal Pregnancy Discrimination Act of 1978 made it clear that sex discrimination includes discrimination "on the basis of pregnancy, childbirth, or related conditions."[5]

The Fetal-Protection Policy of Johnson Controls

Beginning in 1977, Johnson Controls advised women who expected to have children not to take jobs involving exposure to lead, warned women who took such jobs of the risks entailed in having a child while being exposed to lead, and recommended that workers consult their family doctors for advice. The risks were said to include a higher rate of spontaneous abortion as well as unspecified potential risks to the fetus. Between 1979 and 1983, eight employees became pregnant while their blood lead levels were above 30 μg per deciliter (1.45 μmol per liter)(a level the Centers for Disease Control had designated as excessive for children). Although there was no evidence of harm due to lead exposure in any of the children born to the employees, a medical consultant for the company said that he thought hyperactivity in one of the children "could very well be and probably was due to the lead he had."[6]

In 1982, apparently after consulting medical experts about the dangers to the fetus of exposure to lead, the company changed its policy from warning to exclusion:

> . . . women who are pregnant or who are capable of bearing children will not be placed into jobs involving lead exposure or which could expose them to lead through the exercise of job bidding, bumping, transfer, or promotion rights.

The policy defined women capable of bearing children as all women except those who "have medical confirmation that they cannot bear children."

In 1984, a class-action suit was brought challenging the policy as a violation of Title VII of the Civil Rights Act of 1964. In 1988, a federal district court ruled in favor of Johnson Controls, primarily on the basis of depositions and affidavits from physicians and environmental toxicologists regarding the damage that exposure to lead could cause in developing fetuses, children, adults, and animals.[7] The U.S. Court of Appeals for the Seventh Circuit affirmed this decision in 1989 in a seven-to-four opinion.[6] The majority based its opinion primarily on the medical evidence of potential harm to the fetus and on their view that federal law permitted employers to take this potential harm into account in developing employment policies.

The Supreme Court's Decision

The U.S. Supreme Court unanimously reversed the decision in an opinion written by Justice Harry Blackmun. The Court had no trouble finding that the bias in the policy was "obvious," since "fertile men, but not fertile women, are given a choice as to whether they wish to risk their reproductive health for a particular job."[4] The Court noted that the company did not seek to protect all unconceived children, only those of its female employees. The policy was based on the potential for pregnancy and, accordingly, directly in conflict with the Pregnancy Discrimination Act of 1978. The key to the case was determining whether the absence of pregnancy or the absence of the potential to become pregnant was a bona fide occupational qualification for a job in battery manufacturing.

Employment discrimination is permitted "in those certain instances where religion, sex, or national origin is a bona fide occupational qualification reasonably necessary to the normal operation of that particular business or enterprise."[4] The Court's approach was to determine whether Johnson Controls' fetal-protection policy came within the scope of those "certain instances." The statutory language requires that the occupational qualification affect "an employee's ability to do the job."[4]

The Court determined that the defense was available only when it went to the "essence of the business" or was "the core of the employee's job performance."[4]

The Court had previously allowed a maximum-security prison for men to refuse to hire women guards because "the employment of a female guard would create real risks of safety to others if violence broke out because the guard was a woman." Thus, sex was seen as reasonably related to the essence of the guard's job: maintaining prison security. Similarly, other courts had permitted airlines to lay off pregnant flight attendants if it was considered necessary to protect the safety of passengers. The Court agreed that protecting the safety or security of customers was related to the essence of the business and was legitimate.

The welfare of unconceived fetuses, however, did not fit into either category of exception. In the Court's words, "No one can disregard the possibility of injury to future children; the BFOQ [bona fide occupational qualification], however, is not so broad that it transforms this deep social concern into an essential aspect of battery making." Limitations involving pregnancy or sex "must relate to ability to perform the duties of the job. . . . Women as capable of doing their jobs as their male counterparts may not be forced to choose between having a child and having a job." The Court concluded that Congress had left the welfare of the next generation to parents, not employers: "Decisions about the welfare of future children must be left to the parents who conceive, bear, support, and raise them rather than to the employers who hire those parents."[4]

The Court finally addressed potential tort liability should a fetus be injured by its mother's occupational exposure and later sue the company. The Court wrote that since the Occupational Safety and Health Administration (OSHA) had concluded that there was no basis for excluding women of childbearing age from exposure to lead at the minimal levels permitted under its guidelines, the likelihood of fetal injury was slight. And even if injury should occur, the injured child would have to prove that the employer had been negligent. If the employer followed OSHA guidelines and fully informed its workers of the risks involved, the Court concluded that liability seemed "remote at best."

Thus, just as speculation about risks to children not yet conceived has nothing to do with job performance, speculation about future tort liability—at least one step further removed from harm to the fetus—is not job-related.

The Concurring Opinions

Justice Byron White wrote the main concurring opinion for himself, Chief Justice William Rehnquist, and Justice Anthony Kennedy. Although they agreed with the outcome in this case, they dissented from the bona fide occupational-qualification analysis as it applied to tort liability, and warned that the case could be used to undercut certain privacy rights. These three justices believed that under some circumstances it should be permissible for employers to exclude women from employment on the grounds that their fetuses could be injured and sue the employers (the women themselves could not sue because they would be covered by workers' compensation as their exclusive remedy). Their rationale was that parents cannot waive the right of their children to sue, that the parents' negligence will not be imputed to the children, and that even in the absence of negligence, "it is possible that employers will be held strictly liable, if, for example, their manufacturing process is considered."[4] Avoiding such liability was, in the view of these justices, a safety issue relevant to the bona fide occupational-qualification standard.

The other point made by the three justices was relegated to a footnote, but it is of substantial interest. They argued that the Court's opinion could be read to outlaw considerations of privacy as a justification for employment discrimination on the basis of sex because considerations of privacy would not directly relate to the employees' ability to do the job or to customers' safety. They cited cases in which the privacy-related wishes of some patients to be cared for by nurses and nurses' aides of the same sex had been upheld as a bona fide occupational qualification, including an instance regarding the sex of nurses' aides in a retirement home[8] and a policy excluding male nurses from obstetrical practice in one hospital.[9] The justices in the majority responded to this issue by saying simply, "We have never addressed privacy-based sex discrimination and shall not do so here because the sex-based discrimination at issue today does not involve the privacy interests of Johnson Controls' customers."[4] This issue has been left for another day, but it should be noted that the obstetrical-nurse case rests on outmoded judicial stereotyping of obstetricians as men and nurses as women.[10]

Implications of the Decision

The Court took the language of the Pregnancy Discrimination Act seriously, correctly observing that "concern for a woman's existing or potential offspring historically has been the excuse for denying women equal employment opportunities."[4] The purpose of the act was to end such employment discrimination, and the Court's opinion in *Johnson Controls* holds that recasting sex discrimination in the name of fetal protection is illegal. Johnson Controls had argued that its policy was ethical and socially responsible and that it was meant only to prevent exposing the fetus to avoidable risk. Judge Frank Easterbrook probably has the most articulate response to this concern in his dissent from the appeals-court decision:

> There is a strong correlation between the health of the infant and prenatal medical care; there is also a powerful link between the parents' income and infants' health, for higher income means better nutrition, among other things. . . . Removing women from well-paying jobs (and the attendant health insurance), or denying women access to these jobs, may reduce the risk from lead while also reducing levels of medical care and quality of nutrition.[6]

Judge Easterbrook argued that ultimately fetal-protection policies cannot require "zero risk" but must be based on reasonable risk. He correctly noted that it is good and reasonable to worry about the health of workers and their future children. But,

> to insist on *zero* risk . . . is to exclude women from industrial jobs that have been a male preserve. By all means let society lend its energies to improving the prospects of those who come after us. Demanding zero risk produces not progress but paralysis.[6]

The same zero-risk analysis can, of course, be applied to the possibility of tort liability as seen from the industry's perspective. The industry would like its risk to be zero. Six of the nine judges agreed that it is close to zero, or at least remote. As a factual matter, there has been only one recorded case of a child's bringing a lawsuit for injuries suffered while the mother was pregnant and continued to work. In this case, the jury found in favor of the employer, even though there was evidence that the employer had violated OSHA safety standards.[11] Two thirds of the justices on the U.S. Supreme Court think that state tort liability is preempted so long as the employer follows federal law, informs workers of the risks, and is not negligent. Added to this is the extraordinarily difficult issue of causation, even if the employer is negligent. Putting the two together may not eliminate all risk of liability, but the risk is as small as can reasonably be expected.

It has been persuasively suggested that fetal-protection policies that affect only women are based on the view that women are "primarily biologic actors" and not economic ones and that men are only economic actors who have no "biologic connections and responsibilities to their families."[12] The decision in *Johnson Controls* continues the legal and social movement to provide equality of opportunity in the workplace. It does not eliminate the duty to minimize workplace exposure to toxic substances. Indeed, it would be a hollow victory for women to gain the right to be exposed to the same high levels of mutagens and other toxic substances that men are exposed to. The real challenge for public policy remains to turn industry's focus away from new methods of sex discrimination and toward new ways to reduce workplace hazards. In this area, physicians continue to have a prominent role.

Physicians specializing in occupational health should continue to work to reduce exposure to toxic substances in the workplace for all workers (by replacing such agents with other, less toxic substances, reducing their volume, and encouraging the use of protective gear). In addition, all workers should be warned about the health risks of all clinically important exposures that cannot be avoided, and encouraged to be monitored for the early signs of damage. Personal physicians should take a careful occupational history and be sufficiently informed to be able to tell their patients about the risks of exposure to various substances, including what is known about their mutagenicity and teratogenicity.[13] Armed with this information, workers—both men and women—will be able to make informed decisions about their jobs and the risks they are willing to run to keep them, as well as to pressure management intelligently to make the workplace safer.

Congress and the Court have made a strong statement about the use of fetal protection as a rationale to control or restrict the activities and decisions of women: the ultimate decision maker must be the worker herself. This policy is consistent with good medical practice as well—as is evident, for instance, in the policy of the American College of Obstetricians and Gynecologists on "maternal-fetal conflicts."[14] To paraphrase Justice Blackmun, it is no more appropriate for physicians to attempt to control women's opportunities and choices on the basis of their reproductive role than it is for the courts or individual employers to do so.

NOTES

1. Becker ME. From *Muller v. Oregon* to fetal vulnerability policies, 53 U. Chicago Law Rev. 1219 (1986).
2. Muller v. Oregon, 208 U.S. 412 (1908).
3. Fuchs VR. Sex differences in economic well-being. Science 1986; 232:459–64.
4. International Union v. Johnson Controls, 111 S.CT. 1196 (1991).
5. Pregnancy Discrimination Act of 1978, 92 Stat. 2076, 42 U.S.C. sec 2000e (k).
6. International Union v. Johnson Controls, 886 F.2d 871 (7th Cir. 1989) (en banc).
7. International Union v. Johnson Controls, 680 F. Supp. 309 (E.D. Wis. 1988).
8. Fesel v. Masonic Home of Delaware, 447 F. Supp. 1346 (D.Del. 1978).
9. Buckus v. Baptist Medical Center, 510 F. Supp. 1191 (E.D.Ark. 1981).
10. Sex in the delivery room: is the nurse a boy or a girl? In: Annas GJ. Judging medicine. Clifton, N.J.: Humana Press, 1988:53–6.
11. Security National Bank v. Chloride Industrial Battery, 602 F. Supp. 294 (D.Kan. 1985).
12. Becker ME. Can employers exclude women to protect children? JAMA 1990; 264:2113–7.
13. [Mutagenicity is the capacity to cause mutations; teratogenicity is the capacity to cause developmental malformations.—Ed.]
14. American College of Obstetricians and Gynecologists Committee opinion no. 55, Committee on Ethics. Patient choice: maternal-fetal conflict. Washington, D.C.: American College of Obstetricians and Gynecologists, 1987.

Ellison v. Brady

United States Court of Appeals, Ninth Circuit, 1991.
924 F.2d 872.

Before BEEZER AND KOZINSKI, CIRCUIT JUDGES, AND STEPHENS, DISTRICT JUDGE.

BEEZER, CIRCUIT JUDGE:

Kerry Ellison worked as a revenue agent for the Internal Revenue Service in San Mateo, California. During her initial training in 1984 she met Sterling Gray, another trainee, who was also assigned to the San Mateo office. The two co-workers never became friends, and they did not work closely together.

Gray's desk was twenty feet from Ellison's desk, two rows behind and one row over. Revenue agents in the San Mateo office often went to lunch in groups. In June of 1986 when no one else was in the office, Gray asked Ellison to lunch. She accepted. Gray had to pick up his son's forgotten lunch, so they stopped by Gray's house. He gave Ellison a tour of his house.

Ellison alleges that after the June lunch Gray started to pester her with unnecessary questions and hang around her desk. On October 9, 1986, Gray asked Ellison out for a drink after work. She declined, but she suggested that they have lunch the following week. She did not want to have lunch alone with him, and she tried to stay away from the office during lunch time. One day during the following week, Gray uncharacteristically dressed in a three-piece suit and asked Ellison out for lunch. Again, she did not accept.

On October 22, 1986 Gray handed Ellison a note he wrote on a telephone message slip which read:

> I cried over you last night and I'm totally drained today. I have never been in such constant term oil (sic). Thank you for talking with me. I could not stand to feel your hatred for another day.

When Ellison realized that Gray wrote the note, she became shocked and frightened and left the room. Gray followed her into the hallway and demanded that she talk to him but she left the building.

Ellison later showed the note to Bonnie Miller, who supervised both Ellison and Gray. Miller said "this is sexual harassment." Ellison asked Miller not to do anything about it. She wanted to try to handle it herself. Ellison asked a male co-worker to talk to Gray, to tell him that she was not interested in him and to leave her alone. The next day, Thursday, Gray called in sick.

Ellison did not work on Friday, and on the following Monday, she started four weeks of training in St. Louis, Missouri. Gray mailed her a card and a typed, single-spaced, three-page letter. She describes this letter as "twenty times, a hundred times weirder" than the prior note. Gray wrote, in part:

> I know that you are worth knowing with or without sex . . . Leaving aside the hassles and disasters of recent weeks. I have enjoyed you so much over these past few months. Watching you. Experiencing you from O so far away. Admiring your style and elan . . . . Don't you think it odd that two people who have never even talked together, alone, are striking off such intense sparks . . . I will [write] another letter in the near future.[1]

Explaining her reaction, Ellison stated: "I just thought he was crazy. I thought he was nuts. I didn't know what he would do next. I was frightened."

She immediately telephoned Miller. Ellison told her supervisor that she was frightened and really upset. She requested that Miller transfer either her or Gray because she would not be comfortable working in the same office with him. Miller asked Ellison to send a copy of the card and letter to San Mateo.

Miller then telephoned her supervisor, Joe Benton, and discussed the problem. That same day she had a counseling session with Gray. She informed him that he was entitled to union representation. During this meeting, she told Gray to leave Ellison alone.

At Benton's request, Miller apprised the labor relations department of the situation. She also reminded Gray many times over the next few weeks that he must not contact Ellison in any way. Gray subsequently transferred to the San Francisco office on November 24, 1986. Ellison returned from St. Louis in late November and did not discuss the matter further with Miller.

After three weeks in San Francisco, Gray filed union grievances requesting a return to the San Mateo office. The IRS and the union settled the grievances in Gray's favor, agreeing to allow him to transfer back to the San Mateo office provided that he spend four more months in San Francisco and promise not to bother Ellison. On January 28, 1987, Ellison first learned of Gray's request in a letter from Miller explaining that Gray would return to the San Mateo office. The letter indicated that management decided to resolve Ellison's problem with a six-month separation, and that it would take additional action if the problem recurred.

After receiving the letter, Ellison was "frantic." She filed a formal complaint alleging sexual harassment on January 30, 1987 with the IRS. She also obtained permission to transfer to San Francisco temporarily when Gray returned.

Gray sought joint counseling. He wrote Ellison another letter which still sought to maintain the idea that he and Ellison had some type of relationship.[2]

The IRS employee investigating the allegation agreed with Ellison's supervisor that Gray's conduct constituted sexual harassment. In its final decision, however, the Treasury Department rejected Ellison's complaint because it believed that the complaint did not describe a pattern or practice of sexual harassment covered by the EEOC regulations. After an appeal, the EEOC affirmed the Treasury Department's decision on a different ground. It concluded that the agency took adequate action to prevent the repetition of Gray's conduct.

Ellison filed a complaint in September of 1987 in federal district court. The court granted the government's motion for summary judgment on the ground that Ellison had failed to state a prima facie case of sexual harassment due to a hostile working environment. Ellison appeals.

• • •

. . . In *Meritor Savings Bank v. Vinson,* 477 U.S. 57, 106 S.Ct. 2399, 91 L.Ed.2d 49 (1986), the Supreme Court held that sexual harassment constitutes sex discrimination in violation of Title VII.

Courts have recognized different forms of sexual harassment. In "quid pro quo" cases, employers condition employment benefits on sexual favors. In "hostile environment" cases, employees work in offensive or abusive environments. This case, like *Meritor,* involves a hostile environment claim.

• • •

[A] hostile environment exists when an employee can show (1) that he or she was subjected to sexual advances, requests for sexual favors, or other verbal or physical conduct of a sexual nature,[3] (2) that this conduct was unwelcome, and (3) that the conduct was sufficiently severe or pervasive to alter the conditions of the victim's employment and create an abusive working environment.

• • •

The parties ask us to determine if Gray's conduct, as alleged by Ellison, was sufficiently severe or pervasive to alter the conditions of Ellison's employment and create an abusive working environment. The district court, with little Ninth Circuit case law to look to for guidance, held that Ellison did not state a prima facie case of sexual harassment due to a hostile working environment. It believed that Gray's conduct was "isolated and genuinely trivial." We disagree.

• • •

We have closely examined *Meritor* and our previous cases, and we believe that Gray's conduct was sufficiently severe and pervasive to alter the conditions of Ellison's employment and create an abusive working environment. We first note that the required showing of severity or seriousness of the harassing conduct varies inversely with the pervasiveness or frequency of the conduct . . .

Next, we believe that in evaluating the severity and pervasiveness of sexual harassment, we should focus on the perspective of the victim. If we only examined whether a reasonable person would engage in allegedly harassing conduct, we would run the risk of reinforcing the prevailing level of discrimination. Harassers could continue to harass merely because a particular discriminatory practice was common, and victims of harassment would have no remedy . . .

We therefore prefer to analyze harassment from the victim's perspective. A complete understanding of the victim's view requires, among other things, an analysis of the different perspectives of men and women. Conduct that many men consider unobjectionable may offend many women. . . .

We realize that there is a broad range of viewpoints among women as a group, but we believe that many women share common concerns which men do not necessarily share. . . . For example, because women are disproportionately victims of rape and sexual assault, women have a stronger incentive to be concerned with sexual behavior. . . . Women who are victims of mild forms of sexual harassment may understandably worry whether a harasser's conduct is merely a prelude to violent sexual assault. Men, who are rarely victims of sexual assault, may view sexual conduct in a vacuum without a full appreciation of the social setting or the underlying threat of violence that a woman may perceive.

In order to shield employers from having to accommodate the idiosyncratic concerns of the rare hyper-sensitive employee, we hold that a female plaintiff states a prima facie case of hostile environment sexual harassment when she alleges conduct which a reasonable woman would consider sufficiently severe or pervasive to alter the conditions of employment and create an abusive working environment. . . .

We adopt the perspective of a reasonable woman primarily because we believe that a sex-blind reasonable person standard tends to be male-biased and tends to systematically ignore the experiences of women. The reasonable woman standard does not establish a higher level of protection for women than men. . . . Instead, a gender-conscious examination of sexual harassment enables women to participate in the workplace on an equal footing with men. By acknowleding and not trivializing the effects of sexual harassment on reasonable women, courts can work towards ensuring that neither men nor women will have to "run a gauntlet of sexual abuse in return for the privilege of being allowed to work and make a living. . . ."

We note that the reasonable victim standard we adopt today classifies conduct as unlawful sexual harassment even when harassers do not realize that their conduct creates a hostile working environment. Well-intentioned compliments by co-workers or supervisors can form the basis of a sexual harassment cause of action if a reasonable victim of the same sex as the plaintiff would consider the comments sufficiently severe or pervasive to alter a condition of employment and create an abusive working environment. That is because Title VII is not a fault-based tort scheme. "Title VII is aimed at the consequences or effects of an employment practice and not at the . . . motivation" of co-workers or employers. . . . to avoid liability under Title VII, employers may have to educate and sensitize their workforce to eliminate conduct which a reasonable victim would consider unlawful sexual harassment. . . .

The facts of this case illustrate the importance of considering the victim's perspective. Analyzing the facts from the alleged harasser's viewpoint, Gray could be portrayed as a modern-day Cyrano de Bergerac wishing no more than to woo Ellison with his words. . . . There is no evidence that Gray harbored ill will toward Ellison. He even offered in his "love letter" to leave her alone if she wished. Examined in this light, it is not difficult to see why the district court characterized Gray's conduct as isolated and trivial.

Ellison, however, did not consider the acts to be trivial. Gray's first note shocked and frightened her. After receiving the three-page letter, she became really upset and frightened again. She immediately requested that she or Gray be transferred. Her supervisor's prompt response suggests that she too did not consider the conduct trivial. When Ellison learned that Gray arranged to return to San Mateo, she immediately asked to transfer, and she immediately filed an official complaint.

We cannot say as a matter of law that Ellison's reaction was idiosyncratic or hyper-sensitive. We believe that a reasonable woman could have had a similar reaction. After receiving the first bizarre

note from Gray, a person she barely knew, Ellison asked a co-worker to tell Gray to leave her alone. Despite her request, Gray sent her a long, passionate, disturbing letter. He told her he had been "watching" and "experiencing" her; he made repeated references to sex; he said he would write again. Ellison had no way of knowing what Gray would do next. A reasonable woman could consider Gray's conduct, as alleged by Ellison, sufficiently severe and pervasive to alter a condition of employment and create an abusive working environment.

. . . We hope that over time both men and women will learn what conduct offends reasonable members of the other sex. When employers and employees internalize the standard of workplace conduct we establish today, the current gap in perception between the sexes will be bridged.

We reverse the district court's decision that Ellison did not allege a prima facie case of sexual harassment due to a hostile working environment, and we remand for further proceedings consistent with this opinion. . . .

STEPHENS, District Judge, dissenting:

. . . Nowhere in section 2000e of Title VII, the section under which the plaintiff in this case brought suit, is there any indication that Congress intended to provide for any other than equal treatment in the area of civil rights. The legislation is designed to achieve a balanced and generally gender neutral and harmonious workplace which would improve production and the quality of the employees' lives. In fact, the Supreme Court has shown a preference against systems that are not gender or race neutral, such as hiring quotas. . . . While women may be the most frequent targets of this type of conduct that is at issue in this case, they are not the only targets. I believe that it is incumbent upon the courts in this case to use terminology that will meet the needs of all who seek recourse under this section of Title VII. Possible alternatives that are more in line with a gender neutral approach include "victim," "target," or "person." The term "reasonable man" as it is used in the law of torts, traditionally refers to the average adult person, regardless of gender, and the conduct that can reasonably be expected of him or her. For the purposes of the legal issues that are being addressed, such a term assumes that it is applicable to all persons. . . . It takes no stretch of the imagination to envision two complaints emanating from the same workplace regarding the same conditions, one brought by a woman and the other by a man. Application of the "new standard" presents a puzzlement which is born of the assumption that men's eyes do not see what a woman sees through her eyes. I find it surprising that the majority finds no need for evidence on any of these subjects. I am not sure whether the majority also concludes that the woman and the man in question are also reasonable without evidence on this subject. . . .

NOTES

1. In the middle of the long letter Gray did say "I am obligated to you so much that if you want me to leave you alone I will. . . . If you want me to forget you entirely, I can not do that."
2. It is unclear from the record on appeal whether Ellison received the third letter.
3. Here, the government argues that Gray's conduct was not of a sexual nature. The three-page letter, however, makes several references to sex and constitutes verbal conduct of a sexual nature. We need not and do not decide whether a party can state a cause of action for a sexually discriminatory working environment under Title VII when the conduct in question is not sexual. *See Andrews v. City of Philadelphia,* 895 F.2d 1469, 1485 (3d Cir.1990) (conduct need not be sexual); *Hall v. Gus Construction Co.,* 842 F.2d 1010, 1014 (8th Cir.1988) (conduct need not be sexual).

Justice, Sexual Harassment, and the Reasonable Victim Standard

Deborah L. Wells and Beverly J. Kracher

Introduction

The Senate judiciary committee hearings confirming the appointment of Justice Clarence Thomas to the United States Supreme Court provided dramatic testimony that sexual harassment remains a formidable workplace problem. Although the practical impact in the workplace of the Thomas-Hill controversy is difficult to judge, two recent lower court decisions related to sexual harassment should cause managers to take stock of the treatment of sexual harassment within their companies. The impact of these decisions on employers who permit sexually hostile work environments to exist is dubious at this time. This paper presents a compelling moral argument that explains why employers must identify sexually hostile work environments from the perspective of the victim, most often a woman.

Journal of Business Ethics 12/6:423–431, 1993. Copyright © 1993 Kluwer Academic Publishers. With kind permission from Kluwer Academic Publishers.

Forms of Sexual Harassment

There are two generally recognized forms of sexual harassment (EEOC Guidelines, 1980). In *quid pro quo* sexual harassment, the victim is promised an employment benefit or advantage in return for a sexual favor or is denied continued employment or some advantage for refusing to participate in sex (*Arbitration Journal,* 1988). The victim is implicitly or explicitly told that he or she will be selected to fill a position, receive a pay increase, a promotion, or a favorable performance rating, for example, in return for performing a sexual act. Or, the victim is implicitly or explicitly told that he or she will lose his or her job, or receive a low performance rating, for example, if he or she does not perform sexually.

The second widely recognized form of sexual harassment, hostile environment sexual harassment, occurs when an employee's work performance suffers because sex-related behaviors in the work place create an intolerable work environment (EEOC Guidelines, 1980). Co-workers, supervisors, or even customers or clients who continuously ask employees for dates, or make lewd remarks or gestures to employees, can create a hostile working environment. So can the posting of suggestive calendars, posters, or centerfolds or the display of lewd magazines.

Sexual Harassment and the Law: Rulings Prior to Ellison and Jacksonville Shipyards

Section 703(a) (1) of Title VII of the 1964 Civil Rights Act prohibits employment discrimination on the basis of sex. For more than ten years after the passage of the Civil Rights Act, however, the judicial system did not recognize sexual harassment as employment discrimination. Reasoning that sexual attraction would naturally play a role in employment decisions and that perpetrators were acting on their own when they harassed others, courts declined to view sexual harassment as deprivation of employment opportunities to victims, chiefly women (Koen, 1990; Morlacci, 1987). This "boys will be boys" reasoning prevailed until the mid-1970s, when lower courts at last allowed that the most invidious type of sexual harassment, *quid pro quo*, was indeed a form of discrimination. Even so, courts found sexual harassment to be discriminatory only if the victim suffered a tangible economic loss, such as denial of a promotion or pay increase, by refusing the harasser's sexual demands. If the impact of harassment was psychological or otherwise intangible, no discrimination was found to have occurred (Morlacci, 1987).

In 1986, the United States Supreme Court heard its first case dealing with sexual harassment. The high court's ruling in Meritor Savings Bank v. Vinson was particularly important because it recognized hostile environment sexual harassment as a form of employment discrimination that could be as potentially harmful as *quid pro quo* sexual harassment. Although this Supreme Court decision regarding hostile environment sexual harassment was viewed by feminists and interested others as a triumph, the text of the ruling itself leaves much interpretation for the lower courts (Hauck and Pearce, 1987; Hukill, 1991). Specifically missing is a test or decision rule for when a work environment is so contaminated by sexual behavior that it can be considered truly hostile (Koen, 1990).

Hostile Environment Sexual Harassment and the Law: Reasonable Victim Standards in Ellison and Jacksonville Shipyards

A contemporary and controversial legal development in hostile environment sexual harassment employment discrimination litigation is the product of lower court rulings in two states. A California appellate court, in Ellison v. Brady, demanded that hostile environments be judged from the viewpoint of a reasonable victim, not a reasonable person. In Jacksonville Shipyards, a Florida court ruled that the impact of sexually suggestive calendars and other photographs prominently displayed in a workplace be judged from the viewpoint of those negatively affected: women (Murphy *et al.*, 1991; Simon, 1991).

Ellison v. Brady and Jacksonville Shipyards: Brief Description and Implications

Ellison v. Brady

After accompanying colleague Gray to lunch on one occasion, IRS employee Kerry Ellison received a number of letters, in addition to subsequent social invitations, from Gray. Ellison reported Gray's behavior to her supervisor, but attempted to further discourage Gray with the assistance of a coworker who asked Gray to leave Ellison alone. Subsequently, the supervisor, too, asked Gray to stop, but he continued to write letters to Ellison. Although, as the court later acknowledged, many of these letters were innocuous in nature, in one letter Gray stated that he could not stand to feel Ellison's hatred of him, and he continued to write even after she was temporarily relocated in another city for training. When Ellison returned following the completion of her training, Gray agreed to be transferred to a different office, but later changed his mind and successfully protested the transfer through his union's grievance procedure. Upon his return to the office in which Ellison worked, she filed a complaint with the California EEOC (Simon, 1991).

The judge in the federal court that first heard Ellison's case declared that love letters did not constitute sexual harassment, according to any reasonable person. But the decision in Ellison v. Brady rendered by the appeals court overturned the original decision, saying that what does or does not constitute sexual harassment can only be determined by viewing the alleged harassing acts from the perspective of a reasonable victim. This appellate court decision achieved notoriety because it overturned the reasonable person test for judging the impact of one individual's behavior on another.

Jacksonville Shipyards

The Ninth Circuit Court of Appeals, in Ellison v. Brady, was not the only court to recognize the merits of the reasonable victim standard. A federal court in Jacksonville, Florida recognized that by allowing male welders latitude in posting printed materials depicting women in sexually submissive positions, the Jacksonville Shipyards perpetuated a work atmosphere that was degrading to female welders (Hayes, 1991; Murphy *et al.*, 1991). This court, too, declared that the impact of posting sexually demeaning materials should be judged from the perspective of the victim; in this case from the perspective of the female employees.

Reactions to Ellison and Jacksonville Shipyards

Some members of the legal community have labeled the courts in Ellison v. Brady and Jacksonville Shipyards "maverick." These critics discount the impact of the reasonable victim standard, saying that such a standard will not be widely adopted (Larsen, 1991; Epping, 1992). These attorneys narrowly define the reasonable victim standard to mean that only a person who is exactly like the victim (same race, same gender, same age, and so on) is able to judge a situation from that victim's perspective. But it is not necessary to understand the reasonable victim standard in this sense. The reasonable victim standard only requires that a person is able to put himself or herself in the position of the victim in order to judge a situation from that victim's perspective, and it is in this latter sense that we will use the reasonable victim standard in this paper. As of today, there is no agreement within the legal community to use the reasonable victim

standard in either sense to identify hostile environment sexual harassment.

Reasonable Victim Standard: From the Law to Morality

The fact that there is no single set of legally accepted criteria for identifying hostile work environments created by sexual harassment is problematic for business since accepted legal standards often function as adequate guides for constructing policies for the workplace. But this has been overcome with past problems. Many policies, for example smoking policies, have been made without the benefit of legal precedent. That policies must be set without benefit of legal precedent is not surprising, since it often takes years before court edicts, especially Supreme Court edicts, are issued in response to problems arising in day-to-day work life. Given this legal vacuum, it is imperative that businesses look to other sources of standards for conducting their activities. One such source has been, and will be, morality.

Morality is a relevant source of standards for business since, other than legal precedent, it is the only other criterion for determining what is just or fair. Thus, in the case of hostile environment sexual harassment we can look to morality in order to construct a policy that fairly identifies sexually hostile environments. The thesis of this paper is that fair workplace policies regarding sexually hostile environments identify sexually hostile environments from the perspective of the reasonable victim. We use the modern moral theory of John Rawls to defend this thesis.

Rawls' Moral Theory

Heralded as the most ambitious and influential work in social philosophy in the late twentieth century, John Rawls' *A Theory of Justice* (1971) establishes a fair method for arriving at fundamental principles of justice for individuals as well as for the basic institutions of society. Rawls' central idea is that just principles are those principles people, when in a certain fair situation, would unanimously accept. Rawls calls the situation of fairness "the original position" and describes it as a hypothetical situation where free, self-interested, impartial, and rational people agree to principles of conduct they must live by once outside of the original position.

Anyone who has ever tried to get a group of self-interested people to unanimously agree to anything will immediately recognize a problem Rawls faced when constructing his theory. Self-interested people pursue private agendas and thus it is difficult if not impossible to achieve consensus among them. Furthermore, it is difficult to maintain impartiality in self-interested people. Rawls responds to these problems by requiring that we drop all knowledge of our private agendas and, like justice herself, become more or less blindfolded to the qualities that bias our agreements. Thus, in the original position individuals know nothing about who they will be once outside of the original position. That is, in the original position individuals know nothing about what race they will be, their intellectual ability, social status, religion, or class. Rawls calls imposition of the blindfold "the veil of ignorance." This veil of ignorance ensures impartiality and promotes unanimity.

Rawls argues that rationality in the original position dictates use of the maximin strategy. This means that an individual will choose principles where the worst outcome for him or her is the least bad. In *A Theory of Justice* Rawls argues for and systematically explores two social principles of justice he believes would be agreed to in the original position, namely, the equal liberty principle and the difference principle (Rawls, 1971, p. 302).

In particular, the difference principle is the assertion that social and economic inequalities are to be arranged so that they are both:

(A) to the greatest benefit of the least advantaged . . . and,

(B) attached to offices and positions open to all under conditions of fair equality of opportunity (Rawls, 1971, p. 302).

Rawls also argues that in the original position individuals would consent to at least five principles of justice for individuals and individual arrangements (which he calls natural duties). These principles are the duty to uphold just institutions, the duty to give mutual aid, the duty of mutual respect

of persons, the duty not to harm the innocent, and the duty not to injure.

Rawls' principles pertain to hostile environment sexual harassment in two important ways. First, there must be equal opportunity to hold offices and positions in a just society, according to the second part of the difference principle. Since hostile environment sexual harassment violates this principle by closing off to victims the offices and positions they would otherwise hold, hostile environment sexual harassment is shown to be unjust. Second, an understanding of the duty to show respect to persons and the duty not to harm the innocent provides a framework from which we can devise fair workplace policies regarding hostile environment sexual harassment, as we shall show in the following section.

Natural Duties and Hostile Environments

The duty not to harm the innocent and the duty to show mutual respect to persons provide an excellent moral framework for constructing a standard from which to judge whether or not a sexually hostile work environment exists. The rest of this section shows how the duties to show respect to persons and not to harm the innocent provide an identification of sexually hostile environments from the perspective of the victim.

Both duties, namely, to show respect to persons and not harm the innocent, would be agreed to in the original position and thus are important moral constraints. Regarding the duty not to harm the innocent, we can assume that the innocent are persons who are unwilling recipients of harm done to them.

Regarding the duty to show mutual respect Rawls states:

> Mutual respect is shown in several ways: in our willingness to see the situation of others from their point of view, from the perspective of their conception of their good; and in our being prepared to give reasons for our actions whenever the interests of others are materially affected . . . Further, . . . to respect another as a moral person is to try to understand his aims and interests from his standpoint and to pre-

sent him with considerations that enable him to accept the constraints on his conduct . . . Also respect is shown in a willingness to do small favors and courtesies . . . because they are an appropriate expression of our awareness of another person's feelings and aspirations . . . parties in the original positions know that in society they need to be assured by the esteem of their associates. Their self-respect and their confidence in the value of their own system of ends cannot withstand the indifference much less the contempt of others. Everyone benefits from living in a society where the duty of mutual respect is honored (Rawls, 1971, pp. 337–338).

Rawls tells us that respect for persons involves being willing to see things from another's point of view. We need not agree with this other person's perspective, but in order to show respect we must be willing to recognize the other person's perspective and act appropriately. This respect, Rawls tells us, must be mutual and not one-sided. For example, I must be willing to see your perspective and you must be willing to see mine.

Prima facie, there are four ways to identify sexually hostile work environments. First, sexually hostile environments could be identified from the perspective of the reasonable harasser. Second, sexually hostile environments could be identified from the perspective of the reasonable harasser and the reasonable victim (assuming that these perspectives are different from one another). Third, sexually hostile environments could be identified from the perspective of the reasonable person, that is, from the perspective of the reasonable harasser or the reasonable victim (where these perspectives are ultimately the same). Fourth, sexually hostile environments could be identified from the perspective of the reasonable victim. While there are these four possibilities, we assert that only by identifying sexually hostile environments from the perspective of the reasonable victim will a workplace policy be practical and just. Our reasons for not choosing the first three alternatives are the following.

If sexually hostile environments are identified from the perspective of the reasonable harasser, then the duty not to harm the innocent is not fulfilled. For the innocents in this case are the employees being subjected to unwelcome sex-related behavior. They are innocent since they are unwilling participants in the sexually harassing environment in which they find themselves. Innocents are harmed when hostile environments are defined only from the perspective of the harasser since that environment, unproblematic to the harasser who created it, is demeaning to the target or victim and undermines his or her sense of self-esteem. If sexually hostile environments are identified only from the perspective of the harasser, then people are not required to consider the perspective of the victim. This allows harm to occur to the victim, which is morally unacceptable on the grounds of our natural duty not to harm the innocent.

While the duty to show mutual respect may lead us to think that we must identify sexually hostile environments from both perspectives, identifying hostile environments from the perspectives of both the reasonable harasser and the reasonable victim is practically worthless. For while persistent jokes, remarks, and gestures may be perceived as innocuous from the viewpoint of the employee or employer making them, they are threatening or abusive from the viewpoint of the target employee. The duty of mutual respect does require us to take into account another's perspective. But when the perspectives involved are irreconcilable, as in the case of sexually hostile environments, no constructive practical policy can be devised which identifies sexually hostile environments from both perspectives.

If sexually hostile environments are identified from the perspective of the reasonable person, then it does not matter whether the reasonable person assumes the role of the harasser or the victim. For if sexually hostile environments are identified from the perspective of the reasonable person, then there is only one perspective in hostile environment issues, namely, the reasonable person. If there is only one perspective, then as a reasonable person, that individual is able to extrapolate from the particulars of any role assumed and judge whether or not a sexually hostile environment exists in a situation. However, there is more than one perspective in hostile environment issues. As we show in a later section of the paper, men and women generally have different perspectives regarding sexual behavior at work. Since, generally, men are sexual harassers and women are the victims of sexual harassment, then generally harassers have a different perspective than victims. Thus, sexually hostile environments cannot be identified from the reasonable person perspective since there is no *one* reasonable person standard regarding sexually hostile environments.

Since there are reasons for not using the first three alternatives to identify sexually hostile environments, we are left with the alternative of identifying sexually hostile environments from the fourth perspective, namely, through the perspective of the reasonable victim. This alternative is acceptable for the same reasons the others were not. First, it is practically workable since it provides us with a real way to discern instances of sexually hostile environments. For we need only ask reasonable victims if they see a sexual situation as unwelcome and abusive in order to identify sexually hostile environments. Second, it promotes an individual's duty not to harm the innocent because it requires that people identify sexually hostile environments from the perspective of the innocents. Third, it is consistent with current studies which evidence the differences in perspectives between harassers and victims.

Determining the exact qualifications for being a reasonable victim takes us outside the scope of this paper. Nevertheless, assuming that Rawls is correct in arguing that persons in the original position would consent to the duty to show respect to persons, we can say that a reasonable victim's perspective is restricted by the duty to show respect to persons. This is as it should be. The reasonable victim must show respect to others in as much as others must respect the victim. Thus, on the one hand, the reasonable victim must allow some sexual behavior that she finds merely annoying for the sake of the person with a more highly sexual orientation. On the other hand, the reasonable victim can restrict some sexual behavior in the workplace, namely, that sexual behavior that creates an abusive and thus harmful environment. Thus, adhering to the duty to show respect to persons allows us to distinguish between harmful sexual environments and sexual environments which are offensive yet not harmful and to assert that the reasonable victim identifies hostile environments as only those sexual situations that are abusive or harmful.

In summary, we argue that we should identify

sexually hostile environments from the perspective of the reasonable victim. This identification standard is practical, and fulfills the duty not to harm the innocent. In keeping with Rawls, we affirm that a reasonable victim is a person who accepts a duty to show respect to persons. We argue that accepting this duty restricts the reasonable victim's perspective. And this is how it should be. On account of the duty to show respect to persons who are more highly sexually oriented, the reasonable victim allows sexual environments in the workplace that are merely annoying. Yet on account of the duty to show respect to persons with less sexual orientations, the reasonable victim is permitted to restrict sexual environments which are abusive and harmful, that is, which are sexually hostile environments.

Employer Responses to Sexual Harassment

Practitioner-oriented literature is filled with advice on how to avoid sexual harassment claims and costly subsequent litigation. The basic advice, followed by many employers, is to treat sexual harassment in much the same way other serious employee-reported problems are treated: Draft a policy forbidding the behavior, make workers and supervisors aware of the prohibition, establish a reporting procedure, and subject violators to progressive discipline. The persistence of workplace sexual harassment complaints and litigation, however, suggests that employer responses have been inadequate in the past and a revised approach should be taken.

Sexual Harassment Training and the Reasonable Victim Standard

We have used the duty not to harm the innocent and the duty to show respect to persons as a framework from which we arrived at an identification standard for sexually hostile environments. Our thesis is that sexually hostile environments should be identified from the perspective of the reasonable victim. But consideration of the duty to show respect to persons and the duty not to harm the innocent also leads us to say that sexually hostile environments can be curtailed in the workplace through two types of training programs: consciousness-raising, aimed at promoting understanding of the different perspectives men and women hold on sexual behavior in the workplace, and assertiveness training, geared toward teaching potential victims how to respond more forcefully to harassment so that harassers clearly understand there is a perspective other than their own.

Training to Promote Consciousness Raising

Hostile environment sexual harassment training programs must promote mutual respect of persons by changing men's and women's understanding and behavior so that they can perceive, tolerate, and respect their divergent perceptions of the workplace environment. Research shows that men and women experience workplace sexuality quite differently. Men, in general, report a more sexualized work atmosphere than do women (Gutek *et al.,* 1990), in that conversations among men at work are more likely to contain sex-related jokes, comments, and stories of sexual conquests than are conversations among women. Increased contact between the genders, an inevitable consequence of increasing labor force participation rates for women, promotes a more sexualized work environment for women, too, (Gutek *et al.,* 1990) thus increasing the likelihood that sexual harassment will occur. When men and women do encounter sexual behavior at work, they view it very differently. One survey uncovered a stunning dichotomy between men and women: 75 percent of male respondents would be flattered by sexual advances in the workplace; 75 percent of females would be offended (Hayes, 1991).

Sex-related conduct, statements, acts, or events that may not be offensive or harmful to men are offensive and even frightening to women. Women simply have learned to see more of the sexual conduct in the workplace as threatening because they are much more often than men the victims of sexual assault and rape (Simon, 1991). Likewise, men have learned, through sex role socialization, that they should initiate social and sexual activities with women. Men may not turn off this role expectation when they come to work, and so "role spillover" undoubtedly accounts for some sexually harassing behavior (Gutek *et al.,* 1990). Because both of these sets of responses, male and female, are learned, it

makes sense that training can help employees "unlearn" them.

Segal (1990) has developed a training exercise designed to sensitize employees to interpersonal differences in perception of sexual behaviors. He advocates preparing ". . . a list of 20 to 30 examples of conduct which, either alone or in conjunction with other conduct, arguably might give rise to a hostile work environment" (Segal, 1990, p. 176). Participants individually rate the degree to which they believe the conduct gives rise to a hostile work environment. Discussion within mixed gender groups then ensues. In Segal's experience, three patterns have emerged. First, there are wide differences in what women do and do not view as harassing. Second, women are more likely than men to see any given sex-related behavior as giving rise to a hostile environment, and third, when sexual conduct is aimed at women, rather than men, both genders are more likely to see its hostile potential. Participants in this training come away with a heightened awareness of differences between male and female perceptions of workplace sexuality and are more likely to understand the consequences of their sex-related speech and behavior. We recommend this kind of approach to enable employees to see that there are other viewpoints on sexuality and to help them develop a sense of duty to show respect to others.

Assertiveness Training

Workplace training programs must enable individuals to fulfill their duty not to harm the innocent and their duty to show respect to persons. They must reinforce those abilities in individual employees that allow them clearly and forcefully to show how unwelcome particular acts of sexual behavior are, while understanding that the behavior may arise not from malice, but from having a different perspective. Reinforcement of these abilities is necessary since it is questionable whether we can hold a harasser at fault for his or her actions if there is no response from the victim to indicate to the harasser that his or her actions are unwelcome and harmful. That is, the harasser must reasonably be able to know that his or her actions are creating a hostile environment in order to be able to hold the harasser responsible for his or her actions. And since it is sufficient for the harasser's knowledge that his or her actions are creating a hostile environment that the victim clearly states or shows that the actions are unwelcome and harmful, it is beneficial to reinforce the abilities of the victim to make this known.

We recommend that potential victims learn to clearly show their disfavor with particular sexual behaviors through assertiveness training programs. These training programs must accomplish two goals. First, they must determine participants' current levels of assertiveness. The Rathus Assertiveness Schedule, for example, is a diagnostic instrument that has been successfully used for this purpose (Dawley and Wenrich, 1976).

The second goal that must be achieved by training programs is to impart techniques individuals can use to be more assertive when needed. One valuable technique is role playing. Role playing allows individuals to practice being assertive. Role playing may include rehearsing what to say to a harasser. For example, it is valuable to rehearse using "I" statements (e.g., "I am uncomfortable with how you are acting") rather than "you" statements (e.g., "You are making me uncomfortable"). "I" statements are more valuable than "you" statements since they arouse less defensiveness from the listener, evoke feelings of power within the speaker, and encourage discussion of differences of opinion (Drury, 1984).

Teaching a technique called DESC (Bower and Bower, 1976) is also worthwhile in assertiveness training courses. DESC is an acronym for describe the situation, express how you feel, specify what can be done (by both parties) to change the situation, and state rewarding consequences from the change. A DESC script can be used to formulate a letter to a harasser or as the basis of a verbal response to harassment to get a harasser to recognize and change offensive behaviors.

The training we have advocated above is designed to bring about changes in perceptions, attitudes, and behaviors on the part of both potential sexual harassers and their victims. We harbor no illusions regarding the difficulty of producing such changes. In fact, in other contexts, institutionalizing major attitude and behavioral change takes, on the average, eight years (Murray, 1976). Because this is true, the training will have to be offered regularly and be reinforced by strong management support that includes much of the traditional approach to dealing with sexual harassment: clearly written policies, good reporting procedures, and discipline for offenders who resist change even after participation in training.

Conclusion

Although there is no legal consensus on reasonable victim standards, we have shown that employers should adopt this reasonable victim perspective in order to identify sexually hostile work environments. Widespread adoption of the reasonable victim perspective has the potential to curb sexually hostile environments in the workplace as employees seek to fulfill two important moral duties: the duty to show mutual respect and the duty not to harm the innocent.

The most efficacious manner for bringing about this change is to widely sensitize employees to individual perceptual differences on sex-related behaviors through consciousness raising sessions and to increase the assertiveness of potential victims in order to further emphasize that there are two perspectives on sexual harassment in action, not one. Training programs geared to achieve these results must be seriously undertaken and reinforced by repetition and strong management support.

REFERENCES

Bower, S. A. and Bower, G. H.: 1976, *Asserting Yourself: A Practical Guide for Positive Change* (Addison-Wesley, Reading, MA).

Dawley, H. H. and Wenrich, W. W.: 1976, *Achieving Assertive Behavior* (Brooks/Cole, Monterey, CA).

Drury, S. S.: 1984, *Assertive Supervision: Building Involved Teamwork* (Research Press, Champaign, IL).

Epping, A. R.: 1992 (January 16), 'Everything You've Always Wanted to Know About Sexual Harassment but Were Afraid to Ask', *Speech to The Association of Government Accountants Omaha Metro Area Chapter.*

Guidelines on Discrimination on the Basis of Sex: 1980, (Equal Employment Opportunity Commission, Washington, DC).

Gutek, B. A., Cohen, A. G. and Konrad, A. M.: 1990, 'Predicting Social-Sexual Behavior at Work: A Contact Hypothesis', *Academy of Management Journal* **33**, pp. 560–577.

Hauck, V. E. and Pearce, T. G.: 1987, 'Vinson: Sexual Harassment and Employer Response', *Labor Law Journal* **38**, pp. 770–775.

Hayes, A. S.: 1991 (May 28), 'Courts Concede the Sexes Think in Unlike Ways', *Wall Street Journal* **217**, pp. B1 and B5.

Hukill, C.: 1991 (May), 'Significant decisions in labor cases', *Monthly Labor Review* **114**, pp. 32–40.

Koen, Jr., C. M.: 1990 (August), 'Sexual Harassment Claims Stem From a Hostile Work Environment', *Personnel Journal* **69**, pp. 88–99.

Larsen, D. A.: 1991, Personal communication.

Morlacci, M.: 1987, 'Sexual Harassment Law and the Impact of Vinson', *Employee Relations Law Journal* **13**, pp. 501–519.

Murphy, B. S., Barlow, W. E. and Hatch, D. D.: 1991 (May), '"Reasonable Woman" is New Standard for Sexual Harassment', *Personnel Journal* **67**, pp. 34–36.

Murray, E. A.: 1976 (July), 'The Social Response Process in Commercial Banks: An Empirical Investigation', *Academy of Management Review*, **1**, pp. 5–15.

Rawls, J.: 1971, *A Theory of Justice* (Harvard University Press, Cambridge, MA).

Nowlin, W. A.: 1988 (December), 'Sexual Harassment in the Workplace', *The Arbitration Journal* **43**, pp. 32–40.

Segal, J. A.: 1990 (June), 'Safe Sex: A Workplace Oxymoron?', *HRMagazine* **35**, pp. 175–176, 178, 180.

Simon, H. A.: 1991, 'Ellison v. Brady: A "Reasonable Woman" Standard for Sexual Harassment', *Employee Relations Law Journal* **17**, pp. 71–80.

Sexual Harassment: Why the Corporate World Still Doesn't "Get It"

Vaughana Macy Feary

Introduction

With the widely publicized charges of sexual harassment brought by neurosurgeon Dr. Frances Conley against Stanford Medical School, the electrifying allegations of Professor Anita Hill against Judge Clarence Thomas, and the sordid Tailhook scandal involving sexual misconduct in the military, the problem of sexual harassment finally exploded into the headlines. As yesterday's silent victims began joining a swelling chorus of protest from today's working women, corporate America suddenly began admitting that sexual harassment is an explosive communication problem. Yet despite all the recent ballyhoo over sexual harassment in the workplace, corporate America still doesn't really "get it" much less understand how to put an end to it.

If sexual harassment in the workplace is to be understood and eliminated, then not only corporate America, but the entire international business community must recognize and discard some old myths about the nature of ethics, and about the relationship between ethics, law and business, as well as some newer myths about sexual harassment, itself. It must recognize that sexual harassment in the workplace is not simply a snag in communication resulting from factual ignorance or

factual disagreement, or from cultural or gender differences, or from confusions about an especially murky concept. Sexual harassment is not merely a communication problem. It is a moral problem for everyone in the corporate world and, to recognize this is finally to get to the root of the problem and to understand what measures need to be taken to eliminate it.

Sexual Harassment as a Widespread Moral Problem

Why has the business community taken so long to admit that sexual harassment in the workplace is a serious problem? The reason seems to be that it still believes Myth Number One—the tired old joke that business ethics is an oxymoron; business should not really take ethics seriously.

There are numerous statistical studies which show that sexual harassment is an old problem. One of the earliest surveys, conducted by *Redbook* magazine in 1976, found that nine out of ten women responding to the survey had encountered sexual harassment on the job.[1] In 1978, Cornell University found that 70% of women workers surveyed reported sexual harassment. In 1981, The National Merit Systems Protection Board conducted the largest study of sexual harassment yet available and found that 42% of 23,000 people surveyed believed they had been sexually harassed.[2] In 1981, another study conducted by *Redbook*, in col-

Journal of Business Ethics 13:649–662, 1994. Copyright © 1994 Kluwer Academic Publishers. With kind permission from Kluwer Academic Publishers.

laboration with Harvard Business Review, found that 63% of managers responding to the survey reported sexual harassment at their companies.[3] In 1984, Dziech and Weiner reported that 30% of undergraduate women experience sexual harassment during their college careers (a staggering 2,000,000 students) and Gutek (1985) reported that 53.1% of private sector workers surveyed believed that they had suffered economic hardship because of refusing to satisfy sexual demands.[4] In 1991, there was little improvement. In October of that year, following the Thomas hearings, a *Time* magazine poll found that 34% of the women polled had experienced sexual harassment at work.[5] Such findings corroborated the findings of another recent poll conducted by the National Association for Female Executives which found that 53% of the members surveyed had been sexually harassed, or knew of someone who had been harassed.[6] A *Working Woman* survey published in June, 1992 found that 60% of the respondents had been victimized; it attributed this still higher percentage to the fact that the women polled held positions as executives, for "women in managerial and professional positions, as well as those working in male dominated companies are more likely to experience harassment."[7]

Although studies show that some women are more likely to be harassed than others, they also confirm that no group of women (or men) has remained wholly exempt from sexual harassment.[8] One tenth of sexual harassment complaints are now being filed by men.[9] Studies also show that workers may be victimized by supervisors or peers, individuals or groups. The most recent June 1992 *Working Woman* study, however, found that 83% of the harassers enjoy more powerful positions than the victims.[10]

Finally, no work environment seems to be immune. Sexual harassment is a problem in government, in the military, in corporations, in small businesses, and in academe.

Despite all the evidence indicating that sexual harassment was a major problem in the workplace, the business community remained largely indifferent. Although a 1988 *Working Woman* survey of sexual harassment found that 86% of the respondents believed that mandatory training programs would alleviate the problem, only 58% yet offered such programs. In 1988, the United States Merit Systems Protection Board also issued an update on

sexual harassment with a series of recommendations for employers which included such topics as training, policy statements, enforcement action, complaint and investigation procedures, and additional preventative efforts (e.g., random surveys and follow up interviews with parties involved in harassment claims).[11] A few companies such as Corning, which began its attempts to combat sexual harassment as early as the 1970s, and DuPont which has long held workshops designed to sensitize managers to the problem, were responsive.[12] Few other companies followed their leadership. It took the Thomas hearings to finally galvanize the business community into recognizing that sexual harassment was rapidly becoming the communication problem of the '90s.

If the business community had not been as busy repeating the same tired jokes and had taken business ethics seriously, it would not have been caught napping. If business leaders had done their ethics homework, they would have recognized that when women reported being sexually harassed they were not merely supplying factual reports about the conduct of their supervisors or describing the features of their work environment. "Sexual harassment" like the term "rude" is not merely a descriptive term. It is a quasi-moral term. To say "X has been sexually harassed" is not merely to imply that certain descriptive conditions have been met, but also to contextually imply that some moral standard has been violated and that the victim disapproves of the action on moral grounds. Moral claims, unlike purely factual claims, are prescriptive in character, which is to say that they are tied to action in ways that purely descriptive claims are not. Thus to say "X is being sexually harassed" is also to contextually imply that something ought to be done about it. This explains why business leaders should discard Myth Number One. Moral problems do not fade away in a whimper. As the Thomas hearings indicated, they tend to erupt with a bang.

Sexual Harassment in the Workplace—An Historical Overview

In the wake of the Thomas hearings, the corporate world has been forced to acknowledge that sexual harassment is a serious problem. Unfortunately, however, this epiphany is no harbinger of increased moral sensitivity in corporate America. The source of the change is best explained as a natural outgrowth of Myth Number Two—the belief that the only time moral problems are business problems is when they become legal problems.

Given the business community's allegiance to Myth Number Two, it is understandable that corporations have been lethargic in responding to the problem of sexual harassment. Law has moved very slowly in this area. Although Title VII of the Civil Rights Act of 1964 prohibited discrimination on the basis of sex, it was not until 1972 that an amendment was added to explicitly prohibit sexual harassment. Even then, women were reluctant to complain or sue.[13] When women did sue, they were initially unsuccessful, probably because many judges concurred with the view expressed by Judge Frey who remarked, in finding against the plaintiff in a sexual harassment case, that he was unwilling to set a precedent which would encourage a flood of lawsuits because, "the only way an employer could avoid such charges would be to have employees who were asexual."[14]

It was not until *Barnes v. Train* 13 Fair Empl. Prac. Cas. (BNA) 123 (D.D.C.) 1974, rev'd sub nom. *Barnes v. Costle,* 561 F. 2d 983 (D.C. Cir. 1977) that the court agreed that sexual harassment was prohibited under Title VII. The judge found in favor of the plaintiff who had complained of discrimination on the grounds that she had been belittled, harassed, and ultimately fired because she had refused to have sex with her supervisor.[15] The case was important in finding that what was defined in the EEOC guidelines as "quid pro quo sexual harassment" (cases of "unwelcome sexual conduct" in which "submission to such conduct is made either explicitly or implicitly a term or condition of an individual's employment") was prohibited under Title VII and by establishing some precedent for vicarious employer responsibility for the conduct of a supervisor, at least where the employer was aware of the harassment and took no action.

In most cases, however, the emotional, professional, and financial costs of conducting even a successful suit seemed sufficiently high to insure that few women would even sue, particularly as general compensatory and punitive damages are not available to plaintiffs under Title VII.[16] Despite Judge Frey's assumption that providing legal

recognition of sexual harassment would put employers at risk of incurring a flood of suits, in 1980, fully three years after *Barnes,* only 75 charges were filed.[17]

It was not until *Meritor Saving Bank v. Vinson* 447 U.S. 57 (1986), a case in which the plaintiff alleged that she had been harassed, raped, threatened, and forced to acquiesce to further sexual contacts for fear of losing her job, that the Supreme Court, relying heavily upon the 1980 EEOC guidelines, affirmed that "quid pro quo sexual harassment" AND "environmental harassment" ("unwelcome" sexual conduct that "unreasonably interferes with an individual's job performance" or sustains an "intimidating, hostile or offensive working environment") both constitute violations of Title VII. *Meritor* was important in reaffirming the decision in *Barnes* that quid pro quo harassment is illegal and in establishing, for the first time, that sexual harassment which creates a hostile work environment (even in the absence of quid pro quo harassment) is sufficient to make such conduct illegal under Title VII. It was also important because it emphasized that the crucial issue in deciding whether conduct constitutes sexual harassment is whether it is "unwelcome," rather than whether it is "voluntary."[18]

Following *Meritor,* subsequent cases continued a trend (begun even before *Meritor*) of expanding the scope of illegal sexual harassment. A series of decisions extended sexual harassment to cover harassment by coworkers, non-employees (e.g., clients) and third parties (e.g., cases in which employees complain because they are denied benefits accorded to others who acquiesce to sexual harassment).[19] Further decisions extended protection from sexual harassment to homosexuals and to heterosexual men.[20] Other decisions have clarified and extended employer liability. EEOC guidelines, revised in 1988, summarized and incorporated these developments.[21]

Still more significantly, although state and federal antidiscrimination laws were the initial vehicle for legal change vis-à-vis sexual harassment, significant cases have been considered under common law on such grounds as: tort claims based on sexual harassment, worker compensation statutes, intentional infliction of emotional distress, assault and battery, tortious interference with contracts, invasion of privacy, false imprisonment, wrongful discharge, and even on the peculiar grounds of loss of consortium (the loss of a husband's ability to protect his right to his wife's sexual services).[22] The advantage of claims brought under common law is that they may result in heavy punitive damages for employers.

Finally law began to give recognition to prevention, as well as remediation, and to assess higher punitive damages. As an AP release in the October 18, 1991 *Wall Street Journal* noted, at the time of the allegations against Judge Thomas, Maine had just passed a law requiring employers to educate workers about sexual harassment. The first state law of its kind, it may serve as model for other states. Maine also raised fines for violations of the Maine Human Rights Act to $10,000 for the first offense, to $25,000 for the second and to $50,000 for a third offense.

Theoretically, given the legal developments just cited, sexual harassment should have become an explosive communication problem in the '80s. Only two catalysts were missing: power and politics. Despite the much ballyhooed progress of women during the past decades, women still have significantly less political and economic power than men. In 1990, women between the ages of 35–44 (their prime earning years), working full time, only garnered 69% of what men earned, and 37% of female heads of households had incomes in the bottom fifth of the income distribution.[23] At the time of the Thomas hearings, there were still only two women in the U.S. Senate. Finally, as Susan Faludi (author of *Backlash, The Undeclared War Against American Women*) also pointed out, in a biting article in *The Wall Street Journal* following the Thomas fiasco, Thomas' reign at the EEOC during the Reagan years insured that the issue of sexual harassment, as well as sexual discrimination, would be kept firmly under political wraps.[24]

In the wake of the furor created by the Thomas hearings, the corporate world belatedly recognized that the legal machinery for a full fledged assault on the problem was now in place and that political winds had shifted. Women still lack economic power and adequate political representation, but in a close election, they will wield considerable political power at the ballot box. Women's issues are likely to be at the forefront of national politics for some time to come.[25]

The lesson to be learned from all this is that Myth Number Two—the idea that moral problems are serious only when they become legal problems—should have been relinquished a long time ago. Morality and legality are not coextensive; only the most harmful forms of immoral conduct are illegal. If corporations are anxious to avoid public relations fiascos and expensive litigation, they must make moral education part of their business.

Legal guidelines which regulate the work place should emerge, in part, from concern and debate in the business community itself. Simply because sexual harassment has so recently emerged from the shadows of corporate inertia into the glare of judicial scrutiny, it is unlikely that the courts have yet shed any final light upon this matter. Now that sexual harassment has become a subject of public moral and political debate, new cases will be heard, new precedents set, and new laws will be forthcoming. Already punitive damages are soaring. In 1986, an Ohio woman won a 3.1 million dollar verdict against her employer whose quid pro quo offer involved oral sex in order to retain her job.[26] In September 1991, a California court awarded another 3.1 million to two women police officers for being subjected to a hostile work environment.[27] Still more legal problems are emerging because now even alleged perpetrators are suing on the grounds of wrongful discharge. Corporations who have faced, or are facing, such suits include: Polaroid, Newsday, General Motors, AT&T, DuPont, Boeing, and Rockwell International.[28] According to the most recent 1992 *Working Woman* survey, it may cost corporate America more than $1 billion over the next five years to settle existing lawsuits. The business community has paid a high price for its allegiance to outworn myths, not only in punitive damages, but also in marred corporate images. Any lessons learned, have been learned at too high a cost.

Why Corporations Still Don't Get It

As *Business Week* proclaimed in its 1991 October issue, sexual harassment is finally "Top of the News." Corporations STILL don't get it, but they are trying. Most corporations have adopted the recommendations of the United States Merit Systems

Protections Board, enunciated in 1988. As a headline in *The Wall Street Journal* December 2, 1991 points out, "Sexual Harassment is Topping Agenda in Many Executive Education Programs." According to that article, of 495 companies surveyed, 40.2% now provide training programs about sexual harassment. One management consultant in the field estimates that 90% of Fortune 500 companies will offer such programs within the year—despite the fact that her package can cost as much as $100,000.[29] Ironically, sexual harassment has now become a thriving business.

Unfortunately, it is doubtful that most of the existing types of sexual harassment education currently being offered by human resource consultants are likely to be very effective because such programs overlook the role of power in organizations and the potential for the abuse of organizational power in today's job market. An effective educational program should result in the reduction and eventual elimination of harassing behaviors without inflicting further damage upon the groups most likely to be victimized, but it is doubtful that even where there is a clearly defined corporate policy about sexual harassment, a formal grievance procedure, and strictly enforced sanctions for non-compliance that incidents of sexual harassment will be fully reported or greatly reduced.

Managers wield enormous power over subordinates through their ability to hire, fire, demote, or promote employees and through their authority (based upon the law of agency) which recognizes and enforces their managerial decisions. As I will show in the concluding sections of this paper, sexual harassment is a flagrant abuse of power because it violates the moral rights of employees. In practice, however, it is very difficult for employees in subordinate positions to insist upon their rights. Sexual harassment is often subtle and difficult to prove. Even if victims do prove their case, they have every reason to fear subtle forms of retaliation in their current positions and subtle forms of discrimination if they attempt to secure other positions. Claims about unfair hiring and promotion decisions are difficult to substantiate, especially in a climate where there are too many equally well qualified applicants for the few positions available. In a recessive economy almost all employees are desperate to retain the jobs they have and to avoid even the semblance of "making waves." Under such conditions, it is almost impossible for those most likely to be victimized to protect themselves without incurring further harms. As a consequence, an effective educational program must focus not only upon educating the potential victim, but also upon the task of deterring the potential victimizers. In sum, it must educate those who hold and exercise the power in the business community about the reasons why sexual harassment is morally wrong and why they have ethical responsibilities to eliminate it.

The kinds of sexual harassment education currently being offered in most corporations are not likely to deter potential victimizers because they are still based on old myths. Myth Number Three—the belief that most moral problems result from ignorance about facts, explains why corporations are hiring consultants to deluge employees with facts about sexual harassment. Of course we need to know the facts, but a lot of this information is old news, and educating people about facts is simply not enough. Moral problems occur not only when there is ignorance or disagreement about facts, but also when there is disagreement about values. There is no logical inconsistency between acknowledging legal and statistical facts about sexual harassment and refusing to take a moral stand. Only moral education can bridge the gap by providing reasons for giving up deeply entrenched ideas that, at best, the issue of sexual harassment is "much ado about nothing" or, at worst, a "legal menace" to which many managers may deeply resent being subjected.

Myth Number Four—the belief that the problem of sexual harassment results primarily from either cultural differences, or from differences in the way men and women feel and communicate, also acccounts, in part, for the current influx of psychologists and management consultants into the workplace to conduct trendy little workshops designed to educate people about cultural and gender difference. Thanks to Deborah Tannen *et al.*, we are all supposed to believe that "You Just Don't Understand," and that a little psychodrama will clear up the problem.[30] It won't.

Of course there is some truth in old myths or they wouldn't retain such a tenacious hold on our thinking. There may be cultural differences in attitudes about sex and there may be differences between the way the two genders feel and communicate about sex, and some of these differences may serve to causally explain the incidence of sexual harassment—and probably rape as well.

There may also be considerable truth in all three popular models for understanding sexual harassment. According to the natural/biological model, sexual harassment is attributable to biological differences between genders. Men have stronger sexual drives and feel differently about sexual interaction than women do. According to the sociocultural model, sexual harassment is a product of a patriarchal system in which men learn to use and to enjoy the exercise of personal power based on sex. According to the organizational model sexual harassment results from asymmetrical relationships of power and authority which derive from hierarchical organizational structures.[31]

Taken together, culture and gender based approaches to sexual harassment do a great deal to causally explain the widespread incidence of sexual harassment. Unfortunately, they do not provide any rational moral reasons which might convince potential victimizers to make any commitment to changing attitudes, beliefs, communication styles, or behavior which perpetuate it.

The almost exclusive emphasis on culture, gender, or communication can also have damaging side effects. Hiring women consultants to explain facts and to explore differences in feelings and communication styles between the genders can only encourage the notion that sexual harassment is a woman's problem and that all women understand it. It can only reinforce old stereotypes that women form some monolithic group who think and feel alike. This is simply not the case. Moral problems are everyone's problem and everyone, including women, needs to understand their character. Sexual harassment stress syndrome results, in part, from the fact that women, themselves, don't always understand, which is why they lose self confidence and why they feel worthless and at fault. Some women like feminist attorney, Catherine MacKinnon, do understand that "objection to sexual harassment is not a neo-puritan protest"; other women like revisionist Camille Paglia, who believes "this psychodrama is puritanism reborn," don't understand at all.[32] Analogously, emphasizing cultural differences in communication styles

may reinforce old stereotypes, or create new ones encouraging the mistaken idea that all members of ethnic groups supposedly think and behave alike.

The problem of sexual harassment is a moral problem and moral problems do not merely result from differences in feelings or cultural values, nor should human behavior and communication in this area (or any other) properly be understood as mere knee jerk reactions to biological or cultural drives. Biological drives can be restrained and cultures, including corporate cultures, can be changed. The changes we need are not merely changes in the way people feel and communicate, but rather changes in the way people think about what constitutes appropriate moral conduct.

The Definition of Sexual Harassment

Undoubtedly one of the biggest obstacles to "getting" sexual harassment is Myth Number Five—the belief that the concept of sexual harassment (like most moral concepts) is "murky." Some people worry that there are such deep cultural and gender based differences about the topic that no satisfactory definition can ever be provided. It is now fashionable for Europeans to laugh and talk condescendingly about American puritanism, and for people in our own country to act as if the goal of combatting sexual harassment is equivalent to some Machiavellian scheme to "desexualize the workplace" and to deny fellow employees dating and courtship rites.[33] Some people claim to be completely bewildered by what the term means and worry hysterically that a sympathetic hug might be misconstrued as "sexual touching."[34] As one attorney for an employer remarked, "If one woman's interpretation sets the legal standard, then it is virtually up to every woman in the workplace to define if she's been sexually harassed."[35] A great deal of this popular wisdom, however, seems to stem from ignorance about the sophistication of EEOC guidelines, or from deliberate attempts on the part of some members of the political, business, or legal communities to prey on such ignorance and to create a backlash.

Surprisingly, some philosophers have encouraged the supposition that sexual harassment is a murky concept by treating the whole problem of defining it as a complex philosophical problem.

Two recent philosophical articles devoted to defining sexual harassment deserve especial comment. Both articles, one would presume, offer definitions which their respective authors believe to be superior to existing EEOC definitions, but although both articles mention EEOC guidelines in passing, neither supplies any exhaustive criticism or sustained argument to show why their definitions constitute any improvement.

Susan M. Dodds, Lucy Frost, Robert Pargetter and Elizabeth W. Prior (1988) and Edmund Wall (1991) represent diametrically opposed views about how sexual harassment should be defined.[36] Dodds *et al.* propose a behavioral definition, because they believe that sexual harassment can occur even when an individual woman is not offended (e.g., as in cases of women who just shrug off being propositioned). According to Dodds *et al.*, there are no mental states on the part of the victim which are necessary conditions of sexual harassment. They seem to believe that this sharply differentiates their view from the view expressed in EEOC guidelines, and they insist that a behavioral definition is necessary for the administration of public policy.[37]

Wall, by contrast with Dodds *et al.*, believes that the mental states of both the perpetrator and the victim are essential defining elements of sexual harassment.[38] He believes that subjective features are essential in defining sexual harassment because, although a range of behaviors can, on occasion, be identified as sexual harassment, almost any of the behaviors, given different mental states of alleged victimizers and victims, may not qualify as sexual harassment at all. Perhaps a quid pro quo offer was only "banter" or perhaps the alleged victim really welcomed the offer as a "career opportunity."[39] Wall seems very concerned with preventing the much popularized innocent man/paranoid woman scenario.[40] Certainly, his inclusion of the perpetrator's mental states differs from EEOC guidelines which focus on the mental states of a victim, or more accurately, a reasonable victimized person.

Both Dodds *et al.* and Wall agree, however, that certain features which have been proposed as necessary and sufficient conditions of sexual harassment do not so qualify. Some theorists, such as Larry May and John C. Hughes, as well as EEOC guidelines, hold that sexual harassment always constitutes discrimination.[41] Both Dodds *et al.* and Wall disagree because, they argue, a bisexual might sexually harass both sexes without the action being discriminatory.[42] This line of argument seems rather silly as an objection to EEOC guidelines and does nothing to establish that sexual harassment is not discriminatory. The whole purpose of Title VII was to prevent invidious discrimination against any employee in the work place, not merely women. Where sexual issues (gender, sexual preferences, sexual orientation, sexual bias, willingness to succumb to sexual advances etc.) are used as a basis for making hiring, firing, or promotion decisions, or for any differences in treatment in the workplace, there is invidious discrimination among employees, because sex (in any of the senses just indicated) constitutes a morally inappropriate basis for such decisions.

Dodds *et al.* and Wall are also in agreement that the presence of coercion and/or negative consequences resulting from harassment, are not necessary conditions for the existence of sexual harassment because the victim's personality and values contribute to the effect that a sexual offer will have upon that person. Dodds *et al.* and Wall are no doubt correct, but they fail to appreciate that the revised EEOC guidelines are compatible with their position. EEOC guidelines do not define sexual harassment in terms of coercion. EEOC guidelines hold that for behavior to constitute sexual harassment, it must be "unwelcome," and decisions about whether a victim found conduct to be unwelcome are to be based upon facts about her conduct.[43] Furthermore, where the victim has submitted to the sexual conduct, the pivotal issue in determining whether the conduct was harassment is whether the conduct was unwelcome; the issue of whether the conduct was voluntary has been ruled to have "no materiality" whatever.

EEOC guidelines do not define sexual harassment in terms of negative consequences for actual victims. The section dealing with "hostile work environment" specifically acknowledges that certain conditions constitute sexual harassment even when "they lead to no tangible or economic job consequences."[44] Emotional consequences are an issue in EEOC guidelines in determining whether certain types of conduct create a hostile work environment, but the responses are not those of the particular victim, but the hypothetical responses of a reasonable person.[45] By contrast, Wall believes that distress on the part of the actual victim is one of the necessary conditions for sexual harassment.[46] Wall simply seems to be wrong here. Women have been conditioned to stoically accept a great deal of sexual behavior which may harm them professionally. Nevertheless, a reasonable person who had not been so conditioned, might be quite justifiably distressed. It is the issue of whether it would be rational to be distressed, rather than the issue of actual distress which seems central to defining sexual harassment, and this issue is already accommodated within EEOC guidelines.

If we examine the definitions finally proposed by Dodds *et al.* and Wall, we will see that neither definition is any improvement over the definition already proposed by the EEOC. Dodds *et al.* end up defining sexual harassment as:

> behavior which is typically associated with a mental state representing an attitude which seeks sexual ends without any concern for the person from whom those ends are sought, and which typically produces an unwanted and unpleasant response in the person who is the object of that behavior . . . even if the mental states of the harasser or the harassed (or both) are different from those typically associated with such behavior. The behavior constitutes a necessary and sufficient condition for sexual harassment.[47]

The definition proposed by Dodds *et al.* does (as they claim) possess a number of advantages, but most of those advantages can also be claimed for the EEOC definition which invokes "a reasonable person standard" in deciding whether the victim's response is appropriate, as well as in deciding "the more basic issue of whether challenged conduct is of a sexual nature."[48] Moreover, the EEOC definition has a major advantage that Dodds *et al.*'s definition does not possess. The EEOC definition, by appealing to the attitudes of the reasonable person (i.e., any reasonable victim) escapes the trap of cultural relativism. Dodds *et al.*, by contrast, provide an account which they acknowledge to be culture relative, for they claim that "it will be a culture-relative kind of behavior that determines sexual harassment." What counts as sexual harassment will vary from society to society and "behavior which may be sexual harassment in one need

not be in another."[49] While admittedly the kind of behavior which is recognized as sexual harassment will vary to some extent from culture to culture, and while admittedly employees of multinational corporations should respect the views of those from different cultures who feel harassed, even under conditions under which typically Americans would not feel harassed, there is no reason to think (as Dodds *et al.* apparently do) that it is the *fact* that the behavior/attitude correlation is typical in a given culture, or any culture, which justifies classifying the behavior as sexual harassment.

The EEOC guidelines which refer to a "reasonable person" standard avoid the trap of both subjective and cultural relativism; what makes behavior count as sexual harassment is not what a particular woman thinks about the behavior, or even what most people think about the behavior, but rather what a *reasonable* victim would think about it. No doubt there are some (perhaps even Dodds *et al.*) who might contend that what is regarded as a "reasonable person" is also culture relative, but this is simply not true. Reasonable people employ rational grounds for making moral judgments, and what constitutes a rational ground cannot be decided simply by invoking cultural standards. Behavior is morally wrong, not merely because it is typically regarded as morally wrong in a particular culture, but because there are rational grounds for contending that it violates human rights, inflicts harm, or contributes to social injustice. Morality, as Lawrence Kohlberg and numerous philosophers have pointed out, is not a descriptive term. Pari passu, the same is true of the terms "reasonable person" and "sexual harassment."[50]

Even if sexual harassment were a purely descriptive term, the definition provided by Dodds *et al.* is too broad, too narrow, and too vague. It is too broad because the definition they provide would apply equally well to selfish sexual behavior on the part of males toward females in many unhappy consensual relationships ranging from affairs to marriages. It also seems too narrow in that it would exclude conduct in which the perpetrator did have some concern for his victim (e.g., he's in love with her for messianic reasons and thinks that she would be better off succumbing to his advances). It also seems too vague to be any improvement on the EEOC definition. What behaviors in our society would be identified as sexual harassment using their definition? Suppose men and women disagree. How is their definition supposed to help? In particular, how is their definition supposed to serve as a basis for proposing uniform guidelines about sexual harassment for multi-national corporations?

Wall's proposed definition seems equally unlikely to be an improvement upon that already available in EEOC guidelines. Wall believes that the essence of sexual harassment is wrongful communication which violates the privacy rights of the victim. These rights are violated "not by the content of the offender's proposal, but in the inappropriateness of the approach to the victim."[51]

Wall proposes that:

Wherein *X* is the sexual harasser and *Y* the victim, the following are offered as jointly necessary and sufficient conditions of sexual harassment:

1. *X* does not attempt to obtain *Y*'s consent to communicate to *Y*, *X*'s or someone else's purported sexual interest in *Y*.
2. *X* communicates to *Y*, *X*'s or someone else's purported sexual interest in *Y*. *X*'s motives for communicating this is some perceived benefit that he expects to obtain through the communication.
3. *Y* does not consent to discuss with *X*, *X*'s or someone else's purported sexual interest in *Y*.
4. *Y* feels emotionally distressed because *X* did not attempt to obtain *Y*'s consent to this discussion and/or because *Y* objected to the content of *X*'s sexual comments.[52]

There seem to be a number of difficulties with Wall's definition. The worst difficulty is that it is too narrow. It excludes sexist harassment (e.g., demeaning remarks about women in general) and a great deal of environmental harassment (e.g., the display of objectionable sexual objects, discussions of sexual matters unrelated to work, etc.) which most people would want to include. Certainly excluding those elements requires considerably more argument than the perfunctory claim that "girlie" posters probably are better classified as bad taste rather than sexual harassment.[53] Wall's definition does not seem to accord with our basic intuitions. If indeed Judge Thomas did discuss the kinds of

topics (e.g., his sexual endowments and prowess, pornographic movies, and the Coke can incident) with Professor Hill that she alleges he did, most people would agree that she was certainly being subjected to a hostile work environment, even if he never said that he had an interest in engaging in sex with her or suggested that anyone else had such an interest. This seems to contradict Wall's belief that the content of what is communicated is immaterial.

There could also be cases of even quid pro quo sexual harassment in which few of the four conditions Wall specifies obtain. Wall simply fails to recognize that, in the case of sexual harassment, communication fails, not merely because the message is not communicated in an appropriate manner, but because, given the inequalities in status and income between employees, many employees (most of them women) do not feel at liberty to communicate honestly; few can afford to pay the price of honest communication.[54]

If Dodds' *et al.* and Wall's definitions won't do, how should sexual harassment be defined? Don't their difficulties provide still more justification for all the current ballyhoo about the "murkiness" of sexual harassment and the new dangers perfectly well intentioned men and employers may face now that the problem of sexual harassment is being publicly acknowledged? Quite the contrary, defining sexual harassment for the purposes of business ethics is NOT a major philosophical problem. Although, given the difficulty of honest communication, one can hope that the courts will ultimately employ the reasonable person standards in deciding whether conduct is "welcome," the meaning of sexual harassment is reasonably well defined in EEOC guidelines.

Sexual harassment seems to be one of those concepts like the concept "game," to use Wittgenstein's famous example, which form a family.[55] Family members have family resemblances, but there is no shared feature all members of a family necessarily have in common. As a consequence, trying to set out necessary and sufficient conditions for sexual harassment is a thoroughly futile enterprise. The futility of that enterprise, however, does nothing to support the myth that the concept of sexual harassment is hopelessly murky. We are clear enough in paradigm cases about what people mean when they claim they are being sexually harassed. The paradigm cases have already been clearly spelled out by the revised 1985 EEOC guidelines which comprise a twenty page document incorporating references to cases up to that year. In the absence of some better definition, or in the absence of some sustained philosophical argument for adding or subtracting from the sorts of paradigms those guidelines include, they seem to provide better definitions than those Dodds *et al.* and Wall have suggested to replace them.

Of course, in addition to paradigmatic cases of sexual harassment identified by law, there are also borderline cases about which corporations, and in some cases the courts, will have to make decisions. As sexual harassment is a quasi-moral term, legal decisions about borderline cases will almost certainly be based upon whether the questionable behavior is sufficiently morally objectionable to count as sexual harassment in the legal sense. All of this suggests that, for the purpose of business ethics, corporations would be well advised not only to educate their employees about EEOC guidelines, but also to educate them about the moral reasons which justify the belief that sexual harassment is genuinely immoral and ought to be legally prohibited. Given that education, employees will be encouraged not only to refrain from sexual harassment in the paradigm sense defined by law, but also to identify the sorts of borderline cases which the courts may find to be illegal in the future, and to refrain from subtle forms of sexual harassment which violate the spirit, if not the letter of existing law.

Why Sexual Harassment in the Workplace Is Morally Wrong and Why It Ought to Be Legally Prohibited

Sexual harassment is not a murky concept, but in the absence of an adequate theory which provides rational grounds for concluding that sexual harassment is morally wrong, many members of the business community will continue to believe that sexual harassment is "much ado about nothing" from the moral point of view. Moreover, given the difficulty of proving the truth of sexual harassment claims, they may believe that courts would have been well advised to treat the problem with benign neglect.

In order to show that the corporate world must make some genuine moral commitment to ending sexual harassment in the workplace, one final myth must be discarded. Myth Number Six (the Neutrality Myth)—is the mistaken belief, still widely held by corporate America, that moral beliefs are based upon feelings or cultural values, and therefore one moral theory is as good as any other moral theory and equally deserving of respect. Allegiance to this outworn myth explains why corporations are reluctant to bring in professional philosophers to provide a moral education for their employees. It's all right to bring in business consultants to teach facts and to bring in psychologists to explore feelings, but in a multi-cultural society, moral education and moral stands are supposedly inappropriate.

The neutrality myth is a piece of outmoded nonsense. Moral education is now a part of the public school curriculum and an essential part of correctional education. Philosophers disagree among themselves about numerous ethical issues, but there is almost universal agreement about the following elementary points of meta-ethics. A moral theory does not merely express feelings nor is it based merely upon cultural values. A good moral theory provides good moral reasons for actions and beliefs and it must meet certain requirements: (1) *Logical coherence*—it must be clear and not generate contradictions; (2) *Impartiality*—any moral decision one person makes for himself on the basis of the theory must be a decision that person would be willing for others to make in similar circumstances; (3) *Consistency with Basic Moral Intuitions*—the use of the theory should not generate consequences any reasonable person would regard as morally objectionable (e.g., increased physical harm and suffering); (4) *Explanatory Adequacy*—the theory should provide reasons for moral judgements and serve as a basis for resolving conflicts; and (5) *Concern for the Facts*—the theory should take into account relevant facts about people, society, and existing circumstances. Inadequate moral theories do not satisfy these requirements, and some moral theories are better than others because they satisfy these requirements better than other theories. People are equally deserving of respect, but their moral views are not equally deserving of respect. The purpose of moral education is to teach people why some moral theories, and a lot of popular wisdom, simply don't hold water.

If we discard the old neutrality myth, and suggest good moral reasons why sexual harassment is NOT "much ado about nothing," corporations will have lost their last excuse for refusing to take a stand about sexual harassment and for failing to provide some moral education about the topic for their employees. What follows is a very brief outline of some good moral reasons for taking the problem of sexual harassment in the workplace seriously, for regarding it as morally objectionable, and for believing that it should be illegal.

First, sexual harassment is morally wrong because it physically and psychologically harms victims, and because environments which permit sexual harassment seem to encourage such harms. Even the most liberal moral theories acknowledge that harm to others is our strongest moral reason for restricting liberty. As the majority of victims in the past have been women, most of the evidence in support of the claim that sexual harassment is harmful is based upon evidence about women, but presumably any group which was habitually so victimized would suffer similar effects.

Some sexual harassment cases associated with "intimidating, hostile, or offensive working environment" involve rape or physical assault. Furthermore, both quid pro quo harassment and environmental harassment can cause sexual harassment trauma syndrome.[56] This syndrome involves both physical and psychological symptoms. According to Peggy Crull, a member of the New York Commission on Human Rights, an analysis of case material gathered from clients of Working Women's Institute's Information, Referral and Counseling Service showed that 90% of the cases experienced psychological stress symptoms (nervousness, fear, and anger) while 63% experienced physical symptoms (headaches, nausea, tiredness, etc.).[57] State common law claims of intentional infliction of emotional distress often accompany suits under Title VII; both require medical and psychiatric testimony to substantiate such claims.[58]

Some sexual touching which qualifies as sexual harassment under EEOC guidelines (even when it is confined to a single severe incident) may not inflict any direct physical harm on women, but permitting unwanted touching may encourage physical violence against women. As feminist philosopher, Carole Sheffield has pointed out, America's women live with sexual terrorism.[59] There were

103,000 reported rapes in 1990. As most rapes are unreported, the actual number may have been fifteen times that figure.[60] Every year over one million children are physically abused and the average number of assaults per year is 10.5. The majority of teenage victims are female. The incidence of sexual abuse is difficult to determine, but one survey of women found that 38% had experienced intra- or extra-familial sexual abuse by the time they reached age 18.[61] Finally 60–70% of evening calls to police departments concern domestic violence. One study found that 16% of the families surveyed had experienced husband/wife assaults. John Makepeace, in a survey of college students, found that 20% of female college students had experienced violence during dating and courtship.[62] Common sense suggests that, as physical violence against women is already a national disgrace, unwanted sexual touching in the workplace should be prohibited by law, and that cultures and institutions which fail to set limits upon unwanted sexual touching (i.e., touching parts of the body associated with sexual response) are encouraging further physical abuse and disrespect for women.

EEOC guidelines also hold that non physical conduct (e.g., sexual jokes, sexual conversation, the display of pornographic materials, etc.) in cases where it forms a repeated pattern does qualify as sexual harassment. The courts have been divided about this matter.[63] The 1986 Attorney General's Commission on Pornography did conclude that, although there is no general connection between pornography and violence, exposure to sexually degrading and violent materials does contribute to sexual violence against women.[64] The EEOC guidelines can be justified, in part, on the grounds of preventing physical harm to women.

Second, Wall is quite correct in emphasizing that sexual harassment violates privacy rights. Privacy, like pornography is a controversial subject. Suffice it to say here that there is a constitutional right to privacy first recognized by the Supreme Court in Griswold v. State of Connecticut 381 US 479.85 S Ct. 1678 (1965), a case involving the sale of contraceptives. In that case the Court found that there is a right to privacy emanating from penumbras surrounding the First, Third, Fourth, Fifth, Ninth and Fourteenth Amendments which create zones of privacy. Presumably unwanted sexual touching would violate zones of privacy emanating from the Third and Fourth Amendments; if our homes cannot be invaded, presumably our bodies should be doubly sacrosanct. There are also moral rights to specific types of privacy in the workplace.[65] William Brenkert, for example, analyzes privacy as a "three place relationship between a person *A*, some information *X*, and another person *Z*, such that the right to privacy is violated only when *Z* comes to possess information *X* and no relationship exists between *A* and *Z* which would justify *Z*'s coming to know *X*."[66] Given this conception of privacy, Brenkert, as well as Joseph DesJardins, argue that the information a person (or institution) is entitled to know about an employee is confined to the sort of information which pertains to the employee's ability to perform his job. Given that sexual matters are irrelevant in assessing an individual's ability to perform a job, privacy rights seem to preclude any inquiries by managers about the sexual lives of their employees outside of the workplace, and to provide a clear moral justification for discouraging sexual conversations within it.

Third, there are certainly historical and causal correlations between sexual harassment and discrimination. It was no accident that the issue was catapulted into national prominence by a black man and a black woman. While sexual harassment is an emotionally charged issue in every community, it is especially charged in those which have suffered from discrimination. Judge Thomas quite justifiably invoked the lynching metaphor to remind his accusers that black men have been victims of vicious sexual stereotypes which have led to lynchings resulting from wholly unjustified sexual allegations. Professor Hill might equally well have invoked "The Color Purple" to remind skeptics that historically black women have been targets of sexual abuse not only by white men, but also by men of their own race perhaps because, as William Oliver has suggested, black on black sexual violence may be a "function of minority males adopting a 'tough guy, player of women' image in order to deal with the pressure of urban problems."[67] Recent studies verify that women, and especially women of color, are still the group most likely to be victimized by sexual harassment, and that they are usually harassed by men occupying positions of superior authority. Given the complicated connections between discrimination, violence, inequalities in power, and sexual misconduct, corporations

have a duty to insist upon sexual propriety in the workplace in order to protect any employee from becoming a victim of further discrimination.

Fourth, sexual harassment violates liberty rights. Many philosophers, like John Rawls, believe that in a just society "Each person is to have an equal right to the most extensive total system of basic liberties compatible with a similar system for all."[68] Sexual harassment restricts liberty. A 1979 Working Women's Institute study found that 24% of sexual harassment victims were fired for complaining while another 42% left their jobs. Bailey and Richards (1985) found that 21% of women graduate students surveyed reported that they had not enrolled in a course in order to avoid sexual harassment.[69] The Merit Board survey found that between 1985 and 1987 approximately 36,647 employees left their jobs because of sexual harassment. To suggest that women should leave their jobs and deviate from their career tracks when confronted with sexual harassment is only to add injury to injury. Worse yet, it plays into vicious stereotypes that victims of sexual abuse "ask for it."

Fifth, sexual harassment violates rights to fair equality of opportunity. Rawls has argued persuasively that in a just society there should be "roughly equal prospects of culture and achievement for everyone similarly motivated and endowed."[70] There is a wealth of evidence to suggest that women do not enjoy fair equality in the workplace and that sexual harassment is part of the problem. Sexual harassment stress syndrome, resulting from quid pro quo and environmental harassment, impairs job performance. A hostile work environment undermines respect for women making it difficult for them to exercise authority and command respect. Pornography, sexual conversation, sexual and sexist jokes, girlie posters, and the like, are morally objectionable because they violate women's rights to enjoy fair equality of opportunity. They are especially objectionable in any workplace associated with criminal justice; the very life of a woman police or correctional officer may depend upon her ability to command respect from sexually abusive people. To insist that women protest sexual harassment in a public forum, and to fail to institute grievance procedures which protect their privacy only exacerbates the damage already done. It may create resentment among male colleagues, discourage men in positions of authority from serving as mentors to women, irreparably damage victims' prospects from developing warm working relationships with colleagues and for expanding their professional networks, and impair their prospects for securing employment elsewhere.

Sixth, sexual harassment demonstrates the kind of disrespect for persons which is incompatible with Kantian conceptions of the moral point of view. Respect for persons involves respecting every person's rights to be unharmed by others, and to enjoy rights to liberty, privacy, and equality of opportunity.

Seventh, sexual harassment is morally objectionable because it undermines utilitarian justifications for the very free enterprise system upon which the business community depends. The moral justification for such a system is that it supposedly maximizes freedom and efficiency.[71] We have already seen that sexual harassment curtails freedom. It is also inefficient. According to the Merit Board survey, sexual harassment cost the federal government at least 267 million dollars in a two year period. The estimate was based upon conservative conclusions about the costs of job turnover, sick leave and loss of productivity. The 1985 *Working Woman* survey estimated the cost of harassment for a typical Fortune 400 company of 23,784 employees to be nearly $7 million per year. It also estimated that the costs of permitting sexual harassment were over thirty-one times the initial costs of preventing it.[72] Finally, the traditional argument for insisting that the socio-economic inequalities of capitalism are morally justifiable consists in claiming that there is fair equality of opportunity and that permitting inequalities ultimately contributes to the benefit of all. Sexual harassment violates rights to fair equality of opportunity and, by doing so, creates inequalities which are disadvantageous to all. Sexual harassment is not merely a woman's problem. It is a problem for the entire business community.

Conclusion

Sexual harassment is not merely an abuse of power resulting from ignorance about facts or law. It is not merely a legal problem, a cultural problem, a gender problem or a communication problem. Sexual harassment is not "murky" and it is not "much ado about nothing."

Sexual harassment is a serious moral problem. To get to the root of the problem, the corporate world must begin to reason critically, to relinquish old myths, to take a strong moral stand, and to provide moral education for employees. It must then assess the effectiveness of that education by conducting anonymous surveys of those groups with the least powerful positions or with the most complaints in the past to determine whether there is a reduction of complaints among those respondents. Until then, sexual harassment will be a potentially explosive communication problem.

NOTES

1. Conte, Alba. *Sexual Harassment in the Workplace: Law and Practice.* New York: Wiley Law Publications, John Wiley and Sons, Inc., 1990, p. 2.
2. Paludi, Michele A. and Richard B. Barickman. *Academic and Workplace Sexual Harassment, A Resources Manual.* Albany, New York: State University of New York Press, 1991, p. 12.
3. Conte, p. 2.
4. Paludi and Barickman, p. 12.
5. Gibbs, Nancy. 'Office Crimes,' *Time* (October 21, 1991): 52–64.
6. Galen, Michele, Joseph Weber, Alice Cuneo. 'Out of the Shadows, The Thomas Hearings Force Business to Confront an Ugly Reality,' *Business Week* (October 28, 1991): 30–31.
7. Sandoff, Ronni. "Sexual Harassment: The Inside Story,' (Working Woman Survey.) *Working Woman,* June 1992.
8. Conte, p. 4.
9. Templin, Neal. 'As Women Assume More Power, Charges Filed by Men May Rise,' *The Wall Street Journal* (October 18, 1991): B3.
10. Sandroff, p. 8.
11. Conte, pp. 425–6.
12. Segal, Troy and Zachary Schiller. 'Six Experts Suggest Ways to Negotiate the Minefield,' *Business Week* (October 12, 1991): 33.
13. Conte. p. 2.
14. *Ibid.,* p. 18.
15. *Ibid.,* pp. 20–23.
16. *Ibid.,* p. 212.
17. *Ibid.,* p. 3.
18. *Ibid.,* pp. 52–61.
19. *Ibid.,* pp. 37–40, 71–74.
20. *Ibid.,* pp. 41, 70 and Templin, B3.
21. Conte, pp. 67–69 and 493–501.

22. *Ibid.*, pp. 261–279.
23. Faludi, Susan. 'Women Lost Ground in the 1980's and the EEOC Didn't Help,' *The Wall Street Journal* (October 18, 1991; B4).
24. Faludi, Susan. *Backlash, The Undeclared War Against American Women.* New York; Crown Publishing Inc., 1991.
25. Painton, Priscilla. 'Woman Power,' *Time* (October 28, 1991): 24–26.
26. Gibbs, p. 53.
27. Gest, Ted and Amy Saltzman with Betsy Carpenter and Dorian Friedman. *U.S. News & World Report* (October 21, 1991): 38–40.
28. Lublin, JoAnn. 'As Harassment Charges Rise, More Men Fight Back,' *The Wall Street Journal* (October 18, 1991; B4).
29. Lublin, JoAnn. 'Sexual Harassment is Topping Agenda in Many Executive Education Programs,' *The Wall Street Journal* (December 2, 1991): B1.
30. Tannen, Deborah. *You Just Don't Understand, Women and Men in Conversation.* New York: Ballantine Books, 1990.
31. Paludi and Barickman, pp. 61–62.
32. Gest and Saltzman with Carpenter and Freidman, p. 40.
33. Leo, John. 'Harassment's Murky Edges,' *U.S. News & World Report* (October 21, 1991): 26.
34. Crossen, Cynthia. 'Are You From Another Planet, or What?,' *The Wall Street Journal* (October 18, 1991): B1.
35. Leo, p. 26.
36. Dodds, Susan M., Lucy Frost, Robert Pargetter and Elizabeth W. Prior. 'Sexual Harassment,' *Moral Issues in Business.* 5th ed. William W. Shaw and Vincent Barry. Belmont, California: Wadsworth Publishing Co., 1992, 464–471. Wall, Edmund. 'The Definition of Sexual Harassment,' *Public Affairs Quarterly* Vol. 5, No. 4 (October 1991): 371–385.
37. Dodds *et al.*, pp. 466–468.
38. Wall, p. 371.
39. *Ibid.*, pp. 380–1.
40. *Ibid.*, pp. 376–378.
41. Hughes, Larry and May, John C. 'Is Sexual Harassment Coercive?,' in Gertrude Ezorsky, Ed., *Moral Rights in the Workplace.* New York: State of New York Press, 1982, pp. 115–22.
42. Dodds *et al.*, p. 466 and Wall, p. 381.
43. Conte, p. 446.
44. *Ibid.*, p. 482.
45. *Ibid.*, pp. 489–80.
46. *Ibid.*, p. 374.
47. Dodds *et al.*, p. 468.
48. Conte, p. 490.
49. Dodds *et al.*, p. 469.
50. Kohlberg, Lawrence. 'From Ought to Is: How to Commit the Naturalistic Fallacy and Get Away With It in the Study of Moral Development,' *Cognitive Development and Epistemology.* New York: Academic Press, 1971, 151–232.
51. Wall, p. 378.
52. *Ibid.*, p. 374.
53. *Ibid.*, p. 383.
54. Marx, Linda, Gail Wescot, Gayle Vernet and Marilyn Balmaci. 'The Price of Saying No,' *People* (October 28, 1991: 44–49.
55. Wittgnestein, Ludwig. *Philosophical Investigations.* NY: The MacMillan Co., 1953.
56. Conte, p. 9 and Paludi and Barickman, p. 29.
57. Crull, Peggy. 'The Stress Effects of Sexual Harassment on the Job,' *Academic and Workplace Sexual Harassment, A Resources Manual.* ed. Michele A. Paludi and Richard B. Barickman. Albany, New York: State University of New York Press, 1991, 133–144.
58. Conte, p. 9.
59. Sheffield, Carole. 'Sexual Terrorism,' *Feminist Philosophies, Problems, Theories, and Applications.* ed. Janet A. Kourany, James P. Sterba, Rosemarie Tong. Englewood Cliffs, New Jersey: Prentice Hall, 1992, 60–72.
60. Siegel, Larry J. *Criminology,* 4th ed. St. Paul, Minnesota: West Publishing Co., 1989.
61. *Ibid.*, p. 306.
62. *Ibid.*, p. 308.
63. Conte, pp. 491–493.
64. Siegel, p. 406.
65. Brenkert, George G. 'Privacy, Polygraphs and Work,' *Contemporary Issues in Business Ethics.* ed. Joseph R. DesJardins and John J. McCall. Belmont, California: Wadsworth Publishing Co., 1985, 227–237. DesJardins, Joseph R. 'An Employee's Right to Privacy,' *Contemporary Issues in Business Ethics.* ed. Joseph R. DesJardins and John J. McCall. Belmont, California: Wadsworth Publishing Co., 1985, 221–227. Wasserstrom, Richard A. 'Privacy,' *Contemporary Issues in Business Ethics.* 2nd ed., ed. Joseph J. DesJardins and John J. McCall. Belmont, California: Wadsworth Publishing Co., 1990, 196–201.
66. Brenkert, p. 229.
67. Siegel, p. 292.
68. Rawls, John. *A Theory of Justice.* Cambridge: Harvard University Press, The Belknapp Press, 1971.
69. Paludi and Barickman, p. 149.
70. Rawls, p. 73.
71. Velasquez, Manuel. *Business Ethics, Concepts and Cases.* 2nd ed. Englewood Cliffs, New Jersey: Prentice Hall, 1988.
72. Conte, pp. 8–9.

Exaggerating the Extent of Sexual Harassment

Ellen Frankel Paul

Women in American society are victims of sexual harassment in alarming proportions. Sexual harassment is an inevitable corollary to class exploitation; as capitalists exploit workers, so do males in positions of authority exploit their female subordinates. Male professors, supervisors, and apartment managers in ever increasing numbers take advantage of the financial dependence and vulnerability of women to extract sexual concessions.

Valid Assertions?

These are the assertions that commonly begin discussions of sexual harassment. For reasons that will be adumbrated below, dissent from the prevailing view is long overdue. Three recent episodes will serve to frame this disagreement.

Valerie Craig, an employee of Y & Y Snacks, Inc., joined several co-workers and her supervisor for drinks after work one day in July of 1978. Her supervisor drove her home and proposed that they become more intimately acquainted. She refused his invitation for sexual relations, whereupon he said that he would "get even" with her. Ten days after the incident she was fired from her job. She soon filed a complaint of sexual harassment with the Equal Employment Opportunity Commission (EEOC), and the case wound its way through the courts. Craig prevailed, the company was held liable for damages, and she received back pay, reinstatement, and an order prohibiting Y & Y from taking reprisals against her in the future.

Carol Zabowicz, one of only two female forklift operators in a West Bend Co. warehouse, charged that her co-workers over a four-year period from 1978–1982 sexually harassed her by such acts as: asking her whether she was wearing a bra; two of the men exposing their buttocks between ten and twenty times; a male co-worker grabbing his crotch

and making obscene suggestions or growling; subjecting her to offensive and abusive language; and exhibiting obscene drawings with her initials on them. Zabowicz began to show symptoms of physical and psychological stress, necessitating several medical leaves, and she filed a sexual harassment complaint with the EEOC. The district court judge remarked that "the sustained, malicious, and brutal harassment meted out . . . was more than merely unreasonable; it was malevolent and outrageous." The company knew of the harassment and took corrective action only after the employee filed a complaint with the EEOC. The company was, therefore, held liable, and Zabowicz was awarded back pay for the period of her medical absence, and a judgment that her rights were violated under the Civil Rights Act of 1964.

On September 17, 1990, Lisa Olson, a sports reporter for the *Boston Herald*, charged five football players of the just-defeated New England Patriots with sexual harassment for making sexual suggestive and offensive remarks to her when she entered their locker room to conduct a post-game interview. The incident amounted to nothing short of "mind rape," according to Olson. After vociferous lamentations in the media, the National Football League fined the team and its players $25,000 each. The National Organization of Women called for a boycott of Remington electric shavers because the owner of the company, Victor Kiam, also owns the Patriots and who allegedly displayed insufficient sensitivity at the time when the episode occurred.

Utopian Treatment for Women

All these incidents are indisputably disturbing. In an ideal world—one needless to say far different from the one that we inhabit or are ever likely to inhabit—women would not be subjected to such treatment in the course of their work. Women, and men as well, would be accorded respect by co-workers and supervisors, their feelings would be taken into account, and their dignity would be left intact. For women to expect reverential treatment in the workplace is utopian, yet they should not have to tolerate outrageous, offensive sexual overtures and threats as they go about earning a living.

One question that needs to be pondered is: What kinds of undesired sexual behavior women should be protected against by law? That is, what kind of actions are deemed so outrageous and violate a woman's rights to such extent that the law should intervene, and what actions should be considered inconveniences of life, to be morally condemned but not adjudicated? A subsidiary question concerns the type of legal remedy appropriate for the wrongs that do require redress. Before directly addressing these questions, it might be useful to diffuse some of the hyperbole adhering to the sexual harassment issue.

Harassment Surveys

Surveys are one source of this hyperbole. If their results are accepted at face value, they lead to the conclusion that women are disproportionately victims of legions of sexual harassers. A poll by the Albuquerque *Tribune* found that nearly 80 percent of the respondents reported that they or someone they knew had been victims of sexual harassment. The Merit Systems Protection Board determined that 42 percent of the women (and 14 percent of men) working for the federal government had experienced some form of unwanted sexual attention between 1985 and 1987, with unwanted "sexual teasing" identified as the most prevalent form. A Defense Department survey found that 64 percent of women in the military (and 17 percent of the men) suffered "uninvited and unwanted sexual attention" within the previous year. The United Methodist Church established that 77 percent of its clergywomen experienced incidents of sexual harassment, with 41 percent of these naming a pastor or colleague as the perpetrator, and 31 percent mentioning church social functions as the setting.

A few caveats concerning polls in general, and these sorts of polls in particular, are worth considering. Pollsters looking for a particular social ill tend to find it, usually in gargantuan proportions. (What fate would lie in store for a pollster who concluded that child abuse, or wife beating, or mistreatment of the elderly had dwindled to the point of negligibility!) Sexual harassment is a notoriously ill-defined and almost infinitely expandable concept, including everything from rape to unwelcome neck massaging, discomfiture upon witnessing sexual overtures directed at others, yelling at and blowing smoke in the ears of female subordinates, and displays of pornographic pictures in the workplace. Defining sexual harassment, as the United Methodists did, as "any sexually related behavior that is unwelcome, offensive or which fails to respect the rights of others," the concept is broad enough to include everything from "unsolicited suggestive looks or leers [or] pressures for dates" to "actual sexual assaults or rapes." Categorizing everying from rape to "looks" as sexual harassment makes us all victims, a state of affairs satisfying to radical feminists, but not very useful for distinguishing serious injuries from the merely trivial.

Yet, even if the surveys exaggerate the extent of sexual harassment, however defined, what they do reflect is a great deal of tension between the sexes. As women in ever increasing numbers entered the workplace in the last two decades, as the women's movement challenged alleged male hegemony and exploitation with ever greater intemperance, and as women entered previously all-male preserves from the board rooms to the coal pits, it is lamentable, but should not be surprising, that this tension sometimes takes sexual form. Not that sexual harassment on the job, in the university, and in other settings is a trivial or significant matter, but a sense of proportion needs to be restored and, even more important, distinctions need to be made. In other words, sexual harassment must be de-ideologized. Statements that paint nearly all women as victims and all men and their patriarchal, capitalist system as perpetrators, are ideological fantasy. Ideology blurs the distinction between being injured—being a genuine victim—and merely being offended. An example is this statement by Catharine A. MacKinnon, a law professor and feminist activist:

> Sexual harassment perpetuates the interlocked structure by which women have been kept sexually in thrall to men and at the bottom of the labor market. Two forces of American society converge: men's control over women's sexuality and capital's control over employees' work lives. Women historically have been required to exchange sexual services for mate-

rial survival, in one form or another. Prostitution and marriage as well as sexual harassment in different ways institutionalize this arrangement.

Such hyperbole needs to be diffused and distinctions need to be drawn. Rape, a nonconsensual invasion of a person's body, is a crime clear and simple. It is a violation of the right to the physical integrity of the body (the right to life, as John Locke or Thomas Jefferson would have put it). Criminal law should and does prohibit rape. Whether it is useful to call rape "sexual harassment" is doubtful, for it makes the latter concept overly broad while trivializing the former.

Extortion of Sexual Favors

Intimidation in the workplace of the kind that befell Valerie Craig—that is, extortion of sexual favors by a supervisor from a subordinate by threatening to penalize, fire, or fail to reward—is what the courts term *quid pro quo* sexual harassment. Since the mid-1970s, the federal courts have treated this type of sexual harassment as a form of sex discrimination in employment proscribed under Title VII of the Civil Rights Act of 1964. A plaintiff who prevails against an employer may receive such equitable remedies as reinstatement and back pay, and the court can order the company to prepare and disseminate a policy against sexual harassment. Current law places principal liability on the company, not the harassing supervisor, even when higher management is unaware of the harassment and, thus, cannot take any steps to prevent it.

Quid pro quo sexual harassment is morally objectionable and analogous to extortion: The harasser extorts property (i.e., use of the woman's body) through the leverage of fear for her job. The victim of such behavior should have legal recourse, but serious reservations can be held about rectifying these injustices through the blunt instrument of Title VII. In egregious cases the victim is left less than whole (for back pay will not compensate her for ancillary losses), and no prospect for punitive damages are offered to deter would-be harassers. Even more distressing about Title VII is the fact that the primary target of litigation is not the actual harasser, but rather the employer. This places a double burden on a company. The employer is swindled by the supervisor because he spent his time pursuing sexual gratification and thereby impairing the efficiency of the workplace by mismanaging his subordinates, and the employer must endure lengthy and expensive litigation, pay damages, and suffer loss to its reputation. It would be fairer to both the company and the victim to treat sexual harassment as a tort—that is, as a private wrong or injury for which the court can assess damages. Employers should be held vicariously liable only when they know of an employee's behavior and do not try to redress it.

Defining Harassment Is Difficult

As for the workplace harassment endured by Carol Zabowicz—the bared buttocks, obscene portraits, etc.—that too should be legally redressable. Presently, such incidents also fall under the umbrella of Title VII, and are termed hostile environment sexual harassment, a category accepted later than *quid pro quo* and with some judicial reluctance. The main problem with this category is that it has proven too elastic: cases have reached the courts based on everything from off-color jokes to unwanted, persistent sexual advances by co-workers. A new tort of sexual harassment would handle these cases better. Only instances above a certain threshold of egregiousness or outrageousness would be actionable. In other words, the behavior that the plaintiff found offensive would also have to be offensive to the proverbial "reasonable man" of the tort law. That is, the behavior would have to be objectively injurious rather than merely subjectively offensive. The defendant would be the actual harasser, not the company, unless it knew about the problem and failed to act. Victims of scatological jokes, leers, unwanted offers of dates, and other sexual annoyances would no longer have their day in court.

A distinction must be restored between morally offensive behavior and behavior that causes serious harm. Only the latter should fall under the jurisdiction of criminal or tort law. Do we really want legislators and judges delving into our most intimate private lives, deciding when a look is a leer, and when a leer is a Civil Rights Act offense? Do we really want courts deciding, as one recently did, whether a school principal's disparaging remarks about a female school district administrator was sexual harassment and, hence, a breach of Title VII, or merely the act of a spurned and vengeful lover? Do we want judges settling disputes such as the one that arose at a car dealership after a female employee turned down a male co-worker's offer of a date and his colleages retaliated by calling her offensive names and embarrassing her in front of customers? Or another case in which a female shipyard worker complained of an "offensive working environment" because of the prevalence of pornographic material on the docks? Do we want the state to prevent or compensate us for any behavior that someone might find offensive? Should people have a legally enforceable right not to be offended by others? At some point, the price for such protection is the loss of both liberty and privacy rights.

No Perfect Working Environment Exists

Workplaces are breeding grounds of envy, personal grudges, infatuation, and jilted loves, and beneath a fairly high threshold of outrageousness, these travails should be either suffered in silence, complained of to higher management, or left behind as one seeks other employment. No one, female or male, can expect to enjoy a working environment that is perfectly stress-free, or to be treated always and by everyone with kindness and respect. To the extent that sympathetic judges have encouraged women to seek monetary compensation for slights and annoyances, they have not done them a great service. Women need to develop a thick skin in order to survive and prosper in the workforce. It is patronizing to think that they need to be recompensed by male judges for seeing a few pornographic pictures on a wall. By their efforts to

extend sexual harassment charges to even the most trivial behavior, the radical feminists send a message that women are not resilient enough to ignore the run-of-the-mill, churlish provocation from male co-workers. It is difficult to imagine a suit by a longshoreman complaining of mental stress due to the display of nude male centerfolds by female co-workers. Women cannot expect to have it both ways: equality where convenient, but special dispensations when the going gets rough. Equality has its price and that price may include unwelcome sexual advances, irritating and even intimidating sexual jests, and lewd and obnoxious colleagues.

Egregious acts—sexual harassment per se—must be legally redressable. Lesser but not trivial offenses, whether at the workplace or in other more social settings, should be considered moral lapses for which the offending party receives opprobrium, disciplinary warnings, or penalties, depending on the setting and the severity. Trivial offenses, dirty jokes, sexual overtures, and sexual innuendoes do make many women feel intensely discomfited, but, unless they become outrageous through persistence or content, these too should be taken as part of life's annoyances. The perpetrators should be either endured, ignored, rebuked, or avoided, as circumstances and personal inclination dictate. Whether Lisa Olson's experience in the locker room of the Boston Patriots falls into the second or third category is debatable. The media circus triggered by the incident was certainly out of proportion to the event.

As the presence of women on road gangs, construction crews, and oil rigs becomes a fact of life, the animosities and tensions of this transition period are likely to abate gradually. Meanwhile, women should "lighten up," and even dispense a few risqué barbs of their own, a sure way of taking the fun out of it for offensive male bores.

Study Questions

1. Imagine that you are Jerry Tarkwell in "The Case of the Hidden Harassment." How would you handle the case of Jill McNair? In what ways do you agree or disagree with the advice of each of the commentators?

2. List some of the ways in which, according to Burns, women are discriminated against in academic employment.

3. According to Burns, how do women who work in temporary academic positions often get trapped into them?

4. What arguments does Finneran give for claiming that women can legitimately be excluded from working in industries involving the use of substances that can deform or destroy a growing fetus? Do you find his arguments convincing? Why or why not?

5. Why, according to Annas, did the Supreme Court in *Johnson Controls* conclude that fetal protection policy violated the Pregnancy Discrimination Act?

6. In your opinion, should the majority of the Supreme Court in *Johnson Controls* have found that being male is a "bona fide occupational qualification" for working on lead batteries, especially given the possible liability of the company for injuries to children born to female workers exposed to lead?

7. Wells and Kracher employ John Rawls's moral theory as a mean of deriving two natural duties clearly relevant to the issue of sexual harassment. What are these two duties and how are they derivable from Rawls's conception of the original position?

8. There are four ways, say Wells and Kracher, to identify sexually hostile work environments. Which of these is the best perspective and why?

9. How might behavioral definition of sexual harassment lead to a kind of cultural relativism? Why, according to Feary, is the EEOC definition preferable?

10. Summarize Feary's arguments to the conclusion that sexual harassment is morally wrong and should be legally prohibited in the workplace.

11. According to Ellen Frankel Paul, what is the distinction between morally offensive behavior and behavior that causes serious harm? Couldn't the victim of a dirty joke claim that he or she had been seriously harmed by the joke?

12. Do Paul and authors Wells and Kracher differ on what is meant by the "reasonable person" standard for sexual harassment?

CASE SCENARIO 1   Grooming, Dress, and Discrimination

Employers often set guidelines for employees regarding dress and personal appearance, seeking thereby to maintain a chosen level of professionalism or to project the proper image. But such guidelines can give rise to charges of discrimination. How would you resolve the following types of claims?

1. ABC Bank requires all female bank tellers, office workers, and managerial employees to wear a "career ensemble," consisting of a color-coordinated skirt or slacks and a choice of jacket, sweater, or vest. No dress requirements are set for male employees, other than that they wear customary business attire. Is this practice discriminatory? Assuming that "customary business attire" means a suit and tie, can male employees claim that they are also being forced to wear a "uniform"? Suppose an employer had a dress code applicable to all male and female employees in clerical and teller positions, but not to managers. If nearly all of the bank's female employees are tellers and clerks, has the bank discriminated against the female workers?

2. XYZ Technics, Inc., has a policy that forbids its female employees from wearing pants in the company's corporate offices. Does this policy constitute workplace discrimination?
3. L-P Corporation has a rule prohibiting male employees from wearing facial jewelry, including earrings; female employees are permitted to wear facial jewelry that is not "unusual or overly large." Does this rule constitute sex discrimination agaitns L-P's male workers?
4. Television station KXYZ, located in a major city, employs newscasters to anchor its local evening news program. Alicia Thomas had been hired as the female co-anchor of KXYZ's evening newscast. One year after hiring her, however, the station reassigned her to work as a reporter after its ratings and other data indicated a significant negative audience reaction to her dress and appearance. Many of the station's viewers, it seems, found her "too old, too unattractive, and not deferential enough to men," according to a KXYZ spokesperson. Thomas alleges that she is the victim of sex discrimination and that the station is pandering to the sexist bias prevalent among its viewers. Do you agree? To what extent is it legitimate for a broadcaster to take into account its viewers' biases?

CASE SCENARIO 2   Discrimination and Pension Funds

The Los Angeles Department of Water and Power required its female employees to make larger contributions to its pension fund than its male employees. Based on a study of statistics reported on standard mortality tables, the department determined that its two thousand female employees would, on average, live several years longer than its ten thousand male employees. The department reasoned that, since it could not know in advance which of its female employees would have shorter lives than the "average woman," unless women were assessed an extra charge, they would end up being subsidized, to some degree, by the male employees. In fairness to its male employees, the department concluded, it should require its female workers to make monthly contributions that were 14.8 percent higher than contributions required of males. Because employee contributions were withheld from paychecks, a female employee took home less pay than a male employee earning the same salary. Female workers at the department challenged this practice in court, asserting that it constituted sex discrimination. The department countered that it was not basing its practice on myths or stereotypes about women, but rather on a generalization that is unquestionably true—that women, as a class, do live longer than men. The case was finally resolved by the U.S. Supreme Court, which held for the female employees.

The Court argued that the law mandates that employers treat workers as individuals, not "simply as components of a racial, religious, sexual, or national class. If height is required for a job," the Court reasoned, "a tall woman may not be refused employment merely because, on the average, women are too short. Even a true generalization about the class is an insufficient reason for disqualifying an individual to whom the generalization does not apply." The Court went on to apply this reasoning to the department's policy, finding that, since there was no assurance that any individual woman working for the department would actually fit the generalizations of the mortality tables, it was discriminatory to force an employee to contribute more to the fund merely because she is a woman.

1. Does the policy at issue in this case discriminate on the basis of sex? Or does it discriminate on the basis of longevity? If the latter, should the policy be illegal?
2. Do you agree with the department in its argument that the Court's decision will compel it to discriminate against its male employees by effectively requiring them to subsidize the extra pension benefits of its longer-living female workers?
3. How might Burns's analysis of discrimination apply to this case?

4. Compare the actions of the Department of Water and Power to the fetal protection policy of Johnson Controls, Inc. What similarities do you see? What differences?
5. What would likely be the effect of the Court's ruling on the employment practices of businesses like the Department of Water and Power? If the company can argue that it will now cost more to hire women than men, will employers find ways to prefer men?

CASE SCENARIO 3   Discrimination in Prison

Many states are currently experiencing a sharp rise in prison populations; many new prisons are under construction, and states are hiring to fill a variety of jobs associated with these facilities. A number of women have recently applied with the state Department of Corrections for positions as correctional officers, whose basic role is to serve as prison guards. Correctional officer jobs are highly sought after, since they are much better compensated than other positions with the department. The state, however, refuses to hire the female applicants, pointing to a state policy that assigns guards to maximum security facilities based on gender; since the overwhelming majority of the state's prisoners are men, women are virtually excluded altogether from correctional officer positions.

The state defends its policy by arguing that the essence of a correctional officer's job is to maintain prison security, and that this job simply could not be adequately performed by a woman, regardless of her size, strength, and ability. Sex offenders, for example, who have assaulted women before might do so again if access to female guards was possible; and other inmates, "deprived of the normal heterosexual environment," might assault women guards "just because they were women."

The department's female applicants insist that the state's reasoning is simply a rationalization for its perpetuation of sexist thinking: namely, that women are little more than unwitting sex objects who need to be protected. This assumption is paternalistic, they claim, and degrades women. Moreover, it effectively punishes women (who are excluded from the better-paying jobs) for the depraved conduct of the male inmates.

1. Does the state policy at issue here discriminate against women? How would you decide that question?
2. Suppose the job of a correctional officer were to include observing prisoners while taking showers. Is it justifiable to limit this duty to members of the same sex as the prisoners?
3. Compare the actions of the Department of Corrections to the fetal protection policy of Johnson Controls, Inc. What similarities do you see? What differences?

CASE SCENARIO 4   The Sears Case

The Equal Employment Opportunity Commission is the federal agency charged with enforcing federal anti-discrimination laws. After a lengthy investigation, the EEOC brought charges against the Sears, Roebuck & Co., alleging that the giant retailer had, over a period of a decade or more, engaged in a nationwide pattern of discrimination against women by failing to promote its female employees into commission sales positions on the same basis as males, and by paying female checklist management employees less than similarly situated male employees. Commission selling at Sears typically involved "big ticket" items—high-cost merchandise such as major appliances, furnaces, roofing, sewing machines, and vacuums. Merchandise sold on a noncommission basis was generally low-cost and included such items as clothing, jewelry, paint, and cosmetics.

Sears paid commission salespersons a nominal salary plus a 3 percent commission. Noncommission salespersons were paid a straight hourly wage. Commission sales offered greater financial reward.

To support its case against Sears, the EEOC relied heavily upon statistical evidence based on information gathered from employment applications for sales positions that had been rejected by Sears management, and on Sears's computerized payroll records. These data revealed, according to the EEOC, a significant gender disparity among Sears's sales positions, with the great majority of the commission sales positions being held by men. Such a disparity went beyond what would be expected under fair employment conditions, the EEOC concluded. Sears sought to counter the allegation that it intentionally discriminated against women in hiring and promotion into commission sales jobs by arguing that women had little interest in commission sales. Women generally prefer to sell soft-line products, Sears contended. They are more interest in selling clothing and housewares than fencing, refrigeration equipment, and tires. Women also like jobs that are less stressful, risky, and competitive than commission selling tended to be, and women prefer social contact and the cooperative aspects of the workplace. The EEOC responded that the image of women as less greedy, competitive, or daring than men was itself one of the stereotypes that sex discrimination laws were designed to combat. The courts sided with Sears.

1. Does evidence of the disparity betwen men and women in commission sales jobs reflect a sexist bias on the part of Sears, resulting in far fewer opportunities presented to women than men? Or does the evidence merely reflect the general preferences of most women in society?
2. Sears had developed a statement of qualifications for commission sales: The salesperson should be a person who is aggressive and competitive, a person who has lots of drive, and someone with technical knowledge and fluency. Does this profile accurately state the qualifications necessary for the job? Or does it describe the type of people who had been doing the job up to that point, almost all of whom were men?

CASE SCENARIO 5   Harassment in the Locker Room

The early morning, at five or six o'clock, is when sportswriter Lisa Olson can leave her apartment with the least worry. She can walk the empty streets of her Boston neighborhood and buy her newspapers and her groceries. No one will gawk or point or shout at her. No one will notice her. This is her small window of freedom.

She usually has been awake for most of the night. She has worried and thought and worried some more. The phone? Who can that be? For a while she used a system of rings for friends and co-workers, just to know if a stranger was calling, but she has changed her number often and the latest number seems to be safe. For now. Who knows when that new number will land in strange hands?

"I have your number," a voice might say again. "I know where you live. I have battery acid that I will throw on your face. I know the way you go to work."

The whole thing is crazy. What did she do to anyone? The letters. The hate. A man wrote recently that she should jump off the Mystic River bridge, just as Chuck Stuart, the alleged murderer, had done.

She does not answer the doorbell. She mostly does not go out to dinner or to the movies. She does not do anything, really, except work and go home. She is covering the Bruins now for

---

the *Boston Herald,* and the Bruins are in the Stanley Cup playoffs and this should be a wonderful time. But she covers only the games that are played on the road. There has been too much trouble at the Boston Garden, where she has been spit upon and otherwise demeaned and where the two mailboxes on Causeway Street have graffiti addressed to her written on them: LISA IS A CLASSIC BITCH . . . LISA IS A SLUT.

She stays in her apartment during the Bruins' home games, watches them on television, thinks of the stories that she would have written about them. The games end and the news ends and the scoreboard shows end, and she is left to fret through the night. At five or six, she can buy her papers and her groceries and come back to the apartment and close her eyes. Just for a little bit.

How did all this happen?

"She appeared one day in my office," *Herald* executive sports editor Bob Sales says. "She said she was taking some grad school classes at Harvard, but what she always wanted to do was become a sportswriter. She asked if I had any jobs. I did have one. It wasn't much. I needed someone to do the horse racing agate part time at night. She took it."

She was from Phoenix, 22 years old then, in 1986, and as convinced as anyone could be about what she wanted from life. She had been writing sports since she was seven, when she made up her own little newsletter that reported on neighborhood sports events. She almost learned to read with SPORTS ILLUSTRATED and her brothers' *Boy's Life.* This would be the greatest job, writing sports.

She continued with school and worked at the *Herald* and sometimes did some stringing for United Press International. Her big chance to write came from doing the anonymous roundups of sports news that the *Herald* ran daily. She wrote them, Sales noticed, with a nice touch.

In August 1987, when he decided to expand coverage of scholastic sports, Sales hired Olson full time. It wasn't an affirmative-action hire, bringing in another female name for public display; it was a talent hire. "She did nice stories portraying athletes as human beings," Sales says. "These were stories about high school volleyball players and swimmers, and she made you want to read them. I liked what she did a lot."

Olson wrote scholastic and collegiate sports for a year and a half. Sales thought she wrote the best scholastic stories in the city. When a Bruin beat writer became ill in the middle of the 1988–89 season, Sales turned the job over to Olson. He liked her hockey stories and began to expand her range. He told her to continue what she had been doing, to write about athletes in human terms. He sent her to a prizefight and included her on the team of reporters that covered the 1990 Super Bowl. Human stories. Last summer, Sales promoted Michael Gee, who was covering the Patriots, to columnist and that opened up a spot on the Pats' beat. The choice to fill it was Olson.

She started covering the Pats in training camp. For two months, there were no problems. On Sept. 17, she was working on a story on cornerback Maurice Hurst, who had intercepted two passes in a game the day before. Olson said later that she had asked twice to get Hurst to meet her in the media room at Foxboro Stadium. Hurst said he would do the interview after practice, in the locker room, where Olson had been only twice before. This was the beginning of her ordeal. The human stories, alas, became stories about the woman who wrote human stories.

The events of Sept. 17 are old news now, but their effects do not seem to end. Especially for Olson. The story—studied, debated, played across the pages of virtually every newspaper and magazine in the country—was that at least three Patriots players, Zeke Mowatt, Robert Perryman and Michael Timpson, gathered around her and made lewd suggestions while she interviewed Hurst. This was a locker room. The players were naked. The reporter was a woman. The story took off in that cheesy, wink-wink style that some newspapers like to print and readers like to read. Jim Bakker meets Donna Rice at Au Pair Bar in Palm Beach. Or something like that. Sports-page version.

There was a three-day stutter at the beginning, the time frame in which the Pats could have closed the gates. Olson had reported the incident to Sales, who had contacted the Patriots, but nothing happened. "The sad thing is how easily all of this could have been avoided," Sales says. "All she wanted was a chance to sit down with the players involved and explain herself, to explain that she was doing a job and she should be treated that way. That's all the Patriots would have had to do. Get the players together and meet with her."

The Boston Globe printed an account of the lockerroom incident first, on Sept. 21, and the *Herald* followed suit, and then two sportswriters overheard Pats owner Victor Kiam calling Olson "a classic bitch," and there was no stopping this story. The Boston chapter of the National Organization for Women urged a boycott of products by Remington Products, Kiam's company. Kiam apologized for the remark through paid newspaper ads. The issue of "a woman in the locker room," supposedly decided a decade earlier, was rehashed.

Oprah wanted Olson. Phil wanted Olson. Geraldo wanted Olson. She went on none of the shows. She did NBC's *NFL Live* and *CBS This Morning,* appearing uneasy and timid, and then stopped doing TV. She did not have to defend herself. What did she do? She was a reporter who was doing her job and had been insulted, if not actually threatened.

This did not seem to matter. *Playboy* called asking if she was interested in doing a "pictorial layout." Representatives for producers Aaron Spelling and Steven Bochco called asking about the chances of filming her story. She did not return the calls. Andrew Dice Clay did a routine about her. *Saturday Night Live* did a routine. The local disc jockeys did routines. The White House sent a telegram urging her to hang tough on the same day she received her first death threat. The sickos of the land moved to their desks and began to type with two fingers.

"I do a lot of civil-rights cases, so I've seen a lot of things that have gone through the mails, but this was the worst stuff I've ever read," says Michael Avery, one of Olson's lawyers. "The sexual references, the obscene drawings. Things that make you sick."

For a few weeks, Olson continued covering the Pats. It was ridiculous. At a Sept. 30 game against the New York Jets at Foxboro, fans chanted her name and bounced one of those inflated rubber women around the stands. She walked a gauntlet of abuse as she went to the locker room for interviews. She has electric red hair and is easily recognizable. How could she hide? Following the game, Sales moved her off the beat, told her to take a vacation and get away from the noise.

The NFL was strangely quiet for the longest time, and when commissioner Paul Tagliabue finally took action on Oct. 1 by appointing Philip Heymann as special counsel to investigate the locker room incident and its aftermath, the story stayed alive as a lengthy study was conducted. The investigation culminated in the Heymann Report, a 60-page indictment of the Pats players' behavior and their team's handling of the situation, which was released on Nov. 27. The three players and Pats management were fined. Olson supposedly was vindicated. Vindicated? When she had returned to work in mid-October, she covered the Celtics and Bruins, but reporting on NBA games brought her to courtside at Boston Garden, where she still was jostled and touched and hooted at. The words were graphic. At an exhibition game in Worcester, a man poured a beer on her.

In early December, Sales moved Olson exclusively to the Bruin beat, partly because the hockey press box is located almost at the top of the Garden. On Feb. 4, Kiam, continuing in his buffoon's role, told a joke at a dinner in Stamford, Conn., saying that what Olson and the Iraqi army had in common was that they both had seen Patriot missiles up close. Kiam apologized again. Nothing changed. People spit on her head from the luxury boxes, the only seats in the Garden located above the hockey press box. She started to wear a hat for protection. Someone spray-painted *classic bitch* on the front of her apartment house. Her tires were slashed. The letters continued. She changed her phone number again and again. In Hartford, a group of male fans seated in front of the press box chanted all night at her, asking her to show them her breasts.

"Isn't the thing in America supposed to be that you can be whatever you want to be?" asks Bruin public relations director Heidi Holland. "What do these people tell their daughters? That you can't do it because of idiots like me who are missing a chromosome somewhere?"

On April 25, Olson filed suit in Suffolk (County) Superior Court against the Patriots, Kiam, former general manager Pat Sullivan, former media relations director Jimmy Oldham, Mowatt, Perryman and Timpson. She asked for unspecified monetary damages for sexual harassment, civil-rights violations, intentional infliction of emotional distress and intentional damage to her professional reputation. The Patriots have declined to comment on the situation.

The news now is that Olson is leaving Boston. She will finish covering the NHL playoffs and then she will leave the city, leave the country, go work in a foreign country for another paper owned by Rupert Murdoch, proprietor of the *Herald*. She probably will not cover sports, but she will be able to walk the streets and answer the phone and sleep. She has to wonder if she ever will cover sports again.

The suit probably will not be heard for two years, maybe three. It is not one of her great worries. She never wanted to sue anybody in the first place. The continual harassment, sparked anew by Kiam's tasteless dinner joke, forced her hand. She never wanted to be especially famous or rich. She wanted only to do a job that she always wanted to hold. Is that a crime? The rage around her is a puzzle. The buzz wherever she goes is a puzzle. What did she do?

"I'm working on a story about you for SPORTS ILLUSTRATED," a reporter says to her.

"Do you have to?" Lisa Olson says, politely refusing to be quoted in the magazine she read as a child.

The whole thing does not end.

1. Those who defended the actions of the Boston Patriot athletes in the Lisa Olson case argued that she was exposed to nothing more than typical "locker room" humor and that if her job took her into the locker room, she needed to be prepared for some crude behavior. Do you agree?
2. Should newspapers and television stations that hire sports reporters employ only men to cover male-dominated sports like hockey and football?
3. Would it be discriminatory to refuse to hire a male sportswriter to cover a women's basketball team, on the grounds that the job might require the writer to enter the women's locker room?

CHAPTER 7

Advertising and Marketing

It will hardly be a surprise to anyone reading this text that the marketing of products and services in our culture is everywhere. It is next to impossible to pick up a newspaper, listen to the radio or television, or even drive through town without encountering many forms of advertising. Advertising and marketing are so commonplace, in fact, that we rarely stop to think much about the forms they take or the impact that they have upon us. Yet in both ways, as we shall see, the advertising and marketing of goods raises serious moral questions. Consider the existing powers of the federal government. Section 5 of the Federal Trade Commission Act grants the government broad consumer-protection powers: to forbid "unfair or deceptive acts or practices." Under this authority, government agencies may, for example, prohibit altogether any advertising that poses a substantial harm to the consumer or that is misleading in some way. But how is it to be decided whether an ad is deceptive? And why shouldn't consumers be responsible for their own choices, even if unwise or foolish? This chapter begins by exploring these questions. It then looks at a related set of questions about the impact of advertising upon consumers generally.

Those who defend advertising often do so on the grounds that ads aim merely to inform consumers about goods and services that are available in the marketplace. Critics of advertising claim that marketing techniques frequently go beyond simply being informative and become manipulative. Claims about the undue or improper influence of ads are sometimes made in regard to particular target audiences. Advertising directed toward children, for example, is viewed with moral suspicion by those who insist that vulnerable minds are being seduced by TV programming based upon toy characters or through saturation of Saturday-morning TV with ads for sugared breakfast cereal and candy. Other critics of advertising make similar claims with regard to all members of contemporary society. Readings reflecting many of these views are included in this chapter.

ADVERTISING AND FREEDOM OF EXPRESSION

Advertising relies, of course, upon claims made in support of a product or service. The claims may be direct; but they need not be directly stated—they could, for example, be implied by other things said in the ad, or conveyed through visual images. Consider these ads:

- In one familiar ad campaign, the makers of the headache remedy Anacin insisted that its product contained more of "the pain reliever doctors recommend most." An-

---

✍ Surveys and Advertising Deception

In her book *Tainted Truth*, author Cynthia Crossen relates several examples of the deceptive use of consumer surveys. Advertisers are adept, Crossen argues, at framing the questions asked and reporting the results obtained from such surveys in a way that reflects well on their product. Some of Crossen's findings include the following:

- "Ninety percent of college students say Levi's 501 jeans are "in" on campus." The students chose from this list: Levi's 501 jeans; T-shirts with graphics; 1960s-inspired clothing; Lycra/spandex clothing; overalls; patriotic-themed clothing; decorated denim; printed pull-on beach pants; long-sleeved hooded T-shirts; and neon-colored clothing. In other words, there was no way to vote for blue jeans except Levi's 501s . . .

- USAir had the best on-time record of "any of the seven largest airlines," the company's advertising bragged in 1991. USAir conveniently stopped counting at seven; the eighth-largest airline, Pan Am, had the best on-time record of all.

- Hospitals recommend "acetaminophen, the aspirin-free pain reliever in Anacin-3, more than any other pain reliever," said an American Home Products ad. In fact, hospitals did recommend pain relievers containing acetaminophen more than other pain relievers. But acetaminophen is also the active ingredient in Tylenol, and hospitals recommended Tylenol even more than they recommended Anacin-3.

The selective omission of survey data was recently also undertaken, Crossen reports, by the tobacco industry:

- TRIUMPH BEATS MERIT, crowed Lorillard about a taste test pitting its low-tar cigarette against Merit. "An amazing 60 percent said Triumph tastes as good as or better than Merit." Here were the real figures on taste: 36 percent had preferred Triumph, 24 percent said the brands were equal, and 40 percent preferred Merit. In other words, MERIT BEAT TRIUMPH. The lesson here is clear, wrote two marketing experts about another Triumph ad claim that was ruled to be misleading: "If you commission a survey in support of a comparative claim, collect only those data that pertain to the claim and are likely to support it."

Cynthia Crossen, *Tainted Truth: The Manipulation of Fact in America* (New York: Simon and Schuster: 1994).

---

other Anacin advertisement claimed that "Anacin reduces inflammation as Anacin relieves pain fast. These [referring to Tylenol and other brands of acetaminophen] do not."

- In another ad, the makers of Black Flag roach killer claimed that Black Flag kills roaches while "the other leading brand" failed.

The Federal Trade Commission (FTC), the federal agency charged with regulating the marketplace and protecting the public against deceptive and unfair marketing practices, sought to prohibit each of these ads. The first Anacin ad falsely implied, according to the FTC, that Anacin's active ingredient (which is just aspirin) is somehow different from and similar to aspirin (which is what the doctors were recommending). The second Anacin spot was correct in claiming that aspirin products (like Anacin) seem to be more effective against inflammation than acetaminophen; but the ad also suggested that acetaminophen products do not relieve pain as fast as Anacin, and this is false. Black Flag did kill some roaches that the other brand didn't; but only because the tests were performed on roaches bred to be resistant to the type of poison used by the competitor.

Whether these ads were deceptive or unfair in some sense is an issue we will come to in a moment. But first it might be useful to consider what power the federal government has to prevent such forms of advertising, even if they do involve deception or trickery. After all, one might argue, advertisers, like everyone else, have a right to say what they want, a right protected by the First Amendment to the Constitution. How can government regulation of advertising activity be justified at all, in view of the fact that each of us enjoys considerable freedom to speak our minds. The question is one of *free speech* versus *commercial speech*. The answer lies in the fact that, under existing law, the right of "free speech" is not absolute—and this is particularly true for businesses engaged in "commercial speech," that is, speech or expression proposing an economic transaction. Courts, beginning in the 1940s, have consistently held that commercial speech is less deserving of full free-speech protection than is, say, political, religious, or artistic speech or expression. Although the Supreme Court has said recently that truthful, nonmisleading commercial speech is almost always protected to some degree,[1] the Court has also affirmed that a state's interest in restricting certain types of advertising (for example, ads promoting gambling or lotteries) overrides the advertiser's right of free speech.[2] Exactly what justifies this lesser status for commercial speech is less clear. Supporters of the prevailing position often claim that commercial speech is "hardier" than, say, political expression, since the principal motive behind it is economic. Critics challenge this reasoning by pointing out that money certainly plays a large role in political speech as well. Others argue that commercial speech simply does not deal with matters that are as fundamental as political or religious speech. Critics of this argument respond that, in a consumer culture such as ours, commercial speech is every bit as fundamental as religious discourse.

DECEPTION, "PUFFERY," AND THE CONSUMER

But let's leave the debate about the legal status of commercial speech to one side. Assuming that government can and should regulate and restrict commercial speech to a greater extent than other forms of expression, what should it regulate? And why? It might be useful to array marketing techniques along a spectrum, from harmless, truthful claims at one end, to damaging lies at the other. Suppose that the manufacturer and distributor of corn oil says in its ads that its product is "pure vegetable oil." Because corn is obviously a vegetable, no one is likely to be misled or confused by such a straightforward claim. Imagine, by contrast, a maker of salted potato chips who is concerned that health-conscious consumers will not purchase its product. It therefore advertises its product as "sodium free." This statement is a lie, and as it is deliberate fraud, few of us would feel any sympathy for the manufacturer when it is ordered to cease running such an ad.

Neither of the foregoing cases is controversial: Most of us would agree that simple, truthful ads ought not to be banned and that malicious and false ads should be forbidden. One theory that both explains and supports this reaction says that advertising regulation should be based upon the advertiser's intent. We must ask, this theory would say, whether the advertiser intended to mislead or deceive its audience. Lies, or intentional forms of deception, are morally wrong, since they amount to using others (those lied to) as a means to further the interests of the liar. But few ads are outright lies. What then of the large gray area between allowable forms of persuasion, on the one hand, and outright deception, on the other? It is here that we find the vast majority of advertising claims, replete with sug-

> ### ∽ PowerMaster, Buz, and "Draft" Root Beer
>
> Advertising directed at children and teens has been challenged on various grounds. One of the most recent advertising trends to focus public attention has been the effort to promote alcohol and tobacco products among the young. In the early 1990s, Heilman Brewing Company announced that it would introduce a new malt-liquor. Called PowerMaster, the brew was slated to be sold principally in inner-city, urban neighborhoods, targeting young blacks and Hispanics. After an uproar from church leaders and other members of the minority communities in question, Heilman abandoned its plan. The obvious effort to attract disempowered urban youth with appeals to the "power" of liquor amounted, critics contended, to an unconscionable tactic. Similar criticisms have been leveled against Philip Morris, Inc., regarding its "Joe Camel" ads, depicting a cartoonish camel in colorful situations, allegedly aimed at promoting recognition of its Camel cigarettes among children. The more recent introduction of so-called "microsmokes" by some of the large tobacco companies has also drawn criticism from those claiming that the new, alternative cigarette brands are again aimed specifically at young teens. Brands such as American Spirit, Buz, Gunsmoke, Dunhill, Export A, and Beedies rely upon youthful, creative, stylish campaigns directed at fashion-conscious youths. In a related twist to such youthful appeals, the Royal Crown Cola Co. came under fire in 1995 for its decision to boost its sagging sales by introducing a premium "draft" root beer. Sold in amber, long-necked bottles and labeled much like a bottle of beer, critics alleged that R.C. was trying to gain young customers by reinforcing the idea that drinking alcohol is "cool." A six-pack of R.C. Draft Root beer was to retail for about $4— the same as low-end beer.
>
> *Los Angeles Times* 1/26/96:A1.

gestion and innuendo, vague and ambiguous appeals, and deceptive implications. Let's look more closely at these types of ads.

Much of what falls in the middle region of our spectrum is often referred to as "puffery"—harmless exaggeration or colorful "hype"—perhaps false, but nonetheless legally nondeceptive statements. We have all seen the ads for the gadget that "makes life easy," for the clothes that "look good" and "feel great," for the food that is the "best tasting," for the car that is the "most comfortable." Because the claims they make are so ill-defined and subject to varying interpretations, such phrases are nearly always found to be innocuous. Vague and ambiguous phrases and constructions are often used in ads. Brand X toothpaste "helps prevent cavities" and "fights tooth decay." Words like *helps* and *fights* convey little meaning in such contexts. "Four out of five doctors recommend" this remedy. But who are the doctors? What are they doctors of? How many of them were asked about the product? Without answers to these obvious questions, the recommendation is pretty empty. "No preservatives added" says the wrapping on a loaf of bread. None added—since when? Since the baker finished putting them in? No preservatives added—to what? The ones that were already there? The statement may be true, but this claim is also empty, as it actually says nothing about the nature or quantity of preservatives in your bread. One famous hamburger chain asserts that its burgers are "made with 100% pure beef." This claim is meant to suggest that the burger itself is all-beef. But, of course, it doesn't say that—it only says that 100% pure beef is *an ingredient* from which the burger has been made: It's merely the beef, not the burger, that is pure. Such cleverly worded ads might fool some, but what they say is technically true.

Consider several further examples of allegedly deceptive ads:

- In one ad for a hair-coloring product, the manufacturer states that the dye used "colors hair permanently." Consumer A watches the ad, buys and uses the product, but complains when her hair later starts to grow out in its original color.

- The pain reliever Excedrin maintains in one of its ads that "it takes twice as many aspirin tablets to get as much pain relief as in one Excedrin." B sees this ad, assumes that Excedrin is a more powerful pain reliever than aspirin, and buys a bottle of Excedrin for his headache; he subsequently concludes, however, that it is no better, gram-for-gram, than aspirin.

- Volvo Cars of North America runs a TV commercial in which a huge truck is depicted driving over a Volvo. C sees that ad and assumes that it establishes that Volvo is indeed "a car you can believe in." C buys a Volvo.

Are any of these ads deceptive? A's complaint would very likely be dismissed by most, since everyone understands that no hair-coloring product can alter the color of hair before it grows out of the scalp. The same may well be the case with B's purchase of Excedrin. After all, we could say, had he researched a bit before his purchase, he would have realized that the ad compared one 500 mg. Excedrin capsule with two 250 mg. aspirin tablets—proving that 500 is indeed twice 250. Was C deceived by the Volvo ad? The FTC thought so. For, upon investigating, it found that Volvo had specially reinforced the frame of the car used in the commercial—C's Volvo has no such extra protection. In each of these cases, of course, the advertiser could argue that is was not intending to mislead its customers, that any false or incorrect implications drawn from such ads by consumers is their responsibility, not that of the advertiser.

The Volvo case suggests to some another theory of advertising regulation: Ads should be regulated based, not upon the advertiser's intent, but upon the likely impact on the consumer. If the ad misleads a consumer, who then relies upon the content of the ad in making his or her purchase, the moral blame resides with the maker of the ad. Yet this theory seems unduly harsh: Is Clairol really to be forbidden to use the word *permanent* just because a few consumers might think this applies to hair as it grows, and not just the hair to which the coloring has been applied? The question now is what audience of consumers the regulators should be seeking to protect. Not all consumers are alike. Some are well educated and wise to the clever ways of marketing; others are inexperienced and gullible, unaware of the way the game is played. Should regulatory controls apply to all ads that might deceive even the inexperienced consumer? Or should such controls be limited to those ads that would deceive only a "reasonable" consumer? Those who support the first view argue that expecting everyone to operate at the level of the "reasonable" or "average" consumer is unfair, since some are simply not capable of doing so (a fact already recognized, say, in the case of children). Those who favor the second position insist that banning any ad that might deceive even the most naive could well lead to the suppression of information useful to the majority of consumers.

ADVERTISING, MANIPULATION, AND CONSUMER AUTONOMY

As we have already seen, advertising raises serious moral questions about deception and trickery. Many of these questions are specific, asking whether this or that ad is dishonest or misleading. A distinct but more global constellation of issues concerning advertising re-

---

✐ᔫ   Are There Subliminal Messages in Your Computer?

In 1995 Time Warner announced that it would market a new computer video game. Called Endorfun, the game was unique in its use of 100 subaudible messages, embedded in the background music. The messages—"I am powerful"; "I am at peace"; "I am in harmony": "I love being alive"—are intended "to uplift the heart and mind of [Endorfun's] users," according to a Times Warner spokesperson. Makers of Endorfun, a game similar in concept to the popular Tetris, claimed to be capitalizing on the intensity with which video games often rivet the attention of their players. Other software companies are alleged to be experimenting with subliminal messages in their screen-saver programs, with the embedded messages intended to inspire employees to work harder and be more productive. Endorfun's makers reportedly are considering a children's game, into which such messages as "I am healthy" and "I am good at algebra" would be inserted.

Los Angeles Times 12/18/95: C120

---

volves around the nature of advertising's influence upon consumers generally. The concern animating this debate is illustrated by the worries that occasionally surface regarding so-called subliminal advertising.

Beginning with the infamous "popcorn ads" in the 1950s (in which theater operators allegedly inserted split-second images of hot dogs or popcorn into movies) and continuing through more recently alleged abuses (for example, embedding subaudible messages into the Muzak of department stores), the clamor over the existence and use of *subliminal advertising*—visual or audible images or sounds that register only at a subconscious level— strikes a certain moral chord with many people. Regardless of the efficacy of such subliminal techniques (and they are debated), the worry here is not that consumers are being consciously deceived, but that they might be wrongfully influenced into purchasing a product. More generally, this chapter considers the claim that, through advertising, manufacturers and retailers are improperly influencing consumer interests, wants, and desires. Are these worries legitimate? How, if at all, are advertisers influencing my behavior?

As before, it might be useful to array along a spectrum the range of ways in which people can be moved to do something. At one end of this spectrum would lie what might be called *rational persuasion:* the giving of reasons, forthrightly and directly, in an effort to convince another to accept the truth of some claim. Such persuasion is rational because it tries to give cogent arguments in favor of the claim. So, for instance, a physician uses rational persuasion when he gives his patient reasons for having a certain operation. One virtue often claimed for rational persuasion is that it respects the autonomy of the person to whom it is directed. *Autonomy* refers to the ability to be self-determining: to think and act for oneself, not at the whim of another. According to some philosophers, to say that I am autonomous is to say both that my choices are mine and that they are made freely by me. If, after consulting with my doctor, weighing the pros and cons, assessing the medical evidence, and so on, I decide to go ahead and have the operation, I have acted freely (no one forced me into the decision) and my choice is "authentic," consistent with who I am as a person. At the opposite end of the spectrum lie ways of getting people to do something that are antithetical to their autonomy. One clear example of this is *coercion:* the deliberate use of force (or the threat of force) to compel one to act in a certain way. If my doctor distrusts my own judgment to the point that he threatens to have me institutionalized if I don't agree that the operation is the right course, he has not respected my autonomy.

Few, if any, ads involve outright coercion. On the other hand, advertisers rarely seek to be dispassionate rational persuaders. Much advertising again falls into the large, middle region of the spectrum, occupied by what most ethicists call *manipulation:* the attempt to elicit a desired response from the person targeted by adjusting the available alternative or by altering the person's perception in certain ways. Concealment of relevant facts is one obvious way to manipulate consumers, though it is not the only one. But is manipulation in advertising a serious problem? Some critics of advertising have insisted that it is. In an influential book,[3] economist John Kenneth Galbraith argued that manipulation routinely occurs in our market economy and on a grand scale. Galbraith turned the classic economic model of consumer/producer relations upside-down. The classic model assumed that producers create and market what consumers indicate they want or need—supply follows demand. The truth, Galbraith contended, was just the reverse. Representing what he called a *dependence effect,* Galbraith insisted that consumer demand is largely a function of production—producers sell the products they have and use marketing techniques to influence consumers to buy those products. Those in agreement with Galbraith argue that it is profitable for manufacturers to "manage" consumer preferences through the medium of advertising: Tobacco manufacturers want people to keep smoking; auto manufacturers want consumers to stick with gas-powered vehicles for meeting their transportation needs; the fashion industry wants to convince us to wear the latest styles the industry has created. Marketing research, in this view, is done to determine how best to maneuver consumers into buying what the industry has. Critics of advertising insist that the dependence effect is an enduring affront to the dignity and autonomy of consumers.

Is the dependence effect a genuine phenomenon, as the critics of advertising maintain? Defenders of advertising have raised several objections to Galbraith's thesis. First, they assert, the dependence effect it vastly overstated. Producers do not control consumer preferences: If you absolutely do not want a motorcycle, no amount of advertising is going to change your mind. No single message can dominate one's attention in the way the dependence effect seems to suppose. If I do decide to buy a motorcycle, it is because I wanted one already. Which brand or type of bike I buy, of course, may turn on what I have gleaned from ads; but that, say advertisers, just shows that advertising performs the useful function of informing consumers of the options available to satisfy their wants. Finally, proponents of advertising attack the dependence effect hypothesis by arguing that it makes false predictions. The dependence effect, were it genuine, would mean that new products, heavily advertised, ought rarely to fail. Yet, say Galbraith's critics, the failure rate among new products is high. Nor does product success correlate with advertising dollars spent, which the dependence effect would seem to imply. Galbraith's critics believe that he has unfairly singled-out advertising as a sinister force in people's lives, planting in their heads desires that they would not otherwise have had. But, say the critics, how do we decide what my "real" interests or desires are? Isn't it true that my wants or interests have been influenced by many factors, of which advertising is but one? And if I do select a product because it fulfills some fantasy of mine, why is that illegitimate or irrational?

THE READINGS

This chapter begins with a recent case illustrating the power of the Federal Trade Commission (FTC) to ban advertising that is "unfair or deceptive." TV commercials for "Sistema Silueta" urged consumers to purchase a lotion, claiming that it eliminated cellulite and thus made the consumer appear slimmer and more attractive. The owner and distributor of the product, Stanley Klavir, shipped more than ten thousand units of Sistema Silueta before the

FTC interceded to stop further sales. The court argues that the commercials for Sistema Silueta were deceptive and that Klavir can be held personally liable for losses incurred by customers who, in effect, wasted their money.

The readings continue with a selection by author Ivan Preston, who examines the issue of deceptiveness in advertising and the role of government agencies like the FTC in protecting consumers from deceptive marketing techniques. Preston specifically addresses the question of whether government should set standards to protect "ignorant" consumers who are so gullible as to be deceived by advertising ploys that a reasonably intelligent consumer would reject. If the former standard were followed by the FTC—as was the case in the past—the agency would enjoin advertising that conceivably could deceive anyone—the ignorant and even the stupid. Preston notes that such regulation would be extremely expensive to administer and violates the legal precedent for a reasonable-person standard embodied in the common law. Preston's article outlines the historical standing of these two criteria by the FTC and in the courts. He outlines how the FTC has moved away from a standard intended to protect those individuals who were deceived by far-fetched or outlandish advertising claims. The law now aims to protect against those cases of foolishness that are likely to be believed by a significant number of persons. Preston's essay ends with the story of one particular, allegedly deceptive ad campaign and how the FTC dealt with it.

All sides in the debate over advertising grant that advertising conveys messages and that at least some of these messages contain information about products. But some would contend that this information is useful even if it is not weighed critically. Economist Phillip Nelson argues that the point of advertising is to convey information, and that it does this in a number of different and sometimes unapparent ways. Most provocative is his argument that the sheer quantity of advertising itself provides information to consumers—namely, that one product is a better buy than less-advertised products. Nelson contends that, given the economic nature of producers and the existence of the market, it pays to advertise winners and it does not pay producers to advertise losers: In other words, it is profitable to expend advertising dollars for a product that consumers will purchase repeatedly, a product that guarantees repeat sales. Thus, a heavily advertised product is almost certainly a good product. Nelson realizes that there are many good products on the market that are not heavily advertised. A good consumer could discover these with the help of the abundant consumer guides now on the market. This would be a time-consuming endeavor; but, Nelson argues, what really matters is that the heavily advertised product is more likely to satisfy consumer preferences than an unknown one. Again, a profit-motivated producer has risked sometimes millions of dollars on its promotion, and this would be foolish if the product were inferior. If this were true, it might really be less important that consumers develop critical skills to assess their purchases. What they should be clear about is their own preferences; that done, they could most safely satisfy their preferences by simply purchasing the heavily advertised goods.

Opposing Nelson, Richard Lippke urges that advertising poses a threat to consumer freedom because its techniques thwart the critical capacities necessary to make rational choices about the acceptability of its content. The reasons for this state of affairs, according to Lippke, include the following: Many individuals in our society do not encounter advertising with the "finely honed" critical skills necessary to evaluate its claims. This is particularly problematic when one considers children who find advertising's content irresistible (see also the selection by Lynn Sharp Paine in this regard), and who are daily inundated, like many adults, with countless consumer messages. According to Lippke, advertising encourages the abdication of reason, and in so doing undermines consumer freedom. It does this by employing shoddy argument, appealing to emotion, presenting information selectively, and (typically) purveying much misinformation. The effects of advertising's onslaught on individual freedom is compounded by implicit value judgments contained within advertising's message—its propensity to dictate "lifestyle" by suggesting standards of conduct and leisure that ought to be accepted if, for example, the consumer wishes to avoid the disapproval of peers. It is of course true that some individuals are capable of staunchly resisting these ploys and of assessing ads critically. But, for Lippke, this is not enough since, as other ethicists have observed, a source of influence need not be controlling in order for it to be an object of concern.

Lynn Sharp Paine shares many of Lippke's concerns about advertising's potentially pernicious influence on consumer sovereignty. But her particular focus is upon the effect of advertising on children, and she endeavors in her selection to outline the ethical reasons why advertisers should refrain from directing advertising at children. Some sellers tend to view children as (what she calls) "miniature adults" who, like real adults, have a distinctive set of product preferences. But, unlike adults, children lack those analytical skills and psychological capacities requisite for making reasonable consumer judgments. In view of these facts, well documented in the psychological literature on children, Paine suggests three general ethical principles by which children's advertising could be evaluated.

Often advertisers appeal to the emotions in order to motivate consumers to behave in certain ways, for example, to purchase a certain good or service, or, in the case of so-called public service commercials, to refrain from certain behaviors. Some of these advertisements can arouse in viewers feelings of hostility, anxiety, or even loss of self-esteem. In the final reading for this chapter, Michael R. Hyman and Richard Tansey refer to such advertisements as *psychoactive*. The term is meant to refer to the sometimes unintentional effects of the advertisements on a particular individual or group. So, for example, an ad intended to reduce the incidence of child abuse might cause certain sufferers of postpartum depression to feel hostile toward a newborn—a hostility that might result in harm. Hyman and Tansey argue that advertisers should guard against perpetrating such harms, and they suggest certain rules that advertisers should follow to avoid these.

NOTES

1. See the Court's decision in *44 Liquormart v. Rhode Island*.
2. See *Posadas de Puerto Rico v. Tourism Co.*, 478 U.S. 328; and *U.S. v. Edge Broadcasting Co.*
3. John Kenneth Galbraith, *The Affluent Society* (Boston: Houghton Mifflin, 1958).

CASE STUDY   ***FTC. v. Silueta Distributors, Inc., and***
Stanley Klavir

United States District Court
California
1995 WL 215313

ARMSTRONG, District Judge

FACTS

Defendants promoted the sale of a product known as Sistema Silueta through advertisement broadcasts on KDTV, Channel 14, and on other Spanish-language stations across the country. Sistema Silueta consists of a moisture lotion and diuretic tablets. . . . [T]he advertisement represents that Sistema Silueta will eliminate cellulite from the body and that consumer testimonials support this assertion.

The Sistema Silueta advertisement features an unidentified man sitting on the edge of a desk, positioned in front of book-lined shelves. The man states: "I would like to talk to you for a few moments. Sistema Silueta is the scientific miracle of the moment." During this introduction, there is a subscript which reads: "We do not specify a determined weight loss with this product." The subscript disappears as the man continues: "Silueta is an astonishing treatment in two steps which penetrates the skin and attacks and dissolves the fat cells which are the cause of those ugly cellulite bumps, and later expels them from your body."

The commercial then switches to a swimsuit-clad woman who states: "We all know that neither diets nor strenuous exercises can get rid of cellulite, but with Sistema Silueta I did achieve it when I applied it on those areas I wanted to reduce." During the time the woman speaks, there is a subscript that reads: "To lose weight with this product, you need to eat less and follow the instructions."

The advertisement then moves into its third phase, which is comprised of illustration and narration. The illustration is of an overweight woman's body in a swimsuit. The figure rubs a cream onto corpulent and bumpy thighs. The figure then transforms and becomes thin. The next illustration apparently represents fat cells. Arrows are depicted entering into the spaces between the fat cells and the cells become smaller. Then a liquid pours over the picture, apparently washing the residue away. During this illustration phase, the narration is as follows: Step number one—the Silueta cream penetrates underneath the surface of the skin breaking those fat and cellulite deposits and converts them into liquids that step number two takes care of by expelling them from your body.

The advertisement then returns to the unidentified man's office. He is now sitting behind the desk and the swimsuit-clad woman is perched on the edge of the desk. The woman states: "Nothing could be easier. Start today to get the figure you have always dreamed about." During this last scene, there is a subscript that reads: "Testimonials on file."

At this point, the advertisement shows an 800 number. When a consumer calls the 800 number, the consumer is told that it is possible to order the Sistema Silueta products by C.O.D. Although the advertised cost of the Sistema Silueta regimen is $34.95 plus $5.00 shipping and handling, the C.O.D. cost of the regimen is $43.95.

DISCUSSION

1. Liability

Section 5(a) of the FTC Act declares unlawful "unfair or deceptive acts or practices in or affecting commerce" and empowers the Federal Trade Commission (the "Commission") to prevent such acts or practices. Section 12 of the FTC Act is specifically directed to false advertising. This section prohibits the dissemination of "any false advertisement" in order to induce the purchase of "food, drugs, devices, or cosmetics. . . ." The FTC Act defines "false advertisement" as "an advertisement, other than labeling, which is misleading in a material respect." An advertisement is misleading or deceptive if (1) there is a representation, omission, or practice that (2) is likely to mislead consumers acting reasonably under the circumstances, and (3) the representation, omission, or practice is material. Express product claims are presumed to be material. Furthermore, the use of a consumer endorsement violates Section 5 if the endorsement misrepresents that the alleged results are what consumers typically achieve.

FTC asserts that defendants' advertisement violated the FTC Act because it expressly and falsely represented that Sistema Silueta will eliminate cellulite, that Sistema Silueta has caused cellulite elimination in actual use, and that consumer testimonials support the conclusion that Sistema Silueta eliminates cellulite. Because these representations were expressly made in the advertisement, the materiality of the representations is presumed. Furthermore, because these representations relate to the very reason a consumer would purchase the product (i.e., to eliminate cellulite), these representations, if false, would clearly mislead consumers acting reasonably under the circumstances. Thus, the only issue here is whether the representations are false. . . .

Plaintiff provides ample evidence by way of expert declaration testimony establishing that Sistema Silueta cannot eliminate cellulite. This evidence reveals that the "cream is nothing more than a moisturizer, the ingredients of which are those found in body lotions and creams generally." Furthermore, the diuretic tablets contain an herbal diuretic that cannot cause the loss of cellulite, only water loss, which will be replaced immediately upon the ingestion of water.

Because defendants have presented no evidence contradicting plaintiff's contentions regarding any of the three representations, no genuine issue of fact exists as to whether defendants' Sistema Silueta advertisement was false and violated the FTC Act. Thus, this Court grants summary judgment in favor of plaintiff on this issue.

2. Klavir's Liability

Klavir asserts that he is not individually liable for the violations because he did not know and should not have known of the misrepresentations. Klavir maintains that he bought Silueta from Juan Perez, who created the advertisement for Sistema Silueta. Klavir claims that Perez stated he had verified the statements in the advertisement and Klavir had no reasons to believe that Perez's verification was not accurate. Klavir claims that, except for products returned under the money-back guarantee, Klavir received no complaints about the product. Finally, he asserts that, as soon as plaintiff notified him of possible infractions of the FTC Act, defendants voluntarily stopped advertising the product. Based on these contentions, Klavir disclaims any individual liability in this case.

The policy behind the imposition of individual liability is to ensure than an individual defendant does not benefit from deceptive activity and then hide behind the corporation. Individual liability . . . can be predicated either on (1) having participated directly in the violative conduct, or (2) having had the authority to control the conduct. The parties do not dispute Klavir's authority to control Silueta's conduct, as he is the sole owner of Silueta. Disputed here is the issue of whether Klavir must have had knowledge of the conduct before liability attached. . . .

. . . . Courts requiring a showing of knowledge before imposition of individual liability apply the following standard: The Commission must show that the individual defendant possessed one of the following: (1) actual knowledge of material misrepresentations, (2) reckless indifference to the truth or falsity of such misrepresentations, or (3) an awareness of a high probability of fraud along with an intentional avoidance of truth. . . .

The evidence presented here reveals that 63 percent of the consumers who ordered Sistema Silueta returned the product. Such an extraordinarily high rate of return should have placed Klavir on notice that the product did not eliminate cellulite as claimed by the advertisements. This evidence causes the Court to conclude that Klavir acted with a reckless indifference to the truth or falsity of the advertisement's misrepresentations, or, at a minimum, that Klavir had an awareness of a high probability of fraud and intentionally avoided the truth. Consequently, the Court finds that imposition of individual liability on Klavir is appropriate. . . .

Before moving on, the Court addresses Klavir's assertions that his reasonable reliance on the alleged verification made by Perez saves him from individual liability. The Court finds Klavir's argument to be unpersuasive for several reasons. . . . [N]othing in the record establishes Perez as a reliable source for an endorsement of Sistema Silueta. . . . [I]t was unreasonable for Klavir to rely on Perez's alleged verification, as this took place during a sales transaction between Klavir and Perez. It is unlikely that Perez would have informed Klavir, a prospective purchaser, that the advertisement was deceptive. . . . [T]he evidence reveals that the advertisement being challenged here was not the one created by Perez, but was one that was materially altered by Klavir. Klavir significantly edited the advertisement from a 1-minute running time to a 30-second running time. Finally, good faith reliance on another's representation is no defense to liability under the FTC Act.

[The defendant also objected to the remedy the government was seeking: not just a permanent injuction preventing Klavir from deceptively selling his product, but also "restitution and disgorgement—" forcing him to give back his profits. The court ruled against Klavir on this issue also. Restitution and disgorgement is intended to avoid unjust enrichment, to keep a company from benefitting from a deceptive trade practice. Klavir's firm had shipped 10,399 units of Silueta, but 6,546 were returned. Multiplying the unreturned shipments times the cost of each, the court required Klavir to "disgorge" $169,339.35. Then, using names and addresses provided by the defendant, the government would reimburse cheated consumers and keep in the U.S. Treasury whatever was left over.]

The Elements of Deceptiveness Law
Ivan Preston

Let's look first at the process that regulates advertising claims. I have said that the law permits many falsities, but it also prohibits many. First I'll devote some time to showing how the law stops what it stops. Eventually I'll use that background to show why it allows what it allows.

I identify the regulators, who are the principal actors in our story, a bit broadly in this book. I use the term here to include all those who make decisions on deceptiveness. At the Federal Trade Commission (FTC), the U.S. government agency headquartered in Washington, D.C., the key regulators are its commissioners and judges. Comparable officials run the states' consumer protection offices, which typically follow FTC procedures.

I'm also including as regulators the federal trial judges in whose courts advertisers bring private suits against each other. The suits are called Lanham cases because they are authorized by the federal Lanham Trademark Act. The cases involve the plaintiff advertiser, who brings the complaint, and the defendant advertiser. Advertisers need not use this procedure, because they are always free to seek action from the FTC, which protects competitors as well as consumers. However, advertisers frequently volunteer to become Lanham plaintiffs at their own expense because they are not certain that the FTC or the states will pursue the precise action and speed they desire.

Included as regulators as well are the courts that hear appeals. Advertisers may have their cases reviewed if the FTC, the states, or the Lanham trial courts find violations. Appeals occasionally advance to the U.S. Supreme Court. The National Advertising Division of the Council of Better Business Bureaus is also a regulator in a sense because it carries out advertising's self-regulation program. Virtually all advertisers honor their industry's request to submit voluntarily to this program's judgments. Although its decisions have no force of law, they have resulted in stopping many questioned claims.

Asked what regulators regulate, many readers will say "false advertising." That's fine for ordinary usage, but technically it's better to use the term *deceptive advertising*. By strict definition *false* means only claims that are explicitly, literally false. However, ads also make claims that are explicitly true but produce false meanings. Suppose an ad for diet food claims the product can reduce your weight. Could it be suggesting falsely, for example, that the product alone will reduce your weight without your doing anything else?

Consumers often see an ad make such an additional claim even though the ad doesn't explicitly state it. In this case the added claim is false because

From Ivan L. Preston, *The Tangled Web They Weave: Truth, Falsity, and Advertisers;* 1994. The University of Wisconsin Press. Reprinted by permission of the publisher.

you can't accomplish weight reduction without also reducing your calorie intake. Along with eating the diet food, you must stop eating other things. The ad is not "false on its face," yet what it conveys to consumers is false. For that reason the law finds it necessary to prosecute both explicit and conveyed falsity. Since the phrase *false advertising* might imply only the first kind, we customarily use the broader term deceptive advertising.

What the FTC may prohibit is defined by law as "deceptive acts or practices." The commission interprets an *act* as not noticeably different from a *practice,* in practice. The law often uses two terms where one might do, apparently seeing differences most of us would hardly recognize. The custom is no doubt encouraged by the Ways and Means Committee. Deceptive acts or practices are sometimes called *misleading,* which creates another set of virtual twins. The same thing happens with *cease and desist,* which is what the regulators tell advertisers to do with their deceptive acts or practices. I looked up *desist* in my dictionary and found that it means "cease."

The FTC may prohibit *unfair* as well as deceptive acts or practices, and those two terms are really different. Of course it's unfair to be deceptive, but the former is interpreted as referring to other unfairness. Such unfairness is not often applied, however, so this book ignores it.

An act or practice is legally deceptive when it deceives people, or when it is merely likely to do so. Regulators choose most often to show the latter because it's easier to prove. Also, they want to stop the acts and practices before anybody gets hurt. The need to prove only the potential means in theory that they can open a case on the first day an ad appears. In practice, of course, bureaucratic procedures take many days or months, sometimes years, so in reality any ad that may deceive has probably done so with numerous people by the time it's prohibited. Nevertheless, the law need prove only the likeliness of deception, the potential to deceive, deceptive*ness.*

Of course a mere potential may not create harm, which happens only after consumers believe a false claim and act on it. Sometimes, as with slapstick jokes that are obviously false, belief by consumers seems utterly unlikely; actual deceptiveness would be impossible. So, when the regulators examine a false claim that they assume consumers

will disbelieve, they typically dismiss it as having no potential to deceive.

To make their case, the regulators must first show evidence of what advertising was run. Getting print copies or tapes of ads is not a problem because legal rights to investigation require advertisers to supply such things on request. In addition, the FTC monitors many magazines and some newspapers and receives copies in pictureboard form of television ads run by the major networks. The states do similar monitoring in their own areas.

While national advertising is easy for the FTC to track, local advertising is less so. Car dealers and other retailers get heavy scrutiny around Washington, where it's not unusual for congressmen to call in complaints. Elsewhere local advertising will often escape federal notice. Although the FTC has offices in several major cities, large areas remain outside its ability to monitor. Furthermore a federal agency may not act unless violations affect business in more than one state. For these reasons, the consumer protection offices of the individual states play a heavy role in handling local ads.

Once they establish what the ads say, you might think the regulators need only to compare the claim to the item advertised. If they find that the claim matches the actual features, they call it true and acceptable. If they find a contradiction, the claim is false and illegal, and they may prohibit it. That would be simple indeed, but that's not what they do. Instead, they must decide what is inside consumers' heads, what consumers saw the ad to be claiming. Naive advertisers may think they're responsible for no more than what they specifically stated, their literal words. On dealing with the regulators they quickly find that what the public saw and heard them saying is what counts.

Naturally, looking for the claims that ads convey makes the job more complicated. It's much harder to see inside the head of a human being than to identify what a piece of print or tape is saying. Advertisers often exploit this difficulty by protesting that they did not convey a certain message, and occasionally they win such arguments. They can never escape the rule, however, that any message consumers get from an ad is just as much its real message as if the ad had explicitly stated it.

After the regulators determine what the ad conveyed, they sometimes also determine whether consumers believed it and relied upon it. Such information could help show whether the claim will harm consumers if false. However, the regulators need not prove actual belief and reliance, nor is evidence on such points often available anyway. Unless they see that the claim is a joke or other variety of obvious falsity, they typically assume that it has a potential to be believed and relied upon by consumers.

Such an assumption could lead to erros, because straightforward nonjoking claims can be factual but have little or no chance of being believed. Perhaps consumers have prior information from other sources that prompts them to disbelieve the claim. Although the regulators detect such a situation occasionally, they most often persist in assuming the potential for belief. Advertisers typically have not challenged the regulators to produce proof rather than presumption on this matter.

After finding what's conveyed, the regulators examine the relevant facts about the product or service. If those facts are contrary to the conveyed claim, the law may call the claim illegally deceptive and prohibit its further use. The advertiser pays no penalty for its actions up to the time of such an order. It can be punished, however, if it runs the claim later in violation of that order. Although a few such violations occur and result in fines, most advertisers permanently cease the claim.

Thus the law has eliminated a great deal of potentially harmful advertising. It has greatly reduced the cheating.

How Many Consumers Must Be Deceived?

The process just described sounds so simple! The ad regulators merely find what consumers see an ad to be telling them and find whether that conveyed claim is true or false. If it's true, everything's okay. If it's false, it's unlawfully deceptive and the advertiser must stop. Basically that's it, but we must absorb some additional details that make it a little less simple.

For one thing, the regulators may decide that an ad conveys a claim to consumers, though not to all consumers. Let's say an ad stated explicitly, "Our car has the new X-10 engine." While the regulators find that all consumers saw that message conveyed, they also find that 99 percent saw the ad making another claim that was not explicitly stated. The second claim, which is that the new engine has features that no other engine has, is false and the regulators want to prohibit it.

Will they have any problem, though, with the fact that 1 percent of the car-buying public did not see the ad conveying that second message? That small minority agreed with everyone else that the engine had a new name, but they did not see the ad as stating that the engine had any other new feature. What do the regulators do about these people to whom no falsity was conveyed?

The answer to that question is easy: The 1 percent won't matter. The law will rule that the claim was conveyed to consumers generally, and the regulatory process will advance predictably to the finding of a violation. But what if just 80 percent saw the false claim conveyed? The 80 percent is almost as overwhelming a number as 99 percent, but the remaining 20 percent is certainly more significant than a mere 1 percent.

Let's make the example even harder: What if only 40 percent saw the claim? That's still a lot of people, but it's no longer a majority. Can the law treat such a smaller percentage as a fair representation of the whole population of consumers? It's becoming more difficult to decide. We are being forced to recognize that consumers aren't all alike, which means we must reflect the typical or average response they make to ads. Advertising claims hardly ever seem true or false to everybody, although often they will seem to be one or the other for nearly everybody. Other times, the group seeing truth and the group seeing falsity will both be large enough to be important.

What should the rule be when the people seeing a false claim are only a minority, although a significantly large one? Should we say that a majority is necessary, as in electing candidates? Should we require a larger percentage, such as two-thirds or three-quarters? Legislatures often do the latter, to assure that decisions more closely represent the true will of the people.

The FTC, which by law must act in the public interest, follows another line of argument. It decides that it will best fulfill that mandate by recognizing quite small percentages, often in the area of 20 to 25 percent. The federal trial courts adopt an even smaller minimum for Lanham Act cases, 15 percent. The result is that the law may interpret an ad claim as conveyed for legal purposes even though it is not seen conveyed by 75 to 80 percent of the public, for the FTC, or 85 percent, for Lanham cases. Advertising people have yelled bloody murder about that, and certainly have some basis for doing so.

If only a few consumers see a claim conveyed, it might be through what could fairly be called their faulty response. It could be inattention, poor listening, carelessness, stupidity, ill will toward the advertiser, whatever. If it is the consumers who are committing such actions, why should the law hold the advertisers responsible? The FTC has a ready answer for that. It says its mandate is to prevent the possible deception of any group that is large enough, even though a minority, to represent the public interest.

The Supreme Court has validated the FTC's thumbing-of-the-nose at past precedent in this area. To explain the process, I want to tell a story that goes far back in legal lore to examine a traditional way of defining the public interest. It lies in a rule called, in all its current political incorrectness, the reasonable man standard. I will take you back in time to it, bring you up to date on it, and use another name for it.

The *reasonable person standard* of Anglo-American law has held for centuries that citizens must act sensibly and rationally. They must do what a reasonable person ought to do. If they do not, they deserve and will receive no protection from the law. It means the regulators may find consumers to see an ad conveying a claim only if it also finds them acting reasonably in doing so.

The standard suggests that the FTC should choose a high percentage figure. It would not act on a low percentage because it would not interpret a small number of consumers as acting reasonably. There should be no good reason for a legal decision that the new name "X-10" implies new engine features if only 1 or 2 percent saw that claim conveyed. On the other hand, a high percentage would mean the claim must have been conveyed not just to unreasonable consumers but to many reasonable ones as well. You can't argue that the conveyance is only to unreasonable persons if the figure is 99 or even 80 percent.

The regulators do not necessarily use precise percentage figures in stating their conclusions. However, the reasonable person standard's general drift implies the requirement of some minimum percentage, which presumably is much higher than the FTC's 20–25 percent level. Let's assume, very conservatively, that over the centuries it has implied at least 51 percent.

When the FTC was created in 1914 it had to consider this prior legal rule. If it followed the rule, it could not call a claim deceptive unless the ad conveyed it to more than half the consumers. The early commissioners decided they did not like that. The commission had been born under a congressional mandate telling it to get serious about consumer protection. Members of Congress had specifically encouraged the FTC to interpret the law in new ways rather than clinging to old precedent. Accordingly, the first commissioners decided that the public interest required action even when a fairly low percentage of consumers saw a claim being made.

I think of this new approach as the ignorant person standard. *Ignorant* may mean different things, referring in some cases to just plain stupidity. It can also refer, though, to consumers acting sensibly to the extent of their knowledge, while having quite limited knowledge. Reflecting that, ignorant as I use it here simply means uninformed. Certainly many consumers are in that category, because numerous products, such as cars and electronics items, are very complex.

The FTC switched to the ignorant standard in part because the reasonable standard may actually be unreasonable in today's marketplace. We cannot sensibly expect that consumers will always act rationally, using all relevant information and interpreting it accurately. Most of us probably can't do that no matter how hard we try. We would need far more extensive knowledge and experience than we could possibly find the time to acquire. We may have the capacity to acquire much information, but in practice we simply won't get around to it.

Consequently, the FTC decided to judge our behavior by what we *do* do rather than what we ought to do. It recognized that requiring us to do what we ought to do, although it's an ancient legal expectation, is unrealistic in today's world. What we do accomplish, even though it might often be dumber than it could be, should be the proper modern standard for evaluating our behavior.

A Supreme court case confirmed this approach. An encyclopedia claimed that its basic set of books was free even though the consumer would have to pay for ten years' worth of annual update volumes.

The Court agreed with the seller's protest that very few consumers would take the claim of "free" literally. Most consumers, the Court found, would understand that the price covered everything. Nonetheless, the Court ruled that the perception of the few was reasonable because of consumers' lack of familiarity with such offers.

As Justice Hugo Black said in that decision, "The fact that a false statement may be obviously false to those who are trained and experienced does not change its character, nor take away its power to deceive others less experienced. There is no duty resting upon a citizen to suspect the honesty of those with whom he transacts business." That was a strong step toward achieving for consumers what they so badly need. As I said in the Introduction, consumers must be able to rely on advertisers rather than being prompted to distrust them.

For a decade or so the FTC interpreted Black broadly, prohibiting claims almost no one would see an ad to be saying. When Clairol advertised that it would "color hair permanently," the commission decided that the phrase conveyed to consumers the false claim of coloring all hair to be grown for the rest of the user's entire lifetime. The available evidence was that one person—not 1 percent, just one person—testified that some consumers, although not herself, would see that message.

Such cases have not been frequent in recent times and do not accurately indicate current practice. The commission soon cut back that very ignorant person standard to what we might think of as a normally ignorant person standard. It said in effect that a certain number of ignorant persons would have to see the false claim conveyed. The regulators endorse no exact number and determine each case separately on its unique circumstances.

However, the generalization from many decisions is that the required minimum percentage lies in the range of 20 to 25 in FTC cases, and as low as 15 in Lanham Act cases. An advertisement that conveys nothing false to the great majority of its readers can get in trouble for what the rest see. The ad community may find this infuriating but it knows it must live with it.

•   •   •

Ads also convey claims without making them explicitly. These *implied* claims are even harder to determine by looking at the ad alone. Because an implication is by definition not present in specific words, a sensible presumption could be that the consumer won't see what's not there to be seen. Advertisers enjoy that presumption; they use it to argue that what is conveyed consists of nothing more than what is stated explicitly.

Although winning that argument would keep the advertisers out of a lot of trouble, the law does not let them win it very often. Considerable expert evidence shows that consumers see advertisements conveying many claims that aren't specifically present. The regulators, although permitted to decide conveyed content by looking at nothing but the ad, have frequently used expert evidence to identify implied claims. . . .

Why do we see messages sent to us that are different from the messages actually sent? If they typically tell us much more than they actually state to us, it's because we do more with them than just see them. We also interpret their words and pictures; we take them to mean certain additional things because of the overall context.

In a recent television spot, a beer bottle as huge as a ship was floating in the ocean. A tugboat took it in tow to the delight of thirsty drinkers gathered on shore. The depiction defied reality; it was an impossible event in the context of the world as we know it. Presumably virtually all viewers disbelieved that such a bottle actually existed. We see the words and pictures of such a message, but we also see the total ad telling us it's only a joke. Most of us would take a dim view of anyone who thought a real event was being reported.

While that example involves taking a meaning away from the message, it's more common for our interpretations to create added meanings. Remember the claim, "Our car now has the X-10 engine." We may see that as saying the engine has features the previous model didn't have. Maybe it does, or maybe it has only one new feature, the name "X-10." The ad doesn't explicitly say that the claim means anything more than that.

Another ad discussed a feature of a new computer. Consumers might reasonably have seen such an ad to be claiming that the feature was for sale and they could buy the computer having it. Usually that would be true, but the FTC found that this particular computer had not yet been manufactured. The computer industry has a term for hardware or software items that exist only in the advertising—*vaporware*.

How does the FTC decide that an advertisement conveys a certain unstated claim? In the computer example we probably would not object if the FTC found the implied claim by looking only at the ad. Certainly the advertising of an item should ordinarily mean it's for sale—why else would it be advertised? The number of consumers who would see such a claim conveyed is surely many more than the minimum of 20–25 percent that the FTC requires.

However, not all cases are so easy. Suppose a brand of a product is claimed to be superior on one attribute; for example, a car's brakes are said to stop more quickly than those of any competitor. Does that imply the car is better overall? Does it convey the message that the car is better on some other attribute, such as giving a more comfortable ride? Does it imply that the car is better on all other attributes? These questions are harder to assess.

It's reasonable to expect some people would think those things. On the other hand, they aren't as obvious as the implication about the advertised item being for sale. Moreover, we must find how many people saw the claim conveyed, and then compare it to the percentage criteria specified by FTC or Lanham decisions (chap. 2). The difficulty these questions pose eventually forces us to remember that the only real way to see a meaning, a conveyed claim, is to look in the consumer's head, not in the ad.

The Aspercreme (Thompson Medical) Case

What does the name Aspercreme convey to you? Your first hint is that it's a product, although that won't help much. The "creme" portion may indicate a creamy substance of some sort. What about the "Asper" part? We better move on to the next hint: it's a pain relief product. Well, then, "Asper" must mean "aspirin." What else can you think when you see Aspercreme and pain relief associated! It's aspirin in the form of a creamy substance. I guess you rub it in, or rub it on, rather than swallowing it like regular aspirin.

Of course. If that's so, however, why did the Thompson Medical Company, Aspercreme's maker and inventor of its fascinating name, go to great lengths to argue before the FTC that the name and advertising do not convey to consumers that As-

percreme contains aspirin? Do you think maybe it's because Aspercreme *doesn't* contain aspirin?

Of course. Aspercreme's active ingredient was found to be triethanolamine salicylate, or trolamine salicylate, TEA/S for short. Its components are similar to those of aspirin, which chemically is acetylsalicylic acid, or acetylated salicylate. TEA/S has equal amounts of triethanolamine and salicylic acid. It's thus a salicylate with no acetyl group added—a nonacetylated salicylate. Do you think, however, that Thompson Medical saw a possible advantage in claiming that Aspercreme and aspirin, both being salicylates, were similar in their effects?

Once again: of course. Yet the FTC found no evidence that different salicylates work similarly. You simply can't claim that TEA/S does what aspirin does. Even if you could, it could be only under the assumption that both chemicals arrive in equal degrees at the muscle or other bodily component that hurts. But how else are aspirin and Aspercreme different? Ah, it's the matter of being a creamy substance. The FTC found that when people rubbed Aspercreme onto their bodies, most of the salicylate penetrated no farther than the dermis. That's the inner layer of skin, in contrast to the outer layer, the epidermis.

Thompson ran claims that Aspercreme "concentrates all the strong relief of aspirin directly at the point of pain." But Aspercreme got little or no salicylate beneath the skin and into the hurting body parts that a medicine must reach to relieve pain. It had what the scientists call a limited bioavailability. Further, it showed no sign of bioactivity, which in layman's terms means it doesn't work. Apparently any delivery that Aspercreme achieved was in quantities too small to relieve pain to a measurable degree.

Additional ad copy interpreted the reference to concentration as making a comparison that was negative to ordinary aspirin. Aspirin takes a long detour into the mouth and down the throat and into the stomach and into the bloodstream, meandering all over the body before it finally reaches your sore muscle. It's a wonder it ever gets there! Then, having dissipated its effects from all that travel, the aspirin presumably can have little impact at the one place where a person hurts. What's more, it upsets some stomachs!

The only problem with all that analysis, the FTC found, is that aspirin works and Aspercreme just plain doesn't. The faster delivery and avoidance of upset stomachs were technically true, but were being used as smoke screens, irrelevant to the main point. Aspercreme's claim to be superior to regular aspirin was false, cheating consumers and prompting them to distrust advertisers even though consumers need to be able to rely on them.

Did Thompson Medical know it was making these claims without evidence? Did it deliberately lie about them? Of course. That's a serious charge, so I'm going to quote exactly what the FTC said:

> Thompson has known or should have known for some time now that its efficacy claims for Aspercreme are unsubstantiated. . . . Thompson has deliberately continued making efficacy claims despite this fact.
>
> Likewise, it seems clear that Thompson deliberately sought to lead consumers into the belief that Aspercreme contains aspirin. . . . Thompson has known full well for some time that consumers misunderstood the identity of the principal ingredient in Aspercreme and has continued to advertise in a manner that creates more such misunderstanding.

Aspercreme was a phony product and its maker knew it. It also knew, or should have known as an expert in drugs, that the research it offered in defense of its false claims was equally phony. This research came to light in the FTC hearing in which Thompson defended against charges that it had no valid evidence of Aspercreme's effectiveness. It said it did have such evidence, consisting of clinical tests that compared drugs with each other by using them on patients and observing the results.

Thompson's tests found that users reported no difference in pain relief between Aspercreme and aspirin. That finding superficially would make Aspercreme equally as effective as aspirin, and it would support a claim that Aspercreme was superior to aspirin if it were also true that Aspercreme was delivered more quickly. However, we've already seen that the delivery claim was false, because Aspercreme didn't deliver the medicine in sufficient quantity.

The claim of being equally effective turned out to be unsupported, too. The logic Thompson offered was defective, because for a test to show no difference doesn't mean there is no difference. It was a matter of sampling in one test in which

Thompson gave Aspercreme and aspirin to only twenty persons each. That's so few that equal effects are likely to result even if the two drugs really are different. The test was unable to reveal any differences.

Other Thompson research tested Aspercreme alone. Medical experts know that people are highly subjective and variable in reporting increase or decrease of pain. They also know that pain will spontaneously disappear in a short time even when people take no drug. Therefore a test is of no value if it simply measures pain both before and after use of the drug. A decrease in pain is not proof that the drug caused the decrease.

The scientific solution is to control the results by testing both the product and a placebo, the latter looking exactly like the product but lacking the active drug ingredient. Pain often disappears after people use such an item, and this "placebo effect" casts doubt on what happens when they use the active drug. If the test uses both drug and placebo, and the same pain relief occurs with both, the test shows the drug made no contribution. Only if the pain decreased with the drug and not with the placebo can the drug be proved effective.

You might suppose that in a test of two drugs, such as aspirin and Aspercreme, each could be the placebo for the other. However, the experts say that a finding of no difference between the two cannot distinguish between whether they were both equally effective or simply both ineffective. So that type of test needs a placebo, too. It can then prove one drug superior to another if that drug is superior to both the other and to the placebo.

Of course the users must be blinded so that they do not know whether they're getting the drug or the placebo. Better yet, they shouldn't even know that two versions exist. It's necessary also that the doctors who make the judgments be blinded; that's called double-blinding. The doctors should not know who gets what, and of course they should not know who is sponsoring the research and what results are sought.

The Thompson Medical tests lacked these various safeguards and thus were invalid. They did not produce legitimate evidence to support the advertising claim. The company also failed with reports it introduced about consumers indicating satisfaction with Aspercreme. The law considers such testimonial evidence worthless also, among other reasons because there is no way to eliminate the chance that the placebo effect influenced the results. Uncontrolled comments by consumers are no way to find out anything about drugs.

Thompson's tests also lacked adequate record keeping and reporting. That defect produced uncertainty about what kinds of people were involved, what drugs were given, what questions were asked or observations made, and what results really occurred. In some cases, the tested persons used or may have used other drugs that could have interacted with the test drugs and thus affected the results improperly. One research study involved two investigators in different locations, with the results later combined. Thompson, however, was unable to show that those two researchers followed the same instructions or conducted the test in the same manner.

In another Thompson test, the researcher developed a set of categories for analyzing the results only after seeing the data and determining how to manipulate them to favor Aspercreme. Fairness in testing requires the researchers to specify all aspects of their methodology in advance and to follow them without change to prevent a biased impact on the results.

In summary, the company offered no tests that were scientifically adequate. It simply had no support, and the FTC said it knew it had none, for its claims of Aspercreme's performance.

The quality of Thompson's research on the conveyed claim was equally low. It tried to show, by surveying consumers on what they see ads to be saying, that its ads had not claimed that Aspercreme contained aspirin. In two surveys conducted by the same research firm, Thompson asked consumers to name the ingredient in Aspercreme. That question was open-ended, that is, it invited people to give whatever answer they chose with no hints as to possible answers. Five percent or fewer said aspirin, probably because the ads had not mentioned aspirin explicitly. That favored Thompson's position.

The first of those two surveys also asked whether the ad said the product contained aspirin. That was a forced-choice question, making people choose from answers supplied by the surveyor—in this case Yes, No, or Don't Know. The FTC calls forced-choice questions more valid because they get people to respond specifically about the topic in question. Open-ended questions don't reliably get people to say what they know about the specific topic. Because the second question mentioned aspirin specifically, you would expect more affirmative answers than the 5 percent obtained from the first question. That was confirmed, with 22 percent answering Yes on the second question.

However, in the second survey Thompson omitted that question. Do you think maybe the higher figure had something to do with it? Of course. As the FTC decision said, "The evidence is consistent with the conclusion that the direct ingredient question was dropped because it had produced results unfavorable to Thompson." The commission thereupon accepted the 22 percent figure, which met the minimum requirement of 20–25 percent discussed in chapter 2. Thus it found that the surveying showed a significant number of persons saw the message that Aspercreme contained aspirin.

Another Thompson trick was to criticize a survey as unreliable for determining conveyed meanings. The FTC rejected the argument because Thompson had used that research for making an important business decision—picking which of a group of commercials to put on the air. The commission wouldn't allow Thompson to call research unsuitable that it had earlier treated as acceptable.

Thompson took its case to a U.S. court of appeals, claiming consumers didn't care whether Aspercreme contained aspirin, and besides, the labeling had always indicated the actual ingredient. The court said, "One wonders why Thompson is upset about being ordered to disclose that its product does not contain aspirin if no one cares and everyone has always known anyway." Thompson's argument, it said, "borders on the frivolous."

The court also had this rejoinder to Thompson's complaint that the FTC order would destroy its business: "Allowing firms to continue such advertising because to stop would hurt the firm's economic interests is obviously not part of [what] Congress intended the FTC to consider. Thompson has no right to stay in business if the only way it can do so is to engage in false and misleading advertising."

As with Sears, Thompson's cheating in the FTC hearing had a potential to further disadvantage consumers. Had the effort succeeded, Thompson would have been able to continue making claims that would prompt the public to spend money for a benefit that did not exist.

The company, with its Slim-Fast Food Cos. affiliate, was the seventy-first largest national advertiser recently, spending $137.5 million. Its major brands were Slim-Fast, Ultra Slim-Fast, and Dexatrim diet and nutrition products. It also marketed NP27, Cortizone-5, Cortizone-10, Sports-creme, Sleepinal, Aqua-Ban, Breathe Free, Tempo, Lactogest, Silk Solutions, and Arthritis Hot.

And it still sells Aspercreme. By that name. The FTC did not stop the usage because it decided that requiring an accompanying disclosure would be sufficient to dispel the falsity. The disclosure must state prominently and conspicuously that Aspercreme does not contain aspirin.

Advertising and Ethics

Phillip Nelson

The Market System and Advertising

There are two possible routes one can take to ethics. One can exhort others to take account of social well-being in their behavior—"to love one another" and act accordingly. Or one can try to design institutions such that people will, indeed, benefit society, given the motivations that presently impel their behavior. Most economists, whatever their political position, adopt the latter view; ethical behavior is behavior that, in fact, benefits society, not necessarily behavior that is motivated to benefit society.

Those of us who advocate the market as an appropriate institution are following the lead of Adam Smith: that the market, more or less, acts as if there were an invisible hand, converting individual actions motivated by the pursuit of private gain into social benefit. The selfish employer, for example, callously firing employees when he no longer needs them, helps in the reallocation of labor to activities where it is more useful.

This is not the stuff of poetry. In novels—and quite possibly in the interpersonal relations upon which novels generally focus—selfish people act in ways disastrous to those around them. But novels are hardly the basis for determining social policy, though novelists and their compatriots, literary critics, are often in the forefront in the espousal of "social causes." They have been the consciences of

society. Because of their focus on motivation, they have generated a guilt complex when guilt is totally unjustified.

It must be admitted that the market is not a perfect instrument, that the invisible hand wavers a bit. Some individual actions will not lead to social well-being. However, popular perceptions tend to exaggerate market imperfections. For example, the available evidence indicates that the monopoly problem is not terribly serious in the United States. More importantly, the popular view fails to evaluate the problems of alternative institutions. The record of government regulation to make the market behave has been distinguished by case after case where the cure has been worse than the disease, where often there has been no disease at all.

I want to look at the ethics of advertising, given this perspective. Advertising is ethical not because of the motivations of its practitioners but because of the consequences of its operation. The invisible hand strikes again! The market power of consumers will force advertisers to act in ways that benefit society. Advertising will by no means be an "ideal" institution. But it will do an effective job of getting information to consumers.

Advertising bothers its critics not only because its practitioners are selfishly motivated. The advertising itself is often distasteful. Celebrities endorse that brand that pays them the highest price. Advertisers lie if it pays. Advertisers often make empty statements. Nobel prizes for literature have not yet been awarded to the classics of the advertising art. But the crucial question is not whether advertising is aesthetically satisfying, or whether its practitioners are noble, or even whether they occasionally lie.

The question is whether advertising generates social well-being. Some of the former questions are not irrelevant in determining the answer to the latter question. In particular, as I discuss later, the role that truth plays in generating socially useful advertising is an important question.

Advertising and Information

Before resolving the fundamental ethical issue about advertising, it is important to understand how advertising behaves. I support a simple proposition about the behavior of advertising: that all advertising is information. This is not a statement with which the critics of advertising would agree. What bothers them is that advertising is paid for by the manufacturers of the brands whose products are being extolled. How can information be generated by such a process? Clearly, some kind of mechanism is required to make the self-interested statements of manufacturers generate information. But such a mechanism exists—consumer power in the product markets.

The nature of consumer control over advertising varies with the character of consumer information. Consumers can get some information about certain qualities of products prior to purchase. For example, they can try on a dress, find out about the price of a product, or see how new furniture looks. I call these "search qualities." In the case of search qualities, a manufacturer is almost required by the nature of his business to tell the truth. The consumer can determine before he buys the product whether indeed this is the dress or the piece of furniture that has been advertised; and in consequence, it will pay the advertiser to be truthful. This is a situation where the famous ditty of Gilbert and Sullivan would be appropriate:

> This haughty youth, he tells the truth
> Whenever he finds it pays;
> And in this case, it all took place
> Exactly like he says.

Now, there are other qualities that the consumer cannot determine prior to purchase. It is very difficult for the consumer to determine the taste of a brand of tuna fish before he buys the tuna fish, or to determine how durable a car will be

until he's experienced it; but even in these cases, the consumer can get information about a product. The character of his experiences when using the brand will generate information to the consumer. This information will not be useful for initial purchases, but it will govern whether the consumer repeatedly purchases the brand or not. The repeat purchase of consumers provides the basis of consumer control of the market in the case of "experience qualities."

In this case, there will be certain characteristics of the advertising which are truthful. It will pay the advertiser to relate correctly the function of the brand. It pays the manufacturer of Pepto-Bismol to advertise his brand as a stomach remedy rather than as a cure for athlete's foot because, obviously, he is going to be able to get repeat purchases if Pepto-Bismol does something for stomachs and people are taking it for stomachs. If they're taking the stomach remedy for athlete's foot, they're in trouble. So the effort to get repeat purchasers will generate a lot of truthfulness in advertising. Another example: it pays the manufacturer of unsweetened grapefruit juice to advertise the product as unsweetened. This is the effective way to get repeat purchases; hence people can believe it.

There are other qualities about the brand for which the incentive of truthfulness does not exist. It pays the manufacturer of Pepto-Bismol to advertise his brand as the most soothing stomach remedy even if it were the least soothing stomach remedy around. It pays somebody to say that a piece of candy tastes best even if the candy has an unpleasant taste. Even here, however, there is information for the consumer to obtain through advertising. The advertising message is not credible, but the fact that the brand is advertised is a valuable piece of information to the consumer. The consumer rightly believes that there is a positive association between advertising and the better buy. The more advertising he sees of the product, the more confidence he has prior to purchasing the product. Simply put, it pays to advertise winners. It does not pay to advertise losers. In consequence, the brands that are advertised the most heavily are more likely to be the winners.

The mechanism that is operating is the repeat purchasing power of the consumer. Brands that are good after purchase will be brands that consumers buy more. In consequence, there is a negatively sloped demand curve. People buy more as the price per unit of utility of a good goes down, even when it takes experience on the part of consumers to determine this utility. As quantity goes up, the amount of advertising will also go up. This is a well-established relationship.[1] The positive association between quantity and advertising and the negative association between quantity and price per unit of utility generates a negative association between advertising and price per unit of utility. In other words, the "better buys" advertise more; and, in consequence, the *amount* of advertising provides information to consumers.

Considering that we have no direct measure of "better buys," there is a good deal of evidence to support this proposition. First, it pays a firm to expand its sales if it can produce what consumers want more cheaply than other firms. It can increase its sales either by increasing advertising or lowering prices. I maintain that it does both at the same time, just as plants usually increase both their capital and their labor when they expand output on a permanent basis. But the critics say that the larger selling brand advertises more; therefore, it charges more to cover the costs of advertising.

The only way the critics could be right is if diminishing returns in advertising did not exist. By diminishing returns in advertising, I mean that the more a manufacturer spends on advertising, the less he gets in additional sales per dollar of advertising. When there are diminishing returns, the advertising of the larger selling brand is less efficient; it gets fewer sales per dollar. When advertising is less efficient in that sense, the larger advertiser will have a greater incentive to get additional sales by lowering the price. With diminishing returns in advertising, then, the larger selling brand both advertises more and gives greater value per dollar. There is considerable evidence that there are, indeed, diminishing returns in advertising.[2]

There is a second strand of evidence in support of my position. One can successfully predict which products get advertised more intensively by assuming that advertising provides information in the way I have described. It can be shown that it requires more advertising to provide the indirect advertising for experience goods than the direct advertising of search goods. Indeed, the advertising/sales ratios are greater for experience goods than search goods.

There is another important piece of evidence that winners are advertised more. If it is true that the larger-selling brand provides better value per dollar on the average than smaller-selling brands, wouldn't it pay a brand to advertise its rank in its product class more, the higher the rank? Consumers would prefer to buy top sellers rather than bottom sellers. The evidence is overwhelming that more brands say that they are Number One than declare any other rank.

One could argue, I suppose, that consumers are brainwashed into believing that larger-selling brands are better, when the contrary is true. But how could this be? A lot more advertisers have an interest in brainwashing the consumers into believing the contrary. Yet, the "big is beautiful" message wins. The only reasonable explanation is that this is the message which is confirmed by the consumers' own experiences. The brainwashing explanation is particularly hard to accept, given the industries in which brands most frequently advertise their Number One status. It pays consumers to make much more thoughtful decisions about durables than non-durables because the cost to them of making a mistake is so much greater in that case. Yet, the "I am Number One" advertising occurs more frequently for durables than for non-durables.[3] Even more convincing is the evidence that the advertising of Number One rank is not confined to possibly gullible consumers. That same message is used in advertising directed to businessmen. They too must have been brainwashed if the critics are right. But such soft-headed businessmen could hardly survive in the market.

The evidence seems inescapable: larger-selling brands do, on the whole, provide the better value per dollar. The evidence also shows—and all would admit—that larger-selling brands advertise more. In consequence, the more advertised brands are likely to be the better buys.

It is frequently alleged that advertised brands are really no better than non-advertised brands. A case that is often cited in this connection is Bayer Aspirin. But aspirins do, indeed, vary in their physical characteristics. Soft aspirins dissolve in the stomach both more rapidly and more certainly than hard aspirins. In consequence, the soft aspirins are better. They are also more expensive to produce. It is no accident that the most heavily advertised brand of aspirin is a soft aspirin. Of course, there are also non-advertised soft aspirins that sell for less than Bayer Aspirin. But the issue is not whether the best unadvertised aspirin is as good as the most heavily advertised aspirin. The issue is whether purchasing one of the more heavily advertised aspirins at random gives one a better product, on the average, than getting an unadvertised aspirin at random. The existence of unadvertised soft aspirin, when the consumer does not know which aspirin fits into that category, is of little help to the consumer.

Advertising can provide this information without consumers being aware of its doing so. Advertising as information does not require intelligent consumer response to advertising, though it provides a basis for such intelligent response. Consumers who actually believe paid endorsements are the victims of the most benign form of deception. They are deceived into doing what they should do anyhow.

It does not pay consumers to make very thoughtful decisions about advertising. They can respond to advertising for the most ridiculous, explicit reasons and still do what they would have done if they made the most careful judgments about their behavior. "Irrationality" is rational if it is cost-free.

Whatever their explicit reasons, consumers' ultimate reason for responding to advertising is their self-interest in so doing. That is, it is no mere coincidence that thoughtful and unthoughtful judgments lead to the same behavior. If it were not in consumers' self-interest to respond to advertising, they would no longer pay attention to advertising. . . .

NOTES

1. This is borne out by data from the Internal Revenue Service *Source Book of Income,* 1957. For every industry, firms with larger sales advertise more.
2. See Phillip Nelson, "Advertising as Information Once More," *Journal of Political Economy* 4 (1982), 729-774.
3. In the May, 1955, issue of *Life* magazine, there were twelve durable and three non-durable, "I am Number One" advertisements.

Advertising and the Social Conditions of Autonomy

Richard L. Lippke

In *The New Industrial State,* John Kenneth Galbraith charged that advertising creates desires rather than responds to them.[1] His thesis raised in stark terms the issue of who is controlling whom in the marketplace. Yet, Galbraith did not provide a rigorous analysis of autonomy, and his remarks about the effects of advertising on individuals were often more suggestive than carefully worked out.

The claim that advertising is inimical to the autonomy of individuals has been taken up and discussed by philosophers, economists, and social theorists. Typically, these discussions provide first, an analysis of autonomy, and second, some empirical conjecture about whether or not advertising can be said to subvert it. The focus of most of these discussions has been on whether or not advertising can be justly accused of manipulating individuals

Business and Professional Ethics Journal, vol. 8, #4, 35–58, 1988. Reprinted by permission of the author.

into wanting and therefore purchasing specific products or services. Less attention has been paid to what I believe is another major theme in Galbraith's writings—that mass-advertising induces in individuals beliefs, wants, and attitudes conducive to the economic and political interests of corporations in advanced capitalist societies like the United States. Galbraith's concern seems to be not only that advertising is hostile to individual autonomy, but that it is an aspect of the ability of corporations to dominate the lives of other members of society.

What the effects of mass-advertising are on individuals is, it must be admitted, ultimately an empirical question. In spite of this, I will try to show how we might reasonably conclude that advertising undermines autonomy, especially under the social conditions that exist in advanced capitalist countries like the United States.[2] Recent discussions of advertising have not only failed to consider one crucial way in which advertising might subvert autonomy; they have also ignored important aspects of the broader social context of advertising. Specifically, they have paid scant attention to the ways in which other social conditions also undermine autonomy. My analysis will emphasize the complex interplay between and amongst the various social conditions that affect the autonomy of individuals.

In addition to providing an analysis of autonomy, I will show how autonomy requires social conditions for its development and continued viability. I will show how the content and methods of *persuasive* mass-advertising are likely to suppress the development of the abilities, attitudes and knowledge constitutive of dispositional autonomy. Yet, my view is that its full impact on autonomy should be considered in light of the ways in which political and economic institutions distribute the other social conditions of autonomy.

My primary focus will be on persuasive as opposed to informational advertising. Though the distinction is not a sharp one, I take the latter to involve information about the features, price, and availability of a product or service. Persuasive advertising, in contrast, often contains very little direct informational content about a product or service. Whereas the former presupposes some interest on the part of individuals in the product or service, the latter seeks to cultivate an interest. This typically involves tying the product or service to the satisfaction of individuals' other, sometimes subconscious desires. It seems fair to say that current informational advertising is woefully deficient. The information that is presented is often incomplete or misleading, or both. As a result, even informational ads are deceptive or manipulative at times.[3] To that extent, they undercut the abilities of persons to make informed choices and may be destructive to the intellectual honesty that is one of the constituents of dispositional autonomy. Also, in the context of massive persuasive advertising, informational advertising is likely to reinforce the content of its persuasive counterpart. Nonetheless, the two can be roughly distinguished and my remarks will be predominantly directed against persuasive advertising.

Implicit in my analysis will be the claim that one criterion for judging social orders is the extent to which they provide all of their members with the social conditions of autonomy. I will not attempt to argue for this claim here, though it is by no means an uncontroversial one. I note only that my claim is a relatively modest one—that this is *one* criterion for judging social orders. Critics of my approach may point out that many individuals seem to lack a strong desire for the sort of autonomous life I elucidate. We should not, however, be misled by this appearance. Many persons will assent to the principle that, *ceteris paribus,* the choices of individuals ought to be respected. Yet, as Lawrence Haworth shows, it makes little sense to urge such respect where peoples' choices do not reflect an autonomous way of living.[4] This suggests there may be sound reasons to hold that autonomy is a central value. Its value may be obscured for many people by, among other things, persuasive mass-advertising.

One reason that we value autonomy is relevant to Galbraith's thesis that advertising is an aspect of the dominance of large corporations over the lives of individuals in advanced capitalist societies. Persons who are nonautonomous seem much more likely to be dominated by others. Such domination need not be consciously intended or effected by the more powerful.[5] They may simply act in ways that they perceive to be in their own interests. Nonautonomous individuals may respond by passively assimilating the interests of the more powerful. I suspect that something like this is true when it comes to corporations, advertising, and its effects on individuals. Though I cannot hope to fully support Galbraith's thesis here, I will touch on it in numerous places throughout my discussion.[6]

I

Recent discussions of advertising and autonomy are inadequate because they fail to isolate the crucial way in which the content of advertising might be subversive to autonomy. Roger Crisp, a critic of advertising, develops and tries to support the claim that ads are manipulative in an objectionable fashion. He argues that advertising "links, by suggestion, the product with my unconscious desires for [for instance] power and sex."[7] Crisp claims that persuasive advertising leaves persons unaware of their real reasons for purchasing a product, and so precludes their making rational purchasing decisions. Crisp then argues that "many of us have a strong second-order desire not to be manipulated by others without our knowledge, and for no good reason."[8] If persons become aware of how persuasive advertising affects them, by locking onto their unconscious desires, they will likely repudiate the desires induced by advertising. Such repudiated desires will not be regarded by individuals as theirs. Hence, Crisp believes he has shown how advertising is subversive to autonomy.

Crisp's approach seems to attribute both too much and too little power to advertising. Too much, because there is reason to doubt that most adults are manipulated by particular ads in the way Crisp describes. Perhaps children are so manipulated at times, and this is cause for concern. Most adults, though, seem quite able to resist what I will call the "explicit content" of ads. The explicit content of ads is the message to "buy X," along with information about where it may be purchased, its features, and how much it costs. Most individuals learn at an early age that many ads are out to persuade them, even manipulate them. They become wary of ads and this explains why they often resist their explicit content quite easily. Even if persons do have the second-order desire Crisp attributes to them, it is not the explicit content of ads that manipulates them *without their knowledge*. The challenge is to develop an account of how advertising can have power over individuals who very often realize ads are designed to manipulate them.

This brings us to the way in which Crisp's account attributes too little power to advertising. In addition to encouraging persons to buy Brand X, many ads have what I will term an "implicit content" that consists of messages about, broadly speaking, the consumer lifestyle. This lifestyle consists of a set of beliefs, attitudes, norms, expectations, and aspirations that I will, in due course, attempt to summarize. While individuals may be aware that they are being sold particular products, the crucial issue is the extent to which they are aware of being "sold" this implicit content. As Samuel Gorovitz remarks, "it is an error to focus too narrowly on the cognitive content of advertising by looking at the truth of its claims and the validity of its inferences."[9] Instead, we should consider how the images and emotional content of ads affect our beliefs, aspirations, expectations, and attitudes. Crisp does not really consider where some

of the unconscious desires ads supposedly lock onto might originate.

In an important defense of advertising, Robert Arrington argues that it rarely, if ever, subverts the autonomy of individuals. He maintains that a desire is autonomous so long as it is endorsed by an individual on reflection. In other words, the (first-order) desire is autonomous if the person has a second-order desire to have and satisfy it.[10] Advertising, he contends, rarely leads persons to have first-order desires for products that they subsequently repudiate. Perhaps, as we saw earlier, this is because many individuals resist the explicit content of even the most manipulative ads.

Arrington also argues that ads do not violate autonomy by inducing persons to make irrational choices based on faulty or inadequate information. The only information needed for a rational choice, on his view, is information relevant to the satisfaction of individuals' particular desires. He claims that ads often provide the information relevant to the satisfaction of such desires.

Even if we accept his arguments as stated, Arrington's defense of advertising is seriously incomplete. He ignores the very real possibility that it violates autonomy *not* by manipulating persons' desires and choices with respect to particular products, but by suppressing their capacities to make rational choices about the implicit content of ads. If advertising induces uncritical acceptance of the consumer lifestyle as a whole, then Arrington's vindication of it with respect to the formation of particular desires or the making of particular choices *within* that lifestyle is hardly comforting. Arrington consistently ignores the possibility that the beliefs, attitudes, and desires particular ads cater to may themselves be influenced by ads in ways that ought to trouble anyone who values human autonomy.

II

As a first step in building my case, I offer an account of autonomy that draws on recent work on the concept. Robert Young notes that a person has "dispositional autonomy" to the extent that the person's life is "ordered according to a plan or conception which fully expresses [that person's] own will."[11] In a similar vein, Gerald Dworkin suggests that autonomy is a "global" concept: "It is a feature that evaluates a whole way of living one's life and can only be assessed over extended periods of a person's life. . . ."[12] Autonomy is a matter of degree, an achievement that depends in part on the capacities and virtues of individuals, and in part, as we shall see, on the existence of certain social conditions.[13]

Dworkin's analysis employs the well-known distinction between first and second-order desires and abilities. He summarizes his account as follows:

> Putting the various pieces together, autonomy is conceived of as a second-order capacity of persons to reflect critically upon their first-order preferences, desires, wishes, and so forth and the capacity to accept or attempt to change these in light of higher-order preferences and values.[14]

Similarly, Lawrence Haworth interprets autonomy in terms of the notion of "critical competence."[15] Autonomous persons are competent in the sense of being active and generally successful in giving effect to their intentions. They are critical in that they deliberate not only about means to their ends, but about the ends themselves, including those of central significance in their lives. While not engaged in continuous ratiocination, they are nonetheless disposed to critically examine their beliefs, desires, attitudes, and motivations. They subject claims they are confronted with and norms others urge on them to rational scrutiny.

Importantly for our purposes, autonomous individuals should be understood as ones who scrutinize the political, social, and economic institutions under which they live. These institutions, and the patterns of habit and expectation they establish, shape the possibilities individuals can envision and determine the areas in which they can exercise their autonomy. Autonomous individuals want to shape their own lives. Hence, of necessity they will be interested in the social forces and institutions that significantly affect their lives, especially since these forces and institutions are often humanly alterable.

Autonomy is not a capacity that develops in isolation from the social conditions that surround individuals. It requires individuals to have certain abilities, motivations, and knowledge (or at least awareness) of alternative belief-systems and life-styles. It also requires venues in which they can reasonably expect to display these abilities and act on these motivations. Obviously, individuals must not be subjected to things like coercion, deception, brainwashing, and harassment. Being shielded from these is a necessary social condition of the development and exercise of autonomy. Yet, there are other social conditions that while perhaps not, strictly speaking, necessary ones, are such that they foster and support autonomy in vital ways. Societies differ in the extent to which they provide these conditions for all individuals, and thus in the extent to which they enable autonomy.

III

What is the importance of noting the numerous social conditions of autonomy in the context of an analysis of persuasive mass-advertising? Very simply that advertising, as a possible threat to autonomy, does not exist in a social vacuum. We cannot assume that individuals encounter mass-advertising with already finely-honed skills of critical competence. The extent to which they do so is a function of the distribution of other social conditions of autonomy. The absence of social conditions of autonomy in one area will often reinforce or exacerbate the effects of their absence in other areas. Thus, in any attempt to gauge how much of a threat to autonomy persuasive mass-advertising represents, we must consider these and other background social conditions of autonomy.

In advanced capitalist countries like the United States, many individuals spend significant portions of their working lives in conditions destructive to autonomy. As Adina Schwartz and others have argued, hierarchical, authoritarian management structures, typical in such industrialized countries, thwart the autonomy of workers in obvious ways.[16] Very few have meaningful input into the decisions affecting their working lives. The tasks they perform are determined by management, as are the methods used in carrying them out. Work technology is decided by management, as are productivity quotas, discipline procedures, and criteria for evaluation. Workers are not allowed or expected to exercise even the *minimal* autonomy of determining the ends they will pursue or the means used to pursue them. This is one way in which the institutions of advanced capitalism enable corporations to impose their interests on individuals.

Often connected with the character of work is unequal access to quality education. While certain ways of organizing work may simply deny individuals avenues along which to exercise their autonomy, lack of education or poor quality education undermines it in more basic ways.[17] Reduced educational and cultural experiences often result in restricted intellectual abilities and dispositions. The kinds of rational skills needed for autonomy and the motivation to employ them seem to be the products of a liberal education in the classic sense. Individuals who lack ready access to such education are likely to have an impoverished awareness of different ways of conceiving of their lives and their social relations. This makes them ideal candidates for the tutelage in the consumer lifestyle effected by mass-advertising.

Much of that which is sponsored by advertising on TV, radio, and in magazines is hardly such as to encourage the development of autonomy.[18] Program content on commercial networks is often mindless, melodramatic, simplistic in its approach to the problems of human life—or worse, violent, sexist, or subtly racist. Even commercial network news programs seem to emphasize entertainment. Dramatic visual images, "sound bites," and fifteen second summaries of events are the rule. Commercial sponsorship of the media opens the way for the exercise of subtle control over program content. But the more likely effect of that sponsorship is an emphasis on gaining and holding an audience. That which cannot do so does not get sponsored. Yet, I think we should be wary of those who claim that what the public does not choose to consume in the way of mass media reflects its autonomous choices. Other factors, such as lack of education, mindless work, and the impact of advertising may figure in such choices. In any case, what ads are wrapped around must be factored into any analysis of their likely effects.

We should also pay attention to the ways in which institutions distribute political power, and therefore the abilities of individuals to act on and realize their interests. In this regard, the existence of formally democratic political structures is often misleading. Notoriously, access to political power

depends on wealth or economic power in various ways. Here again, the political and economic institutions of advanced capitalism facilitate the dominance of corporations and their constituents.

IV

I come, at last, to the central argument of my paper. My strategy in what follows will be to amass considerations that make a plausible case for the claim that persuasive mass-advertising is detrimental to autonomy. If there is a case to be made, it is not one that can be made by showing how advertising falls into categories that are traditionally viewed as hostile to autonomy—coercion, deception, manipulation, and brainwashing. While advertising is sometimes deceptive and often manipulative, and in some ways akin to brainwashing, its overall character is not easily assimilable to any of these. I am inclined to think that the way to conceptualize its character is in terms of the notion of *suppression*. Advertising suppresses autonomy by discouraging the emergence of its constitutive skills, knowledge, attitudes, and motivations.

One general feature of mass-advertising is simply its pervasiveness. Individuals are inundated with ads, no matter where they go or what activities they engage in. David Braybrooke refers to the "aggregative and cumulative effects" of ads.[19] The quantity of ads and their near inescapability are such that even the most diligent will be hard-pressed to avoid absorbing some of their implicit content. Many television shows and magazines feature or cater to the consumer lifestyle and this reinforces the implicit content.

The pervasiveness of ads is often coupled with an absence of views that challenge or reject their implicit content. In assessing the likely impact of mass-advertising, we must pay attention to societal measures to counter its effects. For instance, in the United States, there are few if any public service announcements urging individuals to be wary of ads, exposing the tactics of manipulation and seduction ads employ. Also, it is unlikely that such announcements would ever be repeated often enough, or have anything like the appeal of ads which promise persons sex, power, prestige, etc., if only they will buy the associated products. It seems clear that our society's educational and religious institutions, which might serve to counter ads, are ill-equipped to raise and deal with complex issues such as the nature of the good life. These are issues which ads greatly oversimplify and offer a virtual unanimity of opinion about. In many cases, attempts to educate children (and adults) about ads are sporadic and unsophisticated. To the extent that this is so, it is unlikely that such education will be forceful enough to effectively counter the advertising barrage.

Stanley Benn writes that one of the unique features of rational suasion is that it invites response and criticism.[20] It presupposes the possibility of a dialogue between or amongst the parties involved. Yet, we might wonder how far most individuals are from having a meaningful dialogue in their lives with advertising. What competing conceptions of the good life has advertising vanquished in an open, rational dialogue? If individuals lack appealing and coherent alternatives to what ads tell them about how to live, they cannot make critical, rational choices about such matters.

It is bad enough that advertising has the character of a loud, persistent bully. What is worse is that it often is not directed only at adults who might be capable of responding critically. The concern about the effects of advertising on the vulnerable, especially children, is not simply that many ads are so manipulative that they trick the vulnerable into wanting things they do not need or which are not good for them. It is also that the implicit content of ads gets absorbed by children, and habits are set up that *carry forward* into their adult lives. The ways in which they habitually perceive their lives and the social world, the alternatives they see as open to them, and the standards they use to judge themselves and others, are all shaped by advertising, perhaps without their ever being aware of it.[21]

I now turn to an analysis of the implicit content of persuasive mass-advertising. This content is a function of both the methods of conveying messages in ads and the messages conveyed. What follows are some of the key facets of this implicit content. I do not claim that my analysis is exhaustive, only that it is thorough enough to support my contention that the character of advertising is such as to suppress autonomy.

I begin with that facet of the content and methods of ads that Jules Henry refers to as the encouragement of "woolly mindedness."[22] Ads subtly encourage the propensity to accept emotional appeals, oversimplification, superficiality, and shoddy standards of proof for claims. Evidence and arguments of the most ridiculous sorts are offered in support of advertising claims. Information about products is presented selectively (i.e. bad or questionable features are ignored), the virtues of products are exaggerated, and deception and misinformation are commonplace. The meanings of words are routinely twisted so that they are either deceptive or wholly lost (e.g. consider the use of words like 'sale' or 'new and improved'). Also, ads encourage the belief that important information about our lives must be entertainly purveyed and such that it can be passively absorbed.

All of these are what we might term "meta-messages." They are messages about how to deal with messages, or more precisely, about how to approach claims made by others. They are messages that tell individuals, among other things, that they cannot believe or trust what others say, that anything (or nothing!) can be proved, that evidence contrary to one's claims may be ignored, and that words can mean whatever anyone wants them to mean. They tell persons that success in communication is a matter of persuading others *no matter how it is done*. Such attitudes about thought and communication starkly oppose the habits and attitudes constitutive of critical competence: clarity, rigor, precision, patience, honesty, effort, etc. Henry remarks that advertising would never succeed in a world filled with logicians.[23] Though we may not want such a world, we should be aware of how advertising promotes sophistry and attitudes supportive of it.

Complementing the meta-messages is the pervasive emphasis on ease and gratification. As Henry points out, austerity and self-restraint are anathema to advertisers.[24] Mass production requires the existence or ready and willing consumers. Lifestyles contrary to consumption are either absent from ads (and from TV shows) or are ridiculed in them. Predominant messages in ads are "take it easy," "relax and enjoy yourself," and most especially, "buy it now!" In moderation, there may be nothing objectionable about such messages. However, where not balanced by other messages, and so not made liable to critical examination, they encourage attitudes subversive to autonomy. In order to formulate, assess, and carry out life-plans of their own choosing, individuals must possess self-control and seriousness of purpose. They must also have the capacity to resist temptations or momentary distractions.

More insidious, though, is a further implied message—that persons ought to let advertisers show them how to live the good life. What could be more inviting than a life that demands so little beyond ease and gratification (especially to children, who are less attuned to the values of self-control and delayed gratification)? Freedom is divorced from self-direction and equated with passivity and consumption. Control over one's life becomes simply the ability to satisfy one's consumer desires. Alternative conceptions of freedom are drowned out. Opposing lifestyles are saddled with a burden of justification. Those who resist the easy gratifications of the consumer marketplace are likely to be perceived as square, eccentric, boring, or life-denying. The scorn of others thus becomes a barrier to the critical examination of life.

While one of the main messages of advertising is to accept a lifestyle of ease and gratification, individuals who buy into that lifestyle cannot be allowed to relax if that means not buying products. Fear and insecurity are the motifs of advertising. There are always new products and services to be sold and individuals must be convinced that they will not experience true or complete gratification until they buy this or that product. As John Waide remarks, advertising cultivates and thrives on "sneer group pressure."[25] Other persons are portrayed as constantly ready to judge negatively those who have not tried the newest product that promises to make their lives more appealing in some fashion. Advertising is fundamentally divisive in this regard. It encourages the view that social relationships are competitive, that persons are out to "top" one another rather than help and support one another. The internalization of this competitive model is likely to deprive individuals of the care and counsel of others, two things that vitally contribute to the sustained critical examination of their lives. Individuals need others to provide them feedback about their conduct and projects, as well as to present them with alternative beliefs, outlooks, and commitments.[26]

Numerous writers have commented on the confusion about values ads promote. Many ads tell individuals that if they will only buy X, they will acquire friendship, self-esteem, sex appeal, power, etc. Collectively, these ads tell individuals that they will be able to satisfy some of their most important desires (ones Waide refers to as being for "nonmarket goods"[27]) through the purchase and use of consumer products. Where they have bought these products and still not found the relevant satisfaction, advertising has a ready answer: buy more or better products!

It is doubtful that there are areas of peoples' lives where clear thinking is of more importance. It is equally doubtful that consumer products can make a significant contribution to the satisfaction of the desires for such nonmarket goods. More to the point, at best ads can only *distract* individuals from clear thinking about such things as why they lack self-esteem, or why they feel powerless, or why their friendships or marriages are unsatisfactory. At worst, they can fill individuals' minds with pseudo-truths or pseudo-values bearing on issues of central significance in their lives. Numerous examples come to mind: how women are encouraged by ads to conceive of their self-worth in terms of unrealistic standards of physical beauty; how having fun is portrayed in ads for beer, wine, and alcohol; ideas about nutrition courtesy of the junk food industry; how racial disharmony, homosexuality, and poverty are missing from the social world of ads; and so on.

Finally, in light of my earlier claim that autonomous individuals will be disposed to critically scrutinize the institutions they live under, it is important to point out how the portrayal of consumption as the good life serves a political function. This portrayal provides individuals with standards and expectations against which to judge not only their own lives, but the institutions that shape and mold their lives. Consumption is presented as the reward for "making it," and as a way of ameliorating, if not curing, boredom, powerlessness, lack of self-esteem, etc. Political and economic institutions then come to be measured by the extent to which they provide individuals access to consumer goods. Of course, there is no guarantee that, judged against this criterion, a society's political and economic institutions will fare well. In this way, even mass-advertising may provide individuals with a basis for criticizing their institutions.

However, the basis is a very limited one. Individuals may only be concerned with whether they might get more or less consumer goods if institutions were organized differently (or run by members of a different political party). Other, competing criteria against which to judge institutions are likely to have a hard time getting a hearing in societies dominated by mass-advertising. In this way, advertising serves as a force that *legitimizes* the political and economic status quo. It deadens individuals to a more extensive critical scrutiny of the institutions they live under. The ways in which their political and economic institutions distribute the social conditions of autonomy, and therefore allow the economic interests of corporations to dominate their lives, are rarely considered or seriously discussed.

One of the supposed virtues of advanced capitalist societies where mass-advertising is ubiquitous is that they afford individuals a wide range of choices. Within the ambit of the consumer lifestyle, that may be so. But, what about some of the more basic choices individuals have about how to live their lives or about how to organize their political and economic affairs? Are these choices many individuals in such societies realize they have, let alone can conceive of an array of alternatives about? My contention is that many in such societies are in no position to make critically competent choices about these more basic issues and that advertising significantly contributes to their inability to do so.

V

It is not enough for defenders of advertising to respond to the preceding analysis by pointing out that *some* individuals seem to resist absorbing much of its implicit content. No doubt this is true. It is also true that many interactions of a more mundane sort between and amongst individuals fall short of being fully autonomous ones. The use of emotional appeals is widespread, as are other forms of manipulation. There are many insecure or servile individuals who are influenced by others in ways that likely fail the tests of critical competence. Few would suggest that societies be judged harshly for allowing such interactions to go on. Yet, it might be argued, why should we think societies ought to treat persuasive mass-advertising any differently? Why not, instead, think it reasonable to let individuals watch out for themselves in the face of mass-advertising? After all, some seem to.

This is a formidable objection, but it fails to take account of the differences between individuals' encounters with advertising and their encounters with other individuals. The latter typically have three features that the former lack. First, encounters with other individuals are often either voluntarily sought out or at least voluntarily maintained. Yet, advertising is not easily avoided. It begins to work its influence on individuals when they are young and it never lets up. It is omni-present. Second, even where individual encounters with other individuals are not fully voluntary (e.g. familial or work relationships), they typically serve some important value or function in individuals' lives. This is less obviously true with respect to persuasive mass-advertising. Third, encounters with other individuals, if found unsatisfactory, can be altered by the participants. Individuals can ask, or insist, that others not deceive or manipulate them. Sometimes this works. With advertising, individuals can, at best, try to shut it out or be wary of it. It is not an agent whose "conduct" can be altered by direct appeals.

Also, the fact that some individuals manage to resist the effects of persuasive mass-advertising might be explained by their having greater access to the other social conditions of autonomy (e.g. education). Surely that does not show that a society need do nothing about an institution in its midst that arguably plays a very significant role in suppressing the autonomy of what is perhaps a very large majority of its members. As Tom Beauchamp notes, a source of influence need not be completely controlling in order to be an object of concern.[28]

Defenders of advertising might at this point argue that the actions of corporations are protected by the moral right of free speech. Joseph DesJardins and John McCall maintain, however, that we should distinguish commercial speech from moral, religious, and political speech. They argue that some types of speech are more valuable to human life than others. Moral, religious, and political speech "contribute to the pursuit of meaning and value in human existence," while commercial speech "in offering an item for sale appears a rather mundane concern."[29] The latter only encourages persons to deliberate about various and competing consumer choices.

DesJardins and McCall and mostly concerned about providing a rationale for governmental efforts to regulate deceptive commercial speech.

Their argument relies on a conception of human autonomy similar to my own. Still, it seems to me that there exists a simpler and more straightforward justification for attempts to regulate deceptive commercial speech, one that appeals to the notion of the sorts of voluntary informed exchanges which are supposed to be the backbone of free enterprise economic systems. Deceptive commercial speech vitiates the *informedness* of such exchanges and it is often possible to prove ads deceptive.

Additionally, DesJardins and McCall fail to distinguish between the explicit and implicit content of persuasive mass-advertising. The latter, as we have seen, is rich in moral and political content. Thus, by their argument, if we should reject restrictions on political, religious, and moral speech, we should equally reject the curtailment of persuasive mass-advertising.[30] Nevertheless, I think that most of the traditional arguments for free speech will not serve defenders of persuasive advertising. Frederick Schauer develops and assesses several of these arguments.[31] I will concentrate on three central ones.

First, there is what Schauer calls the "argument from truth." This argument alleges that there is a causal link between freedom of speech and the discovery of truth. Schauer suggests we modify this argument to emphasize the elimination of error so as to avoid the complications that attend the notion of "objective truth."[32] The modified argument suggests that allowing the expression of contrary views is the only rational way of recognizing human fallibility, thus making possible the rejection or modification of erroneous views. It holds that we can increase the level of rational confidence in our views by comparing them to other views and seeing whether ours survive all currently available attacks. The suppression of speech, as John Stuart Mill noted, is inconsistent with a recognition of human fallibility.

A second argument is what Schauer refers to as the "argument from democracy." It is an argument that presupposes the acceptance of democratic principles for the organization of the state. It then consists of two parts:

1. In order for the people as sovereign electorate to vote intelligently, all relevant information must be available to them; and
2. as political leaders are to serve their citizens'

wishes, the latter must be able to communicate their wishes on all matters to the government.

In short, since democracy implies that government is the servant of the people, the people must retain the right to reject and criticize their government. Yet, this requires no prior restrictions by the government on information available to the citizens.

A third argument has been developed by Thomas Scanlon, and is referred to by Schauer as the "argument from autonomy."[33] This argument claims that the province of thought and decision-making is morally beyond the reach of the state's powers. The state is alleged to have no ultimate authority to decide matters of religious, moral, political, or scientific doctrine. Autonomous persons cannot accept, without independent consideration, the judgment of others as to what they should believe or do, especially on these matters. Thus, it is held that individuals must be free from governmental intrusion into the process of choice.

It is important to note, in general, that all three of these arguments presuppose that it is government suppression of speech that threatens individual thought-processes and choices. Historically, this may have been true, but the development of persuasive mass-advertising poses a different sort of threat. Schauer repeatedly claims that the province of individual thought and decision-making is inherently (as a causal matter) beyond the control of the state. He claims that the area of individual conscience is "under the exclusive control of the individual" because of the "internal" nature of thought.[34] While this may only underestimate the power of the state to influence thoughts and feelings, it surely ignores the possibility that persuasive mass-advertising significantly influences these in the ways detailed earlier.

With regard to the argument from truth, it is not fair to portray advertising as simply offering "truths" for consideration that compete against other beliefs in the marketplace of ideas. Whatever "truths" it offers (and I suspect they are small ones) threaten to drown out all other claims, or to render them tedious or irrelevant by comparison. Worse, as we have seen, its implicit content encourages beliefs and attitudes about thought and decision-making that are hostile to those necessary to sort through claims and weed out the false or misleading ones.

Similar remarks hold for the argument from democracy. Especially relevant here is the political content of persuasive mass-advertising, with its emphasis on consumption-as-the-good-life as *the* standard against which to measure political and economic systems. More insidious than its insistence on this essentially status quo-preserving standard is its implicit denial of the value of political debate and activity. Consumption is where individuals are told they will find satisfaction, and a host of pseudo-issues about such a life are offered as the central focus for individuals' care and concern.

Finally, if advertising is inimical to autonomy in the ways I have claimed throughout this paper, it is obvious that the argument from autonomy cannot be invoked on its behalf. Those who defend persuasive mass-advertising on the basis of its contribution to individual choice would seem to have an extremely limited notion of the range of choices that individuals have about their lives.

Virginia Held makes the important point that in societies like the United States, it is no longer adequate to construe the right to free expression simply as a right not to be interfered with:

> But in a contemporary context this leaves those with economic resources free to express themselves through the media: they can buy time on TV or own a station, they can buy up or start a newspaper, and so on. At the same time, those without economic resources can barely be heard.[35]

Held's concern is with a society's taking steps to *enable* its members to freely express themselves. Though she does not directly address the issue of persuasive mass-advertising, it is likely that she would view the nearly unchecked power of corporations to express their interests through the media with alarm.

VI

What to do about persuasive mass-advertising is, I think, a daunting problem. Throughout my analysis, I have insisted that we consider the effects of advertising in conjunction with the effects of other social conditions that might impact on autonomy.

The question we must ask ourselves, then, is what changes in our political and economic institutions are necessary in order to provide all persons with the social conditions of autonomy. Since advanced capitalist countries like the United States are now plagued in various ways by the dominance of corporate interests, we might hope that enhancing the social conditions of autonomy for all persons will result in the cultivation, expression, and realization of more varied (and autonomous) interests.

While some will think that the only way to accomplish this result is to abandon capitalism altogether, I want to consider changes that are somewhat more modest. First, in order to modify the organization of work so as to provide a venue for the realization of worker autonomy, we might adopt the sorts of worker participation mechanisms institutionalized in countries like West Germany and Sweden.[36] These mechanisms guarantee workers participation in the economic decisions that vitally affect their lives. Second, we would need to guarantee to all individuals the level and quality of education necessary for them to develop the skills, dispositions, and knowledge constitutive of dispositional autonomy. Third, we would need to take steps to lessen if not eliminate the influence of wealth and economic power over the decisions of democratically elected political officials. This might include such things as the development of a public financing scheme for all political campaigns and the institutionalization of mechanisms to guarantee the independence of government officials from those they regulate or purchase products and services from. Fourth, steps must be taken to divorce the media from their almost exclusive reliance on commercial financial support and to provide individuals with increased access to the means of expression. Virginia Held offers a number of valuable proposals about how to effect these ends.[37] These include having more public financing of the media and having commercial sponsors buy nonspecific time on the airwaves. Both measures would reduce the pressure to produce programming that is successful according to narrow commercial criteria. The hope is that this will lead to greater experimentation in the media, and thus to the creation of a more diverse cultural life.

Obviously, the preceding changes would need to be considered at greater length. But, let me instead turn to advertising and its role in the suppression of autonomy. As an aspect of the dominance of corporate interests in advanced capitalist societies, it is important to neither over-estimate nor under-estimate its significance. On the one hand, without complementary changes of the sort just discussed, attempts to regulate or restrict advertising seem likely to have only minimal impact on the development and maintenance of autonomy. At most, such regulation or restriction would eliminate one barrier to autonomy. On the other hand, it may be argued that the salutary effects of such complementary changes will be undermined if no steps are taken to regulate or restrict persuasive mass-advertising. Workers might remain imbued with the mentality promulgated in ads and so unwittingly express views conducive to corporate interests. Attempts to cultivate a more educated populace would still be opposed by the barrage of ads with its implicit content.

Unfortunately, it is hard to come up with a feasible approach to the regulation or restriction of advertising. Since the thrust of my argument has been against persuasive advertising, it might be suggested that we attempt to legislate a distinction between it and informational advertising. The idea would then be to restrict if not eliminate the former while permitting the latter. Perhaps simply providing information about the price, character, and availability of products and services poses little threat to autonomy and may even facilitate it.

One serious problem with this approach will be that of defining "persuasive." For instance, if individuals are shown using and enjoying a product, will that have to be considered an attempt at persuasion? Or, if a product is displayed in a pictorially pleasing manner, will that be considered persuasive? Also, assuming this difficulty can be overcome in a reasonable manner, won't the amount of regulation required necessitate the creation of a massive bureaucracy? It should be noted that corporations confronted with restrictions on persuasive advertising are likely to respond creatively in attempts to circumvent the rules.

An alternative approach would be to try to restrict the overall quantity of advertising without regard to a distinction between informational and persuasive types. It might be feasible to restrict the number of ads on TV to a certain number per hour, but can we do something similar with magazines,

radio, and newspapers? Even if we had the will to do so, at least two serious problems remain:

1. a mere reduction in the quantity of ads (persuasive and otherwise) may not greatly lessen their impact in terms of selling the consumer lifestyle—especially in the absence of steps to counter this implicit content;
2. the difficulties in formulating and enforcing such restrictions would be formidable.

On the latter point, think about the enormous number of venues for advertising (currently existing as well as those that might soon be available) that we would have to regulate.

It is not easy to avoid drawing a pessimistic conclusion from the preceding remarks. Perhaps those more inventive than I can come up with proposals to restrict persuasive advertising that evade these problems and others like them. What cannot be evaded is the political reality that any proposed restrictions will be steadfastly, and I suspect effectively, resisted by corporations and advertisers. On this score, the only hope may lie with the sorts of institutional changes sketched earlier. It is possible that a better educated populace with more democratic control over its corporations can take the necessary steps to curtail the suppression of autonomy effected by current mass-advertising.

NOTES

1. John Kenneth Galbraith, *The New Industrial State* (Boston, MA: Houghton Mifflin, 1967), especially pp. 198–218. See also the selection by Galbraith, "Persuasion—and Power," in Joseph R. DesJardins and John J. McCall (eds.), *Contemporary Issues in Business Ethics* (Belmont, CA: Wadsworth, 1985): 142–147.
2. I will limit my claims to countries with schemes of political and economic organization like those in the United States. Obviously, my claims would have to be weakened or modified if they were to be made applicable to countries with significantly different institutions.
3. On the ways in which many ads deceive by presenting information in misleading ways, see, for instance, Tom L. Beauchamp, "Manipulative Advertising," *Business and Professional Ethics Journal* 3 (Spring/Summer 1984): 1–22.
4. Lawrence Haworth, *Autonomy: An Essay in Philo-*

sophical Psychology and Ethics* (New Haven, CT: Yale University Press, 1986), especially Chapter 8.

5. Tom Beauchamp distinguishes between the responses of individuals to advertising and the intentions of those who create the advertising. My remarks in what follows concern the responses of individuals. I do not wish to suggest that corporations consciously intend all of the effects I delineate. See Beauchamp, "Manipulative Advertising," p. 7.

6. Virginia Held has also touched on the theme of the dominance of corporate interests. See her *Rights and Goods: Justifying Social Action* (New York: The Free Press, 1984), especially Chapter 12.

7. Roger Crisp, "Persuasive Advertising, Autonomy, and the Creation of Desire," *Journal of Business Ethics* 6 (1987): 413–418, p. 414.

8. Ibid., p. 414.

9. Samuel Gorovitz, "Advertising Professional Success Rates," *Business and Professional Ethics Journal* 3 (Spring/Summer 1984): 31–45, p. 41.

10. Robert Arrington, "Advertising and Behavior Control," reprinted in DesJardins and McCall, *Contemporary Issues in Business Ethics,* pp. 167–175.

11. Robert Young, *Personal Autonomy: Beyond Negative and Positive Liberty* (New York: St. Martin's Press, 1986), p. 8.

12. Gerald Dworkin, *The Theory and Practice of Autonomy* (Cambridge: Cambridge University Press, 1988), pp. 15–16.

13. Young distinguishes between internal constraints on autonomy (e.g. lack of self-control) and external constraints (e.g. lack of liberty). See his *Personal Autonomy,* p. 35.

14. Dworkin, *The Theory and Practice of Autonomy,* p. 20.

15. Dworkin, *Autonomy,* pp. 42–43.

16. Adina Schwartz, "Meaningful Work," *Ethics* 92 (July 1982): 632–646. See also Edward Sankowski, "Freedom, Work, and the Scope of Democracy," *Ethics* 91 (January 1981): 228–242; and Carole Pateman, *Participation and Democratic Theory* (Cambridge: Cambridge University Press, 1970).

17. Of course, the lack of avenues for the exercise of autonomy will often result in atrophy of the abilities and motivations that are its constituents.

18. For more on advertising and program content, see Virginia Held, "Advertising and Program Content," *Business and Professional Ethics Journal* 3 (Spring/Summer 1984): 61–76. See also the accompanying commentaries by Clifford Christians and Norman Bowie.

19. David Braybrooke, *Ethics and the World of Business* (Totowa, NJ: Rowman and Allanheld, 1983), pp. 327–328.

20. Stanley I. Benn, "Freedom and Persuasion," *Aus-*

tralasian Journal of Philosophy* 45 (December 1967): 259–275.

21. Cf. Linda Sharp Paine, "Children as Consumers," *Business and Professional Ethics Journal* 3 (Spring/Summer 1984): 119–145. Paine argues persuasively that children ought not be viewed as capable of making responsible consumer choices. She does not emphasize the effects of advertising on the habits of thought and perception of children.

22. Jules Henry, *Culture Against Man* (New York: Random House, 1963), p. 49.

23. Ibid., p. 48.

24. Ibid., p. 75.

25. John Waide, "The Making of Self and World in Advertising," *Journal of Business Ethics* 6 (1987): 39–73.

26. Also, if most persons can be induced to fear the judgment of others and adopt the consumer lifestyle, the result will be a remarkably homogenous collection of otherwise isolated individuals. Advertising superficially promotes individuality by telling persons they can only truly find themselves with this or that product. Of course, it tells every individual the same thing. Ethnic or individual diversity is worn away.

27. Waide, "The Making of Self and World in Advertising," p. 73.

28. Beauchamp, "Manipulative Advertising," p. 3.

29. Joseph R. DesJardins and John J. McCall, "Advertising and Free Speech," in DesJardins and McCall, *Contemporary Issues in Business Ethics,* p. 105.

30. Also, Burton Leiser argues that the United States Supreme Court has seen fit to extend constitutional protection to commercial speech. See his "Professional Advertising: Price Fixing and Professional Dignity versus the Public's Right to a Free Market," *Business and Professional Ethics Journal* 3 (Spring/Summer 1984): 93–107.

31. Frederick Schauer, *Free Speech: A Philosophical Inquiry* (Cambridge: Cambridge University Press, 1982). Schauer notes problems with each of these arguments that I will ignore here.

32. Ibid., pp. 24–25.

33. Thomas Scanlon, "A Theory of Freedom of Expression," *Philosophy and Public Affairs* 6 (Winter 1972): 204–226.

34. Schauer, *Freedom of Speech,* p. 68. See also p. 53.

35. Virginia Held, "Advertising and Program Content," *Business and Professional Ethics Journal* 3 (Spring/Summer 1984): 61–76, p. 73.

36. On this, see G. David Garson, *Worker Self-Management in Industry: The West European Experience* (New York: Praeger Publishers, 1977).

37. See her "Advertising and Program Content," pp. 66–74. Also, see *Rights and Goods,* Chapter 12.

Children as Consumers: An Ethical Evaluation of Children's Television Advertising

Lynn Sharp Paine

Television sponsors and broadcasters began to identify children as a special target audience for commercial messages in the mid-1960s.[1] Within only a few years, children's television advertising emerged as a controversial issue. Concerned parents began to speak out and to urge the networks to adopt codes of ethics governing children's advertising. By 1970, the issue had attracted the attention of the Federal Trade Commission (FTC) and the Federal Communications Commission (FCC). The FCC received some 80,000 letters in support of a proposed rule "looking toward the elimination of sponsorship and commercial content in children's programming."[2] Public attention to the controversy over children's television advertising peaked between 1978 and 1980, when the FTC, under its authority to regulate unfair and deceptive advertising, held public hearings on its proposal to ban televised advertising directed to or seen by large numbers of young children. More recently parents have complained to the FCC about so-called program-length commercials, children's programs designed around licensed characters.[3]

As this brief chronology indicates, children's television advertising has had a history of arousing people's ethical sensibilities. In this paper I want to propose some explanations for why this is so and to argue that there are good ethical reasons that advertisers should refrain from directing commercials to young children. However, because so much of the public debate over children's advertising has focused on the FTC's actions rather than explicitly on the ethical aspects of children's advertising, a few preliminary remarks are called for.

First, it is important to bear in mind that the ethical propriety of directing television advertising to young children is distinct from its legality. Even if advertisers have a constitutional right to advertise lawful products to young children in a nondeceptive way, it is not necessarily the right thing to do.[4] Our system of government guarantees us

rights that it may be unethical to exercise on certain occasions. Terminology may make it easy to lose sight of the distinction between "having a right" and the "right thing to do," but the distinction is critical to constitutional governance.[5] In this paper I will take no position on the scope of advertisers' First Amendment rights to freedom of speech. I am primarily interested in the moral status of advertising to young children.

A second preliminary point worth noting is that evaluating the ethical status of a practice, such as advertising to young children, is a different exercise from evaluating the propriety of governmental regulation of that practice. Even if a practice is unethical, there may be legal, social, economic, political, or administrative reasons that the government cannot or should not forbid or even regulate the practice. The public policy issues faced by the FTC or any other branch of government involved in regulating children's advertising are distinct from the ethical issues facing advertisers. The fact that it may be impossible or unwise for the government to restrict children's advertising does not shield advertisers from ethical responsibility for the practice.

Finally, I want to point out that public opinion regarding children's advertising is a measure neither of its ethical value nor of the propriety of the FTC's actions. Two critics of the FTC declared that it had attempted to impose its conception of what is good on an unwilling American public.[6] There is reason to doubt the writers' assumption about the opinions of the American public regarding children's advertising,[7] but the more critical point is the implication of their argument: that the FTC's actions would have been appropriate had there been a social consensus opposing child-oriented advertising. Majority opinion, however, is neither the final arbiter of justified public policy, nor the standard for assaying the ethical value of a practice like children's advertising. As pointed out earlier, constitutional limits may override majority opinion in the public policy arena. And although publicly expressed opinion may signal ethical concerns (as I suggested in mentioning the letters opposing

From *Business & Professional Ethics Journal*, vol. 3, #3/4, 119–125, 1983. Reprinted by permission of the author.

commercial sponsorship of children's television received by the FCC), social consensus is not the test of ethical quality. We cannot simply say that children's advertising is ethically all right because many people do not object to it or because people's objections to it are relatively weak. An ethical evaluation requires that we probe our ethical principles and test their relation to children's advertising. Publicly expressed opposition may signal that such probing is necessary, but it does not establish an ethical judgment one way or the other.

. . . For purposes of this discussion, I will set aside the legal and public policy questions involved in government restrictions on children's advertising. Instead, as promised, I will explore the ethical issues raised by the practice of directing television advertising to young children. In the process of this investigation, I will necessarily turn my attention to the role of consumers in a free market economy, to the capacities of children as they relate to consumer activities, and to the relationships between adults and children within the family.

By *young children* I mean children who lack the conceptual abilities required for making consumer decisions, certainly children under eight. Many researchers have investigated the age at which children can comprehend the persuasive intent of advertising.[8] Depending on the questions employed to test comprehension of persuasive intent, the critical age has been set as low as kindergarten age or as high as nine or ten.[9] Even if this research were conclusive, however, it would not identify the age at which children become capable of making consumer decisions. Comprehending persuasive intent is intellectually less complex than consumer decisionmaking. Even if children appreciate the selling intent behind advertising, they may lack other conceptual abilities necessary for responsible consumer decisions. Child psychologists could perhaps identify the age at which these additional abilities develop. For purposes of this discussion, however, the precise age is not crucial. When I use the term *child* or *children* I am referring to "young children"—those who lack the requisite abilities.

Children's advertising is advertising targeted or directed to young children. Through children's advertising, advertisers attempt to persuade young children to want and, consequently, to request the advertised product.[10] Although current voluntary guidelines for children's advertising prohibit ad-

vertisers from explicitly instructing children to request that their parents buy the advertised product, child-oriented advertising is designed to induce favorable attitudes that result in such requests.[11] Frequently child-oriented ads utilize themes and techniques that appeal particularly to children: animation, clowns, magic, fantasy effects, superheroes, and special musical themes.[12] They may also involve simply the presentation of products, such as cereals, sweets, and toys, that appeal to young children with announcements directed to them.[13] The critical point in understanding child-directed advertising, however, is not simply the product, the particular themes and techniques employed, or the composition of the audience viewing the ad, but whether the advertiser intends to sell to or through children. Advertisers routinely segment their markets and target their advertising.[14] The question at issue is whether children are appropriate targets.

Advertising directed to young children is a subcategory of advertising seen by them, since children who watch television obviously see a great deal of advertising that is not directed toward them—ads for adult consumer products, investment services, insurance, and so on. Occasionally children's products are advertised by means of commercials directed to adults. The toy manufacturer Fisher-Price, for example, at one time advertised its children's toys and games primarily by means of ads directed to mothers.[15] Some ads are designed to appeal to the whole family. Insofar as these ads address young children they fall within the scope of my attention.

My interest in television advertising directed to young children, as distinct from magazine or radio advertising directed to them, is dictated by the nature of the medium. Television ads portray vivid and lively images that engage young children as the printed words and pictures of magazines, or even the spoken words of radio, could never do. Because of their immediacy television ads can attract the attention of young children who have not yet learned to read. Research has shown that young children develop affection for and even personal relationships with heavily promoted product characters appearing on television.[16] At the same time, because of their immaturity, these children are unable to assess the status of these characters as fictional or real, let alone assess whatever minimal product information they may disclose.[17] Technical limitations make magazine advertising and radio advertising inherently less likely to attract young children's attention. Consequently, they are less susceptible to ethical criticisms of the sort generated by television advertising.

Children as Consumers

The introduction of the practice of targeting children for televised commercial messages challenged existing mores. At the obvious level, the practice was novel. But at a deeper level, it called into question traditional assumptions about children and their proper role in the marketplace. The argument advanced on behalf of advertising to children by the Association of National Advertisers (ANA), the American Association of Advertising Agencies (AAAA), and the American Advertising Federation (AAF) reflects the rejection of some of these traditional assumptions:

> Perhaps the single most important benefit of advertising to children is that it provides information to the child himself, information which advertisers try to gear to the child's interests and on an appropriate level of understanding. This allows the child to learn what products are available, to know their differences, and to begin to make decisions about them based on his own personal wants and preferences. . . . Product diversity responds to these product preferences and ensures that it is the consumer himself who dictates the ultimate success or failure of a given product offering.[18]

The most significant aspect of this argument supporting children's advertising is its vision of children as autonomous consumers. Children are represented as a class of consumers possessing the relevant decision-making capacities and differing from adult consumers primarily in their product preferences. Children are interested in toys and candy, while adults are interested in laundry detergent and investment services. That children may require messages tailored to their level of understanding is acknowledged, but children's conceptual abilities are not regarded as having any other special significance. Advocates of children's advertising argue that it gives children "the same access

to the marketplace which adults have, but keyed to their specific areas of interest."[19]

When children are viewed in this way—as miniature adults with a distinctive set of product preferences—the problematic nature of advertising to them is not apparent. Indeed, it appears almost unfair not to provide children with televised information about products available to satisfy their special interests. Why should they be treated differently from any other class of consumers?

There are, however, significant differences between adults and young children that make it inappropriate to regard children as autonomous consumers. These differences, which go far beyond different product preferences, affect children's capacities to function as responsible consumers and suggest several arguments for regarding advertising to them as unethical. For purposes of this discussion, the most critical differences reflect children's understanding of self, time, and money.

Child-development literature generally acknowledges that the emergence of a sense of one's self as an independent human being is a central experience of childhood and adolescence.[20] This vague notion, "having a sense of one's self as an independent human being," encompasses a broad range of capacities—from recognition of one's physical self as distinct from one's mother to acceptance of responsibilty for one's actions and choices. Normally children acquire these capacities gradually in the course of maturation. While this mastery manifests itself as self-confidence and self-control in an ever-widening range of activities and relationships, it depends more fundamentally upon the emergence of an ability to see oneself as oneself. The reflexive nature of consciousness—the peculiar ability to monitor, study, assess, and reflect upon oneself and even upon one's reflections—underlies the ability to make rational choices. It permits people to reflect upon their desires, to evaluate them, and to have desires about what they shall desire. It permits them to see themselves as one among others and as engaging in relationships with others. Young children lack—or have only in nascent form—this ability to take a higher-order perspective on themselves and to see themselves as having desires or preferences they may wish to cultivate, suppress, or modify. They also lack the self-control that would make it possible to act on these higher-order desires if they had them.

Closely related to the sense of self, if not implicit in self-reflection, is the sense of time. Children's understanding of time—both as it relates to their own existence and to the events around them—is another area where their perspectives are special. Preschoolers are intrigued with "time" questions: "When is an hour up?" "Will you be alive when I grow up?" "When did the world begin and when will it end?" "Will I be alive for all the time after I die?" Young children's efforts to understand time are accompanied by a limited ability to project themselves into the future and to imagine themselves having different preferences in the future. It is generally true that children have extremely short time horizons. But children are also struggling with time in a more fundamental sense: they are testing conceptions of time as well as learning to gauge its passage by conventional markers.[21] Young children's developing sense of time goes hand in hand with their developing sense of self. Their capacity for self-reflection, for evaluating their desires, and for making rational choices is ultimately related to their understanding of their own continuity in time.

Young children are in many ways philosophers: they are exploring and questioning the very fundamentals of existence.[22] Since they have not accepted many of the conventions and assumptions that guide ordinary commercial life, they frequently pose rather profound questions and make insightful observations. But although young children are very good at speculation, they are remarkably unskilled in the sorts of calculations required for making consumer judgments. In my experience, many young children are stymied by the fundamentals of arithmetic and do not understand ordinal relations among even relatively small amounts—let alone the more esoteric notions of selling in exchange for money. Research seems to support the observation that selling is a difficult concept for children. One study found that only 48 percent of six-and-a-half- to seven-and-a-half-year-olds could develop an understanding of the exocentric (as distinct from egocentric) verb *to sell*.[23] A five-year-old may know from experience in making requests that a $5.00 trinket is too expensive, but when she concludes that $5.00 is also too much to pay for a piano, it is obvious that she knows neither the exchange value of $5.00, the worth of a piano, nor the meaning of *too expensive*.[24]

What is the significance of the differences between adults and young children I have chosen to highlight—their differing conceptions of self, time, and money? In the argument for advertising quoted earlier, it was stated that advertising to children enables them "to learn what products are available, to know their differences, and to begin to make decisions about them based on [their] own personal wants and preferences." Ignore, for the moment, the fact that existing children's advertising, which concentrates so heavily on sugared foods and toys, does little either to let children know the range of products available or differences among them and assume that children's advertising could be more informative.[25] Apart from this fact, the critical difficulty with the argument is that because of children's, shall we say, "naive" or "unconventional" conceptions of self, time, and money, they know very little about their own personal wants and preferences—how they are related or how quickly they will change—or about how their economic resources might be mobilized to satisfy those wants. They experience wants and preferences but do not seem to engage in critical reflection, which would lead them to assess, modify, or perhaps even curtail their felt desires for the sake of other more important or enduring desires they may have or may expect to have in the future. Young children also lack the conceptual wherewithal to engage in research or deliberative processes that would assist them in knowing which of the available consumer goods would most thoroughly satisfy their preferences, given their economic resources. The fact that children want so many of the products they see advertised is another indication that they do not evaluate advertised products on the basis of their preferences and economic resources.[26]

There is thus a serious question whether advertising really has or can have much at all to do with children's beginning "to make decisions about [products] based on [their] own personal wants and preferences" until they develop the conceptual maturity to understand their own wants and preferences and to assess the value of products available to satisfy them.[27] If children's conceptions of self, time, and money are not suited to making consumer decisions, one must have reservations about ignoring this fact and treating them as if they were capable of making reasonable consumer judgments anyway. . . .

Children's Advertising and Basic Ethical Principles

My evaluation of children's advertising has proceeded from the principle of consumer sovereignty, a principle of rather narrow application. Unlike more general ethical principles, like the principle of veracity, the principle of consumer sovereignty applies in the specialized area of business. Addressing the issue of children's advertising from the perspective of special business norms rather than more general ethical principles avoids the problem of deciding whether the specialized or more general principles should have priority in the moral reasoning of business people.[28] Nevertheless, children's advertising could also be evaluated from the standpoint of the more general ethical principles requiring veracity and fairness and prohibiting harmful conduct.

Veracity

The principle of veracity, understood as devotion to truth, is much broader than a principle prohibiting deception. Deception, the primary basis of the FTC's complaint against children's advertising, is only one way of infringing the principle of veracity. Both critics and defenders of children's advertising agree that advertisers should not intentionally deceive children and that they should engage in research to determine whether children are misled by their ads. The central issue regarding veracity and children's advertising, however, does not relate to deception so much as to the strength of advertisers' devotion to truth. Advertisers generally do not make false statements intended to mislead children. Nevertheless, the particular nature of children's conceptual worlds makes it exceedingly likely that child-oriented advertising will generate false beliefs or highly improbable product expectations.

Research shows that young children have difficulty differentiating fantasy and reality[29] and frequently place indiscriminate trust in commercial characters who present products to them.[30] They also develop false beliefs about the selling characters in ads[31] and in some cases have unreasonably optimistic beliefs about the satisfactions advertised products will bring them.[32]

This research indicates that concern about the misleading nature of children's advertising is legitimate. Any parent knows—even one who has not examined the research—that young children are easily persuaded of the existence of fantasy characters. They develop (what seem to their parents) irrational fears and hopes from stories they hear and experiences they misinterpret. The stories and fantasies children see enacted in television commercials receive the same generous and idiosyncratic treatment as other information. Children's interpretations of advertising claims are as resistant to parental correction as their other fantasies are. One can only speculate on the nature and validity of the beliefs children adopt as a result of watching, for example, a cartoon depicting a pirate captain's magical discovery of breakfast cereal. Certainly, many ads are designed to create expectations that fun, friendship, and popularity will accompany possession of the advertised product. The likelihood that such expectations will be fulfilled is something young children cannot assess.

To the extent that children develop false beliefs and unreasonable expectations as a result of viewing commercials, moral reservations about children's advertising are justified. To the extent advertisers know that children develop false beliefs and unreasonable expectations, advertisers' devotion to truth and to responsible consumerism are suspect.

Fairness and Respect for Children

The fact that children's advertising benefits advertisers while at the same time nourishing false beliefs, unreasonable expectations, and irresponsible consumer desires among children calls into play principles of fairness and respect. Critics have said that child-oriented advertising takes advantage of children's limited capacities and their suggestibility for the benefit of the advertisers. As expressed by Michael Pertschuk, former chairman of the FTC, advertisers "seize on the child's trust and exploit it as weakness for their gain."[33] To employ as the unwitting means to the parent's pocketbook children who do not understand commercial exchange, who are unable to evaluate their own consumer preferences, and who consequently cannot make consumer decisions based on those preferences does indeed reflect a lack of respect for children. Such a practice fails to respect children's limitations as consumers, and instead capitalizes on them. In the language of Kant, advertisers are not treating children as "ends in themselves": they are treating children solely as instruments for their own gain.

In response to the charge of unfairness, supporters of children's advertising sometimes point out that the children are protected because their parents exercise control over the purse strings.[34] This response demonstrates failure to appreciate the basis of the unfairness charge. It is not potential economic harm that concerns critics: it is the attitude toward children reflected in the use of children's advertising that is central. As explained earlier, the attitude is inappropriate or unfitting.

Another frequent response to the charge of unfairness is that children actually do understand advertising.[35] A great deal of research has focused on whether children distinguish programs from commercials, whether they remember product identities, whether they distinguish program characters from commercial characters, and whether they recognize the persuasive intent of commercials.[36] But even showing that children "understand" advertising in all these ways would not demonstrate that children have the consumer capacities that would make it fair to advertise to them. The critical questions are not whether children can distinguish commercial characters from program characters,[37] or even whether they recognize persuasive intent, but whether they have the concepts of self, time, and money that would make it possible for them to make considered consumer decisions about the products they see advertised. Indeed, if children recognize that commercials are trying to sell things but lack the concepts to assess and deliberate about the products advertised, the charge that advertisers are "using" children or attempting to use them to sell their wares is strengthened. Intuitively, it seems that if children were sophisticated enough to realize that the goods advertised on television are for sale, they would be more likely than their younger counterparts to request the products.[38]

Harm to Children

Another principle to which appeal has been made by critics of television advertising is the principle against causing harm. The harmful effects of children's advertising are thought to include the parent-child conflicts generated by parental refusals to buy requested products, the unhappiness and anger suffered by children whose parents deny their product requests, the unhappiness children suffer when advertising-induced expectations of product performance are disappointed, and unhappiness experienced by children exposed to commercials portraying life-styles more affluent than their own.[39]

Replies to the charge that children's advertising is harmful to children have pinpointed weaknesses in the claim. One supporter of children's advertising says that the "harm" to children whose parents refuse their requests has not been adequately documented.[40] Another, claiming that some experts believe conflicts over purchases are instructive in educating children to make choices, denies that parent-child conflict is harmful.[41] As these replies suggest, demonstrating that children's advertising is harmful to children, as distinct from being misleading or unfair to them, involves much more than showing that it has the effects enumerated. Agreement about the application of the principle against causing harm depends on conceptual as well as factual agreement. A conception of harm must first be elaborated, and it must be shown to include these or other effects of advertising. It is not obvious, for example, that unhappiness resulting from exposure to more different life-styles is in the long run harmful.

Research indicates that children's advertising does contribute to the outcomes noted.[42] Certainly, child-oriented television advertising is not the sole cause of these effects, but it does appear to increase their frequency and even perhaps their intensity.[43] I believe that a conception of harm including some of these effects could be developed, but I will not attempt to do so here. I mention this argument rather to illustrate another general ethical principle on which an argument against children's advertising might be based. . . .

Conclusion

How might advertisers implement their responsibilities to promote consumer satisfaction and consumer responsibility and satisfy the principles of veracity, fairness, and nonmaleficence? There are degrees of compliance with these principles: some marketing strategies will do more than others to enhance consumer satisfaction, for example. One way compliance can be improved is by eliminating child-oriented television advertising for children's products and substituting advertising geared to mature consumers. Rather than employing the techniques found in advertising messages targeted to children under eleven,[44] advertisers could include product information that would interest adult viewers and devise ways to let child viewers know that consumer decisions require responsible decision-making skills. If much of the information presented is incomprehensible to the five-year-olds in the audience, so much the better.[45] When they reach the age at which they begin to understand consumer decision-making, they will perhaps have greater respect for the actual complexity of their responsibilities as consumers.

The problems of child-oriented advertising can best be dealt with if advertisers themselves recognize the inappropriateness of targeting children for commercial messages. I have tried to show why, within the context of a free market economy, the responsibilities of advertisers to promote consumer satisfaction and not to discourage responsible consumer decisions should lead advertisers away from child-oriented advertising. The problem of what types of ads are appropriate given these constraints provides a challenging design problem for the many creative people in the advertising industry. With appropriate inspiration and incentives, I do not doubt that they can meet the challenge.

Whether appropriate inspiration and incentives will be forthcoming is more doubtful. Children's advertising seems well entrenched and is backed by powerful economic forces,[46] and it is clear that some advertisers do not recognize, or are unwilling to acknowledge, the ethical problems of child-focused advertising.[47] The trend toward programming designed around selling characters is especially discouraging.

Even advertisers who recognize that eliminating child-oriented advertising will promote consumer satisfaction and consumer responsibility may be reluctant to reorient their advertising campaigns because of the costs and risks of doing so. Theoretically, only advertisers whose products would not withstand the scrutiny of adult consumers should lose sales from such a reorientation. It is clear that in the short run a general retreat from children's advertising would result in some lost revenues for makers, advertisers, and retail sellers of products that do not sell as well when advertised to adults. It is also possible that television networks, stations, and entrenched producers of children's shows would lose revenues and that children's programming might be jeopardized by the lack of advertisers' interest in commercial time during children's programs.

On the other hand, a shift away from children's advertising to adult advertising could result in even more pressure on existing adult commercial time slots, driving up their prices to a level adequate to subsidize children's programming without loss to the networks. And there are alternative means of financing children's television that could be explored.[48] The extent to which lost revenues and diminished profits would result from recognizing the ethical ideals I have described is largely a question of the ability of all the beneficiaries of children's television advertising to respond creatively. The longer-term effect of relinquishing child-focused advertising would be to move manufacturers, advertisers, and retailers in the direction of products that would not depend for their success on the suggestibility and immaturity of children. In the longer run, the result would be greater market efficiency.

NOTES

Some notes have been deleted and the remaining ones renumbered.

An earlier version of this paper was delivered at a workshop on advertising ethics at the University of Florida in April 1984. I want to thank Robert Baum for organizing the workshop and to express my appreciation to all the workshop participants who commented on my paper, but especially to Katherine Clancy, Susan Elliott, Kathleen Henderson, Betsy Hilbert, Craig Shulstad, and Rita Weisskoff. I also want to acknowledge the helpful criticisms of Eric Douglas, Paul Farris, and Anita Niemi.

1. Richard P. Adler, "Children's Television Advertising: History of the Issue," in *Children and the Faces of Television*, ed. Edward L. Palmer and Aimee Dorr (New York: Academic Press, 1980), p. 241; hereafter cited as Palmer and Dorr.

2. Adler, p. 243.

3. Daniel Seligman, "The Commercial Crisis," *Fortune* 108 (November 14, 1983): 39.

4. For discussion of the constitutionality of banning children's advertising, see C. Edwin Baker, "Commercial Speech: A Problem in the Theory of Freedom," *Iowa Law Review* 62 (October 1976): 1;

Martin H. Redish, "The First Amendment in the Marketplace: Commercial Speech and the Values of Free Expression," *George Washington Law Review* 39 (1970–1971): 429; Gerald J. Thain, "The 'Seven Dirty Words' Decision: A Potential Scrubbrush for Commercials on Children's Television?" *Kentucky Law Journal* 67 (1978–79): 947.

5. This point has been made by others. See, e.g., Ronald Dworkin, "Taking Rights Seriously," in *Taking Rights Seriously* (Cambridge, MA: Harvard University Press, 1977), pp. 188ff.

6. Susan Bartlett Foote and Robert H. Mnookin, "The 'Kid Vid' Crusade," *Public Interest* 61 (Fall 1980): 91.

7. One survey of adults found the following attitudes to children's commercials: strongly negative (23%); negative (50%); neutral (23%); positive (4%). These negative attitudes are most pronounced among parents of kindergarten-age children. The survey is cited in Thomas S. Robertson, "Television Advertising and Parent-Child Relations," in *The Effects of Television Advertising on Children*, ed. Richard P. Adler, Gerald S. Lesser, Laurene Krasny Meringoff, et al. (Lexington, MA: Lexington Books, 1980), p. 197; hereafter cited as Adler et al.

8. E.g., M. Carole Macklin, "Do Children Understand TV Ads?" *Journal of Advertising Research* 23 (February–March 1983): 63–70; Thomas Robertson and John Rossiter, "Children and Commercial Persuasion: An Attribution Theory Analysis," *Journal of Consumer Research* 1 (June 1974): 13–20. See also summaries of research in David Pillemer and Scott Ward, "Investigating the Effects of Television Advertising on Children: An Evaluation of the Empirical Studies," Draft read to American Psychological Assn., Div. 23, San Francisco, California, August 1977; John R. Rossiter, "The Effects of Volume and Repetition of Television Commercials," in Adler et al., pp. 160–62; Ellen Wartella, "Individual Differences in Children's Responses to Television Advertising," in Palmer and Dorr, pp. 312–14.

9. Wartella, p. 313.

10. Compare the definition of "child-oriented television advertising" adopted by the FTC in its Final Staff Report and Recommendation: "advertising which is in or adjacent to programs either directed to children or programs where children constitute a substantial portion of the audience." See "FTC Final Staff Report and Recommendation," *In the Matter of Children's Advertising*, 43 *Federal Register* 17967, March 31, 1981, p. 2.

11. *Self-Regulatory Guidelines for Children's Advertising*, by Children's Advertising Review Unit, Council of Better Business Bureau, Inc., 3rd ed. (New York, 1983), p. 6.

12. F. Earle Barcus, "The Nature of Television Advertising to Children," in Palmer and Dorr, pp. 276–77.

13. Barcus, p. 275.

14. Research has been developed to support advertisers targeting child audiences. See, e.g., Gene Reilly Group, Inc., *The Child* (Darien, CT: The Child, Inc., 1973), cited in Robert B. Choate, "The Politics of Change," in Palmer and Dorr, p. 329.

15. Thomas Donaldson and Patricia H. Werhane, *Ethical Issues in Business* (Englewood Cliffs, NJ: Prentice-Hall, Inc., 1979), p. 294. In a telephone interview a representative of Fisher-Price's advertising agency told me that Fisher-Price continues to focus its advertising on parents because most Fisher-Price toys appeal to the very young.

16. See "FTC Final Staff Report and Recommendation," pp. 21–22, n. 51, for a description of studies by Atkin and White. Atkin found that 90% of the three-year-olds studied and 73% of the seven-year-olds thought that selling characters like them. White found that 82% of a group of four- to seven-year-olds thought that the selling figures ate the products they advertised and wanted the children to do likewise.

17. Studies indicate that there is very limited use of product information in children's television advertising. Predominant are "appeals to psychological states, associations with established values, and unsupported assertions about the qualities of the products"; Barcus, p. 279.

18. Submission before the FTC, 1978, quoted in Emilie Griffin, "The Future Is Inevitable: But Can It Be Shaped in the Interest of Children?" in Palmer and Dorr, p. 347.

19. Griffin, p. 344.

20. E.g., Frances L. Ilg, Louise Bates Ames, and Sidney M. Baker, *Child Behavior*, rev. ed. (New York: Harper & Row, 1981).

21. On the child's conception of time, see Jean Piaget, *The Child's Conception of Time* (New York: Basic Books, 1970).

22. Some intriguing illustrations of children's philosophical questions and observations are recounted in Gareth B. Matthews, *Philosophy and the Young Child* (Cambridge, MA: Harvard University Press, 1980).

23. "FTC Final Staff Report and Recommendation," pp. 27–28, citing the work of Geis.

24. My five-year-old son reasoned thus to explain why a five-dollar piano would be too expensive.

25. Toys, cereals, and candies are the products most heavily promoted to children; Barcus, pp. 275–76.

26. The FTC concluded on the basis of relevant literature that children tend to want whatever products are advertised on television; "FTC Final Staff Report and Recommendation," p. 8. For data on the extent to which children want what they see advertised on

television, see Charles K. Atkin, "Effects of Television Advertising on Children," in Palmer and Dorr, pp. 289–90.

27. The results of one study of children's understanding of television advertising messages suggested that although "parents cannot 'force' early sophistication in children's reactions to television advertising, their attention and instruction can enhance the process." Focusing on children's capacities to understand advertising rather than on their capacities to make decisions, the article supports the general proposition that the child's conceptual world differs in many ways from that of the adult. The critical question is, of course: even if we can promote earlier understanding of advertising and consumer decisions, should we do so? See John R. Rossiter and Thomas S. Robertson, "Canonical Analysis of Developmental, Social, and Experimental Factors in Children's Comprehension of Television Advertising," *Journal of Genetic Psychology* 129 (1976): 326.

28. For general discussion of this issue see Alan H. Goldman, *The Moral Foundations of Professional Ethics*, chap. 5 (Totowa, N.J.: Rowman and Littlefield, 1980).

29. See T. G. Bever, M. L. Smith, B. Bengen, and T. G. Johnson, "Young Viewers' Troubling Response to TV Ads," *Harvard Business Review*, November–December 1975, pp. 109–20.

30. "FTC Final Staff Report and Recommendation," pp. 21–22, n. 51, describes the work of Atkin supporting the conclusion that children trust selling characters. Atkin found in a group of three- to seven-year-olds that 70% of the three-year-olds and 60% of the seven-year-olds trusted the characters about as much as they trusted their mothers.

31. "FTC Final Staff Report and Recommendation," at pp. 21–22, no. 51, describes the work of White, who found that many children in a group of four- to seven-year-olds she studied believe that the selling figures eat the advertised products and want the children to do likewise and that the selling figures want the children to eat things that are good for them.

32. Atkin, p. 300.

33. Quoted in Foote and Mnookin, p. 92.

34. June Esserman of Child Research Services, Inc., quoted in *Comments of M & M/Mars, Children's Television Advertising Trade Regulation Rule-Making Proceeding*, Federal Trade Commission (November 1978), p. 4.

35. *Comments of M & M/Mars*, p. 5. See also Macklin, n. 8, *supra*.

36. See n. 8, *supra*.

37. For a similar view of the relevance of children's ability to distinguish commercial characters from program characters, see Scott Ward, "Compromise in Commercials for Children," *Harvard Business Review*, November–December 1978, p. 133.

38. Recent research indicates that as children become more aware of advertising's persuasive intent, the frequency of their requests does not decline. This finding is contrary to earlier research purportedly showing that awareness of persuasive intent leads to a decline in number of requests; Rossiter, pp. 163–65.

39. Atkin, pp. 298–301.

40. Foote and Mnookin, p. 95.

41. *Comments of M & M/Mars*, p. 64. Cf. n. 27, *supra*.

42. Atkin, pp. 298–301. See also Scott Ward and Daniel B. Wackman, "Children's Purchase Influence Attempts and Parental Yielding," *Journal of Marketing Research*, August 1972, p. 318.

43. For example, one study found that heavy viewers of Saturday morning television got into more arguments with their parents over toy and cereal denials than did light viewers; Atkin, pp. 298–301. See also Ward and Wackman, p. 318.

44. The majority of advertising directed to children is targeted to children two-to-eleven or six-to-eleven years of age; "FTC Final Staff Report and Recommendation," p. 46.

45. For the view that children's special capacities and limitations should be respected but that children should not be "contained" in a special children's world isolated from that of adults, see Valerie Polakow Suransky, *The Erosion of Childhood* (Chicago: University of Chicago Press, 1982).

46. It was estimated that the coalition established to fight the FTC proceedings in 1978 put together a "war chest" of $15–30 million. According to news reports the coalition included several huge law firms, the national advertising association, broadcasters and their associations, the U.S. Chamber of Commerce, the Grocery Manufacturers of America, the sugar association, the chocolate and candy manufacturers, cereal companies and their associations, and more; Choate, p. 334. It is interesting to note that supporters of children's advertising tend not to be people who spend a great deal of time with children.

47. "In the area of children's products, the U.S. is an advertiser's paradise compared with many countries"; Christopher Campbell, International Marketing Director at the Parker Brothers subsidiary of General Mills, quoted in Ronald Alsop, "Countries' Different Ad Rules Are Problem for Global Firms," *Wall Street Journal*, September 27, 1984, p. 33. According to Alsop, "The other countries' aim is to protect kids from exploitation."

48. It is interesting to note that in 1949 42% of the children's programs broadcast were presented without advertiser sponsorship; Melody, p. 36.

The Ethics of Psychoactive Ads

Michael R. Hyman and Richard Tansey

No professional, be he doctor, lawyer, or manager, can promise that he will indeed do good for his client. All he can do is try. But he can promise that he will not knowingly do harm. . . .
—Peter F. Drucker, *Management*

. . . [C]oncern for consumer welfare includes an obligation to critically evaluate all marketing techniques that have indeterminate psychological effects,
—Spence and Moinpour, 1972, p. 43

Consider the following three ads:

- An announcer first holds up a raw egg and asks the viewer to pretend that this egg is the viewer's brain. He then performs a demonstration: he breaks the egg and drops it into a hot frying pan, saying that this is what drugs do to brains.
- A boy had graduated from high school, and his father had wanted him to attend college. Instead, the boy had joined the Army. After a year, the son now returns home to visit his family. Dad now realizes that the Army has "turned his boy into a man," and therefore accepts his son's decision with a warm welcome.
- A young black stands beside a rural road, awaiting a bus—the one that will take him to college. It arrives; the driver opens the door; the young man stays beside the road as the bus leaves. The voice-over implies that the young man's family cannot afford to send him to college.

The goal of the first ad, which is a public service announcement, is to discourage teen-agers and adults from using drugs; the goal of the second ad is to encourage young men and women to enlist in the U.S. Army; the goal of the third ad is to solicit funds for the United Negro College Fund (UNCF).

Each goal seems laudable. We assume that advertisers show these ads because they think them effective in furthering these goals by evoking an emotional response from viewers.

Unfortunately, each of these ads may also evoke an extreme, unintended, emotional response from a meaningful, well-defined group of viewers.

- The anti-drug ad employs a high fear-appeal theme to "scare casual users and non-users straight." However, such an appeal can surely cause great anxiety in many addicted viewers; as a result, some may become suicidal and kill themselves.
- The recruiting ad for the U.S. Army employs a common, unambiguous stereotype to portray conditional love and acceptance; the stereotype of the strong father-figure. However, the depth psychologies of Freud, Jung, and Adler suggest that viewing such a figure could so anger some persons, who have a negative image of father, that they would lash out against their friends and family.
- The UNCF ad may anger some blacks: the ad implies that (1) blacks do not or cannot work their way through college, and (2) black parents do not or cannot save for their children's education. Thus, by ignoring the efforts of many proud, independent blacks, the ad could cause some blacks to feel a loss of self-esteem.[1]

These seemingly innocent bits of imagery need, we suggest, more thought than may at first seem necessary.

What Are Psychoactive Ads?

There is a widely-used tool of advertising, the full consequences of which are unknown: the emotion-arousing ad. It may be used by sponsors seeking a specific result, such as the election of a certain politician, or higher sales for their products, or less lung cancer, or more people seeking psychological counseling. Whatever it promotes, it does so by reaching out, grabbing its viewers, and demanding

Journal of Business Ethics 9:105–114, 1990. Copyright © 1990 Kluwer Academic Publishers. With kind permission from Kluwer Academic Publishers.

attention. It need not amuse the viewer: it can annoy; it can anger; it can alarm; it can sadden.

One type of emotion-arousing ad is what we call a *psychoactive ad*. A psychoactive ad is any emotion-arousing ad that causes a meaningful, well-defined group of viewers to feel extremely anxious, to feel hostile toward others, or to feel a loss of self-esteem.

Though all psychoactive ads cause viewers to respond emotionallly, all ads that cause viewers to respond emotionally are not psychoactive ads. Neither upbeat ads nor warm ads are psychoactive. Upbeat ads are ads that cause viewers to feel alive, cheerful, happy, light-hearted, care-free, and so forth (Edell and Burke, 1987, p. 424). Warm ads are ads that cause viewers to feel a ". . . positive, mild, volatile emotion involving physiological arousal and precipitated by experiencing directly or vicariously a love, family, or friendship relationship" (Aaker *et al.*, 1986, p. 366).

Table 68-1 describes psychoactive ads, defined and organized by type. On this view, ads that can cause extreme anxiety rely on appeals using pathos, tragedy or heroism, or fears; ads that can cause hostility toward others rely on appeals that incite Freudian, Jungian, or Adlerian complexes, cater to unfashionable value systems, or promise hatred or contempt of others; ads that can cause a loss of self-esteem employ some myth contrary to the viewer's self-image. The value of this speculative schema is presently under empirical study by the authors.

Our discussion of psychoactive ads proceeds as follows. First, we discuss the reasons that emotion-rousing ads are widely-used. Then, we argue that a type of emotion-rousing ad, the psychoactive ad, can cause harm. Next, we discuss why current pre-testing methods cannot help advertisers distinguish between merely emotion-rousing ads and psychoactive ads. Finally, we propose some common-sense ways to reduce the number of viewers harmed by psychoactive ads.

Emotion-Arousing Ads: Current Practice and Theory

Today's advertiser has to work hard for the attention of viewers: viewers are generally inattentive to ads in the first place, they are besieged by many competing ads, and they use VCRs and remote controls to avoid TV ads. Increasingly, advertisers try to grab a viewer's attention by provoking an emotional response.

Advertisers try to arouse emotions for three distinct purposes (Mizerski and White, 1986; Zeitlin and Westwood, 1986):

1. emotions per se can be an important benefit derived from a product or brand;
2. emotions can sometimes help communicate the benefits of a product or brand; and
3. emotions can directly influence attitudes.

Each of these purposes can help advertisers sell good and services.

Many advertising researchers now recommend using emotion-arousing ads. After years of analyzing consumers in terms of information processing, these researchers have begun to acknowledge the importance of emotion-arousing ads.

> For the marketing company, emotion should be considered as an integral, possibly central, aspect of the communication activity (Zeitlin and Westwood, 1986, p. 35)

Furthermore, Mizerski and White (1986) suggest that:

> Emotions might be profitably used to teach consumers to purchase the brand when they find themselves in emotional states they wish to alter or extend (p. 67).

One increasingly common type of emotion-arousing ad, the so-called fear-appeal ad, seems to be highly effective, under some circumstances, on certain demographic and sociopsychological market segments (Stuteville, 1970; Burnett and Wilkes, 1980; Zeitlin and Westwood, 1986). Empirical studies by Thorson and Friestad indicate that subjects better remember and more frequently recall ads that portray fear than they do warm or upbeat ads or ads with no emotional content (as reported in *Psychology Today*, 1985). LaTour and Zahra (1989) indicate that viewers hold more positive attitudes toward fear-appeal ads, when such ads cause them to feel energized, rather than tense. (Aaker, *et al.*, 1986; Burke and Edell, 1989; and Edell and Burke, 1987 claim that a positive attitude toward an ad enhances any already favorable attitude toward the brand and increases the intention to buy the brand.)

Because advertisers and advertising researchers consider fear-appeal and other emotion-arousing ads to be effective ads, we see such ads frequently. However, some advertisers try to create emotion-arousing ads that work "psychoactively." As Freedman (1988) reports:

Advertisers have long known that commercials that make you feel good are likely to make you feel good about the product. But, more recent research indicates that advertisers might be able to do even better with ads that evoke unpleasant feelings. If get-

Psychoactive Ads: Types, Definitions, and Examples

Category	Definition	Advertising Examples
Pathos	An ad that shows a helpless person, usually a woman or child, crushed by forces beyond her control. This type of ad does not seek viewer identification, only viewer sympathy.	Some ads about drunk driving (MADD), poverty, child abuse, life insurance, and political candidates (e.g., the 1964 Johnson Atomic Daisy ad).
Tragedy or heroism	An ad that shows a noble person crushed is tragic; one that shows the person overcoming opposition is heroic. These ads often imply that the person's fate is in the viewer's hands.	United Negro College Fund; Save the Children; outreach programs; an ad portraying a desperate wife and child trapped in a bleak situation without cash (American Express ad for MoneyGram).
Fear	An ad that arouses fear in the viewer regarding the effect of the viewer's suboptimal lifestyle.	Anti-smoking ads by the American Cancer Society; anti-cavity toothpaste (Crest); breath-freshening mouthwash (Scope); deodorant soap ("Aren't you glad you use Dial?").
Freudian, Jungian, or Adlerian complexes	An ad that sets up a scene which illustrates one of the neuroses identified by these psychologists.	A man who needs a long-distance phone service because he can't leave his mother (AT&T—Freudian Oedipus complex); a father handing down a tradition to his son (Chivas Regal—Jungian Senex/Puer complex); a coffee-spilling nerd who is pushed aside (AT&T—Adlerian Power complex).
Unfashionable value systems	An ad that says, "when the rest of society condemns you for liking this product, it is just sour grapes." This ad is used to fight popular trends.	A man sneering at vegetables on cheeseburgers (Jack in the Box); "75 years and still smoking" (Camel); "for people who like to smoke" (Benson & Hedges).
Hatred or contempt	An ad that assumes a derogatory or chauvinist stereotype. These ads are often tucked away in specialty magazines.	Love 'em and leave 'em (Playboy ad for "Scotch" cologne); NBA basketball star (Michael Jordan) shows contempt for small, intellectual male (Spike Lee) by dunking a basketball in the intellectual's face (Air Jordan sports shoes).
Myth	An ad that ties a product to a mythical figure or lifestyle.	Rough, two-fisted woodsmen (Jack Daniels); party till you drop (some tequilas): "Marlboro country" (Marlboro); pictures of bloodied lineman in football ad with headline, "*You think your* day was tough (ESPN);" Jolly Green Giant; Tony the Tiger (Frosted Flakes).

ting you to suffer will boost sales, don't expect advertisers to shrink from the task (Freedman, 1988, p. 6).

Thus, emotion-arousing ads are widely used because advertisers believe such ads are effective. However, many emotion-arousing ads are also psychoactive ads. Because we believe psychoactive ads can cause harm, we now argue that it is unethical to carelessly or ruthlessly produce such ads.

The Argument

Consider the following hypothetical example: Boris, a misguided social scientist, believes that frequent exposure to emotion-arousing television ads about the horrors of child abuse causes some postpartum depressive mothers to commit infanticide. To test his belief, Boris conducts an experiment. First, he develops the following null hypothesis:

H_O The probability that a mother, suffering from postpartum depression, will commit infanticide is independent of her exposure to emotion-arousing television ads about child abuse.

Boris then produces several 60-second emotion-arousing ads about the horrors of child abuse. Next, he infiltrates the offices of several local hospitals and the TV-Tyme Cable Company. (The TV-Tyme Cable Company operates a sophisticated, uniquely addressable split-cable system with subscriber-monitoring capabilities.) From stolen patient lists and subscriber lists, Boris selects 200 households, each one with (1) a new mother who suffers from postpartum depression, and (2) a subscription to TV-Tyme Cable. He assigns 100 of these households to a control group, and 100 of these households to an experimental group. Next, for one month, he manipulates all advertising televised to each household in the experimental group as follows: for each viewing session, 60 seconds of Boris' child abuse ads replace the first 60 seconds of scheduled advertising. In the homes of the control group, a neutral ad replaces any televised ad against child abuse. After one month, Boris finds, as he expects, that the number of infanticides is significantly higher in the experimental group than in

the control group. Thus, Boris rejects his null hypothesis.

We are morally offended by such an experiment, one which would not be performed by any reputable social scientist. What are the reasons for calling Boris' experiment immoral? First, we already know that women who suffer from postpartum depression are prone to infanticide (O'Hara, 1986). Common sense tells us that subjecting them to such disturbing images and violent thoughts would ensure that at least some of them would hurt themselves or their infants. Second, because we feel certain that any intelligent person could see the danger of such an "experiment," we condemn Boris for his actions. In short, Boris is unethical because he does harm, and because he knew, or should have known, that he was doing harm.

Now consider the following realistic situation. The policy of television superstation KABC is to regularly broadcast emotion-arousing public service announcements designed to reduce child abuse. Many postpartum depressives across America who subscribe to a television cable service do in fact see many of these ads. For these postpartum depressives, such ads are psychoactive ads; such ads may cause them to feel hostile toward their newborn children. Because far more than a hundred postpartum depressive mothers regularly view such ads, KABC's management thoughtlessly replicates Boris' unethical experiment almost every day.

Thus, the argument suggests that the management of superstation KABC is acting at least as unethically as Boris, the misguided scientist.

Is the Argument Reasonable?

Somehow, the parallel between the noble efforts of KABC's management and Boris' highly unethical experiment may seem weak. The argument might seem unfair for any of the following reasons:

- The intentions are different. The public service announcements aim at preventing child abuse, and thus saving children's lives, whereas Boris' experiment invites murder.
- Any ad could provoke some well-defined group of people. Thus, if the argument is taken to its logical conclusion, all advertising

would be immoral. The legal implications would be staggering; advertising as we know it would disappear simply from the prohibitive costs of product liability insurance.

- The argument uses scare tactics; it preys on the reader's pity by using images of women and children. It relies on sentimentality, apparently to muddy the issue, rather than clarify it.

We will examine these objections one at a time.

Scare Tactics

To object to the argument because it uses scare tactics is to object to scare tactics, whether we use them or advertisers use them. Thus, the objection concedes the argument.

Scare tactics are often used by people who have non-substantive arguments. But people who have good arguments also use them to make their point memorable. The presence of scare tactics does not invalidate an argument.

Put aside the image, for a moment, and look at the structure of the argument. The structure is simple and clear:

- Many groups of people are known to be hurt or offended by exposure to certain images.
- Hurting or offending people is wrong.

- Therefore, to show these images publicly, knowing that members of these groups cannot help but see them and be hurt or offended, is wrong.

To circumvent the scare-tactic objection, simply pick another group of highly sensitive people plus an appropriate, but disturbing, image. Then restate the argument in those terms. Some possibilities would be: people who have just lost a spouse, plus a "keep in touch" ad; recent amputees plus a "be all that you can be" ad; and so forth. Pick one that does not seem unfair, yet fits the argument outlined above.

Intended Results

Let us strengthen the example. Suppose that the televising of emotion-arousing child abuse ads by KABC caused five or more infanticides that would have occurred without the televising. Suppose also

that fifty more child-beaters sought professional help than otherwise would have; as a result, ten fewer children died from abuse. The net results of televising the ads would then be that five more children lived than would otherwise have lived. The management of KABC can therefore claim a net benefit to society, whereas Boris has no such defense. How can we say the cases are parallel?

This objection might look powerful on a casual glance, were it not that saving some lives is always a poor excuse for taking others. The objection ignores the issue of whether it is right to expose a person against his or her will to harmful or seriously offensive images. One must suspect that a thoughtful management of KABC could have found a way of doing good without also doing harm. In failing to look for a solution, these managers were not malicious, as was Boris, but negligent.

Taken to Its Logical Conclusion, All Advertising Is Immoral

If any ad could trigger an anti-social response from a group of vulnerable viewers, why wouldn't all ads be dangerous? What would keep the courts from being inundated with complaints about injuries caused by broadcasted or printed ads? Surely ads are not so sinister, surely the argument with such an absurd outcome must be absurd.

Consider the following seemingly parallel example. Bathtubs are dangerous; many people slip and seriously injure themselves in bathtub accidents. Any ad that *increases* the number of baths also increases the number of accidents. The argument seems to lead to the absurd conclusion that advertising bath products is immoral. Aren't the arguments parallel?

No, the cases are very different. A person chooses to take a bath, but emotional responses to psychoactive ads are not freely chosen. Thus, the real issue is not one of producing bad consequences, but of preying on vulnerable innocents.

Furthermore, the bath product company could act morally to reduce the number of bathtub accidents. In fact, the problem of bathtub accidents, if recognized, could even become a marketing opportunity. The ethically-minded bath product company could choose to run this special promotion: mail in five proofs-of-purchase of their product and receive a free bath safety mat. Thus, even the conclusion of the bath argument is not as absurd as it sounded at first. Advertising any dangerous product, whether it be bathtubs, beer, or blasting caps, may be done more or less responsibly.

Protecting Viewers from Psychoactive Ads

Viewers cannot expect government to regulate the use of emotion-arousing ads.

> If the advertising industry gets any better at employing subtle psychological strategies . . . it may become nearly impossible (for viewers) to figure out the ways in which commercials are hitting home. That may be a little frightening, but it's not illegal—so don't expect the government to protect . . . (viewers) from high-tech advertising, at least not in today's climate of deregulation. In the end, it's strictly viewer beware (Freedman, 1988, p. 7).

Thus, the community of advertisers is morally responsible for vulnerable viewers. Perhaps this is just as well; free markets prefer self-regulation to government intervention, *ceteris paribus.*

How should advertisers protect vulnerable viewers from psychoactive ads? An obvious suggestion would be to pretest each emotion-arousing ad. If a pretest suggests that a well-defined, meaningful group of viewers will psychoactively respond to an ad, that ad should not be shown to that group. If it is impossible, even through careful media targeting, to protect these viewers from that ad, then that ad should be discarded.

LaTour and Zahra (1989) advocate using such pretests to identify unethical (i.e., tension-producing) fear-appeal ads.

> Each ad, even those with a supposed "low level" fear appeal, should be evaluated. . . . Extensive pretests of each ad should be performed to ensure effective balance between the message and associated levels of tension (p. 68).

One common pretesting method involves showing an ad to a group and then asking them about it. Unfortunately, such a procedure is problematic.

The mental or cognitive activity prompted by the advertising may often operate at a level below conscious awareness. In other words, the cognitive activity initiated by the emotional cues in an advertisement may occur so rapidly that the individual cannot observe and report on the process as it happens. This has significant implications on the choice of copytesting procedures. Because of the unconscious mental activity, data gathering techniques based on verbal self-reports may be totally ineffective for gauging the intensity of type of emotional experience(s) developed after exposure to the ad (Mizerski and White, 1986, p. 62).

Because viewers may be unable to report psychoactive responses to an ad, such pretests are not the complete answer.

Along similar lines, advertisers could pretest their emotion-arousing ads by exposing them, in a controlled setting, to hundreds of subjects hooked to psychophysiological apparatuses. Unfortunately, these apparatuses only measure a subject's level of activation; they do not identify the activated emotions, nor do they suggest the potential consequences of these emotions. Furthermore, marketing researchers suggest that our present knowledge of psychophysiological responses is too primitive for us to apply them practically (Rothschild *et al.,* 1986; Stewart and Furst, 1982). Therefore, such pretests are not the full answer either.

LaTour and Zahra (1989) suggest another alternative in their discussion of fear-appeal ads:

> To minimize abuse of fear appeals, some effective, functional and practical ethical guidelines need to be adopted by firms sponsoring such advertising (p. 68).

Thus, we propose that advertisers adopt the following simple practices whenever they design and place an emotion-rousing ad.

Three Simple Practices

Carefully Target the Medium as Well as the Market

Obviously, to guard against every possible negative side-effect of an ad would be impossible. First, psychotics cannot be outguessed; because they will interpret even the dullest images to fit their delusions, no amount of care taken over an ad will remove all chances of its doing harm to these people. Second, if a person named Spuds MacKenzie were to die in a freak yachting accident, his bereaved wife might be upset by some recent Budweiser commercials; Anheuser Busch cannot and should not plan for these circumstances.

Instead of worrying over unique psychoses or strange coincidences, advertisers should use common sense and psychological theory to identify large groups of people whose members are prone to be hurt by the images used in emotion-arousing ads.

Advertisers will easily recognize some groups. For example, common sense (as well as psychological research) suggests that the following groups may respond psychoactively to emotion-arousing ads:

1. AIDS victims (Atkinson *et al.* (1988) report that many are deeply psychologically disturbed);
2. Vietnam combat veterans (Pitman *et al.* (1987) report that these veterans are highly susceptible to combat-reminding imagery);
3. young women (Gould (1987) and Regier *et al.* (1988) suggest that many (i.e., 10%) have anxiety disorders because they are prone to be publicly self-conscious and socially anxious);
4. young men (Caprara *et al.* (1987) report that young males who first viewed aggressive ads then acted more aggressivly toward other males); and
5. compulsive gamblers (Roy *et al.* (1988) report that compulsive gamblers are attracted to sensation-seeking events).

It will be more difficult for advertisers to recognize other groups. One not-so-obvious group is non-institutionalized adults with affective disorders or anxiety disorders. (A survey by the National Institute of Mental Health (Regier *et al.,* 1988) found that, of non-institutionalized adults, 5.1% had affective disorders and 7.3% had anxiety disorders.) Persons with affective or anxiety disorders have high levels of *negative affectivity*. Negative affectivity (NA) reflects pervasive individual differences in negative emotionality and in self-concept; high-NA individuals tend toward distress, aggres-

sion (sadistic or masochistic), and negative self-image (Watson and Clark, 1984). Relative to low-NAs, high-NAs are more likely to (1) identify with any aggressive, anti-social behavior shown in ads, (2) read negative things into ads, and (3) dwell on threats and loss of self-esteem posed by ads (Watson and Clark, 1984). Thus, high-NAs are more likely to respond "psychoactively" to emotion-arousing ads.

This leads us to our first recommended practice: *Advertisers should carefully target the medium as well as the market.*

Because the ad rates charged by broadcasters and publishers are based largely on audience size, advertisers have long recognized the economic reasons for advertising in just the media viewed, heard, or read by their current and likely customers. But now, it seems that there are also ethical reasons for targeting.

For example, specialized magazines, such as *Field & Stream, Ebony, American Baby, Soldier of Fortune, Millionaire,* and *Hustler,* to name but a few, have special, fairly well-defined audiences. A reader of one of these magazines comes to expect certain types of ads and certain types of thematic emotional appeals. By recognizing the acceptable appeals for the readers of these magazines, advertisers can create appropriate ads. Such a precaution will not only reduce one source of unwanted side-effects, but it would also cost the advertiser less than the less responsible approach.

Clearly Label Psychoactive Ads

A general rule of thumb for designing emotion-arousing ads is: Give the viewer a fair chance to avoid the climax of the ad. This rule is based on two assumptions: (1) viewers know best which images they can tolerate and which they cannot, and (2) viewers threatened by an image used in an ad will actively avoid it *if they are given a fair chance to do so.* As Caprara *et al.* (1987) suggests,

> [I]n the case of programmes such as movies, cartoons, and championship fights, the audience is always free to select and therefore, to a certain extent, be prepared to see what is portrayed on the screen . . . [I]n the case of commercials, because of their unexpectedness, their effects are usually out of the viewer's control. . . . [In] television advertising one has

the impression that the viewer is often left to the mercy of the advertising agent (Caprara *et al.*, 1987, p. 24).

This rule does not cover every possibility, but it does offer a useful guide for most normal cases.

Thus, our second recommended practice is: *Advertisers should introduce their emotion-arousing ads with an announcement.*

If viewers know of the strong nature of the imagery or themes prior to their onset, they have ample time to decide whether to see or avoid the ad. Advertisers could place brief warnings, in advance of a video or radio ad, or at the heading of printed copy, about the nature of the ad, much as warnings often precede the airings of movies or political announcements. For example,

Due to its emotional subject matter, the following pro-abortion message may be offensive to some people.

This practice requires that the advertiser keeps the element of choice in mind while considering the ethics of a proposed course of action. If the viewer of a visual image has consciously chosen, on the basis of accurate information, to see it, responsibility for the consequences is shared by the maker and the viewer of the image. Many people will not willingly watch a movie which they suspect contains intolerable images. Nonetheless, these same people, in watching an ad, may find themselves besieged by the same images, held off until the last few seconds. People consciously censor what they view, and it is not the legitimate prerogative of an advertiser to override these efforts at psychological self-protection.

On the other hand, such warnings could do no harm. By taking the trouble to warn the audience about the content of a commercial, advertisers could actually draw more attention to their ads—attention, that is, from those people who are the proper targets.

Advertisers should note that content-specific warnings, i.e., warnings that refer to specific ad content, may actually sensitize viewers, and thus increase the negative effects of psychoactive ads. In studying the effect of forewarning on a viewer's emotional response to horror films, Cantor, Ziemke, and Clark (1984) found that the more ex-

plicit the forewarning about the graphic nature of the film, the greater the viewer's fright and upset. Thus, advertisers should be careful, even in their forewarning, to use only the most general warning messages.

Avoid Trick Endings

Trick endings appear often in ads that rely on appeals using pathos, tragedy or heroism, or fear. A trick ending is an unexpected plot twist, such as a MADD ad in which a little girl, happily playing along the side of a road, is suddenly killed by an intoxicated truck driver.

Clearly, such ads are designed to shock viewers into modifying inappropriate attitudes (e.g., it is acceptable to first imbibe, and then drive) and behaviors (e.g., driving while intoxicated). Though shocking ads may save some lives, such ads will also cause many viewers to feel tense (LaTour and Zahra, 1989). When these ads cause many susceptible viewers to feel extreme anxiety, these ads become psychoactive ads. Thus, advertisers should refrain, for ethical reasons, from showing such ads.

If the ending is really a trick, viewers have no chance to avoid it. Although a clever twist may be amusing when used for humor, it should never be used for a powerful, emotion-arousing message.

Thus, our third recommended practice, which also follows from our rule of thumb, is: *Advertisers should avoid trick endings in their ads.* This practice should minimize the abusive use of fear appeals.

Conclusion

Advertisers often use emotion-arousing ads to promote goods, services, and ideas. We have argued that, because emotion-arousing ads are often psychoactive, advertisers should take care when they deploy them. We therefore propose some simple rules for a more responsible use of emotion-arousing ads. These rules would neither hobble such ads nor greatly increase their cost.

NOTE

1. In a pretest designed to help us select the psychoactive ads we would use in a subsequent empirical study, one of the authors received such responses from a large number of black subjects.

RESOURCES

Aaker, David A., Douglas M. Stayman, and Michael R. Hagerty: 1986, "Warmth in Advertising: Measurement, Impact, and Sequence Effects," *Journal of Consumer Research* 12, 365–381.

Atkinson, J. Hampton, Igor Grant, Caroline J. Kennedy, Douglas D. Richman, Stephen A. Spector, and J. Allen McCutchan: 1988, "Prevalence of Psychiatric Disorders among Men Infected with Human Immunodeficiency Virus," *Archives of General Psychiatry* 45, 859–864.

Burke, Marian Chapman, and Julie A. Edell: 1989, "The Impact of Feelings on Ad-Based Affect and Cognition," *Journal of Marketing Research* 26, 69–83.

Burnett, John J., and Robert E. Wilkes: 1980, "Fear Appeals to Segments Only," *Journal of Advertising Research* 20, 21–24.

Cantor, Joanne, Dean Ziemke, and Glenn G. Sparks: 1984, "Effect of Forewarning on Emotional Responses to a Horror Film," *Journal of Broadcasting* 28, 21–31.

Caprara, G. V., G. D'Imperio, A. Gentilomo, A. Mammucari, P. Renzi, and G. Travaglia: 1987, "The Intrusive Commercial: Influence of Aggressive TV Commercials on Aggression," *European Journal of Social Psychology* 17 (1), 23–31.

Drucker, Peter: 1973, *Management: Tasks, Responsibilities, Practices* (Harper and Row, New York).

Edell, Julie A., and Marian Chapman Burke: 1987, "The Power of Feelings in Understanding Advertising Effects," *Journal of Consumer Research* 14, 421–433.

Freedman, David H.: 1988, "Why We Watch Certain Commercials," *TV Guide* 36 (8), 4–7.

Gould, Stephen J.: "Gender Differences in Advertising Response and Self-Consciousness Variables," *Sex Roles* 16, 215–225.

LaTour, Michael S., and Shaker A. Zahra: 1989, "Fear Appeals as Advertising Strategy: Should They Be Used?,"*The Journal of Consumer Marketing* 6 (2), 61–70.

Mizerski, Richard W., and J. Dennis White: 1986, "Understanding and Using Emotions in Advertising," *The Journal of Consumer Marketing* 3 (3), 57–69.

O'Hara, Michael W.: 1986: "Social Support, Life Events, and Depression during Pregnancy and the Puerperium," *Archives of General Psychiatry* 43, 569–573.

Pitman, Roger K., Scott P. Orr, Dennis F. Forgue, Jacob B. deJong, and James M. Claiborn: 1987, "Psychophysiologic Assesssssment of Posttraumatic Stress Disorder Imagery in Vietnam Combat Veterans," *Archives of General Psychiatry* 44, 970–975.

Psychology Today: 1985, "Advertising: Sold on Emotion," 19 (3), 9.

Regier, Darrel A., Jeffrey H. Boyd, Jack D. Burke, Donald S. Rae, Jerome K. Myers, Morton Kramer, Lee N. Robins, Linda K. George, Marvin Karno, and Ben Z. Locke: 1988, "One-Month Prevalence of Mental Disorders in the United States," *Archives of General Psychiatry* 45, 977–986.

Rothschild, Michael L., Ester Thorson, Byron Reeves, Judith E. Hirsch, and Robert Goldstein: 1986, "EEG Activity and the Processing of Television Commercials," *Communication Research* 13, 182–220.

Roy, Alex, Byron Adinoff, Laurie Roehrich, Danuta Lamparski, Robert Custer, Valerie Lorenz, Maria Barbaccia, Alessandro Guidotti, Erminio Costa, and Markku Linnoila: 1988, "Pathological Gambling," *Archives of General Psychiatry* 45, 369–373.

Spence, Homer E., and Resa Moinpour: 1972, "Fear Appeals in Marketing: A Social Perspective," *Journal of Marketing* 36 (3), 39–43.

Stewart, David W., and David H. Furse: 1982, "Applying Psychophysiological Measures to Marketing and Advertising Research Problems," in *Current Issues and Research in Advertising,* James H. Leigh and Claude R. Martin, editors (University of Michigan, Ann Arbor, MI), 1–38.

Stuteville, John R.: 1970, "Psychic Defenses against High Fear *Appeals:* A Key Marketing Variable," *Journal of Marketing* 34, 39–45.

Watson, David, and Lee Anna Clark: 1984, "Negative Affectivity: The Disposition to Experience Aversive Emotional States," *Psychological Bulletin* 96, 465–490.

Zeitlin, David M., and Richard A. Westwood: 1986, "Measuring Emotional Response," *Journal of Advertising Research* 26, 34–44.

Study Questions

1. In the Sistema Silueta case, how did the owner and distributor of the product, Klavir, argue that he should not be held personally liable for the losses of his customers? Why did the court reject his argument?

2. The ads for Sistema Silueta stated that the user of the product had to "eat less" while on the proscribed regimen. If a user were to lose weight in accordance with these

instructions and attribute the weight loss to the use of the lotion, is the overall ad "unfair or deceptive"? Suppose ads for Sistema Silueta had stated only that the product would "make you look and feel years younger." Should such ads be banned?

3. What are the arguments for and against adopting a policy of prohibiting any advertisement that might deceive or fool the "ignorant" consumer? Which arguments do you find most persuasive?

4. In the Supreme Court's opinion in *FTC v. Standard Education* (1937), Justice Hugo Black stated that "there is no duty upon a citizen to suspect the honesty of those with whom he transacts business." Do you agree? Explain your answer. Is this statement consistent with your understanding of the values behind the free-market system?

5. In your view, why is human autonomy in general, and consumer autonomy in particular, a value to be protected?

6. Do you agree that consumers in our society are experienced enough with the techniques of advertising to be aware of and skeptical of even its most subtle messages?

7. Can you imagine a situation in which a seller of a good heavily advertises the good although the seller knows that the product is an inferior one? How would this affect Nelson's argument?

8. What reasons would support Nelson's conclusion that "consumers who actually believe paid endorsements are victims of the most benign form of deception. They are deceived into doing what they should do anyway"? Critically evaluate the argument.

9. According to Richard Lippke, what are the most important skills and abilities that an autonomous person has?

10. How, according to Lippke, does advertising undermine the social conditions necessary to promote the autonomy of individual citizens?

11. Those skeptical of the argument presented by Hyman and Tansey might insist that, given a certain psychological disposition, any advertisement could have a psychoactive effect. Evaluate this claim and discuss its implications for Hyman and Tansey's argument.

12. Hyman and Tansey cite an advertisement by MADD (Mothers Against Drunk Drivers) that could produce extreme anxiety; the authors conclude that advertisers should refrain from this kind of advertising. What would be the consequentialist rebuttal to their argument? Evaluate this response in light of Hyman and Tansey's claims concerning "intentional consequences."

13. Do you agree with the contention that children's advertising treats young people as a means to the goal of profit maximization? How does Paine reply to the point that even if this is so, parents can and ought to control children's spending?

14. How can children's advertising harm children? Explain carefully the sense of "harm" that you are using in your answer.

CASE SCENARIO 1   Sunoco 260
Ivan Preston

In one ad Sunoco's maker, Sun Oil, showed an ordinary automobile pulling three railroad cars. In another ad the car pulled a U-Haul trailer up a ramp laid over a steep bank of seats in the Los

From Ivan Preston, *The Tangled Web They Weave: Truth, Falsity, and Advertisers*, 1994. The University of Wisconsin Press. Reprinted by permission of the publisher.

Angeles Coliseum. The announcer's voice said it showed the power of a gasoline that was unusual in being "blended with the action of Sunoco 260 . . . the highest octane gasoline at any station anywhere. With 260 action the car and trailer go up the ramp just like that. You get that same 260 action at Sunoco."

Gas stations traditionally use different pumps for different grades of gasoline. Sunoco stations innovated for a time with a pump that gave a choice of grades by drawing gasoline from two separate underground tanks. One tank held a higher octane than any competitor sold; Sunoco called it 260. The other tank held 190, the lowest octane that any car on the road could use. The pump had a "custom blending" switch that let the operator dispense pure 260, pure 190, or various mixtures. Thus 200 was mostly 190 with a bit of 260, 240 was mostly 260 with some 190, and so forth. Most cars used 200, regular gasoline, which powered the cars shown in the ads.

Hardly any cars required undiluted 260, which no doubt explains why no competitors sold it. Nor did Sunoco make 260 primarily to sell it, at least not in its pure form. The purpose, rather, was to be able to claim that the blends to which the 260 tank contributed possessed what the ads called "260 action." The idea of 260 action was a farce, designed to make people think they were getting the advantages of the highest octane gasoline when they weren't. Any real advantage obtainable from 260 could exist only if it were undiluted, yet hardly any drivers bought it that way. When the "custom blending" pump mixed in various amounts of 190, consumers of course got a lower octane, a level that was available from competitors.

Suppose your bartender tells you he has the greatest Scotch in the world and is going to give you some "Scotch action." He thereupon pours you a shot having 10 percent of that brand and 90 percent of the world's lowest rated brand. What are your chances of recognizing the taste of that "greatest Scotch" when it comes in that form? They are the same as consumers had of benefiting from Sunoco 260 when their "260 action" blend was 90 percent 190.

The FTC charged Sunoco with claiming falsely that the blends called "260 action" would give users the highest octane benefits of any gasoline available. Other falsities it alleged were that 260 action would give more engine power than competitors, that it was the only gasoline enabling a car to operate at its maximum power, and that the ad demonstrations proved the power claims.

The commission conceded that none of these claims were made explicitly, so it charged they were implied . . .

The principal sources of confusion were the phrases "260" and "260 action," which were so similar that consumers could easily equate them. If they did so, they would think that any "260 action" blend gave the benefits that 260 gave.

The next step was to imply that 260 gave cars greater power. That implication was aided by a false belief many consumers already held that more octane means more power. In truth, more octane gives more power only up to your car's sufficient octane level, and 260 exceeded that level for virtually all cars on the road. You could get the potential benefits of 260 by buying it in pure form at a much higher cost than for regular. If you did, though, in virtually all cases you would get no more power than other brands offered.

As to the demonstration, if the power claims were not true, the boxcar pull or the Coliseum clim certainly could not prove them. In fact, the ads couldn't have proved the claims even if they were true, among other reasons because the demonstration used only Sunoco and no other brand.

1. Were Sun Oil's ads for Sunoco 260 deceptive, in your view? Could the ads have been expected to deceive the average, reasonable consumer? Or only the particularly "ignorant" or inexperienced one? Did the ads falsely imply that Sunoco 260 would give drivers the highest octane benefit of any gasoline available?
2. Would the average consumer assume that the U-Haul demonstrated that the 260 blend gives cars greater power? Is this ad simply an example of "puffery"? Why or why not?
3. Suppose you were the FTC Commissioner. Would you have challenged the Sunoco ads on the grounds that they conveyed false claims?

CASE SCENARIO 2   Tobacco Marketing

A number of recent efforts by the tobacco industry to market cigarettes and other tobacco products have met with the criticism that they are morally suspect. Consider these ad campaigns:

- In 1988 R.J. Reynolds, maker of Camel cigarettes, introduced Joe Camel, a cartoon figure of a camel, who is depicted as a "smooth character": shown variously in sunglasses and a T-shirt, playing an electric guitar, or wearing a baseball cap turned backward, Joe is nearly as recognizable to young children, one study found, as Mickey Mouse. One recent ad was a four-page fold-out featuring a bar full of male and female camels—all holding or smoking cigarettes. Joe Camel merchandise covers the spectrum from tank tops and baseball caps to sunglasses and suede jackets. While Camel's market share for adult smokers has remained at roughly its 1988 level, share among the under-eighteen market has more than tripled. Critics point with alarm to the sharp rise in teen smokers, claiming that almost 75 percent of adult smokers become hooked on tobacco before their thirteenth birthday. Joe Camel's widespread appeal to underage smokers prompted the FTC, in 1997, to seek a "cease and desist" order against Reynolds, prohibiting the use of Joe Camel in ads in magazines and on roadside billboards. Reynolds's use of Joe Camel is deliberately designed, the agency argued, to induce the illegal purchase of cigarettes by minors.

- Stowebridge Brook Distributors recently marketed Menthol X, a cigarette brand allegedly targeted at young, urban blacks. The packaging for the product consisted of a box resembling the poster ads for Spike Lee's film *Malcolm X*—black, red, or green backgrounds with a large white X. R.J. Reynolds had previously announced plans to market to the same target group a cigarette called Uptown. Critics alleged that the companies were using images associated with racial pride to lure consumers from the black community.

- Cigarette advertising has been banned from television since 1971. Recently, however, tobacco company Philip Morris backed a series of TV ads that some claim violate the ban. The company sponsored a patriotic ad highlighting the Bill of Rights. The ad made no reference to tobacco or cigarettes; the Philip Morris name and logo, however, appeared at the close of the commercial (or at the bottom of the print version of the ad). Defenders of the ad point out that political expression is at the core of the freedom of expression protected by the Constitution. Critics argue that because commercial speech receives far less constitutional protection, companies like Philip Morris have incentive to disguise commercial messages as political expression.

1. Are any of these ad campaigns morally objectionable? If so, why?
2. Some argue that ads of the sort described here deliberately target those least able to resist the suasion of the tobacco industry: children, the poor, and the ill-educated. Do you agree?
3. How would Nelson and Lippke each assess the foregoing advertising campaigns? Be specific.

CASE SCENARIO 3   The Selling of T-Man Action Toys
Michael Boylan

We all know about T-Man and T-Woman, the animated characters who top the charts of Saturday morning cartoon television. The unique sounds they make when they fight super criminals and their deadly laser guns make them a hit among the pre-adolescent set.

You work for the Bellevue Advertising Agency on Madison Avenue. Mactold Toys has approached you about the campaign to sell T-Man and T-Woman. What Mactold is interested in is a campaign that links right into the cartoon adventures themselves. "If it is seamless," says Sally Ware, the marketing VP for Mactold, "the children will think they are still within the scenario of that morning's adventure. They will feel as if they must have their own set of T-toys in order to fully appreciate the show. With twenty million viewers, that's a ton of money."

You listen to Ms. Ware tell you what Mactold has in mind and you promise to come up with a marketing plan in two weeks. However, the more you think about it, the more you are troubled. You are not sure that a "seamless" television commercial for children is really such a good thing to do. You decide to ask for a staff meeting.

Two of your top people, Ms. Black and Mr. White take opposite views.

MS. BLACK: We need the Mactold account, but the plan for a "seamless" advertisement program is not the way to do it. The FCC has been very tight about children's advertising, because children are more easily manipulated than adults.

      Seamless advertising blurs the distinction between fact and fiction. Children must know when someone is making a pitch to them instead of confusing TV show and commercial. I know I wouldn't want my child exposed to those sorts of commercials.

      Instead, let's make a point of making it very separate. We can use live child actors who are playing with the toys and having a grand time. By moving from animation to real people we will be letting the children know that there is a break in the show and that now we are in reality.

      I think Mactold will get better results with my idea.

MR. WHITE: I think Ms. Black is making something of nothing. Children are smarter than you think. We shouldn't treat them like moldable clay. If they can't figure out that a commercial is going on when we tell them the price of the toy and that accessories are sold extra—not to mention "batteries not included," then those children need remedial attention.

      I was a kid once and I hated it when TV commercials "dumbed down" to me. Look, the plain truth is that kids like the animation. They are attracted to it. If we don't make our commercial so irresistible that they like it as much as the show, then we will lose them to the donut bag in the kitchen.

      The FCC regs are no problem to "work around." I say, "Give the client what she wants. If she wants seamless advertising, then seamless advertising it is."

You are undecided. The company has been hurting lately due to some large accounts cutting back. You can really use the business. On the other hand you want to so what's "best"—whatever that means.

1. What would be your decision in this case, and why?
2. How would Paine's analysis of children's advertising apply to this case?

CASE SCENARIO 4   Acme Advertising and the "Jordan Look"

The Acme Advertising Agency has just signed a contract with the Jordan Company, a new clothes and cosmetics manufacturer. Jordan wants to capitalize on a lucrative market for new clothes and hair styles: young women in their late teens and early twenties. Their plan for doing so relies on developing a full media advertising campaign, one that will depict "The Awesome Jordan Look." The campaign will consist primarily of TV ads showing young women with the "Jordan Look" in sexy situations, surrounded by adoring guys.

One of the company's new "Jordan Look" product lines is a wave-setting lotion called Natural Wave. After several weeks of brainstorming and tests with the product, the Acme team hits upon an idea for a new TV commercial for advertising Natural Wave: While the voice-over (narration) introduces the viewer to Natural Wave, the camera will show a drinking straw being soaked in a bowl of the lotion. Drinking straws curl up when soaked in Natural Wave, and the camera will show this. The commercial will *not*, however, *actually say* "Natural Wave will curl your hair just like this straw." (Afterward, the camera will depict a wavy-haired "Jordan Look" girl with a handsome man at her side.) Jordan likes the commercial and it is aired in a number of markets across the country.

One of the young women to see the Natural Wave ad is Esther Washington, a nineteen-year-old college student and single mother. Faced with the demands of school and her infant son, Esther's social life has all but vanished. Lately, she has been feeling lonely and not particularly attractive. After seeing a number of ads highlighting the "Jordan Look," and especially the Natural Wave ad, Esther rushes out to buy Natural Wave (and other awesome Jordan products). Esther has straight hair, and even after several applications (following the product's directions) no waves appear. Frustrated, Esther phones a friend who works at the local office of the Better Business Bureau; the friend recommends that Esther write to the Federal Trade Commission concerning Jordan's product. Esther does so; subsequently the FTC performs its own tests and discovers that, although straws do indeed curl in Natural Wave, straight hair normally does not. The Acme team knew this at the time the commercial was made. The FTC must now decide what, if any, action it should take concerning both the Natural Wave commercial in particular, and the entire "Jordan Look" campaign in general.

1. What are the central ethical issues raised by the events depicted in this scenario?
2. How would the authors you read for this chapter analyze the issues raised in this case? Be specific.
3. How would you argue for a position on how each of the issues raised by the scenario should be resolved? Base your argument on the concepts and arguments raised in the readings for this chapter.

CHAPTER 8

Consumer Safety and Product Liability

Certainly one of the most obvious and pervasive ways in which businesses touch all of our lives is in the manufacture, distribution, and sale of consumer goods. And just as certainly it is when the products marketed and sold fail to perform as expected or, worse, injure consumers that difficult questions of morality and public policy arise.

The widely publicized bankruptcy of Dow Chemical, brought on by billions of dollars of claims against it by women allegedly harmed by Dow's silicon breast implants, and the growing number of charges leveled against DuPont in connection with birth defects supposedly linked to the fungicide Benlate, are but the latest examples of consumer outrage over exposure to harmful products. Cigarette lighters; oral contraceptives; all-terrain vehicles (ATVs); asbestos products; silicon implants and IUDs; fungicides, herbicides, and DDT; DES and thalidomide; sport-utility vehicles; car batteries and drain cleaners; power tools, ladders, and lawnmowers; automobiles, airplanes, and forklifts—all have been claimed to be the cause of injury or even death to consumers. In some of these cases, those injured were paid tens of millions of dollars in damages by the companies who made and marketed the offending products. Consumer advocates defend such awards as a necessary check on corporate greed and callousness; business advocates complain that holding the companies liable is not always fair. Some products, such as cigarettes and silicon breast implants, do pose health risks, but they are, say those in business, desired by large numbers of consumers anyway. Businesspeople also point to such high-profile cases as that of BMW, forced to pay $4 million to a doctor whose BMW had been partially repainted prior to delivery due to acid-rain damage, destroying its "original lustre,"[1] and the woman awarded nearly $3 million from McDonald's for burns she suffered after spilling a cup of McDonald's coffee in her lap—the coffee, she claimed, was too hot.[2] Both of these cases involved so-called *punitive* damages, levied in cases where the conduct was so egregious as to both deserve extra punishment and call for extra deterrence of future harmful conduct. Corporate interests decried these punitive awards as wholly unjustified. The case of Connie Daniell, which opens the readings for this chapter, equally illustrates the exasperations of the business community.

The issues joined by such cases as the foregoing raise central moral questions about responsibility and fairness. Given the inevitability of injuries and accidents in a crowded, highly technological society such as ours, who should bear the burden of the costs those injuries and accidents incur? Who is or ought to be responsible for paying for the costs of defective merchandise or products? Is it fair to leave these costs with whomever is unlucky enough to incur them? Or is there a morally defensible basis for shifting the costs over to

---

ॐ   **Liability for Implants and a Shortage of Silicon**

Beginning in the late 1980s, juries began to return verdicts in the millions to women who claimed that their silicon breast implants ruptured and leaked, causing infection, auto-immune diseases, and other problems. By 1992 the Food and Drug Administration (FDA) had imposed a moritorium on the sale of silicon implants. Dow Corning, the largest implant manufacturer, subsequently admitted that it had suppressed evidence of health problems brought on by the devices. In an agreement struck in 1993, Dow and other implant makers agreed to a $4.25 billion settlement for all suits brought against them, but the number of women filing to receive compensation ultimately forced Dow into bankruptcy. In the after-math of the bankruptcy of Dow Corning, one of the nation's leading manufacturers of silicon implants, various biotechnology industries began to complain that the silicon vital to many of their products was no longer available. Dow, along with other silicon suppliers, had agreed to support a multibillion-dollar fund to settle claims by women reportedly injured by silicon breast implants; it severely curtailed its production of other forms of silicon, which is used in many biotech products, from artificial joints and heart valves, to catheters and pacemakers.

SOURCE: *National Law Journal* 2/20/95.

---

the producer? These questions of public policy and ethics are the subject of the readings in this chapter.

CONSUMER PROTECTION LAWS

A *consumer* is simply anyone who uses goods or services marketed and sold by another. There are many ways in which society currently seeks to protect consumers from unfair or dangerous services or products. Some laws, such as the Consumer Product Safety Act of 1972, authorize consumers to sue in court to enforce a product safety rule; and a defendant accused of improper consumer practices can face either civil or criminal penalties. Most consumer legislation does not, however, protect consumers from their own negligence or carelessness; as we shall see in this chapter, just what that means is not entirely clear.

We have already encountered one significant aspect of consumer protection: statutes forbidding false or misleading advertising. Other consumer protection laws cover a wide area: regulating the labeling of products; prohibiting improper sales techniques and requir-ing full disclosure of sales terms; regulating the charges imposed by credit-card companies; banning unfair or discriminatory credit or collection practices; and protecting consumers from inappropriate use of credit information. One of the largest areas of consumer protec-tion deals with product safety, and it is this aspect of consumer protection that is explored in this chapter.

The law currently says that those who make and sell consumer goods may be held re-sponsible for the design and construction of their products, as well as for the labels affixed to them, the instructions that come with them, and the warnings given concerning them. Manufacturers and distributors of consumer goods can be held liable for promises made concerning their products, for products that were carelessly or negligently manufactured or inspected, or even for products that are defective and dangerous, albeit carefully designed and built.

Warranty law protects consumers by requiring manufacturers to live up to promises they have made relating to the nature and quality of what they have to sell. Warranties can arise explicitly or by implication. If the maker of a power tool says, "This drill will penetrate 1-inch steel," the statement will be treated as an express warranty; a bottle of aspirin with a label reading "contains 500 tablets," expressly warrants the quantity of the product. The most common implied warranty is that of merchantability, a guarantee that the product sold is fit for ordinary use. If I buy a hammer and, when I first use it, the handle breaks, revealing that the wood inside had rotted (though this is not apparent to ordinary inspection), the seller has breached an implied warranty.

Warranties were one of the earliest forms of consumer protection, and it was not until the beginning of this century that the law began to impose duties upon manufacturers and retailers of commercial goods in other ways. With the advent of increasingly complex machines and technologies, such as the automobile, courts began to hold businesses liable for their negligence or lack of care in constructing their goods or in inspecting them for latent defects, even in the absence of any applicable warranty. Courts noted that consumer goods have become increasingly complicated and, at the same time, less intelligible to the ordinary consumer; and the risk of harm posed by such products has escalated just as the ability of the ordinary consumer to assess the risk posed by the goods has diminished. As the number of those injured by product defects frequently not detectable by ordinary consumers grew, courts continued to expand the liability of manufacturers, even if they had to stretch the idea of negligence to do it. In one famous case, a bottle of Coca Cola exploded in the hands of a waiter as she moved it from the case to a refrigerator. A defect in the glass, undetectable by visual inspection, was the likely cause of the accident. In its defense, the bottler emphasized that it carefully tested its bottles and that the tests it used were customary and always effective. Accepting the manufacturer's claims, the court nonetheless held the bottler liable in a case that soon gave rise to the doctrine of *strict product liability*. The court reasoned that the manufacturer put the product on the market knowing that a consumer would very likely not inspect it; the manufacturer is, therefore, more responsible for the product than is the consumer. Moreover, the court argued, by placing liability on the manufacturer, the law will be putting the burden on the party that can best guard against such a loss in the future, by designing safer products.

STRICT PRODUCT LIABILITY

Strict product liability claims dominate the current landscape of consumer protection litigation. A seller may be strictly liable for defective products introduced into the stream of commerce even though the seller was in no way negligent. Section 402(A) of the *Restatement of Torts, Second,* is a source of much modern strict-liability law. It states that a seller may be held liable where it makes and sells a product in a "defective" condition, "unreasonably dangerous" to the consumer. What do these terms mean? It is generally accepted that a product is defective if it was manufactured incorrectly, say, with screws missing or parts not in the right place. Manufacturers can also be liable, however, for defects in the *design* of their products. A company that made buses for commercial transit, for example, was held liable when a woman riding in one of its buses fell to the floor and was injured as the bus made a sharp right turn. The bus was defectively designed as there was no "grab bar" or vertical pole for passengers to hold on to next to the plaintiff's seat.[3] What guidelines should

Product Liability and Costly Verdicts

Lawsuits decided in favor of consumers claiming injuries resulting from product use continued to bring in huge jury awards during the 1990s. Here is a sampling of the largest awards
of 1995:

- Four former asbestos workers were awarded $64.65 million, one of the largest asbestos
  awards to date, in a suit filed against several asbestos manufacturers, among them West-
  inghouse Electric Corp. Each of the four workers was expected to die soon from incur-
  able cancer allegedly caused by exposure to asbestos fibers. In a related case, another
  group of asbestos claimants were awarded $42.6 million against Owens-Corning Fiber-
  glass Corp.
- Mark Peterson, an Illinois college student, was awarded $12.65 million in a suit against
  Goodyear Tire and Rubber Co. Peterson was rendered quadriplegic as a result of spinal
  injuries sustained when his Ford Bronco, equipped with an improperly repaired tire, left
  the road and flipped over. Even though a garage worker had incorrectly patched the tire
  before the accident, Peterson claimed that Goodyear was liable for providing poor instructions for fixing tires.
- The family of Sherry Letz, a twenty-year-old waiter, was awarded $70 million in a
  wrongful death suit against the French manufacturer of a helicopter in which Letz had
  been traveling. The helicopter crashed, according to the family, because of a design defect in the engine. The French manufacturer contended that the engine failure was due to
  faulty maintenance.
- Two sisters received $62 million from Ford Motor Co. for injuries resulting when the
  Bronco II in which they were riding as passengers flipped over. The Bronco II, they alleged, has a tendency to roll over in minor accidents or common driving maneuvers.
  Ford had argued that the driver was at fault, as he had attempted to pass two cars on a
  two-lane road by driving off the side of the road. In a related case, a woman severely
  injured when a Suzuki Samuri flipped over received $40 million, $20 million of which
  was levied as punitive damages against Suzuki Motor Co.

SOURCE: *National Law Journal* 2/5/96.

be used to determine whether a design is defective? Here the law has employed at least two
different tests:

- That the product sold was dangerous to an extent beyond what would be contemplated by an ordinary consumer using common knowledge—in other words, that it
  fell below reasonable consumer expectations
- That the product sold creates such a risk of serious injury that the cost to make it safe
  would outweigh its benefit to society

Each test may, of course, have different results. Suppose Adams locks himself in the
trunk of a old car. There is no latch or other device with which the trunk can be opened
from the inside. He can't get out and is injured. Has the car's trunk been defectively designed? To prove his claim under the first test, Adams would have to show that most consumers could not have foreseen the type of injury he suffered. Since most people would

---

◦⌒◦   **Breast Implants: An "Unavoidably Unsafe" Product?**

Section 402A Comment K of the *Restatement of Torts* states that "there are some products which, in the present state of human knowledge, are quite incapable of being made safe for their intended and ordinary use." Citing the example of prescription drugs, the *Restatement* goes on to say that if the seller's products have been "properly prepared" and a "proper warning given," the seller "is not to be held to strict liability for unfortunate consequences attending their use, merely because he has undertaken to supply the public with an apparently useful and desirable product, attended with a known but apparently reasonable risk." Why shouldn't this language apply to breast or penile implants, which are clearly desired by some consumers despite their attendant risks?

---

readily see the danger, however, he probably doesn't have a case. But this first way of unpacking the idea of a design defect has limitations: How, for example, should we handle cases in which consumers simply don't have any clear expectations about how a product should behave or how safe it is? The second of the two tests for design defects asks this question: Does the existence on the market of trunks without inside latches create such a danger that the risk outweighs the utility or value of having such items available at all? The answer here is somewhat less clear than with regard to the first test, and would probably depend on how much interior trunk latches would add to the costs of cars. Assessments of risk and utility are not easy. After all, such common household items as knives and scissors cause many accidents each year, yet few would argue that we would be better off without them. Some products, of course, cannot be made completely safe; such "unavoidably unsafe" goods, such as vaccines, nonetheless have great utility.

A product can be hazardous to consumers, of course, if they are not properly instructed on how to use it. Sellers of goods can also be strictly liable for failing to inform or to warn consumers adequately about the dangers to which their product might be subject. Here the question facing producers is how best to transmit information concerning the risks of their wares. How much of the risk needs to be disclosed? How vivid must a warning be? In one case, a teenager and her friend decided to make a Christmas candle scented by dousing it with Fabergé cologne, a product that was 82 percent alcohol by volume. The cologne instantly ignited and burned the teenager badly. The victim alleged that Fabergé failed to warn of the cologne's flammability.[4] A woman taking birth-control pills was told by the maker, Ortho Pharmaceutical, that there could be side effects from use, "the most severe of which is abnormal blood-clotting." After several years of taking the pills, the woman suffered a stroke and then sued Ortho, arguing that the risk of a "stroke" had not been fully and adequately conveyed to her.[5] Those in favor of holding manufacturers liable in these cases argued that the firm is in the best position to understand the hazards posed by its products and warn of them; others contended that holding companies liable in all cases where a product user has not understood the warnings given will sharply increase the cost of the products in question, such that those consumers who use products safely will wind up subsidizing the careless.

Though the producer of a good may be responsible if the item is dangerous or defective, it seems unfair to insist that the producer is liable even when its commodity is misused by the consumer. A ladder that has been poorly constructed is its builder's problem, but a ladder placed on obviously uneven ground by the user should, most would say, be the user's problem. Consumer misconduct is a frequently invoked defense to product liability lawsuits, though, once again, this defense has been questioned in some cases. Suppose that Seller markets a car capable of going tremendous speeds. Seller can foresee that at least some buyers of its cars will drive them at the (dangerous) speeds of which they are capable. Should such "foreseeable misuses" of a product be Seller's problem as well?

JUSTICE AND STRICT PRODUCT LIABILITY

The general trend in consumer protection for product-related harms has been in the direction of strict product liability. One of the central moral and social questions posed by this trend is whether the move toward strict liability is justifiable. As we have seen, the imposition of strict producer liability is only one of several possible consumer policies. Arrayed along a spectrum, beginning with complete consumer liability (caveat emptor) at one extreme, we can move in the direction of decreasing consumer responsibility for the costs of accidents and injuries related to the goods available on the market. Imposing first negligence and then strict liability upon producers, the other end of the spectrum, represents a completely socialized form of accident care: Everyone injured in a product-related accident is simply compensated out of a general tax-supported fund. Moving along the spectrum in this way, then, has the effect of taking a cost that initially falls on particular consumers and *spreading that cost out*, by asking producers, or even society as a whole (in the socialized care case), to absorb the cost. The idea of spreading costs is, in fact, one of the principal justifications often advanced in support of strict producer liability. Let's examine the arguments for and against strict liability more closely.

Those who support strict product liability generally appeal to the good consequences that adoption of such a policy will likely have. To see what this means, imagine a company

---

✑🝏   Are Lethal Products Defective?

Some consumer goods have desirable social use even though they pose clear risks to the public. But what about products whose only use is one that has high social disvalue? One case confronting this issue concerns so-called Saturday Night Specials—cheap, small, short-barreled handguns, unusable for hunting or target shooting. Such weapons are used almost exclusively in the commision of crimes. In *Richardson v. Holland*, a Missouri court was asked to hold the manufacturer of one such gun liable for shooting injuries sustained by the plaintiff. The plaintiff argued that the manufacturers of cheap handguns know that the only probable use for their product is for improper and dangerous purposes. Unlike alcohol, automobiles, and other products that are often misused, Saturday Night Specials are designed and sold, knowing that the majority of uses will be improper. The court refused to accept this argument. A manufacturer can be held liable only for products that are "defective," and even when a product is inherently dangerous, placing such items into commerce does not mean that the maker should be liable for dangers that an average consumer would certainly recognize. The gun in this case was not defectively designed or built, the court reasoned, since it functioned just as intended: firing a bullet at the plaintiff. Should the makers of these handguns be liable for injuries that they cause?

741 S.W.2d 751 (1987).

that manufactures and sells explosives used in mining and construction. What are the costs of placing such items on the market? Obviously, one such cost is the expense incurred by the company in the process of manufacture: what it costs to buy the raw materials, to process and assemble the explosives, and so on. It also costs the company money to advertise and market its goods. Just as plainly, however, another cost of having explosives on the market is that they may injure those who use them. Because such costs would not otherwise appear on the ledger books of the company, economists call them *externalities*. The basic idea behind a policy of strict liability, say its defenders, is to make the explosives industry (in this case) cover its own costs or absorb its own externalities—to pay its own way in the world. Not only does this seem fair on its face, but it has good consequences as well. By holding the explosives business liable for injuries caused by its products, for example, we give the industry an incentive to make its goods as safe as possible. And strict product liability makes sense economically as well, since, with its knowledge and expertise, the industry can eliminate or avoid accident costs more cheaply (efficiently) than the consumer. Finally, strict liability affords an effective way of ensuring against the costs of accidents, as the industry can simply add the costs of covering injuries to the price of its goods, thus spreading out the costs among the large base of consumers, rather than leaving the burden concentrated on the few who are injured.

Those opposed to strict product liability challenge each of the foregoing arguments. Strict liability is poor economic policy, claim the critics, because it will generate more costs than its proponents acknowledge. Since they do not have to shoulder the responsibility and the costs of injuries, consumers will tend to be less careful, with the result that the number of accidents and court cases will rise steadily. Insurance premiums will increase. Consumers will be less mindful of product instructions and warnings and will have less incentive to use caution with the products they purchase. Critics also attack strict liability on the grounds of basic fairness. Even if it could be shown that strict product liability will lower the number of accidents or will spread costs more efficiently, why is it fair to use a corporate defendant in that way? If a company that makes explosives or chainsaws is as careful as

---

∽ RSI: The New Mass Tort?

Legal observers in 1995 claimed that the case of a thirty-year-old former high school secretary may be the forerunner of thousands of product liability lawsuits into the next century. Nancy Urbanski worked from 1989 to 1993 for a school district in Minnesota. She began suffering from "shooting pains" in her arms, was transferred to several jobs, and was eventually released. Claiming that she was unable to work, or even tie her children's shoes, Urbanski filed a lawsuit against Apple Computer and IBM Corp., alleging that she sustained repetitive stress injuries (RSIs) from typing on both IBM and Apple computers. According to the U.S. Bureau of Labor Statistics, RSI now accounts for 60 percent of all workplace illness and has cost more than $20 billion in worker's compensation settlements. IBM alone faced as many as 350 RSI lawsuits across the country by 1995. Urbanski alleged that the computer manufacturers failed to adequately test the design of their computers and failed to warn users of the dangers attendant to typing on a keyboard and the injuries that might result from years of use.

Source: *National Law Journal* 2/20/95.

possible in the design and construction of its wares, why is it nonetheless fair to force it to pay for harms to consumers? Sometimes bad things just happen to consumers that are not the manufacturer's fault.

THE READINGS

The readings for this chapter open with two case studies, each of which illustrates the use of the major theories of product liability for consumer injuries: negligence, strict liability, and breach of warranty. In the first case, the court considers and rejects Connie Daniell's contention that Ford Motor Company is liable for injuries she sustained after locking herself in the trunk of a Ford automobile. The second case deals with the facts surrounding the death of nine-year-old Marlo Banks. The boy, playing behind a counter at a local Boys Club, ate rat poison pellets which he mistook for candy. His parents subsequently sued the maker of the pellet—ICI Americas—as well as the exterminating company and the Boys Club for wrongful death. The jury awarded the parents $1 million in punitive damages against ICI, and the manufacturer appealed this judgment. In its argument, reprinted here, the state appellate court reversed the award for the parents, reasoning that the maker of the poison could not be held liable, because it had effectively complied with all applicable federal laws dealing with the labeling and sale of such products.

The selection by Manuel Velasquez steps back from the law to examine more generally how society can best respond to consumer product injuries and fairly determine the level of responsibility for those injuries borne by the businesses that produce consumer goods. Velasquez first considers and rejects a thoroughly free-market approach to the problem of product-related harms. He then weighs the pros and cons of several competing visions of producer responsibility: the "contract," "due care," and "social costs" views. Velasquez's aim is to clarify as much as possible the comparative merits of each approach. Velasquez's essay is followed by one by George Brenkert. Brenkert argues in support of strict producer liability, but he does so on grounds different from the standard appeals to economic efficiency and long-run benefit to society. Arguing that the standard reasons given for strict liability are inadequate, Brenkert insists that strict liability is the most just and fair policy of apportioning costs among consumers and producers, quite apart from whether it brings other good consequences in its wake. Brenkert endeavors to spell out the notion of *compensatory justice* as the guiding principle justifying continued adherence to the strict-liability position.

In the final reading for this chapter, law professor Roger Cramton outlines the challenges posed by the emergence of so-called mass exposure torts. Some of the most difficult moral and policy issues since the widespread imposition of strict liability are raised by society's efforts to handle tens of thousands of similar, product-related injuries by permitting manufacturers of tobacco, asbestos, IUDs, and breast implants to be sued by both actual and prospective victims in a single proceeding. Cramton examines the tension between the societal goals of such class-action lawsuits and the need for each individual victim to seek compensatory justice. Cramton believes that the current system for dealing with large-scale consumer injuries leaves many questions unanswered.

NOTES

1. See *BMW of North America v. Gore* 64 U.S.L.W. 4335 (1996).

2. See *Lieback v. McDonald's Restaurants, Jury Verdict Research,* #CV 932419.

3. See *Campbell v. General Motors*, 32 Cal.3d 112 (1982).

4. See *Moran v. Fabergé, Inc.*, 332 A.2d 11 (1975).

5. See *MacDonald v. Ortho Pharmaceutical Corp.*, 475 N.E.2d 65 (1985).

CASE STUDY *Daniell v. Ford Motor Co., Inc.*

581 F.Supp.728 (1984) Memorandum Opinion and Order

BALDOCK, District Judge.

In 1980, the plaintiff became locked inside the trunk of a 1973 Ford LTD automobile, where she remained for some nine days. Plaintiff now seeks to recover for psychological and physical injuries arising from that occurrence. She contends that the automobile had a design defect in that the trunk lock or latch did not have an internal release or opening mechanism. She also maintains that the manufacturer is liable based on a failure to warn of this condition. Plaintiff advances several theories for recovery: (1) strict products liability under § 402A of the Restatement 2d of Torts (1965), (2) negligence, and (3) breach of express warranty and implied warranties of merchantability and fitness for a particular purpose.

Three uncontroverted facts bar recovery under any of these theories. First, the plaintiff ended up in the trunk compartment of the automobile because she felt "overburdened" and was attempting to commit suicide. Deposition of Connie Daniell at 4–5 (May 25, 1983). Second, the purposes of an automobile trunk are to transport, stow and secure the automobile spare tire, luggage and other goods and to protect those items from elements of the weather. Third, the plaintiff never considered the possibility of exit from the inside of the trunk when the automobile was purchased. Deposition of Connie Daniell at 16 (May 25, 1983). Plaintiff has not set forth evidence indicating that these facts are controverted.

The overriding factor barring plaintiff's recovery is that she intentionally sought to end her life by crawling into an automobile trunk from which she could not escape. This is not a case where a person inadvertently became trapped inside an automobile trunk. The plaintiff was aware of the natural and probable consequences of her perilous conduct. Not only that, the plaintiff, at least initially, sought those dreadful consequences. Plaintiff, not the manufacturer of the vehicle, is responsible for this unfortunate occurrence.

Recovery under strict products liability and negligence will be discussed first because the concept of duty owed by the manufacturer to the consumer or user is the same under both theories in this case. As a general principle, a design defect is actionable only where the condition of the product is unreasonably dangerous to the user or consumer. Restatement 2d of Torts, § 402A (1965). Under strict products liability or negligence, a manufacturer has a duty to consider only those risks of injury which are foreseeable. A risk is not foreseeable by a manufacturer where a product is used in a manner which could not reasonably be anticipated by the manufacturer and that use is the cause of the plaintiff's injury. The plaintiff's injury would not be foreseeable by the manufacturer.

The purposes of an automobile trunk are to transport, stow and secure the automobile spare tire, luggage and other goods and to protect those items from elements of the weather. The design features of an automobile trunk make it well near impossible that an adult intentionally would enter the trunk and close the lid. The dimensions of a trunk, the height of its sill and its load floor and the efforts to first lower the trunk lid and then to engage its latch, are among the design features which encourage closing and latching the trunk lid while standing outside the vehicle. The court holds that the plaintiff's use of the trunk compartment as a means to attempt suicide was an unforeseeable use as a matter of law. Therefore, the manufacturer had no duty to design an internal release or opening mechanism that might have prevented this occurrence.

Nor did the manufacturer have a duty to warn the plaintiff of the danger of her conduct, given the plaintiff's unforeseeable use of the product. Another reason why the manufacturer had no duty to warn the plaintiff of the risk inherent in crawling into an automobile trunk and closing the trunk lid is because such a risk is obvious. There is no duty to warn of known dangers in strict products liability or tort. Moreover, the potential efficacy of any warning, given the plaintiff's use of the automobile trunk compartment for a deliberate suicide attempt, is questionable.

The court notes that the automobile trunk was not defective under these circumstances. The automobile trunk was not unreasonably dangerous within the contemplation of the ordinary consumer or user of such a trunk when used in the ordinary ways and for the ordinary purposes for which such a trunk is used.

Having held that the plaintiff's conception of the manufacturer's duty is in error, the court need not reach the issues of the effect of comparative negligence or other defenses such as assumption of the risk on the products liability claim. (In adopting comparative negligence, the New Mexico Supreme Court indicated that in strict products liability a plaintiff's "misconduct" would be a defense, but not a complete bar to recovery.) The court also does not reach the comparative negligence defense on the negligence claim.

Having considered the products liability and negligence claims, plaintiff's contract claims for breach of warranty are now analyzed. Plaintiff has come forward with no evidence of any express warranty regarding exit from the inside of the trunk. Summary judgment on the express warranty claim is appropriate.

Any implied warranty of merchantability in this case requires that the product must be fit for the ordinary purposes for which such goods are used. The implied warranty of merchantability does not require that the buyer must prove reliance on the skill and judgment of the manufacturer. Still, the usual and ordinary purpose of an automobile trunk is to transport and store goods, including the automobile's spare tire. Plaintiff's use of the trunk was highly extraordinary, and there is no evidence that that trunk was not fit for the ordinary purpose for which it was intended.

Lastly, plaintiff's claim for a breach of implied warranty of fitness for a particular purpose cannot withstand summary judgment because the plaintiff has admitted that, at the time she purchased the automobile neither she nor her husband gave any particular thought to the trunk mechanism. Plaintiff has admitted that she did not even think about getting out from inside of the trunk when purchasing the vehicle. Plaintiff did not rely on the seller's skill or judgment to select or furnish an automobile suitable for the unfortunate purpose for which the plaintiff used it.

WHEREFORE,

IT IS ORDERED that defendant's Motion for Summary Judgment is granted.

CASE STUDY   *ICI Americas, Inc. v. Banks et al.*

Court of Appeals of Georgia
440 S.E.2d 38 (1994)

ANDREWS, Judge.

. . . ICI manufactured a rat poison called Talon-G, which was registered by the Environmental Protection Agency (EPA). . . . As part of the [federal] packaging and labeling requirements, Talon-G was packaged in a container with EPA-approved labeling, which displayed warnings cautioning users that it should be kept out of reach of children; that it may be harmful or fatal if swallowed, and that it be stored in its original container in a location inaccessible to children. ICI sold Talon-G only to professional pest control operators. . . . [A] pest control company servicing the Boys Club placed the Talon-G in an unmarked, unlabeled container stored in an unlocked cabinet at the Boys Club. The poison was apparently found in the container at the Boys Club by the child, who consumed a quantity of it.

. . . There was evidence that the danger the rat poison would be misused by being consumed by children was foreseeable to ICI. . . . Other evidence showed that the danger could have been reduced, and the product made safer by the addition of ingredients which would cause humans, but not rats, to reject it as bitter tasting, or vomit after ingesting it.

Rat poison is a useful rodent control product. . . . Because of its poisonous character, it may also harm or kill human beings who eat it. The poisonous character of rat poison is an inherent characteristic necessary to the usefulness of the product as a rat killer. The product is not defectively or negligently designed simply because it is poisonous, nor solely because it may be possible for the manufacturer to make the product safer by reducing the danger resulting from its poisonous character. . . . Strict liability [for a defective product] is not imposed under the [Georgia] statute merely because a product may be dangerous. Many products can not be made completely safe for use and some can not be made safe at all. However, such products may be useful and desirable. If they are properly prepared, manufactured, packaged and accompanied with adequate warnings and instructions, they can not be said to be defective. To hold otherwise would discourage the marketing of many products because some danger attended their use. We find nothing in [Georgia law] that makes a manufacturer strictly liable for such products absent a defect. . . . "In a products liability case predicated on negligence, the duty imposed is the traditional one of reasonable care. . . . Georgia law does not require a manufacturer to occupy the status of an insurer with respect to product design. . . . The manufacturer is under no obligation to make a [product] accident proof or foolproof, or even more safe. . . ."

"Generally, [i]f a manufacturer does everything necessary to make the [product] function properly for the purpose for which it is designed, if the [product] is without any latent defect, and if its functioning creates no danger or peril that is not known to the user, then the manufacturer has satisfied the law's demands. . . .

The manufacturer is generally not liable for injury resulting from an abnormal use of the product, unless the particular unintended use was foreseeably probable. . . . [But] the manufacturer of a product which, to its actual or constructive knowledge, involves danger to users has a duty to give warning of such danger. . . ." "A duty to warn of danger in the use of a product extends only to the use of the product in the manner reasonably contemplated and anticipated by the manufacturer. . . ."

From the foregoing principles it may be gathered that, where a product in its normal functioning, as designed, creates a latent danger, arising from a foreseeably probable unintended use, and the user or injured party could not from an objective point of view appreciate the latent danger, the manufacturer may be held liable on a claim of defective or negligent design for failing to adequately warn of the foreseeable danger. . . .

. . . [U]nder Georgia law, whether ICI may be liable under the negligence and strict liability claims made by plaintiffs depends on whether it gave adequate warning of the foreseeable danger. Evidence of a foreseeable latent danger, combined with other evidence that ICI could have made the product safer by reducing the danger of misuse by children, was not alone sufficient to support a finding that the product was defectively or negligently designed. There is no requirement imposed by statute or common law that would support the claim that Talon-G was defectively or negligently designed solely because ICI did not make the product safer, or attempt to incorporate the safety features [described by plaintiff's experts]. There is no evidence that the product, as designed, failed to comply with any specific federal or state standard. "To impose upon a manufacturer the duty of producing an accident-proof product may be a desirable aim, but no such obligation has been—or, in our view, may be—imposed by judicial decision."

. . . Labeling of rodenticides is governed by [federal law]. . . . If a pesticide manufacturer places EPA-approved warnings on the label and packaging of its product, its duty to warn is satisfied, and the adequate warning issue ends. . . .

[Judgment for the plaintiff reversed.]

POPE, Chief Judge, Dissenting.

Plaintiffs' nine-year-old son, Marlo, discovered some rat poison pellets in a container behind a counter at a Boys Club and thought they were candy. The poison, an anticoagulant that kills by thinning the blood and breaking down the walls of the blood vessels, was slow acting by design. Marlo showed no symptoms until four days later, when his nose began to bleed. After several more days, Marlo's condition continued to worsen and he was put in the hospital for blood transfusions. By the time the doctors discovered that Marlo had ingested rat poison, it was too late for the antidote to work.

Although it was foreseeable that the rat poison would be consumed by children who mistook it for candy, ICI failed to add an emetic or an aversive agent to the product. Plaintiffs produced expert testimony that an emetic will cause any human who ingests the poison to immediately vomit, thereby expelling the poison, but will not have the same effect on rats because they do not have a vomit reflex. They also submitted expert evidence that the aversive agent Bitrex would make the poison taste bad to children but would not keep rats from eating it; that Bitrex was in use in a variety of products as early as the late 1970s; and that there was no reason ICI could not have begun testing its use in rat poison at that time. . . . [A] jury could find that ICI's failure to add an emetic or aversive agent was unreasonable.

The majority nonetheless holds that ICI cannot be liable because its product had an adequate warning label . . . [based on an earlier case]. . . . *Center Chemical* holds that a manufacturer should not be liable for producing a necessarily dangerous but useful product as long as the product is packaged with an adequate warning label; it does not hold that a manufacturer who can take reasonable steps to make its dangerous product safer can avoid liability by instead placing a warning label on its package. . . .

[The dissent concludes that the jury verdict on the grounds of strict liability and negligence should have been upheld.]

The Ethics of Consumer Production and Marketing

Manuel Velasquez

Introduction

In April 1988, staff members of the Food and Drug Administration announced the results of a study that, they claimed, showed that the drug Accu-

From *Business Ethics: Concepts and Cases,* Third Edition, by Manual Velasquez. Copyright © 1982. Prentice-Hall, Inc. Reprinted by permission of the publisher.

tane, a treatment for acne produced by Hoffman–LaRoche, Inc., was being widely misused.[1] High doses of Accutane, they pointed out, can cause severe damage to fetuses and pregnant women, including birth defects and miscarriages. Yet their study, they claimed, showed that 52 percent of the women to whom Accutane had been administered had been pregnant at some point during their treatment. They estimated the drug was responsible for about 1,000 birth defects nationwide, 1,000 miscarriages, and thousands of voluntary abortions. Hoffman–LaRoche charged that the study was "invalid" but agreed to impose future "restrictions" on uses of the drug.[2]

In 1985, Ethel Smith flicked on a Bic Corporation lighter to light her cigarette. It exploded in her hands, killing her and severely burning her husband. Earlier, Cynthia Littlejohn suffered severe burns about her torso that required seven painful skin grafts when a Bic lighter in her pocket spontaneously ignited and enveloped her in flames.[3] The company later confessed that its own tests showed that 1.2 percent of its lighters were faulty. Experts claimed that the defects could have been corrected for "a couple of pennies a lighter." Some 200 people a year, half of them children, are killed in lighter-related injuries.[4]

In March 1984, Christa Berlin was hospitalized with abdominal pain and fever. Twenty days later, she was dead. Her death was attributed to a pelvic abscess caused by the "Dalkon Shield," a birth control device inserted into her uterus that was produced by A. H. Robins Company, a pharmaceutical manufacturer.[5] As a result of using the birth control device, dozens of other women died similar deaths, thousands suffered the life-threatening infections known as pelvic inflammatory disease, some 10,000 suffered miscarriages, and hundreds gave birth prematurely to babies with congenital defects including blindness, cerebral palsy, and mental retardation.[6] Yet as early as 1973 the company had been aware of the deaths of six women associated with infected abortions.[7] A. H. Robins, however, continued to aggressively market the product until over 2.2 million women in the United States and 1 million women abroad were wearing them.

By 1986, all-terrain vehicles (ATVs) introduced in 1982 by Honda (with about 60 percent of the market), Kawasaki, Suzuki, and Yamaha had killed well over 600 people and injured 275,000, leaving many crippled for life. About half of the casualties inflicted by the three-wheeled motorcyles involved children.[8] Although concerned consumer advocates claimed that the machines incorporated design flaws that rendered them inherently unstable, that they were inappropriate for marketing to children, and that the companies should recall the risky three-wheelers, the companies continued to market the machines and refused to hear of a recall.

Americans are exposed daily to astonishingly high levels of risk from the use of consumer products. Each year thirty-four million people are injured in accidents involving consumer items; of these, 28,000 are killed and perhaps 100,000 are permanently disabled.[9] Product-related accidents are the major cause of death for people between the ages of one and thirty-six, outstripping the deaths caused by cancer or heart disease. The total cost of these injuries is estimated to be about $12 billion per year.[10]

But product injuries make up only one category of costs imposed on unwary consumers. Consumers must also bear the costs of deceptive selling practices, of shoddy product construction, of products that immediately break down, and of warranties that are not honored. For example, a few years ago, the engine of Martha and George Rose's Chevrolet station wagon began missing and white smoke poured out of the tailpipe as she drove it six miles to work.[11] Two non-Chevrolet mechanics who then checked the car later testified that the radiator and cooling system were "in satisfactory condition," that the radiator "was not boiling over," and that the temperature light on the dashboard "was not burning." Upon taking the engine apart, a mechanic found that a hairline crack in the engine block had allowed water to enter the cylinder head, meaning that the car would need an expensive new engine. The engine was still under a "5-year or 50,000-mile" warranty, so the Roses thought the Chevrolet division of General Motors would bear the large costs of repairing what they concluded was an inherently defective engine block. However, when a Chevrolet service manager examined the dismantled car, he insisted that the problem was that the radiator thermostat had stuck shut so no coolant had reached the engine. Since the thermostat was only under a "12-month or 12,000-mile" warranty that had by then expired, and since, the Chevrolet manager claimed, the faulty thermostat had caused the engine to overheat and the engine block to crack, Chevrolet had no responsibility under the warranty. Moreover, the car had been torn down and worked on by unauthorized mechanics. Although the Roses pointed out that the other mechanics had found no evidence of overheating and that no Chevrolet mechanic had suggested replacing the thermostat at any of their regular maintenance servicings, the General Motors field manager and his superiors, both in New Orleans and in Detroit, refused to honor the warranty. Without the engine, the car that General Motors had sold them for $5000 was now worth only $600. Because they could not afford an attorney for a trial they might lose, the Roses could not file suit against General Motors.

The sales practices of Pacific Bell Telephone Company, which serves California telephone customers, provide another illustration of the difficulties that face consumers. On April 23, 1986, the Pacific Utilities Commission of California released a report stating that Pacific Bell service representatives were duping new telephone customers into buying expensive optional features by quoting a fee for new telephone service that included the expensive features, but without telling the new customer that the features were optional, that the consumer was being charged extra for them, and that basic service was available at a much cheaper monthly fee. A sales representative of the telephone company described the way that she approached a new customer calling to get a new telephone hook-up:

> I'm going to tell you that "You will get unlimited local calling, Touchtone service, our four, custom-calling services and a 20 percent discount in the Pacific Bell service area; the central office fee to turn the services on is $37.50 and I have all of these things available and it's only $22.20 a month." Most customers will say, "That's fine." It really isn't a bad deal, but how many people know they don't have to buy all those things, that they can get basic service for $9.95? The company says, "People should be intelligent enough to ask; why should it be PacBell's job to tell them?" People who don't speak English, well, they end up with those services. Sometimes they call back and say, "What is this? I didn't want this." [Pacific Telephone sales representative][12]

According to the Utilities Commission report, 65 percent of Pacific Bell's phone order centers did not quote the basic $9.95 monthly rate that allowed unlimited local calls, but instead quoted only a "standard price" which included extra features (such as a device that tells a customer another call is waiting, automatic forwarding of a call to an-

other phone, equipment for three-way or conference calls, codes that automatically dial a preset number, and extra charges for call discounts at certain times or certain areas) that cost as much as $27.20 a month. The sales representatives pleaded that the company's marketing managers imposed stiff sales quotas on them and would put them on probation if they failed to meet the quotas. In one city, for example, they were expected to sell $197 to $238 worth of services each hour they spent on the telephone with customers. A Utilities Commission staff member remarked that "Marketing management appears to be more concerned about generating revenues than they are about ethical and fair treatment of customers."[13]

Consumers are also bombarded daily by an endless series of advertisements urging them to buy certain products. Although sometimes defended as sources of information, advertisements are also criticized on the grounds that they rarely do more than give the barest indications of the basic function a product is meant to serve and sometimes misrepresent and exaggerate its virtues. Economists argue that advertising expenditures are a waste of resources, while sociologists bemoan the cultural effects of advertising.[14]

This [reading] examines various ethical issues raised by product quality and advertising. The first few sections discuss various approaches to consumer issues and the last sections deal with consumer advertising. We will begin with a focus on what is perhaps the most urgent issue: consumer product injuries and the responsibilities of manufacturers.

Markets and Consumer Protection

Consumer analysts point out that in 1986 alone there were more than 400,000 injuries requiring hospital treatment inflicted on youngsters and adults using toys, nursery equipment, and playground equipment; more than 292,000 people were mangled using home workshop equipment and over 200 of these were killed; 1,425,000 people needed emergency treatment for injuries involving home furnishings and over 1,000 of these injuries resulted in death; 2,722,000 more people required treatment for injuries involving home construction materials that killed at least 1,500 of them.[15] Injuries from auto-related accidents average 70,000 each week; deaths average 1,000 per week; financial losses are estimated at $30 million per day.

Many people believe that consumers will be automatically protected from injury by the operations of free and competitive markets, and that neither governments nor businesspeople have to take special steps to deal with these issues. As [some argue], free markets promote an allocation, use, and distribution of goods that is, in a certain sense, just, respectful of rights, and efficiently productive of maximum utility for those who participate in the market. Moreover, in such markets, the consumer is said to be "sovereign." When consumers want and will willingly pay for something, sellers have an incentive to cater to their wishes. If sellers do not provide what consumers want, then sellers will suffer losses. But when sellers provide what consumers want, they will profit. As the author of a leading textbook on economics writes, "Consumers direct by their innate or learned tastes, as expressed in their dollar votes, the ultimate uses to which society's resources are channeled."[16]

In the "market" approach to consumer protection, consumer safety is seen as a good that is most efficiently provided through the mechanism of the free market whereby sellers must respond to consumer demands. If consumers want products to be safer, then they will indicate this preference in markets by willingly paying more for safer products and by showing a preference for manufacturers of safe products while turning down the goods of manufacturers of unsafe products. Producers will have to respond to this demand by building more safety into their products or they risk losing customers to competitors who cater to the preferences of consumers. Thus, the market ensures that producers respond adequately to consumers' desires for safety. On the other hand, if consumers do not place a high value on safety and demonstrate neither a willingness to pay more for safety nor a preference for safer products, then it is wrong to push increased levels of safety down their throats through government regulations that force producers to build more safety into their products than consumers demand. Such government interference . . . distorts markets, making them unjust, disrespectful of rights, and inefficient. It is just as wrong for businesspeople to decide on their own that consumers should have more protection than they are demanding, and to force on them costly safety devices that they would not buy on their own. Only consumers can say what value they place on safety, and they should be allowed to register their preferences through their free choices in markets and not be coerced by businesses or governments into paying for safety levels they may not want.

For example, an appliance selling for $100 may indicate that it will overheat if it is used for more than an hour and a half, while one selling for $400 may indicate that it can be run safely all day and night continuously. Some buyers will prefer the cheaper model, willingly trading the somewhat higher risk for the $300 cut in price, while others will prefer the more expensive one. If government regulations forced all appliance makers to make only the safer model, or if manufacturers voluntarily decided to make only the safer model, then consumers who do not feel that the increase in safety is worth $300 extra to them will be out of luck. If they cannot do without the appliance, they will be forced to pay the extra $300 even if they would have preferred spending it on something else that is more valuable to them. They are thus unjustly forced to pay money for something they do not want, and their resources are inefficiently wasted on something that produces little utility for anyone.

Critics to this market approach respond, however, that the benefits of free markets obtain with certainty only when markets have the seven characteristics that define them: (1) there are numerous buyer and sellers, (2) everyone can freely enter and exit the market, (3) everyone has full and perfect information, (4) all goods in the market are exactly similar, (5) there are no external costs, (6) all buyers and sellers are rational utility maximizers, and (7) the market is unregulated. Critics of the market approach to consumer issues argue that these characteristics are absent in consumer markets, focusing especially on characteristics (3) and (6).

Markets are efficient, critics point out, only if condition (3) obtains—that is, only if participants have full and perfect information about the goods they are buying. But obviously, consumers are frequently not well informed about the products they buy simply because the sophisticated consumer products on contemporary market shelves are too complex for anyone but an expert to be knowledgeable about them. Not surprisingly, manufacturers, who are knowledgeable about their products, might not voluntarily provide information about the safety levels or defective characteristics of their products to consumers. And, since gathering information is expensive, a consumer may not have the resources to acquire the information on his or her own by, for example, testing several competing brands to determine which provides the most safety for the cost.

In theory it would be possible for consumers who want information to turn to organizations such as the Consumers Union that make a business of acquiring and selling product information. That is, market mechanisms should create a market in consumer information if that is what consumers want. But for two reasons related to the nature of information, it is difficult for such organizations to cover their costs by selling information to consumers. First, as several economists have pointed out, once information is provided to one person who pays for it, it is easily leaked to many others who do not pay, especially in this age of photocopiers.[17] Since people know they can become "free riders" and acquire the information compiled by others without paying for it themselves, the number of people who willingly pay for the information is too small to allow the organization to cover its costs. Second, consumers are often unwilling to pay for information because they do not know what its value to them will be until after they get it and then they no longer need to pay for it since it is already in their possession. For example, a consumer may pay for the information contained in a research report and then find that he or she already knew what was in the report, or that it is about products other than those he or she wants to buy, or that it is irrelevant information about those products. Since consumers cannot know in advance precisely what they are buying when they buy information, they are unwilling to pay the costs organizations must charge to gather the information.[18] Markets alone, then, are not able to support organizations that can provide consumers with the information they need. Instead, such organizations must rely on charitable contributions or on government grants.

A second criticism of the argument that free markets can deal with all consumer issues takes aim at characteristic (6) of free markets: the assumption that the consumer is a "rational utility maximizer."

As one author put it, the consumer assumed by such arguments is "a budget-minded, rational individual, relentlessly pushing toward maximizing his satisfaction . . . [who is able] to think well ahead, to "wait," to consider. The consumer defined by the theory watches every penny."[19] More precisely, the "rational utility maximizer" that the consumer is assumed to be, is a person who has a well-defined and consistent set of preferences, and who is certain how his or her choices will affect those preferences.

Unfortunately, virtually all consumer choices are based on probability estimates we make concerning the chances that the products we buy will function as we think they will. And all the research available shows that we become highly inept, irrational, and inconsistent when we make choices based on probability estimates.

First, as is obvious to any observer, few of us are good at estimating probabilities. We typically underestimate the risks of personal life-threatening activities—such as driving, smoking, eating fried foods—and of being injured by the products we use, and we overestimate the probabilities of unlikely but memorable events such as tornados or attacks by grizzly bears in national parks.[20] Studies have shown that our probability judgments go astray for a number of reasons, including the following:

1. Prior probabilities are ignored when new information becomes available, even if the new information is irrelevant.
2. Emphasis on "causation" results in the underweighting of evidence that is relevant to probability but is not perceived as "causal."
3. Generalizations are made on the basis of small sample findings.
4. Belief is placed in a self-correcting but nonexistent "law of averages."
5. People believe that they exert control over purely chance events.[21]

Second, as a number of researchers have shown, people are irrational and inconsistent when weighing choices based on probability estimates of future costs or payoffs. For example, one set of researchers found that when people are asked to rank probable payoffs, they inconsistently will rank one payoff as being *both* better and worse than another. Another investigator found that when people were asked which of two probable payoffs they preferred, they would often say that they would pay *more* for the payoff that they *least* preferred. Yet another set of studies found that in many cases, a majority of persons would prefer one probable payoff to another in one context, but reversed their preferences in a different context although the probable payoffs were identical in both contexts.[22]

On balance, then, it does not appear that market forces by themselves can deal with all consumer concerns for safety and freedom from risk. Market failures, characterized by inadequate consumer information and by irrationality in the choices of consumers, undercut arguments that try to show that markets alone can provide adequate consumer protection. Instead, consumers must be protected through the legal structures of government and through the voluntary initiatives of responsible businesspeople. We will turn, then, to examining several views about the responsibilities of businesses toward consumers, views that have formed the basis of many of our consumer laws and of increased calls for greater acceptance of responsibility for consumer protection on the part of business.

It is clear, of course, that part of the responsibility for consumer injuries must rest on consumers themselves. Individuals are often careless in their use of products. "Do-it-yourselfers" use power saws without guards attached or inflammable liquids near open flames. People often use tools and instruments that they do not have the skill, the knowledge, or the experience to handle.

But injuries also arise from flaws in product design, in the materials out of which products are made, or in the processes used to construct products. Insofar as manufacturing defects are the source of product-related injuries, consumer advocates claim, the duty of minimizing injuries should lie with the manufacturer. The producer is in the best position to know the hazards raised by a certain product and to eliminate the hazards at the point of manufacture. In addition, the producer's expertise makes the producer knowledgeable about the safest materials and manufacturing methods and enables him to build adequate safeguards into the design of the product. Finally, because the producer is intimately acquainted with the workings of the product, he or she can best inform the con-

sumer on the safest way to use the product and on what precautions to be taken.

Where, then, does the consumer's duties to protect his or her own interests end, and where does the manufacturer's duty to protect consumers' interests begin? Three different theories on the ethical duties of manufacturers have been developed, each one of which strikes a different balance between the consumer's duty to himself or herself and the manufacturer's duty to the consumer: the contract view, the "due care" view, and the social costs view. The contract view would place the greater responsibility on the consumer, while the "due care" and social costs views place the larger measure of responsibility on the manufacturer. We will examine each of these views.

The Contract View of Business's Duties to Consumers

According to the contract view of the business firm's duties to its customers, the relationship between a business firm and its customers is essentially a contractual relationship, and the firm's moral duties to the customer are those created by this contractual relationship.[23] When a consumer buys a product, this view holds, the consumer voluntarily enters into a "sales contract" with the business firm. The firm freely and knowingly agrees to give the consumer a product with certain characteristics and the consumer in turn freely and knowingly agrees to pay a certain sum of money to the firm for the product. In virtue of having voluntarily entered this agreement, the firm then has a duty to provide a product with those characteristics, and the consumer has a correlative right to get a product with those characteristics.

The contract theory of the business firm's duties to its customers rests on the view that a contract is a free agreement that imposes on the parties the basic duty of complying with the terms of the agreement. [There are at least] two justifications Kant provided for the view: A person has a duty to do what he or she contracts to do, because failure to adhere to the terms of a contract is a practice (1) that cannot be universalized, and (2) that treats the other person as a means and not as an end.[24] Rawls's theory also provides a justification for the view, but one that is based on the idea that our freedom is expanded by the recognition of contractual rights and duties: An enforced system of social rules that requires people to do what they contract to do will provide them with the assurance that contracts will be kept. Only if they have such assurance will people feel able to trust each other's word, and on that basis to secure the benefits of the institution of contracts.[25]

[T]raditional moralists have argued that the act of entering into a contract is subject to several secondary moral constraints:

1. Both of the parties to the contract must have full knowledge of the nature of the agreement they are entering.
2. Neither party to a contract must intentionally misrepresent the facts of the contractual situation to the other party.
3. Neither party to a contract must be forced to enter the contract under duress or undue influence.

These secondary constraints can be justified by the same sorts of arguments that Kant and Rawls use to justify the basic duty to perform one's contracts. Kant, for example, easily shows that misrepresentation in the making of a contract cannot be universalized, and Rawls argues that if misrepresentation were not prohibited, fear of deception would make members of a society feel less free to enter contracts. But these secondary constraints can also be justified on the grounds that a contract cannot exist unless these constraints are fulfilled. For a contract is essentially a *free agreement* struck between two parties. Since an agreement cannot exist unless both parties know what they are agreeing to, contracts require full knowledge and the absence of misrepresentation. And since freedom implies the absence of coercion, contracts must be made without duress or undue influence.

The contractual theory of business's duties to consumers, then, claims that a business has four main moral duties: The basic duty of (1) complying with the terms of the sales contract, and the secondary duties of (2) disclosing the nature of the product, (3) avoiding misrepresentation, and (4) avoiding the use of duress and undue influence. By acting in accordance with these duties, a business respects the right of consumers to be treated as free and equal persons, that is, in accordance with their right to be treated only as they have freely consented to be treated.

The Duty to Comply

The most basic moral duty that a business firm owes its customers, according to the contract view, is the duty to provide consumers with a product that lives up to those claims that the firm expressly made about the product, which led the customer to enter the contract freely, and which formed the customer's understanding concerning what he or she was agreeing to buy. In the early 1970s, for example, Winthrop Laboratories marketed a painkiller that the firm advertised as "nonaddictive." Subsequently, a patient using the painkiller became addicted to it and shortly died from an overdose. A court in 1974 found Winthrop Laboratories liable for the patient's death because, although it had expressly stated that the drug was nonaddictive, Winthrop Laboratories had failed to live up to its duty to comply with this express contractual claim.[26]

As the above example suggests, our legal system has incorporated the moral view that firms have a duty to live up to the express claims they make about their products. The Uniform Commercial Code, for example, states in Section 2-314:

> Any affirmation of fact or promise made by the seller to the buyer that related to the goods and becomes part of the basis of the bargain creates an express warranty that the goods shall conform to the affirmation or promise.

In addition to the duties that result from the *express* claim a seller makes about the product, the contract view also holds that the seller has a duty to carry through on any *implied* claims he or she knowingly makes about the product. The seller, for example, has the moral duty to provide a product that can be used safely for the ordinary and special purposes for which the customer, relying on the seller's judgment, has been led to believe it can be used. The seller is morally bound to do whatever he or she knows the buyer understood the seller was promising, since at the point of sale sellers should have corrected any misunderstandings they were aware of.[27]

This idea of an "implied agreement" has also been incorporated into the law. Section 2-315 of the Uniform Commercial Code, for example, reads:

> Where the seller at the time of contracting has reason to know any particular purpose for which the goods are required and that the buyer is relying on the seller's skill or judgment to select or furnish suitable goods, there is . . . an implied warranty that the goods shall be fit for such purpose.

The express or implied claims that a seller might make about the qualities possessed by the product range over a variety of areas and are affected by a number of factors. Frederick Sturdivant classifies these areas in terms of four variables: "The definition of product quality used here is: the degree to which product performance meets predetermined expectation with respect to (1) reliability, (2) service life, (3) maintainability, and (4) safety."[28]

RELIABILITY Claims of reliability refer to the probability that a product will function as the consumer is led to expect that it will function. If a product incorporates a number of interdependent components, then the probability that it will function properly is equal to the result of multiplying together each component's probability of proper functioning.[29] As the number of components in a product multiplies, therefore, the manufacturer has a corresponding duty to ensure that each component functions in such a manner that the total product is as reliable as he or she implicitly or expressly claims it will be. This is especially the case when malfunction poses health or safety hazards. The U.S. Consumer Product Safety Commission lists hundreds of examples of hazards from product malfunctions in its yearly report.[30]

SERVICE LIFE Claims concerning the life of a product refer to the period of time during which the product will function as effectively as the consumer is led to expect it to function. Generally, the consumer implicitly understands that service life will depend on the amount of wear and tear to which one subjects the product. In addition, consumers also base some of their expectations of

service life on the explicit guarantees the manufacturer attaches to the product.

A more subtle factor that influences service life is the factor of obsolescence.[31] Technological advances may render some products obsolete when a new product appears that carries out the same functions more efficiently. Or purely stylistic changes may make last year's product appear dated and less desirable. The contract view implies that a seller who knows that a certain product will become obsolete has a duty to correct any mistaken beliefs he or she knows buyers will form concerning the service life they may expect from the product.

MAINTAINABILITY Claims of maintainability are claims concerning the ease with which the product can be repaired and kept in operating condition. Claims of maintainability are often made in the form of an express warranty. Whirlpool Corporation, for example, appended this express warranty on one of its products:

> During your first year of ownership, all parts of the appliance (except the light bulbs) that we find are defective in materials or workmanship will be repaired or replaced by Whirlpool free of charge, and we will pay all labor charges. During the second year, we will continue to assume the same responsibility as stated above except you pay any labor charges.[32]

But sellers often also imply that a product may be easily repaired even after the expiration date of an express warranty. In fact, however, product repairs may be costly, or even impossible, due to the unavailability of parts.

PRODUCT SAFETY Implied and express claims of product safety refer to the degree of risk associated with using a product. Since the use of virtually any product involves some degree of risk, questions of safety are essentially questions of *acceptable known levels* of risk. That is, a product is safe if its attendant risks are known and judged to be "acceptable" or "reasonable" by the *buyer* in view of the benefits the buyer expects to derive from using the product. This implies that the seller complies with his or her part of a free agreement if the seller provides a product that involves only those risks he or she says it involves, and the buyer purchases it with that understanding. The National Commission on Product Safety, for example, characterized "reasonable risk" in these terms:

> Risks of bodily harm to users are not unreasonable when consumers understand that risks exist, can appraise their probability and severity, know how to cope with them, and voluntarily accept them to get benefits they could not obtain in less risky ways. When there is a risk of this character, consumers have reasonable opportunity to protect themselves; and public authorities should hesitate to substitute their value judgments about the desirability of the risk for those of the consumers who choose to incur it. But preventable risk is not reasonable (a) when consumers do not know that it exists; or (b) when, though aware of it, consumers are unable to estimate its frequency and severity; or (c) when consumers do not know how to cope with it, and hence are likely to incur harm unnecessarily; or (d) when risk is unnecessary in that it could be reduced or eliminated at a cost in money or in the performance of the product that consumers would willingly incur if they knew the facts and were given the choice.[33]

Thus the seller of a product (according to the contractual theory) has a moral duty to provide a product whose use involves *no greater risks* than those the seller *expressly* communicates to the buyer or those the seller *implicitly* communicates by the implicit claims made when marketing the product for a use whose normal risk level is well known. If the label on a bottle, for example, indicates only that the contents are highly toxic ("Danger: Poison"), the product should not include additional risks from flammability. Or, if a firm makes and sells skis, use of the skis should not embody any unexpected additional risks other than the well-known risks which attend skiing (it should not, for example, involve the added possibility of being pierced by splinters should the skis fracture). In short, the seller has a duty to provide a product with a level of risk which is no higher than he or she expressly or implicitly claims it to be, and which the consumer freely and knowingly contracts to assume.

The Duty of Disclosure

An agreement cannot bind unless both parties to the agreement know what they are doing and freely choose to do it. This implies that the seller who intends to enter a contract with a customer has a duty to disclose exactly what the customer is buying and what the terms of the sale are. At a minimum, this means the seller has a duty to inform the buyer of any facts about the product that would affect the customer's decision to purchase the product. For example, if the product the consumer is buying possesses a defect that poses a risk to the user's health or safety, the consumer should be so informed. Some have argued that sellers should also disclose a product's components or ingredients, its performance characteristics, costs of operation, product ratings, and any other applicable standards.[34]

Behind the claim that entry into a sales contract requires full disclosure is the idea that an agreement is free only to the extent that one knows what alternatives are available: Freedom depends on knowledge. The more the buyer knows about the various products available on the market and the more comparisons the buyer is able to make among them, the more one can say that the buyer's agreement is voluntary.[35]

The view that sellers should provide a great deal of information for buyers, however, has been criticized on the grounds that information is costly and therefore should itself be treated as a product for which the consumer should either pay or do without. In short, consumers should freely contract to purchase information as they freely contract to purchase goods, and producers should not have to provide it for them.[36] The problem with the criticism is that the information on which a person bases his or her decision to enter a contract is a rather different kind of entity from the product exchanged through the contract. Since a contract must be entered into freely, and since free choice depends on knowledge, contractual transactions must be based on an open exchange of information. If consumers had to bargain for such information, the resulting contract would hardly be free.

The Duty Not to Misrepresent

Misrepresentation, even more than the failure to disclose information, renders freedom of choice impossible. That is, misrepresentation is coercive: The person who is intentionally misled acts as the deceiver wants the person to act and not as the person would freely have chosen to act if he or she had known the truth. Since free choice is an essential ingredient of a binding contract, intentionally misrepresenting the nature of a commodity is wrong.

A seller misrepresents a commodity when he or she represents it in a way deliberately intended to deceive the buyer into thinking something about the product that the seller knows is false. The deception may be created by a verbal lie, as when a used model is described as "new," or it may be created by a gesture, as when an unmarked used model is displayed together with several new models. That is, the deliberate intent to misrepresent by false implication is as wrong as the explicit lie.

The varieties of misrepresentation seem to be limited only by the ingenuity of the greed that creates them.[37] A manufacturer may give a product a name that the manufacturer knows consumers will confuse with the brand-name of a higher-quality competing product; the manufacturer may write "wool" or "silk" on material made wholly or partly of cotton; the manufacturer may mark a fictitious "regular price" on an article that is always sold at a much lower "sale" price; a business may advertise an unusually low price for an object which the business actually intends to sell at a much higher price once the consumer is lured into the store; a store may advertise an object at an unusually low price, intending to "bait and switch" the unwary buyer over to a more expensive product; a producer may solicit paid "testimonials" from professionals who have never really used the product. We shall return to some of these issues below when we discuss advertising.

The Duty Not to Coerce

People often act irrationally when under the influence of fear or emotional stress. When a seller takes advantage of a buyer's fear or emotional stress to extract consent to an agreement that the buyer would not make if the buyer were thinking rationally, the seller is using duress or undue influence to coerce. An unscrupulous funeral director, for example, may skillfully induce guilt-ridden and grief-stricken survivors to invest in funeral services they cannot afford. Since entry into a contract re-

quires *freely* given consent, the seller has a duty to refrain from exploiting emotional states that may induce the buyer to act irrationally against his or her own best interests. For similar reasons, the seller also has the duty not to take advantage of gullibility, immaturity, ignorance, or any other factors that reduce or eliminate the buyer's ability to make free rational choices.

Problems with the Contractual Theory

The main objections to the contract theory focus on the unreality of the assumptions on which the theory is based. First, critics argue, the theory unrealistically assumes that manufacturers make direct agreements with consumers. Nothing could be further from the truth. Normally, a series of wholesalers and retailers stand between the manufacturer and the ultimate consumer. The manufacturer sells the product to the wholesaler, who sells it to the retailer, who finally sells it to the consumer. The manufacturer never enters into any direct contract with the consumer. How then can one say that manufacturers have contractual duties to the consumer?

Advocates of the contract view of manufacturers' duties have tried to respond to this criticism by arguing that manufacturers enter into "indirect" agreements with consumers. Manufacturers promote their products through their own advertising campaigns. These advertisements supply the promises that lead people to purchase products from retailers who merely function as "conduits" for the manufacturer's product. Consequently, through these advertisements, the manufacturer forges an indirect contractual relationship not only with the immediate retailers who purchase the manufacturer's product but also with the ultimate consumers of the product. The most famous application of this doctrine of broadened indirect contractual relationships is to be found in a 1960 court opinion, *Henningsen v. Bloomfield Motors.*[38] Mrs. Henningsen was driving a new Plymouth when it suddenly gave off a loud cracking noise. The steering wheel spun out of her hands, the car lurched to the right and crashed into a brick wall. Mrs. Henningsen sued the manufacturer, Chrysler Corporation. The court opinion read:

> Under modern conditions the ordinary layman, on responding to the importuning of

colorful advertising, has neither the opportunity nor the capacity to inspect or to determine the fitness of an automobile for use; he must rely on the manufacturer who has control of its construction, and to some degree on the dealer who, to the limited extent called for by the manufacturer's instructions, inspects and services it before delivery. In such a marketing milieu his remedies and those of persons who properly claim through him should not depend "upon the intricacies of the law of sales. The obligation of the manufacturer should not be based alone on privity of contract [that is, on a direct contractual relationship]. It should rest, as was once said, upon 'the demands of social justice'." *Mazetti* v. *Armous & Co. (1913).* "If privity of contract is required," then, under the circumstances of modern merchandising, "privity of contract exists in the consciousness and understanding of all right-thinking persons . . ." Accordingly, we hold that under modern marketing conditions, when a manufacturer puts a new automobile in the stream of trade and promotes its purchase by the public, an implied warranty that it is reasonably suitable for use as such accompanies it into the hands of the ultimate purchaser. Absence of agency between the manufacturer and the dealer who makes the ultimate sale is immaterial.

Thus, Chrysler Corporation was found liable for Mrs. Henningsen's injuries on the grounds that its advertising had created a contractual relationship with Mrs. Henningsen and on the grounds that this contract created an "implied warranty" about the car which Chrysler had a duty to fulfill.

A second objection to the contract theory focuses on the fact that a contract is a two-edged sword. If a consumer can freely agree to buy a product *with* certain qualities, the consumer can also freely agree to buy a product *without* those qualities. That is, freedom of contract allows a manufacturer to be released from his or her contractual obligations by explicitly *disclaiming* that the product is reliable, serviceable, safe, etc. Many manufacturers fix such disclaimers on their products. The Uniform Commercial Code, in fact, stipulates in Section 2-316:

a. Unless the circumstances indicate otherwise, all implied warranties are excluded by expressions like "as is," "with all faults," or other language that in common understanding calls the buyer's attention to the exclusion of warranties and makes plain that there is no warranty, and

b. When the buyer before entering into the contract has examined the goods or the sample or model as fully as he desired, or has refused to examine the goods, there is no implied warranty with regard to defects that on examination ought in the circumstances to have been revealed to him.

The contract view, then, implies that if the consumer has ample opportunity to examine the product and the disclaimers and voluntarily consents to buy it anyway, he or she assumes the responsibility for the defects disclaimed by the manufacturer, as well as for any defects the customer may carelessly have overlooked. Disclaimers can effectively nullify all contractual duties of the manufacturer.

A third objection to the contract theory criticizes the assumption that buyer and seller meet each other as equals in the sales agreement. The contractual theory assumes that buyers and sellers are equally skilled at evaluating the quality of a product and that buyers are able to adequately protect their interests against the seller. This is the assumption built into the requirement that contracts must be freely and knowingly entered into: Both parties must know what they are doing and neither must be coerced into doing it. This equality between buyer and seller that the contractual theory assumes, derives from the laissez-faire ideology that accompanied the historical development of contract theory.[39] Classical laissez-faire ideology held that the economy's markets are competitive and that in competitive markets the consumer's bargaining power is equal to that of the seller. Competition forces the seller to offer the consumer as good or better terms than the consumer could get from other competing sellers, so the consumer has the power to threaten to take his or her business to other sellers. Because of this equality between buyer and seller, it was fair that each be allowed to try to out-bargain the other and unfair to place restrictions on either. In practice, this laissez-faire ideology gave birth to the doctrine of "caveat emptor": let the buyer take care of himself.

In fact, sellers and buyers do not exhibit the equality these doctrines assume. A consumer who must purchase hundreds of different kinds of commodities cannot hope to be as knowledgeable as a manufacturer who specializes in producing a single product. Consumers have neither the expertise nor the time to acquire and process the information on which they must base their purchase decisions. Consumers, as a consequence, must usually rely on the judgment of the seller in making their purchase decisions, and are particularly vulnerable to being harmed by the seller. Equality, far from being the rule, as the contract theory assumes, is usually the exception.

The Due Care Theory

The "due care" theory of the manufacturer's duties to consumers is based on the idea that consumers and sellers do not meet as equals and that the consumer's interests are particularly vulnerable to being harmed by the manufacturer who has a knowledge and an expertise that the consumer does not have. Because manufacturers are in a more advantaged position, they have a duty to take special "care" to ensure that consumers' interests are not harmed by the products that they offer them. The doctrine of "caveat emptor" is here replaced with a weak version of the doctrine of "caveat vendor": let the seller take care. A New York court decision neatly described the advantaged position of the manufacturer and the consequent vulnerability of the consumer:

> Today as never before the product in the hands of the consumer is often a most sophisticated and even mysterious article. Not only does it usually emerge as a sealed unit with an alluring exterior rather than as a visible assembly of component parts, but its functional validity and usefulness often depend on the application of electronic, chemical, or hydraulic principles far beyond the ken of the average consumer. Advances in the technologies of materials, of processes, of operational means have put it almost entirely out of the reach of

the consumer to comprehend why or how the article operates, and thus even farther out of his reach to detect when there may be a defect or a danger present in its design or manufacture. In today's world it is often only the manufacturer who can fairly be said to know and to understand when an article is suitably designed and safely made for its intended purpose. Once floated on the market, many articles in a very real practical sense defy detection of defect, except possibly in the hands of an expert after laborious, and perhaps even destructive, disassembly. By way of direct illustration, how many automobile purchasers or users have any idea how a power steering mechanism operates or is intended to operate, with its "circulating work and piston assembly and its cross shaft splined to the Pitman arm"? We are accordingly persuaded that from the standpoint of justice as regards the operating aspect of today's products, responsibility should be laid on the manufacturer, subject to the limitations we set forth.[40]

The "due care" view holds, then, that because consumers must depend upon the greater expertise of the manufacturer, the manufacturer not only has a duty to deliver a product that lives up to the express and implied claims about it, but in addition the manufacturer has a duty to exercise due care to prevent others from being injured by the product, *even if the manufacturer explicitly disclaims such responsibility and the buyer agrees to the disclaimer.* The manufacturer violates this duty and is "negligent" when there is a failure to exercise the care that a reasonable person could have foreseen would be necessary to prevent others from being harmed by use of the product. Due care must enter into the design of the product, into the choice of reliable materials for constructing the product, into the manufacturing processes involved in putting the product together, into the quality control used to test and monitor production, and into the warnings, labels, and instructions attached to the product. In each of these areas, according to the due care view, the manufacturer, in virtue of a greater expertise and knowledge, has a positive duty to take whatever steps are necessary to ensure that when the product leaves the plant it is as safe as possible, and the customer has a right to such assurance. Failure to take such steps is a breach of the moral duty to exercise due care and a violation of the injured person's right to expect such care, a right that rests on the consumer's need to rely on the manufacturer's expertise. Edgar Schein sketched out the basic elements of the "due care" theory several years ago when he wrote:

> . . . a professional is someone who knows better what is good for his client than the client himself does. . . . If we accept this definition of professionalism . . . we may speculate that it is the *vulnerability of the client* that has necessitated the development of moral and ethical codes surrounding the relationship. The client must be protected from exploitation in a situation in which he is unable to protect himself because he lacks the relevant knowledge to do so . . . If [a manufacturer] is . . . a professional, who is his client? With respect to whom is he exercising his expert knowledge and skills? Who needs protection against the possible misuse of these skills? . . . Many economists argue persuasively . . . that the consumer has not been in a position to know what he was buying and hence was, in fact, in a relatively vulnerable position . . . Clearly, then, one whole area of values deals with the relationship between the [manufacturer] and consumers.[41]

The due care view, of course, rests on the principle that individuals have a moral duty not to harm or injure others by their acts and that others have a moral right to expect such care from individuals. This principle has been justified from a variety of different positions. Rule-utilitarians have defended it on the grounds that if the rule is accepted, everyone's welfare will be advanced.[42] It has been argued for on the basis of Kant's theory, since it seems to follow from the categorical imperative that people should be treated as ends and not merely as means, that is, that they have a *positive* right to be helped when they cannot help themselves.[43] And Rawls has argued that individuals in the "original position" would agree to the principle because it would provide the basis for a secure social environment.[44] The judgment that individual producers have a duty not to harm or

injure, therefore, is solidly based on several ethical principles.

The Duty to Exercise Due Care

According to the due care theory, manufacturers exercise sufficient care when they take adequate steps to prevent whatever injurious effects they can foresee that the use of their product may have on consumers after having conducted inquiries into the way the product will be used and after having attempted to anticipate any possible misuses of the product. A manufacturer, then, is *not* morally negligent when others are harmed by a product and the harm was not one that the manufacturer could possibly have foreseen or prevented. Nor is a manufacturer morally negligent after having taken all reasonable steps to protect the consumer and to ensure that the consumer is informed of any irremovable risks that might still attend the use of the product. A car manufacturer, for example, cannot be said to be negligent from a moral point of view when people carelessly misuse the cars the manufacturer produces. A car manufacturer would be morally negligent only if the manufacturer had allowed unreasonable dangers to remain in the design of the car that consumers cannot be expected to know about or that they cannot guard against by taking their own precautionary measures.

What specific responsibilities does the duty to exercise due care impose on the producer? In general, the producer's responsibilities would extend to three areas:[45]

DESIGN The manufacturer should ascertain whether the design of an article conceals any dangers, whether it incorporates all feasible safety devices, and whether it uses materials that are adequate for the purposes the product is intended to serve. The manufacturer is responsible for being thoroughly acquainted with the design of the item, and to conduct research and tests extensive enough to uncover any risks that may be involved in employing the article under various conditions of use. This requires researching consumers and analyzing their behavior, testing the product under different conditions of consumer use, and selecting materials strong enough to stand up to all probable usages. The effects of aging and of wear should also be analyzed and taken into account in designing an article. Engineering staff should acquaint themselves with hazards that might result from prolonged use and wear, and should warn the consumer of any potential dangers. There is a duty to take the latest technological advances into account in designing a product, especially where advances can provide ways of designing a product that is less liable to harm or injure its users.

PRODUCTION The production manager should control the manufacturing processes to eliminate any defective items, to identify any weaknesses that become apparent during production, and to ensure that short-cuts, substitution of weaker materials, or other economizing measures are not taken during manufacture that would compromise the safety of the final product. To ensure this, there should be adequate quality controls over materials that are to be used in the manufacture of the product and over the various stages of manufacture.

INFORMATION The manufacturer should fix labels, notices, or instructions on the product that will warn the user of all dangers involved in using or misusing the item and that will enable the user to adequately guard himself or herself against harm or injury. These instructions should be clear and simple, and warnings of any hazards involved in using or misusing the product should also be clear, simple, and prominent. In the case of drugs, manufacturers have a duty to warn physicians of any risks or of any dangerous side-effects that research or prolonged use have revealed. It is a breach of the duty not to harm or injure if the manufacturer attempts to conceal or down-play the dangers related to drug usage.

In determining the safeguards that should be built into a product, the manufacturer must also take into consideration the *capacities* of the persons who will use the product. If a manufacturer anticipates that a product will be used by persons who are immature, mentally deficient, or too inexperienced to be aware of the dangers attendant on the use of the product, then the manufacturer owes them a greater degree of care than if the anticipated users were of ordinary intelligence and prudence. Children, for example, cannot be expected to realize the dangers involved in using electrical equipment. Consequently, if a manufacturer anticipates that an electrical item will probably be used by

children, steps must be taken to ensure that a person with a child's understanding will not be injured by the product.

If the possible harmful effects of using a product are serious, or if they cannot be adequately understood without expert opinion, then sale of the product should be carefully controlled. A firm should not oppose regulation of the sale of a product when regulation is the only effective means of ensuring that the users of the product are fully aware of the risks its use involves.

Problems with "Due Care"

The basic difficulty raised by the "due care" theory is that there is no clear method for determining when one has exercised enough "due care." That is, there is no hard and fast rule for determining how far a firm must go to ensure the safety of its product. Some authors have proposed the general utilitarian rule that the greater the probability of harm and the larger the population that might be harmed, the more the firm is obligated to do. But this fails to resolve some important issues. Every product involves at least some small risk of injury. If the manufacturer should try to eliminate even low-level risks, this would require that the manufacturer invest so much in each product that the product would be priced out of reach of most consumers. Moreover, even *attempting* to balance higher risks against added costs involves measurement problems: How does one quantify risks to health and life?

A second difficulty raised by the "due care" theory is that it assumes that the manufacturer can discover the risks that attend the use of a product before the consumer buys and uses it. In fact, in a technologically innovative society new products whose defects cannot emerge until years or decades have passed will continually be introduced into the market. Only years after thousands of people were using and being exposed to asbestos, for example, did a correlation emerge between the incidence of cancer and exposure to asbestos. Although manufacturers may have greater expertise than consumers, their expertise does not make them omniscient. Who, then, is to bear the costs of injuries sustained from products whose defects neither the manufacturer nor the consumer could have uncovered beforehand?

Third, the due care view appears to some to be paternalistic. For it assumes that the *manufacturer* should be the one who makes the important decisions for the consumer, at least with respect to the levels of risks that are proper for consumers to bear. But one may wonder whether such decisions should not be left up to the free choice of consumers who can decide for themselves whether or not they want to pay for additional risk reduction.

The Social Costs View of the Manufacturer's Duties

A third theory on the duties of the manufacturer would extend the manufacturer's duties beyond those imposed by contractual relationships and beyond those imposed by the duty to exercise due care in preventing injury or harm. This third theory holds that a manufacturer should pay the costs of *any* injuries sustained through any defects in the product, *even when the manufacturer exercised all due care in the design and manufacture of the product and has taken all reasonable precautions to warn users of every foreseen danger.* According to this third theory a manufacturer has a duty to assume the risks of even those injuries that arise out of defects in the product that no one could reasonably have foreseen or eliminated. The theory is a very strong version of the doctrine of "caveat vendor": let the seller take care.

This third theory, which has formed the basis of the legal doctrine of "strict liability," is founded on utilitarian arguments.[46] The utilitarian arguments for this third theory hold that the "external" costs of injuries resulting from unavoidable defects in the design of an artifact constitute part of the costs society must pay for producing and using an artifact. By having the manufacturer bear the external costs that result from these injuries as well as the ordinary internal costs of design and manufacture, all costs will be internalized and added on as part of the price of the product. Internalizing all costs in this way, according to proponents of this theory, will lead to a more efficient use of society's resources. First, since the price will reflect *all* the costs of producing and using the artifact, market forces will ensure that the product is not overproduced, and that resources are not wasted on it. (Whereas if some costs were not included in the

price, then manufacturers would tend to produce more than is needed.) Second, since manufacturers have to pay the costs of injuries, they will be motivated to exercise greater care and to thereby reduce the number of accidents. Manufacturers will therefore strive to cut down the social costs of injuries, and this means a more efficient care for our human resources. In order to produce the maximum benefits possible from our limited resources, therefore, the social costs of injuries from defective products should be internalized by passing them on to the manufacturer, even when the manufacturer has done all that could be done to eliminate such defects. And third, internalizing the costs of injury in this way enables the manufacturer to distribute losses among all the users of a product instead of allowing losses to fall on individuals who may not be able to sustain the loss by themselves.

Underlying this third theory on the duties of the manufacturer are the standard utilitarian assumptions about the values of efficiency. The theory assumes that an efficient use of resources is so important for society that social costs should be allocated in whatever way will lead to a more efficient use and care of our resources. On this basis, the theory argues that a manufacturer should bear the social costs for injuries caused by defects in a product, even when no negligence was involved and no contractual relationship existed between the manufacturer and the user.

Problems with the Social Costs View

The major criticism of the social costs view of the manufacturer's duties is that it is unfair.[47] It is unfair, the critics charge, because it violates the basic canons of compensatory justice. Compensatory justice implies that a person should be forced to compensate an injured party only if the person could foresee and could have prevented the injury. By forcing manufacturers to pay for injuries that they could neither foresee nor prevent, the social costs theory (and the legal theory of 'strict liability' that flows from it) treats manufacturers unfairly. Moreover, insofar as the social costs theory encourages passing the costs of injuries on to all consumers (in the form of higher prices), consumers are also being treated unfairly.

A second criticism of the social costs theory attacks the assumption that passing the costs of all injuries on to manufacturers will reduce the number of accidents.[48] On the contrary, critics claim, by relieving consumers of the responsibility of paying for their own injuries, the social costs theory will encourage carelessness in consumers. And an increase in consumer carelessness will lead to an increase in consumer injuries.

A third argument against the social costs theory focuses on the financial burdens the theory imposes on manufacturers and insurance carriers. Critics claim that a growing number of consumers successfully sue manufacturers for compensation for any injuries sustained while using a product, even when the manufacturer took all due care to ensure that the product was safe.[49] Not only have the number of "strict liability" suits increased, critics claim, but the amounts awarded to injured consumers have also escalated. Moreoever, they continue, the rising costs of the many liability suits that the theory of "strict liability" has created have precipitated a crisis in the insurance industry because insurance companies end up paying the liability suits brought against manufacturers. These high costs have imposed heavy losses on insurance companies and have forced many insurance companies to raise their rates to levels that are so high that many manufacturers can no longer afford insurance. Thus, critics claim, the social costs or "strict liability" theory wreaks havoc with the insurance industry; it forces the costs of insurance to climb to unreasonable heights; and it forces many valuable firms out of business because they can no longer afford liability insurance nor can they afford to pay for the many and expensive liability suits they must now face.

Defenders of the social costs view, however, have replied that in reality the costs of consumer liability suits are not large. Studies have shown, they say, that the number of liability suits filed in state courts increased only 9 percent between 1978 and 1984 (when population grew by 6 percent).[50] Less than 1 percent of product-related injuries result in suits and successful suits average payments of only a few thousand dollars.[51] Defenders of the social cost theory also point out that insurance companies and the insurance industry as a whole have remained profitable (with overall profits of $1.7 billion in 1985) and claim that higher insurance costs are due to factors other than an increase in the amount of liability claims.[52]

The arguments for and against the social costs

theory deserve much more discussion than we can give them here. The theory is essentially an attempt to come to grips with the problem of allocating the costs of injuries between two morally innocent parties: The manufacturer who could not foresee or prevent a product-related injury, and the consumer who could not guard himself or herself against the injury because the hazard was unknown. This allocation problem will arise in any society that, like ours, has come to rely upon a technology whose effects do not become evident until years after the technology is introduced. Unfortunately, it is also a problem that may have no "fair" solution.

NOTES

1. Michael Waldolz, "Study of Accutane and Birth Defects Stirs Debate on Use," *Wall Street Journal,* 25 April 1988, p. 4.
2. Philip M. Boffey, "Maker of Drug for Acne Calls Birth-Defect Report 'Invalid,'" *New York Times,* 23 April 1988, pp. 1, 9.
3. Frederick D. Sturdivant and Heidi Vernon-Wortzel, *Business and Society: A Managerial Approach,* 4th ed. (Homewood, IL: Irwin, 1990), pp. 310–11.
4. *Ibid.*
5. Morton Mintz, "At Any Cost: Corporate Greed, Women, and the Dalkon Shield," in Stuart L. Hills, ed., *Corporate Violence: Injury and Death for Profit* (Totowa, NJ: Rowman & Littlefield, 1987), p. 37.
6. *Ibid.*, p. 31.
7. Rogene A. Buchholz, William D. Evans, and Robert A. Wagley, *Management Response to Public Issues* (Englewood Cliffs, NJ: Prentice-Hall, 1989), p. 303.
8. John R. Emshwiller, "All-Terrain Vehicles Spark Debate as User Deaths and Injuries Mount," *Wall Street Journal,* 11 February 1987, p. 29.
9. Consumer Product Safety Commission, *1983 Annual Report,* part 1, (Washington, DC: U.S. Government Printing Office, 1983), p. 11.
10. *Ibid.*
11. The facts summarized in this paragraph are drawn from Penny Addis, "The Life History Complaint Case of Martha and George Rose: 'Honoring the Warranty,'" in *No Access to Law,* Laura Nader, ed. (New York: Academic Press, Inc., 1980), pp. 171–89.
12. Quoted in Ed Pope, "PacBell's Sales Quotas," *San Jose Mercury News,* 24 April 1986, p. 1C; see also "PacBell Accused of Sales Abuse," *San Jose Mercury News,* 24 April 1986, p. 1A; "PacBell Offers Refund for Unwanted Services," *San Jose Mercury News,* 17 May 1986, p. 1A.
13. *Ibid.*, p. 134.

14. Several of these criticisms are surveyed in Stephen A. Greyser, "Advertising: Attacks and Counters," *Harvard Business Review,* 50 (10 March 1972): 22–28.

15. National Safety Council, *Accident Facts, 1988 Edition* (Chicago, IL: National Safety Council, 1988), p. 95.

16. Paul A. Samuelson and William D. Nordhaus, *Macroeconomics,* 13th ed. (New York: McGraw-Hill Book Company, 1989), p. 41.

17. See Robert N. Mayer, *The Consumer Movement: Guardians of the Marketplace* (Boston: Twayne Publishers, 1989), p. 67; and Peter Asch, *Consumer Safety Regulation* (New York: Oxford University Press, 1988), p. 50.

18. Peter Asch, *Consumer Safety Regulation,* p. 51.

19. Lucy Black Creighton, *Pretenders to the Throne: The Consumer Movement in the United States* (Lexington, MA: Lexington Books, 1976), p. 85.

20. Peter Asch, *Consumer Safety Regulation,* pp. 74, 76.

21. *Ibid.*

22. For references to these studies see *ibid.,* pp. 70–73.

23. See Thomas Garrett and Richard J. Klonoski, *Business Ethics,* 2nd ed. (Englewood Cliffs, New Jersey: Prentice-Hall, 1986), p. 88.

24. Immanuel Kant, *Groundwork of the Metaphysic of Morals,* H. J. Paton, ed. (New York: Harper & Row, Publishers, Inc., 1964), pp. 90, 97; see also, Alan Donagan, *The Theory of Morality* (Chicago: The University of Chicago Press), 1977, p. 92.

25. John Rawls, *A Theory of Justice* (Cambridge: Harvard University Press, Belknap Press, 1971), pp. 344–50.

26. *Crocker v. Winthrop Laboratories, Division of Sterling Drug, Inc.,* 514 Southwestern 2d 429 (1974).

27. See Donagan, *Theory of Morality,* p. 91.

28. Frederick D. Sturdivant, *Business and Society,* 3rd ed. (Homewood, IL: Richard D. Irwin, Inc., 1985), p. 392.

29. *Ibid.,* p. 393.

30. U.S. Consumer Products Safety Commission, *1979 Annual Report* (Washington, DC: U.S. Government Printing Office, 1979), pp. 81–101.

31. A somewhat dated but still incisive discussion of this issue is found in Vance Packard, *The Wastemakers* (New York: David McKay Co., Inc., 1960).

32. Quoted in address by S. E. Upton (vice-president of Whirlpool Corporation) to the American Marketing Association in Cleveland, OH: 11 December 1969.

33. National Commission on Product Safety, *Final Report,* quoted in William W. Lowrance, *Of Acceptable Risk* (Los Altos, CA: William Kaufmann, Inc., 1976), p. 80.

34. See Louis Stern, "Consumer Protection via Increased Information," *Journal of Marketing,* 31, no. 2 (April 1967).

35. Lawrence E. Hicks, *Coping with Packaging Laws* (New York: AMACOM, 1972), p. 17.

36. See the discussions in Richard Posner, *Economic Analysis of Law,* 2nd ed. (Boston: Little, Brown and Company, 1977), p. 83; and R. Posner, "Strict Liability: A Comment," *Journal of Legal Studies,* 2, no. 1 (January 1973): 21.

37. See, for example, the many cases cited in George J. Alexander, *Honesty and Competition* (Syracuse, NY: Syracuse University Press, 1967).

38. *Henningsen v. Bloomfield Motors, Inc.,* 32 New Jersey 358, 161 Atlantic 2d 69 (1960).

39. See Friedrich Kessler and Malcolm Pitman Sharp, *Contracts* (Boston: Little, Brown and Company, 1953), pp. 1–9.

40. *Codling v. Paglia,* 32 New York 2d 330, 298 Northeastern 2d 622, 345 New York Supplement 2d 461 (1973).

41. Edgar H. Schein, "The Problem of Moral Education for the Business Manager," *Industrial Management Review,* 8 (1966): 3–11.

42. See W. D. Ross, *The Right and the Good* (Oxford: The Clarendon Press, 1930), ch. 2.

43. Donagan, *Theory of Morality,* p. 83.

44. Rawls, *Theory of Justice,* pp. 114–17; 333–42.

45. Discussions of the requirements of "due care" may be found in a variety of texts, all of which, however, approach the issues from the point of view of legal liability: Irwin Gray, *Product Liability: A Management Response* (New York: AMACOM, 1975), ch. 6; Eugene R. Carrubba, *Assuring Product Integrity* (Lexington, MA: Lexington Books, 1975); Frank Nixon, *Managing to Achieve Quality and Reliability* (New York: McGraw-Hill Book Co., 1971).

46. See, for example, Michael D. Smith, "The Morality of Strict Liability In Tort," *Business and Professional Ethics,* 3, no. 1 (December 1979): 3–5; for a review of the rich legal literature on this topic, see Richard A. Posner, "Strict Liability: A Comment," *The Journal of Legal Studies,* 2, no. 1 (January 1973): 205–21.

47. George P. Fletcher, "Fairness and Utility in Tort Theory," *Harvard Law Review,* 85, no. 3 (January 1972): 537–73.

48. Posner, *Economic Analysis of Law,* pp. 139–42.

49. See "Unsafe Products: The Great Debate Over Blame and Punishment," *Business Week,* 30 April 1984; Stuart Taylor, "Product Liability: the New Morass," *New York Times,* 10 March 1985; "The Product Liability Debate," *Newsweek,* 10 September 1984.

50. "Sorting Out the Liability Debate,"*Newsweek,* 12 May 1986.

51. Ernest F. Hollings, "No Need for Federal Product-Liability Law," *Christian Science Monitor,* 20 September 1984; see also Harvey Rosenfield, "The Plan to Wrong Consumer Rights," *San Jose Mercury News,* 3 October 1984.

52. Irvin Molotsky, "Drive to Limit Product Liability Awards Grows as Consumer Groups Object," *New York Times,* 6 March 1986.

Strict Products Liability and Compensatory Justice

George G. Brenkert

I

Strict products liability is the doctrine that the seller of a product has legal responsibilities to compensate the user of that product for injuries suffered due to a defective aspect of the product, even though the seller has not been negligent in permitting that defect to occur.[1] Thus, even though a manufacturer, for example, has reasonably applied the existing techniques of manufacture and has anticipated and cared for nonintended uses of the product, he may still be held liable for injuries a product user suffers if it can be shown that the product was defective when it left the manufacturer's hands.[2] To say that there is a crisis today concerning this doctrine would be to utter a commonplace observation which few in the business community would deny. The development of the doctrine of strict products liability, they say, financially threatens many businesses.[3] Further, strict products liability is said to be a morally questionable doctrine since the manufacturer or seller has not been negligent in the occurrence of the injury-causing defect in the product. On the other hand, victims of defective products complain that they deserve full compensation for injuries sustained in using a defective product whether or not the seller is at fault. Medical expenses and time lost from one's job are costs no individual should have to bear by himself. It is only fair that the seller share such burdens.

In general, discussions of this crisis focus on the limits to which a business ought to be held responsible to compensate the injured product user. Much less frequently do discussions of strict products liability consider the underlying question of whether the doctrine of strict products liability is rationally justifiable. But unless this question is answered it would seem premature to seek to determine the

limits to which businesses ought to be held liable in such cases. In the following paper I discuss this underlying philosophical question and argue that there is a rational justification for strict products liability which links it to the very nature of the free enterprise system.

II

It should be noted at the outset that strict products liability is not absolute liability. To hold a manufacturer legally (and morally) responsible for any and all injuries which product users might sustain would be morally perverse. First, it would deny the product user's own responsibility to take care in his actions and to suffer the consequences when he does not. As such, it would constitute an extreme form of moral and legal paternalism. Second, if the product is not defective, there is no signficant moral connection between anything that the manufacturer has done or not done and the user's injuries other than the production and sale of the product to its user. But this provides no basis to hold the manufacturer responsible for the user's injuries. If, because of my own carelessness, I cut myself with my pocket knife, the fact that I just bought my knife from Blade Manufacturing Company provides no moral reason to hold Blade Manufacturing responsible for my injury. Finally, though the manufacturer's product might be said to have harmed the person,[4] it is wholly implausible, when the product is not defective and the manufacturer not negligent, to say that the manufacturer has harmed the user. Thus, again there would seem to be no moral basis upon which to maintain that the manufacturer has any liability to the product user. Strict products liability, on the other hand, is the view that the manufacturer can be held liable when the product can be shown to be defective even though the manufacturer himself is not negligent.[5]

There are two justifications of strict products liability which are predominant in the literature. Both justifications are, I believe, untenable. They are:

a. To hold producers strictly liable for defective products will cut down on the number of accidents and injuries which occur, by forcing manufacturers to make their products safer.
b. The manufacturer is best able to distribute to others the costs of injuries which users of his defective products suffer.

There are several reasons why the first justification is unacceptable. First, it has been plausibly argued that almost everything that can be attained through the use of strict liability to force manufacturers to make their products safer can also be attained in other ways through the law.[6] Hence, to hold manufacturers strictly liable will not necessarily help reduce the number of accidents. The incentive to produce safer products already exists without invoking the doctrine of strict products liability.

Second, at least some of the accidents which have been brought under strict liability have been due to features of the products which the manufacturers could not have foreseen or controlled. At the time the product was designed and manufactured, the technological knowledge required to discover the hazard and take steps to minimize its effects was not available. It is doubtful that, in such cases, the imposition of strict liability upon the manufacturer could reduce accidents.[7] Thus, again, this justification for strict products liability fails.[8]

Third, the fact that the imposition of legal restraints and/or penalties would have a certain positive effect, viz., the reduction of accidents, does not show that the imposition of those penalties would be just. It has been pointed out before that the rate of crime might be cut significantly if the law would imprison the wives and children of men who break the law. Regardless of how correct that claim may be, to use these means in order to achieve a significant reduction in the rate of crime would be unjust. Thus, the fact, if fact it be, that strict liability would cut down on the amount of dangerous and/or defective products placed on the market, and thus reduce the amount of accidents and injuries, does not thereby justify the imposition of strict liability on manufacturers.

Finally, the above justification is essentially a utilitarian appeal which emphasizes the welfare of the product users. It is not obvious, however, that those who use this justification have ever undertaken the utilitarian analysis which would show that greater protection of the product user's safety would further the welfare of product users. If emphasis on product user safety would cut down on the number and variety of products produced, the imposition of strict liability might not, in fact, enhance product user welfare but rather lower it. Furthermore, if the safety of product users is the predominant concern, massive public and private education safety campaigns might just as well lower the level of accidents and injuries as strict products liability.

The second justification given for strict products liability is also utilitarian in nature. Among the considerations given in favor of this justification are the following:

a. "An individual harmed by his/her use of a defective product is often unable to bear the loss individually";
b. "Distribution of losses among all users of a product would minimize both individual and aggregate loss";
c. "The situation of producers and marketers in the marketplace enables them conveniently to distribute losses among all users of a product by raising prices sufficiently to compensate those harmed (which is what in fact occurs where strict liability is force)."[9]

This justification is also defective.

First, the word "best" in the phrase "best able to distribute to others the cost" is usually understood in a non-moral sense; it is used to signify that the manufacturer can most efficiently pass on the costs of injuries to others. Once this use of "best" is recognized, then surely the question may correctly be asked: Why ought these costs be passed on to other consumers and/or users of the same product or line of products? Even if the imposition of strict liability did maximize utility, it might be the case that it was still unjust to use the producer as the distributor of losses.[10] Indeed, it has been objected that to pass along the costs of such accidents to other consumers of products of a manufacturer is unjust to them.[11] The above justification is silent to these legitimate questions.

Second, it may not be, as a matter of fact, that manufacturers are always in the best (i.e., most efficient and economical) position to pass costs on to customers. This might be possible in monopoly areas, but even there there are limitations. Further, some products are subject to an "elastic demand" and as such the manufacturer could not pass along the costs.[12] Finally, the present justification could justify far more than is plausible. If the reason for holding the manufacturer liable is that the manufacturer is the "best" administrator of costs, then one might plausibly argue that the manufacturer should pay for injuries suffered not simply when he is not negligent but also when the product is not defective. That is, theoretically this argument could be extended from cases of strict liability to absolute liability. Whether this argument could plausibly be made would depend upon contingent facts concerning the nature and frequency of injuries people suffer using products, the financial strength of businesses, and the kinds and levels of products liability insurance available to them. The argument would not depend on any morally significant elements in the producer/product user relation. Such an implication, I believe, undercuts the purported moral nature of this justification. It reveals it for what it is: an economic, not a moral justification.

Accordingly, neither of the major, current justifications for the imposition of strict liability appears to be acceptable. If this is the case, is strict products liability a groundless doctrine, willfully and unjustly imposed on manufacturers?

III

This question can be asked in two different ways. On the one hand, it can be asked within the assumptions of the free enterprise system. On the other hand, it could be raised such that the fundamental assumptions of that socio-economic system are also open to revision and change. In the following, I will discuss the question *within* the general assumptions of the free enterprise system. Since these are the assumptions which are broadly made in legal and business circles it is interesting to determine what answer might be given within these constraints. Indeed, I suggest, it is only within these general assumptions that strict products liability can be justified.

To begin with, it is crucial to remember that what we have to consider is the relation between an entity doing business and an individual.[13] The

strict liability attributed to business would not be attributed to an individual who happened to sell some particular product he had made to his neighbor or a stranger. If Peter sold an article which he had made to Paul, and Paul hurt himself because the article had a defect which occurred through no negligence of Peter's, we would not normally hold Peter morally responsible to pay for Paul's injuries. Peter did not claim, we may assume, that the product was absolutely risk free. Had he kept it himself, he too might have been injured by it. Paul, on the other hand, bought it. He was not pressured, forced, or coerced to do so. Peter mounted no advertising campaign. Though Paul might not have been injured if the product had been made differently, he supposedly bought it with open eyes. Peter did not seek to deceive Paul about its qualities. The product, both its good and bad qualities, became his through his purchase of it. In short, we assume that both Peter and Paul are morally autonomous individuals capable of knowing their own interests, that such individuals can legitimately exchange their ownership of various products, that the world is not free of risks, and that not all injuries one suffers in such a world can be blamed on others. To demand that Peter protect Paul from such dangers and/or compensate him for injuries resulting from such dangers, is to demand that Peter significantly reduce the risks of the product he offers to Paul. He would have to protect Paul from encountering those risks himself. However, this smacks of paternalism, and undercuts our basic moral assumptions about such relations. Hence, in such a case, Peter is not morally responsible for Paul's injuries, or, due to this transaction, obligated to aid him. Perhaps Peter owes Paul aid because Paul is an injured neighbor or person. Perhaps simply for reasons of charity Peter ought to aid Paul. But Peter has no moral obligation, stemming from the sale itself, to provide aid.

It is different in the case of businesses. They have been held to be legally and morally obliged to pay the victim for his injuries. Why? What is the difference? The difference has to do with the fact that when Paul is hurt by a defective product from corporation X, he is hurt by something produced in a socio-economic system purportedly embodying free enterprise. To say this is to say, among other things, that (a) each business and/or corporation produces articles or services which they sell for profit; (b) each member of this system competes with other members of the system in trying to do as well as he can for himself not simply in each exchange but through each exchange for his other values and desires; (c) competition is to be "open and free, without deception or fraud"; (d) exchanges are to be voluntary and undertaken when each party believes he can thereby benefit. One party provides the means for another party's ends if the other party will provide the first party the means to his ends[14]; (e) the acquisition and disposition of ownership rights, i.e., of private property, is permitted in such exchanges; (f) no market or series of markets constitutes the whole of a society; (g) law, morality, and government play a role in setting acceptable limits to the nature and kinds of exchange in which people may engage.[15]

What is it about such a system which would justify claims of strict products liability against businesses? Calabresi has suggested that the free enterprise system is essentially a system of strict liability.[16] Thus, the very nature of the free enterprise system justifies such liability claims. His argument has two parts. First, he claims that "bearing risks is both the function of, and justification for, private enterprise in a free enterprise society."[17] Free enterprise is prized, in classical economics, precisely because it fosters the creation of entrepreneurs who will take such uninsurable risks, who will, in other words, "gamble on uncertainty and demonstrate their utility by surviving—by winning more than others."[18] Accordingly, the nature of private enterprise requires that individual businesses assume the burden of risk in the production and distribution of its products. However, even if it be granted that this characterization of who must bear the risks "in deciding what goods are worth producing and what new entrants into an industry are worth having" is correct, it would not follow that individual businesses ought to bear the burden of risk in cases of accidents. Calabresi himself recognises this. Thus, he maintains, in the second part of his argument, that there is a close analogy which lets us move from the regular risk bearing businesses must accept in the marketplace to the bearing of risks in accidents: "although . . . (the above characterization) has concerned *regular* entrepreneurial-product risks, not accident risks, the analogy is extremely close."[19] He proceeds,

however, to draw the analogy in the following brief sentence: "As with product-accident risks, our society starts out by allocating ordinary product-production risks in ways which try to maximize the chances that incentives will be placed on those most suited to 'manage' these risks."[20] In short, he simply asserts that the imposition of strict products liability on business will be the most effective means of reducing such risks. But such a view does not really require, as we have seen in the previous section, any assumptions about the nature of the free enterprise system. It could be held independently of such assumptions. Further, this view is simply a form of the first justificatory argument we discussed and rejected in the previous section. We can hardly accept it here under the guise of being attached to the nature of free enterprise.

Nevertheless, Calabresi's initial intuitions about a connection between the assumptions of the free enterprise system and the justification of strict products liability are correct. However, they must be developed in the following, rather different, manner. In the free enterprise system, each person and/or business is obligated to follow the rules and understandings which define this socio-economic system. Following the rules is expected to channel competition among individual persons and businesses so that the results are socially positive. In providing the means to fulfill the ends of others, the means to one's own ends also get fulfilled. Though this does not happen in every case, it is supposed that, in general, this happens. Those who fail in their competition with others may be the object of charity, but not of other duties. Those who succeed, *qua* members of this socio-economic system, do not have moral duties to aid those who fail. Analogously, the team which loses the game may receive our sympathy but the winning team is not obligated to help it so that it may win the next game, or even play better the next game. Those who violate the rules, however, may be punished or penalized, whether or not the violation was intentional and whether or not it redounds to the benefit of the violator. Thus, a team may be assessed a penalty for something a team member unintentionally did to a member of the other team but which, by violating the rules, nevertheless injured the other team's chances of competition in the game.

This point may be emphasized by another instance involving a game but one which brings us closer to strict products liability. Imagine that you are playing table tennis with another person in his newly constructed table tennis room. You are both avid table tennis players and the game means a lot to both of you. Suppose that after play has begun, you are suddenly and quite obviously blinded by the light over the table—the light shade has a hole in it which, when it turned in your direction, sent a shaft of light unexpectedly into your eyes. You lose a crucial point as a result. Surely it would be unfair of your opponent to seek to maintain his point because he was faultless—i.e., he had not intended to blind you when he installed that light shade. You would correctly object that he had gained the point unfairly, that you should not have to give up the point lost, and that the light shade should be modified so that the game could continue on a fair basis. It is only fair that the point be played over.

Businesses and their customers in a free enterprise system are also engaged in competition with each other.[21] The competition here, however, is multifaceted as each tries to gain the best agreement he can from the other with regard to the buying and selling of raw materials, products, services, and labor. Such agreements, however, must be voluntary. The competition which leads to them cannot involve coercion. In addition, such competition must be fair and ultimately result in the benefit of the entire society through the operation of the proverbial "invisible hand." Crucial to the notion of fairness of competition is not simply the demands that the competition itself be open, free, and honest, but also that each person in a society be given an equal opportunity to participate in the system in order to fulfill his own particular ends. Friedman formulates this notion in the following manner: "the priority given to equality of opportunity in the hierarchy of values . . . is manifested particularly in economic policy. The catchwords were free enterprise, competition, laissez-faire. Everyone was free to go into any business, follow any occupation, buy any property, subject only to the agreement of the other parties to the transaction. Each was to have the opportunity to reap the benefits if he succeeded, to suffer the costs if he failed. There were to be no arbitrary obstacles. Performance, not birth, religion, or nationality, was the touchstone."[22]

What is obvious in Friedman's comments is that he is thinking primarily of a person as a producer. Equality of opportunity requires that one not be prevented by arbitrary obstacles from participating (by engaging in a productive role of some kind or other) in the system of free enterprise, competition, etc. in order to fulfill one's own ends ("reap the benefits"). Accordingly, monopolies are restricted, discriminatory hiring policies have been condemned, and price collusion is forbidden. However, each person participates in the system of free enterprise *both* as a worker/producer *and* as a consumer. The two roles interact; if the person could not consume he would not be able to work, and if there were no consumers there would be no work to be done. Even if a particular individual is only (what is ordinarily considered) a consumer, he too plays a theoretically significant role in the competitive free enterprise system. The fairness of the system depends upon the access to information, which is available to him, about goods and services on the market, the lack of coercion imposed on him to buy goods, as well as the lack of arbitrary restrictions imposed by the market and/or government on his behavior. In short, equality of opportunity is a doctrine with two sides which applies both to producers and to consumers. If, then, a person as a consumer or a producer is injured by a defective product, which is one way in which his activities might be arbitrarily restricted by the action of (one of the members of) the market system, surely his free and voluntary participation in the system of free enterprise will be seriously affected. Specifically, his equal opportunity to participate in the system in order to fulfill his own ends will be diminished.

It is here that strict products liability enters the picture. In cases of strict liability the manufacturer does not intend that a certain aspect of his product injures a person. Nevertheless, the person is injured. As a result, his activity both as a consumer and as a producer is disadvantaged. He cannot continue to play the role he might wish either as a producer or consumer. As such he is denied that equality of opportunity which is basic to the economic system in question just as surely as he would be if he were excluded from employment by various unintended consequences of the economic system which nevertheless had certain racially or sexually prejudicial implications. Accordingly, it is fair that the manufacturer compensate the person for his losses before proceeding with business as usual. That is, the user of a manufacturer's product may justifiably demand compensation from the manufacturer when a product of his which can be shown to be defective has injured him and harmed his chances of participation in the system of free enterprise.

Hence, strict liability finds a basis in the notion of equality of opportunity which plays a central role in the notion of a free enterprise system. This is why a business which does *not* have to pay for the injuries which an individual suffers in the use of a defective article made by that business is felt to be unfair to its customers. Its situation is analogous to a player's unintentional violation of a game rule which is intended to foster equality of competitive opportunity. A soccer player, for example, may unintentionally trip an opposing player. He did not mean to do it: perhaps he himself had stumbled and consequently tripped the other player. Still, he is to be penalized. If the referee looked the other way, the tripped player would rightfully object that he had been treated unfairly. Similarly, the manufacturer of a product may be held strictly liable for a product of his which injures a person who uses that product. Even though he be faultless, it is a causal consequence of his activities that renders the user of his product less capable of equal participation in the socio-economic system so as to fulfill his (the user's) own ends. The manufacturer too should be penalized by way of compensating the victim. Thus, the basis upon which manufacturers are held strictly liable is compensatory justice.

In a society which refuses to resort to paternalism or to central direction of the economy and which turns, instead, to competition in order to allocate scarce positions and resources, compensatory justice requires that the competition be fair and losers be protected.[23] Specifically no one who loses should be left so destitute that he cannot re-enter the competition. Further, those who suffer injuries traceable to the defective results of the activities of others which restrict their participation in the competitive system should also be compensated. As such, compensatory justice does not presuppose negligence or evil intentions on the part of those to whom the injuries might ultimately be causally traced. It is not perplexed or incapacitated by the relative innocence of all parties involved. Rather it is concerned with correcting the disadvantaged situation an individual experiences due to accidents or failures which occur in the normal working of that competitive system. It is on this basis that other compensatory programs which alleviate the disabilities of various minority groups are founded. It is also on compensatory justice that strict products liability finds its foundation.

An implication of the preceding argument is that business is not morally obliged to pay, as such, for the physical injury a person suffers. Rather, it must pay for the loss of equal competitive opportunity—even though it usually is the case that it is because of a (physical) injury that there is a loss of such equal opportunity. This, however, corresponds to actual legal cases in which the injury which prevents a person from going about his/her daily activities may be emotional or mental as well as physical. If it were the case that a person were neither mentally nor physically harmed, but still rendered less capable of competitively participating due to a defective aspect of a product, then there would still be grounds for holding the company liable. For example, suppose I purchased and used a cosmetic product guaranteed to last a month. When used by most people it is odorless. On me, however, it has a terrible smell. I can stand the smell, but my co-workers, and most other people, find it intolerable. My employer sends me home from work until it wears off. The product has not physically or mentally harmed me. Still, on the above argument, I would have reason to hold the manufacturer liable. Any cosmetic product with this result is defective. As a consequence my opportunity to participate in the socio-economic system so as to fulfill my own ends is disadvantaged. I should be compensated. . . .

NOTES

1. This characterization of strict products liability is adapted from Weinstein et al., *Products Liability and the Reasonably Safe Product* (New York: John Wiley & Sons, 1978), ch. 1. I understand "the seller" to include the manufacturer, the retailer, as well as distributors and wholesalers. For convenience sake, I will generally refer simply to the manufacturer.

2. Cf. John W. Wade, "On Product 'Design Defects' and Their Actionability," 33 *Vanderbilt Law Review* 553 (1980). Weinstein, et al., *Products Liability and the Reasonably Safe Product*, 8, 28–32. Reed Dickerson, "Products Liability: How Good Does a Product Have to Be?" 42 *Indiana Law Journal* 308–316 (1967). Section 402A of the Restatement (Second) of Torts characterises the seller's situation in this fashion: "the seller has exercised all possible care in the preparation and sale of his product."

3. Cf. John C. Perham, "The Dilemma in Product Liability," *Dun's Review*, 109 (1977), 48–50, 76. W. Page Keeton, "Products Liability—Design Hazards and the Meaning of Defect," 10 *Cumberland Law Review* 293–316 (1979). Alvin S. Weinstein et al., *Products Liability and the Reasonably Safe Product* (New York: John Wiley & Sons, 1978), ch. 1.

4. More properly, of course, the person's use of the manufacturer's product harmed the product user.

5. Clearly one of the central questions confronting the notion of strict liability is what is to count as "defective." With few exceptions, it is held that a product is defective if and only if it is unreasonably dangerous. There have been several different standards proposed as measures of the defectiveness or unreasonably dangerous nature of a product. However, in terms of logical priorities, it really does not matter what the particular standard for defectiveness is unless we know whether we may justifiably hold manufacturers strictly liable for defective products. It is for this reason that I concentrate in this paper on the justifiability of strict products liability.

6. Marcus L. Plant, "Strict Liability of Manufacturers for Injuries Caused by Defects in Products—An Opposing View," 24 *Tennessee Law Review* 945 (1957). William L. Prosser, "The Assault Upon the Citadel (Strict Liability to the Consumer)," 1114, 1115, 1119.

7. Keeton, "The Meaning of Defect in Products Liability—A Review of Basic Principles," 594–595. Weinstein, et al., *Products Liability and the Reasonably Safe Product*, 55.

8. It might be objected that such accidents ought not to fall under strict products liability and hence do not constitute a counterexample to the above justification. This objection is answered in Sections III and IV. [Section IV is not included in this reading.]

9. These three considerations are formulated by Michael D. Smith, "The Morality of Strict Liability in Tort," *Business and Professional Ethics Newsletter*, 3 (1979), 4. Smith himself, however, was drawing upon Guido Calabresi, "Some Thoughts on Risk Distribution and the Law of Torts," 70 *Yale Law Journal* 499–553 (1961).

10. Michael D. Smith, "The Morality of Strict Liability in Tort," 4. Cf. George P. Fletcher, "Fairness and Utility in Tort Theory," 85 *Harvard Law Review* 537–573 (1972).

11. Rev. Francis E. Lucey, S. J., "Liability Without Fault and the Natural Law," 24 *Tennessee Law Review* 952–962 (1957). Perham, "The Dilemma in Product Liability," 48–49.

12. Marcus L. Plant, "Strict Liability of Manufacturers for Injuries Caused by Defects in Products—An Opposing View," 946–947. By "elastic demand" is meant "a slight increase in price will cause a sharp reduction in demand or will turn consumers to a substitute product" (946–947).

13. Cf. William L. Prosser, "The Assault Upon the Citadel," 69 *Yale Law Journal* 1140–1141 (1960). Wade, "On Product 'Design Defects' and Their Actionability," 569. Michel A. Coccio, John W. Dondanville, Thomas R. Nelson, *Products Liability: Trends and Implications* (AMA, 1970), 19.

14. F. A. Hayek emphasizes this point in "The Moral Element in Free Enterprise," in *Studies in Philosophy, Politics, and Economics* (New York: Simon and Schuster, 1967), 229.

15. Several of these characteristics have been drawn from Milton Friedman and Rose Friedman, *Free to Choose* (New York: Avon Books, 1980).

16. Calabresi, "Product Liability: Curse or Bulwark of Free Enterprise," 325.

17. Ibid., 321.

18. Ibid.

19. Ibid., 324.

20. Ibid.

21. Cf. H. B. Acton, *The Morals of Markets* (London: Longman Group Limited, 1971), 1–7, 33–37. Milton Friedman and Rose Friedman, *Free to Choose*.

22. Milton Friedman and Rose Friedman, *Free to Choose*, 123–124.

23. I have heavily drawn, in this paragraph, on the fine article by Bernard Boxhill, "The Morality of Reparation," reprinted in *Reverse Discrimination*, ed. Barry R. Gross (Buffalo, New York: Prometheus Books, 1977), 270–278.

Individualized Justice, Mass Torts, and "Settlement Class Actions": An Introduction

Roger C. Cramton

The tension between individual justice (party autonomy in an adversary system) and collective justice (aggregated handling of legal claims) is the basic theme of [this essay]. Nowhere is this tension more evident than in recent efforts to use "settlement class actions" as a means for large-scale resolution of personal injury or property damage claims arising out of exposure to defective products or toxic substances. Important and novel issues of tort law, civil procedure, constitutional due process, and lawyer behavior are presented by settlements resolving the tort claims of future as well as current claimants. Pending cases provide a number of examples: (1) a class containing millions of persons occupationally exposed to asbestos, (2) a class of more than one million women who received breast implants, (3) a class containing all of the owners of Ford Bronco all-terrain vehicles, (4) a class of owners of GM pickups with saddlebag gas tanks, and (5) a class of current and future owners of homes that have a polybutylene plumbing system, an allegedly defective plumbing material that has been installed in three million mobile homes and an estimated four to five million site-built homes.

This use of the class action device, like most other new developments, has both long- and short-term antecedents. Yet, the recent class actions mentioned above, which contain a novel combination of features, illustrate something quite new in degree and kind. For example, the cases were either brought or certified for settlement purposes rather than to be tried; the plaintiff class includes future victims, many of whom have yet to suffer a legally cognizable injury; approved settlements will bind absent class members, many of whom may not have had an effective opportunity to opt out of the class; the settlements affect claims nationwide and may have the effect of a federal decree eliminating claims governed by state law or a state decree eliminating claims governed by federal law; and in some of the cases, the plaintiffs' lawyers representing the class entered into side settlements with the defendants, giving their current clients different and more favorable relief than the class settlement provides to future claimants. A class action settlement with these features would have been unthinkable to lawyers of a decade or so ago. . . .

Recent class action settlements such as those previously mentioned raise several questions. Some of the most central are:

(1) Is the individual justice provided by tort law in the courts so delayed, erratic, and inefficient that it should be replaced by schemes of collective justice molded by self-interested parties and approved by a single federal district judge? If administrative schemes are to be substituted for the tort system, should this be accomplished by legislation rather than by private settlements approved by a single judge?

(2) Does a federal district court have authority to enter a decree that eliminates or displaces the personal injury rights, otherwise governed by state law, of individuals who have been exposed to a product or substance but have not yet suffered a legal injury (future claimants whose claims have not yet matured when notice is given of the opportunity to opt out)?

(3) How can adequate notice of opportunity to opt out of a class action, required by due process, be provided to "exposure only" persons who do not and cannot know that they will suffer an injury in the future? Is "adequate representation" provided when a lawyer negotiates cash settlements for the lawyer's current clients simultaneously with a class action settlement providing different terms for future claimants? Do the virtues of private settlement and alternative dispute resolution justify departures from general principles of legal ethics?

The American common-law system emphasizes party control of litigation rather than judicial prosecution and investigation. The adversary system presupposes opposing parties who exercise a wide range of choice on whether, where, and when a lawsuit is filed; what claims and defenses are asserted; what resources should be devoted to the litigation; and whether the case is settled or tried. The common-law judge is envisioned as a neutral, relatively passive arbiter of conflicting private interests who rules on questions of law and supervises the conduct of the litigation. Party initiative and the underlying principle of individual autonomy are supported by the constitutional right of trial by jury, which presupposes a detailed evaluation of particularistic facts bearing on the plaintiff's claim and the defendant's defenses.

The American tort system reflects the same values by requiring proof of fault, causation, and harm before one person's loss is shifted to someone else. The injured plaintiff must establish by a preponderance of the evidence that the defendant's wrongful acts caused the plaintiff's harm. Although tort law serves mixed goals—compensating accident victims, deterring conduct that is wrongful or involves unreasonable risks to the health or safety of others, and punishing wrongdoers—the central notion until quite recently has been one of corrective justice—repairing, to the extent possible with a money award, the harm that one individual's wrongful act has caused another. Proof that the defendant's wrongful act has caused the plaintiff's injury inevitably requires a particularistic assessment of the plaintiff's and defendant's conduct, a causal relationship between their actions and the claimed harm, and a valuation of the plaintiff's resulting injury.

Two developments in the twentieth century threaten to displace the traditional model of individual rights and party autonomy. First, many judges participate more actively in the management, conduct, and settlement of litigation. Second, pressures flow from the volume, complexity, cost, and interrelatedness of what are referred to here as "mass exposure torts."

Since the development of negligence doctrine in the nineteenth century, the paradigm case of the traditional tort is an accident in which an actor's vehicle—whether stage coach, railroad, or automobile—has injured a stranger. The individualized approach to adjudicating such disputes seemed natural, if not inevitable, given the premises of American law and the constitutional right to a jury trial. In today's world, however, America's market economy encourages mass distribution of products of new, and perhaps untested, technology. Thousands of strangers may be injured by the dissemination and use of a single product. Mass exposure to these products or substances creates situations in which a large number of people believe, or are led to believe, that the defendant's product caused their injuries. The resulting volume of litigation poses problems that threaten both the tort system's reliance on individual responsibility and the procedural system's reliance on party initiative and control.

Mass exposure torts threaten these aspects of the tort system for several reasons. First, proving or determining whether exposure to the product or substance caused the claimed injury is difficult. Frequently, the exposure that leads to claims of injury occurs over a substantial period of time, and the injury itself may have a long latency period. Often there is scientific uncertainty as to whether the exposure caused the alleged harm or whether the condition was the result of the individual's conduct (smoking, for example) or the presence of background substances in the natural environment. Frequently, expert witnesses will be able to testify about causation only in terms of statistical probabilities based on scattered or inconclusive epidemiological studies.

Second, in many cases it is difficult or impossible to determine which of multiple actors caused the claimed injury. If the harm has a long latency period, evidence of whose product or substance caused the harm may be unavailable fifteen or thirty years after the product's distribution and consumption. A related problem arises in cases involving long-term occupational exposure, such as in the asbestos field. The worker may have been exposed to several products, each with somewhat different injury characteristics, manufactured by a number of companies over a lengthy period of time. In such a case, it may be difficult for the plaintiff to establish that the named defendant or defendants were responsible for the plaintiff's harm.

Third, it is doubtful whether individualized justice can be provided when thousands or even millions of claims flow from mass exposure to a product or substance. For example, millions of Americans were exposed occupationally to asbestos products from the 1930s through the 1970s, before regulatory and safety controls reduced the future danger. Many of those exposed have died or suffered injuries, and the exposure will claim further victims well into the twenty-first century. As another example, over one million women had silicone gel breast implants between 1979 and 1994. As of yet, only a small portion of this group has suffered injury, and the causal relationship between implants and some injuries remains uncertain.

The sheer number of claims in cases like these creates troublesome problems of judicial delay, repetitive trials, high transaction costs, and an inevitable interrelationship among claimants. As indicated earlier, claimants may suffer from a "disease" rather than the type of immediate physical injury associated with a traumatic accident. Causation may be established only by reliance on probabilistic methods. Publicity given to the dangers of use or exposure to the product gives rise to new claims, such as the emotional harm flowing from fear of contracting the disease in the future, and increases the percentage of victims who assert claims. Evidence that defendants knew of the products' risks but failed to warn those exposed to them supports punitive damage claims that threaten producers with large, unpredictable, and recurring judgments based on the same conduct.

Individual trials that replicate evidence of exposure, causation, and injury in case after case burden the courts, create judicial delay, and carry high transaction costs. In conventional tort litigation, approximately sixty percent of amounts paid go to accident victims. A study of asbestos litigation estimates that plaintiffs only receive about forty percent of each litigation dollar. Critics assert that lawyers, insurance companies, and litigation expenses consume too much of the amounts available to compensate victims. If fault and causation requirements were eliminated entirely from complex, difficult cases of mass tort exposure, as was done in social security disability or workers' compensation cases, transaction costs could be greatly reduced.

The model of individualized justice posits that each claimant should make all relevant decisions with respect to her claim. The existence of a host of other similar claims inevitably affects these decisions because a claimant will "now have to take into account the existence of the other claimants, the extent to which the other claims may deplete the assets of the tortfeasor, and the possible savings which may be achieved by sharing the costs of litigation." If payment of compensatory and punitive damages to early claimants results in a producer's insolvency, future claimants will receive little or nothing. Some courts assume that maintaining the solvency of corporate actors is a desirable objective wholly apart from its effect on future claimants.

The high costs of proving causation in the individual case may be reduced by a collective action that spreads the costs of discovery, expert testimony, and litigation among many claimants. Thus, collective justice appeals to all parties to some degree and to courts and judges almost without exception. Plaintiffs avoid the "free rider" problem by sharing the costs of discovering evidence and proving causation and fault. Defendants benefit from reduced transaction costs and fixed liability, displacing the uncertainty of unpredictable future liability. Courts similarly benefit from reduced caseloads because thousands of individual cases are combined into one large class action, and claims are processed outside the courts.

These characteristics of mass exposure torts produce pressures that result in efforts at aggregative or collective justice. The class action is a procedural technique in which representatives of a group (class representatives) may assert against the defendants both their own claims and similar claims of other persons who share a common interest. [The law] requires that class actions meet four prerequisites, generally referred to as numerosity, commonality, typicality, and adequacy. First, the class must be so numerous that joinder of all members is impracticable. Second, questions of law or fact must be common to the class. Third, the claims or defenses of the representative parties must be typical of the class as a whole. Finally, the representative plaintiffs and their lawyers must "fairly and adequately protect the interests of the class." . . .

Although the legislative history of the [rules creating class actions] states that the class action device is "ordinarily not appropriate" for "[a] 'mass accident' resulting in injuries to numerous persons," federal courts in recent years have authorized class actions in a number of single-incident mass accident cases and a smaller number of mass exposure tort cases. The Agent Orange class action, involving the claimed injuries of Vietnam veterans from battlefield exposure to dioxin manufactured by the defendants, was the first such case. Bankruptcy situations involving a major asbestos defendant and the manufacturer of the Dalkon Shield intrauterine device had class action aspects.

Collective justice . . . has its distinctive vices as well as its virtues. To the extent that compensating victims becomes a major goal, considerations of fault, responsibility, and deterrence are muted or eliminated. Collective action may solve the "free rider" problem of individualized justice—some litigants benefitting from, but not contributing to, the expensive efforts of another litigant in discovering causation and fault. But collective action creates the new and serious problem of the "kidnapped rider," an individual deprived of any freedom of action by being drawn involuntarily into collective litigation. Collective action may also deprive individuals of meaningful control over their own legal claims, pushing them involuntarily into compensation grids and administrative claims-handling processes to whose ministrations they have not consented.

Collective justice also departs from the normal lawyer-client relationship in which the client makes decisions concerning objectives and the client's lawyer makes tactical and procedural decisions. The plaintiff's lawyer in traditional tort litigation is probably more in charge of the case than traditional theory would suggest. But an individual plaintiff represented by a lawyer retained on a contingent-fee basis may discharge the lawyer at will and may decide whether or not to accept a settlement offer. In most class actions, especially those involving large classes of absent persons whose claims are of limited worth or future creation, the lawyers representing the class ("class counsel") are clearly in charge. Class counsel typically pick the class representatives, frame the issues, push or abandon particular claims, and make settlement decisions. Class action law even permits class counsel to submit a settlement to the court that some or all of the class representatives oppose. Class action lawyers, even more than government lawyers who represent an amorphous "public," are their own clients in the sense that their fiduciary responsibilities to class members are what they determine them to be in the absence of court supervision and scrutiny.

During the last year or two, a spate of mass exposure class actions have raised novel and interesting questions. The major current cases [include] two class action settlements in the asbestos field; the settlement of the silicone gel breast implants litigation; the *Ford Bronco II* property damage case; the similar litigation involving General Motors pickup trucks; and the polybutylene plumbing case in a Texas state court. In each of these cases, defendants facing mass tort claims have combined with class action plaintiffs' lawyers in efforts to settle the claims of current and future claimants. Some of these proposed settlements have been approved by district courts as fair and reasonable, but have not been reviewed by appellate courts. The proposed settlements have been rejected in the two motor vehicle cases. The breast implants case and other class action filings are pending before trial courts. Appellate review has occurred in only one case. These legal innovations will be tested over the next few years until authoritative decisions, new procedural rules, or legislative solutions replace conflicting arguments with stable law—innovations which may be a long time coming.

Study Questions

1. What three distinct legal theories did Connie Daniell invoke to seek damages from Ford?

2. State in your own words the reasons given by the court in rejecting the plaintiff's claim in *Daniell v. Ford*.

3. Manufacturers and sellers of consumer goods are not generally liable for injuries resulting from misuse of their products. Only if the misuse was foreseeable will courts im-

pose liability. Was the Talon-G rat poison "misused" by Marlo Banks in this case? Did someone else misuse the poison? Was that misuse foreseeable? Could it have been prevented?

4. Why, according to Manuel Velasquez, is it unreasonable to expect that the operation of the free market alone will adequately protect the public from dangerous consumer products?

5. State as precisely as you can in your own words the differences among each of the three theories of producer responsibility outlined by Velasquez—the contract, due care, and social costs theories.

6. George Brenkert argues that the free enterprise system is a mutually cooperative venture between individual consumers and the businesses and corporations that supply the goods the public uses. Brenkert believes that this venture is based on the notion of equality of opportunity. Why, according to Brenkert, does this mean that producers must be strictly liable for consumer injuries?

7. Assuming that Brenkert is correct in claiming that compensation must be forthcoming to those consumers whose participation in the free-market system has been compromised due to a product-related injury, why must the compensation come from the manufacturer of the product? What answer does Brenkert give to this question?

8. What, according to Cramton, are the aspects of mass exposure torts that threaten to undermine what he calls the "traditional" model of product-related tort lawsuits?

CASE SCENARIO 1   *LeBouf v. Goodyear Tire & Rubber Co.*

The following opinion was handed down by a U.S. federal circuit court in 1980.

Reavley, Circuit Judge:

In the early morning hours of June 6, 1976, Shelby Leleux was killed and his passenger, Floyd Dugas, was seriously injured when the Mercury Cougar driven by Leleux veered off the Louisiana back road on which it had been travelling at over 100 miles per hour and crashed into a cement culvert. The accident occurred when the tread separated from the body of the Cougar's left rear tire. Dugas and Leleux's mother, Lillie Mae Duhon, brought this products liability action against Goodyear Tire & Rubber Company, the manufacturer of the tire, and Ford Motor Company, the maker of the automobile, alleging that the accident was attributable to the products' defective designs and the failure of the defendants to warn of the danger of tread separation at high speeds. The district court, sitting without a jury, agreed and held defendants liable jointly. Ford Motor Company appeals, arguing that: (1) it had no duty to warn of or otherwise to guard against the danger of tread separation in situations like that involved here; (2) the district court erred in holding it liable as manufacturer of the tire; and (3) the court should have held Leleux and Dugas to be barred from recovery on the basis of their own conduct in connection with the accident. We affirm.

•   •   •

Ford contends that the circumstances under which product failure occurred in this case constituted a misuse, outside the "normal use" of the Cougar and the tires. Therefore, Ford argues that it had no duty to warn or otherwise to guard against the dangers involved here, and that it, consequently, should not have been held liable for injuries flowing from product failure in that setting.

The only aspect of the accident that raises the question of misuse versus normal use is the excessive speed of the Cougar. There is no evidence that the hazards of speed were exacerbated by poor highway pavement or other road hazards, or that the car or tires had otherwise been subjected to abuse on the night of the accident or before. Moreover, aside from the fact that it may have impaired his judgment in deciding to drive at an excessive speed, there is no indication that Leleux's intoxication constituted an independent element of misuse pertinent to this case.

[2, 3] Certainly the operation of the Cougar in excess of 100 miles per hour was not "normal" in the sense of being a routine or intended use. The sports car involved here was marketed with an intended and recognized appeal to youthful drivers. The 425 horsepower engine with which Ford had equipped it provided a capability of speeds over 100 miles per hour, and the car's allure, no doubt exploited in its marketing, lay in no small measure in this power and potential speed. It was not simply foreseeable, but was to be readily expected, that the Cougar would, on occasion, be driven in excess of the 85 mile per hour proven maximum safe operating speed of its Goodyear tires. Consequently, Ford cannot, on the basis of abnormal use, escape its duty either to provide an adequate warning of the specific danger of tread separation at such high speeds or to ameliorate the danger in some other way. *See Bradco Oil & Gas Co. v. Youngstown Sheet & Tube Co.*, 532 F.2d 501, 503–04 (5th Cir. 1976), *cert. denied*, 429 U.S. 1095, 97 S.Ct. 111, 51 L.Ed.2d 542 (1977) (duty to warn if product, though not otherwise defective, may not be safely used in certain foreseeable ways).

[4] Ford contends, further, that it had no duty to warn—that is, that the car was not "unreasonably dangerous" without a warning—even if the Cougar was in "normal use" at the time of the accident, since the danger involved was obvious or at least should have been known to Leleux, who dabbled in amateur stock car racing. . . . While the hazards generally of high-speed driving would have been as obvious to Leleux as to any other driver, the particular risk in question here—*viz.*, that the tread would separate from a tire and the danger that this would present—would not have been obvious. Moreover, the evidence concerning Leleux's amateur racing background is insufficient to indicate a sophistication on his part regarding tire capabilities such that he, apart from the average purchaser, should have been aware of the danger of tread separation.

1. The court in this case finds that Goodyear and Ford are liable for having marketed a car that they knew (or should have known) would be driven at high speeds. Do you agree with the court's reasoning in support of this conclusion? Is driving at speeds in excess of one hundred miles per hour a "misuse" of this product? Why or why not?
2. According to testimony accepted at trial, the driver, Shelby Leleux, had been drinking throughout the night prior to the morning of the accident; an autopsy revealed that his blood alcohol level was 0.18 percent, well above the legal limit for intoxication. Should this fact nullify Ford's responsibility for the accident? Why or why not?
3. How would the models of responsibility for product-related harms discussed by Velasquez apply to this case? How would Brenkert's theory of strict liability apply?

CASE SCENARIO 2   *Sindell v. Abbott Laboratories*

The following case was decided by the Supreme Court of California in 1980. Judith Sindell brought a suit against eleven manufacturers of a drug known as diethylstilbesterol (DES). The drug was widely used from the early 1940s until 1971 (when it was banned) for the purpose of preventing miscarriages. As many as 3 million women used DES during the period of its availability. Only after several decades on the market did it become clear that the drug caused vaginal and cervical cancer in the daughters of the women who took it. Sindell, one of those daughters afflicted with cancer, filed a class-action lawsuit, seeking both compensatory and punitive damages. The major stumbling block for similar cases had been the legal requirement that the plaintiff show that the defective or unreasonably dangerous product made by the defendants named in the suit caused the plaintiff's injuries. Because DES was a generic drug and thus manufactured and distributed by hundreds of companies, DES daughters frequently could not satisfy the causation requirement, as they could not identify which company had made the DES that their mothers had taken. The California court in this case faced the question of whether to continue insisting that this requirement be met in DES cases. In holding that the requirement could be dropped and the suit could proceed, the court advanced a new theory of recovery known as *market-share liability.*

> In our contemporary complex industrialized society, advances in science and technology create fungible goods which may harm consumers and which cannot be traced to any specific producer. The response of the courts can be either to adhere rigidly to prior doctrine, denying recovery to those injured by such products, or to fashion remedies to meet these changing needs. Just as Justice Traynor in his landmark concurring opinion in *Escola v. Coca Cola Bottling Company* (1944) . . . , recognized that in an era of mass production and complex marketing methods the traditional standard of negligence was insufficient to govern the obligations of manufacturer to consumer, so should we acknowledge that some adaptation of the rules of causation and liability may be appropriate in these recurring circumstances. . . .
>
> The most persuasive reason for finding plaintiff states a cause of action is that . . . : as between an innocent plaintiff and negligent defendants, the latter should bear the cost of the injury. Here, . . . plaintiff is not at fault in failing to provide evidence of causation, and although the absence of such evidence is not attributable to the defendants either, their conduct in marketing a drug the effects of which are delayed for many years played a significant role in creating the unavailability of proof.
>
> From a broader policy standpoint, defendants are better able to bear the cost of injury resulting from the manufacturer of a defective product. As was said by Justice Traynor in *Escola,* "[t]he cost of an injury and the loss of time or health may be an overwhelming misfortune to the person injured, and a needless one, for the risk of injury can be insured by the manufacturer and distributed among the public as a cost of doing business." . . . The manufacturer is in the best position to discover and guard against defects in its products and to warn of harmful effects; thus, holding it liable for defects and failure to warn of harmful effects will provide an incentive to product safety. . . . These considerations are particularly significant where medication is involved, for the consumer is virtually helpless to protect himself from serious, sometimes permanent, sometimes fatal, injuries caused by deleterious drugs.
>
> Where, as here, all defendants produced a drug from an identical formula and the manufacturer of the DES which caused plaintiff's injuries cannot be identified through no fault of plaintiff, a modification of the rule [requiring causation] is warranted. . . .

(W)e hold it to be reasonable in the present context to measure the likelihood that any of the defendants supplied the product which allegedly injured plaintiff by the percentage which the DES sold by each of them for the purpose of preventing miscarriage bears to the entire production of the drug sold by all for that purpose. Plaintiff asserts in her briefs that Eli Lilly and Company and 5 or 6 other companies produced 90 percent of the DES marketed. If at trial this is established to be the fact, then there is a corresponding likelihood that this comparative handful of producers manufactured the DES which caused plaintiff's injuries, and only a 10 percent likelihood that the offending producer would escape liability.

If plaintiff joins in the action the manufacturers of a substantial share of the DES which her mother might have taken, the injustice of shifting the burden of proof to defendants to demonstrate that they could not have made the substance which injured plaintiff is significantly diminished. . . .

The presence in the action of a substantial share of the appropriate market also provides a ready means to apportion damages among the defendants. Each defendant will be held liable for the proportion of the judgment represented by its share of that market unless it demonstrates that it could not have made the product which caused plaintiff's injuries.

1. Is the court's reasoning in support of such market-share liability convincing? Why or why not?
2. The court holds here that the degree of liability incurred by each of the former DES manufacturers should be geared to the share of the market that each had at the time. This might mean, of course, that a particular company would be liable in damages even though the DES responsible for the plaintiff's injuries was sold by someone else. Is this result fair, in your view?

CASE SCENARIO 3   Tobacco Under Attack

Consumer advocates have long argued that cigarettes and other tobacco products are dangerous and that the costs associated with tobacco use should be borne by the tobacco industry. The much-publicized revelations throughout the 1990s of efforts by the industry to conceal knowledge of the addictive nature of its nicotine products are but the latest battles in a long-standing clash between cigarette manufacturers and consumers. A brief summary of the war:

- The earliest lawsuits alleging injury from tobacco use were filed by consumers who began smoking in the forties and fifties, well before warning labels were required on tobacco products. The industry successfully fought these suits by insisting that there was, at the time these consumers began smoking, no clear evidence linking tobacco use with heart, lung, and other diseases. Without such hard data, cigarette makers reasoned, they could not fairly be held liable for the illnesses for which smokers demanded compensation.

- Subsequent to laws passed in the sixties and early seventies requiring warnings and banning television advertising of cigarettes, tobacco manufacturers argued in court that smoking injuries were the result of "contributory negligence," in effect, the consumer's own fault: If consumers take up smoking despite the obvious and mandated warning, cigarette makers insisted, they "assume the risk" of any resulting injury. The users' own personal freedom of choice, and not the product, was the cause of injuries sustained.

- In the early eighties, smokers suffering from tobacco-related injuries began arguing that cigarette makers were effectively failing to comply with mandated warning requirements. Typified by the closely followed *Cippolone* case,[1] these plaintiffs alleged that the tobacco companies used misleading marketing techniques in a way that undercut the very warning labels appearing on their products. Ads associating smoking with youthful, active people in happy, social situations conveyed the message that tobacco use is just good, clean fun. Because this implied claim is false, plaintiffs argued, tobacco manufacturers had breached an express warranty concerning the quality of their product.

- The most recent legal actions against cigarette makers directly attack the industry's "freedom of choice" defense. These lawsuits focus, not on the degree to which the product is linked with disease or the adequacy of the warning given concerning that danger, but rather with the alleged addictive qualities of tobacco's central ingredient—nicotine. Plaintiffs in the massive class-action case *Castano v. American Tobacco,*[2] for example, accused the industry of fraud in connection with a number of allegedly related activities: suppressing the industry's own research revealing that nicotine is an addictive substance; refusing to fund development of a "safer" cigarette; attempting to conceal knowledge of the addictiveness of cigarettes; and adjusting or manipulating the level of nicotine in cigarettes in order to keep smokers hooked. Though the *Castano* case was not permitted to go forward as a class-action suit, arguments quite similar to those advanced in *Castano* are now being used by a number of individual states, each suing the major tobacco manufacturers. By mid-1997 numerous states, counties, and cities had filed suit to recover the Medicaid dollars spent to treat tobacco-related illnesses in the poor and elderly.

- Internal tobacco-industry documents, leaked by whistleblowers and purporting to substantiate the claims of fraud and deliberate manipulation of nicotine levels, became the basis of a decision by the federal Food and Drug Administration (FDA) to classify and regulate cigarettes as a "drug delivery system," signed into law by President Clinton in August 1996. The regulations require anyone younger than twenty-seven to show proof of age before buying cigarettes, ban most vending-machine sales, prohibit tobacco company sponsorship of sporting events, and severely restrict tobacco advertising.

- Finally, a Florida jury in August 1996 handed the tobacco industry its first real courtroom defeat, holding cigarette maker Brown and Williamson liable for the lung cancer contracted by a Florida smoker. The victim was awarded $750,000. Brown and Williamson appealed the decision.

- In 1997 the two largest tobacco manufacturers, R.J. Reynolds and Philip Morris, entered into negotiations with many states that had filed suits against the industry to recover health-care dollars spent on smoking-related illnesses, as well as with private trial lawyers and some public health groups. The proposed settlement, announced in June 1997 and submitted for congressional and presidential approval, would require the tobacco industry to pay $368.5 billion over the next twenty-five years to settle pending litigation and to finance antismoking campaigns and efforts to curb teenage smoking. The tobacco companies would also agree to curtail outdoor advertising and to strengthen health warnings appearing on tobacco products. In exchange the industry would settle hundreds of currently pending lawsuits and obtain immunity from most future suits.

1. Do any of the consumer arguments canvassed here convince you that cigarettes are an "unreasonably dangerous" or "defective" product? Why or why not?
2. Should cigarettes be treated on a par with silicon breast implants or the Dalkon Shield IUD—dangerous products whose manufacturers were held liable for billions of dollars

worth of injuries? Ought tobacco companies be held strictly liable for harms resulting from cigarettes? How would Brenkert's defense of strict liability apply here?

3. The proposed "global settlement" between the tobacco industry and its adversaries, negotiated in 1997, was sharply criticized as deeply immoral, given that it excluded any current or future overseas victims of smoking-related illnesses, by most estimates the fastest-growing segment of smokers worldwide. By 1997 Philip Morris and R.J. Reynolds were selling nearly two-thirds of their cigarettes overseas, and almost half of their 1996 profits came from foreign sales. Should such a settlement be approved? Why or why not?

NOTES

1. 112 S.Ct. 2608 (1992).
2. 95-30725.

CASE SCENARIO 4   Baby Luv and Strict Liability

Baby Luv, Inc., manufactures inexpensive baby furniture and toys. One of its products is an infant crib. Betty Brown had been shopping for a crib for her newborn, and she settled on the Baby Luv crib, largely because it was the least expensive. Only a few weeks after her purchase of the crib, a terrible accident occurred: Betty's infant managed to slide his head between the slats on the crib's side (which were 3⅜ inches apart) and was permanently injured due to near strangulation. (Cribs with slats no more than 2 inches apart, a safe distance, were available on the market at the time Betty bought the Baby Luv.) Betty decides to take Baby Luv to court, alleging that the crib is defective in its design and claiming that the corporation should be held strictly liable. While the parties are preparing to go to trial, the FTC, under pressure from consumer groups, issues a regulation prohibiting the sale of cribs with slats more than 2 inches apart. Before the court, Baby Luv argues two claims: (1) it should *not* be held strictly liable for the infant's injury, and (2) the FTC regulation is an impermissible instance of paternalism.

Imagine that you are a philosophical judge thinking about this case. How would you rule on each of Baby Luv's claims and why? Consider carefully the arguments that can be made on both sides of each issue.

1. What are the central ethical issues raised by the events depicted in this scenario?
2. How would the authors that you read for this chapter analyze the issues raised in this case? Be specific.
3. How would you argue for a position on how each of the issues raised by the scenario should be resolved? Base your argument on the concepts and arguments raised in the readings for this chapter.

⠀CHAPTER 9

Business and
the Environment

Most of us are all too aware of at least some ways in which human activity has damaged the natural environment: We work in cities with bad air, play on beaches polluted with garbage, and buy bottled water instead of drinking what comes out of the tap. But the degree to which humans have adversely altered the natural world is often not fully appreciated. Not only is some of our air and water polluted, but our industries generate tons of hazardous waste—from toxic solvents to spent nuclear material; our wetlands are being drained and filled; our planet may gradually be warming; and our forests are shrinking while deserts expand. These and other examples of environmental destruction result both from beliefs many of us share about the natural world and the practices that form our consumer culture—beliefs and practices that are carried over into the business world.

The tension between the business world and those concerned with protecting the environment has become a frequent feature of the nightly news; and battles between the two groups are being fought out in legislatures. In California, for example, recent efforts by the conservative governor and legislators have centered on streamlining the state's environmental safeguards—redefining wildlife habitat, relaxing deadlines for introduction of electric cars, permitting continued use of potentially dangerous agricultural pesticides—in order to make environmental compliance cheaper and thus more friendly to business and industry in the state. Property rights advocates in many states have taken to the courts to seek the overturn of environmental regulations (for example, wetlands and endangered-species laws) and to obtain compensation for a reduction in the value of their land due to the effects of governmental environmental regulation.

BIODIVERSITY AND PROPERTY RIGHTS

Some of the clearest examples of the conflicts increasingly common between businesses and those concerned with protecting the environment center on laws passed in the 1970s to ensure environmental quality—statutes like the Clean Water Act, the Clean Air Act, and the Endangered Species Act (ESA). The ESA established protected categories of animals, designating some as "endangered" and others as "threatened." Hunting or killing such designated species was forbidden, and land-use restrictions were implemented to support these provisions. Many point to the success of the ESA in returning more than a few species from the brink of extinction. More recently, attention has shifted away from the dangers posed by hunting rare species to the widespread destruction of wildlife habitat, as it gives way to

---

✑ Business and the Superfund Law

In 1980 Congress passed the Comprehensive Environmental Response, Compensation, and Liability Act (CERCLA), widely known as the "Superfund" law. The law was intended to ensure efficient cleanup of sites contaminated by toxic and hazardous waste across the country by identifying parties who would be responsible for "remediation," taking care of the problem. For any given site, the law imposes liability on any or all of a group of "potentially responsible parties," meaning anyone who has either owned or operated a facility at which hazardous substances were disposed of, who arranged for the disposal of such waste, or who accepted waste for transport to the site. The liability imposed by CERCLA is both retroactive and "joint and several." This means that companies that contributed waste to a Superfund site prior to the enactment of the Superfund law are still liable for cleanup costs, even if the storage or dumping of the waste was legal at the time; and each and every responsible party can be held liable for the entire costs of cleanup, assuming the cost cannot be apportioned among two or more parties. Under the law, the current owner of a site, if unable to locate those who polluted it, may be forced to bear all of the cleanup costs. Critics in business and industry complain that such liability requirements are unjust and contribute to the proliferation of "brownfields"—abandoned and decaying industrial sites in urban centers to which redevelopers cannot be attracted for fear of massive liability for cleanup of pollution caused years or even decades earlier. While some studies have shown that CERCLA has been responsible for the removal of toxic or hazardous wastes at thousands of sites nationwide, critics contend the average time between identification of a site and completion of cleanup efforts has averaged more than fifteen years and has cost the responsible parties involved more than $8.3 billion. Recently, conservatives in Congress have pushed to pass wide-ranging reforms of the Superfund law, including prohibiting the retroactive application of the law and eliminating joint and several liability. Should CERCLA be reformed? And if so, how?

---

the relentless encroachment of expanding human populations. The imperative to preserve "biodiversity" has led some environmentalists to campaign for severe restrictions on the draining of wetlands and the clear-cutting of old-growth forests. The continued existence of a diverse range of interdependent species, say defenders of environmental regulation, is itself a value to be pursued, apart from whatever practical benefits (economic, medical, agricultural, and so on) might accrue to human beings by guaranteeing the continuation of the rich diversity evident in the biosphere.

But now such environmental regulations have increasingly come under attack by those who contend that environmental laws are being used unfairly to restrict the legitimate use of natural resources and to violate the land-use rights of property owners. The most widely publicized of such recent controversies pitted efforts by the federal government to protect the habitat of the northern spotted owl against the owners and employees of timber mills anxious to harvest old-growth forests that serve as the bird's habitat. The opening case in this chapter, *Babbitt v. Sweet Home*, deals with the effort of the United States Supreme Court to resolve this dispute.

As the *Sweet Home* case and other readings in this chapter make clear, environmental disputes raise deep questions. The beliefs and values central to the debate over many environmental issues are brought to light by questions like these: What value does the natural environment have? What does it matter if we despoil it? Don't we have to make a living?

What will it cost to clean up a polluted stream or lake? Should the industry who caused the pollution pay to clean it up? But don't we all contribute to pollution? Shouldn't business-people worry about doing business? Why should they have to be concerned with the environment? Those of us who live in the northern, highly industrialized nations of the world disproportionately consume the world's scarce resources, and our lifestyle contributes much to environmental degradation. How should responsibility for ameliorating global environmental problems be allocated? Should our approach to environmental problems be completely human-centered? Is it wrong to wipe out an entire species of plant or animal from the planet? Do natural objects have a worth or value apart from the fact that having them around suits our needs? And even if they do have an intrinsic value, what are the responsibilities of corporations concerning them? Shouldn't a business be concerned only with making a profit? These are just a few of the questions that naturally come to mind when thinking about our responsibilities concerning the environment, and they form the focus of this chapter.

COST/BENEFIT ANALYSIS

One obvious way of beginning to think about environmental problems from the standpoint of business is by treating them as a kind of economic problem, insisting that environmental problems are issues best treated by economic analysis. From this point of view, the question of the sustainability of a viable environment becomes a question of how to allocate valuable but unowned natural resources such as clean air and water. The answer to such questions, from the economic perspective, lies in government or private control of such resources. Looking at things in this way, proponents of economic analysis say, allows society to strike a balance between cost and benefit that will promote the welfare of society as a whole. What these answers presuppose, point out critics of the economic perspective, is a conception of the environment as an economic commodity—a means for promoting the happiness of human beings. Trees, lakes, and animals are valuable only if they promote that happiness, and in that regard they are really not any different from automobiles, VCRs, and personal computers. The economic conception contrasts with the view that non-human forms of life have an intrinsic worth aside from whatever value we invest in them. This view is argued by some environmentalists and philosophers, who believe that such non-human forms of life have as much right to their continued existence as we do to ours, that they deserve to have that right protected from the encroachment of business just as we do. The debate joined by these two distinct perspectives is raised by several of the readings in this chapter.

The economic approach to environmental issues relies upon two assumptions which need to be made explicit. The first is the assumption of *anthropomorphism:* that environmental issues and their solutions are exclusively human-centered. All that matters in deciding environmental issues is that human desires are satisfied; nothing else counts, even if it could be shown that animals (or even trees) had preferences or interests. So the moral question of whether a lake or a river is to be polluted becomes a question of which humans could be harmed by the pollutants (for example, recreational users) and which humans might benefit by the pollution (for example, the businesses that use the lake as an expedient way of disposing of their waste). How ought cases like this to be decided? Economic analysis proposes a tool for the resolution of this and all other conflicts of a similar type. The tool, introduced in chapter 1, is *cost-benefit analysis.* To use this tool, we simply tally the number of preferences that would be satisfied by maintaining the lake's pristine condition (benefit) and compare this with the frustrated desires of the business owners (costs). If the costs are less than the benefits, the lake remains a recreational resource; if not, it becomes a dumping ground.

✐   A New Use for Cost/Benefit Analysis?

A dispute between environmentalists and consumers of electricity over proposed changes in the management of the Glen Canyon Dam, on the Colorado River, recently became the focus for a new form of cost/benefit analysis. Damage to the ecology of the Grand Canyon has resulted, environmentalists contend, from increased water flow as colder water from behind the dam is released to generate additional electricity for peak demand by consumers in southwestern metropolitan areas of the United States. In response to these concerns, the U.S. Interior Department in 1995 proposed to make changes to the water-release policy, changes expected to boost electricity rates throughout the West by nearly $3 billion a year. As part of its procedure in finalizing the proposed changes, the federal government planned to conduct a survey across the country, asking Americans how much they value the Grand Canyon by indicating how much each American would be willing to pay to restore the ecosystem of the canyon, reversing the environmental damage there. Such questions are meant to assess the value Americans attach to leaving a given natural resource unexploited, apart, for example, from the benefit one might get from actually going to the Grand Canyon and enjoying its benefits directly. Some environmentalists praised the effort to factor the "psychic value" people attach to knowing that some natural areas are protected from environmental degradation; others, however, insisted that such analyses still function, ultimately, by placing a price tag on the Grand Canyon's ecological balance. Assessing the "non-use value" of a resource in this way has been used previously. After the *Exxon Valdez* oil spill in Alaska, for example, non-use analysis was employed to attach a figure of $3 billion to Prince William Sound (where the spill occurred) in an unspoiled state. Should non-use analysis be used more widely in setting environmental protection policies? What is such an analysis actually measuring? Does the "willingness-to-pay" criterion adequately capture the value that I attach to knowing that a treasured resource is being protected? Can the non-use value of an item be accurately measured, given that such things are not traded in the marketplace?

One obvious assumption of this method is that all environmental policies should be determined using such consequentialist reasoning. The advantage of such a reasoning is obvious: simplicity. Cost-versus-benefit analysis seems to provide a simple algorithm for deciding difficult cases. But there are significant conceptual and ethical questions that critics and proponents alike find troubling.

One problem has to do with the terminology of "cost" and "benefit." Again, these are to be understood in terms of the satisfaction or frustration of human preferences. Couldn't a critic coherently object that the destruction of an environmental resource imposes a "cost" on non-human animals, or that the benefit of satisfying some desires by allowing pollution doesn't deserve to be counted as a benefit for society? What does the analyst do when there is no easy way of tallying the full range of satisfied and frustrated preferences? Do we count the people who regularly use the lake for recreation, or those who anticipate using the lake, or those who want to preserve the lake for their offspring but who don't intend to use it themselves? Do we count only the desires of the business managers? Or the shareholders and workers as well? Do all these desires count, or should only some of them be considered? One possible solution to such quandaries, advanced by cost/benefit analysis, is the "willingness-to-pay" criterion. Assuming we can settle on whose desires should be considered, the analyst can ask what the desiring parties are willing to pay for the use of the resource in question. Proponents claim that this is an accurate measure of how intensely people desire to use the resource. Those who have the strongest preference will pay the most money. In this case, the strongest preference wins out. So, in the case of the lake, ask the polluters what they would be willing to pay to dump their waste and compare this figure with what those who want to preserve the lake are willing to invest to see that their desires are satisfied. As critics have argued, there are two obvious problems here—one conceptual and one ethical. For the people who seek a recreational use of the resource, how would they estimate the economic value of the recreational activity? Or how would they put a price on the peace and beauty of the place? Additionally, doesn't the willingness-to-pay criterion in reality mean that the party with the most money always wins out? The criticism here is that willingness to pay really means ability to pay. If so, the critics conclude, this criterion is unfair and discriminates against the desires of those who simply don't have the money to compete with the heavily subsidized desires of others.

The final ethical point to be made regarding cost/benefit analysis has to do with value-of-life assessments. Imagine a slightly modified scenario from the foregoing, wherein the parties involved are the polluters and the people living around the lake whose safety is affected by the dumping. How would we assess the potential harm to the latter group? Cost/benefit analysis suggests that we again look at those potential harms from the perspective of economics. To determine the potential costs of pollution on the residents, one could calculate the harm done to them and to society in terms of how disability or death from the pollutants would affect their contributions to the economy. For example, one might attempt to determine the cost of a resident's death in terms of loss of his net earnings, which otherwise could have been used for the purchase of goods and services in the economy. These costs could then be measured against the economic benefits of dumping the pollutants in the lake instead of disposing of them by other conventional means. Critics maintain that the problem with the analysis proceeding in this manner is transparent: It seems to imply that the earning power of an individual is an indication of a person's worth, so poor people would be worth less than wealthier individuals, blacks less than whites, and women less than men. As with the willingness-to-pay criterion, the preferences matter only insofar as they are backed up by money. But, of course, nearly everyone believes that earning power has nothing to do with moral worth or human dignity—the sense of worth our nation's founders appealed to when they wrote that all are created equal and possess inalienable rights. All of the foregoing difficulties notwithstanding, cost/benefit analysis is a primary tool for creating environmental policy today and will continue to be until our perspective on the natural environment and human life changes drastically.

BUSINESS DECISIONS AND ENVIRONMENTAL RACISM

Many businesses, as we have seen, are critical of the efforts of environmentalists to protect the natural world at the expense of jobs and economic growth. But environmental groups like the Sierra Club and Greenpeace, long at the forefront of environmental activism, have recently come under attack from another quarter. The most pressing environmental problem of the next century, say the critics, will be that of *environmental justice*—a problem that the critics contend has largely been ignored by the traditional environmental mainstream. *Environmental justice* refers to the moral imperative to eliminate discrimination in the distribution of benefits and burdens produced by such decisions as where to locate a landfill or a solid-waste incinerator. The duty imposed by such an imperative is to eradicate what has been called *environmental racism*.

The term *environmental racism* was coined in the late 1980s as a way of referring to the allegedly racist distribution of environmental hazards: Communities that are predominately non-white, it was argued, suffer disproportionate exposure to sources of air and water pollution and other environmental hazards. Those concerned about environmental racism point to various statistics in support of their case. A report of the General Accounting Office found that three out of four commercial hazardous landfills in the southeast United States were located in predominately black communities; the number of minority communities nationwide in which hazardous waste sites are to be found is double that of communities without such sites; government enforcement of the Superfund cleanup law is selective, with white communities consistently receiving faster action in dealing with dangerous sites. In sum, most "locally unwanted land uses" (Lulus) tend to be in poor, politically disempowered communities.

Those skeptical of charges of environmental racism argue that minority communities are systematically targeted for a variety of unwanted land uses because planners and business leaders choose the path of least resistance: Minority neighborhoods, because they are generally poorer and less well-organized politically, are unlikely to mount a serious challenge to a siting decision. Business leaders and local governments respond that decisions on where to place a waste incinerator, for example, are legitimately based upon economic criteria, such as land values, proximity to markets and suppliers, zoning laws, and tax rates. This debate raises serious questions: How should environmental impacts be distributed throughout society? Can they be spread equitably? And what would that mean?

THE READINGS

This chapter opens with the decision of the U.S. Supreme Court in the *Sweet Home* case, involving a battle over the proper scope of concern for endangered species and their habitats. The readings then turn to a core question concerning the environment and how humans—in or out of business—view it. This question can be illustrated by an example. Suppose that ABC Manufacturing, Inc., discharges pollutants into a river as a by-product of its plant operations. The pollutants kill fish and other wildlife and damage plants, trees, and flora along the waterway. Assuming ABC is doing something wrong in continuing to dump toxic waste into the river, whom has its actions wronged? Is ABC's conduct wrong because it will ultimately hurt humans, since people will no longer be able to eat the river's fish and enjoy its trees and scenery? Or has ABC done something wrong in harming the fish or trees themselves, apart from how people will be impacted? In the first of our readings on this issue, William Baxter insists that ABC's actions can be assessed only in terms of how they impact people. And it is not necessarily true, according to Baxter, that ABC is acting wrongly. To say that it is, as Baxter makes plain, is to draw conclusions from certain premises about what kinds of things have or don't have moral value, and from the fact of scarcity of basic resources. Fish, trees, and penguins have no value in and of themselves, Baxter believes, and no right to exist apart from the good that having them around will do for human beings. And to protect nature from the hazards of pollution, for example, means that we must devote to that task resources that could be expended elsewhere. It is for this reason, Baxter argues, that the issue is not "pollution or no pollution" but, rather, how much pollution we are going to have to tolerate in order to have the other things that members of a consumer society want.

Mark Sagoff would view the case of ABC Manufacturing quite differently. Putting up with the occasional spill of toxic debris might be worth it, if what mattered to us was having a river that was polluted (because we want the things that cause pollution) but still usable for, say, boating. But this is not, says Sagoff, how we view pollution. We view polluting the planet as an evil, and clean water as a good, apart from and sometimes even in spite of our own selfish goals and desires. Sagoff introduces and explains the distinction drawn by philosophers between a thing's having *intrinsic* versus *instrumental* value. He then proceeds to build an argument for the claim that the concerns many humans share for clean water, unspoiled rain forests, and the survival of endangered species reflect an underlying, though often unacknowledged, commitment to the intrinsic, moral, and aesthetic value of the natural environment. Environmentalists would be wise, he concludes, to argue for environmental protection on moral and aesthetic rather than self-interested and instrumental grounds.

The essay by Gretchen Morgenson and Gale Eisenstodt provides an argument for a free-market approach to problems of environmental pollution. The argument proceeds in two parts: First, the authors contend that government regulation is inefficient and consistently influenced by powerful special-interest lobbies that influence lawmaking for their own gain and to the detriment of society; second, the authors argue that pollution problems can be best addressed through the mechanism of markets, ensuring that the costs of pollution are borne by the producers of polluting technologies and the consumers who benefit from them. The specific proposals that Morgenson and Eisenstodt make do not mean the end of government regulation; the government might, for instance, be involved in the creation of markets for environmentally beneficial goods. Rather, they propose a redirection of environmental efforts in keeping with the free-market principle that individuals are motivated by self-interest.

Norman Bowie's essay begins with the acknowledgment that corporations do have an obligation to protect the environment. This obligation should not be construed, however, as requiring that firms do more than is mandated by law. Bowie reminds us that, with respect to corporations, obligations must be balanced by considerations of profitability. Although it might be technically possible to produce nonpolluting factories or maximally safe automobiles, such endeavors, when undertaken by a corporation, might make it uncompetitive or even threaten its viability. With respect to issues of pollution and safety, Bowie agrees that governmental regulation is the key to revealing what citizens believe to be the proper balance between safety and costs; and businesses have an obligation to heed such a balance. Bowie points out, however, that much unethical conduct occurs when corporations attempt to effect the creation of environmental regulations through lobbyists and political action committees. They attempt "to have their cake and eat it too" by using their influence either to defeat or to weaken these very same laws. The primary obligation of business, Bowie declares, is to stay out of the political arena. He admits that this conclusion is tentative; but it is an extremely interesting point of departure for those who see the interests of business and of environmentalists continually at loggerheads. W. Michael Hoffman responds to Bowie. Hoffman argues that Bowie's focus on obedience to law as the locus of corporate social responsibility is too narrow. Coming to grips with the environmental crisis requires the cooperation and creative efforts of all the affected parties, including business. Yet Hoffman is critical of solutions that amount to little more than designing and marketing environmentally friendly goods and services. He worries that, although markets might currently exist for such goods and services, they may be greatly reduced or even eliminated by the corporate requirement that profits be maximized. At bottom, he suggests, responsible environmental actions may be inconsistent with that self-interested goal.

The last set of readings explores the larger global and environmental concerns that businesses will encounter in the twenty-first century. What should the global environmental priorities be? Will such priorities be viewed differently by multinational corporations based in the largely industrialized countries of the northern hemisphere than by the peoples of the lesser-developed nations in the south? In his essay, Indian author Ramachandra Guha develops a critique of "deep ecology," a movement whose principles and assumptions are increasingly accepted among environmentalists in America. Guha tries to identify the central tenets or precepts of this distinctive form of American environmentalism. The deep ecologists, according to Guha, are non-anthropocentric, believing that the value of nature resides, not in the enjoyment humans derive from it, but in its intrinsic worth; and it is for this reason that deep ecologists rank wilderness preservation among their top priorities. Deep ecologists also borrow from Eastern religions and philosophies in an effort to build a universal basis for environmental initiatives. Guha attacks each of these assumptions. The anthropocentric or human-centered view of life is not the real culprit in many cases of environmental destruction, Guha maintains; rather, such destruction is a result of uncontrolled consumerism among people in nations like the United States. Moreover, the preoccupation of American environmentalists with wilderness preservation leads to neglect of environmental problems facing many poor people in developing nations. The program of deep ecology, Guha concludes, does not fundamentally challenge the premises and larger impacts of modern consumerism and growth.

The final reading, by noted sociologist Robert Bullard, explores the issue of environmental racism. The case for the existence of environmental racism can be made in several ways, according to Bullard. The procedures for enforcing existing environmental protections are not, he claims, followed even-handedly: Communities that are affluent and predominately white, for example, generally receive faster and better action by government authorities to address environmental hazards. And the criteria routinely used by business and industry, and approved by local and state governments, for the siting of unwanted land uses often unfairly target minority communities. Bullard marshals empirical and statistical evidence to support these claims and to argue for a number of steps designed to enable poor, minority communities to reverse the incidence of environmental injustice.

✒︎   "Natural Resource Damages" and the Value of the Environment

In the aftermath of the devastating oil spill in Alaska's Prince William Sound, caused when the tanker *Exxon Valdez* went aground, Exxon Corp. agreed to pay $900 million to the State of Alaska and to the U.S. government. This sum did not reflect the cost of cleanup (for which Exxon paid as well); rather, the $900 million was intended to compensate for damage to the sound itself. Such "natural resource damages" (NRDs) are increasingly common in environmental law and they raise significant issues. Destruction or degradation of "natural resources," defined in federal law to include "land, fish, wildlife, biota, air, water" and other resources, may themselves be the basis for requiring firms to pay monetary damages. Recovery can include the costs of restoring, replacing, or acquiring the equivalent of the injured resource, as well as the diminished value of the resource in the time between injury and restoration. Proponents of imposing such liability on businesses argue that it forces those responsible to more fully absorb the true cost of their environmentally unsafe practices; critics contend that such damages cannot be accurately measured. A typical device for measuring the value to which a bay or a woodland has been degraded is *contingent valuation methodology,* or non-use analysis, which seeks to measure an individual's willingness to pay for the preservation of an endangered species or an unspoiled coastline (see the "A New Use for Cost/Benefit Analysis?" sidebar). Should natural resource damages be imposed? Why or why not?

CASE STUDY   *Babbitt v. Sweet Home Chapter of Communities for a Great Oregon*

United States Supreme Court
115 S. Ct. 2407 (1995)

Justice STEVENS delivered the opinion of the Court.

I

Section 9 of the Endangered Species Act provides [that it is unlawful for any person to] "take" any endangered species "within the United States or the territorial sea of the United States." [T]he Act defines the statutory term "take": ". . . to harass, harm, pursue, hunt, shoot, wound, kill, trap, capture, or collect, or to attempt to engage in any such conduct. . . ." The Interior Department regulations that implement the statute, however, define the statutory term "harm": "Harm . . . means an act which actually kills or injures wildlife. Such act may include significant habitat modification or degradation where it actually kills or injures wildlife by significantly impairing essential behavioral patterns, including breeding, feeding, or sheltering." This regulation has been in place since 1975.

. . .[S]ection 10 of the Act . . . authorizes the Secretary to grant a permit for any taking otherwise prohibited by [the Act] "if such taking is incidental to, and not the purpose of, the carrying out of an otherwise lawful activity."

In addition . . . [the ESA] authorizes the Secretary, in cooperation with the States . . . to acquire land to aid in preserving such species. . . .

Respondents in this action are small landowners, logging companies, and families dependent on the forest products industries in the Pacific Northwest and in the Southeast, and organizations that represent their interests. They brought this . . . action . . . to challenge the statutory validity of the Secretary's regulation defining "harm," particularly the inclusion of habitat modification and degradation in the definition. . . . Their complaint alleged that application of the "harm" regulation to the red-cockaded woodpecker, an endangered species, and the northern spotted owl, a threatened species, had injured them economically.

Respondents advanced three arguments. . . . First, they correctly noted that language in the Senate's original version of the ESA would have defined "take" to include "destruction, modification, or curtailment of [the] habitat or range" of fish or wildlife, but the Senate deleted that language from the bill before enacting it. Second, respondents argued that Congress intended the Act's express authorization for the Federal Government to buy private land in order to prevent habitat degradation . . . to be the exclusive check against habitat modification on private property. Third, because the Senate added the term "harm" to the definition of "take" in a floor amendment without debate, respondents argued that the court should not interpret the term so expansively as to include habitat modification. . . .

II

. . . First, we assume respondents have no desire to harm either the red-cockaded woodpecker or the spotted owl; they merely wish to continue logging activities that would be entirely proper if not prohibited by the ESA. On the other hand, we must assume arguendo that those activities will have the effect, even though unintended, of detrimentally changing the natural habitat of both listed species and that, as a consequence, members of those species will be killed or injured. Under respondents' view of the law, the Secretary's only means of forestalling that grave result— even when the actor knows it is certain to occur—is to use his . . . authority to purchase the lands on which the survival of the species depends. The Secretary, on the other hand, submits that the

. . . prohibition on takings, which Congress defined to include "harm," places on respondents a duty to avoid harm that habitat alteration will cause the birds unless respondents first obtain a permit. . . .

The text of the Act provides three reasons for concluding that the Secretary's interpretation is reasonable. First, an ordinary understanding of the word "harm" supports it. The dictionary definition of the verb form of "harm" is "to cause hurt or damage to: injure." *Webster's Third New International Dictionary* 1034 (1966). In the context of the ESA, that definition naturally encompasses habitat modification that results in actual injury or death to members of an endangered or threatened species.

. . .[U]nless the statutory term "harm" encompasses indirect as well as direct injuries, the word has no meaning that does not duplicate the meaning of other words . . . use[d] to define "take." A reluctance to treat statutory terms as surplusage supports the reasonableness of the Secretary's interpretation.

Second, the broad purpose of the ESA supports the Secretary's decision to extend protection against activities that cause the precise harms Congress enacted the statute to avoid. In *TVA v. Hill* [a 1978 case], we described the Act as "the most comprehensive legislation for the preservation of endangered species ever enacted by any nation. . . ." [A]mong its central purposes is "to provide a means whereby the ecosystems upon which endangered species and threatened species depend may be conserved. . . ."

In *Hill,* we construed [a different section of the Act] as precluding the completion of the Tellico Dam because of its predicted impact on the survival of the snail darter. Both our holding and the language in our opinion stressed the importance of the statutory policy. "The plain intent of Congress in enacting this statute," we recognized, "was to halt and reverse the trend toward species extinction, whatever the cost. . . ."

III

Our conclusion . . . gains further support from the legislative history of the statute. . . . The Senate Report stressed that " '[t]ake' is defined . . . in the broadest possible manner to include every conceivable way in which a person can 'take' or attempt to 'take' any fish or wildlife. . . ." The House Report underscored the breadth of the "take" definition by noting that it included "harassment, whether intentional or not." The Report explained that the definition "would allow, for example, the Secretary to regulate or prohibit the activities of birdwatchers where the effect of those activities might disturb the birds and make it difficult for them to hatch or raise their young." These comments, ignored in the dissent's welcome but selective foray into legislative history, support the Secretary's interpretation that the term "take" in [the Act] reached far more than the deliberate actions of hunters and trappers.

Two endangered species bills . . . were introduced in the Senate and referred to the Commerce Committee. Neither bill included the word "harm" in its definition of "take," although the definitions otherwise closely resembled the one that appeared in the bill as ultimately enacted. Senator Tunney, the floor manager of the bill in the Senate, subsequently introduced a floor amendment that added "harm" to the definition, noting that this and accompanying amendments would "help to achieve the purposes of the bill." Respondents argue that the lack of debate about the amendment that added "harm" counsels in favor of a narrow interpretation. We disagree. An obviously broad word that the Senate went out of its way to add to an important statutory definition is precisely the sort of provision that deserves a respectful reading. . . .

IV

When it enacted the ESA, Congress delegated broad administrative and interpretive power to the Secretary. The task of defining and listing endangered and threatened species requires an expertise and attention to detail that exceeds the normal province of Congress. Fashioning appropriate standards for issuing permits . . . for takings that would otherwise violate . . . [the Act] necessarily requires the exercise of broad discretion. The proper interpretation of a term such as "harm" involves a complex policy choice. When Congress has entrusted the Secretary with broad discretion, we are especially reluctant to substitute our views of wise policy for his. In this case, that reluctance accords with our conclusion, based on the text, structure, and legislative history of the ESA, that the Secretary reasonably construed the intent of Congress when he defined "harm" to include "significant habitat modification or degradation that actually kills or injures wildlife."

Justice O'CONNOR, concurring.

[It is my understanding that] the challenged regulation is limited to significant habitat modification that causes actual, as opposed to hypothetical or speculative, death or injury to identifiable protected animals. . . .

In my view, the regulation is limited by its terms to actions that actually kill or injure individual animals. . . .

. . . As an initial matter, I do not find it as easy as [dissenting] Justice Scalia does to dismiss the notion that significant impairment of breeding injures living creatures. To raze the last remaining ground on which the piping plover currently breeds, thereby making it impossible for any piping plovers to reproduce, would obviously injure the population (causing the species' extinction in a generation). But by completely preventing breeding, it would also injure the individual living bird, in the same way that sterilizing the creature injures the individual living bird. To "injure" is, among other things, "to impair." *Webster's Ninth New Collegiate Dictionary* 623 (1983). One need not subscribe to theories of "psychic harm," [referring to Scalia's response to her], to recognize that to make it impossible for an animal to reproduce is to impair its most essential physical functions and to render that animal, and its genetic material, biologically obsolete. This, in my view, is actual injury.

In any event, even if impairing an animal's ability to breed were not, in and of itself, an injury to that animal, interference with breeding can cause an animal to suffer other, perhaps more obvious, kinds of injury. The regulation has clear application, for example, to significant habitat modification that kills or physically injures animals which, because they are in a vulnerable breeding state, do not or cannot flee or defend themselves, or to environmental pollutants that cause an animal to suffer physical complications during gestation. Breeding, feeding, and sheltering are what animals do. If significant habitat modification, by interfering with these essential behaviors, actually kills or injures an animal protected by the Act, it causes "harm" within the meaning of the regulation. . . .

Justice SCALIA, with whom The CHIEF JUSTICE and Justice THOMAS join, dissenting.

I think it unmistakably clear that the legislation at issue here (1) forbade the hunting and killing of endangered animals, and (2) provided federal lands and federal funds for the acquisition of private lands, to preserve the habitat of endangered animals. The Court's holding that the hunting and killing prohibition incidentally preserves habitat on private lands imposes unfairness to the point of financial ruin—not just upon the rich, but upon the simplest farmer who finds his land conscripted to national zoological use. I respectfully dissent.

The regulation has three features which . . . do not comport with the statute. First, it interprets the statute to prohibit habitat modification that is no more than the cause-in-fact of death or injury to wildlife. Any "significant habitat modification" that in fact produces that result by "impairing essential behavioral patterns" is made unlawful, regardless of whether that result is intended or even foreseeable, and no matter how long the chain of causality between modification and injury. See, e.g., *Palila v. Hawaii Dept. of Land and Natural Resources (Palila II)*, (9th Circuit 1988) (sheep grazing constituted "taking" of palila birds, since although sheep do not destroy full-grown mamane trees, they do destroy mamane seedlings, which will not grow to full-grown trees, on which the palila feeds and nests).

Second, the regulation does not require an "act": the Secretary's officially stated position is that an omission will do. . . .

The third and most important unlawful feature of the regulation is that it encompasses injury inflicted, not only upon individual animals, but upon populations of the protected species. "Injury" in the regulation includes "significantly impairing essential behavioral patterns, including breeding." Impairment of breeding does not "injure" living creatures; it prevents them from propagating, thus "injuring" a population of animals which would otherwise have maintained or increased its numbers. . . .

None of these three features of the regulation can be found in the statutory provisions supposed to authorize it. . . . If "take" were not elsewhere defined in the Act, none could dispute what it means, for the term is as old as the law itself. To "take," when applied to wild animals, means to reduce those animals, by killing or capturing, to human control. See, e.g., 11 *Oxford English Dictionary* (1933) ("Take . . . To catch, capture (a wild beast, bird, fish, etc.)"); *Webster's New International Dictionary of the English Language* (2d ed. 1949) (take defined as "to catch or capture by trapping, snaring, etc., or as prey"). . . . It is obvious that "take" in this sense—a term of art deeply embedded in the statutory and common law concerning wildlife—describes a class of acts (not omissions) done directly and intentionally (not indirectly and by accident) to particular animals (not populations of animals). . . .

Second, the Court maintains that the legislative history of the 1973 Act supports the Secretary's definition. . . .

Both the Senate and House floor managers of the bill explained it in terms which leave no doubt that the problem of habitat destruction on private lands was to be solved principally by the land acquisition program, . . . while [the other provision] solved a different problem altogether—the problem of takings. Senator Tunney stated: "Through [the] land acquisition provisions, we will be able to conserve habitats necessary to protect fish and wildlife from further destruction. "Although most endangered species are threatened primarily by the destruction of their natural habitats, a significant portion of these animals are subject to predation by man for commercial, sport, consumption, or other purposes. The provisions of [the bill] would prohibit the commerce in or the importation, exportation, or taking of endangered species. . . ." The House floor manager, Representative Sullivan, put the same thought in this way: "[T]he principal threat to animals stems from destruction of their habitat. . . . [The bill] will meet this problem by providing funds for acquisition of critical habitat. . . . It will also enable the Department of Agriculture to cooperate with willing landowners who desire to assist in the protection of endangered species, but who are understandably unwilling to do so at excessive cost to themselves. Another hazard to endangered species arises from those who would capture or kill them for pleasure or profit. There is no way that Congress can make it less pleasurable for a person to take an animal, but we can certainly make it less profitable for them to do so." Habitat modification and takings, in other words, were viewed as different provisions of the Act. . . .

Justice O'Connor supposes that an "impairment of breeding" intrinsically injures an animal. . . . [But] surely the only harm to the individual animal from impairment of that "essential function" is not the failure of issue (which harms only the issue), but the psychic harm of perceiving that it will leave this world with no issue (assuming, of course, that the animal in question, perhaps an endangered species of slug, is capable of such painful sentiments). If it includes that psychic harm, then why not the psychic harm of not being able to frolic about—so that the draining of a pond used for an endangered animal's recreation, but in no way essential to its survival, would be prohibited by the Act? . . .

But since the Court is reading the regulation and the statute incorrectly in other respects, it may as well introduce this novelty as well—law a la carte. As I understand the regulation that the

Court has created and held consistent with the statute that it has also created, habitat modification can constitute a "taking," but only if it results in the killing or harming of individual animals, and only if that consequence is the direct result of the modification. This means that the destruction of privately owned habitat that is essential, not for the feeding or nesting, but for the breeding, of butterflies, would not violate the Act, since it would not harm or kill any living butterfly. I, too, think it would not violate the Act—not for the utterly unsupported reason that habitat modifications fall outside the regulation if they happen not to kill or injure a living animal, but for the textual reason that only action directed at living animals constitutes a "take."

The Endangered Species Act is a carefully considered piece of legislation that forbids all persons to hunt or harm endangered animals, but places upon the public at large, rather than upon fortuitously accountable individual landowners, the cost of preserving the habitat of endangered species. There is neither textual support for, nor even evidence of congressional consideration of, the radically different disposition contained in the regulation that the Court sustains. For these reasons, I respectfully dissent.

People or Penguins

William Baxter

I start with the modest proposition that, in dealing with pollution, or indeed with any problem, it is helpful to know what one is attempting to accomplish. Agreement on how and whether to pursue a particular objective, such as pollution control, is not possible unless some more general objective has been identified and stated with reasonable precision. We talk loosely of having clean air and clean water, of preserving our wilderness areas, and so forth. But none of these is a sufficiently general objective: each is more accurately viewed as a means rather than as an end.

With regard to clean air, for example, one may ask, "how clean?" and "what does clean mean?" It is even reasonable to ask, "why have clean air?" Each of these questions is an implicit demand that a more general community goal be stated—a goal sufficiently general in its scope and enjoying sufficiently general assent among the community of actors that such "why" questions no longer seem admissible with respect to that goal.

If, for example, one states as a goal the proposition that "every person should be free to do what-

William F. Baxter, *People or Penguins: The Case for Optimal Pollution* (New York: Columbia University Press: 1974). © 1974 Columbia University Press. Reprinted with permission of the publisher.

ever he wishes in contexts where his actions do not interfere with the interests of other human beings," the speaker is unlikely to be met with a response of "why." The goal may be criticized as uncertain in its implications or difficult to implement, but it is so basic a tenet of our civilization—it reflects a cultural value so broadly shared, at least in the abstract—that the question "why" is seen as impertinent or imponderable or both.

I do not mean to suggest that everyone would agree with the "spheres of freedom" objective just stated. Still less do I mean to suggest that a society could subscribe to four or five such general objectives that would be adequate in their coverage to serve as testing criteria by which all other disagreements might be measured. One difficulty in the attempt to construct such a list is that each new goal added will conflict, in certain applications, with each prior goal listed; and thus each goal serves as a limited qualification on prior goals.

Without any expectation of obtaining unanimous consent to them, let me set forth four goals that I generally use as ultimate testing criteria in attempting to frame solutions to problems of human organization. My position regarding pollution stems from these four criteria. If the criteria appeal to you and any part of what appears hereafter does not, our disagreement will have a helpful focus: which of us is correct, analytically, in supposing that his position on pollution would better serve these general goals. If the criteria do not seem acceptable to you, then it is to be expected that our more particular judgments will differ, and the task will then be yours to identify the basic set of criteria upon which your particular judgments rest.

My criteria are as follows:

1. The spheres of freedom criterion stated above.
2. Waste is a bad thing. The dominant feature of human existence is scarcity—our available resources, our aggregate labors, and our skill in employing both have always been, and will continue for some time to be, inadequate to yield to every man all the tangible and intangible satisfactions he would like to have. Hence, none of those resources, or labors, or skills, should be wasted—that is, employed so as to yield less than they might yield in human satisfactions.
3. Every human being should be regarded as an end rather than as a means to be used for the betterment of another. Each should be afforded dignity and regarded as having an absolute claim to an evenhanded application of such rules as the community may adopt for its governance.
4. Both the incentive and the opportunity to improve his share of satisfactions should be preserved to every individual. Preservation of incentive is dictated by the "no waste" criterion and enjoins against the continuous, totally egalitarian redistribution of satisfactions, or wealth; but subject to that constraint, everyone should receive, by continuous redistribution if necessary, some minimal share of aggregate wealth so as to avoid a level of privation from which the opportunity to improve his situation becomes illusory.

The relationship of these highly general goals to the more specific environmental issues at hand may not be readily apparent, and I am not yet ready to demonstrate their pervasive implications. But let me give one indication of their implications. Recently scientists have informed us that use of DDT in food production is causing damage to the penguin population. For the present purposes let us accept that assertion as an indisputable scientific fact. The scientific fact is often asserted as if the correct implication—that we must stop agricultural

use of DDT—followed from the mere statement of the fact of penguin damage. But plainly it does not follow if my criteria are employed.

My criteria are oriented to people, not penguins. Damage to penguins, or sugar pines, or geological marvels is, without more, simply irrelevant. One must go further, by my criteria, and say: Penguins are important because people enjoy seeing them walk about rocks; and furthermore, the well-being of people would be less impaired by halting use of DDT than by giving up penguins. In short, my observations about environmental problems will be people-oriented, as are my criteria. I have no interest in preserving penguins for their own sake.

It may be said by way of objection to this position, that it is very selfish of people to act as if each person represented one unit of importance and nothing else was of any importance. It is undeniably selfish. Nevertheless I think it is the only tenable starting place for analysis for several reasons. First, no other position corresponds to the way most people really think and act—i.e., corresponds to reality.

Second, this attitude does not portend any massive destruction of nonhuman flora and fauna, for people depend on them in many obvious ways, and they will be preserved because and to the degree that humans do depend on them.

Third, what is good for humans is, in many respects, good for penguins and pine trees—clean air for example. So that humans are, in these respects, surrogates for plant and animal life.

Fourth, I do not know how we could administer any other system. Our decisions are either private or collective. Insofar as Mr. Jones is free to act privately, he may give such preferences as he wishes to other forms of life: he may feed birds in winter and do with less himself, and he may even decline to resist an advancing polar bear on the ground that the bear's appetite is more important than those portions of himself that the bear may choose to eat. In short my basic premise does not rule out private altruism to competing life-forms. It does rule out, however, Mr. Jones' inclination to feed Mr. Smith to the bear, however hungry the bear, however despicable Mr. Smith.

Insofar as we act collectively on the other hand, only humans can be afforded an opportunity to participate in the collective decisions. Penguins cannot vote now and are unlikely subjects for the franchise—pine trees more unlikely still. Again each individual is free to cast his vote so as to benefit sugar pines if that is his inclination. But many of the more extreme assertions that one hears from some conservationists amount to tacit assertions that they are specially appointed representatives of sugar pines, and hence that their preferences should be weighted more heavily than the preferences of other humans who do not enjoy equal rapport with "nature." The simplistic assertion that agricultural use of DDT must stop at once because it is harmful to penguins is of that type.

Fifth, if polar bears or pine trees or penguins, like men, are to be regarded as ends rather than means, if they are to count in our calculus of social organization, someone must tell me how much each one counts, and someone must tell me how these life-forms are to be permitted to express their preferences, for I do not know either answer. If the answer is that certain people are to hold their proxies, then I want to know how those proxy-holders are to be selected: self-appointment does not seem workable to me.

Sixth, and by way of summary of all the foregoing, let me point out that the set of environmental issues under discussion—although they raise very complex technical questions of how to achieve any objective—ultimately raise a normative question: what *ought* we to do. Questions of *ought* are unique to the human mind and world—they are meaningless as applied to a nonhuman situation.

I reject the proposition that we *ought* to respect the "balance of nature" or to "preserve the environment" unless the reason for doing so, express or implied, is the benefit of man.

I reject the idea that there is a "right" or "morally correct" state of nature to which we should return. The word "nature" has no normative connotation. Was it "right" or "wrong" for the earth's crust to heave in contortion and create mountains and seas? Was it "right" for the first amphibian to crawl up out of the primordial ooze? Was it "wrong" for plants to reproduce themselves and alter the atmospheric composition in favor of oxygen? For animals to alter the atmosphere in favor of carbon dioxide both by breathing oxygen and eating plants? No answers can be given to these questions because they are meaningless questions.

All this may seem obvious to the point of being

tedious, but much of the present controversy over environment and pollution rests on tacit normative assumptions about just such nonnormative phenomena: that it is "wrong" to impair penguins with DDT, but not to slaughter cattle for prime rib roasts. That it is wrong to kill stands of sugar pines with industrial fumes, but not to cut sugar pines and build housing for the poor. Every man is entitled to his own preferred definition of Walden Pond, but there is no definition that has any moral superiority over another, except by reference to the selfish needs of the human race.

From the fact that there is no normative definition of the natural state, it follows that there is no normative definition of clean air or pure water—hence no definition of polluted air—or of pollution—except by reference to the needs of man. The "right" composition of the atmosphere is one which has some dust in it and some lead in it and some hydrogen sulfide in it—just those amounts that attend a sensibly organized society thoughtfully and knowledgeably pursuing the greatest possible satisfaction for its human members.

The first and most fundamental step toward solution of our environmental problems is a clear recognition that our objective is not pure air or water but rather some optimal state of pollution. That step immediately suggests the question: How do we define and attain the level of pollution that will yield the maximum possible amount of human satisfaction?

Low levels of pollution contribute to human satisfaction but so do food and shelter and education and music. To attain ever lower levels of pollution, we must pay the cost of having less of these other things. I contrast that view of the cost of pollution control with the more popular statement that pollution control will "cost" very large numbers of dollars. The popular statement is true in some senses, false in others; sorting out the true and false senses is of some importance. The first step in that sorting process is to achieve a clear understanding of the difference between dollars and resources. Resources are the wealth of our nation; dollars are merely claim checks upon those resources. Resources are of vital importance; dollars are comparatively trivial.

Four categories of resources are sufficient for our purposes: At any given time a nation, or a planet if you prefer, has a stock of labor, of technological skill, of capital goods, and of natural resources (such as mineral deposits, timber, water, land, etc.). These resources can be used in various combinations to yield goods and services of all kinds—in some limited quantity. The quantity will be larger if they are combined efficiently, smaller if combined inefficiently. But in either event the resource stock is limited, the goods and services that they can be made to yield are limited; even the most efficient use of them will yield less than our population, in the aggregate, would like to have.

If one considers building a new dam, it is appropriate to say that it will be costly in the sense that it will require x hours of labor, y tons of steel and concrete, and z amount of capital goods. If these resources are devoted to the dam, then they cannot be used to build hospitals, fishing rods, schools, or electric can openers. That is the meaningful sense in which the dam is costly.

Quite apart from the very important question of how wisely we can combine our resources to produce goods and services, is the very different question of how they get distributed—who gets how many goods? Dollars constitute the claim checks which are distributed among people and which control their share of national output. Dollars are nearly valueless pieces of paper except to the extent that they do represent claim checks to some fraction of the output of goods and services. Viewed as claim checks, all the dollars outstanding during any period of time are worth, in the aggregate, the goods and services that are available to be claimed with them during that period—neither more nor less.

It is far easier to increase the supply of dollars than to increase the production of goods and services—printing dollars is easy. But printing more dollars doesn't help because each dollar then simply becomes a claim to fewer goods, i.e., becomes worth less.

The point is this: many people fall into error upon hearing the statement that the decision to build a dam, or to clean up a river, will cost $X million. It is regrettably easy to say: "It's only money. This is a wealthy country, and we have lots of money." But you cannot build a dam or clean a river with $X million—unless you also have a match, you can't even make a fire. One builds a dam or cleans a river by diverting labor and steel and trucks and factories from making one kind of goods to

making another. The cost in dollars is merely a shorthand way of describing the extent of the division necessary. If we build a dam for $X million, then we must recognize that we will have $X million less housing and food and medical care and electric can openers as a result.

Similarly, the costs of controlling pollution are best expressed in terms of the other goods we will have to give up to do the job. This is not to say the job should not be done. Badly as we need more housing, more medical care, and more can openers, and more symphony orchestras, we could do with somewhat less of them, in my judgment at least, in exchange for somewhat cleaner air and rivers. But that is the nature of the trade-off, and analysis of the problem is advanced if that unpleasant reality is kept in mind. Once the trade-off relationship is clearly perceived, it is possible to state in a very general way what the optimal level of pollution is. I would state it as follows:

People enjoy watching penguins. They enjoy relatively clean air and smog-free vistas. Their health is improved by relatively clean water and air. Each of these benefits is a type of good or service. As a society we would be well advised to give up one washing machine if the resources that would have gone into that washing machine can yield greater human satisfaction when diverted into pollution control. We should give up one hospital if the resources thereby freed would yield more human satisfaction when devoted to elimination of noise in our cities. And so on, trade-off by trade-off, we should divert our productive capacities from the production of existing goods and services to the production of a cleaner, quieter, more pastoral nation up to—and no further than—the point at which we value more highly the next washing machine or hospital that we would have to do without than we value the next unit of environmental improvement that the diverted resources would create.

Now this proposition seems to me unassailable but so general and abstract as to be unhelpful—at least unadministerable in the form stated. It assumes we can measure in some way the incremental units of human satisfaction yielded by very different types of goods. The proposition must remain a pious abstraction until I can explain how this measurement process can occur. In [other works] I attempt to show that we can do this—in some contexts with great precision and in other contexts only by rough approximation. But I insist that the proposition stated describes the result for which we should be striving—and again, that it is always useful to know what your target is even if your weapons are too crude to score a bull's eye.

Zuckerman's Dilemma: A Plea for Environmental Ethics

Mark Sagoff

Many of us recall from childhood—or from reading to our own children—E. B. White's story of the spider Charlotte and her campaign to save Wilbur, a barnyard pig.[1] Charlotte wove webs above Wilbur's sty proclaiming the pig's virtues in words—"TERRIFIC," "RADIANT," and "HUMBLE"—she copied from newspaper advertisements salvaged by a helpful rat. Wilbur won a special prize at the county fair. Moved by these events, Zuckerman, the farmer who owned Wilbur, spared him from being sent to market. Charlotte saved Wilbur's life.

"Why did you do all this for me?" the pig asks at the end of *Charlotte's Web*. "I don't deserve it. I've never done anything for you."

"You have been my friend," Charlotte replied. "That in itself is a tremendous thing. I wove my webs for you because I liked you. After all, what's a life anyway? We're born, we live a little while, we die. A spider's life can't help being something of a mess, what with all this trapping and eating flies. By helping you, perhaps I was trying to lift up my life a little. Heaven knows, anyone's life can stand a little of that" (p. 164).

The Varieties of Goodness

Charlotte's Web illustrates three ways we value nature. First, nature benefits us. Nature is useful: it serves a purpose, satisfies a preference, or meets a need. This is the *instrumental* good. Traders have this kind of value in mind when they bid on pork belly futures. Price is the usual measure of the instrumental good.

Second, we may value nature as an object of

Hastings Center Report, vol. 21, no. 5 (Sept.–Oct. 1991), 32–40. Reprinted by permission. Copyright © 1991 The Hastings Center.

knowledge and perception. This is the *aesthetic* good.[2] While the basis of instrumental value lies in our wants and inclinations, the basis of aesthetic value lies in the object itself—in qualities that demand an appreciative response from informed and discriminating observers. The judges who awarded Wilbur a prize recognized in him superb qualities—qualities that made him a pig to be appreciated rather than a pig to be consumed.

Third, we may regard an object (as Charlotte did Wilbur) with love or affection. Charlotte's love for Wilbur included feelings of altruism, as we would expect, since anyone who loves a living object (we might include biological systems and communities) will take an interest in its well-being or welfare. Love might also attach to objects that exemplify ideals, aspirations, and commitments that "lift up" one's life by presenting goals that go beyond one's own welfare. We might speak of "love of country" in this context. Objects of our love and affection have a *moral* good, and, if they are living, *a good of their own.*

Aesthetic value depends on qualities that make an object admirable of its kind; when these qualities change, the aesthetic value of the object may change with them. With love, it is different. Shakespeare wrote that love alters not where it alteration finds, and even if this is not strictly true, love still tolerates better than aesthetic appreciation changes that may occur in its object.

Although love is other-regarding in that it promotes the well-being of its object, it does not require actions to be entirely altruistic. Only saints are completely selfless, and it is hardly obvious that we should try to be like them.[3] Nevertheless, anyone's life can stand some dollop of idealistic or altruistic behavior, as Charlotte says.

When we regard an object with appreciation or with love, we say it has *intrinsic* value, by which we mean that we value the object itself rather than just the benefits it confers on us. This essay concerns the intrinsic value of nature in its relation to environmental policy. The two forms of intrinsic value—aesthetic and moral—differ in important ways, as one would expect, since moral value arises in the context of action, while aesthetic value has to do with perception. I shall touch on these differences, but I do not have space to explicate them here.

The Value of Nature

Those of us who wish to protect estuaries, forests, species, and other aspects of nature may give any of three kinds of arguments—instrumental, aesthetic, or moral—to support our conviction. We might argue on instrumental grounds, for example, that we should save species for their possible medicinal applications, or rain forests because they add to global oxygen budgets. An aesthetic argument, in contrast, would point to the magnificent qualities a ten-thousand-year-old forest or estuary may possess. In nature we find perhaps for the last time in history objects commensurate with our capacity to wonder.

A moral argument describes obligations we have toward objects of nature insofar as we regard them with reverence, affection, and respect. Such an argument may contend that humanity confronts a great responsibility in learning to share the world with other species. Love of or respect for the natural world increases our stature as moral beings, and it may teach us to be critical of and to change our preferences and desires. By taking an interest in the welfare of some creature beside herself, Charlotte too found there is more to life than "all this trapping and eating flies."

Within the next decade or two, we shall decide the fate of many estuaries, forests, species, and other wonderful aspects of the natural world. How can we justify efforts to protect them? Will instrumental or prudential arguments do the trick? If not, how will we justify the sacrifices we must make to save our evolutionary and ecological heritage?

Why Save the Whales?

Consider, as a real-world example, whales. Two centuries ago, whale oil fetched a high price because people used it in lamps. Whales had instru-mental value. Electric lights are better and cheaper than oil lamps; accordingly, there is little or no market for whale oil today.

Why, then, do so many people care about saving whales? Is it for instrumental reasons? Are they concerned about maintaining a strategic reserve of blubber? Do they worry that the seas might fill up with krill? No; as whales have lost their instrumental value, their aesthetic and moral worth has become all the more evident.

Whale oil has substitutes in a way that whales do not. We get along easily without whale oil because electricity lights our lamps. The extinction of whales, in contrast, represents an aesthetic and moral loss—something like the destruction of a great painting or the death of a friend. Life goes on, of course, but we mourn such a loss and, if we caused it, we should feel guilty or ashamed of it. No one cares about the supply of whale oil, but we do care about the abundance of whales. Aesthetic and moral value attaches to those animals themselves rather than to any function they serve or benefit they confer on us. When they perish, all that was valuable about them will perish with them.

Fungibility as the Mark of the Instrumental

Insofar as we care about an object for instrumental reasons, we would accept a substitute—for example, ball point pens in place of quills—if it performs the same function at a lower cost. The market price of any object should in theory not exceed that of the cheapest substitute.

With intrinsic value, it is different. When we see, for example, a Jacques Cousteau film about the ability of humpback whales to communicate with each other over hundreds of miles, we are properly moved to admire this impressive species. That we can fax junk mail faster and farther is irrelevant. We admire the ability of these whales to do what they do. It is *this* species we admire; *its* qualities demand admiration and attention.

Similarly, love is not transferable but attaches to the individuals one happens to love. At one time, people had children, in part, because they needed them as farm hands. Today, we think the relation between parents and children should be primarily moral rather than instrumental. One can purchase the services of farmhands and even of sexual partners, but our relationship to hired labor or sex is nothing like our relationship to children or spouses.

We would not think of trading a child, for example, for a good tractor.

Technology, though still in its infancy, promises to do for many aspects of nature what it has done for whales and for children, namely, to make us economically less dependent on them. This need not concern us. That we no longer require whales for oil or children for tending bobbins does not imply that we cease to value them. The less we depend on nature economically, the more we may find that the reasons to value species, forests, estuaries, and other aspects of nature are not instrumental but aesthetic and moral.

Why Protect the Natural Environment?

We undertake many environmental programs primarily to protect the well-being of nature, even if we defend them as necessary to promote the welfare of human beings. Why, for example, did the Environmental Protection Agency ban DDT in the 1970s? The pesticide killed pelicans and other wildlife; that was the reason to prohibit its use. EPA banned it, however, as a human carcinogen—which it is not.[4] Today we should make no such pretense.[5] The new Clean Air Act undertakes an expensive program to control acid rain. The law does not pretend that acid rain causes cancer. It answers directly to moral and aesthetic concerns about what coal-burning power plants are doing to trees and fish.

We environmentalists often appeal to instrumental arguments for instrumental reasons, i.e., not because we believe them, but because we think that they work. I submit, however, that advances in technology will continue to undermine these arguments. The new biotechnologies, for example, seem poised to replace nature as the source of many agricultural commodities. As one environmentalist observes: "In the years to come, an increasing number of agricultural activities are going to be taken indoors and enclosed in vats and caldrons, sealed off from the outside world."[6]

When machinery replaced child labor in mills and mines, people did not stop raising children. Society found it possible to treat children as objects of love rather than as factors of production. As biotechnology industrializes agriculture, we may protect farmland for its aesthetic and symbolic value rather than for its products. We may measure wealth not in terms of what we can consume but in terms of what we can do without—what we treasure for its own sake.

Poverty is one of today's greatest environmental and ecological problems. This is because people who do not share in the wealth technology creates must live off nature; in their need to exploit the natubral commons, they may destroy it. Analogously, in an urban context, poor people have had to send their children to work in sweat shops—to survive. The problem, of course, is not that poor people have the wrong values. Extreme and deplorable inequalities in the distribution of wealth lead to the mistreatment of children and to the destruction of the environment.

Accordingly, I question the adequacy of the argument environmentalists often make that we must protect nature to provide for the welfare of human beings. I think it is also true that we must provide for the welfare of human beings if we are to protect the natural environment.

Zuckerman's Dilemma

Zuckerman faced a dilemma. He had to choose whether to butcher Wilbur (the slaughterhouse would have paid for the pig) or on moral and aesthetic grounds to spare his life.

What reasons have we to preserve biodiversity, protect rain forests, and maintain the quality of lakes, rivers, and estuaries? I should like to suggest that we confront Zuckerman's dilemma with respect to many of the most wonderful aspects of nature. As we come to depend on nature less and less for instrumental reasons, we may recognize more and more the intrinsic reasons for preserving it.

Water Pollution

Consider, as an example, the problem of water pollution. The question I wish to ask here is whether instrumental arguments would justify the expenditure of the roughly $200 billion Americans invested between 1970 and 1984 in controlling water pollution.[7] Did this investment pay off in terms of our health, safety, or welfare? Could we conclude that, in this instance, instrumental as well as intrinsic values justify the protection of the environment?

I think it fair to say that the large public investment in water pollution control cannot be justified on instrumental grounds alone. The same money put into public clinics, education, or anti-smoking campaigns might have led to greater improvements in public safety and health. This is true in part because the major uses of water—commercial, industrial, agricultural, and municipal—are not very sensitive to water quality. Drinking water can be treated very cheaply and thus can tolerate many common pollutants. "Much of what has been said about the need for high quality water supplies," two experts write, "is more a product of emotion than logic . . . [A] plant at Düsseldorf, Germany, withdraws water from the Rhine River, which is of far lower quality than the Delaware, the Hudson, or the Missouri, treats it . . . and produces quite potable drinking water."[8]

The Value of an Estuary

In the Chesapeake Bay, as in other prominent aquatic ecosystems, pollution must concern us deeply for moral and aesthetic reasons. It is not clear, however, that the harm pollution does to nature translates into damage to human health, safety, or welfare. Indeed, more pollution might be better from a strictly instrumental point of view.

The reason is that the major uses of the Bay are fairly insensitive to water quality. The Chesapeake possesses instrumental value as a liquid highway (Baltimore is a major port), as a sewer (tributaries drain several major cities), and as a site for a huge naval base (Norfolk). These uses affect but are not greatly affected by water quality or, for that matter, by the biological health, integrity, richness, or diversity of the Chesapeake ecosystem.

How does pollution affect the health of commercial and recreational fisheries in estuaries? Consider rockfish (striped bass). Environmentalists for many years deplored the pollution of the Hudson off Manhattan; they pronounced that portion of the estuary—one of the most degraded in the world—biologically dead. Developers of the Westway Project, who wished to fill the offshore waters to build condos, hired scientists who confirmed that rockfish did not and probably could not visit the polluted lower Hudson.

Environmentalists were able to stop the project, however, by arguing in the nick of time that even though the "interpier" area may be the most polluted ecosystem in the world, it functions as perhaps the most important, healthy, and thriving hatchery for rockfish on the Atlantic coast. The well-being of fish populations—at least as we view it—can have more to do with politics than with pollution.[9]

In the Chesapeake, rockfish populations rebounded after a moratorium on fishing. One might surmise, then, that while fisheries have been hurt by overharvesting, the effects of pollution are harder to prove. Bluefish, crabs, and other "scavengers" abound in polluted waters, including the Chesapeake. And organic pollutants, primarily compounds of nitrogen and phosphorus, could support oysters and other filter feeders if their populations (depleted by overfishing and natural disease) returned to the Bay.

Maryland's former director of tidal fisheries, recognizing the benefits of genetic engineering, argued that the Chesapeake Bay "should be run more like a farm than a wilderness."[10] He believed that the state should subsidize efforts to fabricate fish the way Frank Perdue manufactures chickens. Many experts agree that industrial mariculture, by pushing fish populations far beyond the carrying capacity of ecosystems, will render capture fisheries obsolete.[11]

Pollution at present levels hardly bothers boaters, which is why there are so many "stinkpots" out there. Even in a "sick" estuary, a 347 Evinrude outboard gives people what they apparently want: plenty of noise and plenty of wake. Many recreational fish remain plentiful, and biotechnologists are engineering others to withstand pollutants to which they now succumb. They have perfected a nonmigrating rockfish that need not transit the anoxic stem of the Bay. (They have also perfected an acid-tolerant trout that does well in acidified lakes.) It may not be efficient to regulate pollution to accommodate species. It may be cheaper to regulate species to accommodate pollution.

Since a nasty jellyfish occurring naturally in the Bay makes swimming too painful, recreational interest in the Chesapeake is limited in any case. Most vacationers experience the Bay from bridges, where they sit in terrific traffic jams on their way to resorts on the Atlantic shore. They seem willing to pay a lot to visit the Ho Jos, discos, go gos, peep shows, and condos that stretch from Atlantic City to Virginia Beach. If you are looking for recreational benefits people are willing to pay for, look for them there.

Why Not Pollute?

We may find acts of environmental destruction to be aesthetically and morally outrageous even if they do no damage to human health, safety, or welfare. News reports tell us that Prince William Sound, now "sparkling with sea life and renewed health," has produced a record salmon catch in a little more than a year after the tragic Valdez spill.[12] From a strictly instrumental point of view, that spill was not nearly so detrimental as many environmentalists thought. The immediate victims, more than 36,000 waterfowls, at least 1,016 sea otters, and 144 bald eagles, have no commercial value. Populations of wildlife will be detrimentally affected probably forever. These animals have enormous aesthetic and moral—but little instrumental—worth.

I do not mean to suggest that water pollution, especially when it is illegal or careless, is anything but morally and aesthetically outrageous. I do not mean to minimize the harm it does. I am arguing only that pollution may represent a failure in aesthetic appreciation and moral responsibility without representing a market-failure, that is, without impairing any of the uses we make of an estuary. The Chesapeake will perform its major economic tasks: to function as a sewer, a liquid highway, and a place for boating. If it were only the beneficial use rather than the intrinsic value of the Bay that concerned us, controlling pollution further might not be worth the cost.

The Problem of Scale

"What's wrong with this argument," a reader might object, "is that it leaves out the question of scale. We can get away with polluting an estuary here and there if elsewhere healthy ecosystems support the global processes essential to life. At a local scale, an instrumental calculus may argue for industrializing a particular environment. The problem, though, is that when we apply the same calculus to every ecosystem, we end up by destroying the crucial services nature provides."

This argument has weight with respect to activities that affect the atmosphere. Scientists have shown a connection between the use of CFCs and changes in stratospheric ozone. Likewise, the excessive combustion of coal and oil threatens to change the world's climate. That we should follow policies that prudence recommends, I have no doubt. The Montreal Protocol concerning CFCs represents an important first step. Prudence also recommends that we reach similar international agreements to decrease the amount of fuel we burn and, perhaps, to increase our reliance on those forms of energy that do not involve combustion.

While it is urgent that we limit atmospheric pollution, this does not give us a reason to protect intrinsically valuable species or ecosystems. The pollution, degradation, and exploitation of the Chesapeake Bay, for example, has no cognizable effect on global biochemical processes. One may argue, indeed, that the more eutrophic the Bay becomes, the more carbon it will store, thus helping to counter the "greenhouse" effect. By solving the problems of the Chesapeake, we do little to solve the problems of the atmosphere. The two sets of problems arise from different causes, involve different sorts of values, and require different solutions.

Rain Forests

Consider the rain forests, which seem doomed by economic progress. One can argue persuasively that humanity has no more important ethical or aesthetic task than to keep these magnificent ecosystems from being turned into particle boards and disposable diapers. Popular arguments to the effect that rain forests store net carbon or add to global oxygen budgets, however, may not be convincing.

Since rain forests are climax ecosystems, they absorb through the cold burning of decay as much oxygen as they release through respiration; thus the popular belief that these forests add to global oxygen budgets betrays a naivete about how climax ecosystems work.[13] One way to get a rain forest to store net carbon may be to chop it down and plant instead of trees fast-growing crops genetically designed to do very nicely in the relevant soil and climatic conditions. (The biologist Dan Janzen has described this dreadful possibility.)[14] The trees could be used to make disposable diapers which, after use, would go to landfills where they would store carbon nearly forever.

Biodiversity

Anyone with any moral or aesthetic sense must agree that another of humanity's greatest responsibilities today is to arrest shameful and horrendous rates of extinction. Yet one is hard pressed to find credible instrumental arguments for protecting endangered species in their habitats. The reason that we produce Thanksgiving turkeys by the millions while letting the black-footed boobie become extinct is that one bird has instrumental value while the other has not. The boobie had no ecological function; it was epiphenomenal even in its own habitat. Its demise in no way contributed, for example, to the loss of stratospheric ozone or to the "greenhouse" effect.

Environmentalists, to justify their efforts to protect biological diversity, sometimes speculate that exotic species might prove useful for medical purposes, for instance. No public health professional, as far as I know, has vouched for this proposition. Pharmaceutical companies are not known for contributing to the Nature Conservancy or for otherwise encouraging efforts to preserve biodiversity. They are interested in learning from folk medicine, but they cannot even think of tracking down, capturing, and analyzing the contents of millions of species (many of them unidentified) each of which may contain thousands of compounds.

If pharmaceutical companies wanted to mine exotic species, they would not preserve them in their habitats. They might trap and freeze them or sequence their genes for later reconstruction. Seed companies would likewise store germ tissue in banks, not leave it in the wild. Capturing and freezing specimens, not preserving habitats, would be the way to go, to make biodiversity benefit us.

Even a single endangered species enlists our respect and admiration, since (as one observer has said) it would require another heaven and earth to produce such a being. The grand diversity of life, particularly the existence of rare and exotic species, presents a profound moral obligation for civilization, which is to share the earth peaceably with other species. This obligation exists whether or not we can defend the preservation of species on grounds of self-interest rather than morality. The

destruction of biodiversity may be immoral, even sinful, without being irrational or imprudent.

A Plea for Environmental Ethics

In an old movie, a character played by W. C. Fields, having, it appears, negligently killed a baby, confronts its hysterical mother. Eyeing her youthful figure, he says: "No matter, madam; I would be happy to get you with another."

What we find chilling in this scene is Fields's appeal wholly to instrumental value. He sees nothing wrong with killing a baby as long as he can "get" its mother with another child who, one day, will be equally capable of supporting her in her old age. To Fields, objects have only instrumental value; we can evaluate all our actions in terms of costs and benefits. They have no other meaning.

Moral Value—a Benefit or Cost?

The scene in the movie might remind us of the way the EXXON Corporation dealt with public outrage over the recent unpleasantness in Prince William Sound. The corporation assured everyone that the salmon fishery would bounce back. If anyone was out of pocket, EXXON would lavishly compensate them. EXXON said to the outraged public: "No matter, madam; we will be happy to make you at least as well off."

From the point of view of instrumental value alone, both Fields and EXXON were correct. They could replace whatever was lost with equally beneficial or useful substitutes. Another baby could grow up to plow land or tend bobbins as well as the first. The mother's income in old age would not decrease. EXXON too would make up lost income. Isn't it irrational, then, for people to complain when children are killed or wildlife is destroyed? From the point of view of instrumental value, they aren't worth much. They may have meaning, but they confer few benefits on us. They make demands on us. They are mostly costs.

Indeed, raising children, preserving nature, cherishing art, and practicing the virtues of civil life are all costs—the costs of being the people we are. Why do we pay these costs? We can answer only that these costs are benefits; these actions justify themselves; these virtues are their own reward.

I wonder, therefore, whether we environmentalists do well to argue for environmental protection primarily on instrumental rather than on moral and aesthetic grounds. Are the possible medicinal or agricultural uses of rare and endangered species really what we care about? We might as well argue that we should protect whales for the sake of their oil or sea otters to harvest their teeth. I think the destruction and extinction of wildlife would horrify us even if we knew sea otter, murres, and eagles would never benefit us. How do we differ from Charlotte, then, who saved Wilbur even though he did nothing for her?

Preference versus Judgment

"The distinction between instrumental and intrinsic value," someone may object, "lies beside the point of environmental policy, since a cost-benefit analysis, based in willingness-to-pay estimates, can take both sorts of preferences into account. Whether people are willing to pay to protect wildlife for moral, aesthetic, or self-interested reasons (hunting, for example) is their business; all the policy maker needs to know is what their preferences are and how much they are willing to pay to satisfy them."

This objection misses the crucial importance of the way we choose to make decisions. Consider, for example, how we determine whether a person is innocent or guilty of a crime. We might do this by sending questionnaires to a random sample of citizens to check off whether they prefer a guilty or innocent verdict and, perhaps, how much they are willing to pay for each. This method of reaching a verdict would be "rational" in the sense that it aggregates "given" preferences (data) to mathematical principles laid down in advance. The method is also "neutral" in that it translates a data set into a social choice without itself entering, influencing, or affecting the outcome.

On the other hand, we may trust the finding of innocence or guilt to a jury who are steeped in the evidence, who hear the arguments, and then, by deliberation, reach a collective judgment. This procedure, since it involves discussion and even persuasion, would not proceed from "given" preferences according to rules laid down in advance. The process or method itself is *supposed* to affect the result.

Which model would be most appropriate for environmental policy? Consider erosion. Public officials must assess instrumental reasons for protecting soil: they must determine how much arable land we need for crops, how much we are losing, and how best to conserve what we have. They also weigh intrinsic values, for example, what soil and its protection expresses about us or means to us as a community. Our policy, presumably, should be based not on the revealed or expressed preferences of a random sample of people, no matter how rigorous our techniques of sampling and aggregating may be, but on the judgment of responsible authorities after appropriate public consideration and debate.

Similarly, policies for civil rights, education, the arts, child labor, and the environment depend on judgment—often moral and aesthetic judgment—concerning facts about the world and about ourselves, that is, about our goals and intentions as a community. People who believe we ought to save the whales, for example, do not tell us simply what they prefer; rather, they call for the reasoned agreement or disagreement of others. That is why public policy is always argued in public terms—in terms of what *we* ought to do, not what *I* happen to want.

With respect to aesthetic experience, anyone can tell you what he or she likes, but not everyone can tell you what is worth appreciating. A person judges aesthetically not for himself or herself only but on the basis of reasons, arguments, or ideas that he or she believes would lead others to the same conclusion. Knowledge, experience, sensitivity, discernment—these distinguish judgments of taste from expressions of preference.

To be sure, we enjoy objects we appreciate, but we do not value these objects because we enjoy them. Rather, we enjoy them because we find them valuable or, more precisely, enjoyment is one way of perceiving their value. To enjoy ecological communities aesthetically or to value them morally is to find directly in them or in their qualities the reasons that justify their protection. This is not a matter of personal preference. It is a matter of judgment and perception, which one might believe correct or mistaken, and thus argue for or against, within an open political process.

The contrast I have drawn between instrumental and intrinsic value borrows a great deal, of course, from Kant, who summed up the distinction as follows. "That which is related to general human inclination and needs has a *market price* . . . But that which constitutes . . . an end in itself does not have a mere relative worth, i.e., a price, but an intrinsic worth, i.e., a *dignity*." [15] Kant believed that dignity attaches to objects because of what they are and, therefore, how we judge them. The discovery of what things are—whether it is their moral, aesthetic, or scientific properties—has to do with knowledge. Like any form of knowledge it is intersubjective: it represents not the preference of individuals but the will, the perception, or the considered opinion of a community.

Are Values Relative?

While many Americans may share an environmental ideology—the United States has been described as Nature's Nation[16]—this does not apply everywhere. Even if the love of nature belongs to most cultures, moreover, it might express itself in different ways. The Japanese may not experience whales as we do; *Moby Dick* is one of our classics. Italians, who treasure their artistic heritage, might as soon eat as listen to a song bird. How can we expect other cultures to respond to nature in the ways we do?

This kind of question may lead environmentalists to suppose that instrumental arguments for protecting nature have a universality that intrinsic arguments do not. Yet instrumental arguments depend on interpretations of fact—models of climate change, for example—that invite all kinds of disagreement. And ethical issues arise, moreover, even when instrumental concerns are paramount, such as when determining how much industrialized and developing nations should cut back combustion to counter global warming. It may be easier to persuade, attract, or cajole other nations to cooperate (if not agree) with our moral and aesthetic concerns than with our reading of prudence or self-interest. The process of reaching agreement is the same, however, whether instrumental or intrinsic values are at stake.

Living with Nature

I have argued that we ought to preserve nature for its sake and not simply our benefit. How far, however, should we go? The Chesapeake Bay commends itself to us for intrinsic but also for instrumental reasons. How can we balance our need to use with our desire to protect this ecosystem?

We confront this kind of question, I believe, also in relation to people whom we love and whose freedom and spontaneity we respect but with whom we have to live. Children are examples. We could treat our children—as we might treat nature—completely as means to our own ends. We would then simply use them to take out the empties, perform sexual favors, tend bobbins, or whatever it is that benefits us. This would be despicable as well as criminal. We know that morality requires that we treat our children as ends in themselves and not merely as means to our own ends.

At the same time, we have to live with our kids, and this allows us to make certain demands on them, like not to wake us up too early in the morning, no matter how much we love them for their own sake. While we insist on protecting our children's innate character, independence, and integrity, we have to socialize the little devils or they will destroy us and themselves. I think this is true of nature: we can respect the integrity of ecosystems even if we change them in ways that allow us all to share the same planet.

No clear rules determine how far one should go in disciplining one's children or in modifying their behavior; socialization may have fairly broad limits. But there are limits; we recognize child abuse when we see it. Have we such a conception of the abuse of nature? I think we need one. At least we should regard as signs of environmental abuse the typical results of egregious assaults on ecosystems, such as eutrophication, pandemic extinctions, and so on. We might then limit changes we make in nature by keeping this notion of ecological health—or disease—in mind.

Zuckerman's Response

William Reilly, administrator of the Environmental Protection Agency, recently wrote: "Natural ecosystems . . . have intrinsic values independent of human use that are worthy of protection." He cited an advisory scientific report that urged the agency to attach as much importance to intrinsic ecological values as to risks to human health and welfare. Mr. Reilly added:

> Whether it is Long Island Sound or Puget Sound, San Francisco Bay or the Chesapeake, the Gulf of Mexico or the Arctic tundra, it is

time to get serious about protecting what we love. Clearly we do love our great water bodies: . . . They are part of our heritage, part of our consciousness. Let us vow not to let their glory pass from this good Earth.[17]

In 1991 the State of Maryland offered anyone registering an automobile the option of paying $20 (which would go to an environmental fund) to receive a special license plate bearing the motto: "Treasure the Chesapeake." A surprising number of registrants bought the plate. How many of us would have ponied up the $20 for a plate that read: "Use the Chesapeake Efficiently" or "The Chesapeake: It Satisfies Your Revealed and Expressed Preferences"?

To treasure the Chesapeake is to see that it has a good of its own—and therefore a "health" or "integrity"—that we should protect even when to do so does not benefit us. "Why did you do all this for me?" Wilbur asked. "I've never done anything for you." Even when nature does not do anything for us—one might think, for example, of the eagles and otters destroyed in Prince William Sound—we owe it protection for moral and aesthetic reasons. Otherwise our civilization and our lives will amount to little more than the satisfaction of private preferences: what Charlotte described as "all this trapping and eating flies."

In this essay, I have proposed that we may lift up our lives a little by seeing nature as Charlotte did, not just as an assortment of resources to be managed and consumed, but also as a setting for collective moral and aesthetic judgment. I have also suggested that our evolutionary heritage—the diversity of species, the miracle of life—confronts us with the choice Zuckerman had to make: whether to butcher nature for the market or to protect it as an object of moral attention and aesthetic appreciation.

If Zuckerman had not learned to appreciate Wilbur for his own sake, he would have converted the pig to bacon and chops. Likewise, if we do not value nature for ethical and aesthetic reasons, then we might well pollute and degrade it for instrumental ones. If a spider could treat a pig as a friend, however, then we should be able to treat a forest, an estuary, or any other living system in the same way.

NOTES

1. E. B. White, *Charlotte's Web* (New York: Harper & Row, 1952).
2. In defining the instrumental and aesthetic good, I follow the analysis of Georg Henrik von Wright, *The Varieties of Goodness* (London: Routledge & Kegan Paul, 1963), pp. 19–40. Von Wright, however, uses the term *technical good* where I use the term *aesthetic good.*
3. See Susan Wolf, "Moral Saints," *Journal of Philosophy* 79 (1982): 419–39.
4. During the early 1970s an enormous investment in research led to completely inconclusive findings based on animal studies, although one prominent pharmacologist summed up the available evidence by saying that at then-current levels DDT was not a human carcinogen. For documentation, see Thomas R. Dunlap, *DDT: Scientists, Citizens, and Public Policy* (Princeton: Princeton University Press, 1981), esp. pp. 214–17. Oddly, there have been few epidemiological studies during the 1980s, but those that were done show no clear link between DDT exposure and cancer risk. For a review with citations, see Harold M. Schmeck, Jr., "Study Finds No Link Between Cancer Risk and DDT Exposure," *New York Times,* 14 February 1989, reporting a decade-long study of nearly 1,000 people with higher than average exposure to DDT; it found no statistically significant link between the amount of DDT in their bodies and the risk of death by cancer.
5. Scholars argue correctly, I believe, that "in the 1970s, the prevention of cancer risks was accepted as a proxy for all environmental damage." A. Dan Tarlock, "Earth and Other Ethics: The Institutional Issues," *Tennessee Law Review* 56, no. 1 (1988): 63 (citing the DDT controversy as an example). See also, *Regulating Pesticides,* National Academy of Sciences (Washington, D.C.: NAS Press, National Research Council, 1980), pp. 18–28.
6. Jeremy Rifkin, *Biosphere Politics: A New Consciousness for a New Century* (New York: Crown, 1991), p. 69.
7. Office of Policy Analysis, EPA, *The Cost of Clean Air and Water,* Executive Summary (1984), p. 3. For an overview of the disappointing results of water quality protection, see William Pedersen, "Turning the Tide on Water Quality," *Ecology Law Quarterly* 15 (1988): 69–73.
8. A. Kneese and B. Bower, *Managing Water Quality: Economics, Technology, Institutions* (Baltimore: Johns Hopkins Press, Resources for the Future, 1968), p. 125.
9. For details about the Westway Project, see *The Westway Project: A Study of Failure of Federal/State Rela-*

tions, Sixty-Sixth Report by the Committee on Government Operations, 98th Cong. 2d Sess., HR 98-1166, Washington, D.C., U.S.G.P.O., 1984. See also *Action for a Rational Transit v. West Side Highway Project,* 536 F. Supp. 1225 (S.D.N.Y. 1982); *Sierra Club v. U.S. Army Corps of Engineers,* 541 F. Supp. 1327 (S.D.N.Y. 1982) and 701 R2d 1011 (2d Cir. 1983). For another case history exemplifying the same point farther up the Hudson, see L. W. Barnhouse et al., "Population Biology in the Courtroom: The Hudson River Controversy," *BioScience* 34, no. 1 (1984): 14–19.

10. George Krantz is quoted in the *Washington Post,* 26 September 1984.

11. See, for example, Harold Webber, "Aquabusiness," in *Biotechnology and the Marine Sciences,* ed. R. Colwell, A. Sinskey, and E. Pariser (New York: Wiley, 1984), pp. 115–16. Webber believes we depend on traditional fisheries only because the "results of recent research and development in the biotechnological sciences have not yet been integrated into the broader context of large scale, vertically integrated, high technology, centrally controlled, aquabusiness food production systems." He calls the substitution of industrial for "natural" methods of fish production in aquatic environments "Vertically Integrated Aquaculture (VIA)."

12. Jay Mathews, "In Alaska, Oil Spill Has Lost Its Sheen," *Washington Post,* 9 February 1991.

13. For discussion, see T. C. Whitmore, "The Conservation of Tropical Rain Forests," in *Conservation Biology: An Evolutionary Perspective,* ed. M. Soulé and B. A. Wilcox (Sunderland, Mass.: Sinauer, 1980),

p. 313: "The suggestion, sometimes made, that atmospheric oxygen levels would be lowered by the removal of tropical rain forests rests on a mistaken view of climax ecosystems."

14. See William Allen, "Penn Prof Views Biotechnology as Potential Threat to Tropical Forests," *Genetic Engineering News* 7, no. 10 (1987): 10. The article quotes a letter by Janzen: "Tropical wildlands and most of the earth's contemporary species still exist because humanity has not had organisms capable of converting all tropical land surfaces to profitable agriculture and animal husbandry. Within one to three decades, organisms modified through genetic engineering will be capable of making agriculture or animal husbandry, or both, profitable on virtually any land surface. Agricultural inviability, the single greatest tropical conservation force, will be gone."

   Some commentators have speculated that transpiration from rain forests may play some role in the atmosphere. Since more than 85 percent of water absorbed into the atmosphere comes from the oceans, however, the marginal difference—if any—in transpiration between natural and biotech species in rain forests is unlikely to be consequential.

15. Immanuel Kant, *Foundations of the Metaphysics of Morals,* ed. R. P. Wolff, trans. L. W. Beck (Indianapolis: Bobbs-Merrill, 1959), p. 53. Emphasis in original.

16. Perry Miller, *Nature's Nation* (Cambridge, Mass.: Harvard University Press, 1967).

17. William K. Reilly, "A Strategy to Save the Great Water Bodies," *EPA Journal* 16, no. 6 (1990): 4.

Profits Are for Rape and Pillage

Gretchen Morgenson with Gale Eisenstodt

Against all experience the belief persists: Increased government spending and reams of new regulations are the only solutions to the problems of a polluted planet. Although President Bush, in a speech delivered to the U.S. Environment Program last month, argued in favor of free market approaches to environmental issues, he has nonetheless decided to raise the Environmental Protection Agency to Cabinet level. As EPA's political

clout grows, so does its budget. Just five years ago EPA bagged $4.4 billion annually. Gramm-Rudman-Hollings notwithstanding, its yearly budget is now $5 billion and rising.

At the very time when government regulation is discredited and out of favor nearly everywhere, it is making a comeback in the environmental field. Although political and economic arguments for socialism are derided around the world—and the power of the market to allocate resources intelligently is widely acclaimed—environmentalism is being used as an excuse for the government to move back into managing the minutiae of our lives.

Reprinted by permission of *Forbes* magazine, March 5, 1990. © 1990 Forbes, Inc.

Consider what's going on in California. The South Coast Air Quality Management District, a regional regulatory agency, announced a plan last year that advocates, among other things, banning the sale and manufacture of lighter fluids in outdoor cooking. The California plan has 123 measures that ban or restrict various practices or items, including automobile tires, and would cost buckets of money. Putting just 58 of the measures into effect would cost industry and taxpayers around $3.4 billion a year.

And that's just in California. At the federal level, the costs are higher. Take the disastrous $8.5 billion Superfund. Created with taxpayers' money to clean up toxic waste sites, in ten years the fund has cleaned up just 50 of the thousands of sites it considers dangerous. What's taking the EPA so long to exorcise the toxics? Litigation. Superfund legislation gives the EPA authority to go after polluters and make them pay: Much of Superfund's money has been spent trying to find the deepest pockets around a given waste site and litigating to reap damages. While it looks for someone to whom it can assign liability, the cleanups languish.

Then there's the Resource Conservation & Recovery Act, a 14-year-old bit of legislation administered by the EPA covering the storage, transportation and disposal of hazardous wastes. RCRA has required some companies to clean up and maintain their industrial sites at so-called background levels—that is, levels at which chemicals occur naturally in the surrounding environment. Even if a chemical is found to be nonthreatening to human health, it must be reduced to background levels if the company is to comply with regulations and avoid fines. RCRA recent regulations will cost industry—and ultimately the consumer—tens of billions of dollars for compliance.

Why is the government so woefully bad at creating environmentally responsible legislation that doesn't waste money? A crusading Congress has no incentive to weigh the costs of its laws against the benefits. As Robert Crandall, a senior fellow at Washington's Brookings Institution, says: "When you're carrying out a crusade, you don't ask what's the cost of the religion."

But there's another reason the politically driven approach isn't the best way to clean up the environment. It substitutes the actions of a relatively small number of bureaucrats for the actions of tens of millions of freely acting individuals, and so loses the market's stunning ability to harness a great deal of information. Moreover, if individual consumer choice is circumvented, abuse of the political system grows. The peoples of Eastern Europe have spent half a century learning this. Californians may spend the next half-century learning it.

Examples? A key part of the Clean Air Act of 1977 effectively required new power plants to install expensive scrubbers to cut down on sulfur dioxide emissions from their plants. Cost to the industry: $3 billion, even though a solution such as the use of low-sulfur coal would have achieved the same emission-reduction goal at a fraction of the cost. Why scrubbers? Successful lobbying by high-sulfur-coal producers and the United Mine Workers.

A more recent example of special interests' clout can be found in the Clean Fuels Program, part of the amendment to the Clean Air Act being debated in Congress now. In an attempt to reduce smog, one plan pushes the use of alternative fuels such as methanol and ethanol in nine major U.S. cities by 1997. This plan would also compel automakers to produce up to 1 million alternative-fuel cars per year by 1997.

Will people buy such cars? Will they be efficient? Affordable? These are not questions bureaucrats ask themselves.

Conspicuously absent from the Clean Air Act: nuclear power. Nuclear-generated electricity causes neither the acid rain nor greenhouse gases that coal-fired plants do. Safe methods of storing nuclear waste have been developed and are now being used in France. Nuclear power is the best feasible solution to dependence on other countries for our energy. Yet nuclear power is so politicized in this country that few politicians are courageous enough even to discuss it.

The alternative fuels that are offered by the Clean Air Act, it turns out, are no great alternative. Take ethanol, an alcohol fuel made primarily from corn. Although its use would reduce lead and carbon monoxide emissions, ethanol would also produce four times the aldehyde emissions of gasoline. Aldehyde adds to ozone formation and, unlike gasoline, damages plant life. Other negatives: Ethanol costs between 11 cents and 17 cents more per gallon than gasoline, and widespread production of the fuel would raise food prices between an estimated $6 billion and $9 billion a year, according to the House Energy & Commerce Committee, because corn that could otherwise be used for food would be used for fuel. Of course, if the government phases in ethanol production, as planned, midwestern corn producers would win big. No surprise that Representative Richard Durbin (D-Ill.) introduced a bill mandating production of 5.5 billion gallons of ethanol each year. Result: an estimated windfall of $1.1 billion a year for farmers.

Well-meaning though they may be, government solutions are almost always long on costs and short on benefits. If the amendments to the Clean Air Act now before Congress are passed as is, the legislation will, according to the Business Roundtable in New York, cost consumers and taxpayers some $54 billion a year. This without taking into consideration the cost to the U.S.' international competitiveness.

The politicians, of course, can cite the polls. Several recent polls show that most Americans would pay higher taxes for a cleaner environment. [Such polls are inherently elitist: Were they taken widely in Brazil and other developing countries whose peoples do not enjoy high living standards, the results would be entirely different.] But growth *or* a cleaner environment is not putting the alternatives correctly. The two are not mutually exclusive. The real question is: How should environmental decisions be made? By many millions of consumers acting in their own interests in the marketplace? Or a few thousand powerful political operatives bending and swaying to pressure group lobbying?

Environmentalists, many of them old-time business-bashers, like to blame environmental despoliation on corporate greed. Listen to Roger Featherstone, an independent organizer with the environmental group Earth First: "It's more economically viable in the long run to run a corporation environmentally benignly, but in the short term, profits are better for rape and pillage."

Sadly, governments in Hungary and the U.S.S.R. are showing greater interest today in free market approaches to environmental issues than our own bureaucrats are. Zachary Willey, senior economist at the Environmental Defense Fund, a free market environmental group, is scheduled shortly to speak on market-based solutions to environmental prob-

lems at Karl Marx University in Budapest. Sighs Willey: "I wish the EPA was as open to ideas as the Hungarian government is."

Willey will bring this message to the Hungarians: The state should set financial and other incentives that producers and consumers can factor into their decisions about what to make and buy. Once the incentives have been set, the state should step aside and let the market allocate resources. If given the right incentives, the private sector—entrepreneurs, private investors, and nonprofit organizations—can be the environment's best friend.

Note that Willey is not saying the state does not have a positive role to play. The environment is what economists call a "public good": like national defense, education and a sound legal system, "the environment" is not something that can be produced and consumed by self-interested individuals at a profit. Yet society depends upon the production of such goods.

To resolve this paradox, market-oriented economists have long agreed that the state, as Adam Smith wrote in *The Wealth of Nations,* has a "duty of erecting and maintaining certain public institutions, which it can never be for the interest of any individual, or small number of individuals, to erect and maintain"—but to do so in such ways the preferences and desires of self-interested individuals will not be trampled by an omnipotent state apparatus. Setting overall standards and then letting the market prevail, said Smith, would free the state from an impossible task: "the duty of superintending the industry of private people, and of directing it towards the employments most suitable to the interest of the society."

In other words, environmental policy can and should work through the market. Only if it does can we hope to leave a healthy globe to our grandchildren without forcing them to go back to riding bicycles and scrubbing diapers on an old-fashioned washboard.

One of the greatest flaws in the current system is that new regulatory standards must be met by the entire nation, even though pollution levels vary from state to state. It would be fairer, in some cases, to set standards that address regional differences: Why should a new-car buyer in Montana pay thousands of dollars more for a car with auto-emissions equipment when pollution from automobiles isn't even an issue where he lives?

Another problem with our setup now: Congress, EPA and other agencies often mandate which technologies must be used to achieve a given pollution-reduction standard. Both House and Senate Clean Air bills, for example, would require installation of special canisters on autos to cut down on emissions, even though these systems pose fire risks. Rather than tell automakers how to reduce air pollution, the government should work with industry to set reasonably achievable standards, then police industry's activities to ensure that standards are met. The tricky business of R&D, however, should be left to those with expertise in it—corporations and entrepreneurs.

The government can also encourage private industry to come up with new solutions to pollution problems by creating markets for environmentally beneficial goods, such as recycled paper. How? If Congress required all the government's paper suppliers to use 25% recycled materials in their products, a powerful market for recycled paper would be created.

Is the benefit commensurate with the cost? The answer really depends on knowing more about environmental costs. Hence the intelligence of the Bush Administration's emphasis on stepped-up environmental research.

If we are to achieve progress on cleanup problems, we must shed the easy belief that pollution is caused solely by corporate greed. It is not. It is caused by us, all of us, because we want convenient products and we want them cheap. We want low jet fares, safe and comfortable cars, we want to toss away our toddlers' diapers, drink soft drinks from lightweight plastic jugs. We live in a world of relative leisure because energy-consuming products do so much work for us. The polluter is not acting out of greed; he is acting out of an imperative to give us the goods we want at a price we are willing to pay.

Events such as the *Exxon Valdez* spill in Alaska and the company's more recent oil seepage in Staten Island's Arthur Kill waterway make big headlines. What doesn't make the news? Most water pollution today isn't a by-product of manufacturing at all. The greatest volume of pollution comes instead from thousands of farms nationwide that use pesticides which seep into the water table and run off into nearby streams. Easy to abuse Exxon, but down-home farmers make less interesting targets.

Fred Smith Jr., president of the Competitive Enterprise Institute, a public interest group in Washington, points out: "Current policy assigns virtually no responsibility for pollution to the individual. He's viewed as the helpless victim of a willful technology implemented by an immoral market system."

Exxon is forced to pay for the cleanup of the Arthur Kill. Fair enough. So why shouldn't Americans who drive polluting cars have to pay for the damage they do?

How would such an arrangement work? Through economic incentives and disincentives set up to ensure that a product bears its social costs. Offending material—whether it's pesticides, plastics or disposable diapers—imposes cleanup and disposal costs on society. Wouldn't it make sense to tack these cleanup costs onto the original price of the products—through earmarked taxes or user charges?

Take cars, for example. Instead of mandating that manufacturers install expensive pollution-control equipment on all cars, the costs of which would be paid by every car buyer nationwide, why not tax those drivers, old and new, whose cars exceed federally set emission limits? That way, one could still drive one's favorite polluter-on-wheels. Freedom of choice would still exist. But choosing the high-pollution vehicle would cost one more. Making pollution more expensive would also create a vibrant market for new, more efficient pollution-control technologies.

Disposable diapers, one of America's favorite convenience items, are a huge contributor to our nation's burgeoning solid waste problem. Pampers, Luvs, Huggies et al. now account for 2% of the nation's municipal solid waste—in 1988, 18 billion paper and plastic diapers were landfilled in the U.S. That's 3.6 million tons of waste that, researchers believe, will take 500 years to decompose.

What's the solution to this mounting problem? A tax on single-use diapers that will pay the true costs of their disposal. Dumping costs are increasing dramatically, thanks to the fact that most old landfills are glutted and new ones are difficult to site. Tipping fees, costs levied on dumpers by landfill operators, now run an average of about $27 per ton. This means that, on average, parents who use disposable diapers are paying about $50 a year per child to have these diapers dumped, or some

10 cents on every diaper dollar spent. But since tipping fees are expected to cost $100 per ton in ten years, that will jack up the annual cost of disposal to $200 per child.

Cloth diapers are the obvious solution to the Pampers problem: They cost about half of what the single-use variety does and they decompose in six months. To encourage more parents to use cloth diapers, a tax should be slapped on disposables that is roughly equivalent to tipping fees of $100 a ton. The added cost, about 40 cents on every diaper dollar spent, might just convince some mothers to return to cloth. Those who want to continue to use Pampers can, but must pay the full price, including the environmental component.

Pollution taxes like these can be levied on anything—even foam containers and bags of garbage. Where would pollution taxes go? To the town or municipality that handles the waste. Plus, a portion of the revenues could go toward funding private sector development of new ways to recycle or manage the waste. Where such taxes have been tried, results have been good. In 1981 the city of Seattle began charging residents variable rates to cart away their garbage every month. The more refuse you put out, the more you pay. Since the system was implemented, the amount of refuse generated has declined substantially—from 3.5 cans per family to 1.4—and recycling has picked up. Economic incentives work wonders.

What about industrial air pollution? An interesting, and proven, market-based solution to the problem involves trading in Emission Reduction Credits. So-called tradable permit systems begin with a total allowable level of pollution in a given area—as defined by the EPA. Manufacturers in that area can buy and sell permits among themselves based on how much pollution they generate and how much pollution is allowed.

Here's how it works. Let's say Neon Paint Co., of Louisville, Ky., has retrofitted one of its plants in order to bring its annual pollution emissions to a level further below its legal limit. Neon's emission reduction qualifies it for an Emission Reduction Credit. The company can either hang on to this valuable credit to offset an increase in emissions that occurs at another of its plants or that it may expect in coming years, or sell its emissions credit to another firm in the area.

Who would such a buyer be? It could be Petro Chemical, also in Louisville. Petro is exceeding its air pollution limits and therefore has a debit that must be offset. In buying Neon's credit, Petro would be properly penalized for being an excessive polluter. As long as Petro exceeds pollution limits, the company will be forced to pay for credits—a strong incentive to clean up its act.

Such trading, although on a small scale, is going on now. Corporate giants 3M, Armco, GE, Exxon and Texaco have executed ERC trades. The same type of system, although somewhat more costly, could be used to control water pollution as well. John Palmisano is a broker who trades Emission Reduction Credits at AERX, a firm he started six years ago. According to Palmisano, hydrocarbon emissions, a by-product of dry cleaning processes, plastics manufacturing and painting, are the most commonly traded pollutant. He says: "The going price for a hydrocarbon credit is from $750 to $2,500 a pound; the price for these credits has been going up about 30% a year since 1984." Futures on the emissions credits can be traded as well.

Trading in ERCs exemplifies a free market approach to pollution. The system is based on the self-interest and intelligence of millions of individuals. It rewards those who should be rewarded, penalizes offenders and, once markets are established, does not require additional government regulation or staffing.

So far, emissions trading has been small in scale, but President Bush's clean air legislation includes a plan to reduce acid rain through the use of such credits. If passed, the law would force electric power plants to cut sulfur dioxide emissions by 10 million tons and nitrogen oxide emissions by 2 million tons. But the Administration's program would allow the utilities to decide for themselves how to meet those goals. If one utility reduced its pollution to levels below its allocation, it could sell its credit to firms exceeding the limits. "This could be the first large-scale demonstration showing that markets can function for environmental goods, just as they do for computers or anything else," says Daniel Dudek, senior economist at the Environmental Defense Fund.

In the ten years or so that Emission Reduction Credits have been traded, the cost savings to industry and government is estimated at $5 billion. Joshua Margolis, director of trading operations at AERX, explains that with ERCs "you can make money on pollution control. Companies no longer look at it as a fixed cost but as an opportunity."

By contrast, the present system tends to make pollution control more of a risk than an opportunity. As Superfund is structured now, almost any party associated with a waste site—even those only remotely linked to it, like a bank that forecloses on the property, or a company that leased equipment for use at the site—can be held liable for the cleanup of toxics found there. Says Roger Feldman, head of project finance at the Washington law firm of McDermott, Will & Emery: "If the government paid more attention to the mitigation of risk—if it didn't leave Superfund liability hanging over everyone's head—new companies would emerge to clean up."

The state of California is beginning to see the wisdom in this. Richard Stroup, senior associate at the Political Economy Research Center in Bozeman, Mont., has been discussing with state officials how to clean up waste dumps through privatization. How does privatization work? Take an orphan toxic waste site, so called because the polluter responsible for the mess has abandoned it. First authorities would decide what must be done to sanitize or seal the site. Then an auction among companies who may be interested in the site is arranged, and it's sold to the highest bidder, who puts money in escrow against future problems at the site. Therefore, the firm with the best technology for cleaning up a given site—maybe a biotech company with a new waste-treatment technique—takes on the risk attendant with cleaning up the site and profits by managing it properly. Says Stroup: "Rather than let the bureaucrats decide what and how to do these cleanups, let's let entrepreneurs figure out how."

Can entrepreneurs do the job? Edwin Hafner, president of Hafner Industries, Inc. in New Haven, Conn., is a career chemicals man who has found a way to recycle polyvinylchloride (PVC) and other plastics. It has taken 20 years for Hafner to perfect his process and attract necessary funding from corporations to build his PVC recycling plants, but his tenacity should pay off. Hafner says: "I can recycle PVC into a quality that's exactly as good as virgin, for 20% of the energy cost of creating new PVC."

To provide funding for such projects, project finance lawyer Feldman suggests that municipalities give partial guarantees—a sort of bridge loan—to environmental facilities that would help finance their construction and startup until cash flow is sufficient to cover the debt. He says: "Fiscal devices to enhance private sector investment must be refined." Is there potential for abuse in such fiscal enhancements? Of course. But the potential is far less than it would be if the state completely elbowed aside the market.

Advocates of let-the-government-do-it have a lot to answer for in our society. Not the least is the mess in land management. The trouble with public, or common, ownership of lands is that because no one really owns the property, no one has a stake in keeping that property from deteriorating. Land that is tended to and cared for generally increases in value, so when property is privately held, incentives to maintain its beauty are strong. When the government is the owner these incentives disappear.

Consider what the Nature Conservancy Hawaiian chapter, an 8,500-member nonprofit organization, has done. Since it was established in 1980, the conservancy has protected more than 43,000 acres in Hawaii. These lands will be aggressively managed by conservancy staffers and protected from introduced species such as pigs, which uproot mosses and trees from the forest floor. The state of Hawaii, which owns 40% of the land on the islands, has only now begun to understand that its increasingly damaged holdings must be managed.

In fact, voluntary conservation organizations like the Nature Conservancy are some of the best land managers around. Some allow oil drilling or other corporate activities to take place on their land, proving that commercial and environmental interests can coexist. The Welder Wildlife Foundation, near Corpus Christi, Tex. is an example. On its 7,800 acres, students learn wildlife ecology and management; also on-site are an active oilfield and a cattle ranch that help pay to maintain the land. James Teer, director of the foundation, says: "If you don't have the constraints of public organizations, you can do things more efficiently. Our land is used profitably, but we also have fantastic wildlife."

Two centuries ago Adam Smith wrote: "It is not from the benevolence of the butcher, the brewer, or the baker, that we expect our dinner, but from their regard to their own interest." He might have said the same thing about the environment. Instead of seeking to curb the profit motive and freedom of individual choice, we would do well to stimulate them both in ways that let the free market reconcile the industrial revolution with the age of environmentalism.

Morality, Money, and Motor Cars

Norman Bowie

Environmentalists frequently argue that business has special obligations to protect the environment. Although I agree with the environmentalists on this point, I do not agree with them as to where the obligations lie. Business does not have an obligation to protect the environment over and above what is required by law; however, it does have a moral obligation to avoid intervening in the political arena in order to defeat or weaken environmental legislation. In developing this thesis, several points are in order. First, many businesses have violated important moral obligations, and the violation has had a severe negative impact on the environment. For example, toxic waste haulers have illegally dumped hazardous material, and the environment has been harmed as a result. One might argue that those toxic waste haulers who have illegally dumped have violated a special obligation to the environment. Isn't it more accurate to say that these toxic waste haulers have violated their obligation to obey the law and that in this case the law that has been broken is one pertaining to the environment? Businesses have an obligation to obey the law—environmental laws and all others. Since there are many well-publicized cases of business having broken environmental laws, it is easy to think that business has violated some special obligations to the environment. In fact, what business has done is to disobey the law. Environmentalists do not need a special obligation to the environment

to protect the environment against illegal business activity; they need only insist that business obey the laws.

Business has broken other obligations beside the obligation to obey the law and has harmed the environment as a result. Consider the grounding of the Exxon oil tanker *Valdez* in Alaska. That grounding was allegedly caused by the fact that an inadequately trained crewman was piloting the tanker while the captain was below deck and had been drinking. What needs to be determined is whether Exxon's policies and procedures were sufficiently lax so that it could be said Exxon was morally at fault. It might be that Exxon is legally responsible for the accident under the doctrine of respondent superior, but Exxon is not thereby morally responsible. Suppose, however, that Exxon's policies were so lax that the company could be characterized as morally negligent. In such a case, the company would violate its moral obligation to use due care and avoid negligence. Although its negligence was disastrous to the environment, Exxon would have violated no special obligation to the environment. It would have been morally negligent.

A similar analysis could be given to the environmentalists' charges that Exxon's cleanup procedures were inadequate. If the charge is true, either Exxon was morally at fault or not. If the procedures had not been implemented properly by Exxon employees, then Exxon is legally culpable, but not morally culpable. On the other hand, if Exxon lied to government officials by saying that its policies were in accord with regulations and/or were ready for emergencies of this type, then Exxon violated its moral obligation to tell the truth. Exxon's immoral conduct would have harmed the environment, but it violated no special obligation to the environment. More important, none is needed. Environmentalists, like government officials, employ-

---

From *Business, Ethics, and the Environment: The Public Policy Debate,* edited by W. Michael Hoffman, Robert Frederick, and Edward S. Petry, Jr. (Westport, CT: Quorum Books, 1990). Copyright © Center for Business Ethics at Bentley College, Waltham, MA. Reprinted by permission of the Center for Business Ethics. Norman Bowie is the Anderson chair in Corporate Responsibility at the University of Minnesota.

ees, and stockholders, expect that business firms and officials have moral obligations to obey the law, avoid negligent behavior, and tell the truth. In sum, although many business decisions have harmed the environment, these decisions violated no environmental moral obligations. If a corporation is negligent in providing for worker safety, we do not say the corporation violated a special obligation to employees: we say that it violated its obligation to avoid negligent behavior.

The crucial issues concerning business obligations to the environment focus on the excess use of natural resources (the dwindling supply of oil and gas, for instance) and the externalities of production (pollution, for instance). The critics of business want to claim that business has some special obligation to mitigate or solve these problems. I believe this claim is largely mistaken. If business does have a special obligation to help solve the environmental crisis, that obligation results from the special knowledge that business firms have. If they have greater expertise than other constituent groups in society, then it can be argued that, other things being equal, business's responsibilities to mitigate the environmental crisis are somewhat greater. Absent this condition, business's responsibility is no greater than and may be less than that of other social groups. What leads me to think that the critics of business are mistaken?

William Frankena distinguished obligations in an ascending order of the difficulty in carrying them out: avoiding harm, preventing harm, and doing good.[1] The most stringent requirement, to avoid harm, insists no one has a right to render harm on another unless there is a compelling, overriding moral reason to do so. Some writers have referred to this obligation as the moral minimum. A corporation's behavior is consistent with the moral minimum if it causes no avoidable harm to others.

Preventing harm is a less stringent obligation, but sometimes the obligation to prevent harm may be nearly as strict as the obligation to avoid harm. Suppose you are the only person passing a 2-foot-deep working pool where a young child is drowning. There is no one else in the vicinity. Don't you have a strong moral obligation to prevent the child's death? Our obligation to prevent harm is not unlimited, however. Under what conditions must we be good samaritans? Some have argued that four conditions must exist before one is obligated

to prevent harm: capability, need, proximity, and last resort.[2] These conditions are all met with the case of the drowning child: There is obviously a need that you can meet since you are both in the vicinity and have the resources to prevent the drowning with little effort; you are also the last resort.

The least strict moral obligation is to do good—to make contributions to society or to help solve problems (inadequate primary schooling in the inner cities, for example). Although corporations may have some minimum obligation in this regard based on an argument from corporate citizenship, the obligations of the corporation to do good cannot be expanded without limit. An injunction to assist in solving societal problems makes impossible demands on a corporation because at the practical level, it ignores the impact that such activities have on profit.

It might seem that even if this descending order of strictness of obligations were accepted, obligations toward the environment would fall into the moral minimum category. After all, the depletion of natural resources and pollution surely harm the environment. If so, wouldn't the obligations business has to the environment be among the strictest obligations a business can have?

Suppose, however, that a businessperson argues that the phrase "avoid harm" usually applies to human beings. Polluting a lake is not like injuring a human with a faulty product. Those who coined the phrase *moral minimum* for use in the business context defined harm as "particularly including activities which violate or frustrate the enforcement of rules of domestic or institutional law intended to protect individuals against prevention of health, safety or basic freedom."[3] Even if we do not insist that the violations be violations of a rule of law, polluting a lake would not count as a harm under this definition. The environmentalists would respond that it would. Polluting the lake may be injuring people who might swim in or eat fish from it. Certainly it would be depriving people of the freedom to enjoy the lake. Although the environmentalist is correct, especially if we grant the legitimacy of a human right to a clean environment, the success of this reply is not enough to establish the general argument.

Consider the harm that results from the production of automobiles. We know statistically that about 50,000 persons per year will die and that nearly 250,000 others will be seriously injured in automobile accidents in the United States alone. Such death and injury, which is harmful, is avoidable. If that is the case, doesn't the avoid-harm criterion require that the production of automobiles for profit cease? Not really. What such arguments point out is that some refinement of the moral minimum standard needs to take place. Take the automobile example. The automobile is itself a good-producing instrument. Because of the advantages of automobiles, society accepts the possible risks that go in using them. Society also accepts many other types of avoidable harm. We take certain risks—ride in planes, build bridges, and mine coal—to pursue advantageous goals. It seems that the high benefits of some activities justify the resulting harms. As long as the risks are known, it is not wrong that some avoidable harm be permitted so that other social and individual goals can be achieved. The avoidable-harm criterion needs some sharpening.

Using the automobile as a paradigm, let us consider the necessary refinements for the avoid-harm criterion. It is a fundamental principle of ethics that "ought" implies "can." That expression means that you can be held morally responsible only for events within your power. In the ought-implies-can principle, the overwhelming majority of highway deaths and injuries is not the responsibility of the automaker. Only those deaths and injuries attributable to unsafe automobile design can be attributed to the automaker. The ought-implies-can principle can also be used to absolve the auto companies of responsibility for death and injury from safety defects that the automakers could not reasonably know existed. The company could not be expected to do anything about them.

Does this mean that a company has an obligation to build a car as safe as it knows how? No. The standards for safety must leave the product's cost within the price range of the consumer ("ought implies can" again). Comments about engineering and equipment capability are obvious enough. But for a business, capability is also a function of profitability. A company that builds a maximally safe car at a cost that puts it at a competitive disadvantage and hence threatens its survival is building a safe car that lies beyond the capability of the company.

Critics of the automobile industry will express horror at these remarks, for by making capability a function of profitability, society will continue to have avoidable deaths and injuries: however, the situation is not as dire as the critics imagine. Certainly capability should not be sacrificed completely so that profits can be maximized. The decision to build products that are cheaper in cost but are not maximally safe is a social decision that has widespread support. The arguments occur over the line between safety and cost. What we have is a classical trade-off situation. What is desired is some appropriate mix between engineering safety and consumer demand. To say there must be some mix between engineering safety and consumer demand is not to justify all the decisions made by the automobile companies. Ford Motor Company made a morally incorrect choice in placing Pinto gas tanks where it did. Consumers were uninformed, the record of the Pinto in rear-end collisions was worse than that of competitors, and Ford fought government regulations.

Let us apply the analysis of the automobile industry to the issue before us. That analysis shows that an automobile company does not violate its obligation to avoid harm and hence is not in violation of the moral minimum if the trade-off between potential harm and the utility of the products rests on social consensus and competitive realities.

As long as business obeys the environmental laws and honors other standard moral obligations, most harm done to the environment by business has been accepted by society. Through their decisions in the marketplace, we can see that most consumers are unwilling to pay extra for products that are more environmentally friendly than less friendly competitive products. Nor is there much evidence that consumers are willing to conserve resources, recycle, or tax themselves for environmental causes.

Consider the following instances reported in the *Wall Street Journal*.[4] The restaurant chain Wendy's tried to replace foam plates and cups with paper, but customers in the test markets balked. Procter and Gamble offered Downey fabric softener in concentrated form that requires less packaging than ready-to-use products; however the concentrate version is less convenient because it has to be mixed with water. Sales have been poor. Procter and Gamble manufactures Vizir and Lenor brands of detergents in concentrate form, which the customer mixes at home in reusable bottles. Europeans will take the trouble; Americans will not. Kodak tried to eliminate its yellow film boxes but met customer resistance. McDonald's has been testing mini-incinerators that convert trash into energy but often meets opposition from community groups that fear the incinerators will pollute the air. A McDonald's spokesperson points out that the emissions are mostly carbon dioxide and water vapor and are "less offensive than a barbecue." Exxon spent approximately $9,200,000 to "save" 230 otters ($40,000 for each otter). Otters in captivity cost $800. Fishermen in Alaska are permitted to shoot otters as pests.[5] Given these facts, doesn't business have every right to assume that public tolerance for environmental damage is quite high, and hence current legal activities by corporations that harm the environment do not violate the avoid-harm criterion?

Recently environmentalists have pointed out the environmental damage caused by the widespread use of disposable diapers. Are Americans ready to give them up and go back to cloth diapers and the diaper pail? Most observers think not. Procter and Gamble is not violating the avoid-harm criterion by manufacturing Pampers. Moreover, if the public wants cloth diapers, business certainly will produce them. If environmentalists want business to produce products that are friendlier to the environment, they must convince Americans to purchase them. Business will respond to the market. It is the consuming public that has the obligation to make the trade-off between cost and environmental integrity.

Data and arguments of the sort described should give environmental critics of business pause. Nonetheless, these critics are not without counterresponses. For example, they might respond that public attitudes are changing. Indeed, they point out, during the Reagan deregulation era, the one area where the public supported government regulations was in the area of environmental law. In addition, *Fortune* predicts environmental integrity as the primary demand of society on business in the 1990s.[6]

More important, they might argue that environmentally friendly products are at a disadvantage in the marketplace because they have public good characteristics. After all, the best situation for the individual is one where most other people use environmentally friendly products but he or she does not, hence reaping the benefit of lower cost and convenience. Since everyone reasons this way, the real demand for environmentally friendly products cannot be registered in the market. Everyone is understating the value of his or her preference for environmentally friendly products. Hence, companies cannot conclude from market behavior that the environmentally unfriendly products are preferred.

Suppose the environmental critics are right that the public goods characteristic of environmentally friendly products creates a market failure. Does that mean the companies are obligated to stop producing these environmentally unfriendly products? I think not, and I propose that we use the four conditions attached to the prevent-harm obligation to show why not. There is a need, and certainly corporations that cause environmental problems are in proximity. However, environmentally clean firms, if there are any, are not in proximity at all, and most business firms are not in proximity with respect to most environmental problems. In other words, the environmental critic must limit his or her argument to the environmental damage a business actually causes. The environmentalist might argue that Procter and Gamble ought to do something about Pampers; I do not see how an environmentalist can use the avoid-harm criterion to argue that Procter and Gamble should do something about acid rain. But even narrowing the obligation to damage actually caused will not be sufficient to establish an obligation to pull a product from the market because it damages the environment or even to go beyond what is legally required to protect the environment. Even for damage actually done, both the high cost of protecting the environment and the competitive pressures of business make further action to protect the environment beyond the capability of business. This conclusion would be more serious if business were the last resort, but it is not.

Traditionally it is the function of the government to correct for market failure. If the market cannot register the true desires of consumers, let them register their preferences in the political arena. Even fairly conservative economic thinkers allow government a legitimate role in correcting market failure. Perhaps the responsibility for energy conservation and pollution control belongs with the government.

Although I think consumers bear a far greater responsibility for preserving and protecting the environment than they have actually exercised, let us assume that the basic responsibility rests with the government. Does that let business off the hook? No. Most of business's unethical conduct regarding the environment occurs in the political arena.

Far too many corporations try to have their cake and eat it too. They argue that it is the job of government to correct for market failure and then use their influence and money to defeat or water down regulations designed to conserve and protect the environment.[7] They argue that consumers should decide how much conservation and protection the environment should have, and then they try to interfere with the exercise of that choice in the political arena. Such behavior is inconsistent and ethically inappropriate. Business has an obligation to avoid intervention in the political process for the purpose of defeating and weakening environmental regulations. Moreover, this is a special obligation to the environment since business does not have a general obligation to avoid pursuing its own parochial interests in the political arena. Business need do nothing wrong when it seeks to influence tariffs, labor policy, or monetary policy. Business does do something wrong when it interferes with the passage of environmental legislation. Why?

First, such a noninterventionist policy is dictated by the logic of the business's argument to avoid a special obligation to protect the environment. Put more formally:

1. Business argues that it escapes special obligations to the environment because it is willing to respond to consumer preferences in this matter.
2. Because of externalities and public goods considerations, consumers cannot express their preferences in the market.
3. The only other viable forum for consumers to express their preferences is in the political arena.
4. Business intervention interferes with the expression of these preferences.

5. Since point 4 is inconsistent with point 1, business should not intervene in the political process.

The importance of this obligation in business is even more important when we see that environmental legislation has special disadvantages in the political arena. Public choice reminds us that the primary interest of politicians is being reelected. Government policy will be skewed in favor of policies that provide benefits to an influential minority as long as the greater costs are widely dispersed. Politicians will also favor projects where benefits are immediate and where costs can be postponed to the future. Such strategies increase the likelihood that a politician will be reelected.

What is frightening about the environmental crisis is that both the conservation of scarce resources and pollution abatement require policies that go contrary to a politician's self-interest. The costs of cleaning up the environment are immediate and huge, yet the benefits are relatively long range (many of them exceedingly long range). More-over, a situation where the benefits are widely dispersed and the costs are large presents a twofold problem. The costs are large enough so that all voters will likely notice them and in certain cases are catastrophic for individuals (e.g., for those who lose their jobs in a plant shutdown).

Given these facts and the political realities they entail, business opposition to environmental legislation makes a very bad situation much worse. Even if consumers could be persuaded to take environmental issues more seriously, the externalities, opportunities to free ride, and public goods characteristics of the environment make it difficult for even enlightened consumers to express their true preference for the environment in the market. The fact that most environmental legislation trades immediate costs for future benefits makes it difficult for politicians concerned about reelection to support it. Hence it is also difficult for enlightened consumers to have their preferences for a better environment honored in the political arena. Since lack of business intervention seems necessary, and might even be sufficient, for adequate environmental legislation, it seems business has an obligation not to intervene. Nonintervention would prevent the harm of not having the true preferences of consumers for a clean environment revealed. Given business's commitment to satisfying preferences, opposition to having these preferences expressed seems inconsistent as well.

The extent of this obligation to avoid intervening in the political process needs considerable discussion by ethicists and other interested parties. Businesspeople will surely object that if they are not permitted to play a role, Congress and state legislators will make decisions that will put them at a severe competitive disadvantage. For example, if the United States develops stricter environmental controls than other countries do, foreign imports will have a competitive advantage over domestic products. Shouldn't business be permitted to point that out? Moreover, any legislation that places costs on one industry rather than another confers advantages on other industries. The cost to the electric utilities from regulations designed to reduce the pollution that causes acid rain will give advantages to natural gas and perhaps even solar energy. Shouldn't the electric utility industry be permitted to point that out?

These questions pose difficult questions, and my answer to them should be considered highly tentative. I believe the answer to the first question is "yes" and the answer to the second is "no." Business does have a right to insist that the regulations apply to all those in the industry. Anything else would seem to violate norms of fairness. Such issues of fairness do not arise in the second case. Since natural gas and solar do not contribute to acid rain and since the costs of acid rain cannot be fully captured in the market, government intervention through regulation is simply correcting a market failure. With respect to acid rain, the electric utilities do have an advantage they do not deserve. Hence they have no right to try to protect it.

Legislative bodies and regulatory agencies need to expand their staffs to include technical experts, economists, and engineers so that the political process can be both neutral and highly informed about environmental matters. To gain the respect of business and the public, its performance needs to improve. Much more needs to be said to make any contention that business ought to stay out of the political debate theoretically and practically possible. Perhaps these suggestions point the way for future discussion.

Ironically business might best improve its situation in the political arena by taking on an additional obligation to the environment. Businesspersons often have more knowledge about environmental harms and the costs of cleaning them up. They may often have special knowledge about how to prevent environmental harm in the first place. Perhaps business has a special duty to educate the public and to promote environmentally responsible behavior.

Business has no reticence about leading consumer preferences in other areas. Advertising is a billion-dollar industry. Rather than blaming consumers for not purchasing environmentally friendly products, perhaps some businesses might make a commitment to capture the environmental niche. I have not seen much imagination on the part of business in this area. Far too many advertisements with an environmental message are reactive and public relations driven. Recall those by oil companies showing fish swimming about the legs of oil rigs. An educational campaign that encourages consumers to make environmentally friendly decisions in the marketplace would limit the necessity for business activity in the political arena. Voluntary behavior that is environmentally friendly is morally preferable to coerced behavior. If business took greater responsibility for educating the public, the government's responsibility would be lessened. An educational campaign aimed at consumers would likely enable many businesses to do good while simultaneously doing very well.

Hence business does have obligations to the environment, although these obligations are not found where the critics of business place them. Business has no special obligation to conserve natural resources or to stop polluting over and above its legal obligations. It does have an obligation to avoid intervening in the political arena to oppose environmental regulations, and it has a positive obligation to educate consumers. The benefits of honoring these obligations should not be underestimated.

NOTES

The title for this [reading] was suggested by Susan Bernick, a graduate student in the University of Minnesota philosophy department.

1. William Frankena, *Ethics*, 2d ed. (Englewood Cliffs, N.J.: Prentice-Hall, 1973), p. 47. Actually Frankena

has four principles of prima facie duty under the principle of beneficence: one ought not to inflict evil or harm; one ought to prevent evil or harm; one ought to remove evil; and one ought to do or promote good.

2. John G. Simon, Charles W. Powers, and Jon P. Gunneman. *The Ethical Investor: Universities and Corporate Responsibility* (New Haven, Conn.: Yale University Press, 1972), pp. 22–25.

3. Ibid., p. 21.

4. Alicia Swasy, "For Consumers, Ecology Comes Second," *Wall Street Journal*, August 23, 1988, p. B1.

5. Jerry Alder, "Alaska after Exxon," *Newsweek*, September 18, 1989, p. 53.

6. Andrew Kupfer, "Managing Now for the 1990s," *Fortune*, September 26, 1988, pp. 46–47.

7. I owe this point to Gordon Rands, a Ph.D. student in the Carlson School of Management. Indeed the tone of the chapter has shifted considerably as a result of his helpful comments.

Business and Environmental Ethics

W. Michael Hoffman

The business ethics movement, from my perspective, is still on the march. And the environmental movement, after being somewhat silent for the past twenty years, has once again captured our attention—promising to be a major social force in the 1990s. Much will be written in the next few years trying to tie together these two movements. This is one such effort.

Concern over the environment is not new. Warnings came out of the 1960s in the form of burning rivers, dying lakes, and oil-fouled oceans. Radioactivity was found in our food, DDT in mother's milk, lead and mercury in our water. Every breath of air in the North American hemisphere was reported as contaminated. Some said these were truly warnings from Planet Earth of eco-catastrophe, unless we could find limits to our growth and changes in our lifestyle.

Over the past few years Planet Earth began to speak to us even more loudly than before, and we began to listen more than before. The message was ominous, somewhat akin to God warning Noah. It spoke through droughts, heat waves, and forest fires, raising fears of global warming due to the buildup of carbon dioxide and other gases in the atmosphere. It warned us by raw sewage and medical wastes washing up on our beaches, and by devastating oil spills—one despoiling Prince William

Sound and its wildlife to such an extent that it made us weep. It spoke to us through increased skin cancers and discoveries of holes in the ozone layer caused by our use of chlorofluorocarbons. It drove its message home through the rapid and dangerous cutting and burning of our primitive forests at the rate of one football field a second, leaving us even more vulnerable to greenhouse gases like carbon dioxide and eliminating scores of irreplaceable species daily. It rained down on us in the form of acid, defoliating our forests and poisoning our lakes and streams. Its warnings were found on barges roaming the seas for places to dump tons of toxic incinerator ash. And its message exploded in our faces at Chernobyl and Bhopal, reminding us of past warnings at Three Mile Island and Love Canal.

Senator Albert Gore said in 1988: "The fact that we face an ecological crisis without any precedent in historic times is no longer a matter of any dispute worthy of recognition."[1] The question, he continued, is not whether there is a problem, but how we will address it. This will be the focal point for a public policy debate which requires the full participation of two of its major players—business and government. The debate must clarify such fundamental questions as: (1) What obligation does business have to help with our environmental crisis? (2) What is the proper relationship between business and government, especially when faced with a social problem of the magnitude of the environment crisis? And (3) what rationale should be used for making and justifying decisions to protect the environment? Corporations, and society in

From *Business Ethics Quarterly*, vol. 1, no. 2 (1991) 169–184. Reprinted by permission of the author. W. Michael Hoffman is the executive director of the Center for Business Ethics at Bentley College in Waltham, Massachusetts.

general for that matter, have yet to answer these questions satisfactorily. In the first section of this paper I will briefly address the first two questions. In the final two sections I will say a few things about the third question.

I.

In a 1989 keynote address before the "Business, Ethics and the Environment" conference at the Center for Business Ethics, Norman Bowie offered some answers to the first two questions.

> Business does not have an obligation to protect the environment over and above what is required by law; however, it does have a moral obligation to avoid intervening in the political arena in order to defeat or weaken environmental legislation.[2]

I disagree with Bowie on both counts.

Bowie's first point is very Friedmanesque.[3] The social responsibility of business is to produce goods and services and to make profit for its shareholders, while playing within the rules of the market game. These rules, including those to protect the environment, are set by the government and the courts. To do more than is required by these rules is, according to this position, unfair to business. In order to perform its proper function, every business must respond to the market and operate in the same arena as its competitors. As Bowie puts this:

> An injunction to assist in solving societal problems [including depletion of natural resources and pollution] makes impossible demands on a corporation because, at the practical level, it ignores the impact that such activities have on profit.[4]

If, as Bowie claims, consumers are not willing to respond to the cost and use of environmentally friendly products and actions, then it is not the responsibility of business to respond or correct such market failure.

Bowie's second point is a radical departure from this classical position in contending that business should not lobby against the government's process to set environmental regulations. To quote Bowie:

Far too many corporations try to have their cake and eat it too. They argue that it is the job of government to correct for market failure and then they use their influence and money to defeat or water down regulations designed to conserve and protect the environment.[5]

Bowie only recommends this abstinence of corporate lobbying in the case of environmental regulations. He is particularly concerned that politicians, ever mindful of their reelection status, are already reluctant to pass environmental legislation which has huge immediate costs and in most cases very long-term benefits. This makes the obligations of business to refrain from opposing such legislation a justified special case.

I can understand why Bowie argues these points. He seems to be responding to two extreme approaches, both of which are inappropriate. Let me illustrate these extremes by the following two stories.

At the Center's First National Conference on Business Ethics, Harvard Business School Professor George Cabot Lodge told of a friend who owned a paper company on the banks of a New England stream. On the first Earth Day in 1970, his friend was converted to the cause of environmental protection. He became determined to stop his company's pollution of the stream, and marched off to put his new-found religion into action. Later, Lodge learned his friend went broke, so he went to investigate. Radiating a kind of ethical purity, the friend told Lodge that he spent millions to stop the pollution and thus could no longer compete with other firms that did not follow his example. So the company went under, 500 people lost their jobs, and the stream remained polluted.

When Lodge asked why his friend had not sought help from the state or federal government for stricter standards for everyone, the man replied that was not the American way, that government should not interfere with business activity, and that private enterprise could do the job alone. In fact, he felt it was the social responsibility of business to solve environmental problems, so he was proud that he had set an example for others to follow.

The second story portrays another extreme. A few years ago "Sixty Minutes" interviewed a manager of a chemical company that was discharging effluent into a river in upstate New York. At the time, the dumping was legal, though a bill to prevent it was pending in Congress. The manager remarked that he hoped the bill would pass, and that he certainly would support it as a responsible citizen. However, he also said he approved of his company's efforts to defeat the bill and of the firm's policy of dumping wastes in the meantime. After all, isn't the proper role of business to make as much profit as possible within the bounds of law? Making the laws—setting the rules of the game—is the role of government, not business. While wearing his business hat the manager had a job to do, even if it meant doing something that he strongly opposed as a private citizen.

Both stories reveal incorrect answers to the questions posed earlier, the proof of which is found in the fact that neither the New England stream nor the New York river was made any cleaner. Bowie's points are intended to block these two extremes. But to avoid these extremes, as Bowie does, misses the real managerial and ethical failure of the stories. Although the paper company owner and the chemical company manager had radically different views of the ethical responsibilities of business, both saw business and government performing separate roles, and neither felt that business ought to cooperate with government to solve environmental problems.[6]

If the business ethics movement has led us anywhere in the past fifteen years, it is to the position that business has an ethical responsibility to become a more active partner in dealing with social concerns. Business must creatively find ways to become a part of solutions, rather than being a part of problems. Corporations can and must develop a conscience, as Ken Goodpaster and others have argued—and this includes an environmental conscience.[7] Corporations should not isolate themselves from participation in solving our environmental problems, leaving it up to others to find the answers and to tell them what not to do.

Corporations have special knowledge, expertise, and resources which are invaluable in dealing with the environmental crisis. Society needs the ethical vision and cooperation of all its players to solve its most urgent problems, especially one that involves the very survival of the planet itself. Business must work with government to find appropriate solutions. It should lobby for good environmental legislation and lobby against bad legisla-

tion, rather than isolating itself from the legislative process as Bowie suggests. It should not be ethically quixotic and try to go it alone, as our paper company owner tried to do, nor should it be ethically inauthentic and fight against what it believes to be environmentally sound policy, as our chemical company manager tried to do. Instead business must develop and demonstrate moral leadership.

There are examples of corporations demonstrating such leadership, even when this has been a risk to their self-interest. In the area of environmental moral leadership one might cite DuPont's discontinuing its Freon products, a $750-million-a-year-business, because of their possible negative effects on the ozone layer, and Procter and Gamble's manufacture of concentrated fabric softener and detergents which require less packaging. But some might argue, as Bowie does, that the real burden for environmental change lies with consumers, not with corporations. If we as consumers are willing to accept the harm done to the environment by favoring environmentally unfriendly products, corporations have no moral obligation to change so long as they obey environmental law. This is even more the case, so the argument goes, if corporations must take risks or sacrifice profits to do so.

This argument fails to recognize that we quite often act differently when we think of ourselves as *consumers* than when we think of ourselves as *citizens*. Mark Sagoff, concerned about our overreliance on economic solutions, clearly characterizes this dual nature of our decision making.[8] As consumers, we act more often than not for ourselves; as citizens, we take on a broader vision and do what is in the best interests of the community. I often shop for things I don't vote for. I might support recycling referendums, but buy products in nonreturnable bottles. I am not proud of this, but I suspect this is more true of most of us than not. To stake our environmental future on our consumer willingness to pay is surely shortsighted, perhaps even disastrous.

I am not saying that we should not work to be ethically committed citizen consumers, and investors for that matter. I agree with Bowie that "consumers bear a far greater responsibility for preserving and protecting the environment than they have actually exercised,"[9] but activities which affect the environment should not be left up to what we, acting as consumers, are willing to tolerate or accept. To do this would be to use a market-based method of reasoning to decide on an issue which should be determined instead on the basis of our ethical responsibilities as a member of a social community.

Furthermore, consumers don't make the products, provide the services, or enact the legislation which can be either environmentally friendly or unfriendly. Grass roots boycotts and lobbying efforts are important, but we also need leadership and mutual cooperation from business and government in setting forth ethical environmental policy. Even Bowie admits that perhaps business has a responsibility to educate the public and promote environmentally responsible behavior. But I am suggesting that corporate moral leadership goes far beyond public educational campaigns. It requires moral vision, commitment, and courage, and involves risk and sacrifice. I think business is capable of such a challenge. Some are even engaging in such a challenge. Certainly the business ethics movement should do nothing short of encouraging such leadership. I feel morality demands such leadership.

II.

If business has an ethical responsibility to the environment which goes beyond obeying environmental law, what criterion should be used to guide and justify such action? Many corporations are making environmentally friendly decisions where they see there are profits to be made by doing so. They are wrapping themselves in green where they see a green bottom line as a consequence. This rationale is also being used as a strategy by environmentalists to encourage more businesses to become environmentally conscientious. In December 1989 the highly respected Worldwatch Institute published an article by one of its senior researchers entitled "Doing Well by Doing Good" which gives numerous examples of corporations improving their pocketbooks by improving the environment. It concludes by saying that "fortunately, businesses that work to preserve the environment can also make a buck." [10]

In a recent Public Broadcast Corporation documentary entitled "Profit the Earth," several efforts are depicted of what is called the "new environmentalism" which induces corporations to do things for the environment by appealing to their self-interest. The Environmental Defense Fund is shown encouraging agribusiness in Southern California to irrigate more efficiently and profit by selling the water saved to the city of Los Angeles. This in turn will help save Mono Lake. EDF is also shown lobbying for emissions trading that would allow utility companies which are under their emission allotments to sell their "pollution rights" to those companies which are over their allotments. This is for the purpose of reducing acid rain. Thus the frequent strategy of the new environmentalists is to get business to help solve environmental problems by finding profitable or virtually costless ways for them to participate. They feel that compromise, not confrontation, is the only way to save the earth. By using the tools of the free enterprise system, they are in search of win-win solutions, believing that such solutions are necessary to take us beyond what we have so far been able to achieve.

I am not opposed to these efforts; in most cases I think they should be encouraged. There is certainly nothing wrong with making money while protecting the environment, just as there is nothing wrong with feeling good about doing one's duty. But if business is adopting or being encouraged to adopt the view that good environmentalism is good business, then I think this poses a danger for the environmental ethics movement—a danger which has an analogy in the business ethics movement.

As we all know, the position that good ethics is good business is being used more and more by corporate executives to justify the building of ethics into their companies and by business ethics consultants to gain new clients. For example, the Business Roundtable's *Corporate Ethics* report states:

> The corporate community should continue to refine and renew efforts to improve performance and manage change effectively through programs in corporate ethics . . . corporate ethics is a strategic key to survival and profitability in this era of fierce competitiveness in a global economy. [11]

And, for instance, the book *The Power of Ethical Management* by Kenneth Blanchard and Norman Vincent Peale states in big red letters on the cover jacket that "Integrity Pays! You Don't Have to Cheat to Win." The blurb on the inside cover promises that the book "gives hard-hitting, practical, *ethical* strategies that build profits, productivity, and long-term success."[12] Who would have guessed that business ethics could deliver all that! In such ways business ethics gets marketed as the newest cure for what ails corporate America.

Is the rationale that good ethics is good business a proper one for business ethics? I think not. One thing that the study of ethics has taught us over the past 2500 years is that being ethical may on occasion require that we place the interests of others ahead of or at least on par with our own interests. And this implies that the ethical thing to do, the morally right thing to do, may not be in our own self-interest. What happens when the right thing is not the best thing for the business?

Although in most cases good ethics may be good business, it should not be advanced as the only or even the main reason for doing business ethically. When the crunch comes, when ethics conflicts with the firm's interests, any ethics program that has not already faced up to this possibility is doomed to fail because it will undercut the rationale of the program itself. We should promote business ethics, not because good ethics is good business, but because we are morally required to adopt the moral point of view in all our dealings— and business is no exception. In business, as in all other human endeavors, we must be prepared to pay the costs of ethical behavior.

There is a similar danger in the environmental movement with corporations choosing or being wooed to be environmentally friendly on the grounds that it will be in their self-interest. There is the risk of participating in the movement for the wrong reasons. But what does it matter if business cooperates for reasons other than the right reasons, as long as it cooperates? It matters if business believes or is led to believe that it only has a duty to be environmentally conscientious in those cases where such actions either require no sacrifice or actually make a profit. And I am afraid this is exactly what is happening. I suppose it wouldn't matter if the environmental cooperation of business was only needed in those cases where it was also in business' self-interest. But this is surely not the case, unless one begins to really reach and talk about that amorphous concept "long-term" self-interest. Moreover, long-term interests, I suspect, are not what corporations or the new environmentalists have in mind in using self-interest as a reason for environmental action.

I am not saying we should abandon attempts to entice corporations into being ethical, both environmentally and in other ways, by pointing out and providing opportunities where good ethics is good business. And there are many places where such attempts fit well in both the business and environmental ethics movements. But we must be careful not to cast this as the proper guideline for business' ethical responsibility. Because when it is discovered that many ethical actions are not necessarily good for business, at least in the short-run, then the rationale based on self-interest will come up morally short, and both ethical movements will be seen as deceptive and shallow.

NOTES

1. Albert Gore, "What Is Wrong With Us?" *Time* (January 2, 1989), 66.
2. Norman Bowie, "Morality, Money, and Motor Cars," *Business, Ethics, and the Environment: The Public Policy Debate*, edited by W. Michael Hoffman, Robert Frederick, and Edward S. Petry, Jr. (New York: Quorum Books, 1990), p. 89.
3. See Milton Friedman, "The Social Responsibility of Business Is to Increase Its Profits," *The New York Times Magazine* (September 13, 1970).
4. Bowie, p. 91.
5. Bowie, p. 94.
6. Robert Frederick, Assistant Director of the Center for Business Ethics, and I have developed and written these points together. Frederick has also provided me with invaluable assistance on other points in this paper.
7. Kenneth E. Goodpaster, "Can a Corporation have an Environmental Conscience," *The Corporation, Ethics, and the Environment*, edited by W. Michael Hoffman, Robert Frederick, and Edward S. Petry, Jr. (New York: Quorum Books, 1990).
8. Mark Sagoff, "At the Shrine of Our Lady of Fatima, or Why Political Questions Are Not All Economic," found in *Business Ethics: Readings and Cases in Corporate Morality*, 2nd edition, edited by W. Michael Hoffman and Jennifer Mills Moore (New York: McGraw-Hill, 1990), pp. 494–503.
9. Bowie, p. 94.
10. Cynthia Pollock Shea, "Doing Well By Doing Good," *World-Watch* (November/December, 1989), p. 30.
11. *Corporate Ethics: A Prime Business Asset*, a report by The Business Roundtable, February, 1988, p. 4.
12. Kenneth Blanchard, and Norman Vincent Peale, *The Power of Ethical Management* (New York: William Morrow and Company, Inc., 1988).

Radical American Environmentalism and Wilderness Preservation: A Third World Critique

Ramachandra Guha

Introduction

The respected radical journalist Kirkpatrick Sale recently celebrated "the passion of a new and growing movement that has become disenchanted with the environmental establishment and has in recent years mounted a serious and sweeping attack on it—style, substance, systems, sensibilities and all."[1] The vision of those whom Sale calls the "New Ecologists"—and what I refer to in this article as deep ecology—is a compelling one. Decrying the narrowly economic goals of mainstream environmentalism, this new movement aims at nothing less than a philosophical and cultural revolution in human attitudes toward nature. In contrast to the conventional lobbying efforts of environmental professionals based in Washington, it proposes a militant defence of "Mother Earth," an unflinching opposition to human attacks on undisturbed wilderness. With their goals ranging from the spiritual to the political, the adherents of deep ecology span a wide spectrum of the American environmental movement. As Sale correctly notes, this emerging strand has in a matter of a few years made its presence felt in a number of fields: from academic philosophy (as in the journal *Environmental Ethics*) to popular environmentalism (e.g., the group Earth First!).

In this article I develop a critique of deep ecology from the perspective of a sympathetic outsider. I critique deep ecology not as a general (or even a foot soldier) in the continuing struggle between the ghosts of Gifford Pinchot and John Muir over control of the U.S. environmental movement, but as an outsider to these battles. I speak admittedly as a partisan, but of the environmental movement in India, a country with an ecological diversity comparable to [that of] the United States, but with a radically dissimilar cultural and social history.

My treatment of deep ecology is primarily historical and sociological, rather than philosophical, in nature. Specifically, I examine the cultural rootedness of a philosophy that likes to present itself in universalistic terms. I make two main arguments: first, that deep ecology is uniquely American, and despite superficial similarities in rhetorical style, the social and political goals of radical environmentalism in other cultural contexts (e.g., West Germany and India) are quite different; second, that the social consequences of putting deep ecology into practice on a worldwide basis (what its practitioners are aiming for) are very grave indeed.

The Tenets of Deep Ecology

While I am aware that the term *deep ecology* was coined by the Norwegian philosopher Arne Naess, this article refers specifically to the American variant. Adherents of the deep ecological perspective in this country, while arguing intensely among themselves over its political and philosophical implications, share some fundamental premises about human–nature interactions. As I see it, the defining characteristics of deep ecology are fourfold.

First, deep ecology argues that the environmental movement must shift from an "anthropocentric" to a "biocentric" perspective. In many respects, an acceptance of the primacy of this distinction constitutes the litmus test of deep ecology. A considerable effort is expended by deep ecologists in showing that the dominant motif in Western philosophy has been anthropocentric—the belief that man and his works are the center of the universe—and conversely, in identifying those lonely thinkers (Leopold, Thoreau, Muir, Aldous Huxley, Santayana, etc.) who, in assigning man a more humble place in the natural order, anticipated deep ecological thinking. In the political realm, meanwhile, establishment environmentalism (shallow ecology) is chided for casting its arguments in human-centered terms. Preserving nature, the deep ecologists say, has an intrinsic worth quite apart from

From *Environmental Ethics*, vol. 11, Spring 1989. Used by permission of the publisher and author.

any benefits preservation may convey to future human generations. The anthropocentric-biocentric distinction is accepted as axiomatic by deep ecologists, it structures their discourse, and much of the present discussion remains mired within it.

The second characteristic of deep ecology is its focus on the preservation of unspoilt wilderness and the restoration of degraded areas to a more pristine condition—to the relative (and sometimes absolute) neglect of other issues on the environmental agenda. I later identify the cultural roots and portentous consequences of this obsession with wilderness. For the moment, let me indicate three distinct sources from which it springs. Historically, it represents a playing out of the preservationist (read *radical*) and utilitarian (read *reformist*) dichotomy that has plagued American environmentalism since the turn of the century. Morally, it is an imperative that follows from the biocentric perspective; other species of plants and animals, and nature itself, have an intrinsic right to exist. And finally, the preservation of wilderness also turns on a scientific argument—viz., the value of biological diversity in stabilizing ecological regimes and in retaining a gene pool for future generations. Truly radical policy proposals have been put forward by deep ecologists on the basis of these arguments. The influential poet Gary Snyder, for example, would like to see a 90 percent reduction in human populations to allow a restoration of pristine environments, while others have argued forcefully that a large portion of the globe must be immediately cordoned off from human beings.[2]

Third, there is a widespread invocation of Eastern spiritual traditions as forerunners of deep ecology. Deep ecology, it is suggested, was practiced both by major religious traditions and at a more popular level by "primal" peoples in non-Western settings. This complements the search for an authentic lineage in Western thought. At one level, the task is to recover those dissenting voices within the Judeo-Christian tradition; at another, to suggest that religious traditions in other cultures are, in contrast, dominantly if not exclusively "biocentric" in their orientation. This coupling of (ancient) Eastern and (modern) ecological wisdom seemingly helps consolidate the claim that deep ecology is a philosophy of universal significance.

Fourth, deep ecologists, whatever their internal differences, share the belief that they are the "leading edge" of the environmental movement. As the polarity of the shallow–deep and anthropocentric–biocentric distinctions makes clear, they see themselves as the spiritual, philosophical, and political vanguard of American and world environmentalism.

Toward a Critique

Although I analyze each of these tenets independently, it is important to recognize, as deep ecologists are fond of remarking in reference to nature, the interconnectedness and unity of these individual themes.

1. Insofar as it has begun to act as a check on man's arrogance and ecological hubris, the transition from an anthropocentric (human-centered) to a biocentric (humans as only one element in the ecosystem) view in both religious and scientific traditions is only to be welcomed. What is unacceptable are the radical conclusions drawn by deep ecology, in particular, that intervention in nature should be guided primarily by the need to preserve biotic integrity rather than by the needs of humans. The latter for deep ecologists is anthropocentric, the former biocentric. This dichotomy is, however, of very little use in understanding the dynamics of environmental degradation. The two fundamental ecological problems facing the globe are (i) overconsumption by the industrialized world and by urban elites in the Third World and (ii) growing militarization, both in a short-term sense (i.e., ongoing regional wars) and in a long-term sense (i.e., the arms race and the prospect of nuclear annihilation). Neither of these problems has any tangible connection to the anthropocentric-biocentric distinction. Indeed, the agents of these processes would barely comprehend this philosophical dichotomy. The proximate causes of the ecologically wasteful characteristics of industrial society and of militarization are far more mundane: at an aggregate level, the dialectic of economic and political structures, and at a micro-level, the life style choices of individuals. These causes cannot be reduced, whatever the level of analysis, to a deeper anthropocentric attitude toward nature; on the contrary, by constituting a grave threat to human survival, the ecological degradation they cause does not even serve the best interests of human beings! If my identifi-

cation of the major dangers to the integrity of the natural world is correct, invoking the bogy of anthropocentricism is at best irrelevant and at worst a dangerous obfuscation.

2. If the above dichotomy is irrelevant, the emphasis on wilderness is positively harmful when applied to the Third World. If in the United States the preservationist–utilitarian division is seen as mirroring the conflict between "people" and "interests," in countries such as India the situation is very nearly the reverse. Because India is a long settled and densely populated country in which agrarian populations have a finely balanced relationship with nature, the setting aside of wilderness areas has resulted in a direct transfer of resources from the poor to the rich. Thus, Project Tiger, a network of parks hailed by the international conservation community as an outstanding success, sharply posits the interests of the tiger against those of poor peasants living in and around the reserve. The designation of tiger reserves was made possible only by the physical displacement of existing villages and their inhabitants; their management requires the continuing exclusion of peasants and livestock. The initial impetus for setting up parks for the tiger and other large mammals such as the rhinoceros and elephant came from two social groups, first, a class of ex-hunters turned conservationists belonging mostly to the declining Indian feudal elite and second, representatives of international agencies, such as the World Wildlife Fund (WWF) and the International Union for the Conservation of Nature and Natural Resources (IUCN), seeking to transplant the American system of national parks onto Indian soil. In no case have the needs of the local population been taken into account, and as in many parts of Africa, the designated wildlands are managed primarily for the benefit of rich tourists. Until very recently, wildlands preservation has been identified with environmentalism by the state and the conservation elite; in consequence, environmental problems that impinge far more directly on the lives of the poor— e.g., fuel, fodder, water shortages, soil erosion, and air and water pollution—have not been adequately addressed.[3]

Deep ecology provides, perhaps unwittingly, a justification for the continuation of such narrow and inequitable conservation practices under a newly acquired radical guise. Increasingly, the international conservation elite is using the philosophical, moral, and scientific arguments used by deep ecologists in advancing their wilderness crusade. A striking but by no means atypical example is the recent plea by a prominent American biologist for the takeover of large portions of the globe by the author and his scientific colleagues. Writing in a prestigious scientific forum, the *Annual Review of Ecology and Systematics,* Daniel Janzen argues that only biologists have the competence to decide how the tropical landscape should be used. As "the representatives of the natural world," biologists are "in charge of the future of tropical ecology," and only they have the expertise and mandate to "determine whether the tropical agroscape is to be populated only by humans, their mutualists, commensals, and parasites, or whether it will also contain some islands of the greater nature—the nature that spawned humans, yet has been vanquished by them." Janzen exhorts his colleagues to advance their territorial claims on the tropical world more forcefully, warning that the very existence of these areas is at stake: "if biologists want a tropics in which to biologize, they are going to have to buy it with care, energy, effort, strategy, tactics, time, and cash."[4]

This frankly imperialist manifesto highlights the multiple dangers of the preoccupation with wilderness preservation that is characteristic of deep ecology. As I have suggested, it seriously compounds the neglect by the American movement of far more pressing environmental problems within the Third World. But perhaps more importantly, and in a more insidious fashion, it also provides an impetus to the imperialist yearning of Western biologists and their financial sponsors, organizations such as the WWF and IUCN. The wholesale transfer of a movement culturally rooted in American conservation history can only result in the social uprooting of human populations in other parts of the globe.

3. I come now to the persistent invocation of Eastern philosophies as antecedent in point of time but convergent in their structure with deep ecology. Complex and internally differentiated religious traditions—Hinduism, Buddhism, and Taoism—are lumped together as holding a view of nature believed to be quintessentially biocentric. Individual philosophers such as the Taoist Lao Tzu are identified as being forerunners of deep ecology. Even

an intensely political, pragmatic, and Christian-influenced thinker such as Gandhi has been accorded a wholly undeserved place in the deep ecological pantheon. Thus the Zen teacher Robert Aitken Roshi makes the strange claim that Gandhi's thought was not human-centered and that he practiced an embryonic form of deep ecology which is "traditionally Eastern and is found with differing emphasis in Hinduism, Taoism and in Theravada and Mahayana Buddhism."[5] Moving away from the realm of high philosophy and scriptural religion, deep ecologists make the further claim that at the level of material and spiritual practice "primal" peoples subordinated themselves to the integrity of the biotic universe they inhabited.

I have indicated that this appropriation of Eastern traditions is in part dictated by the need to construct an authentic lineage and in part a desire to present deep ecology as a universalistic philosophy. Indeed, in his substantial and quixotic biography of John Muir, Michael Cohen goes so far as to suggest that Muir was the "Taoist of the [American] West."[6] This reading of Eastern traditions is selective and does not bother to differentiate between alternate (and changing) religious and cultural traditions; as it stands, it does considerable violence to the historical record. Throughout most recorded history the characteristic form of human activity in the "East" has been a finely tuned but nonetheless conscious and dynamic manipulation of nature. Although mystics such as Lao Tzu did reflect on the spiritual essence of human relations with nature, it must be recognized that such ascetics and their reflections were supported by a society of cultivators whose relationship with nature was a far more *active* one. Many agricultural communities do have a sophisticated knowledge of the natural environment that may equal (and sometimes surpass) codified "scientific" knowledge; yet, the elaboration of such traditional ecological knowledge (in both material and spiritual contexts) can hardly be said to rest on a mystical affinity with nature of a deep ecological kind. Nor is such knowledge infallible; as the archaeological record powerfully suggests, modern Western man has no monopoly on ecological disasters.

In a brilliant article, the Chicago historian Ronald Inden points out that this romantic and essentially positive view of the East is a mirror image of the scientific and essentially pejorative view nor-

mally upheld by Western scholars of the Orient. In either case, the East constitutes the Other, a body wholly separate and alien from the West; it is defined by a uniquely spiritual and nonrational "essence," even if this essence is valorized quite differently by the two schools. Eastern man exhibits a spiritual dependence with respect to nature—on the one hand, this is symptomatic of his pre-scientific and backward self, on the other, of his ecological wisdom and deep ecological consciousness. Both views are monolithic, simplistic, and have the characteristic effect—intended in one case, perhaps unintended in the other—of denying agency and reason to the East and making it the privileged orbit of Western thinkers.

The two apparently opposed perspectives have then a common underlying structure of discourse in which the East merely serves as a vehicle for Western projections. Varying images of the East are raw material for political and cultural battles being played out in the West; they tell us far more about the Western commentator and his desires than about the "East." Inden's remarks apply not merely to Western scholarship on India, but to Orientalist constructions of China and Japan as well:

> Although these two views appear to be strongly opposed, they often combine together. Both have a similar interest in sustaining the Otherness of India. The holders of the dominant view, best exemplified in the past in imperial administrative discourse (and today probably by that of "development economics"), would place a traditional, superstition-ridden India in a position of perpetual tutelage to a modern, rational West. The adherents of the romantic view, best exemplified academically in the discourses of Christian liberalism and analytic psychology, concede the realm of the public and impersonal to the positivist. Taking their succour not from governments and big business, but from a plethora of religious foundations and self-help institutes, and from allies in the "consciousness industry," not to mention the important industry of tourism, the romantics insist that India embodies a private realm of the imagination and the religious which modern, western man lacks but needs. They, therefore, like the positivists, but for just the opposite reason, have a vested

interest in seeing that the Orientalist view of India as "spiritual," "mysterious," and "exotic" is perpetuated.[7]

4. How radical, finally, are the deep ecologists? Notwithstanding their self-image and strident rhetoric (in which the label "shallow ecology" has an opprobrium similar to that reserved for "social democratic" by Marxist-Leninists), even within the American context their radicalism is limited and it manifests itself quite differently elsewhere.

To my mind, deep ecology is best viewed as a radical trend within the wilderness preservation movement. Although advancing philosophical rather than aesthetic arguments and encouraging political militancy rather than negotiation, its practical emphasis—viz., preservation of unspoilt nature—is virtually identical. For the mainstream movement, the function of wilderness is to provide a temporary antidote to modern civilization. As a special institution within an industrialized society, the national park "provides an opportunity for respite, contrast, contemplation, and affirmation of values for those who live most of their lives in the workaday world."[8] Indeed, the rapid increase in visitations to the national parks in postwar America is a direct consequence of economic expansion. The emergence of a popular interest in wilderness sites, the historian Samuel Hays points out, was "not a throwback to the primitive, but an integral part of the modern standard of living as people sought to add new 'amenity' and 'aesthetic' goals and desires to their earlier preoccupation with necessities and conveniences."[9]

Here, the enjoyment of nature is an integral part of the consumer society. The private automobile (and the life style it has spawned) is in many respects the ultimate ecological villain, and an untouched wilderness the prototype of ecological harmony; yet, for most Americans it is perfectly consistent to drive a thousand miles to spend a holiday in a national park. They possess a vast, beautiful, and sparsely populated continent and are also able to draw upon the natural resources of large portions of the globe by virtue of their economic and political dominance. In consequence, America can simultaneously enjoy the material benefits of an expanding economy and the aesthetic benefits of unspoilt nature. The two poles of "wilderness" and "civilization" mutually coexist in an internally coherent whole, and philosophers of both

poles are assigned a prominent place in this culture. Paradoxically as it may seem, it is no accident that Star Wars technology and deep ecology both find their fullest expression in that leading sector of Western civilization, California.

Deep ecology runs parallel to the consumer society without seriously questioning its ecological and socio-political basis. In its celebration of American wilderness, it also displays an uncomfortable convergence with the prevailing climate of nationalism in the American wilderness movement. For spokesmen such as the historian Roderick Nash, the national park system is America's distinctive cultural contribution to the world, reflective not merely of its economic but of its philosophical and ecological maturity as well. In what Walter Lippmann called the American century, the "American invention of national parks" must be exported worldwide. Betraying an economic determinism that would make even a Marxist shudder, Nash believes that environmental preservation is a "full stomach" phenomenon that is confined to the rich, urban, and sophisticated. Nonetheless, he hopes that "the less developed nations may eventually evolve economically and intellectually to the point where nature preservation is more than a business."[10]

The error which Nash makes (and which deep ecology in some respects encourages) is to equate environmental protection with the protection of wilderness. This is a distinctively American notion, borne out of a unique social and environmental history. The archetypal concerns of radical environmentalists in other cultural contexts are in fact quite different. The German Greens, for example, have elaborated a devastating critique of industrial society which turns on the acceptance of environmental limits to growth. Pointing to the intimate links between industrialization, militarization, and conquest, the Greens argue that economic growth in the West has historically rested on the economic and ecological exploitation of the Third World. Rudolf Bahro is characteristically blunt:

> The working class here [in the West] is the richest lower class in the world. And if I look at the problem from the point of view of the whole of humanity, not just from that of Europe, then I must say that the metropolitan working class is the worst exploiting class in history. . . . What made poverty bearable in

eighteenth- or nineteenth-century Europe was the prospect of escaping it through exploitation of the periphery. But this is no longer a possibility, and continued industrialism in the Third World will mean poverty for whole generations and hunger for millions.[11]

Here the roots of global ecological problems lie in the disproportionate share of resources consumed by the industrialized countries as a whole *and* the urban elite within the Third World. Since it is impossible to reproduce an industrial monoculture worldwide, the ecological movement in the West must begin by cleaning up its own act. The Greens advocate the creation of a "no growth" economy, to be achieved by scaling down current (and clearly unsustainable) consumption levels. This radical shift in consumption and production patterns requires the creation of alternate economic and political structures—smaller in scale and more amenable to social participation—but it rests equally on a shift in cultural values. The expansionist character of modern Western man will have to give way to an ethic of renunciation and self-limitation, in which spiritual and communal values play an increasing role in sustaining social life. This revolution in cultural values, however, has as its point of departure an understanding of environmental processes quite different from deep ecology.

Many elements of the Green program find a strong resonance in countries such as India, where a history of Western colonialism and industrial development has benefited only a tiny elite while exacting tremendous social and environmental costs. The ecological battles presently being fought in India have as their epicenter the conflict over nature between the subsistence and largely rural sector and the vastly more powerful commercial-industrial sector. Perhaps the most celebrated of these battles concerns the Chipko (Hug the Tree) movement, a peasant movement against deforestation in the Himalayan foothills. Chipko is only one of several movements that have sharply questioned the nonsustainable demand being placed on the land and vegetative base by urban centers and industry. These include opposition to large dams by displaced peasants, the conflict between small artisan fishing and large-scale trawler fishing for export, the countrywide movements against commercial forest operations, and opposition to industrial

pollution among downstream agricultural and fishing communities.[12]

Two features distinguish these environmental movements from their Western counterparts. First, for the sections of society most critically affected by environmental degradation—poor and landless peasants, women, and tribals—it is a question of sheer survival, not of enhancing the quality of life. Second, and as a consequence, the environmental solutions they articulate deeply involve questions of equity as well as economic and political redistribution. Highlighting these differences, a leading Indian environmentalist stresses that "environmental protection per se is of least concern to most of these groups. Their main concern is about the use of the environment and who should benefit from it."[13] They seek to wrest control of nature away from the state and the industrial sector and place it in the hands of rural communities who live within that environment but are increasingly denied access to it. These communities have far more basic needs, their demands on the environment are far less intense, and they can draw upon a reservoir of cooperative social institutions and local ecological knowledge in managing the "commons"—forests, grasslands, and the waters—on a sustainable basis. If colonial and capitalist expansion has both accentuated social inequalities and signaled a precipitous fall in ecological wisdom, an alternate ecology must rest on an alternate society and polity as well.

This brief overview of German and Indian environmentalism has some major implications for deep ecology. Both German and Indian environmental traditions allow for a greater integration of ecological concerns with livelihood and work. They also place a greater emphasis on equity and social justice (both within individual countries and on a global scale) on the grounds that in the absence of social regeneration environmental regeneration has very little chance of succeeding. Finally, and perhaps most significantly, they have escaped the preoccupation with wilderness preservation so characteristic of American cultural and environmental history.

A Homily

In 1958, the economist, J. K. Galbraith referred to overconsumption as the unasked question of the American conservation movement. There is a marked selectivity, he wrote, "in the conservationists approach to materials consumption. If we are concerned about our great appetite for materials, it is plausible to seek to increase the supply, to decrease waste, to make better use of the stocks available, and to develop substitutes. But what of the appetite itself? Surely this is the ultimate source of the problem. If it continues its geometric course, will it not one day have to be restrained? Yet in the literature of the resource problem this is the forbidden question. Over it hangs a nearly total silence."[14]

The consumer economy and society have expanded tremendously in the three decades since Galbraith penned these words; yet his criticisms are nearly as valid today. I have said "nearly," for there are some hopeful signs. Within the environmental movement several dispersed groups are working to develop ecologically benign technologies and to encourage less wasteful life styles. Moreover, outside the self-defined boundaries of American environmentalism, opposition to the permanent war economy is being carried on by a peace movement that has a distinguished history and impeccable moral and political credentials.

It is precisely these (to my mind, most hopeful) components of the American social scene that are missing from deep ecology. In their widely noticed book, Bill Devall and George Sessions make no mention of militarization or the movements for peace, while activists whose practical focus is on developing ecologically responsible life styles (e.g., Wendell Berry) are derided as "falling short of deep ecological awareness."[15] A truly radical ecology in the American context ought to work toward a synthesis of the appropriate technology, alternate life style, and peace movements. By making the (largely spurious) anthropocentric–biocentric distinction central to the debate, deep ecologists may have appropriated the moral high ground, but they are at the same time doing a serious disservice to American and global environmentalism.[16]

NOTES

I am grateful to Mike Bell, Tom Birch, Bill Burch, Bill Cronon, Diane Mayerfeld, David Rothenberg, Kirkpatrick Sale, Joel Seton, Tim Weiskel, and Don Worster for helpful comments.

1. K. Sale, "The Forest for the Trees: Can Today's Environmentalists Tell the Difference," *Mother Jones* 11 (November 1986): 26.

2. Quoted in ibid., 32.

3. See Centre for Science and Environment, *India: The State of the Environment 1982: A Citizens Report* (New Delhi: Centre for Science and Environment, 1982), and R. Sukumar, "Elephant-Man Conflict in Karnataka," in *The State of Karnataka's Environment*, ed. C. Saldanha (Bangalore: Centre for Taxonomic Studies, 1985). For Africa, see the brilliant analysis by (H. Kjekshus, *Ecology Control and Economic Development in East African History* (Berkeley: University of California Press, 1977).

4. D. Janzen, "The Future of Tropical Ecology," *Annual Review of Ecology and Systematics* 17 (1986): 305–6.

5. R. A. Roshi, "Gandhi, Dogen, and Deep Ecology," reprinted as appendix C in B. Devall and G. Sessions, *Deep Ecology: Living as if Nature Mattered* (Salt Lake City: Peregrine Smith, 1985). For Gandhi's own views on social reconstruction, see the excellent three-volume collection edited by R. Iyer, *The Moral and Political Writings of Mahatma Gandhi* (Oxford: Clarendon Press, 1986–1987).

6. M. Cohen, *The Pathless Way* (Madison: University of Wisconsin Press, 1984), 120.

7. R. Inden, "Orientalist Constructions of India," *Modern Asian Studies* 20 (1986): 442. Inden draws inspiration from E. Said's forceful polemic, *Orientalism* (New York: Basic Books, 1980). It must be noted, however, that there is a salient difference between Western perceptions of Middle Eastern and Far Eastern cultures, respectively. Due perhaps to the long history of Christian conflict with Islam, Middle Eastern cultures (as Said documents) are consistently presented in pejorative terms. The juxtaposition of hostile and worshipping attitudes that Inden talks of applies only to Western attitudes toward Buddhist and Hindu societies.

8. J. Sax, *Mountains Without Handrails: Reflections on the National Parks* (Ann Arbor: University of Michigan Press, 1980), 42.

9. S. P. Hays, "From Conservation to Environment: Environmental Politics in the United States since World War Two," *Environmental Review* 6 (1982): 21. See also S. P. Hays, *Beauty, Health, and Permanence: Environmental Politics in the United States, 1955–1985* (Cambridge: Cambridge University Press, 1987).

10. R. Nash, *Wilderness and the American Mind*, 3rd ed. (New Haven, Conn.: Yale University Press, 1982).

11. R. Bahro, *From Red to Green* (London: Verso Books, 1984).

12. For an excellent review, see A. Agarwal and S. Narain, eds., *India: The State of the Environment, 1984–1985: A Citizens Report* (New Delhi: Centre for Science and Environment, 1985). See also R. Guha, *The Unquiet Woods: Ecological Change and Peasant Resistance in the Indian Himalaya* (Berkeley: University of California Press, 1990).

13. A. Agarwal, "Human–Nature Interactions in a Third World Country," *Environmentalist* 6 (1986): 167.

14. J. K. Galbraith, "How Much Should a Country Consume?" in *Perspectives on Conservation,* ed. Henry Jarrett (Baltimore: Johns Hopkins University Press, 1958), 91–92.

15. Devall and Sessions, *Deep Ecology,* 122. For Wendell Berry's own assessment of deep ecology, see his "Amplications: Preserving Wildness," *Wilderness* 50 (1987): 39–40, 50–54.

16. In this sense, my critique of deep ecology, although that of an outsider, may facilitate the reassertion of those elements in the American environmental tradition for which there is a profound sympathy in other parts of the globe. A global perspective may also lead to a critical reassessment of figures such as Aldo Leopold and John Muir, the two patron saints of deep ecology. As Donald Worster has pointed out, the message of Muir (and, I would argue, of Leopold as well) makes sense only in an American context; he has very little to say to other cultures. See Worster's review of Stephen Fox's *John Muir and His Legacy,* in *Environmental Ethics* 5 (1983): 277–81.

Decision Making

Robert D. Bullard

Despite the recent attempts by federal agencies to reduce environmental and health threats in the United States, inequities persist.[1] If a community is poor or inhabited largely by people of color, there is a good chance that it receives less protection than a community that is affluent or white.[2] This situation is a result of the country's environmental policies, most of which "distribute the costs in a regressive pattern while providing disproportionate benefits for the educated and wealthy."[3] Even the Environmental Protection Agency (EPA) was not designed to address environmental policies and practices that result in unfair outcomes. The agency has yet to conduct a single piece of disparate impact research using primary data. In fact, the current environmental protection paradigm has institutionalized unequal enforcement, traded human health for profit, placed the burden of proof on the "victims" rather than on the polluting industry, legitimated human exposure to harmful substances, promoted "risky" technologies such as incinerators, exploited the vulnerability of economically and politically disenfranchised communities, subsidized ecological destruction, created an industry around risk assessment, delayed cleanup actions, and failed to develop pollution prevention as the overarching and dominant strategy. As a result, low-income and minority communities continue to bear greater health and environmental burdens, while the more affluent and white communities receive the bulk of the benefits.[4]

The geographic distribution of both minorities and the poor has been found to be highly correlated to the distribution of air pollution, municipal landfills and incinerators, abandoned toxic waste dumps, lead poisoning in children, and contaminated fish consumption.[5] Virtually all studies of exposure to outdoor air pollution have found significant differences in exposure by income and race. Moreover, the race correlation is even stronger than the class correlation.[6] The National Wildlife Federation recently reviewed some sixty-four studies of environmental disparities; in all but one, disparities were found by either race or income, and disparities by race were more numerous than those by income. When race and income were compared for significance, race proved to be the more important factor in twenty-two out of thirty tests.[7] And researchers at Argonne National Laboratory recently found that

> in 1990, 437 of the 3,109 counties and independent cities failed to meet at least one of the EPA ambient air quality standards. . . . 57 percent of whites, 65 percent of African-Americans, and 80 percent of Hispanics live in 437 counties with substandard air quality. Out of the whole population, a total of 33 percent of whites, 50 percent of African-Americans, and 60 percent of Hispanics live in the 136 counties in which two or more air

Environment 36, no. 4 (May 1994), 11–20, 39–44. Reprinted with permission.

pollutants exceed standards. The percentage living in the 29 counties designated as non-attainment areas for three or more pollutants are 12 percent of whites, 20 percent of African-Americans, and 31 percent of Hispanics.[8]

The public health community has very little information on the magnitude of many air pollution-related health problems. For example, scientists are at a loss to explain the rising number of deaths from asthma in recent years. However, it is known that persons suffering from asthma are particularly sensitive to the effects of carbon monoxide, sulfur dioxide, particulate matter, ozone, and oxides of nitrogen.[9]

Current environmental decision making operates at the juncture of science, technology, economics, politics, special interests, and ethics and mirrors the larger social milieu where discrimination is institutionalized. Unequal environmental protection undermines three basic types of equity: procedural, geographic, and social.

Procedural Equity

Procedural equity refers to fairness—that is, to the extent that governing rules, regulations, evaluation criteria, and enforcement are applied in a nondiscriminatory way. Unequal protection results from nonscientific and undemocratic decisions, such as exclusionary practices, conflicts of interest, public hearings held in remote locations and at inconvenient times, and use of only English to communicate with and conduct hearings for non-English-speaking communities.

A 1992 study by staff writers from the *National Law Journal* uncovered glaring inequities in the way EPA enforces its Superfund laws: "There is a racial divide in the way the U.S. government cleans up toxic waste sites and punishes polluters. White communities see faster action, better results and stiffer penalties than communities where blacks, Hispanics and other minorities live. This unequal protection often occurs whether the community is wealthy or poor."[10]

After examining census data, civil court dockets, and EPA's own record of performance at 1,177 Superfund toxic waste sites, the authors of the *National Law Journal* reported the following:

- Penalties applied under hazardous waste laws at sites having the greatest white population were 500 percent higher than penalties at sites with the greatest minority population. Penalties averaged out at $335,566 at sites in white areas but just $55,318 at sites in minority areas.
- The disparity in penalties applied under the toxic waste law correlates with race alone, not income. The average penalty in areas with the lowest median income is $113,491—3 percent more than the average penalty in areas with the highest median income.
- For all the federal environmental laws aimed at protecting citizens from air, water, and waste pollution, penalties for non-compliance were 46 percent higher in white communities than in minority communities.
- Under the Superfund cleanup program, abandoned hazardous waste sites in minority areas take 20 percent longer to be placed on the National Priority List than do those in white areas.
- In more than half of the ten autonomous regions that administer EPA programs around the country, action on cleanup at Superfund sites begins from 12 to 42 percent later at minority sites than at white sites.
- For minority sites, EPA chooses "containment," the capping or walling off of a hazardous waste dump site, 7 percent more frequently than the cleanup method preferred under the law: permanent "treatment" to eliminate the waste or rid it of its toxins. For white sites, EPA orders permanent treatment 22 percent more often than containment.[11]

These findings suggest that unequal environmental protection is placing communities of color at risk. The *National Law Journal* study supplements the findings of several earlier studies and reinforces what grassroots activists have been saying all along: Not only are people of color differentially affected by industrial pollution but also they can expect different treatment from the government.[12]

Geographic Equity

Geographic equity refers to the location and spatial configuration of communities and their proximity to environmental hazards and locally unwanted land uses (LULUs), such as landfills, incinerators, sewage treatment plants, lead smelters, refineries, and other noxious facilities. Hazardous waste incinerators are not randomly scattered across the landscape. Communities with hazardous waste incinerators generally have large minority populations, low incomes, and low property values.[13]

A 1990 Greenpeace report (*Playing with Fire*) found that communities with existing incinerators have 89 percent more people of color than the national average; communities where incinerators are proposed for construction have minority populations that are 60 percent higher than the national average; the average income in communities with existing incinerators is 15 percent lower than the national average; property values in communities that host incinerators are 38 percent lower than the national average; and average property values are 35 percent lower in communities where incinerators have been proposed.[14]

The industrial encroachment into Chicago's Southside neighborhoods is a classic example of geographic inequity. Chicago is the nation's third largest city and one of the most racially segregated cities in the country. More than 92 percent of the city's 1.1 million African American residents live in racially segregated areas. The Altgeld Gardens housing project, located on the city's southeast side, is one of these segregated enclaves. The neighborhood is home to 150,000 residents, of whom 70 percent are African American and 11 percent are Latino.

Altgeld Gardens is encircled by municipal and hazardous waste landfills, toxic waste incinerators, grain elevators, sewage treatment facilities, smelters, steel mills, and a host of other polluting industries.[15] Because of its location, the area has been dubbed a "toxic doughnut" by Hazel Johnson, a community organizer in the neighborhood. There are 50 active or closed commercial hazardous waste landfills; 100 factories, including 7 chemical plants and 5 steel mills; and 103 abandoned toxic waste dumps.[16]

Currently, health and risk assessment data collected by the state of Illinois and the EPA for facility permitting have failed to take into account the cumulative and synergistic effects of having so many "layers" of poison in one community. Altgeld Gardens residents wonder when the govern-

ment will declare a moratorium on permitting any new noxious facilities in their neighborhood and when the existing problems will be cleaned up. All of the polluting industries imperil the health of nearby residents and should be factored into future facility-permitting decisions.

In the Los Angeles air basin, 71 percent of African Americans and 50 percent of Latinos live in areas with the most polluted air, whereas only 34 percent of whites live in highly polluted areas.[17] The "dirtiest" zip code in California (90058) is sandwiched between South-Central Los Angeles and East Los Angeles.[18] The one-square-mile area is saturated with abandoned toxic waste sites, freeways, smokestacks, and wastewater pipes from polluting industries. Some eighteen industrial firms in 1989 discharged more than 33 million pounds of waste chemicals into the environment.

Unequal protection may result from land-use decisions that determine the location of residential amenities and disamenities. Unincorporated communities of poor African Americans suffer a "triple" vulnerability to noxious facility siting.[19] For example, Wallace, Louisiana, a small unincorporated African American community located on the Mississippi River, was rezoned from residential to industrial use by the mostly white officials of St. John the Baptist Parish to allow construction of a Formosa Plastics Corporation plant. The company's plants have been major sources of pollution in Baton Rouge, Louisiana; Point Comfort, Texas; Delaware City, Delaware; and its home country of Taiwan.[20] Wallace residents have filed a lawsuit challenging the rezoning action as racially motivated.

Environmental justice advocates have sought to persuade federal, state, and local governments to adopt policies that address distributive impacts, concentration, enforcement, and compliance concerns. Some states have tried to use a "fair share" approach to come closer to geographic equity. In 1990, New York City adopted a fair share legislative model designed to ensure that every borough and every community within each borough bears its fair share of noxious facilities. Public hearings have begun to address risk burdens in New York City's boroughs.

Testimony at a hearing on environmental disparities in the Bronx points to concerns raised by African Americans and Puerto Ricans who see their neighborhoods threatened by garbage transfer stations, salvage yards, and recycling centers.

On the Hunts Point peninsula alone there are at least thirty private transfer stations, a large-scale Department of Environmental Protection (DEP) sewage treatment plant and a sludge dewatering facility, two Department of Sanitation (DOS) marine transfer stations, a city-wide privately regulated medical waste incinerator, a proposed DOS resource recovery facility and three proposed DEP sludge processing facilities. That all of the facilities listed above are located immediately adjacent to the Hunts Point Food Center, the biggest wholesale food and meat distribution facility of its kind in the United States, and the largest source of employment in the South Bronx, is disconcerting. A policy whereby low-income and minority communities have become the "dumping grounds" for unwanted land uses, works to create an environment of disincentives to community-based development initiatives. It also undermines existing businesses.[21]

Some communities form a special case for environmental justice. For example, Native American reservations are geographic entities but are also quasi-sovereign nations. Because of less-stringent environmental regulations than those at the state and federal levels, Native American reservations from New York to California have become prime targets for risky technologies.[22] Indian natives do not fall under state jurisdiction. Similarly, reservations have been described as the "lands the feds forgot."[23] More than one hundred industries, ranging from solid waste landfills to hazardous waste incinerators and nuclear waste storage facilities, have targeted reservations.[24]

Social Equity

Social equity refers to the role of sociological factors, such as race, ethnicity, class, culture, lifestyles, and political power, in environmental decision making. Poor people and people of color often work in the most dangerous jobs and live in the most polluted neighborhoods, and their children are exposed to all kinds of environmental toxins on the playgrounds and in their homes and schools.

Some government actions have created and exacerbated environmental inequity. More stringent environmental regulations have driven noxious facilities to follow the path of least resistance toward poor, overburdened communities. Governments have even funded studies that justify targeting economically disenfranchised communities for noxious facilities. Cerrell Associates, Inc., a Los Angeles-based consulting firm, advised the state of California on facility siting and concluded that "ideally . . . officials and companies should look for lower socio-economic neighborhoods that are also in a heavy industrial area with little, if any, commercial activity."[25]

The first state-of-the-art solid waste incinerator slated to be built in Los Angeles was proposed for the south-central Los Angeles neighborhood. The city-sponsored project was defeated by local residents.[26] The two permits granted by the California Department of Health Services for state-of-the-art toxic waste incinerators were proposed for mostly Latino communities: Vernon, near East Los Angeles, and Kettleman City, a farm-worker community in the agriculturally rich Central Valley. Kettleman City has 1,200 residents of which 95 percent are Latino. It is home to the largest hazardous waste incinerator west of the Mississippi River. The Vernon proposal was defeated, but the Kettleman City proposal is still pending.

Principles of Environmental Justice

To end unequal environmental protection, governments should adopt five principles of environmental justice: guaranteeing the right to environmental protection, preventing harm before it occurs, shifting the burden of proof to the polluters, obviating proof of intent to discriminate, and redressing existing inequities.

The Right to Protection

Every individual has a right to be protected from environmental degradation. Protecting this right will require enacting a federal "fair environmental protection act." The act could be modeled after the various federal civil rights acts that have promoted nondiscrimination—with the ultimate goal of achieving "zero tolerance"—in such areas as housing, education, and employment. The act ought to address both the intended and unintended effects of public policies and industrial practices that have a disparate impact on racial and ethnic minorities and other vulnerable groups. The precedents for this framework are the Civil Rights Act of 1964, which attempted to address both *de jure* and *de facto* school segregation, the Fair Housing Act of 1968, the same act as amended in 1988, and the Voting Rights Act of 1965.

For the first time in the agency's twenty-three-year history, EPA's Office of Civil Rights has begun investigating charges of environmental discrimination under Title VI of the 1964 Civil Rights Act. The cases involve waste facility siting disputes in Michigan, Alabama, Mississippi, and Louisiana. Similarly, in September 1993, the U.S. Civil Rights Commission issued a report entitled *The Battle for Environmental Justice in Louisiana: Government, Industry, and the People.* This report confirmed what most people who live in "Cancer Alley"—the 85-mile stretch along the Mississippi River from Baton Rouge to New Orleans—already knew: African American communities along the Mississippi River bear disproportionate health burdens from industrial pollution.[27]

A number of bills have been introduced into Congress that address some aspect of environmental justice:

- The Environmental Justice Act of 1993 (H.R. 2105) would provide the federal government with the statistical documentation and ranking of the top one hundred "environmental high impact areas" that warrant attention.
- The Environmental Equal Rights Act of 1993 (H.R. 1924) seeks to amend the Solid Waste Act and would prevent waste facilities from being sited in "environmentally disadvantaged communities."
- The Environmental Health Equity Information Act of 1993 (H.R. 1925) seeks to amend the Comprehensive Environmental Response, Compensation, and Liability Act of 1990 (CERCLA) to require the Agency for Toxic Substances and Disease Registry to collect and maintain information on the race, age, gender, ethnic origin, income level, and educational level of persons living in communities adjacent to toxic substance contamination.

- The Waste Export and Import Prohibition Act (H.R. 3706) banned waste exports as of 1 July 1994 to countries that are not members of the Organization for Economic Cooperation and Development (OECD); the bill would also ban waste exports to and imports from OECD countries as of 1 January 1999.

The states are also beginning to address environmental justice concerns. Arkansas and Louisiana were the first two to enact environmental justice laws. Virginia has passed a legislative resolution on environmental justice. California, Georgia, New York, North Carolina, and South Carolina have pending legislation to address environmental disparities.

Environmental justice groups have succeeded in getting President Clinton to act on the problem of unequal environmental protection, an issue that has been buried for more than three decades. On 11 February 1994, Clinton signed an executive order entitled "Federal Actions to Address Environmental Justice in Minority Populations and Low-Income Populations." This new executive order reinforces what has been law since the passage of the 1964 Civil Rights Act, which prohibits discriminatory practices in programs receiving federal financial assistance.

The executive order also refocuses attention on the National Environmental Policy Act of 1970 (NEPA), which established national policy goals for the protection, maintenance, and enhancement of the environment. The express goal of NEPA is to ensure for all U.S. citizens a safe, healthful, productive, and aesthetically and culturally pleasing environment. NEPA requires federal agencies to prepare detailed statements on the environmental effects of proposed federal actions significantly affecting the quality of human health. Environmental impact statements prepared under NEPA have routinely downplayed the social impacts of federal projects on racial and ethnic minorities and low-income groups.

Under the new executive order, federal agencies and other institutions that receive federal monies have a year to implement an environmental justice strategy. For these strategies to be effective, agencies must move away from the "DAD" (decide, announce, and defend) modus operandi. EPA cannot address all of the environmental injustices alone but must work in concert with other stakeholders, such as state and local governments and private industry. A new interagency approach might include the following:

- Grassroots environmental justice groups and their networks must become full partners, not silent or junior partners, in planning the implementation of the new executive order.
- An advisory commission should include representatives of environmental justice, civil rights, legal, labor, and public health groups, as well as the relevant governmental agencies, to advise on the implementation of the executive order.
- State and regional education, training, and outreach forums and workshops on implementing the executive order should be organized.
- The executive order should become part of the agenda of national conferences and meetings of elected officials, civil rights and environmental groups, public health and medical groups, educators, and other professional organizations.

The executive order comes at an important juncture in this nation's history: Few communities are willing to welcome LULUs or to become dumping grounds for other people's garbage, toxic waste, or industrial pollution. In the real world, however, if a community happens to be poor and inhabited by persons of color, it is likely to suffer from a "double whammy" of unequal protection and elevated health threats. This is unjust and illegal.

The civil rights and environmental laws of the land must be enforced even if it means the loss of a few jobs. This argument was a sound one in the 1860s, when the Thirteenth Amendment to the Constitution, which freed the slaves in the United States, was passed over the opposition of proslavery advocates who posited that the new law would create unemployment (slaves had a zero unemployment rate), drive up wages, and inflict undue hardship on the plantation economy.

Prevention of Harm

Prevention, the elimination of the threat before harm occurs, should be the preferred strategy of governments. For example, to solve the lead problem, the primary focus should be shifted from

treating children who have been poisoned to eliminating the threat by removing lead from houses.

Overwhelming scientific evidence exists on the ill effects of lead on the human body. However, very little action has been taken to rid the nation's housing of lead even though lead poisoning is a preventable disease tagged the "number one environmental health threat to children."[28]

Lead began to be phased out of gasoline in the 1970s. It is ironic that the "regulations were initially developed to protect the newly developed catalytic converter in automobiles, a pollution-control device that happens to be rendered inoperative by lead, rather than to safeguard human health."[29] In 1971, a child was not considered "at risk" unless he or she had 40 micrograms of lead per deciliter of blood (μg/dl). Since that time, the amount of lead that is considered safe has continually dropped. In 1991, the U.S. Public Health Service changed the official definition of an unsafe level to 10 μg/dl. Even at that level, a child's IQ can be slightly diminished and physical growth stunted.

Lead poisoning is correlated with both income and race. In 1988, the Agency for Toxic Substances and Disease Registry found that among families earning less than $6,000, 68 percent of African American children had lead poisoning, as opposed to 36 percent of white children.[30] In families with incomes exceeding $15,000, more than 38 percent of African American children suffered from lead poisoning, compared with 12 percent of white children. Thus, even when differences in income are taken into account, middle-class African American children are three times more likely to be poisoned with lead than are their middle-class white counterparts.

A 1990 report by the Environmental Defense Fund estimated that under the 1991 standard of 10 μg/dl, 96 percent of African American children and 80 percent of white children of poor families who live in inner cities have unsafe amounts of lead in their blood—amounts sufficient to reduce IQ somewhat, harm hearing, reduce the ability to concentrate, and stunt physical growth.[31] Even in families with annual incomes greater than $15,000, 85 percent of urban African American children have unsafe lead levels, compared to 47 percent of white children.

In the spring of 1991, the Bush administration announced an ambitious program to reduce lead exposure of children, including widespread testing of homes, certification of those who remove lead from homes, and medical treatment for affected children. Six months later, the Centers for Disease Control announced that the administration "does not see this as a necessary federal role to legislate or regulate the cleanup of lead poisoning, to require that homes be tested, to require home owners to disclose results once they are known, or to establish standards for those who test or clean up lead hazards."[32]

According to the *New York Times*, the National Association of Realtors pressured President Bush to drop his lead initiative because it feared that forcing homeowners to eliminate lead hazards would add from $5,000 to $10,000 to the price of those homes, further harming a real estate market already devastated by the aftershocks of Reaganomics.[33] The public debate has pitted real estate and housing interests against public health interests. Right now, the housing interests appear to be winning.

For more than two decades, Congress and the nation's medical and public health establishments have waffled, procrastinated, and shuffled papers while the lead problem steadily grows worse. During the years of President Reagan's "benign neglect," funding dropped very low. Even in the best years, when funding has risen to as much as $50 million per year, it has never reached levels that would make a real dent in the problem.

Much could be done to protect at-risk populations if the current laws were enforced. For example, a lead smelter operated for fifty years in a predominantly African American West Dallas neighborhood, where it caused extreme health problems for nearby residents. Dallas officials were informed as early as 1972 that lead from three lead smelters was finding its way into the bloodstreams of children who lived in two mostly African American and Latino neighborhoods: West Dallas and East Oak Cliff.[34]

Living near the RSR and Dixie Metals smelters was associated with a 36 percent increase in childhood blood lead levels. The city was urged to restrict the emissions of lead into the atmosphere and to undertake a large screening program to determine the extent of the public health problem. The city failed to take immediate action to protect the residents who lived near the smelters.

In 1980, EPA, informed about possible health risks associated with the Dallas lead smelters, commissioned another lead-screening study. This study confirmed what was already known a decade earlier. Children living near the Dallas smelters were likely to have greater lead concentrations in their blood than children who did not live near the smelters.[35]

The city only took action after the local newspapers published a series of headline-grabbing stories in 1983 on the "potentially dangerous" lead levels discovered by EPA researchers in 1981.[36] The articles triggered widespread concern, public outrage, several class-action lawsuits, and legal action by the Texas attorney general.

Although EPA was armed with a wealth of scientific data on the West Dallas lead problem, the agency chose to play politics with the community by scrapping a voluntary plan offered by RSR to clean up the "hot spots" in the neighborhood. John Hernandez, EPA's deputy administrator, blocked the cleanup and called for yet another round of tests to be designed by the Centers for Disease Control with EPA and the Dallas Health Department. The results of the new study were released in February 1983. This study again established the smelter as the source of elevated lead levels in West Dallas children.[37] Hernandez's delay of cleanup actions in West Dallas was tantamount to waiting for a body count.[38]

After years of delay, the West Dallas plaintiffs negotiated an out-of-court settlement worth more than $45 million. The lawsuit was settled in June 1983 as RSR agreed to pay for cleaning up the soil in West Dallas, a blood-testing program for children and pregnant women, and the installation of new antipollution equipment. The settlement was made on behalf of 370 children—almost all of whom were poor black residents of the West Dallas public housing project—and forty property owners. The agreement was one of the largest community lead-contamination settlements ever awarded in the United States.[39] The settlement, however, did not require the smelter to close. Moreover, the pollution equipment for the smelter was never installed.

In May 1984, however, the Dallas Board of Adjustments, a city agency responsible for monitoring land-use violations, asked the city attorney to close the smelter permanently for violating the city's zoning code. The lead smelter had operated in the mostly African American West Dallas neighborhood for fifty years without having the necessary use permits. Just four months later, the West

Dallas smelter was permanently closed. After repeated health citations, fines, and citizens' complaints against the smelter, one has to question the city's lax enforcement of health and land-use regulations in African American and Latino neighborhoods.

The smelter is now closed. Although an initial cleanup was carried out in 1984, the lead problem has not gone away.[40] On 31 December 1991, EPA crews began a cleanup of the West Dallas neighborhood. It is estimated that the crews will remove between 30,000 and 40,000 cubic yards of lead-contaminated soil from several West Dallas sites, including school property and about 140 private homes. The project will cost EPA from $3 million to $4 million. The lead content of the soil collected from dump sites in the neighborhood ranged from 8,060 to 21,000 parts per million.[41] Under federal standards, levels of 500 to 1,000 parts per million are considered hazardous. In April 1993, the entire West Dallas neighborhood was declared a Superfund site.

There have been a few other signs related to the lead issue that suggest a consensus on environmental justice is growing among coalitions of environmental, social justice, and civil libertarian groups. The Natural Resources Defense Council, the National Association for the Advancement of Colored People Legal Defense and Education Fund, the American Civil Liberties Union, and the Legal Aid Society of Alameda County joined forces and won an out-of-court settlement worth between $15 million and $20 million for a blood-testing program in California. The lawsuit (*Matthews v. Coye*) arose because the state of California was not performing the federally mandated testing of some 557,000 poor children who receive Medicaid. This historic agreement will likely trigger similar actions in other states that have failed to perform federally mandated screening.[42]

Lead screening is important but it is not the solution. New government-mandated lead abatement initiatives are needed. The nation needs a "Lead Superfund" clean-up program. Public health should not be sacrificed even in a sluggish housing market. Surely, if termite inspections (required in both booming and sluggish housing markets) can be mandated to protect individual home investment, a lead-free home can be mandated to protect human health. Ultimately, the lead debate—public

health (who is affected) versus property rights (who pays for cleanup)—is a value conflict that will not be resolved by the scientific community.

Shift the Burden of Proof

Under the current system, individuals who challenge polluters must prove that they have been harmed, discriminated against, or disproportionately affected. Few poor or minority communities have the resources to hire the lawyers, expert witnesses, and doctors needed to sustain such a challenge. Thus, the burden of proof must be shifted to the polluters who do harm, discriminate, or do not give equal protection to minorities and other overburdened classes.

Environmental justice would require the entities that are applying for operating permits for landfills, incinerators, smelters, refineries, and chemical plants, for example, to prove that their operations are not harmful to human health, will not disproportionately affect minorities or the poor, and are nondiscriminatory.

A case in point is Louisiana Energy Services' proposal to build the nation's first privately owned uranium enrichment plant. The proposed plant would handle about 17 percent of the estimated U.S. requirement for enrichment services in the year 2000. Clearly, the burden of proof should be on Louisiana Energy Services, the state government, and the Nuclear Regulatory Commission to demonstrate that local residents' rights would not be violated in permitting the plant. At present, the burden of proof is on local residents to demonstrate that their health would be endangered and their community adversely affected by the plant.

According to the Nuclear Regulatory Commission's 1993 draft environmental impact statement, the proposed site for the facility is Claiborne Parish, Louisiana, which has a per capita income of only $5,800 per year—just 45 percent of the national average.[43] The enrichment plant would be just one-quarter mile from the almost wholly African American community of Center Springs, founded in 1910, and one and one-quarter miles from Forest Grove, which was founded by freed slaves. However, the draft statement describes the socioeconomic and community characteristics of Homer, a town that is five miles from the proposed site and whose population is more than 50 percent white, rather than those of Center Springs or Forest

Grove. As far as the draft is concerned, the communities of Center Springs and Forest Grove do not exist; they are invisible.

The racial composition of Claiborne Parish is 53.43 percent white, 46.09 percent African American, 0.16 percent American Indian, 0.07 percent Asian, 0.23 percent Hispanic, and 0.01 percent "other."[44] Thus, the parish's percentage population of African Americans is nearly four times greater than that of the nation and nearly two and one-half times greater than that of Louisiana. (African Americans composed 12 percent of the U.S. population and 29 percent of Louisiana's population in 1990.)

Clearly, Clairborne Parish's current residents would receive fewer of the plant's potential benefits—high-paying jobs, home construction, and an increased tax base—than would those who moved into the area or commuted to it to work at the facility. An increasing number of migrants will take jobs at the higher end of the skill and pay scale. These workers are expected to buy homes outside of the parish. Residents of Claiborne Parish, on the other hand, are likely to get the jobs at the low end of the skill and pay scale.[45]

Ultimately, the plant's social costs would be borne by nearby residents, while the benefits would be more dispersed. The potential social costs include increased noise and traffic, threats to public safety and to mental and physical health, and LULUs.

The case of Richmond, California, provides more evidence of the need to shift the burden of proof. A 1989 study, *Richmond at Risk,* found that the African American residents of this city bear the brunt of toxic releases in Contra Costa County and the San Francisco Bay area.[46] At least, thirty-eight industrial sites in and around the city store up to ninety-four million pounds of forty-five different chemicals, including ammonia, chlorine, hydrogen fluoride, and nitric acid. However, the burden of proof is on Richmond residents to show that they are harmed by nearby toxic releases.

On 26 July 1993, sulfur trioxide escaped from the General Chemical plant in Richmond, where people of color make up a majority of the residents. More than twenty thousand citizens were sent to the hospital. A September 1993 report by the Bay Area Air Quality Management District confirmed that "the operation was conducted in a negligent manner without due regard to the potential consequences of a miscalculation or equipment malfunction, and without required permits from the District."[47]

When Richmond residents protested the planned expansion of a Chevron refinery, they were asked to prove that they had been harmed by Chevron's operation. Recently, public pressure has induced Chevron to set aside $4.2 million to establish a new health clinic and help the surrounding community.

A third case involves conditions surrounding the 1,900 *maquiladoras,* assembly plants operated by U.S., Japanese, and other countries' companies along the 2,000-mile U.S.-Mexican border.[48] A 1983 agreement between the United States and Mexico requires U.S. companies in Mexico to export their waste products to the United States, and plants must notify EPA when they are doing so. However, a 1986 survey of 772 *maquiladoras* revealed that only twenty of the plants informed EPA when they were exporting waste to the United States, even though 86 percent of the plants used toxic chemicals in their manufacturing processes. And in 1989, only ten waste-shipment notices were filed with EPA.[49]

Much of the waste from the *maquiladoras* is illegally dumped in sewers, ditches, and the desert. All along the Rio Grande, plants dump toxic wastes into the river, from which 95 percent of the region's residents get their drinking water. In the border cities of Brownsville, Texas, and Matamoros, Mexico, the rate of anencephaly—being born without a brain—is four times the U.S. national average.[50] Affected families have filed lawsuits against eighty-eight of the area's one hundred *maquiladoras* for exposing the community to xylene, a cleaning solvent that can cause brain hemorrhages and lung and kidney damage. However, as usual, the burden of proof rests with the victims. Unfortunately, Mexico's environmental regulatory agency is understaffed and ill equipped to enforce the country's environmental laws adequately.

Obviate Proof of Intent

Laws must allow disparate impact and statistical weight—as opposed to "intent"—to infer discrimination because proving intentional or purposeful discrimination in a court of law is next to impossible. The first lawsuit to charge environmental discrimination in the placement of a waste facility,

Bean v. Southwestern Waste, was filed in 1979. The case involved residents of Houston's Northwood Manor, an urban, middle-class neighborhood of homeowners, and Browning-Ferris Industries, a private disposal company based in Houston.

More than 83 percent of the residents in the subdivision owned their single-family, detached homes. Thus, the Northwood Manor neighborhood was an unlikely candidate for a municipal landfill except that, in 1978, it was more than 82 percent black. An earlier attempt had been made to locate a municipal landfill in the same general area in 1970, when the subdivision and local school district had a majority white population. The 1970 landfill proposal was killed by the Harris County Board of Supervisors as being an incompatible land use; the site was deemed to be too close to a residential area and a neighborhood school. In 1978, however, the controversial sanitary landfill was built only 1,400 feet from a high school, football stadium, track field, and the North Forest Independent School District's administration building.[51] Because Houston has been and continues to be highly segregated, few Houstonians are unaware of where the African American neighborhoods end and the white ones begin. In 1970, for example, more than 90 percent of the city's African American residents lived in mostly black areas. By 1980, 82 percent of Houston's African American population lived in mostly black areas.[52]

Houston is the only major U.S. city without zoning. In 1992, the city council voted to institute zoning, but the measure was defeated at the polls in 1993. The city's African American neighborhoods have paid a high price for the city's unrestrained growth and lack of a zoning policy. Black Houston was allowed to become the dumping ground for the city's garbage. In every case, the racial composition of Houston's African American neighborhoods had been established before the waste facilities were sited.[53]

From the early 1920s through the late 1970s, all five of the city-owned sanitary landfills and six out of eight of Houston's municipal solid-waste incinerators were located in mostly African American neighborhoods.[54] The other two incinerator sites were located in a Latino neighborhood and a white neighborhood. One of the oldest waste sites in Houston was located in Freedmen's Town, an African American neighborhood settled by former slaves in the 1860s. The site has been built over with a charity hospital and a low-income public housing project.

Private industry took its lead from the siting pattern established by the city government. From 1970 to 1978, three of the four privately owned landfills used to dispose of Houston's garbage were located in mostly African American neighborhoods. The fourth privately owned landfill, which was sited in 1971, was located in the mostly white Chattwood subdivision. A residential part, or "buffer zone," separates the white neighborhood from the landfill. Both government and industry responded to white neighborhood associations and their NIMBY (not in my backyard) organizations by siting LULUs according to the PIBBY (place in blacks backyards) strategy.[55]

The statistical evidence in *Bean v. Southwestern Waste* overwhelmingly supported the disproportionate impact argument. Overall, fourteen of the seventeen (82 percent) solid-waste facilities used to dispose of Houston's garbage were located in mostly African American neighborhoods. Considering that Houston's African American residents comprised only 28 percent of the city's total population, they clearly were forced to bear a disproportionate burden of the city's solid-waste facilities.[56] However, the federal judge ruled against the plaintiffs on the grounds that "purposeful discrimination" was not demonstrated.

Although the Northwood Manor residents lost their lawsuit, they did influence the way the Houston city government and the state of Texas addressed race and waste facility siting. Acting under intense pressure from the African American community, the Houston city council passed a resolution in 1980 that prohibited city-owned trucks from dumping at the controversial landfill. In 1981, the Houston city council passed an ordinance restricting the construction of solid-waste disposal sites near public facilities such as schools. And the Texas Department of Health updated its requirements of landfill permit applicants to include detailed land-use, economic, and sociodemographic data on areas where they proposed to site landfills. Black Houstonians had sent a clear signal to the Texas Department of Health, the city of Houston, and private disposal companies that they would fight any future attempts to place waste disposal facilities in their neighborhoods.

Since *Bean v. Southwestern Waste,* not a single landfill or incinerator has been sited in an African American neighborhood in Houston. Not until nearly a decade after that suit did environmental discrimination resurface in the courts. A number of recent cases have challenged siting decisions using the environmental discrimination argument: *East Bibb Twiggs Neighborhood Association v. Macon-Bibb County Planning and Zoning Commission* (1989), *Bordeaux Action Committee v. Metro Government of Nashville* (1990), *R.I.S.E. v. Kay* (1991), and *El Pueblo para El Aire y Agua Limpio v. County of Kings* (1991). Unfortunately, these legal challenges are also confronted with the test of demonstrating "purposeful" discrimination.

Redress Inequities

Disproportionate impacts must be redressed by targeting action and resources. Resources should be spent where environmental and health problems are greatest, as determined by some ranking scheme—but one not limited to risk assessment. The EPA already has geographic targeting that involves selecting a physical area, often a naturally defined area such as a watershed; assessing the condition of the natural resources and range of environmental threats, including risks to public health; formulating and implementing integrated, holistic strategies for restoring or protecting living resources and their habitats within that area; and evaluating the progress of those strategies toward their objectives.[57]

Relying solely on proof of a cause-and-effect relationship as defined by traditional epidemiology disguises the exploitative way the polluting industries have operated in some communities and condones a passive acceptance of the status quo.[58] Because it is difficult to establish causation, polluting industries have the upper hand. They can always hide behind "science" and demand "proof" that their activities are harmful to humans or the environment.

A 1992 EPA report, *Securing Our Legacy,* described the agency's geographic initiatives as "protecting what we love."[59] The strategy emphasized "pollution prevention, multimedia enforcement, research into causes and cures of environmental stress, stopping habitat loss, education, and constituency building."[60] Examples of geographic initiatives under way include the Chesapeake Bay,

Great Lakes, Gulf of Mexico, and Mexican Border programs.

Such targeting should channel resources to the hot spots, communities that are burdened with more than their fair share of environmental problems. For example, EPA's Region VI has developed geographic information systems and comparative risk methodologies to evaluate environmental equity concerns in the region. The methodology combines susceptibility factors, such as age, pregnancy, race, income, preexisting disease, and lifestyle, with chemical release data from the Toxic Release inventory and monitoring information; state health department vital statistics data; and geographic and demographic data—especially from areas around hazardous waste sites—for its regional equity assessment.

Region VI's 1992 Gulf Coast Toxics Initiatives project is an out-growth of its equity assessment. The project targets facilities on the Texas and Louisiana coast, a "sensitive . . . eco-region where most of the releases in the five-state region occur."[61] Inspectors will spend 38 percent of their time in this "multimedia enforcement effort."[62] It is not clear how this percentage was determined, but, for the project to move beyond the "first-step" phase and begin addressing real inequities, most of its resources (not just inspectors) must be channeled to the areas where most of the problems occur.

A 1993 EPA study of Toxic Release Inventory data from Louisiana's petrochemical corridor found that "populations within two miles of facilities releasing 90% of total industrial corridor air releases feature a higher proportion of minorities than the state average; facilities releasing 88% have a higher proportion than the Industrial Corridor parishes' average."[63]

To no one's surprise, communities in Corpus Christi, neighborhoods that run along the Houston Ship Channel and petrochemical corridor, and many unincorporated communities along the 85-mile stretch of the Mississippi River from Baton Rouge to New Orleans ranked at or near the top in terms of pollution discharges in EPA Region VI's Gulf Coast Toxics Initiatives equity assessment. It is very likely that similar rankings would be achieved using the environmental justice framework. However, the question that remains is one of resource allocation—the level of resources that Region VI will channel into solving the pollution problem in communities that have a disproportionately large share of poor people, working-class people, and people of color.

Health concerns raised by Louisiana's residents and grassroots activists in such communities as Alsen, St. Gabriel, Geismer, Morrisonville, and Lions—all of which are located in close proximity to polluting industries—have not been adequately addressed by local parish supervisors, state environmental and health officials, or the federal and regional offices of EPA.[64]

A few contaminated African American communities in southeast Louisiana have been bought out or are in the process of being bought out by industries under their "good neighbor" programs. Moving people away from the health threat is only a partial solution, however, as long as damage to the environment continues. For example, Dow Chemical, the state's largest chemical plant, is buying out residents of mostly African American Morrisonville.[65] The communities of Sun Rise and Reveilletown, which were founded by freed slaves, have already been bought out.

Many of the community buyout settlements are sealed. The secret nature of the agreements limits public scrutiny, community comparisons, and disclosure of harm or potential harm. Few of the recent settlement agreements allow for health monitoring or surveillance of affected residents once they are dispersed.[66] Some settlements have even required the "victims" to sign waivers that preclude them from bringing any further lawsuits against the polluting industry.

A Framework for Environmental Justice

The solution to unequal protection lies in the realm of environmental justice for all people. No community—rich or poor, black or white—should be allowed to become a "sacrifice zone." The lessons from the civil rights struggles around housing, employment, education, and public accommodations over the past four decades suggest that environmental justice requires a legislative foundation. It is not enough to demonstrate the existence of unjust and unfair conditions; the practices that cause the conditions must be made illegal.

The five principles already described—the right to protection, prevention of harm, shifting the burden of proof, obviating proof of intent to discriminate, and targeting resources to redress inequities—constitute a framework for environmental justice. The framework incorporates a legislative strategy, modeled after landmark civil rights mandates, that would make environmental discrimination illegal and costly.

Although enforcing current laws in a nondiscriminatory way would help, a new legislative initiative is needed. Unequal protection must be attacked via a federal "fair environmental protection act" that redefines protection as a right rather than a privilege. Legislative initiatives must also be directed at states because many of the decisions and problems lie with state actions.

Noxious facility siting and cleanup decisions involve very little science and a lot of politics. Institutional discrimination exists in every social arena, including environmental decision making. Burdens and benefits are not randomly distributed. Reliance solely on "objective" science for environmental decision making—in a world shaped largely by power politics and special interests—often masks institutional racism. For example, the assignment of "acceptable" risk and use of "averages" often results from value judgments that serve to legitimate existing inequities. A national environmental justice framework that incorporates the five principles presented above is needed to begin addressing environmental inequities that result from procedural, geographic, and societal imbalances.

The antidiscrimination and enforcement measures called for here are no more regressive than the initiatives undertaken to eliminate slavery and segregation in the United States. Opponents argued at the time that such actions would hurt the slaves by creating unemployment and destroying black institutions, such as businesses and schools. Similar arguments were made in opposition to sanctions against the racist system of apartheid in South Africa. But people of color who live in environmental "sacrifice zones"—from migrant farm workers who are exposed to deadly pesticides to the parents of inner-city children threatened by lead poisoning—will welcome any new approaches that will reduce environmental disparities and eliminate the threats to their families' health.

NOTES

1. U.S. Environmental Protection Agency, *Environmental Equity: Reducing Risk for All Communities* (Washington, D.C., 1992); and K. Sexton and Y. Banks Anderson, eds., "Equity in Environmental Health: Research Issues and Needs," *Toxicology and Industrial Health* 9 (September/October 1993).

2. R. D. Bullard, "Solid Waste Sites and the Black Houston Community," *Sociological Inquiry* 53, nos. 2 and 3 (1983): 273–88; idem., *Invisible Houston: The Black Experience in Boom and Bust* (College Station, Tex.: Texas A&M University Press, 1987); idem., *Dumping in Dixie: Race, Class and Environmental Quality* (Boulder, Colo.: Westview Press, 1990); idem., *Confronting Environmental Racism: Voices from the Grassroots* (Boston, Mass.: South End Press, forthcoming); D. Russell, "Environmental Racism," *Amicas Journal* 11, no. 2 (1989): 22–32; M. Lavelle and M. Coyle. "Unequal Protection," *National Law Journal*, 21 September 1992, 1–2; R. Austin and M. Schill, "Black, Brown, Poor, and Poisoned: Minority Grassroots Environmentalism and the Quest for Eco-Justice," *Kansas Journal of Law and Public Policy* 1 (1991): 69–82; R. Godsil, "Remedying Environmental Racism," *Michigan Law Review* 90 (1991): 394–427; and B. Bryant and P. Mohai, eds., *Race and the Incidence of Environmental Hazards: A Time for Discourse* (Boulder, Colo.: Westview Press, 1992).

3. R. B. Stewart, "Paradoxes of Liberty, Integrity, and Fraternity: The Collective Nature of Environmental Quality and Judicial Review of Administration Action," *Environmental Law* 7, no. 3 (1977): 474–76; M. A. Freeman, "The Distribution of Environmental Quality," in *Environmental Quality Analysis,* ed. by A. V. Kneese and B. T. Bower (Baltimore: Md.: Johns Hopkins University Press for Resources for the Future, 1972); W. J. Kruvant, "People, Energy, and Pollution," in *American Energy Consumer,* ed. by D. K. Newman and D. Day (Cambridge, Mass.: Ballinger, 1975), 125–67; and L. Gianessi, H. M. Peskin, and E. Wolff, "The Distributional Effects of Uniform Air Pollution Policy in the U.S.," *Quarterly Journal of Economics* 56, no. 1 (1979): 281–301.

4. Freeman, note 3 above; Kruvant, note 3 above; Bullard, 1983 and 1990, note 2 above; P. Asch and J. J. Seneca, "Some Evidence on the Distribution of Air Quality," *Land Economics* 54, no. 3 (1978): 278–97; United Church of Christ Commission for Racial Justice, *Toxic Wastes and Race in the United States: A National Study of the Racial and Socioeconomic Characteristics of Communities with Hazardous Waste Sites* (New York: United Church of Christ, 1987); Russell, note 2 above; R. D. Bullard and B. H. Wright, "Environmentalism and the Politics of Equity: Emergent Trends in the Black Community," *Mid-American Review of Sociology* 12, no. 2 (1987): 21–37; idem, "The Quest for Environmental Equity: Mobilizing the African American Community for Social Change," *Society and Natural Resources* 3, no. 4 (1990): 301–11; M. Gelobter, "The Distribution of Air Pollution by Income and Race" (paper presented at the Second Symposium on Social Science in Resource Management, Urbana, Ill., June 1988); R. D. Bullard and J. R. Reagin, "Racism and the City," in *Urban Life in Transition,* ed. by M. Gottdiener and C. V. Pickvance (Newbury Park, Calif.; Sage, 1991): 55–76; R. D. Bullard, "Urban Infrastructure: Social, Environmental, and Health Risks to African Americans," in *The State of Black America 1992,* ed. by B. J. Tidwell (New York: National Urban League, 1992): 183–96; P. Ong and E. Blumenberg, "Race and Environmentalism" (paper presented for the Graduate School of Architecture and Urban Planning, University of California at Los Angeles, 14 March 1990); and B. H. Wright and R. D. Bullard, "Hazards in the Workplace and Black Health," *National Journal of Sociology* 4, no. 1 (1990): 45–62.

5. Freeman, note 3 above; Gianessi, Peskin, and Wolff, note 3 above; Gelobter, note 4 above; D. R. Wernette and L. A. Nieves, "Breathing Polluted Air," *EPA Journal* 18, no. 1 (1992): 16–17; Bullard, 1983, 1987, and 1990, note 2 above; R. D. Bullard, "Environmental Racism," *Environmental Protection* 2 (June 1991): 25–26; L. A. Nieves, "Not in Whose Backyard? Minority Population Concentrations and Noxious Facility Sites" (paper presented at the Annual Meeting of the American Association for the Advancement of Science, Chicago, 9 February 1992); United Church of Christ, note 4 above; Agency for Toxic Substances and Disease Registry, *The Nature and Extent of Lead Poisoning in Children in the United States: A Report to Congress* (Atlanta, Ga.: U.S. Department of Health and Human Services, 1988); K. Florini et al., *Legacy of Lead: America's Continuing Epidemic of Childhood Lead Poisoning* (Washington, D.C.: Environmental Defense Fund, 1990); and P. West, J. M. Fly, F. Larkin, and P. Marans, "Minority Anglers and Toxic Fish Consumption: Evidence of the State-Wide Survey of Michigan," in *The Proceedings of the Michigan Conference on Race and the Incidence of Environmental Hazards,* ed. by B. Bryant and P. Mohai (Ann Arbor, Mich.: University of Michigan School of Natural Resources, 1990): 108–22.

6. Gelobter, note 4 above; and M. Gelobter, "Toward a Model of Environmental Discrimination," in Bryant and Mohai, eds., note 5 above, 87–107.

7. B. Goldman, *Not Just Prosperity: Achieving Sustain-*

ability with Environmental Justice (Washington, D.C.: National Wildlife Federation Corporate Conservation Council, 1994), 8.

8. Wernette and Nieves, note 5 above, 16–17.

9. H. P. Mak, P. Johnson, H. Abbey, and R. C. Talamo, "Prevalence of Asthma and Health Service Utilization of Asthmatic Children in an Inner City," *Journal of Allergy and Clinical Immunology* 70 (1982): 367–72; I. F. Goldstein and A. L. Weinstein, "Air Pollution and Asthma: Effects of Exposure to Short-Term Sulfur Dioxide Peaks," *Environmental Research* 40 (1986): 332–45; J. Schwartz et al., "Predictors of Asthma and Persistent Wheeze in a National Sample of Children in the United States," *American Review of Respiratory Disease* 142 (1990): 555–62; U.S. Environmental Protection Agency, note 1 above; and E. Mann, *L.A.'s Lethal Air: New Strategies for Policy, Organizing and Action* (Los Angeles: Labor/Community Strategy Center, 1991).

10. Lavelle and Coyle, note 2 above, 1–2.

11. Ibid., 2.

12. Bullard, 1983 and 1990, note 2 above; Gelobter, note 4 above; and United Church of Christ, note 4 above.

13. Bullard, 1983 and 1990, note 2 above; P. Costner and J. Thornton, *Playing with Fire* (Washington, D.C.: Greenpeace, 1990); and United Church of Christ, note 4 above.

14. Costner and Thornton, note 13 above.

15. M. H. Brown, *The Toxic Cloud: The Poisoning of America's Air* (New York: Harper and Row, 1987); and J. Summerhays, *Estimation and Evaluation of Cancer Risks Attributable to Air Pollution in Southeast Chicago* (Washington, D.C.: U.S. Environmental Protection Agency, 1989).

16. "Home Street, USA: Living with Pollution," *Greenpeace Magazine,* October/November/December 1991, 8–13.

17. Mann, note 9 above; and Ong and Blumenberg, note 4 above.

18. Mann, note 9 above; and J. Kay, "Fighting Toxic Racism: L.A.'s Minority Neighborhood Is the 'Dirtiest' in the State," *San Francisco Examiner,* 7 April 1991, A1.

19. Bullard, 1990, note 2 above.

20. K. C. Colquette and E. A. Henry Robertson, "Environmental Racism: The Causes, Consequences, and Commendations," *Tulane Environmental Law Journal* 5, no. 1 (1991): 153–207.

21. F. Ferrer, "Testimony by the Office of Bronx Borough President," in *Proceedings from the Public Hearing on Minorities and the Environment: An Exploration into the Effects of Environmental Policies, Practices, and Conditions on Minority and Low-Income Communities* (Bronx, N.Y.: Bronx Planning Office, 20 September 1991).

22. B. Angel, *The Toxic Threat to Indian Lands: A Greenpeace Report* (San Francisco, Calif.: Greenpeace, 1992);

J. Kay, "Indian Lands Targeted for Waste Disposal Sites," *San Francisco Examiner,* 10 April 1991, A1.

23. M. Ambler, "The Lands the Feds Forgot," *Sierra,* May/June 1989, 44.

24. Angel, note 22 above; C. Beasley, "Of Poverty and Pollution: Deadly Threat on Native Lands," *Buzzworm* 2, no. 5 (1990): 39–45; and R. Tomsho, "Dumping Grounds: Indian Tribes Contend with Some of the Worst of America's Pollution," *Wall Street Journal,* 29 November 1990, A1.

25. Cerrell Associates, Inc., *Political Difficulties Facing Waste-to-Energy Conversion Plant Siting* (Los Angeles: California Waste Management Board, 1984).

26. L. Blumberg and R. Gottlieb, *War on Waste: Can American Win Its Battle with Garbage?* (Washington, D.C.: Island Press, 1989).

27. U.S. Commission on Civil Rights, *The Battle for Environmental Justice in Louisiana: Government, Industry and the People* (Kansas City, Mo., 1993).

28. Agency for Toxic Substances and Diseases Registry, note 5 above.

29. P. Reich, *The Hour of Lead* (Washington, D.C.: Environmental Defense Fund, 1992).

30. Agency for Toxic Substances and Disease Registry, note 5 above.

31. Florini et al., note 5 above.

32. P. J. Hilts, "White House Shuns Key Role in Lead Exposure," *New York Times,* 24 August 1991, 14.

33. Ibid.

34. Dallas Alliance Environmental Task Force, *Alliance Final Report* (Dallas, Tex.: Dallas Alliance, 1983).

35. J. Lash, K. Gillman, and D. Sheridan, *A Season of Spoils: The Reagan Administration's Attack on the Environment* (New York: Pantheon Books, 1984), 131–39.

36. D. W. Nauss, "EPA Official: Dallas Lead Study Misleading," *Dallas Times Herald,* 20 March 1983, 1; idem, "The People vs. the Lead Smelter," *Dallas Times Herald,* 17 July 1983, 18; B. Lodge, "EPA Official Faults Dallas Lead Smelter," *Dallas Morning News,* 20 March 1983, A1; and Lash, Gillman, and Sheridan, note 35 above.

37. U.S. Environmental Protection Agency Region VI, *Report of the Dallas Area Lead Assessment Study* (Dallas, Tex., 1993).

38. Lash, Gillman, and Sheridan, note 35 above.

39. Bullard, 1990, note 2 above.

40. S. Scott and R. L. Loftis, "'Slag Sites' Health Risks Still Unclear," *Dallas Morning News,* 23 July 1991, A1.

41. Ibid.

42. B. L. Lee, "Environmental Litigation on Behalf of Poor, Minority Children: *Matthews v. Coye: A Case Study*" (paper presented at the Annual Meeting of the American Association for the Advancement of Science, Chicago, 9 February 1992).

43. Nuclear Regulatory Commission, *Draft Environmental Impact Statement for the Construction and Operation*

of Claiborne Enrichment Centre, Homer, Louisiana (Washington, D.C., 1993), 3–108.

44. See U.S. Census Bureau, *1990 Census of Population General Population Characteristics-Louisiana* (Washington, D.C.: U.S. Government Printing Office, May 1992).

45. Nuclear Regulatory Commission, note 43 above, pages 4–38.

46. Citizens for a Better Environment, *Richmond at Risk* (San Francisco, Calif., 1992).

47. Bay Area Air Quality Management District, *General Chemical Incident of July 26, 1993* (San Francisco, Calif., 15 September 1993), 1.

48. R. Sanchez, "Health and Environmental Risks of the Maquiladora in Mexicali," *National Resources Journal 30* (Winter 1990): 163–86.

49. Center for Investigative Reporting, *Global Dumping Grounds: The International Traffic in Hazardous Waste* (Washington, D.C.: Seven Locks Press, 1989), 59.

50. Working Group on Canada-Mexico Free Trade, "Que Pasa? A Canada-Mexico 'Free' Trade Deal," *New Solutions: A Journal of Environmental and Occupational Health Policy 2* (1991): 10–25.

51. Bullard, 1983, note 2 above.

52. Bullard, 1987, note 2 above.

53. Bullard, 1983, 1987, and 1990, note 2 above. The unit of analysis for the Houston waste study was the neighborhood, not the census tract. The concept of neighborhood predates census tract geography, which became available only in 1950. Neighborhood studies date back nearly a century. *Neighborhood* as used here is defined as "a social/spatial unit of social organization . . . larger than a household and smaller than a city." See A. Hunter, "Urban Neighborhoods: Its Analytical and Social Contexts," *Urban Affairs Quarterly 14* (1979): 270. The neighborhood is part of a city's geography, a place defined by specific physical boundaries and block groups. Similarly, the black neighborhood is a "highly diversified set of in-terrelated structures and aggregates of people who are held together by forces of white oppression and racism." See J. E. Blackwell, *The Black Community: Diversity and Unity* (New York: Harper & Row, 1985), xiii.

54. Bullard, 1983, 1987, and 1990, note 2 above.

55. Ibid.

56. Ibid.

57. U.S. Environmental Protection Agency, *Strategies and Framework for the Future: Final Report* (Washington, D.C., 1992), 12.

58. K. S. Shrader-Frechette, *Risk and Rationality: Philosophical Foundations for Populist Reform* (Berkeley, Calif.: University of California Press, 1992), 98.

59. U.S. Environmental Protection Agency, "Geographic Initiatives: Protecting What We Love," *Securing Our Legacy: An EPA Progress Report, 1989–1991* (Washington, D.C., 1992), 32.

60. Ibid.

61. U.S. Environmental Protection Agency, note 1 above, vol. 2, *Supporting Documents,* 60.

62. Ibid.

63. U.S. Environmental Protection Agency, *Toxic Release Inventory and Emission Reduction, 1987–1990, in the Lower Mississippi River Industrial Corridor* (Washington, D.C., 1993), 25.

64. Bullard, 1990, note 2 above: C. Beasley, "Of Pollution and Poverty: Keeping Watch in Cancer Alley," *Buzzworm 2,* no. 4 (1990): 39–45; and S. Lewis, B. Keating, and D. Russell, *Inconclusive by Design: Waste, Fraud, and Abuse in Federal Environmental Health Research* (Boston, Mass.: National Toxics Campaign, 1992).

65. J. O'Byrne, "The Death of a Town," *Times Picayune,* 20 February 1991, A1.

66. Bullard, 1990, note 2 above; J. O'Byrne and M. Schleitstein, "Invisible Poisons," *Times Picayune,* 18 February 1991, A1; and Lewis, Keating, and Russell, note 64 above.

Study Questions

1. On what grounds does the majority of the Supreme Court in *Babbitt v. Sweet Home* argue that the Secretary of the Interior's regulation is justifiable under the Endangered Species Act?

2. Do you agree with Baxter's four criteria for handling environmental questions? Why or why not?

3. Do you agree with Baxter that any standards for dealing with problems of pollution should be exclusively "people-oriented"?

4. In what way, according to Sagoff, do we currently face an environmental "Zuckerman's dilemma"?

5. Is Sagoff correct in claiming that many of our current attitudes toward and practices concerning the environment (for example, saving whales, banning pesticides, or combating water pollution) show that we attach intrinsic value to non-human forms of life? How would Baxter explain these actions and attitudes?

6. Morgenson and Eisenstodt make several arguments against the efficacy of government regulation. Are you convinced by their arguments? Why or why not?

7. Morgenson and Eisenstodt state that pollution is not the product of corporate greed, but of consumer desire for cheap and convenient goods. Do you agree with this claim?

8. Consider the proposal of Morgenson and Eisenstodt to use emission reduce credits (ERCs) and a pollution tax on automobiles as a means of addressing some air pollution problems. Does the use of ERCs and the tax have a moral consequences for the parties affected by pollution and the tax? Whom might such parties be?

9. To what extent do you think Bowie sees consumers as bearing primary responsibility for environmental problems?

10. Why, according to Bowie, can business have an active role in legislation affecting the conduct of business (for example, tariffs) but not a role in environmental legislation? Is his reasoning sound?

11. Contrast Hoffman and Bowie on the role of the consumer in promoting environmentally responsible business. Which would give a greater role to consumers?

12. Why does Hoffman believe that the environmental movement and the business ethics movement might "come up morally short" and be viewed as "deceptive and shallow"?

13. Guha claims that the emphasis of American environmentalists upon wilderness preservation has proved harmful in application to the Third World. In what ways, according to Guha, has this happened?

14. Some critics of Bullard argue that the disproportionate impact of environmental hazards upon certain communities, even if established, does not show that such an impact is racial; rather, the impact is upon poor people because they are poor, not because they are ethnic minorities. How would Bullard respond to this argument? Do you agree?

15. Imagine the following: It has been proposed by members of a state legislature that fifty-thousand acres of virgin timberland be set aside for a national park. An analysis reveals that the proposed legislation will cost the local town approximately 150 jobs and will have an adverse impact on the local economy. The legislation is presently being debated in the state assembly. What parties will be immediately affected by the decision on this legislation? Over time, what other parties might be affected? What arguments might environmental groups make in support of preservation of this land? What might be the arguments of the timber industry and the local community? How would the authors represented in this chapter assess this case?

CASE SCENARIO 1   To Kill a River

On July 14, 1991, a Southern Pacific freight train derailed as it was crossing a bridge over the Sacramento River in northern California. One of its tank cars was carrying metam sodium, a liquid herbicide. The derailment punctured the tank car and spilled twenty thousand gallons of this chemical into the Sacramento River. As the resulting ten-mile-long spill drifted slowly downstream, it killed virtually every living thing in its path. Nearly a forty-mile stretch of the river's ecosystem was destroyed by this spill: Aquatic plants, flies, nymphs, small fish, and more than a hundred thousand trout were killed. In effect, an ecologist argued, the spill killed the river itself.

The Sacramento is a fast-flowing river and soon flushed itself clean of the toxin. By the end of the summer, the river was clean enough to support life once again. The spill also posed little danger to humans. The river flows into Lake Shasta, the state's largest artificial reservoir. The spill was so dispersed throughout the 550 billion gallons of water in the lake that health officials determined that the water remained safe to drink. Humans were affected by the spill, however, in that fishing, boating, and other recreational uses of the river—along with a strong tourism business that depends on these activities—were devastated.

Society has worked out fairly straightforward ways to determine when humans have been harmed by acts of negligence. We also have well-established ways for determining compensation. We might, for example, require the railroad to compensate merchants for lost revenues. Property owners might require compensation for cleanup costs.

But what about the river itself?

1. Has the railroad incurred a debt to the river, or to any life-forms destroyed by the spill? Has the river been harmed in any morally significant way? What about the fish and plant life destroyed by the spill?
2. How would Baxter and Sagoff respond to the previous question?

CASE SCENARIO 2   Species Habitat Versus Profits

Acme Farms, Inc., owns large tracts of range and ranch land in several western states. On this land Acme raises sheep and goats, among other animals. Business has been good for Acme in recent years; last month, however, the company was hit with a potentially devastating lawsuit brought by the federal government. The suit was aimed at preventing Acme from allowing its sheep and goats to graze on significant portions of the range land, much of which had been identified as habitat for a bird currently listed as an endangered species. Acme, the government charged, was in violation of the Endangered Species Act (ESA) because its sheep and goats, by eating tree seedlings that might, when grown, have provided food and shelter for the birds, had caused some of the birds to die. Such activity amounted to a prohibited "taking" of the bird, defined as a conduct that will "harm" members of the protected species.

In response to the charges, Acme maintained that it in no way attempted to harm the birds in question: It did not hunt, trap, or kill them; it merely made use of land for legitimate business purposes. The government supported its case by appealing to a recent ruling handed down by the U.S. Supreme Court in *Babbit v. Sweet Home Chapter of Communities for a Great Oregon*.[1] In that case the Court held that a "taking," under the Endangered Species Act, can include conduct that causes "significant habitat modification or degradation" resulting in killing or injuring wildlife "by impairing essential behavior patterns, including breeding, feeding, and sheltering." Destruction of habitat, the argument went, was tantamount to destruction of the species.

Both Acme and the government sought to marshal arguments to support their respective positions. Acme argued that requiring it to curtail its ranching operations to avoid causing a harm it never intended effectively places upon landowning businesses the cost of protecting endangered-species habitat, regardless of the degree to which the law would thus reduce the economic value of the land. That is unfair, Acme insisted: If protecting habitat works to the

---

[1] 115 S.Ct. 2407 (1995).

benefit of all Americans, the burden should not fall on a few. The government countered that to al-
low landowners to destroy critical habitat, so long as they don't actually shoot the animal in question, makes a mockery of the ESA, since the law could easily be evaded through an indirect method of eliminating a species. Moreover, the government pointed out, the principle expressed by the Court's interpretation of the ESA is often followed in other areas of environmental policy. Take pollution, for example. It is well established that industries generating pollutants as an unintended by-product of their manufacturing processes must "pay their own way," covering the costs of pollution control or prevention out of their own pockets. Why should this case be different? Acme challenged the strength of this analogy: It is not responsible for the fact that important wildlife habitat fortuitously exists on its property in the way that a polluting industry is responsible for the by-products it decides to generate.

1. Which of the parties involved in this case has the better argument? How should the ESA be interpreted? How would the views represented in the readings apply to this case?
2. How would Morgenson and Eisenstodt weigh the arguments in this case? What resolution do you think they would suggest?

CASE SCENARIO 3   Toxic Waste and Social Responsibility

Z Corp is a computer-chip manufacturer residing in the fictional city of Gilbane. The production process for Z Corp's components results in the creation of certain toxins (lead and arsenic) which are discharged into the city's sewer system and then extracted at a waste treatment facility. The city regulates the amount of toxins that may be discharged, since the treated sewer waste is sold by the city to local farmers for fertilizer. The sales are lucrative. To ensure that the fertilizer is free of contamination, the regulations are ten times more restrictive than comparable federal standards.

Recent tests by a Z Corp environmental engineer indicate that Z Corp might be in violation of the city regulations. The engineer believes that the situation can be remedied by investing in a better pollution control system. Management disagrees and argues that since the city has not notified Z Corp of any violation, there is no cause for action on its part. The situation is further complicated when Z Corp announces a joint venture with another firm, which will increase production 500 percent—which means a fivefold increase in toxins. The environmental engineering department thinks that this production increase means that Z Corp now *must* make the investment in the pollution control system. But management again disagrees, arguing that the city regulations state a permissible standard of one ounce of toxins per million gallons of water. The solution to the problem of increased concentrations of lead and arsenic is simply more filtration: Release enough water so that the city standard of one ounce per million gallons is satisfied. But the problem with this resolution is that it is doubtful whether the city's treatment facility can handle these concentrations. The long-term problem is that lead and arsenic concentrations do not break down, and it is admitted by all that it might threaten the viability of the city's fertilizer enterprise. Management's attitude toward this issue is that it is the city's problem. After all, the company is in compliance with the flawed city regulations. Furthermore, if the corporation is forced to invest in pollution control equipment, the facility might face layoffs or a complete shutdown. The result would be unemployment for many local residents.

1. Can Z Corp claim that it is acting in a morally responsible manner because it is in legal compliance with the flawed city regulations? If a tangible harm results from the sale of contaminated fertilizer, who bears the moral responsibility? Management suggests that

the investment in pollution control equipment will mean the loss of the production line and unemployment, which in turn will lead to lower tax revenues. Does this argument exemplify cost/benefit analysis? Explain.

2. Explain how the perspectives of Bowie and of Hoffman would view this case.

CASE SCENARIO 4   Environmental Racism

No wonder the folks at Chemical Waste Management Inc. were pumped up after winning approval in January to build California's first commercial toxic-waste incinerator. Since 1987, they had been haggling with state and county officials to get permission to burn hazardous waste at their Kettleman Hills dump site in the rural San Joaquin Valley.

But weeks after winning the nod, the nation's largest hazardous-waste company, the state, and the county were slapped with a novel suit alleging they had discriminated by placing the incinerator near mostly Hispanic Kettleman City. Filed by People for Clean Air & Water, the suit claims the Oak Brook (Ill.) company's decision was part of a national pattern of siting hazardous-waste facilities near minority areas.

PROFIT PLUNGE

Lawsuits are routine in the $10 billion hazardous-waste business. But this one is unusually worrisome. The suit marks one of the first uses of the civil rights laws to fight a waste facility. If successful, it would give activists another weapon to attack "Lulus"—locally unpopular land uses. "We are taking this lawsuit very seriously," says Chem Waste Senior Counsel Philip L. Comella.

Chem Waste hardly needs more woes. On Apr. 16, it reported a 31% plunge in first-quarter earnings, to $24 million. Last year, it agreed to pay the Environmental Protection Agency a record civil penalty—$3.75 million—for polluting as its Chicago South Side facility. And the EPA just disclosed its intent to fine Chem Waste $7.1 million for improprieties at its landfill in Model City, N.Y.

At a minimum, the Kettleman suit could delay construction of the facility. Kay Hahn, a Chicago Corp. analyst, estimates that the incinerator would burn 100,000 tons of toxic waste annually and add $25 million to Chem Waste's $1.1 billion in yearly revenues. She says the incinerator is key to the company's long-term strategy because federal rules last year began barring untreated land disposal of hazardous wastes. Now, it must ship its untreated waste in California to another state to be processed.

While the Kettleman suit tests the theory of "environmental racism," the issue isn't just local. The EPA is studying whether minorities bear the brunt of the nation's toxic pollution. And studies by the General Accounting Office, the United Church of Christ, and others show that waste sites are mostly in black or Hispanic communities.

Sometimes poor areas welcome the sites—they bring jobs and more taxes. But mostly, "it's a pattern of picking the path of least resistance," argues Robert D. Bullard, a University of California at Riverside professor. "Minority communities are the least likely to fight."

Chem Waste doesn't dispute that its incinerator sites are in largely minority areas (table). But it says it didn't engage in discriminatory siting, because the sites had incinerators or landfills when it bought them.

PROTRACTED BATTLE

Chances are Chem Waste will defeat the civil rights claims. In the only prior case alleging civil rights violations over a dump siting, the plaintiffs failed in 1979 to prove the company intentionally discriminated. But even if the industry avoids such awards, it can expect more battles.

"We're just not ready to accept them at their word that these incinerators are a safe method of disposal," says plaintiff Joe Maya.

In one sense, the Kettleman suit is just a variation of the "not in my backyard" syndrome. The poor and minorities, like everyone else, don't want to live next to toxic dumps. And that's a key reason few incinerators have been built lately—despite federal laws designating incineration as the preferred destruction method for most toxic waste. Building the sites near nobody's backyard would seem to be the optimal solution. But even that's no guarantee: A few years ago, Chem Waste abandoned plans to burn toxic waste at sea because of environmentalists' protests. A more practical fix? Set national policies for deciding where to put the Lulus.

1. What are some of the reasons for constructing the Chemical Waste Management Inc. facility near Kettleman City?
2. How could it be argued that the decision to place the Chemical Waste facility near Kettleman City is not discriminatory? What argument could be given to show that the siting of the plant is an instance of environmental racism?
3. Assuming that society needs such facilities, how would you recommend that the location of such plants be made? Explain your reasons.

CHAPTER 10

The Moral Dimensions
of Information Technology

Home computers, modems, and "web browsers" are now as much a staple of the American household as the telephone. We balance our checkbooks and pay our taxes with the help of quick and easy software, use modems to invest in mutual funds, engage in chat about the latest movies, and research using an online *Reader's Guide*. In idle moments, "surfing the Internet" has replaced television channel-surfing. As we write this, it is estimated conservatively that more than 2 million people are wired to the Internet, as are countless businesses.

It is obvious that computing technology has changed ordinary life and the way in which business is conducted. The breathtaking possibilities of the information superhighway have created some new and worrisome ethical problems. In 1996 a student at the California Institute of Technology was expelled for allegedly harassing a female student via e-mail, apparently one of the first cases in which such disciplinary action was taken based almost entirely on e-mail data. The case raised questions about the authentication of e-mail (the accused insisted that the message had been manipulated to appear as though he had sent it) and about how "electronic harassment" should be defined. In another case, a student at the University of Texas at El Paso was charged with making terrorist threats over the Internet. The student, upset over the political stance of a California state senator, allegedly posted a message to several environmental and political discussion groups, suggesting that the senator be "hunted down and skinned." Law enforcement officials argued that such speech, sent instantly to millions of people, could incite violence; critics of the arrest argued that freedom of speech over the "net" must be protected, even if the speech is offensive. Both of these cases involved activities in what has come to be called *cyberspace*: a vast matrix of interconnected computer systems, accessible from remote physical locations. Cyberspace comprises numerous computing networks, from commercial services such as Prodigy and America Online to privately operated bulletin board systems and databases. The Internet, and its multimedia component—the World Wide Web—constitute the largest presence in cyberspace. The rapid expansion of cyberspace has brought with it many questions that both society and the business community must now tackle. Computer ethicist Deborah Johnson points out some of these questions:

> Who should have access to Cyberspace? Should Cyberspace be considered private or public? What should count as authorized (or unauthorized) access? What should be considered criminal behavior? Should First Amendment rights be extended to Cyberspace? . . . How should we view unauthorized access and disruptive

---

∽ **Trademarks and the Internet**

The extraordinary growth of cyberspace has outpaced the ability of the business and legal communities to deal adequately with trademark violations in the use of Internet addresses. A standard Internet address consists of a name, followed by the @ symbol and two more designators, known as *domain* names. The suffix of an address, or *top-level domain* (following the dot), groups users into categories: *edu* for educational users, *com* for commercial users, *gov* for government users, and so on. The term between the @ and the dot is the *second-level domain* name and is chosen by the user. Network Solutions, Inc. (NSI), a private organization, registers all such domain names. But what if the domain name you choose is the name of a company owned by someone else? In 1994 Joshua Quittner registered the address *mcdonalds.com* and began using *ronald@mcdonalds.com* as his e-mail address. He offered to sell the name back to McDonald's Restaurants in exchange for a donation by the hamburger giant of computers for a local school; McDonald's reluctantly complied. NSI subsequently implemented a policy allowing holders of registered trademarks and trade names to challenge the use of a domain name identical to their trademark. But observers agree that the problem has not been solved. For example, Roadrunner Computer Systems of Santa Fe registered the domain name *roadrunner.com*. Time Warner, Inc., asked NSI to put a hold on the company's use of the name, as *roadrunner* is also the trademarked name of a Warner cartoon character. As of June 1996, the computer firm had filed suit against Time Warner to lift the hold. As a further example, the word *Eagle* is part of trademarks registered to a pretzel company, an insurance service, a chain of hardware stores, and a pencil manufacturer. The Internet has room for only one *eagle.com* address. Which one of the companies should get to use that address?

Source: *National Law Journal* 2/12/96, C17–18; 6/3/96, B1–2.

---

activities such as virus planting? How seriously should we punish these activities? Should malicious intent play a role in determining the guilt or innocence or amount of punishment? . . . Should we constrain what law enforcement officials can do in pursuit of computer crimes? What should we do if it turns out that in protecting freedom of speech on-line, we are protecting viruses and worms?[1]

This chapter addresses two central issues affecting cyberspace: Who should have access to the computer systems constituting cyberspace and the vast amount of information they contain? How has computing and information technology affected the quality of work life?

HACKERS, BREAK-INS, AND THE FREEDOM OF INFORMATION

Hackers are computer enthusiasts with expert knowledge about software and information systems. As the complexity of these systems increases, the hacker's status is enhanced. The efforts of hackers can be beneficial, for example, by ferreting out glitches in new systems of software. But sometimes they can be mischievous and even destructive. In August 1996 it was reported that Russian hackers had broken through the security system of Citibank Corporation, using only a 2400 baud modem and a laptop computer. Citibank alleges that the

> ### ✎ Online Services and Liability for User Conduct
>
> The rapid proliferation of a variety of online services has posed questions about the responsibility of those providing the service when a subscriber uses the service to wrong another. Recent court decisions reveal an unsettled area of moral and legal debate, and uncertainty about how to conceive of online services. In 1991 a federal court held that CompuServe could not be held responsible for an allegedly libelous statement appearing in a newsletter posted on the service. In 1995 two other federal courts ruled in similar cases, one involving the Prodigy online service, the other dealing with Netcom. In the Prodigy case, the service was accused of permitting a defamatory statement to appear and remain for several weeks on a bulletin board maintained by Prodigy; in the Netcom case, portions of a copyrighted book were posted without permission from the authors. A central question in each of these cases turned on the nature of an online service: Is such a service akin to a traditional newspaper or magazine publisher? Or is it merely a passive conduit for information provided by others? CompuServe was found to be merely a distributor, and thus not liable for defamation; Prodigy, by contrast, was likened more to a standard publisher: Prodigy sought to present a "family-oriented" image and thus exercised editorial control in several ways, including use of software to prescreen user messages for profanity and refusal to allow sexually explicit bulletin boards or discussion groups. By virtue of these steps, it was reasoned, Prodigy had already assumed a degree of control that implies responsibility. Netcom was found partly liable: While it neither created nor controlled the content of postings on its newsgroups, it was made aware of the possible copyright infringement and failed to act by removing the posting.
>
> SOURCE: *National Law Journal* 10/31/94, C9–11; 7/10/95, B7–9; 2/12/96, C4–6.

motivation for the break-in was theft. But the hackers tell a different story. They claim that the reason for this unauthorized intrusion was plain curiosity. One claimed that in Russia sophisticated computer systems are rare, and he simply wanted to explore a network with a complex operating system.

It is important to note that a hacker break-in may not result in theft or sabotage, as in the case of implanting a "worm" or computer virus in a system. In fact, the hacker's intrusion might result only in a temporary system slowdown. Although the intrusion is unauthorized, the motive of intellectual curiosity is often used to justify actions that we ordinarily would not tolerate. What harm is done if a hacker surreptitiously explores a system, doing no damage to the system and stealing nothing? This is not a rhetorical question. You would certainly object if an unauthorized person disassembled your car's motor to further her interest in learning more about the functioning of internal combustion engines—and this even if she reassembled your engine and changed the oil. You would object that the intrusion was one to which you did not consent. But the hacker might deny that this analogy is appropriate, since many hackers apparently hold the view that the information contained within computer systems, as well as information about the systems themselves, ought to be free. In other words, unlike traditional private property, information that can be gained about a system and its contents through a computer network should be available to anyone who has the means to access it. No one has an exclusive-use right to this data. Unlike traditional private property, the data of the "net," the argument goes, should be treated as a kind of public good, like the air. No one has to consent to your breathing air, since no one owns it.

To some it is far-fetched to abandon the idea of private property rights in collected data, yet the government's National Information Initiative promotes universal access to the Internet. What does such "access" mean? As author Clifford Stoll notes, "At one extreme, universal access means that every citizen will be trained in the use of the network, given a workstation, a modem and an account. At the other extreme, universal access may mean that everyone is welcome on line, as long as they pay the fare."[2]

Presumably, many hackers opt for a version of the second extreme, adding that access to whatever is contained on the network be available without cost: There should be no "fare" whatsoever. Richard Stallman, a proponent of this approach, has suggested that hackers do not believe in absolute property rights. A property owner (for example, a corporation that "owns" its system, like Citibank) has a right to use the system and its computers without interference; but when the systems or computers are inactive, the network ought to be accessible without fee to anyone who wants to learn from its programs (like the Russian hackers).[3] Critics argue that this position is implausible. We currently do not provide all information for free: Information in databases must often be purchased; system information is proprietary, protected by intellectual property laws; commercial servers like CompuServe and Prodigy charge for their services; and software is copyrighted. What the hacker claims is that all information contained in or gatherable from the Internet ought to be free and available and that, in fact, society would be better off if this were so.

Reflection reveals that there are ways in which free access to the information of cyberspace is or would be desirable. The marketplace is one example. A decision to make an

---

✍ Software and Copyright: The *Lotus* Case

In a much anticipated ruling in January 1996, the U.S. Supreme Court let stand a lower court decision that all sides agree will significantly affect the software industry. The case pitted Lotus Development Corporation, creators of the popular Lotus 1-2-3 spreadsheet program, against Borland International. Borland had incorporated elements of the Lotus program into its own competing Quattro and Quattro Pro spreadsheets, so that Lotus users could more readily use the Borland product. Specifically, Borland had copied the structure of menus and commands used in Lotus 1-2-3—459 commands in all, arranged in more than fifty trees or submenus. Borland hoped that incorporating Lotus's "menu command hierarchy," or user interface, would lure Lotus users to Quattro. Lotus stated that Borland had committed copyright infringement and filed suit. Although basic concepts or ideas (for example, laws of physics or mathematics) cannot be copyrighted, the expression given to an idea may receive such protection. Lotus argued that its particular structure of commands constituted a creative form of expression, giving the program its unique, user-friendly appeal. Borland countered that the structure of menus and commands was similar to the function buttons on a VCR, so basic a concept that no copyright could attach. The courts sided with Borland. Critics of the ruling complained that it would have an adverse affect on the software industry. User interfaces are often the most creative contribution a developer makes, and as such should be protected. The decision will encourage software companies to copy the successful parts of other programs rather than provide incentives to creativity. Supporters of the decision believe that it will break the potential monopoly of certain developers and allow competitors to create works that employ a standard set of commands familiar to users.

Source: *National Law Journal* 2/12/96, C8–11.

informed purchase is more likely to satisfy a consumer's desires than one that is not so informed. If the data is obtained without cost, so much the better. Furthermore, free access to information is viewed by some as a desirable condition for democratic institutions. The Internet allows for quick and inexpensive exchanges of ideas. People can express their political opinions through bulletin boards and e-mail, find out about important legislation pending in Congress, encounter informed perspectives about the state of the nation or of the environment, and so on. Free access to such opinions and information will spur democratic decision making by helping to create an educated electorate. Finally, imagine the technological boon to society if access to information really were to be free. The degree of interconnected communication afforded by the Internet means that research results would be available to anyone, corporations would not have the need to employ expensive cohorts of lawyers to protect proprietary information, and the number of cooperative ventures would likely increase. So, the argument concludes, the data of cyberspace should be free.

SOFTWARE AND INTELLECTUAL PROPERTY

Pursued to its fullest, the free-information argument would entail a wholesale reconsideration of the market, since it would mean the abandonment of our current conceptions of private property, particularly the rules of intellectual property—rules established by laws protecting copyrights, patents, and trade secrets. But the notion of intellectual property is also challenged by the burgeoning forms of information technology in other ways. These issues are also dealt with in this chapter.

One of the basic rules underlying the major forms of intellectual property protection—patents and copyrights—is that abstract ideas, concepts, and principles are not subject to proprietary protection. I cannot patent the laws of physics, nor can I copyright the idea of a love affair. I might, however, be able to obtain a patent for a device that utilizes the laws of physics, or a copyright for a novel dealing with a particular love affair. More generally, intellectual property rights may attach to the particular expression given to an abstract idea (my telling of the love affair story), as well as to a process or invention incorporating that idea (say, a patent on an oven based on a particular utilization of the principles of solar energy). Patents are more difficult to secure than copyrights, since the applicant must show that the invention of a machine is "novel and unique"; copyright protection is available to any work of authorship that gives a particular expression to a more general idea.

It is clear that many components of information technology are protectable by intellectual property rights. A new and innovative microprocessor or unique fiber-optic communications device could be covered by a patent; and a book on how to "surf the net" is subject to copyright laws. Much of the recent controversy concerning intellectual property in new information technologies has focused on computer software, and this for several reasons. To begin with, the intangible nature of software leaves it unclear as to what forms of intellectual property protection should be accorded to software. Is a spreadsheet program a "process" or "invention" subject to patent law? Or is it a work of authorship, akin to a book or script, and so covered by copyright? The courts have ruled inconsistently on these questions, occasionally favoring one side, then the other. Underlying this dispute is a deeper uncertainty: Should the mathematical formulas and ideas forming the basis of a software program be regarded as a public good, freely available to all? Or should they be viewed as private property? Recent cases have faced this question in the context of the user interfaces—the way in which a program configures what appears on the computer screen, arranges windows, and sequences menus. Should the "look and feel" of such programs, from the user's point of view, be thought of as proprietary?

✑   TDDs and Confidentiality

In an effort to assist customers who suffer from hearing and speech disabilities, and to comply with provisions of the Americans with Disabilities Act (ADA), many regional telephone companies now offer a service utilizing the technology of TDDs: telecommunication devices for the deaf. The service provides a hearing-impaired customer with a special terminal, including monitor and keyboard, along with a standard telephone. Using the keyboard and the screen, the disabled customer can "converse" over phone lines. When a TDD customer places a call, he or she types a message on the keyboard. The message is read by a relay operator, who then translates the message, conveying it verbally to the receiving party. One of the most sensitive issues raised by this technology concerns the confidentiality of the conversations relayed. Under the terms of the ADA, all calls must be relayed, regardless of their content; and relay operators are forbidden to disclose the content of any relayed conversation. Some states even require relay operators to take an oath of confidentiality as a condition of employment. Yet some states have made exceptions, permitting, for instance, the disclosure of conversations dealing with illegal acts, such as child abuse. The absence of uniform ethical and legal guidelines leaves unclear the degree to which users of TDDs can expect that their calls will be private.

SOURCE: *National Law Journal* 7/8/91, 13–14.

Regardless of how these issues are to be resolved, it is clear that developers of software currently have rights to at least some aspects of what they have created. If I borrow, say, your copy of Microsoft Word or a popular game program and install them on the hard disk of my computer without the authorization of the developer, it is clear that I have thereby violated the rights of the programs' makers. Software piracy, of course, is neither a recent phenomenon nor an uncommon one. Unauthorized copying of software is so pervasive, in fact, that some question whether it really is wrong after all. The readings for this chapter explore this issue.

PRIVACY AND TECHNOLOGY

As already explained, more and more computers, both commercial and private, are interconnected via the Internet. The ability of cyberspace to collect, store, and retrieve personal information is seemingly limitless. There are database firms that collect medical histories, credit histories, worker's compensation claims, criminal records, and even records of magazine subscriptions. The information from such databases can be collected to manufacture an electronic dossier of prospective employees or customers. Because such databases are in use today, with very little regulation concerning how the information contained within them is to be collected or used, some have asked how we are properly to balance the interests of these firms with the individual's desire for privacy. Employers might argue that information about a prospective employee is a legitimate business interest, and perhaps even a necessity. Marketing firms would argue that compilations of consumer buying patterns would allow firms to produce goods and services that consumers desire. Surely this is true but, as we saw in Chapter 5, individuals do have a legitimate interest in what kind of information is collected about them and how this information is put to use. To lose control over this infor-

Privacy and the ECPA

The primary source of protection of privacy with regard to various forms of communication in cyberspace is the Electronic Communications Privacy Act (ECPA), passed by Congress in 1986. The ECPA's prohibitions are outlined in the table below.

ECPA Prohibition	Examples of Violations
Interception of electronic communication	• Keystroke monitoring • Tapping a data line • Rerouting an electronic communication to provide simultaneous acquisition
Unauthorized access to electronic communication service	• Obtaining an account through "hacking" • Using inadvertently granted authority to read or alter another's e-mail • Using a bug or other system flaw to read other users' private messages • Preventing others from accessing their stored private messages
Disclosure of electronic communications	• Divulging the contents of e-mail to which you were not a party

SOURCE: Edward Cavazos and Gavino Morin, *Cyberspace and the Law* (Cambridge: MIT Press, 1994), 23.

mation is to lose control over how the relationships with these organizations is shaped. As Deborah Johnson notes,

> Information about us is what allows an organization such as a marketing firm, a credit card company, or a law enforcement agency to establish a relationship with us. And information determines how we are treated in that relationship. You are sent an offer to sign up for a credit card when the credit card company gets your name and address and finds out how much you earn or own. How much credit is extended depends on this information. . . . The nature of the relationship depends on the information received.[4]

The question of how to shape the nature of the relationship between individual and institution is particularly acute when one thinks of the relationship between an employer and an employee. Employers regularly use computers as surveillance devices of an employee's work performance. A program may measure the amount of time an employee spends at a terminal, or the number of keystrokes registered within a given period of time. These quantitative measures may be used to evaluate performance, to decide on raises or promotions, or to determine whether the employee should be replaced by a computer. Many complain that such practices overlook the qualitative aspects of work performance—whether the employee is inputting garbage or producing good work. Particularly alarming to some civil rights activists is the current practice by some firms of inspecting e-mail messages composed in-house. Should these messages be regarded as off-limits to supervisors? Do they deserve the same protection as ordinary mail? This question is pursued in the readings.

TECHNOLOGY AND THE QUALITY OF WORK LIFE

A final concern explored in this chapter addresses the question of how computer technology might affect the conditions of work itself. In March 1996 the National Commission for Employment Policy presented a report intended to assess the employment consequences of the computer revolution. The commission determined something obvious to us now in this decade, at least to anyone who has called the bank and tried to speak to a human being or carried on a monologue at the local ATM: The new technology can displace workers. Whether this happens or not is usually something beyond the workers' control. Often it happens that such decisions are made unilaterally by management, motivated by perceived market pressures. Sometimes the easiest way to increase profits is to diminish labor costs, and computerization can help in this regard. Workers may find their jobs "de-skilled" with the help of computers: Computerized cash registers, for example, eliminate the need for checkers to make change; automated directory assistance removes the need for telephone operators to speak to anyone. The end result for workers might be drab and unsatisfying jobs.

But to others the personal computer and inexpensive access to the Internet or telephone lines is a benefit for workers. Many jobs presently are dependent only on devices of this kind. This fact has allowed for the tremendous growth of telecommuting: the substitution

---

⌘ Computers and Interactions Within the Workplace

To a large extent, business communications are now mediated by new computer technology. Rather than engage in time-consuming meetings and other forms of face-to-face interaction, employees are increasingly relying upon e-mail for speedy albeit impersonal communication. According to Michael Shrage, a research associate at MIT, "If an organization isn't setting up its own 'intranet' with each and every employee having his own World Wide Web home page, it's using IBM/Lotus Notes or GroupWise to share information across the enterprise." Digital networks are quickly becoming the dominant medium for managing work. Boeing Corporation used a high-level computer to manage the development of one of its new passenger jets. This software had the capacity to alert engineers whenever their proposed design changes interfered with other design requirements, for example, when a hydraulic system modification interfered with the electrical system. Boeing management discovered that some of its engineers were deliberately making modifications that would interfere with other systems. This wasn't industrial sabotage; the point was to discover who the other engineers were so that they could all get together (face-to-face) to talk about their designs. Shrage comments: "The irony . . . is that as it becomes ever easier and cheaper to automate various facets of face-to-face relationships, what's seemingly left behind becomes even more important. Those casual chats in the cafeteria, the chance encounter in the elevator, the upper-management retreat at the resort—all assume disproportionate significance precisely because they are part of the dwindling share of organizational time devoted to physical interaction." Shrage thinks that cases like this show that certain human interactions should not be mediated by computers. Yet, he concludes, computer mediation does force members of an organization to reconsider the question of how they want to communicate with each other and the quality of those communications.

Source: *Los Angeles Times* 10/19/96: D1.

of telecommunication by modem and phone line for physical travel to work.[5] Indeed, telecommuting can save time and gasoline. Nice as this might be for professionals and employers, others are concerned about the effects of this technology upon lesser-skilled workers. Telecommuting holds out the promise of making virtually anyone who has the requisite skills an entrepreneur. Some have touted telecommuting as a means of preserving the nuclear family, since it could allow at least one parent the opportunity to stay home with the children and still produce an additional income. Yet telecommuting can amount to an establishment of a cottage industry in which workers buy their own tools and absorb overhead costs (such as energy usage, software, and dedicated phone lines) in order to perform relatively low-level and de-skilled tasks (such as data entry), perhaps under the continual scrutiny of computer programs monitoring their every keystroke. Of course, this arrangement would diminish employer costs, and if the employee complains, there is the threat of moving an operation to "offshore offices," where the same work could be done at an even lower cost.

THE READINGS

The selections for this chapter begin with a case study that illustrates the resources that current information technology makes available to employers to monitor the communications of their workers. Following this case is a pair of essays that take very different views of the impact of the revolution in information technology upon the nature of work in the twenty-first century. Bill Gates, the billionaire president of software giant Microsoft Corporation, shares his optimistic vision of the dawning Information Age. According to Gates, such devices as "wallet PCs" and "personal agents" will allow workers to travel the information superhighway in ways now scarcely imaginable. Author Jeremy Rifkin is less sanguine about the benefits the Information Age will bring to the workplace. Rifkin details the many ways in which he believes that information technology is just beginning to work a fundamental change in the economy. An elite labor force, Rifkin argues, is rapidly replacing many more-traditional niches in the economy, leaving an increasing number of people without steady, full-time employment. Rifkin suggests ways in which the plight of workers can be alleviated in the twenty-first century.

The readings then turn to more-specific moral issues raised by information and computing technology. Eugene Spafford critically examines the reasons commonly offered justifying unauthorized computer intrusions. Spafford is unconvinced by the arguments typically given for such break-ins. Hackers are rarely in a position, Spafford points out, to reliably forecast the long-term effects of their intrusions; moreover, Spafford believes, no computer break-in can ever truly be said to be harmless. Spafford's essay is followed by one from Helen Nissenbaum, who discusses the dilemma posed by users of computer programs who wish to make unauthorized copies of them. Are such actions innocent? Or are they wrongful violations of the rights of the software developers? Nissenbaum contends that a strongly "no copy" regime serves only the interests of the software makers. At least some unauthorized copying, she argues, is morally permissible, though she does not endorse the entire abandonment of proprietary protection for software products.

Problems of privacy in cyberspace are taken up by Richard Spinello. Central to Spinello's discussion is the concept of informed consent. If we are committed to the view that privacy is a significant human interest, the informed consent of those from who information is gathered can at least help safeguard their privacy. Spinello argues that even if employers construe e-mail as corporate property, employees should be informed that their e-mail messages are being monitored. Doing so will help obviate the legal difficulties and potential morale problems, for such surveillance, argues Spinello, creates an "Orwellian atmosphere" that most employees will find oppressive and stressful.

The final reading for this chapter focuses on the implications of telecommuting technology for women in the workplace. Jan Zimmerman argues that telecommuting is not an unalloyed benefit to working women, but can in fact impose additional burdens upon them. The women who occupy these low-level positions, Zimmerman contends, often must balance this labor against their role as child-care givers.

NOTES

1. Deborah G. Johnson, *Computer Ethics,* 2d ed. (Upper Saddle River, N.J.: Prentice-Hall, 1994), 106, 107.
2. Clifford Stoll, *Silicon Snake Oil* (New York: Anchor Books, 1995), 51.
3. Richard Stallman, "Are Computer Property Rights Absolute?" in *Computers, Ethics, and Social Values,* edited by Deborah Johnson and Helen Nissenbaum (Englewood Cliffs, N.J.: Prentice-Hall, 1995).
4. Johnson, *Computer Ethics,* 91.
5. This definition is taken from Margrethe Olson and Sophia B. Primps, "Working at Home with Computers," reprinted in *Computers, Ethics, and Society,* edited by M. David Erdman, Mary B. Williams, and Claudio Gutierrez (New York: Oxford University Press, 1990).

CASE STUDY   E-Mail Policy at Johnson & Dresser

Richard A. Spinello

Jason Perry left the executive office suite of Johnson & Dresser shortly after 3:30 p.m. and returned to his own office on the floor below. He had made a rare visit to the company's Chief Operating Officer (COO) in order to discuss the company's questionable e-mail policies. The meeting had gone reasonably well and Perry was wondering about his next steps. As he checked over his notes and waited for his next appointment he reviewed the events leading up to this meeting.

Perry had joined Johnson & Dresser, a moderate sized retail brokerage firm, about seven years ago. He was hired as a senior systems analyst but within two years he was promoted to the position of Information Systems (IS) Director. He was relatively well known in the industry and aspired to work for one of the major brokerage houses on Wall Street.

A year or two after Perry's promotion he oversaw the purchase and installation of an advanced electronic mail system that would be used throughout the company. Although many were slow to make the transition to an on-line communication system, within a short time almost the entire organization became dependent on e-mail.

The new product had been introduced at several training sessions where electronic mail was frequently compared to regular postal mail and where the confidentiality of one's communications was certainly intimated. Users were not told that all of the company's e-mail messages were archived and available for future inspection at any time. Moreover, users were strongly encouraged to use e-mail for communicating with their fellow employees. The firm clearly saw this form of electronic communication as preferable to the use of phone calls or quick office visits.

Perry did not expect that Johnson & Dresser would make much use of the archived messages, but when an insider trading scandal broke at the firm it was decided to check the e-mail of sev-

---

eral brokers who had been implicated. All of the brokers involved resigned quietly and nothing further came of the matter. The brokerage house had a strong reputation on Wall Street for integrity, and always acted quickly when there were problems of this nature. The company was keenly aware of the importance of an unimpeachable reputation in order to maintain its current clients and attract new business.

In the aftermath of this potential scandal senior managers at the firm decided to routinely inspect employee e-mail. This was to make sure that no one else was involved in the insider trading scandal and to ferret out any other compliance problems or suspicious behavior. As a result some managers regularly asked for a compilation of e-mail messages before an employee's annual review. In the vast majority of cases they found nothing incriminating or damaging in these messages and the individuals never knew that anyone had been checking their electronic mail messages.

But there were some exceptions to this. One incident that bothered Perry a great deal involved a young analyst named Lisa Curry. She was a 10-year veteran at the company responsible for following the utility industry. She worked closely with brokers, providing reports and advice on various utility stocks. Like others at Johnson & Dresser, she was a little wary at first of using the e-mail system. Soon, however, she came to heavily rely on electronic mail for a large portion of her communications with her fellow employees. Indeed over time she felt much less inhibited when she composed e-mail messages. Thus, although she was usually pretty diffident around the company, she found herself engaging in some intense e-mail discussions with one of the few women brokers at the firm, Margaret Leonard. She often sent Leonard messages that complained about sexist corporate policies or messages that conveyed the latest company gossip. None of these messages were especially incendiary or provocative but they were fairly critical of Johnson & Dresser. Also, on occasion she criticized her boss for his lack of sensitivity on certain issues; she was perturbed, for example, at his condescending attitude toward some of the other women analysts.

Curry never dreamed that anyone would ever see these messages. Leonard assured her that she promptly erased the messages right after she read them. Curry let her know that she did the same with Leonard's messages. Both of them assumed that when they hit the delete key the messages would be permanently erased from the system. When Curry was due for her annual review her manager decided to check her e-mail communications and found the messages which she sent to Leonard. He was furious that she was so critical of Johnson & Dresser and also chastised her for wasting so much time sending "trivial, gossipy" e-mail messages. He told her that she did not seem to be a real team player and that maybe she should look around for a company that had a philosophy closer to her own. The end result was that despite her excellent track record as an analyst Curry received a small salary increment and a mixed performance review.

Curry was completely shocked by this. She could not believe that her messages were not considered completely confidential. She expected such confidentiality especially since she was not told anything to the contrary. Indeed, in her view she had been led to believe by the IS department that her privacy would be protected.

Among those she called in the company to complain about her treatment was Perry. She told him that his department's training sessions had duped people into believing that their e-mail messages would be confidential. She also pointed out that users should be told that messages would be archived and might be available for future scrutiny. Finally she stressed that she would be loath to continue using e-mail if everything she wrote would one day be scrutinized by her manager and "God knows who else at this paranoid company!"

Perry was sympathetic. He had received a few other complaints, and was beginning to question the company's fairness. He told Curry that he would look into the matter and try to craft a more open and responsible policy. He could make no promises since he knew that others in the company would need to be involved in any such policy emendations. Perry felt sorry for what happened to Curry, and he did not want to see other employees get blindsided in the same way that she did.

Consequently, Perry decided to ask for a meeting with the Chief Operating Officer in order to broach the issue of a revised e-mail policy that would better protect the privacy of Johnson & Dresser employees. During this session Perry argued that the company should probably at least take steps to inform employees that their messages were being stored and might be intercepted. However, while the COO did not disagree, he was worried about the ramifications of announcing to everyone that e-mail was being monitored. For one thing users might be less inclined to use e-mail, and the productivity gains realized by adopting this technology would be lost.

When asked about the legal implications of all this, Perry noted that according to current law the company was well within its rights to read an employee's e-mail. He wondered, however, if the company was living up to its high moral ideals by inspecting these messages. Isn't it a violation of confidentiality to read someone's postal letters? Why should electronic mail be any different? Should the company be proactive and declare electronic mail off limits except under unusual circumstances? Should it even continue to collect and store the large volume of e-mail messages generated by its many employees?

The COO was ambivalent about these suggestions, and he pointed out to Perry how the policy of archiving and inspecting e-mail helped the firm to uncover the insider trading scandal and take swift action. Maybe it needed to compromise employee privacy sometimes in order to protect the company against such abuses in the future. The more sources it could tap, the better it could discover problems and ensure that everyone at Johnson & Dresser was complying with the regulations of the Securities and Exchange Commission (SEC).

As the meeting came to a conclusion Perry was told to propose and defend a tenable and responsible e-mail policy that could be presented to the Executive Committee. He now began to think about what that policy should be. Clearly, there were many complex issues to untangle and key decisions to make.

Information and Our Interactive Future

Bill Gates

What do you carry on your person now? Probably at least keys, identification, money, and a watch. Quite possibly you also carry credit cards, a checkbook, traveler's checks, an address book, an appointment book, a notepad, reading material, a camera, a pocket tape recorder, a cellular phone, a pager, concert tickets, a map, a compass, a calculator, an electronic entry card, photographs, and perhaps a loud whistle to summon help.

You'll be able to keep all these and more in an information appliance we call the wallet PC. It will be about the same size as a wallet, which means you'll be able to carry it in your pocket or purse. It

will display messages and schedules and also let you read or send electronic mail and faxes, monitor weather and stock reports, and play both simple and sophisticated games. At a meeting you might take notes, check your appointments, browse information if you're bored, or choose from among thousands of easy-to-call-up photos of your kids.

Rather than holding paper currency, the new wallet will store unforgeable digital money. Today when you hand someone a dollar bill, check, gift certificate, or other negotiable instrument, the transfer of paper represents a transfer of funds. But money does not have to be expressed on paper. Credit card charges and wired funds are exchanges of digital financial information. Tomorrow the wallet PC will make it easy for anyone to spend and accept digital funds. Your wallet will link into a store's computer to allow money to be transferred without any physical exchange at a cash register. Digital cash will be used in interpersonal transactions, too. If your son needs money, you might digitally slip five bucks from your wallet PC to his.

When wallet PCs are ubiquitous, we can eliminate the bottlenecks that now plague airport terminals, theaters, and other locations where people queue to show identification or a ticket. As you pass through an airport gate, for example, your wallet PC will connect to the airport's computers and verify that you have paid for a ticket. You won't need a key or magnetic card key to get through doors either. Your wallet PC will identify you to the computer controlling the lock.

As cash and credit cards begin to disappear, criminals may target the wallet PC, so there will have to be safeguards to prevent a wallet PC from being used in the same manner as a stolen charge card. The wallet PC will store the "keys" you'll use to identify yourself. You will be able to invalidate your keys easily, and they will be changed regularly. For some important transactions, just having the key in your wallet PC won't be enough. One solution is to have you enter a password at the time of the transaction. Automatic teller machines ask you to provide a personal identification number, which is just a very short password. Another option, which would eliminate the need for you to remember a password, is the use of biometric measurements. Individual biometric measurements are more secure and almost certainly will be included eventually in some wallet PCs.

A biometric security system records a physical trait, such as a voiceprint or a fingerprint. For example, your wallet PC might demand that you read aloud a random word that it flashes on its screen or that you press your thumb against the side of the device whenever you are about to conduct a transaction with significant financial implications. The wallet will compare what it "heard" or "felt" with its digital record of your voice- or thumbprint.

Wallet PCs with the proper equipment will be able to tell you exactly where you are anyplace on the face of Earth. The Global Positioning System (GPS) satellites in an orbit around Earth broadcast signals that permit jetliners, oceangoing boats, and cruise missiles, or hikers with handheld GPS receivers, to know their exact location to within a few hundred feet. Such devices are currently available

for a few hundred dollars, and they will be built into many wallet PCs.

The wallet PC will connect you to the information highway while you travel a real highway, and tell you where you are. Its built-in speaker will be able to dictate directions to let you know that a freeway exit is coming up or that the next intersection has frequent accidents. It will monitor digital traffic reports and warn you that you'd better leave for an airport early, or suggest an alternate route. The wallet PC's color maps will overlay your location with whatever kinds of information you desire—road and weather conditions, campgrounds, scenic spots, even fast-food outlets. You might ask, "Where's the nearest Chinese restaurant that is still open?" and the information requested will be transmitted to the wallet by wireless network. Off the roads, on a hike in the woods, it will be your compass and as useful as your Swiss Army knife. . . .

Prices will vary, but generally wallet PCs will be priced about the way cameras are today. Simple, single-purpose "smart cards" for digital currency will cost about what a disposable camera does now, whereas, like an elaborate camera, a really sophisticated wallet PC might cost $1,000 or more, but it will outperform the most exotic computer of just a decade ago. Smart cards, the most basic form of the wallet PC, look like credit cards and are popular now in Europe. Their microprocessors are embedded within the plastic. The smart card of the future will identify its owner and store digital money, tickets, and medical information. It won't have a screen, audio capabilities, or any of the more elaborate options of the more expensive wallet PCs. It will be handy for travel or as a backup, and may be sufficient by itself for some people's uses. . . .

No matter what form the PC takes, users will still have to be able to navigate their way through its applications. Think of the way you use your television remote control today to choose what you want to watch. Future systems with more choices will have to do better. They'll have to avoid making you go step-by-step through all the options. Instead of having to remember which channel number to use to find a program, you will be shown a graphical menu and be able to select what you want by pointing to an easy-to-understand image.

You won't necessarily have to point to make your point. Eventually we'll also be able to speak to our televisions, personal computers, or other information appliances. At first we'll have to keep to a limited vocabulary, but eventually our exchanges will become quite conversational. This capability requires powerful hardware and software, because conversation that a human can understand effortlessly is very hard for a computer to interpret. Already, voice recognition works fine for a small set of predefined commands, such as "Call my sister." It's much more difficult for a computer to decipher an arbitrary sentence, but in the next ten years this too will become possible. . . .

One of the worries most often expressed about the highway concerns "information overload." It is usually voiced by someone who imagines, rather aptly, that the fiber-optic cables of the information highway will be like enormous pipes spewing out large quantities of information.

Information overload is not unique to the highway, and it needn't be a problem. We already cope with astonishing amounts of information by relying on an extensive infrastructure that has evolved to help us be selective—everything from library catalogs to movie reviews to the Yellow Pages to recommendations from friends. When people worry about the information-overload problem, ask them to consider how they choose what to read. When we visit a bookstore or a library we don't worry about reading every volume. We get by without reading everything because there are navigational aids that point to information of interest and help us find the print material we want. These pointers include the corner newsstand, the Dewey decimal system in libraries, and book reviews in the local newspaper.

On the information highway, technology and editorial services will combine to offer a number of ways to help us find information. The ideal navigation system will be powerful, expose seemingly limitless information, and yet remain very easy to use. Software will offer queries, filters, spatial navigation, hyperlinks, and agents as the primary selection techniques. . . .

Here's how the different systems will work. A query, as its name indicates, is a question. You will be able to ask a wide range of questions and get complete answers. If you can't recall the name of a movie but you remember that it starred Spencer Tracy and Katharine Hepburn and that there is a scene in which he's asking a lot of questions and she's shivering, then you could type in a query that

asks for all movies that match: "Spencer Tracy," "Katharine Hepburn," "cold," and "questions." In reply, a server on the highway would list the 1957 romantic comedy *Desk Set*, in which Tracy quizzes a shivering Hepburn on a rooftop terrace in the middle of winter. You could watch the scene, watch the whole film, read the script, examine reviews of the movie, and read any comments that Tracy or Hepburn might have made publicly about the scene. If a dubbed or subtitled print had been made for release outside English-speaking countries, you could watch the foreign versions. They might be stored on servers in various countries but would be instantly available to you.

The system will accommodate straightforward queries such as "Show me all the articles that ran worldwide about the first test-tube baby," or "List all the stores that carry two or more kinds of dog food and will deliver a case within sixty minutes to my home address," or "Which of my relatives have I been out of touch with for more than three months?" It will also be able to deliver answers to much more complex queries. You might ask, "Which major city has the greatest percentage of the people who watch rock videos and regularly read about international trade?" Generally, queries won't require much response time, because most of the questions are likely to have been asked before and the answers will already have been computed and stored.

You'll also be able to set up "filters," which are really just standing queries. Filters will work around the clock, watching for new information that matches an interest of yours, filtering out everything else. You will be able to program a filter to gather information on your particular interests, such as news about local sports teams or particular scientific discoveries. If the most important thing to you is the weather, your filter will put that at the top of your personalized newspaper. Some filters will be created automatically by your computer, based on its information about your background and areas of interest. Such a filter might alert me to an important event regarding a person or institution from my past: "Meteorite crashes into Lakeside School." You will also be able to create an explicit filter. That will be an ongoing request for something particular, such as "Wanted: 1990 Nissan Maxima for parts," or "Tell me about anybody selling memorabilia from the last World Cup," or

"Is anyone around here looking for someone to bi-cycle with on Sunday afternoons, rain or shine?" The filter will keep looking until you call off the search. If a filter finds a potential Sunday bicycling companion, for instance, it will automatically check on any other information the person might have published on the network. It will try to answer the question "What's he like?"—which is the first question you'd be likely to ask about a potential new friend.

Spatial navigation will be modeled on the way we locate information today. When we want to find out about some subject now, it's natural to go to a labeled section of a library or bookstore. Newspapers have sports, real estate, and business sections where people "go" for certain kinds of news. In most newspapers, weather reports appear in the same general location day after day.

Spatial navigation, which is already being used in some software products, will let you go where the information is by enabling you to interact with a visual model of a real or make-believe world. You can think of such a model as a map—an illustrated, three-dimensional table of contents. Spatial navigation will be particularly important for interacting with televisions and small, portable PCs, which are unlikely to have conventional keyboards. To do some banking, you might go to a drawing of a main street, then point, using a mouse or a remote control or even your finger, at the drawing of a bank. You will point to a courthouse to find out which cases are being heard by which judges or what the backlog is. You will point to the ferry terminal to learn the schedule and whether the boats are running on time. If you are considering visiting a hotel, you will be able to find out when rooms are available and look at a floor plan, and if the hotel has a video camera connected to the highway, you might be able to look at its lobby and restaurant and see how crowded it is at the moment. . . .

Spatial navigation can also be used for touring. If you want to see reproductions of the artwork in a museum or gallery, you'll be able to "walk" through a visual representation, navigating among the works much as if you were physically there. For details about a painting or sculpture, you would use a hyperlink. No crowds, no rush, and you could ask anything without worrying about seeming uninformed. You would bump into interesting things, just as you do in a real gallery. Navigat-

ing through a virtual gallery won't be like walking through a real art gallery, but it will be a rewarding approximation—just as watching a ballet or basketball game on television can be entertaining even though you're not in the theater or stadium.

If other people are visiting the same "museum," you will be able to choose to see them and interact with them or not, as you please. Your visits needn't be solitary experiences. Some locations will be used purely for cyberspace socialization; in others no one will be visible. Some will force you to appear to some degree as you are; others won't. The way you look to other users will depend on your choices and the rules of the particular location.

If you are using spatial navigation, the place you're moving around in won't have to be real. You'll be able to set up imaginary places and return to them whenever you want. In your own museum, you'll be able to move walls, add imaginary galleries, and rearrange the art. You might want all still lifes to displayed together, even if one is a fragment of a Pompeian fresco that hangs in a gallery of ancient Roman art and one is a Cubist Picasso from a twentieth-century gallery. You will be able to play curator and gather images of your favorite artworks from around the world to "hang" in a gallery of your own. Suppose you want to include a warmly remembered painting of a man asleep being nuzzled by a lion, but you can't recall either the artist or where you saw it. The information highway won't make you go looking for the information. You'll be able to describe what you want by posing a query. The query will start your computer or other information appliance sifting through a reservoir of information to deliver those pieces that match your request. . . .

The last type of navigational aid, and in many ways the most useful of all, is an agent. This is a filter that has taken on a personality and seems to show initiative. An agent's job is to assist you. In the Information Age, that means the agent is there to help you find information.

To understand the ways an agent can help with a variety of tasks, consider how it could improve today's PC interface. The present state of the art in user interface is the graphical user interface, such as Apple's Macintosh and Microsoft Windows, which depicts information and relationships on the screen instead of just describing them in text. Graphical interfaces also allow the user to point to and move objects—including pictures—around on the screen.

But the graphical user interface isn't easy enough for future systems. We've put so many options on the screen that programs or features that are not used regularly have become daunting. The features are great and fast for people familiar with the software, but for the average user not enough guidance comes from the machine for him or her to feel comfortable. Agents will remedy that.

Agents will know how to help you partly because the computer will remember your past activities. It will be able to find patterns of use that will help it work more effectively with you. Through the magic of software, information appliances connected to the highway will appear to learn from your interactions and will make suggestions to you. I call this "softer software."

Software allows hardware to perform a number of functions, but once the program is written, it stays the same. Softer software will appear to get smarter as you use it. It will learn about your requirements in pretty much the same way a human assistant does and, like a human assistant, will become more helpful as it learns about you and your work. The first day a new assistant is on the job, you can't simply ask him to format a document like another memo you wrote a few weeks ago. You can't say, "Send a copy to everybody who should know about this." But over the course of months and years, the assistant becomes more valuable as he picks up on what is typical routine and how you like things done.

The computer today is like a first-day assistant. It needs explicit first-day instructions all the time. And it remains a first-day assistant forever. It will never make one iota of adjustment as a response to its experience with you. We're working to perfect softer software. No one should be stuck with an assistant, in this case software, that doesn't learn from experience.

If an agent that could learn were available now, I would want it to take over certain functions for me. For instance, it would be very helpful if it could scan every project schedule, note the changes, and distinguish the ones I had to pay attention to from the ones I didn't. It would learn the criteria for what needed my attention: the size of the project, what other projects are dependent on it, the cause and the length of any delay. It would learn when a two-week slip could be ignored, and when such a

slip indicates real trouble and I'd better look into it right away before it gets worse. It will take time to achieve this goal, partly because it's difficult, as with an assistant, to find the right balance between initiative and routine. We don't want to overdo it. If the built-in agent tries to be too smart and anticipates and confidently performs unrequested or undesired services, it will be annoying to users who are accustomed to having explicit control over their computers.

When you use an agent, you will be in a dialogue with a program that behaves to some degree like a person. It could be that the software mimics the behavior of a celebrity or a cartoon character as it assists you. An agent that takes on a personality provides a "social user interface." A number of companies, including Microsoft, are developing agents with social-user-interface capabilities. Agents won't replace the graphical-user-interface software, but, rather, will supplement it by providing a character of your choosing to assist you. The character will disappear when you get to the parts of the product you know very well. But if you hesitate or ask for help, the agent will reappear and offer assistance. You may even come to think of the agent as a collaborator, built right into the software. It will remember what you're good at and what you've done in the past, and try to anticipate problems and suggest solutions. It will bring anything unusual to your attention. If you work on something for a few minutes and then decide to discard the revision, the agent might ask if you're sure you want to throw the work away. Some of today's software already does that. But if you were to work for two hours and then give an instruction to delete what you'd just done, the social interface would recognize that as unusual and possibly a serious mistake on your part. The agent would say, "You've worked on this for two hours. Are you really, really sure you want to delete it?"

Some people hearing about softer software and social interface, find the idea of a humanized computer creepy. But I believe even they will come to like it, once they have tried it. We humans tend to anthropomorphize. Animated movies take advantage of this tendency. *The Lion King* is not very realistic, nor does it try to be. Anybody could distinguish little Simba from a live lion cub on film. When a car breaks down or a computer crashes, we are apt to yell at it, or curse it, or even ask why it let us down. We know better, of course, but still tend to treat inanimate objects as if they were alive and had free will. Researchers at universities and software companies are exploring how to make computer interfaces more effective, using this human tendency. In programs such as Microsoft Bob, they have demonstrated that people will treat mechanical agents that have personalities with a surprising degree of deference. It has also been found that users' reactions differed depending on whether the agent's voice was female or male. Recently we worked on a project that involved users rating their experience with a computer. When we had the computer the users had worked with ask for an evaluation of its performance, the responses tended to be positive. But when we had a second computer ask the same people to evaluate their encounters with the first machine, the people were significantly more critical. Their reluctance to criticize the first computer "to its face" suggested that they didn't want to hurt its feelings, even though they knew it was only a machine. Social interfaces may not be suitable for all users or all situations, but I think that we'll see lots of them in the future because they "humanize" computers.

Will There Be a Job for Me in the New Information Age?

Jeremy Rifkin

This is the question that most worries American voters—and the question that American politicians seem most determined to sidestep. President Bill Clinton warns workers that they will have to be retrained six or seven times during their work lives to match the dizzying speed of technological change. Speaker of the House Newt Gingrich talks about the "end of the traditional job" and advises every American worker to become his or her own independent contractor.

But does the president really think 124 million Americans can reinvent themselves every five years to keep up with a high-tech marketplace? Does Gingrich honestly believe every American can become a freelance entrepreneur, continually hustling contracts for short-term work assignments?

Buffeted by these unrealistic employment expectations, American workers are increasingly sullen and pessimistic. . . . While corporate profits are heading through the roof, average families struggle to keep a roof over their heads. More than one-fifth of the workforce is trapped in temporary assignments or works only part time. Millions of others have slipped quietly out of the economy and into an underclass no longer counted in the permanent employment figures. A staggering 15 percent of the population now lives below the official poverty line.

Both Clinton and Gingrich have asked American workers to remain patient. They explain that declining incomes represent only short-term adjustments. Democrats and Republicans alike beseech the faithful to place their trust in the high-tech future—to journey with them into cyberspace and become pioneers on the new electronic frontier. Their enthusiasm for technological marvels has an almost camp ring to it. If you didn't know better, you might suspect Mickey and Pluto were taking you on a guided tour through the Epcot Center.

Jittery and genuinely confused over the yawning gap between the official optimism of the politicians and their own personal plight, middle- and working-class American families seem to be holding on to a tiny thread of hope that the vast productivity gains of the high-tech revolution will somehow "trickle down" to them in the form of better jobs, wages, and benefits.

Few politicians and economists are paying attention to the underlying causes of—dare we say it?—the new "malaise" gripping the country. Throughout the welfare reform debate, for example, members of both parties trotted onto the House and Senate floors to urge an end to welfare and demand that all able-bodied men and women find jobs. Maverick Sen. Paul Simon (D-Ill.) was virtually alone in raising the troubling question: "What jobs?"

Jeremy Rifkin, "Vanishing Jobs." From *Mother Jones* magazine, © 1995, Foundation for National Progress. Reprinted by permission.

The hard reality is that the global economy is in the midst of a transformation as significant as the Industrial Revolution. We are in the early stages of a shift from "mass labor" to highly skilled "elite labor," accompanied by increasing automation in the production of goods and the delivery of services. Sophisticated computers, robots, telecommunications, and other Information Age technologies are replacing human beings in nearly every sector. Factory workers, secretaries, receptionists, clerical workers, salesclerks, bank tellers, telephone operators, librarians, wholesalers, and middle managers are just a few of the many occupations destined for virtual extinction. In the United States alone, as many as 90 million jobs in a labor force of 124 million are potentially vulnerable to displacement by automation.

A few mainstream economists pin their hopes on increasing job opportunities in the knowledge sector. Secretary of Labor Robert Reich, for example, talks incessantly of the need for more highly skilled technicians, computer programmers, engineers, and professional workers. He barnstorms the country urging workers to retrain, retool, and reinvent themselves in time to gain a coveted place on the high-tech express.

The secretary ought to know better. Even if the entire workforce could be retrained for very skilled, high-tech jobs—which, of course, it can't—there will never be enough positions in the elite knowledge sector to absorb the millions let go as automation penetrates into every aspect of the production process.

It's not as if this is a revelation. For years the Tofflers of the world have lectured the rest of us that the end of the industrial age also means the end of "mass production" and "mass labor." What they never mention is what "the masses" should do after they become redundant.

Laura D'Andrea Tyson, of the National Economic Council, argues that the Information Age will bring a plethora of new technologies and products that we can't as yet even anticipate, and therefore it will create many new kinds of jobs. After a debate with me on CNN, Tyson noted that when the automobile replaced the horse and buggy, some people lost their jobs in the buggy trade but many more found work on the assembly line. Tyson believes that the same operating rules will govern the information era.

Tyson's argument is compelling. Still, I can't help but think that she may be wrong. Even if thousands of new products come along, they are likely to be manufactured in near-workerless factories and marketed by near-virtual companies requiring ever-smaller, more highly skilled workforces.

This steady decline of mass labor threatens to undermine the very foundations of the modern American state. For nearly 200 years, the heart of the social contract and the measure of individual human worth have centered on the value of each person's labor. How does society even begin to adjust to a new era in which labor is devalued or even rendered worthless?

This is not the first time the issue of devalued human labor has arisen in the history of the United States. The first group of Americans to be marginalized by the automation revolution was black men, more than 40 years ago. Their story is a bellwether.

In the mid-1950s, automation began to take a toll on the nation's factories. Hardest hit were unskilled jobs in the industries where black workers concentrated. Between 1953 and 1962, 1.6 million blue-collar manufacturing jobs were lost. In an essay, "Problems of the Negro Movement," published in 1964, civil rights activist Tom Kahn quipped, "It's as if racism, having put the Negro in his economic place, stepped aside to watch technology destroy that 'place.'"

Millions of African-American workers and their families became part of a perpetually unemployed "underclass" whose unskilled labor was no longer required in the mainstream economy. Vanquished and forgotten, many urban blacks vented their frustration and anger by taking to the streets. The rioting began in Watts in 1965 and spread east to Detroit and other Northern industrial cities.

Today, the same technological and economic forces are beginning to affect large numbers of white male workers. Many of the disaffected white men who make up ultraright-wing organizations are high school or community college graduates with limited skills who are forced to compete for a diminishing number of agricultural, manufacturing, and service jobs. While they blame affirmative action programs, immigrant groups, and illegal aliens for their woes, these men miss the real cause of their plight—technological innovations that devalue their labor. Like African-American men in the 1960s, the new militants view the government and law enforcement agencies as the enemy. They see a grand conspiracy to deny them their basic freedoms and constitutional rights. And they are arming themselves for a revolution.

The Information Age may present difficulties for the captains of industry as well. By replacing more and more workers with machines, employers will eventually come up against the two economic Achilles' heels of the Information Age. The first is a simple problem of supply and demand: If mass numbers of people are underemployed or unemployed, who's going to buy the flood of products and services being churned out?

The second Achilles' heel for business—and one never talked about—is the effect on capital accumulation when vast numbers of employees are let go or hired on a temporary basis so that employers can avoid paying out benefits—especially pension fund benefits. As it turns out, pension funds, now worth more than $5 trillion in the United States alone, keep much of the capitalist system afloat. For nearly 25 years, the pension funds of millions of workers have served as a forced savings pool that has financed capital investments.

Pension funds account for 74 percent of net individual savings, more than one-third of all corporate equities, and nearly 40 percent of all corporate bonds. Pension assets exceed the assets of commercial banks and make up nearly one-third of the total financial assets of the U.S. economy. In 1993 alone, pension funds made new investments of between $1 trillion and $1.5 trillion.

If too many workers are let go or marginalized into jobs without pension benefits, the capitalist system is likely to collapse slowly in on itself as employers drain it of the workers' funds necessary for new capital investments. In the final analysis, sharing the vast productivity gains of the Information Age is absolutely essential to guarantee the well-being of management, stockholders, labor, and the economy as a whole.

Sadly, while our politicians gush over the great technological breakthroughs that lie ahead in cyberspace, not a single elected official, in either political party, is raising the critical question of how we can ensure that the productivity gains of the Information Age are shared equitably.

In the past, when new technology increased productivity—such as in the 1920s when oil and electricity replaced coal- and steam-powered plants—American workers organized collectively to demand a shorter workweek and better pay and benefits. Today, employers are shortening not the

workweek, but the workforce—effectively preventing millions of American workers from enjoying the benefits of the technology revolution.

Organized labor has been weakened by 40 years of automation, a decline in union membership, and a growing temp workforce that is difficult to organize. In meetings with union officials, I have found that they are universally reluctant to deal with the notion that mass labor—the very basis of trade unionism—will continue to decline and may even disappear altogether. Several union leaders confided to me off the record that the labor movement is in survival mode and trying desperately to prevent a rollback of legislation governing basic rights to organize. Union leaders cannot conceive that they may have to rethink their mission in order to accommodate a fundamental change in the nature of work. But the unions' continued reluctance to grapple with a technology revolution that might eliminate mass labor could spell their own elimination from American life over the next three or four decades.

Working women may hold the key to whether organized labor can reinvent itself in time to survive the Information Age. Women now make up about half of the U.S. workforce, and a majority of employed women provide half or more of their household's income.

In addition to holding down a 40-hour job, working women often manage the household as well. Significantly, nearly 44 percent of all employed women say they would prefer more time with their family to more money.

This is one reason many progressive labor leaders believe the rebirth of the American labor movement hinges on organizing women workers. The call for a 30-hour workweek is a powerful rallying cry that could unite trade unions, women's groups, parenting organizations, churches, and synagogues. Unfortunately, the voice of trade union women is not often heard inside the inner sanctum of the AFL-CIO executive council. Of the 83 unions in the AFL-CIO, only one is headed by a woman.

The women's movement, trapped in struggles over abortion, discriminatory employment practices, and sexual harassment, has also failed to grasp the enormous opportunity brought on by the Information Age. Betty Friedan, the venerable founder of the modern women's movement and someone always a step or two ahead of the crowd, is convinced that the reduction of work hours offers a way to revitalize the women's movement, and take women's interests to the center of public policy discourse.

Of course, employers will argue that shortening the workweek is too costly and would threaten their ability to compete both domestically and abroad. That need not be so. Companies like Hewlett-Packard in France and BMW in Germany have reduced their workweek while continuing to pay workers at the same weekly rate. In return, the workers have agreed to work shifts. Management executives reason that, if they can operate the new high-tech plants on a 24-hour basis, they can double or triple productivity and thus afford to pay workers the same.

In France, government officials are playing with the idea of forgiving the payroll taxes for employers who voluntarily reduce their workweek. While the government will lose tax revenue, economists argue that fewer people will be on welfare, and the new workers will be taxpayers with purchasing power. Employers, workers, the economy, and the government all benefit.

In this country, generous tax credits could be extended to any company willing both to reduce its workweek voluntarily and implement a profit-sharing plan so that its employees will benefit directly from productivity gains.

The biggest surprise I've encountered in the fledgling debate over rethinking work has been the response of some business leaders. I have found genuine concern among a small but growing number of business executives over the critical question of what to do with the millions of people whose labor will be needed less, or not at all, in an increasingly automated age. Many executives have close friends who have been re-engineered out of a job—replaced by the new technologies of the Information Age. Others have had to take part in the painful process of letting employees go in order to optimize the bottom line. Some tell me they worry whether their own children will be able to find a job when they enter the high-tech labor market in a few years.

To be sure, I hear moans and groans from some corporate executives when I zero in on possible solutions—although there are also more than a few nods of agreement. But still, they are willing—even eager—to talk about these critical questions. They are hungry for engagement—the kind that has been absent in the public policy arena. Until now, politicians and economists have steadfastly refused to entertain a discussion of how we prepare for a new economic era characterized by the diminishing need for mass human labor. Until we have that conversation, the fear, anger, and frustration of millions of Americans are going to grow in intensity and become manifest through increasingly hostile and extreme social and political venues.

We are long overdue for public debate over the future of work and how to share the productivity gains of the Information Age.

Are Computer Hacker Break-ins Ethical?*

Eugene H. Spafford

Introduction

On November 2, 1988, a program was run on the Internet that replicated itself on thousands of machines, often loading them to the point where they were unable to process normal requests [2–4]. This Internet Worm program was stopped in a matter of

*An earlier version of this paper appeared as [1].

Reprinted with permission from *Journal of Systems and Software* 17(1); 1992; 41–48. Elsevier Science, Inc.

hours, but the controversy engendered by its release has raged ever since. Other incidents, such as the "wily hackers"† tracked by Cliff Stoll [5], the "Legion of Doom" members who are alleged to have stolen telephone company 911 software

---

† Many law-abiding individuals consider themselves *hackers*—a term formerly used as a compliment. The press and general public have co-opted the term, however, and it is now commonly viewed as pejorative. Here, I will use the word as the general public now uses it.

[6], and the growth of the computer virus problem [7–10] have added to the discussion. What constitutes improper access to computers? Are some break-ins ethical? Is there such a thing as a "moral hacker" [11]?

It is important that we discuss these issues. The continuing evolution of our technological base and our increasing reliance on computers for critical tasks suggest that future incidents may well have more serious consequences than those we have seen to date. With human nature as varied and extreme as it is, and with the technology as available as it is, we must expect to experience more of these incidents.

In this article, I will introduce a few of the major issues that these incidents have raised, and present some arguments related to them. For clarification, I have separated several issues that often have been combined when debated, it is possible that most people agree on some of these points once they are viewed as individual issues.

What Is Ethical?

Webster's Collegiate Dictionary defines ethics as "the discipline dealing with what is good and bad and with moral duty and obligation." More simply, it is the study of what is right to do in a given situation—what we ought to do. Alternatively, it is sometimes described as the study of what is good and how to achieve that good. To suggest whether an act is right or wrong we need to agree on an ethical system that is easy to understand and apply as we consider the ethics of computer break-ins.

Philosophers have been trying for thousands of years to define right and wrong, and I will not make yet another attempt at such a definition. Instead, I will suggest that we make the simplifying assumption that we can judge the ethical nature of an act by applying a deontological assessment: regardless of the effect, is the act itself ethical? Would we view that act as sensible and proper if everyone were to engage in it? Although this may be too simplistic a model (and it can certainly be argued that other ethical philosophies may also be applied), it is a good first approximation for purposes of discussion. If you are unfamiliar with any other formal ethical evaluation method, try applying this assessment to the points I raise later in this article.

If the results are obviously unpleasant or dangerous in the large, then they should be considered unethical as individual acts.

Note that this philosophy assumes that right is determined by actions, not results. Some ethical philosophies assume that the ends justify the means: our society does not operate by such a philosophy, although many individuals do. As a society, we profess to believe that "it isn't whether you win or lose, it's how you play the game." This is why we are concerned with issues of due process and civil rights, even for those espousing repugnant views and committing heinous acts. The process is important no matter the outcome, although the outcome may help to resolve a choice between two almost equal courses of action.

Philosophies that consider the results of an act as the ultimate measure of good are often impossible to apply because of the difficulty in understanding exactly what results from any arbitrary activity. Consider an extreme example: the government orders 100 cigarette smokers, chosen at random, to be beheaded on live nationwide television. The result might well be that many hundreds of thousands of other smokers would quit cold turkey, thus prolonging their lives. It might also prevent hundreds of thousands of people from ever starting to smoke, thus improving the health and longevity of the general populace. The health of millions of other people would improve because they would no longer be subjected to secondary smoke, and the overall impact on the environment would be favorable as tons of air and ground pollutants would no longer be released by smokers or tobacco companies.

Yet, despite the great good this might hold for society, everyone, except for a few extremists, would condemn such an act as immoral. We would likely object even if only one person were executed. It would not matter what the law might be on such an issue: we would not feel that the act was morally correct, nor would we view the ends as justifying the means.

Note that we would be unable to judge the morality of such an action by evaluating the results, because we would not know the full scope of those results. Such an act might have effects, favorable or otherwise, on issues of law, public health, tobacco use, and daytime TV shows for decades or centuries to follow. A system of ethics that considered primarily only the results of our actions could not allow us to evaluate our current activities at the time when we would need such guidance: if we are unable to discern the appropriate course of action prior to its commission, then our system of ethics is of little or no value to us. To obtain ethical guidance, we must base our actions primarily on evaluations of the actions and not on the possible results.

More to the point here, if we attempt to judge the morality of a computer break-in based on the sum total of all future effect, we would be unable to make such a judgment, either for a specific incident or for the general class of acts. In part, this is because it is so difficult to determine the long-term effects of various actions and to discern their causes. We cannot know, for instance, if increased security awareness and restrictions are better for society in the long term, or whether these additional restrictions will result in greater costs and annoyance when using computer systems. We also do not know how many of these changes are directly traceable to incidents of computer break-ins.

One other point should be made here: it is undoubtedly possible to imagine scenarios where a computer break-in would be considered to be the preferable course of action. For instance, if vital medical data were on a computer and necessary to save someone's life in an emergency, but the authorized users of the system could not be located, breaking into the system might well be considered the right thing to do. However, that action does not make the break-in ethical. Rather, such situations occur when a greater wrong would undoubtedly occur if the unethical act were not committed. Similar reasoning applies to situations such as killing in self defense. In the following discussion, I will assume that such conflicts are not the root cause of the break-ins: such situations should very rarely present themselves.

Motivations

Individuals who break into computer systems or who write vandalware usually use one of several rationalizations for their actions. (See, for example, [12] and the discussion in [13].) Most of these individuals would never think to walk down a street, trying every door to find one unlocked, then search through the drawers of the furniture inside. Yet these same people seem to give no second thought to making repeated attempts at guessing passwords to accounts they do not own, and once into a system, browsing through the files on disk.

These computer burglars often give the same reasons for their actions in an attempt to rationalize their activities as morally justified. I present and refute some of the most commonly used ones: motives involving theft and revenge are not uncommon, and their moral nature is simple to discern, so I shall not include them here.

The Hacker Ethic

Many hackers argue that they follow an ethic that both guides their behavior and justifies their break-ins. This hacker ethic states, in part, that all information should be free [11]. This view holds that information belongs to everyone and there should be no boundaries or restraints to prevent anyone from examining information. Richard Stallman states much the same thing in his GNU Manifesto [14]. He and others have stated in various forums that if information is free, it logically follows that there should be no such thing as intellectual property, and no need for security.

What are the implications and consequences of such a philosophy? First and foremost, it raises some disturbing questions of privacy. If all information is (or should be) free, then privacy is no longer a possibility. For information to be free to everyone and for individuals to no longer be able to claim it as property means that anyone may access the information if they please. Furthermore, as it is no longer property of any individual, anyone can alter the information. Items such as bank balances, medical records, credit histories, employment records, and defense information all cease to be controlled. If someone controls information and controls who may access it, the information is obviously not free. But without that control, we would no longer be able to trust the accuracy of the information.

In a perfect world, this lack of privacy and control might not be cause for concern. However, if all information were to be freely available and modifiable, imagine how much damage and chaos would be caused in our real world! Our whole society is based on information whose accuracy must be assured. This includes information held by banks and other financial institutions, credit bureaus, medical agencies and professionals, government agencies such as the IRS, law enforcement agencies, and educational institutions. Clearly, treating all their information as "free" would be unethical in any world where there might be careless and unethical individuals.

Economic arguments can be made against this philosophy, too, in addition to the overwhelming need for privacy and control of information accuracy. Information is not universally free. It is held as property because of privacy concerns, and because it is often collected and developed at great expense. Development of a new algorithm or program or collection of a specialized data base may involve the expenditure of vast sums of time and effort. To claim that it is free or should be free is to express a naive and unrealistic view of the world. To use this to justify computer break-ins is clearly unethical. Although not all information currently treated as private or controlled as proprietary needs such protection, that does not justify unauthorized access to it or to any other data.

The Security Arguments

These arguments are the most common ones offered within the computer community. One argument is the same as that used most often to defend the author of the Internet Worm program in 1988: break-ins illustrate security problems to a community that will otherwise not note the problems.

In the Worm case, one of the first issues to be discussed widely in Internet mailing lists dealt with the intent of the perpetrator—exactly why the worm program had been written and released. Explanations put forth by members of the community ranged from simple accident to the actions of a sociopath. Many said that the Worm was designed to reveal security defects to a community that would not otherwise pay attention. This was not supported by the testimony of the author during his trial, nor is it supported by past experience of system administrators.

The Worm author, Robert T. Morris, appears to have been well known at some universities and major companies, and his talents were generally respected. Had he merely explained the problems or offered a demonstration to these people, he would have been listened to with considerable attention. The month before he released the Worm program on the Internet, he discovered and disclosed a bug in the file transfer program *ftp*; news of the flaw spread rapidly, and an official fix was announced and available within a matter of weeks. The argument that no one would listen to his report of security weaknesses is clearly fallacious.

In the more general case, this security argument is also without merit. Although some system administrators might have been complacent about the security of their systems before the Worm incident, most computer vendors, managers of government computer installations, and system administrators at major colleges and universities have been attentive to reports of security problems. People wishing to report a problem with the security of a system need not exploit it to report it. By way of analogy, one does not set fire to the neighborhood shopping center to bring attention to a fire hazard in one of the stores, and then try to justify the act by claiming that firemen would otherwise never listen to reports of hazards.

The most general argument that some people make is that the individuals who break into systems are performing a service by exposing security flaws, and thus should be encouraged or even rewarded. This argument is severely flawed in several ways. First, it assumes that there is some compelling need to force users to install security fixes on their systems, and thus computer burglars are justified in "breaking and entering" activities. Taken to extremes, it suggests that it would be perfectly acceptable to engage in such activities on a continuing basis, so long as they might expose security flaws. This completely loses sight of the purpose of the computers in the first place—to serve as tools and resources, not as exercises in security. The same reasoning would imply that vigilantes have the right to attempt to break into the homes in my neighborhood on a continuing basis to demonstrate that they are susceptible to burglars.

Another flaw with this argument is that it completely ignores the technical and economic factors that prevent many sites from upgrading or correcting their software. Not every site has the resources to install new system software or to correct existing software. At many sites, the systems are run as turnkey systems—employed as tools and maintained by the vendor. The owners and users of these machines simply do not have the ability to correct or maintain their systems independently, and they are unable to afford custom software support from their vendors. To break into such systems, with or without damage, is effectively to trespass into places of business: to do so in a vigilante effort to force the owners to upgrade their security structure is presumptuous and reprehensible. A burglary is not justified, morally or legally, by an argument that the victim has poor locks and was therefore "asking for it."

A related argument has been made that vendors are responsible for the maintenance of their software, and that such security breaches should immediately require vendors to issue corrections to their customers, past and present. The claim is made that without highly-visible break-ins, vendors will not produce or distribute necessary fixes to software. This attitude is naive, and is neither economically feasible nor technically workable. Certainly, vendors should bear some responsibility for the adequacy of their software [15], but they should not be responsible for fixing every possible flaw in every possible configuration.

Many sites customize their software or otherwise run systems incompatible with the latest vendor releases. For a vendor to be able to provide quick response to security problems, it would be necessary for each customer to run completely standardized software and hardware mixes to ensure the correctness of vendor-supplied updates. Not only would this be considerably less attractive for many customers and contrary to their usual practice, but the increased cost of such "instant" fix distribution would add to the price of such a system and greatly increase the cost borne by the customer. It is unreasonable to expect the user community to sacrifice flexibility and pay a much higher cost per unit simply for faster corrections to the occasional security breach, assuming it is possible for the manufacturer to find those customers and supply them with fixes in a timely manner— something unlikely in a market where machines and software are often repackaged, traded, and resold.

The case of the Internet Worm is a good example of the security argument and its flaws. It further stands as a good example of the conflict between ends and means valuation of ethics. Various people have argued that the Worm's author did us a favor by exposing security flaws. At Mr. Morris's trial on Federal charges stemming from the incident, the defense attorneys also argued that their client should not be punished because of the good the Worm did in exposing those flaws. Others, including the prosecuting attorneys, argued that the act itself was wrong no matter what the outcome. Their contention has been that the result does not justify the act itself, nor does the defense's argument encompass all the consequences of the incident.

This is certainly true: the complete results of the incident are still not known. There have been many other break-ins and network worms since November 1988, perhaps inspired by the media coverage of that incident. More attempts will possibly be made, in part inspired by Mr. Morris's act. Some sites on the Internet have restricted access to their machines, and others were removed from the network; other sites have decided not to pursue a connection, even though it will hinder research and operations. Combined with the many decades of person-hours devoted to cleaning up after the worm, this seems a high price to pay for a claimed "favor."

The legal consequences of this act are also not yet known. For instance, many bills have been introduced into Congress and state legislatures over the last three years in part because of these incidents. One piece of legislation introduced into the House of Representatives, HR-5061, entitled "The Computer Virus Eradication Act of 1988," was the first in a series of legislative actions that have the potential to affect significantly the computer profession. In particular, HR-5061 was notable because its wording would prevent it from being applied to true computer viruses.* The passage of similar well-intentioned but poorly defined legislation could have a major negative effect on the computing profession as a whole.

The Idle System Argument

Another argument put forth by system hackers is that they are simply making use of idle machines. They argue that because some systems are not used at a level near their capacity, the hacker is somehow entitled to use them.

This argument is also flawed. First of all, these systems are usually not in service to provide a

---

*It provided penalities only in cases where programs were introduced into computer systems: a computer virus is a segment of code attached to an existing program that modifies other programs to include a copy of itself [7].

general-purpose user environment. Instead, they are in use in commerce, medicine, public safety, research, and government functions. Unused capacity is present for future needs and sudden surges of activity, not for the support of outside individuals. Imagine if large numbers of people without a computer were to take advantage of a system with idle processor capacity: the system would quickly be overloaded and severely degraded or unavailable for the rightful owners. Once on the system, it would be difficult (or impossible) to oust these individuals if sudden extra capacity were needed by the rightful owners. Even the largest machines available today would not provide sufficient capacity to accommodate such activity on any large scale.

I am unable to think of any other item that someone may buy and maintain, only to have others claim a right to use it when it is idle. For instance, the thought of someone walking up to my expensive car and driving off in it simply because it is not currently being used is ludicrous. Likewise, because I am away at work, it is not proper to hold a party at my house because it is otherwise not being used. The related positions that unused computing capacity is a shared resource, and that my privately developed software belongs to everyone, are equally silly (and unethical) positions.

The Student Hacker Argument

Some trespassers claim that they are doing no harm and changing nothing—they are simply learning about how computer systems operate. They argue that computers are expensive, and that they are merely furthering their education in a cost-effective manner. Some authors of computer viruses claim that their creations are intended to be harmless, and that they are simply learning how to write complex programs.

There are many problems with these arguments. First, as an educator, I claim that writing vandalware or breaking into a computer and looking at the files has almost nothing to do with computer education. Proper education in computer science and engineering involves intensive exposure to fundamental aspects of theory, abstraction, and design techniques. Browsing through a system does not expose someone to the broad scope of theory and practice in computing, nor does it provide the critical feedback so important to a good education

[16, 17]; neither does writing a virus or worm program and releasing it into an unsupervised environment provide any proper educational experience. By analogy, stealing cars and joyriding does not provide one with an education in mechanical engineering, nor does pouring sugar in the gas tank.

Furthermore, individuals "learning" about a system cannot know how everything operates and what results from their activities. Many systems have been damaged accidently by ignorant (or careless) intruders; most of the damage from computer viruses (and the Internet Worm) appear to be caused by unexpected interactions and program faults. Damage to medical systems, factory control, financial information, and other computer systems could have drastic and far-ranging effects that have nothing to do with education, and could certainly not be considered harmless.

A related refutation of the claim has to do with knowledge of the extent of the intrusion. If I am the person responsible for the security of a critical computer system, I cannot assume that *any* intrusion is motivated solely by curiosity and that nothing has been harmed. If I know that the system has been compromised, I must fear the worst and perform a complete system check for damages and changes. I cannot take the word of the intruder, for any intruder who actually caused damage would seek to hide it by claiming that he or she was "just looking." To regain confidence in the correct behavior of my system, I must expend considerable energy to examine and verify every aspect of it.

Apply our universal approach to this situation and imagine if this "educational" behavior was widespread and commonplace. The result would be that we would spend all our time verifying our systems and never be able to trust the results fully. Clearly, this is not good, and thus we must conclude that these "educational" motivations are also unethical.

The Social Protector Argument

One last argument, more often heard in Europe than the United States, is that hackers break into systems to watch for instances of data abuse and to help keep "Big Brother" at bay. In this sense, the hackers are protectors rather than criminals. Again, this assumes that the ends justify the means. It also assumes that the hackers are actually able to achieve some good end.

Undeniably, there is some misuse of personal data by corporations and by the government. The increasing use of computer-based record systems and networks may lead to further abuses. However, it is not clear that breaking into these systems will aid in righting the wrongs. If anything, it may cause those agencies to become even more secretive and use the break-ins as an excuse for more restricted access. Break-ins and vandalism have not resulted in new open-records laws, but they have resulted in the introduction and passage of new criminal statutes. Not only has such activity failed to deter "Big Brother," but it has also resulted in significant segments of the public urging more laws and more aggressive law enforcement—the direct opposite of the supposed goal.

It is also not clear that these hackers are the individuals we want "protecting" us. We need to have the designers and users of the systems—trained computer professionals—concerned about our rights and aware of the dangers involved with the inappropriate use of computer monitoring and record keeping. The threat is a relatively new one, as computers and networks have become widely used only in the last few decades. It will take some time for awareness of the dangers to spread throughout the profession. Clandestine efforts to breach the security of computer systems do nothing to raise the consciousness of the appropriate individuals. Worse, they associate that commendable goal (heightened concern) with criminal activity (computer break-ins), thus discouraging proactive behavior by the individuals in the best positions to act in our favor. Perhaps it is in this sense that computer break-ins and vandalism are most unethical and damaging.

Conclusion

I have argued here that computer break-ins, even when no obvious damage results, are unethical. This must be the considered conclusion even if the result is an improvement in security, because the activity itself is disruptive and immoral. The results of the act should be considered separately from the act itself, especially when we consider how difficult it is to understand all the effects resulting from such an act.

Of course, I have not discussed every possible reason for a break-in. There might well be an in-stance where a break-in might be necessary to save a life or to preserve national security. In such cases, to perform one wrong act to prevent a greater wrong may be the right thing to do. It is beyond the scope or intent of this paper to discuss such cases, especially as no known hacker break-ins have been motivated by such instances.

Historically, computer professionals as a group have not been overly concerned with questions of ethics and propriety as they relate to computers. Individuals and some organizations have tried to address these issues, but the whole computing community needs to be involved to address the problems in any comprehensive manner. Too often, we view computers simply as machines and algorithms, and we do not perceive the serious ethical questions inherent in their use.

However, when we consider that these machines influence the quality of life of millions of individuals, both directly and indirectly, we understand that there are broader issues. Computers are used to design, analyze, support, and control applications that protect and guide the lives and finances of people. Our use (and misuse) of computing systems may have effects beyond our wildest imagining. Thus, we must reconsider our attitudes about acts demonstrating a lack of respect for the rights and privacy of other people's computers and data.

We must also consider what our attitudes will be towards future security problems. In particular, we should consider the effect of widely publishing the source code for worms, viruses, and other threats to security. Although we need a process for rapidly disseminating corrections and security information as they become known, we should realize that widespread publication of details will imperil sites where users are unwilling or unable to install updates and fixes.* Publications should serve a useful purpose: endangering the security of other people's machines or attempting to force them into making changes they are unable to make or afford is not ethical.

Finally, we must decide these issues of ethics as a community of professionals and then present

---

*To anticipate the oft-used comment that the "bad guys" already have such information: not every computer burglar knows or will know *every* system weakness—unless we provide them with detailed analyses.

them to society as a whole. No matter what laws are passed, and no matter how good security measures might become, they will not be enough for us to have completely secure systems. We also need to develop and act according to some shared ethical values. The members of society need to be educated so that they understand the importance of respecting the privacy and ownership of data. If locks and laws were all that kept people from robbing houses, there would be many more burglars than there are now; the shared mores about the sanctity of personal property are an important influence in the prevention of burglary. It is our duty as informed professionals to help extend those mores into the realm of computers.

REFERENCES

1. Spafford, E. H. Is a computer break-in ever ethical? *Info. Tech. Quart.* IX:9–14 (1990).
2. Seeley, D. A tour of the worm. In *Proceedings of the Winter 1989 Usenix Conference,* The Usenix Association, Berkeley, CA, 1989.
3. Spafford, E. H. The internet worm: crisis and aftermath. *Commun. ACM* 32, 678–698 (1989).
4. Spafford, E. H. An analysis of the internet work. In *Proceedings of the 2nd European Software Engineering Conference* (C. Ghezzi and J. A. McDermid. eds.), Springer-Verlag, Berlin, Germany, 1989, pp. 446–468.
5. Stoll, C. *Cuckoo's Egg,* Doubleday, New York. 1989.
6. Schwartz, John. The hacker dragnet. *Newsweek* 65, (April, 1990).
7. Spafford, E. H., K. A. Heaphy, and D. J. Ferbrache. *Computer Viruses: Dealing with Electronic Vandalism and Programmed Threats.* Arlington, Virginia: ADAPSO, 1989.
8. Hoffman, L., ed., *Rogue Programs: Viruses, Worms, and Trojan Horses.* Van Nostrand Reinhold, 1990.
9. Stang, D. J., *Computer Viruses,* 2nd ed., National Computer Security Association, Washington, DC, 1990.
10. Denning, P. J., ed., *Computers Under Attack: Intruders, Worms, and Viruses.* Reading, MA: ACM Books/Addison-Wesley, 1991.
11. Baird, B. J., L. L. Baird, Jr., and R. P. Ranauro. 1987. The moral cracker? *Comp. Sec.* 6:471–478.
12. Landreth, W. *Out of the Inner Circle: a Hacker's Guide to Computer Security,* Microsoft Press, New York. 1984.
13. Adelaide, J. P. Barlow, R. J. Bluefire, R. Brand, C. Stoll, D. Hughes, F. Drake, E. J. Homeboy, E. Goldstein, H. Roberts, J. Gasperini (JIMG), J. Carroll (JRC), L. Felsenstein, T. Mandel, R. Horvitz (RH), R. Stallman (RMS), G. Tenney, Acid Phreak, and Phiber Optik, Is computer hacking a crime? *Harper's Magazine* 280, 45–57 (March 1990).
14. Stallman, R. The GNU manifesto. In *GNU EMacs Manual.* Free Software Foundation, Cambridge, MA: pp. 239–248 (1986).
15. McIlroy, M. D. Unsafe at any price. *Info. Techn. Quart.* IX, 21–23 (1990).
16. P. J. Denning, D. E. Comer, D. Gries, M. C. Mulder, A. Tucker, A. J. Turner, and P. R. Young, Computing as a discipline, *Commun. ACM* 32, 9–23 (1989).
17. Tucker, A. B., et al. *Computing Curricula 1991,* IEEE Society Press, Piscataway, NJ, 1991.

Should I Copy My Neighbor's Software?[1]

Helen Nissenbaum

Introduction

Consider the following situation: Millie Smith is pleased with the way the home bookkeeping application, Quicken, organizes her financial records, even printing checks. Knowing how useful this would be to a good friend of hers, Max Jones, who lives precariously from one paycheck to the next,

From *Computer Ethics and Social Values,* Deborah G. Johnson and Helen Nissenbaum, eds., Prentice-Hall, Inc., 1995. Used with permission of Association for Computing Machinery.

and yet knowing that the program's price tag puts it outside of Max's financial reach, Millie is tempted to help Max out by offering him a copy of hers. She has read the lease agreement on the outside package which prohibits making copies of the diskette for any purpose other than archival backup, so she suspects she might be breaking the law. However, Millie is not as concerned about breaking the law (nor about the second-order question of the morality of law breaking) as she is about violating moral principles. If she is to copy Quicken for Max would her doing so be justifible "not so much in a court of law as in the court of conscience"?[2] For private consumers of commercial software Millie's situation is all too familiar.

Although the majority of these private end-users admit to frequently making and sharing unauthorized copies, they experience a nagging and unresolved sense of wrong-doing. Posing as the "conscience" of these wayward software copiers, a vocal group, whom I refer to as supporters of a "strong no-copy view," urges users like Millie Smith to refrain from unauthorized copying[3] saying that it is always wrong. Jon Barwise, for example, in promoting a strong no-copy position, concludes in a series of scenarios whose protagonists must decide whether or not to copy an $800 piece of software, that even in the case of a professor providing a copy of his diskette to a student who needs it to finish a dissertation, "we should answer all of the (above) questions no."[4] Green and Gilbert, in an article directed specifically to users in educational institutions, recommend that "campuses should view and treat illegal copying as a form of plagiarism or theft" and that they should pursue ways of reducing "illegal and unethical copying."[5]

In the following discussion I challenge the no-copy position, arguing that it emphasizes the moral claims and interests of software producers while failing to consider other morally relevant claims—most notably, those of the private end-user. Accordingly, Millie would not be violating moral principles if she were to share a copy with Max. I show that there are morally compelling factors that motivate many acts of software copying, not simply brazen self-interest, irrationality, or weakness of the will. Although I argue that in *some* cases copying is not a violation, I do not support the position on the other end of the ideological spectrum, which completely rejects the constraints of software copy protection. Rather, we need to judge distinct types of situations according to their individual merits. In some situations there will be an overriding case in favor of copying, in others not. In still others, agents confront a genuine dilemma, trying to respond to equally convincing sets of opposing claims.

To reach this conclusion I focused on the arguments, both consequentialist and rights based, that have been proffered in support of the strong no-copy position. Upon analysis I find that, as a universal position, a strong no-copy position is not defensible.

Two Caveats

First, a word on how I set about recreating the justifications for a strong no-copy position. I've drawn from pieces written for computing trade publications, other non-philosophical journals, electronic-mail communications, as well as conversations. Although the arguments given in favor of a moral prohibition on copying are generally not presented here in a framework of traditional ethical theory, I find this framework useful in organizing and evaluating them. For example, I classify the arguments that predict undesirable consequences of unauthorized copying under the general heading "consequentialist arguments." In a second working category, I classify arguments that claim unauthorized copying to be violations of moral rights and respect for persons. Although this group is more of a grab bag, the label "deontological/rights-based" captures its hybrid spirit. My first caveat, however, is that while the philosophical categories are enlightening, suggestive of potential strengths and weaknesses of the arguments, they should be viewed as rough guides only. Moreover, because few of the commentators offer explicit or complete treatments, I've taken liberties in filling in steps. While I fleshed out the arguments and filled in gaps, I tried to stay strictly within the parameters set by their originators.

Second, in order to simplify the discussion I assume throughout this discussion that programs are written and owned by a single programmer. In the real world of commercial software, teams of software developers rather than single programmers create software products. And for many products, the title usually goes to the software corporation, rather than directly to its employees, the program's authors. In other instances, it goes to intermediate agents such as marketing firms, or vendors. The assumption of a single programmer should not affect the substantive moral thesis.

Consequentialist Arguments

According to the arguments in this category, it is morally wrong to make unauthorized copies because doing so would have negative consequences. Although copying might appear to offer a short-term gain for the copier, the longer term and broader ramifications will be a loss for both consumers and producers alike. Barwise, for example, charges, ". . . software copying is a very serious problem. It is discouraging the creation of courseware and other software, and is causing artificially high prices for what software that does appear."[6]

Barwise's remarks suggest that we can expect at least two types of negative consequences. The first is a probable decline in software production. Because copying reduces the volume of software sales it deprives programmers of income. With an erosion of potential revenues, fewer individuals will be attracted into software production. A smaller population of programmers and other software personnel will result in a reduction of available software. Furthermore, a slowing in software development would have a dampening effect on general welfare. The second negative impact of copying is a projected rise in software prices. Wishing to recoup anticipated losses caused by unauthorized copying, programmers will charge high prices for their software. Giving as an example Wolfram's *Mathematica,* which in 1989 was priced at $795, Barwise blames copying for the artificially high prices of software applications. How good are these arguments?

Embodied in the consequentialist line of arguments are a number of empirical assumptions and predictions which, I contend, are open to challenge. For consequentialist arguments to provide a moral as well as a prudential rationale, they must demonstrate links between copying and reduced income, between reduced income and decline in the software industry, and decline in production and an overall decline in society's welfare. If copying hurts the software industry but has no effect on general welfare a prohibition is not morally justifiable on consequentialist grounds. If copying is not directly related to income, nor income to a decline in the industry, then too, the argument breaks down. On close scrutiny these links don't stick. Furthermore, even if some damage could be attributed to unauthorized copying, I conclude that it's insufficient to warant the all-out prohibition of the strong no-copy position.

Consider the claim that unauthorized copying leads to loss of sales. Although on the face of it, the argument is compelling, the implied link between copying and reduced sales is not always direct. Imagine a situation in which you are deciding whether to buy software application A or copy it from a friend. Although the consequentialists would have us think of all instances of copying as situations in which an agent must decide between the exclusive alternatives, buy A, or copy A, in many real-life situations this is not so. Computer users copy software that they would not buy for a number of reasons: because they could not afford it; are not yet sure that they want the product; or quite simply, have placed higher priority on other needs. For them, the choice is: copy A, or not have A.

Moreover, copying can actually lead to an increase in overall spending on computer software, at least for some individuals. Software sharing opens opportunities for trial and experimentation to otherwise timid users who thereby grow more comfortable with computers and software. As a result they become more active and diversified consumers of software than they would have been without those opportunities. We also find that users who are impressed by a particular piece of copied software, in order to own the manual and enjoy some of the additional benefits of "registered users," will go on to buy the application. In other words, much unauthorized copying would not result in loss of sales and some, in fact, would lead to increases.

The prediction that reduced income will discourage further creation of software belies a complicated story about motivation, action, and reward. Whereas wholesale fluctuations and extreme reductions probably would discourage would-be programmers, the effects of smaller fluctuations are not clear. Richard Stallman[7] ably makes the point that directly tying software production to monetary reward paints an overly simplistic picture of the rewards that motivate programmers. Well-known for his active support of an open environment for information technology, Stallman suggests that besides the satisfaction of contributing to a social good, the fascination with programming itself will keep many of the most talented programmers working. He also raises the question of how much is enough. Although we would not expect many good programmers to have a monk-like devotion to programming and can agree that people work better when rewarded, it's not clear that any increment in reward will make them work proportionately better. (Furthermore, as suggested earlier, we still do not have a realistic idea of the extent to which cases like Millie Smith's actually affects potential earnings.)

Turning the tables on the usual consequentialist chain of reasoning, Stallman counters that prohibitions on copying, and other restrictions on the free distribution of computer code, has the opposite effect on computer technology. It is slowing progress rather than encouraging it. He and others suggest that the free exchange of ideas and code characteristic of the early days of systems and software development was responsible for the remarkable pace of progress, whereas limiting free exchange would dampen innovation and progress, moreover, laws restricting access to software would favor large, powerful and generally more conservative software producers. With a greater capacity to exert legal clout, they could control the production, development, and distribution of software, gradually squeezing out of the commercial arena the independent-minded, creative software-engineer, or "hacker." Even if we see a proliferation of commercially available software, we may also see a slowing of the cutting edge. If Stallman's predictions are sound, they offer moral justification for promoting free copying of software, and not the reverse.

So far, I have questioned the empirical basis for the claims that link copying with loss of revenue: claims that link loss of revenue with a decrease in software production; and, more generally, claims that link copying with a loss to the software industry as a whole. What about effects on general welfare? At this level of generality it is probably impossible to draw a meaningful connection between software and welfare. To the extent that software is a social good, it is surely through high-quality, well-directed software and not sheer quantity.[8] To discourage a potential copier, an extreme no-copy position must show the clear social benefits of abstaining without which there is little to offset the immediate loss. This question deserves more thorough exploration than I'm able to give it here because the connection between software production and overall utility or welfare, is complex. It does suggest, however, that the effects on general welfare of a particular act of copying would vary according not only to the context of copying, but also to the type of software being copied. It would also need to be measured against the projected utility to the potential copier.

Let us now consider the alleged connection between copying and cost and the claim that producers are forced to charge high prices in anticipation of losses through copying. An obvious rejoinder to software producers, like Wolfram, is that if software applications were more reasonably priced, consumers would be less tempted to copy. If products were appropriately priced, the marginal utility of buying over copying would increase. This pattern holds true in the case of recorded music which could provide a model for computer software.[9] Because the cost of a tape, for example, fits many budgets, it is more convenient to buy the tape than search for someone who might have it. Though both the claim and rejoinder appear to hold genuine insights, they leave us in an uncomfortable standoff. Looking at high prices, pointing at consumers, critics say: "It's your fault for copying." Whereas consumers point back claiming: "It's your fault for charging such high prices." The average user apparently cannot afford to buy software at the current rates, and the programmer cannot afford to drop his or her price. Though we may agree that this is not a desirable equilibrium, it's not easy to see who should take the first step out of this circle of accusations. Resolving the standoff requires asking difficult questions about burden. Upon whom do we place the burden of maintaining a healthy software industry—consumer or producer? The question brings me to my concluding comments.

I agree with defenders of a consequentialist line that a prolific software industry with a high-quality ouput, which provides genuine choices to a wide variety of consumers, is a goal worth striving for. I disagree, however, that prohibiting copying is the only, or best, way of ensuring this. First, I have tried to show that the empirical grounds upon which they support their claims are open to dispute. Moreover, if a consequentialist approach is to be at all useful in guiding decisions about unauthorized copying, then it must distinguish among different types of copying—for their consequences surely differ. For example, cases like Millie's sharing a copy with Max would have a vastly different effect than cases in which a user places a copy of the software on a public network. Consequentialist moral injunctions should recognize these differences.

Finally, the no-copy position unreasonably focuses on private end-users, placing on their shoulders the onus of maintaining the health of the software market. But consumer copying is but one variable, among many, that affect the software industry. Holding fixed the other variables might serve some interests, but it gives disproportionate weight to the effects of copying. Decisions by commercial hardware manufacturers and even government agencies can significantly impact software. For example, if a hardware manufacturer perceives that a particular software product is critical to the sale of its machines it may, quite rationally, decide to support the software.[10] In addition, software companies have the capability to influence the actions of potential users by offering not only a good product as code on a diskette, but by also including attractive services such as consulting, good documentation, and software updates. In this way they make it worthwhile for the user to buy software, rather than copy it. The many flourishing software companies stand as evidence that good products and marketing works, despite alleged copying. Because other players—namely, government, hardware producers, software companies—have the power to significantly affect the software industry, we should not ignore their responsibilities when we assess the burden of maintaining the strength of software production. It is wrong for the private consumer to be unfairly burdened with responsibility.

Deontological/Rights-Based Arguments

In urging individual consumers not to make unauthorized copies some supporters refer to the "rights of programmers" and "respect for their labor." Regardless of its effects on the general welfare, or on the software industry, copying software without permission is immoral because it constitutes a violation of a moral right, a neglect of moral obligations. Depriving a programmer of earnings is wrong not only because of its undesirable ramifications, but because it is unjust and unfair. And even if programmers' earnings are not appreciably affected by copying, we have an obligation to respect their desire that we not make unauthorized copies. The obligation is absolute, not broken merely at the discretion of the private end-user.[11] Millie ought not make a copy of Quicken for Max because doing so would be unfair, it would violate the programmers' rights. But what are the rights to

which these commentators refer; and does all copying, in fact, violate them?

Rights-based justifications of no-copy require a satisfactory resolution to both questions. They not only must identify the rights of programmers relevant to the question of unauthorized copying, but must demonstrate that copying always violates these rights. Supporters usually cite property rights as relevant to the question of copying. A justification of the position should, accordingly, ask whether programmers do in fact qualify as owners of their programs so that they would have the appropriate rights of private property over them. But justification does not stop here. For even if we resolve that programmers do own their programs, it doesn't follow necessarily that all copying will violate their property rights. Or to put it another way, it is not obvious that property rights over programs include the right to restrict copying to the extent desired. A justification of the no-copy position needs a second step, to follow the finding that programmers own their programs. And that is, to show that copying violates these property rights. Many commentators fail to recognize the need for the second step, simply concluding that owning implies an unlimited right to restrict copying.

In the discussion that follows I will spell out the two steps in a rights-based position beginning with the question of private ownership, and then moving to the question of whether owning a program implies the right to place absolute limits on reproduction. I will conclude that the second step is the weak one. As before, in recreating the arguments I've worked from informal written pieces, electronic mail messages, and verbal communications. In some cases this has meant filling in missing steps; steps that I judge necessary to making the best possible case for a rights-based justification. Finally, though recognizing that some might object to the very fabric of rights-based justifications of moral injunctions, I offer my criticisms from within this framework, and will not challenge the very idea of a rights-based approach.

Programming and Private Property

First, let's examine the following claim: Because a programmer writes, or creates, software he or she owns it. For some, this claim is so obvious as to not even need justification. To them, a program is an extension of the person's self and so, obviously, belongs to that person. For others, labor theories of property such as John Locke's, which claims that when individuals invest labor in a previously unowned item they earn property rights over it, offer a more traditional and moral grounding for private ownership over programs. Locke writes, "Thus Labour, in the beginning, gave a right of property, wherever any one was pleased to employ it upon what was common."[12] Because programmers invest labor in creating a program, they are entitled to the "fruits of their labor." Although Locke's theory addresses the somewhat different issue of private acquisition of physical property, such as parcels of land and harvests, and focuses on the taking of initial title over a previously unowned item (or one held in common), his theory adapts well to intellectual labor. In fact, the case of intellectual property is somewhat easier for a labor theory in that it avoids a common pitfall identified by Locke's critics who, in the context of physical items, worry about the morally "correct" mix of labor with the physical entity.[13] I will concede then, that a programmer, in producing a program, accrues property rights over it, accepting as justification for this claim—if it is even needed—basic ideas of a labor theory of property.

Some have questioned the justice of extensive property rights over programs claiming that software creation is an essentially cumulative activity. Most programs draw heavily on work that has preceded them so that giving rights to the programmer who happened to write the line of code in question rests on the unwarranted assumption that we can tell accurately where one programmer's labor really begins and the other's ends. For example, most commercial software on today's market is the product of a long line of cumulative work most notably Lotus 1–2–3.[14] However, this objection does not challenge, rather it implicitly adopts, a form of the labor theory because it suggests that *all* those who contributed their effort toward creating a software product deserve proprietary rights over it, and not just those who happen to cross some arbitrary finishing line first. Just because they have made a bigger marketing effort, happen to be more worldly, belong to a large organization, or have good legal representation, does not vest in them a stronger moral claim. Although the question of just rewards for joint labor is an important one in light

of the history of the development of computer software, for the remainder of my discussion, I will assume that we can talk meaningfully about *the* programmer who contributed most significantly to a program's creation. It is about this programmer that the discussion about property rights that follows applies.

As stated earlier, showing that programmers own their programs is not sufficient for a no-copy position. Its supporters must still demonstrate that owning a piece of software implies a moral right to restrict copying to the extent desired (and thus the duty in others to refrain from copying). How might I demonstrate this "second step," required a rights-based justification of strong no-copy? In the next section I will examine whether a universal prohibition on copying software necessarily follows from general property rights over it.

Owning Software and Prohibiting Copying

In general, ownership implies a set of rights, rights defining the relationship between an owner and a piece of property. Typically the rights of an owner over private property fall into a number of set categories including: one that covers conditions on initial acquisition over a previously unowned object;[15] another that refers to the extent of use and enjoyment an owner may exercise over that property; a third that determines the extent to which an owner may restrict access to her property (or alienate others from her property), and a fourth that endows upon an owner the power to determine the terms of transfer of title. Thus abstractly conceived, the concept of private ownership yields a fairly well-defined set of rights. When instantiating these rights in actual cases of owning a specific given item, the specific rights an owner has over that item can vary considerably according to a host of factors. First, at the most general level, certain social, economic, political, and cultural factors greatly affect our ideas about private property rights, their nature and extent, and what sorts of objects can be owned privately in the first place. To simplify matters, for purposes of this discussion, I will assume a common background of roughly Western, free-market, principles. A second variable that also significantly determines the specific rights an owner can have over an item[16] is its metaphysical character, or type. For example, the specific rights a child has over his peanut butter sandwich might include the rights to consume it, to chop it into twenty pieces and to decide whether to share it or not with a friend. But such rights make no sense in the case of landowners and plots of land, pet owners and their pets, car owners and their vehicles, and so forth. When we determine the appropriate set of rights instantiating the general rights of use and enjoyment, restricting access, terms of sale, on items of varying metaphysical character, we come up with distinct sets of specific rights. Whereas intellectual property stretches classical ideas of locking away or fencing ("restricting access"), consuming ("use and enjoyment"), and bartering ("transfer of title") deciding what it means to own software poses an even harder puzzle.

Computer software has raised a host of challenges to property theory, testing the traditional concepts and rationales in novel ways. Because even relatively simple programs have numerous components and moreover have various aspects, the first problem is to define, or identify, the "thing" that is *the* program, the thing that is the proper subject of private ownership. A program can be identified by its source code and object code, a formal specification defining what the program does, its underlying algorithm, and its user interface, or "look and feel." Each of the various components—or aspects—has a distinct metaphysical character and consequently suggests a distinct set of property rights. For example, because a program's source code is considered similar to a written work, it is considered by most to be covered by copyright laws. By contrast some judge a program's algorithm to be a process (and not a mathematical formula) and thus claim that it is patentable. Legal debates address the issue of whether one can abstract a program's so-called look and feel and claim to own that, in addition to, and independently of, the code, algorithm, and so on. And if so, they argue over whether legal protection ought to be through copyright, patent, or something else. There are many instructive works dedicated to the question of the optimal form of legal protection of all these aspects of software in a growing literature which is written from legal, philosophical, and technical perspective.[17]

Fortunately, we need not wait for a resolution to the entire range of puzzles that software ownership raises in order to gain a better understanding of Millie's dilemma. We acknowledge, in her case, that she explicitly duplicated object code, and thus we bypass many of the complexities. However, it is important to note the existing backdrop of uncertainty over how to categorize the metaphysics of software, and thus, how to fit it into our network of ideas on property rights. We are drawing conclusions about software ownership on the basis of imperfect analogies to other forms of private property. This leaves open the possibility of significant differences.

We are ready now to return to this section's central question of how one might derive a prohibition on copying from ownership. On the basis of earlier observations about private property we can conclude that a programmer, or owner, has rights over the program including rights to restrict access and rights of use and enjoyment. Presumably, the programmer's right to generate earnings from his program would instantiate the latter. The programmer could choose to give others limited access to her program by selling diskettes, upon which she has copied the program, at a price she determines. But because the programmer still owns the program itself, she may impose restrictions on its use—in particular she retains the right to prevent buyers of the diskettes from making copies of the program that she has not explicitly authorized. Thus, we derive the programmer's specific right to restrict unauthorized copying from the general right property owners have to restrict access by others to their property. To distinguish transactions of this type from other types of sales, commercial software vendors adopt the jargon "software license" rather than "software sale." Thus, the argument from rights would dictate that Millie not copy because doing so would violate a programmer's valid claim to both use and enjoy his or her property (by depriving them earnings) and restrict access by others to it (by making unauthorized copies).

But this picture leaves out an important component of property theory. Like other rights, property rights restrict the freedoms of others by imposing certain obligations on them. For example a promisee's rights imply an obligation on the part of the promiser to keep the promise; a landowner's rights implies an obligation on would-be trespassers not to cross his or her land. As I stated earlier, the precise nature of property restrictions will vary according to the metaphysical character of the property. But there is yet another factor that shapes the extent and nature of property—and in fact all—rights. Even theorists of a libertarian bent, who support extensive rights over private property, recognize that these rights are not absolute. For example, Locke argued that morality allowed the appropriation of previously unowned property only "where there is enough, and as good, left in common for others."[18] And Nozick, also recognizing limitations on property rights, illustrates one source of these restrictions with his colorful example: "My property rights in my knife allow me to leave it where I will, but not in your chest."[19] In other words, although owning a knife implies extensive rights of use and enjoyment, these rights are constrained by justified claims, or rights, of others—in this case, their right not to be harmed. While I wish to avoid either endorsing or criticizing the more far-reaching agendas of these two authors, I want to draw attention to an important insight they offer about private property rights: that property rights are subject to the limitations of countervailing claims of others.

Actual practice demonstrates that, as a rule rather than an exception, when we determine the nature and extent of property rights, we acknowledge the justified claims of others. For example, in determining the rights of the owner of a lethal weapon we're influenced not only by its general metaphysical features (when we determine the types of actions that constitute use and enjoyment), but are concerned about the well-being of others. And so we restrict the way people may carry lethal weapons—either concealed or unconcealed depending on the accepted wisdom of the city or state in which they happen to live. We regulate construction projects of urban property owners for far less concrete counterclaims than freedom from bodily harm, but in the interest of values like aesthetic integrity of a neighborhood, effects on the quality of life of immediate neighbors, and so forth. We restrict the rights of landowners over water traversing their land, preventing them, for example, from damming a flowing river. We also constrain the behavior of motor vehicle drivers. In all these cases where we perceive a threat to justified claims of other individuals, or of a social order, we limit the extent of owners' rights over their property. It makes sense to carry this principle over to the case

of software asking not only about the claims of programmers, but the claims of end-users.

Does Millie Smith have a reasonable counter-claim that might limit the extent to which Quicken's owners can constrain her actions. She would like to duplicate her Quicken software for Max, an act of generosity, helping satisfy a friend's need. Despite the programmer's preferring that Millie not share a copy, Millie is motivated by other values. She views making a copy as a generous act which would help a friend in need. Copying software is a routine part of computer use. Millie's proposed action is limited: she has no intention of making multiple copies and going into competition with the programmer, she wouldn't dream of plagiarizing the software or passing it off as a product of her own creation. The entire transaction takes place within the private domain of friends and family. She would view offering a copy to Max as a simple act of kindness, neither heroic nor extraordinary. Interfering with the normal flow of behavior, especially as pursued in the private realm, would constitute unreasonable restriction of an agent's liberty. Thus, Millie's countervailing claim is the freedom to pursue the virtue of generosity within the private circle of friends and family.

The conclusion of this line of reasoning is *not* that, from a perspective of rights, *all* unauthorized duplication of software is morally permissible. I am suggesting merely that we decide the question whether to share or not to share in a case by case fashion. Although in some cases a programmer's desire that the user not copy software is a defensible instantiation of the right to restrict access to private property, in others the restriction will not be defensible because it conflicts with the valid claims of another agent. And even in the cases where making a copy would not be immoral it would not follow that the programmer has somehow lost all the property rights over his or her program. Commentators like Green and Gilbert are right to draw attention to programmers' claims over their software, and to encourage respect for intellectual labor; but they overlook the possibility of relevant, conflicting, counterclaims. When, at the beginning of the paper, I referred to the copier's dilemma, it was the dilemma created by conflicting obligations: on the one hand an obligation to respect a programmer's property rights, which in some cases includes the right to restrict copying; and on the other an obligation to help others, tempered by the belief that one ought not have one's behavior unduly restricted within the private domain.

Consider some objections. One objection is that no matter what Millie might think about helping Max, you just cannot get away from the fact that she's violating the programmer's property rights. And this is the reason that her copying—and all unauthorized copying—is immoral.

This objection fails to recognize that counterclaims can substantively affect what counts as a moral (property) right, in any given situation. Consider the rights of a landlord with respect to a leased apartment. When that apartment is vacant, the owner may come and go as he wishes; he may renovate it, choose to rent it, or to let it stand empty. However, once the apartment is leased, the landlord's rights of entry are limited by a tenant's competing right to privacy. Even if it would suit a landlord to stipulate in his lease the right to make surprise checks, this wish would be over-ridden by the justified claims of his tenants not to be disturbed, not to have their privacy violated. We would not say that the landlord's property rights are violated by the tenant; we would say that the landlord no longer has the right of free entry into his leased property. Consider another example. Let's say someone buys a word-processing package. On the outside of the customary sealed envelope containing the diskette, the buyer finds not only the usual terms of a lease agreement, but one further condition. The programmers stipulate that consumers are free to use the word processor any way they want, except to produce a document that promotes abortion. They reason that the abortion stipulation is merely an additional instantiation of their rights as owners to restrict access by others to their property. However, I think that the buyer could quite reasonably object that despite the programmer's intellectual property rights over the word processor, these rights do not include the right to control its use to the extent that it overrides valid, competing claims to freedom of expression. Similarly, Millie, judging that in the private domain she should be largely unrestricted, could argue that the moral arm of the programmer does not extend into the private domain. We conclude, therefore, that in copying for Max she does not violate a moral right.

In a second objection, a critic could charge that if we judge Millie Smith's copying to be morally permissible, this would open the door to a total disregard for the rights of programmers. There would be no stopping agents from making multiple, unauthorized, copies and selling them in competition with the original programmer.

This objection doesn't hold because Millie's case, being significantly different from those other cases, would not lead us down a slippery slope. A potential copier must show a justifiable claim that conflicts with the programmer's. In the objector's example, and even in the case of a do-gooder who decides to place a piece of privately owned software on a public domain network,[20] copying takes place in a public domain lacking Millie's personal and private motivations. They lack the compelling counterclaim. Specifically for the public, commercial arena, we would expect to generate a network of laws and regulations to cover the many cases which moral principles alone could not decide.

Another objection asserts that Millie would be acting immorally in making a copy for Max because copying is stealing. But this objection begs the question because it *assumes* that copying is stealing. In this section we've been examining whether or not copying always violates property rights and therefore constitutes wrongful seizure of another's possession. In other words, whether copying is stealing. This objection assumes that we've satisfactorily established that copying is theft, and thus assumes the issue we're trying to establish.

Conclusion

There is a prevailing presumption—in my opinion a disturbing one—that were we to follow the dictates of moral conscience, we would cease completely to make unauthorized copies of software. Yet when we examine the arguments given in support of that presumption we find that they fall short of their universal scope. The soundness of a rights-based rationale depends on successfully showing that owning software entails a right to restrict copying. I have argued that this step is not obvious, and that at least in some well-defined cases the entailment fails—notably, cases in which there are strong counterclaims. In practice this means that we should give equal consideration to the rights of end-users as well as to those of programmers. To simply insist that property rights override end-user freedoms is to beg the issue at hand.

Consequentialist rationales are also equivocal

in that they rest on a number of sweeping empirical assumptions—many of which exaggerate the effects of copying, some of which are open to doubt. Moreover, it places squarely on the shoulders of private end-users the onus of maintaining a flourishing industry when in fact there are other agents well placed to share the burden. Many software manufacturers who have been vocal in their complaints, despite current levels of copying, appear to be enjoying overwhelming successes. Perhaps because they offer incentives like good consulting services, free upgrades, and reasonable prices they raise the marginal utility of buying over copying.

Finding that there are insufficiently strong moral grounds for universally prohibiting copying, I conclude not that all unauthorized copying is morally acceptable, but that that some copying is acceptable. There is sufficient variability in the types of situations in which software users copy to suggest that we ought to evaluate them case-by-case. In cases like Millie's and Max's, the argument against copying is not a compelling one.

Finally, some critics insist that the best approach to solving this issue is a hard-line economic one. Clearly, a rights-based approach, which unearths the usual set of conflicting rights is not helpful and leads us to a deadlock. Let the free market decide. We ought to allow software producers to place any conditions whatever on the sale of their software, and in particular, any limits on duplication. Consumers will soon make their preferences known. Defenders of no-copy say that current commercial software conditions are more or less in that position today, except that users are not keeping up their end of the bargain when they make copies of software. But even from this hard-line economic standpoint, a no-copy line is disturbing because it lets the robustness of a market depend on a mode of behavior to which most do not conform, and many find distasteful, that is, restricting the inclination to private acts of beneficence and generosity. Unless we alter human nature, experience suggests that this would be a shaky equilibrium.

On a final idealistic note, I echo strains of Richard Stallman in observing that if we can eradicate copying only when individuals ignore a natural tendency to respond to the needs of those close to them, we may not be maximizing expected utility after all.

NOTES

1. An earlier version of this paper was presented at the Fifth Annual Computers and Philosophy Conference, Stanford University, August 8–11, 1990. Several members of the audience, with their sharp criticisms and suggestions, helped clarify my thinking a great deal. I'd also like to thank members of Partha Dasgupta's Applied Ethics Seminar at Stanford (1989) for useful and creative comments.

2. David Lyons, "The New Indian Claims and Original Rights to Land" in *Reading Nozick: Essays on Anarchy, State and Utopia,* (ed.), edited by Jeffrey Paul, Rowman and Littlefield, Totowa, New Jersey. 1981.

3. I will not be dealing with unlikely cases in which copying software might save a life or avert a war. I assume that even those committed to a no-copy position would find rationale to permit those acts.

4. Jon Barwise, "Computers and Mathematics: Editorial Notes," in *Notices of the A.M.S.*

5. K. Green and S. W. Gilbert, "Software Piracy: Its Cost and Consequences" in *Change,* pp. 47–49. January/February 1987.

6. Jon Barwise, "Computers and Mathematics: Editorial Notes," in *Notices of the A.M.S.,* 1989.

7. R. Stallman, "The GNU Manifesto" in *GNU Emacs Manual.* Copyright 1987 Richard Stallman.

8. Joseph Weizenbaum in Chapter 1 of *Computer Power and Human Reason,* San Francisco, Freeman, 1976, makes suggestive comments arguing that consumerism needn't necessarily lead to greater choices among genuinely distinct products. A conservative market might remain unimaginatively "safe," coming up with only trivially diverse products.

9. Although some claim that the loss in sound-quality is a major reason for recorded music being less frequently copied, this doesn't tell the story for all (the average) listeners.

10. Both Stallman, *ibid.* and Barwise, *ibid.* (and probably others) have made similar points.

11. Though strictly speaking, a rule-based approach could ultimately be grounded in utilitarian terms, the ones I consider here merge the rights-based and deontological styles of moral reasoning. They cite programmers' rights, inferring from them absolute obligations on the parts of software users.

12. John Locke, Section 45 in *Second Treatise of Government,* originally published 1690. Hackett Publishing Company, Indianapolis, 1980.

13. Nozick discusses this problem quite extensively in *Anarchy, State and Utopia,* Basic Books, Inc., 1974.

14. For an interesting history of software inter-dependence see Bill Machrone's "The Look-and-Feel Issue: The Evolution of Innovation" in *Computers, Ethics, & Society,* M. D. Ermann, M. B. Williams, C. Gutierrez, Oxford University Press, New York, 1990.

15. This was Locke's central preoccupation.
16. Metaphysical character can co-vary with cultural–social factors to make for an even more complex picture. Consider the potentially diverse views of descendants of European traditions and those of Native American traditions on property rights over land, sea, and air.
17. See, for example: M. Gemignani, "The Regulation of Software," *Abacus*, vol. 5, no. 1, Fall 1987, pp. 57–59; D. G. Johnson, "Should Computer Programs Be Owned?", *Metaphilosophy*, vol. 16, no. 4, October

1985, pp. 276–288; P. Samuelson, "Why the Look and Feel of Software User Interfaces Should Not Be Protected by Copyright Law," *Communications of the ACM*, vol. 32, no. 5, May 1989, pp. 563–572.
18. Locke, *ibid.* Chapter 5 Section 27.
19. *Anarchy, State and Utopia* by Robert Nozick, p. 171.
20. I confess to being stymied by cases such as that of a school teacher in a poor ghetto school deciding to make unauthorized copies of a software applications that he believes would help his students, who would not ordinarily be able to afford it.

Privacy in the Information Age

Richard A. Spinello

Consumer Privacy

As we consider the moral and legal aspects of the right to privacy, it becomes evident that a key element of the moral basis for privacy is the right to control information about oneself. It is precisely this right that is most threatened by new computer technologies. Advances in these technologies have appreciably increased the volume of information that is collected, stored, and distributed, and also the efficiency with which that information is compiled and disseminated. As one prescient observer wrote, "The foundation is being laid for a dossier society, in which computers could be used to infer individuals' life-styles, habits, whereabouts, and associations from data collected in ordinary customer transactions."[1]

Among the plethora of recent challenges to consumer privacy, two stand out as especially noteworthy. In a highly publicized case in late 1990, Lotus Development Corporation abruptly cancelled the release of a product called *Marketplace: Households* because of unexpected and intense public pressure (see the case study at the end of this chapter). This product, which was developed in conjunction with Equifax, a large credit reporting company, was designed to provide a targeted mailing list drawn from a mammoth database of 120 million names. The purchaser of this list would have permanent use of these names. The lists would

be generated on the basis of specific demographic questions about age, income level, marital status, and so forth. Thus, for example, a retailer in Newton, Massachusetts, could buy a list, on a CD-ROM, of all the residents of Newton who are unmarried and over 65 years old with an annual income exceeding $50,000.

Marketplace did not receive a warm reception among consumer groups or right-to-privacy advocates. According to these critics, this product raised serious questions about the use of Equifax's detailed credit information for marketing purposes. They were also alarmed because, unlike the case with the other methods, which permitted only one-time use of mailing lists, the information on the CD-ROM was permanently owned by the user. Despite certain safeguards, there would be little control over how the owners used this information and how they redistributed it to others.

More recently, AT&T has stirred controversy over its project to distribute 800-number directories targeted to carefully selected prospects. For example, one directory might be devoted to travel, and would contain the toll-free 800-numbers of travel agencies, hotels, airlines and so forth. The consumer group for this directory would be those who call such numbers with some frequency. Thus, if a household has made several phone calls within the previous year or two to travel agencies, hotels, or airlines, it would be considered a likely prospect for future travel and hence would receive a copy of this specialized directory. This procedure may sound innocuous, but it presents a problem. The compilation of this directory would require that AT&T search through its electronic phone records to ferret out individuals who have recently called these 800-numbers (this is possible since phone companies record the numbers you have dialed along with how long you were connected). This possibility raises the ethical question of whether such records should be considered private and off limits for marketing and other nonessential purposes. As technological advances make phone records more accessible, where and how does one draw the line in their use? Will the phone companies continue to examine customer dialing records to determine new kinds of information services that could be marketed to the consumer?

Both of these cases highlight the trend to expand the domain of public information. In the Lotus case, information supplied for credit purposes was to be transformed into pseudo-public marketing data that could be sold for a small fee. In the second example, the strong industry tradition of protecting phone numbers appears to be disintegrating. They both make manifest the porosity of our environment in the "information age" and the apparent need for restrictions and carefully crafted guidelines.

The fundamental problem illustrated by these two cases is that society's assumptions about the proprietary nature of information are undergoing a radical transformation—and often without the participation of those who are directly affected. Most of us have assumed that when we provide information about ourselves for a specific purpose, such information is reasonably confidential. For example, when I apply for a car loan, I expect the transaction to be a private affair between me and the bank. In the past, vendors and others saw no value in this information beyond the immediate transaction. However, as such information can more efficiently be collected, stored, retrieved, and disseminated, it now assumes some value, especially as a marketing tool. As a result, collectors of information, both in the corporate and government sectors, now consider much of the information they gather to be suitable for widespread dissemination in the public domain. For many organizations, information has become a commodity that can be collected and redistributed with very little overhead.

Indeed, even state government agencies routinely sell information they have collected about their residents. For example, the Department of Motor Vehicles, in the process of issuing a driver's license, obtains a person's name, height, weight, date of birth, use of corrective lenses, and so forth. Many states now sell this information to credit agencies such as TRW and Trans Union and to direct mail companies such as R. L. Polk, who in turn use these data to draw up targeted marketing lists for resale. Also, in his controversial book *Privacy for Sale,* Jeffrey Rothfeder reveals that agencies of the federal government have about 2,000 data banks on millions of citizens. Many of these agencies "share" this information rather freely or use it to target people suspected of some wrongdoing such as failure to pay taxes.[2]

The upshot of all these unsettling developments is that the boundary separating confidential and public information has shifted dramatically in favor of the public. However, corporations, state agencies, and even the federal government have made this transformation with little or no input from major stakeholders such as citizens and consumers. They have often acted unilaterally to change the status of information so that very little of what is provided to them is now regarded as confidential and unavailable for other uses. Moreover, they have seemingly ignored the idea that by turning information into a low-cost commodity, they have infringed upon the important rights of individual citizens.

Indeed, this subtle but relentless shift in assumptions about confidential information raises many ethical issues. The primary question is whether privacy rights are being violated by the various practices described here. To begin with, what is proprietary information and when should information remain confidential? For example, if I supply information on a loan application, do I have the right to dictate how that information will be used or do I surrender control over such information? Can information disclosed for one purpose be used for another, *secondary* purpose without the individual's consent? Or does this practice constitute an invasion of privacy? And, if it does, how can an individual retain control over such information?

For corporations, such questions also raise a key management issue: What are the legal and moral ramifications if managers do not take these questions seriously and consider more explicitly the problem of protecting privacy?

Corporations and certain government agencies that buy and sell these lists have maintained that the consumer's right to privacy is not compromised. The argument that such practices allow them to target customers efficiently certainly has some merit. Indeed, a well-targeted direct mail effort through a DBM campaign or some other mechanism is vital for the success of many companies, especially those with limited financial resources. In addition, some of these target prospects will welcome the promotional material, while others will simply ignore it. If the only adverse consequence is more unwanted mail for some people, where is the real harm? The benefits of these mailings would certainly appear to outweigh the costs. Also, nonprofit groups and political organizations rely on direct mail campaigns for financial or volunteer support.

Moreover, those who buy and sell this type of information justify their actions by appealing to the argument of commercial property rights. They contend that they "own" this information and hence have an unambiguous right to dispose of it as they see fit. It is by no means clear, however, that providing someone with information confers this sort of property right. When a consumer provides personal information, he or she does not assign to that vendor a right to use that information for other purposes. Unless there were such an explicit agreement, the "property rights" argument does not seem persuasive.

Defenders of the direct mail industry and the treatment of information as a commodity also tend to oversimplify the repercussions of these practices. For one thing, consumers legitimately worry that despite safeguards this information will fall into the wrong hands. This is possible since it is virtually impossible to keep track of data once they are sold to another organization. In addition, although many legitimate businesses use direct mail campaigns to sell their products, information could easily be sold to unscrupulous direct mail companies that engage in fraudulent marketing campaigns or other scams. Such fraudulent solicitations have bilked consumers out of millions of dollars.

Another difficulty concerns the integrity of the data collectors. Can they always be trusted to use the data appropriately and provide safeguards against potential abuses? For instance, it is now fairly common practice for physicians and pharmacists to sell computerized patient records to specialized data collectors, who in turn sell them to pharmaceutical companies interested in tracking how well their products are selling. These data collectors dial into the PC's of physicians and pharmacists and extract information from confidential records. They contend that the use of these records does not violate privacy since patient names are supposedly deleted. However, physicians and pharmacists who entrust their data to these firms have no way of knowing exactly what information is being extracted. Presently there is significant potential for abuse. There are serious questions as to whether the safeguards protecting privacy are adequate. In this embryonic and unregulated data collection industry what is to stop an unscrupulous firm from extracting and using patient names along with the other data? Moreover, once these companies have collected these data there is no control over their subsequent use. Therefore should the custodians of medical records containing such sensitive information sell them to companies even though they are not certain what information is being extracted or how it will be used? The potential for breaches of confidentiality and considerable harm befalling some patients seems to demand tighter controls and closer scrutiny of how such records can be protected.

Still another problem emanates from the power of *data recombination,* which is the correlation of information from different sources to create *new information.* For example, a data collector can purchase data from a credit agency such as TRW or Equifax and combine those data with files purchased from a state agency such as a motor vehicle bureau. The end result might be a revealing profile of an individual's personal and financial background.

The final problem concerns the accuracy of the data that are being transmitted, resold, or recombined with other data. It is well-known that data files contain outdated and inaccurate information. In addition, the larger the database the more likely there will be mistakes and anomalies. Furthermore, as these data are shared, the inaccurate information can be propagated in many different files, until it is virtually impossible to correct. In short, then, errors could take on a life of their own and cause innumerable problems for the subject of those errors.

We can summarize as follows the most salient problems with shuffling data around as if they were just a commodity:

- Potential for data to be sold to unscrupulous vendors

- Problems with insuring the trustworthiness and care of the data collectors
- Potential for data recombination to create detailed, composite profiles of individuals
- The difficulty of correcting inaccurate information once it has been propagated into many different files

It is fair to conclude, then, that the negative consequences of information sharing are more extensive and serious than industry participants are willing to admit. As these data collectors, credit unions, and direct mailers continue to cast their nets wider, consumers will lose more and more control over the information about themselves that was once thought to be confidential. At the same time the harm caused by inaccurate information will be accentuated through this free flow of data. Thus there is real danger that our personal privacy will gradually become more illusion than reality.

Given our previous discussion on the intimate connection between privacy and freedom, it would be instructive to consider how the erosion of privacy through redistributing data adversely affects our autonomy. How is our freedom impaired if our name, address, and other personal information are sold and resold and then end up on junk mailing lists?

One problem in this regard is that under these circumstances almost every transaction assumes greater significance. In our information-sharing society the consumer not only applies for a car loan at the local bank but in the process divulges important information about his or her driving habits and financial history. A consumer making a phone call to a hotel or travel agency is recording an interest in travel for the potential benefit of marketers eager for such information. A serious consequence of these practices, therefore, is that people will think more carefully before engaging in such transactions and leaving behind a permanent record of important personal data. As Richard Wasserstrom observed when privacy is so circumscribed, "life would to this degree become less spontaneous and more measured."[3] As people come to realize that information they provide will be used for other purposes, it is likely that to some extent they will be inhibited from providing that information.

Consider, for example, consumers who apply to banks or finance agencies for credit. They may become loath to make the application when they learn that all the information they provide will be listed on Equifax's Credit Seekers Hotline and subsequently sold to various vendors. Also, they may develop a reluctance to pay with a credit card when they learn that those who use Visa and Mastercard with some frequency will be put on Trans Union's "Bankcard Hotline." They may even hesitate to make certain phone calls if calling records are peddled to different proprietors.

To be sure, as isolated events these may not appear to be so serious, but the cumulative effect is likely to be a powerful constraint on the consumer's hitherto unlimited freedom in this sphere of activity. Clearly, then, the indiscriminate sharing of information and the lack of privacy and confidentiality can impair one's commercial relationships and interfere with important business transactions. Without protection in both their commercial and personal relationships, there will be real limits to their autonomy. The consumer should be free to conduct his or her affairs without the burden of an unwanted observer who tracks purchases, buying habits, phone calls, and other activities.

In summary, there are serious adverse consequences for the consumer when his or her privacy is compromised in commercial transactions. Perhaps the most serious consequence is the diminution of freedom in this area. We have been at pains to insist here that privacy is a fundamental natural right because it is an essential condition for the exercise of our self-determination. The extensive sharing of personal data is a clear example of how the erosion of privacy leads to the diminution of that freedom. Once the shield of privacy has been penetrated, the capacity of individuals to control their destiny in small and large affairs is in grave peril.

The Principle of Informed Consent and Privacy

If we take the right of privacy seriously, it seems evident that some of the policies and practices delineated here must be terminated or at least modified. It may ultimately be necessary to develop new laws and regulations to prevent the steady erosion of this basic right, but the absence of such laws should not inhibit organizations from becoming more socially responsible in this area. They should strive to be proactive in fulfilling their moral obligation to respect the privacy of others.

How, then, can organizations fulfill their obligation to respect the right of privacy? Can we discern a practical principle to guide their activities in this controversial area?

A good starting point is the assumption that the consumer prefers personal information to be regarded as confidential and not available to be traded as a commodity. To some extent the truth of this assumption depends on the nature of the information. Most people are sensitive about medical, credit, or financial information; however, some may be a bit more lenient when it comes to less significant information such as their purchasing habits. Nevertheless, a vast majority of individuals do desire to control all types of information about themselves by having some say in how that information will be shared with others. This desire imposes on the corporation the burden of seeking the consumer's permission to use that information for other purposes. But what is an appropriate method for seeking such permission?

Before answering this question, we cannot overlook the other side of this equation, that is, the need for various types of information. Targeted mailing lists, marketing surveys, and other types of data about customer prospects are the lifeblood of many organizations, especially smaller organizations and startup firms with limited resources. As was noted earlier, the DBM is an efficient marketing tool that benefits both marketers and consumers. Hence there are substantial economic benefits to the activities of data collection and sharing. In addition, as Deborah Johnson has perceptively observed, "the case for information gathering and exchange of information is made . . . on the grounds that they lead to better decision making."[4] Hence reforms that would unduly restrict the access of information could have grave negative consequences for many corporations and their stakeholders. To be sure, it would be a logistical nightmare to require marketers and DBM users to obtain explicit written permission each time they wanted to use personal data or add someone's name to a mailing list that is to be sold to other proprietors. This extreme a reform would make the use of direct mail campaigns prohibitively expensive. In short, the requirement of *affirmative consent* or explicit permission would practically destroy the direct mail and data collection industries.

However, an alternative to affirmative consent is the principle of *implicit informed consent,* which still safeguards privacy and is more economically viable. This is a slight variation of the principle of informed consent. . . . According to Carol Gould, in the context of privacy issues this principle "imposes upon the institution or agency that has or wants information the burden of seeking the consent of the subject and of informing him or her; thus the information remains under the control ab initio of the person whom it is about."[5] The normative justification for this principle is clearly based on the right to privacy and the derived right to participate in decisions affecting one's personal life and one's exercise of free choice.

According to this principle, companies that have collected data about customers must diligently inform them about the primary and secondary uses of those data. Consumers must be given an opportunity to consent to these uses or withhold their consent; but the burden is on the consumer to respond, and a lack of response implies consent. Moreover, companies must provide these customers with the opportunity to grant consent for any *subsequent* uses of these data. For example, they must give customers the option to delete their names from mailing lists designed to be sold to other organizations. Those whose names are on such lists must be notified of this fact and be given the opportunity to have their names removed by sending in a response within a certain time frame. If no response is forthcoming, it is assumed that they do not object to having their name and personal data used in this way.

We can summarize this principle of *implicit informed consent* as follows: Corporations must inform consumers about all the various uses of their personal data and refrain from using these data in ways for which consent is withheld; it is understood that no response to a request for the use of information is equivalent to the consumer's implicit consent.

It is worth noting that many conscientious publishers already engage in a similar practice out of respect for the privacy of their subscribers. For example, *The Economist* frequently rents its subscriber list to organizations seeking qualified prospects for its products or services, but it sends a booklet to all its subscribers notifying them that they have the right to have their name deleted.

Clearly, the principle of implicit informed consent is far less burdensome than the requirement of affirmative consent, since marketers will not have to wait for explicit permission. This principle is a moral minimum for those who take privacy rights seriously. It seeks to balance the need for information and the protection of informational privacy, as it offers a tenable mechanism for allowing individuals to gain control over how personal information is being used. To be sure, it is a pragmatic approach to the problem and is not without some deficiencies. It will be somewhat costly and raises several practical problems. One concerns the scope of permission granted by the consumer. Should the corporation seek unrestricted permission for the use of someone's name or do so on an ad hoc basis? The latter approach would certainly pose some logistical difficulties. Companies must also be diligent about contacting customers and providing them with a convenient way to respond. Despite these potential problems, however, this approach offers many benefits. It puts the burden on the consumer and yet gives that consumer a measure of control over personal information.

It is also worth noting that the European Economic Community is planning to adopt a wide array of rules to protect the privacy of its citizens, and a key provision entails strict restrictions on the use and exchange of computerized information. According to the European proposals, known as the Privacy Directive, "corporations using personal data must tell subjects of their use; a magazine publisher that wanted to sell its circulation list to advertisers, for example, would have to notify subscribers of its plans."[6] It has not yet been determined whether the subject must grant explicit permission or simply be notified with an option for deletion. European companies would also be required to register all commercial databases with each country in the European Community. These and other proposals incorporate principles of data protection that are seen as critical for safeguarding privacy.

Privacy Within the Corporation

Consumers, of course, are not the only group that has a basic right to privacy. Most philosophers and ethicians would insist that the right of personal privacy and other civil liberties also extend to the workplace. Patricia Werhane, for example, includes

privacy in her comprehensive list of employee rights. She maintains that the right to privacy in the workplace includes but is not restricted to the following spheres of activity:

- The employee has the right to control or limit access to the personal information that he or she provides to an employer.
- An employee has a right "to activities of his or her choice outside the workplace."
- An employee has the right to privacy of thought.[7]

In addition, as we argued earlier, the right to privacy is important because it safeguards another basic right that exists in the workplace: the right to autonomy and free expression.

How is workplace privacy threatened by advances in computer technology? One such threat involves the growing use of network management programs that allow system administrators of a PC network to read the files and documents in users' directories. More advanced programs will even allow these administrators to monitor what is being typed on an employee's computer screen. In addition, communications among different offices and even remote locations are now vulnerable to interception and scrutiny. Obviously this capacity will make it increasingly difficult for someone to send confidential memos or develop confidential files of electronic information, a constraint that could lead to serious abuses of an employee's civil liberties.

One of the most controversial issues regarding employee privacy involves the status of electronic mail (e-mail) software, which is a popular form of communication in many organizations. Through electronic mail, users can communicate with their colleagues throughout the organization as long as their computers are networked in some fashion. E-mail permits a user to send a single message simultaneously to hundreds of other users, and so it can increase efficiency by reducing paperwork and phone calls.

But as one might surmise, e-mail raises some critical concerns about privacy. For one thing, most e-mail systems generate archives of messages that can be inspected by anyone with the authority or technical acumen to do so. Should these messages be regarded as private, off limits for perusals by supervisors? Or is any form of communication over a network the property of the corporation that owns that system? In other words, do e-mail messages deserve the same privacy protection as regular mail? Are they public, private, or somewhere in between? This is a difficult question to resolve; there are cogent arguments on all sides of the debate. Also there are several lawsuits pending about this issue, and when they are settled we may have a clearer picture of the legal status of e-mail. For example, former employees of Nissan Motor Corp. U.S.A. filed a suit in 1991 claiming invasion of privacy after they were terminated because of the content of some e-mail messages that were intercepted by Nissan's management.

Most corporations would strongly insist that e-mail communications are public and hence subject to inspection at any time without any notice. They contend that the e-mail facility should be used only for business purposes and that the company has the prerogative to monitor those messages when and if it sees fit. The rationale for this policy is that e-mail is like any other business communication. Furthermore, the employer owns *all* resources in the workplace and has the right to determine how those resources will be deployed.

On the other hand, users and privacy experts contend that reading someone's e-mail is a violation of privacy. What's the difference, they say, between reading someone's handwritten mail or combing through someone's desk to find paper documents and reading the same type of information in a digital format? Hence many unions and independent organizations such as the ACLU contend that companies should not open their employees' electronic mail. In addition, the policy of checking on employees' e-mail creates a "Big Brother" atmosphere which dilutes trust in the organization and ultimately has a corrosive effect on morale. Thus a policy of monitoring e-mail may be costly in the long run and not worth the effort.

Regardless of how employers regard this controversial issue, however, they should have a clearly articulated policy regarding some of these questions. If the corporation considers e-mail messages public information, their employees should be informed that their messages are being monitored. Likewise, corporations should stipulate the legitimate uses of e-mail. A carefully worded policy regarding e-mail will go a long way to correct any false expectations on the part of employees and

can help avoid legal problems as well as negative effects on morale. There is also a need for a comprehensive policy regarding the examining of all forms of corporate communications such as paper files, electronic mail, and telephone conversations. The more employees are informed about these matters, the better off they will be and the less likely the employer will confront legal problems for its actions.

An even greater threat to privacy and autonomy in the workplace is the prevalence of broad-based electronic monitoring programs that track a worker's productivity and work habits. This technology is currently most widely utilized in service industries such as banking and insurance as well as major segments of the travel industry. There may be some disagreement about exactly what constitutes electronic monitoring, but the following is a concise and accurate definition:

> Electronic work monitoring is the computerized collection, storage, analysis, and reporting of information about employees' productive activities.[8]

Electronic monitoring is normally combined with work measurement systems that set a standard for how long a task should take, compares that standard with the actual completion time, and then issues reports showing variances for each employee. For example, the system may set a standard of one minute for a data entry clerk in a given application, that is, it should take the clerk one minute to enter a record. At the end of a given time period a report will be generated showing the list of variances for each record entered along with a summary or average variance. Similar applications might be used by a firm using telemarketing personnel. In this case it would monitor the time spent on each customer or prospect by calculating the time taken to make and complete each phone call.

It is evident from these examples that routine jobs are most conducive for electronic monitoring and work measurement. Thus, in addition to data entry clerks, customer service workers, telephone operators, word processors, and similar jobs are most frequently subjected to this computerized evaluation. One of the most popular applications is known as "telephone call accounting." Systems are designed "to measure efficiency as well as verify the legitimacy of the call."[9] By checking the time, destination, and duration of telephone calls some organizations hope to eliminate long-distance personal calls and other types of abuses that can be expensive. Some systems allow employers to go even further and listen in on phone calls between employees or between an employee and an outside party.

Beyond any doubt, the primary benefit of electronic monitoring systems is their ability to help increase efficiency and reduce waste in an organization. However, these systems may lead to unrealistic and burdensome work standards, which dehumanize workers, increase turnover, and in the long run may militate against achieving real efficiency. These systems may also go too far in invading personal privacy. It can be argued that telephone accounting is necessary to keep spiraling costs under control. However, if corporations seek to achieve this goal by listening in to employee conversations, a case can surely be made that they are violating the employee's right to privacy. If an organization systematically monitors its workers' conversations, it cannot avoid listening to personal conversations in addition to those that are work related. Sometimes in an emergency such conversations with family members or others are simply unavoidable; in these cases the corporation will be privy to information about an employee's personal life that it has no right to possess.

By monitoring work-related conversations and electronic mail in the workplace, the corporation stifles free expression and creates an Orwellian atmosphere that most employees will find oppressive and stressful. One serious problem, of course, is that the information gleaned from such monitoring can be unfairly used against these employees. If the rights of privacy and free expression are to be respected, such surveillance methods must be restricted.

Thus it is not surprising that union leaders and other labor advocates have expressed strong opposition to computerized monitoring systems. They are concerned about invasions of privacy and an overreliance on quantitative data as the basis of performance evaluations. The problem, they contend, is that many aspects of an employee's work are not conducive to such strict quantitative measures. For example, a travel agent may process many more travel reservations than his or her peers but in the process be abrupt and discourteous and thereby alienate some of the agency's customers. Of course, there are benefits to relying on quantitative data, since their use will reduce subjectivity and biases and in the long run could yield a fairer evaluation system.

There are considerable empirical data about the effects of computerized monitoring systems, but they are rather inconclusive. One study, focusing on a monitoring system at a large insurance company, concluded that the system produced fear and resentment among the employees and significantly elevated their stress level. Another exploratory study of several insurance companies and financial institutions concluded that "the introduction of computerized performance monitoring may result in a workplace that is less satisfying to many employees." The study also concluded that "extensive use of numerical performance feedback seems to create a more competitive environment which may decrease the quality of social relationships between peers and between supervisors and subordinates."[10] But the authors of this study also found that most workers were not opposed in principle to such systems, but only to how they were used by management. Also a government study of electronic monitoring reaches an even more disturbing conclusion. According to Dr. Michael Smith of the Office of Technology Assessment:

> Electronic monitoring may create adverse working conditions such as paced work, lack of involvement, reduced task variety and clarity, reduced peer social support, reduced supervisory support, fear of job loss, routinized work activity, and lack of control over tasks.[11]

Other studies, on the other hand, illustrate more positive effects from these systems, such as an improvement in employee evaluations, especially the timeliness and quality of feedback to individual employees.[12] Thus, in general it seems evident that companies contemplating the introduction of these systems should proceed with caution to avoid some of the undesirable effects noted here. Further, at a minimum, companies should clearly state their monitoring policies.

Finally, it should be pointed out that the notion of employee rights such as privacy and free expression is not universally accepted. Many still cling to the traditional doctrine of Employment at Will (EAW), stating that employers may hire, fire, promote, or demote "at will." According to this viewpoint, which has been supported even in recent court cases, "in freely taking a job, an employee voluntarily commits herself to role responsibilities and company loyalty, both of which are undermined by the intrusion of certain employee rights."[13] Advocates of this position would likely claim that employees do not enjoy the rights of privacy and autonomy in the workplace, especially if that right interferes with the efficiency and productivity of the organization. For those who take this position, the electronic monitoring and work measurement methods described here will probably be less problematic.

Summary

One of the primary by-products of the information revolution seems to be the attendant loss of personal privacy. This is a critical issue, since privacy is an important natural right. Although the right to privacy is protected by a patchwork of federal privacy laws and regulations, there is no comprehensive set of such regulations. Hence there are many loopholes and shortcomings in the current laws and regulations that protect privacy. Despite the law's failure to keep up with technology, corporations should seriously consider the importance of respecting the natural right of privacy. Privacy is not only important in itself but also as a condition for the exercise of freedom and self-determination. Without privacy, our lives become more controlled and our dignity as human persons can be impaired.

A key aspect of the moral basis for privacy is the right to control information about oneself. It is this right that is most in jeopardy from advances in digital technology. Information has become a commodity that is collected and stored in huge databases and sold to vendors for direct mail purposes. Sometimes this information is recombined with other information, allowing a vendor to develop a composite profile of individual consumers. All of these activities raise important ethical questions for which there are no easy answers: What exactly constitutes confidential, proprietary information in the age of digital disclosure? Can information disclosed for one purpose be used for secondary purposes without an individual's consent?

Many defenders of the direct mail industry and database marketing are quick to point out that the only harm of these practices is more unwanted mail for some people. We have maintained, however, that there are more serious adverse consequences, including the difficulty of correcting any inaccurate information that has been propagated in files, the dangerous power of data recombination, and the possibility that such data will be sold to unscrupulous vendors for use in direct mail scams. We have also claimed that another serious consequence of these information-sharing practices will be some diminution of the consumer's freedom; many will have reservations about engaging in transactions (such as using credit cards) that leave behind a permanent record of personal data.

However, one must also consider the need for information as a basis for good decision making and the importance of targeted direct mail campaigns, especially for companies with limited resources. Given this situation, perhaps a principle of *implicit informed consent* represents a viable compromise between the needs of business and the privacy of consumers. According to this principle, companies must inform consumers about the primary and secondary uses of their personal information and refrain from using these data if consent is withheld; it is understood that a lack of response to a request for the use of this information is equivalent to the consumer's implicit consent. For instance, companies must give customers the option to delete their names from mailing lists destined to be sold to other organizations. The burden is on the consumer to respond, but this practice will nevertheless enable consumers to regain some control over how their personal information is used.

In future years we may find clever technological solutions to the problem of protecting personal privacy. For instance, some have suggested that a system be devised whereby one's electronic identity is simply a number that is not connected to one's physical self. Account numbers would be attached to encrypted identities, so, for example, data collectors could never determine that Sally Jones was connected with account number 2378125.[14]

Privacy is also an issue for employees, who must now face an array of monitoring devices and other technologies that allow corporations to read their files and monitor their work habits. There is also considerable controversy about employees' use of e-mail and whether these electronic communications are public or private. Many organizations regard these communications as public because they are transmitted across company-owned networks, but privacy advocates maintain that they should be considered as private and confidential communications. As we observed, those corporations that do choose to monitor electronic mail will create a "big brother," Orwellian atmosphere that many employees will find quite demoralizing.

We also discussed other types of electronic monitoring and work measurement systems that track employee work patterns. Such systems are often utilized to set a standard for how long a task should take; they then compare that standard with the actual completion time. Although there are some positive effects of such systems such as better and faster feedback, they can also increase employee stress levels and generate considerable apprehension and loss of morale in the workplace. In addition, electronic monitoring systems may go too far when they lead to the establishment of unrealistic and onerous work standards. Indeed, these systems are designed to enhance efficiency, but they could backfire if they end up dehumanizing workers and increasing employee turnover. At a minimum, corporations should make their monitoring policies as clear and comprehensive as possible.

NOTES

1. David Chaum, "Security without Identification: Transaction Systems to Make Big Brother Obsolete," *Communications of the ACM*, 21 (1985), p. 1030.
2. Jeffrey Rothfeder, *Privacy for Sale* (New York: Simon & Schuster, 1992), pp. 124–52.
3. Richard Wasserstrom, "Privacy: Some Arguments and Assumptions," in *Philosophical Dimensions of Privacy: An Anthology*, ed. Ferdinand Schoeman (New York: Cambridge University Press, 1984), p. 328.
4. Deborah Johnson, *Computer Ethics* (Englewood Cliffs, NJ: Prentice-Hall, 1985), p. 62.
5. Gould, "Network Ethics," p. 27.
6. John Markoff, "Europe's Plans to Protect Privacy Worry Business," *The New York Times*, April 11, 1991, p. A1. Copyright © 1991 by The New York Times Company. Reprinted by permission.
7. Patricia Werhane, *Persons, Rights, and Corporations* (Englewood Cliffs, NJ: Prentice-Hall, 1985), p. 119.
8. John Chalykoff and Nitin Nohria, "Note on Electronic Monitoring," (Cambridge, MA: *Harvard Business School Publications*, 1990), p. 1.
9. Ibid., p. 3.
10. R. H. Irving, C. A. Higgins, F. R. Safayeni, "Computerized Performance Monitoring Systems: Use and Abuse," *Communications of the ACM*, August 1986, p. 800.
11. Quoted in Karen Nussbaum, "Computer Monitoring: A Threat to the Right to Privacy," *Ethical Issues in Information Systems*, ed. Roy Dejoie, George Fowler, and David Paradice (Boston: Boyd & Fraser Publishing, 1991), p. 136.
12. See the article by Irving, Higgins, and Safayeni for a discussion of these studies.
13. Werhane, *Persons, Rights, and Corporations*, p. 83.
14. John Perry Barlow, "Private Life in Cyberspace," *Communications of the ACM*, August 1991, pp. 23–25.

Some Effects of the New Technology on Women

Jan Zimmerman

Caretaking functions, like day care for children of working mothers, adult day care for the dependent segment of the senior population, and reha-

bilitative services for the physically or mentally handicapped, are being reinterpreted as chores that should be handled in a "loving family atmosphere"—and that means women—mothers, grandmothers, daughters or wives—at home. Very, very rarely have men undertaken such unpaid, labor-intensive activities.

With this twist of the prism, the disadvantages

of telecommuting—working by computer from the home—suddenly appear. Telecommuting, lauded as a means of saving gasoline and saving time, encourages the transmutation of societal obligations into women's obligations, while simultaneously serving the ends of the pro-family movement, which seeks to re-create the nuclear family. With electronic homework, the elderly can become self-supporting and "more desirable to have around," says a National Science Foundation Report.[1] With electronic homework, says futurist Alvin Toffler, citing an Institute for the Future prediction, "married secretaries caring for small children at home [can] continue to work."[2] (Nowhere is there any mention of telecommuting fathers caring for small children or the elderly.)

The values behind these images are trebly discriminatory. First, the assumption that women should be the ones to stay home and care for the young, the old, and the infirm reinforces socialization patterns that link gender and nurturance. Second, the statement implies that neither women's worklife nor their caretaking function is important enough to demand full-time attention. (A woman cannot concentrate on meaningful work with an infant on her lap. Nor can a woman working on a computer at home keep a toddler away from the stove or read to an elderly parent; day care is still essential.) And third, it presumes that women will continue to hold routine, low-paying data entry jobs, thus completing the vicious circle that makes those jobs the only ones caretaking mothers can hold. These assumptions run counter to two recent social changes: women's surge into the labor force (women composed nearly 45 percent of the U.S. and over 40 percent of the U.K. work force in 1983, and contributed to the financial support of 97 percent of the U.S. families and 88 percent of British ones); and the increasing variety of family forms (less than 7 percent of American households in 1980 were composed of the traditional homemaker Mom, breadwinner Dad, two or more kids, and a dog; in the U.K. the figure is about 11 percent).[3] By reinforcing these outdated assumptions, however, electronic homework is manipulated to re-create the past.

Telecommuting promises two very different types of work experiences for those at the upper and lower ends of the occupational scale: data entry clerks and secretaries will handle routine tasks under continuous computer scrutiny of their performance and hours, while professionals will have discretionary working hours and unrestricted freedom to use the computer for personal tasks, such as home accounting and data base access.[4] As long as job segregation persists (women make up more than 95 percent of all secretaries and data entry personnel in the U.S. but less than 30 percent of all managers and administrators[5]), telecommuting will be much less tantalizing for women than it is for men in managerial positions, to whom it offers greater independence.

For immigrant, sometimes undocumented, third world women, who constitute the majority of electronics assemblers, computer homework has a different meaning. Those minimally skilled Asian women and Latinas who hope to earn a living in high-tech environments like "Silicon Valley" in California find themselves packing circuit boards on a piecework basis in their kitchens and garages, often pressing their children into service, even if dangerous chemicals are involved. Manufacturers, who generally hire subcontractors to manage such "electronics sweatshops," appreciate this system: they can pay below minimum wages, eliminate benefits, and avoid occupational health and safety regulations. Labor contractors frequently collect kickbacks from the women, who are grateful for the work, willing to accept overhead costs as their own, and too terrified of immigration authorities to report abuses.[6]

If these obviously exploitative conditions could be eliminated, home-based assembly work *could* be of real benefit. Since low-paid assembly workers often cannot afford day care, second cars, or housing near their jobs, homework offers these women a chance to reduce the cost and time of commuting long distances by public transit, and an escape from hostile, often racially discriminatory work environments. Because they do not address those needs, the efforts of some labor unions to outlaw homework meet with resistance from female workers.[7]

There are alternatives that would both avoid the abuses of piecework practices and meet justifiable labor union concerns. Unions, for instance, could act as hiring halls, monitoring pay scales to assure that fair wages and benefits are paid. Or assembly workers could form collectives to establish decentralized, neighborhood-based, miniworksites, with day care on the premises and oc-cupational safety and health conditions regulated. Electronics assembly or computer workstation sites could be shared by people working for many differ-ent companies. As independent contractors, these women could set their own hours, work without su-pervision, and elect their own facilities coordinator.

Rose-Colored Glasses, Rose-Covered Cottages

Cottage industry, or "putting out," first became popular during the early stages of the Industrial Revolution. Prior to that time, each household manufactured fabric and clothing from start to fin-ish, with all members of the household sharing both the work and the money made by selling sur-plus goods. Spinning wheels and looms [were] owned by the family, which controlled the tempo and quality of its work; housework [was] a visible part of the seamless web of tasks whose completion allowed the family to survive. But by the mid-eighteenth century, entrepreneurs who owned the new carding machines and water-powered spin-ning frames that had been developed to speed up textile manufacture took control of the production process.[8]

The entrepreneurs rationalized production by "putting out" the separate tasks of cleaning, spin-ning, drying, weaving, and sewing to different households, which then competed to provide the greatest output at the lowest prices. Initially, the cash income of the cottage industry household rose, but at the cost of reduced activity in the bar-ter economy.[9] As the Industrial Revolution con-tinued, new inventions like water- and steam-powered looms provided the impetus to centralize production in factories. By 1790 the brief age of "putting out" was over. Centralized factories in-creased output, as expected, but they also further divided textile work into the specific, repetitive tasks done by speeders, drawers, dressers, and warpers. In the process, workers lost money and entrepreneurs and investors made it.

Under the factory system, the family wage dis-appeared and the net purchasing power of the household decreased.[10] Employers paid low wages for relatively unskilled tasks, continually reduced piecework pay rates to keep earnings down, and at least one former cash-earner, often the wife, had to remain at home to provide child care and support services for all the family members employed out-side the home.[11] (Even at that time, single women working in the mills earned, on the average, only 57 cents for every male dollar. The lowest factory wage for men was almost invariably greater than the highest wage for women.)[12]

On the other hand, the investors who put up capital to buy equipment earned enormous profits. For one textile firm, the Boston Manufacturing Company, sales skyrocketed from $3,000 annually in 1814 to more than 100 times that figure eight years later. Between 1814 and 1823 the company's assets grew almost twentyfold, increasing from $39,000 to $771,000.[13] The company paid its inves-tors 20 percent dividends every year between 1817 and 1825, but laborers' wages—and household income—did not keep pace.[14] Textile technology spread its impact throughout the entire society, but its rewards were distributed more narrowly.

Although the cottage industry mentality com-pared rather favorably to factory-based, mass-production techniques, it still separated house-work from "productive" labor. In many cases, housework that had been shared by all members of the artisan family devolved solely upon women, while other family members concentrated on pro-ducing goods that brought in cash. Since cash pay-ment was associated with textile labor inside the home, but not with the effort women expended on housework, cottage industries contributed to the devaluation of women's work. The much-acclaimed computerized retreat to the electronic cottage thus appears less a vision of "progress" than a backward glance through a rearview mirror. Rather than a stop en route to an even better artisan age, the electronic cottage heralds another form of owner-controlled, supervised, and rationalized la-bor. Perhaps poet Paul Valery, who said that "the future is not what it used to be," had only the half of it; the past doesn't seem to be what it used to be, either.

The Global Assembly Line

In the decentralized factory of the future, the worker will buy her/his own tools (i.e. a computer and peripherals) and absorb all overhead costs—

rent, heat, equipment insurance, telephone connection charges and installation fees (if one line is continually tied up for computer transmission, the worker must install another line for calls), electrical usage, and installation of a power supply that is more stable than the one electrical utilities usually provide to residences. In addition, employees are likely to lose opportunities for promotion (promotion usually means becoming a supervisor, but there will be fewer workers to supervise), to receive lower earnings because of competitive, piecework payment or flat-rate, contract wage schemes, and forfeit benefits (for example, will a company pay worker's compensation for an employee working at home? Will home workers become self-employed, independent subcontractors liable for all social security taxes, instead of half? Revisions in the 1983 U.S. tax code cite these very consequences as a definition of the term "independent contractor.")

If workers don't accept the wonderful way in which new technology decreases employers' costs, they will be out of luck. Already, "offshore offices" are following runaway factories to the cheap labor of the Sunbelt and the third world. George R. Simpson, chairman of Satellite Data Corporation, says his company relays printed materials by satellite from New York to Barbados, where data entry clerks are paid only $1.50 an hour. As he told *Business Week* magazine, "We can do the work in Barbados for less than it costs in New York to pay for floor space. . . . The economics are so compelling that a company could take a whole building in Hartford, Connecticut, and transfer the whole function to India or Pakistan."[15]

Already, similar economic arguments have been used to justify transferring electronics assembly jobs to the export processing zone (EPZs) of developing countries. Eighty-five to 90 percent of the workers on the global assembly line are female; since most are single and under the age of 25, they are expected to submit docilely to patterns of domination within the factory that mimic traditional patriarchal family relationships.[16] For the manufacturer, the global assembly line offers great savings. Hourly wages that average $4.50 in the United States are typically reduced to hourly rates of $1.15 in Hong Kong, 90 cents in Mexico, 48 cents in Malaysia, or 19 cents in Indonesia.[17] Shipping costs on lightweight components are low, and the components are taxed only on the value added in the overseas assembly process (for example, soldering fine gold wires to the microscopic integrated circuits etched on a silicon chip). For large production runs, "packing" various chips onto a board is usually done overseas, but small runs are often "jobbed out" to minority women in industrial nations. The seemingly endless supply of cheap, female labor in Asia and Latin America obviates any need to provide decent benefits, good working conditions, protection for workers' health, promotional opportunities, or job enrichment; the resulting high job turnover rate is welcomed as a means of discouraging unionization.[18]

As long as the profits of new technology return primarily to those who finance it, rather than to those who produce it, international capital will continue to flow to third world countries so those profits can be maximized. Manufacturers argue that cheap overseas labor is the only way to produce competitively priced goods, a red herring that distracts attention from the millions of dollars spent on advertising, marketing, packaging, promotion, executive salaries, bonuses, "golden parachutes" (benefits for executives who lose their jobs), and dividends. There are, in fact, many other ways to produce competitively priced goods; the question is: from whose pocket will the competitive edge be picked?

• • •

Dividing the World: Hands

Robots for factory automation . . . computers for office automation . . . techniques for manufacturing silicon chips and solar cells . . . gene splicing . . . nuclear power plants. New jobs in new technologies, all right, but not for women. By 1979 these fields had opened up more than 13 million jobs in the United States,[19] but women hold very few of them, especially at the technical level. (Depending on the field, women's participation ranges roughly from 5–25 percent of all engineers, scientists and technicians.)[20] As in more traditional job categories, women's jobs are concentrated at the lower end of the pay scale. Whether a woman assembles circuit boards or plucks chickens, she still makes only about $4.50 or £3 an hour, and she still makes less than men doing the same job.[21]

Neither women's increased participation in the labor force nor the loss of high-paying, unionized, male jobs in the old industrial fields of coal mining, steel production, and car manufacture has appreciably narrowed the wage gap; U.S. women earned 64 cents to the male dollar in 1955, 59 cents in 1981, and 62 cents in 1982. In the U.K. women have not fared much better. In 1983, women working full-time earned 64.5 percent of what men were paid.[22] On a broad social level, this situation will not improve in the short term. Although high-technology industries forecast phenomenal growth over the next ten years, the expansion for low-paying, predominantly female, service jobs will be more than five times the projected growth in high-technology employment.[23] Unless the concept of equal pay for work of comparable worth becomes a reality, new technology will not erase the boundary between women's work and men's work, but rather will redraw it in indelible ink.

For instance, three-quarters of women's jobs in the computer field are in the low-paying categories of keypunch, data entry, and computer operations, while three-quarters of men's jobs are in the much more remunerative fields of machine repair, programming, systems analysis, and other computer specialties. Female computer professionals in the U.S. earn only 75 percent of men's wages; the average wage disparity over all computer occupations is $5,000 to $7,000 each year—enough for a small car, a year's rent, or an annual college tuition bill.[24] Only one percent of female computer professionals earn more than $50,000 a year, which is generally considered the dividing line between middle management and the executive suite.

Although Ada Byron Lovelace programmed the world's first computer (Charles Babbage's differential engine) in 1840 and women like Captain Grace Hopper (U.S. Naval Reserves) programmed the Mark I, one of the first modern computers, during and after World War II, their contributions were considered exceptional. At first, programming was considered a routine, clerical task (female), but later, as a computer technology matured, programming was elevated to an esoteric realm for "wizards" (male). Partly because there were few formal opportunities to learn computer science in schools (learning took place on an *ad hoc* basis in science and engineering centers where computers were plentiful and women were scarce), women's participation was set back nearly twenty years. When colleges started to offer training in computer science

in the late 1960s, women began to enter the field in greater numbers. Now that women constitute nearly 30 percent of all programmers, programming is once again becoming a routine clerical job through the use of automatic program generators, structured programming techniques, and packaged applications software.[25] A July 1980 issue of *Computerworld* unintentionally headlined the irony. One story read, "Programmers seen needing fewer skills," while another in the same issue announced, "Project opens computer science jobs to women."[26]

Computing is not alone, of course. Even the young, nontraditional practitioners of appropriate technologies in the Aquarian age can't avoid pervasive job segregation. Anecdotal evidence shows women in charge of gardening, food preservation, aquaculture, and worm farming, men in charge of alternative energy sources—solar, wind, hydro, and biomass.[27] The biological sciences have always been friendlier to women than the physical sciences, but even here there is segregation. Genetic engineering and molecular biology sport tweedy "masculine" labels, whereas physiology and botany flirt with "feminine" tags. (This fact makes 1983 Nobel laureate Barbara McClintock's achievement in elucidating the role of "jumping genes" of Indian corn all the more spectacular; her recognition was thirty years late.)

Partially as a consequence of discriminatory employment in many fields, new technology encourages its own discriminatory application. The ubiquitous computer enables management to record keystroke and error rates for typists and data entry personnel, to pay piecework rates for information processing, and to implement work speedups. In 1981 the National Institute for Occupational Safety and Health found that clerical workers using video display terminals (VDTs) exhibit higher levels of job stress than any other category of workers ever studied, including air traffic controllers. By comparison, professional writers and editors using VDTs, who control the pace of their own work and receive recognition for it, have the lowest stress.[28] Women, of course, hold 95 percent of those high-stress clerical VDT job slots.[29]

Similarly, women suffer disproportionately from the work rationalization or deskilling effects of most office automation schemes. Rationalization is the division of labor into ever finer, more specialized tasks. In many automated offices secretarial work is now divided so that one person does word processing all day, another does electronic filing, and a third answers the phone.[30] Women who have recently entered middle management are equally vulnerable. Writer Barbara Garson quotes an executive who describes the future corporate structure quite graphically:[31]

> We are moving from the pyramid shape to the Mae West. The employment chart of the future will still show those swellings on the top, and we'll never completely get rid of those big bulges of clerks on the bottom. What we're trying to do right now is pull in that waistline (expensive middle management and skilled secretaries).

Computers and other new forms of office technology—electronic mail, telefacsimile, voice store-and-forward message systems, voice and optical character recognizers—offer management new opportunities to control a female work force that has just started to organize; the technology itself does not demand that those opportunities be seized. A sensitive company could implement office automation in humanitarian ways to increase productivity and reduce error rates, but still offer job diversification, create career ladders, and save jobs. In reality, though, the men at the top who control the process are increasingly distant from the women controlled by it.

Other technologies find different razors to slice labor into similar gender divisions. In the case of hazardous new manufacturing processes, for example, women of childbearing age may be excluded from employment unless they agree to be sterilized. In 1978 five women needed their jobs at American Cyanamid's Willow Bend, West Virginia, pigment plant so badly that they underwent sterilization rather than be demoted to lower-paying jobs.[32] Focusing on women's unsuitability as a class whether or not they intend to have children diverts attention from the fact that jobs hazardous to women's reproductive systems may be just as hazardous to men's; efforts should be directed to make the jobs safe for both.

Genetic screening offers another means of excluding women from the workplace. Seventeen companies in the United States have already begun using this technique (and forty-two more intend to), ostensibly to identify workers who may be susceptible to occupational diseases caused by environmental pollutants. This rather inaccurate screening method can be used to discriminate against women with "faulty genes."[33]

Robotics, which is seen as a threat to "male" jobs on assembly lines in heavy industry, is concurrently identified as a new career opportunity for displaced male workers. Robotics will also displace the predominantly female workers who assemble electronics, manufacture textiles, inspect and test products, or pack and wrap goods,[34] but no one talks about retraining women to produce or supervise their robotic replacements. In a typical catch-22, women are offered no training opportunities, yet they are excluded from this new field because they lack appropriate skills.

The New Automation: Who Puts the Coffee in the Coffee Pot?

"I thought we spent all that money on the machine because they said the operators never had to sit around and do nothing." Typist Ellen Levy still shudders when she thinks of that remark, made by her boss's wife while Ellen waited for the computer to finish printing out a job.[35] The temptation is so great to identify the worker with her equipment that the person behind the work disappears in a fog of words: "When can your machine do this?" Human beings become the machines they operate: word processors, keypunchers, spinners, stampers. The identification becomes so pervasive that supervisors wonder, "If the machine is doing all the work, why is it taking so long?"

When computers, electric weed clippers, robots, microwave ovens, and digitally controlled coffee makers are taken for granted, the labor involved becomes invisible. But someone still has to run the weed clipper, prepare the meal, enter data, put coffee in the coffee maker, and throw away the old grounds. Particularly when that someone is a woman, whose labor is likely to be either unpaid or underpaid, we forget that work is even required. Such invisibility is particularly destructive to women since new technologies disperse the work done by paid female labor to unpaid female consumers.

Banking or paying bills by computer, touch-tone phone, or videotex, for instance, will result in extensive job loss for bank tellers, bookkeepers, record keepers, and clerical workers, all female jobs. We know that the work these women do is valuable: Citibank in New York charges customers who have less than $500 in their accounts twenty-five cents for every transaction with a human being, instead of with an automatic teller machine (ATM). (The bank tried to limit "live" teller service to customers whose minimum balance was $5,000, but public outrage forced them to devise a less offensive, but equally income-discriminatory, formula. Can you imagine waiting outside on a cold, rainy day to use an ATM?)[36]

Companies whose accounts will be electronically credited when clients "dial-their-dollars-direct" from home will collectively save millions of dollars that they now spend on clerical and book-keeping services. They ought to *pay* their customers for the savings they will realize, but of course they won't. Hey, we're supposed to be grateful for the convenience; after all, we're not standing in the rain waiting in line, are we?

When people start checking out their food, shoes, and jogging suits on home TV screens, retail clerks and grocery checkers will join the unemployment line, right behind the tellers and billing clerks. Hard-working librarians will be next, since videotex will offer a handy substitute for the library services cut during an era of tight budgets. And don't forget the airplane reservation clerk and ticket sellers, whose jobs will also fall prey to the green screen. The telephone company already has replaced live voices and real people with speech synthesizers that provide forwarding numbers, time, weather, and directory assistance.

Unpaid consumers, primarily women, will be doing the work women used to be paid to do. In 1982 females in the U.S. made up 60 percent of all retail sales clerks, 85 percent each of librarians, billing clerks, and cashiers, 92 percent of telephone operators, 94 percent of bank tellers, and 98 percent of telephone receptionists—all occupations that will become obsolete in the Information Age. On the other half of the great gender divide, men will come out ahead with new technology. In 1982 in the U.S. they held the overwhelming percentage of jobs for which demand will rise as home information services proliferate: 78 percent of all ship-

ping clerks; 90 percent of electronic technicians; 94 percent of delivery services and route workers, 95 percent each of TV, computer, and home appliance repair and installation technicians.[37] Look at it this way: all those unpaid female consumers will have been really well trained!

NOTES

1. R. Rheinhold, "Study Says Technology Could Transform Society," *New York Times,* June 14, 1982, p. A16.
2. A. Toffler, *The Third Wave* (New York: William Morrow, 1980), p. 215; (London, Pan Books, 1981).
3. "Women and the Family" and "Women and the Economy," *WEAL Washington Report,* 12 (June/July 1983), p. 1, 3; and Matrix, *Making Space: Women and the Man-made Environment* (London: Pluto Press, 1984), p. 5: "About one in nine of all households consist of a man *with* a paid job, a woman *without* one and children under the age of 16." M. Harris, *America Now: The Anthropology of a Changing Culture* (New York: Simon & Schuster, 1981), p. 97.
4. B. A. Gutek, "Women's Work in the Office of the Future," in J. Zimmerman, *The Technological Woman: Interfacing with Tomorrow* (New York, Praeger, 1983), pp. 159–68.
5. N. F. Rytina, "Earnings of Men and Women: A Look at Specific Occupations," *Monthly Labor Review,* April 1983, pp. 25–31.
6. For this and the following paragraph, see: R. Morales, "Cold Shoulder on a Hot Stove," in Zimmerman, pp. 169–80. P. Mattera, "Home Computer Sweatshop," *The Nation,* 2 (April 1983): pp. 390–92.
7. Morales, op. cit., pp. 173–79. "Worksteaders' Clean Up," *Newsweek,* January 9, 1984, pp. 86–87. N. Katz, "Join the Future Now: Women and Work in the Electronics Industry," San Francisco State University, 1981, photocopy. Ursula Huws discusses union participation in the U.K. in her book *The New Homeworkers* (London: Low Pay Unit, 1984).
8. T. Dublin, *Women at Work* (New York: Columbia University Press, 1979), pp. 5, 14–16. R. Baxautall *et al.,* eds., *America's Working Women* (New York: Random House, 1976), pp. 13–15, 20–21. A. Oakley, *Woman's Work: The Housewife Past and Present* (New York: Vintage Books, 1976), pp. 32–36.
9. Ibid., pp. 35–36.
10. J. Pinchbeck, *Women Workers and the Industrial Revolution* (New York: August M. Kelley, reprinted 1969), p. 4; (London: Virago, 1981).
11. Dublin, op. cit., p. 109. E. Abbott, *Women in Industry: A study in American Economic History* (New York: Arno Press, reprinted 1969), p. 269.
12. Ibid., 279. Dublin, op. cit., p. 66. See also A. Clark,

The Working Life of Women in the Seventeenth Century
(London: Routledge & Kegan Paul, 1982; first published 1919).

13. Dublin, op. cit., p. 18.
14. According to Dublin, op. cit., p. 137, "Output per worker averaged across these firms rose by almost 49% from 1836 to 1850, while daily wages increased only 4%."
15. "The Instant Offshore Office," *Business Week,* March 15, 1982, p. 136E.
16. M.P. Fernadez-Kelly, "Gender and Industry on Mexico's New Frontier," in J. Zimmerman, ed., *The Technological Woman: Interfacing with Tomorrow* (New York: Praeger, 1983), pp. 18–29.
17. Hourly wages from *Semiconductor International,* February 1982, chart shown in: A. Fuentes and B. Enrenreich, *Women in the Global Factory,* INC pamphlet no. 2, Institute for New Communications, (New York: South End Press, 1983), p. 9.
18. R. Morales, "Cold Shoulder on a Hot Stove," in Zimmerman, ed., op. cit., pp. 169–80.
19. "America Rushes to High Tech for Growth," *Business Week,* March 28, 1983, pp. 84–87, 90.
20. N. F. Rytina, "Earnings of Men and Women: A Look at Specific Occupations," *Monthly Labor Review,* April 1982, pp. 25–31.
21. Rytina, op. cit., pp. 26–29.
22. "Consumer income report," *Current Population Reports,* P-60, U.S. Department of Commerce, Bureau of the Census, Washington, D.C., 1983. *Employment Gazette,* U.K., October 1983.
23. "America Rushes to High Tech Jobs for Growth," op. cit. E. Rothschild, "Reagan and the Real America," *The New York Review,* February 15, 1981, pp. 12–17.
24. J. Zimmerman, "Women in Computing: Meeting the Challenge in an Automated Industry," *Interface Age* 12 (December 1983): 79, 86–88.
25. P. Kraft, *Programmers and Managers* (New York: Springer Verlag, 1977).
26. B. Schulz, "Programmers Seen Needing Fewer Skills," *Computerworld,* July 28, 1980, pp. 1, 6.
27. "Funded by National Science Foundation: Project Opens Computer Science Jobs to Women," *Computerworld,* July 28, 1980, p. 17.
27. J. Smith, *Something Old, Something New, Something Borrowed, Something Due: Women and Appropriate Technology* (Missoula, Montana: Women and Technology Project, 1978).
28. U.S. Department of Health and Human Services, "Potential Health Hazards of Video Display Terminals," DHSS (NIOSH), no. 81-129, Cincinnati, Ohio, 1981.
29. J. Gregory, "The Next Move: Organizing Women in the Office," in J. Zimmerman, ed., *The Technological Woman: Interfacing with Tomorrow* (New York: Praeger, 1983), p. 260.
30. Ibid., pp. 260–72.
31. Quoted in B. Garson, "The Electronic Sweatshop: Scanning the Office of the Future," *Mother Jones* 6 (July 1981): 41.
32. A. Mereson, "The New Fetal Protectionism: Women Workers Are Sterilized or Lose Their Jobs," *Civil Liberties,* July 1982, pp. 6–7. See also: R. Petchesky, "Workers, Reproductive Hazards, and the Politics of Protection: An Introduction," *Feminist Studies* 5 (Summer 1979): pp. 233–45. W. Chavkin, "Occupational Hazards to Reproduction: A Review Essay and Annotated Bibliography, *Feminist Studies* 5 (Summer 1979): 311–25.
33. "Genes on the Job," *Science for the People,* November/December 1982, pp. 7–8.
34. B. Cornish, "Robots See, Hear, Feel," *The Futurist,* August 1981, pp. 11–13. O. Friedrich, "The Robot Revolution," *Time,* December 8, 1980, pp. 72–83. Rytina, op. cit.
35. S. Otos and E. Levy, "Word Processing: This Is Not a Final Draft," in Zimmerman, ed., *The Technological Woman,* op. cit., p. 152.
36. Citibank, New York, telephone conversation with author's research associate to confirm fees, February 24, 1984. "Citibank relents on rule limiting live-teller access," Los Angeles Times, May 31, 1983, p. IV-2.
37. All statistics from Rytina, op. cit.

Study Questions

1. Based on your reading of the case study "E-Mail Policy at Johnson & Dresser," how would you advise Jason Perry to formulate a comprehensive policy governing use of and access to e-mail messages at Johnson & Dresser? How would you defend your advice?

2. What new technologies does Bill Gates envision will be available to workers in the twenty-first century? How does he believe those devices will improve our lives?

3. How, according to Jeremy Rifkin, can the mass unemployment he foresees for the early part of the twenty-first century be forestalled or prevented? Are his suggestions defensible?

4. Why does Spafford reject consequentialist justifications for computer break-ins? Explain his preferred moral perspective in your own words.

5. Make explicit what Spafford calls "the social protector" argument. What does he find objectionable in this argument?

6. According to Nissenbaum, what are the likely negative consequences of permitting unauthorized copying of proprietary software? Why does she discount these consequences?

7. What objections does Nissenbaum raise to the claim that software developers have a right to place absolute limits on the reproduction of their programs? Do you agree with those reasons?

8. Explain as best you can in your own words the distinction between affirmative consent and implied informed consent. Why does Spinello think that the latter is more "economically viable"?

9. Employers argue that in certain circumstances employee surveillance is a business necessity. For what jobs might this be a plausible claim? For what jobs is the claim less plausible? Can computerized surveillance mechanisms undermine employee loyalty? If so, could you argue that they are inefficient? Discuss.

10. Zimmerman cites a National Science Foundation report and quotes Alvin Toffler regarding the effects of telecommuting on women. Why does she find the images discussed in these sources discriminatory?

11. According to Zimmerman, what effect will automation have on women? Speculate upon what could be done to mollify these tendencies.

CASE SCENARIO 1   The Robert Morris Case

Around 6 PM EST on Wednesday, November 2, 1988, a computer "worm" was discovered in a system in Pennsylvania. Soon the worm was spreading itself across Internet, which connects many research and university systems. By 10 PM the worm had managed to infect the Bay Area Research Network (BARnet), which is one of the fastest and most sophisticated in the nation. At this time, the worm exploded quickly throughout Internet, and teams of computer wizards combined forces to stop the threat.

The worm attacked the system in three different ways. First, it simply cracked various passwords by force. Next, it attacked the core of UNIX, a program widely used in the network, by attacking a main function known as "send-mail" and adjusting its commands. Finally, it overstacked data into a status report function known as "finger demon" or "fingerd." The worm did this without attracting notice by making itself look like legitimate commands. After completing infection of a site, the worm replicated itself and went to another system. When a site was successfully infected, the worm sent a signal to "Ernie," a popular computer system at Berkeley. In order to avoid quick detection, the worm program rolled a fifteen-sided die to see if it could infect a new system. A positive roll, a one-in-fifteen chance, instructed the worm to go ahead.

From Deborah Johnson, *Computer Ethics,* 2d ed. (Upper Saddle River, N.J.: Prentice-Hall, 1994), 103.

Unfortunately, the program was faulty and was infecting on a fourteen-in-fifteen chance instead. This caused systems to slow down and operators to take notice.

The infector was eventually identified as Robert T. Morris, Jr., a Cornell computer science graduate student. Within forty-eight hours, the worm had been isolated and decompiled, and notices had gone out explaining how to destroy the pest. Although the worm did no permanent damage, it slowed systems to a standstill and acquired passwords into these systems.

Morris was suspended from Cornell by a university board of inquiry for irresponsible acts, and he went to trial in January of 1990. A federal court in Syracuse charged him with violating the Federal Computer Fraud and Abuse Act of 1986. The Morris case was unprecedented in United States courts; it was the first to test the 1986 act. During the trial, Morris revealed that he had realized he had made a mistake and tried to stop the worm. He contacted various friends at Harvard to help him. Andrew Sudduth testified at the trial that he had sent messages out with the solution to kill the program, but the networks were already clogged with the worm.

Morris was found guilty, placed on three years' probation, fined $10,000, and ordered to perform 400 hours of community service. He could have been jailed up to five years and fined $250,000.

During the trial, the seriousness of Morris's behavior was debated in newspapers and magazines. On one side, some said that his crime was not serious and that release of the worm had managed to alert many systems managers to the vulnerability of their computers. Those who thought this also thought that no jail time was appropriate, but community service was. On the other side, some argued that Morris should go to jail. The argument put forth was that a jail sentence would send a clear message to those attempting similar actions on computer systems.[1]

1. What would Spafford say about this case? Consider in particular the fact that the worm alerted many data managers to the vulnerability of their computers.
2. Morris attempted to stop the worm, and no permanent damage occurred. Does his penalty fit the crime? Defend your answer.

CASE SCENARIO 2   Surveillance and E-mail Messages

Surveillance is an issue not only for lower-echelon employees but also for management. A few years ago, Tower Systems International offered corporations an e-mail monitoring system aptly called Surveillance, which monitored e-mail transmissions. The system permitted companies to obtain reports on the following:

■ All electronic messages sent and received

■ All electronic messages sent but not yet opened

■ All operators' sign-ins and sign-offs

■ All attempted security violations, including information on the operator, location, and time of the infraction

---

1. This case summary was written by Dave Colantonio based on the following: "The Worm's Aftermath," *Science,* November 11, 1988, p. 1121; "Hacker's Case May Shape Computer Security Law," *The Washington Post,* January 9, 1990, p. A4; "Student Testifies His Error Jammed Computer Network," *The New York Times,* January 19, 1990, p. A19; "From Hacker to Symbol," *The New York Times,* January 24, 1990, "Revenge on the Nerds," *The Washington Post,* February 11, 1990; "U.S. Accepts Hacker's Sentence," *The New York Times,* June 2, 1990; "No Jail Time Imposed in Hacker Case," *The Washington Post,* May 5, 1990, p. A1; "Computer Intruder Is Put on Probation and Fined $10,000," *The New York Times,* May 5, 1990, p. 1.

Any employee making e-mail transmissions would be subject to monitoring.[1]

1. According to Spinello, what are some of the problems attendant to the use of a system like Surveillance?
2. Should employees be informed of the existence and operation of such programs? Why or why not?
3. Are systems such as Surveillance appropriate for some employees in a firm, even if not for all? If so, for which employees would the use of such monitoring be permissible, in your view?

CASE SCENARIO 3   Lotus/Equifax "Marketplace"

Lotus Development Corporation (makers of Lotus 1-2-3 spreadsheet software) developed, in conjunction with the billion-dollar credit corporation Equifax, a CD-ROM database called Lotus Marketplace: Household. The CD-ROM contained consumer information on some 120 million individuals and 80 million households. This information was actual and inferred, and included names, addresses, marital status, household incomes, purchasing tendencies, and so on. The CD was to be marketed to small businesses and bundled with software that would allow companies to compile mailing lists of prospective clients. At a retail price of $695, owning such software would be advantageous to direct-mail businesses with limited marketing budgets. Many individuals and organizations objected to this offering, pointing out that the data would be collected without notifying the affected parties. Furthermore, the objection went, there was no ready mechanism whereby individuals could assess the data and correct inaccuracies. Lotus/Equifax replied that the data on the CD-ROM was information that could be obtained from other sources and that the parties could remove their names and data from the CD by writing to Lotus/Equifax.

1. As a consumer, would you be satisfied with the reply by Lotus/Equifax regarding the privacy concerns expressed above? Explain. Is it practical to demand that the developers receive the informed consent of all the parties about whom information was to be gathered for the CD?
2. If the same information as would have been contained on the projected CD were already available to large corporations through other avenues, could a credible argument be made that preventing Lotus-Equifax from marketing their disk would discriminate against small businesses?

---

1. See Barbara Garson, *The Electronic Sweatshop* (New York: Penguin Books, 1989).

Epilogue: International Competition and Corporate Social Responsibility

How should a socially responsible corporation address the problems discussed in these chapters? This epilogue offers some reflections upon the question of what structure a socially responsible multinational might have. We begin by considering two scenarios of recent international business practices. The first involves labor practices in Indonesia, the second, sales practices of pharmaceutical firms in poorer nations. Following the scenarios, we suggest how two prominent models of corporate social responsibility might address the moral issues the scenarios raise. Our purpose here is not to define multinational corporate social responsibility, but simply to explore some of the implications of the models.

SCENARIOS

Nike manufactures and sells fashionable, high-quality athletic equipment and clothing. Its athletic shoe industry accounts for almost $2 billion in sales per annum. Virtually all of its shoe production is done offshore in Asia through independent local contractors. Nike is not unique in this respect. The Indonesian shoe industry, for instance, employs twenty-five thousand workers, who produce shoes for Nike, Reebok, L.A. Gear, and Addidas. The plight of these workers, who are for the most part young girls, is pitiable. They earn less than $0.15 per hour and live in company-run dormitories or settlements, often sharing their small quarters with six other workers.[1] Overtime is mandatory, and often this results in an eleven-hour workday. Workers are subject to abusive treatment by the factory owners, who hold contracts with leading U.S. manufacturers. Labor laws do exist but they are violated with impunity because of the eagerness of the governments to attract foreign capital.

The United States has not been blind to these offenses and recently threatened to repeal tariff preferences if Indonesia did not improve its labor conditions. The threat resulted in an official minimum wage of $1.80 per hour and a decree that forbade the military from intervening in labor disputes (e.g., wildcat strikes). But many factories fail to comply with these dictates, in part because the very same military officers who command the soldiers sit on the boards of directors of the offending factories. These officers stood to benefit from the existing labor practices. Furthermore, the penalties for noncompliance are minimal; failure to comply with the new wage standard, for example, means a fine of $50.

Endorsements paid to Michael Jordan, Nike's spokesperson, exceed what the entire twenty-five-thousand-person workforce earns in a year. In this system of labor, it costs $5.60 to produce a pair of basketball shoes that retail in the United States for more than $70.[2]

In his text *Ethics and the Conduct of Business,* John R. Boatright outlines some of the more widely criticized practices of the pharmaceutical industry when it sells abroad. One problem is lack of information. A study of the Office of Technology Assessment indicated that many American-made drugs had labels with medically important information missing and unsupported claims added. One example is Lomotril, marketed by G. D. Searle. Used for the treatment of diarrhea (which can be a life-threatening condition, particularly for children in poorer countries), the drug treats the symptoms of diarrhea by producing constipation, but it does not treat the causes. The World Health Organization has declared Lomotril to be of no medical value. Furthermore, the drug is dangerous when used by children under two years of age. But Searle has recommended the drug for infants in Hong Kong, Thailand, the Philippines, and Central America. Boatright also cites a book by Richard J. Barnet and Ronald Muller entitled *Global Reach,* which shows that the market price for tranquilizers in Columbia was more than sixty times higher than in other places in the world. The only reason for this is that the markets will bear these prices.[3]

MULTINATIONAL RESPONSES

How would a socially responsible multinational respond to cases like these? Let's consider first the canonical position of corporate social responsibility introduced in chapter 1. According to this framework, a multinational should maximize profits while obeying the law. The interesting question in this context is whose law the multinational should use as a limiting condition for profit maximization. Should a company like Nike insist that its Indonesian contractors adhere to U.S. labor laws and practices with respect to wages, hours, and working conditions? Should G. D. Searle provide to Third World markets the same warnings about side effects and indications for a drug that it provides in the United States? Or should these multinationals adopt the standards of the host nation, or do anything they wish in the absence of any host country standards?

Many corporations faced with this decision adopt the second option—the "When in Rome, do as the Romans do" option—with the following justifications.

Using the host nation's standards respects the autonomy of the host nation, for example, its freedom of self-determination. In choosing the host nation's standards, the multinational respects the host nation's freedom to choose for itself those conditions of labor and commerce that it understands to be in the best interests of its citizenry. In addition, a proponent of this justification might add that FDA regulations are not sacred laws, but peculiarities of our own country in which over-regulation is a problem.

As it stands, this justification is weak. It presupposes a kind of moral relativism which, as explored in an earlier chapter, is subject to serious criticisms. It is conceivable that the commercial standards of a host nation are consistent with egregious violations of human rights, such as child and forced labor and dangerous working conditions. We do not countenance such practices in our society because of our respect for persons. By parity of reasoning, we should not countenance these practices in another society since the victims are persons also.

The price paid for host nation autonomy in this sense may be a loss of freedom and security for the workers of the host nation. This is a particularly acute problem when the host nation is not a democracy, but a repressive dictatorship or a corrupt plutocracy which shows no regard at all for the interests of its citizenry. Surely the practices of such regimes cannot be defended on the grounds of national autonomy. It might be argued plausibly that if the host nation is not a representative democracy, the multinational has no business seeking it out as a trading partner.

Still there is another common argument that can support morally objectionable labor practices in Indonesia and other parts of the Third World. It may be argued that any reform of the existing practices actually injures the parties whom it is designed to help.[4] Reforms, such as safer working conditions, shorter hours, higher wages, and so forth, result in an imposition of costs on the multinational; it would be more expensive to do business in the host nation. If these costs were great, the reforms could stop investment in the host nation altogether, which in turn would frustrate the host nation's attempts to industrialize and raise the standard of living. Presumably, the heightened standard of living would be enjoyed by the workers, not just their bosses, as the argument would be moot. Still the argument implies that national prosperity depends on members of the society who are most vulnerable to exploitation.

At first glance, this argument seems more like a rationalization for the exploitation of the workers. According to some critics of multinationals, the adoption of host country standards, however repressive, is not founded on "respect"; rather the standards are adopted because they are conducive to multinational profit maximization. But the argument is more subtle than this. It implies that the absence of protective regulation is the price that must be paid by a poorer nation if it is eventually to join the ranks of wealthy nations. Some people must suffer for the poor nation to become a player in the global market. Without addressing the knotty question of why the burden of suffering must be borne exclusively by the poor, it is interesting to speculate about whether this is a conceptual or a historical claim; that is, are the labor conditions in China, Indonesia, and Central America a necessary condition for industrialization and eventual prosperity, or could these goals be achieved in some other way? It is true that there is a historical precedent for the claim—the labor conditions during the industrial revolution in Britain and the United States were typically harsh. But it is conceivable that moving from a poor agrarian society to a wealthy industrialized one could be accomplished without harming the interests of the workers. For a transition of this kind to occur in our world economy, cooperation of the multinational would be critical. Countries hungry for foreign dollars are only too willing to accede to the demands of multinationals; therefore, part of the responsibility of avoiding the kinds of harms discussed in the foregoing scenarios rests with them. The multinationals' power to effect change is significant. If U.S. shoe manufacturers insisted that their contractors adopt labor standards that improved working conditions, the factory owners would comply or else lose their businesses. Similarly, if the U.S. garment industry refused to deal with Central American facilities that use child labor, the factories would change their labor practices. But none of this is possible if the multinational's goal is simply profit maximization and where the only interests that matter are those of the profit-maximizing shareholders. We conclude that the canonical position in which obeying the law meant relativism would merely perpetuate the existing deplorable conditions.

A second model of multinational corporate social responsibility is *stakeholder theory.* This model differs radically from the canonical view. Here, the scope of social responsibility includes not only the shareholders but also stakeholders, who are "those groups which have a stake or claim on the firm. Specifically . . . suppliers, customers, employees, stockholders, and the local community as well as management in its role as agent for these groups."[5] Stakeholders are those parties whose actions have an effect on or can be affected by the corporation. On this model, management acts as the agent of all stakeholders, not just the shareholders, and the interests of those diverse groups must be taken into account when the firm acts. Any traditional manager, of course, does take into account the interests of these parties when considering a corporate action. When she lowers the price of goods, for example, she considers how the action might affect annual returns or how a new product will be received by customers in the market. But stakeholder theory goes further than this.

On this account the business of the firm is to be conducted for the benefit of *all* stakeholders; that is, the corporation is an instrument not for profit maximization, but for promoting and coordinating the interests of the stakeholders.

The moral foundation for this theory of the corporation is (typically) Kantian. The individuals who make up the stakeholder groups are persons of intrinsic worth whose interests require respect. Their interests cannot be compromised without serious and proper consideration.

This conception of corporate social responsibility might seem strange, since it gives a radically different answer to the question *For whose benefit does the corporation exist?* But recently (i.e., in the past sixty years), corporations have been made to recognize the legitimate interests of stakeholders other than the shareholders. That recognition is by way of legislation. Corporations are held liable for faulty products, employees have the right to bargain collectively, and communities are protected from industrial pollution by environmental regulation. Legislation like this indicates an unwillingness by society to have its economic institutions directed simply by self-interest and competition. Other interests, for instance in a clean environment, in safety, in a good wage and working conditions, can be frustrated if society relies upon the "invisible hand." But as indicated in chapter 1, regulation is reactive—demands for it arise only after society has been injured. Stakeholder theory, on the other hand, is proactive and interweaves societal interests into the fabric of the corporation itself.

Stakeholder theory as applied to a multinational would expand the range of individual stakeholders (e.g., individual workers, managers, and customers) to include foreign nationals. Some may object to this extension, but it is a direct implication of the meaning of *stakeholder* according to traditional definitions. For example, workers as a group are an important stakeholder. They are vital to the success and the survival of the firm. But what about contract workers like those in Indonesia? One might argue that they are really not employees of Nike or Reebok, but rather employees of the factory owners with whom they hold their contract. Still they are stakeholders since their actions can affect the well-being of the multinational (e.g., by striking), and reciprocally the multinational can affect their well-being (e.g., by closing up shop). The community is also a traditional stakeholder. It may provide land and infrastructure (e.g., roads and power lines) that are necessary for the operation of a factory. Reciprocally, the factory provides incomes and other benefits that support the community. In the context of our discussion of multinationals, *community* would include communities in the host nation. Applying stakeholder theory to multinationals would mean including constituencies of the host nation; that they live in foreign lands is irrelevant. What is important is that they can affect and be affected by the multinational. In consequence, their interests, like those of domestic management, domestic workers, and the shareholders, would have to be respected.

There are some troubling questions about stakeholder theory. Here we address one obvious question which has both a practical and moral basis. How does a manager direct the corporation for the benefit of all the stakeholders? Suppose Nike decided to require that its contractors give higher wages to their workers. That might mean lower returns to the shareholders or higher costs to Nike's customers. Pharmaceutical firms are charged by critics with selling drugs at much higher prices in South America than retail in the United States. The market there will bear a much greater markup. Clearly, if they dropped prices to their U.S. levels, customers would benefit. But wouldn't profit-minded shareholders (who are also stakeholders) suffer? Because stakeholder theory does not favor the interests of one constituency over another, it is difficult to know how management would settle these conflicts. It seems that some principle, or set of principles is necessary for adjudicating among the conflicting claims of stakeholders.

How would management balance the diverse and often conflicting interests of the stakeholders? Without a framework a manager might find that task impossible. One way of approaching this problem is to attempt to articulate a set of basic and fundamental interests of the stakeholders. Such fundamental interests would be those of the multinational insofar as they are fundamental interests of the stakeholders it comprises. Sacrificing these would mean jeopardizing the moral status of the stakeholder multinational. We will leave it to you to determine just what might compose this list for all the stakeholders. Still, we can suggest what conditions must be satisfied for an interest to be a fundamental stakeholder interest.

For this we turn to Tom Donaldson's discussion of fundamental international rights from his excellent book *The Ethics of International Business*. Donaldson argues that multinationals are morally required to recognize certain fundamental international rights which no corporation may violate. But how are these be identified? Donaldson suggests that they must satisfy the following conditions:

- They must protect something of very great importance.

- They must be subject to substantial and recurrent threats.

- The obligations that they impose must be affordable and distributed fairly.[6]

From these conditions Donaldson generates a list of individual rights, including the rights to physical security, property, subsistence, and minimal education. The existence of these individual rights imposes significant limitations on the actions of multinationals. For example, the right to physical security would be violated by a multinational's failure to provide safety equipment, and the employment of child labor would be a violation of the right to minimal education.

We believe that a set of conditions similar to Donaldson's might be useful in specifying fundamental stakeholder interests. Like Donaldson's rights they would place limitations on the actions of the multinational and on the competing interests of the stakeholders. A fundamental interest must be of great importance to the stakeholder, must be subject to substantial and recurrent threats, and may impose on other stakeholders only those burdens that are affordable and distributed fairly.

For example, from these conditions it is clear that Indonesian workers have a substantial interest in at least a subsistence wage and tolerable working conditions. This interest is subject to recurrent threat from both investment-poor host nations and profit-maximizing multinationals alike. But could the burdens of supporting this interest be distributed fairly among the other stakeholders? To ameliorate the working conditions would impose costs. Customers might find that athletic shoes are more expensive, and shareholders might find that their returns are diminished. To answer this question, one would have to articulate the fundamental interests of these groups. Here we can only speculate. Shareholders have a fundamental interest in profitability, but not necessarily maximum profitability. Customers have a fundamental interest in high-quality products at competitive prices. It would seem likely that in many cases (certainly the Nike case) the interest in subsistence wages and safe working conditions could be compatible with both the shareholder and customer interests. Ideally, an equilibrium could be struck between the competing interests. The result would be a cost imposition on customers and shareholders which would not be burdensome (perhaps in the Nike case, Nike could defray some of these costs by hiring a spokesperson with a less-inflated salary). The company would still be profitable, and shoes could still be competitively priced. This outcome is preferable to the current situation in which the workers are made to bear the full costs of high earnings and cheap products; it is a fairer distribution. On the other hand, workers could not demand benefits that would make the venture unprofitable, violating the fundamental interest of the investors. Nor could acceding to workers' demands result in products that are not affordable to consumers. Of course, this would also result in the demise of the corporation. A multinational that could not equitably satisfy the fundamental interests of its constituent shareholders would lose its right to be described as a stakeholder firm.

There are certainly some difficult problems that this brief sketch does not address, such as the distinction between profitability and maximum profitability, a clear articulation of fundamental stakeholder interests, and the role of management. Still, the stakeholder theory seems to be a fruitful area for research and is clearly preferable to the canonical view of corporate social responsibility.

Study Questions

1. From the stakeholder perspective, what are the fundamental interests of community and suppliers?

2. Could a stakeholder multinational ever hope to compete against a multinational that adopted the canonical view of corporate social responsibility? What would be the primary difficulties? Explain.

3. How would the canonical position on corporate social responsibility respond to G. D. Searle's marketing practices? What about the stakeholder multinational?

CASE SCENARIO 1   Part-Time Workers vs. Profitability

In August of 1997, the Teamsters union squared off against delivery giant, UPS (United Parcel Service). The strike effectively crippled the world's largest parcel shipment company—its 12 million daily package deliveries were reduced by 90 percent—and it disrupted the affairs of thousands of businesses and workers. The Teamsters, who represent 185,000 of UPS's 308,000 employees, called the strike over two issues of great concern to all American workers: pensions and part-time jobs.

UPS wanted to stop contributing to the Teamster-controlled pension plan and set up its own pension plan. It claimed that by doing so it could increase monthly benefits of UPS employees by an average of 50 percent. But a withdrawal by such a big contributor as UPS (1 billion dollars a year) would weaken the Teamster pension program itself and could conceivably jeopardize the pensions of non-UPS Teamsters. Additionally, Teamster president Ron Carey alleged that the proposed pension plan was simply a ruse for siphoning money back into the corporation. Whatever profits the pension fund makes on its investments over and above what it needs to pay employee benefits would be funneled "back into their [UPS's] pockets, not back into the funds for the participants, for the members who worked hard" (*The New York Times,* Aug. 8, 1997). On the multi-employer plan, the surpluses could be used to increase employee benefits.

But perhaps the most important issue in the strike concerned the nationwide worry about the status of part-time workers. Businesses that wish to remain flexible, perhaps fearing an end to economic expansion, claim that large numbers of such workers are essential to their interest in profitability and competitiveness. That's plausible. But we have all heard horror stories of people stringing together part-time jobs to make ends meet. According to labor statistics published in *The Los Angeles Times* (August 14, 1997), as many as two million people in the work force are doing this today, working fulltime at two or more part-time jobs, often at low salaries and without benefits. Is part-time employment the new tendency in the labor market, or is it a temporary phenomenon?

UPS has lots of part-timers—a full 57 percent of its labor force. By market standards, the position of these part-timers is good. Their salaries average over $11.00 an hour, and they receive the same generous health care benefits as full-time employees.

But many of these workers are "part-time" in name only. UPS has 10,000 employees who work more than 35 hours a week and many who work over 40 hours per week. That's virtually full-time work. At an average of $11.00 an hour, it's a little more than half of what a full-time UPS employee gets. Another issue is that many part-timers wish they could work more. Some may work as few as twelve hours a week—the midnight-to-4 A.M. shift as a loader of the formerly ubiquitous brown vans. The general problem, according to the union officials, is that many of these workers wish they were full-time UPS employees. Since 1993, 38,000 of the 46,000 union jobs that UPS created have been part-time. In the present negotiation with the Teamsters. UPS has offered to create 200 new full-time jobs a year for the next five years.

The Teamsters claimed that UPS's job creation practice is just another case of a big service corporation shifting from full-time labor to "throwaway" jobs. It pointed out that UPS made more than 1 billion dollars in profits last year. It demanded that UPS create more full-time employment opportunities by combining existing part-time positions. UPS claims that its part-time jobs are hardly "throwaways." Unskilled workers start at $8.00 per hour and receive health and retirement benefits. Furthermore, UPS denies that most of these employees want full-time work.

1. Daniel Pedersen of *Newsweek* has noted that the structure of many modern corporations has two tiers: an upper tier of elite workers who enjoy the best pay and benefits and a second tier of lower-paid contract workers (part-time or temporary workers). The structure allows the corporation to remain flexible and competitive, for example, in economic downturns, the second-tier workers can be laid off without damaging the infrastructure of the corporation. In your opinion, what are the implications of this structure for labor (for example, do you think that at some point in time a full-time job will become a status symbol)? Is this structure justified if it increases profitability?
2. Does UPS have an obligation to offer full-time employment status to those part-time workers who are working over 35 hours per week? Are the Teamsters justified in their demands that UPS combine existing part-time positions?
3. In proposing the creation of its own pension fund, arguably UPS is acting in the best interests of its employees. Are the Teamsters' objections to the UPS proposal out of line?
4. State in your own words how you think the canonical and stakeholder models of corporate social responsibility would evaluate the respective arguments of UPS and the Teamsters.

NOTES

1. William Greider, *One World Ready or Not: The Manic Logic of Global Capitalism* (New York: Simon & Schuster, 1977), 390.
2. John R. Boatright, *Ethics and the Conduct of Business,* 2d ed. (New York: Prentice Hall, 1997), 390.
3. Boatright, *Ethics and Conduct,* 373–374.
4. Grieder, *One World Ready or Not,* p. 409.
5. William M. Evan and R. Edward Freeman, "A Stakeholder Theory of the Modern Corporation: Kantian Capitalism" reprinted in *Contemporary Issues in Business Ethics,* 3d ed., Joseph R. DesJardins and John J. McCall eds., (Belmont, CA: Wadsworth, 1966), 77.
6. Thomas Donaldson, *The Ethics of International Business* (New York: Oxford University Press, 1989), 75–76.

 APPENDIX

Information on the World Wide Web

A rapidly growing amount of information relating to many of the issues covered in this text is now available on the World Wide Web (WWW). The Web sites listed here can serve as useful starting points for those who wish to research topics of interest. Sites are grouped into five categories: Law, Business Ethics, Privacy Rights, Government Agencies, and Other.

■ Law

Cornell Legal Information Institute
http://www.law.cornell.edu
General legal information

FindLaw
http://www.findlaw.com
General legal information

Thomas
http://thomas.loc.gov
Federal legislation

CataLaw
http://www.catalaw.com
Consumer law, advertising law,
information technology law,
women and the law

■ Business Ethics

Institute for Business and
Professional Ethics
http://www.depaul.edu

Centre for Applied Ethics
http://www.ethics.ubc.ca

Olsson Center for Applied Ethics
http://www.darden.virginia.edu

■ Privacy Rights

American Civil Liberties Union
http://www.aclu.org

Privacy International
http://www.privacy.org

■ Government Agencies

Equal Employment Opportunity
Commission (EEOC)
http://gsa.gov/eeo

Federal Trade Commission (FTC)
http://www.gopher.ftc.gov

Environmental Protection Agency (EPA)
http://www.epa.gov

Occupational Safety and Health
Administration (OSHA)
http://www.osha-slc.gov

Consumer Product Safety Commission
http://www.epsc.gov

■ Other

Cato Institute
http://www.cato.org

National Organization for Women
http://www.now.org

Consumer Law Page
http://www.consumerlawpage.com

Information Technology Law Page
http://www.smithLyons.ca

Warren Gorham & Lamont
http://www.wgl
Employment law